THE HERITAGE SHAKESPEARE

EDITED, WITH AN INTRODUCTION TO EACH PLAY
AND A GLOSSARY, BY

PETER ALEXANDER

Regius Professor of English Language and Literature
in the University of Glasgow

TRAGEDIES

William Shakespeare

THE TRAGEDIES

with an introduction by George Rylands

and wood-engravings by Agnes Miller Parker

NEW YORK · THE HERITAGE PRESS

The text of the Heritage Shakespeare is that of
Collins Tudor Shakespeare, edited by PROFESSOR PETER ALEXANDER,
and first published in 1951; it is here used with the permission of
Wm. Collins Sons & Co., Ltd., Glasgow, Scotland.
This volume of *Tragedies* is one of three presenting
the complete plays of Shakespeare. The volume of *Comedies* contains
Professor Alexander's General Introduction,
and reproduces the preliminary matter of the First Folio.
The second volume comprises the *Histories.*

Contents

Preface

BY GEORGE RYLANDS

All tragedies are finish'd by a death,
  All comedies are ended by a marriage;
The future states of both are left to faith,
  For authors fear description might disparage
The worlds to come of both, or fall beneath,
  And then both worlds would punish their
    miscarriage;
So leaving each their priest and prayer-book ready,
They say no more of Death or of the Lady.

So muses the disillusioned Byron, while Don Juan sleeps upon the happy breast of Haidée. His own marriage was a tragedy. And on his death-bed he exclaimed, smiling through his pain: 'Che bella Scena!' Few poets have learnt so hardly the truth of Horace Walpole's axiom, that life is a tragedy to those who feel, a comedy to those who think.

Shakespeare is a tragic comedian. His strength lies in the union of thought and feeling. There is laughter in his tragedy, in his comedy tenderness and tears. The gravedigger holds up Yorick's skull to Hamlet, relishing in memory the jests of the mad rogue. A Fool and a beggar sit in judgement on two wooden stools arraigned by Lear as his hard-hearted daughters. A drunken porter bears the keys of hell-gate in *Macbeth*. Romeo in Juliet's monument meditates:

How oft when men are at the point of death
Have they been merry! which their keepers call
A lightning before death.

And Mercutio dies with a pun upon his lips.

'Come away, come away, death,' sings the Clown in *Twelfth Night;* 'I am slain by a fair cruel maid.' And when we turn from the tragic heroes to the heroines of comedy, we remember that Rosaline sets the mocking Berowne,

To move wild laughter in the throat of death . . .
[And] jest a twelvemonth in a hospital.

Beatrice, seeing her cousin slandered and undone, bursts forth: 'Kill Claudio.' Viola lets 'concealment, like a worm i' the bud, feed on her damask cheek.' Rosalind knows that 'men have died from time to time, and worms have eaten them, but not for love.' Thought and feeling, romance and realism, truth and beauty, intermingle and, to use Donne's felicitous word, *inter-inanimate* one another.

The supreme example comes with the consummation of the tragic period. Royal Egypt, herself the serpent of old Nile, receives in a basket of figs the worm whose 'biting is immortal.' 'Will it eat me?' asks Cleopatra. And the Warwickshire rustic replies: 'You must not think I am so simple but I know the devil himself will not eat a woman.' The asp is both the 'poor venomous fool' whose sharp teeth must

> this knot intrinsicate
> Of life at once untie,

and the baby at the breast that sucks the nurse asleep. When the Clown departs, wishing the Queen joy of the worm, she soars into the empyrean of poetry. A last pang of jealousy touches her when, as she embraces her girls in farewell, Iras falls dead. Curled Antony will spend on Iras that kiss which it is her heaven to have. The eastern star sets. Death is as sweet as balm, as soft as air. And then Charmian catches up Cleopatra's phrase for Cæsar: 'ass unpolicied,' and matches it with her tribute, 'lass unparallel'd.' These eighty lines—from the entry of the rural fellow to Charmian's magical

> Your crown's awry;
> I'll mend it and then play,

are the quintessence of Shakespeare. Here is the reconciliation of opposites: the fusion of comedy and tragedy, of the physical and spiritual, of prose and poetry, of the eternal feminine with the enigma of death, of generation and dissolution:

> The stroke of death is as a lover's pinch
> Which hurts, and is desired.

* * * * *

'What is death,' asked Sir Walter Raleigh on the scaffold, 'but an opinion and imagination?' The opinions and imaginations, the fantasies and fashions of mortality, at divers times and in divers places, have been manifold. From the *Dies irae* to Omar Khayyam; from 'The wages of sin is death' to 'And Death shall be no more, Death, thou shalt die'; from the Stoicism of Marcus Aurelius to the mortification of the Trappist monk; from Homer's Achilles in the phantom kingdom, yearning after the life of a starving churl, to Mr. Boswell's 'It is a curious turn but I never can resist seeing executions.' The Middle Ages set a grinning skeleton at Everyman's feast; Ferdinand, a great Renaissance prince, weeps over the sister whom he has had strangled: 'Cover her face. Mine eyes dazzle. She died young.' The *oraison funèbre* of the seventeenth century, clothed in purple and fine linen, gives place to the gothic glooms and gravestone truisms of the eighteenth. The ecstasies and morbidities of the romantic revival lead naturally to the tear-floods of the Victorian novel, to Dickens weeping for the death of Little Nell. Between all such things and ourselves there intervene the trenches of Flanders, the concentration camps, the air-raid shelter, and the H-bomb. Yet the Elizabethans and Jacobeans were as familiar with death as we are. The plague might carry off thirty thousand Londoners in a hot season. Traitors were drawn upon a hurdle through the open streets, hanged, cut down alive, the heart and bowels plucked out, the body divided into four quarters to be disposed of at the King's pleasure. In tavern and alley there were sudden stabbings; in great men's houses duels and assassinations; in palaces Italian devilry:

> I learned in Naples how to poison flowers,
> To strangle with a lawn thrust through the throat,
> To pierce the windpipe with a needle's point,
> Or whilst one is asleep, to take a quill
> And blow a little powder in his ears,
> Or open his mouth, and pour quick silver down,
> And yet I have a braver way than these.

No wonder that Donne and Webster are obsessed with death and that so many of the poets, preachers, and playwrights see 'the skull beneath the skin,' in Eliot's phrase. But with Shakespeare, always the exception, it is otherwise. Nevertheless he is a tragedian: and death is and must be the tragedian's proper subject. Man's exit from the world's stage rings down the curtain. *Finis coronat opus.*

* * * * *

Hamlet, Othello, Brutus, and Macbeth are all murderers. Antony, Brutus, Othello, Juliet, Lady Macbeth, Cleopatra take their own lives. Coriolanus and Hamlet are done to death by treachery. Timon and Lear, titanic figures, outstretch their mortal span until they but usurp their life. They are crushed by fate and their own passionate pride. These are the hard facts. But our response is surprising, paradoxical. It does not tally with the facts. The note which is struck again and again is the note of exultation. Even in *Hamlet*, Fortinbras can exclaim:

O proud death!
What feast is toward in thine eternal cell?

Romeo runs his sea-sick weary bark with desperate eagerness upon the dashing rocks. Antony sees himself as the greatest prince of the world, 'a Roman by a Roman valiantly vanquished.' Brutus, the noblest Roman of them all, falls upon his sword, and no man else has honour by his death. Othello, foiled of revenge, stabs himself with joy, as once he stabbed the Turk in Aleppo, malignant traducer of the state. Macbeth will die with harness on his back:

And damn'd be him that first cries 'Hold, enough!'

More splendid still is the exultation of Caius Marcius, when his rival calls him 'Boy' and sets the conspirators on him:

Cut me to pieces, Volsces; men and lads,
Stain all your edges on me. 'Boy'! False hound!
If you have writ your annals true, 'tis there
That, like an eagle in a dovecote, I
Flutter'd your Volscians in Corioli.
Alone I did it! 'Boy'!

Timon, less arrogant and no less proud, outmatches him:

Come not to me again; but say to Athens,
Timon hath made his everlasting mansion
Upon the beached verge of the salt flood;
Who once a day with his embossed froth
The turbulent surge shall cover.

In Shakespearean tragedy again and again we lift up our hearts when the wages of sin is paid. In the death of the hero we find no sting. There is victory in the grave.

> Thou are not conquered. Beauty's ensign yet
> Is crimson in thy lips and in thy cheeks,
> And death's pale flag is not advanced there!

There are two notable exceptions. As night falls upon the plains of Troy, and Æneas rallies a scattered remnant of the vanquished, Troilus enters with the news of Hector's death, Hector 'the gallant war-man,' exemplar of heroism.

> TROILUS. Hector is slain!
> ALL. Hector! the gods forbid!
> TROILUS. He's dead, and at the murderer's horse's tail,
> In beastly sort, dragg'd through the shameful field.
> . . . Hector is gone:
> Who shall tell Priam so, or Hecuba?
> Let him that will a screech-owl aye be call'd
> Go in to Troy, and say there 'Hector's dead.'
> There is a word will Priam turn to stone,
> Make wells and Niobes of the maids and wives,
> Cold statues of the youth; and, in a word,
> Scare Troy out of itself. But, march away;
> Hector is dead; there is no more to say.

It is the knell of chivalry. No resignation or exultation here. Only a pitiful hope of revenge hides the defiant boy's inward misery.

Troilus is a political play, a problem play. Some would even call it a comedy and the editors of the First Folio were in two minds where to print it. It is Shakespeare's only highbrow play; caviare to the general. Hamlet might have written it; Tennyson and Goethe put it in the first rank. As an analyst of war Shakespeare shows himself as searching as Tolstoi. But it is also an allegory and a dirge. The modern world defeats the mediaeval. Lancelot and Galahad, Sir Philip Sidney, Spenser's Sir Guyon and the Redcross Knight are brought low by the politician and the malcontent, by the *Inglese italianato*, by the despot:

> Then everything includes itself in power,
> Power into will, will into appetite;
> And appetite, a universal wolf,

> So doubly seconded with will and power,
> Must make perforce a universal prey,
> And last eat up himself.

Shakespeare mourns the passing of Elizabeth I, Spenser's Gloriana, as Edmund Burke mourned the revolution which brought low the head of Marie Antoinette:

> The age of Chivalry is gone. That of sophisters, economists, and calculators has succeeded, and the glory of Europe is extinguished for ever. . . . The unbought grace of life, the cheap defence of nations, the nurse of manly sentiments and heroic enterprise is gone.

Hector is dead; there is no more to say.

Even more terrible and baffling is the hanging of Cordelia. 'Shakespeare,' says Samuel Johnson sternly, 'has suffered the virtue of Cordelia to perish in a just cause, contrary to the natural ideas of justice, to the hope of the reader, and, what is yet more strange, to the faith of chronicles.' And he goes on to confess: 'I was many years ago so shocked by Cordelia's death, that I know not whether I ever endured to read again the last scenes of the play till I undertook to revise them as an editor.' More than fifty years have passed since Professor A. C. Bradley, whose writ on Shakespearean tragedy is holy, asked the question, Why does Cordelia die? and found an answer to satisfy himself. He felt that when the curtain falls on a Shakespearean tragedy, the implicit moral is that the waste and wickedness of the world are not the final reality but only a part of reality taken as a whole, and when so taken, illusive. The artist so transmutes the tragic facts that 'suffering and death count for little or nothing, nobility of spirit, heroism and sacrifice for much or all. What happens to such a being as Cordelia does not matter in comparison to what she is.' In short, the 'moral' of *King Lear* lies in the irony of this collocation:

> ALBANY. The gods defend her!
>
> *Enter Lear with Cordelia dead in his arms*

The gods care nothing for prosperity and power. It is the renunciation of them which they approve. Indeed Lear forearms us for the catastrophe to come when he is taken prisoner:

Upon such sacrifices, my Cordelia,
The gods themselves throw incense.

The Gospels abound in such spiritual paradoxes. 'He that humbleth himself shall be exalted.' 'What shall it profit a man, if he shall gain the whole world, and lose his own soul?' 'He that findeth his life shall lose it: and he that loseth his life for my sake shall find it.' 'He saved others; himself he cannot save.'

Bacon tells us that prosperity is the blessing of the Old Testament, adversity is the blessing of the New; and that 'prosperity doth best discover vice, but adversity doth best discover virtue.' We can adapt the distinction thus: 'Comedy doth best discover vice. Tragedy doth best discover virtue.' Comedy corrects and purges with a perpetual fountain of good sense, with laughter and ridicule. Comedy is concerned with man in his social relationships—domestic, sexual, political, national. Tragedy lays bare the individual soul; man suffering amid awful forms and powers; man battling with the forces of evil outside himself or within, and

Triumphing over Death and Chance and thee, O Time.

King Lear then, if Bradley is right, is not an exception, as *Troilus and Cressida* is. *Troilus* is often coupled with *Measure for Measure* but they have little in common. In the latter play however there is much which is relevant to the tragic period, in that Shakespeare explores the two themes of sex and death which, as Byron suggested, are proper to comedy and tragedy respectively. Pompey the bawd and Lucio the libertine are lords of life. Their opposites are Abhorson the executioner and Barnardine, the condemned felon, who swears he 'will not die today for any man's persuasion.' Angelo, the sexual ascetic, has power over life and death and sentences Claudio for getting his betrothed with child. He can only be saved if his sister Isabella, who would dedicate herself to the death-in-life of conventual vows, will yield up the treasures of her body to the outward-sainted deputy Angelo and forfeit her immortal soul. At the heart of the play lies the homily on death delivered in the prison by the just Duke in a friar's habit. Living and dying is the double theme, expounded in theatrical terms, of this tragicomedy, so characteristic of Shakespeare, whose last Act insists upon the lesson of forgiveness.

The lesson is relevant to *Cymbeline*, which we find printed among the tragedies but which inaugurated Shakespeare's final period and which is usually defined as a romance. Perhaps he essayed this new genre a little earlier, when he rehandled an old play, *Pericles, Prince of Tyre*—a genre which the younger generation, notably Beaumont and Fletcher, were to exploit, and which was to contribute, along with the Masque, to the Restoration theatre. The world of the three final romances is a world of adventure and *coups de théâtre*, of vision and dream and oracle and 'music i' th' air,' of shepherds and pagan deities and lost princesses, of sudden reversals, discoveries and encounters, of evil passions and ancient wrongs; above all, of repentance and redemption, of expiation and forgiveness. If *Cymbeline* is not a complete success, at any rate it creates the most vital of all the heroines in Imogen. The romantic experiment becomes more controlled and more profound in *The Winter's Tale*. Practice has made perfect in *The Tempest*.

The spiritual purport of the romances is adumbrated in *Lear*, when father and daughter kneel to one another in reconciliation and more especially in the speech which immediately precedes the quotation (given above) of the sacrifices which the gods themselves approve. Cordelia would yet 'outfrown false fortune's frown' and face her callous sisters: But Lear will not have it so:

> No, no, no, no. Come, let's away to prison;
> We two alone will sing like birds i' the cage;
> When thou dost ask me blessing, I'll kneel down,
> And ask of thee forgiveness: so we'll live,
> And pray, and sing, and tell old tales, and laugh
> At gilded butterflies, and hear poor rogues
> Talk of court news; and we'll talk with them too,
> Who loses and who wins; who's in, who's out;
> And take upon's the mystery of things,
> As if we were God's spies: and we'll wear out,
> In a wall'd prison, packs and sects of great ones
> That ebb and flow by the moon.

In the three romances the vision is realised, the prophecy comes true. Within a prison of song and prayer, of time remembered and time suspended, youth and age observe the gilded and the great, the beggar and the rogue, with the all-seeing eye of Providence. 'Pardon's the word for all.' Prospero learns from Ariel that the rarer action is in virtue, rather than in vengeance:

> And my ending is despair,
> Unless I be relieved by prayer,
> Which pierces so that it assaults
> Mercy itself and frees all faults.

* * * * *

To think and speak in a general way of 'the poetry of Donne,' 'the music of Brahms,' 'the painting of Picasso,' is unprofitable. One must start from the individual poem, composition, or design. So it is with Shakespeare's tragedies. Each play is distinct; a work of art with its own conditions, means, and purpose. The differences are more illuminating than the common factors; the differences dividing Romeo and Troilus, both young lovers and idealists: or the two ageing lovers and soldiers, Othello and Antony; the differences between Juliet and Imogen, Brutus and Macbeth, Claudius and Iachimo, Iago and Edmund. The function of the prose varies from tragedy to tragedy. The poetry differs in kind. Romeo is a poetic mouthpiece. In *Othello* the poetry is essential to the conception of the Moor. Antony and Cleopatra are gilded over with poetry yet they themselves are not poets. And then again the rhetoric of Ulysses is very different from that of Macbeth or Coriolanus or Iachimo.

Titus Andronicus (1593) is apprentice work. It is a very far cry from that Senecan melodrama to *Antony and Cleopatra* (1609). Yet it is not mere Grand Guignol. The rhetoric in the manner of Marlowe, Kyd, and Peele is powerful. There are gleams of poetry. We can look on from Tamora to Goneril, from Aaron to Edmund, from Titus himself to Lear. The stage revival or resurrection of the tragedy by Laurence Olivier and Peter Brook not only made theatrical history but proved also that *Titus Andronicus* is good theatre. *Romeo and Juliet*, which Shakespeare wrote some two years later perhaps, is as much a poem as it is a play. But the idealisation of the heroine is set off by the Nurse and that of the hero by Mercutio. Mercutio's death in a noonday scuffle in the streets is more tragic than the suicides of Romeo and Juliet in the Monument, where their passion is made as eternal as that of the lovers on the Grecian Urn of Keats:

> For ever wilt thou love, and she be fair.

Hamlet, a name synonymous with Shakespeare's, belongs to the year 1600 or thereabouts. Shakespeare's career lasted for a little less than ten years before *Hamlet*, and a little more than ten years after it; and roughly the same number of plays belong to each decade. Round about *Hamlet* cluster close a bunch of wonders; a history, a Roman tragedy, the three most Shakespearean comedies, a problem play (or perhaps two), and a farce. All may have been composed in less than thirty-six months. *Credo quia impossibile est.*

* * * * *

The tragedies proper—and they are Shakespeare's masterpieces—belong to the years 1599 to 1609. The sequence begins and ends with Rome, as he discovered it in Sir Thomas North's translation of a French translation of Plutarch's *Lives of the Noble Grecians and Romans*. He had got and used all he wanted in the English chroniclers, and hard on the heels of Henry V, the man of action, comes Brutus, the philosopher, a man divided against himself, anticipating both Hamlet and Macbeth:

> Between the acting of a dreadful thing
> And the first motion, all the interim is
> Like a phantasma, or a hideous dream:
> The genius and the mortal instruments
> Are then in council; and the state of man,
> Like to a little kingdom, suffers then
> The nature of an insurrection.

Two other points are to be noted. First, he turns in *Cæsar* from chronicle form to classical form. The play is admirably constructed in a movement and counter-movement. The former begins and ends with the mob; the latter begins and ends with the dictators. The cunningly composed temptation scene in the first movement, in which Cassius realises that although Brutus is noble his 'honourable metal may be wrought from that it is disposed'—an anticipation of Iago and the Moor—is matched in the second movement by their quarrel. Secondly, we note Shakespeare's skill in characterising a group and conveying their relations with one another. The main interest is divided between Brutus, Cassius, Antony, and Cæsar. But Casca also is very much alive and so is Octavius. Even the small parts are rewarding. And this is the secret of the tragedy that followed *Cæsar*. Polonius, Osric, the Gravedigger, the First Player, Marcellus, are evidence that Shakespeare had now a talented and expert company at his command. It is a play about young men. Fortinbras, Horatio, Laertes, Rosencrantz and Guildenstern, and Osric do much, by contrast and comparison, towards the creation of the central figure, for whose completion Shakespeare exploits to the full the convention of soliloquy, which he had tried out on occasion already, with varying success, for Berowne and Romeo, for his Kings, and (unforgettably) for Falstaff.

If Shakespeare over-reached himself in *Hamlet* by putting everything in, he followed that romantic melodrama with a tragedy in which he tried to leave everything out. *Othello*, if we omit the first act, as Verdi was to do in his masterpiece, observes the unities. But Verdi's Iago is the Miltonic Satan rather than the hail-fellow well-met, *faux bonhomme* soldier whom Shakespeare conceived. The part is invariably misinterpreted by readers, critics, and actors, although Charles Lamb bears witness to Bensley's understanding of it. Despite the explicit statement confirmed by Iago himself that the Moor is not easily jealous, the hero too often arouses incredulity or disapprobation. The first act of the tragedy is essential because Desdemona's deception of her father, which is indeed to be the death of him, is the trump card in Iago's hand. She is to lie again, about the handkerchief, and yet again, most pitifully, on her death-bed. Iago is no monster of motiveless malignity. He relates to the mediaeval Envy; to Chaucer's 'smiler with the knyf under the cloke'; to the Ironical Man of Theophrastus; to the Malcontent; to Bacon's essay on Dissimulation. Herman Melville marvellously resurrected him in Claggart, the master-at-arms, who destroys the handsome sailor, Billy Budd. Shakespeare, as so often, gives us the clue in the first few minutes, when Iago says 'I am not what I am.' The disparity between the exterior and the inward man, between semblance and truth, is a constant theme in the plays. A man can smile and smile and be a villain. There's no art to find the mind's construction in the face:

Seems, madam: nay, it is. I know not seems.

In *Macbeth* Shakespeare returns to the device of the soliloquy but more subtly, allying it with its sworn brother the 'aside.' But whereas in *Hamlet* all the other characters are flesh and blood endowed with a life of their own, in *Macbeth* they seem to be projections of the hero. Macduff is what he could and should have been. Banquo is the mean between the two. Lady Macbeth is flesh of his flesh. The witches are symbols of his imaginative power; for he is a poet. The bloody sergeant is a symbol of his prowess as a warrior and his ruthlessness as a butcher. The structure of the play is unusual. It falls into three parts. Banquo has the central Act; Duncan the first two; Macduff Acts IV and V. The first three Acts which haunt us from childhood as we read are always a disappointment in the theatre itself, but the last two discover a vitality and significance on the stage which we miss in the study. Shakespeare experiments in another way also; that is, in a kind of shorthand, both in the rapid highly-charged scene which only plays for a few moments; and in concentration, pregnancy, economy of phrase. The combination of abstract and concrete, of the general and the particular, the imaginative and the sensory, makes this one of the most stylistically remarkable of all the plays, seeming to oscillate between enigmatic, suggestive phrases and direct concise homely images and idioms.

King Lear, last of the great four, is a parable. It is also a first-rate acting play, in which Garrick and Edmund Kean were as breath-taking as Mrs. Siddons in the part of Lady Macbeth. Lear poses the question—and at the heart of every great tragedy lies an unanswerable interrogative—'Is there any cause in nature which makes these hard hearts?' The hog, the lion, the wolf, the vulture, the gilded fly are what they are by nature; they act according to their kind. Nor can we tax the elements with *unkindness;* it is the nature of the rain to wet and the wind to blow. What then of man, the poor, bare, forked animal? Is he more bestial and savage than the brute creation? Is mankind kind? Set against this is the world which proud man, drest in a little brief authority, makes for himself;

a world of degrees, customs, prerogatives and laws; of courtiers, flatterers, parasites, justicers, and beadles; of rustling silks, furred gowns, rich perfumes, gold plate; a world of luxury, sophistication, and perjury. The King and the Bastard both invoke the goddess, Nature. Is this a natural or an unnatural world? Shakespeare had explored the theme in his crude *Timon of Athens*, where the first three Acts present the vices and affectations of society, while the last two show the hero as a savage in a wooded cavern by the sea shore. Here, such is the irony of fate, digging for a natural root, he lights upon the great corrupter of man, gold, which will make 'black white, base noble, old young, coward valiant.' And here will Timon find

The unkindest beast more kinder than mankind.

From eleventh-century Scotland and from legendary Wessex—Thomas Hardy liked to think that Lear's conflict with the heavens was joined on Egdon heath—Shakespeare returned to Plutarch and to Rome to complete his tragic sequence. Neither *Antony* nor *Coriolanus* has the classical restraint of *Julius Cæsar*. They are less effective in performance and less tragic to the critic and common reader. *Coriolanus* is favoured by the French but we feel it to be lacking in colour and warmth and order. The hero is an arrogant, passionate, overgrown boy—a soldier of genius and a patriot. He is at the mercy of three distinct forces; the Volscian general who is his professional adversary but whose emulation is mitigated by admiring love; the garlic-breathing mutable mob whom he disdains, together with their creatures, the two demagogues; and his mother, prouder even than he, who lives for him alone and is his undoing. The player of Aufidius must dominate the first movement which is contained in Act I. The political triumph of 'the rank-scented many' and their agitators fills the second movement and ends at Act IV, Scene 2 with the hero's exile. In the final movement Coriolanus rises again only to be brought down by Volumnia and Aufidius, in innocent but unholy alliance, and assassinated. The play, like *Troilus*, has not had its deserts. In Menenius we have the most rounded of all Shakespeare's old men. Volumnia's great oration, lifted almost word for word from North's Plutarch, is one of the noblest things in the whole canon. The audacity of idiom and syntax, the energy of verse and speech, anticipate the virtuosity of style in *Cymbeline* and *The Winter's Tale*.

What is all nerve, muscle, sinew, bone in *Coriolanus* takes on high colour, glowing flesh, and rich attire in *Antony and Cleopatra*. Here the audacity is equalled by the felicity and ease. As with *Hamlet*, this is romantic art, not classical; a panorama rather than a play. If our hearts are not moved, if we do not suffer, it is because the hero and heroine have no illusions about themselves or each other and no moral sense. In a word they are not heroic. Our moral sense is now blinded by their glamour, and now identified with the priggish vain efficient egoist, Octavius, who is fatally revealed both to the Egyptian Queen and to us when he asks the assembled court: 'Which is the Queen of Egypt?' The eternal feminine has no power upon him until she is lying dead.

> As she would catch another Antony
> In her strong toil of grace.

The eternal feminine, we must remember, was enacted by a boy player; a fact which Shakespeare never forgets. His tact and taste and cunning are impeccable. But it is a condition of the play.

* * * * *

'Shakespeare's plays are not in the rigorous and critical sense either tragedies or comedies, but compositions of a distinct kind; exhibiting the real state of sublunary nature, which partakes of good and evil, joy and sorrow, mingled with endless variety of proportion and innumerable modes of combination; and expressing the course of the world, in which the loss of the one is the gain of the other; in which, at the same time, the reveller is hasting to his wine, and the mourner burying his friend; in which the malignity of one is sometimes defeated by the frolick of another; and many mischiefs and many benefits are done and hindered without design. . . . Shakespeare has united the powers of exciting laughter and sorrow not only in one mind, but in one composition.'

Such is the pronouncement of Samuel Johnson, Shakespeare's justest critic, although we shall hardly agree with him that the dramatist writes tragedy with a great appearance of toil and study, while in comedy he seems to luxuriate as in a mode of thinking congenial to his nature. But that Shakespeare is a tragi-comedian is true. And Shakespeare knew it. For he tells us that 'the web of our life is of a mingled yarn, good and ill together; our virtues would be proud if our faults whipped them not; and our crimes would despair if they were not cherished by our virtues.' The web of his drama is 'of a mingled yarn' and although the deaths which bring down the curtain on his tragedies may have this in common, that they lift up our hearts, yet we must not seek for any cut-and-dried philosophy, any moral simplifications. His admonition on that score has Johnsonian common sense:

> 'Tis all men's office to speak patience
> To those that wring under the load of sorrow,
> But no man's virtue or sufficiency
> To be so moral when he shall endure
> The like himself. . . .
>   I will be flesh and blood;
> For there was never yet philosopher
> That could endure the toothache patiently,
> However they have writ the style of gods
> And made a push at chance and sufferance.

A Note on the Illustrations

BY AGNES MILLER PARKER

IN WRITING his plays for the living stage, Shakespeare had no thought of setting them down as a permanent record to be read as literature years later. And yet, unquestionably, more people have read Shakespeare's dramas in the intervening three and a half centuries than have ever seen them enacted on a stage.

As an artist, devoted to the illustration of skilfully produced works of fine literature, it is natural that I should have taken the *literary* approach to the *Tragedies*, giving primary consideration to the reader. He is thus free to make his own wide-screen moving pictures as he goes along. What I have tried to add to this broad image, in my two wood-engravings for each play, has been a comment on a momentary situation, or a crystallization of the mood of the play.

Inevitably the life-and-death theme runs through these tragedies, and whenever this idea lent itself to illustration, I used it. But I frequently found the actual death scene ill-suited to pictorial composition or less dramatic than some other moment in the play. In these cases, the more potent stimuli proved to be the masterfully developed contrasts in Shakespeare's characterizations. One example is Timon of Athens: rich and golden in one picture, stripped and desolate in the other.

To a great extent, I reserved the symbols and visual imagery of the tragedies for the title-page engraving and for the introductory plate. The latter is based mostly on the speeches in Julius Cæsar (Casca's in Act I, Scene 3, and Calpurnia's in Act II, Scene 2) dealing with the violent thunderstorm that presages the death of Cæsar. From *King Lear* comes the symbol of the oak cleaved by lightning, and from *Macbeth* the hawk as a symbol of the sudden and violent striking down of an innocent victim.

On the title page the sword represents violence against the crown, the sea the uncertainty of fortune, while the comet and storm, as in the introductory plate, complete a design stemming from Calpurnia's cry:

> When beggars die there are no comets seen;
> The heavens themselves blaze forth the death of princes.

The History of Troilus and Cressida

TROILUS AND CRESSIDA

TROILUS AND CRESSIDA stands at the head of the Tragedies in the First Folio, but only by accident. It was originally to come after *Romeo and Juliet;* when Jaggard had printed three pages, however, the press was stopped, the pages withdrawn, and *Timon of Athens* put in its place. Only after the section given to the Tragedies had been completed did the printer insert *Troilus and Cressida* in a kind of no-man's land between the Histories and Tragedies, and at too late an hour in the make-up of the volume to include its title in the list of contents.

An explanation for this unusual proceeding bibliographers have found in the history of the play's publication.

Under 7th February 1603 the Stationers' Register notes that on that day at a 'Full Court' of the Company the printer Roberts obtained the right to print *The booke of Troilus and Cressida as yt is acted by my lo: Chamberlens Men,* always provided *he hath gotten sufficient aucthority for yt.* As Roberts made no further move towards printing, the assumption that he was acting for Shakespeare's company and shutting out any piratical attempt at publication is most plausible. Six years later, however, two stationers Richard Bonian and Henry Walley put an edition, duly entered in the Register, on the market, apparently in defiance of the actors' wishes. This at least seems the meaning we must put on a phrase from the preface which they inserted before the text of the piece. This preface does not stand in what is now recognized as the first state of their publication. In that state they had put on the title-page the information that the play *was acted at the Globe;* someone on whose authority they relied must have pointed out to them that this was an error, and on their learning that the play had never appeared on the public stage, they replaced the original title-page with another, and, to give the public an idea of the exclusive nature of their publication, inserted the following notice:

A neuer writer, to an euer reader. Newes.

Eternall reader, you have heere a new play, neuer stal'd with the Stage, neuer clapper-clawd with the palmes of the vulger, and yet passing full of the palme comicall; for it is a birth of your braine, that neuer under-tooke any thing commicall, vainely: And were but the vaine names of commedies changde for the titles of Commodities, or of Playes for Pleas; you should see all those grand censors, that now stile them such vanities, flock to them for the maine grace of their grauities: especially this authors Commedies, that are so fram'd to the life, that they serue for the most common Commentaries, of all the actions of our liues, shewing such a dexteritie, and power of witte, that the most displeased with Playes, are pleasd with his Commedies. And all such dull and heavy-witted worldlings, as were neuer capable of the witte of a Commedie, comming by report of them to his representations, haue found that witte there, that they neuer found in themselves, and have parted better wittied then they came: feeling an edge of witte set upon them, more than euer they dreamd they had braine to grinde it on. So much and such sauored salt of witte is in his Commedies, that they seeme (for their height of pleasure) to be borne in that sea that brought forth *Venus*. Amongst all there is none more witty than this: And had I time I would comment upon it, though I know it needs not, (for so much as will make you thinke your testerne well bestowd) but for so much worth, as euen poor I know to be stuft in it. It deserues such a labour, as well as the best Commedy in *Terence* or *Plautus*. And beleeve this, that when hee is gone, and his Commedies out of sale, you will scramble for them, and set up a new English Inquisition. Take this for a warning, and at the perrill of your pleasures losse, and Iudgements, refuse not, nor like this the lesse, for not being sullied, with the smoaky breath of the multitude; but thanke fortune for the scape it hath made amongst you. Since by the grand possessor's wills I beleeue you should have prayd for them rather then beene prayd. And so I leaue all such to bee prayd for (for the states of their wits healths) that will not praise it.

Vale.

Bonian and Walley would not have gone to the expense of a new title-page and a preface unless they had been sure of their informant; for the statement that the play had never appeared on the public stage, if mistaken, would certainly have been open, as Bonian and Walley must have known, to public correction. There would not have been wanting frequenters of the Globe to put them right about it. Further the 'neuer writer,' in spite of his flourishes, obviously knows what he is talking about. We may then safely accept his assurance that the play was produced on some private occasion, especially as the peculiarities of the piece itself lend support to his statement. Further, his assertion that 'the grand possessors' were opposed to publication seems borne out by the trouble that delayed the printing of the play in the First Folio. Taking the grand possessors as the actors, we may see their opposition to the quarto publication of the play recoiling on them when they in their turn came to reprint it; Walley, the surviving partner from the original venture, could easily have made himself a nuisance by disputing the actors' right to print what the Stationers' Register had assigned to him as his copy.

The preface to the Quarto thus explains the peculiar position of *Troilus and Cressida* in the Folio; it also indicates how Bonian and Walley were able to print a sound version of the play without the actors' co-operation. Aristocratic supporters of the theatre would naturally wish to have copies of such a private piece, and that the Quarto was printed from such a transcript is confirmed by the nature of the stage directions and other details.

Once corroboration is found for the factual detail in the preface, the writer's critical opinions must be taken as those of one who was a well-informed and enthusiastic admirer of Shakespeare's work; and the question at once arises why this critic's judgment on the piece should conflict with that of so many later interpreters and commentators. *Troilus and Cressida* stands in modern criticism with the dark comedies or with the comical satires that are supposed to mark the transition from the times of Elizabeth to the more cynical and disillusioned attitude of the Jacobeans. Here Shakespeare, many would have us believe, reveals his disgust and disillusion, deliberately reversing the values of tradition by imposing on a heroic story, and a romantic episode attached to it, a realistic and scathing treatment that emphasizes the emptiness of what passes for honour and the hollowness of woman's love. Why were Shakespeare's contemporary admirers so blind to all this?

That the play glances cynically at Homer's story and that Shakespeare deliberately reverses Chaucer's verdict on his Criseyde would be obvious to those with any pretensions to a literary education. To regard this as the very height of comedy the Jacobean critic must have recalled the occasion when it was all very much in keeping and the audience would sense in such literary heresy a kind of dexterity they could enjoy. To find such an audience in 1602 except at one or other of the Inns of Court seems impossible, and the interpretation of Shakespeare's play, unless the observations of a well-informed contemporary are to go for nothing, should allow for the unusual occasion and the dexterity with which Shakespeare plays the physician to a group with their own peculiar kind of humour.

PRIAM, *King of Troy*
HECTOR, TROILUS, PARIS, DEIPHOBUS, HELENUS — *his sons*
MARGARELON, *a bastard son of Priam*
ÆNEAS, ANTENOR — *Trojan commanders*
CALCHAS, *a Trojan priest, taking part with the Greeks*
PANDARUS, *uncle to Cressida*
AGAMEMNON, *the Greek general*
MENELAUS, *his brother*
ACHILLES, AJAX, ULYSSES, NESTOR, DIOMEDES, PATROCLUS — *Greek commanders*
THERSITES, *a deformed and scurrilous Greek*
ALEXANDER, *servant to Cressida*
SERVANT *to Troilus*
SERVANT *to Paris*
SERVANT *to Diomedes*

HELEN, *wife to Menelaus*
ANDROMACHE, *wife to Hector*
CASSANDRA, *daughter to Priam, a prophetess*
CRESSIDA, *daughter to Calchas*

Trojan *and* Greek Soldiers, *and* Attendants

SCENE:

Troy and the Greek camp before it

Troilus and Cressida

PROLOGUE

In Troy, there lies the scene. From isles of Greece
The princes orgillous, their high blood chaf'd,
Have to the port of Athens sent their ships
Fraught with the ministers and instruments
Of cruel war. Sixty and nine that wore
Their crownets regal from th' Athenian bay
Put forth toward Phrygia; and their vow is made
To ransack Troy, within whose strong immures
The ravish'd Helen, Menelaus' queen,
With wanton Paris sleeps—and that's the quarrel.
To Tenedos they come,
And the deep-drawing barks do there disgorge
Their war-like fraughtage. Now on Dardan plains
The fresh and yet unbruised Greeks do pitch
Their brave pavilions: Priam's six-gated city,
Dardan, and Tymbria, Helias, Chetas, Troien,
And Antenorides, with massy staples
And corresponsive and fulfilling bolts,
Sperr up the sons of Troy.
Now expectation, tickling skittish spirits
On one and other side, Troyan and Greek
Sets all on hazard—and hither am I come
A Prologue arm'd, but not in confidence
Of author's pen or actor's voice, but suited
In like conditions as our argument,
To tell you, fair beholders, that our play
Leaps o'er the vaunt and firstlings of those broils,
Beginning in the middle; starting thence away
To what may be digested in a play.
Like or find fault; do as your pleasures are;
Now good or bad, 'tis but the chance of war.

TROILUS AND CRESSIDA

ACT I. SCENE 1

Troy. Before PRIAM'S *palace*

Enter TROILUS *armed, and* PANDARUS

TROILUS. Call here my varlet; I'll unarm again.
Why should I war without the walls of Troy
That find such cruel battle here within?
Each Troyan that is master of his heart,
Let him to field; Troilus, alas, hath none!
PANDARUS. Will this gear ne'er be mended?
TROILUS. The Greeks are strong, and skilful to their strength,
Fierce to their skill, and to their fierceness valiant;
But I am weaker than a woman's tear,
Tamer than sleep, fonder than ignorance,
Less valiant than the virgin in the night,
And skilless as unpractis'd infancy.

PANDARUS. Well, I have told you enough of this; for my part, I'll not meddle nor make no farther. He that will have a cake out of the wheat must needs tarry the grinding.

TROILUS. Have I not tarried?

PANDARUS. Ay, the grinding; but you must tarry the bolting.

TROILUS. Have I not tarried?

PANDARUS. Ay, the bolting; but you must tarry the leavening.

TROILUS. Still have I tarried.

PANDARUS. Ay, to the leavening; but here's yet in the word 'hereafter' the kneading, the making of the cake, the heating of the oven, and the baking; nay, you must stay the cooling too, or you may chance to burn your lips.

TROILUS. Patience herself, what goddess e'er she be,
Doth lesser blench at suff'rance than I do.
At Priam's royal table do I sit;
And when fair Cressid comes into my thoughts—
So, traitor, then she comes when she is thence.

PANDARUS. Well, she look'd yesternight fairer than ever I saw her look, or any woman else.

TROILUS. I was about to tell thee: when my heart,
As wedged with a sigh, would rive in twain,
Lest Hector or my father should perceive me,

I have, as when the sun doth light a storm,
Buried this sigh in wrinkle of a smile.
But sorrow that is couch'd in seeming gladness
Is like that mirth fate turns to sudden sadness.

PANDARUS. An her hair were not somewhat darker than Helen's—well, go to—there were no more comparison between the women. But, for my part, she is my kinswoman; I would not, as they term it, praise her, but I would somebody had heard her talk yesterday, as I did. I will not dispraise your sister Cassandra's wit; but—

TROILUS. O Pandarus! I tell thee, Pandarus—
When I do tell thee there my hopes lie drown'd,
Reply not in how many fathoms deep
They lie indrench'd. I tell thee I am mad
In Cressid's love. Thou answer'st 'She is fair'—
Pourest in the open ulcer of my heart—
Her eyes, her hair, her cheek, her gait, her voice,
Handlest in thy discourse. O, that her hand,
In whose comparison all whites are ink
Writing their own reproach; to whose soft seizure
The cygnet's down is harsh, and spirit of sense
Hard as the palm of ploughman! This thou tell'st me,
As true thou tell'st me, when I say I love her;
But, saying thus, instead of oil and balm,
Thou lay'st in every gash that love hath given me
The knife that made it.

PANDARUS. I speak no more than truth.

TROILUS. Thou dost not speak so much.

PANDARUS. Faith, I'll not meddle in it. Let her be as she is: if she be fair, 'tis the better for her; an she be not, she has the mends in her own hands.

TROILUS. Good Pandarus! How now, Pandarus!

PANDARUS. I have had my labour for my travail, ill thought on of her and ill thought on of you; gone between and between, but small thanks for my labour.

TROILUS. What, art thou angry, Pandarus? What, with me?

PANDARUS. Because she's kin to me, therefore she's not so fair as Helen. An she were not kin to me, she would be as fair a Friday as Helen is on Sunday. But what care I? I care not an she were a blackamoor; 'tis all one to me.

TROILUS. Say I she is not fair?

PANDARUS. I do not care whether you do or no. She's a fool to stay behind her father. Let her to the Greeks; and so I'll tell her the next time I see her. For my part, I'll meddle nor make no more i' th' matter.

TROILUS. Pandarus!

PANDARUS. Not I.

TROILUS. Sweet Pandarus!

PANDARUS. Pray you, speak no more to me: I will leave all as I found it, and there an end. *Exit. Sound alarum*

TROILUS. Peace, you ungracious clamours! Peace, rude sounds!
Fools on both sides! Helen must needs be fair,
When with your blood you daily paint her thus.
I cannot fight upon this argument;
It is too starv'd a subject for my sword.
But Pandarus—O gods, how do you plague me!
I cannot come to Cressid but by Pandar;
And he's as tetchy to be woo'd to woo
As she is stubborn-chaste against all suit.
Tell me, Apollo, for thy Daphne's love,
What Cressid is, what Pandar, and what we?
Her bed is India; there she lies, a pearl;
Between our Ilium and where she resides
Let it be call'd the wild and wand'ring flood;
Ourself the merchant, and this sailing Pandar
Our doubtful hope, our convoy, and our bark.

Alarum. Enter ÆNEAS

ÆNEAS. How now, Prince Troilus! Wherefore not afield?

TROILUS. Because not there. This woman's answer sorts,
For womanish it is to be from thence.
What news, Æneas, from the field to-day?

ÆNEAS. That Paris is returned home, and hurt.

TROILUS. By whom, Æneas?

ÆNEAS. Troilus, by Menelaus.

TROILUS. Let Paris bleed: 'tis but a scar to scorn;
Paris is gor'd with Menelaus' horn. [*Alarum*]

ÆNEAS. Hark what good sport is out of town to-day!

TROILUS. Better at home, if 'would I might' were 'may.'

But to the sport abroad. Are you bound thither?
ÆNEAS. In all swift haste.
TROILUS. Come, go we then together. *Exeunt*

SCENE 2

Troy. A street

Enter CRESSIDA *and her man* ALEXANDER

CRESSIDA. Who were those went by?
ALEXANDER. Queen Hecuba and Helen.
CRESSIDA. And whither go they?
ALEXANDER. Up to the eastern tower,
Whose height commands as subject all the vale,
To see the battle. Hector, whose patience
Is as a virtue fix'd, to-day was mov'd.
He chid Andromache, and struck his armourer;
And, like as there were husbandry in war,
Before the sun rose he was harness'd light,
And to the field goes he; where every flower
Did as a prophet weep what it foresaw
In Hector's wrath.
CRESSIDA. What was his cause of anger?
ALEXANDER. The noise goes, this: there is among the Greeks
A lord of Troyan blood, nephew to Hector;
They call him Ajax.
CRESSIDA. Good; and what of him?
ALEXANDER. They say he is a very man per se,
And stands alone.
CRESSIDA. So do all men, unless they are drunk, sick, or have no legs.
ALEXANDER. This man, lady, hath robb'd many beasts of their particular additions: he is as valiant as a lion, churlish as the bear, slow as the elephant—a man into whom nature hath so crowded humours that his valour is crush'd into folly, his folly sauced with discretion. There is no man hath a virtue that he hath not a glimpse of, nor any man an attaint but he carries some stain of it; he is melancholy without cause and merry against the hair; he hath

the joints of every thing; but everything so out of joint that he is a gouty Briareus, many hands and no use, or purblind Argus, all eyes and no sight.

CRESSIDA. But how should this man, that makes me smile, make Hector angry?

ALEXANDER. They say he yesterday cop'd Hector in the battle and struck him down, the disdain and shame whereof hath ever since kept Hector fasting and waking.

Enter PANDARUS

CRESSIDA. Who comes here?

ALEXANDER. Madam, your uncle Pandarus.

CRESSIDA. Hector's a gallant man.

ALEXANDER. As may be in the world, lady.

PANDARUS. What's that? What's that?

CRESSIDA. Good morrow, uncle Pandarus.

PANDARUS. Good morrow, cousin Cressid. What do you talk of?—Good morrow, Alexander.—How do you, cousin? When were you at Ilium?

CRESSIDA. This morning, uncle.

PANDARUS. What were you talking of when I came? Was Hector arm'd and gone ere you came to Ilium? Helen was not up, was she?

CRESSIDA. Hector was gone; but Helen was not up.

PANDARUS. E'en so. Hector was stirring early.

CRESSIDA. That were we talking of, and of his anger.

PANDARUS. Was he angry?

CRESSIDA. So he says here.

PANDARUS. True, he was so; I know the cause too; he'll lay about him today, I can tell them that. And there's Troilus will not come far behind him; let them take heed of Troilus, I can tell them that too.

CRESSIDA. What, is he angry too?

PANDARUS. Who, Troilus? Troilus is the better man of the two.

CRESSIDA. O Jupiter! there's no comparison.

PANDARUS. What, not between Troilus and Hector? Do you know a man if you see him?

CRESSIDA. Ay, if I ever saw him before and knew him.

PANDARUS. Well, I say Troilus is Troilus.

CRESSIDA. Then you say as I say, for I am sure he is not Hector.

PANDARUS. No, nor Hector is not Troilus in some degrees.

CRESSIDA. 'Tis just to each of them: he is himself.

PANDARUS. Himself! Alas, poor Troilus! I would he were!

CRESSIDA. So he is.

PANDARUS. Condition I had gone barefoot to India.

CRESSIDA. He is not Hector.

PANDARUS. Himself! no, he's not himself. Would 'a were himself! Well, the gods are above; time must friend or end. Well, Troilus, well! I would my heart were in her body! No, Hector is not a better man than Troilus.

CRESSIDA. Excuse me.

PANDARUS. He is elder.

CRESSIDA. Pardon me, pardon me.

PANDARUS. Th' other's not come to't; you shall tell me another tale when th' other's come to't. Hector shall not have his wit this year.

CRESSIDA. He shall not need it if he have his own.

PANDARUS. Nor his qualities.

CRESSIDA. No matter.

PANDARUS. Nor his beauty.

CRESSIDA. 'Twould not become him: his own's better.

PANDARUS. You have no judgment, niece. Helen herself swore th' other day that Troilus, for a brown favour, for so 'tis, I must confess—not brown neither—

CRESSIDA. No, but brown.

PANDARUS. Faith, to say truth, brown and not brown.

CRESSIDA. To say the truth, true and not true.

PANDARUS. She prais'd his complexion above Paris.

CRESSIDA. Why, Paris hath colour enough.

PANDARUS. So he has.

CRESSIDA. Then Troilus should have too much. If she prais'd him above, his complexion is higher than his; he having colour enough, and the other higher, is too flaming a praise for a good complexion. I had as lief Helen's golden tongue had commended Troilus for a copper nose.

PANDARUS. I swear to you I think Helen loves him better than Paris.

CRESSIDA. Then she's a merry Greek indeed.

PANDARUS. Nay, I am sure she does. She came to him th' other day into the compass'd window—and you know he has not past three or four hairs on his chin—

CRESSIDA. Indeed a tapster's arithmetic may soon bring his particulars therein to a total.

PANDARUS. Why, he is very young, and yet will he within three pound lift as much as his brother Hector.

CRESSIDA. Is he so young a man and so old a lifter?

PANDARUS. But to prove to you that Helen loves him: she came and puts me her white hand to his cloven chin—

CRESSIDA. Juno have mercy! How came it cloven?

PANDARUS. Why, you know, 'tis dimpled. I think his smiling becomes him better than any man in all Phrygia.

CRESSIDA. O, he smiles valiantly!

PANDARUS. Does he not?

CRESSIDA. O yes, an 'twere a cloud in autumn!

PANDARUS. Why, go to, then! But to prove to you that Helen loves Troilus—

CRESSIDA. Troilus will stand to the proof, if you'll prove it so.

PANDARUS. Troilus! Why, he esteems her no more than I esteem an addle egg.

CRESSIDA. If you love an addle egg as well as you love an idle head, you would eat chickens i' th' shell.

PANDARUS. I cannot choose but laugh to think how she tickled his chin. Indeed, she has a marvell's white hand, I must needs confess.

CRESSIDA. Without the rack.

PANDARUS. And she takes upon her to spy a white hair on his chin.

CRESSIDA. Alas, poor chin! Many a wart is richer.

PANDARUS. But there was such laughing! Queen Hecuba laugh'd that her eyes ran o'er.

CRESSIDA. With millstones.

PANDARUS. And Cassandra laugh'd.

CRESSIDA. But there was a more temperate fire under the pot of her eyes. Did her eyes run o'er too?

PANDARUS. And Hector laugh'd.

CRESSIDA. At what was all this laughing?

PANDARUS. Marry, at the white hair that Helen spied on Troilus' chin.

CRESSIDA. An't had been a green hair I should have laugh'd too.

PANDARUS. They laugh'd not so much at the hair as at his pretty answer.

CRESSIDA. What was his answer?

PANDARUS. Quoth she 'Here's but two and fifty hairs on your chin, and one of them is white.'

CRESSIDA. This is her question.

PANDARUS. That's true; make no question of that. 'Two and fifty hairs,' quoth he 'and one white. That white hair is my father, and all the rest are his sons.' 'Jupiter!' quoth she 'which of these hairs is Paris my husband?' 'The forked one,' quoth he, 'pluck't out and give it him.' But there was such laughing! and Helen so blush'd, and Paris so chaf'd; and all the rest so laugh'd that it pass'd.

CRESSIDA. So let it now; for it has been a great while going by.

PANDARUS. Well, cousin, I told you a thing yesterday; think on't.

CRESSIDA. So I do.

PANDARUS. I'll be sworn 'tis true; he will weep you, and 'twere a man born in April.

CRESSIDA. And I'll spring up in his tears, an 'twere a nettle against May. [*Sound a retreat*]

PANDARUS. Hark! they are coming from the field. Shall we stand up here and see them as they pass toward Ilium? Good niece, do, sweet niece Cressida.

CRESSIDA. At your pleasure.

PANDARUS. Here, here, here's an excellent place; here we may see most bravely. I'll tell you them all by their names as they pass by; but mark Troilus above the rest.

ÆNEAS *passes*

CRESSIDA. Speak not so loud.

PANDARUS. That's Æneas. Is not that a brave man? He's one of the flowers of Troy, I can tell you. But mark Troilus; you shall see anon.

ANTENOR *passes*

CRESSIDA. Who's that?

PANDARUS. That's Antenor. He has a shrewd wit, I can tell you; and he's a man good enough; he's one o' th' soundest judgments in Troy, whosoever, and a proper man of person. When comes Troilus? I'll show you Troilus anon. If he see me, you shall see him nod at me.

CRESSIDA. Will he give you the nod?

PANDARUS. You shall see.

CRESSIDA. If he do, the rich shall have more.

HECTOR *passes*

PANDARUS. That's Hector, that, that, look you, that; there's a fellow! Go thy way, Hector! There's a brave man, niece. O brave Hector! Look how he looks. There's a countenance! Is't not a brave man?

CRESSIDA. O, a brave man!

PANDARUS. Is 'a not? It does a man's heart good. Look you what hacks are on his helmet! Look you yonder, do you see? Look you there. There's no jesting; there's laying on; take't off who will, as they say. There be hacks.

CRESSIDA. Be those with swords?

PANDARUS. Swords! anything, he cares not; an the devil come to him, it's all one. By God's lid, it does one's heart good. Yonder comes Paris, yonder comes Paris.

PARIS *passes*

Look ye yonder, niece; is't not a gallant man too, is't not? Why, this is brave now. Who said he came hurt home to-day? He's not hurt. Why, this will do Helen's heart good now, ha! Would I could see Troilus now! You shall see Troilus anon.

HELENUS *passes*

CRESSIDA. Who's that?

PANDARUS. That's Helenus. I marvel where Troilus is. That's Helenus. I think he went not forth to-day. That's Helenus.

CRESSIDA. Can Helenus fight, uncle?

PANDARUS. Helenus! no. Yes, he'll fight indifferent well. I marvel where Troilus is. Hark! do you not hear the people cry 'Troilus'? Helenus is a priest.

CRESSIDA. What sneaking fellow comes yonder?

TROILUS *passes*

PANDARUS. Where? yonder? That's Deiphobus. 'Tis Troilus. There's a man, niece. Hem! Brave Troilus, the prince of chivalry!

CRESSIDA. Peace, for shame, peace!

PANDARUS. Mark him; note him. O brave Troilus! Look well upon him, niece; look you how his sword is bloodied, and his helm more hack'd than Hector's; and how he looks, and how he goes! O admirable youth! he never saw three and twenty. Go thy way, Troilus, go thy way. Had I a sister were a grace or a daughter a goddess, he should take his choice. O admirable man! Paris? Paris is dirt to him; and, I warrant, Helen, to change, would give an eye to boot.

CRESSIDA. Here comes more.

Common soldiers pass

PANDARUS. Asses, fools, dolts! chaff and bran, chaff and bran! porridge after meat! I could live and die in the eyes of Troilus. Ne'er look, ne'er look; the eagles are gone. Crows and daws, crows and daws! I had rather be such a man as Troilus than Agamemnon and all Greece.

CRESSIDA. There is amongst the Greeks Achilles, a better man than Troilus.

PANDARUS. Achilles? A drayman, a porter, a very camel!

CRESSIDA. Well, well.

PANDARUS. Well, well! Why, have you any discretion? Have you any eyes? Do you know what a man is? Is not birth, beauty, good shape, discourse, manhood, learning, gentleness, virtue, youth, liberality, and such like, the spice and salt that season a man?

CRESSIDA. Ay, a minc'd man; and then to be bak'd with no date in the pie, for then the man's date is out.

PANDARUS. You are such a woman! A man knows not at what ward you lie.

CRESSIDA. Upon my back, to defend my belly; upon my wit, to defend my wiles; upon my secrecy, to defend mine honesty; my mask, to defend my beauty; and you, to defend all these; and at all these wards I lie at, at a thousand watches.

PANDARUS. Say one of your watches.

CRESSIDA. Nay, I'll watch you for that; and that's one of the chiefest of them too. If I cannot ward what I would not have hit, I can watch you for telling how I took the blow; unless it swell past hiding, and then it's past watching.

PANDARUS. You are such another!

Enter TROILUS' BOY

BOY. Sir, my lord would instantly speak with you.

PANDARUS. Where?

BOY. At your own house; there he unarms him.

PANDARUS. Good boy, tell him I come. *Exit* BOY
I doubt he be hurt. Fare ye well, good niece.

CRESSIDA. Adieu, uncle.

PANDARUS. I will be with you, niece, by and by.

CRESSIDA. To bring, uncle.

PANDARUS. Ay, a token from Troilus.

CRESSIDA. By the same token, you are a bawd.

Exit PANDARUS

Words, vows, gifts, tears, and love's full sacrifice,
He offers in another's enterprise;
But more in Troilus thousand-fold I see
Than in the glass of Pandar's praise may be,
Yet hold I off. Women are angels, wooing:
Things won are done; joy's soul lies in the doing.
That she belov'd knows nought that knows not this:
Men prize the thing ungain'd more than it is.
That she was never yet that ever knew
Love got so sweet as when desire did sue;
Therefore this maxim out of love I teach:
Achievement is command; ungain'd, beseech.
Then though my heart's content firm love doth bear,
Nothing of that shall from mine eyes appear. *Exit*

SCENE 3

The Grecian camp. Before AGAMEMNON'S *tent*

Sennet. Enter AGAMEMNON, NESTOR, ULYSSES, DIOMEDES, MENELAUS, *and others*

AGAMEMNON. Princes,
What grief hath set these jaundies o'er your cheeks?
The ample proposition that hope makes
In all designs begun on earth below
Fails in the promis'd largeness; checks and disasters
Grow in the veins of actions highest rear'd,
As knots, by the conflux of meeting sap,
Infects the sound pine, and diverts his grain
Tortive and errant from his course of growth.
Nor, princes, is it matter new to us
That we come short of our suppose so far
That after seven years' siege yet Troy walls stand;
Sith every action that hath gone before,
Whereof we have record, trial did draw
Bias and thwart, not answering the aim,
And that unbodied figure of the thought
That gave't surmised shape. Why then, you princes,
Do you with cheeks abash'd behold our works
And call them shames, which are, indeed, nought else
But the protractive trials of great Jove
To find persistive constancy in men;
The fineness of which metal is not found
In fortune's love? For then the bold and coward,
The wise and fool, the artist and unread,
The hard and soft, seem all affin'd and kin.
But in the wind and tempest of her frown
Distinction, with a broad and powerful fan,
Puffing at all, winnows the light away;
And what hath mass or matter by itself
Lies rich in virtue and unmingled.

NESTOR. With due observance of thy godlike seat,
Great Agamemnon, Nestor shall apply
Thy latest words. In the reproof of chance

Lies the true proof of men. The sea being smooth,
How many shallow bauble boats dare sail
Upon her patient breast, making their way
With those of nobler bulk!
But let the ruffian Boreas once enrage
The gentle Thetis, and anon behold
The strong-ribb'd bark through liquid mountains cut,
Bounding between the two moist elements
Like Perseus' horse. Where's then the saucy boat,
Whose weak untimber'd sides but even now
Co-rivall'd greatness? Either to harbour fled
Or made a toast for Neptune. Even so
Doth valour's show and valour's worth divide
In storms of fortune; for in her ray and brightness
The herd hath more annoyance by the breeze
Than by the tiger; but when the splitting wind
Makes flexible the knees of knotted oaks,
And flies fled under shade—why, then the thing of courage,
As rous'd with rage, with rage doth sympathise,
And with an accent tun'd in self-same key
Retorts to chiding fortune.

ULYSSES. Agamemnon,
Thou great commander, nerve and bone of Greece,
Heart of our numbers, soul and only spirit
In whom the tempers and the minds of all
Should be shut up—hear what Ulysses speaks.
Besides the applause and approbation
The which, [*To* AGAMEMNON] most mighty, for thy place and sway,
[*To* NESTOR] And, thou most reverend, for thy stretch'd-out life,
I give to both your speeches—which were such
As Agamemnon and the hand of Greece
Should hold up high in brass; and such again
As venerable Nestor, hatch'd in silver,
Should with a bond of air, strong as the axle-tree
On which heaven rides, knit all the Greekish ears
To his experienc'd tongue—yet let it please both,
Thou great, and wise, to hear Ulysses speak.

AGAMEMNON. Speak, Prince of Ithaca; and be't of less expect
That matter needless, of importless burden,
Divide thy lips than we are confident,
When rank Thersites opes his mastic jaws,
We shall hear music, wit, and oracle.
ULYSSES. Troy, yet upon his basis, had been down,
And the great Hector's sword had lack'd a master,
But for these instances:
The specialty of rule hath been neglected;
And look how many Grecian tents do stand
Hollow upon this plain, so many hollow factions.
When that the general is not like the hive,
To whom the foragers shall all repair,
What honey is expected? Degree being vizarded,
Th' unworthiest shows as fairly in the mask.
The heavens themselves, the planets, and this centre,
Observe degree, priority, and place,
Insisture, course, proportion, season, form,
Office, and custom, in all line of order;
And therefore is the glorious planet Sol
In noble eminence enthron'd and spher'd
Amidst the other, whose med'cinable eye
Corrects the ill aspects of planets evil,
And posts, like the commandment of a king,
Sans check, to good and bad. But when the planets
In evil mixture to disorder wander,
What plagues and what portents, what mutiny,
What raging of the sea, shaking of earth,
Commotion in the winds! Frights, changes, horrors,
Divert and crack, rend and deracinate,
The unity and married calm of states
Quite from their fixture! O, when degree is shak'd,
Which is the ladder of all high designs,
The enterprise is sick! How could communities,
Degrees in schools, and brotherhoods in cities,
Peaceful commerce from dividable shores,
The primogenity and due of birth,
Prerogative of age, crowns, sceptres, laurels,
But by degree, stand in authentic place?

Take but degree away, untune that string,
And hark what discord follows! Each thing melts
In mere oppugnancy: the bounded waters
Should lift their bosoms higher than the shores,
And make a sop of all this solid globe;
Strength should be lord of imbecility,
And the rude son should strike his father dead;
Force should be right; or, rather, right and wrong—
Between whose endless jar justice resides—
Should lose their names, and so should justice too.
Then everything includes itself in power,
Power into will, will into appetite;
And appetite, an universal wolf,
So doubly seconded with will and power,
Must make perforce an universal prey,
And last eat up himself. Great Agamemnon,
This chaos, when degree is suffocate,
Follows the choking.
And this neglection of degree it is
That by a pace goes backward, with a purpose
It hath to climb. The general's disdain'd
By him one step below, he by the next,
That next by him beneath; so ever step,
Exampl'd by the first pace that is sick
Of his superior, grows to an envious fever
Of pale and bloodless emulation.
And 'tis this fever that keeps Troy on foot,
Not her own sinews. To end a tale of length,
Troy in our weakness stands, not in her strength.

NESTOR. Most wisely hath Ulysses here discover'd
The fever whereof all our power is sick.

AGAMEMNON. The nature of the sickness found, Ulysses,
What is the remedy?

ULYSSES. The great Achilles, whom opinion crowns
The sinew and the forehand of our host,
Having his ear full of his airy fame,
Grows dainty of his worth, and in his tent
Lies mocking our designs; with him Patroclus
Upon a lazy bed the livelong day
Breaks scurril jests;

And with ridiculous and awkward action–
Which, slanderer, he imitation calls–
He pageants us. Sometime, great Agamemnon,
Thy topless deputation he puts on;
And like a strutting player whose conceit
Lies in his hamstring, and doth think it rich
To hear the wooden dialogue and sound
'Twixt his stretch'd footing and the scaffoldage–
Such to-be-pitied and o'er-wrested seeming
He acts thy greatness in; and when he speaks
'Tis like a chime a-mending; with terms unsquar'd,
Which, from the tongue of roaring Typhon dropp'd,
Would seem hyperboles. At this fusty stuff
The large Achilles, on his press'd bed lolling,
From his deep chest laughs out a loud applause;
Cries 'Excellent! 'tis Agamemnon just.
Now play me Nestor; hem, and stroke thy beard,
As he being drest to some oration.'
That's done–as near as the extremest ends
Of parallels, as like Vulcan and his wife;
Yet god Achilles still cries 'Excellent!
'Tis Nestor right. Now play him me, Patroclus,
Arming to answer in a night alarm.'
And then, forsooth, the faint defects of age
Must be the scene of mirth: to cough and spit
And, with a palsy-fumbling on his gorget,
Shake in and out the rivet. And at this sport
Sir Valour dies; cries 'O, enough, Patroclus;
Or give me ribs of steel! I shall split all
In pleasure of my spleen.' And in this fashion
All our abilities, gifts, natures, shapes,
Severals and generals of grace exact,
Achievements, plots, orders, preventions,
Excitements to the field or speech for truce,
Success or loss, what is or is not, serves
As stuff for these two to make paradoxes.

NESTOR. And in the imitation of these twain–
Who, as Ulysses says, opinion crowns
With an imperial voice–many are infect.
Ajax is grown self-will'd and bears his head

In such a rein, in full as proud a place
As broad Achilles; keeps his tent like him;
Makes factious feasts; rails on our state of war
Bold as an oracle, and sets Thersites,
A slave whose gall coins slanders like a mint,
To match us in comparisons with dirt,
To weaken and discredit our exposure,
How rank soever rounded in with danger.

ULYSSES. They tax our policy and call it cowardice,
Count wisdom as no member of the war,
Forestall prescience, and esteem no act
But that of hand. The still and mental parts
That do contrive how many hands shall strike
When fitness calls them on, and know, by measure
Of their observant toil, the enemies' weight—
Why, this hath not a finger's dignity:
They call this bed-work, mapp'ry, closet-war;
So that the ram that batters down the wall,
For the great swinge and rudeness of his poise,
They place before his hand that made the engine,
Or those that with the fineness of their souls
By reason guide his execution.

NESTOR. Let this be granted, and Achilles' horse
Makes many Thetis' sons. [*Tucket*]

AGAMEMNON. What trumpet? Look, Menelaus.

MENELAUS. From Troy.

Enter ÆNEAS

AGAMEMNON. What would you fore our tent?

ÆNEAS. Is this great Agamemnon's tent, I pray you?

AGAMEMNON. Even this.

ÆNEAS. May one that is a herald and a prince
Do a fair message to his kingly eyes?

AGAMEMNON. With surety stronger than Achilles' arm
Fore all the Greekish heads, which with one voice
Call Agamemnon head and general.

ÆNEAS. Fair leave and large security. How may
A stranger to those most imperial looks
Know them from eyes of other mortals?

AGAMEMNON. How?

ÆNEAS. Ay;
I ask, that I might waken reverence,
And bid the cheek be ready with a blush
Modest as Morning when she coldly eyes
The youthful Phœbus.
Which is that god in office, guiding men?
Which is the high and mighty Agamemnon?
AGAMEMNON. This Troyan scorns us, or the men of Troy
Are ceremonious courtiers.
ÆNEAS. Courtiers as free, as debonair, unarm'd,
As bending angels; that's their fame in peace.
But when they would seem soldiers, they have galls,
Good arms, strong joints, true swords; and, Jove's accord,
Nothing so full of heart. But peace, Æneas,
Peace, Troyan; lay thy finger on thy lips.
The worthiness of praise distains his worth,
If that the prais'd himself bring the praise forth;
But what the repining enemy commends,
That breath fame blows; that praise, sole pure, transcends.
AGAMEMNON. Sir, you of Troy, call you yourself Æneas?
ÆNEAS. Ay, Greek, that is my name.
AGAMEMNON. What's your affair, I pray you?
ÆNEAS. Sir, pardon; 'tis for Agamemnon's ears.
AGAMEMNON. He hears nought privately that comes from Troy.
ÆNEAS. Nor I from Troy come not to whisper with him;
I bring a trumpet to awake his ear,
To set his sense on the attentive bent,
And then to speak.
AGAMEMNON. Speak frankly as the wind;
It is not Agamemnon's sleeping hour.
That thou shalt know, Troyan, he is awake,
He tells thee so himself.
ÆNEAS. Trumpet, blow loud,
Send thy brass voice through all these lazy tents;
And every Greek of mettle, let him know
What Troy means fairly shall be spoke aloud.
[*Sound trumpet*]
We have, great Agamemnon, here in Troy
A prince called Hector—Priam is his father—

Who in this dull and long-continued truce
Is resty grown; he bade me take a trumpet
And to this purpose speak: Kings, princes, lords!
If there be one among the fair'st of Greece
That holds his honour higher than his ease,
That seeks his praise more than he fears his peril,
That knows his valour and knows not his fear,
That loves his mistress more than in confession
With truant vows to her own lips he loves,
And dare avow her beauty and her worth
In other arms than hers—to him this challenge.
Hector, in view of Troyans and of Greeks,
Shall make it good or do his best to do it:
He hath a lady wiser, fairer, truer,
Than ever Greek did couple in his arms;
And will to-morrow with his trumpet call
Mid-way between your tents and walls of Troy
To rouse a Grecian that is true in love.
If any come, Hector shall honour him;
If none, he'll say in Troy, when he retires,
The Grecian dames are sunburnt and not worth
The splinter of a lance. Even so much.

AGAMEMNON. This shall be told our lovers, Lord Æneas.
If none of them have soul in such a kind,
We left them all at home. But we are soldiers;
And may that soldier a mere recreant prove
That means not, hath not, or is not in love.
If then one is, or hath, or means to be,
That one meets Hector; if none else, I am he.

NESTOR. Tell him of Nestor, one that was a man
When Hector's grandsire suck'd. He is old now;
But if there be not in our Grecian mould
One noble man that hath one spark of fire
To answer for his love, tell him from me
I'll hide my silver beard in a gold beaver,
And in my vantbrace put this wither'd brawn,
And, meeting him, will tell him that my lady
Was fairer than his grandame, and as chaste
As may be in the world. His youth in flood,
I'll prove this truth with my three drops of blood.

ÆNEAS. Now heavens forfend such scarcity of youth!
ULYSSES. Amen.
AGAMEMNON. Fair Lord Æneas, let me touch your hand;
To our pavilion shall I lead you, first.
Achilles shall have word of this intent;
So shall each lord of Greece, from tent to tent.
Yourself shall feast with us before you go,
And find the welcome of a noble foe.

Exeunt all but ULYSSES *and* NESTOR

ULYSSES. Nestor!
NESTOR. What says Ulysses?
ULYSSES. I have a young conception in my brain;
Be you my time to bring it to some shape.
NESTOR. What is't?
ULYSSES. This 'tis:
Blunt wedges rive hard knots. The seeded pride
That hath to this maturity blown up
In rank Achilles must or now be cropp'd
Or, shedding, breed a nursery of like evil
To overbulk us all.
NESTOR. Well, and how?
ULYSSES. This challenge that the gallant Hector sends,
However it is spread in general name,
Relates in purpose only to Achilles.
NESTOR. True. The purpose is perspicuous even as substance
Whose grossness little characters sum up;
And, in the publication, make no strain
But that Achilles, were his brain as barren
As banks of Libya–though, Apollo knows,
'Tis dry enough–will with great speed of judgment,
Ay, with celerity, find Hector's purpose
Pointing on him.
ULYSSES. And wake him to the answer, think you?
NESTOR. Why, 'tis most meet. Who may you else oppose
That can from Hector bring those honours off,
If not Achilles? Though't be a sportful combat,
Yet in this trial much opinion dwells;
For here the Troyans taste our dear'st repute
With their fin'st palate; and trust to me, Ulysses,
Our imputation shall be oddly pois'd

In this vile action; for the success,
Although particular, shall give a scantling
Of good or bad unto the general;
And in such indexes, although small pricks
To their subsequent volumes, there is seen
The baby figure of the giant mass
Of things to come at large. It is suppos'd
He that meets Hector issues from our choice;
And choice, being mutual act of all our souls,
Makes merit her election, and doth boil,
As 'twere from forth us all, a man distill'd
Out of our virtues; who miscarrying,
What heart receives from hence a conquering part,
To steel a strong opinion to themselves?
Which entertain'd, limbs are his instruments,
In no less working than are swords and bows
Directive by the limbs.

ULYSSES. Give pardon to my speech.
Therefore 'tis meet Achilles meet not Hector.
Let us, like merchants, show our foulest wares
And think perchance they'll sell; if not, the lustre
Of the better yet to show shall show the better,
By showing the worst first. Do not consent
That ever Hector and Achilles meet;
For both our honour and our shame in this
Are dogg'd with two strange followers.

NESTOR. I see them not with my old eyes. What are they?

ULYSSES. What glory our Achilles shares from Hector,
Were he not proud, we all should wear with him;
But he already is too insolent;
And it were better parch in Afric sun
Than in the pride and salt scorn of his eyes,
Should he scape Hector fair. If he were foil'd,
Why, then we do our main opinion crush
In taint of our best man. No, make a lott'ry;
And, by device, let blockish Ajax draw
The sort to fight with Hector. Among ourselves
Give him allowance for the better man;
For that will physic the great Myrmidon,
Who broils in loud applause, and make him fall

His crest, that prouder than blue Iris bends.
If the dull brainless Ajax come safe off,
We'll dress him up in voices; if he fail,
Yet go we under our opinion still
That we have better men. But, hit or miss,
Our project's life this shape of sense assumes—
Ajax employ'd plucks down Achilles' plumes.

NESTOR. Now, Ulysses, I begin to relish thy advice;
And I will give a taste thereof forthwith
To Agamemnon. Go we to him straight.
Two curs shall tame each other: pride alone
Must tarre the mastiffs on, as 'twere their bone. *Exeunt*

ACT II. SCENE 1

The Grecian camp

Enter AJAX *and* THERSITES

AJAX. Thersites!

THERSITES. Agamemnon—how if he had boils full, all over, generally?

AJAX. Thersites!

THERSITES. And those boils did run—say so. Did not the general run then? Were not that a botchy core?

AJAX. Dog!

THERSITES. Then there would come some matter from him; I see none now.

AJAX. Thou bitch-wolf's son, canst thou not hear? Feel, then. [*Strikes him*]

THERSITES. The plague of Greece upon thee, thou mongrel beef-witted lord!

AJAX. Speak, then, thou whinid'st leaven, speak. I will beat thee into handsomeness.

THERSITES. I shall sooner rail thee into wit and holiness; but I think thy horse will sooner con an oration than thou learn a prayer without book. Thou canst strike, canst thou? A red murrain o' thy jade's tricks!

AJAX. Toadstool, learn me the proclamation.

THERSITES. Dost thou think I have no sense, thou strikest me thus?

AJAX. The proclamation!

THERSITES. Thou art proclaim'd, a fool, I think.

AJAX. Do not, porpentine, do not; my fingers itch.

THERSITES. I would thou didst itch from head to foot and I had the scratching of thee; I would make thee the loathsomest scab in Greece. When thou art forth in the incursions, thou strikest as slow as another.

AJAX. I say, the proclamation.

THERSITES. Thou grumblest and railest every hour on Achilles; and thou art as full of envy at his greatness as Cerberus is at Proserpina's beauty—ay, that thou bark'st at him.

AJAX. Mistress Thersites!

THERSITES. Thou shouldst strike him.

AJAX. Cobloaf!

THERSITES. He would pun thee into shivers with his fist, as a sailor breaks a biscuit.

AJAX. You whoreson cur! [*Strikes him*]

THERSITES. Do, do.

AJAX. Thou stool for a witch!

THERSITES. Ay, do, do; thou sodden-witted lord! Thou hast no more brain than I have in mine elbows; an assinico may tutor thee. You scurvy valiant ass! Thou art here but to thrash Troyans, and thou art bought and sold among those of any wit like a barbarian slave. If thou use to beat me, I will begin at thy heel and tell what thou art by inches, thou thing of no bowels, thou!

AJAX. You dog!

THERSITES. You scurvy lord!

AJAX. You cur! [*Strikes him*]

THERSITES. Mars his idiot! Do, rudeness; do, camel; do, do.

Enter ACHILLES *and* PATROCLUS

ACHILLES. Why, how now, Ajax! Wherefore do you thus?
How now, Thersites! What's the matter, man?

THERSITES. You see him there, do you?

ACHILLES. Ay; what's the matter?

THERSITES. Nay, look upon him.

ACHILLES. So I do. What's the matter?

THERSITES. Nay, but regard him well.

ACHILLES. Well! why, so I do.

THERSITES. But yet you look not well upon him; for who some ever you take him to be, he is Ajax.

ACHILLES. I know that, fool.

THERSITES. Ay, but that fool knows not himself.

AJAX. Therefore I beat thee.

THERSITES. Lo, lo, lo, lo, what modicums of wit he utters! His evasions have ears thus long. I have bobb'd his brain more than he has beat my bones. I will buy nine sparrows for a penny, and his pia mater is not worth the ninth part of a sparrow. This lord, Achilles, Ajax—who wears his wit in his belly and his guts in his head—I'll tell you what I say of him.

ACHILLES. What?

THERSITES. I say this Ajax— [AJAX *offers to strike him*]

ACHILLES. Nay, good Ajax.

THERSITES. Has not so much wit—

ACHILLES. Nay, I must hold you.

THERSITES. As will stop the eye of Helen's needle, for whom he comes to fight.

ACHILLES. Peace, fool.

THERSITES. I would have peace and quietness, but the fool will not—he there; that he; look you there.

AJAX. O thou damned cur! I shall—

ACHILLES. Will you set your wit to a fool's?

THERSITES. No, I warrant you, the fool's will shame it.

PATROCLUS. Good words, Thersites.

ACHILLES. What's the quarrel?

AJAX. I bade the vile owl go learn me the tenour of the proclamation, and he rails upon me.

THERSITES. I serve thee not.

AJAX. Well, go to, go to.

THERSITES. I serve here voluntary.

ACHILLES. Your last service was suff'rance; 'twas not voluntary. No man is beaten voluntary. Ajax was here the voluntary, and you as under an impress.

THERSITES. E'en so; a great deal of your wit too lies in your sinews, or else there be liars. Hector shall have a great catch an he knock out either of your brains: 'a were as good crack a fusty nut with no kernel.

ACHILLES. What, with me too, Thersites?

THERSITES. There's Ulysses and old Nestor—whose wit was mouldy ere your grandsires had nails on their toes—yoke you like draught oxen, and make you plough up the wars.

ACHILLES. What, what?

THERSITES. Yes, good sooth. To Achilles, to Ajax, to—

AJAX. I shall cut out your tongue.

THERSITES. 'Tis no matter; I shall speak as much as thou afterwards.

PATROCLUS. No more words, Thersites; peace!

THERSITES. I will hold my peace when Achilles' brach bids me, shall I?

ACHILLES. There's for you, Patroclus.

THERSITES. I will see you hang'd like clotpoles ere I come any more to your tents. I will keep where there is wit stirring, and leave the faction of fools. *Exit*

PATROCLUS. A good riddance.

ACHILLES. Marry, this, sir, is proclaim'd through all our host,
That Hector, by the fifth hour of the sun,
Will with a trumpet 'twixt our tents and Troy,
To-morrow morning, call some knight to arms
That hath a stomach; and such a one that dare
Maintain I know not what; 'tis trash. Farewell.

AJAX. Farewell. Who shall answer him?

ACHILLES. I know not; 'tis put to lott'ry. Otherwise
He knew his man.

AJAX. O, meaning you! I will go learn more of it. *Exeunt*

SCENE 2

Troy. PRIAM'S *palace*

Enter PRIAM, HECTOR, TROILUS, PARIS, *and* HELENUS

PRIAM. After so many hours, lives, speeches, spent,
Thus once again says Nestor from the Greeks:
'Deliver Helen, and all damage else—

As honour, loss of time, travail, expense,
Wounds, friends, and what else dear that is consum'd
In hot digestion of this cormorant war–
Shall be struck off.' Hector, what say you to't?

HECTOR. Though no man lesser fears the Greeks than I,
As far as toucheth my particular,
Yet, dread Priam,
There is no lady of more softer bowels,
More spongy to suck in the sense of fear,
More ready to cry out 'Who knows what follows?'
Than Hector is. The wound of peace is surety,
Surety secure; but modest doubt is call'd
The beacon of the wise, the tent that searches
To th' bottom of the worst. Let Helen go.
Since the first sword was drawn about this question,
Every tithe soul 'mongst many thousand dismes
Hath been as dear as Helen–I mean, of ours.
If we have lost so many tenths of ours
To guard a thing not ours, nor worth to us,
Had it our name, the value of one ten,
What merit's in that reason which denies
The yielding of her up?

TROILUS. Fie, fie, my brother!
Weigh you the worth and honour of a king,
So great as our dread father's, in a scale
Of common ounces? Will you with counters sum
The past-proportion of his infinite,
And buckle in a waist most fathomless
With spans and inches so diminutive
As fears and reasons? Fie, for godly shame!

HELENUS. No marvel though you bite so sharp at reasons,
You are so empty of them. Should not our father
Bear the great sway of his affairs with reasons,
Because your speech hath none that tells him so?

TROILUS. You are for dreams and slumbers, brother priest;
You fur your gloves with reason. Here are your reasons:
You know an enemy intends you harm;
You know a sword employ'd is perilous,
And reason flies the object of all harm.
Who marvels, then, when Helenus beholds

A Grecian and his sword, if he do set
The very wings of reason to his heels
And fly like chidden Mercury from Jove,
Or like a star disorb'd? Nay, if we talk of reason,
Let's shut our gates and sleep. Manhood and honour
Should have hare hearts, would they but fat their thoughts
With this cramm'd reason. Reason and respect
Make livers pale and lustihood deject.

HECTOR. Brother, she is not worth what she doth cost
The keeping.

TROILUS. What's aught but as 'tis valued?

HECTOR. But value dwells not in particular will:
It holds his estimate and dignity
As well wherein 'tis precious of itself
As in the prizer. 'Tis mad idolatry
To make the service greater than the god;
And the will dotes that is attributive
To what infectiously itself affects,
Without some image of th' affected merit.

TROILUS. I take to-day a wife, and my election
Is led on in the conduct of my will;
My will enkindled by mine eyes and ears,
Two traded pilots 'twixt the dangerous shores
Of will and judgment: how may I avoid,
Although my will distaste what it elected,
The wife I chose? There can be no evasion
To blench from this and to stand firm by honour.
We turn not back the silks upon the merchant
When we have soil'd them; nor the remainder viands
We do not throw in unrespective sieve,
Because we now are full. It was thought meet
Paris should do some vengeance on the Greeks;
Your breath with full consent bellied his sails;
The seas and winds, old wranglers, took a truce,
And did him service. He touch'd the ports desir'd;
And for an old aunt whom the Greeks held captive
He brought a Grecian queen, whose youth and freshness
Wrinkles Apollo's, and makes stale the morning.
Why keep we her? The Grecians keep our aunt.
Is she worth keeping? Why, she is a pearl

Whose price hath launch'd above a thousand ships,
And turn'd crown'd kings to merchants.
If you'll avouch 'twas wisdom Paris went–
As you must needs, for you all cried 'Go, go'–
If you'll confess he brought home worthy prize–
As you must needs, for you all clapp'd your hands,
And cried 'Inestimable!'–why do you now
The issue of your proper wisdoms rate,
And do a deed that never fortune did–
Beggar the estimation which you priz'd
Richer than sea and land? O theft most base,
That we have stol'n what we do fear to keep!
But thieves unworthy of a thing so stol'n
That in their country did them that disgrace
We fear to warrant in our native place!

CASSANDRA. [*Within*] Cry, Troyans, cry.

PRIAM. What noise, what shriek is this?

TROILUS. 'Tis our mad sister; I do know her voice.

CASSANDRA. [*Within*] Cry, Troyans.

HECTOR. It is Cassandra.

Enter CASSANDRA, *raving*

CASSANDRA. Cry, Troyans, cry. Lend me ten thousand eyes,
And I will fill them with prophetic tears.

HECTOR. Peace, sister, peace.

CASSANDRA. Virgins and boys, mid-age and wrinkled eld,
Soft infancy, that nothing canst but cry,
Add to my clamours. Let us pay betimes
A moiety of that mass of moan to come.
Cry, Troyans, cry. Practise your eyes with tears.
Troy must not be, nor goodly Ilion stand;
Our firebrand brother, Paris, burns us all.
Cry, Troyans, cry, A Helen and a woe!
Cry, cry. Troy burns, or else let Helen go. *Exit*

HECTOR. Now, youthful Troilus, do not these high strains
Of divination in our sister work
Some touches of remorse, or is your blood
So madly hot that no discourse of reason,
Nor fear of bad success in a bad cause,
Can qualify the same?

TROILUS. Why, brother Hector,
We may not think the justness of each act
Such and no other than event doth form it;
Nor once deject the courage of our minds
Because Cassandra's mad. Her brain-sick raptures
Cannot distaste the goodness of a quarrel
Which hath our several honours all engag'd
To make it gracious. For my private part,
I am no more touch'd than all Priam's sons;
And Jove forbid there should be done amongst us
Such things as might offend the weakest spleen
To fight for and maintain.

PARIS. Else might the world convince of levity
As well my undertakings as your counsels;
But I attest the gods, your full consent
Gave wings to my propension, and cut off
All fears attending on so dire a project.
For what, alas, can these my single arms?
What propugnation is in one man's valour
To stand the push and enmity of those
This quarrel would excite? Yet, I protest,
Were I alone to pass the difficulties,
And had as ample power as I have will,
Paris should ne'er retract what he hath done
Nor faint in the pursuit.

PRIAM. Paris, you speak
Like one besotted on your sweet delights.
You have the honey still, but these the gall;
So to be valiant is no praise at all.

PARIS. Sir, I propose not merely to myself
The pleasures such a beauty brings with it;
But I would have the soil of her fair rape
Wip'd off in honourable keeping her.
What treason were it to the ransack'd queen,
Disgrace to your great worths, and shame to me,
Now to deliver her possession up
On terms of base compulsion! Can it be
That so degenerate a strain as this
Should once set footing in your generous bosoms?
There's not the meanest spirit on our party

Without a heart to dare or sword to draw
When Helen is defended; nor none so noble
Whose life were ill bestow'd or death unfam'd
Where Helen is the subject. Then, I say,
Well may we fight for her whom we know well
The world's large spaces cannot parallel.

HECTOR. Paris and Troilus, you have both said well;
And on the cause and question now in hand
Have gloz'd, but superficially; not much
Unlike young men, whom Aristotle thought
Unfit to hear moral philosophy.
The reasons you allege do more conduce
To the hot passion of distemp'red blood
Than to make up a free determination
'Twixt right and wrong; for pleasure and revenge
Have ears more deaf than adders to the voice
Of any true decision. Nature craves
All dues be rend'red to their owners. Now,
What nearer debt in all humanity
Than wife is to the husband? If this law
Of nature be corrupted through affection;
And that great minds, of partial indulgence
To their benumbed wills, resist the same;
There is a law in each well-order'd nation
To curb those raging appetites that are
Most disobedient and refractory.
If Helen, then, be wife to Sparta's king—
As it is known she is—these moral laws
Of nature and of nations speak aloud
To have her back return'd. Thus to persist
In doing wrong extenuates not wrong,
But makes it much more heavy. Hector's opinion
Is this, in way of truth. Yet, ne'er the less,
My spritely brethren, I propend to you
In resolution to keep Helen still;
For 'tis a cause that hath no mean dependence
Upon our joint and several dignities.

TROILUS. Why, there you touch'd the life of our design.
Were it not glory that we more affected
Than the performance of our heaving spleens,

I would not wish a drop of Troyan blood
Spent more in her defence. But, worthy Hector,
She is a theme of honour and renown,
A spur to valiant and magnanimous deeds,
Whose present courage may beat down our foes,
And fame in time to come canonize us;
For I presume brave Hector would not lose
So rich advantage of a promis'd glory
As smiles upon the forehead of this action
For the wide world's revenue.

HECTOR. I am yours,
You valiant offspring of great Priamus.
I have a roisting challenge sent amongst
The dull and factious nobles of the Greeks
Will strike amazement to their drowsy spirits.
I was advertis'd their great general slept,
Whilst emulation in the army crept.
This, I presume, will wake him. *Exeunt*

SCENE 3

The Grecian camp. Before the tent of ACHILLES

Enter THERSITES, *solus*

THERSITES. How now, Thersites! What, lost in the labyrinth of thy fury? Shall the elephant Ajax carry it thus? He beats me, and I rail at him. O worthy satisfaction! Would it were otherwise: that I could beat him, whilst he rail'd at me! 'Sfoot, I'll learn to conjure and raise devils, but I'll see some issue of my spiteful execrations. Then there's Achilles, a rare engineer! If Troy be not taken till these two undermine it, the walls will stand till they fall of themselves. O thou great thunder-darter of Olympus, forget that thou art Jove, the king of gods, and, Mercury, lose all the serpentine craft of thy caduceus, if ye take not that little little less-than-little wit from them that they have! which short-arm'd ignorance itself knows is so abundant scarce, it will not in circumvention deliver a fly from a spider without drawing their massy irons and cutting the web. After this, the vengeance on the whole camp! or, rather, the Neapolitan bone-ache! for that, methinks, is the curse depending on those that war for a placket. I have said my prayers; and devil Envy say 'Amen.' What ho! my Lord Achilles!

Enter PATROCLUS

PATROCLUS. Who's there? Thersites! Good Thersites, come in and rail.

THERSITES. If I could 'a rememb'red a gilt counterfeit, thou wouldst not have slipp'd out of my contemplation; but it is no matter; thyself upon thyself! The common curse of mankind, folly and ignorance, be thine in great revenue! Heaven bless thee from a tutor, and discipline come not near thee! Let thy blood be thy direction till thy death. Then if she that lays thee out says thou art a fair corse, I'll be sworn and sworn upon't she never shrouded any but lazars. Amen. Where's Achilles?

PATROCLUS. What, art thou devout? Wast thou in prayer?

THERSITES. Ay, the heavens hear me!

PATROCLUS. Amen.

Enter ACHILLES

ACHILLES. Who's there?

PATROCLUS. Thersites, my lord.

ACHILLES. Where, where? O, where? Art thou come? Why, my cheese, my digestion, why hast thou not served thyself in to my table so many meals? Come, what's Agamemnon?

THERSITES. Thy commander, Achilles. Then tell me, Patroclus, what's Achilles?

PATROCLUS. Thy lord, Thersites. Then tell me, I pray thee, what's Thersites?

THERSITES. Thy knower, Patroclus. Then tell me, Patroclus, what art thou?

PATROCLUS. Thou must tell that knowest.

ACHILLES. O, tell, tell!

THERSITES. I'll decline the whole question. Agamemnon commands Achilles; Achilles is my lord; I am Patroclus' knower; and Patroclus is a fool.

PATROCLUS. You rascal!

THERSITES. Peace, fool! I have not done.

ACHILLES. He is a privileg'd man. Proceed, Thersites.

THERSITES. Agamemnon is a fool; Achilles is a fool; Thersites is a fool; and, as aforesaid, Patroclus is a fool.

ACHILLES. Derive this; come.

THERSITES. Agamemnon is a fool to offer to command Achilles; Achilles is a fool to be commanded of Agamemnon; Thersites is a fool to serve such a fool; and this Patroclus is a fool positive.

PATROCLUS. Why am I a fool?

THERSITES. Make that demand of the Creator. It suffices me thou art. Look you, who comes here?

ACHILLES. Come, Patroclus, I'll speak with nobody. Come in with me, Thersites. *Exit*

THERSITES. Here is such patchery, such juggling, and such knavery. All the argument is a whore and a cuckold—a good quarrel to draw emulous factions and bleed to death upon. Now the dry serpigo on the subject, and war and lechery confound all! *Exit*

Enter AGAMEMNON, ULYSSES, NESTOR, DIOMEDES, AJAX, *and* CALCHAS

AGAMEMNON. Where is Achilles?

PATROCLUS. Within his tent; but ill-dispos'd, my lord.

AGAMEMNON. Let it be known to him that we are here.
He shent our messengers; and we lay by
Our appertainings, visiting of him.
Let him be told so; lest, perchance, he think
We dare not move the question of our place
Or know not what we are.

PATROCLUS. I shall say so to him. *Exit*

ULYSSES. We saw him at the opening of his tent.
He is not sick.

AJAX. Yes, lion-sick, sick of proud heart. You may call it melancholy, if you will favour the man; but, by my head, 'tis pride. But why, why? Let him show us a cause. A word, my lord. [*Takes* AGAMEMNON *aside*]

NESTOR. What moves Ajax thus to bay at him?

ULYSSES. Achilles hath inveigled his fool from him.

NESTOR. Who, Thersites?

ULYSSES. He.

NESTOR. Then will Ajax lack matter, if he have lost his argument.

ULYSSES. No; you see he is his argument that has his argument—Achilles.

NESTOR. All the better; their fraction is more our wish than their faction. But it was a strong composure a fool could disunite!

ULYSSES. The amity that wisdom knits not, folly may easily untie.

Re-enter PATROCLUS

Here comes Patroclus.

NESTOR. No Achilles with him.

ULYSSES. The elephant hath joints, but none for courtesy; his legs are legs for necessity, not for flexure.

PATROCLUS. Achilles bids me say he is much sorry
If any thing more than your sport and pleasure
Did move your greatness and this noble state
To call upon him; he hopes it is no other
But for your health and your digestion sake,
An after-dinner's breath.

AGAMEMNON. Hear you, Patroclus.
We are too well acquainted with these answers;
But his evasion, wing'd thus swift with scorn,
Cannot outfly our apprehensions.
Much attribute he hath, and much the reason
Why we ascribe it to him. Yet all his virtues,
Not virtuously on his own part beheld,
Do in our eyes begin to lose their gloss;
Yea, like fair fruit in an unwholesome dish,
Are like to rot untasted. Go and tell him
We come to speak with him; and you shall not sin
If you do say we think him over-proud
And under-honest, in self-assumption greater
Than in the note of judgment; and worthier than himself
Here tend the savage strangeness he puts on,
Disguise the holy strength of their command,
And underwrite in an observing kind

His humorous predominance; yea, watch
His pettish lunes, his ebbs, his flows, as if
The passage and whole carriage of this action
Rode on his tide. Go tell him this, and add
That if he overhold his price so much
We'll none of him, but let him, like an engine
Not portable, lie under this report:
Bring action hither; this cannot go to war.
A stirring dwarf we do allowance give
Before a sleeping giant. Tell him so.

PATROCLUS. I shall, and bring his answer presently. *Exit*

AGAMEMNON. In second voice we'll not be satisfied;
We come to speak with him. Ulysses, enter you.

Exit ULYSSES

AJAX. What is he more than another?

AGAMEMNON. No more than what he thinks he is.

AJAX. Is he so much? Do you not think he thinks himself a better man than I am?

AGAMEMNON. No question.

AJAX. Will you subscribe his thought and say he is?

AGAMEMNON. No, noble Ajax; you are as strong, as valiant, as wise, no less noble, much more gentle, and altogether more tractable.

AJAX. Why should a man be proud? How doth pride grow? I know not what pride is.

AGAMEMNON. Your mind is the clearer, Ajax, and your virtues the fairer. He that is proud eats up himself. Pride is his own glass, his own trumpet, his own chronicle; and whatever praises itself but in the deed devours the deed in the praise.

Re-enter ULYSSES

AJAX. I do hate a proud man as I do hate the engend'ring of toads.

NESTOR. [*Aside*] And yet he loves himself: is't not strange?

ULYSSES. Achilles will not to the field to-morrow.

AGAMEMNON. What's his excuse?

ULYSSES. He doth rely on none;
But carries on the stream of his dispose,
Without observance or respect of any,

In will peculiar and in self-admission.

AGAMEMNON. Why will he not, upon our fair request,
Untent his person and share the air with us?

ULYSSES. Things small as nothing, for request's sake only,
He makes important; possess'd he is with greatness,
And speaks not to himself but with a pride
That quarrels at self-breath. Imagin'd worth
Holds in his blood such swol'n and hot discourse
That 'twixt his mental and his active parts
Kingdom'd Achilles in commotion rages,
And batters down himself. What should I say?
He is so plaguy proud that the death tokens of it
Cry 'No recovery.'

AGAMEMNON. Let Ajax go to him.
Dear lord, go you and greet him in his tent.
'Tis said he holds you well; and will be led
At your request a little from himself.

ULYSSES. O Agamemnon, let it not be so!
We'll consecrate the steps that Ajax makes
When they go from Achilles. Shall the proud lord
That bastes his arrogance with his own seam
And never suffers matter of the world
Enter his thoughts, save such as doth revolve
And ruminate himself—shall he be worshipp'd
Of that we hold an idol more than he?
No, this thrice-worthy and right valiant lord
Shall not so stale his palm, nobly acquir'd,
Nor, by my will, assubjugate his merit,
As amply titled as Achilles is,
By going to Achilles.
That were to enlard his fat-already pride,
And add more coals to Cancer when he burns
With entertaining great Hyperion.
This lord go to him! Jupiter forbid,
And say in thunder 'Achilles go to him.'

NESTOR. [*Aside*] O, this is well! He rubs the vein of him.

DIOMEDES. [*Aside*] And how his silence drinks up this applause!

AJAX. If I go to him, with my armed fist I'll pash him o'er the face.

AGAMEMNON. O, no, you shall not go.

AJAX. An 'a be proud with me I'll pheeze his pride.
  Let me go to him.

ULYSSES. Not for the worth that hangs upon our quarrel.

AJAX. A paltry, insolent fellow!

NESTOR. [*Aside*] How he describes himself!

AJAX. Can he not be sociable?

ULYSSES. [*Aside*] The raven chides blackness.

AJAX. I'll let his humours blood.

AGAMEMNON. [*Aside*] He will be the physician that should be the patient.

AJAX. An all men were a my mind—

ULYSSES. [*Aside*] Wit would be out of fashion.

AJAX. 'A should not bear it so, 'a should eat's words first. Shall pride carry it?

NESTOR. [*Aside*] An 'twould, you'd carry half.

ULYSSES. [*Aside*] 'A would have ten shares.

AJAX. I will knead him, I'll make him supple.

NESTOR. [*Aside*] He's not yet through warm. Force him with praises; pour in, pour in; his ambition is dry.

ULYSSES. [*To* AGAMEMNON] My lord, you feed too much on this dislike.

NESTOR. Our noble general, do not do so.

DIOMEDES. You must prepare to fight without Achilles.

ULYSSES. Why 'tis this naming of him does him harm.
  Here is a man—but 'tis before his face;
  I will be silent.

NESTOR. Wherefore should you so?
  He is not emulous, as Achilles is.

ULYSSES. Know the whole world, he is as valiant.

AJAX. A whoreson dog, that shall palter with us thus! Would he were a Troyan!

NESTOR. What a vice were it in Ajax now—

ULYSSES. If he were proud.

DIOMEDES. Or covetous of praise.

ULYSSES. Ay, or surly borne.

DIOMEDES. Or strange, or self-affected.

ULYSSES. Thank the heavens, lord, thou art of sweet composure;
  Praise him that gat thee, she that gave thee suck;

Fam'd be thy tutor, and thy parts of nature
Thrice-fam'd beyond, beyond all erudition;
But he that disciplin'd thine arms to fight—
Let Mars divide eternity in twain
And give him half; and, for thy vigour,
Bull-bearing Milo his addition yield
To sinewy Ajax. I will not praise thy wisdom,
Which, like a bourn, a pale, a shore, confines
Thy spacious and dilated parts. Here's Nestor,
Instructed by the antiquary times—
He must, he is, he cannot but be wise;
But pardon, father Nestor, were your days
As green as Ajax' and your brain so temper'd,
You should not have the eminence of him,
But be as Ajax.

AJAX. Shall I call you father?

NESTOR. Ay, my good son.

DIOMEDES. Be rul'd by him, Lord Ajax.

ULYSSES. There is no tarrying here; the hart Achilles
Keeps thicket. Please it our great general
To call together all his state of war;
Fresh kings are come to Troy. To-morrow
We must with all our main of power stand fast;
And here's a lord—come knights from east to west
And cull their flower, Ajax shall cope the best.

AGAMEMNON. Go we to council. Let Achilles sleep.
Light boats sail swift, though greater hulks draw deep.

Exeunt

ACT III. SCENE 1

Troy. PRIAM'S *palace*

Music sounds within. Enter PANDARUS *and a* SERVANT

PANDARUS. Friend, you—pray you, a word. Do you not follow the young Lord Paris?

SERVANT. Ay, sir, when he goes before me.

PANDARUS. You depend upon him, I mean?

SERVANT. Sir, I do depend upon the lord.

PANDARUS. You depend upon a notable gentleman; I must needs praise him.

SERVANT. The lord be praised!

PANDARUS. You know me, do you not?

SERVANT. Faith, sir, superficially.

PANDARUS. Friend, know me better: I am the Lord Pandarus.

SERVANT. I hope I shall know your honour better.

PANDARUS. I do desire it.

SERVANT. You are in the state of grace.

PANDARUS. Grace! Not so, friend; honour and lordship are my titles. What music is this?

SERVANT. I do but partly know, sir; it is music in parts.

PANDARUS. Know you the musicians?

SERVANT. Wholly, sir.

PANDARUS. Who play they to?

SERVANT. To the hearers, sir.

PANDARUS. At whose pleasure, friend?

SERVANT. At mine, sir, and theirs that love music.

PANDARUS. Command, I mean, friend.

SERVANT. Who shall I command, sir?

PANDARUS. Friend, we understand not one another: I am too courtly, and thou art too cunning. At whose request do these men play?

SERVANT. That's to't, indeed, sir. Marry, sir, at the request of Paris my lord, who is there in person; with him the mortal Venus, the heart-blood of beauty, love's invisible soul–

PANDARUS. Who, my cousin, Cressida?

SERVANT. No, sir, Helen. Could not you find out that by her attributes?

PANDARUS. It should seem, fellow, that thou hast not seen the Lady Cressida. I come to speak with Paris from the Prince Troilus; I will make a complimental assault upon him, for my business seethes.

SERVANT. Sodden business! There's a stew'd phrase indeed!

Enter PARIS *and* HELEN, *attended*

PANDARUS. Fair be to you, my lord, and to all this fair company! Fair desires, in all fair measure, fairly guide them—especially to you, fair queen! Fair thoughts be your fair pillow.

HELEN. Dear lord, you are full of fair words.

PANDARUS. You speak your fair pleasure, sweet queen. Fair prince, here is good broken music.

PARIS. You have broke it, cousin; and by my life, you shall make it whole again; you shall piece it out with a piece of your performance.

HELEN. He is full of harmony.

PANDARUS. Truly, lady, no.

HELEN. O, sir—

PANDARUS. Rude, in sooth; in good sooth, very rude.

PARIS. Well said, my lord. Well, you say so in fits.

PANDARUS. I have business to my lord, dear queen. My lord, will you vouchsafe me a word?

HELEN. Nay, this shall not hedge us out. We'll hear you sing, certainly.

PANDARUS. Well, sweet queen, you are pleasant with me. But, marry, thus, my lord: my dear lord and most esteemed friend, your brother Troilus—

HELEN. My Lord Pandarus, honey-sweet lord—

PANDARUS. Go to, sweet queen, go to—commends himself most affectionately to you—

HELEN. You shall not bob us out of our melody. If you do, our melancholy upon your head!

PANDARUS. Sweet queen, sweet queen; that's a sweet queen, i' faith.

HELEN. And to make a sweet lady sad is a sour offence.

PANDARUS. Nay, that shall not serve your turn; that shall it not, in truth, la. Nay, I care not for such words; no, no. —And, my lord, he desires you that, if the King call for him at supper, you will make his excuse.

HELEN. My Lord Pandarus!

PANDARUS. What says my sweet queen, my very very sweet queen?

PARIS. What exploit's in hand? Where sups he to-night?

HELEN. Nay, but, my lord—

PANDARUS. What says my sweet queen?—My cousin will fall out with you.

HELEN. You must not know where he sups.

PARIS. I'll lay my life, with my disposer Cressida.

PANDARUS. No, no, no such matter; you are wide. Come, your disposer is sick.

PARIS. Well, I'll make's excuse.

PANDARUS. Ay, good my lord. Why should you say Cressida? No, your poor disposer's sick.

PARIS. I spy.

PANDARUS. You spy! What do you spy?—Come, give me an instrument. Now, sweet queen.

HELEN. Why, this is kindly done.

PANDARUS. My niece is horribly in love with a thing you have, sweet queen.

HELEN. She shall have it, my lord, if it be not my Lord Paris.

PANDARUS. He! No, she'll none of him; they two are twain.

HELEN. Falling in, after falling out, may make them three.

PANDARUS. Come, come. I'll hear no more of this; I'll sing you a song now.

HELEN. Ay, ay, prithee now. By my troth, sweet lord, thou hast a fine forehead.

PANDARUS. Ay, you may, you may.

HELEN. Let thy song be love. This love will undo us all. O Cupid, Cupid, Cupid!

PANDARUS. Love! Ay, that it shall, i' faith.

PARIS. Ay, good now, love, love, nothing but love.

PANDARUS. In good troth, it begins so. [*Sings*]

Love, love, nothing but love, still love, still more!
For, oh, love's bow
Shoots buck and doe;
The shaft confounds
Not that it wounds,
But tickles still the sore.
These lovers cry, O ho, they die!
Yet that which seems the wound to kill
Doth turn O ho! to ha! ha! he!
So dying love lives still.
O ho! a while, but ha! ha! ha!
O ho! groans out for ha! ha! ha!—hey ho!

HELEN. In love, i' faith, to the very tip of the nose.

PARIS. He eats nothing but doves, love; and that breeds hot blood, and hot blood begets hot thoughts, and hot thoughts beget hot deeds, and hot deeds is love.

PANDARUS. Is this the generation of love: hot blood, hot thoughts, and hot deeds? Why, they are vipers. Is love a generation of vipers? Sweet lord, who's a-field today?

PARIS. Hector, Deiphobus, Helenus, Antenor, and all the gallantry of Troy. I would fain have arm'd to-day, but my Nell would not have it so. How chance my brother Troilus went not?

HELEN. He hangs the lip at something. You know all, Lord Pandarus.

PANDARUS. Not I, honey-sweet queen. I long to hear how they spend to-day. You'll remember your brother's excuse?

PARIS. To a hair.

PANDARUS. Farewell, sweet queen.

HELEN. Commend me to your niece.

PANDARUS. I will, sweet queen. *Exit. Sound a retreat*

PARIS. They're come from the field. Let us to Priam's hall
To greet the warriors. Sweet Helen, I must woo you
To help unarm our Hector. His stubborn buckles,
With these your white enchanting fingers touch'd,
Shall more obey than to the edge of steel
Or force of Greekish sinews; you shall do more
Than all the island kings—disarm great Hector.

HELEN. 'Twill make us proud to be his servant, Paris;
Yea, what he shall receive of us in duty
Gives us more palm in beauty than we have,
Yea, overshines ourself.

PARIS. Sweet, above thought I love thee. *Exeunt*

SCENE 2

Troy. PANDARUS' *orchard*

Enter PANDARUS *and* TROILUS' BOY, *meeting*

PANDARUS. How now! Where's thy master? At my cousin Cressida's?

BOY. No, sir; he stays for you to conduct him thither.

Enter TROILUS

PANDARUS. O, here he comes. How now, how now!
TROILUS. Sirrah, walk off. *Exit* BOY
PANDARUS. Have you seen my cousin?
TROILUS. No, Pandarus. I stalk about her door
Like a strange soul upon the Stygian banks
Staying for waftage. O, be thou my Charon,
And give me swift transportance to these fields
Where I may wallow in the lily beds
Propos'd for the deserver! O gentle Pandar,
From Cupid's shoulder pluck his painted wings,
And fly with me to Cressid!
PANDARUS. Walk here i' th' orchard, I'll bring her straight. *Exit*
TROILUS. I am giddy; expectation whirls me round.
Th' imaginary relish is so sweet
That it enchants my sense; what will it be
When that the wat'ry palate tastes indeed
Love's thrice-repured nectar? Death, I fear me;
Swooning destruction; or some joy too fine,
Too subtle-potent, tun'd too sharp in sweetness,
For the capacity of my ruder powers.
I fear it much; and I do fear besides
That I shall lose distinction in my joys;
As doth a battle, when they charge on heaps
The enemy flying.

Re-enter PANDARUS

PANDARUS. She's making her ready, she'll come straight; you must be witty now. She does so blush, and fetches her wind so short, as if she were fray'd with a sprite. I'll fetch her. It is the prettiest villain; she fetches her breath as short as a new-ta'en sparrow. *Exit*
TROILUS. Even such a passion doth embrace my bosom.
My heart beats thicker than a feverous pulse,
And all my powers do their bestowing lose,
Like vassalage at unawares encount'ring

The eye of majesty.

Re-enter PANDARUS *with* CRESSIDA

PANDARUS. Come, come, what need you blush? Shame's a baby.—Here she is now; swear the oaths now to her that you have sworn to me.—What, are you gone again? You must be watch'd ere you be made tame, must you? Come your ways, come your ways; an you draw backward, we'll put you i' th' fills.—Why do you not speak to her? —Come, draw this curtain and let's see your picture. Alas the day, how loath you are to offend daylight! An 'twere dark, you'd close sooner. So, so; rub on, and kiss the mistress. How now, a kiss in fee-farm! Build there, carpenter; the air is sweet. Nay, you shall fight your hearts out ere I part you. The falcon as the tercel, for all the ducks i' th' river. Go to, go to.

TROILUS. You have bereft me of all words, lady.

PANDARUS. Words pay no debts, give her deeds; but she'll bereave you o' th' deeds too, if she call your activity in question. What, billing again? Here's 'In witness whereof the parties interchangeably.' Come in, come in; I'll go get a fire. *Exit*

CRESSIDA. Will you walk in, my lord?

TROILUS. O Cressid, how often have I wish'd me thus!

CRESSIDA. Wish'd, my lord! The gods grant—O my lord!

TROILUS. What should they grant? What makes this pretty abruption? What too curious dreg espies my sweet lady in the fountain of our love?

CRESSIDA. More dregs than water, if my fears have eyes.

TROILUS. Fears make devils of cherubims; they never see truly.

CRESSIDA. Blind fear, that seeing reason leads, finds safer footing than blind reason stumbling without fear. To fear the worst oft cures the worse.

TROILUS. O, let my lady apprehend no fear! In all Cupid's pageant there is presented no monster.

CRESSIDA. Nor nothing monstrous neither?

TROILUS. Nothing, but our undertakings when we vow to weep seas, live in fire, eat rocks, tame tigers; thinking it harder for our mistress to devise imposition enough than for us to undergo any difficulty imposed. This is the monstruosity in love, lady, that the will is infinite, and the execution confin'd; that the desire is boundless, and the act a slave to limit.

CRESSIDA. They say all lovers swear more performance than they are able, and yet reserve an ability that they never perform; vowing more than the perfection of ten, and discharging less than the tenth part of one. They that have the voice of lions and the act of hares, are they not monsters?

TROILUS. Are there such? Such are not we. Praise us as we are tasted, allow us as we prove; our head shall go bare till merit crown it. No perfection in reversion shall have a praise in present. We will not name desert before his birth; and, being born, his addition shall be humble. Few words to fair faith: Troilus shall be such to Cressid as what envy can say worst shall be a mock for his truth; and what truth can speak truest not truer than Troilus.

CRESSIDA. Will you walk in, my lord?

Re-enter PANDARUS

PANDARUS. What, blushing still? Have you not done talking yet?

CRESSIDA. Well, uncle, what folly I commit, I dedicate to you.

PANDARUS. I thank you for that; if my lord get a boy of you, you'll give him me. Be true to my lord; if he flinch, chide me for it.

TROILUS. You know now your hostages: your uncle's word and my firm faith.

PANDARUS. Nay, I'll give my word for her too: our kindred, though they be long ere they are wooed, they are constant being won; they are burs, I can tell you; they'll stick where they are thrown.

CRESSIDA. Boldness comes to me now and brings me heart.
Prince Troilus, I have lov'd you night and day
For many weary months.

TROILUS. Why was my Cressid then so hard to win?

CRESSIDA. Hard to seem won; but I was won, my lord,
With the first glance that ever—pardon me.

If I confess much, you will play the tyrant.
I love you now; but till now not so much
But I might master it. In faith, I lie;
My thoughts were like unbridled children, grown
Too headstrong for their mother. See, we fools!
Why have I blabb'd? Who shall be true to us,
When we are so unsecret to ourselves?
But, though I lov'd you well, I woo'd you not;
And yet, good faith, I wish'd myself a man,
Or that we women had men's privilege
Of speaking first. Sweet, bid me hold my tongue,
For in this rapture I shall surely speak
The thing I shall repent. See, see, your silence,
Cunning in dumbness, from my weakness draws
My very soul of counsel. Stop my mouth.

TROILUS. And shall, albeit sweet music issues thence.

PANDARUS. Pretty, i' faith.

CRESSIDA. My lord, I do beseech you, pardon me;
'Twas not my purpose thus to beg a kiss.
I am asham'd. O heavens! what have I done?
For this time will I take my leave, my lord.

TROILUS. Your leave, sweet Cressid!

PANDARUS. Leave! An you take leave till to-morrow morning—

CRESSIDA. Pray you, content you.

TROILUS. What offends you, lady?

CRESSIDA. Sir, mine own company.

TROILUS. You cannot shun yourself.

CRESSIDA. Let me go and try.
I have a kind of self resides with you;
But an unkind self, that itself will leave
To be another's fool. I would be gone.
Where is my wit? I know not what I speak.

TROILUS. Well know they what they speak that speak so wisely.

CRESSIDA. Perchance, my lord, I show more craft than love;
And fell so roundly to a large confession
To angle for your thoughts; but you are wise—
Or else you love not; for to be wise and love
Exceeds man's might; that dwells with gods above.

TROILUS. O that I thought it could be in a woman—

As, if it can, I will presume in you—
To feed for aye her lamp and flames of love;
To keep her constancy in plight and youth,
Outliving beauty's outward, with a mind
That doth renew swifter than blood decays!
Or that persuasion could but thus convince me
That my integrity and truth to you
Might be affronted with the match and weight
Of such a winnowed purity in love.
How were I then uplifted! but, alas,
I am as true as truth's simplicity,
And simpler than the infancy of truth.

CRESSIDA. In that I'll war with you.

TROILUS. O virtuous fight,
When right with right wars who shall be most right!
True swains in love shall in the world to come
Approve their truth by Troilus, when their rhymes,
Full of protest, of oath, and big compare,
Want similes, truth tir'd with iteration—
As true as steel, as plantage to the moon,
As sun to day, as turtle to her mate,
As iron to adamant, as earth to th' centre—
Yet, after all comparisons of truth,
As truth's authentic author to be cited,
'As true as Troilus' shall crown up the verse
And sanctify the numbers.

CRESSIDA. Prophet may you be!
If I be false, or swerve a hair from truth,
When time is old and hath forgot itself,
When waterdrops have worn the stones of Troy,
And blind oblivion swallow'd cities up,
And mighty states characterless are grated
To dusty nothing—yet let memory
From false to false, among false maids in love,
Upbraid my falsehood when th' have said 'As false
As air, as water, wind, or sandy earth,
As fox to lamb, or wolf to heifer's calf,
Pard to the hind, or stepdame to her son'—
Yea, let them say, to stick the heart of falsehood,
'As false as Cressid.'

PANDARUS. Go to, a bargain made; seal it, seal it; I'll be the witness. Here I hold your hand; here my cousin's. If ever you prove false one to another, since I have taken such pains to bring you together, let all pitiful goers-between be call'd to the world's end after my name—call them all Pandars; let all constant men be Troiluses, all false women Cressids, and all brokers between Pandars. Say 'Amen.'

TROILUS. Amen.

CRESSIDA. Amen.

PANDARUS. Amen. Whereupon I will show you a chamber and a bed; which bed, because it shall not speak of your pretty encounters, press it to death. Away!
And Cupid grant all tongue-tied maidens here,
Bed, chamber, pander, to provide this gear! *Exeunt*

SCENE 3

The Greek camp

Flourish. Enter AGAMEMNON, ULYSSES, DIOMEDES, NESTOR, AJAX, MENELAUS, *and* CALCHAS

CALCHAS. Now, Princes, for the service I have done,
Th' advantage of the time prompts me aloud
To call for recompense. Appear it to your mind
That, through the sight I bear in things to come,
I have abandon'd Troy, left my possession,
Incurr'd a traitor's name, expos'd myself
From certain and possess'd conveniences
To doubtful fortunes, sequest'ring from me all
That time, acquaintance, custom, and condition,
Made tame and most familiar to my nature;
And here, to do you service, am become
As new into the world, strange, unacquainted—
I do beseech you, as in way of taste,
To give me now a little benefit
Out of those many regist'red in promise,
Which you say live to come in my behalf.

AGAMEMNON. What wouldst thou of us, Troyan? Make demand.

CALCHAS. You have a Troyan prisoner call'd Antenor,
Yesterday took; Troy holds him very dear.
Oft have you—often have you thanks therefore—
Desir'd my Cressid in right great exchange,
Whom Troy hath still denied; but this Antenor,
I know, is such a wrest in their affairs
That their negotiations all must slack
Wanting his manage; and they will almost
Give us a prince of blood, a son of Priam,
In change of him. Let him be sent, great Princes,
And he shall buy my daughter; and her presence
Shall quite strike off all service I have done
In most accepted pain.

AGAMEMNON. Let Diomedes bear him,
And bring us Cressid hither. Calchas shall have
What he requests of us. Good Diomed,
Furnish you fairly for this interchange;
Withal, bring word if Hector will to-morrow
Be answer'd in his challenge. Ajax is ready.

DIOMEDES. This shall I undertake; and 'tis a burden
Which I am proud to bear.

Exeunt DIOMEDES *and* CALCHAS

ACHILLES *and* PATROCLUS *stand in their tent*

ULYSSES. Achilles stands i' th' entrance of his tent.
Please it our general pass strangely by him,
As if he were forgot; and, Princes all,
Lay negligent and loose regard upon him.
I will come last. 'Tis like he'll question me
Why such unplausive eyes are bent, why turn'd on him?
If so, I have derision med'cinable
To use between your strangeness and his pride,
Which his own will shall have desire to drink.
It may do good. Pride hath no other glass
To show itself but pride; for supple knees
Feed arrogance and are the proud man's fees.

AGAMEMNON. We'll execute your purpose, and put on
A form of strangeness as we pass along.
So do each lord; and either greet him not,
Or else disdainfully, which shall shake him more

Than if not look'd on. I will lead the way.

ACHILLES. What comes the general to speak with me?
You know my mind. I'll fight no more 'gainst Troy.

AGAMEMNON. What says Achilles? Would he aught with us?

NESTOR. Would you, my lord, aught with the general?

ACHILLES. No.

NESTOR. Nothing, my lord.

AGAMEMNON. The better.

Exeunt AGAMEMNON *and* NESTOR

ACHILLES. Good day, good day.

MENELAUS. How do you? How do you? *Exit*

ACHILLES. What, does the cuckold scorn me?

AJAX. How now, Patroclus?

ACHILLES. Good morrow, Ajax.

AJAX. Ha?

ACHILLES. Good morrow.

AJAX. Ay, and good next day too. *Exit*

ACHILLES. What mean these fellows? Know they not Achilles?

PATROCLUS. They pass by strangely. They were us'd to bend,
To send their smiles before them to Achilles,
To come as humbly as they us'd to creep
To holy altars.

ACHILLES. What, am I poor of late?
'Tis certain, greatness, once fall'n out with fortune,
Must fall out with men too. What the declin'd is,
He shall as soon read in the eyes of others
As feel in his own fall; for men, like butterflies,
Show not their mealy wings but to the summer;
And not a man for being simply man
Hath any honour, but honour for those honours
That are without him, as place, riches, and favour,
Prizes of accident, as oft as merit;
Which when they fall, as being slippery standers,
The love that lean'd on them as slippery too,
Doth one pluck down another, and together
Die in the fall. But 'tis not so with me:
Fortune and I are friends; I do enjoy
At ample point all that I did possess

Save these men's looks; who do, methinks, find out
Something not worth in me such rich beholding
As they have often given. Here is Ulysses.
I'll interrupt his reading.
How now, Ulysses!

ULYSSES. Now, great Thetis' son!

ACHILLES. What are you reading?

ULYSSES. A strange fellow here
Writes me that man—how dearly ever parted,
How much in having, or without or in—
Cannot make boast to have that which he hath,
Nor feels not what he owes, but by reflection;
As when his virtues shining upon others
Heat them, and they retort that heat again
To the first giver.

ACHILLES. This is not strange, Ulysses.
The beauty that is borne here in the face
The bearer knows not, but commends itself
To others' eyes; nor doth the eye itself—
That most pure spirit of sense—behold itself,
Not going from itself; but eye to eye opposed
Salutes each other with each other's form;
For speculation turns not to itself
Till it hath travell'd, and is mirror'd there
Where it may see itself. This is not strange at all.

ULYSSES. I do not strain at the position—
It is familiar—but at the author's drift;
Who, in his circumstance, expressly proves
That no man is the lord of anything,
Though in and of him there be much consisting,
Till he communicate his parts to others;
Nor doth he of himself know them for aught
Till he behold them formed in th' applause
Where th' are extended; who, like an arch, reverb'rate
The voice again; or, like a gate of steel
Fronting the sun, receives and renders back
His figure and his heat. I was much rapt in this;
And apprehended here immediately
Th' unknown Ajax. Heavens, what a man is there!
A very horse that has he knows not what!

Nature, what things there are
Most abject in regard and dear in use!
What things again most dear in the esteem
And poor in worth! Now shall we see to-morrow—
An act that very chance doth throw upon him—
Ajax renown'd. O heavens, what some men do,
While some men leave to do!
How some men creep in skittish Fortune's hall,
Whiles others play the idiots in her eyes!
How one man eats into another's pride,
While pride is fasting in his wantonness!
To see these Grecian lords!—why, even already
They clap the lubber Ajax on the shoulder,
As if his foot were on brave Hector's breast,
And great Troy shrinking.

ACHILLES. I do believe it; for they pass'd by me
As misers do by beggars—neither gave to me
Good word nor look. What, are my deeds forgot?

ULYSSES. Time hath, my lord, a wallet at his back,
Wherein he puts alms for oblivion,
A great-siz'd monster of ingratitudes.
Those scraps are good deeds past, which are devour'd
As fast as they are made, forgot as soon
As done. Perseverance, dear my lord,
Keeps honour bright. To have done is to hang
Quite out of fashion, like a rusty mail
In monumental mock'ry. Take the instant way;
For honour travels in a strait so narrow
Where one but goes abreast. Keep then the path,
For emulation hath a thousand sons
That one by one pursue; if you give way,
Or hedge aside from the direct forthright,
Like to an ent'red tide they all rush by
And leave you hindmost;
Or, like a gallant horse fall'n in first rank,
Lie there for pavement to the abject rear,
O'er-run and trampled on. Then what they do in present,
Though less than yours in past, must o'ertop yours;
For Time is like a fashionable host,
That slightly shakes his parting guest by th' hand;

And with his arms out-stretch'd, as he would fly,
Grasps in the comer. The welcome ever smiles,
And farewell goes out sighing. O, let not virtue seek
Remuneration for the thing it was;
For beauty, wit,
High birth, vigour of bone, desert in service,
Love, friendship, charity, are subjects all
To envious and calumniating Time.
One touch of nature makes the whole world kin—
That all with one consent praise new-born gawds,
Though they are made and moulded of things past,
And give to dust that is a little gilt
More laud than gilt o'er-dusted.
The present eye praises the present object.
Then marvel not, thou great and complete man,
That all the Greeks begin to worship Ajax,
Since things in motion sooner catch the eye
Than what stirs not. The cry went once on thee,
And still it might, and yet it may again,
If thou wouldst not entomb thyself alive
And case thy reputation in thy tent,
Whose glorious deeds but in these fields of late
Made emulous missions 'mongst the gods themselves,
And drave great Mars to faction.

ACHILLES. Of this my privacy
I have strong reasons.

ULYSSES. But 'gainst your privacy
The reasons are more potent and heroical.
'Tis known, Achilles, that you are in love
With one of Priam's daughters.

ACHILLES. Ha! known!

ULYSSES. Is that a wonder?
The providence that's in a watchful state
Knows almost every grain of Plutus' gold;
Finds bottom in th' uncomprehensive deeps;
Keeps place with thought, and almost, like the gods,
Do thoughts unveil in their dumb cradles.
There is a mystery—with whom relation
Durst never meddle—in the soul of state,
Which hath an operation more divine

Than breath or pen can give expressure to.
All the commerce that you have had with Troy
As perfectly is ours as yours, my lord;
And better would it fit Achilles much
To throw down Hector than Polyxena.
But it must grieve young Pyrrhus now at home,
When fame shall in our island sound her trump,
And all the Greekish girls shall tripping sing
'Great Hector's sister did Achilles win;
But our great Ajax bravely beat down him.'
Farewell, my lord. I as your lover speak.
The fool slides o'er the ice that you should break. *Exit*

PATROCLUS. To this effect, Achilles, have I mov'd you.
A woman impudent and mannish grown
Is not more loath'd than an effeminate man
In time of action. I stand condemn'd for this;
They think my little stomach to the war
And your great love to me restrains you thus.
Sweet, rouse yourself; and the weak wanton Cupid
Shall from your neck unloose his amorous fold,
And, like a dew-drop from the lion's mane,
Be shook to airy air.

ACHILLES. Shall Ajax fight with Hector?

PATROCLUS. Ay, and perhaps receive much honour by him.

ACHILLES. I see my reputation is at stake;
My fame is shrewdly gor'd.

PATROCLUS. O, then, beware:
Those wounds heal ill that men do give themselves;
Omission to do what is necessary
Seals a commission to a blank of danger;
And danger, like an ague, subtly taints
Even then when they sit idly in the sun.

ACHILLES. Go call Thersites hither, sweet Patroclus.
I'll send the fool to Ajax, and desire him
T' invite the Troyan lords, after the combat,
To see us here unarm'd. I have a woman's longing,
An appetite that I am sick withal,
To see great Hector in his weeds of peace;
To talk with him, and to behold his visage,
Even to my full of view.

Enter THERSITES

A labour sav'd!

THERSITES. A wonder!

ACHILLES. What?

THERSITES. Ajax goes up and down the field asking for himself.

ACHILLES. How so?

THERSITES. He must fight singly to-morrow with Hector, and is so prophetically proud of an heroical cudgelling that he raves in saying nothing.

ACHILLES. How can that be?

THERSITES. Why, 'a stalks up and down like a peacock–a stride and a stand; ruminates like an hostess that hath no arithmetic but her brain to set down her reckoning, bites his lip with a politic regard, as who should say 'There were wit in this head, an 'twould out'; and so there is; but it lies as coldly in him as fire in a flint, which will not show without knocking. The man's undone for ever; for if Hector break not his neck i' th' combat, he'll break't himself in vainglory. He knows not me. I said 'Good morrow, Ajax'; and he replies 'Thanks, Agamemnon.' What think you of this man that takes me for the general? He's grown a very land fish, languageless, a monster. A plague of opinion! A man may wear it on both sides, like a leather jerkin.

ACHILLES. Thou must be my ambassador to him, Thersites.

THERSITES. Who, I? Why, he'll answer nobody; he professes not answering. Speaking is for beggars: he wears his tongue in's arms. I will put on his presence. Let Patroclus make his demands to me, you shall see the pageant of Ajax.

ACHILLES. To him, Patroclus. Tell him I humbly desire the valiant Ajax to invite the most valorous Hector to come unarm'd to my tent; and to procure safe conduct for his person of the magnanimous and most illustrious six-or-seven-times-honour'd Captain General of the Grecian army, et cetera, Agamemnon. Do this.

PATROCLUS. Jove bless great Ajax!

THERSITES. Hum!

PATROCLUS. I come from the worthy Achilles–

THERSITES. Ha!

PATROCLUS. Who most humbly desires you to invite Hector to his tent–

THERSITES. Hum!

PATROCLUS. And to procure safe conduct from Agamemnon.

THERSITES. Agamemnon!

PATROCLUS. Ay, my lord.

THERSITES. Ha!

PATROCLUS. What you say to't?

THERSITES. God buy you, with all my heart.

PATROCLUS. Your answer, sir.

THERSITES. If to-morrow be a fair day, by eleven of the clock it will go one way or other. Howsoever, he shall pay for me ere he has me.

PATROCLUS. Your answer, sir.

THERSITES. Fare ye well, with all my heart.

ACHILLES. Why, but he is not in this tune, is he?

THERSITES. No, but he's out a tune thus. What music will be in him when Hector has knock'd out his brains I know not; but, I am sure, none; unless the fiddler Apollo get his sinews to make catlings on.

ACHILLES. Come, thou shalt bear a letter to him straight.

THERSITES. Let me carry another to his horse; for that's the more capable creature.

ACHILLES. My mind is troubled, like a fountain stirr'd;
And I myself see not the bottom of it.

Exeunt ACHILLES *and* PATROCLUS

THERSITES. Would the fountain of your mind were clear again, that I might water an ass at it. I had rather be a tick in a sheep than such a valiant ignorance. *Exit*

ACT IV. SCENE 1

Troy. A street

Enter, at one side, Æneas, *and servant with a torch; at another,* Paris, Deiphobus, Antenor, Diomedes *the Grecian, and others, with torches*

Paris. See, ho! Who is that there?
Deiphobus. It is the Lord Æneas.
Æneas. Is the Prince there in person?
Had I so good occasion to lie long
As you, Prince Paris, nothing but heavenly business
Should rob my bed-mate of my company.
Diomedes. That's my mind too. Good morrow, Lord Æneas.
Paris. A valiant Greek, Æneas—take his hand:
Witness the process of your speech, wherein
You told how Diomed, a whole week by days,
Did haunt you in the field.
Æneas. Health to you, valiant sir,
During all question of the gentle truce;
But when I meet you arm'd, as black defiance
As heart can think or courage execute.
Diomedes. The one and other Diomed embraces.
Our bloods are now in calm; and so long health!
But when contention and occasion meet,
By Jove, I'll play the hunter for thy life
With all my force, pursuit, and policy.
Æneas. And thou shalt hunt a lion, that will fly
With his face backward. In humane gentleness,
Welcome to Troy! now, by Anchises' life,
Welcome indeed! By Venus' hand I swear
No man alive can love in such a sort
The thing he means to kill, more excellently.
Diomedes. We sympathise. Jove let Æneas live,
If to my sword his fate be not the glory,
A thousand complete courses of the sun!
But in mine emulous honour let him die
With every joint a wound, and that to-morrow!

ÆNEAS. We know each other well.
DIOMEDES. We do; and long to know each other worse.
PARIS. This is the most despiteful'st gentle greeting
The noblest hateful love, that e'er I heard of.
What business, lord, so early?
ÆNEAS. I was sent for to the King; but why, I know not.
PARIS. His purpose meets you: 'twas to bring this Greek
To Calchas' house, and there to render him,
For the enfreed Antenor, the fair Cressid.
Let's have your company; or, if you please,
Haste there before us. I constantly believe–
Or rather call my thought a certain knowledge–
My brother Troilus lodges there to-night.
Rouse him and give him note of our approach,
With the whole quality wherefore; I fear
We shall be much unwelcome.
AENEAS. That I assure you:
Troilus had rather Troy were borne to Greece
Than Cressid borne from Troy.
PARIS. There is no help;
The bitter disposition of the time
Will have it so. On, lord; we'll follow you.
ÆNEAS. Good morrow, all. *Exit with servant*
PARIS. And tell me, noble Diomed–faith, tell me true,
Even in the soul of sound good-fellowship–
Who in your thoughts deserves fair Helen best,
Myself or Menelaus?
DIOMEDES. Both alike:
He merits well to have her that doth seek her,
Not making any scruple of her soilure,
With such a hell of pain and world of charge;
And you as well to keep her that defend her,
Not palating the taste of her dishonour,
With such a costly loss of wealth and friends.
He like a puling cuckold would drink up
The lees and dregs of a flat tamed piece;
You, like a lecher, out of whorish loins
Are pleas'd to breed out your inheritors.
Both merits pois'd, each weighs nor less nor more;
But he as he, the heavier for a whore.

PARIS. You are too bitter to your country-woman.
DIOMEDES. She's bitter to her country. Hear me, Paris:
For every false drop in her bawdy veins
A Grecian's life hath sunk; for every scruple
Of her contaminated carrion weight
A Troyan hath been slain; since she could speak,
She hath not given so many good words breath
As for her Greeks and Troyans suff'red death.
PARIS. Fair Diomed, you do as chapmen do,
Dispraise the thing that you desire to buy;
But we in silence hold this virtue well:
We'll not commend what we intend to sell.
Here lies our way. *Exeunt*

SCENE 2

Troy. The court of PANDARUS' *house*

Enter TROILUS *and* CRESSIDA

TROILUS. Dear, trouble not yourself; the morn is cold.
CRESSIDA. Then, sweet my lord, I'll call mine uncle down;
He shall unbolt the gates.
TROILUS. Trouble him not;
To bed, to bed! Sleep kill those pretty eyes,
And give as soft attachment to thy senses
As infants' empty of all thought!
CRESSIDA. Good morrow, then.
TROILUS. I prithee now, to bed.
CRESSIDA. Are you aweary of me?
TROILUS. O Cressida! but that the busy day,
Wak'd by the lark, hath rous'd the ribald crows,
And dreaming night will hide our joys no longer,
I would not from thee.
CRESSIDA. Night hath been too brief.
TROILUS. Beshrew the witch! with venomous wights she stays
As tediously as hell, but flies the grasps of love
With wings more momentary-swift than thought.
You will catch cold, and curse me.

CRESSIDA. Prithee tarry.
You men will never tarry.
O foolish Cressid! I might have still held off,
And then you would have tarried. Hark! there's one up.

PANDARUS. [*Within*] What's all the doors open here?

TROILUS. It is your uncle.

Enter PANDARUS

CRESSIDA. A pestilence on him! Now will he be mocking.
I shall have such a life!

PANDARUS. How now, how now! How go maidenheads? Here, you maid! Where's my cousin Cressid?

CRESSIDA. Go hang yourself, you naughty mocking uncle.
You bring me to do, and then you flout me too.

PANDARUS. To do what? to do what? Let her say what. What have I brought you to do?

CRESSIDA. Come, come, beshrew your heart! You'll ne'er be good,
Nor suffer others.

PANDARUS. Ha, ha! Alas, poor wretch! a poor capocchia! hast not slept to-night? Would he not, a naughty man, let it sleep? A bugbear take him!

CRESSIDA. Did not I tell you? Would he were knock'd i' th' head! [*One knocks*]
Who's that at door? Good uncle, go and see.
My lord, come you again into my chamber.
You smile and mock me, as if I meant naughtily.

TROILUS. Ha! ha!

CRESSIDA. Come, you are deceiv'd, I think of no such thing. [*Knock*]
How earnestly they knock! Pray you come in:
I would not for half Troy have you seen here.

Exeunt TROILUS *and* CRESSIDA

PANDARUS. Who's there? What's the matter? Will you beat down the door? How now? What's the matter?

Enter ÆNEAS

ÆNEAS. Good morrow, lord, good morrow.

PANDARUS. Who's there? My lord Æneas? By my troth,
I knew you not. What news with you so early?

ÆNEAS. Is not Prince Troilus here?

PANDARUS. Here! What should he do here?

ÆNEAS. Come, he is here, my lord; do not deny him.
It doth import him much to speak with me.

PANDARUS. Is he here, say you? It's more than I know, I'll be sworn. For my own part, I came in late. What should he do here?

ÆNEAS. Who!—nay, then. Come, come, you'll do him wrong ere you are ware; you'll be so true to him to be false to him. Do not you know of him, but yet go fetch him hither; go.

Re-enter TROILUS

TROILUS. How now! What's the matter?

ÆNEAS. My lord, I scarce have leisure to salute you,
My matter is so rash. There is at hand
Paris your brother, and Deiphobus,
The Grecian Diomed, and our Antenor
Deliver'd to us; and for him forthwith,
Ere the first sacrifice, within this hour,
We must give up to Diomedes' hand
The Lady Cressida.

TROILUS. Is it so concluded?

ÆNEAS. By Priam, and the general state of Troy.
They are at hand and ready to effect it.

TROILUS. How my achievements mock me!
I will go meet them; and, my lord Æneas,
We met by chance; you did not find me here.

ÆNEAS. Good, good, my lord, the secrets of neighbour Pandar
Have not more gift in taciturnity.

Exeunt TROILUS *and* ÆNEAS

PANDARUS. Is't possible? No sooner got but lost? The devil take Antenor! The young prince will go mad. A plague upon Antenor! I would they had broke's neck.

Re-enter CRESSIDA

CRESSIDA. How now! What's the matter? Who was here?

PANDARUS. Ah, ah!

CRESSIDA. Why sigh you so profoundly? Where's my lord?
Gone? Tell me, sweet uncle, what's the matter?

PANDARUS. Would I were as deep under the earth as I am above!

CRESSIDA. O the gods! What's the matter?

PANDARUS. Pray thee, get thee in. Would thou hadst ne'er been born! I knew thou wouldst be his death! O, poor gentleman! A plague upon Antenor!

CRESSIDA. Good uncle, I beseech you, on my knees I beseech you, what's the matter?

PANDARUS. Thou must be gone, wench, thou must be gone; thou art chang'd for Antenor; thou must to thy father, and be gone from Troilus. 'Twill be his death; 'twill be his bane; he cannot bear it.

CRESSIDA. O you immortal gods! I will not go.

PANDARUS. Thou must.

CRESSIDA. I will not, uncle. I have forgot my father;
I know no touch of consanguinity,
No kin, no love, no blood, no soul so near me
As the sweet Troilus. O you gods divine,
Make Cressid's name the very crown of falsehood,
If ever she leave Troilus! Time, force, and death,
Do to this body what extremes you can,
But the strong base and building of my love
Is as the very centre of the earth,
Drawing all things to it. I'll go in and weep–

PANDARUS. Do, do.

CRESSIDA. Tear my bright hair, and scratch my praised cheeks,
Crack my clear voice with sobs and break my heart,
With sounding 'Troilus.' I will not go from Troy.

Exeunt

SCENE 3

Troy. A street before PANDARUS' *house*

Enter PARIS, TROILUS, ÆNEAS, DEIPHOBUS, ANTENOR, *and* DIOMEDES

PARIS. It is great morning; and the hour prefix'd
For her delivery to this valiant Greek
Comes fast upon. Good my brother Troilus,
Tell you the lady what she is to do

And haste her to the purpose.
TROILUS. Walk into her house.
I'll bring her to the Grecian presently;
And to his hand when I deliver her,
Think it an altar, and thy brother Troilus
A priest, there off'ring to it his own heart. *Exit*
PARIS. I know what 'tis to love,
And would, as I shall pity, I could help!
Please you walk in, my lords. *Exeunt*

SCENE 4

Troy. PANDARUS' *house*

Enter PANDARUS *and* CRESSIDA

PANDARUS. Be moderate, be moderate.
CRESSIDA. Why tell you me of moderation?
The grief is fine, full, perfect, that I taste,
And violenteth in a sense as strong
As that which causeth it. How can I moderate it?
If I could temporize with my affections
Or brew it to a weak and colder palate,
The like allayment could I give my grief.
My love admits no qualifying dross;
No more my grief, in such a precious loss.

Enter TROILUS

PANDARUS. Here, here, here he comes. Ah, sweet ducks!
CRESSIDA. O Troilus! Troilus! [*Embracing him*]
PANDARUS. What a pair of spectacles is here! Let me embrace too. 'O heart,' as the goodly saying is,
O heart, heavy heart,
Why sigh'st thou without breaking?
where he answers again
Because thou canst not ease thy smart
By friendship nor by speaking.
There was never a truer rhyme. Let us cast away nothing, for we may live to have need of such a verse. We see it, we see it. How now, lambs!

TROILUS. Cressid, I love thee in so strain'd a purity
That the bless'd gods, as angry with my fancy,
More bright in zeal than the devotion which
Cold lips blow to their deities, take thee from me.
CRESSIDA. Have the gods envy?
PANDARUS. Ay, ay, ay; 'tis too plain a case.
CRESSIDA. And is it true that I must go from Troy?
TROILUS. A hateful truth.
CRESSIDA. What, and from Troilus too?
TROILUS. From Troy and Troilus.
CRESSIDA. Is't possible?
TROILUS. And suddenly; where injury of chance
Puts back leave-taking, justles roughly by
All time of pause, rudely beguiles our lips
Of all rejoindure, forcibly prevents
Our lock'd embrasures, strangles our dear vows
Even in the birth of our own labouring breath.
We two, that with so many thousand sighs
Did buy each other, must poorly sell ourselves
With the rude brevity and discharge of one.
Injurious time now with a robber's haste
Crams his rich thievery up, he knows not how.
As many farewells as be stars in heaven,
With distinct breath and consign'd kisses to them,
He fumbles up into a loose adieu,
And scants us with a single famish'd kiss,
Distasted with the salt of broken tears.
ÆNEAS. [*Within*] My lord, is the lady ready?
TROILUS. Hark! you are call'd. Some say the Genius so
Cries 'Come' to him that instantly must die.
Bid them have patience; she shall come anon.
PANDARUS. Where are my tears? Rain, to lay this wind, or my heart will be blown up by th' root? *Exit*
CRESSIDA. I must then to the Grecians?
TROILUS. No remedy.
CRESSIDA. A woeful Cressid 'mongst the merry Greeks!
When shall we see again?
TROILUS. Hear me, my love. Be thou but true of heart—
CRESSIDA. I true! how now! What wicked deem is this?
TROILUS. Nay, we must use expostulation kindly,

For it is parting from us.
I speak not 'Be thou true' as fearing thee,
For I will throw my glove to Death himself
That there's no maculation in thy heart;
But 'Be thou true' say I to fashion in
My sequent protestation: be thou true,
And I will see thee.

CRESSIDA. O, you shall be expos'd, my lord, to dangers
As infinite as imminent! But I'll be true.

TROILUS. And I'll grow friend with danger. Wear this sleeve.

CRESSIDA. And you this glove. When shall I see you?

TROILUS. I will corrupt the Grecian sentinels
To give thee nightly visitation.
But yet be true.

CRESSIDA. O heavens! 'Be true' again!

TROILUS. Hear why I speak it, love.
The Grecian youths are full of quality;
They're loving, well compos'd with gifts of nature,
And flowing o'er with arts and exercise.
How novelties may move, and parts with person,
Alas, a kind of godly jealousy,
Which I beseech you call a virtuous sin,
Makes me afeard.

CRESSIDA. O heavens! you love me not.

TROILUS. Die I a villain, then!
In this I do not call your faith in question
So mainly as my merit. I cannot sing,
Nor heel the high lavolt, nor sweeten talk,
Nor play at subtle games—fair virtues all,
To which the Grecians are most prompt and pregnant;
But I can tell that in each grace of these
There lurks a still and dumb-discoursive devil
That tempts most cunningly. But be not tempted.

CRESSIDA. Do you think I will?

TROILUS. No.
But something may be done that we will not;
And sometimes we are devils to ourselves,
When we will tempt the frailty of our powers,
Presuming on their changeful potency.

ÆNEAS. [*Within*] Nay, good my lord!
TROILUS. Come, kiss; and let us part.
PARIS. [*Within*] Brother Troilus!
TROILUS. Good brother, come you hither;
And bring Æneas and the Grecian with you.
CRESSIDA. My lord, will you be true?
TROILUS. Who, I? Alas, it is my vice, my fault!
Whiles others fish with craft for great opinion,
I with great truth catch mere simplicity;
Whilst some with cunning gild their copper crowns,
With truth and plainness I do wear mine bare.

Enter ÆNEAS, PARIS, ANTENOR, DEIPHOBUS, *and* DIOMEDES

Fear not my truth: the moral of my wit
Is 'plain and true'; there's all the reach of it.
Welcome, Sir Diomed! Here is the lady
Which for Antenor we deliver you;
At the port, lord, I'll give her to thy hand,
And by the way possess thee what she is.
Entreat her fair; and, by my soul, fair Greek,
If e'er thou stand at mercy of my sword,
Name Cressid, and thy life shall be as safe
As Priam is in Ilion.
DIOMEDES. Fair Lady Cressid,
So please you, save the thanks this prince expects.
The lustre in your eye, heaven in your cheek,
Pleads your fair usage; and to Diomed
You shall be mistress, and command him wholly.
TROILUS. Grecian, thou dost not use me courteously
To shame the zeal of my petition to thee
In praising her. I tell thee, lord of Greece,
She is as far high-soaring o'er thy praises
As thou unworthy to be call'd her servant.
I charge thee use her well, even for my charge;
For, by the dreadful Pluto, if thou dost not,
Though the great bulk Achilles be thy guard,
I'll cut thy throat.
DIOMEDES. O, be not mov'd, Prince Troilus.
Let me be privileg'd by my place and message
To be a speaker free: when I am hence

I'll answer to my lust. And know you, lord,
I'll nothing do on charge: to her own worth
She shall be priz'd. But that you say 'Be't so,'
I speak it in my spirit and honour, 'No.'

TROILUS. Come, to the port. I'll tell thee, Diomed,
This brave shall oft make thee to hide thy head.
Lady, give me your hand; and, as we walk,
To our own selves bend we our needful talk.

Exeunt TROILUS, CRESSIDA, *and* DIOMEDES
[*Sound trumpet*]

PARIS. Hark! Hector's trumpet.

ÆNEAS. How have we spent this morning!
The Prince must think me tardy and remiss,
That swore to ride before him to the field.

PARIS. 'Tis Troilus' fault. Come, come to field with him.

DEIPHOBUS. Let us make ready straight.

ÆNEAS. Yea, with a bridegroom's fresh alacrity
Let us address to tend on Hector's heels.
The glory of our Troy doth this day lie
On his fair worth and single chivalry. *Exeunt*

SCENE 5

The Grecian camp. Lists set out

Enter AJAX, *armed;* AGAMEMNON, ACHILLES, PATROCLUS, MENELAUS, ULYSSES, NESTOR, *and others*

AGAMEMNON. Here art thou in appointment fresh and fair,
Anticipating time with starting courage.
Give with thy trumpet a loud note to Troy,
Thou dreadful Ajax, that the appalled air
May pierce the head of the great combatant,
And hale him hither.

AJAX. Thou, trumpet, there's my purse.
Now crack thy lungs and split thy brazen pipe;
Blow, villain, till thy sphered bias cheek
Out-swell the colic of puff Aquilon'd.
Come, stretch thy chest, and let thy eyes spout blood:
Thou blowest for Hector. [*Trumpet sounds*]

ULYSSES. No trumpet answers.
ACHILLES. 'Tis but early days.

Enter DIOMEDES, *with* CRESSIDA

AGAMEMNON. Is not yond Diomed, with Calchas' daughter?
ULYSSES. 'Tis he, I ken the manner of his gait:
He rises on the toe. That spirit of his
In aspiration lifts him from the earth.
AGAMEMNON. Is this the lady Cressid?
DIOMEDES. Even she.
AGAMEMNON. Most dearly welcome to the Greeks, sweet lady.
NESTOR. Our general doth salute you with a kiss.
ULYSSES. Yet is the kindness but particular;
'Twere better she were kiss'd in general.
NESTOR. And very courtly counsel: I'll begin.
So much for Nestor.
ACHILLES. I'll take that winter from your lips, fair lady.
Achilles bids you welcome.
MENELAUS. I had good argument for kissing once.
PATROCLUS. But that's no argument for kissing now;
For thus popp'd Paris in his hardiment,
And parted thus you and your argument.
ULYSSES. O deadly gall, and theme of all our scorns!
For which we lose our heads to gild his horns.
PATROCLUS. The first was Menelaus' kiss; this, mine—
[*Kisses her again*]
Patroclus kisses you.
MENELAUS. O, this is trim!
PATROCLUS. Paris and I kiss evermore for him.
MENELAUS. I'll have my kiss, sir. Lady, by your leave.
CRESSIDA. In kissing, do you render or receive?
PATROCLUS. Both take and give.
CRESSIDA. I'll make my match to live,
The kiss you take is better than you give;
Therefore no kiss.
MENELAUS. I'll give you boot; I'll give you three for one.
CRESSIDA. You are an odd man; give even or give none.
MENELAUS. An odd man, lady? Every man is odd.
CRESSIDA. No, Paris is not; for you know 'tis true

That you are odd, and he is even with you.
MENELAUS. You fillip me o' th' head.
CRESSIDA. No, I'll be sworn.
ULYSSES. It were no match, your nail against his horn.
May I, sweet lady, beg a kiss of you?
CRESSIDA. You may.
ULYSSES. I do desire it.
CRESSIDA. Why, beg then.
ULYSSES. Why then, for Venus' sake give me a kiss
When Helen is a maid again, and his.
CRESSIDA. I am your debtor; claim it when 'tis due.
ULYSSES. Never's my day, and then a kiss of you.
DIOMEDES. Lady, a word. I'll bring you to your father.
Exit with CRESSIDA
NESTOR. A woman of quick sense.
ULYSSES. Fie, fie upon her!
There's language in her eye, her cheek, her lip,
Nay, her foot speaks; her wanton spirits look out
At every joint and motive of her body.
O these encounters so glib of tongue
That give a coasting welcome ere it comes,
And wide unclasp the tables of their thoughts
To every ticklish reader! Set them down
For sluttish spoils of opportunity,
And daughters of the game. [*Trumpet within*]
ALL. The Troyans' trumpet.

Enter HECTOR, *armed;* ÆNEAS, TROILUS, PARIS, HELENUS, *and other Trojans, with attendants*

AGAMEMNON. Yonder comes the troop.
ÆNEAS. Hail, all the state of Greece! What shall be done
To him that victory commands? Or do you purpose
A victor shall be known? Will you the knights
Shall to the edge of all extremity
Pursue each other, or shall they be divided
By any voice or order of the field?
Hector bade ask.
AGAMEMNON. Which way would Hector have it?
ÆNEAS. He cares not; he'll obey conditions.
ACHILLES. 'Tis done like Hector; but securely done,

A little proudly, and great deal misprizing
The knight oppos'd.

ÆNEAS. If not Achilles, sir,
What is your name?

ACHILLES. If not Achilles, nothing.

ÆNEAS. Therefore Achilles. But whate'er, know this:
In the extremity of great and little
Valour and pride excel themselves in Hector;
The one almost as infinite as all,
The other blank as nothing. Weigh him well,
And that which looks like pride is courtesy.
This Ajax is half made of Hector's blood;
In love whereof half Hector stays at home;
Half heart, half hand, half Hector comes to seek
This blended knight, half Troyan and half Greek.

ACHILLES. A maiden battle then? O, I perceive you!

Re-enter DIOMEDES

AGAMEMNON. Here is Sir Diomed. Go, gentle knight,
Stand by our Ajax. As you and Lord Æneas
Consent upon the order of their fight,
So be it; either to the uttermost,
Or else a breath. The combatants being kin
Half stints their strife before their strokes begin.
[AJAX *and* HECTOR *enter the lists*]

ULYSSES. They are oppos'd already.

AGAMEMNON. What Troyan is that same that looks so heavy?

ULYSSES. The youngest son of Priam, a true knight;
Not yet mature, yet matchless; firm of word;
Speaking in deeds and deedless in his tongue;
Not soon provok'd, nor being provok'd soon calm'd;
His heart and hand both open and both free;
For what he has he gives, what thinks he shows,
Yet gives he not till judgment guide his bounty,
Nor dignifies an impair thought with breath;
Manly as Hector, but more dangerous;
For Hector in his blaze of wrath subscribes
To tender objects, but he in heat of action
Is more vindicative than jealous love.

They call him Troilus, and on him erect
A second hope as fairly built as Hector.
Thus says Æneas, one that knows the youth
Even to his inches, and, with private soul,
Did in great Ilion thus translate him to me.
[*Alarum.* HECTOR *and* AJAX *fight*]

AGAMEMNON. They are in action.

NESTOR. Now, Ajax, hold thine own!

TROILUS. Hector, thou sleep'st;
Awake thee.

AGAMEMNON. His blows are well dispos'd. There, Ajax!
[*Trumpets cease*]

DIOMEDES. You must no more.

ÆNEAS. Princes, enough, so please you.

AJAX. I am not warm yet; let us fight again.

DIOMEDES. As Hector pleases.

HECTOR. Why, then will I no more.
Thou art, great lord, my father's sister's son,
A cousin-german to great Priam's seed;
The obligation of our blood forbids
A gory emulation 'twixt us twain:
Were thy commixtion Greek and Troyan so
That thou could'st say 'This hand is Grecian all,
And this is Troyan; the sinews of this leg
All Greek, and this all Troy; my mother's blood
Runs on the dexter cheek, and this sinister
Bounds in my father's'; by Jove multipotent,
Thou shouldst not bear from me a Greekish member
Wherein my sword had not impressure made
Of our rank feud; but the just gods gainsay
That any drop thou borrow'dst from thy mother,
My sacred aunt, should by my mortal sword
Be drained! Let me embrace thee, Ajax.
By him that thunders, thou hast lusty arms;
Hector would have them fall upon him thus.
Cousin, all honour to thee!

AJAX. I thank thee, Hector.
Thou art too gentle and too free a man.
I came to kill thee, cousin, and bear hence
A great addition earned in thy death.

HECTOR. Not Neoptolemus so mirable,
On whose bright crest Fame with her loud'st Oyes
Cries 'This is he' could promise to himself
A thought of added honour torn from Hector.
ÆNEAS. There is expectance here from both the sides
What further you will do.
HECTOR. We'll answer it:
The issue is embracement. Ajax, farewell.
AJAX. If I might in entreaties find success,
As seld I have the chance, I would desire
My famous cousin to our Grecian tents.
DIOMEDES. 'Tis Agamemnon's wish; and great Achilles
Doth long to see unarm'd the valiant Hector.
HECTOR. Æneas, call my brother Troilus to me,
And signify this loving interview
To the expecters of our Troyan part;
Desire them home. Give me thy hand, my cousin;
I will go eat with thee, and see your knights.

AGAMEMNON *and the rest of the Greeks come forward*

AJAX. Great Agamemnon comes to meet us here.
HECTOR. The worthiest of them tell me name by name;
But for Achilles, my own searching eyes
Shall find him by his large and portly size.
AGAMEMNON. Worthy all arms! as welcome as to one
That would be rid of such an enemy.
But that's no welcome. Understand more clear,
What's past and what's to come is strew'd with husks
And formless ruin of oblivion;
But in this extant moment, faith and troth,
Strain'd purely from all hollow bias-drawing,
Bids thee with most divine integrity,
From heart of very heart, great Hector, welcome.
HECTOR. I thank thee, most imperious Agamemnon.
AGAMEMNON. [*To* TROILUS] My well-fam'd lord of Troy, no less to you.
MENELAUS. Let me confirm my princely brother's greeting.
You brace of warlike brothers, welcome hither.
HECTOR. Who must we answer?
ÆNEAS. The noble Menelaus.

HECTOR. O you, my lord? By Mars his gauntlet, thanks!
Mock not that I affect the untraded oath;
Your quondam wife swears still by Venus' glove.
She's well, but bade me not commend her to you.
MENELAUS. Name her not now, sir; she's a deadly theme.
HECTOR. O, pardon; I offend.
NESTOR. I have, thou gallant Troyan, seen thee oft,
Labouring for destiny, make cruel way
Through ranks of Greekish youth; and I have seen thee,
As hot as Perseus, spur thy Phrygian steed,
Despising many forfeits and subduements,
When thou hast hung thy advanced sword i' th' air,
Not letting it decline on the declined;
That I have said to some my standers-by
'Lo, Jupiter is yonder, dealing life!'
And I have seen thee pause and take thy breath,
When that a ring of Greeks have hemm'd thee in,
Like an Olympian wrestling. This have I seen;
But this thy countenance, still lock'd in steel,
I never saw till now. I knew thy grandsire,
And once fought with him. He was a soldier good,
But, by great Mars, the captain of us all,
Never like thee. O, let an old man embrace thee;
And, worthy warrior, welcome to our tents.
ÆNEAS. 'Tis the old Nestor.
HECTOR. Let me embrace thee, good old chronicle,
That hast so long walk'd hand in hand with time.
Most reverend Nestor, I am glad to clasp thee.
NESTOR. I would my arms could match thee in contention
As they contend with thee in courtesy.
HECTOR. I would they could.
NESTOR. Ha!
By this white beard, I'd fight with thee to-morrow.
Well, welcome, welcome! I have seen the time.
ULYSSES. I wonder now how yonder city stands,
When we have here her base and pillar by us.
HECTOR. I know your favour, Lord Ulysses, well.
Ah, sir, there's many a Greek and Troyan dead,
Since first I saw yourself and Diomed
In Ilion on your Greekish embassy.

ULYSSES. Sir, I foretold you then what would ensue.
My prophecy is but half his journey yet;
For yonder walls, that pertly front your town,
Yond towers, whose wanton tops do buss the clouds,
Must kiss their own feet.
HECTOR. I must not believe you.
There they stand yet; and modestly I think
The fall of every Phrygian stone will cost
A drop of Grecian blood. The end crowns all;
And that old common arbitrator, Time,
Will one day end it.
ULYSSES. So to him we leave it.
Most gentle and most valiant Hector, welcome.
After the General, I beseech you next
To feast with me and see me at my tent.
ACHILLES. I shall forestall thee, Lord Ulysses, thou!
Now, Hector, I have fed mine eyes on thee;
I have with exact view perus'd thee, Hector,
And quoted joint by joint.
HECTOR. Is this Achilles?
ACHILLES. I am Achilles.
HECTOR. Stand fair, I pray thee; let me look on thee.
ACHILLES. Behold thy fill.
HECTOR. Nay, I have done already.
ACHILLES. Thou art too brief. I will the second time,
As I would buy thee, view thee limb by limb.
HECTOR. O, like a book of sport thou'lt read me o'er;
But there's more in me than thou understand'st.
Why dost thou so oppress me with thine eye?
ACHILLES. Tell me, you heavens, in which part of his body
Shall I destroy him? Whether there, or there, or there?
That I may give the local wound a name,
And make distinct the very breach whereout
Hector's great spirit flew. Answer me, heavens.
HECTOR. It would discredit the blest gods, proud man,
To answer such a question. Stand again.
Think'st thou to catch my life so pleasantly
As to prenominate in nice conjecture
Where thou wilt hit me dead?
ACHILLES. I tell thee yea.

HECTOR. Wert thou an oracle to tell me so,
I'd not believe thee. Henceforth guard thee well;
For I'll not kill thee there, nor there, nor there;
But, by the forge that stithied Mars his helm,
I'll kill thee everywhere, yea, o'er and o'er.
You wisest Grecians, pardon me this brag.
His insolence draws folly from my lips;
But I'll endeavour deeds to match these words,
Or may I never—
AJAX. Do not chafe thee, cousin;
And you, Achilles, let these threats alone
Till accident or purpose bring you to't.
You may have every day enough of Hector,
If you have stomach. The general state, I fear,
Can scarce entreat you to be odd with him.
HECTOR. I pray you let us see you in the field;
We have had pelting wars since you refus'd
The Grecians' cause.
ACHILLES. Dost thou entreat me, Hector?
To-morrow do I meet thee, fell as death;
To-night all friends.
HECTOR. Thy hand upon that match.
AGAMEMNON. First, all you peers of Greece, go to my tent;
There in the full convive we; afterwards,
As Hector's leisure and your bounties shall
Concur together, severally entreat him.
Beat loud the tabourines, let the trumpets blow,
That this great soldier may his welcome know.
Exeunt all but TROILUS *and* ULYSSES
TROILUS. My Lord Ulysses, tell me, I beseech you,
In what place of the field doth Calchas keep?
ULYSSES. At Menelaus' tent, most princely Troilus.
There Diomed doth feast with him to-night,
Who neither looks upon the heaven nor earth,
But gives all gaze and bent of amorous view
On the fair Cressid.
TROILUS. Shall I, sweet lord, be bound to you so much,
After we part from Agamemnon's tent,
To bring me thither?
ULYSSES. You shall command me, sir.

As gentle tell me of what honour was
This Cressida in Troy? Had she no lover there
That wails her absence?

TROILUS. O, sir, to such as boasting show their scars
A mock is due. Will you walk on, my lord?
She was belov'd, she lov'd; she is, and doth;
But still sweet love is food for fortune's tooth. *Exeunt*

ACT V. SCENE 1

The Grecian camp. Before the tent of ACHILLES

Enter ACHILLES *and* PATROCLUS

ACHILLES. I'll heat his blood with Greekish wine to-night,
Which with my scimitar I'll cool to-morrow.
Patroclus, let us feast him to the height.

PATROCLUS. Here comes Thersites.

Enter THERSITES

ACHILLES. How now, thou core of envy!
Thou crusty batch of nature, what's the news?

THERSITES. Why, thou picture of what thou seemest, and idol of idiot worshippers, here's a letter for thee.

ACHILLES. From whence, fragment?

THERSITES. Why, thou full dish of fool, from Troy.

PATROCLUS. Who keeps the tent now?

THERSITES. The surgeon's box or the patient's wound.

PATROCLUS. Well said, Adversity! and what needs these tricks?

THERSITES. Prithee, be silent, boy; I profit not by thy talk; thou art said to be Achilles' male varlet.

PATROCLUS. Male varlet, you rogue! What's that?

THERSITES. Why, his masculine whore. Now, the rotten diseases of the south, the guts-griping ruptures, catarrhs, loads o' gravel in the back, lethargies, cold palsies, raw eyes, dirt-rotten livers, wheezing lungs, bladders full of imposthume, sciaticas, limekilns i' th' palm, incurable bone-ache, and the rivelled fee-simple of the tetter, take and take again such preposterous discoveries!

Patroclus. Why, thou damnable box of envy, thou, what meanest thou to curse thus?

Thersites. Do I curse thee?

Patroclus. Why, no, you ruinous butt; you whoreson indistinguishable cur, no.

Thersites. No! Why art thou, then, exasperate, thou idle immaterial skein of sleid silk, thou green sarcenet flap for a sore eye, thou tassel of a prodigal's purse, thou? Ah, how the poor world is pest'red with such water-flies—diminutives of nature!

Patroclus. Out, gall!

Thersites. Finch egg!

Achilles. My sweet Patroclus, I am thwarted quite
From my great purpose in to-morrow's battle.
Here is a letter from Queen Hecuba,
A token from her daughter, my fair love,
Both taxing me and gaging me to keep
An oath that I have sworn. I will not break it.
Fall Greeks; fail fame; honour or go or stay;
My major vow lies here, this I'll obey.
Come, come, Thersites, help to trim my tent;
This night in banqueting must all be spent.
Away, Patroclus! *Exit with* Patroclus

Thersites. With too much blood and too little brain these two may run mad; but, if with too much brain and too little blood they do, I'll be a curer of madmen. Here's Agamemnon, an honest fellow enough, and one that loves quails, but he has not so much brain as ear-wax; and the goodly transformation of Jupiter there, his brother, the bull, the primitive statue and oblique memorial of cuckolds, a thrifty shoeing-horn in a chain, hanging at his brother's leg—to what form but that he is, should wit larded with malice, and malice forced with wit, turn him to? To an ass, were nothing: he is both ass and ox. To an ox, were nothing: he is both ox and ass. To be a dog, a mule, a cat, a fitchew, a toad, a lizard, an owl, a puttock, or a herring without a roe, I would not care; but to be Menelaus, I would conspire against destiny. Ask me not what I would be, if I were not Thersites; for I care not to be the louse of a lazar, so I were not Menelaus. Hey-day! sprites and fires!

Enter HECTOR, TROILUS, AJAX, AGAMEMNON, ULYSSES, NESTOR, MENELAUS, *and* DIOMEDES, *with lights*

AGAMEMNON. We go wrong, we go wrong.
AJAX. No, yonder 'tis;
There, where we see the lights.
HECTOR. I trouble you.
AJAX. No, not a whit.

Re-enter ACHILLES

ULYSSES. Here comes himself to guide you.
ACHILLES. Welcome, brave Hector; welcome, Princes all.
AGAMEMNON. So now, fair Prince of Troy, I bid good night;
Ajax commands the guard to tend on you.
HECTOR. Thanks, and good night to the Greeks' general.
MENELAUS. Good night, my lord.
HECTOR. Good night, sweet Lord Menelaus.
THERSITES. Sweet draught! 'Sweet' quoth 'a?
Sweet sink, sweet sewer!
ACHILLES. Good night and welcome, both at once, to those
That go or tarry.
AGAMEMNON. Good night.

Exeunt AGAMEMNON *and* MENELAUS

ACHILLES. Old Nestor tarries; and you too, Diomed,
Keep Hector company an hour or two.
DIOMEDES. I cannot, lord; I have important business,
The tide whereof is now. Good night, great Hector.
HECTOR. Give me your hand.
ULYSSES. [*Aside to* TROILUS] Follow his torch; he goes to Calchas' tent;
I'll keep you company.
TROILUS. Sweet sir, you honour me.
HECTOR. And so, good night.

Exit DIOMEDES; ULYSSES *and* TROILUS *following*

ACHILLES. Come, come, enter my tent.

Exeunt all but THERSITES

THERSITES. That same Diomed's a false-hearted rogue, a most unjust knave; I will no more trust him when he leers than I will a serpent when he hisses. He will spend his mouth and promise, like Brabbler the hound; but when he performs, astronomers foretell it: it is prodigious, there will come some change; the sun borrows of the moon when Diomed keeps his word. I will rather leave to see Hector than not to dog him. They say he keeps a Troyan drab, and uses the traitor Calchas' tent. I'll after. Nothing but lechery! All incontinent varlets! *Exit*

SCENE 2

The Grecian camp. Before CALCHAS' *tent*

Enter DIOMEDES

DIOMEDES. What, are you up here, ho? Speak.
CALCHAS. [*Within*] Who calls?
DIOMEDES. Diomed. Calchas, I think. Where's your daughter?
CALCHAS. [*Within*] She comes to you.

Enter TROILUS *and* ULYSSES, *at a distance; after them* THERSITES

ULYSSES. Stand where the torch may not discover us.

Enter CRESSIDA

TROILUS. Cressid comes forth to him.
DIOMEDES. How now, my charge!
CRESSIDA. Now, my sweet guardian! Hark, a word with you. [*Whispers*]
TROILUS. Yea, so familiar!
ULYSSES. She will sing any man at first sight.
THERSITES. And any man may sing her, if he can take her cliff; she's noted.
DIOMEDES. Will you remember?
CRESSIDA. Remember? Yes.
DIOMEDES. Nay, but do, then;
And let your mind be coupled with your words.

TROILUS. What shall she remember?
ULYSSES. List!
CRESSIDA. Sweet honey Greek, tempt me no more to folly.
THERSITES. Roguery!
DIOMEDES. Nay, then—
CRESSIDA. I'll tell you what—
DIOMEDES. Fo, fo! come, tell a pin; you are a forsworn—
CRESSIDA. In faith, I cannot. What would you have me do?
THERSITES. A juggling trick, to be secretly open.
DIOMEDES. What did you swear you would bestow on me?
CRESSIDA. I prithee, do not hold me to mine oath;
Bid me do anything but that, sweet Greek.
DIOMEDES. Good night.
TROILUS. Hold, patience!
ULYSSES. How now, Troyan!
CRESSIDA. Diomed!
DIOMEDES. No, no, good night; I'll be your fool no more.
TROILUS. Thy better must.
CRESSIDA. Hark! a word in your ear.
TROILUS. O plague and madness!
ULYSSES. You are moved, Prince; let us depart, I pray,
Lest your displeasure should enlarge itself
To wrathful terms. This place is dangerous;
The time right deadly; I beseech you, go.
TROILUS. Behold, I pray you.
ULYSSES. Nay, good my lord, go off;
You flow to great distraction; come, my lord.
TROILUS. I prithee stay.
ULYSSES. You have not patience; come.
TROILUS. I pray you, stay; by hell and all hell's torments,
I will not speak a word.
DIOMEDES. And so, good night.
CRESSIDA. Nay, but you part in anger.
TROILUS. Doth that grieve thee? O withered truth!
ULYSSES. How now, my lord?
TROILUS. By Jove, I will be patient.
CRESSIDA. Guardian! Why, Greek!
DIOMEDES. Fo, fo! adieu! you palter.
CRESSIDA. In faith, I do not. Come hither once again.
ULYSSES. You shake, my lord, at something; will you go?

You will break out.
TROILUS. She strokes his cheek.
ULYSSES. Come, come.
TROILUS. Nay, stay; by Jove, I will not speak a word:
There is between my will and all offences
A guard of patience. Stay a little while.
THERSITES. How the devil luxury, with his fat rump and potato finger, tickles these together! Fry, lechery, fry!
DIOMEDES. But will you, then?
CRESSIDA. In faith, I will, lo; never trust me else.
DIOMEDES. Give me some token for the surety of it.
CRESSIDA. I'll fetch you one. *Exit*
ULYSSES. You have sworn patience.
TROILUS. Fear me not, my lord;
I will not be myself, nor have cognition
Of what I feel. I am all patience.

Re-enter CRESSIDA

THERSITES. Now the pledge; now, now, now!
CRESSIDA. Here, Diomed, keep this sleeve.
TROILUS. O beauty! where is thy faith?
ULYSSES. My lord!
TROILUS. I will be patient; outwardly I will.
CRESSIDA. You look upon that sleeve; behold it well.
He lov'd me—O false wench!—Give't me again.
DIOMEDES. Whose was't?
CRESSIDA. It is no matter, now I ha't again.
I will not meet with you to-morrow night.
I prithee, Diomed, visit me no more.
THERSITES. Now she sharpens. Well said, whetstone.
DIOMEDES. I shall have it.
CRESSIDA. What, this?
DIOMEDES. Ay, that.
CRESSIDA. O all you gods! O pretty, pretty pledge!
Thy master now lies thinking on his bed
Of thee and me, and sighs, and takes my glove,
And gives memorial dainty kisses to it,
As I kiss thee. Nay, do not snatch it from me;
He that takes that doth take my heart withal.
DIOMEDES. I had your heart before; this follows it.

TROILUS. I did swear patience.
CRESSIDA. You shall not have it, Diomed; faith, you shall not;
I'll give you something else.
DIOMEDES. I will have this. Whose was it?
CRESSIDA. It is no matter.
DIOMEDES. Come, tell me whose it was.
CRESSIDA. 'Twas one's that lov'd me better than you will.
But, now you have it, take it.
DIOMEDES. Whose was it?
CRESSIDA. By all Diana's waiting women yond,
And by herself, I will not tell you whose.
DIOMEDES. To-morrow will I wear it on my helm,
And grieve his spirit that dares not challenge it.
TROILUS. Wert thou the devil and wor'st it on thy horn,
It should be challeng'd.
CRESSIDA. Well, well, 'tis done, 'tis past; and yet it is not;
I will not keep my word.
DIOMEDES. Why, then farewell;
Thou never shalt mock Diomed again.
CRESSIDA. You shall not go. One cannot speak a word
But it straight starts you.
DIOMEDES. I do not like this fooling.
THERSITES. Nor I, by Pluto; but that that likes not you
Pleases me best.
DIOMEDES. What, shall I come? The hour—
CRESSIDA. Ay, come—O Jove! Do come. I shall be plagu'd.
DIOMEDES. Farewell till then.
CRESSIDA. Good night. I prithee come. *Exit* DIOMEDES
Troilus, farewell! One eye yet looks on thee;
But with my heart the other eye doth see.
Ah, poor our sex! this fault in us I find,
The error of our eye directs our mind.
What error leads must err; O, then conclude,
Minds sway'd by eyes are full of turpitude. *Exit*
THERSITES. A proof of strength she could not publish more,
Unless she said 'My mind is now turn'd whore.'
ULYSSES. All's done, my lord.
TROILUS. It is.
ULYSSES. Why stay we, then?

TROILUS. To make a recordation to my soul
Of every syllable that here was spoke.
But if I tell how these two did coact,
Shall I not lie in publishing a truth?
Sith yet there is a credence in my heart,
An esperance so obstinately strong,
That doth invert th' attest of eyes and ears;
As if those organs had deceptious functions
Created only to calumniate.
Was Cressid here?

ULYSSES. I cannot conjure, Troyan.

TROILUS. She was not, sure.

ULYSSES. Most sure she was.

TROILUS. Why, my negation hath no taste of madness.

ULYSSES. Nor mine, my lord. Cressid was here but now.

TROILUS. Let it not be believ'd for womanhood.
Think, we had mothers; do not give advantage
To stubborn critics, apt, without a theme,
For depravation, to square the general sex
By Cressid's rule. Rather think this not Cressid.

ULYSSES. What hath she done, Prince, that can soil our mothers?

TROILUS. Nothing at all, unless that this were she.

THERSITES. Will 'a swagger himself out on's own eyes?

TROILUS. This she? No; this is Diomed's Cressida.
If beauty have a soul, this is not she;
If souls guide vows, if vows be sanctimonies,
If sanctimony be the god's delight,
If there be rule in unity itself,
This was not she. O madness of discourse,
That cause sets up with and against itself!
Bifold authority! where reason can revolt
Without perdition, and loss assume all reason
Without revolt: this is, and is not, Cressid.
Within my soul there doth conduce a fight
Of this strange nature, that a thing inseparate
Divides more wider than the sky and earth;
And yet the spacious breadth of this division
Admits no orifex for a point as subtle
As Ariachne's broken woof to enter.

Instance, O instance! strong as Pluto's gates:
Cressid is mine, tied with the bonds of heaven.
Instance, O instance! strong as heaven itself:
The bonds of heaven are slipp'd, dissolv'd, and loos'd;
And with another knot, five-finger-tied,
The fractions of her faith, orts of her love,
The fragments, scraps, the bits, and greasy relics
Of her o'er-eaten faith, are bound to Diomed.

ULYSSES. May worthy Troilus be half-attach'd
With that which here his passion doth express?

TROILUS. Ay, Greek; and that shall be divulged well
In characters as red as Mars his heart
Inflam'd with Venus. Never did young man fancy
With so eternal and so fix'd a soul.
Hark, Greek: as much as I do Cressid love,
So much by weight hate I her Diomed.
That sleeve is mine that he'll bear on his helm;
Were it a casque compos'd by Vulcan's skill
My sword should bite it. Not the dreadful spout
Which shipmen do the hurricano call,
Constring'd in mass by the almighty sun,
Shall dizzy with more clamour Neptune's ear
In his descent than shall my prompted sword
Falling on Diomed.

THERSITES. He'll tickle it for his concupy.

TROILUS. O Cressid! O false Cressid! false, false, false!
Let all untruths stand by thy stained name,
And they'll seem glorious.

ULYSSES. O, contain yourself;
Your passion draws ears hither.

Enter ÆNEAS

ÆNEAS. I have been seeking you this hour, my lord.
Hector, by this, is arming him in Troy;
Ajax, your guard, stays to conduct you home.

TROILUS. Have with you, Prince. My courteous lord, adieu.
Fairwell, revolted fair!—and, Diomed,
Stand fast and wear a castle on thy head.

ULYSSES. I'll bring you to the gates.

TROILUS. Accept distracted thanks.

Exeunt TROILUS, ÆNEAS, *and* ULYSSES

THERSITES. Would I could meet that rogue Diomed! I would croak like a raven; I would bode, I would bode. Patroclus will give me anything for the intelligence of this whore; the parrot will not do more for an almond than he for a commodious drab. Lechery, lechery! Still wars and lechery! Nothing else holds fashion. A burning devil take them! *Exit*

SCENE 3

Troy. Before PRIAM'S *palace*

Enter HECTOR *and* ANDROMACHE

ANDROMACHE. When was my lord so much ungently temper'd
To stop his ears against admonishment?
Unarm, unarm, and do not fight to-day.
HECTOR. You train me to offend you; get you in.
By all the everlasting gods, I'll go.
ANDROMACHE. My dreams will, sure, prove ominous to the day.
HECTOR. No more, I say.

Enter CASSANDRA

CASSANDRA. Where is my brother Hector?
ANDROMACHE. Here, sister, arm'd, and bloody in intent.
Consort with me in loud and dear petition,
Pursue we him on knees; for I have dreamt
Of bloody turbulence, and this whole night
Hath nothing been but shapes and forms of slaughter.
CASSANDRA. O, 'tis true!
HECTOR. Ho! bid my trumpet sound.
CASSANDRA. No notes of sally, for the heavens, sweet brother!
HECTOR. Be gone, I say. The gods have heard me swear.
CASSANDRA. The gods are deaf to hot and peevish vows;
They are polluted off'rings, more abhorr'd
Than spotted livers in the sacrifice.

ANDROMACHE. O, be persuaded! Do not count it holy
To hurt by being just. It is as lawful,
For we would give much, to use violent thefts
And rob in the behalf of charity.
CASSANDRA. It is the purpose that makes strong the vow;
But vows to every purpose must not hold.
Unarm, sweet Hector.
HECTOR. Hold you still, I say.
Mine honour keeps the weather of my fate.
Life every man holds dear; but the dear man
Holds honour far more precious dear than life.

Enter TROILUS

How now, young man! Mean'st thou to fight to-day?
ANDROMACHE. Cassandra, call my father to persuade.
Exit CASSANDRA
HECTOR. No, faith, young Troilus; doff thy harness, youth;
I am to-day i' th' vein of chivalry.
Let grow thy sinews till their knots be strong,
And tempt not yet the brushes of the war.
Unarm thee, go; and doubt thou not, brave boy,
I'll stand to-day for thee and me and Troy.
TROILUS. Brother, you have a vice of mercy in you
Which better fits a lion than a man.
HECTOR. What vice is that, good Troilus?
Chide me for it.
TROILUS. When many times the captive Grecian falls,
Even in the fan and wind of your fair sword,
You bid them rise and live.
HECTOR. O, 'tis fair play!
TROILUS. Fool's play, by heaven, Hector.
HECTOR. How now! how now!
TROILUS. For th' love of all the gods,
Let's leave the hermit Pity with our mother;
And when we have our armours buckled on,
The venom'd vengeance ride upon our swords,
Spur them to ruthful work, rein them from ruth!
HECTOR. Fie, savage, fie!
TROILUS. Hector, then 'tis wars.
HECTOR. Troilus, I would not have you fight to-day.

TROILUS. Who should withhold me?
Not fate, obedience, nor the hand of Mars
Beck'ning with fiery truncheon my retire;
Not Priamus and Hecuba on knees,
Their eyes o'ergalled with recourse of tears;
Nor you, my brother, with your true sword drawn,
Oppos'd to hinder me, should stop my way,
But by my ruin.

Re-enter CASSANDRA, *with* PRIAM

CASSANDRA. Lay hold upon him, Priam, hold him fast;
He is thy crutch; now if thou lose thy stay,
Thou on him leaning, and all Troy on thee,
Fall all together.
PRIAM. Come, Hector, come, go back.
Thy wife hath dreamt; thy mother hath had visions;
Cassandra doth foresee; and I myself
Am like a prophet suddenly enrapt
To tell thee that this day is ominous.
Therefore, come back.
HECTOR. Æneas is a-field;
And I do stand engag'd to many Greeks,
Even in the faith of valour, to appear
This morning to them.
PRIAM. Ay, but thou shalt not go.
HECTOR. I must not break my faith.
You know me dutiful; therefore, dear sir,
Let me not shame respect; but give me leave
To take that course by your consent and voice
Which you do here forbid me, royal Priam.
CASSANDRA. O Priam, yield not to him!
ANDROMACHE. Do not, dear father.
HECTOR. Andromache, I am offended with you.
Upon the love you bear me, get you in.

Exit ANDROMACHE

TROILUS. This foolish, dreaming, superstitious girl
Makes all these bodements.
CASSANDRA. O, farewell, dear Hector!
Look how thou diest. Look how thy eye turns pale.
Look how thy wounds do bleed at many vents.

Hark how Troy roars; how Hecuba cries out;
How poor Andromache shrills her dolours forth;
Behold distraction, frenzy, and amazement,
Like witless antics, one another meet,
And all cry, Hector! Hector's dead! O Hector!

TROILUS. Away, away!

CASSANDRA. Farewell!—yet, soft! Hector, I take my leave.
Thou dost thyself and all our Troy deceive. *Exit*

HECTOR. You are amaz'd, my liege, at her exclaim.
Go in, and cheer the town; we'll forth, and fight,
Do deeds worth praise and tell you them at night.

PRIAM. Farewell. The gods with safety stand about thee!

Exeunt severally PRIAM *and* HECTOR. *Alarums*

TROILUS. They are at it, hark! Proud Diomed, believe,
I come to lose my arm or win my sleeve.

Enter PANDARUS

PANDARUS. Do you hear, my lord? Do you hear?

TROILUS. What now?

PANDARUS. Here's a letter come from yond poor girl.

TROILUS. Let me read.

PANDARUS. A whoreson tisick, a whoreson rascally tisick so troubles me, and the foolish fortune of this girl, and what one thing, what another, that I shall leave you one o' th's days; and I have a rheum in mine eyes too, and such an ache in my bones that unless a man were curs'd I cannot tell what to think on't. What says she there?

TROILUS. Words, words, mere words, no matter from the heart;
Th' effect doth operate another way.

[*Tearing the letter*]

Go, wind, to wind, there turn and change together.
My love with words and errors still she feeds,
But edifies another with her deeds. *Exeunt severally*

SCENE 4

The plain between Troy and the Grecian camp

Enter THERSITES. *Excursions*

THERSITES. Now they are clapper-clawing one another; I'll go look on. That dissembling abominable varlet, Diomed, has got that same scurvy doting foolish young knave's sleeve of Troy there in his helm. I would fain see them meet, that that same young Troyan ass that loves the whore there might send that Greekish whoremasterly villain with the sleeve back to the dissembling luxurious drab of a sleeve-less errand. A th' t'other side, the policy of those crafty swearing rascals–that stale old mouse-eaten dry cheese, Nestor, and that same dog-fox, Ulysses –is not prov'd worth a blackberry. They set me up, in policy, that mongrel cur, Ajax, against that dog of as bad a kind, Achilles; and now is the cur Ajax prouder than the cur Achilles, and will not arm to-day; whereupon the Grecians begin to proclaim barbarism, and policy grows into an ill opinion.

Enter DIOMEDES, TROILUS *following*

Soft! here comes sleeve, and t'other.

TROILUS. Fly not; for shouldst thou take the river Styx
I would swim after.

DIOMEDES. Thou dost miscall retire.
I do not fly; but advantageous care
Withdrew me from the odds of multitude.
Have at thee.

THERSITES. Hold thy whore, Grecian; now for thy whore, Troyan–now the sleeve, now the sleeve!

Exeunt TROILUS *and* DIOMEDES *fighting*

Enter HECTOR

HECTOR. What art thou, Greek? Art thou for Hector's match?
Art thou of blood and honour?

THERSITES. No, no—I am a rascal; a scurvy railing knave; a very filthy rogue.

HECTOR. I do believe thee. Live. *Exit*

THERSITES. God-a-mercy, that thou wilt believe me; but a plague break thy neck for frighting me! What's become of the wenching rogues? I think they have swallowed one another. I would laugh at that miracle. Yet, in a sort, lechery eats itself. I'll seek them. *Exit*

SCENE 5

Another part of the plain

Enter DIOMEDES *and a* SERVANT

DIOMEDES. Go, go, my servant, take thou Troilus' horse;
Present the fair steed to my lady Cressid.
Fellow, commend my service to her beauty;
Tell her I have chastis'd the amorous Troyan,
And am her knight by proof.

SERVANT. I go, my lord. *Exit*

Enter AGAMEMNON

AGAMEMNON. Renew, renew! The fierce Polydamus
Hath beat down Menon; bastard Margarelon
Hath Doreus prisoner,
And stands colossus-wise, waving his beam,
Upon the pashed corses of the kings
Epistrophus and Cedius. Polixenes is slain;
Amphimacus and Thoas deadly hurt;
Patroclus ta'en, or slain; and Palamedes
Sore hurt and bruis'd. The dreadful Sagittary
Appals our numbers. Haste we, Diomed,
To reinforcement, or we perish all.

Enter NESTOR

NESTOR. Go, bear Patroclus' body to Achilles,
And bid the snail-pac'd Ajax arm for shame.
There is a thousand Hectors in the field;
Now here he fights on Galathe his horse,

And there lacks work; anon he's there afoot,
And there they fly or die, like scaled sculls
Before the belching whale; then is he yonder,
And there the strawy Greeks, ripe for his edge,
Fall down before him like the mower's swath.
Here, there, and everywhere, he leaves and takes;
Dexterity so obeying appetite
That what he will he does, and does so much
That proof is call'd impossibility.

Enter ULYSSES

ULYSSES. O, courage, courage, Princes! Great Achilles
Is arming, weeping, cursing, vowing vengeance.
Patroclus' wounds have rous'd his drowsy blood,
Together with his mangled Myrmidons,
That noseless, handless, hack'd and chipp'd, come to him,
Crying on Hector. Ajax hath lost a friend
And foams at mouth, and he is arm'd and at it,
Roaring for Troilus; who hath done to-day
Mad and fantastic execution,
Engaging and redeeming of himself
With such a careless force and forceless care
As if that luck, in very spite of cunning,
Bade him win all.

Enter AJAX

AJAX. Troilus! thou coward Troilus! *Exit*
DIOMEDES. Ay, there, there.
NESTOR. So, so, we draw together. *Exit*

Enter ACHILLES

ACHILLES. Where is this Hector?
Come, come, thou boy-queller, show thy face;
Know what it is to meet Achilles angry.
Hector! where's Hector? I will none but Hector. *Exeunt*

SCENE 6

Another part of the plain

Enter AJAX

AJAX. Troilus, thou coward Troilus, show thy head.

Enter DIOMEDES

DIOMEDES. Troilus, I say! Where's Troilus?
AJAX. What wouldst thou?
DIOMEDES. I would correct him.
AJAX. Were I the general, thou shouldst have my office
Ere that correction. Troilus, I say! What, Troilus!

Enter TROILUS

TROILUS. O traitor Diomed! Turn thy false face, thou traitor,
And pay thy life thou owest me for my horse.
DIOMEDES. Ha! art thou there?
AJAX. I'll fight with him alone. Stand, Diomed.
DIOMEDES. He is my prize. I will not look upon.
TROILUS. Come, both, you cogging Greeks; have at you both. *Exeunt fighting*

Enter HECTOR

HECTOR. Yea, Troilus? O, well fought, my youngest brother!

Enter ACHILLES

ACHILLES. Now do I see thee, ha! Have at thee, Hector!
HECTOR. Pause, if thou wilt.
ACHILLES. I do disdain thy courtesy, proud Troyan.
Be happy that my arms are out of use;
My rest and negligence befriends thee now,
But thou anon shalt hear of me again;
Till when, go seek thy fortune. *Exit*
HECTOR. Fare thee well.
I would have been much more a fresher man,
Had I expected thee.

Re-enter TROILUS

How now, my brother!
TROILUS. Ajax hath ta'en Æneas. Shall it be?
No, by the flame of yonder glorious heaven,
He shall not carry him; I'll be ta'en too,
Or bring him off. Fate, hear me what I say:
I reck not though thou end my life to-day. *Exit*

Enter one in armour

HECTOR. Stand, stand, thou Greek; thou art a goodly mark.
No? wilt thou not? I like thy armour well;
I'll frush it and unlock the rivets all
But I'll be master of it. Wilt thou not, beast, abide?
Why then, fly on; I'll hunt thee for thy hide. *Exeunt*

SCENE 7

Another part of the plain

Enter ACHILLES, *with Myrmidons*

ACHILLES. Come here about me, you my Myrmidons;
Mark what I say. Attend me where I wheel;
Strike not a stroke, but keep yourselves in breath;
And when I have the bloody Hector found,
Empale him with your weapons round about;
In fellest manner execute your arms.
Follow me, sirs, and my proceedings eye.
It is decreed Hector the great must die. *Exeunt*

Enter MENELAUS *and* PARIS, *fighting; then* THERSITES

THERSITES. The cuckold and the cuckold-maker are at it. Now, bull! now, dog! 'Loo, Paris, 'loo! now my double-horn'd Spartan! 'loo, Paris, 'loo! The bull has the game. Ware horns, ho! *Exeunt* PARIS *and* MENELAUS

Enter MARGARELON

MARGARELON. Turn, slave, and fight.
THERSITES. What art thou?

MARGARELON. A bastard son of Priam's.

THERSITES. I am a bastard too; I love bastards. I am a bastard begot, bastard instructed, bastard in mind, bastard in valour, in everything illegitimate. One bear will not bite another, and wherefore should one bastard? Take heed, the quarrel's most ominous to us: if the son of a whore fight for a whore, he tempts judgment. Farewell, bastard. *Exit*

MARGARELON. The devil take thee, coward! *Exit*

SCENE 8

Another part of the plain

Enter HECTOR

HECTOR. Most putrified core so fair without,
Thy goodly armour thus hath cost thy life.
Now is my day's work done; I'll take good breath:
Rest, sword; thou hast thy fill of blood and death!
[*Disarms*]

Enter ACHILLES *and his Myrmidons*

ACHILLES. Look, Hector, how the sun begins to set;
How ugly night comes breathing at his heels;
Even with the vail and dark'ning of the sun,
To close the day up, Hector's life is done.

HECTOR. I am unarm'd; forego this vantage, Greek.

ACHILLES. Strike, fellows, strike; this is the man I seek.
[HECTOR *falls*]
So, Ilion, fall thou next! Come, Troy, sink down;
Here lies thy heart, thy sinews, and thy bone.
On, Myrmidons, and cry you all amain
'Achilles hath the mighty Hector slain.'
[*A retreat sounded*]
Hark! a retire upon our Grecian part.

MYRMIDON. The Troyan trumpets sound the like, my lord.

ACHILLES. The dragon wing of night o'erspreads the earth
And, stickler-like, the armies separates.
My half-supp'd sword, that frankly would have fed,

Pleas'd with this dainty bait, thus goes to bed.
[*Sheathes his sword*]
Come, tie his body to my horse's tail;
Along the field I will the Troyan trail. *Exeunt*

SCENE 9

Another part of the plain

Sound retreat. Shout. Enter AGAMEMNON, AJAX, MENELAUS, NESTOR, DIOMEDES, *and the rest, marching*

AGAMEMNON. Hark! hark! what shout is this?
NESTOR. Peace, drums!
SOLDIERS. [*Within*] Achilles! Achilles! Hector's slain. Achilles!
DIOMEDES. The bruit is Hector's slain, and by Achilles.
AJAX. If it be so, yet bragless let it be;
Great Hector was as good a man as he.
AGAMEMNON. March patiently along. Let one be sent
To pray Achilles see us at our tent.
If in his death the gods have us befriended;
Great Troy is ours, and our sharp wars are ended.
Exeunt

SCENE 10

Another part of the plain

Enter ÆNEAS, PARIS, ANTENOR, *and* DEIPHOBUS

ÆNEAS. Stand, ho! yet are we masters of the field.
Never go home; here starve we out the night.

Enter TROILUS

TROILUS. Hector is slain.
ALL. Hector! The gods forbid!
TROILUS. He's dead, and at the murderer's horse's tail,
In beastly sort, dragg'd through the shameful field.
Frown on, you heavens, effect your rage with speed.

ACHILLES. *Look, Hector, how the sun begins to set;*
How ugly night comes breathing at his heels;
Even with the vail and dark'ning of the sun,
To close the day up, Hector's life is done.
HECTOR. *I am unarm'd; forego this vantage, Greek.*
ACHILLES. *Strike, fellows, strike; this is the man I seek.*
(ACT V. Scene 8)

Sit, gods, upon your thrones, and smile at Troy.
I say at once let your brief plagues be mercy,
And linger not our sure destructions on.

ÆNEAS. My lord, you do discomfort all the host.

TROILUS. You understand me not that tell me so.
I do not speak of flight, of fear of death,
But dare all imminence that gods and men
Address their dangers in. Hector is gone.
Who shall tell Priam so, or Hecuba?
Let him that will a screech-owl aye be call'd
Go in to Troy, and say there 'Hector's dead.'
There is a word will Priam turn to stone;
Make wells and Niobes of the maids and wives,
Cold statues of the youth; and, in a word,
Scare Troy out of itself. But, march away;
Hector is dead; there is no more to say.
Stay yet. You vile abominable tents,
Thus proudly pight upon our Phrygian plains,
Let Titan rise as early as he dare,
I'll through and through you. And, thou great-siz'd coward,
No space of earth shall sunder our two hates;
I'll haunt thee like a wicked conscience still,
That mouldeth goblins swift as frenzy's thoughts.
Strike a free march to Troy. With comfort go;
Hope of revenge shall hide our inward woe.

Enter PANDARUS

PANDARUS. But hear you, hear you!

TROILUS. Hence, broker-lackey. Ignominy and shame
Pursue thy life and live aye with thy name!

Exeunt all but PANDARUS

PANDARUS. A goodly medicine for my aching bones! O world! world! world! thus is the poor agent despis'd! O traitors and bawds, how earnestly are you set a work, and how ill requited! Why should our endeavour be so lov'd, and the performance so loathed? What verse for it? What instance for it? Let me see—

Full merrily the humble-bee doth sing
Till he hath lost his honey and his sting;

And being once subdu'd in armed trail,
Sweet honey and sweet notes together fail.

Good traders in the flesh, set this in your painted cloths.
As many as be here of pander's hall,
Your eyes, half out, weep out at Pandar's fall;
Or, if you cannot weep, yet give some groans,
Though not for me, yet for your aching bones.
Brethren and sisters of the hold-door trade,
Some two months hence my will shall here be made.
It should be now, but that my fear is this,
Some galled goose of Winchester would hiss.
Till then I'll sweat and seek about for eases,
And at that time bequeath you my diseases. *Exit*

The Tragedy of Coriolanus

CORIOLANUS

HEMINGE AND CONDELL intended that *Coriolanus* should stand in their edition first among the Tragedies, but the accident that delayed the printing of *Troilus and Cressida* forced the printer to place that piece between the Histories and Tragedies, and so just before *Coriolanus*. Why Heminge and Condell should have selected *Coriolanus* for first place is not clear; it was so far unpublished and the editors may have wished to give unpublished pieces a prominent position in their arrangement. It was not because of its chronological order in Shakespeare's work, for *Coriolanus* is the last of his Tragedies, coming immediately after *Antony and Cleopatra*. The external evidence for date is slight: Ben Jonson's *Silent Woman* contains the remark, 'you have lurched your friends of the better half of the garland,' which has all the appearance of being a hit at Shakespeare's use of 'lurch' in Act II, Scene 2, 'He lurch'd all swords of the garland.' As the *Silent Woman* went on the stage about January 1610, *Coriolanus* must date not later than 1609. 'The coal of fire upon the ice' has been taken as a reminiscence of the great frost of 1607-8 in which the Thames was so frozen that coal could be used in braziers on it. But though the external evidence is slight, the internal evidence is such that there can be little question of the place of the piece. Shakespeare's style in the last years of his work for the stage shows certain features in the versification that can be expressed in figures, figures that, taken in conjunction with the external evidence, indicate with some precision the sequence of composition. While lines in which the ending is 'light,' concluding with auxiliaries, pronouns, and monosyllabic adverbs, are found in plays before *Antony and Cleopatra*, it is only with that play that they become really numerous; and at the same time the 'weak' endings, having in the final place prepositions such as 'by,' 'at,' or conjunctions like 'and' or 'as' on which the voice hardly falls, are now noticeable for the first time. This evidence places *Coriolanus* just after *Antony and Cleopatra* and before *Cymbeline*, which, though included by Heminge and Condell in the same section as the Tragedies, modern criticism takes with *The Winter's Tale* and *The Tempest* and treats as one of the Romances.

In *Coriolanus*, as in *Antony and Cleopatra*, Shakespeare found his story in Plutarch. To criticize Plutarch, who has preserved for us so much of the antique world, would be presumptuous and ungrateful, but when Shakespeare's play is put beside the narrative, we can see how Shakespeare has regrouped the figures and changed the emphasis so that we have a much more definite picture of their natures and a clearer perception of where the responsibility for the tragic confusion lies. It may be objected, however, that Plutarch's *Life of Coriolanus* is designed as history, although most historians regard it as more myth than history, and that Shakespeare's version can have no claim to present us with a more truthful or trustworthy account of what happened. That is true; all that is suggested, however, is that taking Plutarch's account as history Shakespeare has proposed a clearer and more likely interpretation of the relations between the individuals; Plutarch was interested in the personal drama in which his heroes each in turn played their part rather than in the social or economic problems that so often provided the background for his hero's action. Shakespeare carries this treatment much further and gives to the personal drama a clarity and relief beside which Plutarch's narrative has the charm and quality of a splendid tapestry. It would be absurd to say that Shakespeare and Plutarch were devoid of interest in social and cognate problems but neither approaches them as a social or economic specialist; their first business is with the man; all else is in keeping with the proportions assigned to the human figure.

In these democratic days *Coriolanus* does not have what is called a good press; his class-consciousness is felt as an offence against good fellowship, aggravated by the solitariness, as Plutarch calls it, which isolates him even from some of his fellow patricians. His mother rounds off the unfavourable impression the man and his loyalties leave on the commentator whose humanitarian notions react angrily to such pretensions. Nor does the æsthetic spectator viewing his actions from what once was the shelter of Bloomsbury find this soldier more endurable. Lytton Strachey felt that *Coriolanus* was an intolerable play and that the hero was no longer human but the creation of an artist who had given up his interest in the tedious business of life and now presents us with the statue of a demi-god cast in bronze roaring its perfect periods through a melodious megaphone. Strachey at least has some feeling for the heroic aspects of his subject, though he betrays a sad lack of self-knowledge when he thinks he can see how much better the theme could have been developed by a treatment very different from Shakespeare's.

In spite of Strachey's attempt to transport the play into the never-never land of what he regarded as Shakespeare's final refuge from the horrors of existence, modern spectators are conscious of the realities in the contest between Coriolanus and the tribunes of the people, and that the tensions of the play are present in all times and more especially in what we now like to regard as the developing forms of social evolution. The tendency to feel critical of the high-handed honesty of the soldier is natural, but to prefer to it the underhand treachery of the tribunes is not only unnatural but impolitic. Such chicanery delivers society to its enemies, and to say that it is the soldier only who is a traitor to his country is to ignore the cowardly betrayal inherent in the vanity and malice of the policy of his opponents. All have faults, but there emerges from the terrible confusion a magnanimity and self-sacrifice that gives the play its splendid severity, and for all his faults these are the virtues that make Coriolanus its protagonist.

CAIUS MARCIUS, *afterwards* CAIUS MARCIUS CORIOLANUS

TITUS LARTIUS
COMINIUS } *Generals against the Volscians*

MENENIUS AGRIPPA, *friend to Coriolanus*

SICINIUS VELUTUS
JUNIUS BRUTUS } *Tribunes of the People*

YOUNG MARCIUS, *son to Coriolanus*

A ROMAN HERALD

NICANOR, *a Roman*

TULLUS AUFIDIUS, *General of the Volscians*

LIEUTENANT *to Aufidius*

CONSPIRATORS *with Aufidius*

ADRIAN, *a Volscian*

A CITIZEN *of Antium*

TWO VOLSCIAN GUARDS

VOLUMNIA, *mother to Coriolanus*

VIRGILIA, *wife to Coriolanus*

VALERIA, *friend to Virgilia*

GENTLEWOMAN *attending on Virgilia*

Roman *and* Volscian Senators, Patricians, Ædiles, Lictors, Soldiers, Citizens, Messengers, Servants *to Aufidius, and other* Attendants

SCENE:

Rome and the neighbourhood; Corioli and the neighbourhood; Antium

Coriolanus

ACT I. SCENE 1

Rome. A street

Enter a company of mutinous citizens, with staves, clubs, and other weapons

FIRST CITIZEN. Before we proceed any further, hear me speak.

ALL. Speak, speak.

FIRST CITIZEN. You are all resolv'd rather to die than to famish?

ALL. Resolv'd, resolv'd.

FIRST CITIZEN. First, you know Caius Marcius is chief enemy to the people.

ALL. We know't, we know't.

FIRST CITIZEN. Let us kill him, and we'll have corn at our own price. Is't a verdict?

ALL. No more talking on't; let it be done. Away, away!

SECOND CITIZEN. One word, good citizens.

FIRST CITIZEN. We are accounted poor citizens, the patricians good. What authority surfeits on would relieve us; if they would yield us but the superfluity while it were wholesome, we might guess they relieved us humanely; but they think we are too dear. The leanness that afflicts us, the object of our misery, is as an inventory to particularize their abundance; our sufferance is a gain to them. Let us revenge this with our pikes ere we become rakes; for the gods know I speak this in hunger for bread, not in thirst for revenge.

SECOND CITIZEN. Would you proceed especially against Caius Marcius?

FIRST CITIZEN. Against him first; he's a very dog to the commonalty.

SECOND CITIZEN. Consider you what services he has done for his country?

FIRST CITIZEN. Very well, and could be content to give him good report for't but that he pays himself with being proud.

SECOND CITIZEN. Nay, but speak not maliciously.

FIRST CITIZEN. I say unto you, what he hath done famously he did it to that end; though soft-conscienc'd men can be content to say it was for his country, he did it to please his mother and to be partly proud, which he is, even to the altitude of his virtue.

SECOND CITIZEN. What he cannot help in his nature you account a vice in him. You must in no way say he is covetous.

FIRST CITIZEN. If I must not, I need not be barren of accusations; he hath faults, with surplus, to tire in repetition. [*Shouts within*] What shouts are these? The other side o' th' city is risen. Why stay we prating here? To th' Capitol!

ALL. Come, come.

FIRST CITIZEN. Soft! who comes here?

Enter MENENIUS AGRIPPA

SECOND CITIZEN. Worthy Menenius Agrippa; one that hath always lov'd the people.

FIRST CITIZEN. He's one honest enough; would all the rest were so!

MENENIUS. What work's, my countrymen, in hand? Where go you
With bats and clubs? The matter? Speak, I pray you.

FIRST CITIZEN. Our business is not unknown to th' Senate; they have had inkling this fortnight what we intend to do, which now we'll show 'em in deeds. They say poor suitors have strong breaths; they shall know we have strong arms too.

MENENIUS. Why, masters, my good friends, mine honest neighbours,
Will you undo yourselves?

FIRST CITIZEN. We cannot, sir; we are undone already.

MENENIUS. I tell you, friends, most charitable care
Have the patricians of you. For your wants,
Your suffering in this dearth, you may as well

Strike at the heaven with your staves as lift them
Against the Roman state; whose course will on
The way it takes, cracking ten thousand curbs
Of more strong link asunder than can ever
Appear in your impediment. For the dearth,
The gods, not the patricians, make it, and
Your knees to them, not arms, must help. Alack,
You are transported by calamity
Thither where more attends you; and you slander
The helms o' th' state, who care for you like fathers,
When you curse them as enemies.

FIRST CITIZEN. Care for us! True, indeed! They ne'er car'd for us yet. Suffer us to famish, and their storehouses cramm'd with grain; make edicts for usury, to support usurers; repeal daily any wholesome act established against the rich, and provide more piercing statutes daily to chain up and restrain the poor. If the wars eat us not up, they will; and there's all the love they bear us.

MENENIUS. Either you must
Confess yourselves wondrous malicious,
Or be accus'd of folly. I shall tell you
A pretty tale. It may be you have heard it;
But, since it serves my purpose, I will venture
To stale't a little more.

FIRST CITIZEN. Well, I'll hear it, sir; yet you must not think to fob off our disgrace with a tale. But, an't please you, deliver.

MENENIUS. There was a time when all the body's members
Rebell'd against the belly; thus accus'd it:
That only like a gulf it did remain
I' th' midst o' th' body, idle and unactive,
Still cupboarding the viand, never bearing
Like labour with the rest; where th' other instruments
Did see and hear, devise, instruct, walk, feel,
And, mutually participate, did minister
Unto the appetite and affection common
Of the whole body. The belly answer'd—

FIRST CITIZEN. Well, sir, what answer made the belly?

MENENIUS. Sir, I shall tell you. With a kind of smile,
Which ne'er came from the lungs, but even thus—

For look you, I may make the belly smile
As well as speak–it tauntingly replied
To th' discontented members, the mutinous parts
That envied his receipt; even so most fitly
As you malign our senators for that
They are not such as you.

FIRST CITIZEN. Your belly's answer–What?
The kingly crowned head, the vigilant eye,
The counsellor heart, the arm our soldier,
Our steed the leg, the tongue our trumpeter,
With other muniments and petty helps
Is this our fabric, if that they–

MENENIUS. What then?
Fore me, this fellow speaks! What then? What then?

FIRST CITIZEN. Should by the cormorant belly be restrain'd,
Who is the sink o' th' body–

MENENIUS. Well, what then?

FIRST CITIZEN. The former agents, if they did complain,
What could the belly answer?

MENENIUS. I will tell you;
If you'll bestow a small–of what you have little–
Patience awhile, you'st hear the belly's answer.

FIRST CITIZEN. Y'are long about it.

MENENIUS. Note me this, good friend:
Your most grave belly was deliberate,
Not rash like his accusers, and thus answered.
'True is it, my incorporate friends,' quoth he
'That I receive the general food at first
Which you do live upon; and fit it is,
Because I am the storehouse and the shop
Of the whole body. But, if you do remember,
I send it through the rivers of your blood,
Even to the court, the heart, to th' seat o' th' brain;
And, through the cranks and offices of man,
The strongest nerves and small inferior veins
From me receive that natural competency
Whereby they live. And though that all at once
You, my good friends'–this says the belly; mark me.

FIRST CITIZEN. Ay, sir; well, well.

MENENIUS. 'Though all at once cannot

See what I do deliver out to each,
Yet I can make my audit up, that all
From me do back receive the flour of all,
And leave me but the bran.' What say you to't?

FIRST CITIZEN. It was an answer. How apply you this?

MENENIUS. The senators of Rome are this good belly,
And you the mutinous members; for, examine
Their counsels and their cares, digest things rightly
Touching the weal o' th' common, you shall find
No public benefit which you receive
But it proceeds or comes from them to you,
And no way from yourselves. What do you think,
You, the great toe of this assembly?

FIRST CITIZEN. I the great toe? Why the great toe?

MENENIUS. For that, being one o' th' lowest, basest, poorest,
Of this most wise rebellion, thou goest foremost.
Thou rascal, that art worst in blood to run,
Lead'st first to win some vantage.
But make you ready your stiff bats and clubs.
Rome and her rats are at the point of battle;
The one side must have bale.

Enter CAIUS MARCIUS

Hail, noble Marcius!

MARCIUS. Thanks. What's the matter, you dissentious rogues
That, rubbing the poor itch of your opinion,
Make yourselves scabs?

FIRST CITIZEN. We have ever your good word.

MARCIUS. He that will give good words to thee will flatter
Beneath abhorring. What would you have, you curs,
That like nor peace nor war? The one affrights you,
The other makes you proud. He that trusts to you,
Where he should find you lions, finds you hares;
Where foxes, geese; you are no surer, no,
Than is the coal of fire upon the ice
Or hailstone in the sun. Your virtue is
To make him worthy whose offence subdues him,
And curse that justice did it. Who deserves greatness
Deserves your hate; and your affections are
A sick man's appetite, who desires most that

Which would increase his evil. He that depends
Upon your favours swims with fins of lead,
And hews down oaks with rushes. Hang ye! Trust ye?
With every minute you do change a mind
And call him noble that was now your hate,
Him vile that was your garland. What's the matter
That in these several places of the city
You cry against the noble Senate, who,
Under the gods, keep you in awe, which else
Would feed on one another? What's their seeking?

MENENIUS. For corn at their own rates, whereof they say
The city is well stor'd.

MARCIUS. Hang 'em! They say!
They'll sit by th' fire and presume to know
What's done i' th' Capitol, who's like to rise,
Who thrives and who declines; side factions, and give out
Conjectural marriages, making parties strong,
And feebling such as stand not in their liking
Below their cobbled shoes. They say there's grain enough!
Would the nobility lay aside their ruth
And let me use my sword, I'd make a quarry
With thousands of these quarter'd slaves, as high
As I could pick my lance.

MENENIUS. Nay, these are almost thoroughly persuaded;
For though abundantly they lack discretion,
Yet are they passing cowardly. But, I beseech you,
What says the other troop?

MARCIUS. They are dissolv'd. Hang 'em!
They said they were an-hungry; sigh'd forth proverbs—
That hunger broke stone walls, that dogs must eat,
That meat was made for mouths, that the gods sent not
Corn for the rich men only. With these shreds
They vented their complainings; which being answer'd,
And a petition granted them—a strange one,
To break the heart of generosity
And make bold power look pale—they threw their caps
As they would hang them on the horns o' th' moon,
Shouting their emulation.

MENENIUS. What is granted them?

MARCIUS. Five tribunes, to defend their vulgar wisdoms,

Of their own choice. One's Junius Brutus—
Sicinius Velutus, and I know not. 'Sdeath!
The rabble should have first unroof'd the city
Ere so prevail'd with me; it will in time
Win upon power and throw forth greater themes
For insurrection's arguing.

MENENIUS. This is strange.

MARCIUS. Go get you home, you fragments.

Enter a MESSENGER, *hastily*

MESSENGER. Where's Caius Marcius?

MARCIUS. Here. What's the matter?

MESSENGER. The news is, sir, the Volsces are in arms.

MARCIUS. I am glad on't; then we shall ha' means to vent
Our musty superfluity. See, our best elders.

Enter COMINIUS, TITUS LARTIUS, *with other* SENATORS; JUNIUS BRUTUS *and* SICINIUS VELUTUS

FIRST SENATOR. Marcius, 'tis true that you have lately told us:
The Volsces are in arms.

MARCIUS. They have a leader,
Tullus Aufidius, that will put you to't.
I sin in envying his nobility;
And were I anything but what I am,
I would wish me only he.

COMINIUS. You have fought together?

MARCIUS. Were half to half the world by th' ears, and he
Upon my party, I'd revolt, to make
Only my wars with him. He is a lion
That I am proud to hunt.

FIRST SENATOR. Then, worthy Marcius,
Attend upon Cominius to these wars.

COMINIUS. It is your former promise.

MARCIUS. Sir, it is;
And I am constant. Titus Lartius, thou
Shalt see me once more strike at Tullus' face.
What, art thou stiff? Stand'st out?

LARTIUS. No, Caius Marcius;
I'll lean upon one crutch and fight with t'other

Ere stay behind this business.

MENENIUS. O, true bred!

FIRST SENATOR. Your company to th' Capitol; where, I know,
Our greatest friends attend us.

LARTIUS. [*To* COMINIUS] Lead you on.
[*To* MARCIUS] Follow Cominius; we must follow you;
Right worthy you priority.

COMINIUS. Noble Marcius!

FIRST SENATOR. [*To the Citizens*] Hence to your homes; be gone.

MARCIUS. Nay, let them follow.
The Volsces have much corn: take these rats thither
To gnaw their garners. Worshipful mutineers,
Your valour puts well forth; pray follow.

Citizens steal away. Exeunt all but SICINIUS *and* BRUTUS

SICINIUS. Was ever man so proud as is this Marcius?

BRUTUS. He has no equal.

SICINIUS. When we were chosen tribunes for the people–

BRUTUS. Mark'd you his lip and eyes?

SICINIUS. Nay, but his taunts!

BRUTUS. Being mov'd, he will not spare to gird the gods.

SICINIUS. Bemock the modest moon.

BRUTUS. The present wars devour him! He is grown
Too proud to be so valiant.

SICINIUS. Such a nature,
Tickled with good success, disdains the shadow
Which he treads on at noon. But I do wonder
His insolence can brook to be commanded
Under Cominius.

BRUTUS. Fame, at the which he aims–
In whom already he is well grac'd–cannot
Better be held nor more attain'd than by
A place below the first; for what miscarries
Shall be the general's fault, though he perform
To th' utmost of a man, and giddy censure
Will then cry out of Marcius 'O, if he
Had borne the business!'

SICINIUS. Besides, if things go well,
Opinion, that so sticks on Marcius, shall

Of his demerits rob Cominius.
BRUTUS. Come.
Half all Cominius' honours are to Marcius,
Though Marcius earn'd them not; and all his faults
To Marcius shall be honours, though indeed
In aught he merit not.
SICINIUS. Let's hence and hear
How the dispatch is made, and in what fashion,
More than his singularity, he goes
Upon this present action.
BRUTUS. Let's along. *Exeunt*

SCENE 2

Corioli. The Senate House

Enter TULLUS AUFIDIUS *with* SENATORS *of Corioli*

FIRST SENATOR. So, your opinion is, Aufidius,
That they of Rome are ent'red in our counsels
And know how we proceed.
AUFIDIUS. Is it not yours?
What ever have been thought on in this state
That could be brought to bodily act ere Rome
Had circumvention? 'Tis not four days gone
Since I heard thence; these are the words—I think
I have the letter here; yes, here it is:
[*Reads*] 'They have press'd a power, but it is not known
Whether for east or west. The dearth is great;
The people mutinous; and it is rumour'd,
Cominius, Marcius your old enemy,
Who is of Rome worse hated than of you,
And Titus Lartius, a most valiant Roman,
These three lead on this preparation
Whither 'tis bent. Most likely 'tis for you;
Consider of it.'
FIRST SENATOR. Our army's in the field;
We never yet made doubt but Rome was ready
To answer us.
AUFIDIUS. Nor did you think it folly

To keep your great pretences veil'd till when
They needs must show themselves; which in the hatching,
It seem'd, appear'd to Rome. By the discovery
We shall be short'ned in our aim, which was
To take in many towns ere almost Rome
Should know we were afoot.

SECOND SENATOR. Noble Aufidius,
Take your commission; hie you to your bands;
Let us alone to guard Corioli.
If they set down before's, for the remove
Bring up your army; but I think you'll find
Th' have not prepar'd for us.

AUFIDIUS. O, doubt not that!
I speak from certainties. Nay more,
Some parcels of their power are forth already,
And only hitherward. I leave your honours.
If we and Caius Marcius chance to meet,
'Tis sworn between us we shall ever strike
Till one can do no more.

ALL. The gods assist you!

AUFIDIUS. And keep your honours safe!

FIRST SENATOR. Farewell.

SECOND SENATOR. Farewell.

ALL. Farewell. *Exeunt*

SCENE 3

Rome. MARCIUS' *house*

Enter VOLUMNIA *and* VIRGILIA, *mother and wife to* MARCIUS; *they set them down on two low stools and sew*

VOLUMNIA. I pray you, daughter, sing, or express yourself in a more comfortable sort. If my son were my husband, I should freelier rejoice in that absence wherein he won honour than in the embracements of his bed where he would show most love. When yet he was but tender-bodied, and the only son of my womb; when youth with comeliness pluck'd all gaze his way; when, for a day of kings' entreaties, a mother should not sell him an hour from her beholding; I, considering how honour would become such a person—that it was no better than picture-like to hang by th' wall, if renown made it not stir—was pleas'd to let him seek danger where he was to find fame. To a cruel war I sent him, from whence he return'd his brows bound with oak. I tell thee, daughter, I sprang not more in joy at first hearing he was a man-child than now in first seeing he had proved himself a man.

VIRGILIA. But had he died in the business, madam, how then?

VOLUMNIA. Then his good report should have been my son; I therein would have found issue. Hear me profess sincerely: had I a dozen sons, each in my love alike, and none less dear than thine and my good Marcius, I had rather had eleven die nobly for their country than one voluptuously surfeit out of action.

Enter a GENTLEWOMAN

GENTLEWOMAN. Madam, the Lady Valeria is come to visit you.

VIRGILIA. Beseech you give me leave to retire myself.

VOLUMNIA. Indeed you shall not.
Methinks I hear hither your husband's drum;
See him pluck Aufidius down by th' hair;
As children from a bear, the Volsces shunning him.
Methinks I see him stamp thus, and call thus:
'Come on, you cowards! You were got in fear,
Though you were born in Rome.' His bloody brow
With his mail'd hand then wiping, forth he goes,
Like to a harvest-man that's task'd to mow
Or all or lose his hire.

VIRGILIA. His bloody brow? O Jupiter, no blood!

VOLUMNIA. Away, you fool! It more becomes a man
Than gilt his trophy. The breasts of Hecuba,
When she did suckle Hector, look'd not lovelier
Than Hector's forehead when it spit forth blood
At Grecian sword, contemning. Tell Valeria
We are fit to bid her welcome. *Exit* GENTLEWOMAN

VIRGILIA. Heavens bless my lord from fell Aufidius!

VOLUMNIA. He'll beat Aufidius' head below his knee
And tread upon his neck.

Re-enter GENTLEWOMAN, *with* VALERIA *and an usher*

VALERIA. My ladies both, good day to you.

VOLUMNIA. Sweet madam!

VIRGILIA. I am glad to see your ladyship.

VALERIA. How do you both? You are manifest housekeepers. What are you sewing here? A fine spot, in good faith. How does your little son?

VIRGILIA. I thank your ladyship; well, good madam.

VOLUMNIA. He had rather see the swords and hear a drum than look upon his schoolmaster.

VALERIA. O' my word, the father's son! I'll swear 'tis a very pretty boy. O' my troth, I look'd upon him a Wednesday half an hour together; has such a confirm'd countenance! I saw him run after a gilded butterfly; and when he caught it he let it go again, and after it again, and over and over he comes, and up again, catch'd it again; or whether his fall enrag'd him, or how 'twas, he did so set his teeth and tear it. O, I warrant, how he mammock'd it!

VOLUMNIA. One on's father's moods.

VALERIA. Indeed, la, 'tis a noble child.

VIRGILIA. A crack, madam.

VALERIA. Come, lay aside your stitchery; I must have you play the idle huswife with me this afternoon.

VIRGILIA. No, good madam; I will not out of doors.

VALERIA. Not out of doors!

VOLUMNIA. She shall, she shall.

VIRGILIA. Indeed, no, by your patience; I'll not over the threshold till my lord return from the wars.

VALERIA. Fie, you confine yourself most unreasonably; come, you must go visit the good lady that lies in.

VIRGILIA. I will wish her speedy strength, and visit her with my prayers; but I cannot go thither.

VOLUMNIA. Why, I pray you?

VIRGILIA. 'Tis not to save labour, nor that I want love.

VALERIA. You would be another Penelope; yet they say all the yarn she spun in Ulysses' absence did but fill Ithaca full of moths. Come, I would your cambric were sensible as your finger, that you might leave pricking it for pity. Come, you shall go with us.

VIRGILIA. No, good madam, pardon me; indeed I will not forth.

VALERIA. In truth, la, go with me; and I'll tell you excellent news of your husband.

VIRGILIA. O, good madam, there can be none yet.

VALERIA. Verily, I do not jest with you; there came news from him last night.

VIRGILIA. Indeed, madam?

VALERIA. In earnest, it's true; I heard a senator speak it. Thus it is: the Volsces have an army forth; against whom Cominius the general is gone, with one part of our Roman power. Your lord and Titus Lartius are set down before their city Corioli; they nothing doubt prevailing and to make it brief wars. This is true, on mine honour; and so, I pray, go with us.

VIRGILIA. Give me excuse, good madam; I will obey you in everything hereafter.

VOLUMNIA. Let her alone, lady; as she is now, she will but disease our better mirth.

VALERIA. In troth, I think she would. Fare you well, then. Come, good sweet lady. Prithee, Virgilia, turn thy solemness out o' door and go along with us.

VIRGILIA. No, at a word, madam; indeed I must not. I wish you much mirth.

VALERIA. Well then, farewell. *Exeunt*

SCENE 4

Before Corioli

Enter MARCIUS, TITUS LARTIUS, *with drum and colours, with* CAPTAINS *and soldiers. To them a* MESSENGER

MARCIUS. Yonder comes news; a wager—they have met.

LARTIUS. My horse to yours—no.

MARCIUS. 'Tis done.

LARTIUS. Agreed.

MARCIUS. Say, has our general met the enemy?

MESSENGER. They lie in view, but have not spoke as yet.
LARTIUS. So, the good horse is mine.
MARCIUS. I'll buy him of you.
LARTIUS. No, I'll nor sell nor give him; lend you him I will
For half a hundred years. Summon the town.
MARCIUS. How far off lie these armies?
MESSENGER. Within this mile and half.
MARCIUS. Then shall we hear their 'larum, and they ours.
Now, Mars, I prithee, make us quick in work,
That we with smoking swords may march from hence
To help our fielded friends! Come, blow thy blast.

They sound a parley. Enter two SENATORS *with others, on the walls of Corioli*

Tullus Aufidius, is he within your walls?
FIRST SENATOR. No, nor a man that fears you less than he:
That's lesser than a little. [*Drum afar off*] Hark, our drums
Are bringing forth our youth. We'll break our walls
Rather than they shall pound us up; our gates,
Which yet seem shut, we have but pinn'd with rushes;
They'll open of themselves. [*Alarum far off*] Hark you far off!
There is Aufidius. List what work he makes
Amongst your cloven army.
MARCIUS. O, they are at it!
LARTIUS. Their noise be our instruction. Ladders, ho!

Enter the army of the Volsces

MARCIUS. They fear us not, but issue forth their city.
Now put your shields before your hearts, and fight
With hearts more proof than shields. Advance, brave Titus.
They do disdain us much beyond our thoughts,
Which makes me sweat with wrath. Come on, my fellows.
He that retires, I'll take him for a Volsce,
And he shall feel mine edge.

Alarum. The Romans are beat back to their trenches. Re-enter MARCIUS, *cursing*

MARCIUS. All the contagion of the south light on you,
You shames of Rome! you herd of—Boils and plagues
Plaster you o'er, that you may be abhorr'd
Farther than seen, and one infect another
Against the wind a mile! You souls of geese
That bear the shapes of men, how have you run
From slaves that apes would beat! Pluto and hell!
All hurt behind! Backs red, and faces pale
With flight and agued fear! Mend and charge home,
Or, by the fires of heaven, I'll leave the foe
And make my wars on you. Look to't. Come on;
If you'll stand fast we'll beat them to their wives,
As they us to our trenches. Follow me.

Another alarum. The Volsces fly, and MARCIUS *follows them to the gates*

So, now the gates are ope; now prove good seconds;
'Tis for the followers fortune widens them,
Not for the fliers. Mark me, and do the like.
[MARCIUS *enters the gates*]

FIRST SOLDIER. Fool-hardiness; not I.
SECOND SOLDIER. Not I. [MARCIUS *is shut in*]
FIRST SOLDIER. See, they have shut him in.
ALL. To th' pot, I warrant him. [*Alarum continues*]

Re-enter TITUS LARTIUS

LARTIUS. What is become of Marcius?
ALL. Slain, sir, doubtless.
FIRST SOLDIER. Following the fliers at the very heels,
With them he enters; who, upon the sudden,
Clapp'd to their gates. He is himself alone,
To answer all the city.
LARTIUS. O noble fellow!
Who sensibly outdares his senseless sword,
And when it bows stand'st up. Thou art left, Marcius;
A carbuncle entire, as big as thou art,
Were not so rich a jewel. Thou wast a soldier
Even to Cato's wish, not fierce and terrible
Only in strokes; but with thy grim looks and
The thunder-like percussion of thy sounds

Thou mad'st thine enemies shake, as if the world
Were feverous and did tremble.

Re-enter MARCIUS, *bleeding, assaulted by the enemy*

FIRST SOLDIER. Look, sir.
LARTIUS. O, 'tis Marcius!
Let's fetch him off, or make remain alike.
[*They fight, and all enter the city*]

SCENE 5

Within Corioli. A street

Enter certain Romans, with spoils

FIRST ROMAN. This will I carry to Rome.
SECOND ROMAN. And I this.
THIRD ROMAN. A murrain on't! I took this for silver.
[*Alarum continues still afar off*]

Enter MARCIUS *and* TITUS LARTIUS *with a trumpeter*

MARCIUS. See here these movers that do prize their hours
At a crack'd drachma! Cushions, leaden spoons,
Irons of a doit, doublets that hangmen would
Bury with those that wore them, these base slaves,
Ere yet the fight be done, pack up. Down with them!
Exeunt pillagers
And hark, what noise the general makes! To him!
There is the man of my soul's hate, Aufidius,
Piercing our Romans; then, valiant Titus, take
Convenient numbers to make good the city;
Whilst I, with those that have the spirit, will haste
To help Cominius.
LARTIUS. Worthy sir, thou bleed'st;
Thy exercise hath been too violent
For a second course of fight.
MARCIUS. Sir, praise me not;
My work hath yet not warm'd me. Fare you well;
The blood I drop is rather physical
Than dangerous to me. To Aufidius thus

I will appear, and fight.

LARTIUS. Now the fair goddess, Fortune,
Fall deep in love with thee, and her great charms
Misguide thy opposers' swords! Bold gentleman,
Prosperity be thy page!

MARCIUS. Thy friend no less
Than those she placeth highest! So farewell.

LARTIUS. Thou worthiest Marcius! *Exit* MARCIUS
Go sound thy trumpet in the market-place;
Call thither all the officers o' th' town,
Where they shall know our mind. Away! *Exeunt*

SCENE 6

Near the camp of COMINIUS

Enter COMINIUS, *as it were in retire, with soldiers*

COMINIUS. Breathe you, my friends. Well fought; we are come off
Like Romans, neither foolish in our stands
Nor cowardly in retire. Believe me, sirs,
We shall be charg'd again. Whiles we have struck,
By interims and conveying gusts we have heard
The charges of our friends. The Roman gods,
Lead their successes as we wish our own,
That both our powers, with smiling fronts encount'ring,
May give you thankful sacrifice!

Enter a MESSENGER

Thy news?

MESSENGER. The citizens of Corioli have issued
And given to Lartius and to Marcius battle;
I saw our party to their trenches driven,
And then I came away.

COMINIUS. Though thou speak'st truth,
Methinks thou speak'st not well. How long is't since?

MESSENGER. Above an hour, my lord.

COMINIUS. 'Tis not a mile; briefly we heard their drums.
How couldst thou in a mile confound an hour,

And bring thy news so late?
MESSENGER. Spies of the Volsces
Held me in chase, that I was forc'd to wheel
Three or four miles about; else had I, sir,
Half an hour since brought my report.

Enter MARCIUS

COMINIUS. Who's yonder
That does appear as he were flay'd? O gods!
He has the stamp of Marcius, and I have
Before-time seen him thus.
MARCIUS. Come I too late?
COMINIUS. The shepherd knows not thunder from a tabor
More than I know the sound of Marcius' tongue
From every meaner man.
MARCIUS. Come I too late?
COMINIUS. Ay, if you come not in the blood of others,
But mantled in your own.
MARCIUS. O! let me clip ye
In arms as sound as when I woo'd, in heart
As merry as when our nuptial day was done,
And tapers burn'd to bedward.
COMINIUS. Flower of warriors,
How is't with Titus Lartius?
MARCIUS. As with a man busied about decrees:
Condemning some to death and some to exile;
Ransoming him or pitying, threat'ning th' other;
Holding Corioli in the name of Rome
Even like a fawning greyhound in the leash,
To let him slip at will.
COMINIUS. Where is that slave
Which told me they had beat you to your trenches?
Where is he? Call him hither.
MARCIUS. Let him alone;
He did inform the truth. But for our gentlemen,
The common file—a plague! tribunes for them!
The mouse ne'er shunn'd the cat as they did budge
From rascals worse than they.
COMINIUS. But how prevail'd you?
MARCIUS. Will the time serve to tell? I do not think.

Where is the enemy? Are you lords o' th' field?
If not, why cease you till you are so?

COMINIUS. Marcius,
We have at disadvantage fought, and did
Retire to win our purpose.

MARCIUS. How lies their battle? Know you on which side
They have plac'd their men of trust?

COMINIUS. As I guess, Marcius,
Their bands i' th' vaward are the Antiates,
Of their best trust; o'er them Aufidius,
Their very heart of hope.

MARCIUS. I do beseech you,
By all the battles wherein we have fought,
By th' blood we have shed together, by th' vows
We have made to endure friends, that you directly
Set me against Aufidius and his Antiates;
And that you not delay the present, but,
Filling the air with swords advanc'd and darts,
We prove this very hour.

COMINIUS. Though I could wish
You were conducted to a gentle bath
And balms applied to you, yet dare I never
Deny your asking: take your choice of those
That best can aid your action.

MARCIUS. Those are they
That most are willing. If any such be here—
As it were sin to doubt—that love this painting
Wherein you see me smear'd; if any fear
Lesser his person than an ill report;
If any think brave death outweighs bad life
And that his country's dearer than himself;
Let him alone, or so many so minded,
Wave thus to express his disposition,
And follow Marcius. [*They all shout and wave their swords, take him up in their arms and cast up their caps*]
O, me alone! Make you a sword of me?
If these shows be not outward, which of you
But is four Volsces? None of you but is
Able to bear against the great Aufidius
A shield as hard as his. A certain number,

Though thanks to all, must I select from all; the rest
Shall bear the business in some other fight,
As cause will be obey'd. Please you to march;
And four shall quickly draw out my command,
Which men are best inclin'd.

COMINIUS. March on, my fellows;
Make good this ostentation, and you shall
Divide in all with us. *Exeunt*

SCENE 7

The gates of Corioli

TITUS LARTIUS, *having set a guard upon Corioli, going with drum and trumpet toward* COMINIUS *and* CAIUS MARCIUS, *enters with a* LIEUTENANT, *other soldiers, and a scout*

LARTIUS. So, let the ports be guarded; keep your duties
As I have set them down. If I do send, dispatch
Those centuries to our aid; the rest will serve
For a short holding. If we lose the field
We cannot keep the town.

LIEUTENANT. Fear not our care, sir.

LARTIUS. Hence, and shut your gates upon's.
Our guider, come; to th' Roman camp conduct us. *Exeunt*

SCENE 8

A field of battle between the Roman and the Volscian camps

Alarum, as in battle. Enter MARCIUS *and* AUFIDIUS *at several doors*

MARCIUS. I'll fight with none but thee, for I do hate thee
Worse than a promise-breaker.

AUFIDIUS. We hate alike:
Not Afric owns a serpent I abhor
More than thy fame and envy. Fix thy foot.

MARCIUS. Let the first budger die the other's slave,

And the gods doom him after!

AUFIDIUS. If I fly, Marcius,
Halloa me like a hare.

MARCIUS. Within these three hours, Tullus,
Alone I fought in your Corioli walls,
And made what work I pleas'd. 'Tis not my blood
Wherein thou seest me mask'd. For thy revenge
Wrench up thy power to th' highest.

AUFIDIUS. Wert thou the Hector
That was the whip of your bragg'd progeny,
Thou shouldst not scape me here.

Here they fight, and certain Volsces come in the aid of AUFIDIUS. MARCIUS *fights till they be driven in breathless*

Officious, and not valiant, you have sham'd me
In your condemned seconds. *Exeunt*

SCENE 9

The Roman camp

Flourish. Alarum. A retreat is sounded. Enter, at one door, COMINIUS *with the Romans; at another door,* MARCIUS, *with his arm in a scarf*

COMINIUS. If I should tell thee o'er this thy day's work,
Thou't not believe thy deeds; but I'll report it
Where senators shall mingle tears with smiles;
Where great patricians shall attend, and shrug,
I' th' end admire; where ladies shall be frighted
And, gladly quak'd, hear more; where the dull tribunes,
That with the fusty plebeians hate thine honours,
Shall say against their hearts 'We thank the gods
Our Rome hath such a soldier.'
Yet cam'st thou to a morsel of this feast,
Having fully din'd before.

Enter TITUS LARTIUS, *with his power, from the pursuit*

LARTIUS. O General,

Here is the steed, we the caparison.
Hadst thou beheld–

MARCIUS. Pray now, no more; my mother,
Who has a charter to extol her blood,
When she does praise me grieves me. I have done
As you have done–that's what I can; induc'd
As you have been–that's for my country.
He that has but effected his good will
Hath overta'en mine act.

COMINIUS. You shall not be
The grave of your deserving; Rome must know
The value of her own. 'Twere a concealment
Worse than a theft, no less than a traducement,
To hide your doings and to silence that
Which, to the spire and top of praises vouch'd,
Would seem but modest. Therefore, I beseech you,
In sign of what you are, not to reward
What you have done, before our army hear me.

MARCIUS. I have some wounds upon me, and they smart
To hear themselves rememb'red.

COMINIUS. Should they not,
Well might they fester 'gainst ingratitude
And tent themselves with death. Of all the horses–
Whereof we have ta'en good, and good store–of all
The treasure in this field achiev'd and city,
We render you the tenth; to be ta'en forth
Before the common distribution at
Your only choice.

MARCIUS. I thank you, General,
But cannot make my heart consent to take
A bribe to pay my sword. I do refuse it,
And stand upon my common part with those
That have beheld the doing.

A long flourish. They all cry 'Marcius, Marcius!' cast up their caps and lances. COMINIUS *and* LARTIUS *stand bare*

May these same instruments which you profane
Never sound more! When drums and trumpets shall
I' th' field prove flatterers, let courts and cities be

Made all of false-fac'd soothing. When steel grows
Soft as the parasite's silk, let him be made
An overture for th' wars. No more, I say.
For that I have not wash'd my nose that bled,
Or foil'd some debile wretch, which without note
Here's many else have done, you shout me forth
In acclamations hyperbolical,
As if I lov'd my little should be dieted
In praises sauc'd with lies.

COMINIUS. Too modest are you;
More cruel to your good report than grateful
To us that give you truly. By your patience,
If 'gainst yourself you be incens'd, we'll put you—
Like one that means his proper harm—in manacles,
Then reason safely with you. Therefore be it known,
As to us, to all the world, that Caius Marcius
Wears this war's garland; in token of the which,
My noble steed, known to the camp, I give him,
With all his trim belonging; and from this time,
For what he did before Corioli, call him
With all th' applause and clamour of the host,
Caius Marcius Coriolanus.
Bear th' addition nobly ever!

[*Flourish. Trumpets sound, and drums*]

ALL. Caius Marcius Coriolanus!

CORIOLANUS. I will go wash;
And when my face is fair you shall perceive
Whether I blush or no. Howbeit, I thank you;
I mean to stride your steed, and at all times
To undercrest your good addition
To th' fairness of my power.

COMINIUS. So, to our tent;
Where, ere we do repose us, we will write
To Rome of our success. You, Titus Lartius,
Must to Corioli back. Send us to Rome
The best, with whom we may articulate
For their own good and ours.

LARTIUS. I shall, my lord.

CORIOLANUS. The gods begin to mock me. I, that now
Refus'd most princely gifts, am bound to beg

Of my Lord General.
COMINIUS. Take't—'tis yours; what is't?
CORIOLANUS. I sometime lay here in Corioli
At a poor man's house; he us'd me kindly.
He cried to me; I saw him prisoner;
But then Aufidius was within my view,
And wrath o'erwhelm'd my pity. I request you
To give my poor host freedom.
COMINIUS. O, well begg'd!
Were he the butcher of my son, he should
Be free as is the wind. Deliver him, Titus.
LARTIUS. Marcius, his name?
CORIOLANUS. By Jupiter, forgot!
I am weary; yea, my memory is tir'd.
Have we no wine here?
COMINIUS. Go we to our tent.
The blood upon your visage dries; 'tis time
It should be look'd to. Come. *Exeunt*

SCENE 10

The camp of the Volsces

A flourish. Cornets. Enter TULLUS AUFIDIUS *bloody, with two or three soldiers*

AUFIDIUS. The town is ta'en.
FIRST SOLDIER. 'Twill be deliver'd back on good condition.
AUFIDIUS. Condition!
I would I were a Roman; for I cannot,
Being a Volsce, be that I am. Condition?
What good condition can a treaty find
I' th' part that is at mercy? Five times, Marcius,
I have fought with thee; so often hast thou beat me;
And wouldst do so, I think, should we encounter
As often as we eat. By th' elements,
If e'er again I meet him beard to beard,
He's mine or I am his. Mine emulation
Hath not that honour in't it had; for where
I thought to crush him in an equal force,

True sword to sword, I'll potch at him some way,
Or wrath or craft may get him.

First Soldier. He's the devil.

Aufidius. Bolder, though not so subtle. My valour's poison'd
With only suff'ring stain by him; for him
Shall fly out of itself. Nor sleep nor sanctuary,
Being naked, sick, nor fane nor Capitol,
The prayers of priests nor times of sacrifice,
Embarquements all of fury, shall lift up
Their rotten privilege and custom 'gainst
My hate to Marcius. Where I find him, were it
At home, upon my brother's guard, even there,
Against the hospitable canon, would I
Wash my fierce hand in's heart. Go you to th' city;
Learn how 'tis held, and what they are that must
Be hostages for Rome.

First Soldier. Will not you go?

Aufidius. I am attended at the cypress grove; I pray you—
'Tis south the city mills—bring me word thither
How the world goes, that to the pace of it
I may spur on my journey.

First Soldier. I shall, sir. *Exeunt*

ACT II. SCENE 1

Rome. A public place

Enter Menenius, *with the two Tribunes of the people*, Sicinius *and* Brutus

Menenius. The augurer tells me we shall have news tonight.

Brutus. Good or bad?

Menenius. Not according to the prayer of the people, for they love not Marcius.

Sicinius. Nature teaches beasts to know their friends.

Menenius. Pray you, who does the wolf love?

Sicinius. The lamb.

Menenius. Ay, to devour him, as the hungry plebeians would the noble Marcius.

BRUTUS. He's a lamb indeed, that baes like a bear.

MENENIUS. He's a bear indeed, that lives like a lamb. You two are old men; tell me one thing that I shall ask you.

BOTH TRIBUNES. Well, sir.

MENENIUS. In what enormity is Marcius poor in that you two have not in abundance?

BRUTUS. He's poor in no one fault, but stor'd with all.

SICINIUS. Especially in pride.

BRUTUS. And topping all others in boasting.

MENENIUS. This is strange now. Do you two know how you are censured here in the city–I mean of us o' th' right-hand file? Do you?

BOTH TRIBUNES. Why, how are we censur'd?

MENENIUS. Because you talk of pride now–will you not be angry?

BOTH TRIBUNES. Well, well, sir, well.

MENENIUS. Why, 'tis no great matter; for a very little thief of occasion will rob you of a great deal of patience. Give your dispositions the reins, and be angry at your pleasures –at the least, if you take it as a pleasure to you in being so. You blame Marcius for being proud?

BRUTUS. We do it not alone, sir.

MENENIUS. I know you can do very little alone; for your helps are many, or else your actions would grow wondrous single: your abilities are too infant-like for doing much alone. You talk of pride. O that you could turn your eyes toward the napes of your necks, and make but an interior survey of your good selves! O that you could!

BOTH TRIBUNES. What then, sir?

MENENIUS. Why, then you should discover a brace of unmeriting, proud, violent, testy magistrates–alias fools–as any in Rome.

SICINIUS. Menenius, you are known well enough too.

MENENIUS. I am known to be a humorous patrician, and one that loves a cup of hot wine with not a drop of allaying Tiber in't; said to be something imperfect in favouring the first complaint, hasty and tinder-like upon too trivial motion; one that converses more with the buttock of the night than with the forehead of the morning. What I think I utter, and spend my malice in my breath. Meeting two such wealsmen as you are—I cannot call you Lycurguses—if the drink you give me touch my palate adversely, I make a crooked face at it. I cannot say your worships have deliver'd the matter well, when I find the ass in compound with the major part of your syllables; and though I must be content to bear with those that say you are reverend grave men, yet they lie deadly that tell you you have good faces. If you see this in the map of my microcosm, follows it that I am known well enough too? What harm can your bisson conspectuities glean out of this character, if I be known well enough too?

BRUTUS. Come, sir, come, we know you well enough.

MENENIUS. You know neither me, yourselves, nor any thing. You are ambitious for poor knaves' caps and legs; you wear out a good wholesome forenoon in hearing a cause between an orange-wife and a fosset-seller, and then rejourn the controversy of threepence to a second day of audience. When you are hearing a matter between party and party, if you chance to be pinch'd with the colic, you make faces like mummers, set up the bloody flag against all patience, and, in roaring for a chamber-pot, dismiss the controversy bleeding, the more entangled by your hearing. All the peace you make in their cause is calling both the parties knaves. You are a pair of strange ones.

BRUTUS. Come, come, you are well understood to be a perfecter giber for the table than a necessary bencher in the Capitol.

MENENIUS. Our very priests must become mockers, if they shall encounter such ridiculous subjects as you are. When you speak best unto the purpose, it is not worth the wagging of your beards; and your beards deserve not so honourable a grave as to stuff a botcher's cushion or to be entomb'd in an ass's pack-saddle. Yet you must be saying Marcius is proud; who, in a cheap estimation, is worth all your predecessors since Deucalion; though peradventure some of the best of 'em were hereditary hangmen. God-den to your worships. More of your conversation would infect my brain, being the herdsmen of the beastly plebeians. I will be bold to take my leave of you.

[BRUTUS *and* SICINIUS *go aside*]

Enter VOLUMNIA, VIRGILIA, *and* VALERIA

How now, my as fair as noble ladies—and the moon, were she earthly, no nobler—whither do you follow your eyes so fast?

VOLUMNIA. Honourable Menenius, my boy Marcius approaches; for the love of Juno, let's go.

MENENIUS. Ha! Marcius coming home?

VOLUMNIA. Ay, worthy Menenius, and with most prosperous approbation.

MENENIUS. Take my cap, Jupiter, and I thank thee. Hoo! Marcius coming home!

VOLUMNIA, VIRGILIA. Nay, 'tis true.

VOLUMNIA. Look, here's a letter from him; the state hath another, his wife another; and I think there's one at home for you.

MENENIUS. I will make my very house reel to-night. A letter for me?

VIRGILIA. Yes, certain, there's a letter for you; I saw't.

MENENIUS. A letter for me! It gives me an estate of seven years' health; in which time I will make a lip at the physician. The most sovereign prescription in Galen is but empiricutic and, to this preservative, of no better report than a horse-drench. Is he not wounded? He was wont to come home wounded.

VIRGILIA. O, no, no, no.

VOLUMNIA. O, he is wounded, I thank the gods for't.

MENENIUS. So do I too, if it be not too much. Brings a victory in his pocket? The wounds become him.

VOLUMNIA. On's brows, Menenius, he comes the third time home with the oaken garland.

MENENIUS. Has he disciplin'd Aufidius soundly?

VOLUMNIA. Titus Lartius writes they fought together, but Aufidius got off.

MENENIUS. And 'twas time for him too, I'll warrant him that; an he had stay'd by him, I would not have been so fidius'd for all the chests in Corioli and the gold that's in them. Is the Senate possess'd of this?

VOLUMNIA. Good ladies, let's go. Yes, yes, yes: the Senate has letters from the general, wherein he gives my son the whole name of the war; he hath in this action outdone his former deeds doubly.

VALERIA. In troth, there's wondrous things spoke of him.

MENENIUS. Wondrous! Ay, I warrant you, and not without his true purchasing.

VIRGILIA. The gods grant them true!

VOLUMNIA. True! pow, waw.

MENENIUS. True! I'll be sworn they are true. Where is he wounded? [*To the* TRIBUNES] God save your good worships! Marcius is coming home; he has more cause to be proud. Where is he wounded?

VOLUMNIA. I' th' shoulder and i' th' left arm; there will be large cicatrices to show the people when he shall stand for his place. He received in the repulse of Tarquin seven hurts i' th' body.

MENENIUS. One i' th' neck and two i' th' thigh—there's nine that I know.

VOLUMNIA. He had before this last expedition twenty-five wounds upon him.

MENENIUS. Now it's twenty-seven; every gash was an enemy's grave. [*A shout and flourish*] Hark! the trumpets.

VOLUMNIA. These are the ushers of Marcius. Before him he carries noise, and behind him he leaves tears;
Death, that dark spirit, in's nervy arm doth lie,
Which, being advanc'd, declines, and then men die.

A sennet. Trumpets sound. Enter COMINIUS *the General, and* TITUS LARTIUS; *between them,* CORIOLANUS, *crown'd with an oaken garland; with* CAPTAINS *and soldiers and a* HERALD

HERALD. Know, Rome, that all alone Marcius did fight
Within Corioli gates, where he hath won,
With fame, a name to Caius Marcius; these
In honour follows Coriolanus.
Welcome to Rome, renowned Coriolanus! [*Flourish*]

ALL. Welcome to Rome, renowned Coriolanus!

CORIOLANUS. No more of this, it does offend my heart.
Pray now, no more.

COMINIUS. Look, sir, your mother!

CORIOLANUS. O,
You have, I know, petition'd all the gods
For my prosperity! [*Kneels*]
VOLUMNIA. Nay, my good soldier, up;
My gentle Marcius, worthy Caius, and
By deed-achieving honour newly nam'd–
What is it? Coriolanus must I call thee?
But, O, thy wife!
CORIOLANUS. My gracious silence, hail!
Wouldst thou have laugh'd had I come coffin'd home,
That weep'st to see me triumph? Ah, my dear,
Such eyes the widows in Corioli wear,
And mothers that lack sons.
MENENIUS. Now the gods crown thee!
CORIOLANUS. And live you yet? [*To* VALERIA] O my sweet lady, pardon.
VOLUMNIA. I know not where to turn.
O, welcome home! And welcome, General.
And y'are welcome all.
MENENIUS. A hundred thousand welcomes. I could weep
And I could laugh; I am light and heavy. Welcome!
A curse begin at very root on's heart
That is not glad to see thee! You are three
That Rome should dote on; yet, by the faith of men,
We have some old crab trees here at home that will not
Be grafted to your relish. Yet welcome, warriors.
We call a nettle but a nettle, and
The faults of fools but folly.
COMINIUS. Ever right.
CORIOLANUS. Menenius ever, ever.
HERALD. Give way there, and go on.
CORIOLANUS. [*To his wife and mother*] Your hand, and yours.
Ere in our own house I do shade my head,
The good patricians must be visited;
From whom I have receiv'd not only greetings,
But with them change of honours.
VOLUMNIA. I have lived
To see inherited my very wishes,
And the buildings of my fancy; only

There's one thing wanting, which I doubt not but
Our Rome will cast upon thee.

CORIOLANUS. Know, good mother,
I had rather be their servant in my way
Than sway with them in theirs.

COMINIUS. On, to the Capitol.

[*Flourish. Cornets. Exeunt in state, as before*]

BRUTUS *and* SICINIUS *come forward*

BRUTUS. All tongues speak of him and the bleared sights
Are spectacled to see him. Your prattling nurse
Into a rapture lets her baby cry
While she chats him; the kitchen malkin pins
Her richest lockram 'bout her reechy neck,
Clamb'ring the walls to eye him; stalls, bulks, windows,
Are smother'd up, leads fill'd and ridges hors'd
With variable complexions, all agreeing
In earnestness to see him. Seld-shown flamens
Do press among the popular throngs and puff
To win a vulgar station; our veil'd dames
Commit the war of white and damask in
Their nicely gawded cheeks to th' wanton spoil
Of Phœbus' burning kisses. Such a pother,
As if that whatsoever god who leads him
Were slily crept into his human powers,
And gave him graceful posture.

SICINIUS. On the sudden
I warrant him consul.

BRUTUS. Then our office may
During his power go sleep.

SICINIUS. He cannot temp'rately transport his honours
From where he should begin and end, but will
Lose those he hath won.

BRUTUS. In that there's comfort.

SICINIUS. Doubt not
The commoners, for whom we stand, but they
Upon their ancient malice will forget
With the least cause these his new honours; which
That he will give them make I as little question
As he is proud to do't.

BRUTUS. I heard him swear,
Were he to stand for consul, never would he
Appear i' th' market-place, nor on him put
The napless vesture of humility;
Nor, showing, as the manner is, his wounds
To th' people, beg their stinking breaths.
SICINIUS. 'Tis right.
BRUTUS. It was his word. O, he would miss it rather
Than carry it but by the suit of the gentry to him
And the desire of the nobles.
SICINIUS. I wish no better
Than have him hold that purpose, and to put it
In execution.
BRUTUS. 'Tis most like he will.
SICINIUS. It shall be to him then as our good wills:
A sure destruction.
BRUTUS. So it must fall out
To him or our authorities. For an end,
We must suggest the people in what hatred
He still hath held them; that to's power he would
Have made them mules, silenc'd their pleaders, and
Dispropertied their freedoms; holding them
In human action and capacity
Of no more soul nor fitness for the world
Than camels in their war, who have their provand
Only for bearing burdens, and sore blows
For sinking under them.
SICINIUS. This, as you say, suggested
At some time when his soaring insolence
Shall touch the people—which time shall not want,
If he be put upon't, and that's as easy
As to set dogs on sheep—will be his fire
To kindle their dry stubble; and their blaze
Shall darken him for ever.

Enter a MESSENGER

BRUTUS. What's the matter?
MESSENGER. You are sent for to the Capitol. 'Tis thought
That Marcius shall be consul.
I have seen the dumb men throng to see him and

The blind to hear him speak; matrons flung gloves,
Ladies and maids their scarfs and handkerchers,
Upon him as he pass'd; the nobles bended
As to Jove's statue, and the commons made
A shower and thunder with their caps and shouts.
I never saw the like.

BRUTUS. Let's to the Capitol,
And carry with us ears and eyes for th' time,
But hearts for the event.

SICINIUS. Have with you. *Exeunt*

SCENE 2

Rome. The Capitol

Enter two OFFICERS, *to lay cushions, as it were in the Capitol*

FIRST OFFICER. Come, come, they are almost here. How many stand for consulships?

SECOND OFFICER. Three, they say; but 'tis thought of every one Coriolanus will carry it.

FIRST OFFICER. That's a brave fellow; but he's vengeance proud and loves not the common people.

SECOND OFFICER. Faith, there have been many great men that have flatter'd the people, who ne'er loved them; and there be many that they have loved, they know not wherefore; so that, if they love they know not why, they hate upon no better a ground. Therefore, for Coriolanus neither to care whether they love or hate him manifests the true knowledge he has in their disposition, and out of his noble carelessness lets them plainly see't.

FIRST OFFICER. If he did not care whether he had their love or no, he waved indifferently 'twixt doing them neither good nor harm; but he seeks their hate with greater devotion than they can render it him, and leaves nothing undone that may fully discover him their opposite. Now to seem to affect the malice and displeasure of the people is as bad as that which he dislikes—to flatter them for their love.

SECOND OFFICER. He hath deserved worthily of his country; and his ascent is not by such easy degrees as those who, having been supple and courteous to the people, bonneted, without any further deed to have them at all, into their estimation and report; but he hath so planted his honours in their eyes and his actions in their hearts that for their tongues to be silent and not confess so much were a kind of ingrateful injury; to report otherwise were a malice that, giving itself the lie, would pluck reproof and rebuke from every ear that heard it.

FIRST OFFICER. No more of him; he's a worthy man. Make way, they are coming.

A sennet. Enter the PATRICIANS *and the* TRIBUNES OF THE PEOPLE, LICTORS *before them;* CORIOLANUS, MENENIUS, COMINIUS *the Consul.* SICINIUS *and* BRUTUS *take their places by themselves.* CORIOLANUS *stands*

MENENIUS. Having determin'd of the Volsces, and
To send for Titus Lartius, it remains,
As the main point of this our after-meeting,
To gratify his noble service that
Hath thus stood for his country. Therefore please you,
Most reverend and grave elders, to desire
The present consul and last general
In our well-found successes to report
A little of that worthy work perform'd
By Caius Marcius Coriolanus; whom
We met here both to thank and to remember
With honours like himself. [CORIOLANUS *sits*]

FIRST SENATOR. Speak, good Cominius.
Leave nothing out for length, and make us think
Rather our state's defective for requital
Than we to stretch it out. Masters o' th' people,
We do request your kindest ears; and, after,
Your loving motion toward the common body,
To yield what passes here.

SICINIUS. We are convented
Upon a pleasing treaty, and have hearts
Inclinable to honour and advance

The theme of our assembly.
BRUTUS. Which the rather
We shall be bless'd to do, if he remember
A kinder value of the people than
He hath hereto priz'd them at.
MENENIUS. That's off, that's off;
I would you rather had been silent. Please you
To hear Cominius speak?
BRUTUS. Most willingly.
But yet my caution was more pertinent
Than the rebuke you give it.
MENENIUS. He loves your people;
But tie him not to be their bedfellow.
Worthy Cominius, speak.
[CORIOLANUS *rises, and offers to go away*]
Nay, keep your place.
FIRST SENATOR. Sit, Coriolanus, never shame to hear
What you have nobly done.
CORIOLANUS. Your Honours' pardon.
I had rather have my wounds to heal again
Than hear say how I got them.
BRUTUS. Sir, I hope
My words disbench'd you not.
CORIOLANUS. No, sir; yet oft,
When blows have made me stay, I fled from words.
You sooth'd not, therefore hurt not. But your people,
I love them as they weigh—
MENENIUS. Pray now, sit down.
CORIOLANUS. I had rather have one scratch my head i' th' sun
When the alarum were struck than idly sit
To hear my nothings monster'd. *Exit*
MENENIUS. Masters of the people,
Your multiplying spawn how can he flatter—
That's thousand to one good one—when you now see
He had rather venture all his limbs for honour
Than one on's ears to hear it? Proceed, Cominius.
COMINIUS. I shall lack voice; the deeds of Coriolanus
Should not be utter'd feebly. It is held
That valour is the chiefest virtue and
Most dignifies the haver. If it be,

The man I speak of cannot in the world
Be singly counterpois'd. At sixteen years,
When Tarquin made a head for Rome, he fought
Beyond the mark of others; our then Dictator,
Whom with all praise I point at, saw him fight
When with his Amazonian chin he drove
The bristled lips before him; he bestrid
An o'erpress'd Roman and i' th' consul's view
Slew three opposers; Tarquin's self he met,
And struck him on his knee. In that day's feats,
When he might act the woman in the scene,
He prov'd best man i' th' field, and for his meed
Was brow-bound with the oak. His pupil age
Man-ent'red thus, he waxed like a sea,
And in the brunt of seventeen battles since
He lurch'd all swords of the garland. For this last,
Before and in Corioli, let me say
I cannot speak him home. He stopp'd the fliers,
And by his rare example made the coward
Turn terror into sport; as weeds before
A vessel under sail, so men obey'd
And fell below his stem. His sword, death's stamp,
Where it did mark, it took; from face to foot
He was a thing of blood, whose every motion
Was tim'd with dying cries. Alone he ent'red
The mortal gate of th' city, which he painted
With shunless destiny; aidless came off,
And with a sudden re-enforcement struck
Corioli like a planet. Now all's his.
When by and by the din of war 'gan pierce
His ready sense, then straight his doubled spirit
Re-quick'ned what in flesh was fatigate,
And to the battle came he; where he did
Run reeking o'er the lives of men, as if
'Twere a perpetual spoil; and till we call'd
Both field and city ours he never stood
To ease his breast with panting.

MENENIUS. Worthy man!

FIRST SENATOR. He cannot but with measure fit the honours
Which we devise him.

COMINIUS. Our spoils he kick'd at,
And look'd upon things precious as they were
The common muck of the world. He covets less
Than misery itself would give, rewards
His deeds with doing them, and is content
To spend the time to end it.
MENENIUS. He's right noble;
Let him be call'd for.
FIRST SENATOR. Call Coriolanus.
OFFICER. He doth appear.

Re-enter CORIOLANUS

MENENIUS. The Senate, Coriolanus, are well pleas'd
To make thee consul.
CORIOLANUS. I do owe them still
My life and services.
MENENIUS. It then remains
That you do speak to the people.
CORIOLANUS. I do beseech you
Let me o'erleap that custom; for I cannot
Put on the gown, stand naked, and entreat them
For my wounds' sake to give their suffrage. Please you
That I may pass this doing.
SICINIUS. Sir, the people
Must have their voices; neither will they bate
One jot of ceremony.
MENENIUS. Put them not to't.
Pray you go fit you to the custom, and
Take to you, as your predecessors have,
Your honour with your form.
CORIOLANUS. It is a part
That I shall blush in acting, and might well
Be taken from the people.
BRUTUS. Mark you that?
CORIOLANUS. To brag unto them 'Thus I did, and thus!'
Show them th' unaching scars which I should hide,
As if I had receiv'd them for the hire
Of their breath only!
MENENIUS. Do not stand upon't.
We recommend to you, Tribunes of the People,

Our purpose to them; and to our noble consul
Wish we all joy and honour.

SENATORS. To Coriolanus come all joy and honour!

[*Flourish. Cornets. Then exeunt all but* SICINIUS *and* BRUTUS]

BRUTUS. You see how he intends to use the people.

SICINIUS. May they perceive's intent! He will require them
As if he did contemn what he requested
Should be in them to give.

BRUTUS. Come, we'll inform them
Of our proceedings here. On th' market-place
I know they do attend us. *Exeunt*

SCENE 3

Rome. The Forum

Enter seven or eight citizens

FIRST CITIZEN. Once, if he do require our voices, we ought not to deny him.

SECOND CITIZEN. We may, sir, if we will.

THIRD CITIZEN. We have power in ourselves to do it, but it is a power that we have no power to do; for if he show us his wounds and tell us his deeds, we are to put our tongues into those wounds and speak for them; so, if he tell us his noble deeds, we must also tell him our noble acceptance of them. Ingratitude is monstrous, and for the multitude to be ingrateful were to make a monster of the multitude; of the which we being members should bring ourselves to be monstrous members.

FIRST CITIZEN. And to make us no better thought of, a little help will serve; for once we stood up about the corn, he himself stuck not to call us the many-headed multitude.

THIRD CITIZEN. We have been call'd so of many; not that our heads are some brown, some black, some abram, some bald, but that our wits are so diversely colour'd; and truly I think if all our wits were to issue out of one skull, they would fly east, west, north, south, and their consent of one direct way should be at once to all the points o' th' compass.

SECOND CITIZEN. Think you so? Which way do you judge my wit would fly?

THIRD CITIZEN. Nay, your wit will not so soon out as another man's will—'tis strongly wedg'd up in a block-head; but if it were at liberty 'twould sure southward.

SECOND CITIZEN. Why that way?

THIRD CITIZEN. To lose itself in a fog; where being three parts melted away with rotten dews, the fourth would return for conscience' sake, to help to get thee a wife.

SECOND CITIZEN. You are never without your tricks; you may, you may.

THIRD CITIZEN. Are you all resolv'd to give your voices? But that's no matter, the greater part carries it. I say, if he would incline to the people, there was never a worthier man.

Enter CORIOLANUS, *in a gown of humility, with* MENENIUS

Here he comes, and in the gown of humility. Mark his behaviour. We are not to stay all together, but to come by him where he stands, by ones, by twos, and by threes. He's to make his requests by particulars, wherein every one of us has a single honour, in giving him our own voices with our own tongues; therefore follow me, and I'll direct you how you shall go by him.

ALL. Content, content. *Exeunt citizens*

MENENIUS. O sir, you are not right; have you not known
The worthiest men have done't?

CORIOLANUS. What must I say?
'I pray, sir'—Plague upon't! I cannot bring
My tongue to such a pace. 'Look, sir, my wounds
I got them in my country's service, when
Some certain of your brethren roar'd and ran
From th' noise of our own drums.'

MENENIUS. O me, the gods!
You must not speak of that. You must desire them
To think upon you.

CORIOLANUS. Think upon me? Hang 'em!

I would they would forget me, like the virtues
Which our divines lose by 'em.

MENENIUS. You'll mar all.
I'll leave you. Pray you speak to 'em, I pray you,
In wholesome manner. *Exit*

Re-enter three of the citizens

CORIOLANUS. Bid them wash their faces
And keep their teeth clean. So, here comes a brace.
You know the cause, sir, of my standing here.

THIRD CITIZEN. We do, sir; tell us what hath brought you to't.

CORIOLANUS. Mine own desert.

SECOND CITIZEN. Your own desert?

CORIOLANUS. Ay, not mine own desire.

THIRD CITIZEN. How, not your own desire?

CORIOLANUS. No, sir, 'twas never my desire yet to trouble the poor with begging.

THIRD CITIZEN. You must think, if we give you anything, we hope to gain by you.

CORIOLANUS. Well then, I pray, your price o' th' consulship?

FIRST CITIZEN. The price is to ask it kindly.

CORIOLANUS. Kindly, sir, I pray let me ha't. I have wounds to show you, which shall be yours in private. Your good voice, sir; what say you?

SECOND CITIZEN. You shall ha' it, worthy sir.

CORIOLANUS. A match, sir. There's in all two worthy voices begg'd. I have your alms. Adieu.

THIRD CITIZEN. But this is something odd.

SECOND CITIZEN. An 'twere to give again—but 'tis no matter.
Exeunt the three citizens

Re-enter two other citizens

CORIOLANUS. Pray you now, if it may stand with the tune of your voices that I may be consul, I have here the customary gown.

FOURTH CITIZEN. You have deserved nobly of your country, and you have not deserved nobly.

CORIOLANUS. Your enigma?

FOURTH CITIZEN. You have been a scourge to her enemies;

you have been a rod to her friends. You have not indeed loved the common people.

CORIOLANUS. You should account me the more virtuous, that I have not been common in my love. I will, sir, flatter my sworn brother, the people, to earn a dearer estimation of them; 'tis a condition they account gentle; and since the wisdom of their choice is rather to have my hat than my heart, I will practise the insinuating nod and be off to them most counterfeitly. That is, sir, I will counterfeit the bewitchment of some popular man and give it bountiful to the desirers. Therefore, beseech you I may be consul.

FIFTH CITIZEN. We hope to find you our friend; and therefore give you our voices heartily.

FOURTH CITIZEN. You have received many wounds for your country.

CORIOLANUS. I will not seal your knowledge with showing them. I will make much of your voices, and so trouble you no farther.

BOTH CITIZENS. The gods give you joy, sir, heartily!

Exeunt citizens

CORIOLANUS. Most sweet voices!
Better it is to die, better to starve,
Than crave the hire which first we do deserve.
Why in this wolvish toge should I stand here
To beg of Hob and Dick that do appear
Their needless vouches? Custom calls me to't.
What custom wills, in all things should we do't,
The dust on antique time would lie unswept,
And mountainous error be too highly heap'd
For truth to o'erpeer. Rather than fool it so,
Let the high office and the honour go
To one that would do thus. I am half through:
The one part suffered, the other will I do.

Re-enter three citizens more

Here come moe voices.
Your voices. For your voices I have fought;
Watch'd for your voices; for your voices bear
Of wounds two dozen odd; battles thrice six
I have seen and heard of; for your voices have

Done many things, some less, some more. Your voices?
Indeed, I would be consul.

SIXTH CITIZEN. He has done nobly, and cannot go without any honest man's voice.

SEVENTH CITIZEN. Therefore let him be consul. The gods give him joy, and make him good friend to the people!

ALL. Amen, amen. God save thee, noble consul!

Exeunt citizens

CORIOLANUS. Worthy voices!

Re-enter MENENIUS *with* BRUTUS *and* SICINIUS

MENENIUS. You have stood your limitation, and the tribunes
Endue you with the people's voice. Remains
That, in th' official marks invested, you
Anon do meet the Senate.

CORIOLANUS. Is this done?

SICINIUS. The custom of request you have discharg'd.
The people do admit you, and are summon'd
To meet anon, upon your approbation.

CORIOLANUS. Where? At the Senate House?

SICINIUS. There, Coriolanus.

CORIOLANUS. May I change these garments?

SICINIUS. You may, sir.

CORIOLANUS. That I'll straight do, and, knowing myself again,
Repair to th' Senate House.

MENENIUS. I'll keep you company. Will you along?

BRUTUS. We stay here for the people.

SICINIUS. Fare you well.

Exeunt CORIOLANUS *and* MENENIUS

He has it now; and by his looks methinks
'Tis warm at's heart.

BRUTUS. With a proud heart he wore
His humble weeds. Will you dismiss the people?

Re-enter citizens

SICINIUS. How now, my masters! Have you chose this man?

FIRST CITIZEN. He has our voices, sir.

BRUTUS. We pray the gods he may deserve your loves.

SECOND CITIZEN. Amen, sir. To my poor unworthy notice,
He mock'd us when he begg'd our voices.
THIRD CITIZEN. Certainly;
He flouted us downright.
FIRST CITIZEN. No, 'tis his kind of speech—he did not mock us.
SECOND CITIZEN. Not one amongst us, save yourself, but says
He us'd us scornfully. He should have show'd us
His marks of merit, wounds receiv'd for's country.
SICINIUS. Why, so he did, I am sure.
ALL. No, no; no man saw 'em.
THIRD CITIZEN. He said he had wounds which he could show in private,
And with his hat, thus waving it in scorn,
'I would be consul,' says he; 'aged custom
But by your voices will not so permit me;
Your voices therefore.' When we granted that,
Here was 'I thank you for your voices. Thank you,
Your most sweet voices. Now you have left your voices,
I have no further with you.' Was not this mockery?
SICINIUS. Why either were you ignorant to see't,
Or, seeing it, of such childish friendliness
To yield your voices?
BRUTUS. Could you not have told him—
As you were lesson'd—when he had no power
But was a petty servant to the state,
He was your enemy; ever spake against
Your liberties and the charters that you bear
I' th' body of the weal; and now, arriving
A place of potency and sway o' th' state,
If he should still malignantly remain
Fast foe to th' plebeii, your voices might
Be curses to yourselves? You should have said
That as his worthy deeds did claim no less
Than what he stood for, so his gracious nature
Would think upon you for your voices, and
Translate his malice towards you into love,
Standing your friendly lord.
SICINIUS. Thus to have said,

As you were fore-advis'd, had touch'd his spirit
And tried his inclination; from him pluck'd
Either his gracious promise, which you might,
As cause had call'd you up, have held him to;
Or else it would have gall'd his surly nature,
Which easily endures not article
Tying him to aught. So, putting him to rage,
You should have ta'en th' advantage of his choler
And pass'd him unelected.

BRUTUS. Did you perceive
He did solicit you in free contempt
When he did need your loves; and do you think
That his contempt shall not be bruising to you
When he hath power to crush? Why, had your bodies
No heart among you? Or had you tongues to cry
Against the rectorship of judgment?

SICINIUS. Have you
Ere now denied the asker, and now again,
Of him that did not ask but mock, bestow
Your su'd-for tongues?

THIRD CITIZEN. He's not confirm'd: we may deny him yet.

SECOND CITIZENS. And will deny him;
I'll have five hundred voices of that sound.

FIRST CITIZEN. I twice five hundred, and their friends to piece 'em.

BRUTUS. Get you hence instantly, and tell those friends
They have chose a consul that will from them take
Their liberties, make them of no more voice
Than dogs, that are as often beat for barking
As therefore kept to do so.

SICINIUS. Let them assemble;
And, on a safer judgment, all revoke
Your ignorant election. Enforce his pride
And his old hate unto you; besides, forget not
With what contempt he wore the humble weed;
How in his suit he scorn'd you; but your loves,
Thinking upon his services, took from you
Th' apprehension of his present portance,
Which, most gibingly, ungravely, he did fashion
After the inveterate hate he bears you.

BRUTUS. Lay
  A fault on us, your tribunes, that we labour'd,
  No impediment between, but that you must
  Cast your election on him.
SICINIUS. Say you chose him
  More after our commandment than as guided
  By your own true affections; and that your minds,
  Pre-occupied with what you rather must do
  Than what you should, made you against the grain
  To voice him consul. Lay the fault on us.
BRUTUS. Ay, spare us not. Say we read lectures to you,
  How youngly he began to serve his country,
  How long continued; and what stock he springs of—
  The noble house o' th' Marcians; from whence came
  That Ancus Marcius, Numa's daughter's son,
  Who, after great Hostilius, here was king;
  Of the same house Publius and Quintus were,
  That our best water brought by conduits hither;
  And Censorinus, nobly named so,
  Twice being by the people chosen censor,
  Was his great ancestor.
SICINIUS. One thus descended,
  That hath beside well in his person wrought
  To be set high in place, we did commend
  To your remembrances; but you have found,
  Scaling his present bearing with his past,
  That he's your fixed enemy, and revoke
  Your sudden approbation.
BRUTUS. Say you ne'er had done't—
  Harp on that still—but by our putting on;
  And presently, when you have drawn your number,
  Repair to th' Capitol.
CITIZENS. We will so; almost all
  Repent in their election. *Exeunt plebeians*
BRUTUS. Let them go on;
  This mutiny were better put in hazard
  Than stay, past doubt, for greater.
  If, as his nature is, he fall in rage
  With their refusal, both observe and answer
  The vantage of his anger.

SICINIUS. To th' Capitol, come.
We will be there before the stream o' th' people;
And this shall seem, as partly 'tis, their own,
Which we have goaded onward. *Exeunt*

ACT III. SCENE 1

Rome. A street

Cornets. Enter CORIOLANUS, MENENIUS, *all the* GENTRY, COMINIUS, TITUS LARTIUS, *and other* SENATORS

CORIOLANUS. Tullus Aufidius, then, had made new head?
LARTIUS. He had, my lord; and that it was which caus'd
Our swifter composition.
CORIOLANUS. So then the Volsces stand but as at first,
Ready, when time shall prompt them, to make road
Upon's again.
COMINIUS. They are worn, Lord Consul, so
That we shall hardly in our ages see
Their banners wave again.
CORIOLANUS. Saw you Aufidius?
LARTIUS. On safeguard he came to me, and did curse
Against the Volsces, for they had so vilely
Yielded the town. He is retir'd to Antium.
CORIOLANUS. Spoke he of me?
LARTIUS. He did, my lord.
CORIOLANUS. How? What?
LARTIUS. How often he had met you, sword to sword;
That of all things upon the earth he hated
Your person most; that he would pawn his fortunes
To hopeless restitution, so he might
Be call'd your vanquisher.
CORIOLANUS. At Antium lives he?
LARTIUS. At Antium.
CORIOLANUS. I wish I had a cause to seek him there,
To oppose his hatred fully. Welcome home.

Enter SICINIUS *and* BRUTUS

Behold, these are the tribunes of the people,
The tongues o' th' common mouth. I do despise them,
For they do prank them in authority,
Against all noble sufferance.

SICINIUS. Pass no further.

CORIOLANUS. Ha! What is that?

BRUTUS. It will be dangerous to go on–no further.

CORIOLANUS. What makes this change?

MENENIUS. The matter?

COMINIUS. Hath he not pass'd the noble and the common?

BRUTUS. Cominius, no.

CORIOLANUS. Have I had children's voices?

FIRST SENATOR. Tribunes, give way: he shall to th' market-place.

BRUTUS. The people are incens'd against him.

SICINIUS. Stop,
Or all will fall in broil.

CORIOLANUS. Are these your herd?
Must these have voices, that can yield them now
And straight disclaim their tongues? What are your offices?
You being their mouths, why rule you not their teeth?
Have you not set them on?

MENENIUS. Be calm, be calm.

CORIOLANUS. It is a purpos'd thing, and grows by plot,
To curb the will of the nobility;
Suffer't, and live with such as cannot rule
Nor ever will be rul'd.

BRUTUS. Call't not a plot.
The people cry you mock'd them; and of late,
When corn was given them gratis, you repin'd;
Scandal'd the suppliants for the people, call'd them
Time-pleasers, flatterers, foes to nobleness.

CORIOLANUS. Why, this was known before.

BRUTUS. Not to them all.

CORIOLANUS. Have you inform'd them sithence?

BRUTUS. How? I inform them!

COMINIUS. You are like to do such business.

BRUTUS. Not unlike
Each way to better yours.

CORIOLANUS. Why then should I be consul? By yond clouds,
Let me deserve so ill as you, and make me
Your fellow tribune.
SICINIUS. You show too much of that
For which the people stir; if you will pass
To where you are bound, you must enquire your way,
Which you are out of, with a gentler spirit,
Or never be so noble as a consul,
Nor yoke with him for tribune.
MENENIUS. Let's be calm.
COMINIUS. The people are abus'd; set on. This palt'ring
Becomes not Rome; nor has Coriolanus
Deserved this so dishonour'd rub, laid falsely
I' th' plain way of his merit.
CORIOLANUS. Tell me of corn!
This was my speech, and I will speak't again—
MENENIUS. Not now, not now.
FIRST SENATOR. Not in this heat, sir, now.
CORIOLANUS. Now, as I live, I will.
My nobler friends, I crave their pardons.
For the mutable, rank-scented meiny, let them
Regard me as I do not flatter, and
Therein behold themselves. I say again,
In soothing them we nourish 'gainst our Senate
The cockle of rebellion, insolence, sedition,
Which we ourselves have plough'd for, sow'd, and scatter'd,
By mingling them with us, the honour'd number,
Who lack not virtue, no, nor power, but that
Which they have given to beggars.
MENENIUS. Well, no more.
FIRST SENATOR. No more words, we beseech you.
CORIOLANUS. How? no more!
As for my country I have shed my blood,
Not fearing outward force, so shall my lungs
Coin words till their decay against those measles
Which we disdain should tetter us, yet sought
The very way to catch them.
BRUTUS. You speak o' th' people
As if you were a god, to punish; not

A man of their infirmity.
SICINIUS. 'Twere well
We let the people know't.
MENENIUS. What, what? his choler?
CORIOLANUS. Choler!
Were I as patient as the midnight sleep,
By Jove, 'twould be my mind!
SICINIUS. It is a mind
That shall remain a poison where it is,
Not poison any further.
CORIOLANUS. Shall remain!
Hear you this Triton of the minnows? Mark you
His absolute 'shall'?
COMINIUS. 'Twas from the canon.
CORIOLANUS. 'Shall'!
O good but most unwise patricians! Why,
You grave but reckless senators, have you thus
Given Hydra here to choose an officer
That with his peremptory 'shall,' being but
The horn and noise o' th' monster's, wants not spirit
To say he'll turn your current in a ditch,
And make your channel his? If he have power,
Then vail your ignorance; if none, awake
Your dangerous lenity. If you are learn'd,
Be not as common fools; if you are not,
Let them have cushions by you. You are plebeians,
If they be senators; and they are no less,
When, both your voices blended, the great'st taste
Most palates theirs. They choose their magistrate;
And such a one as he, who puts his 'shall,'
His popular 'shall,' against a graver bench
Than ever frown'd in Greece. By Jove himself,
It makes the consuls base; and my soul aches
To know, when two authorities are up,
Neither supreme, how soon confusion
May enter 'twixt the gap of both and take
The one by th' other.
COMINIUS. Well, on to th' market-place.
CORIOLANUS. Whoever gave that counsel to give forth
The corn o' th' storehouse gratis, as 'twas us'd

Sometime in Greece—
MENENIUS. Well, well, no more of that.
CORIOLANUS. Though there the people had more absolute pow'r—
I say they nourish'd disobedience, fed
The ruin of the state.
BRUTUS. Why shall the people give
One that speaks thus their voice?
CORIOLANUS. I'll give my reasons,
More worthier than their voices. They know the corn
Was not our recompense, resting well assur'd
They ne'er did service for't; being press'd to th' war
Even when the navel of the state was touch'd,
They would not thread the gates. This kind of service
Did not deserve corn gratis. Being i' th' war,
Their mutinies and revolts, wherein they show'd
Most valour, spoke not for them. Th' accusation
Which they have often made against the Senate,
All cause unborn, could never be the native
Of our so frank donation. Well, what then?
How shall this bosom multiplied digest
The Senate's courtesy? Let deeds express
What's like to be their words: 'We did request it;
We are the greater poll, and in true fear
They gave us our demands.' Thus we debase
The nature of our seats, and make the rabble
Call our cares fears; which will in time
Break ope the locks o' th' Senate and bring in
The crows to peck the eagles.
MENENIUS. Come, enough.
BRUTUS. Enough, with over measure.
CORIOLANUS. No, take more.
What may be sworn by, both divine and human,
Seal what I end withal! This double worship,
Where one part does disdain with cause, the other
Insult without all reason; where gentry, title, wisdom,
Cannot conclude but by the yea and no
Of general ignorance—it must omit
Real necessities, and give way the while
To unstable slightness. Purpose so barr'd, it follows

Nothing is done to purpose. Therefore, beseech you—
You that will be less fearful than discreet;
That love the fundamental part of state
More than you doubt the change on't; that prefer
A noble life before a long, and wish
To jump a body with a dangerous physic
That's sure of death without it—at once pluck out
The multitudinous tongue; let them not lick
The sweet which is their poison. Your dishonour
Mangles true judgment, and bereaves the state
Of that integrity which should become't,
Not having the power to do the good it would,
For th' ill which doth control't.

BRUTUS. Has said enough.

SICINIUS. Has spoken like a traitor and shall answer
As traitors do.

CORIOLANUS. Thou wretch, despite o'erwhelm thee!
What should the people do with these bald tribunes,
On whom depending, their obedience fails
To the greater bench? In a rebellion,
When what's not meet, but what must be, was law,
Then were they chosen; in a better hour
Let what is meet be said it must be meet,
And throw their power i' th' dust.

BRUTUS. Manifest treason!

SICINIUS. This a consul? No.

BRUTUS. The ædiles, ho!

Enter an ÆDILE

Let him be apprehended.

SICINIUS. Go call the people, [*Exit* ÆDILE] in whose name myself
Attach thee as a traitorous innovator,
A foe to th' public weal. Obey, I charge thee,
And follow to thine answer.

CORIOLANUS. Hence, old goat!

PATRICIANS. We'll surety him.

COMINIUS. Ag'd sir, hands off.

CORIOLANUS. Hence, rotten thing! or I shall shake thy bones
Out of thy garments.

SICINIUS. Help, ye citizens!

Enter a rabble of plebeians, with the ÆDILES

MENENIUS. On both sides more respect.

SICINIUS. Here's he that would take from you all your power.

BRUTUS. Seize him, ædiles.

PLEBEIANS. Down with him! down with him!

SECOND SENATOR. Weapons, weapons, weapons!

[*They all bustle about* CORIOLANUS]

ALL. Tribunes! patricians! citizens! What, ho! Sicinius! Brutus! Coriolanus! Citizens!

PATRICIANS. Peace, peace, peace; stay, hold, peace!

MENENIUS. What is about to be? I am out of breath;
Confusion's near; I cannot speak. You tribunes
To th' people—Coriolanus, patience!
Speak, good Sicinius.

SICINIUS. Hear me, people; peace!

PLEBEIANS. Let's hear our tribune. Peace! Speak, speak, speak.

SICINIUS. You are at point to lose your liberties.
Marcius would have all from you; Marcius,
Whom late you have nam'd for consul.

MENENIUS. Fie, fie, fie!
This is the way to kindle, not to quench.

FIRST SENATOR. To unbuild the city, and to lay all flat.

SICINIUS. What is the city but the people?

PLEBEIANS. True,
The people are the city.

BRUTUS. By the consent of all we were establish'd
The people's magistrates.

PLEBEIANS. You so remain.

MENENIUS. And so are like to do.

COMINIUS. That is the way to lay the city flat,
To bring the roof to the foundation,
And bury all which yet distinctly ranges
In heaps and piles of ruin.

SICINIUS. This deserves death.

BRUTUS. Or let us stand to our authority
Or let us lose it. We do here pronounce,

Upon the part o' th' people, in whose power
We were elected theirs: Marcius is worthy
Of present death.

SICINIUS. Therefore lay hold of him;
Bear him to th' rock Tarpeian, and from thence
Into destruction cast him.

BRUTUS. Ædiles, seize him.

PLEBEIANS. Yield, Marcius, yield.

MENENIUS. Hear me one word; beseech you, Tribunes,
Hear me but a word.

ÆDILES. Peace, peace!

MENENIUS. Be that you seem, truly your country's friend,
And temp'rately proceed to what you would
Thus violently redress.

BRUTUS. Sir, those cold ways,
That seem like prudent helps, are very poisonous
Where the disease is violent. Lay hands upon him
And bear him to the rock.

[CORIOLANUS *draws his sword*]

CORIOLANUS. No: I'll die here.
There's some among you have beheld me fighting;
Come, try upon yourselves what you have seen me.

MENENIUS. Down with that sword! Tribunes, withdraw awhile.

BRUTUS. Lay hands upon him.

MENENIUS. Help Marcius, help,
You that be noble; help him, young and old.

PLEBEIANS. Down with him, down with him!

[*In this mutiny the* TRIBUNES, *the* ÆDILES, *and the people are beat in*]

MENENIUS. Go, get you to your house; be gone, away.
All will be nought else.

SECOND SENATOR. Get you gone.

CORIOLANUS. Stand fast;
We have as many friends as enemies.

MENENIUS. Shall it be put to that?

FIRST SENATOR. The gods forbid!
I prithee, noble friend, home to thy house;
Leave us to cure this cause.

MENENIUS. For 'tis a sore upon us

You cannot tent yourself; be gone, beseech you.

COMINIUS. Come, sir, along with us.

CORIOLANUS. I would they were barbarians, as they are,
Though in Rome litter'd; not Romans, as they are not,
Though calved i' th' porch o' th' Capitol.

MENENIUS. Be gone.
Put not your worthy rage into your tongue;
One time will owe another.

CORIOLANUS. On fair ground
I could beat forty of them.

MENENIUS. I could myself
Take up a brace o' th' best of them; yea, the two tribunes.

COMINIUS. But now 'tis odds beyond arithmetic,
And manhood is call'd foolery when it stands
Against a falling fabric. Will you hence,
Before the tag return? whose rage doth rend
Like interrupted waters, and o'erbear
What they are us'd to bear.

MENENIUS. Pray you be gone.
I'll try whether my old wit be in request
With those that have but little; this must be patch'd
With cloth of any colour.

COMINIUS. Nay, come away.

Exeunt CORIOLANUS *and* COMINIUS, *with others*

PATRICIANS. This man has marr'd his fortune.

MENENIUS. His nature is too noble for the world:
He would not flatter Neptune for his trident,
Or Jove for's power to thunder. His heart's his mouth;
What his breast forges, that his tongue must vent;
And, being angry, does forget that ever
He heard the name of death. [*A noise within*]
Here's goodly work!

PATRICIANS. I would they were a-bed.

MENENIUS. I would they were in Tiber.
What the vengeance, could he not speak 'em fair?

Re-enter BRUTUS *and* SICINIUS, *with the rabble again*

SICINIUS. Where is this viper
That would depopulate the city and

Be every man himself?

MENENIUS. You worthy Tribunes–

SICINIUS. He shall be thrown down the Tarpeian rock
With rigorous hands; he hath resisted law,
And therefore law shall scorn him further trial
Than the severity of the public power,
Which he so sets at nought.

FIRST CITIZEN. He shall well know
The noble tribunes are the people's mouths,
And we their hands.

PLEBEIANS. He shall, sure on't.

MENENIUS. Sir, sir–

SICINIUS. Peace!

MENENIUS. Do not cry havoc, where you should but hunt
With modest warrant.

SICINIUS. Sir, how comes't that you
Have holp to make this rescue?

MENENIUS. Hear me speak.
As I do know the consul's worthiness,
So can I name his faults.

SICINIUS. Consul! What consul?

MENENIUS. The consul Coriolanus.

BRUTUS. He consul!

PLEBEIANS. No, no, no, no, no.

MENENIUS. If, by the tribunes' leave, and yours, good people,
I may be heard, I would crave a word or two;
The which shall turn you to no further harm
Than so much loss of time.

SICINIUS. Speak briefly, then,
For we are peremptory to dispatch
This viperous traitor; to eject him hence
Were but one danger, and to keep him here
Our certain death; therefore it is decreed
He dies to-night.

MENENIUS. Now the good gods forbid
That our renowned Rome, whose gratitude
Towards her deserved children is enroll'd
In Jove's own book, like an unnatural dam
Should now eat up her own!

SICINIUS. He's a disease that must be cut away.
MENENIUS. O, he's a limb that has but a disease–
Mortal, to cut it off: to cure it, easy.
What has he done to Rome that's worthy death?
Killing our enemies, the blood he hath lost–
Which I dare vouch is more than that he hath
By many an ounce–he dropt it for his country;
And what is left, to lose it by his country
Were to us all that do't and suffer it
A brand to th' end o' th' world.
SICINIUS. This is clean kam.
BRUTUS. Merely awry. When he did love his country,
It honour'd him.
SICINIUS. The service of the foot,
Being once gangren'd, is not then respected
For what before it was.
BRUTUS. We'll hear no more.
Pursue him to his house and pluck him thence,
Lest his infection, being of catching nature,
Spread further.
MENENIUS. One word more, one word
This tiger-footed rage, when it shall find
The harm of unscann'd swiftness, will, too late,
Tie leaden pounds to's heels. Proceed by process,
Lest parties–as he is belov'd–break out,
And sack great Rome with Romans.
BRUTUS. If it were so–
SICINIUS. What do ye talk?
Have we not had a taste of his obedience–
Our ædiles smote, ourselves resisted? Come!
MENENIUS. Consider this: he has been bred i' th' wars
Since 'a could draw a sword, and is ill school'd
In bolted language; meal and bran together
He throws without distinction. Give me leave,
I'll go to him and undertake to bring him
Where he shall answer by a lawful form,
In peace, to his utmost peril.
FIRST SENATOR. Noble Tribunes,
It is the humane way; the other course
Will prove too bloody, and the end of it

Unknown to the beginning.
SICINIUS. Noble Menenius,
Be you then as the people's officer.
Masters, lay down your weapons.
BRUTUS. Go not home.
SICINIUS. Meet on the market-place. We'll attend you there;
Where, if you bring not Marcius, we'll proceed
In our first way.
MENENIUS. I'll bring him to you.
[*To the* SENATORS] Let me desire your company; he must come,
Or what is worst will follow.
FIRST SENATOR. Pray you let's to him. *Exeunt*

SCENE 2

Rome. The house of CORIOLANUS

Enter CORIOLANUS *with* NOBLES

CORIOLANUS. Let them pull all about mine ears, present me
Death on the wheel or at wild horses' heels;
Or pile ten hills on the Tarpeian rock,
That the precipitation might down stretch
Below the beam of sight; yet will I still
Be thus to them.
FIRST PATRICIAN. You do the nobler.
CORIOLANUS. I muse my mother
Does not approve me further, who was wont
To call them woollen vassals, things created
To buy and sell with groats; to show bare heads
In congregations, to yawn, be still, and wonder,
When one but of my ordinance stood up
To speak of peace or war.

Enter VOLUMNIA

I talk of you:
Why did you wish me milder? Would you have me
False to my nature? Rather say I play

The man I am.

VOLUMNIA. O, sir, sir, sir,
I would have had you put your power well on
Before you had worn it out.

CORIOLANUS. Let go.

VOLUMNIA. You might have been enough the man you are
With striving less to be so; lesser had been
The thwartings of your dispositions, if
You had not show'd them how ye were dispos'd,
Ere they lack'd power to cross you.

CORIOLANUS. Let them hang.

VOLUMNIA. Ay, and burn too.

Enter MENENIUS *with the* SENATORS

MENENIUS. Come, come, you have been too rough, something too rough;
You must return and mend it.

FIRST SENATOR. There's no remedy,
Unless, by not so doing, our good city
Cleave in the midst and perish.

VOLUMNIA. Pray be counsell'd;
I have a heart as little apt as yours,
But yet a brain that leads my use of anger
To better vantage.

MENENIUS. Well said, noble woman!
Before he should thus stoop to th' herd, but that
The violent fit o' th' time craves it as physic
For the whole state, I would put mine armour on,
Which I can scarcely bear.

CORIOLANUS. What must I do?

MENENIUS. Return to th' tribunes.

CORIOLANUS. Well, what then, what then?

MENENIUS. Repent what you have spoke.

CORIOLANUS. For them! I cannot do it to the gods;
Must I then do't to them?

VOLUMNIA. You are too absolute;
Though therein you can never be too noble
But when extremities speak. I have heard you say
Honour and policy, like unsever'd friends,
I' th' war do grow together; grant that, and tell me

In peace what each of them by th' other lose
That they combine not there.
CORIOLANUS. Tush, tush!
MENENIUS. A good demand.
VOLUMNIA. If it be honour in your wars to seem
The same you are not, which for your best ends
You adopt your policy, how is it less or worse
That it shall hold companionship in peace
With honour as in war; since that to both
It stands in like request?
CORIOLANUS. Why force you this?
VOLUMNIA. Because that now it lies you on to speak
To th' people, not by your own instruction,
Nor by th' matter which your heart prompts you,
But with such words that are but roted in
Your tongue, though but bastards and syllables
Of no allowance to your bosom's truth.
Now, this no more dishonours you at all
Than to take in a town with gentle words,
Which else would put you to your fortune and
The hazard of much blood.
I would dissemble with my nature where
My fortunes and my friends at stake requir'd
I should do so in honour. I am in this
Your wife, your son, these senators, the nobles;
And you will rather show our general louts
How you can frown, than spend a fawn upon 'em
For the inheritance of their loves and safeguard
Of what that want might ruin.
MENENIUS. Noble lady!
Come, go with us, speak fair; you may salve so,
Not what is dangerous present, but the loss
Of what is past.
VOLUMNIA. I prithee now, my son,
Go to them with this bonnet in thy hand;
And thus far having stretch'd it—here be with them—
Thy knee bussing the stones—for in such business
Action is eloquence, and the eyes of th' ignorant
More learned than the ears—waving thy head,
Which often thus correcting thy stout heart,

Now humble as the ripest mulberry
That will not hold the handling. Or say to them
Thou art their soldier and, being bred in broils,
Hast not the soft way which, thou dost confess,
Were fit for thee to use, as they to claim,
In asking their good loves; but thou wilt frame
Thyself, forsooth, hereafter theirs, so far
As thou hast power and person.

MENENIUS. This but done
Even as she speaks, why, their hearts were yours;
For they have pardons, being ask'd, as free
As words to little purpose.

VOLUMNIA. Prithee now,
Go, and be rul'd; although I know thou hadst rather
Follow thine enemy in a fiery gulf
Than flatter him in a bower.

Enter COMINIUS

Here is Cominius.

COMINIUS. I have been i' th' market-place; and, sir, 'tis fit
You make strong party, or defend yourself
By calmness or by absence; all's in anger.

MENENIUS. Only fair speech.

COMINIUS. I think 'twill serve, if he
Can thereto frame his spirit.

VOLUMNIA. He must and will.
Prithee now, say you will, and go about it.

CORIOLANUS. Must I go show them my unbarb'd sconce? Must I
With my base tongue give to my noble heart
A lie that it must bear? Well, I will do't;
Yet, were there but this single plot to lose,
This mould of Marcius, they to dust should grind it,
And throw't against the wind. To th' market-place!
You have put me now to such a part which never
I shall discharge to th' life.

COMINIUS. Come, come, we'll prompt you.

VOLUMNIA. I prithee now, sweet son, as thou hast said
My praises made thee first a soldier, so,
To have my praise for this, perform a part

Thou hast not done before.
CORIOLANUS. Well, I must do't.
Away, my disposition, and possess me
Some harlot's spirit! My throat of war be turn'd,
Which quier'd with my drum, into a pipe
Small as an eunuch or the virgin voice
That babies lulls asleep! The smiles of knaves
Tent in my cheeks, and schoolboys' tears take up
The glasses of my sight! A beggar's tongue
Make motion through my lips, and my arm'd knees,
Who bow'd but in my stirrup, bend like his
That hath receiv'd an alms! I will not do't,
Lest I surcease to honour mine own truth,
And by my body's action teach my mind
A most inherent baseness.
VOLUMNIA. At thy choice, then.
To beg of thee, it is my more dishonour
Than thou of them. Come all to ruin. Let
Thy mother rather feel thy pride than fear
Thy dangerous stoutness; for I mock at death
With as big heart as thou. Do as thou list.
Thy valiantness was mine, thou suck'dst it from me;
But owe thy pride thyself.
CORIOLANUS. Pray be content.
Mother, I am going to the market-place;
Chide me no more. I'll mountebank their loves,
Cog their hearts from them, and come home belov'd
Of all the trades in Rome. Look, I am going.
Commend me to my wife. I'll return consul,
Or never trust to what my tongue can do
I' th' way of flattery further.
VOLUMNIA. Do your will. *Exit*
COMINIUS. Away! The tribunes do attend you. Arm yourself
To answer mildly; for they are prepar'd
With accusations, as I hear, more strong
Than are upon you yet.
CORIOLANUS. The word is 'mildly.' Pray you let us go.
Let them accuse me by invention; I
Will answer in mine honour.

MENENIUS. Ay, but mildly.
CORIOLANUS. Well, mildly be it then—mildly. *Exeunt*

SCENE 3

Rome. The Forum

Enter SICINIUS *and* BRUTUS

BRUTUS. In this point charge him home, that he affects
Tyrannical power. If he evade us there,
Enforce him with his envy to the people,
And that the spoil got on the Antiates
Was ne'er distributed.

Enter an ÆDILE

What, will he come?
ÆDILE. He's coming.
BRUTUS. How accompanied?
ÆDILE. With old Menenius, and those senators
That always favour'd him.
SICINIUS. Have you a catalogue
Of all the voices that we have procur'd,
Set down by th' poll?
ÆDILE. I have; 'tis ready.
SICINIUS. Have you collected them by tribes?
ÆDILE. I have.
SICINIUS. Assemble presently the people hither;
And when they hear me say 'It shall be so
I' th' right and strength o' th' commons' be it either
For death, for fine, or banishment, then let them,
If I say fine, cry 'Fine!'—if death, cry 'Death!'
Insisting on the old prerogative
And power i' th' truth o' th' cause.
ÆDILE. I shall inform them.
BRUTUS. And when such time they have begun to cry,
Let them not cease, but with a din confus'd
Enforce the present execution
Of what we chance to sentence.
ÆDILE. Very well.

SICINIUS. Make them be strong, and ready for this hint,
When we shall hap to give't them.
BRUTUS. Go about it. *Exit* ÆDILE
Put him to choler straight. He hath been us'd
Ever to conquer, and to have his worth
Of contradiction; being once chaf'd, he cannot
Be rein'd again to temperance; then he speaks
What's in his heart, and that is there which looks
With us to break his neck.

Enter CORIOLANUS, MENENIUS, *and* COMINIUS, *with others*

SICINIUS. Well, here he comes.
MENENIUS. Calmly, I do beseech you.
CORIOLANUS. Ay, as an ostler, that for th' poorest piece
Will bear the knave by th' volume. Th' honour'd gods
Keep Rome in safety, and the chairs of justice
Supplied with worthy men! plant love among's!
Throng our large temples with the shows of peace,
And not our streets with war!
FIRST SENATOR. Amen, amen!
MENENIUS. A noble wish.

Re-enter the ÆDILE, *with the plebeians*

SICINIUS. Draw near, ye people.
ÆDILE. List to your tribunes. Audience! peace, I say!
CORIOLANUS. First, hear me speak.
BOTH TRIBUNES. Well, say. Peace, ho!
CORIOLANUS. Shall I be charg'd no further than this present?
Must all determine here?
SICINIUS. I do demand,
If you submit you to the people's voices,
Allow their officers, and are content
To suffer lawful censure for such faults
As shall be prov'd upon you.
CORIOLANUS. I am content.
MENENIUS. Lo, citizens, he says he is content.
The warlike service he has done, consider; think
Upon the wounds his body bears, which show
Like graves i' th' holy churchyard.

CORIOLANUS. Scratches with briers,
Scars to move laughter only.
MENENIUS. Consider further,
That when he speaks not like a citizen,
You find him like a soldier; do not take
His rougher accents for malicious sounds,
But, as I say, such as become a soldier
Rather than envy you.
COMINIUS. Well, well! No more.
CORIOLANUS. What is the matter,
That being pass'd for consul with full voice,
I am so dishonour'd that the very hour
You take it off again?
SICINIUS. Answer to us.
CORIOLANUS. Say then; 'tis true, I ought so.
SICINIUS. We charge you that you have contriv'd to take
From Rome all season'd office, and to wind
Yourself into a power tyrannical;
For which you are a traitor to the people.
CORIOLANUS. How—traitor?
MENENIUS. Nay, temperately! Your promise.
CORIOLANUS. The fires i' th' lowest hell fold in the people!
Call me their traitor! Thou injurious tribune!
Within thine eyes sat twenty thousand deaths,
In thy hands clutch'd as many millions, in
Thy lying tongue both numbers, I would say
'Thou liest' unto thee with a voice as free
As I do pray the gods.
SICINIUS. Mark you this, people?
PLEBEIANS. To th' rock, to th' rock, with him!
SICINIUS. Peace!
We need not put new matter to his charge.
What you have seen him do and heard him speak,
Beating your officers, cursing yourselves,
Opposing laws with strokes, and here defying
Those whose great power must try him—even this,
So criminal and in such capital kind,
Deserves th' extremest death.
BRUTUS. But since he hath
Serv'd well for Rome—

CORIOLANUS. What do you prate of service?
BRUTUS. I talk of that that know it.
CORIOLANUS. You!
MENENIUS. Is this the promise that you made your mother?
COMINIUS. Know, I pray you–
CORIOLANUS. I'll know no further.
  Let them pronounce the steep Tarpeian death,
  Vagabond exile, flaying, pent to linger
  But with a grain a day, I would not buy
  Their mercy at the price of one fair word,
  Nor check my courage for what they can give,
  To have't with saying 'Good morrow.'
SICINIUS. For that he has–
  As much as in him lies–from time to time
  Envied against the people, seeking means
  To pluck away their power; as now at last
  Given hostile strokes, and that not in the presence
  Of dreaded justice, but on the ministers
  That do distribute it–in the name o' th' people,
  And in the power of us the tribunes, we,
  Ev'n from this instant, banish him our city,
  In peril of precipitation
  From off the rock Tarpeian, never more
  To enter our Rome gates. I' th' people's name,
  I say it shall be so.
PLEBEIANS. It shall be so, it shall be so! Let him away!
  He's banish'd, and it shall be so.
COMINIUS. Hear me, my masters and my common friends–
SICINIUS. He's sentenc'd; no more hearing.
COMINIUS. Let me speak.
  I have been consul, and can show for Rome
  Her enemies' marks upon me. I do love
  My country's good with a respect more tender,
  More holy and profound, than mine own life,
  My dear wife's estimate, her womb's increase
  And treasure of my loins. Then if I would
  Speak that–
SICINIUS. We know your drift. Speak what?
BRUTUS. There's no more to be said, but he is banish'd,
  As enemy to the people and his country.

It shall be so.

PLEBEIANS. It shall be so, it shall be so.

CORIOLANUS. You common cry of curs, whose breath I hate
As reek o' th' rotten fens, whose loves I prize
As the dead carcasses of unburied men
That do corrupt my air—I banish you.
And here remain with your uncertainty!
Let every feeble rumour shake your hearts;
Your enemies, with nodding of their plumes,
Fan you into despair! Have the power still
To banish your defenders, till at length
Your ignorance—which finds not till it feels,
Making but reservation of yourselves
Still your own foes—deliver you
As most abated captives to some nation
That won you without blows! Despising
For you the city, thus I turn my back;
There is a world elsewhere. *Exeunt* CORIOLANUS, COMINIUS, MENENIUS, *with the other* PATRICIANS

ÆDILE. The people's enemy is gone, is gone!

[*They all shout and throw up their caps*]

PLEBEIANS. Our enemy is banish'd, he is gone! Hoo-oo!

SICINIUS. Go see him out at gates, and follow him,
As he hath follow'd you, with all despite;
Give him deserv'd vexation. Let a guard
Attend us through the city.

PLEBEIANS. Come, come, let's see him out at gates; come!
The gods preserve our noble tribunes! Come. *Exeunt*

ACT IV. SCENE 1

Rome. Before a gate of the city

Enter CORIOLANUS, VOLUMNIA, VIRGILIA, MENENIUS, COMINIUS, *with the young* NOBILITY *of Rome*

CORIOLANUS. Come, leave your tears; a brief farewell. The beast

With many heads butts me away. Nay, mother,
Where is your ancient courage? You were us'd
To say extremities was the trier of spirits;
That common chances common men could bear;
That when the sea was calm all boats alike
Show'd mastership in floating; fortune's blows,
When most struck home, being gentle wounded craves
A noble cunning. You were us'd to load me
With precepts that would make invincible
The heart that conn'd them.

VIRGILIA. O heavens! O heavens!

CORIOLANUS. Nay, I prithee, woman—

VOLUMNIA. Now the red pestilence strike all trades in Rome,
And occupations perish!

CORIOLANUS. What, what, what!
I shall be lov'd when I am lack'd. Nay, mother,
Resume that spirit when you were wont to say,
If you had been the wife of Hercules,
Six of his labours you'd have done, and sav'd
Your husband so much sweat. Cominius,
Droop not; adieu. Farewell, my wife, my mother.
I'll do well yet. Thou old and true Menenius,
Thy tears are salter than a younger man's
And venomous to thine eyes. My sometime General,
I have seen thee stern, and thou hast oft beheld
Heart-hard'ning spectacles; tell these sad women
'Tis fond to wail inevitable strokes,
As 'tis to laugh at 'em. My mother, you wot well
My hazards still have been your solace; and
Believe't not lightly—though I go alone,
Like to a lonely dragon, that his fen
Makes fear'd and talk'd of more than seen—your son
Will or exceed the common or be caught
With cautelous baits and practice.

VOLUMNIA. My first son,
Whither wilt thou go? Take good Cominius
With thee awhile; determine on some course
More than a wild exposture to each chance
That starts i' th' way before thee.

VIRGILIA. O the gods!

COMINIUS. I'll follow thee a month, devise with thee
Where thou shalt rest, that thou mayst hear of us,
And we of thee; so, if the time thrust forth
A cause for thy repeal, we shall not send
O'er the vast world to seek a single man,
And lose advantage, which doth ever cool
I' th' absence of the needer.

CORIOLANUS. Fare ye well;
Thou hast years upon thee, and thou art too full
Of the wars' surfeits to go rove with one
That's yet unbruis'd; bring me but out at gate.
Come, my sweet wife, my dearest mother, and
My friends of noble touch; when I am forth,
Bid me farewell, and smile. I pray you come.
While I remain above the ground you shall
Hear from me still, and never of me aught
But what is like me formerly.

MENENIUS. That's worthily
As any ear can hear. Come, let's not weep.
If I could shake off but one seven years
From these old arms and legs, by the good gods,
I'd with thee every foot.

CORIOLANUS. Give me thy hand.
Come. *Exeunt*

SCENE 2

Rome. A street near the gate

Enter the two Tribunes, SICINIUS *and* BRUTUS *with the* ÆDILE

SICINIUS. Bid them all home; he's gone, and we'll no further.
The nobility are vex'd, whom we see have sided
In his behalf.

BRUTUS. Now we have shown our power,
Let us seem humbler after it is done
Than when it was a-doing.

SICINIUS. Bid them home.
  Say their great enemy is gone, and they
  Stand in their ancient strength.
BRUTUS. Dismiss them home. *Exit* ÆDILE
  Here comes his mother.

Enter VOLUMNIA, VIRGILIA, *and* MENENIUS

SICINIUS. Let's not meet her.
BRUTUS. Why?
SICINIUS. They say she's mad.
BRUTUS. They have ta'en note of us; keep on your way.
VOLUMNIA. O, y'are well met; th' hoarded plague o' th' gods
  Requite your love!
MENENIUS. Peace, peace, be not so loud.
VOLUMNIA. If that I could for weeping, you should hear—
  Nay, and you shall hear some. [*To* BRUTUS] Will you be gone?
VIRGILIA. [*To* SICINIUS] You shall stay too. I would I had the power
  To say so to my husband.
SICINIUS. Are you mankind?
VOLUMNIA. Ay, fool; is that a shame? Note but this, fool:
  Was not a man my father? Hadst thou foxship
  To banish him that struck more blows for Rome
  Than thou hast spoken words?
SICINIUS. O blessed heavens!
VOLUMNIA. Moe noble blows than ever thou wise words;
  And for Rome's good. I'll tell thee what—yet go!
  Nay, but thou shalt stay too. I would my son
  Were in Arabia, and thy tribe before him,
  His good sword in his hand.
SICINIUS. What then?
VIRGILIA. What then!
  He'd make an end of thy posterity.
VOLUMNIA. Bastards and all.
  Good man, the wounds that he does bear for Rome!
MENENIUS. Come, come, peace.
SICINIUS. I would he had continued to his country
  As he began, and not unknit himself

The noble knot he made.
BRUTUS. I would he had.
VOLUMNIA. 'I would he had!' 'Twas you incens'd the rabble—
Cats that can judge as fitly of his worth
As I can of those mysteries which heaven
Will not have earth to know.
BRUTUS. Pray, let's go.
VOLUMNIA. Now, pray, sir, get you gone;
You have done a brave deed. Ere you go, hear this:
As far as doth the Capitol exceed
The meanest house in Rome, so far my son—
This lady's husband here, this, do you see?—
Whom you have banish'd does exceed you all.
BRUTUS. Well, well, we'll leave you.
SICINIUS. Why stay we to be baited
With one that wants her wits? *Exeunt* TRIBUNES
VOLUMNIA. Take my prayers with you.
I would the gods had nothing else to do
But to confirm my curses. Could I meet 'em
But once a day, it would unclog my heart
Of what lies heavy to't.
MENENIUS. You have told them home,
And, by my troth, you have cause. You'll sup with me?
VOLUMNIA. Anger's my meat; I sup upon myself,
And so shall starve with feeding. Come, let's go.
Leave this faint puling and lament as I do,
In anger, Juno-like. Come, come, come.
Exeunt VOLUMNIA *and* VIRGILIA
MENENIUS. Fie, fie, fie! *Exit*

SCENE 3

A highway between Rome and Antium

Enter a ROMAN *and a* VOLSCE, *meeting*

ROMAN. I know you well, sir, and you know me; your name, I think, is Adrian.
VOLSCE. It is so, sir. Truly, I have forgot you.

ROMAN. I am a Roman; and my services are, as you are, against 'em. Know you me yet?

VOLSCE. Nicanor? No!

ROMAN. The same, sir.

VOLSCE. You had more beard when I last saw you, but your favour is well appear'd by your tongue. What's the news in Rome? I have a note from the Volscian state, to find you out there. You have well saved me a day's journey.

ROMAN. There hath been in Rome strange insurrections: the people against the senators, patricians, and nobles.

VOLSCE. Hath been! Is it ended, then? Our state thinks not so; they are in a most warlike preparation, and hope to come upon them in the heat of their division.

ROMAN. The main blaze of it is past, but a small thing would make it flame again; for the nobles receive so to heart the banishment of that worthy Coriolanus that they are in a ripe aptness to take all power from the people, and to pluck from them their tribunes for ever. This lies glowing, I can tell you, and is almost mature for the violent breaking out.

VOLSCE. Coriolanus banish'd!

ROMAN. Banish'd, sir.

VOLSCE. You will be welcome with this intelligence, Nicanor.

ROMAN. The day serves well for them now. I have heard it said the fittest time to corrupt a man's wife is when she's fall'n out with her husband. Your noble Tullus Aufidius will appear well in these wars, his great opposer, Coriolanus, being now in no request of his country.

VOLSCE. He cannot choose. I am most fortunate thus accidentally to encounter you; you have ended my business, and I will merrily accompany you home.

ROMAN. I shall between this and supper tell you most strange things from Rome, all tending to the good of their adversaries. Have you an army ready, say you?

VOLSCE. A most royal one: the centurions and their charges, distinctly billeted, already in th' entertainment, and to be on foot at an hour's warning.

ROMAN. I am joyful to hear of their readiness, and am the man, I think, that shall set them in present action. So, sir, heartily well met, and most glad of your company.

VOLSCE. You take my part from me, sir. I have the most cause to be glad of yours.

ROMAN. Well, let us go together.

SCENE 4

Antium. Before AUFIDIUS' *house*

Enter CORIOLANUS, *in mean apparel, disguis'd and muffled*

CORIOLANUS. A goodly city is this Antium. City,
'Tis I that made thy widows: many an heir
Of these fair edifices fore my wars
Have I heard groan and drop. Then know me not.
Lest that thy wives with spits and boys with stones,
In puny battle slay me.

Enter a CITIZEN

Save you, sir.

CITIZEN. And you.

CORIOLANUS. Direct me, if it be your will,
Where great Aufidius lies. Is he in Antium?

CITIZEN. He is, and feasts the nobles of the state
At his house this night.

CORIOLANUS. Which is his house, beseech you?

CITIZEN. This here before you.

CORIOLANUS. Thank you, sir; farewell. *Exit* CITIZEN
O world, thy slippery turns! Friends now fast sworn,
Whose double bosoms seems to wear one heart,
Whose hours, whose bed, whose meal and exercise
Are still together, who twin, as 'twere, in love
Unseparable, shall within this hour,
On a dissension of a doit, break out
To bitterest enmity; so fellest foes,
Whose passions and whose plots have broke their sleep
To take the one the other, by some chance,
Some trick not worth an egg, shall grow dear friends

And interjoin their issues. So with me:
My birthplace hate I, and my love's upon
This enemy town. I'll enter. If he slay me,
He does fair justice: if he give me way,
I'll do his country service.

SCENE 5

Antium. AUFIDIUS' *house*

Music plays. Enter a SERVINGMAN

FIRST SERVANT. Wine, wine, wine! What service is here! I think our fellows are asleep. *Exit*

Enter another SERVINGMAN

SECOND SERVANT. Where's Cotus? My master calls for him. Cotus! *Exit*

Enter CORIOLANUS

CORIOLANUS. A goodly house. The feast smells well, but I
Appear not like a guest.

Re-enter the first SERVINGMAN

FIRST SERVANT. What would you have, friend?
Whence are you? Here's no place for you: pray go to the door. *Exit*

CORIOLANUS. I have deserv'd no better entertainment
In being Coriolanus.

Re-enter second SERVINGMAN

SECOND SERVANT. Whence are you, sir? Has the porter his eyes in his head that he gives entrance to such companions? Pray get you out.

CORIOLANUS. Away!

SECOND SERVANT. Away? Get you away.

CORIOLANUS. Now th' art troublesome.

SECOND SERVANT. Are you so brave? I'll have you talk'd with anon.

Enter a third SERVINGMAN. *The first meets him*

THIRD SERVANT. What fellow's this?

FIRST SERVANT. A strange one as ever I look'd on. I cannot get him out o' th' house. Prithee call my master to him.

THIRD SERVANT. What have you to do here, fellow? Pray you avoid the house.

CORIOLANUS. Let me but stand—I will not hurt your hearth.

THIRD SERVANT. What are you?

CORIOLANUS. A gentleman.

THIRD SERVANT. A marv'llous poor one.

CORIOLANUS. True, so I am.

THIRD SERVANT. Pray you, poor gentleman, take up some other station; here's no place for you. Pray you avoid. Come.

CORIOLANUS. Follow your function, go and batten on cold bits. *[Pushes him away from him]*

THIRD SERVANT. What, you will not? Prithee tell my master what a strange guest he has here.

SECOND SERVANT. And I shall. *Exit*

THIRD SERVANT. Where dwell'st thou?

CORIOLANUS. Under the canopy.

THIRD SERVANT. Under the canopy?

CORIOLANUS. Ay.

THIRD SERVANT. Where's that?

CORIOLANUS. I' th' city of kites and crows.

THIRD SERVANT. I' th' city of kites and crows!
What an ass it is! Then thou dwell'st with daws too?

CORIOLANUS. No, I serve not thy master.

THIRD SERVANT. How, sir! Do you meddle with my master?

CORIOLANUS. Ay; 'tis an honester service than to meddle with thy mistress. Thou prat'st and prat'st; serve with thy trencher; hence! *[Beats him away]*

Enter AUFIDIUS *with the second* SERVINGMAN

AUFIDIUS. Where is this fellow?

SECOND SERVANT. Here, sir; I'd have beaten him like a dog, but for disturbing the lords within.

AUFIDIUS. Whence com'st thou? What wouldst thou? Thy name?
Why speak'st not? Speak, man. What's thy name?

CORIOLANUS. *[Unmuffling]* If, Tullus,

Not yet thou know'st me, and, seeing me, dost not
Think me for the man I am, necessity
Commands me name myself.

AUFIDIUS. What is thy name?

CORIOLANUS. A name unmusical to the Volscians' ears,
And harsh in sound to thine.

AUFIDIUS. Say, what's thy name?
Thou has a grim appearance, and thy face
Bears a command in't; though thy tackle's torn,
Thou show'st a noble vessel. What's thy name?

CORIOLANUS. Prepare thy brow to frown—know'st thou me yet?

AUFIDIUS. I know thee not. Thy name?

CORIOLANUS. My name is Caius Marcius, who hath done
To thee particularly, and to all the Volsces,
Great hurt and mischief; thereto witness may
My surname, Coriolanus. The painful service,
The extreme dangers, and the drops of blood
Shed for my thankless country, are requited
But with that surname—a good memory
And witness of the malice and displeasure
Which thou shouldst bear me. Only that name remains;
The cruelty and envy of the people,
Permitted by our dastard nobles, who
Have all forsook me, hath devour'd the rest,
An suffer'd me by th' voice of slaves to be
Whoop'd out of Rome. Now this extremity
Hath brought me to thy hearth; not out of hope,
Mistake me not, to save my life; for if
I had fear'd death, of all the men i' th' world
I would have 'voided thee; but in mere spite,
To be full quit of those my banishers,
Stand I before thee here. Then if thou hast
A heart of wreak in thee, that wilt revenge
Thine own particular wrongs and stop those maims
Of shame seen through thy country, speed thee straight
And make my misery serve thy turn. So use it
That my revengeful services may prove
As benefits to thee; for I will fight
Against my cank'red country with the spleen

Of all the under fiends. But if so be
Thou dar'st not this, and that to prove more fortunes
Th'art tir'd, then, in a word, I also am
Longer to live most weary, and present
My throat to thee and to thy ancient malice;
Which not to cut would show thee but a fool,
Since I have ever followed thee with hate,
Drawn tuns of blood out of thy country's breast,
And cannot live but to thy shame, unless
It be to do thee service.

AUFIDIUS. O Marcius, Marcius!
Each word thou hast spoke hath weeded from my heart
A root of ancient envy. If Jupiter
Should from yond cloud speak divine things,
And say ' 'Tis true,' I'd not believe them more
Than thee, all noble Marcius. Let me twine
Mine arms about that body, where against
My grained ash an hundred times hath broke
And scarr'd the moon with splinters; here I clip
The anvil of my sword, and do contest
As hotly and as nobly with thy love
As ever in ambitious strength I did
Contend against thy valour. Know thou first,
I lov'd the maid I married; never man
Sigh'd truer breath; but that I see thee here,
Thou noble thing, more dances my rapt heart
Than when I first my wedded mistress saw
Bestride my threshold. Why, thou Mars, I tell thee
We have a power on foot, and I had purpose
Once more to hew thy target from thy brawn,
Or lose mine arm for't. Thou hast beat me out
Twelve several times, and I have nightly since
Dreamt of encounters 'twixt thyself and me–
We have been down together in my sleep,
Unbuckling helms, fisting each other's throat–
And wak'd half dead with nothing. Worthy Marcius,
Had we no other quarrel else to Rome but that
Thou art thence banish'd, we would muster all
From twelve to seventy, and, pouring war
Into the bowels of ungrateful Rome,

Like a bold flood o'erbeat. O, come, go in,
And take our friendly senators by th' hands,
Who now are here, taking their leaves of me
Who am prepar'd against your territories,
Though not for Rome itself.

CORIOLANUS. You bless me, gods!

AUFIDIUS. Therefore, most absolute sir, if thou wilt have
The leading of thine own revenges, take
Th' one half of my commission, and set down—
As best thou art experienc'd, since thou know'st
Thy country's strength and weakness—thine own ways,
Whether to knock against the gates of Rome,
Or rudely visit them in parts remote
To fright them ere destroy. But come in;
Let me commend thee first to those that shall
Say yea to thy desires. A thousand welcomes!
And more a friend than e'er an enemy;
Yet, Marcius, that was much. Your hand; most welcome!

Exeunt CORIOLANUS *and* AUFIDIUS

The two SERVINGMEN *come forward*

FIRST SERVANT. Here's a strange alteration!

SECOND SERVANT. By my hand, I had thought to have strucken him with a cudgel; and yet my mind gave me his clothes made a false report of him.

FIRST SERVANT. What an arm he has! He turn'd me about with his finger and his thumb, as one would set up a top.

SECOND SERVANT. Nay, I knew by his face that there was something in him; he had, sir, a kind of face, methought —I cannot tell how to term it.

FIRST SERVANT. He had so, looking as it were—Would I were hang'd, but I thought there was more in him than I could think.

SECOND SERVANT. So did I, I'll be sworn. He is simply the rarest man i' th' world.

FIRST SERVANT. I think he is; but a greater soldier than he you wot on.

SECOND SERVANT. Who, my master?

FIRST SERVANT. Nay, it's no matter for that.

SECOND SERVANT. Worth six on him.

FIRST SERVANT. Nay, not so neither; but I take him to be the greater soldier.

SECOND SERVANT. Faith, look you, one cannot tell how to say that; for the defence of a town our general is excellent.

FIRST SERVANT. Ay, and for an assault too.

Re-enter the third SERVINGMAN

THIRD SERVANT. O slaves, I can tell you news–news, you rascals!

BOTH. What, what, what? Let's partake.

THIRD SERVANT. I would not be a Roman, of all nations; I had as lief be a condemn'd man.

BOTH. Wherefore? wherefore?

THIRD SERVANT. Why, here's he that was wont to thwack our general–Caius Marcius.

FIRST SERVANT. Why do you say 'thwack our general'?

THIRD SERVANT. I do not say 'thwack our general,' but he was always good enough for him.

SECOND SERVANT. Come, we are fellows and friends. He was ever too hard for him, I have heard him say so himself.

FIRST SERVANT. He was too hard for him directly, to say the troth on't; before Corioli he scotch'd him and notch'd him like a carbonado.

SECOND SERVANT. An he had been cannibally given, he might have broil'd and eaten him too.

FIRST SERVANT. But more of thy news!

THIRD SERVANT. Why, he is so made on here within as if he were son and heir to Mars; set at upper end o' th' table; no question asked him by any of the senators but they stand bald before him. Our general himself makes a mistress of him, sanctifies himself with's hand, and turns up the white o' th' eye to his discourse. But the bottom of the news is, our general is cut i' th' middle and but one half of what he was yesterday, for the other has half by the entreaty and grant of the whole table. He'll go, he says, and sowl the porter of Rome gates by th' ears; he will mow all down before him, and leave his passage poll'd.

SECOND SERVANT. And he's as like to do't as any man I can imagine.

THIRD SERVANT. Do't! He will do't; for look you, sir, he has as many friends as enemies; which friends, sir, as it were, durst not—look you, sir—show themselves, as we term it, his friends, whilst he's in directitude.

FIRST SERVANT. Directitude? What's that?

THIRD SERVANT. But when they shall see, sir, his crest up again and the man in blood, they will out of their burrows, like conies after rain, and revel all with him.

FIRST SERVANT. But when goes this forward?

THIRD SERVANT. To-morrow, to-day, presently. You shall have the drum struck up this afternoon; 'tis as it were a parcel of their feast, and to be executed ere they wipe their lips.

SECOND SERVANT. Why, then we shall have a stirring world again. This peace is nothing but to rust iron, increase tailors, and breed ballad-makers.

FIRST SERVANT. Let me have war, say I; it exceeds peace as far as day does night; it's spritely, waking, audible, and full of vent. Peace is a very apoplexy, lethargy; mull'd, deaf, sleepy, insensible; a getter of more bastard children than war's a destroyer of men.

SECOND SERVANT. 'Tis so; and as war in some sort may be said to be a ravisher, so it cannot be denied but peace is a great maker of cuckolds.

FIRST SERVANT. Ay, and it makes men hate one another.

THIRD SERVANT. Reason: because they then less need one another. The wars for my money. I hope to see Romans as cheap as Volscians. They are rising, they are rising.

BOTH. In, in, in, in! *Exeunt*

SCENE 6

Rome. A public place

Enter the two Tribunes, SICINIUS *and* BRUTUS

SICINIUS. We hear not of him, neither need we fear him.
His remedies are tame. The present peace

And quietness of the people, which before
Were in wild hurry, here do make his friends
Blush that the world goes well; who rather had,
Though they themselves did suffer by't, behold
Dissentious numbers pest'ring streets than see
Our tradesmen singing in their shops, and going
About their functions friendly.

Enter MENENIUS

BRUTUS. We stood to't in good time. Is this Menenius?
SICINIUS. 'Tis he, 'tis he. O, he is grown most kind
Of late. Hail, sir!
MENENIUS. Hail to you both!
SICINIUS. Your Coriolanus is not much miss'd
But with his friends. The commonwealth doth stand,
And so would do, were he more angry at it.
MENENIUS. All's well, and might have been much better if
He could have temporiz'd.
SICINIUS. Where is he, hear you?
MENENIUS. Nay, I hear nothing; his mother and his wife
Hear nothing from him.

Enter three or four citizens

CITIZENS. The gods preserve you both!
SICINIUS. God-den, our neighbours.
BRUTUS. God-den to you all, god-den to you all.
FIRST CITIZEN. Ourselves, our wives, and children, on our knees
Are bound to pray for you both.
SICINIUS. Live and thrive!
BRUTUS. Farewell, kind neighbours; we wish'd Coriolanus
Had lov'd you as we did.
CITIZENS. Now the gods keep you!
BOTH TRIBUNES. Farewell, farewell. *Exeunt citizens*
SICINIUS. This is a happier and more comely time
Than when these fellows ran about the streets
Crying confusion.
BRUTUS. Caius Marcius was
A worthy officer i' the war, but insolent,
O'ercome with pride, ambitious past all thinking,

Self-loving—
SICINIUS. And affecting one sole throne,
Without assistance.
MENENIUS. I think not so.
SICINIUS. We should by this, to all our lamentation,
If he had gone forth consul, found it so.
BRUTUS. The gods have well prevented it, and Rome
Sits safe and still without him.

Enter an ÆDILE

ÆDILE. Worthy tribunes,
There is a slave, whom we have put in prison,
Reports the Volsces with several powers
Are ent'red in the Roman territories,
And with the deepest malice of the war
Destroy what lies before 'em.
MENENIUS. 'Tis Aufidius,
Who, hearing of our Marcius' banishment,
Thrusts forth his horns again into the world,
Which were inshell'd when Marcius stood for Rome,
And durst not once peep out.
SICINIUS. Come, what talk you of Marcius?
BRUTUS. Go see this rumourer whipp'd. It cannot be
The Volsces dare break with us.
MENENIUS. Cannot be!
We have record that very well it can;
And three examples of the like hath been
Within my age. But reason with the fellow
Before you punish him, where he heard this,
Lest you shall chance to whip your information
And beat the messenger who bids beware
Of what is to be dreaded.
SICINIUS. Tell not me.
I know this cannot be.
BRUTUS. Not possible.

Enter a MESSENGER

MESSENGER. The nobles in great earnestness are going
All to the Senate House; some news is come
That turns their countenances.

SICINIUS. 'Tis this slave–
Go whip him fore the people's eyes–his raising,
Nothing but his report.
MESSENGER. Yes, worthy sir,
The slave's report is seconded, and more,
More fearful, is deliver'd.
SICINIUS. What more fearful?
MESSENGER. It is spoke freely out of many mouths–
How probable I do not know–that Marcius,
Join'd with Aufidius, leads a power 'gainst Rome,
And vows revenge as spacious as between
The young'st and oldest thing.
SICINIUS. This is most likely!
BRUTUS. Rais'd only that the weaker sort may wish
Good Marcius home again.
SICINIUS. The very trick on't.
MENENIUS. This is unlikely.
He and Aufidius can no more atone
Than violent'st contrariety.

Enter a second MESSENGER

SECOND MESSENGER. You are sent for to the Senate.
A fearful army, led by Caius Marcius
Associated with Aufidius, rages
Upon our territories, and have already
O'erborne their way, consum'd with fire and took
What lay before them.

Enter COMINIUS

COMINIUS. O, you have made good work!
MENENIUS. What news? what news?
COMINIUS. You have holp to ravish your own daughters and
To melt the city leads upon your pates,
To see your wives dishonour'd to your noses–
MENENIUS. What's the news? What's the news?
COMINIUS. Your temples burned in their cement, and
Your franchises, whereon you stood, confin'd
Into an auger's bore.
MENENIUS. Pray now, your news?
You have made fair work, I fear me. Pray, your news.

If Marcius should be join'd wi' th' Volscians—
COMINIUS. If!
He is their god; he leads them like a thing
Made by some other deity than Nature,
That shapes man better; and they follow him
Against us brats with no less confidence
Than boys pursuing summer butterflies,
Or butchers killing flies.
MENENIUS. You have made good work,
You and your apron men; you that stood so much
Upon the voice of occupation and
The breath of garlic-eaters!
COMINIUS. He'll shake
Your Rome about your ears.
MENENIUS. As Hercules
Did shake down mellow fruit. You have made fair work!
BRUTUS. But is this true, sir?
COMINIUS. Ay; and you'll look pale
Before you find it other. All the regions
Do smilingly revolt, and who resists
Are mock'd for valiant ignorance,
And perish constant fools. Who is't can blame him?
Your enemies and his find something in him.
MENENIUS. We are all undone unless
The noble man have mercy.
COMINIUS. Who shall ask it?
The tribunes cannot do't for shame; the people
Deserve such pity of him as the wolf
Does of the shepherds; for his best friends, if they
Should say 'Be good to Rome'—they charg'd him even
As those should do that had deserv'd his hate,
And therein show'd like enemies.
MENENIUS. 'Tis true;
If he were putting to my house the brand
That should consume it, I have not the face
To say 'Beseech you, cease.' You have made fair hands,
You and your crafts! You have crafted fair!
COMINIUS. You have brought
A trembling upon Rome, such as was never
S' incapable of help.

BOTH TRIBUNES. Say not we brought it.
MENENIUS. How! Was't we? We lov'd him, but, like beasts
And cowardly nobles, gave way unto your clusters,
Who did hoot him out o' th' city.
COMINIUS. But I fear
They'll roar him in again. Tullus Aufidius,
The second name of men, obeys his points
As if he were his officer. Desperation
Is all the policy, strength, and defence,
That Rome can make against them.

Enter a troop of citizens

MENENIUS. Here comes the clusters.
And is Aufidius with him? You are they
That made the air unwholesome when you cast
Your stinking greasy caps in hooting at
Coriolanus' exile. Now he's coming,
And not a hair upon a soldier's head
Which will not prove a whip; as many coxcombs
As you threw caps up will he tumble down,
And pay you for your voices. 'Tis no matter;
If he could burn us all into one coal,
We have deserv'd it.
PLEBEIANS. Faith, we hear fearful news.
FIRST CITIZEN. For mine own part,
When I said banish him, I said 'twas pity.
SECOND CITIZEN. And so did I.
THIRD CITIZEN. And so did I; and, to say the truth, so did very many of us. That we did, we did for the best; and though we willingly consented to his banishment, yet it was against our will.
COMINIUS. Y'are goodly things, you voices!
MENENIUS. You have made
Good work, you and your cry! Shall's to the Capitol?
COMINIUS. O, ay, what else?

Exeunt COMINIUS *and* MENENIUS

SICINIUS. Go, masters, get you home; be not dismay'd;
These are a side that would be glad to have
This true which they so seem to fear. Go home,
And show no sign of fear.

FIRST CITIZEN. The gods be good to us! Come, masters, let's home. I ever said we were i' th' wrong when we banish'd him.

SECOND CITIZEN. So did we all. But come, let's home.

Exeunt citizens

BRUTUS. I do not like this news.

SICINIUS. Nor I.

BRUTUS. Let's to the Capitol. Would half my wealth
Would buy this for a lie!

SICINIUS. Pray let's go. *Exeunt*

SCENE 7

A camp at a short distance from Rome

Enter AUFIDIUS *with his* LIEUTENANT

AUFIDIUS. Do they still fly to th' Roman?

LIEUTENANT. I do not know what witchcraft's in him, but
Your soldiers use him as the grace fore meat,
Their talk at table, and their thanks at end;
And you are dark'ned in this action, sir,
Even by your own.

AUFIDIUS. I cannot help it now,
Unless by using means I lame the foot
Of our design. He bears himself more proudlier,
Even to my person, than I thought he would
When first I did embrace him; yet his nature
In that's no changeling, and I must excuse
What cannot be amended.

LIEUTENANT. Yet I wish, sir–
I mean, for your particular–you had not
Join'd in commission with him, but either
Had borne the action of yourself, or else
To him had left it solely.

AUFIDIUS. I understand thee well; and be thou sure,
When he shall come to his account, he knows not
What I can urge against him. Although it seems,
And so he thinks, and is no less apparent
To th' vulgar eye, that he bears all things fairly

And shows good husbandry for the Volscian state,
Fights dragon-like, and does achieve as soon
As draw his sword; yet he hath left undone
That which shall break his neck or hazard mine
Whene'er we come to our account.

LIEUTENANT. Sir, I beseech you, think you he'll carry Rome?

AUFIDIUS. All places yield to him ere he sits down,
And the nobility of Rome are his;
The senators and patricians love him too.
The tribunes are no soldiers, and their people
Will be as rash in the repeal as hasty
To expel him thence. I think he'll be to Rome
As is the osprey to the fish, who takes it
By sovereignty of nature. First he was
A noble servant to them, but he could not
Carry his honours even. Whether 'twas pride,
Which out of daily fortune ever taints
The happy man; whether defect of judgment,
To fail in the disposing of those chances
Which he was lord of; or whether nature,
Not to be other than one thing, not moving
From th' casque to th' cushion, but commanding peace
Even with the same austerity and garb
As he controll'd the war; but one of these–
As he hath spices of them all–not all,
For I dare so far free him–made him fear'd,
So hated, and so banish'd. But he has a merit
To choke it in the utt'rance. So our virtues
Lie in th' interpretation of the time;
And power, unto itself most commendable,
Hath not a tomb so evident as a chair
T' extol what it hath done.
One fire drives out one fire; one nail, one nail;
Rights by rights falter, strengths by strengths do fail.
Come, let's away. When, Caius, Rome is thine,
Thou art poor'st of all; then shortly art thou mine.

Exeunt

ACT V. SCENE 1

Rome. A public place

Enter MENENIUS, COMINIUS, SICINIUS *and* BRUTUS, *the two Tribunes, with others*

MENENIUS. No, I'll not go. You hear what he hath said
Which was sometime his general, who lov'd him
In a most dear particular. He call'd me father;
But what o' that? Go, you that banish'd him:
A mile before his tent fall down, and knee
The way into his mercy. Nay, if he coy'd
To hear Cominius speak, I'll keep at home.

COMINIUS. He would not seem to know me.

MENENIUS. Do you hear?

COMINIUS. Yet one time he did call me by my name.
I urg'd our old acquaintance, and the drops
That we have bled together. 'Coriolanus'
He would not answer to; forbid all names;
He was a kind of nothing, titleless,
Till he had forg'd himself a name i' th' fire
Of burning Rome.

MENENIUS. Why, so! You have made good work.
A pair of tribunes that have wrack'd for Rome
To make coals cheap—a noble memory!

COMINIUS. I minded him how royal 'twas to pardon
When it was less expected; he replied,
It was a bare petition of a state
To one whom they had punish'd.

MENENIUS. Very well.
Could he say less?

COMINIUS. I offer'd to awaken his regard
For's private friends; his answer to me was,
He could not stay to pick them in a pile
Of noisome musty chaff. He said 'twas folly,
For one poor grain or two, to leave unburnt
And still to nose th' offence.

MENENIUS. For one poor grain or two!
I am one of those. His mother, wife, his child,
And this brave fellow too—we are the grains:

You are the musty chaff, and you are smelt
Above the moon. We must be burnt for you.

SICINIUS. Nay, pray be patient; if you refuse your aid
In this so never-needed help, yet do not
Upbraid's with our distress. But sure, if you
Would be your country's pleader, your good tongue,
More than the instant army we can make,
Might stop our countryman.

MENENIUS. No; I'll not meddle.

SICINIUS. Pray you go to him.

MENENIUS. What should I do?

BRUTUS. Only make trial what your love can do
For Rome, towards Marcius.

MENENIUS. Well, and say that Marcius
Return me, as Cominius is return'd,
Unheard—what then?
But as a discontented friend, grief-shot
With his unkindness? Say't be so?

SICINIUS. Yet your good will
Must have that thanks from Rome after the measure
As you intended well.

MENENIUS. I'll undertake't;
I think he'll hear me. Yet to bite his lip
And hum at good Cominius much unhearts me.
He was not taken well: he had not din'd;
The veins unfill'd, our blood is cold, and then
We pout upon the morning, are unapt
To give or to forgive; but when we have stuff'd
These pipes and these conveyances of our blood
With wine and feeding, we have suppler souls
Than in our priest-like fasts. Therefore I'll watch him
Till he be dieted to my request,
And then I'll set upon him.

BRUTUS. You know the very road into his kindness
And cannot lose your way.

MENENIUS. Good faith, I'll prove him,
Speed how it will. I shall ere long have knowledge
Of my success. *Exit*

COMINIUS. He'll never hear him.

SICINIUS. Not?

ACT V. SCENE 1

COMINIUS. I tell you he does sit in gold, his eye
Red as 'twould burn Rome, and his injury
The gaoler to his pity. I kneel'd before him;
'Twas very faintly he said 'Rise'; dismiss'd me
Thus with his speechless hand. What he would do,
He sent in writing after me; what he would not,
Bound with an oath to yield to his conditions;
So that all hope is vain,
Unless his noble mother and his wife,
Who, as I hear, mean to solicit him
For mercy to his country. Therefore let's hence,
And with our fair entreaties haste them on. *Exeunt*

SCENE 2

The Volscian camp before Rome

Enter MENENIUS *to the* WATCH *on guard*

FIRST WATCH. Stay. Whence are you?
SECOND WATCH. Stand, and go back.
MENENIUS. You guard like men, 'tis well; but, by your leave,
I am an officer of state and come
To speak with Coriolanus.
FIRST WATCH. From whence?
MENENIUS. From Rome.
FIRST WATCH. You may not pass; you must return. Our general
Will no more hear from thence.
SECOND WATCH. You'll see your Rome embrac'd with fire before
You'll speak with Coriolanus.
MENENIUS. Good my friends,
If you have heard your general talk of Rome
And of his friends there, it is lots to blanks
My name hath touch'd your ears: it is Menenius.
FIRST WATCH. Be it so; go back. The virtue of your name
Is not here passable.
MENENIUS. I tell thee, fellow,

Thy general is my lover. I have been
The book of his good acts whence men have read
His fame unparallel'd haply amplified;
For I have ever verified my friends—
Of whom he's chief—with all the size that verity
Would without lapsing suffer. Nay, sometimes,
Like to a bowl upon a subtle ground,
I have tumbled past the throw, and in his praise
Have almost stamp'd the leasing; therefore, fellow,
I must have leave to pass.

FIRST WATCH. Faith, sir, if you had told as many lies in his behalf as you have uttered words in your own, you should not pass here; no, though it were as virtuous to lie as to live chastely. Therefore go back.

MENENIUS. Prithee, fellow, remember my name is Menenius, always factionary on the party of your general.

SECOND WATCH. Howsoever you have been his liar, as you say you have, I am one that, telling true under him, must say you cannot pass. Therefore go back.

MENENIUS. Has he din'd, canst thou tell? For I would not speak with him till after dinner.

FIRST WATCH. You are a Roman, are you?

MENENIUS. I am as thy general is.

FIRST WATCH. Then you should hate Rome, as he does. Can you, when you have push'd out your gates the very defender of them, and in a violent popular ignorance given your enemy your shield, think to front his revenges with the easy groans of old women, the virginal palms of your daughters, or with the palsied intercession of such a decay'd dotant as you seem to be? Can you think to blow out the intended fire your city is ready to flame in with such weak breath as this? No, you are deceiv'd; therefore back to Rome and prepare for your execution. You are condemn'd; our general has sworn you out of reprieve and pardon.

MENENIUS. Sirrah, if thy captain knew I were here, he would use me with estimation.

FIRST WATCH. Come, my captain knows you not.

MENENIUS. I mean thy general.

FIRST WATCH. My general cares not for you. Back, I say;

go, lest I let forth your half pint of blood. Back—that's the utmost of your having. Back.

MENENIUS. Nay, but fellow, fellow—

Enter CORIOLANUS *with* AUFIDIUS

CORIOLANUS. What's the matter?

MENENIUS. Now, you companion, I'll say an errand for you; you shall know now that I am in estimation; you shall perceive that a Jack guardant cannot office me from my son Coriolanus. Guess but by my entertainment with him if thou stand'st not i' th' state of hanging, or of some death more long in spectatorship and crueller in suffering; behold now presently, and swoon for what's to come upon thee. The glorious gods sit in hourly synod about thy particular prosperity, and love thee no worse than thy old father Menenius does! O my son! my son! thou art preparing fire for us; look thee, here's water to quench it. I was hardly moved to come to thee; but being assured none but myself could move thee, I have been blown out of your gates with sighs, and conjure thee to pardon Rome and thy petitionary countrymen. The good gods assuage thy wrath, and turn the dregs of it upon this varlet here; this, who, like a block, hath denied my access to thee.

CORIOLANUS. Away!

MENENIUS. How! away!

CORIOLANUS. Wife, mother, child, I know not. My affairs
Are servanted to others. Though I owe
My revenge properly, my remission lies
In Volscian breasts. That we have been familiar,
Ingrate forgetfulness shall poison rather
Than pity note how much. Therefore be gone.
Mine ears against your suits are stronger than
Your gates against my force. Yet, for I lov'd thee,
Take this along; I writ it for thy sake [*Gives a letter*]
And would have sent it. Another word, Menenius,
I will not hear thee speak. This man, Aufidius,
Was my belov'd in Rome; yet thou behold'st.

AUFIDIUS. You keep a constant temper.

Exeunt CORIOLANUS *and* AUFIDIUS

FIRST WATCH. Now, sir, is your name Menenius?

SECOND WATCH. 'Tis a spell, you see, of much power! You know the way home again.

FIRST WATCH. Do you hear how we are shent for keeping your greatness back?

SECOND WATCH. What cause, do you think, I have to swoon?

MENENIUS. I neither care for th' world nor your general; for such things as you, I can scarce think there's any, y'are so slight. He that hath a will to die by himself fears it not from another. Let your general do his worst. For you, be that you are, long; and your misery increase with your age! I say to you, as I was said to: Away! *Exit*

FIRST WATCH. A noble fellow, I warrant him.

SECOND WATCH. The worthy fellow is our general; he's the rock, the oak not to be wind-shaken. *Exeunt*

SCENE 3

The tent of CORIOLANUS

Enter CORIOLANUS, AUFIDIUS, *and others*

CORIOLANUS. We will before the walls of Rome to-morrow
Set down our host. My partner in this action,
You must report to th' Volscian lords how plainly
I have borne this business.

AUFIDIUS. Only their ends
You have respected; stopp'd your ears against
The general suit of Rome; never admitted
A private whisper—no, not with such friends
That thought them sure of you.

CORIOLANUS. This last old man,
Whom with crack'd heart I have sent to Rome,
Lov'd me above the measure of a father;
Nay, godded me indeed. Their latest refuge
Was to send him; for whose old love I have—
Though I show'd sourly to him—once more offer'd
The first conditions, which they did refuse
And cannot now accept. To grace him only,

That thought he could do more, a very little
I have yielded to; fresh embassies and suits,
Nor from the state nor private friends, hereafter
Will I lend ear to. [*Shout within*] Ha! what shout is this?
Shall I be tempted to infringe my vow
In the same time 'tis made? I will not.

Enter, in mourning habits, VIRGILIA, VOLUMNIA, VALERIA, *young* MARCIUS, *with attendants*

My wife comes foremost, then the honour'd mould
Wherein this trunk was fram'd, and in her hand
The grandchild to her blood. But out, affection!
All bond and privilege of nature, break!
Let it be virtuous to be obstinate.
What is that curtsy worth? or those doves' eyes,
Which can make gods forsworn? I melt, and am not
Of stronger earth than others. My mother bows,
As if Olympus to a molehill should
In supplication nod; and my young boy
Hath an aspect of intercession which
Great nature cries 'Deny not.' Let the Volsces
Plough Rome and harrow Italy; I'll never
Be such a gosling to obey instinct, but stand
As if a man were author of himself
And knew no other kin.

VIRGILIA. My lord and husband!

CORIOLANUS. These eyes are not the same I wore in Rome.

VIRGILIA. The sorrow that delivers us thus chang'd
Makes you think so.

CORIOLANUS. Like a dull actor now
I have forgot my part and I am out,
Even to a full disgrace. Best of my flesh,
Forgive my tyranny; but do not say,
For that, 'Forgive our Romans.' O, a kiss
Long as my exile, sweet as my revenge!
Now, by the jealous queen of heaven, that kiss
I carried from thee, dear, and my true lip
Hath virgin'd it e'er since. You gods! I prate,
And the most noble mother of the world
Leave unsaluted. Sink, my knee, i' th' earth; [*Kneels*]

Coriolanus. *But out, affection!*
All bond and privilege of nature, break!
Let it be virtuous to be obstinate.
What is that curtsy worth? or those doves' eyes,
Which can make gods forsworn? I melt, and am not
Of stronger earth than others.

(Act V. Scene 3)

Of thy deep duty more impression show
Than that of common sons.

VOLUMNIA. O, stand up blest!
Whilst with no softer cushion than the flint
I kneel before thee, and unproperly
Show duty, as mistaken all this while
Between the child and parent. [*Kneels*]

CORIOLANUS. What's this?
Your knees to me, to your corrected son?
Then let the pebbles on the hungry beach
Fillip the stars; then let the mutinous winds
Strike the proud cedars 'gainst the fiery sun,
Murd'ring impossibility, to make
What cannot be slight work.

VOLUMNIA. Thou art my warrior;
I holp to frame thee. Do you know this lady?

CORIOLANUS. The noble sister of Publicola,
The moon of Rome, chaste as the icicle
That's curdied by the frost from purest snow,
And hangs on Dian's temple—dear Valeria!

VOLUMNIA. This is a poor epitome of yours,
Which by th' interpretation of full time
May show like all yourself.

CORIOLANUS. The god of soldiers,
With the consent of supreme Jove, inform
Thy thoughts with nobleness, that thou mayst prove
To shame unvulnerable, and stick i' th' wars
Like a great sea-mark, standing every flaw,
And saving those that eye thee!

VOLUMNIA. Your knee, sirrah.

CORIOLANUS. That's my brave boy.

VOLUMNIA. Even he, your wife, this lady, and myself,
Are suitors to you.

CORIOLANUS. I beseech you, peace!
Or, if you'd ask, remember this before:
The thing I have forsworn to grant may never
Be held by you denials. Do not bid me
Dismiss my soldiers, or capitulate
Again with Rome's mechanics. Tell me not
Wherein I seem unnatural; desire not

T'allay my rages and revenges with
Your colder reasons.

VOLUMNIA. O, no more, no more!
You have said you will not grant us any thing—
For we have nothing else to ask but that
Which you deny already; yet we will ask,
That, if you fail in our request, the blame
May hang upon your hardness; therefore hear us.

CORIOLANUS. Aufidius, and you Volsces, mark; for we'll
Hear nought from Rome in private. Your request?

VOLUMNIA. Should we be silent and not speak, our raiment
And state of bodies would bewray what life
We have led since thy exile. Think with thyself
How more unfortunate than all living women
Are we come hither; since that thy sight, which should
Make our eyes flow with joy, hearts dance with comforts,
Constrains them weep and shake with fear and sorrow,
Making the mother, wife, and child, to see
The son, the husband, and the father, tearing
His country's bowels out. And to poor we
Thine enmity's most capital: thou bar'st us
Our prayers to the gods, which is a comfort
That all but we enjoy. For how can we,
Alas, how can we for our country pray,
Whereto we are bound, together with thy victory,
Whereto we are bound? Alack, or we must lose
The country, our dear nurse, or else thy person,
Our comfort in the country. We must find
An evident calamity, though we had
Our wish, which side should win; for either thou
Must as a foreign recreant be led
With manacles through our streets, or else
Triumphantly tread on thy country's ruin,
And bear the palm for having bravely shed
Thy wife and children's blood. For myself, son,
I purpose not to wait on fortune till
These wars determine; if I can not persuade thee
Rather to show a noble grace to both parts
Than seek the end of one, thou shalt no sooner
March to assault thy country than to tread—

Trust to't, thou shalt not—on thy mother's womb
That brought thee to this world.

VIRGILIA. Ay, and mine,
That brought you forth this boy to keep your name
Living to time.

BOY. 'A shall not tread on me!
I'll run away till I am bigger, but then I'll fight.

CORIOLANUS. Not of a woman's tenderness to be
Requires nor child nor woman's face to see.
I have sat too long. [*Rising*]

VOLUMNIA. Nay, go not from us thus.
If it were so that our request did tend
To save the Romans, thereby to destroy
The Volsces whom you serve, you might condemn us
As poisonous of your honour. No, our suit
Is that you reconcile them: while the Volsces
May say 'This mercy we have show'd,' the Romans
'This we receiv'd,' and each in either side
Give the all-hail to thee, and cry 'Be blest
For making up this peace!' Thou know'st, great son,
The end of war's uncertain; but this certain,
That, if thou conquer Rome, the benefit
Which thou shalt thereby reap is such a name
Whose repetition will be dogg'd with curses;
Whose chronicle thus writ: 'The man was noble,
But with his last attempt he wip'd it out,
Destroy'd his country, and his name remains
To th' ensuing age abhorr'd.' Speak to me, son.
Thou hast affected the fine strains of honour,
To imitate the graces of the gods,
To tear with thunder the wide cheeks o' th' air,
And yet to charge thy sulphur with a bolt
That should but rive an oak. Why dost not speak?
Think'st thou it honourable for a noble man
Still to remember wrongs? Daughter, speak you:
He cares not for your weeping. Speak thou, boy;
Perhaps thy childishness will move him more
Than can our reasons. There's no man in the world
More bound to's mother, yet here he lets me prate
Like one i' th' stocks. Thou hast never in thy life

Show'd thy dear mother any courtesy,
When she, poor hen, fond of no second brood,
Has cluck'd thee to the wars, and safely home
Loaden with honour. Say my request's unjust,
And spurn me back; but if it be not so,
Thou art not honest, and the gods will plague thee,
That thou restrain'st from me the duty which
To a mother's part belongs. He turns away.
Down, ladies; let us shame him with our knees.
To his surname Coriolanus 'longs more pride
Than pity to our prayers. Down. An end;
This is the last. So we will home to Rome,
And die among our neighbours. Nay, behold's!
This boy, that cannot tell what he would have
But kneels and holds up hands for fellowship,
Does reason our petition with more strength
Than thou hast to deny't. Come, let us go.
This fellow had a Volscian to his mother;
His wife is in Corioli, and his child
Like him by chance. Yet give us our dispatch.
I am hush'd until our city be afire,
And then I'll speak a little.

[*He holds her by the hand, silent*]

CORIOLANUS. O mother, mother!
What have you done? Behold, the heavens do ope,
The gods look down, and this unnatural scene
They laugh at. O my mother, mother! O!
You have won a happy victory to Rome;
But for your son—believe it, O, believe it!—
Most dangerously you have with him prevail'd,
If not most mortal to him. But let it come.
Aufidius, though I cannot make true wars,
I'll frame convenient peace. Now, good Aufidius,
Were you in my stead, would you have heard
A mother less, or granted less, Aufidius?

AUFIDIUS. I was mov'd withal.

CORIOLANUS. I dare be sworn you were!
And, sir, it is no little thing to make
Mine eyes to sweat compassion. But, good sir,
What peace you'll make, advise me. For my part,

I'll not to Rome, I'll back with you; and pray you
Stand to me in this cause. O mother! wife!

AUFIDIUS. [*Aside*] I am glad thou hast set thy mercy and thy honour
At difference in thee. Out of that I'll work
Myself a former fortune.

CORIOLANUS. [*To the ladies*] Ay, by and by;
But we will drink together; and you shall bear
A better witness back than words, which we,
On like conditions, will have counter-seal'd.
Come, enter with us. Ladies, you deserve
To have a temple built you. All the swords
In Italy, and her confederate arms,
Could not have made this peace. *Exeunt*

SCENE 4

Rome. A public place

Enter MENENIUS *and* SICINIUS

MENENIUS. See you yond coign o' th' Capitol, yond corner-stone?

SICINIUS. Why, what of that?

MENENIUS. If it be possible for you to displace it with your little finger, there is some hope the ladies of Rome, especially his mother, may prevail with him. But I say there is no hope in't; our throats are sentenc'd, and stay upon execution.

SICINIUS. Is't possible that so short a time can alter the condition of a man?

MENENIUS. There is differency between a grub and a butterfly; yet your butterfly was a grub. This Marcius is grown from man to dragon; he has wings, he's more than a creeping thing.

SICINIUS. He lov'd his mother dearly.

MENENIUS. So did he me; and he no more remembers his mother now than an eight-year-old horse. The tartness of his face sours ripe grapes; when he walks, he moves like an engine and the ground shrinks before his treading. He is able to pierce a corslet with his eye, talks like a knell, and his hum is a battery. He sits in his state as a thing made for Alexander. What he bids be done is finish'd with his bidding. He wants nothing of a god but eternity, and a heaven to throne in.

SICINIUS. Yes—mercy, if you report him truly.

MENENIUS. I paint him in the character. Mark what mercy his mother shall bring from him. There is no more mercy in him than there is milk in a male tiger; that shall our poor city find. And all this is 'long of you.

SICINIUS. The gods be good unto us!

MENENIUS. No, in such a case the gods will not be good unto us. When we banish'd him we respected not them; and, he returning to break our necks, they respect not us.

Enter a MESSENGER

MESSENGER. Sir, if you'd save your life, fly to your house.
The plebeians have got your fellow tribune
And hale him up and down; all swearing if
The Roman ladies bring not comfort home
They'll give him death by inches.

Enter another MESSENGER

SICINIUS. What's the news?

SECOND MESSENGER. Good news, good news! The ladies have prevail'd,
The Volscians are dislodg'd, and Marcius gone.
A merrier day did never yet greet Rome,
No, not th' expulsion of the Tarquins.

SICINIUS. Friend,
Art thou certain this is true? Is't most certain?

SECOND MESSENGER. As certain as I know the sun is fire.
Where have you lurk'd, that you make doubt of it?
Ne'er through an arch so hurried the blown tide
As the recomforted through th' gates. Why, hark you!
[*Trumpets, hautboys, drums beat, all together*]
The trumpets, sackbuts, psalteries, and fifes,
Tabors and cymbals, and the shouting Romans,
Make the sun dance. Hark you! [*A shout within*]

MENENIUS. This is good news.

I will go meet the ladies. This Volumnia
Is worth of consuls, senators, patricians,
A city full; of tribunes such as you,
A sea and land full. You have pray'd well to-day:
This morning for ten thousand of your throats
I'd not have given a doit. Hark, how they joy!
[*Sound still with the shouts*]

SICINIUS. First, the gods bless you for your tidings; next,
Accept my thankfulness.

SECOND MESSENGER. Sir, we have all
Great cause to give great thanks.

SICINIUS. They are near the city?

MESSENGER. Almost at point to enter.

SICINIUS. We'll meet them,
And help the joy. *Exeunt*

SCENE 5

Rome. A street near the gate

Enter two SENATORS *with* VOLUMNIA, VIRGILIA, VALERIA, *passing over the stage, with other* LORDS

FIRST SENATOR. Behold our patroness, the life of Rome!
Call all your tribes together, praise the gods,
And make triumphant fires; strew flowers before them.
Unshout the noise that banish'd Marcius,
Repeal him with the welcome of his mother;
Cry 'Welcome, ladies, welcome!'

ALL. Welcome, ladies, welcome!
[*A flourish with drums and trumpets. Exeunt*]

SCENE 6

Corioli. A public place

Enter TULLUS AUFIDIUS, *with attendants*

AUFIDIUS. Go tell the lords o' th' city I am here;
Deliver them this paper; having read it,

Bid them repair to th' market-place, where I,
Even in theirs and in the commons' ears,
Will vouch the truth of it. Him I accuse
The city ports by this hath enter'd and
Intends t' appear before the people, hoping
To purge himself with words. Dispatch.

Exeunt attendants

Enter three or four CONSPIRATORS *of* AUFIDIUS' *faction*

Most welcome!

FIRST CONSPIRATOR. How is it with our general?

AUFIDIUS. Even so
As with a man by his own alms empoison'd,
And with his charity slain.

SECOND CONSPIRATOR. Most noble sir,
If you do hold the same intent wherein
You wish'd us parties, we'll deliver you
Of your great danger.

AUFIDIUS. Sir, I cannot tell;
We must proceed as we do find the people.

THIRD CONSPIRATOR. The people will remain uncertain whilst
'Twixt you there's difference; but the fall of either
Makes the survivor heir of all.

AUFIDIUS. I know it;
And my pretext to strike at him admits
A good construction. I rais'd him, and I pawn'd
Mine honour for his truth; who being so heighten'd,
He watered his new plants with dews of flattery,
Seducing so my friends; and to this end
He bow'd his nature, never known before
But to be rough, unswayable, and free.

THIRD CONSPIRATOR. Sir, his stoutness
When he did stand for consul, which he lost
By lack of stooping–

AUFIDIUS. That I would have spoken of.
Being banish'd for't, he came unto my hearth,
Presented to my knife his throat. I took him;
Made him joint-servant with me; gave him way
In all his own desires; nay, let him choose

Out of my files, his projects to accomplish,
My best and freshest men; serv'd his designments
In mine own person; holp to reap the fame
Which he did end all his, and took some pride
To do myself this wrong. Till, at the last,
I seem'd his follower, not partner; and
He wag'd me with his countenance as if
I had been mercenary.

FIRST CONSPIRATOR. So he did, my lord.
The army marvell'd at it; and, in the last,
When he had carried Rome and that we look'd
For no less spoil than glory—

AUFIDIUS. There was it;
For which my sinews shall be stretch'd upon him.
At a few drops of women's rheum, which are
As cheap as lies, he sold the blood and labour
Of our great action; therefore shall he die,
And I'll renew me in his fall. But, hark! [*Drums and trumpets sound, with great shouts of the people*]

FIRST CONSPIRATOR. Your native town you enter'd like a post,
And had no welcomes home; but he returns
Splitting the air with noise.

SECOND CONSPIRATOR. And patient fools,
Whose children he hath slain, their base throats tear
With giving him glory.

THIRD CONSPIRATOR. Therefore, at your vantage,
Ere he express himself or move the people
With what he would say, let him feel your sword,
Which we will second. When he lies along,
After your way his tale pronounc'd shall bury
His reasons with his body.

AUFIDIUS. Say no more:
Here come the lords.

Enter the LORDS *of the city*

LORDS. You are most welcome home.

AUFIDIUS. I have not deserv'd it.
But, worthy lords, have you with heed perused
What I have written to you?

LORDS. We have.
FIRST LORD. And grieve to hear't.
What faults he made before the last, I think
Might have found easy fines; but there to end
Where he was to begin, and give away
The benefit of our levies, answering us
With our own charge, making a treaty where
There was a yielding—this admits no excuse.
AUFIDIUS. He approaches; you shall hear him.

Enter CORIOLANUS, *marching with drum and colours; the commoners being with him*

CORIOLANUS. Hail, lords! I am return'd your soldier;
No more infected with my country's love
Than when I parted hence, but still subsisting
Under your great command. You are to know
That prosperously I have attempted, and
With bloody passage led your wars even to
The gates of Rome. Our spoils we have brought home
Doth more than counterpoise a full third part
The charges of the action. We have made peace
With no less honour to the Antiates
Than shame to th' Romans; and we here deliver,
Subscrib'd by th' consuls and patricians,
Together with the seal o' th' Senate, what
We have compounded on.
AUFIDIUS. Read it not, noble lords;
But tell the traitor in the highest degree
He hath abus'd your powers.
CORIOLANUS. Traitor! How now?
AUFIDIUS. Ay, traitor, Marcius.
CORIOLANUS. Marcius!
AUFIDIUS. Ay, Marcius, Caius Marcius! Dost thou think
I'll grace thee with that robbery, thy stol'n name
Coriolanus, in Corioli?
You lords and heads o' th' state, perfidiously
He has betray'd your business and given up,
For certain drops of salt, your city Rome—
I say your city—to his wife and mother;
Breaking his oath and resolution like

A twist of rotten silk; never admitting
Counsel o' th' war; but at his nurse's tears
He whin'd and roar'd away your victory,
That pages blush'd at him, and men of heart
Look'd wond'ring each at others.
CORIOLANUS. Hear'st thou, Mars?
AUFIDIUS. Name not the god, thou boy of tears—
CORIOLANUS. Ha!
AUFIDIUS. —no more.
CORIOLANUS. Measureless liar, thou hast made my heart
Too great for what contains it. 'Boy'! O slave!
Pardon me, lords, 'tis the first time that ever
I was forc'd to scold. Your judgments, my grave lords,
Must give this cur the lie; and his own notion—
Who wears my stripes impress'd upon him, that
Must bear my beating to his grave—shall join
To thrust the lie unto him.
FIRST LORD. Peace, both, and hear me speak.
CORIOLANUS. Cut me to pieces, Volsces; men and lads,
Stain all your edges on me. 'Boy'! False hound!
If you have writ your annals true, 'tis there
That, like an eagle in a dove-cote, I
Flutter'd your Volscians in Corioli.
Alone I did it. 'Boy'!
AUFIDIUS. Why, noble lords,
Will you be put in mind of his blind fortune,
Which was your shame, by this unholy braggart,
Fore your own eyes and ears?
CONSPIRATORS. Let him die for't.
ALL THE PEOPLE. Tear him to pieces. Do it presently. He kill'd my son. My daughter. He kill'd my cousin Marcus. He kill'd my father.
SECOND LORD. Peace, ho! No outrage—peace!
The man is noble, and his fame folds in
This orb o' th' earth. His last offences to us
Shall have judicious hearing. Stand, Aufidius,
And trouble not the peace.
CORIOLANUS. O that I had him,
With six Aufidiuses, or more—his tribe,
To use my lawful sword!

AUFIDIUS. Insolent villain!

CONSPIRATORS. Kill, kill, kill, kill, kill him!

[*The* CONSPIRATORS *draw and kill* CORIOLANUS, *who falls.* AUFIDIUS *stands on him*]

LORDS. Hold, hold, hold, hold!

AUFIDIUS. My noble masters, hear me speak.

FIRST LORD. O Tullus!

SECOND LORD. Thou hast done a deed whereat valour will weep.

THIRD LORD. Tread not upon him. Masters all, be quiet;
Put up your swords.

AUFIDIUS. My lords, when you shall know—as in this rage,
Provok'd by him, you cannot—the great danger
Which this man's life did owe you, you'll rejoice
That he is thus cut off. Please it your honours
To call me to your Senate, I'll deliver
Myself your loyal servant, or endure
Your heaviest censure.

FIRST LORD. Bear from hence his body,
And mourn you for him. Let him be regarded
As the most noble corse that ever herald
Did follow to his urn.

SECOND LORD. His own impatience
Takes from Aufidius a great part of blame.
Let's make the best of it.

AUFIDIUS. My rage is gone,
And I am struck with sorrow. Take him up.
Help, three o' th' chiefest soldiers; I'll be one.
Beat thou the drum, that it speak mournfully;
Trail your steel pikes. Though in this city he
Hath widowed and unchilded many a one,
Which to this hour bewail the injury,
Yet he shall have a noble memory.
Assist. *Exeunt, bearing the body of* CORIOLANUS

[*A dead march sounded*]

The Tragedy of Titus Andronicus

TITUS ANDRONICUS

It is unlikely that there will ever be agreement among scholars about the authorship of *Titus Andronicus*, and that in spite of the unequivocal nature of the external evidence attributing it to Shakespeare.

In 1598 Francis Meres in maintaining that 'Shakespeare among the English is the most excellent in both kinds (tragedy and comedy) for the stage' names as evidence six comedies and six tragedies by Shakespeare, and among them *Titus Andronicus*. Meres was a Cambridge graduate and during a stay in London, between leaving the University and his obtaining a parish, seems to have interested himself in literature and the drama, his *Palladis Tamia or Wits Treasury* being the fruit of this period. Heminge and Condell included this play in the First Folio.

As almost everyone's interest in or study of the plays begins with the acknowledged masterpieces of comedy and tragedy, it is not surprising that the passage to *Titus Andronicus* seems to take us into another world. This is not an impression only of the modern reader or spectator, for as early as 1614 Ben Jonson said something that anticipates the opinion of later generations. In his somewhat elaborate Induction to *Bartholomew Fair* Jonson wrote:

> He that will swear *Jeronimo* or *Andronicus* are the best plays yet, shall pass unexcepted at here as a man whose judgment shows it is constant and hath stood still these five-and-twenty or thirty years.

Taken at its face value this would date Kyd's *Spanish Tragedy* and Shakespeare's *Titus Andronicus* between 1584 and 1589. There is no record of a performance of *Titus* before January 1594, when it was performed at the Rose by the company of the Earl of Sussex. Henslowe marked it in his diary as 'ne'; but it was not a new play, as the title page of the first quarto of 1594 informs us that it was played by Pembroke's company; and this company had broken in the summer of 1593, having failed to pay their way in the provinces where the plague and the closing of the London theatres had driven them. *Titus* must therefore date from before the closing of the London theatres on 23 June 1592; indeed, a play that Henslowe records as performed on 10 June 1592, *A Knack to Know a Knave*, seems to refer to *Titus* in these lines:

> My gracious lord, as welcome shall you be
> To me, my daughter, and my son-in-law,
> As Titus was unto the Roman senators,
> When he had made a conquest of the Goths;
> That, in requital of his service done,
> Did offer him the imperial diadem.
> As they in Titus, we your grace shall find
> The perfect figure of a princely mind.

To avoid concluding that this reference to the opening scene of *Titus Andronicus* must date that piece before June 1592, Professor Dover Wilson is forced to conjecture that the author is here referring to a play he is going to write and doesn't write till the following year. This seems to attribute powers of divination to the audience at the Rose of an exceptional kind, for if they weren't thought-readers what could they make of a reference to a story which, if it existed then, could only have been an obscure pseudo-historical romance? Such an argument is a bit of special pleading to persuade us that Peele was the author who thus anticipated his next play, and that he wrote *Titus Andronicus* in 1593 just before his poem *The Honour of the Garter*, which obviously borrows from the play. With Jonson's reference to *Titus* in mind and his pairing it with *The Spanish Tragedy*, it is more reasonable to suppose that the reference in *A Knack to Know a Knave* to Titus is to Shakespeare's character, and that Peele found it convenient to borrow from the play in 1593. Had *Titus* not been in existence till 1593, how could Pembroke's men come to have it in their repertoire?

Jonson's reference indicates that *Titus* belongs to a type of tragedy long out of date, and *Titus Andronicus* and *The Spanish Tragedy* are the perfect examples of the Senecan revenge type of tragedy that Nashe glances at in the epistle with which he introduced Greene's *Menaphon* in 1589. The early version of *Hamlet* may have been of this type (*see* p. 637) and as fashions in the theatre changed the revenge hero like Kyd's old Hieronimo provided occasion for jesting references, and until Shakespeare revised *Hamlet* even that hero is referred to without due decorum. There is no reason to suppose that Shakespeare would not, and every reason to suppose that he would, try his skill in this once popular style; and a comparison of *Titus* with *The Spanish Tragedy* shows the mastery Shakespeare already brought to his work for the stage. To complain that there are a dozen or so murders, a rape and mutilation, and that the play ends with orders for an execution, is to object to the type of play, not to deny the dexterous and even classical lines on which these horrors are contrived. Shakespeare had as his models Seneca and Ovid: the ghastly banquet at which the children of Tamora are served in a pie is only an elaboration of the scene in the *Thyestes* of Seneca where the father feeds on his children; skilfully adapted now to the conditions of the Elizabethan theatre this scene, alive with the immediate reactions of those sitting at the table, leads to the deaths of the emperor and empress as well as of Titus and his daughter and provides a finale of vengeance as complete and astonishing as that of Kyd's *Spanish Tragedy;* it is the most perfect transposition of the Senecan revenge theme into the idiom of the Elizabethan stage.

Shakespeare was to restore the tragic drama to the dignity it had occupied in the days when those to whom Seneca was a pupil had served the theatre; but to decry Shakespeare's earliest attempt in this mode entirely is to ignore the capacity of the aspirant. To say with one distinguished commentator that this play 'would long since have been relegated to the limbo of half-forgotten drama by the Greene-Peele-Marlowe school' but for some accident that attached it to Shakespeare's work is to ignore the test the Stratford company submitted it to in an extended tour of Europe. Had it not been soundly constructed it could never have stood up to such a voyage, and the firm lines on which it is built show the hand not of Greene or Peele but of the master-craftsman himself.

SATURNINUS, *son to the late Emperor of Rome, afterwards Emperor*

BASSIANUS, *brother to Saturninus*

TITUS ANDRONICUS, *a noble Roman*

MARCUS ANDRONICUS, *Tribune of the People, and brother to Titus*

LUCIUS, QUINTUS, MARTIUS, MUTIUS — *sons to Titus Andronicus*

YOUNG LUCIUS, *a boy, son to Lucius*

PUBLIUS, *son to Marcus Andronicus*

SEMPRONIUS, CAIUS, VALENTINE — *kinsmen to Titus*

ÆMILIUS, *a noble Roman*

ALARBUS, DEMETRIUS, CHIRON — *sons to Tamora*

AARON, *a Moor, beloved by Tamora*

A CAPTAIN

A MESSENGER

A CLOWN

TAMORA, *Queen of the Goths*

LAVINIA, *daughter to Titus Andronicus*

A NURSE, *and a black* CHILD

Romans *and* Goths, Senators, Tribunes, Officers, Soldiers, *and* Attendants

SCENE:

Rome and the neighbourhood

Titus Andronicus

ACT I. SCENE 1

Rome. Before the Capitol

Flourish. Enter the Tribunes *and* Senators *aloft; and then enter below* Saturninus *and his followers at one door, and* Bassianus *and his followers at the other, with drums and trumpets*

Saturninus. Noble patricians, patrons of my right,
Defend the justice of my cause with arms;
And, countrymen, my loving followers,
Plead my successive title with your swords.
I am his first-born son that was the last
That ware the imperial diadem of Rome;
Then let my father's honours live in me,
Nor wrong mine age with this indignity.

Bassianus. Romans, friends, followers, favourers of my right,
If ever Bassianus, Cæsar's son,
Were gracious in the eyes of royal Rome,
Keep then this passage to the Capitol;
And suffer not dishonour to approach
The imperial seat, to virtue consecrate,
To justice, continence, and nobility;
But let desert in pure election shine;
And, Romans, fight for freedom in your choice.

Enter Marcus Andronicus *aloft, with the crown*

Marcus. Princes, that strive by factions and by friends
Ambitiously for rule and empery,
Know that the people of Rome, for whom we stand
A special party, have by common voice
In election for the Roman empery
Chosen Andronicus, surnamed Pius
For many good and great deserts to Rome.

A nobler man, a braver warrior,
Lives not this day within the city walls.
He by the Senate is accited home,
From weary wars against the barbarous Goths,
That with his sons, a terror to our foes,
Hath yok'd a nation strong, train'd up in arms.
Ten years are spent since first he undertook
This cause of Rome, and chastised with arms
Our enemies' pride; five times he hath return'd
Bleeding to Rome, bearing his valiant sons
In coffins from the field; *and at this day*
To the monument of that Andronici
Done sacrifice of expiation,
And slain the noblest prisoner of the Goths.
And now at last, laden with honour's spoils,
Returns the good Andronicus to Rome,
Renowned Titus, flourishing in arms.
Let us entreat, by honour of his name
Whom worthily you would have now succeed,
And in the Capitol and Senate's right,
Whom you pretend to honour and adore,
That you withdraw you and abate your strength,
Dismiss your followers, and, as suitors should,
Plead your deserts in peace and humbleness.

SATURNINUS. How fair the Tribune speaks to calm my thoughts.

BASSIANUS. Marcus Andronicus, so I do affy
In thy uprightness and integrity,
And so I love and honour thee and thine,
Thy noble brother Titus and his sons,
And her to whom my thoughts are humbled all,
Gracious Lavinia, Rome's rich ornament,
That I will here dismiss my loving friends,
And to my fortunes and the people's favour
Commit my cause in balance to be weigh'd.

Exeunt the soldiers of BASSIANUS

SATURNINUS. Friends, that have been thus forward in my right,
I thank you all and here dismiss you all,
And to the love and favour of my country

Commit myself, my person, and the cause.

Exeunt the soldiers of SATURNINUS

Rome, be as just and gracious unto me
As I am confident and kind to thee.
Open the gates and let me in.

BASSIANUS. Tribunes, and me, a poor competitor.

[*Flourish. They go up into the Senate House*]

Enter a CAPTAIN

CAPTAIN. Romans, make way. The good Andronicus,
Patron of virtue, Rome's best champion,
Successful in the battles that he fights,
With honour and with fortune is return'd
From where he circumscribed with his sword
And brought to yoke the enemies of Rome.

Sound drums and trumpets, and then enter MARTIUS *and* MUTIUS, *two of* TITUS' *sons; and then two men bearing a coffin covered with black; then* LUCIUS *and* QUINTUS, *two other sons; then* TITUS ANDRONICUS; *and then* TAMORA *the Queen of Goths, with her three sons,* ALARBUS, DEMETRIUS, *and* CHIRON, *with* AARON *the Moor, and others, as many as can be. Then set down the coffin and* TITUS *speaks*

TITUS. Hail, Rome, victorious in thy mourning weeds!
Lo, as the bark that hath discharg'd her fraught
Returns with precious lading to the bay
From whence at first she weigh'd her anchorage,
Cometh Andronicus, bound with laurel boughs,
To re-salute his country with his tears,
Tears of true joy for his return to Rome.
Thou great defender of this Capitol,
Stand gracious to the rites that we intend!
Romans, of five and twenty valiant sons,
Half of the number that King Priam had,
Behold the poor remains, alive and dead!
These that survive let Rome reward with love;
These that I bring unto their latest home,
With burial amongst their ancestors.

Here Goths have given me leave to sheathe my sword.
Titus, unkind, and careless of thine own,
Why suffer'st thou thy sons, unburied yet,
To hover on the dreadful shore of Styx?
Make way to lay them by their brethren.
[*They open the tomb*]
There greet in silence, as the dead are wont,
And sleep in peace, slain in your country's wars.
O sacred receptacle of my joys,
Sweet cell of virtue and nobility,
How many sons hast thou of mine in store
That thou wilt never render to me more!

LUCIUS. Give us the proudest prisoner of the Goths,
That we may hew his limbs, and on a pile
Ad manes fratrum sacrifice his flesh
Before this earthy prison of their bones,
That so the shadows be not unappeas'd,
Nor we disturb'd with prodigies on earth.

TITUS. I give him you—the noblest that survives,
The eldest son of this distressed queen.

TAMORA. Stay, Roman brethen! Gracious conqueror,
Victorious Titus, rue the tears I shed,
A mother's tears in passion for her son;
And if thy sons were ever dear to thee,
O, think my son to be as dear to me!
Sufficeth not that we are brought to Rome
To beautify thy triumphs, and return
Captive to thee and to thy Roman yoke;
But must my sons be slaughtered in the streets
For valiant doings in their country's cause?
O, if to fight for king and commonweal
Were piety in thine, it is in these.
Andronicus, stain not thy tomb with blood.
Wilt thou draw near the nature of the gods?
Draw near them then in being merciful.
Sweet mercy is nobility's true badge.
Thrice-noble Titus, spare my first-born son.

TITUS. Patient yourself, madam, and pardon me.
These are their brethren, whom your Goths beheld
Alive and dead; and for their brethren slain

Religiously they ask a sacrifice.
To this your son is mark'd, and die he must
T' appease their groaning shadows that are gone.

LUCIUS. Away with him, and make a fire straight;
And with our swords, upon a pile of wood,
Let's hew his limbs till they be clean consum'd.

Exeunt TITUS' SONS, *with* ALARBUS

TAMORA. O cruel, irreligious piety!

CHIRON. Was never Scythia half so barbarous!

DEMETRIUS. Oppose not Scythia to ambitious Rome.
Alarbus goes to rest, and we survive
To tremble under Titus' threat'ning look.
Then, madam, stand resolv'd, but hope withal
The self-same gods that arm'd the Queen of Troy
With opportunity of sharp revenge
Upon the Thracian tyrant in his tent
May favour Tamora, the Queen of Goths—
When Goths were Goths and Tamora was queen—
To quit the bloody wrongs upon her foes.

Re-enter LUCIUS, QUINTUS, MARTIUS, *and* MUTIUS, *the sons of* ANDRONICUS, *with their swords bloody*

LUCIUS. See, lord and father, how we have perform'd
Our Roman rites: Alarbus' limbs are lopp'd,
And entrails feed the sacrificing fire,
Whose smoke like incense doth perfume the sky.
Remaineth nought but to inter our brethren,
And with loud 'larums welcome them to Rome.

TITUS. Let it be so, and let Andronicus
Make this his latest farewell to their souls.

[*Sound trumpets and lay the coffin in the tomb*]

In peace and honour rest you here, my sons;
Rome's readiest champions, repose you here in rest,
Secure from worldly chances and mishaps!
Here lurks no treason, here no envy swells,
Here grow no damned drugs, here are no storms,
No noise, but silence and eternal sleep.
In peace and honour rest you here, my sons!

Enter LAVINIA

LAVINIA. In peace and honour live Lord Titus long;
My noble lord and father, live in fame!
Lo, at this tomb my tributary tears
I render for my brethren's obsequies;
And at thy feet I kneel, with tears of joy
Shed on this earth for thy return to Rome.
O, bless me here with thy victorious hand,
Whose fortunes Rome's best citizens applaud!

TITUS. Kind Rome, that hast thus lovingly reserv'd
The cordial of mine age to glad my heart!
Lavinia, live; outlive thy father's days,
And fame's eternal date, for virtue's praise!

Enter, above, MARCUS ANDRONICUS *and* TRIBUNES; *re-enter* SATURNINUS, BASSIANUS, *and attendants*

MARCUS. Long live Lord Titus, my beloved brother,
Gracious triumpher in the eyes of Rome!

TITUS. Thanks, gentle Tribune, noble brother Marcus.

MARCUS. And welcome, nephews, from successful wars,
You that survive and you that sleep in fame.
Fair lords, your fortunes are alike in all
That in your country's service drew your swords;
But safer triumph is this funeral pomp
That hath aspir'd to Solon's happiness
And triumphs over chance in honour's bed.
Titus Andronicus, the people of Rome,
Whose friend in justice thou hast ever been,
Send thee by me, their Tribune and their trust,
This palliament of white and spotless hue;
And name thee in election for the empire
With these our late-deceased Emperor's sons:
Be candidatus then, and put it on,
And help to set a head on headless Rome.

TITUS. A better head her glorious body fits
Than his that shakes for age and feebleness.
What should I don this robe and trouble you?
Be chosen with proclamations to-day,
To-morrow yield up rule, resign my life,
And set abroad new business for you all?
Rome, I have been thy soldier forty years,

And led my country's strength successfully,
And buried one and twenty valiant sons,
Knighted in field, slain manfully in arms,
In right and service of their noble country.
Give me a staff of honour for mine age,
But not a sceptre to control the world.
Upright he held it, lords, that held it last.

MARCUS. Titus, thou shalt obtain and ask the empery.

SATURNINUS. Proud and ambitious Tribune, canst thou tell?

TITUS. Patience, Prince Saturninus.

SATURNINUS. Romans, do me right.
Patricians, draw your swords, and sheathe them not
Till Saturninus be Rome's Emperor.
Andronicus, would thou were shipp'd to hell
Rather than rob me of the people's hearts!

LUCIUS. Proud Saturnine, interrupter of the good
That noble-minded Titus means to thee!

TITUS. Content thee, Prince; I will restore to thee
The people's hearts, and wean them from themselves.

BASSIANUS. Andronicus, I do not flatter thee,
But honour thee, and will do till I die.
My faction if thou strengthen with thy friends,
I will most thankful be; and thanks to men
Of noble minds is honourable meed.

TITUS. People of Rome, and people's Tribunes here,
I ask your voices and your suffrages:
Will ye bestow them friendly on Andronicus?

TRIBUNES. To gratify the good Andronicus,
And gratulate his safe return to Rome,
The people will accept whom he admits.

TITUS. Tribunes, I thank you; and this suit I make,
That you create our Emperor's eldest son,
Lord Saturnine; whose virtues will, I hope,
Reflect on Rome as Titan's rays on earth,
And ripen justice in this commonweal.
Then, if you will elect by my advice,
Crown him, and say 'Long live our Emperor!'

MARCUS. With voices and applause of every sort,
Patricians and plebeians, we create
Lord Saturninus Rome's great Emperor;

And say 'Long live our Emperor Saturnine!'
[*A long flourish till they come down*]

SATURNINUS. Titus Andronicus, for thy favours done
To us in our election this day
I give thee thanks in part of thy deserts,
And will with deeds requite thy gentleness;
And for an onset, Titus, to advance
Thy name and honourable family,
Lavinia will I make my emperess,
Rome's royal mistress, mistress of my heart,
And in the sacred Pantheon her espouse.
Tell me, Andronicus, doth this motion please thee?

TITUS. It doth, my worthy lord, and in this match
I hold me highly honoured of your Grace,
And here in sight of Rome, to Saturnine,
King and commander of our commonweal,
The wide world's Emperor, do I consecrate
My sword, my chariot, and my prisoners,
Presents well worthy Rome's imperious lord;
Receive them then, the tribute that I owe,
Mine honour's ensigns humbled at thy feet.

SATURNINUS. Thanks, noble Titus, father of my life.
How proud I am of thee and of thy gifts
Rome shall record; and when I do forget
The least of these unspeakable deserts,
Romans, forget your fealty to me.

TITUS. [*To* TAMORA] Now, madam, are you prisoner to an emperor;
To him that for your honour and your state
Will use you nobly and your followers.

SATURNINUS. [*Aside*] A goodly lady, trust me; of the hue
That I would choose, were I to choose anew.–
Clear up, fair Queen, that cloudy countenance;
Though chance of war hath wrought this change of cheer,
Thou com'st not to be made a scorn in Rome–
Princely shall be thy usage every way.
Rest on my word, and let not discontent
Daunt all your hopes. Madam, he comforts you
Can make you greater than the Queen of Goths.

Lavinia, you are not displeas'd with this?

LAVINIA. Not I, my lord, sith true nobility
Warrants these words in princely courtesy.

SATURNINUS. Thanks, sweet Lavinia. Romans, let us go.
Ransomless here we set our prisoners free.
Proclaim our honours, lords, with trump and drum.
[*Flourish*]

BASSIANUS. Lord Titus, by your leave, this maid is mine.
[*Seizing* LAVINIA]

TITUS. How, sir! Are you in earnest then, my lord?

BASSIANUS. Ay, noble Titus, and resolv'd withal
To do myself this reason and this right.

MARCUS. Suum cuique is our Roman justice:
This prince in justice seizeth but his own.

LUCIUS. And that he will and shall, if Lucius live.

TITUS. Traitors, avaunt! Where is the Emperor's guard?
Treason, my lord–Lavinia is surpris'd!

SATURNINUS. Surpris'd! By whom?

BASSIANUS. By him that justly may
Bear his betroth'd from all the world away.

Exeunt BASSIANUS *and* MARCUS *with* LAVINIA

MUTIUS. Brothers, help to convey her hence away,
And with my sword I'll keep this door safe.

Exeunt LUCIUS, QUINTUS, *and* MARTIUS

TITUS. Follow, my lord, and I'll soon bring her back.

MUTIUS. My lord, you pass not here.

TITUS. What, villain boy!
Bar'st me my way in Rome?

MUTIUS. Help, Lucius, help!

TITUS *kills him. During the fray, exeunt* SATURNINUS,
TAMORA, DEMETRIUS, CHIRON, *and* AARON

Re-enter LUCIUS

LUCIUS. My lord, you are unjust, and more than so:
In wrongful quarrel you have slain your son.

TITUS. Nor thou nor he are any sons of mine;
My sons would never so dishonour me.

Re-enter aloft the EMPEROR *with* TAMORA
and her two SONS, *and* AARON *the Moor*

Traitor, restore Lavinia to the Emperor.
LUCIUS. Dead, if you will; but not to be his wife,
That is another's lawful promis'd love. *Exit*
SATURNINUS. No, Titus, no; the Emperor needs her not,
Nor her, nor thee, nor any of thy stock.
I'll trust by leisure him that mocks me once;
Thee never, nor thy traitorous haughty sons,
Confederates all thus to dishonour me.
Was there none else in Rome to make a stale
But Saturnine? Full well, Andronicus,
Agree these deeds with that proud brag of thine
That saidst I begg'd the empire at thy hands.
TITUS. O monstrous! What reproachful words are these?
SATURNINUS. But go thy ways; go, give that changing piece
To him that flourish'd for her with his sword.
A valiant son-in-law thou shalt enjoy;
One fit to bandy with thy lawless sons,
To ruffle in the commonwealth of Rome.
TITUS. These words are razors to my wounded heart.
SATURNINUS. And therefore, lovely Tamora, Queen of Goths,
That, like the stately Phœbe 'mongst her nymphs,
Dost overshine the gallant'st dames of Rome,
If thou be pleas'd with this my sudden choice,
Behold, I choose thee, Tamora, for my bride
And will create thee Emperess of Rome.
Speak, Queen of Goths, dost thou applaud my choice?
And here I swear by all the Roman gods—
Sith priest and holy water are so near,
And tapers burn so bright, and everything
In readiness for Hymenæus stand—
I will not re-salute the streets of Rome,
Or climb my palace, till from forth this place
I lead espous'd my bride along with me.
TAMORA. And here in sight of heaven to Rome I swear,
If Saturnine advance the Queen of Goths,
She will a handmaid be to his desires,
A loving nurse, a mother to his youth.
SATURNINUS. Ascend, fair Queen, Pantheon. Lords, accompany

Your noble Emperor and his lovely bride,
Sent by the heavens for Prince Saturnine,
Whose wisdom hath her fortune conquered;
There shall we consummate our spousal rites.
Exeunt all but Titus

Titus. I am not bid to wait upon this bride.
Titus, when wert thou wont to walk alone,
Dishonoured thus, and challenged of wrongs?

Re-enter Marcus, *and* Titus' *sons*, Lucius, Quintus, *and* Martius

Marcus. O Titus, see, O, see what thou hast done!
In a bad quarrel slain a virtuous son.
Titus. No, foolish Tribune, no; no son of mine—
Nor thou, nor these, confederates in the deed
That hath dishonoured all our family;
Unworthy brother and unworthy sons!
Lucius. But let us give him burial, as becomes;
Give Mutius burial with our bretheren.
Titus. Traitors, away! He rests not in this tomb.
This monument five hundred years hath stood,
Which I have sumptuously re-edified;
Here none but soldiers and Rome's servitors
Repose in fame; none basely slain in brawls.
Bury him where you can, he comes not here.
Marcus. My lord, this is impiety in you.
My nephew Mutius' deeds do plead for him;
He must be buried with his bretheren.
Quintus. Martius. } And shall, or him we will accompany.
Titus. 'And shall!' What villain was it spake that word?
Quintus. He that would vouch it in any place but here.
Titus. What, would you bury him in my despite?
Marcus. No, noble Titus, but entreat of thee
To pardon Mutius and to bury him.
Titus. Marcus, even thou hast struck upon my crest,
And with these boys mine honour thou hast wounded.
My foes I do repute you every one;
So trouble me no more, but get you gone.
Martius. He is not with himself; let us withdraw.

QUINTUS. Not I, till Mutius' bones be buried.
[*The* BROTHER *and the* SONS *kneel*]
MARCUS. Brother, for in that name doth nature plead—
QUINTUS. Father, and in that name doth nature speak—
TITUS. Speak thou no more, if all the rest will speed.
MARCUS. Renowned Titus, more than half my soul—
LUCIUS. Dear father, soul and substance of us all—
MARCUS. Suffer thy brother Marcus to inter
His noble nephew here in virtue's nest,
That died in honour and Lavinia's cause.
Thou art a Roman—be not barbarous.
The Greeks upon advice did bury Ajax,
That slew himself; and wise Laertes' son
Did graciously plead for his funerals.
Let not young Mutius, then, that was thy joy,
Be barr'd his entrance here.
TITUS. Rise, Marcus, rise;
The dismal'st day is this that e'er I saw,
To be dishonoured by my sons in Rome!
Well, bury him, and bury me the next.
[*They put* MUTIUS *in the tomb*]
LUCIUS. There lie thy bones, sweet Mutius, with thy friends,
Till we with trophies do adorn thy tomb.
ALL. [*Kneeling*] No man shed tears for noble Mutius;
He lives in fame that died in virtue's cause.
MARCUS. My lord—to step out of these dreary dumps—
How comes it that the subtle Queen of Goths
Is of a sudden thus advanc'd in Rome?
TITUS. I know not, Marcus, but I know it is—
Whether by device or no, the heavens can tell.
Is she not, then, beholding to the man
That brought her for this high good turn so far?
MARCUS. Yes, and will nobly him remunerate.

Flourish. Re-enter the EMPEROR, TAMORA *and her two* SONS, *with the* MOOR, *at one door; at the other door,* BASSIANUS *and* LAVINIA, *with others*

SATURNINUS. So, Bassianus, you have play'd your prize:
God give you joy, sir, of your gallant bride!

BASSIANUS. And you of yours, my lord! I say no more,
Nor wish no less; and so I take my leave.
SATURNINUS. Traitor, if Rome have law or we have power,
Thou and thy faction shall repent this rape.
BASSIANUS. Rape, call you it, my lord, to seize my own,
My true betrothed love, and now my wife?
But let the laws of Rome determine all;
Meanwhile am I possess'd of that is mine.
SATURNINUS. 'Tis good, sir. You are very short with us;
But if we live we'll be as sharp with you.
BASSIANUS. My lord, what I have done, as best I may,
Answer I must, and shall do with my life.
Only thus much I give your Grace to know:
By all the duties that I owe to Rome,
This noble gentleman, Lord Titus here,
Is in opinion and in honour wrong'd,
That, in the rescue of Lavinia,
With his own hand did slay his youngest son,
In zeal to you, and highly mov'd to wrath
To be controll'd in that he frankly gave.
Receive him then to favour, Saturnine,
That hath express'd himself in all his deeds
A father and a friend to thee and Rome.
TITUS. Prince Bassianus, leave to plead my deeds.
'Tis thou and those that have dishonoured me.
Rome and the righteous heavens be my judge
How I have lov'd and honoured Saturnine!
TAMORA. My worthy lord, if ever Tamora
Were gracious in those princely eyes of thine,
Then hear me speak indifferently for all;
And at my suit, sweet, pardon what is past.
SATURNINUS. What, madam! be dishonoured openly,
And basely put it up without revenge?
TAMORA. Not so, my lord; the gods of Rome forfend
I should be author to dishonour you!
But on mine honour dare I undertake
For good Lord Titus' innocence in all,
Whose fury not dissembled speaks his griefs.
Then at my suit look graciously on him;
Lose not so noble a friend on vain suppose,

Nor with sour looks afflict his gentle heart.
[*Aside to* SATURNINUS] My lord, be rul'd by me, be won at last;
Dissemble all your griefs and discontents.
You are but newly planted in your throne;
Lest, then, the people, and patricians too,
Upon a just survey take Titus' part,
And so supplant you for ingratitude,
Which Rome reputes to be a heinous sin,
Yield at entreats, and then let me alone:
I'll find a day to massacre them all,
And raze their faction and their family,
The cruel father and his traitorous sons,
To whom I sued for my dear son's life;
And make them know what 'tis to let a queen
Kneel in the streets and beg for grace in vain.–
Come, come, sweet Emperor; come, Andronicus.
Take up this good old man, and cheer the heart
That dies in tempest of thy angry frown.

SATURNINUS. Rise, Titus, rise; my Empress hath prevail'd.

TITUS. I thank your Majesty and her, my lord;
These words, these looks, infuse new life in me.

TAMORA. Titus, I am incorporate in Rome,
A Roman now adopted happily,
And must advise the Emperor for his good.
This day all quarrels die, Andronicus;
And let it be mine honour, good my lord,
That I have reconcil'd your friends and you.
For you, Prince Bassianus, I have pass'd
My word and promise to the Emperor
That you will be more mild and tractable.
And fear not, lords–and you, Lavinia.
By my advice, all humbled on your knees,
You shall ask pardon of his Majesty.

LUCIUS. We do, and vow to heaven and to his Highness
That what we did was mildly as we might,
Tend'ring our sister's honour and our own.

MARCUS. That on mine honour here do I protest.

SATURNINUS. Away, and talk not; trouble us no more.

TAMORA. Nay, nay, sweet Emperor, we must all be friends.

The Tribune and his nephews kneel for grace.
I will not be denied. Sweet heart, look back.

SATURNINUS. Marcus, for thy sake, and thy brother's here,
And at my lovely Tamora's entreats,
I do remit these young men's heinous faults.
Stand up.
Lavinia, though you left me like a churl,
I found a friend; and sure as death I swore
I would not part a bachelor from the priest.
Come, if the Emperor's court can feast two brides,
You are my guest, Lavinia, and your friends.
This day shall be a love-day, Tamora.

TITUS. To-morrow, and it please your Majesty
To hunt the panther and the hart with me,
With horn and hound we'll give your Grace bonjour.

SATURNINUS. Be it so, Titus, and gramercy too.

Exeunt. Sound trumpets

ACT II. SCENE 1

Rome. Before the palace

Enter AARON

AARON. Now climbeth Tamora Olympus' top,
Safe out of Fortune's shot, and sits aloft,
Secure of thunder's crack or lightning flash,
Advanc'd above pale envy's threat'ning reach.
As when the golden sun salutes the morn,
And, having gilt the ocean with his beams,
Gallops the zodiac in his glistening coach
And overlooks the highest-peering hills,
So Tamora.
Upon her wit doth earthly honour wait,
And virtue stoops and trembles at her frown.
Then, Aaron, arm thy heart and fit thy thoughts
To mount aloft with thy imperial mistress,
And mount her pitch whom thou in triumph long

Hast prisoner held, fett'red in amorous chains,
And faster bound to Aaron's charming eyes
Than is Prometheus tied to Caucasus.
Away with slavish weeds and servile thoughts!
I will be bright and shine in pearl and gold,
To wait upon this new-made emperess.
To wait, said I? To wanton with this queen,
This goddess, this Semiramis, this nymph,
This siren that will charm Rome's Saturnine,
And see his shipwreck and his commonweal's.
Hullo! what storm is this?

Enter CHIRON *and* DEMETRIUS, *braving*

DEMETRIUS. Chiron, thy years wants wit, thy wits wants edge
And manners, to intrude where I am grac'd,
And may, for aught thou knowest, affected be.
CHIRON. Demetrius, thou dost over-ween in all;
And so in this, to bear me down with braves.
'Tis not the difference of a year or two
Makes me less gracious or thee more fortunate:
I am as able and as fit as thou
To serve and to deserve my mistress' grace;
And that my sword upon thee shall approve,
And plead my passions for Lavinia's love.
AARON. [*Aside*] Clubs, clubs! These lovers will not keep the peace.
DEMETRIUS. Why, boy, although our mother, unadvis'd,
Gave you a dancing-rapier by your side,
Are you so desperate grown to threat your friends?
Go to; have your lath glued within your sheath
Till you know better how to handle it.
CHIRON. Meanwhile, sir, with the little skill I have,
Full well shalt thou perceive how much I dare.
DEMETRIUS. Ay, boy, grow ye so brave? [*They draw*]
AARON. [*Coming forward*] Why, how now, lords!
So near the Emperor's palace dare ye draw
And maintain such a quarrel openly?
Full well I wot the ground of all this grudge:
I would not for a million of gold

The cause were known to them it most concerns;
Nor would your noble mother for much more
Be so dishonoured in the court of Rome.
For shame, put up.

DEMETRIUS. Not I, till I have sheath'd
My rapier in his bosom, and withal
Thrust those reproachful speeches down his throat
That he hath breath'd in my dishonour here.

CHIRON. For that I am prepar'd and full resolv'd,
Foul-spoken coward, that thund'rest with thy tongue,
And with thy weapon nothing dar'st perform.

AARON. Away, I say!
Now, by the gods that warlike Goths adore,
This pretty brabble will undo us all.
Why, lords, and think you not how dangerous
It is to jet upon a prince's right?
What, is Lavinia then become so loose,
Or Bassianus so degenerate,
That for her love such quarrels may be broach'd
Without controlment, justice, or revenge?
Young lords, beware; an should the Empress know
This discord's ground, the music would not please.

CHIRON. I care not, I, knew she and all the world:
I love Lavinia more than all the world.

DEMETRIUS. Youngling, learn thou to make some meaner choice:
Lavinia is thine elder brother's hope.

AARON. Why, are ye mad, or know ye not in Rome
How furious and impatient they be,
And cannot brook competitors in love?
I tell you, lords, you do but plot your deaths
By this device.

CHIRON. Aaron, a thousand deaths
Would I propose to achieve her whom I love.

AARON. To achieve her—How?

DEMETRIUS. Why mak'st thou it so strange?
She is a woman, therefore may be woo'd;
She is a woman, therefore may be won;
She is Lavinia, therefore must be lov'd.
What, man! more water glideth by the mill

Than wots the miller of; and easy it is
Of a cut loaf to steal a shive, we know.
Though Bassianus be the Emperor's brother,
Better than he have worn Vulcan's badge.

AARON. [*Aside*] Ay, and as good as Saturninus may.

DEMETRIUS. Then why should he despair that knows to court it
With words, fair looks, and liberality?
What, hast not thou full often struck a doe,
And borne her cleanly by the keeper's nose?

AARON. Why, then, it seems some certain snatch or so
Would serve your turns.

CHIRON. Ay, so the turn were served.

DEMETRIUS. Aaron, thou hast hit it.

AARON. Would you had hit it too!
Then should not we be tir'd with this ado.
Why, hark ye, hark ye! and are you such fools
To square for this? Would it offend you, then,
That both should speed?

CHIRON. Faith, not me.

DEMETRIUS. Nor me, so I were one.

AARON. For shame, be friends, and join for that you jar.
'Tis policy and stratagem must do
That you affect; and so must you resolve
That what you cannot as you would achieve,
You must perforce accomplish as you may.
Take this of me: Lucrece was not more chaste
Than this Lavinia, Bassianus' love.
A speedier course than ling'ring languishment
Must we pursue, and I have found the path.
My lords, a solemn hunting is in hand;
There will the lovely Roman ladies troop;
The forest walks are wide and spacious,
And many unfrequented plots there are
Fitted by kind for rape and villainy.
Single you thither then this dainty doe,
And strike her home by force if not by words.
This way, or not at all, stand you in hope.
Come, come, our Empress, with her sacred wit
To villainy and vengeance consecrate,

Will we acquaint with all what we intend;
And she shall file our engines with advice
That will not suffer you to square yourselves,
But to your wishes' height advance you both.
The Emperor's court is like the house of Fame,
The palace full of tongues, of eyes, and ears;
The woods are ruthless, dreadful, deaf, and dull.
There speak and strike, brave boys, and take your turns;
There serve your lust, shadowed from heaven's eye,
And revel in Lavinia's treasury.

CHIRON. Thy counsel, lad, smells of no cowardice.

DEMETRIUS. Sit fas aut nefas, till I find the stream
To cool this heat, a charm to calm these fits,
Per Styga, per manes vehor. *Exeunt*

SCENE 2

A forest near Rome

Enter TITUS ANDRONICUS, *and his three sons,* LUCIUS, QUINTUS, MARTIUS, *making a noise with hounds and horns; and* MARCUS

TITUS. The hunt is up, the morn is bright and grey,
The fields are fragrant, and the woods are green.
Uncouple here, and let us make a bay,
And wake the Emperor and his lovely bride,
And rouse the Prince, and ring a hunter's peal,
That all the court may echo with the noise.
Sons, let it be your charge, as it is ours,
To attend the Emperor's person carefully.
I have been troubled in my sleep this night,
But dawning day new comfort hath inspir'd.

Here a cry of hounds, and wind horns in a peal. Then enter SATURNINUS, TAMORA, BASSIANUS, LAVINIA, CHIRON, DEMETRIUS, *and their attendants*

Many good morrows to your Majesty!
Madam, to you as many and as good!
I promised your Grace a hunter's peal.

SATURNINUS. And you have rung it lustily, my lords—
Somewhat too early for new-married ladies.
BASSIANUS. Lavinia, how say you?
LAVINIA. I say no;
I have been broad awake two hours and more.
SATURNINUS. Come on then, horse and chariots let us have,
And to our sport. [*To* TAMORA] Madam, now shall ye see
Our Roman hunting.
MARCUS. I have dogs, my lord,
Will rouse the proudest panther in the chase,
And climb the highest promontory top.
TITUS. And I have horse will follow where the game
Makes way, and run like swallows o'er the plain.
DEMETRIUS. Chiron, we hunt not, we, with horse nor hound,
But hope to pluck a dainty doe to ground. *Exeunt*

SCENE 3

A lonely part of the forest

Enter AARON *alone, with a bag of gold*

AARON. He that had wit would think that I had none,
To bury so much gold under a tree
And never after to inherit it.
Let him that thinks of me so abjectly
Know that this gold must coin a stratagem,
Which, cunningly effected, will beget
A very excellent piece of villainy.
And so repose, sweet gold, for their unrest
[*Hides the gold*]
That have their alms out of the Empress' chest.

Enter TAMORA *alone, to the Moor*

TAMORA. My lovely Aaron, wherefore look'st thou sad
When everything doth make a gleeful boast?
The birds chant melody on every bush;
The snakes lie rolled in the cheerful sun;
The green leaves quiver with the cooling wind

AARON. *Madam, though Venus govern your desires,*
Saturn is dominator over mine.
What signifies my deadly-standing eye,
My silence and my cloudy melancholy,
My fleece of woolly hair that now uncurls
Even as an adder when she doth unroll
To do some fatal execution? . . .
Vengeance is in my heart, death in my hand,
Blood and revenge are hammering in my head.
(ACT II. Scene 3)

And make a chequer'd shadow on the ground;
Under their sweet shade, Aaron, let us sit,
And while the babbling echo mocks the hounds,
Replying shrilly to the well-tun'd horns,
As if a double hunt were heard at once,
Let us sit down and mark their yellowing noise;
And–after conflict such as was suppos'd
The wand'ring prince and Dido once enjoyed,
When with a happy storm they were surpris'd,
And curtain'd with a counsel-keeping cave–
We may, each wreathed in the other's arms,
Our pastimes done, possess a golden slumber,
Whiles hounds and horns and sweet melodious birds
Be unto us as is a nurse's song
Of lullaby to bring her babe asleep.

AARON. Madam, though Venus govern your desires,
Saturn is dominator over mine.
What signifies my deadly-standing eye,
My silence and my cloudy melancholy,
My fleece of woolly hair that now uncurls
Even as an adder when she doth unroll
To do some fatal execution?
No, madam, these are no venereal signs.
Vengeance is in my heart, death in my hand,
Blood and revenge are hammering in my head.
Hark, Tamora, the empress of my soul,
Which never hopes more heaven than rests in thee–
This is the day of doom for Bassianus;
His Philomel must lose her tongue to-day,
Thy sons make pillage of her chastity,
And wash their hands in Bassianus' blood.
Seest thou this letter? Take it up, I pray thee,
And give the King this fatal-plotted scroll.
Now question me no more; we are espied.
Here comes a parcel of our hopeful booty,
Which dreads not yet their lives' destruction.

Enter BASSIANUS *and* LAVINIA

TAMORA. Ah, my sweet Moor, sweeter to me than life!

AARON. No more, great Empress: Bassianus comes.

Be cross with him; and I'll go fetch thy sons
To back thy quarrels, whatsoe'er they be. *Exit*

BASSIANUS. Who have we here? Rome's royal Emperess,
Unfurnish'd of her well-beseeming troop?
Or is it Dian, habited like her,
Who hath abandoned her holy groves
To see the general hunting in this forest?

TAMORA. Saucy controller of my private steps!
Had I the pow'r that some say Dian had,
Thy temples should be planted presently
With horns, as was Actæon's; and the hounds
Should drive upon thy new-transformed limbs,
Unmannerly intruder as thou art!

LAVINIA. Under your patience, gentle Emperess,
'Tis thought you have a goodly gift in horning,
And to be doubted that your Moor and you
Are singled forth to try thy experiments.
Jove shield your husband from his hounds to-day!
'Tis pity they should take him for a stag.

BASSIANUS. Believe me, Queen, your swarth Cimmerian
Doth make your honour of his body's hue,
Spotted, detested, and abominable.
Why are you sequest'red from all your train,
Dismounted from your snow-white goodly steed,
And wand'red hither to an obscure plot,
Accompanied but with a barbarous Moor,
If foul desire had not conducted you?

LAVINIA. And, being intercepted in your sport,
Great reason that my noble lord be rated
For sauciness. I pray you let us hence,
And let her joy her raven-coloured love;
This valley fits the purpose passing well.

BASSIANUS. The King my brother shall have notice of this.

LAVINIA. Ay, for these slips have made him noted long.
Good king, to be so mightily abused!

TAMORA. Why, I have patience to endure all this.

Enter CHIRON *and* DEMETRIUS

DEMETRIUS. How now, dear sovereign, and our gracious mother!

Why doth your Highness look so pale and wan?
TAMORA. Have I not reason, think you, to look pale?
These two have 'ticed me hither to this place.
A barren detested vale you see it is:
The trees, though summer, yet forlorn and lean,
Overcome with moss and baleful mistletoe;
Here never shines the sun; here nothing breeds,
Unless the nightly owl or fatal raven.
And when they show'd me this abhorred pit,
They told me, here, at dead time of the night,
A thousand fiends, a thousand hissing snakes,
Ten thousand swelling toads, as many urchins,
Would make such fearful and confused cries
As any mortal body hearing it
Should straight fall mad or else die suddenly.
No sooner had they told this hellish tale
But straight they told me they would bind me here
Unto the body of a dismal yew,
And leave me to this miserable death.
And then they call'd me foul adulteress,
Lascivious Goth, and all the bitterest terms
That ever ear did hear to such effect;
And had you not by wondrous fortune come,
This vengeance on me had they executed.
Revenge it, as you love your mother's life,
Or be ye not henceforth call'd my children.
DEMETRIUS. This is a witness that I am thy son.
[*Stabs* BASSIANUS]
CHIRON. And this for me, struck home to show my strength.
[*Also stabs*]
LAVINIA. Ay, come, Semiramis—nay, barbarous Tamora,
For no name fits thy nature but thy own!
TAMORA. Give me the poniard; you shall know, my boys,
Your mother's hand shall right your mother's wrong.
DEMETRIUS. Stay, madam, here is more belongs to her;
First thrash the corn, then after burn the straw.
This minion stood upon her chastity,
Upon her nuptial vow, her loyalty,
And with that painted hope braves your mightiness;
And shall she carry this unto her grave?

CHIRON. An if she do, I would I were an eunuch.
Drag hence her husband to some secret hole,
And make his dead trunk pillow to our lust.
TAMORA. But when ye have the honey we desire,
Let not this wasp outlive, us both to sting.
CHIRON. I warrant you, madam, we will make that sure.
Come, mistress, now perforce we will enjoy
That nice-preserved honesty of yours.
LAVINIA. O Tamora! thou bearest a woman's face—
TAMORA. I will not hear her speak; away with her!
LAVINIA. Sweet lords, entreat her hear me but a word.
DEMETRIUS. Listen, fair madam: let it be your glory
To see her tears; but be your heart to them
As unrelenting flint to drops of rain.
LAVINIA. When did the tiger's young ones teach the dam?
O, do not learn her wrath—she taught it thee;
The milk thou suck'dst from her did turn to marble,
Even at thy teat thou hadst thy tyranny.
Yet every mother breeds not sons alike:
[*To* CHIRON] Do thou entreat her show a woman's pity.
CHIRON. What, wouldst thou have me prove myself a bastard?
LAVINIA. 'Tis true, the raven doth not hatch a lark.
Yet have I heard—O, could I find it now!—
The lion, mov'd with pity, did endure
To have his princely paws par'd all away.
Some say that ravens foster forlorn children,
The whilst their own birds famish in their nests;
O, be to me, though thy hard heart say no,
Nothing so kind, but something pitiful!
TAMORA. I know not what it means; away with her!
LAVINIA. O, let me teach thee! For my father's sake,
That gave thee life when well he might have slain thee,
Be not obdurate, open thy deaf ears.
TAMORA. Hadst thou in person ne'er offended me,
Even for his sake am I pitiless.
Remember, boys, I pour'd forth tears in vain
To save your brother from the sacrifice;
But fierce Andronicus would not relent.
Therefore away with her, and use her as you will;

The worse to her the better lov'd of me.
LAVINIA. O Tamora, be call'd a gentle queen,
And with thine own hands kill me in this place!
For 'tis not life that I have begg'd so long;
Poor I was slain when Bassianus died.
TAMORA. What beg'st thou, then? Fond woman, let me go.
LAVINIA. 'Tis present death I beg; and one thing more,
That womanhood denies my tongue to tell:
O, keep me from their worse than killing lust,
And tumble me into some loathsome pit,
Where never man's eye may behold my body;
Do this, and be a charitable murderer.
TAMORA. So should I rob my sweet sons of their fee;
No, let them satisfy their lust on thee.
DEMETRIUS. Away! for thou hast stay'd us here too long.
LAVINIA. No grace? no womanhood? Ah, beastly creature,
The blot and enemy to our general name!
Confusion fall–
CHIRON. Nay, then I'll stop your mouth. Bring thou her husband.
This is the hole where Aaron bid us hide him.

DEMETRIUS *throws the body of* BASSIANUS *into the pit; then exeunt* DEMETRIUS *and* CHIRON, *dragging off* LAVINIA

TAMORA. Farewell, my sons; see that you make her sure.
Ne'er let my heart know merry cheer indeed
Till all the Andronici be made away.
Now will I hence to seek my lovely Moor,
And let my spleenful sons this trull deflower. *Exit*

Re-enter AARON, *with two of* TITUS' *sons,* QUINTUS *and* MARTIUS

AARON. Come on, my lords, the better foot before;
Straight will I bring you to the loathsome pit
Where I espied the panther fast asleep.
QUINTUS. My sight is very dull, whate'er it bodes.
MARTIUS. And mine, I promise you; were it not for shame,
Well could I leave our sport to sleep awhile.
[*Falls into the pit*]

QUINTUS. What, art thou fallen? What subtle hole is this,
Whose mouth is covered with rude-growing briers,
Upon whose leaves are drops of new-shed blood
As fresh as morning dew distill'd on flowers?
A very fatal place it seems to me.
Speak, brother, hast thou hurt thee with the fall?
MARTIUS. O brother, with the dismal'st object hurt
That ever eye with sight made heart lament!
AARON. [*Aside*] Now will I fetch the King to find them here,
That he thereby may have a likely guess
How these were they that made away his brother. *Exit*
MARTIUS. Why dost not comfort me, and help me out
From this unhallow'd and blood-stained hole?
QUINTUS. I am surprised with an uncouth fear;
A chilling sweat o'er-runs my trembling joints;
My heart suspects more than mine eye can see.
MARTIUS. To prove thou hast a true divining heart,
Aaron and thou look down into this den,
And see a fearful sight of blood and death.
QUINTUS. Aaron is gone, and my compassionate heart
Will not permit mine eyes once to behold
The thing whereat it trembles by surmise;
O, tell me who it is, for ne'er till now
Was I a child to fear I know not what.
MARTIUS. Lord Bassianus lies beray'd in blood,
All on a heap, like to a slaughtered lamb,
In this detested, dark, blood-drinking pit.
QUINTUS. If it be dark, how dost thou know 'tis he?
MARTIUS. Upon his bloody finger he doth wear
A precious ring that lightens all this hole,
Which, like a taper in some monument,
Doth shine upon the dead man's earthy cheeks,
And shows the ragged entrails of this pit;
So pale did shine the moon on Pyramus
When he by night lay bath'd in maiden blood.
O brother, help me with thy fainting hand—
If fear hath made thee faint, as me it hath—
Out of this fell devouring receptacle,
As hateful as Cocytus' misty mouth.
QUINTUS. Reach me thy hand, that I may help thee out,

Or, wanting strength to do thee so much good,
I may be pluck'd into the swallowing womb
Of this deep pit, poor Bassianus' grave.
I have no strength to pluck thee to the brink.

MARTIUS. Nor I no strength to climb without thy help.

QUINTUS. Thy hand once more; I will not loose again,
Till thou art here aloft, or I below.
Thou canst not come to me—I come to thee. [*Falls in*]

Enter the EMPEROR *and* AARON *the Moor*

SATURNINUS. Along with me! I'll see what hole is here,
And what he is that now is leapt into it.
Say, who art thou that lately didst descend
Into this gaping hollow of the earth?

MARTIUS. The unhappy sons of old Andronicus,
Brought hither in a most unlucky hour,
To find thy brother Bassianus dead.

SATURNINUS. My brother dead! I know thou dost but jest:
He and his lady both are at the lodge
Upon the north side of this pleasant chase;
'Tis not an hour since I left them there.

MARTIUS. We know not where you left them all alive;
But, out alas! here have we found him dead.

Re-enter TAMORA, *with attendants;* TITUS ANDRONICUS *and* LUCIUS

TAMORA. Where is my lord the King?

SATURNINUS. Here, Tamora; though griev'd with killing grief.

TAMORA. Where is thy brother Bassianus?

SATURNINUS. Now to the bottom dost thou search my wound;
Poor Bassianus here lies murdered.

TAMORA. Then all too late I bring this fatal writ,
The complot of this timeless tragedy;
And wonder greatly that man's face can fold
In pleasing smiles such murderous tyranny.
[*She giveth* SATURNINE *a letter*]

SATURNINUS. [*Reads*] 'An if we miss to meet him handsomely,
Sweet huntsman—Bassianus 'tis we mean—
Do thou so much as dig the grave for him.

Thou know'st our meaning. Look for thy reward
Among the nettles at the elder-tree
Which overshades the mouth of that same pit
Where we decreed to bury Bassianus.
Do this, and purchase us thy lasting friends.'
O Tamora! was ever heard the like?
This is the pit and this the elder-tree.
Look, sirs, if you can find the huntsman out
That should have murdered Bassianus here.

AARON. My gracious lord, here is the bag of gold.

SATURNINUS. [*To* TITUS] Two of thy whelps, fell curs of bloody kind,
Have here bereft my brother of his life.
Sirs, drag them from the pit unto the prison;
There let them bide until we have devis'd
Some never-heard-of torturing pain for them.

TAMORA. What, are they in this pit? O wondrous thing!
How easily murder is discovered!

TITUS. High Emperor, upon my feeble knee
I beg this boon, with tears not lightly shed,
That this fell fault of my accursed sons–
Accursed if the fault be prov'd in them–

SATURNINUS. If it be prov'd! You see it is apparent.
Who found this letter? Tamora, was it you?

TAMORA. Andronicus himself did take it up.

TITUS. I did, my lord, yet let me be their bail;
For, by my fathers' reverend tomb, I vow
They shall be ready at your Highness' will
To answer their suspicion with their lives.

SATURNINUS. Thou shalt not bail them; see thou follow me.
Some bring the murdered body, some the murderers;
Let them not speak a word–the guilt is plain;
For, by my soul, were there worse end than death,
That end upon them should be executed.

TAMORA. Andronicus, I will entreat the King.
Fear not thy sons; they shall do well enough.

TITUS. Come, Lucius, come; stay not to talk with them.

Exeunt

SCENE 4

Another part of the forest

Enter the Empress' sons, DEMETRIUS *and* CHIRON, *with* LAVINIA, *her hands cut off, and her tongue cut out, and ravish'd*

DEMETRIUS. So, now go tell, an if thy tongue can speak,
Who 'twas that cut thy tongue and ravish'd thee.
CHIRON. Write down thy mind, bewray thy meaning so,
An if thy stumps will let thee play the scribe.
DEMETRIUS. See how with signs and tokens she can scrowl.
CHIRON. Go home, call for sweet water, wash thy hands.
DEMETRIUS. She hath no tongue to call, nor hands to wash;
And so let's leave her to her silent walks.
CHIRON. An 'twere my cause, I should go hang myself.
DEMETRIUS. If thou hadst hands to help thee knit the cord.
Exeunt DEMETRIUS *and* CHIRON

Wind horns. Enter MARCUS, *from hunting*

MARCUS. Who is this?—my niece, that flies away so fast?
Cousin, a word: where is your husband?
If I do dream, would all my wealth would wake me!
If I do wake, some planet strike me down,
That I may slumber an eternal sleep!
Speak, gentle niece. What stern ungentle hands
Hath lopp'd, and hew'd, and made thy body bare
Of her two branches—those sweet ornaments
Whose circling shadows kings have sought to sleep in,
And might not gain so great a happiness
As half thy love? Why dost not speak to me?
Alas, a crimson river of warm blood,
Like to a bubbling fountain stirr'd with wind,
Doth rise and fall between thy rosed lips,
Coming and going with thy honey breath.
But sure some Tereus hath deflowered thee,
And, lest thou shouldst detect him, cut thy tongue.
Ah, now thou turn'st away thy face for shame!
And notwithstanding all this loss of blood—

As from a conduit with three issuing spouts—
Yet do thy cheeks look red as Titan's face
Blushing to be encount'red with a cloud.
Shall I speak for thee? Shall I say 'tis so?
O, that I knew thy heart, and knew the beast,
That I might rail at him to ease my mind!
Sorrow concealed, like an oven stopp'd,
Doth burn the heart to cinders where it is.
Fair Philomel, why she but lost her tongue,
And in a tedious sampler sew'd her mind;
But, lovely niece, that mean is cut from thee.
A craftier Tereus, cousin, hast thou met,
And he hath cut those pretty fingers off
That could have better sew'd than Philomel.
O, had the monster seen those lily hands
Tremble like aspen leaves upon a lute
And make the silken strings delight to kiss them,
He would not then have touch'd them for his life!
Or had he heard the heavenly harmony
Which that sweet tongue hath made,
He would have dropp'd his knife, and fell asleep,
As Cerberus at the Thracian poet's feet.
Come, let us go, and make thy father blind,
For such a sight will blind a father's eye;
One hour's storm will drown the fragrant meads,
What will whole months of tears thy father's eyes?
Do not draw back, for we will mourn with thee;
O, could our mourning ease thy misery! *Exeunt*

ACT III. SCENE 1

Rome. A street

Enter the JUDGES, TRIBUNES, *and* SENATORS, *with* TITUS' *two sons* MARTIUS *and* QUINTUS *bound, passing on the stage to the place of execution, and* TITUS *going before, pleading*

TITUS. Hear me, grave fathers; noble Tribunes, stay!

For pity of mine age, whose youth was spent
In dangerous wars whilst you securely slept;
For all my blood in Rome's great quarrel shed,
For all the frosty nights that I have watch'd,
And for these bitter tears, which now you see
Filling the aged wrinkles in my cheeks,
Be pitiful to my condemned sons,
Whose souls are not corrupted as 'tis thought.
For two and twenty sons I never wept,
Because they died in honour's lofty bed.
[ANDRONICUS *lieth down, and the judges pass by him with the prisoners, and exeunt*]
For these, Tribunes, in the dust I write
My heart's deep languor and my soul's sad tears.
Let my tears stanch the earth's dry appetite;
My sons' sweet blood will make it shame and blush.
O earth, I will befriend thee more with rain
That shall distil from these two ancient urns,
Than youthful April shall with all his show'rs.
In summer's drought I'll drop upon thee still;
In winter with warm tears I'll melt the snow
And keep eternal spring-time on thy face,
So thou refuse to drink my dear sons' blood.

Enter LUCIUS *with his weapon drawn*

O reverend Tribunes! O gentle aged men!
Unbind my sons, reverse the doom of death,
And let me say, that never wept before,
My tears are now prevailing orators.
LUCIUS. O noble father, you lament in vain;
The Tribunes hear you not, no man is by,
And you recount your sorrows to a stone.
TITUS. Ah, Lucius, for thy brothers let me plead!
Grave Tribunes, once more I entreat of you.
LUCIUS. My gracious lord, no tribune hears you speak.
TITUS. Why, 'tis no matter, man: if they did hear,
They would not mark me; if they did mark,
They would not pity me; yet plead I must,
And bootless unto them.
Therefore I tell my sorrows to the stones;

Who though they cannot answer my distress,
Yet in some sort they are better than the Tribunes,
For that they will not intercept my tale.
When I do weep, they humbly at my feet
Receive my tears, and seem to weep with me;
And were they but attired in grave weeds,
Rome could afford no tribunes like to these.
A stone is soft as wax: tribunes more hard than stones.
A stone is silent and offendeth not,
And tribunes with their tongues doom men to death.
[*Rises*]
But wherefore stand'st thou with thy weapon drawn?

LUCIUS. To rescue my two brothers from their death;
For which attempt the judges have pronounc'd
My everlasting doom of banishment.

TITUS. O happy man! they have befriended thee.
Why, foolish Lucius, dost thou not perceive
That Rome is but a wilderness of tigers?
Tigers must prey, and Rome affords no prey
But me and mine; how happy art thou then
From these devourers to be banished!
But who comes with our brother Marcus here?

Enter MARCUS *with* LAVINIA

MARCUS. Titus, prepare thy aged eyes to weep,
Or if not so, thy noble heart to break.
I bring consuming sorrow to thine age.

TITUS. Will it consume me? Let me see it then.

MARCUS. This was thy daughter.

TITUS. Why, Marcus, so she is.

LUCIUS. Ay me! this object kills me.

TITUS. Faint-hearted boy, arise, and look upon her.
Speak, Lavinia, what accursed hand
Hath made thee handless in thy father's sight?
What fool hath added water to the sea,
Or brought a fagot to bright-burning Troy?
My grief was at the height before thou cam'st,
And now like Nilus it disdaineth bounds.
Give me a sword, I'll chop off my hands too,
For they have fought for Rome, and all in vain;

And they have nurs'd this woe in feeding life;
In bootless prayer have they been held up,
And they have serv'd me to effectless use.
Now all the service I require of them
Is that the one will help to cut the other.
'Tis well, Lavinia, that thou hast no hands;
For hands to do Rome service is but vain.

LUCIUS. Speak, gentle sister, who hath martyr'd thee?

MARCUS. O, that delightful engine of her thoughts
That blabb'd them with such pleasing eloquence
Is torn from forth that pretty hollow cage,
Where like a sweet melodious bird it sung
Sweet varied notes, enchanting every ear!

LUCIUS. O, say thou for her, who hath done this deed?

MARCUS. O, thus I found her straying in the park,
Seeking to hide herself as doth the deer
That hath receiv'd some unrecuring wound.

TITUS. It was my dear, and he that wounded her
Hath hurt me more than had he kill'd me dead;
For now I stand as one upon a rock,
Environ'd with a wilderness of sea,
Who marks the waxing tide grow wave by wave,
Expecting ever when some envious surge
Will in his brinish bowels swallow him.
This way to death my wretched sons are gone;
Here stands my other son, a banish'd man,
And here my brother, weeping at my woes.
But that which gives my soul the greatest spurn
Is dear Lavinia, dearer than my soul.
Had I but seen thy picture in this plight,
It would have madded me; what shall I do
Now I behold thy lively body so?
Thou hast no hands to wipe away thy tears,
Nor tongue to tell me who hath martyr'd thee;
Thy husband he is dead, and for his death
Thy brothers are condemn'd, and dead by this.
Look, Marcus! Ah, son Lucius, look on her!
When I did name her brothers, then fresh tears
Stood on her cheeks, as doth the honey dew
Upon a gath'red lily almost withered.

MARCUS. Perchance she weeps because they kill'd her husband;
Perchance because she knows them innocent.

TITUS. If they did kill thy husband, then be joyful,
Because the law hath ta'en revenge on them.
No, no, they would not do so foul a deed;
Witness the sorrow that their sister makes.
Gentle Lavinia, let me kiss thy lips,
Or make some sign how I may do thee ease.
Shall thy good uncle and thy brother Lucius
And thou and I sit round about some fountain,
Looking all downwards to behold our cheeks
How they are stain'd, like meadows yet not dry
With miry slime left on them by a flood?
And in the fountain shall we gaze so long,
Till the fresh taste be taken from that clearness,
And made a brine-pit with our bitter tears?
Or shall we cut away our hands like thine?
Or shall we bite our tongues, and in dumb shows
Pass the remainder of our hateful days?
What shall we do? Let us that have our tongues
Plot some device of further misery
To make us wonder'd at in time to come.

LUCIUS. Sweet father, cease your tears; for at your grief
See how my wretched sister sobs and weeps.

MARCUS. Patience, dear niece. Good Titus, dry thine eyes.

TITUS. Ah, Marcus, Marcus! Brother, well I wot
Thy napkin cannot drink a tear of mine,
For thou, poor man, hast drown'd it with thine own.

LUCIUS. Ah, my Lavinia, I will wipe thy cheeks.

TITUS. Mark, Marcus, mark! I understand her signs.
Had she a tongue to speak, now would she say
That to her brother which I said to thee:
His napkin, with his true tears all bewet,
Can do no service on her sorrowful cheeks.
O, what a sympathy of woe is this—
As far from help as Limbo is from bliss!

Enter AARON *the Moor*

AARON. Titus Andronicus, my lord the Emperor

Sends thee this word, that, if thou love thy sons,
Let Marcus, Lucius, or thyself, old Titus,
Or any one of you, chop off your hand
And send it to the King: he for the same
Will send thee hither both thy sons alive,
And that shall be the ransom for their fault.

TITUS. O gracious Emperor! O gentle Aaron!
Did ever raven sing so like a lark
That gives sweet tidings of the sun's uprise?
With all my heart I'll send the Emperor my hand.
Good Aaron, wilt thou help to chop it off?

LUCIUS. Stay, father! for that noble hand of thine,
That hath thrown down so many enemies,
Shall not be sent. My hand will serve the turn,
My youth can better spare my blood than you,
And therefore mine shall save my brothers' lives.

MARCUS. Which of your hands hath not defended Rome
And rear'd aloft the bloody battle-axe,
Writing destruction on the enemy's castle?
O, none of both but are of high desert!
My hand hath been but idle; let it serve
To ransom my two nephews from their death;
Then have I kept it to a worthy end.

AARON. Nay, come, agree whose hand shall go along,
For fear they die before their pardon come.

MARCUS. My hand shall go.

LUCIUS. By heaven, it shall not go!

TITUS. Sirs, strive no more; such with'red herbs as these
Are meet for plucking up, and therefore mine.

LUCIUS. Sweet father, if I shall be thought thy son,
Let me redeem my brothers both from death.

MARCUS. And for our father's sake and mother's care,
Now let me show a brother's love to thee.

TITUS. Agree between you; I will spare my hand.

LUCIUS. Then I'll go fetch an axe.

MARCUS. But I will use the axe.

Exeunt LUCIUS *and* MARCUS

TITUS. Come hither, Aaron, I'll deceive them both;
Lend me thy hand, and I will give thee mine.

AARON. [*Aside*] If that be call'd deceit, I will be honest,

And never whilst I live deceive men so;
But I'll deceive you in another sort,
And that you'll say ere half an hour pass.
[*He cuts off* TITUS' *hand*]

Re-enter LUCIUS *and* MARCUS

TITUS. Now stay your strife. What shall be is dispatch'd.
Good Aaron, give his Majesty my hand;
Tell him it was a hand that warded him
From thousand dangers; bid him bury it.
More hath it merited—that let it have.
As for my sons, say I account of them
As jewels purchas'd at an easy price;
And yet dear too, because I bought mine own.
AARON. I go, Andronicus; and for thy hand
Look by and by to have thy sons with thee.
[*Aside*] Their heads I mean. O, how this villainy
Doth fat me with the very thoughts of it!
Let fools do good, and fair men call for grace:
Aaron will have his soul black like his face. *Exit*
TITUS. O, here I lift this one hand up to heaven,
And bow this feeble ruin to the earth;
If any power pities wretched tears,
To that I call! [*To* LAVINIA] What, would'st thou kneel with me?
Do, then, dear heart; for heaven shall hear our prayers,
Or with our sighs we'll breathe the welkin dim
And stain the sun with fog, as sometime clouds
When they do hug him in their melting bosoms.
MARCUS. O brother, speak with possibility,
And do not break into these deep extremes.
TITUS. Is not my sorrow deep, having no bottom?
Then be my passions bottomless with them.
MARCUS. But yet let reason govern thy lament.
TITUS. If there were reason for these miseries,
Then into limits could I bind my woes.
When heaven doth weep, doth not the earth o'erflow?
If the winds rage, doth not the sea wax mad,
Threat'ning the welkin with his big-swol'n face?
And wilt thou have a reason for this coil?

I am the sea; hark how her sighs do blow.
She is the weeping welkin, I the earth;
Then must my sea be moved with her sighs;
Then must my earth with her continual tears
Become a deluge, overflow'd and drown'd;
For why my bowels cannot hide her woes,
But like a drunkard must I vomit them.
Then give me leave; for losers will have leave
To ease their stomachs with their bitter tongues.

Enter a MESSENGER, *with two heads and a hand*

MESSENGER. Worthy Andronicus, ill art thou repaid
For that good hand thou sent'st the Emperor.
Here are the heads of thy two noble sons;
And here's thy hand, in scorn to thee sent back–
Thy grief their sports, thy resolution mock'd,
That woe is me to think upon thy woes,
More than remembrance of my father's death. *Exit*

MARCUS. Now let hot Ætna cool in Sicily,
And be my heart an ever-burning hell!
These miseries are more than may be borne.
To weep with them that weep doth ease some deal,
But sorrow flouted at is double death.

LUCIUS. Ah, that this sight should make so deep a wound,
And yet detested life not shrink thereat!
That ever death should let life bear his name,
Where life hath no more interest but to breathe!
[LAVINIA *kisses* TITUS]

MARCUS. Alas, poor heart, that kiss is comfortless
As frozen water to a starved snake.

TITUS. When will this fearful slumber have an end?

MARCUS. Now farewell, flatt'ry; die, Andronicus.
Thou dost not slumber: see thy two sons' heads,
Thy warlike hand, thy mangled daughter here;
Thy other banish'd son with this dear sight
Struck pale and bloodless; and thy brother, I,
Even like a stony image, cold and numb.
Ah! now no more will I control thy griefs.
Rent off thy silver hair, thy other hand
Gnawing with thy teeth; and be this dismal sight

The closing up of our most wretched eyes.
Now is a time to storm; why art thou still?

TITUS. Ha, ha, ha!

MARCUS. Why dost thou laugh? It fits not with this hour.

TITUS. Why, I have not another tear to shed;
Besides, this sorrow is an enemy,
And would usurp upon my wat'ry eyes
And make them blind with tributary tears.
Then which way shall I find Revenge's cave?
For these two heads do seem to speak to me,
And threat me I shall never come to bliss
Till all these mischiefs be return'd again
Even in their throats that have committed them.
Come, let me see what task I have to do.
You heavy people, circle me about,
That I may turn me to each one of you
And swear unto my soul to right your wrongs.
The vow is made. Come, brother, take a head,
And in this hand the other will I bear.
And, Lavinia, thou shalt be employ'd in this;
Bear thou my hand, sweet wench, between thy teeth.
As for thee, boy, go, get thee from my sight;
Thou art an exile, and thou must not stay.
Hie to the Goths and raise an army there;
And if ye love me, as I think you do,
Let's kiss and part, for we have much to do.

Exeunt all but LUCIUS

LUCIUS. Farewell, Andronicus, my noble father,
The woefull'st man that ever liv'd in Rome.
Farewell, proud Rome; till Lucius come again,
He leaves his pledges dearer than his life.
Farewell, Lavinia, my noble sister;
O, would thou wert as thou tofore hast been!
But now nor Lucius nor Lavinia lives
But in oblivion and hateful griefs.
If Lucius live, he will requite your wrongs
And make proud Saturnine and his emperess
Beg at the gates like Tarquin and his queen.
Now will I to the Goths, and raise a pow'r
To be reveng'd on Rome and Saturnine. *Exit*

SCENE 2

Rome. TITUS' *house*

A banquet. Enter TITUS, MARCUS, LAVINIA, *and the boy* YOUNG LUCIUS

TITUS. So so, now sit; and look you eat no more
Than will preserve just so much strength in us
As will revenge these bitter woes of ours.
Marcus, unknit that sorrow-wreathen knot;
Thy niece and I, poor creatures, want our hands,
And cannot passionate our tenfold grief
With folded arms. This poor right hand of mine
Is left to tyrannize upon my breast;
Who, when my heart, all mad with misery,
Beats in this hollow prison of my flesh,
Then thus I thump it down.
[*To* LAVINIA] Thou map of woe, that thus dost talk in signs!
When thy poor heart beats with outrageous beating,
Thou canst not strike it thus to make it still.
Wound it with sighing, girl, kill it with groans;
Or get some little knife between thy teeth
And just against thy heart make thou a hole,
That all the tears that thy poor eyes let fall
May run into that sink and, soaking in,
Drown the lamenting fool in sea-salt tears.

MARCUS. Fie, brother, fie! Teach her not thus to lay
Such violent hands upon her tender life.

TITUS. How now! Has sorrow made thee dote already?
Why, Marcus, no man should be mad but I.
What violent hands can she lay on her life?
Ah, wherefore dost thou urge the name of hands?
To bid Æneas tell the tale twice o'er
How Troy was burnt and he made miserable?
O, handle not the theme, to talk of hands,
Lest we remember still that we have none.
Fie, fie, how franticly I square my talk,
As if we should forget we had no hands,

If Marcus did not name the word of hands!
Come, let's fall to; and, gentle girl, eat this:
Here is no drink. Hark, Marcus, what she says–
I can interpret all her martyr'd signs;
She says she drinks no other drink but tears,
Brew'd with her sorrow, mesh'd upon her cheeks.
Speechless complainer, I will learn thy thought;
In thy dumb action will I be as perfect
As begging hermits in their holy prayers.
Thou shalt not sigh, nor hold thy stumps to heaven,
Nor wink, nor nod, nor kneel, nor make a sign,
But I of these will wrest an alphabet,
And by still practice learn to know thy meaning.

BOY. Good grandsire, leave these bitter deep laments;
Make my aunt merry with some pleasing tale.

MARCUS. Alas, the tender boy, in passion mov'd,
Doth weep to see his grandsire's heaviness.

TITUS. Peace, tender sapling; thou art made of tears,
And tears will quickly melt thy life away.
[MARCUS *strikes the dish with a knife*]
What dost thou strike at, Marcus, with thy knife?

MARCUS. At that that I have kill'd, my lord–a fly.

TITUS. Out on thee, murderer, thou kill'st my heart!
Mine eyes are cloy'd with view of tyranny;
A deed of death done on the innocent
Becomes not Titus' brother. Get thee gone;
I see thou art not for my company.

MARCUS. Alas, my lord, I have but kill'd a fly.

TITUS. 'But!' How if that fly had a father and mother?
How would he hang his slender gilded wings
And buzz lamenting doings in the air!
Poor harmless fly,
That with his pretty buzzing melody
Came here to make us merry! And thou hast kill'd him.

MARCUS. Pardon me, sir; it was a black ill-favour'd fly,
Like to the Empress' Moor; therefore I kill'd him.

TITUS. O, O, O!
Then pardon me for reprehending thee,
For thou hast done a charitable deed.
Give me thy knife, I will insult on him,

Flattering myself as if it were the Moor
Come hither purposely to poison me.
There's for thyself, and that's for Tamora.
Ah, sirrah!
Yet, I think, we are not brought so low
But that between us we can kill a fly
That comes in likeness of a coal-black Moor.

MARCUS. Alas, poor man! grief has so wrought on him,
He takes false shadows for true substances.

TITUS. Come, take away. Lavinia, go with me;
I'll to thy closet, and go read with thee
Sad stories chanced in the times of old.
Come, boy, and go with me; thy sight is young,
And thou shalt read when mine begin to dazzle. *Exeunt*

ACT IV. SCENE 1

Rome. TITUS' *garden*

Enter YOUNG LUCIUS *and* LAVINIA *running after him, and the boy flies from her with his books under his arm. Enter* TITUS *and* MARCUS

BOY. Help, grandsire, help! my aunt Lavinia
Follows me everywhere, I know not why.
Good uncle Marcus, see how swift she comes!
Alas, sweet aunt, I know not what you mean.

MARCUS. Stand by me, Lucius; do not fear thine aunt.

TITUS. She loves thee, boy, too well to do thee harm.

BOY. Ay, when my father was in Rome she did.

MARCUS. What means my niece Lavinia by these signs?

TITUS. Fear her not, Lucius; somewhat doth she mean.
See, Lucius, see how much she makes of thee.
Somewhither would she have thee go with her.
Ah, boy, Cornelia never with more care
Read to her sons than she hath read to thee
Sweet poetry and Tully's Orator.

MARCUS. Canst thou not guess wherefore she plies thee thus?

BOY. My lord, I know not, I, nor can I guess,
Unless some fit or frenzy do possess her;
For I have heard my grandsire say full oft
Extremity of griefs would make men mad;
And I have read that Hecuba of Troy
Ran mad for sorrow. That made me to fear;
Although, my lord, I know my noble aunt
Loves me as dear as e'er my mother did,
And would not, but in fury, fright my youth;
Which made me down to throw my books, and fly—
Causeless, perhaps. But pardon me, sweet aunt;
And, madam, if my uncle Marcus go,
I will most willingly attend your ladyship.

MARCUS. Lucius, I will. [LAVINIA *turns over with her stumps the books which* LUCIUS *has let fall*]

TITUS. How now, Lavinia! Marcus, what means this?
Some book there is that she desires to see.
Which is it, girl, of these?—Open them, boy.—
But thou art deeper read and better skill'd;
Come and take choice of all my library,
And so beguile thy sorrow, till the heavens
Reveal the damn'd contriver of this deed.
Why lifts she up her arms in sequence thus?

MARCUS. I think she means that there were more than one
Confederate in the fact; ay, more there was,
Or else to heaven she heaves them for revenge.

TITUS. Lucius, what book is that she tosseth so?

BOY. Grandsire, 'tis Ovid's Metamorphoses;
My mother gave it me.

MARCUS. For love of her that's gone,
Perhaps she cull'd it from among the rest.

TITUS. Soft! So busily she turns the leaves! Help her.
What would she find? Lavinia, shall I read?
This is the tragic tale of Philomel
And treats of Tereus' treason and his rape;
And rape, I fear, was root of thy annoy.

MARCUS. See, brother, see! Note how she quotes the leaves.

TITUS. Lavinia, wert thou thus surpris'd, sweet girl,
Ravish'd and wrong'd as Philomela was,

Forc'd in the ruthless, vast, and gloomy woods?
See, see!
Ay, such a place there is where we did hunt–
O, had we never, never hunted there!–
Pattern'd by that the poet here describes,
By nature made for murders and for rapes.

MARCUS. O, why should nature build so foul a den,
Unless the gods delight in tragedies?

TITUS. Give signs, sweet girl, for here are none but friends,
What Roman lord it was durst do the deed.
Or slunk not Saturnine, as Tarquin erst,
That left the camp to sin in Lucrece' bed?

MARCUS. Sit down, sweet niece; brother, sit down by me.
Apollo, Pallas, Jove, or Mercury,
Inspire me, that I may this treason find!
My lord, look here! Look here, Lavinia!

[*He writes his name with his staff, and guides it with feet and mouth*]

This sandy plot is plain; guide, if thou canst,
This after me. I have writ my name
Without the help of any hand at all.
Curs'd be that heart that forc'd us to this shift!
Write thou, good niece, and here display at last
What God will have discovered for revenge.
Heaven guide thy pen to print thy sorrows plain,
That we may know the traitors and the truth!

[*She takes the staff in her mouth and guides it with her stumps, and writes*]

O, do ye read, my lord, what she hath writ?

TITUS. 'Stuprum–Chiron–Demetrius.'

MARCUS. What, what! the lustful sons of Tamora
Performers of this heinous bloody deed?

TITUS. Magni Dominator poli,
Tam lentus audis scelera? tam lentus vides?

MARCUS. O, calm thee, gentle lord! although I know
There is enough written upon this earth
To stir a mutiny in the mildest thoughts,
And arm the minds of infants to exclaims.
My lord, kneel down with me; Lavinia, kneel;

And kneel, sweet boy, the Roman Hector's hope;
And swear with me—as, with the woeful fere
And father of that chaste dishonoured dame,
Lord Junius Brutus sware for Lucrece' rape—
That we will prosecute, by good advice,
Mortal revenge upon these traitorous Goths,
And see their blood or die with this reproach.

TITUS. 'Tis sure enough, an you knew how;
But if you hunt these bear-whelps, then beware:
The dam will wake; and if she wind ye once,
She's with the lion deeply still in league,
And lulls him whilst she playeth on her back,
And when he sleeps will she do what she list.
You are a young huntsman, Marcus; let alone;
And come, I will go get a leaf of brass,
And with a gad of steel will write these words,
And lay it by. The angry northern wind
Will blow these sands like Sibyl's leaves abroad,
And where's our lesson, then? Boy, what say you?

BOY. I say, my lord, that if I were a man
Their mother's bedchamber should not be safe
For these base bondmen to the yoke of Rome.

MARCUS. Ay, that's my boy! Thy father hath full oft
For his ungrateful country done the like.

BOY. And, uncle, so will I, an if I live.

TITUS. Come, go with me into mine armoury.
Lucius, I'll fit thee; and withal my boy
Shall carry from me to the Empress' sons
Presents that I intend to send them both.
Come, come; thou'lt do my message, wilt thou not?

BOY. Ay, with my dagger in their bosoms, grandsire.

TITUS. No, boy, not so; I'll teach thee another course.
Lavinia, come. Marcus, look to my house.
Lucius and I'll go brave it at the court;
Ay, marry, will we, sir! and we'll be waited on.

Exeunt TITUS, LAVINIA, *and* YOUNG LUCIUS

MARCUS. O heavens, can you hear a good man groan
And not relent, or not compassion him?
Marcus, attend him in his ecstasy,
That hath more scars of sorrow in his heart

Than foemen's marks upon his batt'red shield,
But yet so just that he will not revenge.
Revenge the heavens for old Andronicus! *Exit*

SCENE 2

Rome. The palace

Enter AARON, DEMETRIUS *and* CHIRON, *at one door; and at the other door,* YOUNG LUCIUS *and another with a bundle of weapons, and verses writ upon them*

CHIRON. Demetrius, here's the son of Lucius;
He hath some message to deliver us.
AARON. Ay, some mad message from his mad grandfather.
BOY. My lords, with all the humbleness I may,
I greet your honours from Andronicus–
[*Aside*] And pray the Roman gods confound you both!
DEMETRIUS. Gramercy, lovely Lucius. What's the news?
BOY. [*Aside*] That you are both decipher'd, that's the news,
For villains mark'd with rape.–May it please you,
My grandsire, well-advis'd, hath sent by me
The goodliest weapons of his armoury
To gratify your honourable youth,
The hope of Rome; for so he bid me say;
And so I do, and with his gifts present
Your lordships, that, whenever you have need,
You may be armed and appointed well.
And so I leave you both–[*Aside*] like bloody villains.
Exeunt YOUNG LUCIUS *and attendant*
DEMETRIUS. What's here? A scroll, and written round about.
Let's see:
[*Reads*] 'Integer vitae, scelerisque purus,
Non eget Mauri iaculis, nec arcu.'
CHIRON. O, 'tis a verse in Horace, I know it well;
I read it in the grammar long ago.
AARON. Ay, just–a verse in Horace. Right, you have it.
[*Aside*] Now, what a thing it is to be an ass!

Here's no sound jest! The old man hath found their guilt,
And sends them weapons wrapp'd about with lines
That wound, beyond their feeling, to the quick.
But were our witty Empress well afoot,
She would applaud Andronicus' conceit.
But let her rest in her unrest awhile—
And now, young lords, was't not a happy star
Led us to Rome, strangers, and more than so,
Captives, to be advanced to this height?
It did me good before the palace gate
To brave the Tribune in his brother's hearing.

DEMETRIUS. But me more good to see so great a lord
Basely insinuate and send us gifts.

AARON. Had he not reason, Lord Demetrius?
Did you not use his daughter very friendly?

DEMETRIUS. I would we had a thousand Roman dames
At such a bay, by turn to serve our lust.

CHIRON. A charitable wish and full of love.

AARON. Here lacks but your mother for to say amen.

CHIRON. And that would she for twenty thousand more.

DEMETRIUS. Come, let us go and pray to all the gods
For our beloved mother in her pains.

AARON. [*Aside*] Pray to the devils; the gods have given us over. [*Trumpets sound*]

DEMETRIUS. Why do the Emperor's trumpets flourish thus?

CHIRON. Belike, for joy the Emperor hath a son.

DEMETRIUS. Soft! who comes here?

Enter NURSE, *with a blackamoor* CHILD

NURSE. Good morrow, lords.
O, tell me, did you see Aaron the Moor?

AARON. Well, more or less, or ne'er a whit at all,
Here Aaron is; and what with Aaron now?

NURSE. O gentle Aaron, we are all undone!
Now help, or woe betide thee evermore!

AARON. Why, what a caterwauling dost thou keep!
What dost thou wrap and fumble in thy arms?

NURSE. O, that which I would hide from heaven's eye:
Our Empress' shame and stately Rome's disgrace!
She is delivered, lord; she is delivered.

AARON. To whom?
NURSE. I mean she is brought a-bed.
AARON. Well, God give her good rest! What hath he sent her?
NURSE. A devil.
AARON. Why, then she is the devil's dam;
A joyful issue.
NURSE. A joyless, dismal, black, and sorrowful issue!
Here is the babe, as loathsome as a toad
Amongst the fair-fac'd breeders of our clime;
The Empress sends it thee, thy stamp, thy seal,
And bids thee christen it with thy dagger's point.
AARON. Zounds, ye whore! Is black so base a hue?
Sweet blowse, you are a beauteous blossom sure.
DEMETRIUS. Villain, what hast thou done?
AARON. That which thou canst not undo.
CHIRON. Thou hast undone our mother.
AARON. Villain, I have done thy mother.
DEMETRIUS. And therein, hellish dog, thou hast undone her.
Woe to her chance, and damn'd her loathed choice!
Accurs'd the offspring of so foul a fiend!
CHIRON. It shall not live.
AARON. It shall not die.
NURSE. Aaron, it must; the mother wills it so.
AARON. What, must it, nurse? Then let no man but I
Do execution on my flesh and blood.
DEMETRIUS. I'll broach the tadpole on my rapier's point.
Nurse, give it me; my sword shall soon dispatch it.
AARON. Sooner this sword shall plough thy bowels up.
[*Takes the* CHILD *from the* NURSE, *and draws*]
Stay, murderous villains, will you kill your brother!
Now, by the burning tapers of the sky
That shone so brightly when this boy was got,
He dies upon my scimitar's sharp point
That touches this my first-born son and heir.
I tell you, younglings, not Enceladus,
With all his threat'ning band of Typhon's brood,
Nor great Alcides, nor the god of war,
Shall seize this prey out of his father's hands.
What, what, ye sanguine, shallow-hearted boys!

Ye white-lim'd walls! ye alehouse painted signs!
Coal-black is better than another hue
In that it scorns to bear another hue;
For all the water in the ocean
Can never turn the swan's black legs to white,
Although she lave them hourly in the flood.
Tell the Empress from me I am of age
To keep mine own—excuse it how she can.

DEMETRIUS. Wilt thou betray thy noble mistress thus?

AARON. My mistress is my mistress: this my self,
The vigour and the picture of my youth.
This before all the world do I prefer;
This maugre all the world will I keep safe,
Or some of you shall smoke for it in Rome.

DEMETRIUS. By this our mother is for ever sham'd.

CHIRON. Rome will despise her for this foul escape.

NURSE. The Emperor in his rage will doom her death.

CHIRON. I blush to think upon this ignomy.

AARON. Why, there's the privilege your beauty bears:
Fie, treacherous hue, that will betray with blushing
The close enacts and counsels of thy heart!
Here's a young lad fram'd of another leer.
Look how the black slave smiles upon the father,
As who should say 'Old lad, I am thine own.'
He is your brother, lords, sensibly fed
Of that self-blood that first gave life to you;
And from your womb where you imprisoned were
He is enfranchised and come to light.
Nay, he is your brother by the surer side,
Although my seal be stamped in his face.

NURSE. Aaron, what shall I say unto the Empress?

DEMETRIUS. Advise thee, Aaron, what is to be done,
And we will all subscribe to thy advice.
Save thou the child, so we may all be safe.

AARON. Then sit we down and let us all consult.
My son and I will have the wind of you:
Keep there; now talk at pleasure of your safety.
[*They sit*]

DEMETRIUS. How many women saw this child of his?

AARON. Why, so, brave lords! When we join in league

I am a lamb; but if you brave the Moor,
The chafed boar, the mountain lioness,
The ocean swells not so as Aaron storms.
But say, again, how many saw the child?

NURSE. Cornelia the midwife and myself;
And no one else but the delivered Empress.

AARON. The Emperess, the midwife, and yourself.
Two may keep counsel when the third's away:
Go to the Empress, tell her this I said. [*He kills her*]
Weeke weeke!
So cries a pig prepared to the spit.

DEMETRIUS. What mean'st thou, Aaron? Wherefore didst thou this?

AARON. O Lord, sir, 'tis a deed of policy.
Shall she live to betray this guilt of ours—
A long-tongu'd babbling gossip? No, lords, no.
And now be it known to you my full intent:
Not far, one Muliteus, my countryman—
His wife but yesternight was brought to bed;
His child is like to her, fair as you are.
Go pack with him, and give the mother gold,
And tell them both the circumstance of all,
And how by this their child shall be advanc'd,
And be received for the Emperor's heir
And substituted in the place of mine,
To calm this tempest whirling in the court;
And let the Emperor dandle him for his own.
Hark ye, lords. You see I have given her physic,
[*Pointing to the* NURSE]
And you must needs bestow her funeral;
The fields are near, and you are gallant grooms.
This done, see that you take no longer days,
But send the midwife presently to me.
The midwife and the nurse well made away,
Then let the ladies tattle what they please.

CHIRON. Aaron, I see thou wilt not trust the air
With secrets.

DEMETRIUS. For this care of Tamora,
Herself and hers are highly bound to thee. *Exeunt* DEMETRIUS *and* CHIRON, *bearing off the dead* NURSE

AARON. Now to the Goths, as swift as swallow flies,
There to dispose this treasure in mine arms,
And secretly to greet the Empress' friends.
Come on, you thick-lipp'd slave, I'll bear you hence;
For it is you that puts us to our shifts.
I'll make you feed on berries and on roots,
And feed on curds and whey, and suck the goat,
And cabin in a cave, and bring you up
To be a warrior and command a camp.
Exit with the CHILD

SCENE 3

Rome. A public place

Enter TITUS, *bearing arrows with letters on the ends of them; with him* MARCUS, YOUNG LUCIUS, *and other gentlemen*, PUBLIUS, SEMPRONIUS, *and* CAIUS, *with bows*

TITUS. Come, Marcus, come; kinsmen, this is the way.
Sir boy, let me see your archery;
Look ye draw home enough, and 'tis there straight.
Terras Astrea reliquit,
Be you rememb'red, Marcus; she's gone, she's fled.
Sirs, take you to your tools. You, cousins, shall
Go sound the ocean and cast your nets;
Happily you may catch her in the sea;
Yet there's as little justice as at land.
No; Publius and Sempronius, you must do it;
'Tis you must dig with mattock and with spade,
And pierce the inmost centre of the earth;
Then, when you come to Pluto's region,
I pray you deliver him this petition.
Tell him it is for justice and for aid,
And that it comes from old Andronicus,
Shaken with sorrows in ungrateful Rome.
Ah, Rome! Well, well, I made thee miserable
What time I threw the people's suffrages
On him that thus doth tyrannize o'er me.

Go get you gone; and pray be careful all,
And leave you not a man-of-war unsearch'd.
This wicked Emperor may have shipp'd her hence;
And, kinsmen, then we may go pipe for justice.

MARCUS. O Publius, is not this a heavy case,
To see thy noble uncle thus distract?

PUBLIUS. Therefore, my lords, it highly us concerns
By day and night t'attend him carefully,
And feed his humour kindly as we may
Till time beget some careful remedy.

MARCUS. Kinsmen, his sorrows are past remedy.
Join with the Goths, and with revengeful war
Take wreak on Rome for this ingratitude,
And vengeance on the traitor Saturnine.

TITUS. Publius, how now? How now, my masters?
What, have you met with her?

PUBLIUS. No, my good lord; but Pluto sends you word,
If you will have Revenge from hell, you shall.
Marry, for Justice, she is so employ'd,
He thinks, with Jove in heaven, or somewhere else,
So that perforce you must needs stay a time.

TITUS. He doth me wrong to feed me with delays.
I'll dive into the burning lake below
And pull her out of Acheron by the heels.
Marcus, we are but shrubs, no cedars we,
No big-bon'd men fram'd of the Cyclops' size;
But metal, Marcus, steel to the very back,
Yet wrung with wrongs more than our backs can bear;
And, sith there's no justice in earth nor hell,
We will solicit heaven, and move the gods
To send down Justice for to wreak our wrongs.
Come, to this gear. You are a good archer, Marcus.
[*He gives them the arrows*]
'Ad Jovem' that's for you; here 'Ad Apollinem.'
'Ad Martem' that's for myself.
Here, boy, 'To Pallas'; here 'To Mercury.'
'To Saturn,' Caius—not to Saturnine:
You were as good to shoot against the wind.
To it, boy. Marcus, loose when I bid.
Of my word, I have written to effect;

There's not a god left unsolicited.

MARCUS. Kinsmen, shoot all your shafts into the court;
We will afflict the Emperor in his pride.

TITUS. Now, masters, draw. [*They shoot*] O, well said, Lucius!
Good boy, in Virgo's lap! Give it Pallas.

MARCUS. My lord, I aim a mile beyond the moon;
Your letter is with Jupiter by this.

TITUS. Ha! ha!
Publius, Publius, what hast thou done?
See, see, thou hast shot off one of Taurus' horns.

MARCUS. This was the sport, my lord: when Publius shot,
The Bull, being gall'd, gave Aries such a knock
That down fell both the Ram's horns in the court;
And who should find them but the Empress' villain?
She laugh'd, and told the Moor he should not choose
But give them to his master for a present.

TITUS. Why, there it goes! God give his lordship joy!

Enter the CLOWN, *with a basket and two pigeons in it*

News, news from heaven! Marcus, the post is come.
Sirrah, what tidings? Have you any letters?
Shall I have justice? What says Jupiter?

CLOWN. Ho, the gibbet-maker? He says that he hath taken them down again, for the man must not be hang'd till the next week.

TITUS. But what says Jupiter, I ask thee?

CLOWN. Alas, sir, I know not Jupiter; I never drank with him in all my life.

TITUS. Why, villain, art not thou the carrier?

CLOWN. Ay, of my pigeons, sir; nothing else.

TITUS. Why, didst thou not come from heaven?

CLOWN. From heaven! Alas, sir, I never came there. God forbid I should be so bold to press to heaven in my young days. Why, I am going with my pigeons to the Tribunal Plebs, to take up a matter of brawl betwixt my uncle and one of the Emperal's men.

MARCUS. Why, sir, that is as fit as can be to serve for your oration; and let him deliver the pigeons to the Emperor from you.

TITUS. Tell me, can you deliver an oration to the Emperor with a grace?

CLOWN. Nay, truly, sir, I could never say grace in all my life.

TITUS. Sirrah, come hither. Make no more ado,
But give your pigeons to the Emperor;
By me thou shalt have justice at his hands.
Hold, hold! Meanwhile here's money for thy charges.
Give me pen and ink. Sirrah, can you with a grace deliver up a supplication?

CLOWN. Ay, sir.

TITUS. Then here is a supplication for you. And when you come to him, at the first approach you must kneel; then kiss his foot; then deliver up your pigeons; and then look for your reward. I'll be at hand, sir; see you do it bravely.

CLOWN. I warrant you, sir; let me alone.

TITUS. Sirrah, hast thou a knife? Come let me see it.
Here, Marcus, fold it in the oration;
For thou hast made it like a humble suppliant.
And when thou hast given it to the Emperor,
Knock at my door, and tell me what he says.

CLOWN. God be with you, sir; I will.

TITUS. Come, Marcus, let us go. Publius, follow me. *Exeunt*

SCENE 4

Rome. Before the palace

Enter the EMPEROR, *and the* EMPRESS *and her two sons,* DEMETRIUS *and* CHIRON; LORDS *and others. The* EMPEROR *brings the arrows in his hand that* TITUS *shot at him*

SATURNINUS. Why, lords, what wrongs are these! Was ever seen
An emperor in Rome thus overborne,
Troubled, confronted thus; and, for the extent
Of egal justice, us'd in such contempt?
My lords, you know, as know the mightful gods,
However these disturbers of our peace

Buzz in the people's ears, there nought hath pass'd
But even with law against the wilful sons
Of old Andronicus. And what an if
His sorrows have so overwhelm'd his wits,
Shall we be thus afflicted in his wreaks,
His fits, his frenzy, and his bitterness?
And now he writes to heaven for his redress.
See, here's 'To Jove' and this 'To Mercury';
This 'To Apollo'; this 'To the God of War'–
Sweet scrolls to fly about the streets of Rome!
What's this but libelling against the Senate,
And blazoning our unjustice every where?
A goodly humour, is it not, my lords?
As who would say in Rome no justice were.
But if I live, his feigned ecstasies
Shall be no shelter to these outrages;
But he and his shall know that justice lives
In Saturninus' health; whom, if she sleep,
He'll so awake as he in fury shall
Cut off the proud'st conspirator that lives.

TAMORA. My gracious lord, my lovely Saturnine,
Lord of my life, commander of my thoughts,
Calm thee, and bear the faults of Titus' age,
Th' effects of sorrow for his valiant sons
Whose loss hath pierc'd him deep and scarr'd his heart;
And rather comfort his distressed plight
Than prosecute the meanest or the best
For these contempts. [*Aside*] Why, thus it shall become
High-witted Tamora to gloze with all.
But, Titus, I have touch'd thee to the quick,
Thy life-blood out; if Aaron now be wise,
Then is all safe, the anchor in the port.

Enter CLOWN

How now, good fellow! Wouldst thou speak with us?

CLOWN. Yes, forsooth, an your mistriship be Emperial.

TAMORA. Empress I am, but yonder sits the Emperor.

CLOWN. 'Tis he.–God and Saint Stephen give you godden. I have brought you a letter and a couple of pigeons here.

[SATURNINUS *reads the letter*]

SATURNINUS. Go take him away, and hang him presently.

CLOWN. How much money must I have?

TAMORA. Come, sirrah, you must be hang'd.

CLOWN. Hang'd! by'r lady, then I have brought up a neck to a fair end. [*Exit guarded*]

SATURNINUS. Despiteful and intolerable wrongs!
Shall I endure this monstrous villainy?
I know from whence this same device proceeds.
May this be borne—as if his traitorous sons
That died by law for murder of our brother
Have by my means been butchered wrongfully?
Go drag the villain hither by the hair;
Nor age nor honour shall shape privilege.
For this proud mock I'll be thy slaughterman,
Sly frantic wretch, that holp'st to make me great,
In hope thyself should govern Rome and me.

Enter NUNTIUS ÆMILIUS

What news with thee, Æmilius?

ÆMILIUS. Arm, my lords! Rome never had more cause.
The Goths have gathered head; and with a power
Of high resolved men, bent to the spoil,
They hither march amain, under conduct
Of Lucius, son to old Andronicus;
Who threats in course of this revenge to do
As much as ever Coriolanus did.

SATURNINUS. Is warlike Lucius general of the Goths?
These tidings nip me, and I hang the head
As flowers with frost, or grass beat down with storms.
Ay, now begins our sorrows to approach.
'Tis he the common people love so much;
Myself hath often heard them say—
When I have walked like a private man—
That Lucius' banishment was wrongfully,
And they have wish'd that Lucius were their emperor.

TAMORA. Why should you fear? Is not your city strong?

SATURNINUS. Ay, but the citizens favour Lucius,
And will revolt from me to succour him.

TAMORA. King, be thy thoughts imperious like thy name!
Is the sun dimm'd, that gnats do fly in it?

The eagle suffers little birds to sing,
And is not careful what they mean thereby,
Knowing that with the shadow of his wings
He can at pleasure stint their melody;
Even so mayest thou the giddy men of Rome.
Then cheer thy spirit; for know thou, Emperor,
I will enchant the old Andronicus
With words more sweet, and yet more dangerous,
Than baits to fish or honey-stalks to sheep,
When as the one is wounded with the bait,
The other rotted with delicious feed.

SATURNINUS. But he will not entreat his son for us.

TAMORA. If Tamora entreat him, then he will;
For I can smooth and fill his aged ears
With golden promises, that, were his heart
Almost impregnable, his old ears deaf,
Yet should both ear and heart obey my tongue.
[*To* ÆMILIUS] Go thou before to be our ambassador;
Say that the Emperor requests a parley
Of warlike Lucius, and appoint the meeting
Even at his father's house, the old Andronicus.

SATURNINUS. Æmilius, do this message honourably;
And if he stand on hostage for his safety,
Bid him demand what pledge will please him best.

ÆMILIUS. Your bidding shall I do effectually. *Exit*

TAMORA. Now will I to that old Andronicus,
And temper him with all the art I have,
To pluck proud Lucius from the warlike Goths.
And now, sweet Emperor, be blithe again,
And bury all thy fear in my devices.

SATURNINUS. Then go successantly, and plead to him.

Exeunt

ACT V. SCENE 1

Plains near Rome

Enter LUCIUS *with an army of* GOTHS *with drums and colours*

LUCIUS. Approved warriors and my faithful friends,
I have received letters from great Rome
Which signifies what hate they bear their Emperor
And how desirous of our sight they are.
Therefore, great lords, be, as your titles witness,
Imperious and impatient of your wrongs;
And wherein Rome hath done you any scath,
Let him make treble satisfaction.
FIRST GOTH. Brave slip, sprung from the great Andronicus,
Whose name was once our terror, now our comfort,
Whose high exploits and honourable deeds
Ingrateful Rome requites with foul contempt,
Be bold in us: we'll follow where thou lead'st,
Like stinging bees in hottest summer's day,
Led by their master to the flow'red fields,
And be aveng'd on cursed Tamora.
ALL THE GOTHS. And as he saith, so say we all with him.
LUCIUS. I humbly thank him, and I thank you all.
But who comes here, led by a lusty Goth?

Enter a GOTH, *leading* AARON *with his* CHILD *in his arms*

SECOND GOTH. Renowned Lucius, from our troops I stray'd
To gaze upon a ruinous monastery;
And as I earnestly did fix mine eye
Upon the wasted building, suddenly
I heard a child cry underneath a wall.
I made unto the noise, when soon I heard
The crying babe controll'd with this discourse:
'Peace, tawny slave, half me and half thy dam!
Did not thy hue bewray whose brat thou art,
Had nature lent thee but thy mother's look,
Villain, thou mightst have been an emperor;
But where the bull and cow are both milk-white,

They never do beget a coal-black calf.
Peace, villain, peace!'—even thus he rates the babe—
'For I must bear thee to a trusty Goth,
Who, when he knows thou art the Empress' babe,
Will hold thee dearly for thy mother's sake.'
With this, my weapon drawn, I rush'd upon him,
Surpris'd him suddenly, and brought him hither
To use as you think needful of the man.

LUCIUS. O worthy Goth, this is the incarnate devil
That robb'd Andronicus of his good hand;
This is the pearl that pleas'd your Empress' eye;
And here's the base fruit of her burning lust.
Say, wall-ey'd slave, whither wouldst thou convey
This growing image of thy fiend-like face?
Why dost not speak? What, deaf? Not a word?
A halter, soldiers! Hang him on this tree,
And by his side his fruit of bastardy.

AARON. Touch not the boy, he is of royal blood.

LUCIUS. Too like the sire for ever being good.
First hang the child, that he may see it sprawl—
A sight to vex the father's soul withal.
Get me a ladder.

[*A ladder brought, which* AARON *is made to climb*]

AARON. Lucius, save the child,
And bear it from me to the Emperess.
If thou do this, I'll show thee wondrous things
That highly may advantage thee to hear;
If thou wilt not, befall what may befall,
I'll speak no more but 'Vengeance rot you all!'

LUCIUS. Say on; an if it please me which thou speak'st,
Thy child shall live, and I will see it nourish'd.

AARON. An if it please thee! Why, assure thee, Lucius,
'Twill vex thy soul to hear what I shall speak;
For I must talk of murders, rapes, and massacres,
Acts of black night, abominable deeds,
Complots of mischief, treason, villainies,
Ruthful to hear, yet piteously perform'd;
And this shall all be buried in my death,
Unless thou swear to me my child shall live.

LUCIUS. Tell on thy mind; I say thy child shall live.

AARON. Swear that he shall, and then I will begin.
LUCIUS. Who should I swear by? Thou believest no god;
That granted, how canst thou believe an oath?
AARON. What if I do not?—as indeed I do not;
Yet, for I know thou art religious
And hast a thing within thee called conscience,
With twenty popish tricks and ceremonies
Which I have seen thee careful to observe,
Therefore I urge thy oath. For that I know
An idiot holds his bauble for a god,
And keeps the oath which by that god he swears,
To that I'll urge him. Therefore thou shalt vow
By that same god—what god soe'er it be
That thou adorest and hast in reverence—
To save my boy, to nourish and bring him up;
Or else I will discover nought to thee.
LUCIUS. Even by my god I swear to thee I will.
AARON. First know thou, I begot him on the Empress.
LUCIUS. O most insatiate and luxurious woman!
AARON. Tut, Lucius, this was but a deed of charity
To that which thou shalt hear of me anon.
'Twas her two sons that murdered Bassianus;
They cut thy sister's tongue, and ravish'd her,
And cut her hands, and trimm'd her as thou sawest.
LUCIUS. O detestable villain! Call'st thou that trimming?
AARON. Why, she was wash'd, and cut, and trimm'd, and 'twas
Trim sport for them which had the doing of it.
LUCIUS. O barbarous beastly villains like thyself!
AARON. Indeed, I was their tutor to instruct them.
That codding spirit had they from their mother,
As sure a card as ever won the set;
That bloody mind, I think, they learn'd of me,
As true a dog as ever fought at head.
Well, let my deeds be witness of my worth.
I train'd thy brethren to that guileful hole
Where the dead corpse of Bassianus lay;
I wrote the letter that thy father found,
And hid the gold within that letter mention'd,
Confederate with the Queen and her two sons;

And what not done, that thou hast cause to rue,
Wherein I had no stroke of mischief in it?
I play'd the cheater for thy father's hand,
And, when I had it, drew myself apart
And almost broke my heart with extreme laughter.
I pried me through the crevice of a wall,
When, for his hand, he had his two sons' heads;
Beheld his tears, and laugh'd so heartily
That both mine eyes were rainy like to his;
And when I told the Empress of this sport,
She swooned almost at my pleasing tale,
And for my tidings gave me twenty kisses.

GOTH. What, canst thou say all this and never blush?

AARON. Ay, like a black dog, as the saying is.

LUCIUS. Art thou not sorry for these heinous deeds?

AARON. Ay, that I had not done a thousand more.
Even now I curse the day—and yet, I think,
Few come within the compass of my curse—
Wherein I did not some notorious ill:
As kill a man, or else devise his death;
Ravish a maid, or plot the way to do it;
Accuse some innocent, and forswear myself;
Set deadly enmity between two friends;
Make poor men's cattle break their necks;
Set fire on barns and hay-stacks in the night,
And bid the owners quench them with their tears.
Oft have I digg'd up dead men from their graves,
And set them upright at their dear friends' door
Even when their sorrows almost was forgot,
And on their skins, as on the bark of trees,
Have with my knife carved in Roman letters
'Let not your sorrow die, though I am dead.'
Tut, I have done a thousand dreadful things
As willingly as one would kill a fly;
And nothing grieves me heartily indeed
But that I cannot do ten thousand more.

LUCIUS. Bring down the devil, for he must not die
So sweet a death as hanging presently.

AARON. If there be devils, would I were a devil,
To live and burn in everlasting fire,

So I might have your company in hell
But to torment you with my bitter tongue!
LUCIUS. Sirs, stop his mouth, and let him speak no more.

Enter ÆMILIUS

GOTH. My lord, there is a messenger from Rome
Desires to be admitted to your presence.
LUCIUS. Let him come near.
Welcome, Æmilius. What's the news from Rome?
ÆMILIUS. Lord Lucius, and you Princes of the Goths,
The Roman Emperor greets you all by me;
And, for he understands you are in arms,
He craves a parley at your father's house,
Willing you to demand your hostages,
And they shall be immediately deliver'd.
FIRST GOTH. What says our general?
LUCIUS. Æmilius, let the Emperor give his pledges
Unto my father and my uncle Marcus.
And we will come. March away. *Exeunt*

SCENE 2

Rome. Before TITUS' *house*

Enter TAMORA, *and her two sons,* DEMETRIUS *and* CHIRON, *disguised*

TAMORA. Thus, in this strange and sad habiliment,
I will encounter with Andronicus,
And say I am Revenge, sent from below
To join with him and right his heinous wrongs.
Knock at his study, where they say he keeps
To ruminate strange plots of dire revenge;
Tell him Revenge is come to join with him,
And work confusion on his enemies.

They knock, and TITUS *opens his study door, above*

TITUS. Who doth molest my contemplation?
Is it your trick to make me ope the door,
That so my sad decrees may fly away

And all my study be to no effect?
You are deceiv'd; for what I mean to do
See here in bloody lines I have set down;
And what is written shall be executed.

TAMORA. Titus, I am come to talk with thee.

TITUS. No, not a word. How can I grace my talk,
Wanting a hand to give it that accord?
Thou hast the odds of me; therefore no more.

TAMORA. If thou didst know me, thou wouldst talk with me.

TITUS. I am not mad, I know thee well enough:
Witness this wretched stump, witness these crimson lines;
Witness these trenches made by grief and care;
Witness the tiring day and heavy night;
Witness all sorrow that I know thee well
For our proud Empress, mighty Tamora.
Is not thy coming for my other hand?

TAMORA. Know thou, sad man, I am not Tamora:
She is thy enemy and I thy friend.
I am Revenge, sent from th' infernal kingdom
To ease the gnawing vulture of thy mind
By working wreakful vengeance on thy foes.
Come down and welcome me to this world's light;
Confer with me of murder and of death;
There's not a hollow cave or lurking-place,
No vast obscurity or misty vale,
Where bloody murder or detested rape
Can couch for fear but I will find them out;
And in their ears tell them my dreadful name—
Revenge, which makes the foul offender quake.

TITUS. Art thou Revenge? and art thou sent to me
To be a torment to mine enemies?

TAMORA. I am; therefore come down and welcome me.

TITUS. Do me some service ere I come to thee.
Lo, by thy side where Rape and Murder stands;
Now give some surance that thou art Revenge—
Stab them, or tear them on thy chariot wheels;
And then I'll come and be thy waggoner
And whirl along with thee about the globes.
Provide thee two proper palfreys, black as jet,

To hale thy vengeful waggon swift away,
And find out murderers in their guilty caves;
And when thy car is loaden with their heads,
I will dismount, and by thy waggon wheel
Trot, like a servile footman, all day long,
Even from Hyperion's rising in the east
Until his very downfall in the sea.
And day by day I'll do this heavy task,
So thou destroy Rapine and Murder there.

TAMORA. These are my ministers, and come with me.

TITUS. Are they thy ministers? What are they call'd?

TAMORA. Rape and Murder; therefore called so
'Cause they take vengeance of such kind of men.

TITUS. Good Lord, how like the Empress' sons they are!
And you the Empress! But we worldly men
Have miserable, mad, mistaking eyes.
O sweet Revenge, now do I come to thee;
And, if one arm's embracement will content thee,
I will embrace thee in it by and by.

TAMORA. This closing with him fits his lunacy.
Whate'er I forge to feed his brain-sick humours,
Do you uphold and maintain in your speeches,
For now he firmly takes me for Revenge;
And, being credulous in this mad thought,
I'll make him send for Lucius his son,
And whilst I at a banquet hold him sure,
I'll find some cunning practice out of hand
To scatter and disperse the giddy Goths,
Or, at the least, make them his enemies.
See, here he comes, and I must ply my theme.

Enter TITUS, *below*

TITUS. Long have I been forlorn, and all for thee.
Welcome, dread Fury, to my woeful house.
Rapine and Murder, you are welcome too.
How like the Empress and her sons you are!
Well are you fitted, had you but a Moor.
Could not all hell afford you such a devil?
For well I wot the Empress never wags
But in her company there is a Moor;

And, would you represent our queen aright,
It were convenient you had such a devil.
But welcome as you are. What shall we do?
TAMORA. What wouldst thou have us do, Andronicus?
DEMETRIUS. Show me a murderer, I'll deal with him.
CHIRON. Show me a villain that hath done a rape,
And I am sent to be reveng'd on him.
TAMORA. Show me a thousand that hath done thee wrong,
And I will be revenged on them all.
TITUS. Look round about the wicked streets of Rome,
And when thou find'st a man that's like thyself,
Good Murder, stab him; he's a murderer.
Go thou with him, and when it is thy hap
To find another that is like to thee,
Good Rapine, stab him; he is a ravisher.
Go thou with them; and in the Emperor's court
There is a queen, attended by a Moor;
Well shalt thou know her by thine own proportion,
For up and down she doth resemble thee.
I pray thee, do on them some violent death;
They have been violent to me and mine.
TAMORA. Well hast thou lesson'd us; this shall we do.
But would it please thee, good Andronicus,
To send for Lucius, thy thrice-valiant son,
Who leads towards Rome a band of warlike Goths,
And bid him come and banquet at thy house;
When he is here, even at thy solemn feast,
I will bring in the Empress and her sons,
The Emperor himself, and all thy foes;
And at thy mercy shall they stoop and kneel,
And on them shalt thou ease thy angry heart.
What says Andronicus to this device?
TITUS. Marcus, my brother! 'Tis sad Titus calls.

Enter MARCUS

Go, gentle Marcus, to thy nephew Lucius;
Thou shalt inquire him out among the Goths.
Bid him repair to me, and bring with him
Some of the chiefest princes of the Goths;
Bid him encamp his soldiers where they are.

Tell him the Emperor and the Empress too
Feast at my house, and he shall feast with them.
This do thou for my love; and so let him,
As he regards his aged father's life.

MARCUS. This will I do, and soon return again. *Exit*

TAMORA. Now will I hence about thy business,
And take my ministers along with me.

TITUS. Nay, nay, let Rape and Murder stay with me,
Or else I'll call my brother back again,
And cleave to no revenge but Lucius.

TAMORA. [*Aside to her sons*] What say you, boys? Will you abide with him,
Whiles I go tell my lord the Emperor
How I have govern'd our determin'd jest?
Yield to his humour, smooth and speak him fair,
And tarry with him till I turn again.

TITUS. [*Aside*] I knew them all, though they suppos'd me mad,
And will o'er-reach them in their own devices,
A pair of cursed hell-hounds and their dam.

DEMETRIUS. Madam, depart at pleasure; leave us here.

TAMORA. Farewell, Andronicus, Revenge now goes
To lay a complot to betray thy foes.

TITUS. I know thou dost; and, sweet Revenge, farewell.
Exit TAMORA

CHIRON. Tell us, old man, how shall we be employ'd?

TITUS. Tut, I have work enough for you to do.
Publius, come hither, Caius, and Valentine.

Enter PUBLIUS, CAIUS, *and* VALENTINE

PUBLIUS. What is your will?

TITUS. Know you these two?

PUBLIUS. The Empress' sons, I take them: Chiron, Demetrius.

TITUS. Fie, Publius, fie! thou art too much deceiv'd.
The one is Murder, and Rape is the other's name;
And therefore bind them, gentle Publius—
Caius and Valentine, lay hands on them.
Oft have you heard me wish for such an hour,
And now I find it; therefore bind them sure,

And stop their mouths if they begin to cry. *Exit*

[*They lay hold on* CHIRON *and* DEMETRIUS]

CHIRON. Villains, forbear! we are the Empress' sons.

PUBLIUS. And therefore do we what we are commanded.
Stop close their mouths, let them not speak a word.
Is he sure bound? Look that you bind them fast.

Re-enter TITUS ANDRONICUS *with a knife, and* LAVINIA *with a basin*

TITUS. Come, come, Lavinia; look, thy foes are bound.
Sirs, stop their mouths, let them not speak to me;
But let them hear what fearful words I utter.
O villains, Chiron and Demetrius!
Here stands the spring whom you have stain'd with mud;
This goodly summer with your winter mix'd.
You kill'd her husband; and for that vile fault
Two of her brothers were condemn'd to death,
My hand cut off and made a merry jest;
Both her sweet hands, her tongue, and that more dear
Than hands or tongue, her spotless chastity,
Inhuman traitors, you constrain'd and forc'd.
What would you say, if I should let you speak?
Villains, for shame you could not beg for grace.
Hark, wretches! how I mean to martyr you.
This one hand yet is left to cut your throats,
Whiles that Lavinia 'tween her stumps doth hold
The basin that receives your guilty blood.
You know your mother means to feast with me,
And calls herself Revenge, and thinks me mad.
Hark, villains! I will grind your bones to dust,
And with your blood and it I'll make a paste;
And of the paste a coffin I will rear,
And make two pasties of your shameful heads;
And bid that strumpet, your unhallowed dam,
Like to the earth, swallow her own increase.
This is the feast that I have bid her to,
And this the banquet she shall surfeit on;
For worse than Philomel you us'd my daughter,
And worse than Progne I will be reveng'd.
And now prepare your throats. Lavinia, come,

Receive the blood; and when that they are dead,
Let me go grind their bones to powder small,
And with this hateful liquor temper it;
And in that paste let their vile heads be bak'd.
Come, come, be every one officious
To make this banquet, which I wish may prove
More stern and bloody than the Centaurs' feast.

[*He cuts their throats*]

So.
Now bring them in, for I will play the cook,
And see them ready against their mother comes.

Exeunt, bearing the dead bodies

SCENE 3

The court of TITUS' *house*

Enter LUCIUS, MARCUS, *and the* GOTHS, *with* AARON *prisoner, and his* CHILD *in the arms of an attendant*

LUCIUS. Uncle Marcus, since 'tis my father's mind
That I repair to Rome, I am content.
FIRST GOTH. And ours with thine, befall what fortune will.
LUCIUS. Good uncle, take you in this barbarous Moor,
This ravenous tiger, this accursed devil;
Let him receive no sust'nance, fetter him,
Till he be brought unto the Empress' face
For testimony of her foul proceedings.
And see the ambush of our friends be strong;
I fear the Emperor means no good to us.
AARON. Some devil whisper curses in my ear,
And prompt me that my tongue may utter forth
The venomous malice of my swelling heart!
LUCIUS. Away, inhuman dog, unhallowed slave!
Sirs, help our uncle to convey him in.

Exeunt GOTHS *with* AARON. *Flourish within*

The trumpets show the Emperor is at hand.

Sound trumpets. Enter SATURNINUS *and* TAMORA, *with* ÆMILIUS, TRIBUNES, SENATORS, *and others*

SATURNINUS. What, hath the firmament more suns than one?
LUCIUS. What boots it thee to call thyself a sun?
MARCUS. Rome's Emperor, and nephew, break the parle;
These quarrels must be quietly debated.
The feast is ready which the careful Titus
Hath ordain'd to an honourable end,
For peace, for love, for league, and good to Rome.
Please you, therefore, draw nigh and take your places.
SATURNINUS. Marcus, we will.
[*A table brought in. The company sit down*]

Trumpets sounding, enter TITUS *like a cook, placing the dishes, and* LAVINIA *with a veil over her face; also* YOUNG LUCIUS, *and others*

TITUS. Welcome, my lord; welcome, dread Queen;
Welcome, ye warlike Goths; welcome, Lucius;
And welcome all. Although the cheer be poor,
'Twill fill your stomachs; please you eat of it.
SATURNINUS. Why art thou thus attir'd, Andronicus?
TITUS. Because I would be sure to have all well
To entertain your Highness and your Empress.
TAMORA. We are beholding to you, good Andronicus.
TITUS. An if your Highness knew my heart, you were.
My lord the Emperor, resolve me this:
Was it well done of rash Virginius
To slay his daughter with his own right hand,
Because she was enforc'd, stain'd, and deflower'd?
SATURNINUS. It was, Andronicus.
TITUS. Your reason, mighty lord.
SATURNINUS. Because the girl should not survive her shame,
And by her presence still renew his sorrows.
TITUS. A reason mighty, strong, and effectual;
A pattern, precedent, and lively warrant
For me, most wretched, to perform the like.
Die, die, Lavinia, and thy shame with thee; [*He kills her*]
And with thy shame thy father's sorrow die!
SATURNINUS. What hast thou done, unnatural and unkind?
TITUS. Kill'd her for whom my tears have made me blind.
I am as woeful as Virginius was,
And have a thousand times more cause than he

To do this outrage; and it now is done.
SATURNINUS. What, was she ravish'd? Tell who did the deed.
TITUS. Will't please you eat? Will't please your Highness feed?
TAMORA. Why hast thou slain thine only daughter thus?
TITUS. Not I; 'twas Chiron and Demetrius.
They ravish'd her, and cut away her tongue;
And they, 'twas they, that did her all this wrong.
SATURNINUS. Go, fetch them hither to us presently.
TITUS. Why, there they are, both baked in this pie,
Whereof their mother daintily hath fed,
Eating the flesh that she herself hath bred.
'Tis true, 'tis true: witness my knife's sharp point.
[*He stabs the* EMPRESS]
SATURNINUS. Die, frantic wretch, for this accursed deed!
[*He stabs* TITUS]
LUCIUS. Can the son's eye behold his father bleed?
There's meed for meed, death for a deadly deed.
[*He stabs* SATURNINUS. *A great tumult.* LUCIUS, MARCUS, *and their friends go up into the balcony*]
MARCUS. You sad-fac'd men, people and sons of Rome,
By uproars sever'd, as a flight of fowl
Scatter'd by winds and high tempestuous gusts,
O, let me teach you how to knit again
This scattered corn into one mutual sheaf,
These broken limbs again into one body;
Lest Rome herself be bane unto herself,
And she whom mighty kingdoms curtsy to,
Like a forlorn and desperate castaway,
Do shameful execution on herself.
But if my frosty signs and chaps of age,
Grave witnesses of true experience,
Cannot induce you to attend my words,
[*To* LUCIUS] Speak, Rome's dear friend, as erst our ancestor,
When with his solemn tongue he did discourse
To love-sick Dido's sad attending ear
The story of that baleful burning night,
When subtle Greeks surpris'd King Priam's Troy.
Tell us what Sinon hath bewitch'd our ears,

Or who hath brought the fatal engine in
That gives our Troy, our Rome, the civil wound.
My heart is not compact of flint nor steel;
Nor can I utter all our bitter grief,
But floods of tears will drown my oratory
And break my utt'rance, even in the time
When it should move ye to attend me most,
And force you to commiseration.
Here's Rome's young Captain, let him tell the tale;
While I stand by and weep to hear him speak.

LUCIUS. Then, gracious auditory, be it known to you
That Chiron and the damn'd Demetrius
Were they that murd'red our Emperor's brother;
And they it were that ravished our sister.
For their fell faults our brothers were beheaded,
Our father's tears despis'd, and basely cozen'd
Of that true hand that fought Rome's quarrel out
And sent her enemies unto the grave.
Lastly, myself unkindly banished,
The gates shut on me, and turn'd weeping out,
To beg relief among Rome's enemies;
Who drown'd their enmity in my true tears,
And op'd their arms to embrace me as a friend.
I am the turned forth, be it known to you,
That have preserv'd her welfare in my blood
And from her bosom took the enemy's point,
Sheathing the steel in my advent'rous body.
Alas! you know I am no vaunter, I;
My scars can witness, dumb although they are,
That my report is just and full of truth.
But, soft! methinks I do digress too much,
Citing my worthless praise. O, pardon me!
For when no friends are by, men praise themselves.

MARCUS. Now is my turn to speak. Behold the child.
[*Pointing to the* CHILD *in an attendant's arms*]
Of this was Tamora delivered,
The issue of an irreligious Moor,
Chief architect and plotter of these woes.
The villain is alive in Titus' house,
Damn'd as he is, to witness this is true.

Now judge what cause had Titus to revenge
These wrongs unspeakable, past patience,
Or more than any living man could bear.
Now have you heard the truth: what say you, Romans?
Have we done aught amiss, show us wherein,
And, from the place where you behold us pleading,
The poor remainder of Andronici
Will, hand in hand, all headlong hurl ourselves,
And on the ragged stones beat forth our souls,
And make a mutual closure of our house.
Speak, Romans, speak; and if you say we shall,
Lo, hand in hand, Lucius and I will fall.

ÆMILIUS. Come, come, thou reverend man of Rome,
And bring our Emperor gently in thy hand,
Lucius our Emperor; for well I know
The common voice do cry it shall be so.

ALL. Lucius, all hail, Rome's royal Emperor!

MARCUS. Go, go into old Titus' sorrowful house,
And hither hale that misbelieving Moor
To be adjudg'd some direful slaught'ring death,
As punishment for his most wicked life. *Exeunt some attendants.* LUCIUS, MARCUS, *and the others descend*

ALL. Lucius, all hail, Rome's gracious governor!

LUCIUS. Thanks, gentle Romans! May I govern so
To heal Rome's harms and wipe away her woe!
But, gentle people, give me aim awhile,
For nature puts me to a heavy task.
Stand all aloof; but, uncle, draw you near
To shed obsequious tears upon this trunk.
O, take this warm kiss on thy pale cold lips.
[*Kisses* TITUS]
These sorrowful drops upon thy blood-stain'd face,
The last true duties of thy noble son!

MARCUS. Tear for tear and loving kiss for kiss
Thy brother Marcus tenders on thy lips.
O, were the sum of these that I should pay
Countless and infinite, yet would I pay them!

LUCIUS. Come hither, boy; come, come, and learn of us
To melt in showers. Thy grandsire lov'd thee well;
Many a time he danc'd thee on his knee,

Sung thee asleep, his loving breast thy pillow;
Many a story hath he told to thee,
And bid thee bear his pretty tales in mind
And talk of them when he was dead and gone.

MARCUS. How many thousand times hath these poor lips,
When they were living, warm'd themselves on thine!
O, now, sweet boy, give them their latest kiss!
Bid him farewell; commit him to the grave;
Do them that kindness, and take leave of them.

BOY. O grandsire, grandsire! ev'n with all my heart
Would I were dead, so you did live again!
O Lord, I cannot speak to him for weeping;
My tears will choke me, if I ope my mouth.

Re-enter attendants with AARON

A ROMAN. You sad Andronici, have done with woes;
Give sentence on the execrable wretch
That hath been breeder of these dire events.

LUCIUS. Set him breast-deep in earth, and famish him;
There let him stand and rave and cry for food.
If any one relieves or pities him,
For the offence he dies. This is our doom.
Some stay to see him fast'ned in the earth.

AARON. Ah, why should wrath be mute and fury dumb?
I am no baby, I, that with base prayers
I should repent the evils I have done;
Ten thousand worse than ever yet I did
Would I perform, if I might have my will.
If one good deed in all my life I did,
I do repent it from my very soul.

LUCIUS. Some loving friends convey the Emperor hence,
And give him burial in his father's grave.
My father and Lavinia shall forthwith
Be closed in our household's monument.
As for that ravenous tiger, Tamora,
No funeral rite, nor man in mourning weed,
No mournful bell shall ring her burial;
But throw her forth to beasts and birds to prey.
Her life was beastly and devoid of pity,
And being dead, let birds on her take pity. *Exeunt*

The Tragedy of Romeo and Juliet

ROMEO AND JULIET

LIKE SOME OTHER of Shakespeare's plays founded on novels, *Romeo and Juliet* is the final term in a long series of versions of the story from which the plot is constructed. Unlike, however, his practice at times elsewhere Shakespeare's borrowings here are confined almost entirely to one immediate source; yet even here it would be untrue to say that Shakespeare contented himself with borrowing a plot and making his individual contribution solely in the delineation of the characters. He alters the details of the story in order to devise a plot that will, together with the new and heightened vitality he gives the characters, enable him to achieve the fullest development of his theme. Yet even in *Romeo and Juliet* some of the deviations from his immediate source may have been suggested to him by his reading of a much earlier version of the story.

Shakespeare's main source is Arthur Brooke's *Romeus and Juliet*, described on the title-page as a 'tragical history' which was 'written first in Italian by Bandell, and now in English by Ar. Br.' Matteo Bandello published his novella *Romeo e Giulietta* in 1554, less than ten years before Brooke's metrical version of 1562; Brooke, however, used an intermediate version in French which Pierre Boaistuau adapted from Bandello in 1559. It was from this same French version that William Painter made his translation *Rhomeo and Julietta* which he published in his *Palace of Pleasure*, the second volume, in 1567.

Many of the features of the story can be paralleled in earlier accounts of the adventures of lovers; the sleeping potion is a very ancient device, and the mistake that wrecks the successful issue of the love story is found in diverse forms. The author who first gave the lovers the names by which the world now knows them and the rival houses their familiar appellations was Luigi da Porto in his *Giulietta e Romeo*, published in 1530 or so. The lovers' names he seems to have hit on by himself; the Capulets and Montagues however he borrowed from Dante, who in the *Purgatorio*, vi, 106-8, makes Sordello the troubadour upbraid the emperor for failing to restore order in Italy. Vernon translates:

> Come and see the Montagus and Capulets, the Monaldi and the Filippeschi, thou heedless man, those already sad (*i.e.*, banished and ruined), and those in dread (of becoming so).

Here Dante contrasts the factions already destroyed in former quarrels with those still engaged in mutual destruction. The Monaldi and Filippeschi were apparently warring parties in Orvieto; but the Montagues and the Capulets had belonged to Verona and Cremona respectively and were cited as factions that had been exterminated, not as rivals. Luigi da Porto took over from some commentator the notion that the Montagues and the Capulets were both of Verona and at odds with one another, and made them part of the story.

It is convenient to halt at da Porto the regress into a remoter age to which a study of the motifs of the Romeo-and-Juliet story eventually leads, for it was to da Porto's version that a recent student of the legend (Olin H. Moore: *The Legend of Romeo and Juliet*) thinks Shakespeare had recourse as he refashioned the details of Arthur Brooke's version.

The Argument which Brooke set out before his poem might seem to cover all except one of the features of Shakespeare's play:

Love hath inflaméd twain by sudden sight,
  And both do grant the thing that both desire.
  They wed in shrift by counsel of a friar.
  Young Romeus climbs fair Juliet's bower by night.
Three months he doth enjoy his chief delight.
  By Tybalt's rage provokéd into ire,
  He payeth death to Tybalt for his hire.
  A banished man he 'scapes by secret flight.
New marriage is offered to his wife.
  She drinks a drink that seems to reave her breath:
  They bury her that sleeping yet hath life.
Her husband hears the tidings of her death.
  He drinks his bane. And she with Romeus' knife,
When she awakes, herself, alas! she slay'th.

In Shakespeare the action is compressed into five or six days; otherwise Brooke might be summarizing the play. Shakespeare, however, has by a number of important refinements, some of which suggest that he had considered da Porto's version, adjusted the plot to the conception he has formed of his characters, who are, it need hardly be said, more human and lifelike in every way than those of his sources. Perhaps the most important of these adjustments is the central place in the action he gives to the fatal encounter between Romeo and Tybalt. In Brooke's poem the first mention of Tybalt is at the brawl where he is killed by Romeo; Brooke makes it clear that it was Tybalt's zeal for fighting that forced Romeo to deal with him, and this characteristic of Tybalt Shakespeare develops, preparing for the crisis of the action by introducing Tybalt on two occasions prior to the fight, on each occasion, in the opening scene and at the banquet, as the deliberate trouble-maker who finds in the traditional feud an excuse for his quarrelsome disposition and bad blood.

Many commentators have criticized the play as not conforming to the pattern to which they insist a dramatist must cut his tragedy. Where, they ask, is the tragic flaw? And they are faced with the dilemma of declaring that the sudden and mutual love of Romeo and Juliet is, if not a flaw in itself, at least a disregard of the *convenances* prescribed by the visiting terms on which their families stand, and so the cause of the disaster, or, on the other hand of supposing that the play is not really a tragedy at all and that in spite of the untimely deaths of so many young and promising citizens. The attempt to escape this dilemma by representing the families and not their children as the leading characters, and by making their feud the tragic flaw that leads to the death of their children, attributes our interest in the picture to the background and not to the figures which it merely accommodates.

CHORUS
ESCALUS, *Prince of Verona*
PARIS, *a young nobleman, kinsman to the Prince*
MONTAGUE } *heads of two houses at variance with each other*
CAPULET }
AN OLD MAN, *of the Capulet family*
ROMEO, *son to Montague*
MERCUTIO, *kinsman to the Prince, and friend to Romeo*
BENVOLIO, *nephew to Montague, and friend to Romeo*
TYBALT, *nephew to Lady Capulet*
FRIAR LAWRENCE } *Franciscans*
FRIAR JOHN }
BALTHASAR, *servant to Romeo*
SAMPSON } *servants to Capulet*
GREGORY }
PETER, *servant to Juliet's nurse*
ABRAHAM, *servant to Montague*
AN APOTHECARY
THREE MUSICIANS
AN OFFICER

LADY MONTAGUE, *wife to Montague*
LADY CAPULET, *wife to Capulet*
JULIET, *daughter to Capulet*
NURSE *to Juliet*

Citizens of Verona; Gentlemen *and* Gentlewomen *of both houses;* Maskers, Torchbearers, Pages, Guards, Watchmen, Servants, *and* Attendants

SCENE:

Verona and Mantua

Romeo and Juliet

THE PROLOGUE

Enter CHORUS

Two households, both alike in dignity,
In fair Verona, where we lay our scene,
From ancient grudge break to new mutiny,
Where civil blood makes civil hands unclean.
From forth the fatal loins of these two foes
A pair of star-cross'd lovers take their life;
Whose misadventur'd piteous overthrows
Doth with their death bury their parents' strife.
The fearful passage of their death-mark'd love,
And the continuance of their parents' rage,
Which, but their children's end, nought could remove,
Is now the two hours' traffic of our stage;
The which if you with patient ears attend,
What here shall miss, our toil shall strive to mend. *Exit*

ACT I. SCENE 1

Verona. A public place

Enter SAMPSON *and* GREGORY, *of the house of* CAPULET, *with swords and bucklers on*

SAMPSON. Gregory, on my word, we'll not carry coals.
GREGORY. No, for then we should be colliers.
SAMPSON. I mean, an we be in choler, we'll draw.
GREGORY. Ay, while you live, draw your neck out of collar.
SAMPSON. I strike quickly, being moved.
GREGORY. But thou art not quickly moved to strike.
SAMPSON. A dog of the house of Montague moves me.

GREGORY. To move is to stir, and to be valiant is to stand; therefore, if thou art moved, thou run'st away.

SAMPSON. A dog of that house shall move me to stand. I will take the wall of any man or maid of Montague's.

GREGORY. That shows thee a weak slave; for the weakest goes to the wall.

SAMPSON. 'Tis true; and therefore women, being the weaker vessels, are ever thrust to the wall; therefore I will push Montague's men from the wall and thrust his maids to the wall.

GREGORY. The quarrel is between our masters and us their men.

SAMPSON. 'Tis all one; I will show myself a tyrant. When I have fought with the men, I will be civil with the maids—I will cut off their heads.

GREGORY. The heads of the maids?

SAMPSON. Ay, the heads of the maids, or their maidenheads; take it in what sense thou wilt.

GREGORY. They must take it in sense that feel it.

SAMPSON. Me they shall feel while I am able to stand; and 'tis known I am a pretty piece of flesh.

GREGORY. 'Tis well thou art not fish; if thou hadst, thou hadst been poor-John. Draw thy tool; here comes two of the house of Montagues.

Enter two other servingmen, ABRAHAM *and* BALTHASAR

SAMPSON. My naked weapon is out; quarrel, I will back thee.

GREGORY. How? turn thy back and run?

SAMPSON. Fear me not.

GREGORY. No, marry; I fear thee!

SAMPSON. Let us take the law of our sides; let them begin.

GREGORY. I will frown as I pass by, and let them take it as they list.

SAMPSON. Nay, as they dare. I will bite my thumb at them, which is disgrace to them if they bear it.

ABRAHAM. Do you bite your thumb at us, sir?

SAMPSON. I do bite my thumb, sir.

ABRAHAM. Do you bite your thumb at us, sir?

SAMPSON. [*Aside to* GREGORY] Is the law of our side, if I say ay?

GREGORY. [*Aside to* SAMPSON] No.

SAMPSON. No, sir, I do not bite my thumb at you, sir; but I bite my thumb, sir.

GREGORY. Do you quarrel, sir?

ABRAHAM. Quarrel, sir! No, sir.

SAMPSON. But if you do, sir, I am for you. I serve as good a man as you.

ABRAHAM. No better?

SAMPSON. Well, sir.

Enter BENVOLIO

GREGORY. [*Aside to* SAMPSON] Say 'better'; here comes one of my master's kinsmen.

SAMPSON. Yes, better, sir.

ABRAHAM. You lie.

SAMPSON. Draw, if you be men. Gregory, remember thy swashing blow. [*They fight*]

BENVOLIO. Part, fools! [*Beats down their swords*]
Put up your swords; you know not what you do.

Enter TYBALT

TYBALT. What, art thou drawn among these heartless hinds?
Turn thee, Benvolio; look upon thy death.

BENVOLIO. I do but keep the peace; put up thy sword,
Or manage it to part these men with me.

TYBALT. What, drawn, and talk of peace! I hate the word,
As I hate hell, all Montagues, and thee.
Have at thee, coward! [*They fight*]

Enter an OFFICER, *and three or four citizens with clubs or partisans*

OFFICER. Clubs, bills, and partisans! Strike; beat them down.

CITIZENS. Down with the Capulets! Down with the Montagues!

Enter OLD CAPULET *in his gown, and his* WIFE

CAPULET. What noise is this? Give me my long sword, ho!

LADY CAPULET. A crutch, a crutch! Why call you for a sword?

CAPULET. My sword, I say! Old Montague is come,

And flourishes his blade in spite of me.

Enter OLD MONTAGUE *and his* WIFE

MONTAGUE. Thou villain Capulet!—Hold me not, let me go.
LADY MONTAGUE. Thou shalt not stir one foot to seek a foe.

Enter PRINCE ESCALUS, *with his train*

PRINCE. Rebellious subjects, enemies to peace,
Profaners of this neighbour-stained steel—
Will they not hear? What, ho! you men, you beasts,
That quench the fire of your pernicious rage
With purple fountains issuing from your veins!
On pain of torture, from those bloody hands
Throw your mistempered weapons to the ground,
And hear the sentence of your moved prince.
Three civil brawls, bred of an airy word,
By thee, old Capulet, and Montague,
Have thrice disturb'd the quiet of our streets
And made Verona's ancient citizens
Cast by their grave beseeming ornaments
To wield old partisans, in hands as old,
Cank'red with peace, to part your cank'red hate.
If ever you disturb our streets again,
Your lives shall pay the forfeit of the peace.
For this time all the rest depart away.
You, Capulet, shall go along with me;
And, Montague, come you this afternoon,
To know our farther pleasure in this case,
To old Free-town, our common judgment-place.
Once more, on pain of death, all men depart.

Exeunt all but MONTAGUE, *his* WIFE, *and* BENVOLIO

MONTAGUE. Who set this ancient quarrel new abroach?
Speak, nephew; were you by when it began?
BENVOLIO. Here were the servants of your adversary
And yours, close fighting ere I did approach.
I drew to part them; in the instant came
The fiery Tybalt, with his sword prepar'd;
Which, as he breath'd defiance to my ears,
He swung about his head and cut the winds,
Who, nothing hurt withal, hiss'd him in scorn.

While we were interchanging thrusts and blows,
Came more and more, and fought on part and part,
Till the Prince came, who parted either part.

LADY MONTAGUE. O, where is Romeo? Saw you him today?
Right glad I am he was not at this fray.

BENVOLIO. Madam, an hour before the worshipp'd sun
Peer'd forth the golden window of the east,
A troubled mind drew me to walk abroad;
Where, underneath the grove of sycamore
That westward rooteth from this city side,
So early walking did I see your son.
Towards him I made; but he was ware of me
And stole into the covert of the wood.
I, measuring his affections by my own,
Which then most sought where most might not be found,
Being one too many by my weary self,
Pursu'd my humour, not pursuing his,
And gladly shunn'd who gladly fled from me.

MONTAGUE. Many a morning hath he there been seen,
With tears augmenting the fresh morning's dew,
Adding to clouds more clouds with his deep sighs;
But all so soon as the all-cheering sun
Should in the farthest east begin to draw
The shady curtains from Aurora's bed,
Away from light steals home my heavy son,
And private in his chamber pens himself,
Shuts up his windows, locks fair daylight out,
And makes himself an artificial night.
Black and portentous must his humour prove,
Unless good counsel may the cause remove.

BENVOLIO. My noble uncle, do you know the cause?

MONTAGUE. I neither know it nor can learn of him.

BENVOLIO. Have you importun'd him by any means?

MONTAGUE. Both by myself and many other friends.
But he, his own affections' counsellor,
Is to himself—I will not say how true;
But to himself so secret and so close,
So far from sounding and discovery,
As is the bud bit with an envious worm,
Ere he can spread his sweet leaves to the air,

Or dedicate his beauty to the sun.
Could we but learn from whence his sorrows grow,
We would as willingly give cure as know.

Enter Romeo

Benvolio. See where he comes. So please you step aside;
I'll know his grievance or be much denied.
Montague. I would thou wert so happy by thy stay
To hear true shrift. Come, madam, let's away.
Exeunt Montague *and his* Wife
Benvolio. Good morrow, cousin.
Romeo. Is the day so young?
Benvolio. But new struck nine.
Romeo. Ay me! sad hours seem long.
Was that my father that went hence so fast?
Benvolio. It was. What sadness lengthens Romeo's hours?
Romeo. Not having that which having makes them short.
Benvolio. In love?
Romeo. Out–
Benvolio. Of love?
Romeo. Out of her favour where I am in love.
Benvolio. Alas that love, so gentle in his view,
Should be so tyrannous and rough in proof!
Romeo. Alas that love, whose view is muffled still,
Should without eyes see pathways to his will!
Where shall we dine? O me! What fray was here?
Yet tell me not, for I have heard it all.
Here's much to do with hate, but more with love.
Why then, O brawling love! O loving hate!
O anything, of nothing first create!
O heavy lightness! serious vanity!
Mis-shapen chaos of well-seeming forms!
Feather of lead, bright smoke, cold fire, sick health!
Still-waking sleep, that is not what it is!
This love feel I, that feel no love in this.
Dost thou not laugh?
Benvolio. No, coz, I rather weep.
Romeo. Good heart, at what?
Benvolio. At thy good heart's oppression.
Romeo. Why, such is love's transgression.

Griefs of mine own lie heavy in my breast,
Which thou wilt propagate, to have it prest
With more of thine. This love that thou hast shown
Doth add more grief to too much of mine own.
Love is a smoke rais'd with the fume of sighs;
Being purg'd, a fire sparkling in lovers' eyes;
Being vex'd, a sea nourish'd with loving tears.
What is it else? A madness most discreet,
A choking gall, and a preserving sweet.
Farewell, my coz.

BENVOLIO. Soft! I will go along;
And if you leave me so, you do me wrong.

ROMEO. Tut, I have lost myself; I am not here:
This is not Romeo, he's some other where.

BENVOLIO. Tell me in sadness who is that you love.

ROMEO. What, shall I groan and tell thee?

BENVOLIO. Groan! Why, no;
But sadly tell me who.

ROMEO. Bid a sick man in sadness make his will.
Ah, word ill urg'd to one that is so ill!
In sadness, cousin, I do love a woman.

BENVOLIO. I aim'd so near when I suppos'd you lov'd.

ROMEO. A right good markman! And she's fair I love.

BENVOLIO. A right fair mark, fair coz, is soonest hit.

ROMEO. Well, in that hit you miss: she'll not be hit
With Cupid's arrow. She hath Dian's wit,
And in strong proof of chastity well arm'd,
From Love's weak childish bow she lives unharm'd.
She will not stay the siege of loving terms,
Nor bide th' encounter of assailing eyes,
Nor ope her lap to saint-seducing gold.
O, she is rich in beauty; only poor
That, when she dies, with beauty dies her store.

BENVOLIO. Then she hath sworn that she will still live chaste?

ROMEO. She hath, and in that sparing makes huge waste;
For beauty, starv'd with her severity,
Cuts beauty off from all posterity.
She is too fair, too wise, wisely too fair,
To merit bliss by making me despair.

She hath forsworn to love, and in that vow
Do I live dead that live to tell it now.
BENVOLIO. Be rul'd by me: forget to think of her.
ROMEO. O, teach me how I should forget to think!
BENVOLIO. By giving liberty unto thine eyes.
Examine other beauties.
ROMEO. 'Tis the way
To call hers, exquisite, in question more.
These happy masks that kiss fair ladies' brows,
Being black, puts us in mind they hide the fair.
He that is stricken blind cannot forget
The precious treasure of his eyesight lost.
Show me a mistress that is passing fair,
What doth her beauty serve but as a note
Where I may read who pass'd that passing fair?
Farewell; thou canst not teach me to forget.
BENVOLIO. I'll pay that doctrine or else die in debt. *Exeunt*

SCENE 2

A street

Enter CAPULET, COUNTY PARIS, *and the* CLOWN, *his servant*

CAPULET. But Montague is bound as well as I,
In penalty alike; and 'tis not hard, I think,
For men so old as we to keep the peace.
PARIS. Of honourable reckoning are you both,
And pity 'tis you liv'd at odds so long.
But now, my lord, what say you to my suit?
CAPULET. But saying o'er what I have said before:
My child is yet a stranger in the world,
She hath not seen the change of fourteen years;
Let two more summers wither in their pride
Ere we may think her ripe to be a bride.
PARIS. Younger than she are happy mothers made.
CAPULET. And too soon marr'd are those so early made.
Earth hath swallowed all my hopes but she;
She is the hopeful lady of my earth.

But woo her, gentle Paris, get her heart;
My will to her consent is but a part.
And, she agreed, within her scope of choice
Lies my consent and fair according voice.
This night I hold an old accustom'd feast,
Whereto I have invited many a guest,
Such as I love; and you among the store,
One more, most welcome, makes my number more.
At my poor house look to behold this night
Earth-treading stars that make dark heaven light.
Such comfort as do lusty young men feel
When well-apparell'd April on the heel
Of limping winter treads, even such delight
Among fresh female buds shall you this night
Inherit at my house. Hear all, all see,
And like her most whose merit most shall be;
Which on more view of many, mine, being one,
May stand in number, though in reck'ning none.
Come, go with me. [*To* SERVANT, *giving him a paper*] Go, sirrah, trudge about
Through fair Verona; find those persons out
Whose names are written there, and to them say
My house and welcome on their pleasure stay.

Exeunt CAPULET *and* PARIS

SERVANT. Find them out whose names are written here! It is written that the shoemaker should meddle with his yard and the tailor with his last, the fisher with his pencil and the painter with his nets; but I am sent to find those persons whose names are here writ, and can never find what names the writing person hath here writ. I must to the learned. In good time!

Enter BENVOLIO *and* ROMEO

BENVOLIO. Tut, man, one fire burns out another's burning,
One pain is less'ned by another's anguish;
Turn giddy, and be holp by backward turning;
One desperate grief cures with another's languish.
Take thou some new infection to thy eye,
And the rank poison of the old will die.

ROMEO. Your plantain leaf is excellent for that.

BENVOLIO. For what, I pray thee?
ROMEO. For your broken shin.
BENVOLIO. Why, Romeo, art thou mad?
ROMEO. Not mad, but bound more than a madman is;
Shut up in prison, kept without my food,
Whipt and tormented, and—God-den, good fellow.
SERVANT. God gi' go'den. I pray, sir, can you read?
ROMEO. Ay, mine own fortune in my misery.
SERVANT. Perhaps you have learned it without book. But I pray, can you read anything you see?
ROMEO. Ay, if I know the letters and the language.
SERVANT. Ye say honestly; rest you merry!
ROMEO. Stay, fellow; I can read.
[*He reads the list*] 'Signior Martino and his wife and daughters; County Anselme and his beauteous sisters; the lady widow of Vitruvio; Signior Placentio and his lovely nieces; Mercutio and his brother Valentine; mine uncle Capulet, his wife, and daughters; my fair niece Rosaline and Livia; Signior Valentio and his cousin Tybalt; Lucio and the lively Helena.'
A fair assembly. [*Gives back the paper*] Whither should they come?
SERVANT. Up.
ROMEO. Whither?
SERVANT. To supper. To our house.
ROMEO. Whose house?
SERVANT. My master's.
ROMEO. Indeed, I should have ask'd you that before.
SERVANT. Now I'll tell you without asking: my master is the great rich Capulet; and if you be not of the house of Montagues, I pray come and crush a cup of wine. Rest you merry! *Exit*
BENVOLIO. At this same ancient feast of Capulet's
Sups the fair Rosaline whom thou so loves,
With all the admired beauties of Verona.
Go thither, and with unattainted eye
Compare her face with some that I shall show,
And I will make thee think thy swan a crow.
ROMEO. When the devout religion of mine eye
Maintains such falsehood, then turn tears to fires;

And these, who, often drown'd, could never die,
Transparent heretics, be burnt for liars!
One fairer than my love! The all-seeing sun
Ne'er saw her match since first the world begun.

BENVOLIO. Tut, you saw her fair, none else being by,
Herself pois'd with herself in either eye;
But in that crystal scales let there be weigh'd
Your lady's love against some other maid
That I will show you shining at this feast,
And she shall scant show well that now seems best.

ROMEO. I'll go along, no such sight to be shown,
But to rejoice in splendour of mine own. *Exeunt*

SCENE 3

CAPULET'S *house*

Enter LADY CAPULET *and* NURSE

LADY CAPULET. Nurse, where's my daughter? Call her forth to me.

NURSE. Now, by my maidenhead at twelve year old,
I bade her come. What, lamb! what, ladybird!
God forbid! Where's this girl? What, Juliet.

Enter JULIET

JULIET. How now, who calls?

NURSE. Your mother.

JULIET. Madam, I am here. What is your will?

LADY CAPULET. This is the matter. Nurse, give leave awhile,
We must talk in secret. Nurse, come back again;
I have rememb'red me, thou's hear our counsel.
Thou knowest my daughter's of a pretty age.

NURSE. Faith, I can tell her age unto an hour.

LADY CAPULET. She's not fourteen.

NURSE. I'll lay fourteen of my teeth—
And yet, to my teen be it spoken, I have but four—
She's not fourteen. How long is it now
To Lammas-tide?

LADY CAPULET. A fortnight and odd days.

NURSE. Even or odd, of all days in the year,
Come Lammas Eve at night shall she be fourteen.
Susan and she—God rest all Christian souls!—
Were of an age. Well, Susan is with God;
She was too good for me. But, as I said,
On Lammas Eve at night shall she be fourteen;
That shall she, marry; I remember it well.
'Tis since the earthquake now eleven years;
And she was wean'd—I never shall forget it—
Of all the days of the year, upon that day;
For I had then laid wormwood to my dug,
Sitting in the sun under the dove-house wall;
My lord and you were then at Mantua.
Nay, I do bear a brain. But, as I said,
When it did taste the wormwood on the nipple
Of my dug, and felt it bitter, pretty fool,
To see it tetchy, and fall out with the dug!
Shake, quoth the dove-house. 'Twas no need, I trow,
To bid me trudge.
And since that time it is eleven years;
For then she could stand high-lone; nay, by th' rood,
She could have run and waddled all about;
For even the day before, she broke her brow;
And then my husband—God be with his soul!
'A was a merry man—took up the child.
'Yea,' quoth he 'dost thou fall upon thy face?
Thou wilt fall backward when thou hast more wit,
Wilt thou not, Jule?' And, by my holidam,
The pretty wretch left crying, and said 'Ay.'
To see, now, how a jest shall come about!
I warrant, an I should live a thousand years,
I never should forget it: 'Wilt thou not, Jule?' quoth he,
And, pretty fool, it stinted, and said 'Ay.'

LADY CAPULET. Enough of this; I pray thee hold thy peace.

NURSE. Yes, madam. Yet I cannot choose but laugh
To think it should leave crying and say 'Ay.'
And yet, I warrant, it had upon it brow
A bump as big as a young cock'rel's stone—
A perilous knock; and it cried bitterly.
'Yea,' quoth my husband 'fall'st upon thy face?

Thou wilt fall backward when thou comest to age;
Wilt thou not, Jule?' It stinted, and said 'Ay.'

JULIET. And stint thou too, I pray thee, nurse, say I.

NURSE. Peace, I have done. God mark thee to his grace!
Thou wast the prettiest babe that e'er I nurs'd;
An I might live to see thee married once,
I have my wish.

LADY CAPULET. Marry, that 'marry' is the very theme
I came to talk of. Tell me, daughter Juliet,
How stands your dispositions to be married?

JULIET. It is an honour that I dream not of.

NURSE. An honour! Were not I thine only nurse,
I would say thou hadst suck'd wisdom from thy teat.

LADY CAPULET. Well, think of marriage now. Younger than you,
Here in Verona, ladies of esteem,
Are made already mothers. By my count,
I was your mother much upon these years
That you are now a maid. Thus, then, in brief:
The valiant Paris seeks you for his love.

NURSE. A man, young lady! lady, such a man
As all the world—why, he's a man of wax.

LADY CAPULET. Verona's summer hath not such a flower.

NURSE. Nay, he's a flower; in faith, a very flower.

LADY CAPULET. What say you? Can you love the gentleman?
This night you shall behold him at our feast;
Read o'er the volume of young Paris' face,
And find delight writ there with beauty's pen;
Examine every married lineament,
And see how one another lends content;
And what obscur'd in this fair volume lies
Find written in the margent of his eyes.
This precious book of love, this unbound lover,
To beautify him, only lacks a cover.
The fish lives in the sea, and 'tis much pride
For fair without the fair within to hide.
That book in many's eyes doth share the glory
That in gold clasps locks in the golden story;
So shall you share all that he doth possess,

By having him making yourself no less.
NURSE. No less! Nay, bigger; women grow by men.
LADY CAPULET. Speak briefly, can you like of Paris' love?
JULIET. I'll look to like, if looking liking move;
But no more deep will I endart mine eye
Than your consent gives strength to make it fly.

Enter a SERVANT

SERVANT. Madam, the guests are come, supper serv'd up, you call'd, my young lady asked for, the nurse curs'd in the pantry, and everything in extremity. I must hence to wait; I beseech you, follow straight.
LADY CAPULET. We follow thee. [*Exit* SERVANT] Juliet, the County stays.
NURSE. Go, girl, seek happy nights to happy days. *Exeunt*

SCENE 4

A street

Enter ROMEO, MERCUTIO, BENVOLIO, *with five or six other maskers; torch-bearers*

ROMEO. What, shall this speech be spoke for our excuse?
Or shall we on without apology?
BENVOLIO. The date is out of such prolixity.
We'll have no Cupid hoodwink'd with a scarf,
Bearing a Tartar's painted bow of lath,
Scaring the ladies like a crow-keeper;
Nor no without-book prologue, faintly spoke
After the prompter, for our entrance;
But, let them measure us by what they will,
We'll measure them a measure, and be gone.
ROMEO. Give me a torch; I am not for this ambling;
Being but heavy, I will bear the light.
MERCUTIO. Nay, gentle Romeo, we must have you dance.
ROMEO. Not I, believe me. You have dancing shoes
With nimble soles: I have a soul of lead
So stakes me to the ground I cannot move.
MERCUTIO. You are a lover; borrow Cupid's wings

And soar with them above a common bound.
ROMEO. I am too sore enpierced with his shaft
To soar with his light feathers; and so bound
I cannot bound a pitch above dull woe.
Under love's heavy burden do I sink.
MERCUTIO. And to sink in it should you burden love;
Too great oppression for a tender thing.
ROMEO. Is love a tender thing? It is too rough,
Too rude, too boist'rous, and it pricks like thorn.
MERCUTIO. If love be rough with you, be rough with love;
Prick love for pricking, and you beat love down.
Give me a case to put my visage in. [*Putting on a mask*]
A visor for a visor! What care I
What curious eye doth quote deformities?
Here are the beetle brows shall blush for me.
BENVOLIO. Come, knock and enter; and no sooner in
But every man betake him to his legs.
ROMEO. A torch for me. Let wantons, light of heart,
Tickle the senseless rushes with their heels;
For I am proverb'd with a grandsire phrase;
I'll be a candle-holder and look on;
The game was ne'er so fair, and I am done.
MERCUTIO. Tut, dun's the mouse, the constable's own word;
If thou art Dun, we'll draw thee from the mire
Of this sir-reverence love, wherein thou stickest
Up to the ears. Come, we burn daylight, ho!
ROMEO. Nay, that's not so.
MERCUTIO. I mean, sir, in delay
We waste our lights in vain—like lights by day.
Take our good meaning, for our judgment sits
Five times in that ere once in our five wits.
ROMEO. And we mean well in going to this mask;
But 'tis no wit to go.
MERCUTIO. Why, may one ask?
ROMEO. I dreamt a dream to-night.
MERCUTIO. And so did I.
ROMEO. Well, what was yours?
MERCUTIO. That dreamers often lie.
ROMEO. In bed asleep, while they do dream things true.
MERCUTIO. O, then I see Queen Mab hath been with you.

She is the fairies' midwife, and she comes
In shape no bigger than an agate stone
On the fore-finger of an alderman,
Drawn with a team of little atomies
Athwart men's noses as they lie asleep;
Her waggon-spokes made of long spinners' legs;
The cover, of the wings of grasshoppers;
Her traces, of the smallest spider's web;
Her collars, of the moonshine's wat'ry beams;
Her whip, of cricket's bone; the lash, of film;
Her waggoner, a small grey-coated gnat,
Not half so big as a round little worm
Prick'd from the lazy finger of a maid.
Her chariot is an empty hazel-nut,
Made by the joiner squirrel or old grub,
Time out o' mind the fairies' coachmakers.
And in this state she gallops night by night
Through lovers' brains, and then they dream of love;
O'er courtiers' knees, that dream on curtsies straight;
O'er lawyers' fingers, who straight dream on fees;
O'er ladies' lips, who straight on kisses dream,
Which oft the angry Mab with blisters plagues,
Because their breaths with sweetmeats tainted are.
Sometimes she gallops o'er a courtier's nose,
And then dreams he of smelling out a suit;
And sometime comes she with a tithe-pig's tail,
Tickling a parson's nose as 'a lies asleep,
Then dreams he of another benefice.
Sometime she driveth o'er a soldier's neck,
And then dreams he of cutting foreign throats,
Of breaches, ambuscadoes, Spanish blades,
Of healths five fathoms deep; and then anon
Drums in his ear, at which he starts and wakes,
And, being thus frighted, swears a prayer or two,
And sleeps again. This is that very Mab
That plats the manes of horses in the night;
And bakes the elf-locks in foul sluttish hairs,
Which once untangled much misfortune bodes.
This is the hag, when maids lie on their backs,
That presses them and learns them first to bear,

Making them women of good carriage.
This is she–

ROMEO. Peace, peace, Mercutio, peace!
Thou talk'st of nothing.

MERCUTIO. True, I talk of dreams,
Which are the children of an idle brain,
Begot of nothing but vain fantasy;
Which is as thin of substance as the air,
And more inconstant than the wind, who woos
Even now the frozen bosom of the north,
And, being anger'd, puffs away from thence,
Turning his side to the dew-dropping south.

BENVOLIO. This wind you talk of blows us from ourselves:
Supper is done, and we shall come too late.

ROMEO. I fear, too early; for my mind misgives
Some consequence, yet hanging in the stars,
Shall bitterly begin his fearful date
With this night's revels and expire the term
Of a despised life clos'd in my breast,
By some vile forfeit of untimely death.
But He that hath the steerage of my course
Direct my sail! On, lusty gentlemen.

BENVOLIO. Strike, drum.

They march about the stage. Exeunt

SCENE 5

CAPULET'S *house*

Enter the MASKERS. SERVINGMEN *come forth with napkins*

FIRST SERVANT. Where's Potpan, that he helps not to take away? He shift a trencher! He scrape a trencher!

SECOND SERVANT. When good manners shall lie all in one or two men's hands, and they unwash'd too, 'tis a foul thing.

FIRST SERVANT. Away with join-stools, remove the court-cubbert, look to the plate. Good thou, save me a piece of marchpane; and as thou loves me let the porter let in Susan Grindstone and Nell. Antony, and Potpan!

SECOND SERVANT. Ay, boy, ready.

FIRST SERVANT. You are look'd for and call'd for, ask'd for and sought for, in the great chamber.

THIRD SERVANT. We cannot be here and there too. Cheerly, boys! Be brisk a while, and the longer liver take all!

[SERVANTS *retire*]

Enter CAPULET, *with all the* GUESTS *and* GENTLEWOMEN *to the* MASKERS

CAPULET. Welcome, gentlemen! Ladies that have their toes
Unplagu'd with corns will have a bout with you.
Ah ha, my mistresses! which of you all
Will now deny to dance? She that makes dainty,
She I'll swear hath corns; am I come near ye now?
Welcome, gentlemen! I have seen the day
That I have worn a visor and could tell
A whispering tale in a fair lady's ear,
Such as would please. 'Tis gone, 'tis gone, 'tis gone!
You are welcome, gentlemen. Come, musicians, play.
A hall, a hall! give room; and foot it, girls.

[*Music plays, and they dance*]

More light, you knaves; and turn the tables up,
And quench the fire, the room is grown too hot.
Ah, sirrah, this unlook'd for sport comes well.
Nay, sit, nay, sit, good cousin Capulet,
For you and I are past our dancing days.
How long is't now since last yourself and I
Were in a mask?

SECOND CAPULET. By'r Lady, thirty years.

CAPULET. What, man? 'tis not so much, 'tis not so much.
'Tis since the nuptial of Lucentio,
Come Pentecost as quickly as it will,
Some five and twenty years; and then we mask'd.

SECOND CAPULET. 'Tis more, 'tis more: his son is elder, sir;
His son is thirty.

CAPULET. Will you tell me that?
His son was but a ward two years ago.

ROMEO. [*To a* SERVANT] What lady's that which doth enrich the hand
Of yonder knight?

SERVANT. I know not, sir.

ROMEO. O, she doth teach the torches to burn bright!
It seems she hangs upon the cheek of night
As a rich jewel in an Ethiop's ear–
Beauty too rich for use, for earth too dear!
So shows a snowy dove trooping with crows
As yonder lady o'er her fellows shows.
The measure done, I'll watch her place of stand,
And, touching hers, make blessed my rude hand.
Did my heart love till now? Forswear it, sight;
For I ne'er saw true beauty till this night.

TYBALT. This, by his voice, should be a Montague.
Fetch me my rapier, boy. What, dares the slave
Come hither, cover'd with an antic face,
To fleer and scorn at our solemnity?
Now, by the stock and honour of my kin,
To strike him dead I hold it not a sin.

CAPULET. Why, how now, kinsman! Wherefore storm you so?

TYBALT. Uncle, this is a Montague, our foe;
A villain, that is hither come in spite
To scorn at our solemnity this night.

CAPULET. Young Romeo, is it?

TYBALT. 'Tis he, that villain Romeo.

CAPULET. Content thee, gentle coz, let him alone.
'A bears him like a portly gentleman;
And, to say truth, Verona brags of him
To be a virtuous and well-govern'd youth.
I would not for the wealth of all this town
Here in my house do him disparagement.
Therefore be patient, take no note of him;
It is my will; the which if thou respect,
Show a fair presence and put off these frowns,
An ill-beseeming semblance for a feast.

TYBALT. It fits, when such a villain is a guest.
I'll not endure him.

CAPULET. He shall be endur'd.
What, goodman boy! I say he shall. Go to;
Am I the master here or you? Go to.
You'll not endure him! God shall mend my soul!
You'll make a mutiny among my guests!

You will set cock-a-hoop! You'll be the man!
TYBALT. Why, uncle, 'tis a shame.
CAPULET. Go to, go to;
You are a saucy boy. Is't so, indeed?
This trick may chance to scathe you. I know what:
You must contrary me. Marry, 'tis time.—
Well said, my hearts!—You are a princox; go.
Be quiet, or—More light, more light!—For shame!
I'll make you quiet. What!—Cheerly, my hearts!
TYBALT. Patience perforce with wilful choler meeting
Makes my flesh tremble in their different greeting.
I will withdraw; but this intrusion shall,
Now seeming sweet, convert to bitt'rest gall. *Exit*
ROMEO. [*To* JULIET] If I profane with my unworthiest hand
This holy shrine, the gentle fine is this:
My lips, two blushing pilgrims, ready stand
To smooth that rough touch with a tender kiss.
JULIET. Good pilgrim, you do wrong your hand too much,
Which mannerly devotion shows in this;
For saints have hands that pilgrims' hands do touch,
And palm to palm is holy palmers' kiss.
ROMEO. Have not saints lips, and holy palmers too?
JULIET. Ay, pilgrim, lips that they must use in pray'r.
ROMEO. O, then, dear saint, let lips do what hands do!
They pray; grant thou, lest faith turn to despair.
JULIET. Saints do not move, though grant for prayers' sake.
ROMEO. Then move not while my prayer's effect I take.
Thus from my lips by thine my sin is purg'd.
[*Kissing her*]
JULIET. Then have my lips the sin that they have took.
ROMEO. Sin from my lips? O trespass sweetly urg'd!
Give me my sin again. [*Kissing her*]
JULIET. You kiss by th' book.
NURSE. Madam, your mother craves a word with you.
ROMEO. What is her mother?
NURSE. Marry, bachelor,
Her mother is the lady of the house,
And a good lady, and a wise and virtuous.
I nurs'd her daughter that you talk'd withal.

I tell you, he that can lay hold of her
Shall have the chinks.

ROMEO. Is she a Capulet?
O dear account! my life is my foe's debt.

BENVOLIO. Away, be gone; the sport is at the best.

ROMEO. Ay, so I fear; the more is my unrest.

CAPULET. Nay, gentlemen, prepare not to be gone;
We have a trifling foolish banquet towards.
Is it e'en so? Why, then I thank you all;
I thank you, honest gentlemen; good night.
More torches here! [*Exeunt* MASKERS] Come on then, let's to bed.
Ah, sirrah, by my fay, it waxes late;
I'll to my rest. *Exeunt all but* JULIET *and* NURSE

JULIET. Come hither, nurse. What is yond gentleman?

NURSE. The son and heir of old Tiberio.

JULIET. What's he that now is going out of door?

NURSE. Marry, that I think be young Petruchio.

JULIET. What's he that follows there, that would not dance?

NURSE. I know not.

JULIET. Go ask his name.–If he be married,
My grave is like to be my wedding bed.

NURSE. His name is Romeo, and a Montague;
The only son of your great enemy.

JULIET. My only love sprung from my only hate!
Too early seen unknown, and known too late!
Prodigious birth of love it is to me,
That I must love a loathed enemy.

NURSE. What's this? What's this?

JULIET. A rhyme I learnt even now
Of one I danc'd withal. [*One calls within* 'Juliet']

NURSE. Anon, anon!
Come, let's away; the strangers all are gone. *Exeunt*

ACT II. PROLOGUE

Enter Chorus

Now old desire doth in his death-bed lie,
And young affection gapes to be his heir;
That fair for which love groan'd for and would die,
With tender Juliet match'd, is now not fair.
Now Romeo is belov'd, and loves again,
Alike bewitched by the charm of looks;
But to his foe suppos'd he must complain,
And she steal love's sweet bait from fearful hooks.
Being held a foe, he may not have access
To breathe such vows as lovers use to swear;
And she as much in love, her means much less
To meet her new beloved any where.
But passion lends them power, time means, to meet,
Temp'ring extremities with extreme sweet. *Exit*

SCENE 1

A lane by the wall of Capulet's *orchard*

Enter Romeo

Romeo. Can I go forward when my heart is here?
Turn back, dull earth, and find thy centre out.
[*He climbs the wall and leaps down within it*]

Enter Benvolio *with* Mercutio

Benvolio. Romeo! my cousin, Romeo! Romeo!
Mercutio. He is wise,
And, on my life, hath stol'n him home to bed.
Benvolio. He ran this way, and leapt this orchard wall.
Call, good Mercutio.
Mercutio. Nay, I'll conjure too.
Romeo! humours! madman! passion! lover!
Appear thou in the likeness of a sigh;
Speak but one rhyme and I am satisfied;
Cry but 'Ay me!' pronounce but 'love' and 'dove';
Speak to my gossip Venus one fair word,

One nickname for her purblind son and heir,
Young Adam Cupid, he that shot so trim
When King Cophetua lov'd the beggar-maid!
He heareth not, he stirreth not, he moveth not;
The ape is dead, and I must conjure him.
I conjure thee by Rosaline's bright eyes,
By her high forehead and her scarlet lip,
By her fine foot, straight leg, and quivering thigh,
And the demesnes that there adjacent lie,
That in thy likeness thou appear to us.

BENVOLIO. An if he hear thee, thou wilt anger him.

MERCUTIO. This cannot anger him: 'twould anger him
To raise a spirit in his mistress' circle
Of some strange nature, letting it there stand
Till she had laid it and conjur'd it down;
That were some spite. My invocation
Is fair and honest: in his mistress' name,
I conjure only but to raise up him.

BENVOLIO. Come, he hath hid himself among these trees
To be consorted with the humorous night:
Blind is his love, and best befits the dark.

MERCUTIO. If love be blind, love cannot hit the mark.
Now will he sit under a medlar tree,
And wish his mistress were that kind of fruit
As maids call medlars when they laugh alone.
O Romeo, that she were, O that she were
An open et cetera, thou a pop'rin pear!
Romeo, good night. I'll to my truckle bed;
This field-bed is too cold for me to sleep.
Come, shall we go?

BENVOLIO. Go, then; for 'tis in vain
To seek him here that means not to be found. *Exeunt*

SCENE 2

CAPULET'S *orchard*

Enter ROMEO

ROMEO. He jests at scars that never felt a wound.

Enter JULIET *above at a window*

But, soft! What light through yonder window breaks?
It is the east, and Juliet is the sun.
Arise, fair sun, and kill the envious moon,
Who is already sick and pale with grief
That thou her maid art far more fair than she.
Be not her maid, since she is envious;
Her vestal livery is but sick and green,
And none but fools do wear it; cast it off.
It is my lady; O, it is my love!
O that she knew she were!
She speaks, yet she says nothing. What of that?
Her eye discourses; I will answer it.
I am too bold, 'tis not to me she speaks;
Two of the fairest stars in all the heaven,
Having some business, do entreat her eyes
To twinkle in their spheres till they return.
What if her eyes were there, they in her head?
The brightness of her cheek would shame those stars,
As daylight doth a lamp; her eyes in heaven
Would through the airy region stream so bright
That birds would sing, and think it were not night.
See how she leans her cheek upon her hand!
O that I were a glove upon that hand,
That I might touch that cheek!

JULIET. Ay me!

ROMEO. She speaks.
O, speak again, bright angel, for thou art
As glorious to this night, being o'er my head,
As is a winged messenger of heaven
Unto the white-upturned wond'ring eyes
Of mortals that fall back to gaze on him,
When he bestrides the lazy-pacing clouds
And sails upon the bosom of the air.

JULIET. O Romeo, Romeo! wherefore art thou Romeo?
Deny thy father and refuse thy name;
Or, if thou wilt not, be but sworn my love,
And I'll no longer be a Capulet.

ROMEO. [*Aside*] Shall I hear more, or shall I speak at this?

JULIET. 'Tis but thy name that is my enemy;
Thou art thyself, though not a Montague.
What's Montague? It is nor hand, nor foot,
Nor arm, nor face, nor any other part
Belonging to a man. O, be some other name!
What's in a name? That which we call a rose
By any other name would smell as sweet;
So Romeo would, were he not Romeo call'd,
Retain that dear perfection which he owes
Without that title. Romeo, doff thy name;
And for thy name, which is no part of thee,
Take all myself.

ROMEO. I take thee at thy word:
Call me but love, and I'll be new baptiz'd;
Henceforth I never will be Romeo.

JULIET. What man art thou, that, thus bescreen'd in night,
So stumblest on my counsel?

ROMEO. By a name
I know not how to tell thee who I am:
My name, dear saint, is hateful to myself,
Because it is an enemy to thee;
Had I it written, I would tear the word.

JULIET. My ears have yet not drunk a hundred words
Of thy tongue's uttering, yet I know the sound:
Art thou not Romeo, and a Montague?

ROMEO. Neither, fair maid, if either thee dislike.

JULIET. How cam'st thou hither, tell me, and wherefore?
The orchard walls are high and hard to climb;
And the place death, considering who thou art,
If any of my kinsmen find thee here.

ROMEO. With love's light wings did I o'erperch these walls
For stony limits cannot hold love out;
And what love can do, that dares love attempt.
Therefore thy kinsmen are no stop to me.

JULIET. If they do see thee, they will murder thee.

ROMEO. Alack, there lies more peril in thine eye
Than twenty of their swords; look thou but sweet,
And I am proof against their enmity.

JULIET. I would not for the world they saw thee here.

ROMEO. I have night's cloak to hide me from their eyes;

And but thou love me, let them find me here.
My life were better ended by their hate
Than death prorogued wanting of thy love.

JULIET. By whose direction found'st thou out this place?

ROMEO. By love, that first did prompt me to enquire;
He lent me counsel, and I lent him eyes.
I am no pilot; yet, wert thou as far
As that vast shore wash'd with the farthest sea,
I should adventure for such merchandise.

JULIET. Thou knowest the mask of night is on my face,
Else would a maiden blush bepaint my cheek
For that which thou hast heard me speak to-night.
Fain would I dwell on form, fain, fain deny
What I have spoke; but farewell compliment!
Dost thou love me? I know thou wilt say ay,
And I will take thy word; yet, if thou swear'st,
Thou mayst prove false; at lovers' perjuries
They say Jove laughs. O gentle Romeo,
If thou dost love, pronounce it faithfully.
Or, if thou think'st I am too quickly won,
I'll frown, and be perverse, and say thee nay,
So thou wilt woo; but else, not for the world.
In truth, fair Montague, I am too fond;
And therefore thou mayst think my haviour light;
But trust me, gentleman, I'll prove more true
Than those that have more cunning to be strange.
I should have been more strange, I must confess,
But that thou overheard'st, ere I was ware,
My true love's passion. Therefore pardon me,
And not impute this yielding to light love,
Which the dark night hath so discovered.

ROMEO. Lady, by yonder blessed moon I vow,
That tips with silver all these fruit-tree tops—

JULIET. O, swear not by the moon, th' inconstant moon,
That monthly changes in her circled orb,
Lest that thy love prove likewise variable.

ROMEO. What shall I swear by?

JULIET. Do not swear at all;
Or, if thou wilt, swear by thy gracious self,
Which is the god of my idolatry,

And I'll believe thee.
ROMEO. If my heart's dear love—
JULIET. Well, do not swear. Although I joy in thee,
I have no joy of this contract to-night:
It is too rash, too unadvis'd, too sudden;
Too like the lightning, which doth cease to be
Ere one can say 'It lightens.' Sweet, good night!
This bud of love, by summer's ripening breath,
May prove a beauteous flow'r when next we meet.
Good night, good night! As sweet repose and rest
Come to thy heart as that within my breast!
ROMEO. O, wilt thou leave me so unsatisfied?
JULIET. What satisfaction canst thou have to-night?
ROMEO. Th' exchange of thy love's faithful vow for mine.
JULIET. I gave thee mine before thou didst request it;
And yet I would it were to give again.
ROMEO. Wouldst thou withdraw it? For what purpose, love?
JULIET. But to be frank, and give it thee again.
And yet I wish but for the thing I have.
My bounty is as boundless as the sea,
My love as deep: the more I give to thee,
The more I have, for both are infinite.
[NURSE *calls within*]
I hear some noise within. Dear love, adieu!—
Anon, good nurse!—Sweet Montague, be true.
Stay but a little, I will come again. *Exit*
ROMEO. O blessed, blessed night! I am afeard,
Being in night, all this is but a dream,
Too flattering-sweet to be substantial.

Re-enter JULIET *above*

JULIET. Three words, dear Romeo, and good night indeed.
If that thy bent of love be honourable,
Thy purpose marriage, send me word to-morrow,
By one that I'll procure to come to thee,
Where and what time thou wilt perform the rite;
And all my fortunes at thy foot I'll lay,
And follow thee, my lord, throughout the world.
NURSE. [*Within*] Madam!

JULIET. I come anon.—But if thou meanest not well,
I do beseech thee—

NURSE. [*Within*] Madam!

JULIET. By and by, I come—
To cease thy suit, and leave me to my grief.
To-morrow will I send.

ROMEO. So thrive my soul—

JULIET. A thousand times good night! *Exit*

ROMEO. A thousand times the worse, to want thy light.
Love goes toward love as school-boys from their books;
But love from love, toward school with heavy looks.

Re-enter JULIET *above*

JULIET. Hist! Romeo, hist!—O for a falc'ner's voice,
To lure this tassel-gentle back again!
Bondage is hoarse, and may not speak aloud;
Else would I tear the cave where Echo lies,
And make her airy tongue more hoarse than mine
With repetition of my Romeo's name.
Romeo!

ROMEO. It is my soul that calls upon my name.
How silver-sweet sound lovers' tongues by night,
Like softest music to attending ears!

JULIET. Romeo!

ROMEO. My dear?

JULIET. At what o'clock to-morrow
Shall I send to thee?

ROMEO. By the hour of nine.

JULIET. I will not fail. 'Tis twenty years till then.
I have forgot why I did call thee back.

ROMEO. Let me stand here till thou remember it.

JULIET. I shall forget, to have thee still stand there,
Rememb'ring how I love thy company.

ROMEO. And I'll still stay, to have thee still forget,
Forgetting any other home but this.

JULIET. 'Tis almost morning. I would have thee gone;
And yet no farther than a wanton's bird,
That lets it hop a little from her hand,
Like a poor prisoner in his twisted gyves,
And with a silk thread plucks it back again,

So loving-jealous of his liberty.
ROMEO. I would I were thy bird.
JULIET. Sweet, so would I.
Yet I should kill thee with much cherishing.
Good night, good night! Parting is such sweet sorrow
That I shall say good night till it be morrow. *Exit*
ROMEO. Sleep dwell upon thine eyes, peace in thy breast!
Would I were sleep and peace, so sweet to rest!
Hence will I to my ghostly father's cell,
His help to crave and my dear hap to tell. *Exit*

SCENE 3

FRIAR LAWRENCE'S *cell*

Enter FRIAR LAWRENCE *with a basket*

FRIAR LAWRENCE. The grey-ey'd morn smiles on the frowning night,
Check'ring the eastern clouds with streaks of light;
And fleckel'd darkness like a drunkard reels
From forth day's path and Titan's fiery wheels.
Now, ere the sun advance his burning eye
The day to cheer and night's dank dew to dry,
I must up-fill this osier cage of ours
With baleful weeds and precious-juiced flowers.
The earth that's nature's mother is her tomb;
What is her burying grave, that is her womb.
And from her womb children of divers kind
We sucking on her natural bosom find;
Many for many virtues excellent,
None but for some, and yet all different.
O, mickle is the powerful grace that lies
In plants, herbs, stones, and their true qualities;
For nought so vile that on the earth doth live
But to the earth some special good doth give;
Nor aught so good but, strain'd from that fair use
Revolts from true birth, stumbling on abuse:
Virtue itself turns vice, being misapplied,
And vice sometime's by action dignified.

Within the infant rind of this weak flower
Poison hath residence, and medicine power;
For this, being smelt, with that part cheers each part;
Being tasted, slays all senses with the heart.
Two such opposed kings encamp them still
In man as well as herbs—grace and rude will;
And where the worser is predominant,
Full soon the canker death eats up that plant.

Enter ROMEO

ROMEO. Good morrow, father!
FRIAR LAWRENCE. Benedicite!
What early tongue so sweet saluteth me?
Young son, it argues a distempered head
So soon to bid good morrow to thy bed.
Care keeps his watch in every old man's eye,
And where care lodges sleep will never lie;
But where unbruised youth with unstuff'd brain
Doth couch his limbs, there golden sleep doth reign.
Therefore thy earliness doth me assure
Thou art uprous'd with some distemp'rature;
Or if not so, then here I hit it right—
Our Romeo hath not been in bed to-night.
ROMEO. That last is true; the sweeter rest was mine.
FRIAR LAWRENCE. God pardon sin! Wast thou with Rosaline?
ROMEO. With Rosaline, my ghostly father? No;
I have forgot that name, and that name's woe.
FRIAR LAWRENCE. That's my good son; but where hast thou been then?
ROMEO. I'll tell thee ere thou ask it me again.
I have been feasting with mine enemy;
Where, on a sudden, one hath wounded me
That's by me wounded; both our remedies
Within thy help and holy physic lies.
I bear no hatred, blessed man, for, lo,
My intercession likewise steads my foe.
FRIAR LAWRENCE. Be plain, good son, and homely in thy drift;
Riddling confession finds but riddling shrift.
ROMEO. Then plainly know my heart's dear love is set

On the fair daughter of rich Capulet.
As mine on hers, so hers is set on mine;
And all combin'd, save what thou must combine
By holy marriage. When, and where, and how,
We met, we woo'd, and made exchange of vow,
I'll tell thee as we pass; but this I pray,
That thou consent to marry us to-day.

FRIAR LAWRENCE. Holy Saint Francis! What a change is here!
Is Rosaline, that thou didst love so dear,
So soon forsaken? Young men's love, then, lies
Not truly in their hearts, but in their eyes.
Jesu Maria, what a deal of brine
Hath wash'd thy sallow cheeks for Rosaline!
How much salt water thrown away in waste,
To season love, that of it doth not taste!
The sun not yet thy sighs from heaven clears,
Thy old groans yet ring in mine ancient ears;
Lo, here upon thy cheek the stain doth sit
Of an old tear that is not wash'd off yet.
If e'er thou wast thyself, and these woes thine,
Thou and these woes were all for Rosaline.
And art thou chang'd? Pronounce this sentence, then:
Women may fall, when there's no strength in men.

ROMEO. Thou chid'st me oft for loving Rosaline.

FRIAR LAWRENCE. For doting, not for loving, pupil mine.

ROMEO. And bad'st me bury love.

FRIAR LAWRENCE. Not in a grave
To lay one in, another out to have.

ROMEO. I pray thee chide me not; her I love now
Doth grace for grace and love for love allow;
The other did not so.

FRIAR LAWRENCE. O, she knew well
Thy love did read by rote that could not spell.
But come, young waverer, come, go with me,
In one respect I'll thy assistant be;
For this alliance may so happy prove
To turn your household's rancour to pure love.

ROMEO. O, let us hence; I stand on sudden haste.

FRIAR LAWRENCE. Wisely and slow; they stumble that run fast. *Exeunt*

SCENE 4

A street

Enter BENVOLIO *and* MERCUTIO

MERCUTIO. Where the devil should this Romeo be?
Came he not home to-night?

BENVOLIO. Not to his father's; I spoke with his man.

MERCUTIO. Why, that same pale hard-hearted wench, that Rosaline,
Torments him so that he will sure run mad.

BENVOLIO. Tybalt, the kinsman to old Capulet,
Hath sent a letter to his father's house.

MERCUTIO. A challenge, on my life.

BENVOLIO. Romeo will answer it.

MERCUTIO. Any man that can write may answer a letter.

BENVOLIO. Nay, he will answer the letter's master, how he dares, being dared.

MERCUTIO. Alas, poor Romeo, he is already dead: stabb'd with a white wench's black eye; run through the ear with a love-song; the very pin of his heart cleft with the blind bow-boy's butt-shaft. And is he a man to encounter Tybalt?

BENVOLIO. Why, what is Tybalt?

MERCUTIO. More than Prince of Cats. O, he's the courageous captain of compliments. He fights as you sing prick-song: keeps time, distance, and proportion; he rests his minim rests, one, two, and the third in your bosom; the very butcher of a silk button, a duellist, a duellist; a gentleman of the very first house, of the first and second cause. Ah, the immortal passado! the punto reverso! the hay!—

BENVOLIO. The what?

MERCUTIO. The pox of such antic, lisping, affecting fantasticoes; these new tuners of accent!—'By Jesu, a very good blade! a very tall man! a very good whore!' Why, is not this a lamentable thing, grandsire, that we should be thus afflicted with these strange flies, these fashion-mongers, these pardon me's, who stand so much on the new form that they cannot sit at ease on the old bench? O, their bones, their bones!

ACT II. SCENE 4

Enter ROMEO

BENVOLIO. Here comes Romeo, here comes Romeo.

MERCUTIO. Without his roe, like a dried herring. O flesh, flesh, how art thou fishified! Now is he for the numbers that Petrarch flow'd in; Laura, to his lady, was a kitchen-wench—marry, she had a better love to berhyme her; Dido, a dowdy; Cleopatra, a gipsy; Helen and Hero, hildings and harlots; Thisbe, a grey eye or so, but not to the purpose—Signior Romeo, bon jour! There's a French salutation to your French slop. You gave us the counterfeit fairly last night.

ROMEO. Good morrow to you both. What counterfeit did I give you?

MERCUTIO. The slip, sir, the slip; can you not conceive?

ROMEO. Pardon, good Mercutio; my business was great, and in such a case as mine a man may strain courtesy.

MERCUTIO. That's as much as to say, such a case as yours constrains a man to bow in the hams.

ROMEO. Meaning, to curtsy.

MERCUTIO. Thou hast most kindly hit it.

ROMEO. A most courteous exposition.

MERCUTIO. Nay, I am the very pink of courtesy.

ROMEO. Pink for flower.

MERCUTIO. Right.

ROMEO. Why, then is my pump well flower'd.

MERCUTIO. Sure wit! Follow me this jest now till thou hast worn out thy pump, that, when the single sole of it is worn, the jest may remain, after the wearing, solely singular.

ROMEO. O single-sol'd jest, solely singular for the singleness!

MERCUTIO. Come between us, good Benvolio; my wits faints.

ROMEO. Swits and spurs, swits and spurs; or I'll cry a match.

MERCUTIO. Nay, if our wits run the wild-goose chase, I am done; for thou hast more of the wild goose in one of thy wits than, I am sure, I have in my whole five. Was I with you there for the goose?

ROMEO. Thou wast never with me for anything when thou wast not there for the goose.

MERCUTIO. I will bite thee by the ear for that jest.

ROMEO. Nay, good goose, bite not.

MERCUTIO. Thy wit is a very bitter sweeting; it is a most sharp sauce.

ROMEO. And is it not then well serv'd in to a sweet goose?

MERCUTIO. O, here's a wit of cheveril, that stretches from an inch narrow to an ell broad!

ROMEO. I stretch it out for that word 'broad,' which, added to the goose, proves thee far and wide a broad goose.

MERCUTIO. Why, is not this better now than groaning for love? Now art thou sociable, now art thou Romeo; now art thou what thou art by art as well as by nature; for this drivelling love is like a great natural that runs lolling up and down to hide his bauble in a hole.

BENVOLIO. Stop there, stop there.

MERCUTIO. Thou desirest me to stop in my tale against the hair.

BENVOLIO. Thou wouldst else have made thy tale large.

MERCUTIO. O, thou art deceiv'd: I would have made it short; for I was come to the whole depth of my tale, and meant, indeed, to occupy the argument no longer.

ROMEO. Here's goodly gear!

Enter NURSE *and her man,* PETER

MERCUTIO. A sail, a sail!

BENVOLIO. Two, two; a shirt and a smock

NURSE. Peter!

PETER. Anon.

NURSE. My fan, Peter.

MERCUTIO. Good Peter, to hide her face; for her fan's the fairer face.

NURSE. God ye good morrow, gentlemen.

MERCUTIO. God ye good den, fair gentlewoman.

NURSE. Is it good den?

MERCUTIO. 'Tis no less, I tell ye; for the bawdy hand of the dial is now upon the prick of noon.

NURSE. Out upon you! What a man are you?

ROMEO. One, gentlewoman, that God hath made himself to mar.

NURSE. By my troth, it is well said. 'For himself to mar' quoth 'a! Gentlemen, can any of you tell me where I may find the young Romeo?

ROMEO. I can tell you; but young Romeo will be older when you have found him than he was when you sought him. I am the youngest of that name, for fault of a worse.

NURSE. You say well.

MERCUTIO. Yea, is the worst well? Very well took, i' faith; wisely, wisely.

NURSE. If you be he, sir, I desire some confidence with you.

BENVOLIO. She will indite him to some supper.

MERCUTIO. A bawd, a bawd, a bawd! So ho!

ROMEO. What hast thou found?

MERCUTIO. No hare, sir; unless a hare, sir, in a lenten pie, that is something stale and hoar ere it be spent.

[*He walks by them and sings*]

An old hare hoar,
And an old hare hoar,
Is very good meat in Lent;
But a hare that is hoar
Is too much for a score,
When it hoars ere it be spent.

Romeo, will you come to your father's? We'll to dinner thither.

ROMEO. I will follow you.

MERCUTIO. Farewell, ancient lady; farewell, [*Sings*] lady, lady, lady. *Exeunt* MERCUTIO *and* BENVOLIO

NURSE. I pray you, sir, what saucy merchant was this that was so full of his ropery?

ROMEO. A gentleman, nurse, that loves to hear himself talk, and will speak more in a minute than he will stand to in a month.

NURSE. An 'a speak anything against me, I'll take him down, an 'a were lustier than he is, and twenty such Jacks; and if I cannot, I'll find those that shall. Scurvy knave! I am none of his flirt-gills; I am none of his skains-mates. And thou must stand by too, and suffer every knave to use me at his pleasure?

PETER. I saw no man use you at his pleasure; if I had, my weapon should quickly have been out, I warrant you. I dare draw as soon as another man, if I see occasion in a good quarrel, and the law on my side.

NURSE. Now, afore God, I am so vex'd that every part

about me quivers. Scurvy knave!—Pray you, sir, a word; and as I told you, my young lady bid me enquire you out; what she bid me say I will keep to myself. But first let me tell ye, if ye should lead her in a fool's paradise, as they say, it were a very gross kind of behaviour, as they say; for the gentlewoman is young; and, therefore, if you should deal double with her, truly it were an ill thing to be off'red to any gentlewoman, and very weak dealing.

ROMEO. Nurse, commend me to thy lady and mistress. I protest unto thee—

NURSE. Good heart, and, i' faith, I will tell her as much. Lord, Lord! she will be a joyful woman.

ROMEO. What wilt thou tell her, nurse? Thou dost not mark me.

NURSE. I will tell her, sir, that you do protest; which, as I take it, is a gentleman-like offer.

ROMEO. Bid her devise
Some means to come to shrift this afternoon;
And there she shall at Friar Lawrence' cell
Be shriv'd and married. Here is for thy pains.

NURSE. No, truly, sir; not a penny.

ROMEO. Go to; I say you shall.

NURSE. This afternoon, sir? Well, she shall be there.

ROMEO. And stay, good nurse—behind the abbey wall
Within this hour my man shall be with thee,
And bring thee cords made like a tackled stair;
Which to the high top-gallant of my joy
Must be my convoy in the secret night.
Farewell; be trusty, and I'll quit thy pains.
Farewell; commend me to thy mistress.

NURSE. Now God in heaven bless thee!—
Hark you, sir.

ROMEO. What say'st thou, my dear nurse?

NURSE. Is your man secret? Did you ne'er hear say
Two may keep counsel, putting one away?

ROMEO. I warrant thee my man's as true as steel.

NURSE. Well, sir. My mistress is the sweetest lady—Lord, Lord! when 'twas a little prating thing! O, there is a nobleman in town, one Paris, that would fain lay knife aboard; but she, good soul, had as lief see a toad, a very toad, as see him. I anger her sometimes, and tell her that Paris is the properer man; but, I'll warrant you, when I say so she looks as pale as any clout in the versal world. Doth not rosemary and Romeo begin both with a letter?

ROMEO. Ay, nurse; what of that? Both with an R.

NURSE. Ah, mocker! that's the dog's name. R is for the–no, I know it begins with some other letter. And she hath the prettiest sententious of it, of you and rosemary, that it would do you good to hear it.

ROMEO. Commend me to thy lady.

NURSE. Ay, a thousand times.–Peter!

PETER. Anon.

NURSE. [*Handing him her fan*] Before and apace. *Exeunt*

SCENE 5

CAPULET'S *orchard*

Enter JULIET

JULIET. The clock struck nine when I did send the nurse;
In half an hour she promis'd to return.
Perchance she cannot meet him–that's not so.
O, she is lame! Love's heralds should be thoughts,
Which ten times faster glide than the sun's beams
Driving back shadows over louring hills;
Therefore do nimble-pinion'd doves draw Love,
And therefore hath the wind-swift Cupid wings.
Now is the sun upon the highmost hill
Of this day's journey; and from nine till twelve
Is three long hours, yet she is not come.
Had she affections and warm youthful blood,
She would be as swift in motion as a ball;
My words would bandy her to my sweet love,
And his to me.
But old folks–many feign as they were dead;
Unwieldy, slow, heavy, and pale as lead.

Enter NURSE *and* PETER

O God, she comes! O honey nurse, what news?

Hast thou met with him? Send thy man away.

NURSE. Peter, stay at the gate. *Exit* PETER

JULIET. Now, good sweet nurse—O Lord, why look'st thou sad?
Though news be sad, yet tell them merrily;
If good, thou shamest the music of sweet news
By playing it to me with so sour a face.

NURSE. I am aweary, give me leave a while;
Fie, how my bones ache! What a jaunce have I had!

JULIET. I would thou hadst my bones and I thy news.
Nay, come, I pray thee speak; good, good nurse, speak.

NURSE. Jesu, what haste? Can you not stay a while?
Do you not see that I am out of breath?

JULIET. How art thou out of breath, when thou hast breath
To say to me that thou art out of breath?
The excuse that thou dost make in this delay
Is longer than the tale thou dost excuse.
Is thy news good or bad? Answer to that;
Say either, and I'll stay the circumstance.
Let me be satisfied, is't good or bad?

NURSE. Well, you have made a simple choice; you know not how to choose a man. Romeo! no, not he; though his face be better than any man's, yet his leg excels all men's; and for a hand, and a foot, and a body, though they be not to be talk'd on, yet they are past compare. He is not the flower of courtesy, but I'll warrant him as gentle as a lamb. Go thy ways, wench; serve God. What, have you din'd at home?

JULIET. No, no. But all this did I know before.
What says he of our marriage? What of that?

NURSE. Lord, how my head aches! What a head have I!
It beats as it would fall in twenty pieces.
My back a t' other side—ah, my back, my back!
Beshrew your heart for sending me about
To catch my death with jauncing up and down!

JULIET. I' faith, I am sorry that thou art not well.
Sweet, sweet, sweet nurse, tell me, what says my love?

NURSE. Your love says like an honest gentleman, and a courteous, and a kind, and a handsome, and, I warrant, a virtuous—Where is your mother?

JULIET. Where is my mother! Why, she is within;
Where should she be? How oddly thou repliest!
'Your love says like an honest gentleman,
Where is your mother?'
NURSE. O God's lady dear!
Are you so hot? Marry, come up, I trow;
Is this the poultice for my aching bones?
Henceforward, do your messages yourself.
JULIET. Here's such a coil! Come, what says Romeo?
NURSE. Have you got leave to go to shrift to-day?
JULIET. I have.
NURSE. Then hie you hence to Friar Lawrence' cell;
There stays a husband to make you a wife.
Now comes the wanton blood up in your cheeks;
They'll be in scarlet straight at any news.
Hie you to church; I must another way,
To fetch a ladder, by the which your love
Must climb a bird's nest soon when it is dark.
I am the drudge, and toil in your delight;
But you shall bear the burden soon at night.
Go; I'll to dinner; hie you to the cell.
JULIET. Hie to high fortune! Honest nurse, farewell. *Exeunt*

SCENE 6

FRIAR LAWRENCE'S *cell*

Enter FRIAR LAWRENCE *and* ROMEO

FRIAR LAWRENCE. So smile the heavens upon this holy act
That after-hours with sorrow chide us not!
ROMEO. Amen, amen! But come what sorrow can,
It cannot countervail the exchange of joy
That one short minute gives me in her sight.
Do thou but close our hands with holy words,
Then love-devouring death do what he dare;
It is enough I may but call her mine.
FRIAR LAWRENCE. These violent delights have violent ends,
And in their triumph die; like fire and powder,
Which, as they kiss, consume. The sweetest honey

Is loathsome in his own deliciousness,
And in the taste confounds the appetite.
Therefore love moderately: long love doth so;
Too swift arrives as tardy as too slow.

Enter JULIET

Here comes the lady. O, so light a foot
Will ne'er wear out the everlasting flint.
A lover may bestride the gossamer
That idles in the wanton summer air
And yet not fall, so light is vanity.

JULIET. Good even to my ghostly confessor.

FRIAR LAWRENCE. Romeo shall thank thee, daughter, for us both.

JULIET. As much to him, else is his thanks too much.

ROMEO. Ah, Juliet, if the measure of thy joy
Be heap'd like mine, and that thy skill be more
To blazon it, then sweeten with thy breath
This neighbour air, and let rich music's tongue
Unfold the imagin'd happiness that both
Receive in either by this dear encounter.

JULIET. Conceit, more rich in matter than in words,
Brags of his substance, not of ornament.
They are but beggars that can count their worth;
But my true love is grown to such excess
I cannot sum up sum of half my wealth.

FRIAR LAWRENCE. Come, come with me, and we will make short work;
For, by your leaves, you shall not stay alone
Till holy church incorporate two in one. *Exeunt*

ACT III. SCENE 1

A public place

Enter MERCUTIO, BENVOLIO, PAGE, *and servants*

BENVOLIO. I pray thee, good Mercutio, let's retire.
The day is hot, the Capulets abroad,
And if we meet we shall not scape a brawl;

For now, these hot days, is the mad blood stirring.

MERCUTIO. Thou art like one of these fellows that, when he enters the confines of a tavern, claps me his sword upon the table, and says 'God send me no need of thee!' and by the operation of the second cup draws him on the drawer, when, indeed, there is no need.

BENVOLIO. Am I like such a fellow?

MERCUTIO. Come, come, thou art as hot a Jack in thy mood as any in Italy; and as soon moved to be moody, and as soon moody to be moved.

BENVOLIO. And what to?

MERCUTIO. Nay, an there were two such, we should have none shortly, for one would kill the other. Thou! why, thou wilt quarrel with a man that hath a hair more or a hair less in his beard than thou hast. Thou wilt quarrel with a man for cracking nuts, having no other reason but because thou hast hazel eyes. What eye but such an eye would spy out such a quarrel? Thy head is as full of quarrels as an egg is full of meat; and yet thy head hath been beaten as addle as an egg for quarrelling. Thou has quarrell'd with a man for coughing in the street, because he hath wakened thy dog that hath lain asleep in the sun. Didst thou not fall out with a tailor for wearing his new doublet before Easter? With another for tying his new shoes with old riband? And yet thou wilt tutor me from quarrelling!

BENVOLIO. An I were so apt to quarrel as thou art, any man should buy the fee simple of my life for an hour and a quarter.

MERCUTIO. The fee simple! O simple!

Enter TYBALT *and others*

BENVOLIO. By my head, here comes the Capulets.

MERCUTIO. By my heel, I care not.

TYBALT. Follow me close, for I will speak to them.
Gentlemen, good den; a word with one of you.

MERCUTIO. And but one word with one of us? Couple it with something; make it a word and a blow.

TYBALT. You shall find me apt enough to that, sir, an you will give me occasion.

MERCUTIO. Could you not take some occasion without giving?

TYBALT. Mercutio, thou consortest with Romeo.

MERCUTIO. Consort! What, dost thou make us minstrels? An thou make minstrels of us, look to hear nothing but discords. Here's my fiddlestick; here's that shall make you dance. Zounds, consort!

BENVOLIO. We talk here in the public haunt of men;
Either withdraw unto some private place,
Or reason coldly of your grievances,
Or else depart; here all eyes gaze on us.

MERCUTIO. Men's eyes were made to look, and let them gaze;
I will not budge for no man's pleasure, I.

Enter ROMEO

TYBALT. Well, peace be with you, sir. Here comes my man.

MERCUTIO. But I'll be hang'd, sir, if he wear your livery.
Marry, go before to field, he'll be your follower;
Your worship in that sense may call him man.

TYBALT. Romeo, the love I bear thee can afford
No better term than this: thou art a villain.

ROMEO. Tybalt, the reason that I have to love thee
Doth much excuse the appertaining rage
To such a greeting. Villain am I none;
Therefore, farewell; I see thou knowest me not.

TYBALT. Boy, this shall not excuse the injuries
That thou hast done me; therefore turn and draw.

ROMEO. I do protest I never injur'd thee,
But love thee better than thou canst devise
Till thou shalt know the reason of my love;
And so, good Capulet—which name I tender
As dearly as mine own—be satisfied.

MERCUTIO. O calm, dishonourable, vile submission!
Alla stoccata carries it away. [*Draws*]
Tybalt, you rat-catcher, will you walk?

TYBALT. What wouldst thou have with me?

MERCUTIO. Good King of Cats, nothing but one of your nine lives; that I mean to make bold withal, and, as you shall use me hereafter, dry-beat the rest of the eight. Will you pluck your sword out of his pilcher by the ears? Make haste, lest mine be about your ears ere it be out.

TYBALT. I am for you. [*Draws*]

ROMEO. Gentle Mercutio, put thy rapier up.

MERCUTIO. Come, sir, your passado. [*They fight*]

ROMEO. Draw, Benvolio; beat down their weapons.
Gentlemen, for shame, forbear this outrage!
Tybalt! Mercutio! the Prince expressly hath
Forbid this bandying in Verona streets.
Hold, Tybalt! Good Mercutio!

[TYBALT *under* ROMEO's *arm thrusts* MERCUTIO *in, and flies with his friends*]

MERCUTIO. I am hurt.
A plague a both your houses! I am sped.
Is he gone and hath nothing?

BENVOLIO. What, art thou hurt?

MERCUTIO. Ay, ay, a scratch, a scratch; marry, 'tis enough.
Where is my page? Go, villain, fetch a surgeon.

Exit PAGE

ROMEO. Courage, man; the hurt cannot be much.

MERCUTIO. No, 'tis not so deep as a well, nor so wide as a church door, but 'tis enough, 'twill serve. Ask for me to-morrow, and you shall find me a grave man. I am peppered, I warrant, for this world. A plague a both your houses! Zounds, a dog, a rat, a mouse, a cat, to scratch a man to death! A braggart, a rogue, a villain, that fights by the book of arithmetic! Why the devil came you between us? I was hurt under your arm.

ROMEO. I thought all for the best.

MERCUTIO. Help me into some house, Benvolio, or I shall faint.
A plague a both your houses!
They have made worms' meat of me.
I have it, and soundly too—Your houses!

Exeunt MERCUTIO *and* BENVOLIO

ROMEO. This gentleman, the Prince's near ally,
My very friend, hath got this mortal hurt
In my behalf; my reputation stain'd
With Tybalt's slander—Tybalt, that an hour
Hath been my cousin. O sweet Juliet,
Thy beauty hath made me effeminate,
And in my temper soft'ned valour's steel!

Re-enter BENVOLIO

BENVOLIO. O Romeo, Romeo, brave Mercutio is dead!
That gallant spirit hath aspir'd the clouds,
Which too untimely here did scorn the earth.
ROMEO. This day's black fate on moe days doth depend;
This but begins the woe others must end.

Re-enter TYBALT

BENVOLIO. Here comes the furious Tybalt back again.
ROMEO. Alive in triumph and Mercutio slain!
Away to heaven respective lenity,
And fire-ey'd fury be my conduct now!
Now, Tybalt, take the 'villain' back again
That late thou gav'st me; for Mercutio's soul
Is but a little way above our heads,
Staying for thine to keep him company.
Either thou or I, or both, must go with him.
TYBALT. Thou, wretched boy, that didst consort him here,
Shalt with him hence.
ROMEO. This shall determine that.
[*They fight;* TYBALT *falls*]
BENVOLIO. Romeo, away, be gone.
The citizens are up, and Tybalt slain.
Stand not amaz'd. The Prince will doom thee death
If thou art taken. Hence, be gone, away!
ROMEO. O, I am fortune's fool!
BENVOLIO. Why dost thou stay? *Exit* ROMEO

Enter citizens

FIRST CITIZEN. Which way ran he that kill'd Mercutio?
Tybalt, that murderer, which way ran he?
BENVOLIO. There lies that Tybalt.
FIRST CITIZEN. Up, sir, go with me;
I charge thee in the Prince's name, obey.

Enter PRINCE, *attended;* MONTAGUE, CAPULET, *their* WIVES, *and all*

PRINCE. Where are the vile beginners of this fray?

BENVOLIO. O noble Prince, I can discover all
The unlucky manage of this fatal brawl:
There lies the man, slain by young Romeo,
That slew thy kinsman, brave Mercutio.
LADY CAPULET. Tybalt, my cousin! O my brother's child!
O Prince! O husband! O, the blood is spill'd
Of my dear kinsman! Prince, as thou art true,
For blood of ours shed blood of Montague.
O cousin, cousin!
PRINCE. Benvolio, who began this bloody fray?
BENVOLIO. Tybalt, here slain, whom Romeo's hand did slay;
Romeo that spoke him fair, bid him bethink
How nice the quarrel was, and urg'd withal
Your high displeasure. All this, uttered
With gentle breath, calm look, knees humbly bow'd,
Could not take truce with the unruly spleen
Of Tybalt, deaf to peace, but that he tilts
With piercing steel at bold Mercutio's breast;
Who, all as hot, turns deadly point to point,
And, with a martial scorn, with one hand beats
Cold death aside, and with the other sends
It back to Tybalt, whose dexterity
Retorts it. Romeo he cries aloud
'Hold, friends! friends, part!' and, swifter than his tongue,
His agile arm beats down their fatal points,
And 'twixt them rushes; underneath whose arm
An envious thrust from Tybalt hit the life
Of stout Mercutio; and then Tybalt fled;
But by and by comes back to Romeo,
Who had but newly entertain'd revenge,
And to't they go like lightning; for ere I
Could draw to part them was stout Tybalt slain;
And as he fell did Romeo turn and fly.
This is the truth, or let Benvolio die.
LADY CAPULET. He is a kinsman to the Montague,
Affection makes him false, he speaks not true;
Some twenty of them fought in this black strife,
And all those twenty could but kill one life.
I beg for justice, which thou, Prince, must give:
Romeo slew Tybalt, Romeo must not live.

PRINCE. Romeo slew him; he slew Mercutio.
Who now the price of his dear blood doth owe?
MONTAGUE. Not Romeo, Prince; he was Mercutio's friend;
His fault concludes but what the law should end,
The life of Tybalt.
PRINCE. And for that offence,
Immediately we do exile him hence.
I have an interest in your hate's proceeding,
My blood for your rude brawls doth lie a-bleeding;
But I'll amerce you with so strong a fine
That you shall all repent the loss of mine.
I will be deaf to pleading and excuses,
Nor tears nor prayers shall purchase out abuses;
Therefore use none. Let Romeo hence in haste,
Else when he is found that hour is his last.
Bear hence this body, and attend our will:
Mercy but murders, pardoning those that kill. *Exeunt*

SCENE 2

CAPULET'S *orchard*

Enter JULIET

JULIET. Gallop apace, you fiery-footed steeds
Towards Phœbus' lodging; such a waggoner
As Phaethon would whip you to the west,
And bring in cloudy night immediately.
Spread thy close curtain, love-performing night,
That runaways' eyes may wink, and Romeo
Leap to these arms, untalk'd of and unseen.
Lovers can see to do their amorous rites
By their own beauties; or if love be blind,
It best agrees with night. Come, civil night,
Thou sober-suited matron, all in black,
And learn me how to lose a winning match,
Play'd for a pair of stainless maidenhoods;
Hood my unmann'd blood, bating in my cheeks,
With thy black mantle, till strange love, grown bold,
Think true love acted simple modesty.

Come, night; come, Romeo; come, thou day in night;
For thou wilt lie upon the wings of night
Whiter than new snow on a raven's back.
Come, gentle night, come, loving black-brow'd night,
Give me my Romeo; and, when he shall die,
Take him and cut him out in little stars,
And he will make the face of heaven so fine
That all the world will be in love with night,
And pay no worship to the garish sun.
O, I have bought the mansion of a love,
But not possess'd it; and though I am sold,
Not yet enjoy'd. So tedious is this day
As is the night before some festival
To an impatient child that hath new robes,
And may not wear them. O, here comes my nurse,

Enter NURSE *with cords*

And she brings news; and every tongue that speaks
But Romeo's name speaks heavenly eloquence.
Now, nurse, what news? What has thou there? The cords
That Romeo bid thee fetch?

NURSE. Ay, ay, the cords. [*Throws them down*]

JULIET. Ay, me! what news? Why dost thou wring thy hands?

NURSE. Ah, well-a-day! he's dead, he's dead, he's dead.
We are undone, lady, we are undone.
Alack the day! he's gone, he's kill'd, he's dead.

JULIET. Can heaven be so envious?

NURSE. Romeo can,
Though heaven cannot. O Romeo, Romeo!
Who ever would have thought it? Romeo!

JULIET. What devil art thou that dost torment me thus?
This torture should be roar'd in dismal hell.
Hath Romeo slain himself? Say thou but 'I'
And that bare vowel I shall poison more
Than the death-darting eye of cockatrice.
I am not I if there be such an 'I';
Or those eyes shut that makes thee answer 'I.'
If he be slain, say 'I'; or if not, 'No';
Brief sounds determine of my weal or woe.

NURSE. I saw the wound, I saw it with mine eyes—
God save the mark!—here on his manly breast.
A piteous corse, a bloody piteous corse;
Pale, pale as ashes, all bedaub'd in blood,
All in gore-blood. I swounded at the sight.
JULIET. O, break, my heart! poor bankrupt, break at once!
To prison, eyes; ne'er look on liberty.
Vile earth, to earth resign; end motion here;
And thou and Romeo press one heavy bier!
NURSE. O Tybalt, Tybalt, the best friend I had!
O courteous Tybalt! honest gentleman!
That ever I should live to see thee dead!
JULIET. What storm is this that blows so contrary?
Is Romeo slaught'red, and is Tybalt dead?
My dearest cousin and my dearer lord?
Then, dreadful trumpet, sound the general doom;
For who is living if those two are gone?
NURSE. Tybalt is gone, and Romeo banished;
Romeo that kill'd him, he is banished.
JULIET. O God! Did Romeo's hand shed Tybalt's blood?
NURSE. It did, it did; alas the day, it did!
JULIET. O serpent heart, hid with a flow'ring face!
Did ever dragon keep so fair a cave?
Beautiful tyrant! fiend angelical!
Dove-feather'd raven! wolfish-ravening lamb!
Despised substance of divinest show!
Just opposite to what thou justly seem'st,
A damned saint, an honourable villain!
O nature, what hadst thou to do in hell,
When thou didst bower the spirit of a fiend
In mortal paradise of such sweet flesh?
Was ever book containing such vile matter
So fairly bound? O, that deceit should dwell
In such a gorgeous palace!
NURSE. There's no trust,
No faith, no honesty in men; all perjur'd,
All forsworn, all naught, all dissemblers.
Ah, where's my man? Give me some aqua-vitæ.
These griefs, these woes, these sorrows, make me old.
Shame come to Romeo!

JULIET. Blister'd be thy tongue
For such a wish! He was not born to shame:
Upon his brow shame is asham'd to sit;
For 'tis a throne where honour may be crown'd
Sole monarch of the universal earth.
O, what a beast was I to chide at him!
NURSE. Will you speak well of him that kill'd your cousin?
JULIET. Shall I speak ill of him that is my husband?
Ah, poor my lord, what tongue shall smooth thy name,
When I, thy three-hours wife, have mangled it?
But wherefore, villain, didst thou kill my cousin?
That villain cousin would have kill'd my husband.
Back, foolish tears, back to your native spring;
Your tributary drops belong to woe,
Which you, mistaking, offer up to joy.
My husband lives that Tybalt would have slain,
And Tybalt's dead that would have slain my husband.
All this is comfort; wherefore weep I then?
Some word there was, worser than Tybalt's death,
That murd'red me; I would forget it fain,
But, O, it presses to my memory
Like damned guilty deeds to sinners' minds:
'Tybalt is dead, and Romeo banished.'
That 'banished,' that one word 'banished,'
Hath slain ten thousand Tybalts. Tybalt's death
Was woe enough, if it had ended there;
Or if sour woe delights in fellowship
And needly will be rank'd with other griefs,
Why followed not, when she said 'Tybalt's dead,'
Thy father or thy mother, nay, or both,
Which modern lamentation might have mov'd?
But, with a rear-ward following Tybalt's death,
'Romeo is banished'—to speak that word
Is father, mother, Tybalt, Romeo, Juliet,
All slain, all dead. 'Romeo is banished'—
There is no end, no limit, measure, bound,
In that word's death; no words can that woe sound.
Where is my father and my mother, nurse?
NURSE. Weeping and wailing over Tybalt's corse.
Will you go to them? I will bring you thither.

JULIET. Wash they his wounds with tears! Mine shall be spent,
When theirs are dry, for Romeo's banishment.
Take up those cords. Poor ropes, you are beguil'd,
Both you and I, for Romeo is exil'd;
He made you for a highway to my bed,
But I, a maid, die maiden-widowed.
Come, cords; come, nurse; I'll to my wedding-bed;
And death, not Romeo, take my maidenhead!

NURSE. Hie to your chamber; I'll find Romeo
To comfort you. I wot well where he is.
Hark ye, your Romeo will be here at night.
I'll to him; he is hid at Lawrence' cell.

JULIET. O, find him! give this ring to my true knight,
And bid him come to take his last farewell. *Exeunt*

SCENE 3

FRIAR LAWRENCE'S *cell*

Enter FRIAR LAWRENCE

FRIAR LAWRENCE. Romeo, come forth; come forth, thou fearful man;
Affliction is enamour'd of thy parts,
And thou art wedded to calamity.

Enter ROMEO

ROMEO. Father, what news? What is the Prince's doom?
What sorrow craves acquaintance at my hand
That I yet know not?

FRIAR LAWRENCE. Too familiar
Is my dear son with such sour company;
I bring thee tidings of the Prince's doom.

ROMEO. What less than doomsday is the Prince's doom?

FRIAR LAWRENCE. A gentler judgment vanish'd from his lips—
Not body's death, but body's banishment.

ROMEO. Ha, banishment! Be merciful, say 'death';
For exile hath more terror in his look,

Much more than death. Do not say 'banishment.'
FRIAR LAWRENCE. Here from Verona art thou banished.
Be patient, for the world is broad and wide.
ROMEO. There is no world without Verona walls,
But purgatory, torture, hell itself.
Hence banished is banish'd from the world,
And world's exile is death. Then 'banished'
Is death mis-term'd; calling death 'banished,'
Thou cut'st my head off with a golden axe,
And smilest upon the stroke that murders me.
FRIAR LAWRENCE. O deadly sin! O rude unthankfulness!
Thy fault our law calls death; but the kind Prince,
Taking thy part, hath rush'd aside the law,
And turn'd that black word death to banishment.
This is dear mercy, and thou seest it not.
ROMEO. 'Tis torture, and not mercy; heaven is here
Where Juliet lives, and every cat, and dog,
And little mouse, every unworthy thing,
Live here in heaven and may look on her;
But Romeo may not. More validity,
More honourable state, more courtship lives
In carrion flies than Romeo. They may seize
On the white wonder of dear Juliet's hand,
And steal immortal blessing from her lips;
Who, even in pure and vestal modesty,
Still blush, as thinking their own kisses sin;
But Romeo may not—he is banished.
This may flies do, when I from this must fly;
They are free men, but I am banished.
And sayest thou yet that exile is not death?
Hadst thou no poison mix'd, no sharp-ground knife,
No sudden mean of death, though ne'er so mean,
But 'banished' to kill me—'banished'?
O friar, the damned use that word in hell;
Howling attends it; how hast thou the heart,
Being a divine, a ghostly confessor,
A sin-absolver, and my friend profess'd,
To mangle me with that word 'banished'?
FRIAR LAWRENCE. Thou fond mad man, hear me a little speak.

ROMEO. O, thou wilt speak again of banishment.

FRIAR LAWRENCE. I'll give thee armour to keep off that word;
Adversity's sweet milk, philosophy,
To comfort thee, though thou art banished.

ROMEO. Yet 'banished'? Hang up philosophy;
Unless philosophy can make a Juliet,
Displant a town, reverse a prince's doom,
It helps not, it prevails not. Talk no more.

FRIAR LAWRENCE. O, then I see that madmen have no ears.

ROMEO. How should they, when that wise men have no eyes?

FRIAR LAWRENCE. Let me dispute with thee of thy estate.

ROMEO. Thou canst not speak of that thou dost not feel.
Wert thou as young as I, Juliet thy love,
An hour but married, Tybalt murdered,
Doting like me, and like me banished,
Then mightst thou speak, then mightst thou tear thy hair,
And fall upon the ground, as I do now,
Taking the measure of an unmade grave.
[*Knocking within*]

FRIAR LAWRENCE. Arise; one knocks. Good Romeo, hide thyself.

ROMEO. Not I; unless the breath of heart-sick groans,
Mist-like, enfold me from the search of eyes. [*Knocking*]

FRIAR LAWRENCE. Hark how they knock! Who's there? Romeo, arise;
Thou wilt be taken.—Stay awhile.—Stand up; [*Knocking*]
Run to my study.—By and by.—God's will,
What simpleness is this!—I come, I come. [*Knocking*]
Who knocks so hard? Whence come you? What's your will?

NURSE. [*Within*] Let me come in and you shall know my errand;
I come from Lady Juliet.

FRIAR LAWRENCE. Welcome, then.

Enter NURSE

NURSE. O holy friar, O, tell me, holy friar,
Where's my lady's lord, where's Romeo?

FRIAR LAWRENCE. There on the ground, with his own tears made drunk.
NURSE. O, he is even in my mistress' case,
Just in her case!
FRIAR LAWRENCE. O woeful sympathy!
Piteous predicament!
NURSE. Even so lies she,
Blubb'ring and weeping, weeping and blubb'ring.
Stand up, stand up; stand, an you be a man;
For Juliet's sake, for her sake, rise and stand;
Why should you fall into so deep an O?
ROMEO. Nurse!
NURSE. Ah, sir! ah, sir! Well, death's the end of all.
ROMEO. Spakest thou of Juliet? How is it with her?
Doth not she think me an old murderer,
Now I have stain'd the childhood of our joy
With blood remov'd but little from her own?
Where is she? and how doth she? and what says
My conceal'd lady to our cancell'd love?
NURSE. O, she says nothing, sir, but weeps and weeps;
And now falls on her bed, and then starts up,
And Tybalt calls; and then on Romeo cries,
And then down falls again.
ROMEO. As if that name,
Shot from the deadly level of a gun,
Did murder her; as that name's cursed hand
Murder'd her kinsman. O, tell me, friar, tell me,
In what vile part of this anatomy
Doth my name lodge? Tell me that I may sack
The hateful mansion. [*Drawing his sword*]
FRIAR LAWRENCE. Hold thy desperate hand.
Art thou a man? Thy form cries out thou art:
Thy tears are womanish; thy wild acts denote
The unreasonable fury of a beast.
Unseemly woman in a seeming man!
And ill-beseeming beast in seeming both!
Thou has amaz'd me. By my holy order,
I thought thy disposition better temper'd.
Hast thou slain Tybalt? Wilt thou slay thyself?
And slay thy lady that in thy life lives,

By doing damned hate upon thyself?
Why railest thou on thy birth, the heaven, and earth?
Since birth, and heaven, and earth, all three do meet
In thee at once; which thou at once wouldst lose.
Fie, fie! thou shamest thy shape, thy love, thy wit
Which, like a usurer, abound'st in all,
And usest none in that true use indeed
Which should bedeck thy shape, thy love, thy wit.
Thy noble shape is but a form of wax,
Digressing from the valour of a man;
Thy dear love sworn but hollow perjury,
Killing that love which thou hast vow'd to cherish;
Thy wit, that ornament to shape and love,
Misshapen in the conduct of them both,
Like powder in a skilless soldier's flask,
Is set afire by thine own ignorance,
And thou dismemb'red with thine own defence.
What, rouse thee, man! Thy Juliet is alive,
For whose dear sake thou wast but lately dead;
There art thou happy. Tybalt would kill thee,
But thou slewest Tybalt; there art thou happy too.
The law, that threat'ned death, becomes thy friend,
And turns it to exile; there art thou happy.
A pack of blessings lights upon thy back;
Happiness courts thee in her best array;
But, like a misbehav'd and sullen wench,
Thou pout'st upon thy fortune and thy love.
Take heed, take heed, for such die miserable.
Go, get thee to thy love, as was decreed,
Ascend her chamber, hence and comfort her.
But look thou stay not till the watch be set,
For then thou canst not pass to Mantua,
Where thou shalt live till we can find a time
To blaze your marriage, reconcile your friends,
Beg pardon of the Prince, and call thee back
With twenty hundred thousand times more joy
Than thou went'st forth in lamentation.
Go before, nurse; commend me to thy lady;
And bid her hasten all the house to bed,
Which heavy sorrow makes them apt unto;

Romeo is coming.
NURSE. O Lord, I could have stay'd here all the night
To hear good counsel; O, what learning is!
My lord, I'll tell my lady you will come.
ROMEO. Do so, and bid my sweet prepare to chide.
NURSE. Here, sir, a ring she bid me give you, sir.
Hie you, make haste, for it grows very late. *Exit*
ROMEO. How well my comfort is reviv'd by this!
FRIAR LAWRENCE. Go hence; good night; and here stands all your state:
Either be gone before the watch be set,
Or by the break of day disguis'd from hence.
Sojourn in Mantua; I'll find out your man,
And he shall signify from time to time
Every good hap to you that chances here.
Give me thy hand. 'Tis late; farewell; good night.
ROMEO. But that a joy past joy calls out on me,
It were a grief so brief to part with thee.
Farewell. *Exeunt*

SCENE 4

CAPULET'S *house*

Enter CAPULET, LADY CAPULET, *and* PARIS

CAPULET. Things have fall'n out, sir, so unluckily
That we have had no time to move our daughter.
Look you, she lov'd her kinsman Tybalt dearly,
And so did I. Well, we were born to die.
'Tis very late; she'll not come down to-night.
I promise you, but for your company,
I would have been abed an hour ago.
PARIS. These times of woe afford no time to woo.
Madam, good night; commend me to your daughter.
LADY CAPULET. I will, and know her mind early to-morrow;
To-night, she's mew'd up to her heaviness.
CAPULET. Sir Paris, I will make a desperate tender
Of my child's love. I think she will be rul'd
In all respects by me; nay, more, I doubt it not.
Wife, go you to her ere you go to bed;

Acquaint her here of my son Paris' love
And bid her, mark you me, on Wednesday next—
But, soft! what day is this?
PARIS. Monday, my lord.
CAPULET. Monday! ha, ha! Well, Wednesday is too soon.
A Thursday let it be; a Thursday, tell her,
She shall be married to this noble earl.
Will you be ready? Do you like this haste?
We'll keep no great ado—a friend or two;
For, hark you, Tybalt being slain so late,
It may be thought we held him carelessly,
Being our kinsman, if we revel much;
Therefore we'll have some half a dozen friends,
And there an end. But what say you to Thursday?
PARIS. My lord, I would that Thursday were to-morrow.
CAPULET. Well, get you gone; a Thursday be it then.
Go you to Juliet ere you go to bed;
Prepare her, wife, against this wedding-day.
Farewell, my lord. Light to my chamber, ho!
Afore me, it is so very very late
That we may call it early by and by.
Good night. *Exeunt*

SCENE 5

CAPULET'S *orchard*

Enter ROMEO *and* JULIET, *aloft*

JULIET. Wilt thou be gone? It is not yet near day;
It was the nightingale, and not the lark,
That pierc'd the fearful hollow of thine ear;
Nightly she sings on yond pomegranate tree.
Believe me, love, it was the nightingale.
ROMEO. It was the lark, the herald of the morn,
No nightingale. Look, love, what envious streaks
Do lace the severing clouds in yonder east;
Night's candles are burnt out, and jocund day
Stands tiptoe on the misty mountain tops.
I must be gone and live, or stay and die.

JULIET. Yond light is not daylight; I know it, I:
It is some meteor that the sun exhales
To be to thee this night a torch-bearer,
And light thee on thy way to Mantua;
Therefore stay yet; thou need'st not to be gone.
ROMEO. Let me be ta'en, let me be put to death;
I am content, so thou wilt have it so.
I'll say yon grey is not the morning's eye,
'Tis but the pale reflex of Cynthia's brow;
Nor that is not the lark whose notes do beat
The vaulty heaven so high above our heads.
I have more care to stay than will to go.
Come death, and welcome! Juliet wills it so.
How is't, my soul? Let's talk–it is not day.
JULIET. It is, it is; hie hence, be gone, away!
It is the lark that sings so out of tune,
Straining harsh discords and unpleasing sharps.
Some say the lark makes sweet division;
This doth not so, for she divideth us.
Some say the lark and loathed toad change eyes;
O, now I would they had chang'd voices too!
Since arm from arm that voice doth us affray,
Hunting thee hence with hunts-up to the day.
O, now be gone! More light and light it grows.
ROMEO. More light and light–more dark and dark our woes.

Enter NURSE

NURSE. Madam!
JULIET. Nurse?
NURSE. Your lady mother is coming to your chamber.
The day is broke; be wary, look about. *Exit*
JULIET. Then, window, let day in and let life out.
ROMEO. Farewell, farewell! One kiss, and I'll descend.
[*He goeth down*]
JULIET. Art thou gone so, love–lord, ay, husband, friend!
I must hear from thee every day in the hour,
For in a minute there are many days;
O, by this count I shall be much in years
Ere I again behold my Romeo!
ROMEO. Farewell!

I will omit no opportunity
That may convey my greetings, love, to thee.

JULIET. O, think'st thou we shall ever meet again?

ROMEO. I doubt it not; and all these woes shall serve
For sweet discourses in our times to come.

JULIET. O God, I have an ill-divining soul!
Methinks I see thee, now thou art below,
As one dead in the bottom of a tomb;
Either my eyesight fails or thou look'st pale.

ROMEO. And trust me, love, in my eye so do you;
Dry sorrow drinks our blood. Adieu, adieu! *Exit below*

JULIET. O Fortune, Fortune! all men call thee fickle.
If thou art fickle, what dost thou with him
That is renown'd for faith? Be fickle, Fortune;
For then, I hope, thou wilt not keep him long,
But send him back.

LADY CAPULET. [*Within*] Ho, daughter! are you up?

JULIET. Who is't that calls? It is my lady mother.
Is she not down so late, or up so early?
What unaccustom'd cause procures her hither?

Enter LADY CAPULET

LADY CAPULET. Why, how now, Juliet!

JULIET. Madam, I am not well.

LADY CAPULET. Evermore weeping for your cousin's death?
What, wilt thou wash him from his grave with tears?
An if thou couldst, thou couldst not make him live;
Therefore have done. Some grief shows much of love;
But much of grief shows still some want of wit.

JULIET. Yet let me weep for such a feeling loss.

LADY CAPULET. So shall you feel the loss, but not the friend
Which you weep for.

JULIET. Feeling so the loss,
I cannot choose but ever weep the friend.

LADY CAPULET. Well, girl, thou weep'st not so much for his death
As that the villain lives which slaughter'd him.

JULIET. What villain, madam?

LADY CAPULET. That same villain, Romeo.

JULIET. [*Aside*] Villain and he be many miles asunder!—

God pardon him! I do, with all my heart;
And yet no man like he doth grieve my heart.

LADY CAPULET. That is because the traitor murderer lives.

JULIET. Ay, madam, from the reach of these my hands.
Would none but I might venge my cousin's death!

LADY CAPULET. We will have vengeance for it, fear thou not;
Then weep no more. I'll send to one in Mantua—
Where that same banish'd runagate doth live—
Shall give him such an unaccustom'd dram
That he shall soon keep Tybalt company;
And then I hope thou wilt be satisfied.

JULIET. Indeed I never shall be satisfied
With Romeo till I behold him—dead—
Is my poor heart so for a kinsman vex'd.
Madam, if you could find out but a man
To bear a poison, I would temper it,
That Romeo should, upon receipt thereof,
Soon sleep in quiet. O, how my heart abhors
To hear him nam'd, and cannot come to him,
To wreak the love I bore my cousin Tybalt
Upon his body that hath slaughter'd him!

LADY CAPULET. Find thou the means, and I'll find such a man.
But now I'll tell thee joyful tidings, girl.

JULIET. And joy comes well in such a needy time.
What are they, beseech your ladyship?

LADY CAPULET. Well, well, thou hast a careful father, child;
One who, to put thee from thy heaviness,
Hath sorted out a sudden day of joy
That thou expects not, nor I look'd not for.

JULIET. Madam, in happy time, what day is that?

LADY CAPULET. Marry, my child, early next Thursday morn
The gallant, young, and noble gentleman,
The County Paris, at Saint Peter's Church,
Shall happily make thee there a joyful bride.

JULIET. Now, by Saint Peter's Church, and Peter too,
He shall not make me there a joyful bride.
I wonder at this haste, that I must wed
Ere he that should be husband comes to woo.

I pray you tell my lord and father, madam,
I will not marry yet; and when I do, I swear
It shall be Romeo, whom you know I hate,
Rather than Paris. These are news indeed!

LADY CAPULET. Here comes your father; tell him so yourself,
And see how he will take it at your hands.

Enter CAPULET *and* NURSE

CAPULET. When the sun sets, the air doth drizzle dew;
But for the sunset of my brother's son
It rains downright.
How now! a conduit, girl? What, still in tears?
Evermore show'ring? In one little body
Thou counterfeit'st a bark, a sea, a wind;
For still thy eyes, which I may call the sea,
Do ebb and flow with tears. The bark thy body is,
Sailing in this salt flood; the winds thy sighs,
Who, raging with thy tears, and they with them,
Without a sudden calm will overset
Thy tempest-tossed body. How now, wife!
Have you delivered to her our decree?

LADY CAPULET. Ay, sir; but she will none, she gives you thanks.
I would the fool were married to her grave!

CAPULET. Soft! take me with you, take me with you, wife.
How will she none? Doth she not give us thanks?
Is she not proud? Doth she not count her blest,
Unworthy as she is, that we have wrought
So worthy a gentleman to be her bridegroom?

JULIET. Not proud you have, but thankful that you have.
Proud can I never be of what I hate,
But thankful even for hate that is meant love.

CAPULET. How how, how how, chopt logic! What is this?
'Proud'—and 'I thank you'—and 'I thank you not'—
And yet 'not proud'? Mistress minion, you,
Thank me no thankings, nor proud me no prouds,
But fettle your fine joints 'gainst Thursday next,
To go with Paris to Saint Peter's Church,
Or I will drag thee on a hurdle thither.

Out, you green-sickness carrion! Out, you baggage!
You tallow-face!
LADY CAPULET. Fie, fie! what, are you mad?
JULIET. Good father, I beseech you on my knees,
Hear me with patience but to speak a word.
CAPULET. Hang thee, young baggage! disobedient wretch!
I tell thee what—get thee to church a Thursday,
Or never after look me in the face.
Speak not, reply not, do not answer me;
My fingers itch. Wife, we scarce thought us blest
That God had lent us but this only child;
But now I see this one is one too much,
And that we have a curse in having her.
Out on her, hilding!
NURSE. God in heaven bless her!
You are to blame, my lord, to rate her so.
CAPULET. And why, my Lady Wisdom? Hold your tongue,
Good Prudence; smatter with your gossips, go.
NURSE. I speak no treason.
CAPULET. O, God-i-goden!
NURSE. May not one speak?
CAPULET. Peace, you mumbling fool!
Utter your gravity o'er a gossip's bowl,
For here we need it not.
LADY CAPULET. You are too hot.
CAPULET. God's bread! it makes me mad:
Day, night, hour, tide, time, work, play,
Alone, in company, still my care hath been
To have her match'd; and having now provided
A gentleman of noble parentage,
Of fair demesnes, youthful, and nobly train'd,
Stuff'd, as they say, with honourable parts,
Proportion'd as one's thought would wish a man—
And then to have a wretched puling fool,
A whining mammet, in her fortune's tender,
To answer 'I'll not wed, I cannot love,
I am too young, I pray you pardon me!'
But, an you will not wed, I'll pardon you.
Graze where you will, you shall not house with me.
Look to't, think on't; I do not use to jest.

Thursday is near; lay hand on heart, advise:
An you be mine, I'll give you to my friend;
An you be not, hang, beg, starve, die in the streets,
For, by my soul, I'll ne'er acknowledge thee,
Nor what is mine shall never do thee good.
Trust to't, bethink you, I'll not be forsworn. *Exit*

JULIET. Is there no pity sitting in the clouds
That sees into the bottom of my grief?
O, sweet my mother, cast me not away!
Delay this marriage for a month, a week;
Or, if you do not, make the bridal bed
In that dim monument where Tybalt lies.

LADY CAPULET. Talk not to me, for I'll not speak a word;
Do as thou wilt, for I have done with thee. *Exit*

JULIET. O God!—O nurse! how shall this be prevented?
My husband is on earth, my faith in heaven;
How shall that faith return again to earth,
Unless that husband send it me from heaven
By leaving earth? Comfort me, counsel me.
Alack, alack, that heaven should practise stratagems
Upon so soft a subject as myself!
What say'st thou! Hast thou not a word of joy?
Some comfort, nurse.

NURSE. Faith, here it is:
Romeo is banished; and all the world to nothing
That he dares ne'er come back to challenge you;
Or, if he do, it needs must be by stealth.
Then, since the case so stands as now it doth,
I think it best you married with the County.
O, he's a lovely gentleman!
Romeo's a dishclout to him; an eagle, madam,
Hath not so green, so quick, so fair an eye
As Paris hath. Beshrew my very heart,
I think you are happy in this second match,
For it excels your first; or, if it did not,
Your first is dead, or 'twere as good he were
As living here and you no use of him.

JULIET. Speak'st thou from thy heart?

NURSE. And from my soul too, else beshrew them both.

JULIET. Amen!

NURSE. What?
JULIET. Well, thou hast comforted me marvellous much.
Go in; and tell my lady I am gone,
Having displeas'd my father, to Lawrence' cell
To make confession, and to be absolv'd.
NURSE. Marry, I will; and this is wisely done. *Exit*
JULIET. Ancient damnation! O most wicked fiend!
Is it more sin to wish me thus forsworn,
Or to dispraise my lord with that same tongue
Which she hath prais'd him with above compare
So many thousand times? Go, counsellor;
Thou and my bosom henceforth shall be twain.
I'll to the friar to know his remedy;
If all else fail, myself have power to die. *Exit*

ACT IV. SCENE 1

FRIAR LAWRENCE'S *cell*

Enter FRIAR LAWRENCE *and* COUNTY PARIS

FRIAR LAWRENCE. On Thursday, sir? The time is very short.
PARIS. My father Capulet will have it so,
And I am nothing slow to slack his haste.
FRIAR LAWRENCE. You say you do not know the lady's mind;
Uneven is the course; I like it not.
PARIS. Immoderately she weeps for Tybalt's death,
And therefore have I little talk'd of love;
For Venus smiles not in a house of tears.
Now, sir, her father counts it dangerous
That she do give her sorrow so much sway,
And in his wisdom hastes our marriage,
To stop the inundation of her tears;
Which, too much minded by herself alone,
May be put from her by society.
Now do you know the reason of this haste.
FRIAR LAWRENCE. [*Aside*] I would I knew not why it should be slow'd.—

Look, sir, here comes the lady toward my cell.

Enter JULIET

PARIS. Happily met, my lady and my wife!
JULIET. That may be, sir, when I may be a wife.
PARIS. That may be must be, love, on Thursday next.
JULIET. What must be shall be.
FRIAR LAWRENCE. That's a certain text.
PARIS. Come you to make confession to this father?
JULIET. To answer that, I should confess to you.
PARIS. Do not deny to him that you love me.
JULIET. I will confess to you that I love him.
PARIS. So will ye, I am sure, that you love me.
JULIET. If I do so, it will be of more price
Being spoke behind your back than to your face.
PARIS. Poor soul, thy face is much abus'd with tears.
JULIET. The tears have got small victory by that,
For it was bad enough before their spite.
PARIS. Thou wrong'st it more than tears with that report.
JULIET. That is no slander, sir, which is a truth;
And what I spake, I spake it to my face.
PARIS. Thy face is mine, and thou hast sland'red it.
JULIET. It may be so, for it is not mine own.
Are you at leisure, holy father, now,
Or shall I come to you at evening mass?
FRIAR LAWRENCE. My leisure serves me, pensive daughter, now.
My lord, we must entreat the time alone.
PARIS. God shield I should disturb devotion!
Juliet, on Thursday early will I rouse ye;
Till then, adieu, and keep this holy kiss. *Exit*
JULIET. O, shut the door, and when thou hast done so,
Come weep with me—past hope, past cure, past help.
FRIAR LAWRENCE. O, Juliet, I already know thy grief;
It strains me past the compass of my wits.
I hear thou must, and nothing may prorogue it,
On Thursday next be married to this County.
JULIET. Tell me not, friar, that thou hear'st of this,
Unless thou tell me how I may prevent it;
If, in thy wisdom, thou canst give no help,

Do thou but call my resolution wise,
And with this knife I'll help it presently.
God join'd my heart and Romeo's, thou our hands;
And ere this hand, by thee to Romeo's seal'd,
Shall be the label to another deed,
Or my true heart with treacherous revolt
Turn to another, this shall slay them both.
Therefore, out of thy long-experienc'd time,
Give me some present counsel; or, behold,
'Twixt my extremes and me this bloody knife
Shall play the umpire, arbitrating that
Which the commission of thy years and art
Could to no issue of true honour bring.
Be not so long to speak; I long to die,
If what thou speak'st speak not of remedy.

FRIAR LAWRENCE. Hold, daughter; I do spy a kind of hope,
Which craves as desperate an execution
As that is desperate which we would prevent.
If, rather than to marry County Paris,
Thou hast the strength of will to slay thyself,
Then is it likely thou wilt undertake
A thing like death to chide away this shame,
That cop'st with death himself to scape from it;
And, if thou dar'st, I'll give thee remedy.

JULIET. O, bid me leap, rather than marry Paris,
From off the battlements of any tower,
Or walk in thievish ways, or bid me lurk
Where serpents are; chain me with roaring bears,
Or hide me nightly in a charnel house,
O'er-cover'd quite with dead men's rattling bones,
With reeky shanks and yellow chapless skulls;
Or bid me go into a new-made grave,
And hide me with a dead man in his shroud—
Things that, to hear them told, have made me tremble—
And I will do it without fear or doubt,
To live an unstain'd wife to my sweet love.

FRIAR LAWRENCE. Hold, then; go home, be merry, give consent
To marry Paris. Wednesday is to-morrow;
To-morrow night look that thou lie alone,

Let not the nurse lie with thee in thy chamber.
Take thou this vial, being then in bed,
And this distilled liquor drink thou off;
When presently through all thy veins shall run
A cold and drowsy humour; for no pulse
Shall keep his native progress, but surcease;
No warmth, no breath, shall testify thou livest;
The roses in thy lips and cheeks shall fade
To paly ashes, thy eyes' windows fall,
Like death when he shuts up the day of life;
Each part, depriv'd of supple government,
Shall, stiff and stark and cold, appear like death;
And in this borrow'd likeness of shrunk death
Thou shalt continue two and forty hours,
And then awake as from a pleasant sleep.
Now, when the bridegroom in the morning comes
To rouse thee from thy bed, there art thou dead.
Then, as the manner of our country is,
In thy best robes, uncovered on the bier,
Thou shalt be borne to that same ancient vault
Where all the kindred of the Capulets lie.
In the meantime, against thou shalt awake,
Shall Romeo by my letters know our drift,
And hither shall he come; and he and I
Will watch thy waking, and that very night
Shall Romeo bear thee hence to Mantua.
And this shall free thee from this present shame,
If no inconstant toy nor womanish fear
Abate thy valour in the acting it.

JULIET. Give me, give me! O, tell not me of fear!

FRIAR LAWRENCE. Hold; get you gone, be strong and prosperous
In this resolve. I'll send a friar with speed
To Mantua, with my letters to thy lord.

JULIET. Love give me strength! and strength shall help afford.
Farewell, dear father! *Exeunt*

SCENE 2

CAPULET'S *house*

Enter CAPULET, LADY CAPULET, NURSE, *and two or three servingmen*

CAPULET. So many guests invite as here are writ.

Exit a SERVINGMAN

Sirrah, go hire me twenty cunning cooks.

SERVINGMAN. You shall have none ill, sir; for I'll try if they can lick their fingers.

CAPULET. How canst thou try them so?

SERVINGMAN. Marry, sir, 'tis an ill cook that cannot lick his own fingers; therefore he that cannot lick his fingers goes not with me.

CAPULET. Go, be gone. *Exit second* SERVINGMAN

We shall be much unfurnish'd for this time.
What, is my daughter gone to Friar Lawrence?

NURSE. Ay, forsooth.

CAPULET. Well, he may chance to do some good on her:
A peevish self-will'd harlotry it is.

Enter JULIET

NURSE. See where she comes from shrift with merry look.

CAPULET. How now, my headstrong! Where have you been gadding?

JULIET. Where I have learnt me to repent the sin
Of disobedient opposition
To you and your behests; and am enjoin'd
By holy Lawrence to fall prostrate here,
To beg your pardon. Pardon, I beseech you.
Henceforward I am ever rul'd by you.

CAPULET. Send for the County; go tell him of this.
I'll have this knot knit up to-morrow morning.

JULIET. I met the youthful lord at Lawrence' cell,
And gave him what becomed love I might,
Not stepping o'er the bounds of modesty.

CAPULET. Why, I am glad on't; this is well—stand up—
This is as't should be. Let me see the County;

Ay, marry, go, I say, and fetch him hither.
Now, afore God, this reverend holy friar,
All our whole city is much bound to him.

JULIET. Nurse, will you go with me into my closet
To help me sort such needful ornaments
As you think fit to furnish me to-morrow?

LADY CAPULET. No, not till Thursday; there is time enough.

CAPULET. Go, nurse, go with her. We'll to church to-morrow. *Exeunt* JULIET *and* NURSE

LADY CAPULET. We shall be short in our provision;
'Tis now near night.

CAPULET. Tush, I will stir about,
And all things shall be well, I warrant thee, wife.
Go thou to Juliet, help to deck up her;
I'll not to bed to-night; let me alone.
I'll play the huswife for this once. What, ho!
They are all forth; well, I will walk myself
To County Paris, to prepare up him
Against to-morrow. My heart is wondrous light
Since this same wayward girl is so reclaim'd. *Exeunt*

SCENE 3

JULIET'S *chamber*

Enter JULIET *and* NURSE

JULIET. Ay, those attires are best; but, gentle nurse,
I pray thee, leave me to myself to-night,
For I have need of many orisons
To move the heavens to smile upon my state,
Which well thou knowest is cross and full of sin.

Enter LADY CAPULET

LADY CAPULET. What, are you busy, ho? Need you my help?

JULIET. No, madam; we have cull'd such necessaries
As are behoveful for our state to-morrow.
So please you, let me now be left alone,
And let the nurse this night sit up with you;

For I am sure you have your hands full all
In this so sudden business.

LADY CAPULET. Good night.
Get thee to bed, and rest; for thou hast need.
Exeunt LADY CAPULET *and* NURSE

JULIET. Farewell! God knows when we shall meet again.
I have a faint cold fear thrills through my veins,
That almost freezes up the heat of life;
I'll call them back again to comfort me.
Nurse!—What should she do here?
My dismal scene I needs must act alone.
Come, vial.
What if this mixture do not work at all?
Shall I be married, then, to-morrow morning?
No, no; this shall forbid it. Lie thou there.
[*Laying down her dagger*]
What if it be a poison which the friar
Subtly hath minist'red to have me dead,
Lest in this marriage he should be dishonour'd,
Because he married me before to Romeo?
I fear it is; and yet methinks it should not,
For he hath still been tried a holy man.
How, if, when I am laid into the tomb,
I wake before the time that Romeo
Come to redeem me? There's a fearful point.
Shall I not then be stifled in the vault,
To whose foul mouth no healthsome air breathes in,
And there die strangled ere my Romeo comes?
Or, if I live, is it not very like
The horrible conceit of death and night,
Together with the terror of the place—
As in a vault, an ancient receptacle
Where for this many hundred years the bones
Of all my buried ancestors are pack'd;
Where bloody Tybalt, yet but green in earth,
Lies fest'ring in his shroud; where, as they say,
At some hours in the night spirits resort—
Alack, alack, is it not like that I,
So early waking—what with loathsome smells,
And shrieks like mandrakes' torn out of the earth,

That living mortals, hearing them, run mad—
O, if I wake, shall I not be distraught,
Environed with all these hideous fears,
And madly play with my forefathers' joints,
And pluck the mangled Tybalt from his shroud,
And, in this rage, with some great kinsman's bone,
As with a club, dash out my desp'rate brains?
O, look! methinks I see my cousin's ghost
Seeking out Romeo, that did spit his body
Upon a rapier's point. Stay, Tybalt, stay.
Romeo, I come. This do I drink to thee.
[*She drinks and falls upon her bed within the curtains*]

SCENE 4

CAPULET'S *house*

Enter LADY CAPULET *and* NURSE

LADY CAPULET. Hold, take these keys, and fetch more spices, nurse.

NURSE. They call for dates and quinces in the pastry.

Enter CAPULET

CAPULET. Come, stir, stir, stir! The second cock hath crow'd,
The curfew bell hath rung, 'tis three o'clock.
Look to the bak'd meats, good Angelica;
Spare not for cost.

NURSE. Go, you cot-quean, go,
Get you to bed; faith, you'll be sick to-morrow
For this night's watching.

CAPULET. No, not a whit; what! I have watch'd ere now
All night for lesser cause, and ne'er been sick.

LADY CAPULET. Ay, you have been a mouse-hunt in your time;
But I will watch you from such watching now.
Exeunt LADY CAPULET *and* NURSE

CAPULET. A jealous-hood, a jealous-hood!

ACT IV. SCENE 4

Enter three or four servingmen with spits and logs and baskets

Now, fellow, what is there?

FIRST FELLOW. Things for the cook, sir; but I know not what.

CAPULET. Make haste, make haste. *Exit* FIRST FELLOW
Sirrah, fetch drier logs;
Call Peter; he will show thee where they are.

SECOND FELLOW. I have a head, sir, that will find out logs,
And never trouble Peter for the matter.

CAPULET. Mass, and well said; a merry whoreson, ha!
Thou shalt be logger-head. *Exit* SECOND FELLOW
Good faith, 'tis day;
The County will be here with music straight,
For so he said he would. [*Play music*] I hear him near.
Nurse! Wife! What, ho! What, nurse, I say!

Re-enter NURSE

Go waken Juliet, go and trim her up;
I'll go and chat with Paris. Hie, make haste,
Make haste. The bridegroom he is come already.
Make haste, I say. *Exeunt*

SCENE 5

JULIET's *chamber*

Enter NURSE

NURSE. Mistress! What, mistress! Juliet! Fast, I warrant her, she.
Why, lamb! Why, lady! Fie, you slug-a-bed!
Why, love, I say! madam! sweetheart! Why, bride!
What, not a word? You take your pennyworths now.
Sleep for a week; for the next night, I warrant,
The County Paris hath set up his rest
That you shall rest but little. God forgive me!
Marry, and amen. How sound is she asleep!
I needs must wake her. Madam, madam, madam!

Ay, let the County take you in your bed;
He'll fright you up, i' faith. Will it not be?
[*Draws the curtains*]
What, dress'd, and in your clothes, and down again!
I must needs wake you. Lady! lady! lady!
Alas, alas! Help, help! my lady's dead!
O well-a-day that ever I was born!
Some aqua-vitæ, ho! My lord! My lady!

Enter LADY CAPULET

LADY CAPULET. What noise is here?
NURSE. O lamentable day!
LADY CAPULET. What is the matter?
NURSE. Look, look! O heavy day!
LADY CAPULET. O me, O me! My child, my only life,
Revive, look up, or I will die with thee!
Help, help! Call help.

Enter CAPULET

CAPULET. For shame, bring Juliet forth; her lord is come.
NURSE. She's dead, deceas'd, she's dead; alack the day!
LADY CAPULET. Alack the day, she's dead, she's dead, she's dead!
CAPULET. Ha! let me see her. Out, alas! she's cold;
Her blood is settled, and her joints are stiff.
Life and these lips have long been separated.
Death lies on her like an untimely frost
Upon the sweetest flower of all the field.
NURSE. O lamentable day!
LADY CAPULET. O woeful time!
CAPULET. Death, that hath ta'en her hence to make me wail,
Ties up my tongue and will not let me speak.

Enter FRIAR LAWRENCE *and* COUNTY PARIS, *with musicians*

FRIAR LAWRENCE. Come, is the bride ready to go to church?
CAPULET. Ready to go, but never to return.
O son, the night before thy wedding day
Hath Death lain with thy wife. There she lies,
Flower as she was, deflowered by him.

Death is my son-in-law, Death is my heir;
My daughter he hath wedded; I will die,
And leave him all; life, living, all is Death's.

PARIS. Have I thought long to see this morning's face,
And doth it give me such a sight as this?

LADY CAPULET. Accurs'd, unhappy, wretched, hateful day!
Most miserable hour that e'er time saw
In lasting labour of his pilgrimage!
But one, poor one, one poor and loving child,
But one thing to rejoice and solace in,
And cruel Death hath catch'd it from my sight!

NURSE. O woe! O woeful, woeful, woeful day!
Most lamentable day, most woeful day
That ever, ever, I did yet behold!
O day! O day! O day! O hateful day!
Never was seen so black a day as this.
O woeful day, O woeful day!

PARIS. Beguil'd, divorced, wronged, spited, slain!
Most detestable Death, by thee beguil'd,
By cruel cruel thee quite overthrown!
O love! O life!—not life, but love in death!

CAPULET. Despis'd, distressed, hated, martyr'd, kill'd!—
Uncomfortable time, why cam'st thou now
To murder, murder our solemnity?
O child! O child! my soul, and not my child!
Dead art thou; alack, my child is dead,
And with my child my joys are buried.

FRIAR LAWRENCE. Peace, ho, for shame! Confusion's cure lives not
In these confusions. Heaven and yourself
Had part in this fair maid; now heaven hath all,
And all the better is it for the maid.
Your part in her you could not keep from death,
But heaven keeps his part in eternal life.
The most you sought was her promotion,
For 'twas your heaven she should be advanc'd;
And weep ye now, seeing she is advanc'd
Above the clouds, as high as heaven itself?
O, in this love, you love your child so ill
That you run mad, seeing that she is well.

She's not well married that lives married long,
But she's best married that dies married young.
Dry up your tears, and stick your rosemary
On this fair corse, and, as the custom is,
In all her best array bear her to church;
For though fond nature bids us all lament,
Yet nature's tears are reason's merriment.

CAPULET. All things that we ordained festival
Turn from their office to black funeral:
Our instruments to melancholy bells,
Our wedding cheer to a sad burial feast,
Our solemn hymns to sullen dirges change;
Our bridal flowers serve for a buried corse;
And all things change them to the contrary.

FRIAR LAWRENCE. Sir, go you in; and, madam, go with him;
And go, Sir Paris. Every one prepare
To follow this fair corse unto her grave.
The heavens do lour upon you for some ill;
Move them no more by crossing their high will.

Exeunt all but NURSE *and* MUSICIANS

FIRST MUSICIAN. Faith, we may put up our pipes and be gone.

NURSE. Honest good fellows, ah, put up, put up;
For well you know this a pitiful case. *Exit*

FIRST MUSICIAN. Ay, by my troth, the case may be amended.

Enter PETER

PETER. Musicians, O, musicians, 'Heart's ease,' 'Heart's ease'! O, an you will have me live, play 'Heart's ease.'

FIRST MUSICIAN. Why 'Heart's ease'?

PETER. O, musicians, because my heart itself plays 'My heart is full of woe.' O, play me some merry dump to comfort me.

FIRST MUSICIAN. Not a dump we! 'Tis no time to play now.

PETER. You will not, then?

FIRST MUSICIAN. No.

PETER. I will then give it you soundly.

FIRST MUSICIAN. What will you give us?

PETER. No money, on my faith, but the gleek. I will give you the minstrel.

FIRST MUSICIAN. Then I will give you the serving-creature.

PETER. Then will I lay the serving-creature's dagger on your pate. I will carry no crotchets: I'll re you, I'll fa you; do you note me?

FIRST MUSICIAN. An you re us and fa us, you note us.

SECOND MUSICIAN. Pray you put up your dagger, and put out your wit.

PETER. Then have at you with my wit! I will dry-beat you with an iron wit, and put up my iron dagger. Answer me like men.

'When griping grief the heart doth wound
And doleful dumps the mind oppress,
Then music with her silver sound'—

Why 'silver sound'? Why 'music with her silver sound'? What say you, Simon Catling?

FIRST MUSICIAN. Marry, sir, because silver hath a sweet sound.

PETER. Pretty! What say you, Hugh Rebeck?

SECOND MUSICIAN. I say 'silver sound' because musicians sound for silver.

PETER. Pretty too! What say you, James Soundpost?

THIRD MUSICIAN. Faith, I know not what to say.

PETER. O, I cry you mercy, you are the singer; I will say for you. It is 'music with her silver sound' because musicians have no gold for sounding.

'Then music with her silver sound
With speedy help doth lend redress.' *Exit*

FIRST MUSICIAN. What a pestilent knave is this same!

SECOND MUSICIAN. Hang him, Jack! Come, we'll in here; tarry for the mourners, and stay dinner. *Exeunt*

ACT V. SCENE 1

Mantua. A street

Enter Romeo

Romeo. If I may trust the flattering truth of sleep,
My dreams presage some joyful news at hand.
My bosom's lord sits lightly in his throne,
And all this day an unaccustom'd spirit
Lifts me above the ground with cheerful thoughts.
I dreamt my lady came and found me dead—
Strange dream, that gives a dead man leave to think!—
And breath'd such life with kisses in my lips
That I reviv'd, and was an emperor.
Ah me! how sweet is love itself possess'd,
When but love's shadows are so rich in joy!

Enter Balthasar, Romeo's *man*

News from Verona! How now, Balthasar!
Dost thou not bring me letters from the friar?
How doth my lady? Is my father well?
How fares my Juliet? That I ask again,
For nothing can be ill if she be well.
Balthasar. Then she is well, and nothing can be ill.
Her body sleeps in Capels' monument,
And her immortal part with angels lives.
I saw her laid low in her kindred's vault,
And presently took post to tell it you.
O, pardon me for bringing these ill news,
Since you did leave it for my office, sir.
Romeo. Is it e'en so? Then I defy you, stars.
Thou knowest my lodging: get me ink and paper,
And hire post-horses; I will hence to-night.
Balthasar. I do beseech you, sir, have patience;
Your looks are pale and wild, and do import
Some misadventure.
Romeo. Tush, thou art deceiv'd;
Leave me, and do the thing I bid thee do.
Hast thou no letters to me from the friar?

BALTHASAR. No, my good lord.
ROMEO. No matter; get thee gone,
And hire those horses; I'll be with thee straight.
Exit BALTHASAR
Well, Juliet, I will lie with thee to-night.
Let's see for means. O mischief, thou art swift
To enter in the thoughts of desperate men!
I do remember an apothecary,
And hereabouts 'a dwells, which late I noted
In tatt'red weeds, with overwhelming brows,
Culling of simples. Meagre were his looks;
Sharp misery had worn him to the bones;
And in his needy shop a tortoise hung,
An alligator stuff'd, and other skins
Of ill-shap'd fishes; and about his shelves
A beggarly account of empty boxes,
Green earthen pots, bladders, and musty seeds,
Remnants of packthread, and old cakes of roses,
Were thinly scattered, to make up a show.
Noting this penury, to myself I said
'An if a man did need a poison now,
Whose sale is present death in Mantua,
Here lives a caitiff wretch would sell it him.'
O, this same thought did but forerun my need
And this same needy man must sell it me.
As I remember, this should be the house.
Being holiday, the beggar's shop is shut.
What, ho! Apothecary!

Enter APOTHECARY

APOTHECARY. Who calls so loud?
ROMEO. Come hither, man. I see that thou art poor.
Hold, there is forty ducats; let me have
A dram of poison, such soon-speeding gear
As will disperse itself through all the veins
That the life-weary taker may fall dead,
And that the trunk may be discharg'd of breath
As violently as hasty powder fir'd
Doth hurry from the fatal cannon's womb.
APOTHECARY. Such mortal drugs I have; but Mantua's law

Is death to any he that utters them.
ROMEO. Art thou so bare and full of wretchedness
And fearest to die? Famine is in thy cheeks,
Need and oppression starveth in thy eyes,
Contempt and beggary hangs upon thy back,
The world is not thy friend, nor the world's law;
The world affords no law to make thee rich;
Then be not poor, but break it and take this.
APOTHECARY. My poverty but not my will consents.
ROMEO. I pay thy poverty and not thy will.
APOTHECARY. Put this in any liquid thing you will
And drink it off; and if you had the strength
Of twenty men, it would dispatch you straight.
ROMEO. There is thy gold—worse poison to men's souls,
Doing more murder in this loathsome world
Than these poor compounds that thou mayst not sell.
I sell thee poison: thou hast sold me none.
Farewell; buy food, and get thyself in flesh.
Come, cordial and not poison, go with me
To Juliet's grave; for there must I use thee. *Exeunt*

SCENE 2

FRIAR LAWRENCE'S *cell*

Enter FRIAR JOHN

FRIAR JOHN. Holy Franciscan friar! Brother, ho!

Enter FRIAR LAWRENCE

FRIAR LAWRENCE. This same should be the voice of Friar John.
Welcome from Mantua! What says Romeo?
Or, if his mind be writ, give me his letter.
FRIAR JOHN. Going to find a barefoot brother out,
One of our order, to associate me,
Here in this city visiting the sick,
And finding him, the searchers of the town,
Suspecting that we both were in a house
Where the infectious pestilence did reign,

Seal'd up the doors, and would not let us forth,
So that my speed to Mantua there was stay'd.

FRIAR LAWRENCE. Who bare my letter, then, to Romeo?

FRIAR JOHN. I could not send it—here it is again—
Nor get a messenger to bring it thee,
So fearful were they of infection.

FRIAR LAWRENCE. Unhappy fortune! By my brotherhood,
The letter was not nice, but full of charge
Of dear import; and the neglecting it
May do much danger. Friar John, go hence;
Get me an iron crow, and bring it straight
Unto my cell.

FRIAR JOHN. Brother, I'll go and bring it thee. *Exit*

FRIAR LAWRENCE. Now must I to the monument alone.
Within this three hours will fair Juliet wake;
She will beshrew me much that Romeo
Hath had not notice of these accidents.
But I will write again to Mantua,
And keep her at my cell till Romeo come—
Poor living corse, clos'd in a dead man's tomb! *Exit*

SCENE 3

Verona. A churchyard; in it the tomb of the CAPULETS

Enter PARIS, *and his* PAGE *bearing flowers and a torch*

PARIS. Give me thy torch, boy; hence, and stand aloof;
Yet put it out, for I would not be seen.
Under yond yew trees lay thee all along,
Holding thy ear close to the hollow ground;
So shall no foot upon the churchyard tread—
Being loose, unfirm, with digging up of graves—
But thou shalt hear it. Whistle then to me,
As signal that thou hearest something approach.
Give me those flowers. Do as I bid thee, go.

PAGE. [*Aside*] I am almost afraid to stand alone
Here in the churchyard; yet I will adventure. [*Retires*]

PARIS. Sweet flower, with flowers thy bridal bed I strew—
O woe, thy canopy is dust and stones!—

Which with sweet water nightly I will dew:
Or, wanting that, with tears distill'd by moans.
The obsequies that I for thee will keep,
Nightly shall be to strew thy grave and weep.
[*The* PAGE *whistles*]
The boy gives warning something doth approach.
What cursed foot wanders this way to-night
To cross my obsequies and true love's rite?
What, with a torch! Muffle me, night, awhile. [*Retires*]

Enter ROMEO *and* BALTHASAR, *with a torch, a mattock, and a crow of iron*

ROMEO. Give me that mattock and the wrenching iron.
Hold, take this letter; early in the morning
See thou deliver it to my lord and father.
Give me the light; upon thy life I charge thee,
Whate'er thou hearest or seest, stand all aloof
And do not interrupt me in my course.
Why I descend into this bed of death
Is partly to behold my lady's face,
But chiefly to take thence from her dead finger
A precious ring—a ring that I must use
In dear employment; therefore hence, be gone.
But if thou, jealous, dost return to pry
In what I farther shall intend to do,
By heaven, I will tear thee joint by joint,
And strew this hungry churchyard with thy limbs.
The time and my intents are savage-wild,
More fierce and more inexorable far
Than empty tigers or the roaring sea.
BALTHASAR. I will be gone, sir, and not trouble ye.
ROMEO. So shalt thou show me friendship.
Take thou that;
Live and be prosperous; and farewell, good fellow.
BALTHASAR. [*Aside*] For all this same, I'll hide me hereabout;
His looks I fear, and his intents I doubt. [*Retires*]
ROMEO. Thou detestable maw, thou womb of death,
Gorg'd with the dearest morsel of the earth,
Thus I enforce thy rotten jaws to open,

[*Breaking open the tomb*]

And, in despite, I'll cram thee with more food.

PARIS. This is that banish'd haughty Montague
That murd'red my love's cousin—with which grief
It is supposed the fair creature died—
And here is come to do some villainous shame
To the dead bodies. I will apprehend him.
Stop thy unhallowed toil, vile Montague.
Can vengeance be pursued further than death?
Condemned villain, I do apprehend thee.
Obey, and go with me; for thou must die.

ROMEO. I must indeed; and therefore came I hither.
Good gentle youth, tempt not a desp'rate man;
Fly hence, and leave me. Think upon these gone;
Let them affright thee. I beseech thee, youth,
Put not another sin upon my head
By urging me to fury; O, be gone!
By heaven, I love thee better than myself,
For I come hither arm'd against myself.
Stay not, be gone; live, and hereafter say
A madman's mercy bid thee run away.

PARIS. I do defy thy conjuration,
And apprehend thee for a felon here.

ROMEO. Wilt thou provoke me? Then have at thee, boy!

[*They fight*]

PAGE. O lord, they fight! I will go call the watch.

Exit. PARIS *falls*

PARIS. O, I am slain! If thou be merciful,
Open the tomb, lay me with Juliet. [*Dies*]

ROMEO. In faith, I will. Let me peruse this face.
Mercutio's kinsman, noble County Paris!
What said my man, when my betossed soul
Did not attend him as we rode? I think
He told me Paris should have married Juliet.
Said he not so, or did I dream it so?
Or am I mad, hearing him talk of Juliet,
To think it was so? O, give me thy hand,
One writ with me in sour misfortune's book!
I'll bury thee in a triumphant grave.
A grave? O no! A lantern, slaught'red youth;

For here lies Juliet, and her beauty makes
This vault a feasting presence full of light.
Death, lie thou there, by a dead man interr'd.
[*Laying* PARIS *in the tomb*]
How oft when men are at the point of death
Have they been merry! Which their keepers call
A lightning before death. O, how may I
Call this a lightning? O my love! my wife!
Death, that hath suck'd the honey of thy breath,
Hath had no power yet upon thy beauty.
Thou art not conquer'd; beauty's ensign yet
Is crimson in thy lips and in thy cheeks,
And death's pale flag is not advanced there.
Tybalt, liest thou there in thy bloody sheet?
O, what more favour can I do to thee
Than with that hand that cut thy youth in twain
To sunder his that was thine enemy?
Forgive me, cousin. Ah, dear Juliet,
Why art thou yet so fair? Shall I believe
That unsubstantial Death is amorous,
And that the lean abhorred monster keeps
Thee here in dark to be his paramour?
For fear of that I still will stay with thee,
And never from this palace of dim night
Depart again. Here, here will I remain
With worms that are thy chambermaids. O, here
Will I set up my everlasting rest,
And shake the yoke of inauspicious stars
From this world-wearied flesh. Eyes, look your last.
Arms, take your last embrace. And, lips, O you
The doors of breath, seal with a righteous kiss
A dateless bargain to engrossing death!
Come, bitter conduct, come, unsavoury guide.
Thou desperate pilot, now at once run on
The dashing rocks thy sea-sick weary bark.
Here's to my love! [*Drinks*] O true apothecary!
Thy drugs are quick. Thus with a kiss I die. [*Falls*]

Enter FRIAR LAWRENCE, *with lantern, crow, and spade*

FRIAR LAWRENCE. Saint Francis be my speed! How oft to-night

Have my old feet stumbled at graves! Who's there?

BALTHASAR. Here's one, a friend, and one that knows you well.

FRIAR LAWRENCE. Bliss be upon you! Tell me, good my friend,
What torch is yond that vainly lends his light
To grubs and eyeless skulls? As I discern,
It burneth in the Capels' monument.

BALTHASAR. It doth so, holy sir; and there's my master,
One that you love.

FRIAR LAWRENCE. Who is it?

BALTHASAR. Romeo.

FRIAR LAWRENCE. How long hath he been there?

BALTHASAR. Full half an hour.

FRIAR LAWRENCE. Go with me to the vault.

BALTHASAR. I dare not, sir.
My master knows not but I am gone hence,
And fearfully did menace me with death,
If I did stay to look on his intents.

FRIAR LAWRENCE. Stay, then, I'll go alone; fear comes upon me;
O, much I fear some ill unthrifty thing.

BALTHASAR. As I did sleep under this yew tree here,
I dreamt my master and another fought,
And that my master slew him.

FRIAR LAWRENCE. Romeo!
Alack, alack, what blood is this which stains
The stony entrance of this sepulchre?
What mean these masterless and gory swords
To lie discolour'd by this place of peace?

[*Enters the tomb*]

Romeo! O, pale! Who else? What, Paris too?
And steep'd in blood? Ah, what an unkind hour
Is guilty of this lamentable chance!
The lady stirs. [JULIET *wakes*]

JULIET. O comfortable friar! Where is my lord?
I do remember well where I should be,
And there I am. Where is my Romeo? [*Noise within*]

FRIAR LAWRENCE. I hear some noise. Lady, come from that nest

Of death, contagion, and unnatural sleep;
A greater power than we can contradict
Hath thwarted our intents. Come, come away;
Thy husband in thy bosom there lies dead;
And Paris too. Come, I'll dispose of thee
Among a sisterhood of holy nuns.
Stay not to question, for the watch is coming;
Come, go, good Juliet. I dare no longer stay.

JULIET. Go, get thee hence, for I will not away.

Exit FRIAR LAWRENCE

What's here? A cup, clos'd in my true love's hand?
Poison, I see, hath been his timeless end.
O churl! drunk all, and left no friendly drop
To help me after? I will kiss thy lips;
Haply some poison yet doth hang on them,
To make me die with a restorative. [*Kisses him*]
Thy lips are warm.

FIRST WATCHMAN. [*Within*] Lead, boy. Which way?

JULIET. Yea, noise? Then I'll be brief. O happy dagger!

[*Snatching* ROMEO's *dagger*]

This is thy sheath; there rust, and let me die.

[*She stabs herself and falls on* ROMEO's *body*]

Enter WATCH, *with* PARIS'S PAGE

PAGE. This is the place; there, where the torch doth burn.

FIRST WATCH. The ground is bloody; search about the churchyard.
Go, some of you, whoe'er you find attach.

Exeunt some of the WATCH

Pitiful sight! here lies the County slain;
And Juliet bleeding, warm, and newly dead,
Who here hath lain this two days buried.
Go, tell the Prince; run to the Capulets;
Raise up the Montagues; some others search.

Exeunt others of the WATCH

We see the ground whereon these woes do lie;
But the true ground of all these piteous woes
We cannot without circumstance descry.

Re-enter some of the WATCH *with* BALTHASAR

SECOND WATCH. Here's Romeo's man; we found him in the churchyard.

FIRST WATCH. Hold him in safety till the Prince come hither.

Re-enter FRIAR LAWRENCE *and another* WATCHMAN

THIRD WATCH. Here is a friar that trembles, sighs, and weeps;
We took this mattock and this spade from him,
As he was coming from this churchyard's side.

FIRST WATCH. A great suspicion; stay the friar too.

Enter the PRINCE *and attendants*

PRINCE. What misadventure is so early up,
That calls our person from our morning rest?

Enter CAPULET, LADY CAPULET, *and others*

CAPULET. What should it be that is so shriek'd abroad?

LADY CAPULET. The people in the street cry 'Romeo,'
Some 'Juliet' and some 'Paris'; and all run,
With open outcry, toward our monument.

PRINCE. What fear is this which startles in our ears?

FIRST WATCHMAN. Sovereign, here lies the County Paris slain;
And Romeo dead; and Juliet, dead before,
Warm and new kill'd.

PRINCE. Search, seek, and know how this foul murder comes.

FIRST WATCHMAN. Here is a friar, and slaughter'd Romeo's man,
With instruments upon them fit to open
These dead men's tombs.

CAPULET. O heavens! O wife, look how our daughter bleeds!
This dagger hath mista'en, for, lo, his house
Is empty on the back of Montague,
And it mis-sheathed in my daughter's bosom.

LADY CAPULET. O me! this sight of death is as a bell
That warns my old age to a sepulchre.

Enter MONTAGUE *and others*

PRINCE. Come, Montague, for thou art early up

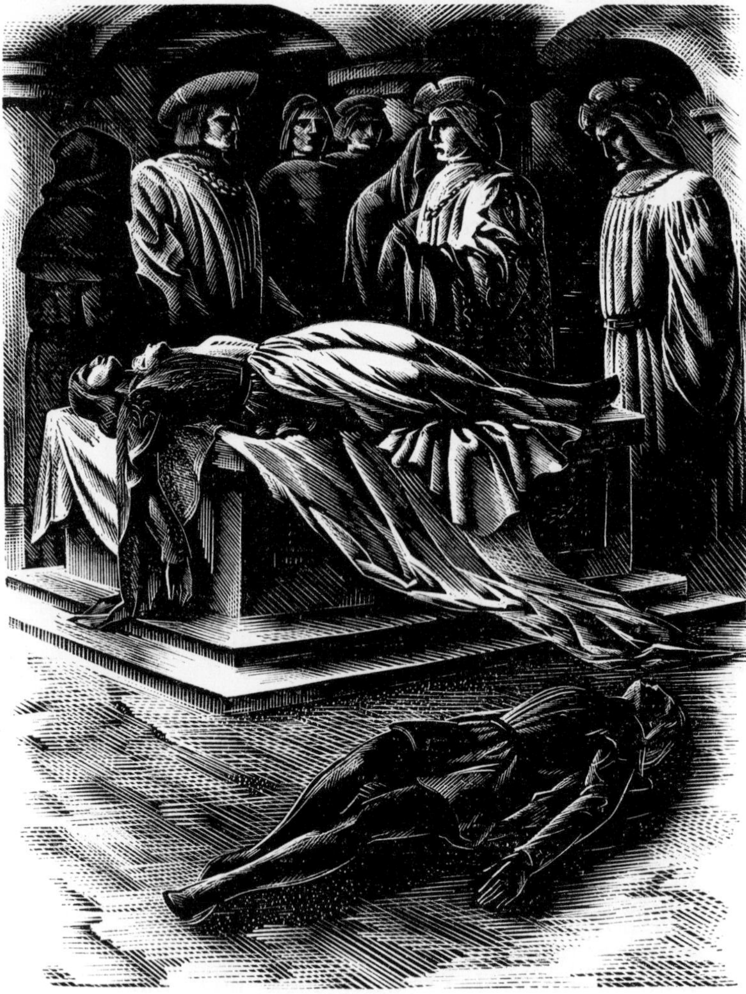

Chorus. *From forth the fatal loins of these two foes*
A pair of star-cross'd lovers take their life;
Whose misadventur'd piteous overthrows
Doth with their death bury their parents' strife.
(Prologue)

To see thy son and heir more early down.

MONTAGUE. Alas, my liege, my wife is dead to-night;
Grief of my son's exile hath stopp'd her breath.
What further woe conspires against mine age?

PRINCE. Look, and thou shalt see.

MONTAGUE. O thou untaught! what manners is in this,
To press before thy father to a grave?

PRINCE. Seal up the mouth of outrage for a while,
Till we can clear these ambiguities,
And know their spring, their head, their true descent;
And then will I be general of your woes,
And lead you even to death. Meantime forbear,
And let mischance be slave to patience.
Bring forth the parties of suspicion.

FRIAR LAWRENCE. I am the greatest, able to do least,
Yet most suspected, as the time and place
Doth make against me, of this direful murder;
And here I stand, both to impeach and purge
Myself condemned and myself excus'd.

PRINCE. Then say at once what thou dost know in this.

FRIAR LAWRENCE. I will be brief, for my short date of breath
Is not so long as is a tedious tale.
Romeo, there dead, was husband to that Juliet;
And she, there dead, that Romeo's faithful wife.
I married them; and their stol'n marriage-day
Was Tybalt's doomsday, whose untimely death
Banish'd the new-made bridegroom from this city
For whom, and not for Tybalt, Juliet pin'd.
You, to remove that siege of grief from her,
Betroth'd, and would have married her perforce,
To County Paris. Then comes she to me,
And with wild looks bid me devise some mean
To rid her from this second marriage,
Or in my cell there would she kill herself.
Then gave I her, so tutor'd by my art,
A sleeping potion; which so took effect
As I intended, for it wrought on her
The form of death. Meantime I writ to Romeo
That he should hither come as this dire night

To help to take her from her borrowed grave,
Being the time the potion's force should cease.
But he which bore my letter, Friar John,
Was stay'd by accident, and yesternight
Return'd my letter back. Then all alone
At the prefixed hour of her waking
Came I to take her from her kindred's vault;
Meaning to keep her closely at my cell
Till I conveniently could send to Romeo.
But when I came, some minute ere the time
Of her awakening, here untimely lay
The noble Paris and true Romeo dead.
She wakes; and I entreated her come forth,
And bear this work of heaven with patience.
But then a noise did scare me from the tomb,
And she, too desperate, would not go with me,
But, as it seems, did violence on herself.
All this I know, and to the marriage
Her nurse is privy; and if ought in this
Miscarried by my fault, let my old life
Be sacrific'd, some hour before his time,
Unto the rigour of severest law.

PRINCE. We still have known thee for a holy man.
Where's Romeo's man? What can he say to this?

BALTHASAR. I brought my master news of Juliet's death;
And then in post he came from Mantua
To this same place, to this same monument.
This letter he early bid me give his father;
And threat'ned me with death, going in the vault,
If I departed not and left him there.

PRINCE. Give me the letter, I will look on it.
Where is the County's page that rais'd the watch?
Sirrah, what made your master in this place?

PAGE. He came with flowers to strew his lady's grave;
And bid me stand aloof, and so I did.
Anon comes one with light to ope the tomb;
And by and by my master drew on him;
And then I ran away to call the watch.

PRINCE. This letter doth make good the friar's words,
Their course of love, the tidings of her death;

And here he writes that he did buy a poison
Of a poor 'pothecary, and therewithal
Came to this vault to die, and lie with Juliet.
Where be these enemies? Capulet, Montague,
See what a scourge is laid upon your hate,
That heaven finds means to kill your joys with love!
And I, for winking at your discords too,
Have lost a brace of kinsmen. All are punish'd.

CAPULET. O brother Montague, give me thy hand.
This is my daughter's jointure, for no more
Can I demand.

MONTAGUE. But I can give thee more;
For I will raise her statue in pure gold,
That whiles Verona by that name is known,
There shall no figure at such rate be set
As that of true and faithful Juliet.

CAPULET. As rich shall Romeo's by his lady's lie—
Poor sacrifices of our enmity!

PRINCE. A glooming peace this morning with it brings;
The sun for sorrow will not show his head.
Go hence, to have more talk of these sad things;
Some shall be pardon'd and some punished;
For never was a story of more woe
Than this of Juliet and her Romeo. *Exeunt*

The Life of Timon of Athens

TIMON OF ATHENS

TIMON OF ATHENS stands in the First Folio immediately after *Romeo and Juliet* and in the place originally assigned to *Troilus and Cressida*. When the printer, after printing three pages of *Troilus*, found it necessary (*see* p. 3) to withdraw that play for the time being he left a space into which he later inserted *Timon of Athens*. As the text of *Timon* is the most irregular and chaotic of those included in the First Folio, the question whether Heminge and Condell ever intended to print this piece has suggested itself; was it dug out from the company's archives to fill a gap? The further question provoked by these irregularities concerns the authorship of the piece.

Many commentators have felt able on various grounds to divide up the play and assign some parts to Shakespeare and others to a collaborator or collaborators. Recent opinion is more conservative; many of the features once taken as explicable only on grounds of multiple authorship are now seen to admit of another explanation. If the play as we have it is a still unfinished work that Shakespeare never brought to the test of presentation on the stage, many of the irregularities, apart from those added by the peculiar circumstances in which it was inserted, could be attributed to the state of the author's draft. The question then arises why Shakespeare left it unfinished.

To the question about the unfinished condition of *Timon* two answers have been offered. E. K. Chambers fancied that it was the last of the Tragedies and that Shakespeare had in what seemed to the learned commentator a succession of studies in disillusion and despair worked himself into so hysterical a condition that he had to abandon his final and most distressing study of the tragic situation. *Timon* seemed to Chambers only intelligible if we supposed Shakespeare to have been mentally distraught at least for a period. The other answer is very different. Raleigh looked upon *Timon* as a preliminary study on the theme of *Lear*. He supposed that Shakespeare put it aside because he was dissatisfied with his material, finding it unable to carry the emphasis he wished to place on it. Its rejection was a purely artistic decision and the preliminary to a more satisfactory attack on the theme in *Lear*.

It is perhaps a mere coincidence that the play Heminge and Condell put in place of *Troilus* should have some of the features of that work. The suggestion that Shakespeare designed *Troilus* not for the public theatre but for a private audience (*see* pp. 3-5) is supported by external as well as internal evidence. The play seems to demand for its appreciation a point of view more specialized than that required in Shakespeare's plays for the Globe; the paradoxical nature of the piece that reduces the Homeric story to most unheroic proportions would make its full appeal only to an audience with some literary pretensions. *Timon of Athens* shares this paradoxical humour but in a contrary sense, for the story which William Painter in his *Palace of Pleasure* can describe as that of 'the strange and beastly nature of Timon of Athens enemy of mankind,' Shakespeare can offer as the life of one who may have acted unwisely but not ignobly. The construction of the piece is equally unusual, for no play by Shakespeare for the regular stage moves so uniformly from interview to interview as does the second half of *Timon.* Whatever Shakespeare's original intention, whether he had the stage of the Globe in mind or some other scene, *Timon* has peculiar features that will doubtless continue to provoke surmise and speculation.

Shakespeare found his source material in the reference to Timon in Plutarch's *Life of Antony*, where Antony deserted by his friends is represented as adopting the part of the Athenian misanthrope; Shakespeare must also have known directly or indirectly the story of Timon as told by Lucian. The relationship between Shakespeare's *Timon* and that of an anonymous and academic play on the same subject is likely to remain a matter of dispute. The anonymous *Timon* remained in manuscript till the Shakespeare Society provided a printed text in 1842. It shares with Shakespeare's play a banquet at which Timon throws things at the guests; in Shakespeare the missiles are generally described by editors as the dishes, but Mr. Maxwell in the Cambridge 'New Shakespeare' has as his stage direction 'throws the stones at them,' for he takes the final line in the scene as his cue,

> One day he gives us diamonds, next day stones

since in the other *Timon* the missiles are described as stones painted as artichokes. This and the presence of a faithful steward in both plays can hardly be explained away as mere coincidence. There must be some common source, if we are not prepared to allow some connection between the academic and Shakespeare's *Timon.*

TIMON *of Athens*

LUCIUS LUCULLUS SEMPRONIUS	*flattering lords*

VENTIDIUS, *one of Timon's false friends*

ALCIBIADES, *an Athenian captain*

APEMANTUS, *a churlish philosopher*

FLAVIUS, *steward to Timon*

FLAMINIUS LUCILIUS SERVILIUS	*Timon's servants*
CAPHIS PHILOTUS TITUS HORTENSIUS	*servants to Timon's creditors*

POET

PAINTER

JEWELLER

MERCHANT

MERCER

AN OLD ATHENIAN

THREE STRANGERS

A PAGE

A FOOL

PHRYNIA TIMANDRA	*mistresses to Alcibiades*
CUPID AMAZONS	*in the Masque*

Lords, Senators, Officers, Soldiers, Servants, Thieves, *and* Attendants

SCENE:

Athens and the neighbouring woods

Timon of Athens

ACT I. SCENE 1

Athens. TIMON'S *house*

Enter POET, PAINTER, JEWELLER, MERCHANT, *and* MERCER, *at several doors*

POET. Good day, sir.
PAINTER. I am glad y'are well.
POET. I have not seen you long; how goes the world?
PAINTER. It wears, sir, as it grows.
POET. Ay, that's well known.
But what particular rarity? What strange,
Which manifold record not matches? See,
Magic of bounty, all these spirits thy power
Hath conjur'd to attend! I know the merchant.
PAINTER. I know them both; th' other's a jeweller.
MERCHANT. O, 'tis a worthy lord!
JEWELLER. Nay, that's most fix'd.
MERCHANT. A most incomparable man; breath'd, as it were,
To an untirable and continuate goodness.
He passes.
JEWELLER. I have a jewel here—
MERCHANT. O, pray let's see't. For the Lord Timon, sir?
JEWELLER. If he will touch the estimate. But for that—
POET. When we for recompense have prais'd the vile,
It stains the glory in that happy verse
Which aptly sings the good.
MERCHANT. [*Looking at the jewel*] 'Tis a good form.
JEWELLER. And rich. Here is a water, look ye.
PAINTER. You are rapt, sir, in some work, some dedication
To the great lord.
POET. A thing slipp'd idly from me.
Our poesy is as a gum, which oozes
From whence 'tis nourish'd. The fire i' th' flint
Shows not till it be struck: our gentle flame

Provokes itself, and like the current flies
Each bound it chafes. What have you there?
PAINTER. A picture, sir. When comes your book forth?
POET. Upon the heels of my presentment, sir.
Let's see your piece.
PAINTER. 'Tis a good piece.
POET. So 'tis; this comes off well and excellent.
PAINTER. Indifferent.
POET. Admirable. How this grace
Speaks his own standing! What a mental power
This eye shoots forth! How big imagination
Moves in this lip! To th' dumbness of the gesture
One might interpret.
PAINTER. It is a pretty mocking of the life.
Here is a touch; is't good?
POET. I will say of it
It tutors nature. Artificial strife
Lives in these touches, livelier than life.

Enter certain SENATORS, *and pass over*

PAINTER. How this lord is followed!
POET. The senators of Athens–happy man!
PAINTER. Look, moe!
POET. You see this confluence, this great flood of visitors.
I have in this rough work shap'd out a man
Whom this beneath world doth embrace and hug
With amplest entertainment. My free drift
Halts not particularly, but moves itself
In a wide sea of tax. No levell'd malice
Infects one comma in the course I hold,
But flies an eagle flight, bold and forth on,
Leaving no tract behind.
PAINTER. How shall I understand you?
POET. I will unbolt to you.
You see how all conditions, how all minds–
As well of glib and slipp'ry creatures as
Of grave and austere quality, tender down
Their services to Lord Timon. His large fortune,
Upon his good and gracious nature hanging,
Subdues and properties to his love and tendance

All sorts of hearts; yea, from the glass-fac'd flatterer
To Apemantus, that few things loves better
Than to abhor himself; even he drops down
The knee before him, and returns in peace
Most rich in Timon's nod.

PAINTER. I saw them speak together.

POET. Sir, I have upon a high and pleasant hill
Feign'd Fortune to be thron'd. The base o' th' mount
Is rank'd with all deserts, all kind of natures
That labour on the bosom of this sphere
To propagate their states. Amongst them all
Whose eyes are on this sovereign lady fix'd
One do I personate of Lord Timon's frame,
Whom Fortune with her ivory hand wafts to her;
Whose present grace to present slaves and servants
Translates his rivals.

PAINTER. 'Tis conceiv'd to scope.
This throne, this Fortune, and this hill, methinks,
With one man beckon'd from the rest below,
Bowing his head against the steepy mount
To climb his happiness, would be well express'd
In our condition.

POET. Nay, sir, but hear me on.
All those which were his fellows but of late–
Some better than his value–on the moment
Follow his strides, his lobbies fill with tendance,
Rain sacrificial whisperings in his ear,
Make sacred even his stirrup, and through him
Drink the free air.

PAINTER. Ay, marry, what of these?

POET. When Fortune in her shift and change of mood
Spurns down her late beloved, all his dependants,
Which labour'd after him to the mountain's top
Even on their knees and hands, let him slip down,
Not one accompanying his declining foot.

PAINTER. 'Tis common.
A thousand moral paintings I can show
That shall demonstrate these quick blows of Fortune's
More pregnantly than words. Yet you do well

To show Lord Timon that mean eyes have seen
The foot above the head.

Trumpets sound. Enter TIMON, *addressing himself courteously to every suitor, a* MESSENGER *from* VENTIDIUS *talking with him;* LUCILIUS *and other servants following*

TIMON. Imprison'd is he, say you?
MESSENGER. Ay, my good lord. Five talents is his debt;
His means most short, his creditors most strait.
Your honourable letter he desires
To those have shut him up; which failing,
Periods his comfort.
TIMON. Noble Ventidius! Well.
I am not of that feather to shake off
My friend when he must need me. I do know him
A gentleman that well deserves a help,
Which he shall have. I'll pay the debt, and free him.
MESSENGER. Your lordship ever binds him.
TIMON. Commend me to him; I will send his ransom;
And being enfranchis'd, bid him come to me.
'Tis not enough to help the feeble up,
But to support him after. Fare you well.
MESSENGER. All happiness to your honour! *Exit*

Enter an OLD ATHENIAN

OLD ATHENIAN. Lord Timon, hear me speak.
TIMON. Freely, good father.
OLD ATHENIAN. Thou hast a servant nam'd Lucilius.
TIMON. I have so; what of him?
OLD ATHENIAN. Most noble Timon, call the man before thee.
TIMON. Attends he here, or no? Lucilius!
LUCILIUS. Here, at your lordship's service.
OLD ATHENIAN. This fellow here, Lord Timon, this thy creature,
By night frequents my house. I am a man
That from my first have been inclin'd to thrift,
And my estate deserves an heir more rais'd
Than one which holds a trencher.
TIMON. Well; what further?

OLD ATHENIAN. One only daughter have I, no kin else,
On whom I may confer what I have got.
The maid is fair, o' th' youngest for a bride,
And I have bred her at my dearest cost
In qualities of the best. This man of thine
Attempts her love; I prithee, noble lord,
Join with me to forbid him her resort;
Myself have spoke in vain.
TIMON. The man is honest.
OLD ATHENIAN. Therefore he will be, Timon.
His honesty rewards him in itself;
It must not bear my daughter.
TIMON. Does she love him?
OLD ATHENIAN. She is young and apt:
Our own precedent passions do instruct us
What levity's in youth.
TIMON. Love you the maid?
LUCILIUS. Ay, my good lord, and she accepts of it.
OLD ATHENIAN. If in her marriage my consent be missing,
I call the gods to witness I will choose
Mine heir from forth the beggars of the world,
And dispossess her all.
TIMON. How shall she be endow'd,
If she be mated with an equal husband?
OLD ATHENIAN. Three talents on the present; in future, all.
TIMON. This gentleman of mine hath serv'd me long;
To build his fortune I will strain a little,
For 'tis a bond in men. Give him thy daughter:
What you bestow, in him I'll counterpoise,
And make him weigh with her.
OLD ATHENIAN. Most noble lord,
Pawn me to this your honour, she is his.
TIMON. My hand to thee; mine honour on my promise.
LUCILIUS. Humbly I thank your lordship. Never may
That state or fortune fall into my keeping
Which is not owed to you!
Exeunt LUCILIUS *and* OLD ATHENIAN
POET. [*Presenting his poem*] Vouchsafe my labour, and long live your lordship!
TIMON. I thank you; you shall hear from me anon;

Go not away. What have you there, my friend?
PAINTER. A piece of painting, which I do beseech
Your lordship to accept.
TIMON. Painting is welcome.
The painting is almost the natural man;
For since dishonour traffics with man's nature,
He is but outside; these pencill'd figures are
Even such as they give out. I like your work,
And you shall find I like it; wait attendance
Till you hear further from me.
PAINTER. The gods preserve ye!
TIMON. Well fare you, gentleman. Give me your hand;
We must needs dine together. Sir, your jewel
Hath suffered under praise.
JEWELLER. What, my lord! Dispraise?
TIMON. A mere satiety of commendations;
If I should pay you for't as 'tis extoll'd,
It would unclew me quite.
JEWELLER. My lord, 'tis rated
As those which sell would give; but you well know
Things of like value, differing in the owners,
Are prized by their masters. Believe't, dear lord,
You mend the jewel by the wearing it.
TIMON. Well mock'd.

Enter APEMANTUS

MERCHANT. No, my good lord; he speaks the common tongue,
Which all men speak with him.
TIMON. Look who comes here; will you be chid?
JEWELLER. We'll bear, with your lordship.
MERCHANT. He'll spare none.
TIMON. Good morrow to thee, gentle Apemantus!
APEMANTUS. Till I be gentle, stay thou for thy good morrow;
When thou art Timon's dog, and these knaves honest.
TIMON. Why dost thou call them knaves? Thou know'st them not.
APEMANTUS. Are they not Athenians?
TIMON. Yes.

APEMANTUS. Then I repent not.

JEWELLER. You know me, Apemantus?

APEMANTUS. Thou know'st I do; I call'd thee by thy name.

TIMON. Thou art proud, Apemantus.

APEMANTUS. Of nothing so much as that I am not like Timon.

TIMON. Whither art going?

APEMANTUS. To knock out an honest Athenian's brains.

TIMON. That's a deed thou't die for.

APEMANTUS. Right, if doing nothing be death by th' law.

TIMON. How lik'st thou this picture, Apemantus?

APEMANTUS. The best, for the innocence.

TIMON. Wrought he not well that painted it?

APEMANTUS. He wrought better that made the painter; and yet he's but a filthy piece of work.

PAINTER. Y'are a dog.

APEMANTUS. Thy mother's of my generation; what's she, if I be a dog?

TIMON. Wilt dine with me, Apemantus?

APEMANTUS. No; I eat not lords.

TIMON. An thou shouldst, thou'dst anger ladies.

APEMANTUS. O, they eat lords; so they come by great bellies.

TIMON. That's a lascivious apprehension.

APEMANTUS. So thou apprehend'st it take it for thy labour.

TIMON. How dost thou like this jewel, Apemantus?

APEMANTUS. Not so well as plain dealing, which will not cost a man a doit.

TIMON. What dost thou think 'tis worth?

APEMANTUS. Not worth my thinking. How now, poet!

POET. How now, philosopher!

APEMANTUS. Thou liest.

POET. Art not one?

APEMANTUS. Yes.

POET. Then I lie not.

APEMANTUS. Art not a poet?

POET. Yes.

APEMANTUS. Then thou liest. Look in thy last work, where thou hast feign'd him a worthy fellow.

POET. That's not feign'd–he is so.

APEMANTUS. Yes, he is worthy of thee, and to pay thee for thy labour. He that loves to be flattered is worthy o' th' flatterer. Heavens, that I were a lord!

TIMON. What wouldst do then, Apemantus?

APEMANTUS. E'en as Apemantus does now: hate a lord with my heart.

TIMON. What, thyself?

APEMANTUS. Ay.

TIMON. Wherefore?

APEMANTUS. That I had no angry wit to be a lord.–Art not thou a merchant?

MERCHANT. Ay, Apemantus.

APEMANTUS. Traffic confound thee, if the gods will not!

MERCHANT. If traffic do it, the gods do it.

APEMANTUS. Traffic's thy god, and thy god confound thee!

Trumpet sounds. Enter a MESSENGER

TIMON. What trumpet's that?

MESSENGER. 'Tis Alcibiades, and some twenty horse,
All of companionship.

TIMON. Pray entertain them; give them guide to us.
Exeunt some attendants
You must needs dine with me. Go not you hence
Till I have thank'd you. When dinner's done
Show me this piece. I am joyful of your sights.

Enter ALCIBIADES, *with the rest*

Most welcome, sir! [*They salute*]

APEMANTUS. So, so, there!
Aches contract and starve your supple joints!
That there should be small love amongst these sweet knaves,
And all this courtesy! The strain of man's bred out
Into baboon and monkey.

ALCIBIADES. Sir, you have sav'd my longing, and I feed
Most hungerly on your sight.

TIMON. Right welcome, sir!
Ere we depart we'll share a bounteous time
In different pleasures. Pray you, let us in.
Exeunt all but APEMANTUS

ACT I. SCENE 1

Enter two Lords

First Lord. What time o' day is't, Apemantus?

Apemantus. Time to be honest.

First Lord. That time serves still.

Apemantus. The more accursed thou that still omit'st it.

Second Lord. Thou art going to Lord Timon's feast.

Apemantus. Ay; to see meat fill knaves and wine heat fools.

Second Lord. Fare thee well, fare thee well.

Apemantus. Thou art a fool to bid me farewell twice.

Second Lord. Why, Apemantus?

Apemantus. Shouldst have kept one to thyself, for I mean to give thee none.

First Lord. Hang thyself.

Apemantus. No, I will do nothing at thy bidding; make thy requests to thy friend.

Second Lord. Away, unpeaceable dog, or I'll spurn thee hence.

Apemantus. I will fly, like a dog, the heels o' th' ass. *Exit*

First Lord. He's opposite to humanity. Come, shall we in
And taste Lord Timon's bounty? He outgoes
The very heart of kindness.

Second Lord. He pours it out: Plutus, the god of gold,
Is but his steward; no meed but he repays
Sevenfold above itself; no gift to him
But breeds the giver a return exceeding
All use of quittance.

First Lord. The noblest mind he carries
That ever govern'd man.

Second Lord. Long may he live in fortunes! shall we in?

First Lord. I'll keep you company. *Exeunt*

SCENE 2

A room of state in TIMON's *house*

Hautboys playing loud music. A great banquet serv'd in; FLAVIUS *and others attending; and then enter* LORD TIMON, *the states, the* ATHENIAN LORDS, VENTIDIUS, *which* TIMON *redeem'd from prison. Then comes, dropping after all,* APEMANTUS, *discontentedly, like himself*

VENTIDIUS. Most honoured Timon,
It hath pleas'd the gods to remember my father's age,
And call him to long peace.
He is gone happy, and has left me rich.
Then, as in grateful virtue I am bound
To your free heart, I do return those talents,
Doubled with thanks and service, from whose help
I deriv'd liberty.
TIMON. O, by no means,
Honest Ventidius! You mistake my love;
I gave it freely ever; and there's none
Can truly say he gives, if he receives.
If our betters play at that game, we must not dare
To imitate them: faults that are rich are fair.
VENTIDIUS. A noble spirit!
TIMON. Nay, my lords, ceremony was but devis'd at first
To set a gloss on faint deeds, hollow welcomes,
Recanting goodness, sorry ere 'tis shown;
But where there is true friendship there needs none.
Pray, sit; more welcome are ye to my fortunes
Than my fortunes to me. [*They sit*]
FIRST LORD. My lord, we always have confess'd it.
APEMANTUS. Ho, ho, confess'd it! Hang'd it, have you not?
TIMON. O, Apemantus, you are welcome.
APEMANTUS. No;
You shall not make me welcome.
I come to have thee thrust me out of doors.
TIMON. Fie, th'art a churl; ye have got a humour there
Does not become a man; 'tis much to blame.

They say, my lords, Ira furor brevis est; but yond man is ever angry. Go, let him have a table by himself; for he does neither affect company nor is he fit for't indeed.

APEMANTUS. Let me stay at thine apperil, Timon.
I come to observe; I give thee warning on't.

TIMON. I take no heed of thee. Th'art an Athenian, therefore welcome. I myself would have no power; prithee let my meat make thee silent.

APEMANTUS. I scorn thy meat; 'twould choke me, for I should ne'er flatter thee. O you gods, what a number of men eats Timon, and he sees 'em not! It grieves me to see so many dip their meat in one man's blood; and all the madness is, he cheers them up too.
I wonder men dare trust themselves with men.
Methinks they should invite them without knives:
Good for their meat and safer for their lives.
There's much example for't; the fellow that sits next him now, parts bread with him, pledges the breath of him in a divided draught, is the readiest man to kill him. 'T has been proved. If I were a huge man I should fear to drink at meals.
Lest they should spy my windpipe's dangerous notes:
Great men should drink with harness on their throats.

TIMON. My lord, in heart! and let the health go round.

SECOND LORD. Let it flow this way, my good lord.

APEMANTUS. Flow this way! A brave fellow! He keeps his tides well. Those healths will make thee and thy state look ill, Timon. Here's that which is too weak to be a sinner, honest water, which ne'er left man i' th' mire.
This and my food are equals; there's no odds.
Feasts are too proud to give thanks to the gods.

APEMANTUS' *Grace*

Immortal gods, I crave no pelf;
I pray for no man but myself.
Grant I may never prove so fond
To trust man on his oath or bond,
Or a harlot for her weeping,
Or a dog that seems a-sleeping,
Or a keeper with my freedom,

Or my friends, if I should need 'em.
Amen. So fall to't.
Rich men sin, and I eat root. [*Eats and drinks*]

Much good dich thy good heart, Apemantus!

TIMON. Captain Alcibiades, your heart's in the field now.

ALCIBIADES. My heart is ever at your service, my lord.

TIMON. You had rather be at a breakfast of enemies than a dinner of friends.

ALCIBIADES. So they were bleeding new, my lord, there's no meat like 'em; I could wish my best friend at such a feast.

APEMANTUS. Would all those flatterers were thine enemies then, that then thou mightst kill 'em, and bid me to 'em.

FIRST LORD. Might we but have that happiness, my lord, that you would once use our hearts, whereby we might express some part of our zeals, we should think ourselves for ever perfect.

TIMON. O, no doubt, my good friends, but the gods themselves have provided that I shall have much help from you. How had you been my friends else? Why have you that charitable title from thousands, did not you chiefly belong to my heart? I have told more of you to myself than you can with modesty speak in your own behalf; and thus far I confirm you. O you gods, think I, what need we have any friends if we should ne'er have need of 'em? They were the most needless creatures living, should we ne'er have use for 'em; and would most resemble sweet instruments hung up in cases, that keep their sounds to themselves. Why, I have often wish'd myself poorer, that I might come nearer to you. We are born to do benefits; and what better or properer can we call our own than the riches of our friends? O, what a precious comfort 'tis to have so many like brothers commanding one another's fortunes! O, joy's e'en made away ere't can be born! Mine eyes cannot hold out water, methinks. To forget their faults, I drink to you.

APEMANTUS. Thou weep'st to make them drink, Timon.

SECOND LORD. Joy had the like conception in our eyes,
And at that instant like a babe sprung up.

APEMANTUS. Ho, ho! I laugh to think that babe a bastard.

THIRD LORD. I promise you, my lord, you mov'd me much.

APEMANTUS. Much! [*Sound tucket*]
TIMON. What means that trump?

Enter a SERVANT

How now?
SERVANT. Please you, my lord, there are certain ladies most desirous of admittance.
TIMON. Ladies! What are their wills?
SERVANT. There comes with them a forerunner, my lord, which bears that office to signify their pleasures.
TIMON. I pray let them be admitted.

Enter CUPID

CUPID. Hail to thee, worthy Timon, and to all
That of his bounties taste! The five best Senses
Acknowledge thee their patron, and come freely
To gratulate thy plenteous bosom. Th' Ear,
Taste, Touch, Smell, pleas'd from thy table rise;
They only now come but to feast thine eyes.
TIMON. They're welcome all; let 'em have kind admittance.
Music, make their welcome. *Exit* CUPID
FIRST LORD. You see, my lord, how ample y'are belov'd.

Music. Re-enter CUPID, *with a Masque of* LADIES *as Amazons, with lutes in their hands, dancing and playing*

APEMANTUS. Hoy-day, what a sweep of vanity comes this way!
They dance? They are mad women.
Like madness is the glory of this life,
As this pomp shows to a little oil and root.
We make ourselves fools to disport ourselves,
And spend our flatteries to drink those men
Upon whose age we void it up again
With poisonous spite and envy.
Who lives that's not depraved or depraves?
Who dies that bears not one spurn to their graves
Of their friends' gift?
I should fear those that dance before me now
Would one day stamp upon me. 'T has been done:

Men shut their doors against a setting sun.

The LORDS *rise from table, with much adoring of* TIMON; *and to show their loves, each single out an Amazon, and all dance, men with women, a lofty strain or two to the hautboys, and cease*

TIMON. You have done our pleasures much grace, fair ladies,
Set a fair fashion on our entertainment,
Which was not half so beautiful and kind;
You have added worth unto't and lustre,
And entertain'd me with mine own device;
I am to thank you for't.
FIRST LADY. My lord, you take us even at the best.
APEMANTUS. Faith, for the worst is filthy, and would not hold taking, I doubt me.
TIMON. Ladies, there is an idle banquet attends you;
Please you to dispose yourselves.
ALL LADIES. Most thankfully, my lord.
Exeunt CUPID *and* LADIES
TIMON. Flavius!
FLAVIUS. My lord?
TIMON. The little casket bring me hither.
FLAVIUS. Yes, my lord. [*Aside*] More jewels yet!
There is no crossing him in's humour,
Else I should tell him—well i' faith, I should—
When all's spent, he'd be cross'd then, an he could.
'Tis pity bounty had not eyes behind,
That man might ne'er be wretched for his mind. *Exit*
FIRST LORD. Where be our men?
SERVANT. Here, my lord, in readiness.
SECOND LORD. Our horses!

Re-enter FLAVIUS, *with the casket*

TIMON. O my friends,
I have one word to say to you. Look you, my good lord,
I must entreat you honour me so much
As to advance this jewel; accept it and wear it,
Kind my lord.
FIRST LORD. I am so far already in your gifts—
ALL. So are we all.

Enter a SERVANT

SERVANT. My lord, there are certain nobles of the Senate newly alighted and come to visit you.

TIMON. They are fairly welcome. *Exit* SERVANT

FLAVIUS. I beseech your honour, vouchsafe me a word; it does concern you near.

TIMON. Near! Why then, another time I'll hear thee. I prithee let's be provided to show them entertainment.

FLAVIUS. [*Aside*] I scarce know how.

Enter another SERVANT

SECOND SERVANT. May it please your honour, Lord Lucius, out of his free love, hath presented to you four milk-white horses, trapp'd in silver.

TIMON. I shall accept them fairly. Let the presents
Be worthily entertain'd. *Exit* SERVANT

Enter a third SERVANT

How now! What news?

THIRD SERVANT. Please you, my lord, that honourable gentleman, Lord Lucullus, entreats your company to-morrow to hunt with him and has sent your honour two brace of greyhounds.

TIMON. I'll hunt with him; and let them be receiv'd,
Not without fair reward. *Exit* SERVANT

FLAVIUS. [*Aside*] What will this come to?
He commands us to provide and give great gifts,
And all out of an empty coffer;
Nor will he know his purse, or yield me this,
To show him what a beggar his heart is,
Being of no power to make his wishes good.
His promises fly so beyond his state
That what he speaks is all in debt; he owes
For ev'ry word. He is so kind that he now
Pays interest for't; his land's put to their books.
Well, would I were gently put out of office
Before I were forc'd out!
Happier is he that has no friend to feed
Than such that do e'en enemies exceed.

I bleed inwardly for my lord. *Exit*

TIMON. You do yourselves much wrong;
You bate too much of your own merits.
Here, my lord, a trifle of our love.

SECOND LORD. With more than common thanks I will receive it.

THIRD LORD. O, he's the very soul of bounty!

TIMON. And now I remember, my lord, you gave good words the other day of a bay courser I rode on. 'Tis yours because you lik'd it.

THIRD LORD. O, I beseech you pardon me, my lord, in that.

TIMON. You may take my word, my lord: I know no man
Can justly praise but what he does affect.
I weigh my friend's affection with mine own.
I'll tell you true; I'll call to you.

ALL LORDS. O, none so welcome!

TIMON. I take all and your several visitations
So kind to heart 'tis not enough to give;
Methinks I could deal kingdoms to my friends
And ne'er be weary. Alcibiades,
Thou art a soldier, therefore seldom rich.
It comes in charity to thee; for all thy living
Is 'mongst the dead, and all the lands thou hast
Lie in a pitch'd field.

ALCIBIADES. Ay, defil'd land, my lord.

FIRST LORD. We are so virtuously bound—

TIMON. And so am I to you.

SECOND LORD. So infinitely endear'd—

TIMON. All to you. Lights, more lights!

FIRST LORD. The best of happiness, honour, and fortunes, keep with you, Lord Timon!

TIMON. Ready for his friends.

Exeunt all but APEMANTUS *and* TIMON

APEMANTUS. What a coil's here!
Serving of becks and jutting-out of bums!
I doubt whether their legs be worth the sums
That are given for 'em. Friendship's full of dregs:
Methinks false hearts should never have sound legs.
Thus honest fools lay out their wealth on curtsies.

TIMON. Now, Apemantus, if thou wert not sullen

I would be good to thee.

APEMANTUS. No, I'll nothing; for if I should be brib'd too, there would be none left to rail upon thee, and then thou wouldst sin the faster. Thou giv'st so long, Timon, I fear me thou wilt give away thyself in paper shortly. What needs these feasts, pomps, and vain-glories?

TIMON. Nay, an you begin to rail on society once, I am sworn not to give regard to you. Farewell; and come with better music. *Exit*

APEMANTUS. So. Thou wilt not hear me now: thou shalt not then. I'll lock thy heaven from thee.
O that men's ears should be
To counsel deaf, but not to flattery! *Exit*

ACT II. SCENE 1

A SENATOR'S *house*

Enter a SENATOR, *with papers in his hand*

SENATOR. And late, five thousand. To Varro and to Isidore
He owes nine thousand; besides my former sum,
Which makes it five and twenty. Still in motion
Of raging waste? It cannot hold; it will not.
If I want gold, steal but a beggar's dog
And give it Timon, why, the dog coins gold.
If I would sell my horse and buy twenty moe
Better than he, why, give my horse to Timon,
Ask nothing, give it him, it foals me straight,
And able horses. No porter at his gate,
But rather one that smiles and still invites
All that pass by. It cannot hold; no reason
Can sound his state in safety. Caphis, ho!
Caphis, I say!

Enter CAPHIS

CAPHIS. Here, sir; what is your pleasure?

SENATOR. Get on your cloak and haste you to Lord Timon;
Importune him for my moneys; be not ceas'd

With slight denial, nor then silenc'd when
'Commend me to your master' and the cap
Plays in the right hand, thus; but tell him
My uses cry to me, I must serve my turn
Out of mine own; his days and times are past,
And my reliances on his fracted dates
Have smit my credit. I love and honour him,
But must not break my back to heal his finger.
Immediate are my needs, and my relief
Must not be toss'd and turn'd to me in words,
But find supply immediate. Get you gone;
Put on a most importunate aspect,
A visage of demand; for I do fear,
When every feather sticks in his own wing,
Lord Timon will be left a naked gull,
Which flashes now a phœnix. Get you gone.

CAPHIS. I go, sir.

SENATOR. Take the bonds along with you,
And have the dates in compt.

CAPHIS. I will, sir.

SENATOR. Go. *Exeunt*

SCENE 2

Before TIMON'S *house*

Enter FLAVIUS, TIMON'S *steward, with many bills in his hand*

FLAVIUS. No care, no stop! So senseless of expense
That he will neither know how to maintain it
Nor cease his flow of riot; takes no account
How things go from him, nor resumes no care
Of what is to continue. Never mind
Was to be so unwise to be so kind.
What shall be done? He will not hear till feel.
I must be round with him. Now he comes from hunting.
Fie, fie, fie, fie!

Enter CAPHIS, *and the* SERVANTS *of* ISIDORE *and* VARRO

CAPHIS. Good even, Varro. What, you come for money?
VARRO'S SERVANT. Is't not your business too?
CAPHIS. It is. And yours too, Isidore?
ISIDORE'S SERVANT. It is so.
CAPHIS. Would we were all discharg'd!
VARRO'S SERVANT. I fear it.
CAPHIS. Here comes the lord.

Enter TIMON *and his train, with* ALCIBIADES

TIMON. So soon as dinner's done we'll forth again,
My Alcibiades.—With me? What is your will?
CAPHIS. My lord, here is a note of certain dues.
TIMON. Dues! Whence are you?
CAPHIS. Of Athens here, my lord.
TIMON. Go to my steward.
CAPHIS. Please it your lordship, he hath put me off
To the succession of new days this month.
My master is awak'd by great occasion
To call upon his own, and humbly prays you
That with your other noble parts you'll suit
In giving him his right.
TIMON. Mine honest friend,
I prithee but repair to me next morning.
CAPHIS. Nay, good my lord—
TIMON. Contain thyself, good friend.
VARRO'S SERVANT. One Varro's servant, my good lord—
ISIDORE'S SERVANT. From Isidore: he humbly prays your speedy payment—
CAPHIS. If you did know, my lord, my master's wants—
VARRO'S SERVANT. 'Twas due on forfeiture, my lord, six weeks and past.
ISIDORE'S SERVANT. Your steward puts me off, my lord; and I am sent expressly to your lordship.
TIMON. Give me breath.
I do beseech you, good my lords, keep on;
I'll wait upon you instantly.
Exeunt ALCIBIADES *and* LORDS
[*To* FLAVIUS] Come hither. Pray you,
How goes the world that I am thus encount'red
With clamorous demands of date-broke bonds

And the detention of long-since-due debts,
Against my honour?

FLAVIUS. Please you, gentlemen,
The time is unagreeable to this business.
Your importunacy cease till after dinner,
That I may make his lordship understand
Wherefore you are not paid.

TIMON. Do so, my friends.
See them well entertain'd. *Exit*

FLAVIUS. Pray draw near. *Exit*

Enter APEMANTUS *and* FOOL

CAPHIS. Stay, stay, here comes the fool with Apemantus. Let's ha' some sport with 'em.

VARRO'S SERVANT. Hang him, he'll abuse us!

ISIDORE'S SERVANT. A plague upon him, dog!

VARRO'S SERVANT. How dost, fool?

APEMANTUS. Dost dialogue with thy shadow?

VARRO'S SERVANT. I speak not to thee.

APEMANTUS. No, 'tis to thyself. [*To the* FOOL] Come away.

ISIDORE'S SERVANT. [*To* VARRO'S SERVANT] There's the fool hangs on your back already.

APEMANTUS. No, thou stand'st single; th'art not on him yet.

CAPHIS. Where's the fool now?

APEMANTUS. He last ask'd the question. Poor rogues and usurers' men! Bawds between gold and want!

ALL SERVANTS. What are we, Apemantus?

APEMANTUS. Asses.

ALL SERVANTS. Why?

APEMANTUS. That you ask me what you are, and do not know yourselves. Speak to 'em, fool.

FOOL. How do you, gentlemen?

ALL SERVANTS. Gramercies, good fool. How does your mistress?

FOOL. She's e'en setting on water to scald such chickens as you are. Would we could see you at Corinth!

APEMANTUS. Good! gramercy.

Enter PAGE

FOOL. Look you, here comes my mistress' page.

PAGE. [*To the* FOOL] Why, how now, Captain? What do you in this wise company? How dost thou, Apemantus?

APEMANTUS. Would I had a rod in my mouth, that I might answer thee profitably!

PAGE. Prithee, Apemantus, read me the superscription of these letters; I know not which is which.

APEMANTUS. Canst not read?

PAGE. No.

APEMANTUS. There will little learning die, then, that day thou art hang'd. This is to Lord Timon; this to Alcibiades. Go; thou wast born a bastard, and thou't die a bawd.

PAGE. Thou wast whelp'd a dog, and thou shalt famish a dog's death. Answer not: I am gone. *Exit* PAGE

APEMANTUS. E'en so thou outrun'st grace.
Fool, I will go with you to Lord Timon's.

FOOL. Will you leave me there?

APEMANTUS. If Timon stay at home. You three serve three usurers?

ALL SERVANTS. Ay; would they serv'd us!

APEMANTUS. So would I—as good a trick as ever hangman serv'd thief.

FOOL. Are you three usurers' men?

ALL SERVANTS. Ay, fool.

FOOL. I think no usurer but has a fool to his servant. My mistress is one, and I am her fool. When men come to borrow of your masters, they approach sadly and go away merry; but they enter my mistress' house merrily and go away sadly. The reason of this?

VARRO'S SERVANT. I could render one.

APEMANTUS. Do it then, that we may account thee a whoremaster and a knave; which notwithstanding, thou shalt be no less esteemed.

VARRO'S SERVANT. What is a whoremaster, fool?

FOOL. A fool in good clothes, and something like thee. 'Tis a spirit. Sometime 't appears like a lord; sometime like a lawyer; sometime like a philosopher, with two stones moe than's artificial one. He is very often like a knight; and, generally, in all shapes that man goes up and down in from fourscore to thirteen, this spirit walks in.

VARRO'S SERVANT. Thou art not altogether a fool.

FOOL. Nor thou altogether a wise man.
As much foolery as I have, so much wit thou lack'st.

APEMANTUS. That answer might have become Apemantus.

VARRO'S SERVANT. Aside, aside; here comes Lord Timon.

Re-enter TIMON *and* FLAVIUS

APEMANTUS. Come with me, fool, come.

FOOL. I do not always follow lover, elder brother, and woman; sometime the philosopher.

Exeunt APEMANTUS *and* FOOL

FLAVIUS. Pray you walk near; I'll speak with you anon.

Exeunt SERVANTS

TIMON. You make me marvel wherefore ere this time
Had you not fully laid my state before me,
That I might so have rated my expense
As I had leave of means.

FLAVIUS. You would not hear me
At many leisures I propos'd.

TIMON. Go to;
Perchance some single vantages you took
When my indisposition put you back,
And that unaptness made your minister
Thus to excuse yourself.

FLAVIUS. O my good lord,
At many times I brought in my accounts,
Laid them before you; you would throw them off
And say you found them in mine honesty.
When, for some trifling present, you have bid me
Return so much, I have shook my head and wept;
Yea, 'gainst th' authority of manners, pray'd you
To hold your hand more close. I did endure
Not seldom, nor no slight checks, when I have
Prompted you in the ebb of your estate
And your great flow of debts. My lov'd lord,
Though you hear now—too late!—yet now's a time:
The greatest of your having lacks a half
To pay your present debts.

TIMON. Let all my land be sold.

FLAVIUS. 'Tis all engag'd, some forfeited and gone;
And what remains will hardly stop the mouth

Of present dues. The future comes apace;
What shall defend the interim? And at length
How goes our reck'ning?

TIMON. To Lacedæmon did my land extend.

FLAVIUS. O my good lord, the world is but a word;
Were it all yours to give it in a breath,
How quickly were it gone!

TIMON. You tell me true.

FLAVIUS. If you suspect my husbandry or falsehood,
Call me before th' exactest auditors
And set me on the proof. So the gods bless me,
When all our offices have been oppress'd
With riotous feeders, when our vaults have wept
With drunken spilth of wine, when every room
Hath blaz'd with lights and bray'd with minstrelsy,
I have retir'd me to a wasteful cock
And set mine eyes at flow.

TIMON. Prithee no more.

FLAVIUS. 'Heavens,' have I said 'the bounty of this lord!
How many prodigal bits have slaves and peasants
This night englutted! Who is not Lord Timon's?
What heart, head, sword, force, means, but is Lord Timon's?
Great Timon, noble, worthy, royal Timon!'
Ah! when the means are gone that buy this praise,
The breath is gone whereof this praise is made.
Feast-won, fast-lost; one cloud of winter show'rs,
These flies are couch'd.

TIMON. Come, sermon me no further.
No villainous bounty yet hath pass'd my heart;
Unwisely, not ignobly, have I given.
Why dost thou weep? Canst thou the conscience lack
To think I shall lack friends? Secure thy heart:
If I would broach the vessels of my love,
And try the argument of hearts by borrowing,
Men and men's fortunes could I frankly use
As I can bid thee speak.

FLAVIUS. Assurance bless your thoughts!

TIMON. And, in some sort, these wants of mine are crown'd
That I account them blessings; for by these

Shall I try friends. You shall perceive how you
Mistake my fortunes; I am wealthy in my friends.
Within there! Flaminius! Servilius!

Enter FLAMINIUS, SERVILIUS, *and another* SERVANT

SERVANTS. My lord! my lord!

TIMON. I will dispatch you severally—you to Lord Lucius; to Lord Lucullus you; I hunted with his honour to-day. You to Sempronius. Commend me to their loves; and I am proud, say, that my occasions have found time to use 'em toward a supply of money. Let the request be fifty talents.

FLAMINIUS. As you have said, my lord. *Exeunt* SERVANTS

FLAVIUS. [*Aside*] Lord Lucius and Lucullus? Humh!

TIMON. Go you, sir, to the senators,
Of whom, even to the state's best health, I have
Deserv'd this hearing. Bid 'em send o' th' instant
A thousand talents to me.

FLAVIUS. I have been bold,
For that I knew it the most general way,
To them to use your signet and your name;
But they do shake their heads, and I am here
No richer in return.

TIMON. Is't true? Can't be?

FLAVIUS. They answer, in a joint and corporate voice,
That now they are at fall, want treasure, cannot
Do what they would, are sorry—you are honourable—
But yet they could have wish'd—they know not—
Something hath been amiss—a noble nature
May catch a wrench—would all were well!—'tis pity—
And so, intending other serious matters,
After distasteful looks, and these hard fractions,
With certain half-caps and cold-moving nods,
They froze me into silence.

TIMON. You gods, reward them!
Prithee, man, look cheerly. These old fellows
Have their ingratitude in them hereditary.
Their blood is cak'd, 'tis cold, it seldom flows;
'Tis lack of kindly warmth they are not kind;
And nature, as it grows again toward earth,

Is fashion'd for the journey dull and heavy.
Go to Ventidius. Prithee be not sad,
Thou art true and honest; ingeniously I speak,
No blame belongs to thee. Ventidius lately
Buried his father, by whose death he's stepp'd
Into a great estate. When he was poor,
Imprison'd, and in scarcity of friends,
I clear'd him with five talents. Greet him from me,
Bid him suppose some good necessity
Touches his friend, which craves to be rememb'red
With those five talents. That had, give't these fellows
To whom 'tis instant due. Nev'r speak or think
That Timon's fortunes 'mong his friends can sink.

FLAVIUS. I would I could not think it.
That thought is bounty's foe;
Being free itself, it thinks all others so. *Exeunt*

ACT III. SCENE 1

LUCULLUS' *house*

FLAMINIUS *waiting to speak with* LUCULLUS. *Enter a* SERVANT *to him*

SERVANT. I have told my lord of you; he is coming down to you.

FLAMINIUS. I thank you, sir.

Enter LUCULLUS

SERVANT. Here's my lord.

LUCULLUS. [*Aside*] One of Lord Timon's men? A gift, I warrant. Why, this hits right; I dreamt of a silver basin and ewer to-night–Flaminius, honest Flaminius, you are very respectively welcome, sir. Fill me some wine. [*Exit* SERVANT] And how does that honourable, complete, free-hearted gentleman of Athens, thy very bountiful good lord and master?

FLAMINIUS. His health is well, sir.

LUCULLUS. I am right glad that his health is well, sir. And what hast thou there under thy cloak, pretty Flaminius?

FLAMINIUS. Faith, nothing but an empty box, sir, which in my lord's behalf I come to entreat your honour to supply; who, having great and instant occasion to use fifty talents, hath sent to your lordship to furnish him, nothing doubting your present assistance therein.

LUCULLUS. La, la, la, la! 'Nothing doubting' says he? Alas, good lord! a noble gentleman 'tis, if he would not keep so good a house. Many a time and often I ha' din'd with him and told him on't; and come again to supper to him of purpose to have him spend less; and yet he would embrace no counsel, take no warning by my coming. Every man has his fault, and honesty is his. I ha' told him on't, but I could ne'er get him from't.

Re-enter SERVANT, *with wine*

SERVANT. Please your lordship, here is the wine.

LUCULLUS. Flaminius, I have noted thee always wise. Here's to thee.

FLAMINIUS. Your lordship speaks your pleasure.

LUCULLUS. I have observed thee always for a towardly prompt spirit, give thee thy due, and one that knows what belongs to reason, and canst use the time well, if the time use thee well. Good parts in thee. [*To* SERVANT] Get you gone, sirrah. [*Exit* SERVANT] Draw nearer, honest Flaminius. Thy lord's a bountiful gentleman; but thou art wise, and thou know'st well enough, although thou com'st to me, that this is no time to lend money, especially upon bare friendship without security. Here's three solidares for thee. Good boy, wink at me, and say thou saw'st me not. Fare thee well.

FLAMINIUS. Is't possible the world should so much differ,
And we alive that liv'd? Fly, damned baseness,
To him that worships thee. [*Throwing the money back*]

LUCULLUS. Ha! Now I see thou art a fool, and fit for thy master. *Exit*

FLAMINIUS. May these add to the number that may scald thee!
Let molten coin be thy damnation,
Thou disease of a friend and not himself!

Has friendship such a faint and milky heart
It turns in less than two nights? O you gods,
I feel my master's passion! This slave
Unto his honour has my lord's meat in him;
Why should it thrive and turn to nutriment
When he is turn'd to poison?
O, may diseases only work upon't!
And when he's sick to death, let not that part of nature
Which my lord paid for be of any power
To expel sickness, but prolong his hour! *Exit*

SCENE 2

A public place

Enter LUCIUS, *with three* STRANGERS

LUCIUS. Who, the Lord Timon? He is my very good friend, and an honourable gentleman.

FIRST STRANGER. We know him for no less, though we are but strangers to him. But I can tell you one thing, my lord, and which I hear from common rumours: now Lord Timon's happy hours are done and past, and his estate shrinks from him.

LUCIUS. Fie, no: do not believe it; he cannot want for money.

SECOND STRANGER. But believe you this, my lord, that not long ago one of his men was with the Lord Lucullus to borrow so many talents; nay, urg'd extremely for't, and showed what necessity belong'd to't, and yet was denied.

LUCIUS. How?

SECOND STRANGER. I tell you, denied, my lord.

LUCIUS. What a strange case was that! Now, before the gods, I am asham'd on't. Denied that honourable man! There was very little honour show'd in't. For my own part, I must needs confess I have received some small kindnesses from him, as money, plate, jewels, and such-like trifles, nothing comparing to his; yet, had he mistook him and sent to me, I should ne'er have denied his occasion so many talents.

Enter SERVILIUS

SERVILIUS. See, by good hap, yonder's my lord; I have sweat to see his honour.—My honour'd lord!

LUCIUS. Servilius? You are kindly met, sir. Fare thee well; commend me to thy honourable virtuous lord, my very exquisite friend.

SERVILIUS. May it please your honour, my lord hath sent—

LUCIUS. Ha! What has he sent? I am so much endeared to that lord: he's ever sending. How shall I thank him, think'st thou? And what has he sent now?

SERVILIUS. Has only sent his present occasion now, my lord, requesting your lordship to supply his instant use with so many talents.

LUCIUS. I know his lordship is but merry with me;
He cannot want fifty-five hundred talents.

SERVILIUS. But in the mean time he wants less, my lord.
If his occasion were not virtuous
I should not urge it half so faithfully.

LUCIUS. Dost thou speak seriously, Servilius?

SERVILIUS. Upon my soul, 'tis true, sir.

LUCIUS. What a wicked beast was I to disfurnish myself against such a good time, when I might ha' shown myself honourable! How unluckily it happ'ned that I should purchase the day before for a little part and undo a great deal of honour! Servilius, now before the gods, I am not able to do—the more beast, I say! I was sending to use Lord Timon myself, these gentlemen can witness; but I would not for the wealth of Athens I had done't now. Commend me bountifully to his good lordship, and I hope his honour will conceive the fairest of me, because I have no power to be kind. And tell him this from me: I count it one of my greatest afflictions, say, that I cannot pleasure such an honourable gentleman. Good Servilius, will you befriend me so far as to use mine own words to him?

SERVILIUS. Yes, sir, I shall.

LUCIUS. I'll look you out a good turn, Servilius.

Exit SERVILIUS

True, as you said, Timon is shrunk indeed;
And he that's once denied will hardly speed. *Exit*

First Stranger. Do you observe this, Hostilius?

Second Stranger. Ay, too well.

First Stranger. Why, this is the world's soul; and just of the same piece
Is every flatterer's spirit. Who can call him his friend
That dips in the same dish? For, in my knowing,
Timon has been this lord's father,
And kept his credit with his purse;
Supported his estate; nay, Timon's money
Has paid his men their wages. He ne'er drinks
But Timon's silver treads upon his lip;
And yet—O, see the monstrousness of man
When he looks out in an ungrateful shape!—
He does deny him, in respect of his,
What charitable men afford to beggars.

Third Stranger. Religion groans at it.

First Stranger. For mine own part,
I never tasted Timon in my life,
Nor came any of his bounties over me
To mark me for his friend; yet I protest,
For his right noble mind, illustrious virtue,
And honourable carriage,
Had his necessity made use of me,
I would have put my wealth into donation,
And the best half should have return'd to him,
So much I love his heart. But I perceive
Men must learn now with pity to dispense;
For policy sits above conscience. *Exeunt*

SCENE 3

Sempronius' *house*

Enter Sempronius *and a* Servant *of* Timon's

Sempronius. Must he needs trouble me in't? Hum! 'Bove all others?
He might have tried Lord Lucius or Lucullus;
And now Ventidius is wealthy too,
Whom he redeem'd from prison. All these

Owe their estates unto him.

SERVANT. My lord,
They have all been touch'd and found base metal, for
They have all denied him.

SEMPRONIUS. How! Have they denied him?
Has Ventidius and Lucullus denied him?
And does he send to me? Three? Humh!
It shows but little love or judgment in him.
Must I be his last refuge? His friends, like physicians,
Thrice give him over. Must I take th' cure upon me?
Has much disgrac'd me in't; I'm angry at him,
That might have known my place. I see no sense for't,
But his occasions might have woo'd me first;
For, in my conscience, I was the first man
That e'er received gift from him.
And does he think so backwardly of me now
That I'll requite it last? No;
So it may prove an argument of laughter
To th' rest, and I 'mongst lords be thought a fool.
I'd rather than the worth of thrice the sum
Had sent to me first, but for my mind's sake;
I'd such a courage to do him good. But now return,
And with their faint reply this answer join:
Who bates mine honour shall not know my coin. *Exit*

SERVANT. Excellent! Your lordship's a goodly villain. The devil knew not what he did when he made man politic—he cross'd himself by't; and I cannot think but, in the end, the villainies of man will set him clear. How fairly this lord strives to appear foul! Takes virtuous copies to be wicked, like those that under hot ardent zeal would set whole realms on fire.
Of such a nature is his politic love.
This was my lord's best hope; now all are fled,
Save only the gods. Now his friends are dead,
Doors that were ne'er acquainted with their wards
Many a bounteous year must be employ'd
Now to guard sure their master.
And this is all a liberal course allows:
Who cannot keep his wealth must keep his house. *Exit*

SCENE 4

A hall in TIMON'S *house*

Enter two of VARRO'S MEN, *meeting* LUCIUS' SERVANT, *and others, all being servants of* TIMON'S *creditors, to wait for his coming out. Then enter* TITUS *and* HORTENSIUS

FIRST VARRO'S SERVANT. Well met; good morrow, Titus and Hortensius.

TITUS. The like to you, kind Varro.

HORTENSIUS. Lucius! What, do we meet together?

LUCIUS' SERVANT. Ay, and I think one business does command us all; for mine is money.

TITUS. So is theirs and ours.

Enter PHILOTUS

LUCIUS' SERVANT. And Sir Philotus too!

PHILOTUS. Good day at once.

LUCIUS' SERVANT. Welcome, good brother, what do you think the hour?

PHILOTUS. Labouring for nine.

LUCIUS' SERVANT. So much?

PHILOTUS. Is not my lord seen yet?

LUCIUS' SERVANT. Not yet.

PHILOTUS. I wonder on't; he was wont to shine at seven.

LUCIUS' SERVANT. Ay, but the days are wax'd shorter with him;
You must consider that a prodigal course
Is like the sun's, but not like his recoverable.
I fear
'Tis deepest winter in Lord Timon's purse;
That is, one may reach deep enough and yet
Find little.

PHILOTUS. I am of your fear for that.

TITUS. I'll show you how t' observe a strange event.
Your lord sends now for money.

HORTENSIUS. Most true, he does.

TITUS. And he wears jewels now of Timon's gift,

For which I wait for money.

HORTENSIUS. It is against my heart.

LUCIUS' SERVANT. Mark how strange it shows
Timon in this should pay more than he owes;
And e'en as if your lord should wear rich jewels
And send for money for 'em.

HORTENSIUS. I'm weary of this charge, the gods can witness;
I know my lord hath spent of Timon's wealth,
And now ingratitude makes it worse than stealth.

FIRST VARRO'S SERVANT. Yes, mine's three thousand crowns; what's yours?

LUCIUS' SERVANT. Five thousand mine.

FIRST VARRO'S SERVANT. 'Tis much deep; and it should seem by th' sum
Your master's confidence was above mine,
Else surely his had equall'd.

Enter FLAMINIUS

TITUS. One of Lord Timon's men.

LUCIUS' SERVANT. Flaminius! Sir, a word. Pray, is my lord ready to come forth?

FLAMINIUS. No, indeed, he is not.

TITUS. We attend his lordship; pray signify so much.

FLAMINIUS. I need not tell him that; he knows you are too diligent. *Exit*

Enter FLAVIUS, *in a cloak, muffled*

LUCIUS' SERVANT. Ha! Is not that his steward muffled so?
He goes away in a cloud. Call him, call him.

TITUS. Do you hear, sir?

SECOND VARRO'S SERVANT. By your leave, sir.

FLAVIUS. What do ye ask of me, my friend?

TITUS. We wait for certain money here, sir.

FLAVIUS. Ay,
If money were as certain as your waiting,
'Twere sure enough.
Why then preferr'd you not your sums and bills
When your false masters eat of my lord's meat?
Then they could smile, and fawn upon his debts,

And take down th' int'rest into their glutt'nous maws.
You do yourselves but wrong to stir me up;
Let me pass quietly.
Believe't, my lord and I have made an end:
I have no more to reckon, he to spend.

LUCIUS' SERVANT. Ay, but this answer will not serve.

FLAVIUS. If 'twill not serve, 'tis not so base as you,
For you serve knaves. *Exit*

FIRST VARRO'S SERVANT. How! What does his cashier'd worship mutter?

SECOND VARRO'S SERVANT. No matter what; he's poor, and that's revenge enough. Who can speak broader than he that has no house to put his head in? Such may rail against great buildings.

Enter SERVILIUS

TITUS. O, here's Servilius; now we shall know some answer.

SERVILIUS. If I might beseech you, gentlemen, to repair some other hour, I should derive much from't; for take't of my soul, my lord leans wondrously to discontent. His comfortable temper has forsook him; he's much out of health and keeps his chamber.

LUCIUS' SERVANT. Many do keep their chambers are not sick;
And if it be so far beyond his health,
Methinks he should the sooner pay his debts,
And make a clear way to the gods.

SERVILIUS. Good gods!

TITUS. We cannot take this for answer, sir.

FLAMINIUS. [*Within*] Servilius, help! My lord! my lord!

Enter TIMON, *in a rage*, FLAMINIUS *following*

TIMON. What, are my doors oppos'd against my passage?
Have I been ever free, and must my house
Be my retentive enemy, my gaol?
The place which I have feasted, does it now,
Like all mankind, show me an iron heart?

LUCIUS' SERVANT. Put in now, Titus.

TITUS. My lord, here is my bill.

LUCIUS' SERVANT. Here's mine.

HORTENSIUS. And mine, my lord.
BOTH VARRO'S SERVANTS. And ours, my lord.
PHILOTUS. All our bills.
TIMON. Knock me down with 'em; cleave me to the girdle.
LUCIUS' SERVANT. Alas, my lord–
TIMON. Cut my heart in sums.
TITUS. Mine, fifty talents.
TIMON. Tell out my blood.
LUCIUS' SERVANT. Five thousand crowns, my lord.
TIMON. Five thousand drops pays that. What yours? and yours?
FIRST VARRO'S SERVANT. My lord–
SECOND VARRO'S SERVANT. My lord–
TIMON. Tear me, take me, and the gods fall upon you!
Exit

HORTENSIUS. Faith, I perceive our masters may throw their caps at their money. These debts may well be call'd desperate ones, for a madman owes 'em. *Exeunt*

Re-enter TIMON *and* FLAVIUS

TIMON. They have e'en put my breath from me, the slaves.
Creditors? Devils!
FLAVIUS. My dear lord–
TIMON. What if it should be so?
FLAMINIUS. My lord–
TIMON. I'll have it so. My steward!
FLAVIUS. Here, my lord.
TIMON. So fitly? Go, bid all my friends again:
Lucius, Lucullus, and Sempronius–all.
I'll once more feast the rascals.
FLAVIUS. O my lord,
You only speak from your distracted soul;
There is not so much left to furnish out
A moderate table.
TIMON. Be it not in thy care.
Go, I charge thee, invite them all; let in the tide
Of knaves once more; my cook and I'll provide. *Exeunt*

SCENE 5

The Senate House

Enter three SENATORS *at one door,* ALCIBIADES *meeting them, with attendants*

FIRST SENATOR. My lord, you have my voice to't: the fault's bloody.
'Tis necessary he should die:
Nothing emboldens sin so much as mercy.
SECOND SENATOR. Most true; the law shall bruise him.
ALCIBIADES. Honour, health, and compassion, to the Senate!
FIRST SENATOR. Now, Captain?
ALCIBIADES. I am an humble suitor to your virtues;
For pity is the virtue of the law,
And none but tyrants use it cruelly.
It pleases time and fortune to lie heavy
Upon a friend of mine, who in hot blood
Hath stepp'd into the law, which is past depth
To those that without heed do plunge into't.
He is a man, setting his fate aside,
Of comely virtues;
Nor did he soil the fact with cowardice–
An honour in him which buys out his fault–
But with a noble fury and fair spirit,
Seeing his reputation touch'd to death,
He did oppose his foe;
And with such sober and unnoted passion
He did behove his anger ere 'twas spent,
As if he had but prov'd an argument.
FIRST SENATOR. You undergo too strict a paradox,
Striving to make an ugly deed look fair;
Your words have took such pains as if they labour'd
To bring manslaughter into form and set
Quarrelling upon the head of valour; which, indeed,
Is valour misbegot, and came into the world
When sects and factions were newly born.
He's truly valiant that can wisely suffer
The worst that man can breathe,

And make his wrongs his outsides,
To wear them like his raiment, carelessly,
And ne'er prefer his injuries to his heart,
To bring it into danger.
If wrongs be evils, and enforce us kill,
What folly 'tis to hazard life for ill!

ALCIBIADES. My lord–

FIRST SENATOR. You cannot make gross sins look clear:
To revenge is no valour, but to bear.

ALCIBIADES. My lords, then, under favour, pardon me
If I speak like a captain:
Why do fond men expose themselves to battle,
And not endure all threats? Sleep upon't,
And let the foes quietly cut their throats,
Without repugnancy? If there be
Such valour in the bearing, what make we
Abroad? Why, then, women are more valiant,
That stay at home, if bearing carry it;
And the ass more captain than the lion; the fellow
Loaden with irons wiser than the judge,
If wisdom be in suffering. O my lords,
As you are great, be pitifully good.
Who cannot condemn rashness in cold blood?
To kill, I grant, is sin's extremest gust;
But, in defence, by mercy, 'tis most just.
To be in anger is impiety;
But who is man that is not angry?
Weigh but the crime with this.

SECOND SENATOR. You breathe in vain.

ALCIBIADES. In vain! His service done
At Lacedæmon and Byzantium
Were a sufficient briber for his life.

FIRST SENATOR. What's that?

ALCIBIADES. Why, I say, my lords, has done fair service,
And slain in fight many of your enemies;
How full of valour did he bear himself
In the last conflict, and made plenteous wounds!

SECOND SENATOR. He has made too much plenty with 'em.
He's a sworn rioter; he has a sin that often
Drowns him and takes his valour prisoner.

If there were no foes, that were enough
To overcome him. In that beastly fury
He has been known to commit outrages
And cherish factions. 'Tis inferr'd to us
His days are foul and his drink dangerous.

FIRST SENATOR. He dies.

ALCIBIADES. Hard fate! He might have died in war.
My lords, if not for any parts in him—
Though his right arm might purchase his own time,
And be in debt to none—yet, more to move you,
Take my deserts to his, and join 'em both;
And, for I know your reverend ages love
Security, I'll pawn my victories, all
My honours to you, upon his good returns.
If by this crime he owes the law his life,
Why, let the war receive't in valiant gore;
For law is strict, and war is nothing more.

FIRST SENATOR. We are for law: he dies. Urge it no more
On height of our displeasure. Friend or brother,
He forfeits his own blood that spills another.

ALCIBIADES. Must it be so? It must not be. My lords,
I do beseech you, know me.

SECOND SENATOR. How!

ALCIBIADES. Call me to your remembrances.

THIRD SENATOR. What!

ALCIBIADES. I cannot think but your age has forgot me;
It could not else be I should prove so base
To sue, and be denied such common grace.
My wounds ache at you.

FIRST SENATOR. Do you dare our anger?
'Tis in few words, but spacious in effect:
We banish thee for ever.

ALCIBIADES. Banish me!
Banish your dotage! Banish usury
That makes the Senate ugly.

FIRST SENATOR. If after two days' shine Athens contain thee,
Attend our weightier judgment. And, not to swell our spirit,
He shall be executed presently. *Exeunt* SENATORS

ALCIBIADES. Now the gods keep you old enough that you
may live

Only in bone, that none may look on you!
I'm worse than mad; I have kept back their foes,
While they have told their money and let out
Their coin upon large interest, I myself
Rich only in large hurts. All those for this?
Is this the balsam that the usuring Senate
Pours into captains' wounds? Banishment!
It comes not ill; I hate not to be banish'd;
It is a cause worthy my spleen and fury,
That I may strike at Athens. I'll cheer up
My discontented troops, and lay for hearts.
'Tis honour with most lands to be at odds;
Soldiers should brook as little wrongs as gods. *Exit*

SCENE 6

A banqueting hall in TIMON'S *house*

Music. Tables set out; servants attending. Enter divers LORDS, *friends of* TIMON, *at several doors*

FIRST LORD. The good time of day to you, sir.

SECOND LORD. I also wish it to you. I think this honourable lord did but try us this other day.

FIRST LORD. Upon that were my thoughts tiring when we encount'red. I hope it is not so low with him as he made it seem in the trial of his several friends.

SECOND LORD. It should not be, by the persuasion of his new feasting.

FIRST LORD. I should think so. He hath sent me an earnest inviting, which many my near occasions did urge me to put off; but he hath conjur'd me beyond them, and I must needs appear.

SECOND LORD. In like manner was I in debt to my importunate business, but he would not hear my excuse. I am sorry, when he sent to borrow of me, that my provision was out.

FIRST LORD. I am sick of that grief too, as I understand how all things go.

SECOND LORD. Every man here's so. What would he have borrowed of you?

FIRST LORD. A thousand pieces.

SECOND LORD. A thousand pieces!

FIRST LORD. What of you?

SECOND LORD. He sent to me, sir—here he comes.

Enter TIMON *and attendants*

TIMON. With all my heart, gentlemen both! And how fare you?

FIRST LORD. Ever at the best, hearing well of your lordship.

SECOND LORD. The swallow follows not summer more willing than we your lordship.

TIMON. [*Aside*] Nor more willingly leaves winter; such summer-birds are men—Gentlemen, our dinner will not recompense this long stay; feast your ears with the music awhile, if they will fare so harshly o' th' trumpet's sound; we shall to't presently.

FIRST LORD. I hope it remains not unkindly with your lordship that I return'd you an empty messenger.

TIMON. O sir, let it not trouble you.

SECOND LORD. My noble lord—

TIMON. Ah, my good friend, what cheer?

SECOND LORD. My most honourable lord, I am e'en sick of shame that, when your lordship this other day sent to me, I was so unfortunate a beggar.

TIMON. Think not on't, sir.

SECOND LORD. If you had sent but two hours before—

TIMON. Let it not cumber your better remembrance. [*The banquet brought in*] Come, bring in all together.

SECOND LORD. All cover'd dishes!

FIRST LORD. Royal cheer, I warrant you.

THIRD LORD. Doubt not that, if money and the season can yield it.

FIRST LORD. How do you? What's the news?

THIRD LORD. Alcibiades is banish'd. Hear you of it?

FIRST AND SECOND LORDS. Alcibiades banish'd!

THIRD LORD. 'Tis so, be sure of it.

FIRST LORD. How? how?

SECOND LORD. I pray you, upon what?

TIMON. My worthy friends, will you draw near?

THIRD LORD. I'll tell you more anon. Here's a noble feast toward.

SECOND LORD. This is the old man still.

THIRD LORD. Will't hold? Will't hold?

SECOND LORD. It does; but time will—and so—

THIRD LORD. I do conceive.

TIMON. Each man to his stool with that spur as he would to the lip of his mistress; your diet shall be in all places alike. Make not a city feast of it, to let the meat cool ere we can agree upon the first place. Sit, sit. The gods require our thanks:

You great benefactors, sprinkle our society with thankfulness. For your own gifts make yourselves prais'd; but reserve still to give, lest your deities be despised. Lend to each man enough, that one need not lend to another; for were your god-heads to borrow of men, men would forsake the gods. Make the meat be beloved more than the man that gives it. Let no assembly of twenty be without a score of villains. If there sit twelve women at the table, let a dozen of them be—as they are. The rest of your foes, O gods, the senators of Athens, together with the common lag of people, what is amiss in them, you gods, make suitable for destruction. For these my present friends, as they are to me nothing, so in nothing bless them, and to nothing are they welcome.

Uncover, dogs, and lap. [*The dishes are uncovered and seen to be full of warm water*]

SOME SPEAK. What does his lordship mean?

SOME OTHER. I know not.

TIMON. May you a better feast never behold,
You knot of mouth-friends! Smoke and lukewarm water
Is your perfection. This is Timon's last;
Who, stuck and spangled with your flatteries,
Washes it off, and sprinkles in your faces
[*Throwing the water in their faces*]
Your reeking villainy. Live loath'd and long,
Most smiling, smooth, detested parasites,
Courteous destroyers, affable wolves, meek bears,

You fools of fortune, trencher friends, time's flies,
Cap and knee slaves, vapours, and minute-jacks!
Of man and beast the infinite malady
Crust you quite o'er! What, dost thou go?
Soft, take thy physic first; thou too, and thou.
Stay, I will lend thee money, borrow none. [*Throws the dishes at them, and drives them out*]
What, all in motion? Henceforth be no feast
Whereat a villain's not a welcome guest.
Burn house! Sink Athens! Henceforth hated be
Of Timon man and all humanity! *Exit*

Re-enter the LORDS

FIRST LORD. How now, my lords!

SECOND LORD. Know you the quality of Lord Timon's fury?

THIRD LORD. Push! Did you see my cap?

FOURTH LORD. I have lost my gown.

FIRST LORD. He's but a mad lord, and nought but humours sways him. He gave me a jewel th' other day, and now he has beat it out of my hat. Did you see my jewel?

THIRD LORD. Did you see my cap?

SECOND LORD. Here 'tis.

FOURTH LORD. Here lies my gown.

FIRST LORD. Let's make no stay.

SECOND LORD. Lord Timon's mad.

THIRD LORD. I feel't upon my bones.

FOURTH LORD. One day he gives us diamonds, next day stones. *Exeunt*

ACT IV. SCENE 1

Without the walls of Athens

Enter TIMON

TIMON. Let me look back upon thee. O thou wall
That girdles in those wolves, dive in the earth
And fence not Athens! Matrons, turn incontinent.
Obedience, fail in children! Slaves and fools,

Pluck the grave wrinkled Senate from the bench
And minister in their steads. To general filths
Convert, o' th' instant, green virginity.
Do't in your parents' eyes. Bankrupts, hold fast;
Rather than render back, out with your knives
And cut your trusters' throats. Bound servants, steal:
Large-handed robbers your grave masters are,
And pill by law. Maid, to thy master's bed:
Thy mistress is o' th' brothel. Son of sixteen,
Pluck the lin'd crutch from thy old limping sire,
With it beat out his brains. Piety and fear,
Religion to the gods, peace, justice, truth,
Domestic awe, night-rest, and neighbourhood,
Instruction, manners, mysteries, and trades,
Degrees, observances, customs and laws,
Decline to your confounding contraries
And let confusion live. Plagues incident to men,
Your potent and infectious fevers heap
On Athens, ripe for stroke. Thou cold sciatica,
Cripple our senators, that their limbs may halt
As lamely as their manners. Lust and liberty,
Creep in the minds and marrows of our youth,
That 'gainst the stream of virtue they may strive
And drown themselves in riot. Itches, blains,
Sow all th' Athenian bosoms, and their crop
Be general leprosy! Breath infect breath,
That their society, as their friendship, may
Be merely poison! Nothing I'll bear from thee
But nakedness, thou detestable town!
Take thou that too, with multiplying bans.
Timon will to the woods, where he shall find
Th' unkindest beast more kinder than mankind.
The gods confound–hear me, you good gods all–
The Athenians both within and out that wall!
And grant, as Timon grows, his hate may grow
To the whole race of mankind, high and low!
Amen. *Exit*

SCENE 2

Athens. TIMON'S *house*

Enter FLAVIUS, *with two or three* SERVANTS

FIRST SERVANT. Hear you, Master Steward, where's our master?
Are we undone, cast off, nothing remaining?
FLAVIUS. Alack, my fellows, what should I say to you?
Let me be recorded by the righteous gods,
I am as poor as you.
FIRST SERVANT. Such a house broke!
So noble a master fall'n! All gone, and not
One friend to take his fortune by the arm
And go along with him?
SECOND SERVANT. As we do turn our backs
From our companion, thrown into his grave,
So his familiars to his buried fortunes
Slink all away; leave their false vows with him,
Like empty purses pick'd; and his poor self,
A dedicated beggar to the air,
With his disease of all-shunn'd poverty,
Walks, like contempt, alone. More of our fellows.

Enter other SERVANTS

FLAVIUS. All broken implements of a ruin'd house.
THIRD SERVANT. Yet do our hearts wear Timon's livery;
That see I by our faces. We are fellows still,
Serving alike in sorrow. Leak'd is our bark;
And we, poor mates, stand on the dying deck,
Hearing the surges threat. We must all part
Into this sea of air.
FLAVIUS. Good fellows all,
The latest of my wealth I'll share amongst you.
Wherever we shall meet, for Timon's sake,
Let's yet be fellows; let's shake our heads and say,
As 'twere a knell unto our master's fortune,
'We have seen better days.' Let each take some.
[*Giving them money*]

Nay, put out all your hands. Not one word more!
Thus part we rich in sorrow, parting poor.
[*Embrace, and part several ways*]
O the fierce wretchedness that glory brings us!
Who would not wish to be from wealth exempt,
Since riches point to misery and contempt?
Who would be so mock'd with glory, or to live
But in a dream of friendship,
To have his pomp, and all what state compounds,
But only painted, like his varnish'd friends?
Poor honest lord, brought low by his own heart,
Undone by goodness! Strange, unusual blood,
When man's worst sin is he does too much good!
Who then dares to be half so kind again?
For bounty, that makes gods, does still mar men.
My dearest lord—blest to be most accurst,
Rich only to be wretched—thy great fortunes
Are made thy chief afflictions. Alas, kind lord!
He's flung in rage from this ingrateful seat
Of monstrous friends; nor has he with him to
Supply his life, or that which can command it.
I'll follow and enquire him out.
I'll ever serve his mind with my best will;
Whilst I have gold, I'll be his steward still. *Exit*

SCENE 3

The woods near the sea-shore. Before TIMON's *cave*

Enter TIMON *in the woods*

TIMON. O blessed breeding sun, draw from the earth
Rotten humidity; below thy sister's orb
Infect the air! Twinn'd brothers of one womb—
Whose procreation, residence, and birth,
Scarce is dividant—touch them with several fortunes:
The greater scorns the lesser. Not nature,
To whom all sores lay siege, can bear great fortune
But by contempt of nature.
Raise me this beggar and deny't that lord:

The senator shall bear contempt hereditary,
The beggar native honour.
It is the pasture lards the rother's sides,
The want that makes him lean. Who dares, who dares,
In purity of manhood stand upright,
And say 'This man's a flatterer'? If one be,
So are they all; for every grise of fortune
Is smooth'd by that below. The learned pate
Ducks to the golden fool. All's oblique;
There's nothing level in our cursed natures
But direct villainy. Therefore be abhorr'd
All feasts, societies, and throngs of men!
His semblable, yea, himself, Timon disdains.
Destruction fang mankind! Earth, yield me roots.
[*Digging*]
Who seeks for better of thee, sauce his palate
With thy most operant poison. What is here?
Gold? Yellow, glittering, precious gold? No, gods,
I am no idle votarist. Roots, you clear heavens!
Thus much of this will make black white, foul fair,
Wrong right, base noble, old young, coward valiant.
Ha, you gods! why this? What, this, you gods? Why, this
Will lug your priests and servants from your sides,
Pluck stout men's pillows from below their heads—
This yellow slave
Will knit and break religions, bless th' accurs'd,
Make the hoar leprosy ador'd, place thieves
And give them title, knee, and approbation,
With senators on the bench. This is it
That makes the wappen'd widow wed again—
She whom the spital-house and ulcerous sores
Would cast the gorge at this embalms and spices
To th' April day again. Come, damn'd earth,
Thou common whore of mankind, that puts odds
Among the rout of nations, I will make thee
Do thy right nature. [*March afar off*]
Ha! a drum? Th'art quick,
But yet I'll bury thee. Thou't go, strong thief,
When gouty keepers of thee cannot stand.
Nay, stay thou out for earnest. [*Keeping some gold*]

Enter ALCIBIADES, *with drum and fife, in warlike manner; and* PHRYNIA *and* TIMANDRA

ALCIBIADES. What art thou there? Speak.

TIMON. A beast, as thou art. The canker gnaw thy heart
For showing me again the eyes of man!

ALCIBIADES. What is thy name? Is man so hateful to thee
That art thyself a man?

TIMON. I am Misanthropos, and hate mankind.
For thy part, I do wish thou wert a dog,
That I might love thee something.

ALCIBIADES. I know thee well;
But in thy fortunes am unlearn'd and strange.

TIMON. I know thee too; and more than that I know thee
I not desire to know. Follow thy drum;
With man's blood paint the ground, gules, gules.
Religious canons, civil laws, are cruel;
Then what should war be? This fell whore of thine
Hath in her more destruction than thy sword
For all her cherubin look.

PHRYNIA. Thy lips rot off!

TIMON. I will not kiss thee; then the rot returns
To thine own lips again.

ALCIBIADES. How came the noble Timon to this change?

TIMON. As the moon does, by wanting light to give.
But then renew I could not, like the moon;
There were no suns to borrow of.

ALCIBIADES. Noble Timon,
What friendship may I do thee?

TIMON. None, but to
Maintain my opinion.

ALCIBIADES. What is it, Timon?

TIMON. Promise me friendship, but perform none. If thou wilt not promise, the gods plague thee, for thou art a man! If thou dost perform, confound thee, for thou art a man!

ALCIBIADES. I have heard in some sort of thy miseries.

TIMON. Thou saw'st them when I had prosperity.

ALCIBIADES. I see them now; then was a blessed time.

TIMON. As thine is now, held with a brace of harlots.

TIMANDRA. Is this th' Athenian minion whom the world
Voic'd so regardfully?
TIMON. Art thou Timandra?
TIMANDRA. Yes.
TIMON. Be a whore still; they love thee not that use thee.
Give them diseases, leaving with thee their lust.
Make use of thy salt hours. Season the slaves
For tubs and baths; bring down rose-cheek'd youth
To the tub-fast and the diet.
TIMANDRA. Hang thee, monster!
ALCIBIADES. Pardon him, sweet Timandra, for his wits
Are drown'd and lost in his calamities.
I have but little gold of late, brave Timon,
The want whereof doth daily make revolt
In my penurious band. I have heard, and griev'd,
How cursed Athens, mindless of thy worth,
Forgetting thy great deeds, when neighbour states,
But for thy sword and fortune, trod upon them—
TIMON. I prithee beat thy drum and get thee gone.
ALCIBIADES. I am thy friend, and pity thee, dear Timon.
TIMON. How dost thou pity him whom thou dost trouble?
I had rather be alone.
ALCIBIADES. Why, fare thee well;
Here is some gold for thee.
TIMON. Keep it: I cannot eat it.
ALCIBIADES. When I have laid proud Athens on a heap—
TIMON. War'st thou 'gainst Athens?
ALCIBIADES. Ay, Timon, and have cause.
TIMON. The gods confound them all in thy conquest;
And thee after, when thou hast conquer'd!
ALCIBIADES. Why me, Timon?
TIMON. That by killing of villains
Thou wast born to conquer my country.
Put up thy gold. Go on. Here's gold. Go on.
Be as a planetary plague, when Jove
Will o'er some high-vic'd city hang his poison
In the sick air; let not thy sword skip one.
Pity not honour'd age for his white beard:
He is an usurer. Strike me the counterfeit matron:
It is her habit only that is honest,

Herself's a bawd. Let not the virgin's cheek
Make soft thy trenchant sword; for those milk paps
That through the window bars bore at men's eyes
Are not within the leaf of pity writ,
But set them down horrible traitors. Spare not the babe
Whose dimpled smiles from fools exhaust their mercy;
Think it a bastard whom the oracle
Hath doubtfully pronounc'd thy throat shall cut,
And mince it sans remorse. Swear against abjects;
Put armour on thine ears and on thine eyes,
Whose proof nor yells of mothers, maids, nor babes,
Nor sight of priests in holy vestments bleeding,
Shall pierce a jot. There's gold to pay thy soldiers.
Make large confusion; and, thy fury spent,
Confounded be thyself! Speak not, be gone.

ALCIBIADES. Hast thou gold yet? I'll take the gold thou givest me,
Not all thy counsel.

TIMON. Dost thou, or dost thou not, heaven's curse upon thee!

PHRYNIA AND TIMANDRA. Give us some gold, good Timon. Hast thou more?

TIMON. Enough to make a whore forswear her trade,
And to make whores a bawd. Hold up, you sluts,
Your aprons mountant; you are not oathable,
Although I know you'll swear, terribly swear,
Into strong shudders and to heavenly agues,
Th' immortal gods that hear you. Spare your oaths;
I'll trust to your conditions. Be whores still;
And he whose pious breath seeks to convert you—
Be strong in whore, allure him, burn him up;
Let your close fire predominate his smoke,
And be no turncoats. Yet may your pains six months
Be quite contrary! And thatch your poor thin roofs
With burdens of the dead—some that were hang'd,
No matter. Wear them, betray with them. Whore still;
Paint till a horse may mire upon your face.
A pox of wrinkles!

PHRYNIA AND TIMANDRA. Well, more gold. What then?
Believe't that we'll do anything for gold.

TIMON. Consumptions sow
In hollow bones of man; strike their sharp shins,
And mar men's spurring. Crack the lawyer's voice,
That he may never more false title plead,
Nor sound his quillets shrilly. Hoar the flamen,
That scolds against the quality of flesh
And not believes himself. Down with the nose,
Down with it flat, take the bridge quite away
Of him that, his particular to foresee,
Smells from the general weal. Make curl'd-pate ruffians bald,
And let the unscarr'd braggarts of the war
Derive some pain from you. Plague all,
That your activity may defeat and quell
The source of all erection. There's more gold.
Do you damn others, and let this damn you,
And ditches grave you all!

PHRYNIA AND TIMANDRA. More counsel with more money, bounteous Timon.

TIMON. More whore, more mischief first; I have given you earnest.

ALCIBIADES. Strike up the drum towards Athens. Farewell, Timon;
If I thrive well, I'll visit thee again.

TIMON. If I hope well, I'll never see thee more.

ALCIBIADES. I never did thee harm.

TIMON. Yes, thou spok'st well of me.

ALCIBIADES. Call'st thou that harm?

TIMON. Men daily find it. Get thee away, and take
Thy beagles with thee.

ALCIBIADES. We but offend him. Strike.

Drum beats. Exeunt all but TIMON

TIMON. That nature, being sick of man's unkindness,
Should yet be hungry! Common mother, thou, [*Digging*]
Whose womb unmeasurable and infinite breast
Teems and feeds all; whose self-same mettle,
Whereof thy proud child, arrogant man, is puff'd,
Engenders the black toad and adder blue,
The gilded newt and eyeless venom'd worm,
With all th' abhorred births below crisp heaven

Whereon Hyperion's quick'ning fire doth shine—
Yield him, who all thy human sons doth hate,
From forth thy plenteous bosom, one poor root!
Ensear thy fertile and conceptious womb,
Let it no more bring out ingrateful man!
Go great with tigers, dragons, wolves, and bears;
Teem with new monsters whom thy upward face
Hath to the marbled mansion all above
Never presented!—O, a root! Dear thanks!—
Dry up thy marrows, vines, and plough-torn leas,
Whereof ingrateful man, with liquorish draughts
And morsels unctuous, greases his pure mind,
That from it all consideration slips—

Enter APEMANTUS

More man? Plague, plague!

APEMANTUS. I was directed hither. Men report
Thou dost affect my manners and dost use them.

TIMON. 'Tis, then, because thou dost not keep a dog,
Whom I would imitate. Consumption catch thee!

APEMANTUS. This is in thee a nature but infected,
A poor unmanly melancholy sprung
From change of fortune. Why this spade, this place?
This slave-like habit and these looks of care?
Thy flatterers yet wear silk, drink wine, lie soft,
Hug their diseas'd perfumes, and have forgot
That ever Timon was. Shame not these woods
By putting on the cunning of a carper.
Be thou a flatterer now, and seek to thrive
By that which has undone thee: hinge thy knee,
And let his very breath whom thou'lt observe
Blow off thy cap; praise his most vicious strain,
And call it excellent. Thou wast told thus;
Thou gav'st thine ears, like tapsters that bade welcome,
To knaves and all approachers. 'Tis most just
That thou turn rascal; hadst thou wealth again
Rascals should have't. Do not assume my likeness.

TIMON. Were I like thee, I'd throw away myself.

APEMANTUS. Thou hast cast away thyself, being like thyself;

A madman so long, now a fool. What, think'st
That the bleak air, thy boisterous chamberlain,
Will put thy shirt on warm? Will these moist trees,
That have outliv'd the eagle, page thy heels
And skip when thou point'st out? Will the cold brook,
Candied with ice, caudle thy morning taste
To cure thy o'ernight's surfeit? Call the creatures
Whose naked natures live in all the spite
Of wreakful heaven, whose bare unhoused trunks,
To the conflicting elements expos'd,
Answer mere nature—bid them flatter thee.
O, thou shalt find—

TIMON. A fool of thee. Depart.

APEMANTUS. I love thee better now than e'er I did.

TIMON. I hate thee worse.

APEMANTUS. Why?

TIMON. Thou flatter'st misery.

APEMANTUS. I flatter not, but say thou art a caitiff.

TIMON. Why dost thou seek me out?

APEMANTUS. To vex thee.

TIMON. Always a villain's office or a fool's.
Dost please thyself in't?

APEMANTUS. Ay.

TIMON. What, a knave too?

APEMANTUS. If thou didst put this sour-cold habit on
To castigate thy pride, 'twere well; but thou
Dost it enforcedly. Thou'dst courtier be again
Wert thou not beggar. Willing misery
Outlives incertain pomp, is crown'd before.
The one is filling still, never complete;
The other, at high wish. Best state, contentless,
Hath a distracted and most wretched being,
Worse than the worst, content.
Thou should'st desire to die, being miserable.

TIMON. Not by his breath that is more miserable.
Thou art a slave whom Fortune's tender arm
With favour never clasp'd, but bred a dog.
Hadst thou, like us from our first swath, proceeded
The sweet degrees that this brief world affords
To such as may the passive drugs of it

Freely command, thou wouldst have plung'd thyself
In general riot, melted down thy youth
In different beds of lust, and never learn'd
The icy precepts of respect, but followed
The sug'red game before thee. But myself,
Who had the world as my confectionary;
The mouths, the tongues, the eyes, and hearts of men
At duty, more than I could frame employment;
That numberless upon me stuck, as leaves
Do on the oak, have with one winter's brush
Fell from their boughs, and left me open, bare
For every storm that blows—I to bear this,
That never knew but better, is some burden.
Thy nature did commence in sufferance; time
Hath made thee hard in't. Why shouldst thou hate men?
They never flatter'd thee. What hast thou given?
If thou wilt curse, thy father, that poor rag,
Must be thy subject; who, in spite, put stuff
To some she-beggar and compounded thee
Poor rogue hereditary. Hence, be gone.
If thou hadst not been born the worst of men,
Thou hadst been a knave and flatterer.

APEMANTUS. Art thou proud yet?

TIMON. Ay, that I am not thee.

APEMANTUS. I, that I was
No prodigal.

TIMON. I, that I am one now.
Were all the wealth I have shut up in thee,
I'd give thee leave to hang it. Get thee gone.
That the whole life of Athens were in this!
Thus would I eat it. [*Eating a root*]

APEMANTUS. Here! I will mend thy feast.
[*Offering him food*]

TIMON. First mend my company: take away thyself.

APEMANTUS. So I shall mend mine own by th' lack of thine.

TIMON. 'Tis not well mended so; it is but botch'd.
If not, I would it were.

APEMANTUS. What wouldst thou have to Athens?

TIMON. Thee thither in a whirlwind. If thou wilt,
Tell them there I have gold; look, so I have.

APEMANTUS. Here is no use for gold.

TIMON. The best and truest;
For here it sleeps and does no hired harm.

APEMANTUS. Where liest a nights, Timon?

TIMON. Under that's above me.
Where feed'st thou a days, Apemantus?

APEMANTUS. Where my stomach finds meat; or rather, where I eat it.

TIMON. Would poison were obedient, and knew my mind!

APEMANTUS. Where wouldst thou send it?

TIMON. To sauce thy dishes.

APEMANTUS. The middle of humanity thou never knewest, but the extremity of both ends. When thou wast in thy gilt and thy perfume, they mock'd thee for too much curiosity; in thy rags thou know'st none, but art despis'd for the contrary. There's a medlar for thee; eat it.

TIMON. On what I hate I feed not.

APEMANTUS. Dost hate a medlar?

TIMON. Ay, though it look like thee.

APEMANTUS. An th' hadst hated medlars sooner, thou shouldst have loved thyself better now. What man didst thou ever know unthrift that was beloved after his means?

TIMON. Who, without those means thou talk'st of, didst thou ever know belov'd?

APEMANTUS. Myself.

TIMON. I understand thee: thou hadst some means to keep a dog.

APEMANTUS. What things in the world canst thou nearest compare to thy flatterers?

TIMON. Women nearest; but men, men are the things themselves. What wouldst thou do with the world, Apemantus, if it lay in thy power?

APEMANTUS. Give it the beasts, to be rid of the men.

TIMON. Wouldst thou have thyself fall in the confusion of men, and remain a beast with the beasts?

APEMANTUS. Ay, Timon.

TIMON. A beastly ambition, which the gods grant thee t' attain to! If thou wert the lion, the fox would beguile thee; if thou wert the lamb, the fox would eat thee; if thou wert the fox, the lion would suspect thee, when, peradventure, thou wert accus'd by the ass. If thou wert the ass, thy dulness would torment thee; and still thou liv'dst but as a breakfast to the wolf. If thou wert the wolf, thy greediness would afflict thee, and oft thou shouldst hazard thy life for thy dinner. Wert thou the unicorn, pride and wrath would confound thee, and make thine own self the conquest of thy fury. Wert thou a bear, thou wouldst be kill'd by the horse; wert thou a horse, thou wouldst be seiz'd by the leopard; wert thou a leopard, thou wert german to the lion, and the spots of thy kindred were jurors on thy life. All thy safety were remotion, and thy defence absence. What beast couldst thou be that were not subject to a beast? And what a beast art thou already, that seest not thy loss in transformation!

APEMANTUS. If thou couldst please me with speaking to me, thou mightst have hit upon it here. The commonwealth of Athens is become a forest of beasts.

TIMON. How has the ass broke the wall, that thou art out of the city?

APEMANTUS. Yonder comes a poet and a painter. The plague of company light upon thee! I will fear to catch it, and give way. When I know not what else to do, I'll see thee again.

TIMON. When there is nothing living but thee, thou shalt be welcome. I had rather be a beggar's dog than Apemantus.

APEMANTUS. Thou art the cap of all the fools alive.

TIMON. Would thou wert clean enough to spit upon!

APEMANTUS. A plague on thee! thou art too bad to curse.

TIMON. All villains that do stand by thee are pure.

APEMANTUS. There is no leprosy but what thou speak'st.

TIMON. If I name thee.
I'll beat thee—but I should infect my hands.

APEMANTUS. I would my tongue could rot them off!

TIMON. Away, thou issue of a mangy dog!
Choler does kill me that thou art alive;
I swoon to see thee.

APEMANTUS. Would thou wouldst burst!

TIMON. Away,
Thou tedious rogue! I am sorry I shall lose

A stone by thee. [*Throws a stone at him*]

APEMANTUS. Beast!

TIMON. Slave!

APEMANTUS. Toad!

TIMON. Rogue, rogue, rogue!
I am sick of this false world, and will love nought
But even the mere necessities upon't.
Then, Timon, presently prepare thy grave;
Lie where the light foam of the sea may beat
Thy gravestone daily; make thine epitaph,
That death in me at others' lives may laugh.
[*Looks at the gold*] O thou sweet king-killer, and dear divorce
'Twixt natural son and sire! thou bright defiler
Of Hymen's purest bed! thou valiant Mars!
Thou ever young, fresh, lov'd, and delicate wooer,
Whose blush doth thaw the consecrated snow
That lies on Dian's lap! thou visible god,
That sold'rest close impossibilities,
And mak'st them kiss! that speak'st with every tongue
To every purpose! O thou touch of hearts!
Think thy slave man rebels, and by thy virtue
Set them into confounding odds, that beasts
May have the world in empire!

APEMANTUS. Would 'twere so!
But not till I am dead. I'll say th' hast gold.
Thou wilt be throng'd to shortly.

TIMON. Throng'd to?

APEMANTUS. Ay.

TIMON. Thy back, I prithee.

APEMANTUS. Live, and love thy misery!

TIMON. Long live so, and so die! [*Exit* APEMANTUS] I am quit. More things like men? Eat, Timon, and abhor them.

Enter the BANDITTI

FIRST BANDIT. Where should he have this gold? It is some poor fragment, some slender ort of his remainder. The mere want of gold and the falling-from of his friends drove him into this melancholy.

SECOND BANDIT. It is nois'd he hath a mass of treasure.

THIRD BANDIT. Let us make the assay upon him; if he care not for't, he will supply us easily; if he covetously reserve it, how shall's get it?

SECOND BANDIT. True; for he bears it not about him. 'Tis hid.

FIRST BANDIT. Is not this he?

BANDITTI. Where?

SECOND BANDIT. 'Tis his description.

THIRD BANDIT. He; I know him.

BANDITTI. Save thee, Timon!

TIMON. Now, thieves?

BANDITTI. Soldiers, not thieves.

TIMON. Both too, and women's sons.

BANDITTI. We are not thieves, but men that much do want.

TIMON. Your greatest want is, you want much of meat.
Why should you want? Behold, the earth hath roots;
Within this mile break forth a hundred springs;
The oaks bear mast, the briars scarlet hips;
The bounteous housewife Nature on each bush
Lays her full mess before you. Want! Why want?

FIRST BANDIT. We cannot live on grass, on berries, water,
As beasts and birds and fishes.

TIMON. Nor on the beasts themselves, the birds, and fishes;
You must eat men. Yet thanks I must you con
That you are thieves profess'd, that you work not
In holier shapes; for there is boundless theft
In limited professions. Rascal thieves,
Here's gold. Go, suck the subtle blood o' th' grape
Till the high fever seethe your blood to froth,
And so scape hanging. Trust not the physician;
His antidotes are poison, and he slays
Moe than you rob. Take wealth and lives together;
Do villainy, do, since you protest to do't,
Like workmen. I'll example you with thievery:
The sun's a thief, and with his great attraction
Robs the vast sea; the moon's an arrant thief,
And her pale fire she snatches from the sun;
The sea's a thief, whose liquid surge resolves
The moon into salt tears; the earth's a thief,
That feeds and breeds by a composture stol'n

From gen'ral excrement—each thing's a thief.
The laws, your curb and whip, in their rough power
Has uncheck'd theft. Love not yourselves; away,
Rob one another. There's more gold. Cut throats;
All that you meet are thieves. To Athens go,
Break open shops; nothing can you steal
But thieves do lose it. Steal not less for this
I give you; and gold confound you howsoe'er!
Amen.

THIRD BANDIT. Has almost charm'd me from my profession by persuading me to it.

FIRST BANDIT. 'Tis in the malice of mankind that he thus advises us; not to have us thrive in our mystery.

SECOND BANDIT. I'll believe him as an enemy, and give over my trade.

FIRST BANDIT. Let us first see peace in Athens. There is no time so miserable but a man may be true. *Exeunt* THIEVES

Enter FLAVIUS, *to* TIMON

FLAVIUS. O you gods!
Is yond despis'd and ruinous man my lord?
Full of decay and failing? O monument
And wonder of good deeds evilly bestow'd!
What an alteration of honour
Has desp'rate want made!
What viler thing upon the earth than friends,
Who can bring noblest minds to basest ends!
How rarely does it meet with this time's guise,
When man was wish'd to love his enemies!
Grant I may ever love, and rather woo
Those that would mischief me than those that do!
Has caught me in his eye; I will present
My honest grief unto him, and as my lord
Still serve him with my life. My dearest master!

TIMON. Away! What art thou?

FLAVIUS. Have you forgot me, sir?

TIMON. Why dost ask that? I have forgot all men;
Then, if thou grant'st th'art a man, I have forgot thee.

FLAVIUS. An honest poor servant of yours.

TIMON. Then I know thee not.

TIMON. *Rogue, rogue, rogue!*
I am sick of this false world, and will love nought
But even the mere necessities upon't.
Then, Timon, presently prepare thy grave;
Lie where the light foam of the sea may beat
Thy gravestone daily; make thine epitaph,
That death in me at others' lives may laugh.
(ACT IV. Scene 3)

I never had honest man about me, I.
All I kept were knaves, to serve in meat to villains.

FLAVIUS. The gods are witness,
Nev'r did poor steward wear a truer grief
For his undone lord than mine eyes for you.

TIMON. What, dost thou weep? Come nearer. Then I love thee
Because thou art a woman and disclaim'st
Flinty mankind, whose eyes do never give
But thorough lust and laughter. Pity's sleeping.
Strange times, that weep with laughing, not with weeping!

FLAVIUS. I beg of you to know me, good my lord,
T' accept my grief, and whilst this poor wealth lasts
To entertain me as your steward still.

TIMON. Had I a steward
So true, so just, and now so comfortable?
It almost turns my dangerous nature mild.
Let me behold thy face. Surely, this man
Was born of woman.
Forgive my general and exceptless rashness,
You perpetual-sober gods! I do proclaim
One honest man—mistake me not, but one;
No more, I pray—and he's a steward.
How fain would I have hated all mankind!
And thou redeem'st thyself. But all, save thee,
I fell with curses.
Methinks thou art more honest now than wise;
For by oppressing and betraying me
Thou mightst have sooner got another service;
For many so arrive at second masters
Upon their first lord's neck. But tell me true,
For I must ever doubt though ne'er so sure,
Is not thy kindness subtle, covetous,
If not a usuring kindness, and as rich men deal gifts,
Expecting in return twenty for one?

FLAVIUS. No, my most worthy master, in whose breast
Doubt and suspect, alas, are plac'd too late!
You should have fear'd false times when you did feast:
Suspect still comes where an estate is least.
That which I show, heaven knows, is merely love,

Duty, and zeal, to your unmatched mind,
Care of your food and living; and believe it,
My most honour'd lord,
For any benefit that points to me,
Either in hope or present, I'd exchange
For this one wish, that you had power and wealth
To requite me by making rich yourself.

TIMON. Look thee, 'tis so! Thou singly honest man,
Here, take. The gods, out of my misery,
Have sent thee treasure. Go, live rich and happy,
But thus condition'd; thou shalt build from men;
Hate all, curse all, show charity to none,
But let the famish'd flesh slide from the bone
Ere thou relieve the beggar. Give to dogs
What thou deniest to men; let prisons swallow 'em,
Debts wither 'em to nothing. Be men like blasted woods,
And may diseases lick up their false bloods!
And so, farewell and thrive.

FLAVIUS. O, let me stay
And comfort you, my master.

TIMON. If thou hat'st curses,
Stay not; fly whilst thou art blest and free.
Ne'er see thou man, and let me ne'er see thee.

Exeunt severally

ACT V. SCENE 1

The woods. Before TIMON'S *cave*

Enter POET *and* PAINTER

PAINTER. As I took note of the place, it cannot be far where he abides.

POET. What's to be thought of him? Does the rumour hold for true that he's so full of gold?

PAINTER. Certain. Alcibiades reports it; Phrynia and Timandra had gold of him. He likewise enrich'd poor straggling soldiers with great quantity. 'Tis said he gave unto his steward a mighty sum.

POET. Then this breaking of his has been but a try for his friends?

PAINTER. Nothing else. You shall see him a palm in Athens again, and flourish with the highest. Therefore 'tis not amiss we tender our loves to him in this suppos'd distress of his; it will show honestly in us, and is very likely to load our purposes with what they travail for, if it be a just and true report that goes of his having.

POET. What have you now to present unto him?

PAINTER. Nothing at this time but my visitation; only I will promise him an excellent piece.

POET. I must serve him so too, tell him of an intent that's coming toward him.

PAINTER. Good as the best. Promising is the very air o' th' time; it opens the eyes of expectation. Performance is ever the duller for his act, and but in the plainer and simpler kind of people the deed of saying is quite out of use. To promise is most courtly and fashionable; performance is a kind of will or testament which argues a great sickness in his judgment that makes it.

Enter TIMON *from his cave*

TIMON. [*Aside*] Excellent workman! Thou canst not paint a man so bad as is thyself.

POET. I am thinking what I shall say I have provided for him. It must be a personating of himself; a satire against the softness of prosperity, with a discovery of the infinite flatteries that follow youth and opulency.

TIMON. [*Aside*] Must thou needs stand for a villain in thine own work? Wilt thou whip thine own faults in other men? Do so, I have gold for thee.

POET. Nay, let's seek him;
Then do we sin against our own estate
When we may profit meet and come too late.

PAINTER. True;
When the day serves, before black-corner'd night,
Find what thou want'st by free and offer'd light.
Come.

TIMON. [*Aside*] I'll meet you at the turn. What a god's gold,
That he is worshipp'd in a baser temple

Than where swine feed!
'Tis thou that rig'st the bark and plough'st the foam,
Settlest admired reverence in a slave.
To thee be worship! and thy saints for aye
Be crown'd with plagues, that thee alone obey!
Fit I meet them. [*Advancing from his cave*]

POET. Hail, worthy Timon!

PAINTER. Our late noble master!

TIMON. Have I once liv'd to see two honest men?

POET. Sir,
Having often of your open bounty tasted,
Hearing you were retir'd, your friends fall'n off,
Whose thankless natures—O abhorred spirits!—
Not all the whips of heaven are large enough—
What! to you,
Whose star-like nobleness gave life and influence
To their whole being! I am rapt, and cannot cover
The monstrous bulk of this ingratitude
With any size of words.

TIMON. Let it go naked: men may see't the better.
You that are honest, by being what you are,
Make them best seen and known.

PAINTER. He and myself
Have travail'd in the great show'r of your gifts,
And sweetly felt it.

TIMON. Ay, you are honest men.

PAINTER. We are hither come to offer you our service.

TIMON. Most honest men! Why, how shall I requite you?
Can you eat roots, and drink cold water—No?

BOTH. What we can do, we'll do, to do you service.

TIMON. Y'are honest men. Y'have heard that I have gold;
I am sure you have. Speak truth; y'are honest men.

PAINTER. So it is said, my noble lord; but therefore
Came not my friend nor I.

TIMON. Good honest men! Thou draw'st a counterfeit
Best in all Athens. Th'art indeed the best;
Thou counterfeit'st most lively.

PAINTER. So, so, my lord.

TIMON. E'en so, sir, as I say. [*To the* POET] And for thy fiction,

Why, thy verse swells with stuff so fine and smooth
That thou art even natural in thine art.
But for all this, my honest-natur'd friends,
I must needs say you have a little fault.
Marry, 'tis not monstrous in you; neither wish I
You take much pains to mend.

BOTH. Beseech your honour
To make it known to us.

TIMON. You'll take it ill.

BOTH. Most thankfully, my lord.

TIMON. Will you indeed?

BOTH. Doubt it not, worthy lord.

TIMON. There's never a one of you but trusts a knave
That mightily deceives you.

BOTH. Do we, my lord?

TIMON. Ay, and you hear him cog, see him dissemble,
Know his gross patchery, love him, feed him,
Keep in your bosom; yet remain assur'd
That he's a made-up villain.

PAINTER. I know not such, my lord.

POET. Nor I.

TIMON. Look you, I love you well; I'll give you gold,
Rid me these villains from your companies.
Hang them or stab them, drown them in a draught,
Confound them by some course, and come to me,
I'll give you gold enough.

BOTH. Name them, my lord; let's know them.

TIMON. You that way, and you this—but two in company;
Each man apart, all single and alone,
Yet an arch-villain keeps him company.
[*To the* PAINTER] If, where thou art, two villains shall not be,
Come not near him. [*To the* POET] If thou wouldst not reside
But where one villain is, then him abandon.—
Hence, pack! there's gold; you came for gold, ye slaves.
[*To the* PAINTER] You have work for me; there's payment; hence!
[*To the* POET] You are an alchemist; make gold of that.—
Out, rascal dogs! [*Beats and drives them out*]

Enter FLAVIUS *and two* SENATORS

FLAVIUS. It is vain that you would speak with Timon;
For he is set so only to himself
That nothing but himself which looks like man
Is friendly with him.
FIRST SENATOR. Bring us to his cave.
It is our part and promise to th' Athenians
To speak with Timon.
SECOND SENATOR. At all times alike
Men are not still the same; 'twas time and griefs
That fram'd him thus. Time, with his fairer hand,
Offering the fortunes of his former days,
The former man may make him. Bring us to him,
And chance it as it may.
FLAVIUS. Here is his cave.
Peace and content be here! Lord Timon! Timon!
Look out, and speak to friends. Th' Athenians
By two of their most reverend Senate greet thee.
Speak to them, noble Timon.

Enter TIMON *out of his cave*

TIMON. Thou sun that comforts, burn. Speak and be hang'd!
For each true word a blister, and each false
Be as a cauterizing to the root o' th' tongue,
Consuming it with speaking!
FIRST SENATOR. Worthy Timon–
TIMON. Of none but such as you, and you of Timon.
FIRST SENATOR. The senators of Athens greet thee, Timon.
TIMON. I thank them; and would send them back the plague,
Could I but catch it for them.
FIRST SENATOR. O, forget
What we are sorry for ourselves in thee.
The senators with one consent of love
Entreat thee back to Athens, who have thought
On special dignities, which vacant lie
For thy best use and wearing.
SECOND SENATOR. They confess
Toward thee forgetfulness too general, gross;
Which now the public body, which doth seldom

Play the recanter, feeling in itself
A lack of Timon's aid, hath sense withal
Of it own fail, restraining aid to Timon,
And send forth us to make their sorrowed render,
Together with a recompense more fruitful
Than their offence can weigh down by the dram;
Ay, even such heaps and sums of love and wealth
As shall to thee blot out what wrongs were theirs
And write in thee the figures of their love,
Ever to read them thine.

TIMON. You witch me in it;
Surprise me to the very brink of tears.
Lend me a fool's heart and a woman's eyes,
And I'll beweep these comforts, worthy senators.

FIRST SENATOR. Therefore so please thee to return with us,
And of our Athens, thine and ours, to take
The captainship, thou shalt be met with thanks,
Allow'd with absolute power, and thy good name
Live with authority. So soon we shall drive back
Of Alcibiades th' approaches wild,
Who, like a boar too savage, doth root up
His country's peace.

SECOND SENATOR. And shakes his threat'ning sword
Against the walls of Athens.

FIRST SENATOR. Therefore, Timon–

TIMON. Well, sir, I will. Therefore I will, sir, thus:
If Alcibiades kill my countrymen,
Let Alcibiades know this of Timon,
That Timon cares not. But if he sack fair Athens,
And take our goodly aged men by th' beards,
Giving our holy virgins to the stain
Of contumelious, beastly, mad-brain'd war,
Then let him know–and tell him Timon speaks it
In pity of our aged and our youth–
I cannot choose but tell him that I care not,
And let him take't at worst; for their knives care not,
While you have throats to answer. For myself,
There's not a whittle in th' unruly camp
But I do prize it at my love before
The reverend'st throat in Athens. So I leave you

To the protection of the prosperous gods,
As thieves to keepers.

FLAVIUS. Stay not, all's in vain.

TIMON. Why, I was writing of my epitaph;
It will be seen to-morrow. My long sickness
Of health and living now begins to mend,
And nothing brings me all things. Go, live still;
Be Alcibiades your plague, you his,
And last so long enough!

FIRST SENATOR. We speak in vain.

TIMON. But yet I love my country, and am not
One that rejoices in the common wreck,
As common bruit doth put it.

FIRST SENATOR. That's well spoke.

TIMON. Commend me to my loving countrymen—

FIRST SENATOR. These words become your lips as they pass through them.

SECOND SENATOR. And enter in our ears like great triumphers
In their applauding gates.

TIMON. Commend me to them,
And tell them that, to ease them of their griefs,
Their fears of hostile strokes, their aches, losses,
Their pangs of love, with other incident throes
That nature's fragile vessel doth sustain
In life's uncertain voyage, I will some kindness do them—
I'll teach them to prevent wild Alcibiades' wrath.

FIRST SENATOR. I like this well; he will return again.

TIMON. I have a tree, which grows here in my close,
That mine own use invites me to cut down,
And shortly must I fell it. Tell my friends,
Tell Athens, in the sequence of degree
From high to low throughout, that whoso please
To stop affliction, let him take his haste,
Come hither, ere my tree hath felt the axe,
And hang himself. I pray you do my greeting.

FLAVIUS. Trouble him no further; thus you still shall find him.

TIMON. Come not to me again; but say to Athens
Timon hath made his everlasting mansion

Upon the beached verge of the salt flood,
Who once a day with his embossed froth
The turbulent surge shall cover. Thither come,
And let my gravestone be your oracle.
Lips, let sour words go by and language end:
What is amiss, plague and infection mend!
Graves only be men's works and death their gain!
Sun, hide thy beams. Timon hath done his reign.

Exit TIMON *into his cave*

FIRST SENATOR. His discontents are unremovably
Coupled to nature.

SECOND SENATOR. Our hope in him is dead. Let us return
And strain what other means is left unto us
In our dear peril.

FIRST SENATOR. It requires swift foot. *Exeunt*

SCENE 2

Before the walls of Athens

Enter two other SENATORS *with a* MESSENGER

FIRST SENATOR. Thou hast painfully discover'd; are his files
As full as thy report?

MESSENGER. I have spoke the least.
Besides, his expedition promises
Present approach.

SECOND SENATOR. We stand much hazard if they bring not Timon.

MESSENGER. I met a courier, one mine ancient friend,
Whom, though in general part we were oppos'd,
Yet our old love had a particular force,
And made us speak like friends. This man was riding
From Alcibiades to Timon's cave
With letters of entreaty, which imported
His fellowship i' th' cause against your city,
In part for his sake mov'd.

Enter the other SENATORS, *from* TIMON

FIRST SENATOR. Here come our brothers.

THIRD SENATOR. No talk of Timon, nothing of him expect.
The enemies' drum is heard, and fearful scouring
Doth choke the air with dust. In, and prepare.
Ours is the fall, I fear; our foes the snare. *Exeunt*

SCENE 3

The woods. TIMON'S *cave, and a rude tomb seen*

Enter a SOLDIER *in the woods, seeking* TIMON

SOLDIER. By all description this should be the place.
Who's here? Speak, ho! No answer? What is this?
Timon is dead, who hath outstretch'd his span.
Some beast rear'd this; here does not live a man.
Dead, sure; and this his grave. What's on this tomb
I cannot read; the character I'll take with wax.
Our captain hath in every figure skill,
An ag'd interpreter, though young in days;
Before proud Athens he's set down by this,
Whose fall the mark of his ambition is. *Exit*

SCENE 4

Before the walls of Athens

Trumpets sound. Enter ALCIBIADES *with his powers before Athens*

ALCIBIADES. Sound to this coward and lascivious town
Our terrible approach.

Sound a parley. The SENATORS *appear upon the walls*

Till now you have gone on and fill'd the time
With all licentious measure, making your wills
The scope of justice; till now, myself, and such
As slept within the shadow of your power,
Have wander'd with our travers'd arms, and breath'd
Our sufferance vainly. Now the time is flush,
When crouching marrow, in the bearer strong,

Cries of itself 'No more!' Now breathless wrong
Shall sit and pant in your great chairs of ease,
And pursy insolence shall break his wind
With fear and horrid flight.

FIRST SENATOR. Noble and young,
When thy first griefs were but a mere conceit,
Ere thou hadst power or we had cause of fear,
We sent to thee, to give thy rages balm,
To wipe out our ingratitude with loves
Above their quantity.

SECOND SENATOR. So did we woo
Transformed Timon to our city's love
By humble message and by promis'd means.
We were not all unkind, nor all deserve
The common stroke of war.

FIRST SENATOR. These walls of ours
Were not erected by their hands from whom
You have receiv'd your griefs; nor are they such
That these great tow'rs, trophies, and schools, should fall
For private faults in them.

SECOND SENATOR. Nor are they living
Who were the motives that you first went out;
Shame, that they wanted cunning, in excess
Hath broke their hearts. March, noble lord,
Into our city with thy banners spread.
By decimation and a tithed death–
If thy revenges hunger for that food
Which nature loathes–take thou the destin'd tenth,
And by the hazard of the spotted die
Let die the spotted.

FIRST SENATOR. All have not offended;
For those that were, it is not square to take,
On those that are, revenge: crimes, like lands,
Are not inherited. Then, dear countryman,
Bring in thy ranks, but leave without thy rage;
Spare thy Athenian cradle, and those kin
Which, in the bluster of thy wrath, must fall
With those that have offended. Like a shepherd
Approach the fold and cull th' infected forth,
But kill not all together.

SECOND SENATOR. What thou wilt,
Thou rather shalt enforce it with thy smile
Than hew to't with thy sword.
FIRST SENATOR. Set but thy foot
Against our rampir'd gates and they shall ope,
So thou wilt send thy gentle heart before
To say thou't enter friendly.
SECOND SENATOR. Throw thy glove,
Or any token of thine honour else,
That thou wilt use the wars as thy redress
And not as our confusion, all thy powers
Shall make their harbour in our town till we
Have seal'd thy full desire.
ALCIBIADES. Then there's my glove;
Descend, and open your uncharged ports.
Those enemies of Timon's and mine own,
Whom you yourselves shall set out for reproof,
Fall, and no more. And, to atone your fears
With my more noble meaning, not a man
Shall pass his quarter or offend the stream
Of regular justice in your city's bounds,
But shall be render'd to your public laws
At heaviest answer.
BOTH. 'Tis most nobly spoken.
ALCIBIADES. Descend, and keep your words.

[*The* SENATORS *descend and open the gates*]

Enter a SOLDIER *as a Messenger*

SOLDIER. My noble General, Timon is dead;
Entomb'd upon the very hem o' th' sea;
And on his grave-stone this insculpture, which
With wax I brought away, whose soft impression
Interprets for my poor ignorance.

ALCIBIADES *reads the Epitaph*

'Here lies a wretched corse, of wretched soul bereft;
Seek not my name. A plague consume you wicked caitiffs left!
Here lie I, Timon, who alive all living men did hate.
Pass by, and curse thy fill; but pass, and stay not here thy gait.'

These well express in thee thy latter spirits.
Though thou abhorr'dst in us our human griefs,
Scorn'dst our brain's flow, and those our droplets which
From niggard nature fall, yet rich conceit
Taught thee to make vast Neptune weep for aye
On thy low grave, on faults forgiven. Dead
Is noble Timon, of whose memory
Hereafter more. Bring me into your city,
And I will use the olive, with my sword;
Make war breed peace, make peace stint war, make each
Prescribe to other, as each other's leech.
Let our drums strike. *Exeunt*

The Tragedy of
Julius Caesar

JULIUS CÆSAR

DURING A VISIT to England the Swiss traveller Thomas Platter saw a performance of this play in London in 1599:

> After lunch on 21 September, round about 2 o'clock, I went with my companions across the water, and in the straw-thatched house saw the tragedy of the first emperor, Julius Cæsar, excellently performed by some fifteen persons. At the end of the play, according to custom, they danced with much grace and in wonderful combination, two clad in men's clothes and two in women's.

The Globe had been completed that summer for the Chamberlain's men, and *Julius Cæsar* is the first of the great tragedies that had their *première* there. The play is also mentioned by John Weever, who took a keen interest in the theatre, in some lines he wrote in 1599, although the volume containing them, *The Mirror of Martyrs*, was published only in 1601:

> The manie-headed multitude were drawne
> By *Brutus* speach, that Cæsar was ambitious;
> When eloquent *Mark Antonie* had showne
> His vertues, who but *Brutus* then was vicious?

Critical opinion has never regarded *Julius Cæsar* as equal to some of the later tragedies, but the play has a clarity of construction and felicity of expression that have made it popular with audiences and readers alike. Even its most vehement critic recognizes the skill that has gone to its making. Bernard Shaw felt that he knew far better than Shakespeare the real significance of this episode of world history, and that Shakespeare's play was a travesty of the truth:

> It is when we turn to Julius Cæsar, the most splendidly written political melodrama we possess, that we realize the apparently immortal author of *Hamlet* as a man, not for all time, but for an age only. . . . It is impossible for even the most judicially minded critic to look without a revulsion of indignant contempt at this travestying of a great man as a

> silly braggart, whilst the pitiful gang of mischief-makers who destroyed him are lauded as statesmen and patriots.

Yet Shaw recognizes at least the dexterity of the playwright:

> Regarded as a crafty stage job, the play is a triumph: rhetoric, claptrap, effective gushes of emotion, all the devices of the popular playwright, are employed with a profusion of power that almost breaks their backs . . . the dramatist's art can be carried no further on that plane.

Shakespeare's picture of Cæsar is certainly difficult to reconcile with the notion that tradition has given us of him; it is different from what references elsewhere in the plays might have prepared us for. No one troubles much about the manner in which Shakespeare has adapted the chronicler's account of Macbeth to the theme of the play, for Macbeth would be unknown but for Shakespeare's creation; it is otherwise, however, with Cæsar, and *Julius Cæsar* presents us with a difficulty common to all literary creations that give a prominent part to an outstanding historical figure; especially when the part is not that already created in the popular imagination.

Shaw is more than unfair when he pretends that Shakespeare represents the conspirators as statesmen, for Shakespeare follows Plutarch in emphasizing the futility of their policy. Plutarch was by tradition a republican, or at least one who regarded the more democratic methods of the old city state as more ideal than the rule of a dictator; yet he does not hesitate to admit that Rome had come to such a pass that only a dictator could maintain internal order and support the external burden that Roman valour and organization had by their triumphs placed on the republic. Indeed Shakespeare actually develops a theme that Plutarch introduces in these words:

> But Cæsar's great prosperity and good fortune that favoured him all his lifetime, did continue afterwards in the revenge of his death, pursuing the murtherers both by sea and land, till they had not left a man more to be executed, of all them that were actors or counsellors in the conspiracy of his death.

That the conspirators killed the man in vain Shakespeare

brings home to us by his references to the 'spirit' of Cæsar and by the use he makes of the apparition that visited Brutus before Philippi. Shakespeare represents the conspirators as fighting against a current in the affairs of men that sweeps them irresistibly to their destruction.

It was doubtless to emphasize this idea that Shakespeare modified the traditional features of Cæsar. The conspirators felt they had only to dispose of an ageing and somewhat ossified individual; they feared and hated what he stood for, but failed to understand where his strength lay. That fear and hatred Shakespeare does not represent as uncoloured by motives that are personal and individual. Brutus alone is exempt from the charge of envy and malice.

It is the position of Brutus between his loyalty to the traditions of his ancestors and of the Republic on the one hand and his loyalty to his friend and benefactor on the other that provides the moral situation that gives its form to the drama. That he may have chosen unwisely Shakespeare does not deny; all that Shakespeare insists on our seeing is that the choice of this compassionate man was prompted by motives that we cannot regard as ignoble or selfish.

Perhaps Shakespeare does not put the tragic choice before us as impartially as we find it presented in the later tragedies, or so we feel because of what we already think we know of the historical Julius Cæsar. If there can be any fault-finding with so fine a piece it must be on this score; but the fault is a fault only when *Julius Cæsar* is compared with the maturer masterpieces.

Julius Cæsar
Octavius Cæsar, Marcus Antonius, M. Æmilius Lepidus — *Triumvirs after the death of Julius Cæsar*
Cicero, Publius, Popilius Lena — *Senators*
Marcus Brutus, Cassius, Casca, Trebonius, Ligarius, Decius Brutus, Metellus Cimber, Cinna — *conspirators against Julius Cæsar*
Flavius *and* Marullus, *tribunes*
Artemidorus, *a sophist of Cnidos*
A Soothsayer
Cinna, *a poet*
Another Poet
Lucilius, Titinius, Messala, Young Cato, Volumnius — *friends to Brutus and Cassius*
Varro, Clitus, Claudius, Strato, Lucius, Dardanius — *servants to Brutus*
Pindarus, *servant to Cassius*

Calpurnia, *wife to Cæsar*
Portia, *wife to Brutus*

Senators, Citizens, Guards, Attendants, &c.

SCENE:

Rome; near Sardis; near Philippi

Julius Caesar

ACT I. SCENE 1

Rome. A street

Enter Flavius, Marullus, *and certain commoners over the stage*

Flavius. Hence! home, you idle creatures, get you home.
Is this a holiday? What! know you not,
Being mechanical, you ought not walk
Upon a labouring day without the sign
Of your profession? Speak, what trade art thou?

First Citizen. Why, sir, a carpenter.

Marullus. Where is thy leather apron and thy rule?
What dost thou with thy best apparel on?
You, sir, what trade are you?

Second Citizen. Truly, sir, in respect of a fine workman, I am but, as you would say, a cobbler.

Marullus. But what trade art thou? Answer me directly.

Second Citizen. A trade, sir, that I hope I may use with a safe conscience, which is indeed, sir, a mender of bad soles.

Marullus. What trade, thou knave? Thou naughty knave, what trade?

Second Citizen. Nay, I beseech you, sir, be not out with me; yet, if you be out, sir, I can mend you.

Marullus. What mean'st thou by that? Mend me, thou saucy fellow!

Second Citizen. Why, sir, cobble you.

Flavius. Thou art a cobbler, art thou?

Second Citizen. Truly, sir, all that I live by is with the awl. I meddle with no tradesman's matters nor women's matters, but with awl. I am indeed, sir, a surgeon to old shoes. When they are in great danger, I re-cover them. As proper men as ever trod upon neat's leather have gone upon my handiwork.

Flavius. But wherefore art not in thy shop to-day?

Why dost thou lead these men about the streets?

SECOND CITIZEN. Truly, sir, to wear out their shoes, to get myself into more work. But indeed, sir, we make holiday to see Cæsar, and to rejoice in his triumph.

MARULLUS. Wherefore rejoice? What conquest brings he home?
What tributaries follow him to Rome,
To grace in captive bonds his chariot wheels?
You blocks, you stones, you worse than senseless things!
O you hard hearts, you cruel men of Rome,
Knew you not Pompey? Many a time and oft
Have you climb'd up to walls and battlements,
To tow'rs and windows, yea, to chimney-tops,
Your infants in your arms, and there have sat
The livelong day, with patient expectation,
To see great Pompey pass the streets of Rome.
And when you saw his chariot but appear,
Have you not made an universal shout,
That Tiber trembled underneath her banks,
To hear the replication of your sounds
Made in her concave shores?
And do you now put on your best attire?
And do you now cull out a holiday?
And do you now strew flowers in his way
That comes in triumph over Pompey's blood?
Be gone!
Run to your houses, fall upon your knees,
Pray to the gods to intermit the plague
That needs must light on this ingratitude.

FLAVIUS. Go, go, good countrymen, and for this fault
Assemble all the poor men of your sort;
Draw them to Tiber banks, and weep your tears
Into the channel, till the lowest stream
Do kiss the most exalted shores of all.

Exeunt all the commoners

See whe'r their basest metal be not mov'd;
They vanish tongue-tied in their guiltiness.
Go you down that way towards the Capitol;
This way will I. Disrobe the images
If you do find them deck'd with ceremonies.

MARULLUS. May we do so?
You know it is the feast of Lupercal.
FLAVIUS. It is no matter; let no images
Be hung with Cæsar's trophies. I'll about,
And drive away the vulgar from the streets;
So do you too, where you perceive them thick.
These growing feathers pluck'd from Cæsar's wing
Will make him fly an ordinary pitch,
Who else would soar above the view of men,
And keep us all in servile fearfulness. *Exeunt*

SCENE 2

Rome. A public place

Music. Enter CÆSAR; ANTONY, *for the course;* CALPURNIA, PORTIA, DECIUS, CICERO, BRUTUS, CASSIUS, *and* CASCA; *a great crowd following, among them a* SOOTHSAYER; *after them,* MARULLUS *and* FLAVIUS

CÆSAR. Calpurnia.
CASCA. Peace, ho! Cæsar speaks. [*Music ceases*]
CÆSAR. Calpurnia.
CALPURNIA. Here, my lord.
CÆSAR. Stand you directly in Antonius' way
When he doth run his course. Antonius!
ANTONY. Cæsar, my lord.
CÆSAR. Forget not in your speed, Antonius,
To touch Calpurnia; for our elders say,
The barren, touched in this holy chase,
Shake off their sterile curse.
ANTONY. I shall remember.
When Cæsar says 'Do this,' it is perform'd.
CÆSAR. Set on, and leave no ceremony out. [*Music*]
SOOTHSAYER. Cæsar!
CÆSAR. Ha! Who calls?
CASCA. Bid every noise be still. Peace yet again.
[*Music ceases*]
CÆSAR. Who is it in the press that calls on me?
I hear a tongue, shriller than all the music,

Cry 'Cæsar!' Speak. Cæsar is turn'd to hear.

SOOTHSAYER. Beware the ides of March.

CÆSAR. What man is that?

BRUTUS. A soothsayer bids you beware the ides of March.

CÆSAR. Set him before me; let me see his face.

CASSIUS. Fellow, come from the throng; look upon Cæsar.

CÆSAR. What say'st thou to me now? Speak once again.

SOOTHSAYER. Beware the ides of March.

CÆSAR. He is a dreamer; let us leave him. Pass.

Sennet. Exeunt all but BRUTUS *and* CASSIUS

CASSIUS. Will you go see the order of the course?

BRUTUS. Not I.

CASSIUS. I pray you do.

BRUTUS. I am not gamesome: I do lack some part
Of that quick spirit that is in Antony.
Let me not hinder, Cassius, your desires;
I'll leave you.

CASSIUS. Brutus, I do observe you now of late;
I have not from your eyes that gentleness
And show of love as I was wont to have.
You bear too stubborn and too strange a hand
Over your friend that loves you.

BRUTUS. Cassius,
Be not deceiv'd. If I have veil'd my look,
I turn the trouble of my countenance
Merely upon myself. Vexed I am
Of late with passions of some difference,
Conceptions only proper to myself,
Which give some soil, perhaps, to my behaviours;
But let not therefore my good friends be griev'd—
Among which number, Cassius, be you one—
Nor construe any further my neglect
Than that poor Brutus, with himself at war,
Forgets the shows of love to other men.

CASSIUS. Then, Brutus, I have much mistook your passion,
By means whereof this breast of mine hath buried
Thoughts of great value, worthy cogitations.
Tell me, good Brutus, can you see your face?

BRUTUS. No, Cassius; for the eye sees not itself
But by reflection, by some other things.

CASSIUS. 'Tis just;
And it is very much lamented, Brutus,
That you have no such mirrors as will turn
Your hidden worthiness into your eye,
That you might see your shadow. I have heard,
Where many of the best respect in Rome—
Except immortal Cæsar—speaking of Brutus,
And groaning underneath this age's yoke,
Have wish'd that noble Brutus had his eyes.

BRUTUS. Into what dangers would you lead me, Cassius,
That you would have me seek into myself
For that which is not in me?

CASSIUS. Therefore, good Brutus, be prepar'd to hear;
And since you know you cannot see yourself
So well as by reflection, I, your glass,
Will modestly discover to yourself
That of yourself which you yet know not of.
And be not jealous on me, gentle Brutus:
Were I a common laughter, or did use
To stale with ordinary oaths my love
To every new protester; if you know
That I do fawn on men and hug them hard,
And after scandal them; or if you know
That I profess myself in banqueting
To all the rout, then hold me dangerous.
[*Flourish and shout*]

BRUTUS. What means this shouting? I do fear the people
Choose Cæsar for their king.

CASSIUS. Ay, do you fear it?
Then must I think you would not have it so.

BRUTUS. I would not, Cassius; yet I love him well.
But wherefore do you hold me here so long?
What is it that you would impart to me?
If it be aught toward the general good,
Set honour in one eye and death i' th' other,
And I will look on both indifferently;
For let the gods so speed me as I love
The name of honour more than I fear death.

CASSIUS. I know that virtue to be in you, Brutus,
As well as I do know your outward favour.

Well, honour is the subject of my story.
I cannot tell what you and other men
Think of this life; but, for my single self,
I had as lief not be as live to be
In awe of such a thing as I myself.
I was born free as Cæsar; so were you.
We both have fed as well, and we can both
Endure the winter's cold as well as he.
For once, upon a raw and gusty day,
The troubled Tiber chafing with her shores,
Cæsar said to me 'Dar'st thou, Cassius, now
Leap in with me into this angry flood,
And swim to yonder point?' Upon the word,
Accoutred as I was, I plunged in
And bade him follow. So indeed he did.
The torrent roar'd, and we did buffet it
With lusty sinews, throwing it aside
And stemming it with hearts of controversy;
But ere we could arrive the point propos'd,
Cæsar cried 'Help me, Cassius, or I sink!'
I, as Æneas, our great ancestor,
Did from the flames of Troy upon his shoulder
The old Anchises bear, so from the waves of Tiber
Did I the tired Cæsar. And this man
Is now become a god; and Cassius is
A wretched creature, and must bend his body
If Cæsar carelessly but nod on him.
He had a fever when he was in Spain,
And when the fit was on him I did mark
How he did shake. 'Tis true, this god did shake.
His coward lips did from their colour fly,
And that same eye, whose bend doth awe the world,
Did lose his lustre. I did hear him groan.
Ay, and that tongue of his, that bade the Romans
Mark him, and write his speeches in their books,
Alas! it cried 'Give me some drink, Titinius'
As a sick girl. Ye gods! it doth amaze me
A man of such a feeble temper should
So get the start of the majestic world,
And bear the palm alone. [*Shout. Flourish*]

BRUTUS. Another general shout!
I do believe that these applauses are
For some new honours that are heap'd on Cæsar.
CASSIUS. Why, man, he doth bestride the narrow world
Like a Colossus, and we petty men
Walk under his huge legs, and peep about
To find ourselves dishonourable graves.
Men at some time are masters of their fates:
The fault, dear Brutus, is not in our stars,
But in ourselves, that we are underlings.
'Brutus' and 'Cæsar.' What should be in that 'Cæsar'?
Why should that name be sounded more than yours?
Write them together; yours is as fair a name.
Sound them: it doth become the mouth as well.
Weigh them: it is as heavy. Conjure with 'em:
'Brutus' will start a spirit as soon as 'Cæsar.'
Now, in the names of all the gods at once,
Upon what meat doth this our Cæsar feed,
That he is grown so great? Age, thou art sham'd!
Rome, thou has lost the breed of noble bloods!
When went there by an age, since the great flood,
But it was fam'd with more than with one man?
When could they say, till now, that talk'd of Rome,
That her wide walls encompass'd but one man?
Now is it Rome indeed, and room enough,
When there is in it but one only man.
O! you and I have heard our fathers say
There was a Brutus once that would have brook'd
Th' eternal devil to keep his state in Rome
As easily as a king.
BRUTUS. That you do love me, I am nothing jealous;
What you would work me to, I have some aim;
How I have thought of this, and of these times,
I shall recount hereafter. For this present,
I would not, so with love I might entreat you,
Be any further mov'd. What you have said
I will consider; what you have to say
I will with patience hear; and find a time
Both meet to hear and answer such high things.
Till then, my noble friend, chew upon this:

Brutus had rather be a villager
Than to repute himself a son of Rome
Under these hard conditions as this time
Is like to lay upon us.

CASSIUS. I am glad that my weak words
Have struck but thus much show of fire from Brutus.

Re-enter CÆSAR *and his train*

BRUTUS. The games are done, and Cæsar is returning.

CASSIUS. As they pass by, pluck Casca by the sleeve,
And he will, after his sour fashion, tell you
What hath proceeded worthy note to-day.

BRUTUS. I will do so. But, look you, Cassius,
The angry spot doth glow on Cæsar's brow,
And all the rest look like a chidden train;
Calpurnia's cheek is pale, and Cicero
Looks with such ferret and such fiery eyes
As we have seen him in the Capitol,
Being cross'd in conference by some senators.

CASSIUS. Casca will tell us what the matter is.

CÆSAR. Antonius!

ANTONY. Cæsar?

CÆSAR. Let me have men about me that are fat;
Sleek-headed men, and such as sleep o' nights.
Yond Cassius has a lean and hungry look;
He thinks too much. Such men are dangerous.

ANTONY. Fear him not, Cæsar, he's not dangerous;
He is a noble Roman, and well given.

CÆSAR. Would he were fatter! But I fear him not.
Yet if my name were liable to fear,
I do not know the man I should avoid
So soon as that spare Cassius. He reads much,
He is a great observer, and he looks
Quite through the deeds of men. He loves no plays,
As thou dost, Antony; he hears no music.
Seldom he smiles, and smiles in such a sort
As if he mock'd himself, and scorn'd his spirit
That could be mov'd to smile at anything.
Such men as he be never at heart's ease
Whiles they behold a greater than themselves,

And therefore are they very dangerous.
I rather tell thee what is to be fear'd
Than what I fear; for always I am Cæsar.
Come on my right hand, for this ear is deaf,
And tell me truly what thou think'st of him.

Sennet. Exeunt CÆSAR *and his train*

CASCA. You pull'd me by the cloak. Would you speak with me?

BRUTUS. Ay, Casca; tell us what hath chanc'd to-day,
That Cæsar looks so sad?

CASCA. Why, you were with him, were you not?

BRUTUS. I should not then ask Casca what had chanc'd.

CASCA. Why, there was a crown offer'd him; and being offer'd him, he put it by with the back of his hand, thus; and then the people fell a-shouting.

BRUTUS. What was the second noise for?

CASCA. Why, for that too.

CASSIUS. They shouted thrice; what was the last cry for?

CASCA. Why, for that too.

BRUTUS. Was the crown offer'd him thrice?

CASCA. Ay, marry, was't, and he put it by thrice, every time gentler than other; and at every putting by mine honest neighbours shouted.

CASSIUS. Who offer'd him the crown?

CASCA. Why, Antony.

BRUTUS. Tell us the manner of it, gentle Casca.

CASCA. I can as well be hang'd as tell the manner of it: it was mere foolery; I did not mark it. I saw Mark Antony offer him a crown yet 'twas not a crown neither, 'twas one of these coronets—and, as I told you, he put it by once; but for all that, to my thinking, he would fain have had it. Then he offered it to him again; then he put it by again; but to my thinking, he was very loath to lay his fingers off it. And then he offered it the third time; he put it the third time by; and still as he refus'd it, the rabblement hooted, and clapp'd their chopt hands, and threw up their sweaty night-caps, and uttered such a deal of stinking breath because Cæsar refus'd the crown, that it had almost choked Cæsar; for he swooned and fell down at it. And for mine own part I durst not laugh, for fear of opening my lips and receiving the bad air.

CASSIUS. But soft, I pray you. What, did Cæsar swoon?

CASCA. He fell down in the market-place, and foam'd at mouth, and was speechless.

BRUTUS. 'Tis very like. He hath the falling sickness.

CASSIUS. No, Cæsar hath it not; but you, and I,
And honest Casca, we have the falling sickness.

CASCA. I know not what you mean by that, but I am sure Cæsar fell down. If the tag-rag people did not clap him and hiss him, according as he pleas'd and displeas'd them, as they use to do the players in the theatre, I am no true man.

BRUTUS. What said he when he came unto himself?

CASCA. Marry, before he fell down, when he perceiv'd the common herd was glad he refus'd the crown, he pluckt me ope his doublet, and offer'd them his throat to cut. An I had been a man of any occupation, if I would not have taken him at a word, I would I might go to hell among the rogues. And so he fell. When he came to himself again, he said, if he had done or said anything amiss, he desir'd their worships to think it was his infirmity. Three or four wenches, where I stood, cried 'Alas, good soul!' and forgave him with all their hearts. But there's no heed to be taken of them; if Cæsar had stabb'd their mothers, they would have done no less.

BRUTUS. And after that, he came thus sad away?

CASCA. Ay.

CASSIUS. Did Cicero say anything?

CASCA. Ay, he spoke Greek.

CASSIUS. To what effect?

CASCA. Nay, an I tell you that, I'll ne'er look you i' th' face again. But those that understood him smil'd at one another, and shook their heads; but for mine own part, it was Greek to me. I could tell you more news too: Marullus and Flavius, for pulling scarfs off Cæsar's images, are put to silence. Fare you well. There was more foolery yet, if I could remember it.

CASSIUS. Will you sup with me to-night, Casca?

CASCA. No, I am promis'd forth.

CASSIUS. Will you dine with me to-morrow?

CASCA. Ay, if I be alive, and your mind hold, and your dinner worth the eating.

CASSIUS. Good; I will expect you.

CASCA. Do so. Farewell, both. *Exit*

BRUTUS. What a blunt fellow is this grown to be!
He was quick mettle when he went to school.

CASSIUS. So is he now, in execution
Of any bold or noble enterprise,
However he puts on this tardy form.
This rudeness is a sauce to his good wit,
Which gives men stomach to digest his words
With better appetite.

BRUTUS. And so it is. For this time I will leave you.
To-morrow, if you please to speak with me,
I will come home to you; or, if you will,
Come home to me, and I will wait for you.

CASSIUS. I will do so. Till then, think of the world.

Exit BRUTUS

Well, Brutus, thou art noble; yet, I see,
Thy honourable metal may be wrought
From that it is dispos'd. Therefore it is meet
That noble minds keep ever with their likes;
For who so firm that cannot be seduc'd?
Cæsar doth bear me hard; but he loves Brutus.
If I were Brutus now and he were Cassius,
He should not humour me. I will this night,
In several hands, in at his windows throw,
As if they came from several citizens,
Writings, all tending to the great opinion
That Rome holds of his name; wherein obscurely
Cæsar's ambition shall be glanced at.
And, after this, let Cæsar seat him sure;
For we will shake him, or worse days endure. *Exit*

SCENE 3

Rome. A street

Thunder and lightning. Enter, from opposite sides, CASCA, *with his sword drawn, and* CICERO

CICERO. Good even, Casca. Brought you Cæsar home?
Why are you breathless? and why stare you so?
CASCA. Are not you mov'd, when all the sway of earth
Shakes like a thing unfirm? O Cicero,
I have seen tempests when the scolding winds
Have riv'd the knotty oaks, and I have seen
Th' ambitious ocean swell, and rage, and foam,
To be exalted with the threat'ning clouds;
But never till to-night, never till now,
Did I go through a tempest dropping fire.
Either there is a civil strife in heaven,
Or else the world, too saucy with the gods,
Incenses them to send destruction.
CICERO. Why, saw you anything more wonderful?
CASCA. A common slave—you know him well by sight—
Held up his left hand, which did flame and burn
Like twenty torches join'd; and yet his hand,
Not sensible of fire, remain'd unscorch'd.
Besides—I ha' not since put up my sword—
Against the Capitol I met a lion,
Who glar'd upon me, and went surly by
Without annoying me; and there were drawn
Upon a heap a hundred ghastly women,
Transformed with their fear, who swore they saw
Men, all in fire, walk up and down the streets.
And yesterday the bird of night did sit,
Even at noon-day, upon the market-place,
Hooting and shrieking. When these prodigies
Do so conjointly meet, let not men say
'These are their reasons—they are natural,'
For I believe they are portentous things
Unto the climate that they point upon.
CICERO. Indeed, it is a strange-disposed time;

But men may construe things after their fashion,
Clean from the purpose of the things themselves.
Comes Cæsar to the Capitol to-morrow?

CASCA. He doth; for he did bid Antonius
Send word to you he would be there to-morrow.

CICERO. Good night, then, Casca; this disturbed sky
Is not to walk in.

CASCA. Farewell, Cicero. *Exit* CICERO

Enter CASSIUS

CASSIUS. Who's there?

CASCA. A Roman.

CASSIUS. Casca, by your voice.

CASCA. Your ear is good. Cassius, what night is this!

CASSIUS. A very pleasing night to honest men.

CASCA. Who ever knew the heavens menace so?

CASSIUS. Those that have known the earth so full of faults.
For my part, I have walk'd about the streets,
Submitting me unto the perilous night,
And, thus unbraced, Casca, as you see,
Have bar'd my bosom to the thunderstone;
And when the cross blue lightning seem'd to open
The breast of heaven, I did present myself
Even in the aim and very flash of it.

CASCA. But wherefore did you so much tempt the heavens?
It is the part of men to fear and tremble
When the most mighty gods by tokens send
Such dreadful heralds to astonish us.

CASSIUS. You are dull, Casca, and those sparks of life
That should be in a Roman you do want,
Or else you use not. You look pale, and gaze,
And put on fear, and cast yourself in wonder,
To see the strange impatience of the heavens;
But if you would consider the true cause—
Why all these fires, why all these gliding ghosts,
Why birds and beasts, from quality and kind;
Why old men, fools, and children calculate;
Why all these things change from their ordinance,
Their natures and preformed faculties,
To monstrous quality—why, you shall find

That heaven hath infus'd them with these spirits,
To make them instruments of fear and warning
Unto some monstrous state.
Now could I, Casca, name to thee a man
Most like this dreadful night
That thunders, lightens, opens graves, and roars
As doth the lion in the Capitol;
A man no mightier than thyself or me
In personal action, yet prodigious grown,
And fearful, as these strange eruptions are.

CASCA. 'Tis Cæsar that you mean, is it not, Cassius?

CASSIUS. Let it be who it is; for Romans now
Have thews and limbs like to their ancestors.
But woe the while! our fathers' minds are dead,
And we are govern'd with our mothers' spirits;
Our yoke and sufferance show us womanish.

CASCA. Indeed they say the senators to-morrow
Mean to establish Cæsar as a king;
And he shall wear his crown by sea and land,
In every place save here in Italy.

CASSIUS. I know where I will wear this dagger then;
Cassius from bondage will deliver Cassius.
Therein, ye gods, you make the weak most strong;
Therein, ye gods, you tyrants do defeat.
Nor stony tower, nor walls of beaten brass,
Nor airless dungeon, nor strong links of iron,
Can be retentive to the strength of spirit;
But life, being weary of these worldly bars,
Never lacks power to dismiss itself.
If I know this, know all the world besides,
That part of tyranny that I do bear,
I can shake off at pleasure. [*Thunder still*]

CASCA. So can I;
So every bondman in his own hand bears
The power to cancel his captivity.

CASSIUS. And why should Cæsar be a tyrant, then?
Poor man! I know he would not be a wolf
But that he sees the Romans are but sheep;
He were no lion, were not Romans hinds.
Those that with haste will make a mighty fire

Begin it with weak straws. What trash is Rome,
What rubbish, and what offal, when it serves
For the base matter to illuminate
So vile a thing as Cæsar! But, O grief,
Where hast thou led me? I perhaps speak this
Before a willing bondman; then I know
My answer must be made. But I am arm'd,
And dangers are to me indifferent.

CASCA. You speak to Casca, and to such a man
That is no fleering tell-tale. Hold, my hand.
Be factious for redress of all these griefs,
And I will set this foot of mine as far
As who goes farthest.

CASSIUS. There's a bargain made.
Now know you, Casca, I have mov'd already
Some certain of the noblest-minded Romans
To undergo with me an enterprise
Of honourable-dangerous consequence;
And I do know by this they stay for me
In Pompey's porch; for now, this fearful night,
There is no stir or walking in the streets,
And the complexion of the element
In favour's like the work we have in hand,
Most bloody, fiery, and most terrible.

Enter CINNA

CASCA. Stand close awhile, for here comes one in haste.

CASSIUS. 'Tis Cinna, I do know him by his gait;
He is a friend. Cinna, where haste you so?

CINNA. To find out you. Who's that? Metellus Cimber?

CASSIUS. No, it is Casca, one incorporate
To our attempts. Am I not stay'd for, Cinna?

CINNA. I am glad on't. What a fearful night is this!
There's two or three of us have seen strange sights.

CASSIUS. Am I not stay'd for? Tell me.

CINNA. Yes, you are. O Cassius, if you could
But win the noble Brutus to our party—

CASSIUS. Be you content. Good Cinna, take this paper,
And look you lay it in the prætor's chair,
Where Brutus may but find it; and throw this

In at his window; set this up with wax
Upon old Brutus' statue. All this done,
Repair to Pompey's porch, where you shall find us.
Is Decius Brutus and Trebonius there?
CINNA. All but Metellus Cimber, and he's gone
To seek you at your house. Well, I will hie,
And so bestow these papers as you bade me.
CASSIUS. That done, repair to Pompey's theatre. *Exit* CINNA
Come, Casca, you and I will yet ere day
See Brutus at his house. Three parts of him
Is ours already, and the man entire
Upon the next encounter yields him ours.
CASCA. O, he sits high in all the people's hearts;
And that which would appear offence in us
His countenance, like richest alchemy,
Will change to virtue and to worthiness.
CASSIUS. Him and his worth and our great need of him
You have right well conceited. Let us go,
For it is after midnight; and ere day
We will awake him and be sure of him. *Exeunt*

ACT II. SCENE 1

Rome

Enter BRUTUS *in his orchard*

BRUTUS. What, Lucius, ho!
I cannot by the progress of the stars
Give guess how near to day. Lucius, I say!
I would it were my fault to sleep so soundly.
When, Lucius, when? Awake, I say! What, Lucius!

Enter LUCIUS

LUCIUS. Call'd you, my lord?
BRUTUS. Get me a taper in my study, Lucius;
When it is lighted, come and call me here.
LUCIUS. I will, my lord. *Exit*

Brutus. It must be by his death; and for my part,
I know no personal cause to spurn at him,
But for the general: he would be crown'd.
How that might change his nature, there's the question.
It is the bright day that brings forth the adder,
And that craves wary walking. Crown him–that!
And then, I grant, we put a sting in him
That at his will he may do danger with.
Th' abuse of greatness is, when it disjoins
Remorse from power; and to speak truth of Cæsar,
I have not known when his affections sway'd
More than his reason. But 'tis a common proof
That lowliness is young ambition's ladder,
Whereto the climber-upward turns his face;
But when he once attains the upmost round,
He then unto the ladder turns his back,
Looks in the clouds, scorning the base degrees
By which he did ascend. So Cæsar may.
Then, lest he may, prevent. And since the quarrel
Will bear no colour for the thing he is,
Fashion it thus–that what he is, augmented,
Would run to these and these extremities;
And therefore think him as a serpent's egg,
Which, hatch'd, would as his kind grow mischievous,
And kill him in the shell.

Re-enter Lucius

Lucius. The taper burneth in your closet, sir.
Searching the window for a flint, I found
This paper, thus seal'd up; and I am sure
It did not lie there when I went to bed.
[*Giving him a letter*]

Brutus. Get you to bed again, it is not day.
Is not to-morrow, boy, the ides of March?

Lucius. I know not, sir.

Brutus. Look in the calendar, and bring me word.

Lucius. I will, sir. *Exit*

Brutus. The exhalations, whizzing in the air,
Give so much light that I may read by them.
[*Opens the letter and reads*]

'Brutus, thou sleep'st. Awake, and see thyself.
Shall Rome, &c. Speak, strike, redress!
Brutus, thou sleep'st; awake.'
Such instigations have been often dropp'd
Where I have took them up.
'Shall Rome, &c.' Thus must I piece it out:
Shall Rome stand under one man's awe? What, Rome?
My ancestors did from the streets of Rome
The Tarquin drive, when he was call'd a king.
'Speak, strike, redress!' Am I entreated
To speak and strike? O Rome, I make thee promise,
If the redress will follow, thou receivest
Thy full petition at the hand of Brutus!

Re-enter LUCIUS

LUCIUS. Sir, March is wasted fifteen days.
[*Knocking within*]

BRUTUS. 'Tis good. Go to the gate; somebody knocks.
Exit LUCIUS

Since Cassius first did whet me against Cæsar,
I have not slept.
Between the acting of a dreadful thing
And the first motion, all the interim is
Like a phantasma or a hideous dream.
The Genius and the mortal instruments
Are then in council; and the state of man,
Like to a little kingdom, suffers then
The nature of an insurrection.

Re-enter LUCIUS

LUCIUS. Sir, 'tis your brother Cassius at the door
Who doth desire to see you.

BRUTUS. Is he alone?

LUCIUS. No, sir, there are moe with him.

BRUTUS. Do you know them?

LUCIUS. No, sir; their hats are pluck'd about their ears
And half their faces buried in their cloaks,
That by no means I may discover them
By any mark of favour.

BRUTUS. Let 'em enter. *Exit* LUCIUS

They are the faction. O conspiracy,
Sham'st thou to show thy dang'rous brow by night,
When evils are most free? O, then by day
Where wilt thou find a cavern dark enough
To mask thy monstrous visage? Seek none, conspiracy;
Hide it in smiles and affability!
For if thou hath thy native semblance on,
Not Erebus itself were dim enough
To hide thee from prevention.

Enter the conspirators, Cassius, Casca, Decius, Cinna, Metellus Cimber, *and* Trebonius

Cassius. I think we are too bold upon your rest.
Good morrow, Brutus. Do we trouble you?
Brutus. I have been up this hour, awake all night.
Know I these men that come along with you?
Cassius. Yes, every man of them; and no man here
But honours you; and every one doth wish
You had but that opinion of yourself
Which every noble Roman bears of you.
This is Trebonius.
Brutus. He is welcome hither.
Cassius. This, Decius Brutus.
Brutus. He is welcome too.
Cassius. This, Casca; this, Cinna;
And this, Metellus Cimber.
Brutus. They are all welcome.
What watchful cares do interpose themselves
Betwixt your eyes and night?
Cassius. Shall I entreat a word? [*They whisper*]
Decius. Here lies the east. Doth not the day break here?
Casca. No.
Cinna. O, pardon, sir, it doth; and yon grey lines
That fret the clouds are messengers of day.
Casca. You shall confess that you are both deceiv'd.
Here, as I point my sword, the sun arises;
Which is a great way growing on the south,
Weighing the youthful season of the year.
Some two months hence up higher toward the north
He first presents his fire; and the high east

Stands as the Capitol, directly here.
BRUTUS. Give me your hands all over, one by one.
CASSIUS. And let us swear our resolution.
BRUTUS. No, not an oath. If not the face of men,
The sufferance of our souls, the time's abuse,
If these be motives weak, break off betimes,
And every man hence to his idle bed.
So let high-sighted tyranny range on,
Till each man drop by lottery. But if these,
As I am sure they do, bear fire enough
To kindle cowards, and to steel with valour
The melting spirits of women, then, countrymen,
What need we any spur but our own cause
To prick us to redress? What other bond
Than secret Romans that have spoke the word
And will not palter? And what other oath
Than honesty to honesty engag'd
That this shall be or we will fall for it?
Swear priests and cowards and men cautelous,
Old feeble carrions and such suffering souls
That welcome wrongs; unto bad causes swear
Such creatures as men doubt; but do not stain
The even virtue of our enterprise,
Nor th' insuppressive mettle of our spirits,
To think that or our cause or our performance
Did need an oath; when every drop of blood
That every Roman bears, and nobly bears,
Is guilty of a several bastardy,
If he do break the smallest particle
Of any promise that hath pass'd from him.
CASSIUS. But what of Cicero? Shall we sound him?
I think he will stand very strong with us.
CASCA. Let us not leave him out.
CINNA. No, by no means.
METELLUS. O, let us have him; for his silver hairs
Will purchase us a good opinion,
And buy men's voices to commend our deeds.
It shall be said his judgment rul'd our hands;
Our youths and wildness shall no whit appear,
But all be buried in his gravity.

BRUTUS. O, name him not! Let us not break with him;
For he will never follow any thing
That other men begin.
CASSIUS. Then leave him out.
CASCA. Indeed he is not fit.
DECIUS. Shall no man else be touch'd but only Cæsar?
CASSIUS. Decius, well urg'd. I think it is not meet
Mark Antony, so well belov'd of Cæsar,
Should outlive Cæsar. We shall find of him
A shrewd contriver; and you know his means,
If he improve them, may well stretch so far
As to annoy us all; which to prevent,
Let Antony and Cæsar fall together.
BRUTUS. Our course will seem too bloody, Caius Cassius,
To cut the head off and then hack the limbs—
Like wrath in death and envy afterwards;
For Antony is but a limb of Cæsar.
Let's be sacrificers, but not butchers, Caius.
We all stand up against the spirit of Cæsar,
And in the spirit of men there is no blood.
O that we then could come by Cæsar's spirit,
And not dismember Cæsar! But, alas,
Cæsar must bleed for it! And, gentle friends,
Let's kill him boldly, but not wrathfully;
Let's carve him as a dish fit for the gods,
Not hew him as a carcase fit for hounds;
And let our hearts, as subtle masters do,
Stir up their servants to an act of rage,
And after seem to chide 'em. This shall make
Our purpose necessary, and not envious;
Which so appearing to the common eyes
We shall be call'd purgers, not murderers.
And for Mark Antony, think not of him;
For he can do no more than Cæsar's arm
When Cæsar's head is off.
CASSIUS. Yet I fear him;
For in the engrafted love he bears to Cæsar—
BRUTUS. Alas, good Cassius, do not think of him!
If he love Cæsar, all that he can do
Is to himself take thought and die for Cæsar;

And that were much he should, for he is given
To sports, to wildness, and much company.
TREBONIUS. There is no fear in him. Let him not die;
For he will live, and laugh at this hereafter.
[*Clock strikes*]
BRUTUS. Peace! Count the clock.
CASSIUS. The clock hath stricken three.
TREBONIUS. 'Tis time to part.
CASSIUS. But it is doubtful yet
Whether Cæsar will come forth to-day or no;
For he is superstitious grown of late,
Quite from the main opinion he held once
Of fantasy, of dreams, and ceremonies.
It may be these apparent prodigies,
The unaccustom'd terror of this night,
And the persuasion of his augurers,
May hold him from the Capitol to-day.
DECIUS. Never fear that. If he be so resolv'd,
I can o'ersway him; for he loves to hear
That unicorns may be betray'd with trees,
And bears with glasses, elephants with holes.
Lions with toils, and men with flatterers;
But when I tell him he hates flatterers,
He says he does, being then most flattered.
Let me work;
For I can give his humour the true bent,
And I will bring him to the Capitol.
CASSIUS. Nay, we will all of us be there to fetch him.
BRUTUS. By the eighth hour. Is that the uttermost?
CINNA. Be that the uttermost, and fail not then.
METELLUS. Caius Ligarius doth bear Cæsar hard,
Who rated him for speaking well of Pompey.
I wonder none of you have thought of him.
BRUTUS. Now, good Metellus, go along by him.
He loves me well, and I have given him reasons;
Send him but hither, and I'll fashion him.
CASSIUS. The morning comes upon's. We'll leave you, Brutus.
And, friends, disperse yourselves; but all remember
What you have said, and show yourselves true Romans.

BRUTUS. Good gentlemen, look fresh and merrily;
Let not our looks put on our purposes,
But bear it as our Roman actors do,
With untir'd spirits and formal constancy.
And so good morrow to you every one.

Exeunt all but BRUTUS

Boy! Lucius! Fast asleep? It is no matter;
Enjoy the honey-heavy dew of slumber.
Thou hast no figures nor no fantasies
Which busy care draws in the brains of men;
Therefore thou sleep'st so sound.

Enter PORTIA

PORTIA. Brutus, my lord!
BRUTUS. Portia, what mean you? Wherefore rise you now?
It is not for your health thus to commit
Your weak condition to the raw cold morning.
PORTIA. Nor for yours neither. Y'have ungently, Brutus,
Stole from my bed; and yesternight at supper
You suddenly arose and walk'd about,
Musing and sighing, with your arms across;
And when I ask'd you what the matter was,
You star'd upon me with ungentle looks.
I urg'd you further; then you scratch'd your head
And too impatiently stamp'd with your foot.
Yet I insisted; yet you answer'd not,
But with an angry wafture of your hand
Gave sign for me to leave you. So I did,
Fearing to strengthen that impatience
Which seem'd too much enkindled; and withal
Hoping it was but an effect of humour,
Which sometime hath his hour with every man.
It will not let you eat, nor talk, nor sleep;
And, could it work so much upon your shape
As it hath much prevail'd on your condition,
I should not know you Brutus. Dear my lord,
Make me acquainted with your cause of grief.
BRUTUS. I am not well in health, and that is all.
PORTIA. Brutus is wise, and, were he not in health,
He would embrace the means to come by it.

BRUTUS. Why, so I do. Good Portia, go to bed.
PORTIA. Is Brutus sick, and is it physical
To walk unbraced and suck up the humours
Of the dank morning? What, is Brutus sick,
And will he steal out of his wholesome bed,
To dare the vile contagion of the night,
And tempt the rheumy and unpurged air
To add unto his sickness? No, my Brutus;
You have some sick offence within your mind,
Which by the right and virtue of my place
I ought to know of; and upon my knees
I charm you, by my once-commended beauty,
By all your vows of love, and that great vow
Which did incorporate and make us one,
That you unfold to me, your self, your half,
Why you are heavy—and what men to-night
Have had resort to you; for here have been
Some six or seven, who did hide their faces
Even from darkness.
BRUTUS. Kneel not, gentle Portia.
PORTIA. I should not need, if you were gentle Brutus.
Within the bond of marriage, tell me, Brutus,
Is it excepted I should know no secrets
That appertain to you? Am I your self
But, as it were, in sort or limitation?
To keep with you at meals, comfort your bed,
And talk to you sometimes? Dwell I but in the suburbs
Of your good pleasure? If it be no more,
Portia is Brutus' harlot, not his wife.
BRUTUS. You are my true and honourable wife,
As dear to me as are the ruddy drops
That visit my sad heart.
PORTIA. If this were true, then should I know this secret.
I grant I am a woman; but withal
A woman that Lord Brutus took to wife.
I grant I am a woman; but withal
A woman well reputed, Cato's daughter.
Think you I am no stronger than my sex,
Being so father'd and so husbanded?
Tell me your counsels, I will not disclose 'em.

I have made strong proof of my constancy,
Giving myself a voluntary wound
Here, in the thigh. Can I bear that with patience,
And not my husband's secrets?

BRUTUS. O ye gods,
Render me worthy of this noble wife! [*Knocking within*]
Hark, hark! one knocks. Portia, go in awhile,
And by and by thy bosom shall partake
The secrets of my heart.
All my engagements I will construe to thee,
All the charactery of my sad brows.
Leave me with haste. *Exit* PORTIA
Lucius, who's that knocks?

Enter LUCIUS *and* LIGARIUS

LUCIUS. Here is a sick man that would speak with you.

BRUTUS. Caius Ligarius, that Metellus spake of.
Boy, stand aside. Caius Ligarius, how?

LIGARIUS. Vouchsafe good morrow from a feeble tongue.

BRUTUS. O, what a time have you chose out, brave Caius,
To wear a kerchief! Would you were not sick!

LIGARIUS. I am not sick, if Brutus have in hand
Any exploit worthy the name of honour.

BRUTUS. Such an exploit have I in hand, Ligarius,
Had you a healthful ear to hear of it.

LIGARIUS. By all the gods that Romans bow before,
I here discard my sickness. [*Pulls off his kerchief*] Soul of Rome!
Brave son, deriv'd from honourable loins!
Thou, like an exorcist, hast conjur'd up
My mortified spirit. Now bid me run,
And I will strive with things impossible;
Yea, get the better of them. What's to do?

BRUTUS. A piece of work that will make sick men whole.

LIGARIUS. But are not some whole that we must make sick?

BRUTUS. That must we also. What it is, my Caius,
I shall unfold to thee, as we are going,
To whom it must be done.

LIGARIUS. Set on your foot,
And with a heart new-fir'd I follow you

To do I know not what; but it sufficeth
That Brutus leads me on. *[Thunder]*
BRUTUS. Follow me, then. *Exeunt*

SCENE 2

Rome. CÆSAR'S *house*

Thunder and lightning. Enter JULIUS CÆSAR *in his night-gown*

CÆSAR. Nor heaven nor earth have been at peace to-night.
Thrice hath Calpurnia in her sleep cried out
'Help, ho! They murder Cæsar!' Who's within?

Enter a SERVANT

SERVANT. My lord?
CÆSAR. Go bid the priests do present sacrifice,
And bring me their opinions of success.
SERVANT. I will, my lord. *Exit*

Enter CALPURNIA

CALPURNIA. What mean you, Cæsar? Think you to walk forth?
You shall not stir out of your house to-day.
CÆSAR. Cæsar shall forth; the things that threaten'd me
Ne'er look'd but on my back. When they shall see
The face of Cæsar, they are vanished.
CALPURNIA. Cæsar, I never stood on ceremonies,
Yet now they fright me. There is one within,
Besides the things that we have heard and seen,
Recounts most horrid sights seen by the watch.
A lioness hath whelped in the streets,
And graves have yawn'd and yielded up their dead;
Fierce fiery warriors fight upon the clouds,
In ranks and squadrons and right form of war,
Which drizzled blood upon the Capitol;
The noise of battle hurtled in the air;
Horses did neigh, and dying men did groan,
And ghosts did shriek and squeal about the streets.

O Cæsar, these things are beyond all use,
And I do fear them!

CÆSAR. What can be avoided,
Whose end is purpos'd by the mighty gods?
Yet Cæsar shall go forth; for these predictions
Are to the world in general as to Cæsar.

CALPURNIA. When beggars die there are no comets seen:
The heavens themselves blaze forth the death of princes.

CÆSAR. Cowards die many times before their deaths:
The valiant never taste of death but once.
Of all the wonders that I yet have heard,
It seems to me most strange that men should fear,
Seeing that death, a necessary end,
Will come when it will come.

Re-enter SERVANT

What say the augurers?

SERVANT. They would not have you to stir forth to-day.
Plucking the entrails of an offering forth,
They could not find a heart within the beast.

CÆSAR. The gods do this in shame of cowardice.
Cæsar should be a beast without a heart,
If he should stay at home to-day for fear.
No, Cæsar shall not. Danger knows full well
That Cæsar is more dangerous than he:
We are two lions litter'd in one day,
And I the elder and more terrible;
And Cæsar shall go forth.

CALPURNIA. Alas, my lord,
Your wisdom is consum'd in confidence.
Do not go forth to-day. Call it my fear
That keeps you in the house, and not your own.
We'll send Mark Antony to the Senate House,
And he shall say you are not well to-day.
Let me, upon my knee, prevail in this.

CÆSAR. Mark Antony shall say I am not well;
And for thy humour I will stay at home.

Enter DECIUS

Here's Decius Brutus, he shall tell them so.

DECIUS. Cæsar, all hail! Good morrow, worthy Cæsar.
I come to fetch you to the Senate House.
CÆSAR. And you are come in very happy time,
To bear my greeting to the senators
And tell them that I will not come to-day.
Cannot, is false; and that I dare not, falser;
I will not come to-day. Tell them so, Decius.
CALPURNIA. Say he is sick.
CÆSAR. Shall Cæsar send a lie?
Have I in conquest stretch'd mine arm so far,
To be afeard to tell greybeards the truth?
Decius, go tell them Cæsar will not come.
DECIUS. Most mighty Cæsar, let me know some cause,
Lest I be laugh'd at when I tell them so.
CÆSAR. The cause is in my will: I will not come.
That is enough to satisfy the Senate.
But for your private satisfaction,
Because I love you, I will let you know:
Calpurnia here, my wife, stays me at home.
She dreamt to-night she saw my statua,
Which, like a fountain with an hundred spouts,
Did run pure blood; and many lusty Romans
Came smiling and did bathe their hands in it.
And these does she apply for warnings and portents
And evils imminent, and on her knee
Hath begg'd that I will stay at home to-day.
DECIUS. This dream is all amiss interpreted;
It was a vision fair and fortunate.
Your statue spouting blood in many pipes,
In which so many smiling Romans bath'd,
Signifies that from you great Rome shall suck
Reviving blood, and that great men shall press
For tinctures, stains, relics, and cognizance.
This by Calpurnia's dream is signified.
CÆSAR. And this way have you well expounded it.
DECIUS. I have, when you have heard what I can say—
And know it now: the Senate have concluded
To give this day a crown to mighty Cæsar.
If you shall send them word you will not come,
Their minds may change. Besides, it were a mock

Apt to be render'd, for some one to say
'Break up the Senate till another time,
When Cæsar's wife shall meet with better dreams.'
If Cæsar hide himself, shall they not whisper
'Lo, Cæsar is afraid'?
Pardon me, Cæsar; for my dear dear love
To your proceeding bids me tell you this,
And reason to my love is liable.

CÆSAR. How foolish do your fears seem now, Calpurnia!
I am ashamed I did yield to them.
Give me my robe, for I will go.

Enter BRUTUS, LIGARIUS, METELLUS, CASCA, TREBONIUS, CINNA, *and* PUBLIUS

And look where Publius is come to fetch me.

PUBLIUS. Good morrow, Cæsar.

CÆSAR. Welcome, Publius.
What, Brutus, are you stirr'd so early too?
Good morrow, Casca. Caius Ligarius,
Cæsar was ne'er so much your enemy
As that same ague which hath made you lean.
What is't o'clock?

BRUTUS. Cæsar, 'tis strucken eight.

CÆSAR. I thank you for your pains and courtesy.

Enter ANTONY

See! Antony, that revels long o' nights,
Is notwithstanding up. Good morrow, Antony.

ANTONY. So to most noble Cæsar.

CÆSAR. Bid them prepare within.
I am to blame to be thus waited for.
Now, Cinna. Now, Metellus. What, Trebonius!
I have an hour's talk in store for you.
Remember that you call on me to-day;
Be near me, that I may remember you.

TREBONIUS. Cæsar, I will. [*Aside*] And so near will I be,
That your best friends shall wish I had been further.

CÆSAR. Good friends, go in and taste some wine with me;
And we, like friends, will straightway go together.

BRUTUS. [*Aside*] That every like is not the same, O Cæsar,
The heart of Brutus yearns to think upon! *Exeunt*

SCENE 3

Rome. A street near the Capitol

Enter ARTEMIDORUS *reading a paper*

ARTEMIDORUS. 'Cæsar, beware of Brutus; take heed of Cassius; come not near Casca; have an eye to Cinna; trust not Trebonius; mark well Metellus Cimber; Decius Brutus loves thee not; thou hast wrong'd Caius Ligarius. There is but one mind in all these men, and it is bent against Cæsar. If thou beest not immortal, look about you. Security gives way to conspiracy. The mighty gods defend thee!

Thy lover,
ARTEMIDORUS.'

Here will I stand till Cæsar pass along,
And as a suitor will I give him this.
My heart laments that virtue cannot live
Out of the teeth of emulation.
If thou read this, O Cæsar, thou mayest live;
If not, the fates with traitors do contrive. *Exit*

SCENE 4

Rome. Before the house of BRUTUS

Enter PORTIA *and* LUCIUS

PORTIA. I prithee, boy, run to the Senate House.
Stay not to answer me, but get thee gone.
Why dost thou stay?
LUCIUS. To know my errand, madam.
PORTIA. I would have had thee there and here again,
Ere I can tell thee what thou shouldst do there.
[*Aside*] O constancy, be strong upon my side!
Set a huge mountain 'tween my heart and tongue!
I have a man's mind, but a woman's might.
How hard it is for women to keep counsel!—
Art thou here yet?

LUCIUS. Madam, what should I do?
Run to the Capitol, and nothing else?
And so return to you, and nothing else?
PORTIA. Yes, bring me word, boy, if thy lord look well,
For he went sickly forth; and take good note
What Cæsar doth, what suitors press to him.
Hark, boy! What noise is that?
LUCIUS. I hear none, madam.
PORTIA. Prithee listen well.
I heard a bustling rumour, like a fray,
And the wind brings it from the Capitol.
LUCIUS. Sooth, madam, I hear nothing.

Enter the SOOTHSAYER

PORTIA. Come hither, fellow.
Which way hast thou been?
SOOTHSAYER. At mine own house, good lady.
PORTIA. What is't o'clock?
SOOTHSAYER. About the ninth hour, lady.
PORTIA. Is Cæsar yet gone to the Capitol?
SOOTHSAYER. Madam, not yet. I go to take my stand,
To see him pass on to the Capitol.
PORTIA. Thou hast some suit to Cæsar, hast thou not?
SOOTHSAYER. That I have, lady. If it will please Cæsar
To be so good to Cæsar as to hear me,
I shall beseech him to befriend himself.
PORTIA. Why, know'st thou any harm's intended towards him?
SOOTHSAYER. None that I know will be, much that I fear may chance.
Good morrow to you. Here the street is narrow;
The throng that follows Cæsar at the heels,
Of senators, of prætors, common suitors,
Will crowd a feeble man almost to death.
I'll get me to a place more void, and there
Speak to great Cæsar as he comes along. *Exit*
PORTIA. I must go in. [*Aside*] Ay me, how weak a thing
The heart of woman is! O Brutus,
The heavens speed thee in thine enterprise!
Sure the boy heard me.—Brutus hath a suit
That Cæsar will not grant.—O, I grow faint.—

Run, Lucius, and commend me to my lord;
Say I am merry. Come to me again,
And bring me word what he doth say to thee.
Exeunt severally

ACT III. SCENE 1

Rome. A street before the Capitol

Flourish. Enter CÆSAR, BRUTUS, CASSIUS, CASCA, DECIUS, METELLUS, TREBONIUS, CINNA, ANTONY, LEPIDUS, ARTEMIDORUS, POPILIUS, PUBLIUS, *and the* SOOTHSAYER

CÆSAR. The ides of March are come.
SOOTHSAYER. Ay, Cæsar, but not gone.
ARTEMIDORUS. Hail, Cæsar! Read this schedule.
DECIUS. Trebonius doth desire you to o'er-read,
At your best leisure, this his humble suit.
ARTEMIDORUS. O Cæsar, read mine first; for mine's a suit
That touches Cæsar nearer. Read it, great Cæsar.
CÆSAR. What touches us ourself shall be last serv'd.
ARTEMIDORUS. Delay not, Cæsar; read it instantly.
CÆSAR. What, is the fellow mad?
PUBLIUS. Sirrah, give place.
CASSIUS. What, urge you your petitions in the street?
Come to the Capitol.

CÆSAR *enters the Capitol, the rest following*

POPILIUS. I wish your enterprise to-day may thrive.
CASSIUS. What enterprise, Popilius?
POPILIUS. Fare you well. [*Advances to* CÆSAR]
BRUTUS. What said Popilius Lena?
CASSIUS. He wish'd to-day our enterprise might thrive.
I fear our purpose is discovered.
BRUTUS. Look how he makes to Cæsar. Mark him.
CASSIUS. Casca, be sudden, for we fear prevention.
Brutus, what shall be done? If this be known,
Cassius or Cæsar never shall turn back,

For I will slay myself.
BRUTUS. Cassius, be constant.
Popilius Lena speaks not of our purposes;
For look, he smiles, and Cæsar doth not change.
CASSIUS. Trebonius knows his time; for look you, Brutus,
He draws Mark Antony out of the way.
Exeunt ANTONY *and* TREBONIUS
DECIUS. Where is Metellus Cimber? Let him go
And presently prefer his suit to Cæsar.
BRUTUS. He is address'd; press near and second him.
CINNA. Casca, you are the first that rears your hand.
CÆSAR. Are we all ready? What is now amiss
That Cæsar and his Senate must redress?
METELLUS. Most high, most mighty, and most puissant Cæsar,
Metellus Cimber throws before thy seat
An humble heart. [*Kneeling*]
CÆSAR. I must prevent thee, Cimber.
These couchings and these lowly courtesies
Might fire the blood of ordinary men,
And turn pre-ordinance and first decree
Into the law of children. Be not fond
To think that Cæsar bears such rebel blood
That will be thaw'd from the true quality
With that which melteth fools—I mean, sweet words,
Low-crooked curtsies, and base spaniel fawning.
Thy brother by decree is banished;
If thou dost bend, and pray, and fawn for him,
I spurn thee like a cur out of my way.
Know, Cæsar doth not wrong; nor without cause
Will he be satisfied.
METELLUS. Is there no voice more worthy than my own
To sound more sweetly in great Cæsar's ear
For the repealing of my banish'd brother?
BRUTUS. I kiss thy hand, but not in flattery, Cæsar,
Desiring thee that Publius Cimber may
Have an immediate freedom of repeal.
CÆSAR. What, Brutus!
CASSIUS. Pardon, Cæsar! Cæsar, pardon!
As low as to thy foot doth Cassius fall,

To beg enfranchisement for Publius Cimber.
CÆSAR. I could be well mov'd, if I were as you;
If I could pray to move, prayers would move me;
But I am constant as the northern star,
Of whose true-fix'd and resting quality
There is no fellow in the firmament.
The skies are painted with unnumb'red sparks,
They are all fire, and every one doth shine;
But there's but one in all doth hold his place.
So in the world: 'tis furnish'd well with men,
And men are flesh and blood, and apprehensive;
Yet in the number I do know but one
That unassailable holds on his rank,
Unshak'd of motion; and that I am he,
Let me a little show it, even in this–
That I was constant Cimber should be banish'd,
And constant do remain to keep him so.
CINNA. O Cæsar!
CÆSAR. Hence! Wilt thou lift up Olympus?
DECIUS. Great Cæsar!
CÆSAR. Doth not Brutus bootless kneel?
CASCA. Speak, hands, for me! [*They stab* CÆSAR. CASCA *strikes the first*, BRUTUS *the last blow*]
CÆSAR. Et tu, Brute?–Then fall, Cæsar!
CINNA. Liberty! Freedom! Tyranny is dead!
Run hence, proclaim, cry it about the streets.
CASSIUS. Some to the common pulpits, and cry out
'Liberty, freedom, and enfranchisement!'
BRUTUS. People and Senators, be not affrighted.
Fly not; stand still. Ambition's debt is paid.
CASCA. Go to the pulpit, Brutus.
DECIUS. And Cassius too.
BRUTUS. Where's Publius?
CINNA. Here, quite confounded with this mutiny.
METELLUS. Stand fast together, lest some friend of Cæsar's
Should chance–
BRUTUS. Talk not of standing. Publius, good cheer!
There is no harm intended to your person,
Nor to no Roman else. So tell them, Publius.
CASSIUS. And leave us, Publius, lest that the people,

Rushing on us, should do your age some mischief.
BRUTUS. Do so; and let no man abide this deed
But we the doers.

Re-enter TREBONIUS

CASSIUS. Where is Antony?
TREBONIUS. Fled to his house amaz'd.
Men, wives, and children, stare, cry out, and run,
As it were doomsday.
BRUTUS. Fates, we will know your pleasures.
That we shall die, we know; 'tis but the time,
And drawing days out, that men stand upon.
CASSIUS. Why, he that cuts off twenty years of life
Cuts off so many years of fearing death.
BRUTUS. Grant that, and then is death a benefit.
So are we Cæsar's friends, that have abridg'd
His time of fearing death. Stoop, Romans, stoop,
And let us bathe our hands in Cæsar's blood
Up to the elbows, and besmear our swords.
Then walk we forth, even to the market-place,
And waving our red weapons o'er our heads,
Let's all cry 'Peace, freedom, and liberty!'
CASSIUS. Stoop then, and wash. How many ages hence
Shall this our lofty scene be acted over
In states unborn and accents yet unknown!
BRUTUS. How many times shall Cæsar bleed in sport,
That now on Pompey's basis lies along
No worthier than the dust!
CASSIUS. So oft as that shall be,
So often shall the knot of us be call'd
The men that gave their country liberty.
DECIUS. What, shall we forth?
CASSIUS. Ay, every man away.
Brutus shall lead, and we will grace his heels
With the most boldest and best hearts of Rome.

Enter a SERVANT

BRUTUS. Soft, who comes here? A friend of Antony's.
SERVANT. Thus, Brutus, did my master bid me kneel;
Thus did Mark Antony bid me fall down;

And, being prostrate, thus he bade me say:
Brutus is noble, wise, valiant, and honest;
Cæsar was mighty, bold, royal, and loving.
Say I love Brutus, and I honour him;
Say I fear'd Cæsar, honour'd him, and lov'd him.
If Brutus will vouchsafe that Antony
May safely come to him, and be resolv'd
How Cæsar hath deserv'd to lie in death,
Mark Antony shall not love Cæsar dead
So well as Brutus living; but will follow
The fortunes and affairs of noble Brutus
Through the hazards of this untrod state
With all true faith. So says my master Antony.

BRUTUS. Thy master is a wise and valiant Roman;
I never thought him worse.
Tell him, so please him come unto this place,
He shall be satisfied and, by my honour,
Depart untouch'd.

SERVANT. I'll fetch him presently. *Exit*

BRUTUS. I know that we shall have him well to friend.

CASSIUS. I wish we may. But yet have I a mind
That fears him much; and my misgiving still
Falls shrewdly to the purpose.

Re-enter ANTONY

BRUTUS. But here comes Antony. Welcome, Mark Antony.

ANTONY. O mighty Cæsar! dost thou lie so low?
Are all thy conquests, glories, triumphs, spoils,
Shrunk to this little measure? Fare thee well.
I know not, gentlemen, what you intend,
Who else must be let blood, who else is rank.
If I myself, there is no hour so fit
As Cæsar's death's hour; nor no instrument
Of half that worth as those your swords, made rich
With the most noble blood of all this world.
I do beseech ye, if you bear me hard,
Now, whilst your purpled hands do reek and smoke,
Fulfil your pleasure. Live a thousand years,
I shall not find myself so apt to die.
No place will please me so, no mean of death,

As here by Cæsar, and by you cut off,
The choice and master spirits of this age.

BRUTUS. O Antony! beg not your death of us.
Though now we must appear bloody and cruel,
As by our hands and this our present act
You see we do; yet see you but our hands,
And this the bleeding business they have done.
Our hearts you see not; they are pitiful;
And pity to the general wrong of Rome,
As fire drives out fire, so pity pity,
Hath done this deed on Cæsar. For your part,
To you our swords have leaden points, Mark Antony;
Our arms in strength of malice, and our hearts
Of brothers' temper, do receive you in
With all kind love, good thoughts, and reverence.

CASSIUS. Your voice shall be as strong as any man's
In the disposing of new dignities.

BRUTUS. Only be patient till we have appeas'd
The multitude, beside themselves with fear,
And then we will deliver you the cause
Why I, that did love Cæsar when I struck him,
Have thus proceeded.

ANTONY. I doubt not of your wisdom.
Let each man render me his bloody hand.
First, Marcus Brutus, will I shake with you;
Next, Caius Cassius, do I take your hand;
Now, Decius Brutus, yours; now yours, Metellus;
Yours, Cinna; and, my valiant Casca, yours.
Though last, not least in love, yours, good Trebonius.
Gentlemen all—alas, what shall I say?
My credit now stands on such slippery ground
That one of two bad ways you must conceit me,
Either a coward or a flatterer.
That I did love thee, Cæsar, O, 'tis true!
If then thy spirit look upon us now,
Shall it not grieve thee dearer than thy death
To see thy Antony making his peace,
Shaking the bloody fingers of thy foes,
Most noble! in the presence of thy corse?
Had I as many eyes as thou hast wounds,

Weeping as fast as they stream forth thy blood,
It would become me better than to close
In terms of friendship with thine enemies.
Pardon me, Julius! Here wast thou bay'd, brave hart;
Here didst thou fall; and here thy hunters stand,
Sign'd in thy spoil, and crimson'd in thy Lethe.
O world, thou wast the forest to this hart;
And this indeed, O world, the heart of thee!
How like a deer strucken by many princes
Dost thou here lie!

CASSIUS. Mark Antony—

ANTONY. Pardon me, Caius Cassius.
The enemies of Cæsar shall say this;
Then, in a friend, it is cold modesty.

CASSIUS. I blame you not for praising Cæsar so;
But what compact mean you to have with us?
Will you be prick'd in number of our friends,
Or shall we on, and not depend on you?

ANTONY. Therefore I took your hands; but was indeed
Sway'd from the point by looking down on Cæsar.
Friends am I with you all, and love you all,
Upon this hope, that you shall give me reasons
Why and wherein Cæsar was dangerous.

BRUTUS. Or else were this a savage spectacle.
Our reasons are so full of good regard
That were you, Antony, the son of Cæsar,
You should be satisfied.

ANTONY. That's all I seek;
And am moreover suitor that I may
Produce his body to the market-place
And, in the pulpit, as becomes a friend,
Speak in the order of his funeral.

BRUTUS. You shall, Mark Antony.

CASSIUS. Brutus, a word with you.
[*Aside to* BRUTUS] You know not what you do. Do not consent
That Antony speak in his funeral.
Know you how much the people may be mov'd
By that which he will utter?

BRUTUS. [*Aside to* CASSIUS] By your pardon—

I will myself into the pulpit first,
And show the reason of our Cæsar's death.
What Antony shall speak, I will protest
He speaks by leave and by permission;
And that we are contented Cæsar shall
Have all true rites and lawful ceremonies.
It shall advantage more than do us wrong.

CASSIUS. I know not what may fall. I like it not.

BRUTUS. Mark Antony, here, take you Cæsar's body.
You shall not in your funeral speech blame us,
But speak all good you can devise of Cæsar;
And say you do't by our permission;
Else shall you not have any hand at all
About his funeral. And you shall speak
In the same pulpit whereto I am going,
After my speech is ended.

ANTONY. Be it so;
I do desire no more.

BRUTUS. Prepare the body then, and follow us.

Exeunt all but ANTONY

ANTONY. O, pardon me, thou bleeding piece of earth,
That I am meek and gentle with these butchers!
Thou art the ruins of the noblest man
That ever lived in the tide of times.
Woe to the hand that shed this costly blood!
Over thy wounds now do I prophesy—
Which like dumb mouths do ope their ruby lips
To beg the voice and utterance of my tongue—
A curse shall light upon the limbs of men;
Domestic fury and fierce civil strife
Shall cumber all the parts of Italy;
Blood and destruction shall be so in use,
And dreadful objects so familiar,
That mothers shall but smile when they behold
Their infants quartered with the hands of war,
All pity chok'd with custom of fell deeds;
And Cæsar's spirit, ranging for revenge,
With Até by his side come hot from hell,
Shall in these confines with a monarch's voice
Cry 'Havoc!' and let slip the dogs of war,

That this foul deed shall smell above the earth
With carrion men, groaning for burial.

Enter OCTAVIUS' SERVANT

You serve Octavius Cæsar, do you not?
SERVANT. I do, Mark Antony.
ANTONY. Cæsar did write for him to come to Rome.
SERVANT. He did receive his letters, and is coming,
And bid me say to you by word of mouth–
O Cæsar! [*Seeing the body*]
ANTONY. Thy heart is big, get thee apart and weep.
Passion, I see, is catching; for mine eyes,
Seeing those beads of sorrow stand in thine,
Began to water. Is thy master coming?
SERVANT. He lies to-night within seven leagues of Rome.
ANTONY. Post back with speed, and tell him what hath chanc'd.
Here is a mourning Rome, a dangerous Rome,
No Rome of safety for Octavius yet;
Hie hence and tell him so. Yet stay awhile;
Thou shalt not back till I have borne this corse
Into the market-place. There shall I try,
In my oration, how the people take
The cruel issue of these bloody men;
According to the which thou shalt discourse
To young Octavius of the state of things.
Lend me your hand. *Exeunt with* CÆSAR'S *body*

SCENE 2

Rome. The Forum

Enter BRUTUS *and* CASSIUS, *with the plebeians*

CITIZENS. We will be satisfied! Let us be satisfied!
BRUTUS. Then follow me, and give me audience, friends.
Cassius, go you into the other street,
And part the numbers.
Those that will hear me speak, let 'em stay here;
Those that will follow Cassius, go with him;

And public reasons shall be rendered
Of Cæsar's death.

FIRST PLEBEIAN. I will hear Brutus speak.

SECOND PLEBEIAN. I will hear Cassius, and compare their reasons,
When severally we hear them rendered. *Exit* CASSIUS, *with some of the plebeians.* BRUTUS *goes into the pulpit*

THIRD PLEBEIAN. The noble Brutus is ascended. Silence!

BRUTUS. Be patient till the last.
Romans, countrymen, and lovers! hear me for my cause, and be silent, that you may hear. Believe me for mine honour, and have respect to mine honour, that you may believe. Censure me in your wisdom, and awake your senses, that you may the better judge. If there be any in this assembly, any dear friend of Cæsar's, to him I say that Brutus' love to Cæsar was no less than his. If then that friend demand why Brutus rose against Cæsar, this is my answer: Not that I lov'd Cæsar less, but that I lov'd Rome more. Had you rather Cæsar were living, and die all slaves, than that Cæsar were dead, to live all free men? As Cæsar lov'd me, I weep for him; as he was fortunate, I rejoice at it; as he was valiant, I honour him; but—as he was ambitious, I slew him. There is tears for his love; joy for his fortune; honour for his valour; and death for his ambition. Who is here so base that would be a bondman? If any, speak; for him have I offended. Who is here so rude that would not be a Roman? If any, speak; for him have I offended. Who is here so vile that will not love his country? If any, speak; for him have I offended. I pause for a reply.

ALL. None, Brutus, none.

BRUTUS. Then none have I offended. I have done no more to Cæsar than you shall do to Brutus. The question of his death is enroll'd in the Capitol; his glory not extenuated, wherein he was worthy; nor his offences enforc'd, for which he suffered death.

Enter MARK ANTONY *and others with* CÆSAR'S *body*

Here comes his body, mourn'd by Mark Antony, who, though he had no hand in his death, shall receive the benefit of his dying, a place in the commonwealth, as which of you shall not? With this I depart, that, as I slew my best lover for the good of Rome, I have the same dagger for myself, when it shall please my country to need my death.

ALL. Live, Brutus! live, live!

FIRST PLEBEIAN. Bring him with triumph home unto his house.

SECOND PLEBEIAN. Give him a statue with his ancestors.

THIRD PLEBEIAN. Let him be Cæsar.

FOURTH PLEBEIAN. Cæsar's better parts
Shall be crown'd in Brutus.

FIRST PLEBEIAN. We'll bring him to his house with shouts and clamours.

BRUTUS. My countrymen—

SECOND PLEBEIAN. Peace, silence! Brutus speaks.

FIRST PLEBEIAN. Peace, ho!

BRUTUS. Good countrymen, let me depart alone,
And for my sake stay here with Antony.
Do grace to Cæsar's corpse, and grace his speech
Tending to Cæsar's glories, which Mark Antony
By our permission, is allow'd to make.
I do entreat you, not a man depart
Save I alone, till Antony have spoke. *Exit*

FIRST PLEBEIAN. Stay, ho! and let us hear Mark Antony.

THIRD PLEBEIAN. Let him go up into the public chair.
We'll hear him. Noble Antony, go up.

ANTONY. For Brutus' sake I am beholding to you. [*Goes up*]

FOURTH PLEBEIAN. What does he say of Brutus?

THIRD PLEBEIAN. He says, for Brutus' sake
He finds himself beholding to us all.

FOURTH PLEBEIAN. 'Twere best he speak no harm of Brutus here.

FIRST PLEBEIAN. This Cæsar was a tyrant.

THIRD PLEBEIAN. Nay, that's certain.
We are blest that Rome is rid of him.

SECOND PLEBEIAN. Peace! let us hear what Antony can say.

ANTONY. You gentle Romans—

ALL. Peace, ho! let us hear him.

ANTONY. Friends, Romans, countrymen, lend me your ears;
I come to bury Cæsar, not to praise him.

The evil that men do lives after them;
The good is oft interred with their bones;
So let it be with Cæsar. The noble Brutus
Hath told you Cæsar was ambitious.
If it were so, it was a grievous fault;
And grievously hath Cæsar answer'd it.
Here, under leave of Brutus and the rest—
For Brutus is an honourable man;
So are they all, all honourable men—
Come I to speak in Cæsar's funeral.
He was my friend, faithful and just to me;
But Brutus says he was ambitious,
And Brutus is an honourable man.
He hath brought many captives home to Rome,
Whose ransoms did the general coffers fill;
Did this in Cæsar seem ambitious?
When that the poor have cried, Cæsar hath wept;
Ambition should be made of sterner stuff.
Yet Brutus says he was ambitious;
And Brutus is an honourable man.
You all did see that on the Lupercal
I thrice presented him a kingly crown,
Which he did thrice refuse. Was this ambition?
Yet Brutus says he was ambitious;
And sure he is an honourable man.
I speak not to disprove what Brutus spoke,
But here I am to speak what I do know.
You all did love him once, not without cause;
What cause withholds you, then, to mourn for him?
O judgment, thou art fled to brutish beasts,
And men have lost their reason! Bear with me;
My heart is in the coffin there with Cæsar,
And I must pause till it come back to me.

FIRST PLEBEIAN. Methinks there is much reason in his sayings.

SECOND PLEBEIAN. If thou consider rightly of the matter,
Cæsar has had great wrong.

THIRD PLEBEIAN. Has he, masters!
I fear there will be a worse come in his place.

FOURTH PLEBEIAN. Mark'd ye his words? He would not take the crown;

Therefore 'tis certain he was not ambitious.

FIRST PLEBEIAN. If it be found so, some will dear abide it.

SECOND PLEBEIAN. Poor soul! his eyes are red as fire with weeping.

THIRD PLEBEIAN. There's not a nobler man in Rome than Antony.

FOURTH PLEBEIAN. Now mark him, he begins again to speak.

ANTONY. But yesterday the word of Cæsar might
Have stood against the world: now lies he there,
And none so poor to do him reverence.
O masters, if I were dispos'd to stir
Your hearts and minds to mutiny and rage,
I should do Brutus wrong, and Cassius wrong,
Who, you all know, are honourable men.
I will not do them wrong; I rather choose
To wrong the dead, to wrong myself and you,
Than I will wrong such honourable men.
But here's a parchment with the seal of Cæsar;
I found it in his closet—'tis his will.
Let but the commons hear this testament,
Which, pardon me, I do not mean to read,
And they would go and kiss dead Cæsar's wounds
And dip their napkins in his sacred blood;
Yea, beg a hair of him for memory
And, dying, mention it within their wills,
Bequeathing it as a rich legacy
Unto their issue.

FOURTH PLEBEIAN. We'll hear the will. Read it, Mark Antony.

ALL. The will, the will! We will hear Cæsar's will.

ANTONY. Have patience, gentle friends, I must not read it;
It is not meet you know how Cæsar lov'd you.
You are not wood, you are not stones, but men;
And being men, hearing the will of Cæsar,
It will inflame you, it will make you mad.
'Tis good you know not that you are his heirs;
For if you should, O, what would come of it?

FOURTH PLEBEIAN. Read the will; we'll hear it, Antony!
You shall read us the will—Cæsar's will.

ANTONY. Will you be patient? Will you stay awhile?
I have o'ershot myself to tell you of it.

I fear I wrong the honourable men
Whose daggers have stabb'd Cæsar; I do fear it.

FOURTH PLEBEIAN. They were traitors. Honourable men!

ALL. The will! the testament!

SECOND PLEBEIAN. They were villains, murderers. The will!
Read the will.

ANTONY. You will compel me, then, to read the will?
Then make a ring about the corpse of Cæsar,
And let me show you him that made the will.
Shall I descend? and will you give me leave?

ALL. Come down.

SECOND PLEBEIAN. Descend. [ANTONY *comes down*]

THIRD PLEBEIAN. You shall have leave.

FOURTH PLEBEIAN. A ring! Stand round.

FIRST PLEBEIAN. Stand from the hearse, stand from the body.

SECOND PLEBEIAN. Room for Antony, most noble Antony!

ANTONY. Nay, press not so upon me; stand far off.

ALL. Stand back. Room! Bear back.

ANTONY. If you have tears, prepare to shed them now.
You all do know this mantle. I remember
The first time ever Cæsar put it on;
'Twas on a summer's evening, in his tent,
That day he overcame the Nervii.
Look! in this place ran Cassius' dagger through;
See what a rent the envious Casca made;
Through this the well-beloved Brutus stabb'd,
And as he pluck'd his cursed steel away,
Mark how the blood of Cæsar follow'd it,
As rushing out of doors, to be resolv'd
If Brutus so unkindly knock'd or no;
For Brutus, as you know, was Cæsar's angel.
Judge, O you gods, how dearly Cæsar lov'd him!
This was the most unkindest cut of all;
For when the noble Cæsar saw him stab,
Ingratitude, more strong than traitors' arms,
Quite vanquish'd him. Then burst his mighty heart;
And in his mantle muffling up his face,
Even at the base of Pompey's statua,
Which all the while ran blood, great Cæsar fell.
O, what a fall was there, my countrymen!

Then I, and you, and all of us fell down,
Whilst bloody treason flourish'd over us.
O, now you weep, and I perceive you feel
The dint of pity. These are gracious drops.
Kind souls, what weep you when you but behold
Our Cæsar's vesture wounded? Look you here,
Here is himself, marr'd as you see with traitors.

FIRST PLEBEIAN. O piteous spectacle!

SECOND PLEBEIAN. O noble Cæsar!

THIRD PLEBEIAN. O woeful day!

FOURTH PLEBEIAN. O traitors, villains!

FIRST PLEBEIAN. O most bloody sight!

SECOND PLEBEIAN. We will be reveng'd.

ALL. Revenge! About! Seek! Burn! Fire! Kill! Slay! Let not a traitor live!

ANTONY. Stay, countrymen.

FIRST PLEBEIAN. Peace there! Hear the noble Antony.

SECOND PLEBEIAN. We'll hear him, we'll follow him, we'll die with him.

ANTONY. Good friends, sweet friends, let me not stir you up
To such a sudden flood of mutiny.
They that have done this deed are honourable.
What private griefs they have, alas, I know not,
That made them do it; they are wise and honourable,
And will, no doubt, with reasons answer you.
I come not, friends, to steal away your hearts;
I am no orator, as Brutus is,
But, as you know me all, a plain blunt man,
That love my friend; and that they know full well
That gave me public leave to speak of him.
For I have neither wit, nor words, nor worth,
Action, nor utterance, nor the power of speech,
To stir men's blood; I only speak right on.
I tell you that which you yourselves do know;
Show you sweet Cæsar's wounds, poor poor dumb mouths,
And bid them speak for me. But were I Brutus,
And Brutus Antony, there were an Antony
Would ruffle up your spirits, and put a tongue
In every wound of Cæsar, that should move
The stones of Rome to rise and mutiny.

ALL. We'll mutiny.
FIRST PLEBEIAN. We'll burn the house of Brutus.
THIRD PLEBEIAN. Away, then! Come seek the conspirators.
ANTONY. Yet hear me, countrymen; yet hear me speak.
ALL. Peace, ho! Hear Antony, most noble Antony.
ANTONY. Why, friends, you go to do you know not what.
Wherein hath Cæsar thus deserv'd your loves?
Alas, you know not! I must tell you, then:
You have forgot the will I told you of.
ALL. Most true. The will! Let's stay and hear the will.
ANTONY. Here is the will, and under Cæsar's seal:
To every Roman citizen he gives,
To every several man, seventy-five drachmas.
SECOND PLEBEIAN. Most noble Cæsar! We'll revenge his death.
THIRD PLEBEIAN. O royal Cæsar!
ANTONY. Hear me with patience.
ALL. Peace, ho!
ANTONY. Moreover, he hath left you all his walks,
His private arbours, and new-planted orchards,
On this side Tiber; he hath left them you,
And to your heirs for ever—common pleasures,
To walk abroad and recreate yourselves.
Here was a Cæsar! When comes such another?
FIRST PLEBEIAN. Never, never! Come away, away!
We'll burn his body in the holy place,
And with the brands fire the traitors' houses.
Take up the body.
SECOND PLEBEIAN. Go, fetch fire.
THIRD PLEBEIAN. Pluck down benches.
FOURTH PLEBEIAN. Pluck down forms, windows, any thing.
Exeunt plebeians with the body
ANTONY. Now let it work. Mischief, thou art afoot,
Take thou what course thou wilt.

Enter a SERVANT

How now, fellow!
SERVANT. Sir, Octavius is already come to Rome.
ANTONY. Where is he?
SERVANT. He and Lepidus are at Cæsar's house.

ANTONY. And thither will I straight to visit him.
He comes upon a wish. Fortune is merry,
And in this mood will give us any thing.
SERVANT. I heard him say Brutus and Cassius
Are rid like madmen through the gates of Rome.
ANTONY. Belike they had some notice of the people,
How I had mov'd them. Bring me to Octavius. *Exeunt*

SCENE 3

Rome. A street

Enter CINNA *the poet, and after him the plebeians*

CINNA. I dreamt to-night that I did feast with Cæsar,
And things unluckily charge my fantasy.
I have no will to wander forth of doors,
Yet something leads me forth.
FIRST PLEBEIAN. What is your name?
SECOND PLEBEIAN. Whither are you going?
THIRD PLEBEIAN. Where do you dwell?
FOURTH PLEBEIAN. Are you a married man or a bachelor?
SECOND PLEBEIAN. Answer every man directly.
FIRST PLEBEIAN. Ay, and briefly.
FOURTH PLEBEIAN. Ay, and wisely.
THIRD PLEBEIAN. Ay, and truly, you were best.
CINNA. What is my name? Whither am I going? Where do I dwell? Am I a married man or a bachelor? Then to answer every man directly and briefly, wisely and truly: wisely, I say I am a bachelor.
SECOND PLEBEIAN. That's as much as to say they are fools that marry. You'll bear me a bang for that, I fear. Proceed directly.
CINNA. Directly, I am going to Cæsar's funeral.
FIRST PLEBEIAN. As a friend or an enemy?
CINNA. As a friend.
SECOND PLEBEIAN. That matter is answered directly.
FOURTH PLEBEIAN. For your dwelling—briefly.
CINNA. Briefly, I dwell by the Capitol.

THIRD PLEBEIAN. Your name, sir, truly.

CINNA. Truly, my name is Cinna.

FIRST PLEBEIAN. Tear him to pieces; he's a conspirator!

CINNA. I am Cinna the poet, I am Cinna the poet.

FOURTH PLEBEIAN. Tear him for his bad verses, tear him for his bad verses!

CINNA. I am not Cinna the conspirator.

FOURTH PLEBEIAN. It is no matter, his name's Cinna; pluck but his name out of his heart, and turn him going.

THIRD PLEBEIAN. Tear him, tear him! Come, brands, ho! fire-brands! To Brutus', to Cassius'! Burn all! Some to Decius' house, and some to Casca's; some to Ligarius'. Away, go! *Exeunt all the plebeians with* CINNA

ACT IV. SCENE 1

Rome. ANTONY'S *house*

Enter ANTONY, OCTAVIUS, *and* LEPIDUS

ANTONY. These many, then, shall die; their names are prick'd.

OCTAVIUS. Your brother too must die. Consent you, Lepidus?

LEPIDUS. I do consent.

OCTAVIUS. Prick him down, Antony.

LEPIDUS. Upon condition Publius shall not live,
Who is your sister's son, Mark Antony.

ANTONY. He shall not live; look, with a spot I damn him.
But, Lepidus, go you to Cæsar's house;
Fetch the will hither, and we shall determine
How to cut off some charge in legacies.

LEPIDUS. What, shall I find you here?

OCTAVIUS. Or here or at the Capitol. *Exit* LEPIDUS

ANTONY. This is a slight unmeritable man,
Meet to be sent on errands. Is it fit,
The threefold world divided, he should stand
One of the three to share it?

OCTAVIUS. So you thought him,

And took his voice who should be prick'd to die
In our black sentence and proscription.

ANTONY. Octavius, I have seen more days than you;
And though we lay these honours on this man,
To ease ourselves of divers sland'rous loads,
He shall but bear them as the ass bears gold,
To groan and sweat under the business,
Either led or driven as we point the way;
And having brought our treasure where we will,
Then take we down his load, and turn him off,
Like to the empty ass, to shake his ears
And graze in commons.

OCTAVIUS. You may do your will;
But he's a tried and valiant soldier.

ANTONY. So is my horse, Octavius, and for that
I do appoint him store of provender.
It is a creature that I teach to fight,
To wind, to stop, to run directly on,
His corporal motion govern'd by my spirit.
And, in some taste, is Lepidus but so:
He must be taught, and train'd, and bid go forth
A barren-spirited fellow; one that feeds
On abjects, orts, and imitations,
Which, out of use and stal'd by other men,
Begin his fashion. Do not talk of him
But as a property. And now, Octavius,
Listen great things: Brutus and Cassius
Are levying powers; we must straight make head;
Therefore let our alliance be combin'd,
Our best friends made, our means stretch'd;
And let us presently go sit in council,
How covert matters may be best disclos'd,
And open perils surest answered.

OCTAVIUS. Let us do so; for we are at the stake,
And bay'd about with many enemies;
And some that smile have in their hearts, I fear,
Millions of mischiefs. *Exeunt*

SCENE 2

The Camp near Sardis. Before the tent of BRUTUS

Drum. Enter BRUTUS, LUCILIUS, LUCIUS, *and the army.*
TITINIUS *and* PINDARUS *meet them*

BRUTUS. Stand, ho!
LUCILIUS. Give the word, ho! and stand.
BRUTUS. What now, Lucilius? Is Cassius near?
LUCILIUS. He is at hand, and Pindarus is come
To do you salutation from his master.
BRUTUS. He greets me well. Your master, Pindarus,
In his own change, or by ill officers,
Hath given me some worthy cause to wish
Things done undone; but if he be at hand
I shall be satisfied.
PINDARUS. I do not doubt
But that my noble master will appear
Such as he is, full of regard and honour.
BRUTUS. He is not doubted. A word, Lucilius,
How he receiv'd you; let me be resolv'd.
LUCILIUS. With courtesy and with respect enough,
But not with such familiar instances
Nor with such free and friendly conference
As he hath us'd of old.
BRUTUS. Thou has describ'd
A hot friend cooling. Ever note, Lucilius,
When love begins to sicken and decay,
It useth an enforced ceremony.
There are no tricks in plain and simple faith;
But hollow men, like horses hot at hand,
Make gallant show and promise of their mettle;
But when they should endure the bloody spur,
They fall their crests, and like deceitful jades
Sink in the trial. Comes his army on?
LUCILIUS. They mean this night in Sardis to be quarter'd.
The greater part, the horse in general,
Are come with Cassius. [*Low march within*]
BRUTUS. Hark! he is arriv'd:

March gently on to meet him.

Enter CASSIUS *and his powers*

CASSIUS. Stand, ho!
BRUTUS. Stand, ho! Speak the word along.
FIRST SOLDIER. Stand!
SECOND SOLDIER. Stand!
THIRD SOLDIER. Stand!
CASSIUS. Most noble brother, you have done me wrong.
BRUTUS. Judge me, you gods! wrong I mine enemies?
And, if not so, how should I wrong a brother?
CASSIUS. Brutus, this sober form of yours hides wrongs;
And when you do them—
BRUTUS. Cassius, be content;
Speak your griefs softly; I do know you well.
Before the eyes of both our armies here,
Which should perceive nothing but love from us,
Let us not wrangle. Bid them move away;
Then in my tent, Cassius, enlarge your griefs,
And I will give you audience.
CASSIUS. Pindarus,
Bid our commanders lead their charges off
A little from this ground.
BRUTUS. Lucilius, do you the like; and let no man
Come to our tent till we have done our conference.
Let Lucius and Titinius guard our door. *Exeunt*

SCENE 3

The Camp near Sardis. Within the tent of BRUTUS

Enter BRUTUS *and* CASSIUS

CASSIUS. That you have wrong'd me doth appear in this:
You have condemn'd and noted Lucius Pella
For taking bribes here of the Sardians;
Wherein my letters, praying on his side,
Because I knew the man, were slighted off.
BRUTUS. You wrong'd yourself to write in such a case.
CASSIUS. In such a time as this it is not meet

That every nice offence should bear his comment.
BRUTUS. Let me tell you, Cassius, you yourself
Are much condemn'd to have an itching palm,
To sell and mart your offices for gold
To undeservers.
CASSIUS. I an itching palm!
You know that you are Brutus that speaks this,
Or, by the gods, this speech were else your last.
BRUTUS. The name of Cassius honours this corruption,
And chastisement doth therefore hide his head.
CASSIUS. Chastisement!
BRUTUS. Remember March, the ides of March remember:
Did not great Julius bleed for justice sake?
What villain touch'd his body, that did stab,
And not for justice? What, shall one of us,
That struck the foremost man of all this world
But for supporting robbers, shall we now
Contaminate our fingers with base bribes,
And sell the mighty space of our large honours
For so much trash as may be grasped thus?
I had rather be a dog and bay the moon
Than such a Roman.
CASSIUS. Brutus, bait not me!
I'll not endure it. You forget yourself,
To hedge me in. I am a soldier, I,
Older in practice, abler than yourself
To make conditions.
BRUTUS. Go to; you are not, Cassius.
CASSIUS. I am.
BRUTUS. I say you are not.
CASSIUS. Urge me no more, I shall forget myself;
Have mind upon your health, tempt me no farther.
BRUTUS. Away, slight man!
CASSIUS. Is't possible?
BRUTUS. Hear me, for I will speak.
Must I give way and room to your rash choler?
Shall I be frighted when a madman stares?
CASSIUS. O ye gods, ye gods! must I endure all this?
BRUTUS. All this? Ay, more! Fret till your proud heart break.

Go show your slaves how choleric you are,
And make your bondmen tremble. Must I budge?
Must I observe you? Must I stand and crouch
Under your testy humour? By the gods,
You shall digest the venom of your spleen
Though it do split you; for from this day forth
I'll use you for my mirth, yea, for my laughter,
When you are waspish.

CASSIUS. Is it come to this?

BRUTUS. You say you are a better soldier.
Let it appear so; make your vaunting true,
And it shall please me well. For mine own part,
I shall be glad to learn of noble men.

CASSIUS. You wrong me every way; you wrong me, Brutus;
I said an elder soldier, not a better.
Did I say 'better'?

BRUTUS. If you did, I care not.

CASSIUS. When Cæsar liv'd, he durst not thus have mov'd me.

BRUTUS. Peace, peace! You durst not so have tempted him.

CASSIUS. I durst not?

BRUTUS. No.

CASSIUS. What, durst not tempt him?

BRUTUS. For your life you durst not.

CASSIUS. Do not presume too much upon my love;
I may do that I shall be sorry for.

BRUTUS. You have done that you should be sorry for.
There is no terror, Cassius, in your threats;
For I am arm'd so strong in honesty
That they pass by me as the idle wind,
Which I respect not. I did send to you
For certain sums of gold, which you denied me;
For I can raise no money by vile means.
By heaven, I had rather coin my heart,
And drop my blood for drachmas, than to wring
From the hard hands of peasants their vile trash
By any indirection. I did send
To you for gold to pay my legions,
Which you denied me; was that done like Cassius?
Should I have answer'd Caius Cassius so?
When Marcus Brutus grows so covetous,

To lock such rascal counters from his friends,
Be ready, gods, with all your thunderbolts,
Dash him to pieces!
CASSIUS. I denied you not.
BRUTUS. You did.
CASSIUS. I did not. He was but a fool
That brought my answer back.
Brutus hath riv'd my heart.
A friend should bear his friend's infirmities,
But Brutus makes mine greater than they are.
BRUTUS. I do not, till you practise them on me.
CASSIUS. You love me not.
BRUTUS. I do not like your faults.
CASSIUS. A friendly eye could never see such faults.
BRUTUS. A flatterer's would not, though they do appear
As huge as high Olympus.
CASSIUS. Come, Antony, and young Octavius, come,
Revenge yourselves alone on Cassius,
For Cassius is aweary of the world:
Hated by one he loves; brav'd by his brother;
Check'd like a bondman; all his faults observ'd,
Set in a notebook, learn'd, and conn'd by rote,
To cast into my teeth. O, I could weep
My spirit from mine eyes! There is my dagger,
And here my naked breast; within, a heart
Dearer than Plutus' mine, richer than gold;
If that thou be'st a Roman, take it forth.
I, that denied thee gold, will give my heart.
Strike as thou didst at Cæsar; for I know,
When thou didst hate him worst, thou lov'dst him better
Than ever thou lov'dst Cassius.
BRUTUS. Sheathe your dagger.
Be angry when you will, it shall have scope;
Do what you will, dishonour shall be humour.
O Cassius, you are yoked with a lamb,
That carries anger as the flint bears fire;
Who, much enforced, shows a hasty spark,
And straight is cold again.
CASSIUS. Hath Cassius liv'd
To be but mirth and laughter to his Brutus,

When grief and blood ill-temper'd vexeth him?
BRUTUS. When I spoke that I was ill-temper'd too.
CASSIUS. Do you confess so much? Give me your hand.
BRUTUS. And my heart too.
CASSIUS. O Brutus!
BRUTUS. What's the matter?
CASSIUS. Have not you love enough to bear with me,
When that rash humour which my mother gave me
Makes me forgetful?
BRUTUS. Yes, Cassius; and from henceforth,
When you are over-earnest with your Brutus,
He'll think your mother chides, and leave you so.

Enter a POET, *followed by* LUCILIUS, TITINIUS, *and* LUCIUS

POET. Let me go in to see the generals.
There is some grudge between 'em; 'tis not meet
They be alone.
LUCILIUS. You shall not come to them.
POET. Nothing but death shall stay me.
CASSIUS. How now! What's the matter?
POET. For shame, you generals! What do you mean?
Love, and be friends, as two such men should be;
For I have seen more years, I'm sure, than ye.
CASSIUS. Ha, ha! How vilely doth this cynic rhyme!
BRUTUS. Get you hence, sirrah; saucy fellow, hence!
CASSIUS. Bear with him, Brutus: 'tis his fashion.
BRUTUS. I'll know his humour when he knows his time.
What should the wars do with these jigging fools?
Companion, hence!
CASSIUS. Away, away, be gone! *Exit* POET
BRUTUS. Lucilius and Titinius, bid the commanders
Prepare to lodge their companies to-night.
CASSIUS. And come yourselves, and bring Messala with you
Immediately to us. *Exeunt* LUCILIUS *and* TITINIUS
BRUTUS. Lucius, a bowl of wine! *Exit* LUCIUS
CASSIUS. I did not think you could have been so angry.
BRUTUS. O Cassius, I am sick of many griefs!
CASSIUS. Of your philosophy you make no use,
If you give place to accidental evils.

BRUTUS. No man bears sorrow better. Portia is dead.
CASSIUS. Ha! Portia?
BRUTUS. She is dead.
CASSIUS. How scap'd I killing when I cross'd you so?
O insupportable and touching loss!
Upon what sickness?
BRUTUS. Impatient of my absence,
And grief that young Octavius with Mark Antony
Have made themselves so strong; for with her death
That tidings came. With this she fell distract,
And, her attendants absent, swallow'd fire.
CASSIUS. And died so?
BRUTUS. Even so.
CASSIUS. O ye immortal gods!

Enter LUCIUS *with wine and tapers*

BRUTUS. Speak no more of her. Give me a bowl of wine.
In this I bury all unkindness, Cassius. [*Drinks*]
CASSIUS. My heart is thirsty for that noble pledge.
Fill, Lucius, till the wine o'erswell the cup;
I cannot drink too much of Brutus' love. [*Drinks*]
Exit LUCIUS

Re-enter TITINIUS, *with* MESSALA

BRUTUS. Come in, Titinius! Welcome, good Messala!
Now sit we close about this taper here,
And call in question our necessities.
CASSIUS. Portia, art thou gone?
BRUTUS. No more, I pray you.
Messala, I have here received letters,
That young Octavius and Mark Antony
Come down upon us with a mighty power,
Bending their expedition toward Philippi.
MESSALA. Myself have letters of the self-same tenour.
BRUTUS. With what addition?
MESSALA. That, by proscription and bills of outlawry,
Octavius, Antony, and Lepidus,
Have put to death an hundred senators.
BRUTUS. Therein our letters do not well agree;

Mine speak of seventy senators that died
By their proscriptions, Cicero being one.
CASSIUS. Cicero one!
MESSALA. Cicero is dead,
And by that order of proscription.
Had you your letters from your wife, my lord?
BRUTUS. No, Messala.
MESSALA. Nor nothing in your letters writ of her?
BRUTUS. Nothing, Messala.
MESSALA. That, methinks, is strange.
BRUTUS. Why ask you? Hear you aught of her in yours?
MESSALA. No, my lord.
BRUTUS. Now, as you are a Roman, tell me true.
MESSALA. Then like a Roman bear the truth I tell:
For certain she is dead, and by strange manner.
BRUTUS. Why, farewell, Portia. We must die, Messala.
With meditating that she must die once,
I have the patience to endure it now.
MESSALA. Even so great men great losses should endure.
CASSIUS. I have as much of this in art as you,
But yet my nature could not bear it so.
BRUTUS. Well, to our work alive. What do you think
Of marching to Philippi presently?
CASSIUS. I do not think it good.
BRUTUS. Your reason?
CASSIUS. This it is:
'Tis better that the enemy seek us;
So shall he waste his means, weary his soldiers,
Doing himself offence, whilst we, lying still,
Are full of rest, defence, and nimbleness.
BRUTUS. Good reasons must, of force, give place to better.
The people 'twixt Philippi and this ground
Do stand but in a forc'd affection;
For they have grudg'd us contribution.
The enemy, marching along by them,
By them shall make a fuller number up,
Come on refresh'd, new-added, and encourag'd;
From which advantage shall we cut him off,
If at Philippi we do face him there,
These people at our back.

CASSIUS. Hear me, good brother.
BRUTUS. Under your pardon. You must note beside
That we have tried the utmost of our friends,
Our legions are brim full, our cause is ripe.
The enemy increaseth every day:
We, at the height, are ready to decline.
There is a tide in the affairs of men
Which, taken at the flood, leads on to fortune;
Omitted, all the voyage of their life
Is bound in shallows and in miseries.
On such a full sea are we now afloat,
And we must take the current when it serves,
Or lose our ventures.
CASSIUS. Then, with your will, go on;
We'll along ourselves and meet them at Philippi.
BRUTUS. The deep of night is crept upon our talk,
And nature must obey necessity,
Which we will niggard with a little rest.
There is no more to say?
CASSIUS. No more. Good night:
Early to-morrow will we rise, and hence.
BRUTUS. Lucius! [*Enter* LUCIUS] My gown. [*Exit* LUCIUS]
Farewell, good Messala.
Good night, Titinius. Noble, noble Cassius,
Good night, and good repose!
CASSIUS. O my dear brother,
This was an ill beginning of the night!
Never come such division 'tween our souls!
Let it not, Brutus.
BRUTUS. Everything is well.
CASSIUS. Good night, my lord.
BRUTUS. Good night, good brother.
TITINIUS AND MESSALA. Good night, Lord Brutus.
BRUTUS. Farewell, every one.
Exeunt CASSIUS, TITINIUS, *and* MESSALA

Re-enter LUCIUS *with the gown*

Give me the gown. Where is thy instrument?
LUCIUS. Here in the tent.
BRUTUS. What, thou speak'st drowsily?

Poor knave, I blame thee not; thou art o'erwatched.
Call Claudius and some other of my men;
I'll have them sleep on cushions in my tent.

LUCIUS. Varro and Claudius!

Enter VARRO *and* CLAUDIUS

VARRO. Calls my lord?

BRUTUS. I pray you, sirs, lie in my tent and sleep;
It may be I shall raise you by and by
On business to my brother Cassius.

VARRO. So please you we will stand and watch your pleasure.

BRUTUS. I will not have it so. Lie down, good sirs;
It may be I shall otherwise bethink me.
Look, Lucius, here's the book I sought for so;
I put it in the pocket of my gown.
[VARRO *and* CLAUDIUS *lie down*]

LUCIUS. I was sure your lordship did not give it me.

BRUTUS. Bear with me, good boy, I am much forgetful.
Canst thou hold up thy heavy eyes awhile,
And touch thy instrument a strain or two?

LUCIUS. Ay, my lord, an't please you.

BRUTUS. It does, my boy.
I trouble thee too much, but thou art willing.

LUCIUS. It is my duty, sir.

BRUTUS. I should not urge thy duty past thy might;
I know young bloods look for a time of rest.

LUCIUS. I have slept, my lord, already.

BRUTUS. It was well done; and thou shalt sleep again;
I will not hold thee long. If I do live,
I will be good to thee.
[*Music and a song.* LUCIUS *falls asleep*]
This is a sleepy tune. O murd'rous slumber!
Layest thou thy leaden mace upon my boy,
That plays thee music? Gentle knave, good night.
I will not do thee so much wrong to wake thee.
If thou dost nod, thou break'st thy instrument;
I'll take it from thee: and, good boy, good night.
Let me see, let me see; is not the leaf turn'd down
Where I left reading? Here it is, I think. [*Sits down*]

Enter the GHOST *of* CÆSAR

How ill this taper burns! Ha! who comes here?
I think it is the weakness of mine eyes
That shapes this monstrous apparition.
It comes upon me. Art thou any thing?
Art thou some god, some angel, or some devil,
That mak'st my blood cold and my hair to stare?
Speak to me what thou art.

GHOST. Thy evil spirit, Brutus.

BRUTUS. Why com'st thou?

GHOST. To tell thee thou shalt see me at Philippi.

BRUTUS. Well; then I shall see thee again?

GHOST. Ay, at Philippi.

BRUTUS. Why, I will see thee at Philippi, then. *Exit* GHOST
Now I have taken heart thou vanishest.
Ill spirit, I would hold more talk with thee.
Boy! Lucius! Varro! Claudius! Sirs, awake!
Claudius!

LUCIUS. The strings, my lord, are false.

BRUTUS. He thinks he still is at his instrument.
Lucius, awake!

LUCIUS. My lord!

BRUTUS. Didst thou dream, Lucius, that thou so criedst out?

LUCIUS. My lord, I do not know that I did cry.

BRUTUS. Yes, that thou didst. Didst thou see any thing?

LUCIUS. Nothing, my lord.

BRUTUS. Sleep again, Lucius. Sirrah Claudius!
[*To* VARRO] Fellow thou, awake!

VARRO. My lord?

CLAUDIUS. My lord?

BRUTUS. Why did you so cry out, sirs, in your sleep?

BOTH. Did we, my lord?

BRUTUS. Ay. Saw you any thing?

VARRO. No, my lord, I saw nothing.

CLAUDIUS. Nor I, my lord.

BRUTUS. Go and commend me to my brother Cassius;
Bid him set on his pow'rs betimes before,
And we will follow.

VARRO AND CLAUDIUS. It shall be done, my lord. *Exeunt*

ACT V. SCENE 1

Near Philippi

Enter OCTAVIUS, ANTONY, *and their army*

OCTAVIUS. Now, Antony, our hopes are answered.
You said the enemy would not come down,
But keep the hills and upper regions;
It proves not so. Their battles are at hand;
They mean to warn us at Philippi here,
Answering before we do demand of them.

ANTONY. Tut, I am in their bosoms, and I know
Wherefore they do it. They could be content
To visit other places, and come down
With fearful bravery, thinking by this face
To fasten in our thoughts that they have courage;
But 'tis not so.

Enter a MESSENGER

MESSENGER. Prepare you, generals:
The enemy comes on in gallant show;
Their bloody sign of battle is hung out,
And something to be done immediately.

ANTONY. Octavius, lead your battle softly on,
Upon the left hand of the even field.

OCTAVIUS. Upon the right hand I: keep thou the left.

ANTONY. Why do you cross me in this exigent?

OCTAVIUS. I do not cross you; but I will do so. [*March*]

Drum. Enter BRUTUS, CASSIUS, *and their army;*
LUCILIUS, TITINIUS, MESSALA, *and others*

BRUTUS. They stand, and would have parley.

CASSIUS. Stand fast, Titinius; we must out and talk.

OCTAVIUS. Mark Antony, shall we give sign of battle?

ANTONY. No, Cæsar, we will answer on their charge.
Make forth; the generals would have some words.

OCTAVIUS. Stir not until the signal.

BRUTUS. Words before blows. Is it so, countrymen?

OCTAVIUS. Not that we love words better, as you do.

BRUTUS. Good words are better than bad strokes, Octavius.
ANTONY. In your bad strokes, Brutus, you give good words;
Witness the hole you made in Cæsar's heart,
Crying 'Long live! Hail, Cæsar!'
CASSIUS. Antony,
The posture of your blows are yet unknown;
But for your words, they rob the Hybla bees,
And leave them honeyless.
ANTONY. Not stingless too?
BRUTUS. O yes, and soundless too;
For you have stol'n their buzzing, Antony,
And very wisely threat before you sting.
ANTONY. Villains, you did not so when your vile daggers
Hack'd one another in the sides of Cæsar.
You show'd your teeth like apes, and fawn'd like hounds,
And bow'd like bondmen, kissing Cæsar's feet;
Whilst damned Casca, like a cur, behind
Struck Cæsar on the neck. O you flatterers!
CASSIUS. Flatterers! Now, Brutus, thank yourself:
This tongue had not offended so to-day
If Cassius might have rul'd.
OCTAVIUS. Come, come, the cause. If arguing make us sweat,
The proof of it will turn to redder drops.
Look,
I draw a sword against conspirators;
When think you that the sword goes up again?
Never till Cæsar's three and thirty wounds
Be well aveng'd, or till another Cæsar
Have added slaughter to the sword of traitors.
BRUTUS. Cæsar, thou canst not die by traitors' hands,
Unless thou bring'st them with thee.
OCTAVIUS. So I hope.
I was not born to die on Brutus' sword.
BRUTUS. O, if thou wert the noblest of thy strain,
Young man, thou couldst not die more honourable.
CASSIUS. A peevish schoolboy, worthless of such honour,
Join'd with a masker and a reveller!
ANTONY. Old Cassius still!
OCTAVIUS. Come, Antony; away!
Defiance, traitors, hurl we in your teeth.

If you dare fight to-day, come to the field;
If not, when you have stomachs.

Exeunt OCTAVIUS, ANTONY, *and their army*

CASSIUS. Why, now, blow wind, swell billow, and swim bark!
The storm is up, and all is on the hazard.

BRUTUS. Ho, Lucilius! hark, a word with you.

LUCILIUS. My lord. [BRUTUS *and* LUCILIUS *converse apart*]

CASSIUS. Messala.

MESSALA. What says my general?

CASSIUS. Messala,
This is my birth-day; as this very day
Was Cassius born. Give me thy hand, Messala.
Be thou my witness that against my will,
As Pompey was, am I compell'd to set
Upon one battle all our liberties.
You know that I held Epicurus strong,
And his opinion; now I change my mind,
And partly credit things that do presage.
Coming from Sardis, on our former ensign
Two mighty eagles fell; and there they perch'd,
Gorging and feeding from our soldiers' hands,
Who to Philippi here consorted us.
This morning are they fled away and gone,
And in their steads do ravens, crows, and kites,
Fly o'er our heads and downward look on us
As we were sickly prey. Their shadows seem
A canopy most fatal, under which
Our army lies, ready to give up the ghost.

MESSALA. Believe not so.

CASSIUS. I but believe it partly;
For I am fresh of spirit and resolv'd
To meet all perils very constantly.

BRUTUS. Even so, Lucilius.

CASSIUS. Now, most noble Brutus,
The gods to-day stand friendly, that we may,
Lovers in peace, lead on our days to age!
But, since the affairs of men rest still incertain,
Let's reason with the worst that may befall.
If we do lose this battle, then is this

The very last time we shall speak together.
What are you then determined to do?
BRUTUS. Even by the rule of that philosophy
By which I did blame Cato for the death
Which he did give himself—I know not how,
But I do find it cowardly and vile,
For fear of what might fall, so to prevent
The time of life—arming myself with patience
To stay the providence of some high powers
That govern us below.
CASSIUS. Then, if we lose this battle,
You are contented to be led in triumph
Thorough the streets of Rome?
BRUTUS. No, Cassius, no. Think not, thou noble Roman,
That ever Brutus will go bound to Rome;
He bears too great a mind. But this same day
Must end that work the ides of March begun,
And whether we shall meet again I know not.
Therefore our everlasting farewell take:
For ever and for ever farewell, Cassius!
If we do meet again, why, we shall smile;
If not, why then this parting was well made.
CASSIUS. For ever and for ever farewell, Brutus!
If we do meet again, we'll smile indeed;
If not, 'tis true this parting was well made.
BRUTUS. Why then, lead on. O that a man might know
The end of this day's business ere it come!
But it sufficeth that the day will end,
And then the end is known. Come, ho! away! *Exeunt*

SCENE 2

Near Philippi. The field of battle

Alarum. Enter BRUTUS *and* MESSALA

BRUTUS. Ride, ride, Messala, ride, and give these bills
Unto the legions on the other side. [*Loud alarum*]
Let them set on at once; for I perceive
But cold demeanour in Octavius' wing,

And sudden push gives them the overthrow.
Ride, ride, Messala; let them all come down. *Exeunt*

SCENE 3

Another part of the field

Alarums. Enter CASSIUS *and* TITINIUS

CASSIUS. O, look, Titinius, look, the villains fly!
Myself have to mine own turn'd enemy.
This ensign here of mine was turning back;
I slew the coward, and did take it from him.
TITINIUS. O Cassius, Brutus gave the word too early,
Who, having some advantage on Octavius,
Took it too eagerly. His soldiers fell to spoil,
Whilst we by Antony are all enclos'd.

Enter PINDARUS

PINDARUS. Fly further off, my lord, fly further off;
Mark Antony is in your tents, my lord;
Fly, therefore, noble Cassius, fly far off.
CASSIUS. This hill is far enough. Look, look, Titinius.
Are those my tents where I perceive the fire?
TITINIUS. They are, my lord.
CASSIUS. Titinius, if thou lovest me,
Mount thou my horse and hide thy spurs in him,
Till he have brought thee up to yonder troops
And here again, that I may rest assur'd
Whether yond troops are friend or enemy.
TITINIUS. I will be here again even with a thought. *Exit*
CASSIUS. Go, Pindarus, get higher on that hill;
My sight was ever thick; regard Titinius,
And tell me what thou not'st about the field.
[PINDARUS *goes up*]
This day I breathed first. Time is come round,
And where I did begin there shall I end;
My life is run his compass. Sirrah, what news?
PINDARUS. [*Above*] O my lord!
CASSIUS. What news?

PINDARUS. Titinius is enclosed round about
With horsemen that make to him on the spur;
Yet he spurs on. Now they are almost on him.
Now Titinius! Now some light. O, he lights too!
He's ta'en. [*Shout*]
And hark! They shout for joy.
CASSIUS. Come down; behold no more.
O, coward that I am to live so long
To see my best friend ta'en before my face!

Enter PINDARUS

Come hither, sirrah.
In Parthia did I take thee prisoner;
And then I swore thee, saving of thy life,
That whatsoever I did bid thee do
Thou shouldst attempt it. Come now, keep thine oath;
Now be a freeman, and with this good sword,
That ran through Cæsar's bowels, search this bosom.
Stand not to answer; here, take thou the hilts;
And when my face is cover'd, as 'tis now,
Guide thou the sword. [PINDARUS *stabs him*]
Cæsar, thou art reveng'd,
Even with the sword that kill'd thee. [*Dies*]
PINDARUS. So, I am free; yet would not so have been,
Durst I have done my will. O Cassius!
Far from this country Pindarus shall run,
Where never Roman shall take note of him. *Exit*

Re-enter TITINIUS, *with* MESSALA

MESSALA. It is but change, Titinius; for Octavius
Is overthrown by noble Brutus' power,
As Cassius' legions are by Antony.
TITINIUS. These tidings will well comfort Cassius.
MESSALA. Where did you leave him?
TITINIUS. All disconsolate,
With Pindarus, his bondman, on this hill.
MESSALA. Is not that he that lies upon the ground?
TITINIUS. He lies not like the living. O my heart!
MESSALA. Is not that he?
TITINIUS. No, this was he, Messala;

But Cassius is no more. O setting sun,
As in thy red rays thou dost sink to night,
So in his red blood Cassius' day is set!
The sun of Rome is set. Our day is gone;
Clouds, dews, and dangers come; our deeds are done.
Mistrust of my success hath done this deed.

MESSALA. Mistrust of good success hath done this deed.
O hateful error, melancholy's child,
Why dost thou show to the apt thoughts of men
The things that are not? O error, soon conceiv'd,
Thou never com'st unto a happy birth,
But kill'st the mother that engend'red thee!

TITINIUS. What, Pindarus! Where art thou, Pindarus?

MESSALA. Seek him, Titinius, whilst I go to meet
The noble Brutus, thrusting this report
Into his ears. I may say 'thrusting' it;
For piercing steel and darts envenomed
Shall be as welcome to the ears of Brutus
As tidings of this sight.

TITINIUS. Hie you, Messala,
And I will seek for Pindarus the while. *Exit* MESSALA
Why didst thou send me forth, brave Cassius?
Did I not meet thy friends, and did not they
Put on my brows this wreath of victory,
And bid me give it thee? Didst thou not hear their shouts?
Alas, thou hast misconstrued every thing!
But hold thee, take this garland on thy brow;
Thy Brutus bid me give it thee, and I
Will do his bidding. Brutus, come apace,
And see how I regarded Caius Cassius.
By your leave, gods. This is a Roman's part.
Come, Cassius' sword, and find Titinius' heart. [*Dies*]

Alarum. Re-enter MESSALA, *with* BRUTUS, YOUNG CATO, STRATO, VOLUMNIUS, *and* LUCILIUS

BRUTUS. Where, where, Messala, doth his body lie?

MESSALA. Lo yonder, and Titinius mourning it.

BRUTUS. Titinius' face is upward.

CATO. He is slain.

BRUTUS. O Julius Cæsar, thou art mighty yet!
Thy spirit walks abroad and turns our swords
In our own proper entrails. [*Low alarums*]
CATO. Brave Titinius!
Look whe'r he have not crown'd dead Cassius!
BRUTUS. Are yet two Romans living such as these?
The last of all the Romans, fare thee well!
It is impossible that ever Rome
Should breed thy fellow. Friends, I owe more tears
To this dead man than you shall see me pay.
I shall find time, Cassius, I shall find time.
Come, therefore, and to Thasos send his body.
His funerals shall not be in our camp,
Lest it discomfort us. Lucilius, come;
And come, young Cato; let us to the field.
Labeo and Flavius set our battles on.
'Tis three o'clock; and, Romans, yet ere night
We shall try fortune in a second fight. *Exeunt*

SCENE 4

Another part of the field

Alarum. Enter BRUTUS, MESSALA, YOUNG CATO, LUCILIUS, *and* FLAVIUS

BRUTUS. Yet, countrymen, O, yet hold up your heads!
CATO. What bastard doth not? Who will go with me?
I will proclaim my name about the field:
I am the son of Marcus Cato, ho!
A foe to tyrants, and my country's friend.
I am the son of Marcus Cato, ho!

Enter soldiers and fight

BRUTUS. And I am Brutus, Marcus Brutus, I!
Brutus, my country's friend! Know me for Brutus!
Exit. YOUNG CATO *falls*
LUCILIUS. O young and noble Cato, art thou down?
Why, now thou diest as bravely as Titinius,
And mayst be honour'd, being Cato's son.

FIRST SOLDIER. Yield, or thou diest.
LUCILIUS. Only I yield to die.
[*Offering money*] There is so much that thou wilt kill me straight.
Kill Brutus, and be honour'd in his death.
FIRST SOLDIER. We must not. A noble prisoner!

Enter ANTONY

SECOND SOLDIER. Room, ho! Tell Antony Brutus is ta'en.
FIRST SOLDIER. I'll tell the news. Here comes the general.
Brutus is ta'en! Brutus is ta'en, my lord!
ANTONY. Where is he?
LUCILIUS. Safe, Antony; Brutus is safe enough.
I dare assure thee that no enemy
Shall ever take alive the noble Brutus.
The gods defend him from so great a shame!
When you do find him, or alive or dead,
He will be found like Brutus, like himself.
ANTONY. This is not Brutus, friend; but, I assure you,
A prize no less in worth. Keep this man safe;
Give him all kindness. I had rather have
Such men my friends than enemies. Go on,
And see whe'r Brutus be alive or dead;
And bring us word unto Octavius' tent
How everything is chanc'd. *Exeunt*

SCENE 5

Another part of the field

Enter BRUTUS, DARDANIUS, CLITUS, STRATO, *and* VOLUMNIUS

BRUTUS. Come, poor remains of friends, rest on this rock.
CLITUS. Statilius show'd the torch-light; but, my lord,
He came not back. He is or ta'en or slain.
BRUTUS. Sit thee down, Clitus. Slaying is the word;
It is a deed in fashion. Hark thee, Clitus. [*Whispering*]
CLITUS. What, I, my lord? No, not for all the world.
BRUTUS. Peace, then, no words.

CLITUS. I'll rather kill myself.
BRUTUS. Hark thee, Dardanius!
DARDANIUS. Shall I do such a deed?
CLITUS. O Dardanius!
DARDANIUS. O Clitus!
CLITUS. What ill request did Brutus make to thee?
DARDANIUS. To kill him, Clitus. Look, he meditates.
CLITUS. Now is that noble vessel full of grief,
That it runs over even at his eyes.
BRUTUS. Come hither, good Volumnius; list a word.
VOLUMNIUS. What says my lord?
BRUTUS. Why, this, Volumnius:
The ghost of Cæsar hath appear'd to me
Two several times by night—at Sardis once,
And this last night here in Philippi fields.
I know my hour is come.
VOLUMNIUS. Not so, my lord.
BRUTUS. Nay, I am sure it is, Volumnius.
Thou seest the world, Volumnius, how it goes;
Our enemies have beat us to the pit; [*Low alarums*]
It is more worthy to leap in ourselves
Than tarry till they push us. Good Volumnius,
Thou know'st that we two went to school together;
Even for that our love of old, I prithee,
Hold thou my sword-hilts whilst I run on it.
VOLUMNIUS. That's not an office for a friend, my lord.
[*Alarum still*]
CLITUS. Fly, fly, my lord; there is no tarrying here.
BRUTUS. Farewell to you; and you; and you, Volumnius.
Strato, thou hast been all this while asleep;
Farewell to thee too, Strato. Countrymen,
My heart doth joy that yet in all my life
I found no man but he was true to me.
I shall have glory by this losing day,
More than Octavius and Mark Antony
By this vile conquest shall attain unto.
So fare you well at once; for Brutus' tongue
Hath almost ended his life's history.
Night hangs upon mine eyes; my bones would rest,
That have but labour'd to attain this hour.

[*Alarum. Cry within* 'Fly, fly, fly!']

CLITUS. Fly, my lord, fly.

BRUTUS. Hence! I will follow.

Exeunt CLITUS, DARDANIUS, *and* VOLUMNIUS

I prithee, Strato, stay thou by thy lord;
Thou art a fellow of a good respect;
Thy life hath had some smatch of honour in it.
Hold then my sword, and turn away thy face,
While I do run upon it. Wilt thou, Strato?

STRATO. Give me your hand first. Fare you well, my lord.

BRUTUS. Farewell, good Strato. Cæsar, now be still.
I kill'd not thee with half so good a will.

[*He runs on his sword, and dies*]

Alarum. Retreat. Enter OCTAVIUS, ANTONY, MESSALA, LUCILIUS, *and the army*

OCTAVIUS. What man is that?

MESSALA. My master's man. Strato, where is thy master?

STRATO. Free from the bondage you are in, Messala.
The conquerors can but make a fire of him;
For Brutus only overcame himself,
And no man else hath honour by his death.

LUCILIUS. So Brutus should be found. I thank thee, Brutus,
That thou hast prov'd Lucilius' saying true.

OCTAVIUS. All that serv'd Brutus, I will entertain them.
Fellow, wilt thou bestow thy time with me?

STRATO. Ay, if Messala will prefer me to you.

OCTAVIUS. Do so, good Messala.

MESSALA. How died my master, Strato?

STRATO. I held the sword, and he did run on it.

MESSALA. Octavius, then take him to follow thee,
That did the latest service to my master.

ANTONY. This was the noblest Roman of them all.
All the conspirators save only he
Did that they did in envy of great Cæsar;
He only in a general honest thought
And common good to all made one of them.
His life was gentle; and the elements
So mix'd in him that Nature might stand up
And say to all the world 'This was a man!'

Brutus. *My heart doth joy that yet in all my life*
I found no man but he was true to me.
I shall have glory by this losing day,
More than Octavius and Mark Antony
By this vile conquest shall attain unto. . . .
Cæsar, now be still.
I kill'd not thee with half so good a will.
(Act V. Scene 5)

OCTAVIUS. According to his virtue let us use him,
With all respect and rites of burial.
Within my tent his bones to-night shall lie,
Most like a soldier, ordered honourably.
So call the field to rest, and let's away
To part the glories of this happy day. *Exeunt*

The Tragedy of Macbeth

MACBETH

SHAKESPEARE may have stood in King's College Chapel, Aberdeen, and looked on the tomb of the historian from whom he was to take, by way of Holinshed, the story of Macbeth. Hector Boece, friend of Erasmus and Professor at the University of Paris, was called by Bishop Elphinstone to be the first Principal of the newly founded University of Aberdeen; and there he wrote his *Chronica Gentis Scotorum*, published in Paris in 1527. He used the Latin chronicle, written about 1385, of an earlier Aberdeen historian John de Fordun and the Scots vernacular verse chronicle of Andrew Wintoun, but incorporated history and fable in a manner that drew from Lord Hailes the jibe: "The Scots had been reformed from Popery, but not from Hector Boece." It was in 1601 that the magistrates of Aberdeen conferred on Fletcher and a company of English actors the freedom of the city, and, as Fletcher was later closely associated with Shakespeare's company, Fletcher's companions may have included members of the Chamberlain's company and Shakespeare himself. Such a visit would explain the local colour so many fancy they detect in *Macbeth*.

Two translations from Boece were made in the vernacular for James V: John Bellenden's is in prose, William Stewart's in verse; the first being published in 1540, the other remaining in manuscript till 1858. Holinshed in his turn translated Bellenden's Scots prose into English, consulting however from time to time the Latin of Boece. Bellenden's translation gives a very free rendering of Boece and contains new material; but it was Boece who introduced or invented some of the main features of the Macbeth legend. In Wintoun, a junior contemporary of Fordun, Macbeth dreams of three women (described by Wintoun as 'thre werd systrys') that foretell his progress to the throne: in Boece they have become actors in the scene who make their prophetic pronouncements not only to Macbeth but also to Banquo. Banquo is the invention of Boece, as is Fleance his son; and it is this historian who makes

Macbeth murder Lady Macduff and her children and perish in his turn at the hands of Macduff.

Shakespeare, taking up the story from Holinshed, has strengthened the shadows with which the Scottish historians had already darkened their portrait of the real King. Macbeth reigned with considerable acceptance from 1040 to 1057, when he was killed in battle at Lumphanan by Malcolm III. Macbeth had obtained the crown by killing Duncan, but of his nine predecessors only two escaped violent death, and the disposal of a weak ruler such as Duncan was at the time regarded as not unnatural, all the more so as Macbeth had a legitimate claim to the throne. According to the ancient Celtic mode of tenure called Tanistry the right of succession lay not with the individual but with the family in which it was hereditary. Duncan in naming Malcolm as his heir was introducing the later right of primogeniture. Macbeth's claim historians in after times ignored, and Shakespeare strengthens the charge against Macbeth of mere usurpation; in addition Shakespeare represents Duncan as an aged and gracious sovereign whom Macbeth kills not in open conflict but by stealth, for Shakespeare makes Macbeth murder his sovereign as some seventy years earlier Donwald, by the hands of agents, had murdered his guest King Duff.

Among Shakespeare's most important changes must be included his treatment of Banquo. In Boece that nobleman is allied with Macbeth in the killing of Duncan; Shakespeare however exonerated Banquo, who had been invented in earlier times as an ancestor of the house of Stewart, from all the complicity in the king's death. This taken in conjunction with the show of eight kings in IV,1, and the touching for the king's evil, has been regarded as dictated by the dramatist's desire to flatter King James; yet each of these episodes is an organic part of the dramatic design which takes us far beyond local and temporal interests and associations.

The heart of the matter for Shakespeare lay not in the compliments, very proper as they were, to his sovereign and patron, but in the tremendous figure that emerged from the dark and chaotic past of Scotland to confront and disturb the dramatist's imagination. Shakespeare's Macbeth is like Donwald the trusted thane who murders his king and his guest, 'though he abhorred the act greatlie in heart'; like Kenneth II who poisoned Duff's son, Macbeth hears the voice that spoke to the murderer in the night:

> Thinke not Kenneth that the wicked slaughter of Malcolme Duffe by thee contrived is kept secret from the knowledge of the eternall God . . . . even at this present are there in hand secret practises to dispatch both thee and thy issue out of the waie, that other maie injoy this Kingdome which thou doost indeuour to assure vnto thine issue.

Macbeth is the man whose force and abilities expose him in times when violence and turmoil are the prevailing conditions to temptations that it would seem cowardly to shun and that he is too much of a man to forget once he has yielded. Like her husband Lady Macbeth is a representative creation; she marshals her partner to the deed as did Donwald's wife only to discover in the end that she is too much of a woman to sustain the part she has imagined for herself. *Macbeth* is a work of the historical imagination.

Shakespeare's play may be dated by the allusions to equivocation in II,3, which were suggested by the trial on 28 March 1606 of Father Garnet the Jesuit for his part in the Gunpowder plot. *The Puritan*, of doubtful authorship, printed in 1607, has a reference to the appearance of Banquo's ghost at the feast, and as this scene in *Macbeth* was Shakespeare's invention, some time in the year 1606 may be taken as almost certainly the date of composition.

The spectacular features of the piece lent themselves to the almost operatic treatment that the play received on the Restoration stage. The songs introduced in the Folio text at III,5, and IV,1, which are also found in Middleton's *The Witch*, suggest that even before 1623 something had already been done in the direction taken by later adaptors. Modern criticism is however less ready to find in the only surviving version we have of Shakespeare's tragedy the extensive interpolation once generally taken for granted.

DUNCAN, *King of Scotland*

MALCOLM, DONALBAIN — *his sons*

MACBETH, BANQUO — *Generals of the King's army*

MACDUFF, LENNOX, ROSS, MENTEITH, ANGUS, CAITHNESS — *Noblemen of Scotland*

FLEANCE, *son to Banquo*

SIWARD, *Earl of Northumberland, General of the English forces*

YOUNG SIWARD, *his son*

SEYTON, *an officer attending on Macbeth*

BOY, *son to Macduff*

A SERGEANT

A PORTER

AN OLD MAN

AN ENGLISH DOCTOR

A SCOTS DOCTOR

LADY MACBETH

LADY MACDUFF

GENTLEWOMAN *attending on Lady Macbeth*

THE WEIRD SISTERS

HECATE

THE GHOST *of Banquo*

Apparitions

Lords, Gentlemen, Officers, Soldiers, Murderers, Attendants, *and* Messengers

SCENE:

Scotland and England

Macbeth

ACT I. SCENE 1

An open place

Thunder and lightning. Enter three WITCHES

FIRST WITCH. When shall we three meet again?
In thunder, lightning, or in rain?
SECOND WITCH. When the hurlyburly's done,
When the battle's lost and won.
THIRD WITCH. That will be ere the set of sun.
FIRST WITCH. Where the place?
SECOND WITCH. Upon the heath.
THIRD WITCH. There to meet with Macbeth.
FIRST WITCH. I come, Graymalkin.
SECOND WITCH. Paddock calls.
THIRD WITCH. Anon!
ALL. Fair is foul, and foul is fair:
Hover through the fog and filthy air. WITCHES *vanish*

SCENE 2

A camp near Forres

Alarum within. Enter KING DUNCAN, MALCOLM, DONALBAIN, LENNOX, *with attendants, meeting a bleeding* SERGEANT

DUNCAN. What bloody man is that? He can report,
As seemeth by his plight, of the revolt
The newest state.
MALCOLM. This is the sergeant
Who like a good and hardy soldier fought
'Gainst my captivity. Hail, brave friend!
Say to the King the knowledge of the broil
As thou didst leave it.
SERGEANT. Doubtful it stood,

As two spent swimmers that do cling together
And choke their art. The merciless Macdonwald—
Worthy to be a rebel, for to that
The multiplying villainies of nature
Do swarm upon him—from the Western Isles
Of kerns and gallowglasses is supplied;
And Fortune, on his damned quarrel smiling,
Show'd like a rebel's whore. But all's too weak;
For brave Macbeth—well he deserves that name—
Disdaining Fortune, with his brandish'd steel
Which smok'd with bloody execution,
Like valour's minion, carv'd out his passage
Till he fac'd the slave;
Which ne'er shook hands, nor bade farewell to him,
Till he unseam'd him from the nave to th' chaps,
And fix'd his head upon our battlements.

DUNCAN. O valiant cousin! worthy gentleman!

SERGEANT. As whence the sun gins his reflection
Shipwrecking storms and direful thunders break,
So from that spring whence comfort seem'd to come
Discomfort swells. Mark, King of Scotland, mark:
No sooner justice had, with valour arm'd,
Compell'd these skipping kerns to trust their heels,
But the Norweyan lord, surveying vantage,
With furbish'd arms and new supplies of men,
Began a fresh assault.

DUNCAN. Dismay'd not this
Our captains, Macbeth and Banquo?

SERGEANT. Yes;
As sparrows eagles, or the hare the lion.
If I say sooth, I must report they were
As cannons overcharg'd with double cracks;
So they doubly redoubled strokes upon the foe.
Except they meant to bathe in reeking wounds,
Or memorize another Golgotha,
I cannot tell—
But I am faint; my gashes cry for help.

DUNCAN. So well thy words become thee as thy wounds;
They smack of honour both.—Go get him surgeons.

Exit SERGEANT, *attended*

ACT I. SCENE 2

Enter Ross

Who comes here?
MALCOLM. The worthy Thane of Ross.
LENNOX. What a haste looks through his eyes!
So should he look that seems to speak things strange.
ROSS. God save the King!
DUNCAN. Whence cam'st thou, worthy thane?
ROSS. From Fife, great King,
Where the Norweyan banners flout the sky
And fan our people cold.
Norway himself, with terrible numbers,
Assisted by that most disloyal traitor
The Thane of Cawdor, began a dismal conflict,
Till that Bellona's bridegroom, lapp'd in proof,
Confronted him with self-comparisons,
Point against point rebellious, arm 'gainst arm,
Curbing his lavish spirit; and to conclude,
The victory fell on us.
DUNCAN. Great happiness!
ROSS. That now
Sweno, the Norways' king, craves composition;
Nor would we deign him burial of his men
Till he disbursed, at Saint Colme's Inch,
Ten thousand dollars to our general use.
DUNCAN. No more that Thane of Cawdor shall deceive
Our bosom interest. Go pronounce his present death,
And with his former title greet Macbeth.
ROSS. I'll see it done.
DUNCAN. What he hath lost, noble Macbeth hath won.
Exeunt

SCENE 3

A blasted heath

Thunder. Enter the three WITCHES

FIRST WITCH. Where hast thou been, sister?
SECOND WITCH. Killing swine.

THIRD WITCH. Sister, where thou?
FIRST WITCH. A sailor's wife had chestnuts in her lap,
And mounch'd, and mounch'd, and mounch'd.
'Give me' quoth I.
'Aroint thee, witch!' the rump-fed ronyon cries.
Her husband's to Aleppo gone, master o' th' Tiger;
But in a sieve I'll thither sail
And, like a rat without a tail,
I'll do, I'll do, and I'll do.
SECOND WITCH. I'll give thee a wind.
FIRST WITCH. Th'art kind.
THIRD WITCH. And I another.
FIRST WITCH. I myself have all the other;
And the very ports they blow,
All the quarters that they know
I' th' shipman's card.
I'll drain him dry as hay:
Sleep shall neither night nor day
Hang upon his pent-house lid;
He shall live a man forbid;
Weary sev'nights, nine times nine,
Shall he dwindle, peak, and pine.
Though his bark cannot be lost,
Yet it shall be tempest-tost.
Look what I have.
SECOND WITCH. Show me, show me.
FIRST WITCH. Here I have a pilot's thumb,
Wreck'd as homeward he did come.

[*Drum within*]

THIRD WITCH. A drum, a drum!
Macbeth doth come.
ALL. The Weird Sisters, hand in hand,
Posters of the sea and land,
Thus do go about, about;
Thrice to thine, and thrice to mine,
And thrice again, to make up nine.
Peace! The charm's wound up.

Enter MACBETH *and* BANQUO

MACBETH. So foul and fair a day I have not seen.

BANQUO. How far is't call'd to Forres? What are these,
So wither'd, and so wild in their attire,
That look not like th' inhabitants o' th' earth,
And yet are on't? Live you, or are you aught
That man may question? You seem to understand me,
By each at once her choppy finger laying
Upon her skinny lips. You should be women,
And yet your beards forbid me to interpret
That you are so.
MACBETH. Speak, if you can. What are you?
FIRST WITCH. All hail, Macbeth! Hail to thee, Thane of Glamis!
SECOND WITCH. All hail, Macbeth! Hail to thee, Thane of Cawdor!
THIRD WITCH. All hail, Macbeth, that shalt be King hereafter!
BANQUO. Good sir, why do you start, and seem to fear
Things that do sound so fair? I' th' name of truth,
Are ye fantastical, or that indeed
Which outwardly ye show? My noble partner
You greet with present grace and great prediction
Of noble having and of royal hope,
That he seems rapt withal. To me you speak not.
If you can look into the seeds of time
And say which grain will grow and which will not,
Speak then to me, who neither beg nor fear
Your favours nor your hate.
FIRST WITCH. Hail!
SECOND WITCH. Hail!
THIRD WITCH. Hail!
FIRST WITCH. Lesser than Macbeth, and greater.
SECOND WITCH. Not so happy, yet much happier.
THIRD WITCH. Thou shalt get kings, though thou be none.
So, all hail, Macbeth and Banquo!
FIRST WITCH. Banquo and Macbeth, all hail!
MACBETH. Stay, you imperfect speakers, tell me more.
By Sinel's death I know I am Thane of Glamis;
But how of Cawdor? The Thane of Cawdor lives,
A prosperous gentleman; and to be King
Stands not within the prospect of belief,

No more than to be Cawdor. Say from whence
You owe this strange intelligence, or why
Upon this blasted heath you stop our way
With such prophetic greeting? Speak, I charge you.
WITCHES *vanish*

BANQUO. The earth hath bubbles, as the water has,
And these are of them. Whither are they vanish'd?
MACBETH. Into the air; and what seem'd corporal melted
As breath into the wind. Would they had stay'd!
BANQUO. Were such things here as we do speak about?
Or have we eaten on the insane root
That takes the reason prisoner?
MACBETH. Your children shall be kings.
BANQUO. You shall be King.
MACBETH. And Thane of Cawdor too; went it not so?
BANQUO. To th' self-same tune and words. Who's here?

Enter ROSS *and* ANGUS

ROSS. The King hath happily receiv'd, Macbeth,
The news of thy success; and when he reads
Thy personal venture in the rebels' fight,
His wonders and his praises do contend
Which should be thine or his. Silenc'd with that,
In viewing o'er the rest o' th' self-same day,
He finds thee in the stout Norweyan ranks,
Nothing afeard of what thyself didst make,
Strange images of death. As thick as tale
Came post with post, and every one did bear
Thy praises in his kingdom's great defence,
And pour'd them down before him.
ANGUS. We are sent
To give thee, from our royal master, thanks;
Only to herald thee into his sight,
Not pay thee.
ROSS. And, for an earnest of a greater honour,
He bade me, from him, call thee Thane of Cawdor;
In which addition, hail, most worthy Thane!
For it is thine.
BANQUO. What, can the devil speak true?
MACBETH. The Thane of Cawdor lives; why do you dress me

In borrowed robes?
ANGUS. Who was the Thane lives yet;
But under heavy judgment bears that life
Which he deserves to lose. Whether he was combin'd
With those of Norway, or did line the rebel
With hidden help and vantage, or that with both
He labour'd in his country's wreck, I know not;
But treasons capital, confess'd and prov'd,
Have overthrown him.
MACBETH. [*Aside*] Glamis, and Thane of Cawdor!
The greatest is behind.—Thanks for your pains.
[*Aside to* BANQUO] Do you not hope your children shall be kings,
When those that gave the Thane of Cawdor to me
Promis'd no less to them?
BANQUO. [*Aside to* MACBETH] That, trusted home,
Might yet enkindle you unto the crown,
Besides the Thane of Cawdor. But 'tis strange;
And oftentimes to win us to our harm,
The instruments of darkness tell us truths,
Win us with honest trifles, to betray 's
In deepest consequence.—
Cousins, a word, I pray you.
MACBETH. [*Aside*] Two truths are told,
As happy prologues to the swelling act
Of the imperial theme.—I thank you, gentlemen.
[*Aside*] This supernatural soliciting
Cannot be ill; cannot be good. If ill,
Why hath it given me earnest of success,
Commencing in a truth? I am Thane of Cawdor.
If good, why do I yield to that suggestion
Whose horrid image doth unfix my hair
And make my seated heart knock at my ribs
Against the use of nature? Present fears
Are less than horrible imaginings.
My thought, whose murder yet is but fantastical,
Shakes so my single state of man
That function is smother'd in surmise,
And nothing is but what is not.
BANQUO. Look how our partner's rapt.

MACBETH. [*Aside*] If chance will have me King, why, chance may crown me,
Without my stir.

BANQUO. New honours come upon him,
Like our strange garments, cleave not to their mould
But with the aid of use.

MACBETH. [*Aside*] Come what come may,
Time and the hour runs through the roughest day.

BANQUO. Worthy Macbeth, we stay upon your leisure.

MACBETH. Give me your favour. My dull brain was wrought
With things forgotten. Kind gentlemen, your pains
Are regist'red where every day I turn
The leaf to read them. Let us toward the King.
[*Aside to* BANQUO] Think upon what hath chanc'd; and, at more time,
The interim having weigh'd it, let us speak
Our free hearts each to other.

BANQUO. [*Aside to* MACBETH] Very gladly.

MACBETH. [*Aside to* BANQUO] Till then, enough.–Come, friends. *Exeunt*

SCENE 4

Forres. The palace

Flourish. Enter DUNCAN, MALCOLM, DONALBAIN, LENNOX *and attendants*

DUNCAN. Is execution done on Cawdor? Are not
Those in commission yet return'd?

MALCOLM. My liege,
They are not yet come back. But I have spoke
With one that saw him die; who did report
That very frankly he confess'd his treasons,
Implor'd your Highness' pardon, and set forth
A deep repentance. Nothing in his life
Became him like the leaving it: he died
As one that had been studied in his death
To throw away the dearest thing he ow'd
As 'twere a careless trifle.

DUNCAN. There's no art
To find the mind's construction in the face.
He was a gentleman on whom I built
An absolute trust.

Enter MACBETH, BANQUO, ROSS, *and* ANGUS

O worthiest cousin!
The sin of my ingratitude even now
Was heavy on me. Thou art so far before
That swiftest wing of recompense is slow
To overtake thee. Would thou hadst less deserv'd,
That the proportion both of thanks and payment
Might have been mine! Only I have left to say,
More is thy due than more than all can pay.

MACBETH. The service and the loyalty I owe,
In doing it, pays itself. Your Highness' part
Is to receive our duties; and our duties
Are to your throne and state children and servants,
Which do but what they should by doing everything
Safe toward your love and honour.

DUNCAN. Welcome hither.
I have begun to plant thee, and will labour
To make thee full of growing. Noble Banquo,
That hast no less deserv'd, nor must be known
No less to have done so, let me infold thee
And hold thee to my heart.

BANQUO. There if I grow,
The harvest is your own.

DUNCAN. My plenteous joys,
Wanton in fulness, seek to hide themselves
In drops of sorrow. Sons, kinsmen, thanes,
And you whose places are the nearest, know
We will establish our estate upon
Our eldest, Malcolm, whom we name hereafter
The Prince of Cumberland; which honour must
Not unaccompanied invest him only,
But signs of nobleness, like stars, shall shine
On all deservers. From hence to Inverness,
And bind us further to you.

MACBETH. The rest is labour, which is not us'd for you.

I'll be myself the harbinger, and make joyful
The hearing of my wife with your approach;
So, humbly take my leave.

DUNCAN. My worthy Cawdor!

MACBETH. [*Aside*] The Prince of Cumberland! That is a step
On which I must fall down, or else o'er-leap,
For in my way it lies. Stars, hide your fires;
Let not light see my black and deep desires.
The eye wink at the hand; yet let that be
Which the eye fears, when it is done, to see. *Exit*

DUNCAN. True, worthy Banquo: he is full so valiant;
And in his commendations I am fed;
It is a banquet to me. Let's after him,
Whose care is gone before to bid us welcome.
It is a peerless kinsman. *Flourish. Exeunt*

SCENE 5

Inverness. MACBETH'S *castle*

Enter LADY MACBETH, *reading a letter*

LADY MACBETH. 'They met me in the day of success; and I have learn'd by the perfect'st report they have more in them than mortal knowledge. When I burn'd in desire to question them further, they made themselves air, into which they vanish'd. Whiles I stood rapt in the wonder of it, came missives from the King, who all-hail'd me "Thane of Cawdor"; by which title, before, these weird sisters saluted me, and referr'd me to the coming on of time, with "Hail, king that shalt be!" This have I thought good to deliver thee, my dearest partner of greatness, that thou mightst not lose the dues of rejoicing by being ignorant of what greatness is promis'd thee. Lay it to thy heart, and farewell.'

Glamis thou art, and Cawdor; and shalt be
What thou art promis'd. Yet do I fear thy nature;
It is too full o' th' milk of human kindness
To catch the nearest way. Thou wouldst be great;

Art not without ambition, but without
The illness should attend it. What thou wouldst highly,
That wouldst thou holily; wouldst not play false,
And yet wouldst wrongly win.
Thou'dst have, great Glamis, that which cries
'Thus thou must do' if thou have it;
And that which rather thou dost fear to do
Than wishest should be undone. Hie thee hither,
That I may pour my spirits in thine ear,
And chastise with the valour of my tongue
All that impedes thee from the golden round
Which fate and metaphysical aid doth seem
To have thee crown'd withal.

Enter a MESSENGER

What is your tidings?

MESSENGER. The King comes here to-night.

LADY MACBETH. Thou'rt mad to say it.
Is not thy master with him? who, were't so,
Would have inform'd for preparation.

MESSENGER. So please you, it is true. Our Thane is coming.
One of my fellows had the speed of him,
Who, almost dead for breath, had scarcely more
Than would make up his message.

LADY MACBETH. Give him tending:
He brings great news. *Exit* MESSENGER
The raven himself is hoarse
That croaks the fatal entrance of Duncan
Under my battlements. Come, you spirits
That tend on mortal thoughts, unsex me here;
And fill me, from the crown to the toe, top-full
Of direst cruelty. Make thick my blood,
Stop up th' access and passage to remorse,
That no compunctious visitings of nature
Shake my fell purpose nor keep peace between
Th' effect and it. Come to my woman's breasts,
And take my milk for gall, you murd'ring ministers,
Wherever in your sightless substances
You wait on nature's mischief. Come, thick night,
And pall thee in the dunnest smoke of hell,

That my keen knife see not the wound it makes,
Nor heaven peep through the blanket of the dark
To cry 'Hold, hold.'

Enter MACBETH

Great Glamis! Worthy Cawdor!
Greater than both, by the all-hail hereafter!
Thy letters have transported me beyond
This ignorant present, and I feel now
The future in the instant.

MACBETH. My dearest love,
Duncan comes here to-night.

LADY MACBETH. And when goes hence?

MACBETH. To-morrow–as he purposes.

LADY MACBETH. O, never
Shall sun that morrow see!
Your face, my Thane, is as a book where men
May read strange matters. To beguile the time,
Look like the time; bear welcome in your eye,
Your hand, your tongue; look like th' innocent flower,
But be the serpent under't. He that's coming
Must be provided for; and you shall put
This night's great business into my dispatch;
Which shall to all our nights and days to come
Give solely sovereign sway and masterdom.

MACBETH. We will speak further.

LADY. MACBETH. Only look up clear.
To alter favour ever is to fear.
Leave all the rest to me. *Exeunt*

SCENE 6

Inverness. Before MACBETH'S *castle*

Hautboys and torches. Enter DUNCAN, MALCOLM, DONALBAIN, BANQUO, LENNOX, MACDUFF, ROSS, ANGUS, *and attendants*

DUNCAN. This castle hath a pleasant seat; the air
Nimbly and sweetly recommends itself

Unto our gentle senses.

BANQUO. This guest of summer,
The temple-haunting martlet, does approve
By his lov'd mansionry that the heaven's breath
Smells wooingly here; no jutty, frieze,
Buttress, nor coign of vantage, but this bird
Hath made her pendent bed and procreant cradle.
Where they most breed and haunt, I have observ'd
The air is delicate.

Enter LADY MACBETH

DUNCAN. See, see, our honour'd hostess!
The love that follows us sometime is our trouble,
Which still we thank as love. Herein I teach you
How you shall bid God 'ield us for your pains,
And thank us for your trouble.

LADY MACBETH. All our service
In every point twice done, and then done double,
Were poor and single business to contend
Against those honours deep and broad wherewith
Your Majesty loads our house; for those of old,
And the late dignities heap'd up to them,
We rest your hermits.

DUNCAN. Where's the Thane of Cawdor?
We cours'd him at the heels and had a purpose
To be his purveyor; but he rides well,
And his great love, sharp as his spur, hath holp him
To his home before us. Fair and noble hostess,
We are your guest to-night.

LADY MACBETH. Your servants ever
Have theirs, themselves, and what is theirs, in compt,
To make their audit at your Highness' pleasure,
Still to return your own.

DUNCAN. Give me your hand;
Conduct me to mine host. We love him highly,
And shall continue our graces towards him.
By your leave, hostess. *Exeunt*

SCENE 7

Inverness. MACBETH'S *castle*

Hautboys, torches. Enter a SEWER, *and divers servants with dishes and service over the stage. Then enter* MACBETH

MACBETH. If it were done when 'tis done, then 'twere well
It were done quickly. If th' assassination
Could trammel up the consequence, and catch,
With his surcease, success; that but this blow
Might be the be-all and the end-all here—
But here upon this bank and shoal of time—
We'd jump the life to come. But in these cases
We still have judgment here, that we but teach
Bloody instructions, which being taught return
To plague th' inventor. This even-handed justice
Commends th' ingredience of our poison'd chalice
To our own lips. He's here in double trust:
First, as I am his kinsman and his subject—
Strong both against the deed; then, as his host,
Who should against his murderer shut the door,
Not bear the knife myself. Besides, this Duncan
Hath borne his faculties so meek, hath been
So clear in his great office, that his virtues
Will plead like angels, trumpet-tongu'd, against
The deep damnation of his taking-off;
And pity, like a naked new-born babe,
Striding the blast, or heaven's cherubin hors'd
Upon the sightless couriers of the air,
Shall blow the horrid deed in every eye,
That tears shall drown the wind. I have no spur
To prick the sides of my intent, but only
Vaulting ambition, which o'er-leaps itself,
And falls on th' other.

Enter LADY MACBETH

How now! What news?

LADY MACBETH. He has almost supp'd. Why have you left the chamber?

MACBETH. Hath he ask'd for me?
LADY MACBETH. Know you not he has?
MACBETH. We will proceed no further in this business.
He hath honour'd me of late; and I have bought
Golden opinions from all sorts of people,
Which would be worn now in their newest gloss,
Not cast aside so soon.
LADY MACBETH. Was the hope drunk
Wherein you dress'd yourself? Hath it slept since,
And wakes it now to look so green and pale
At what it did so freely? From this time
Such I account thy love. Art thou afeard
To be the same in thine own act and valour
As thou art in desire? Wouldst thou have that
Which thou esteem'st the ornament of life,
And live a coward in thine own esteem,
Letting 'I dare not' wait upon 'I would,'
Like the poor cat i' th' adage?
MACBETH. Prithee, peace;
I dare do all that may become a man;
Who dares do more is none.
LADY MACBETH. What beast was't then
That made you break this enterprise to me?
When you durst do it, then you were a man;
And to be more than what you were, you would
Be so much more the man. Nor time nor place
Did then adhere, and yet you would make both;
They have made themselves, and that their fitness now
Does unmake you. I have given suck, and know
How tender 'tis to love the babe that milks me—
I would, while it was smiling in my face,
Have pluck'd my nipple from his boneless gums,
And dash'd the brains out, had I so sworn
As you have done to this.
MACBETH. If we should fail?
LADY MACBETH. We fail!
But screw your courage to the sticking place,
And we'll not fail. When Duncan is asleep—
Whereto the rather shall his day's hard journey
Soundly invite him—his two chamberlains

Will I with wine and wassail so convince
That memory, the warder of the brain,
Shall be a fume, and the receipt of reason
A limbec only. When in swinish sleep
Their drenched natures lie as in a death,
What cannot you and I perform upon
Th' unguarded Duncan? what not put upon
His spongy officers, who shall bear the guilt
Of our great quell?

MACBETH. Bring forth men-children only;
For thy undaunted mettle should compose
Nothing but males. Will it not be receiv'd,
When we have mark'd with blood those sleepy two
Of his own chamber, and us'd their very daggers,
That they have done't?

LADY MACBETH. Who dares receive it other,
As we shall make our griefs and clamour roar
Upon his death?

MACBETH. I am settled, and bend up
Each corporal agent to this terrible feat.
Away, and mock the time with fairest show;
False face must hide what the false heart doth know.

Exeunt

ACT II. SCENE 1

Inverness. Court of MACBETH'S *castle*

Enter BANQUO, *and* FLEANCE *with a torch before him*

BANQUO. How goes the night, boy?

FLEANCE. The moon is down; I have not heard the clock.

BANQUO. And she goes down at twelve.

FLEANCE. I take 't, 'tis later, sir.

BANQUO. Hold, take my sword. There's husbandry in heaven;
Their candles are all out. Take thee that too.
A heavy summons lies like lead upon me,
And yet I would not sleep. Merciful powers
Restrain in me the cursed thoughts that nature

Gives way to in repose!

Enter MACBETH *and a servant with a torch*

Give me my sword.
Who's there?

MACBETH. A friend.

BANQUO. What, sir, not yet at rest? The king's a-bed.
He hath been in unusual pleasure, and
Sent forth great largess to your offices.
This diamond he greets your wife withal,
By the name of most kind hostess; and shut up
In measureless content.

MACBETH. Being unprepar'd,
Our will became the servant to defect;
Which else should free have wrought.

BANQUO. All's well.
I dreamt last night of the three Weird Sisters.
To you they have show'd some truth.

MACBETH. I think not of them;
Yet, when we can entreat an hour to serve,
We would spend it in some words upon that business,
If you would grant the time.

BANQUO. At your kind'st leisure.

MACBETH. If you shall cleave to my consent, when 'tis,
It shall make honour for you.

BANQUO. So I lose none
In seeking to augment it, but still keep
My bosom franchis'd and allegiance clear,
I shall be counsell'd.

MACBETH. Good repose the while!

BANQUO. Thanks, sir; the like to you!

Exeunt BANQUO *and* FLEANCE

MACBETH. Go bid thy mistress, when my drink is ready,
She strike upon the bell. Get thee to bed. *Exit* SERVANT
Is this a dagger which I see before me,
The handle toward my hand? Come, let me clutch thee.
I have thee not, and yet I see thee still.
Art thou not, fatal vision, sensible
To feeling as to sight? or art thou but
A dagger of the mind, a false creation,

Proceeding from the heat-oppressed brain?
I see thee yet, in form as palpable
As this which now I draw.
Thou marshall'st me the way that I was going;
And such an instrument I was to use.
Mine eyes are made the fools o' th' other senses,
Or else worth all the rest. I see thee still;
And on thy blade and dudgeon gouts of blood,
Which was not so before. There's no such thing:
It is the bloody business which informs
Thus to mine eyes. Now o'er the one half-world
Nature seems dead, and wicked dreams abuse
The curtain'd sleep; now witchcraft celebrates
Pale Hecate's offerings; and wither'd murder,
Alarum'd by his sentinel, the wolf,
Whose howl's his watch, thus with his stealthy pace,
With Tarquin's ravishing strides, towards his design
Moves like a ghost. Thou sure and firm-set earth,
Hear not my steps which way they walk, for fear
Thy very stones prate of my whereabout
And take the present horror from the time,
Which now suits with it. Whiles I threat, he lives;
Words to the heat of deeds too cold breath gives.
[*A bell rings*]
I go, and it is done; the bell invites me.
Hear it not, Duncan, for it is a knell
That summons thee to heaven or to hell. *Exit*

SCENE 2

Inverness. MACBETH'S *castle*

Enter LADY MACBETH

LADY MACBETH. That which hath made them drunk hath made me bold;
What hath quench'd them hath given me fire. Hark! Peace!
It was the owl that shriek'd, the fatal bellman,
Which gives the stern'st good-night. He is about it.

The doors are open; and the surfeited grooms
Do mock their charge with snores. I have drugg'd their possets,
That death and nature do contend about them,
Whether they live or die.

MACBETH. [*Within*] Who's there! What, ho!

LADY MACBETH. Alack! I am afraid they have awak'd,
And 'tis not done. Th' attempt, and not the deed,
Confounds us. Hark! I laid their daggers ready;
He could not miss 'em. Had he not resembled
My father as he slept, I had done't.

Enter MACBETH

My husband!

MACBETH. I have done the deed. Didst thou not hear a noise?

LADY MACBETH. I heard the owl scream and the crickets cry.
Did not you speak?

MACBETH. When?

LADY MACBETH. Now.

MACBETH. As I descended?

LADY MACBETH. Ay.

MACBETH. Hark!
Who lies i' th' second chamber?

LADY MACBETH. Donalbain.

MACBETH. This is a sorry sight. [*Looking on his hands*]

LADY MACBETH. A foolish thought to say a sorry sight.

MACBETH. There's one did laugh in's sleep, and one cried 'Murder!'
That they did wake each other. I stood and heard them;
But they did say their prayers, and address'd them
Again to sleep.

LADY MACBETH. There are two lodg'd together.

MACBETH. One cried 'God bless us,' and 'Amen' the other,
As they had seen me with these hangman's hands.
List'ning their fear, I could not say 'Amen'
When they did say 'God bless us!'

LADY MACBETH. Consider it not so deeply.

MACBETH. But wherefore could not I pronounce 'Amen'?

I had most need of blessing, and 'Amen'
Stuck in my throat.

LADY MACBETH. These deeds must not be thought
After these ways: so, it will make us mad.

MACBETH. Methought I heard a voice cry 'Sleep no more;
Macbeth does murder sleep'—the innocent sleep,
Sleep that knits up the ravell'd sleave of care,
The death of each day's life, sore labour's bath,
Balm of hurt minds, great nature's second course,
Chief nourisher in life's feast.

LADY MACBETH. What do you mean?

MACBETH. Still it cried 'Sleep no more' to all the house;
'Glamis hath murder'd sleep; and therefore Cawdor
Shall sleep no more—Macbeth shall sleep no more.'

LADY MACBETH. Who was it that thus cried? Why, worthy Thane,
You do unbend your noble strength to think
So brainsickly of things. Go get some water
And wash this filthy witness from your hand.
Why did you bring these daggers from the place?
They must lie there. Go carry them, and smear
The sleepy grooms with blood.

MACBETH. I'll go no more:
I am afraid to think what I have done;
Look on't again I dare not.

LADY MACBETH. Infirm of purpose!
Give me the daggers. The sleeping and the dead
Are but as pictures; 'tis the eye of childhood
That fears a painted devil. If he do bleed,
I'll gild the faces of the grooms withal,
For it must seem their guilt. *Exit. Knocking within*

MACBETH. Whence is that knocking?
How is't with me, when every noise appals me?
What hands are here? Ha! they pluck out mine eyes.
Will all great Neptune's ocean wash this blood
Clean from my hand? No; this my hand will rather
The multitudinous seas incarnadine,
Making the green one red.

Re-enter LADY MACBETH

LADY MACBETH. My hands are of your colour; but I shame
To wear a heart so white. [*Knock*] I hear a knocking
At the south entry; retire we to our chamber.
A little water clears us of this deed.
How easy is it then! Your constancy
Hath left you unattended. [*Knock*] Hark! more knocking.
Get on your nightgown, lest occasion call us
And show us to be watchers. Be not lost
So poorly in your thoughts.

MACBETH. To know my deed, 'twere best not know myself. [*Knock*]
Wake Duncan with thy knocking! I would thou couldst!

Exeunt

SCENE 3

Inverness. MACBETH'S *castle*

Knocking within. Enter a PORTER

PORTER. Here's a knocking indeed! If a man were porter of hell-gate, he should have old turning the key. [*Knock*] Knock, knock, knock! Who's there, i' th' name of Beelzebub? Here's a farmer that hang'd himself on th' expectation of plenty. Come in time; have napkins enow about you; here you'll sweat for't. [*Knock*] Knock, knock! Who's there, i' th' other devil's name? Faith, here's an equivocator, that could swear in both the scales against either scale; who committed treason enough for God's sake, yet could not equivocate to heaven. O, come in, equivocator. [*Knock*] Knock, knock, knock! Who's there? Faith, here's an English tailor come hither for stealing out of a French hose. Come in, tailor, here you may roast your goose. [*Knock*] Knock, knock; never at quiet! What are you? But this place is too cold for hell. I'll devil-porter it no further. I had thought to have let in some of all professions that go the primrose way to th' everlasting bonfire. [*Knock*] Anon, anon! [*Opens the gate*] I pray you remember the porter.

Enter MACDUFF *and* LENNOX

MACDUFF. Was it so late, friend, ere you went to bed, that you do lie so late?

PORTER. Faith, sir, we were carousing till the second cock; and drink, sir, is a great provoker of three things.

MACDUFF. What three things does drink especially provoke?

PORTER. Marry, sir, nose-painting, sleep, and urine. Lechery, sir, it provokes and unprovokes: it provokes the desire, but it takes away the performance. Therefore much drink may be said to be an equivocator with lechery: it makes him, and it mars him; it sets him on, and it takes him off; it persuades him, and disheartens him; makes him stand to, and not stand to; in conclusion, equivocates him in a sleep, and, giving him the lie, leaves him.

MACDUFF. I believe drink gave thee the lie last night.

PORTER. That it did, sir, i' the very throat on me; but I requited him for his lie; and, I think, being too strong for him, though he took up my legs sometime, yet I made a shift to cast him.

MACDUFF. Is thy master stirring?

Enter MACBETH

Our knocking has awak'd him; here he comes.

LENNOX. Good morrow, noble sir!

MACBETH. Good morrow, both!

MACDUFF. Is the King stirring, worthy Thane?

MACBETH. Not yet.

MACDUFF. He did command me to call timely on him;
I have almost slipp'd the hour.

MACBETH. I'll bring you to him.

MACDUFF. I know this is a joyful trouble to you;
But yet 'tis one.

MACBETH. The labour we delight in physics pain.
This is the door.

MACDUFF. I'll make so bold to call,
For 'tis my limited service. *Exit*

LENNOX. Goes the King hence to-day?

MACBETH. He does; he did appoint so.

LENNOX. The night has been unruly. Where we lay,

Our chimneys were blown down; and, as they say,
Lamentings heard i' th' air, strange screams of death,
And prophesying, with accents terrible,
Of dire combustion and confus'd events
New hatch'd to th' woeful time; the obscure bird
Clamour'd the livelong night. Some say the earth
Was feverous and did shake.

MACBETH. 'Twas a rough night.

LENNOX. My young remembrance cannot parallel
A fellow to it.

Re-enter MACDUFF

MACDUFF. O horror, horror, horror! Tongue nor heart
Cannot conceive nor name thee.

MACBETH. / LENNOX. What's the matter?

MACDUFF. Confusion now hath made his masterpiece.
Most sacrilegious murder hath broke ope
The Lord's anointed temple, and stole thence
The life o' th' building.

MACBETH. What is't you say—the life?

LENNOX. Mean you his Majesty?

MACDUFF. Approach the chamber, and destroy your sight
With a new Gorgon. Do not bid me speak;
See, and then speak yourselves.

Exeunt MACBETH *and* LENNOX

Awake, awake!
Ring the alarum bell. Murder and treason!
Banquo and Donalbain! Malcolm! awake!
Shake off this downy sleep, death's counterfeit,
And look on death itself. Up, up, and see
The great doom's image! Malcolm! Banquo!
As from your graves rise up and walk like sprites
To countenance this horror! Ring the bell. [*Bell rings*]

Enter LADY MACBETH

LADY MACBETH. What's the business,
That such a hideous trumpet calls to parley
The sleepers of the house? Speak, speak!

MACDUFF. O gentle lady,

'Tis not for you to hear what I can speak!
The repetition in a woman's ear
Would murder as it fell.

Enter BANQUO

O Banquo, Banquo,
Our royal master's murder'd!

LADY MACBETH. Woe, alas!
What, in our house?

BANQUO. Too cruel any where.
Dear Duff, I prithee contradict thyself,
And say it is not so.

Re-enter MACBETH, LENNOX, *with* ROSS

MACBETH. Had I but died an hour before this chance,
I had liv'd a blessed time; for, from this instant,
There's nothing serious in mortality–
All is but toys; renown and grace is dead;
The wine of life is drawn, and the mere lees
Is left this vault to brag of.

Enter MALCOLM *and* DONALBAIN

DONALBAIN. What is amiss?

MACBETH. You are, and do not know't.
The spring, the head, the fountain of your blood,
Is stopp'd; the very source of it is stopp'd.

MACDUFF. Your royal father's murder'd.

MALCOLM. O, by whom?

LENNOX. Those of his chamber, as it seem'd, had done't.
Their hands and faces were all badg'd with blood;
So were their daggers, which unwip'd we found
Upon their pillows. They star'd and were distracted;
No man's life was to be trusted with them.

MACBETH. O, yet I do repent me of my fury
That I did kill them.

MACDUFF. Wherefore did you so?

MACBETH. Who can be wise, amaz'd, temp'rate, and furious,
Loyal and neutral, in a moment? No man.
The expedition of my violent love
Outrun the pauser reason. Here lay Duncan,

His silver skin lac'd with his golden blood;
And his gash'd stabs look'd like a breach in nature
For ruin's wasteful entrance: there, the murderers,
Steep'd in the colours of their trade, their daggers
Unmannerly breech'd with gore. Who could refrain,
That had a heart to love, and in that heart
Courage to make's love known?

LADY MACBETH. Help me hence, ho!

MACDUFF. Look to the lady.

MALCOLM. [*Aside to* DONALBAIN] Why do we hold our tongues that most may claim
This argument for ours?

DONALBAIN. [*Aside to* MALCOLM] What should be spoken
Here, where our fate, hid in an auger-hole,
May rush and seize us? Let's away.
Our tears are not yet brew'd.

MALCOLM. [*Aside to* DONALBAIN] Nor our strong sorrow
Upon the foot of motion.

BANQUO. Look to the lady. [LADY MACBETH *is carried out*]
And when we have our naked frailties hid,
That suffer in exposure, let us meet,
And question this most bloody piece of work,
To know it further. Fears and scruples shake us.
In the great hand of God I stand, and thence
Against the undivulg'd pretence I fight
Of treasonous malice.

MACDUFF. And so do I.

ALL. So all.

MACBETH. Let's briefly put on manly readiness
And meet i' th' hall together.

ALL. Well contented.

Exeunt all but MALCOLM *and* DONALBAIN

MALCOLM. What will you do? Let's not consort with them.
To show an unfelt sorrow is an office
Which the false man does easy. I'll to England.

DONALBAIN. To Ireland I; our separated fortune
Shall keep us both the safer. Where we are,
There's daggers in men's smiles; the near in blood,
The nearer bloody.

MALCOLM. This murderous shaft that's shot

Hath not yet lighted; and our safest way
Is to avoid the aim. Therefore to horse;
And let us not be dainty of leave-taking,
But shift away. There's warrant in that theft
Which steals itself, when there's no mercy left. *Exeunt*

SCENE 4

Inverness. Without MACBETH'S *castle*

Enter ROSS *with an* OLD MAN

OLD MAN. Threescore and ten I can remember well;
Within the volume of which time I have seen
Hours dreadful and things strange; but this sore night
Hath trifled former knowings.
ROSS. Ah, good father,
Thou seest, the heavens, as troubled with man's act,
Threatens his bloody stage. By th' clock 'tis day,
And yet dark night strangles the travelling lamp.
Is't night's predominance, or the day's shame,
That darkness does the face of earth entomb,
When living light should kiss it?
OLD MAN. 'Tis unnatural,
Even like the deed that's done. On Tuesday last,
A falcon, tow'ring in her pride of place,
Was by a mousing owl hawk'd at and kill'd.
ROSS. And Duncan's horses—a thing most strange and certain—
Beauteous and swift, the minions of their race,
Turn'd wild in nature, broke their stalls, flung out,
Contending 'gainst obedience, as they would make
War with mankind.
OLD MAN. 'Tis said they eat each other.
ROSS. They did so; to the amazement of mine eyes,
That look'd upon't.

Enter MACDUFF

Here comes the good Macduff.
How goes the world, sir, now?

MACDUFF. Why, see you not?
ROSS. Is't known who did this more than bloody deed?
MACDUFF. Those that Macbeth hath slain.
ROSS. Alas, the day!
What good could they pretend?
MACDUFF. They were suborn'd.
Malcolm and Donalbain, the King's two sons,
Are stol'n away and fled; which puts upon them
Suspicion of the deed.
ROSS. 'Gainst nature still.
Thriftless ambition, that wilt ravin up
Thine own life's means! Then 'tis most like
The sovereignty will fall upon Macbeth.
MACDUFF. He is already nam'd, and gone to Scone
To be invested.
ROSS. Where is Duncan's body?
MACDUFF. Carried to Colmekill,
The sacred storehouse of his predecessors
And guardian of their bones.
ROSS. Will you to Scone?
MACDUFF. No, cousin, I'll to Fife.
ROSS. Well, I will thither.
MACDUFF. Well, may you see things well done there! Adieu,
Lest our old robes sit easier than our new.
ROSS. Farewell, father.
OLD MAN. God's benison go with you, and with those
That would make good of bad, and friends of foes.

Exeunt

ACT III. SCENE 1

Forres. The palace

Enter BANQUO

BANQUO. Thou hast it now—King, Cawdor, Glamis, all
As the weird women promis'd; and I fear
Thou play'dst most foully for't; yet it was said
It should not stand in thy posterity;

But that myself should be the root and father
Of many kings. If there come truth from them–
As upon thee, Macbeth, their speeches shine–
Why, by the verities on thee made good,
May they not be my oracles as well
And set me up in hope? But, hush, no more.

Sennet sounded. Enter MACBETH *as King*, LADY MACBETH *as Queen;* LENNOX, ROSS, LORDS, LADIES, *and attendants*

MACBETH. Here's our chief guest.
LADY MACBETH. If he had been forgotten,
It had been as a gap in our great feast,
And all-thing unbecoming.
MACBETH. To-night we hold a solemn supper, sir,
And I'll request your presence.
BANQUO. Let your Highness
Command upon me; to the which my duties
Are with a most indissoluble tie
For ever knit.
MACBETH. Ride you this afternoon?
BANQUO. Ay, my good lord.
MACBETH. We should have else desir'd your good advice–
Which still hath been both grave and prosperous–
In this day's council; but we'll take to-morrow.
Is't far you ride?
BANQUO. As far, my lord, as will fill up the time
'Twixt this and supper. Go not my horse the better,
I must become a borrower of the night
For a dark hour or twain.
MACBETH. Fail not our feast.
BANQUO. My lord, I will not.
MACBETH. We hear our bloody cousins are bestow'd
In England and in Ireland, not confessing
Their cruel parricide, filling their hearers
With strange invention; but of that to-morrow,
When therewithal we shall have cause of state
Craving us jointly. Hie you to horse; adieu,
Till you return at night. Goes Fleance with you?
BANQUO. Ay, my good lord; our time does call upon's.

MACBETH. I wish your horses swift and sure of foot,
And so I do commend you to their backs.
Farewell. *Exit* BANQUO
Let every man be master of his time
Till seven at night; to make society
The sweeter welcome, we will keep ourself
Till supper-time alone. While then, God be with you!
Exeunt all but MACBETH *and a* SERVANT
Sirrah, a word with you. Attend those men our pleasure?
SERVANT. They are, my lord, without the palace gate.
MACBETH. Bring them before us. *Exit* SERVANT
To be thus is nothing,
But to be safely thus. Our fears in Banquo
Stick deep; and in his royalty of nature
Reigns that which would be fear'd. 'Tis much he dares,
And to that dauntless temper of his mind
He hath a wisdom that doth guide his valour
To act in safety. There is none but he
Whose being I do fear; and under him
My Genius is rebuk'd, as it is said
Mark Antony's was by Cæsar. He chid the Sisters
When first they put the name of King upon me,
And bade them speak to him; then prophet-like,
They hail'd him father to a line of kings.
Upon my head they plac'd a fruitless crown
And put a barren sceptre in my gripe,
Thence to be wrench'd with an unlineal hand,
No son of mine succeeding. If't be so,
For Banquo's issue have I fil'd my mind;
For them the gracious Duncan have I murder'd;
Put rancours in the vessel of my peace
Only for them, and mine eternal jewel
Given to the common enemy of man
To make them kings—the seeds of Banquo kings!
Rather than so, come, Fate, into the list,
And champion me to th' utterance! Who's there?

Re-enter SERVANT *and two* MURDERERS

Now go to the door and stay there till we call.
Exit SERVANT

Was it not yesterday we spoke together?
FIRST MURDERER. It was, so please your Highness.
MACBETH. Well then, now
Have you consider'd of my speeches? Know
That it was he, in the times past, which held you
So under fortune; which you thought had been
Our innocent self. This I made good to you
In our last conference, pass'd in probation with you,
How you were borne in hand, how cross'd, the instruments,
Who wrought with them, and all things else that might
To half a soul and to a notion craz'd
Say 'Thus did Banquo.'
FIRST MURDERER. You made it known to us.
MACBETH. I did so; and went further, which is now
Our point of second meeting. Do you find
Your patience so predominant in your nature
That you can let this go? Are you so gospell'd,
To pray for this good man and for his issue,
Whose heavy hand hath bow'd you to the grave
And beggar'd yours for ever?
FIRST MURDERER. We are men, my liege.
MACBETH. Ay, in the catalogue ye go for men;
As hounds, and greyhounds, mongrels, spaniels, curs,
Shoughs, water-rugs, and demi-wolves, are clept
All by the name of dogs. The valued file
Distinguishes the swift, the slow, the subtle,
The house-keeper, the hunter, every one
According to the gift which bounteous nature
Hath in him clos'd; whereby he does receive
Particular addition, from the bill
That writes them all alike; and so of men.
Now, if you have a station in the file,
Not i' th' worst rank of manhood, say't;
And I will put that business in your bosoms
Whose execution takes your enemy off,
Grapples you to the heart and love of us,
Who wear our health but sickly in his life,
Which in his death were perfect.
SECOND MURDERER. I am one, my liege,

Whom the vile blows and buffets of the world
Hath so incens'd that I am reckless what
I do to spite the world.

FIRST MURDERER. And I another,
So weary with disasters, tugg'd with fortune,
That I would set my life on any chance,
To mend it or be rid on't.

MACBETH. Both of you
Know Banquo was your enemy.

BOTH MURDERERS. True, my lord.

MACBETH. So is he mine; and in such bloody distance
That every minute of his being thrusts
Against my near'st of life; and though I could
With bare-fac'd power sweep him from my sight,
And bid my will avouch it, yet I must not,
For certain friends that are both his and mine,
Whose loves I may not drop, but wail his fall
Who I myself struck down. And thence it is
That I to your assistance do make love,
Masking the business from the common eye
For sundry weighty reasons.

SECOND MURDERER. We shall, my lord,
Perform what you command us.

FIRST MURDERER. Though our lives–

MACBETH. Your spirits shine through you. Within this hour at most,
I will advise you where to plant yourselves,
Acquaint you with the perfect spy o' th' time,
The moment on't; for 't must be done to-night,
And something from the palace; always thought
That I require a clearness; and with him,
To leave no rubs nor botches in the work,
Fleance his son, that keeps him company,
Whose absence is no less material to me
Than is his father's, must embrace the fate
Of that dark hour. Resolve yourselves apart;
I'll come to you anon.

BOTH MURDERERS. We are resolv'd, my lord.

MACBETH. I'll call upon you straight; abide within.

Exeunt MURDERERS

It is concluded: Banquo, thy soul's flight
If it find heaven must find it out to-night. *Exit*

SCENE 2

Forres. The palace

Enter Lady Macbeth *and a* Servant

Lady Macbeth. Is Banquo gone from court?
Servant. Ay, madam, but returns again to-night.
Lady Macbeth. Say to the King I would attend his leisure
For a few words.
Servant. Madam, I will. *Exit*
Lady Macbeth. Nought's had, all's spent,
Where our desire is got without content.
'Tis safer to be that which we destroy,
Than by destruction dwell in doubtful joy.

Enter Macbeth

How now, my lord! Why do you keep alone,
Of sorriest fancies your companions making,
Using those thoughts which should indeed have died
With them they think on? Things without all remedy
Should be without regard. What's done is done.
Macbeth. We have scotch'd the snake, not kill'd it;
She'll close, and be herself, whilst our poor malice
Remains in danger of her former tooth.
But let the frame of things disjoint, both the worlds suffer,
Ere we will eat our meal in fear and sleep
In the affliction of these terrible dreams
That shake us nightly. Better be with the dead,
Whom we, to gain our peace, have sent to peace,
Than on the torture of the mind to lie
In restless ecstasy. Duncan is in his grave;
After life's fitful fever he sleeps well;
Treason has done his worst; nor steel, nor poison,
Malice domestic, foreign levy, nothing,
Can touch him further.
Lady Macbeth. Come on.

Gentle my lord, sleek o'er your rugged looks;
Be bright and jovial among your guests to-night.
MACBETH. So shall I, love; and so, I pray, be you.
Let your remembrance apply to Banquo;
Present him eminence, both with eye and tongue—
Unsafe the while, that we
Must lave our honours in these flattering streams,
And make our faces vizards to our hearts,
Disguising what they are.
LADY MACBETH. You must leave this.
MACBETH. O, full of scorpions is my mind, dear wife!
Thou know'st that Banquo, and his Fleance, lives.
LADY MACBETH. But in them nature's copy's not eterne.
MACBETH. There's comfort yet; they are assailable.
Then be thou jocund. Ere the bat hath flown
His cloister'd flight; ere to black Hecate's summons
The shard-bone beetle with his drowsy hums
Hath rung night's yawning peal, there shall be done
A deed of dreadful note.
LADY MACBETH. What's to be done?
MACBETH. Be innocent of the knowledge, dearest chuck,
Till thou applaud the deed. Come, seeling night,
Scarf up the tender eye of pitiful day,
And with thy bloody and invisible hand
Cancel and tear to pieces that great bond
Which keeps me pale. Light thickens, and the crow
Makes wing to th' rooky wood;
Good things of day begin to droop and drowse,
Whiles night's black agents to their preys do rouse.
Thou marvell'st at my words; but hold thee still:
Things bad begun make strong themselves by ill.
So, prithee go with me. *Exeunt*

SCENE 3

Forres. The approaches to the palace

Enter three MURDERERS

FIRST MURDERER. But who did bid thee join with us?

THIRD MURDERER. Macbeth.

SECOND MURDERER. He needs not our mistrust, since he delivers
Our offices, and what we have to do,
To the direction just.

FIRST MURDERER. Then stand with us.
The west yet glimmers with some streaks of day;
Now spurs the lated traveller apace
To gain the timely inn, and near approaches
The subject of our watch.

THIRD MURDERER. Hark! I hear horses.

BANQUO. [*Within*] Give us a light there, ho!

SECOND MURDERER. Then 'tis he; the rest
That are within the note of expectation
Already are i' th' court.

FIRST MURDERER. His horses go about.

THIRD MURDERER. Almost a mile; but he does usually,
So all men do, from hence to th' palace gate
Make it their walk.

Enter BANQUO, *and* FLEANCE *with a torch*

SECOND MURDERER. A light, a light!

THIRD MURDERER. 'Tis he.

FIRST MURDERER. Stand to 't.

BANQUO. It will be rain to-night.

FIRST MURDERER. Let it come down. [*Stabs* BANQUO]

BANQUO. O, treachery! Fly, good Fleance, fly, fly, fly.
Thou mayst revenge. O slave! [*Dies.* FLEANCE *escapes*]

THIRD MURDERER. Who did strike out the light?

FIRST MURDERER. Was't not the way?

THIRD MURDERER. There's but one down; the son is fled.

SECOND MURDERER. We have lost
Best half of our affair.

FIRST MURDERER. Well, let's away,
And say how much is done. *Exeunt*

SCENE 4

Forres. The palace

Banquet prepared. Enter MACBETH, LADY MACBETH, ROSS, LENNOX, LORDS, *and attendants*

MACBETH. You know your own degrees, sit down.
At first and last the hearty welcome.
LORDS. Thanks to your Majesty.
MACBETH. Our self will mingle with society
And play the humble host.
Our hostess keeps her state; but in best time
We will require her welcome.
LADY MACBETH. Pronounce it for me, sir, to all our friends;
For my heart speaks they are welcome.

Enter FIRST MURDERER *to the door*

MACBETH. See, they encounter thee with their hearts' thanks.
Both sides are even; here I'll sit i' th' midst.
Be large in mirth; anon we'll drink a measure
The table round. [*Going to the door*]
There's blood upon thy face.
MURDERER. 'Tis Banquo's then.
MACBETH. 'Tis better thee without than he within.
Is he dispatch'd?
MURDERER. My lord, his throat is cut;
That I did for him.
MACBETH. Thou art the best o' th' cut-throats;
Yet he's good that did the like for Fleance.
If thou didst it, thou art the nonpareil.
MURDERER. Most royal sir—Fleance is 'scap'd.
MACBETH. Then comes my fit again. I had else been perfect,
Whole as the marble, founded as the rock,
As broad and general as the casing air,
But now I am cabin'd, cribb'd, confin'd, bound in
To saucy doubts and fears. But Banquo's safe?
MURDERER. Ay, my good lord. Safe in a ditch he bides,
With twenty trenched gashes on his head,
The least a death to nature.

MACBETH. Thanks for that.
There the grown serpent lies; the worm that's fled
Hath nature that in time will venom breed,
No teeth for th' present. Get thee gone; to-morrow
We'll hear, ourselves, again. *Exit* MURDERER

LADY MACBETH. My royal lord,
You do not give the cheer; the feast is sold
That is not often vouch'd, while 'tis a-making,
'Tis given with welcome. To feed were best at home:
From thence the sauce to meat is ceremony;
Meeting were bare without it.

Enter the GHOST *of* BANQUO *and sits in* MACBETH'S *place*

MACBETH. Sweet remembrancer!
Now good digestion wait on appetite,
And health on both!

LENNOX. May't please your Highness sit?

MACBETH. Here had we now our country's honour roof'd,
Were the grac'd person of our Banquo present;
Who may I rather challenge for unkindness
Than pity for mischance.

ROSS. His absence, sir,
Lays blame upon his promise. Please 't your Highness
To grace us with your royal company.

MACBETH. The table's full.

LENNOX. Here is a place reserv'd, sir.

MACBETH. Where?

LENNOX. Here, my good lord.
What is't that moves your Highness?

MACBETH. Which of you have done this?

LORDS. What, my good lord?

MACBETH. Thou canst not say I did it; never shake
Thy gory locks at me.

ROSS. Gentlemen, rise; his Highness is not well.

LADY MACBETH. Sit, worthy friends. My lord is often thus,
And hath been from his youth. Pray you, keep seat.
The fit is momentary; upon a thought
He will again be well. If much you note him,
You shall offend him and extend his passion.
Feed, and regard him not.—Are you a man?

MACBETH. Ay, and a bold one that dare look on that
Which might appal the devil.
LADY MACBETH. O proper stuff!
This is the very painting of your fear;
This is the air-drawn dagger which you said
Led you to Duncan. O, these flaws and starts—
Impostors to true fear—would well become
A woman's story at a winter's fire,
Authoriz'd by her grandam. Shame itself!
Why do you make such faces? When all's done,
You look but on a stool.
MACBETH. Prithee see there.
Behold! look! lo! how say you?
Why, what care I? If thou canst nod, speak, too.
If charnel-houses and our graves must send
Those that we bury back, our monuments
Shall be the maws of kites. *Exit* GHOST
LADY MACBETH. What, quite unmann'd in folly?
MACBETH. If I stand here, I saw him.
LADY MACBETH. Fie, for shame!
MACBETH. Blood hath been shed ere now, i' th' olden time,
Ere humane statute purg'd the gentle weal;
Ay, and since too, murders have been perform'd
Too terrible for the ear. The time has been
That when the brains were out the man would die,
And there an end; but now they rise again,
With twenty mortal murders on their crowns,
And push us from our stools. This is more strange
Than such a murder is.
LADY MACBETH. My worthy lord,
Your noble friends do lack you.
MACBETH. I do forget.
Do not muse at me, my most worthy friends;
I have a strange infirmity, which is nothing
To those that know me. Come, love and health to all;
Then I'll sit down. Give me some wine, fill full.

Enter GHOST

I drink to the general joy o' th' whole table,
And to our dear friend Banquo, whom we miss.

Would he were here! To all, and him, we thirst,
And all to all.

LORDS. Our duties, and the pledge.

MACBETH. Avaunt, and quit my sight. Let the earth hide thee.
Thy bones are marrowless, thy blood is cold;
Thou has no speculation in those eyes
Which thou dost glare with!

LADY MACBETH. Think of this, good peers,
But as a thing of custom. 'Tis no other;
Only it spoils the pleasure of the time.

MACBETH. What man dare, I dare.
Approach thou like the rugged Russian bear,
The arm'd rhinoceros, or th' Hyrcan tiger;
Take any shape but that, and my firm nerves
Shall never tremble. Or be alive again,
And dare me to the desert with thy sword;
If trembling I inhabit, then protest me
The baby of a girl. Hence, horrible shadow!
Unreal mock'ry, hence! *Exit* GHOST
Why, so; being gone,
I am a man again. Pray you, sit still.

LADY MACBETH. You have displac'd the mirth, broke the good meeting,
With most admir'd disorder.

MACBETH. Can such things be,
And overcome us like a summer's cloud,
Without our special wonder? You make me strange
Even to the disposition that I owe,
When now I think you can behold such sights
And keep the natural ruby of your cheeks,
When mine is blanch'd with fear.

ROSS. What sights, my lord?

LADY MACBETH. I pray you speak not; he grows worse and worse;
Question enrages him. At once, good night.
Stand not upon the order of your going,
But go at once.

LENNOX. Good night; and better health
Attend his Majesty!

LADY MACBETH. A kind good night to all!

Exeunt LORDS *and attendants*

MACBETH. It will have blood; they say blood will have blood.
Stones have been known to move, and trees to speak;
Augurs and understood relations have
By maggot-pies and choughs and rooks brought forth
The secret'st man of blood. What is the night?

LADY MACBETH. Almost at odds with morning, which is which.

MACBETH. How say'st thou that Macduff denies his person
At our great bidding?

LADY MACBETH. Did you send to him, sir?

MACBETH. I hear it by the way; but I will send–
There's not a one of them but in his house
I keep a servant fee'd–I will to-morrow.
And betimes I will to the Weird Sisters:
More shall they speak; for now I am bent to know
By the worst means the worst. For mine own good
All causes shall give way. I am in blood
Stepp'd in so far that, should I wade no more,
Returning were as tedious as go o'er.
Strange things I have in head that will to hand,
Which must be acted ere they may be scann'd.

LADY MACBETH. You lack the season of all natures, sleep.

MACBETH. Come, we'll to sleep. My strange and self-abuse
Is the initiate fear that wants hard use.
We are yet but young in deed. *Exeunt*

SCENE 5

A heath

Thunder. Enter the three WITCHES, *meeting* HECATE

FIRST WITCH. Why, how now, Hecat! You look angerly.

HECATE. Have I not reason, beldams as you are,
Saucy and overbold? How did you dare
To trade and traffic with Macbeth
In riddles and affairs of death;

And I, the mistress of your charms,
The close contriver of all harms,
Was never call'd to bear my part,
Or show the glory of our art?
And, which is worse, all you have done
Hath been but for a wayward son,
Spiteful and wrathful; who, as others do,
Loves for his own ends, not for you.
But make amends now. Get you gone,
And at the pit of Acheron
Meet me i' the morning; thither he
Will come to know his destiny.
Your vessels and your spells provide,
Your charms, and everything beside.
I am for th' air; this night I'll spend
Unto a dismal and a fatal end.
Great business must be wrought ere noon.
Upon the corner of the moon
There hangs a vap'rous drop profound;
I'll catch it ere it come to ground;
And that, distill'd by magic sleights,
Shall raise such artificial sprites
As, by the strength of their illusion,
Shall draw him on to his confusion.
He shall spurn fate, scorn death, and bear
His hopes 'bove wisdom, grace, and fear;
And you all know security
Is mortals' chiefest enemy.
[*Music and a song within:* 'Come away, come away, etc.']
Hark! I am call'd; my little spirit, see,
Sits in a foggy cloud, and stays for me. *Exit*

FIRST WITCH. Come, let's make haste; she'll soon be back again. *Exeunt*

SCENE 6

Forres. The palace

Enter LENNOX *and another* LORD

LENNOX. My former speeches have but hit your thoughts,
Which can interpret farther. Only I say
Things have been strangely borne. The gracious Duncan
Was pitied of Macbeth. Marry, he was dead.
And the right-valiant Banquo walk'd too late;
Whom, you may say, if't please you, Fleance kill'd,
For Fleance fled. Men must not walk too late.
Who cannot want the thought how monstrous
It was for Malcolm and for Donalbain
To kill their gracious father? Damned fact!
How it did grieve Macbeth! Did he not straight,
In pious rage, the two delinquents tear,
That were the slaves of drink and thralls of sleep?
Was not that nobly done? Ay, and wisely too;
For 'twould have anger'd any heart alive
To hear the men deny't. So that, I say,
He has borne all things well; and I do think
That had he Duncan's sons under his key—
As, an't please heaven, he shall not—they should find
What 'twere to kill a father; so should Fleance.
But peace! For from broad words, and 'cause he fail'd
His presence at the tyrant's feast, I hear,
Macduff lives in disgrace. Sir, can you tell
Where he bestows himself?
LORD. The son of Duncan,
From whom this tyrant holds the due of birth,
Lives in the English court, and is receiv'd
Of the most pious Edward with such grace
That the malevolence of fortune nothing
Takes from his high respect; thither Macduff
Is gone to pray the holy King upon his aid
To wake Northumberland and warlike Siward,
That by the help of these—with Him above
To ratify the work—we may again

Give to our tables meat, sleep to our nights,
Free from our feasts and banquets bloody knives,
Do faithful homage and receive free honours–
All which we pine for now. And this report
Hath so exasperate the King that he
Prepares for some attempt of war.

LENNOX. Sent he to Macduff?

LORD. He did; and with an absolute 'Sir, not I!'
The cloudy messenger turns me his back
And hums, as who should say 'You'll rue the time
That clogs me with this answer.'

LENNOX. And that well might
Advise him to a caution t' hold what distance
His wisdom can provide. Some holy angel
Fly to the court of England and unfold
His message ere he come, that a swift blessing
May soon return to this our suffering country
Under a hand accurs'd!

LORD. I'll send my prayers with him. *Exeunt*

ACT IV. SCENE 1

A dark cave. In the middle, a cauldron boiling

Thunder. Enter the three WITCHES

FIRST WITCH. Thrice the brinded cat hath mew'd.

SECOND WITCH. Thrice and once the hedge-pig whin'd.

THIRD WITCH. Harpier cries; 'tis time, 'tis time.

FIRST WITCH. Round about the cauldron go;
In the poison'd entrails throw.
Toad that under cold stone
Days and nights has thirty-one
Swelt'red venom sleeping got
Boil thou first i' th' charmed pot.

ALL. Double, double toil and trouble;
Fire burn, and cauldron bubble.

SECOND WITCH. Fillet of a fenny snake,
In the cauldron boil and bake;

Eye of newt, and toe of frog,
Wool of bat, and tongue of dog,
Adder's fork, and blind-worm's sting,
Lizard's leg, and howlet's wing—
For a charm of pow'rful trouble,
Like a hell-broth boil and bubble.

ALL. Double, double toil and trouble;
Fire burn, and cauldron bubble.

THIRD WITCH. Scale of dragon, tooth of wolf,
Witch's mummy, maw and gulf
Of the ravin'd salt-sea shark,
Root of hemlock digg'd i' th' dark,
Liver of blaspheming Jew,
Gall of goat, and slips of yew
Sliver'd in the moon's eclipse,
Nose of Turk, and Tartar's lips,
Finger of birth-strangled babe
Ditch-deliver'd by a drab—
Make the gruel thick and slab;
Add thereto a tiger's chaudron,
For th' ingredience of our cauldron.

ALL. Double, double toil and trouble;
Fire burn, and cauldron bubble.

SECOND WITCH. Cool it with a baboon's blood,
Then the charm is firm and good.

Enter HECATE

HECATE. O, well done! I commend your pains;
And every one shall share i' th' gains.
And now about the cauldron sing,
Like elves and fairies in a ring,
Enchanting all that you put in.

[*Music and a song:* 'Black Spirits, etc.' *Exit* HECATE]

SECOND WITCH. By the pricking of my thumbs,
Something wicked this way comes.
Open, locks, whoever knocks.

Enter MACBETH

MACBETH. How now, you secret, black, and midnight hags!
What is't you do?

ALL. A deed without a name.

MACBETH. I conjure you by that which you profess—
Howe'er you come to know it—answer me.
Though you untie the winds and let them fight
Against the churches; though the yesty waves
Confound and swallow navigation up;
Though bladed corn be lodg'd and trees blown down;
Though castles topple on their warders' heads;
Though palaces and pyramids do slope
Their heads to their foundations; though the treasure
Of nature's germens tumble all together,
Even till destruction sicken—answer me
To what I ask you.

FIRST WITCH. Speak.

SECOND WITCH. Demand.

THIRD WITCH. We'll answer.

FIRST WITCH. Say, if thou'dst rather hear it from our mouths,
Or from our masters?

MACBETH. Call 'em; let me see 'em.

FIRST WITCH. Pour in sow's blood that hath eaten
Her nine farrow; grease that's sweaten
From the murderer's gibbet throw
Into the flame.

ALL. Come, high or low;
Thyself and office deftly show.

Thunder. FIRST APPARITION, *an Armed Head*

MACBETH. Tell me, thou unknown power—

FIRST WITCH. He knows thy thought.
Hear his speech, but say thou nought.

APPARITION. Macbeth! Macbeth! Macbeth! Beware Macduff;
Beware the Thane of Fife. Dismiss me. Enough.
[*He descends*]

MACBETH. Whate'er thou art, for thy good caution, thanks;
Thou hast harp'd my fear aright. But one word more—

FIRST WITCH. He will not be commanded. Here's another,
More potent than the first.

Thunder. SECOND APPARITION, *a Bloody Child*

MACBETH. *How now, you secret, black, and midnight hags!*
What is't you do?
ALL. *A deed without a name.*
MACBETH. *I conjure you by that which you profess—*
Howe'er you come to know it—answer me. . . .
Though castles topple on their warders' heads;
Though palaces and pyramids do slope
Their heads to their foundations . . . —answer me
To what I ask you. (ACT IV. Scene 1)

APPARITION. Macbeth! Macbeth! Macbeth!
MACBETH. Had I three ears, I'd hear thee.
APPARITION. Be bloody, bold, and resolute; laugh to scorn
The pow'r of man, for none of woman born
Shall harm Macbeth. [*Descends*]
MACBETH. Then live, Macduff; what need I fear of thee?
But yet I'll make assurance double sure
And take a bond of fate. Thou shalt not live;
That I may tell pale-hearted fear it lies,
And sleep in spite of thunder.

Thunder. THIRD APPARITION, *a Child Crowned, with a tree in his hand*

What is this
That rises like the issue of a king,
And wears upon his baby brow the round
And top of sovereignty?
ALL. Listen, but speak not to't.
APPARITION. Be lion-mettled, proud, and take no care
Who chafes, who frets, or where conspirers are;
Macbeth shall never vanquish'd be until
Great Birnam wood to high Dunsinane Hill
Shall come against him. [*Descends*]
MACBETH. That will never be.
Who can impress the forest, bid the tree
Unfix his earth-bound root? Sweet bodements, good!
Rebellion's head rise never till the wood
Of Birnam rise, and our high-plac'd Macbeth
Shall live the lease of nature, pay his breath
To time and mortal custom. Yet my heart
Throbs to know one thing; tell me, if your art
Can tell so much—shall Banquo's issue ever
Reign in this kingdom?
ALL. Seek to know no more.
MACBETH. I will be satisfied. Deny me this,
And an eternal curse fall on you! Let me know.
Why sinks that cauldron, and what noise is this?
[*Hautboys*]
FIRST WITCH. Show!
SECOND WITCH. Show!

THIRD WITCH. Show!
ALL. Show his eyes, and grieve his heart;
Come like shadows, so depart!

A SHOW OF EIGHT KINGS, *and* BANQUO *last; the last king with a glass in his hand*

MACBETH. Thou art too like the spirit of Banquo; down!
Thy crown does sear mine eye-balls. And thy hair,
Thou other gold-bound brow, is like the first.
A third is like the former. Filthy hags!
Why do you show me this? A fourth? Start, eyes.
What, will the line stretch out to th' crack of doom?
Another yet? A seventh? I'll see no more.
And yet the eighth appears, who bears a glass
Which shows me many more; and some I see
That twofold balls and treble sceptres carry.
Horrible sight! Now I see 'tis true;
For the blood-bolter'd Banquo smiles upon me,
And points at them for his. [*The show vanishes*] What! is this so?
FIRST WITCH. Ay, sir, all this is so. But why
Stands Macbeth thus amazedly?
Come, sisters, cheer we up his sprites,
And show the best of our delights;
I'll charm the air to give a sound,
While you perform your antic round;
That this great king may kindly say,
Our duties did his welcome pay.

Music. The WITCHES *dance, and vanish*

MACBETH. Where are they? Gone? Let this pernicious hour
Stand aye accursed in the calendar.
Come in, without there.

Enter LENNOX

LENNOX. What's your Grace's will?
MACBETH. Saw you the Weird Sisters?
LENNOX. No, my lord.
MACBETH. Came they not by you?
LENNOX. No, indeed, my lord.

MACBETH. Infected be the air whereon they ride;
And damn'd all those that trust them! I did hear
The galloping of horse. Who was't came by?
LENNOX. 'Tis two or three, my lord, that bring you word
Macduff is fled to England.
MACBETH. Fled to England!
LENNOX. Ay, my good lord.
MACBETH [*Aside*] Time, thou anticipat'st my dread exploits.
The flighty purpose never is o'ertook
Unless the deed go with it. From this moment
The very firstlings of my heart shall be
The firstlings of my hand. And even now,
To crown my thoughts with acts, be it thought and done:
The castle of Macduff I will surprise,
Seize upon Fife, give to the edge o' th' sword
His wife, his babes, and all unfortunate souls
That trace him in his line. No boasting like a fool:
This deed I'll do before this purpose cool.
But no more sights!—Where are these gentlemen?
Come, bring me where they are. *Exeunt*

SCENE 2

Fife. MACDUFF'S *castle*

Enter LADY MACDUFF, *her* SON, *and* ROSS

LADY MACDUFF. What had he done to make him fly the land?
ROSS. You must have patience, madam.
LADY MACDUFF. He had none;
His flight was madness. When our actions do not,
Our fears do make us traitors.
ROSS. You know not
Whether it was his wisdom or his fear.
LADY MACDUFF. Wisdom! To leave his wife, to leave his babes,
His mansion, and his titles, in a place
From whence himself does fly? He loves us not;
He wants the natural touch; for the poor wren,

The most diminutive of birds, will fight,
Her young ones in her nest, against the owl.
All is the fear, and nothing is the love;
As little is the wisdom, where the flight
So runs against all reason.

ROSS. My dearest coz,
I pray you, school yourself. But, for your husband,
He is noble, wise, judicious, and best knows
The fits o' th' season. I dare not speak much further;
But cruel are the times, when we are traitors
And do not know ourselves; when we hold rumour
From what we fear, yet know not what we fear,
But float upon a wild and violent sea
Each way and none. I take my leave of you;
Shall not be long but I'll be here again.
Things at the worst will cease, or else climb upward
To what they were before.–My pretty cousin,
Blessing upon you!

LADY MACDUFF. Father'd he is, and yet he's fatherless.

ROSS. I am so much a fool, should I stay longer,
It would be my disgrace and your discomfort.
I take my leave at once. *Exit*

LADY MACDUFF. Sirrah, your father's dead;
And what will you do now? How will you live?

SON. As birds do, mother.

LADY MACDUFF. What, with worms and flies?

SON. With what I get, I mean; and so do they.

LADY MACDUFF. Poor bird! thou'dst never fear the net nor lime,
The pitfall nor the gin.

SON. Why should I, mother? Poor birds they are not set for.
My father is not dead, for all your saying.

LADY MACDUFF. Yes, he is dead. How wilt thou do for a father?

SON. Nay, how will you do for a husband?

LADY MACDUFF. Why, I can buy me twenty at any market.

SON. Then you'll buy 'em to sell again.

LADY MACDUFF. Thou speak'st with all thy wit; and yet, i' faith,
With wit enough for thee.

SON. Was my father a traitor, mother?

LADY MACDUFF. Ay, that he was.

SON. What is a traitor?

LADY MACDUFF. Why, one that swears and lies.

SON. And be all traitors that do so?

LADY MACDUFF. Every one that does so is a traitor, and must be hang'd.

SON. And must they all be hang'd that swear and lie?

LADY MACDUFF. Every one.

SON. Who must hang them?

LADY MACDUFF. Why, the honest men.

SON. Then the liars and swearers are fools; for there are liars and swearers enow to beat the honest men and hang up them.

LADY MACDUFF. Now, God help thee, poor monkey! But how wilt thou do for a father?

SON. If he were dead, you'd weep for him; if you would not, it were a good sign that I should quickly have a new father.

LADY MACDUFF. Poor prattler, how thou talk'st!

Enter a MESSENGER

MESSENGER. Bless you, fair dame! I am not to you known,
Though in your state of honour I am perfect.
I doubt some danger does approach you nearly.
If you will take a homely man's advice,
Be not found here; hence, with your little ones.
To fright you thus, methinks, I am too savage;
To do worse to you were fell cruelty,
Which is too nigh your person. Heaven preserve you!
I dare abide no longer. *Exit*

LADY MACDUFF. Whither should I fly?
I have done no harm. But I remember now
I am in this earthly world, where to do harm
Is often laudable, to do good sometime
Accounted dangerous folly. Why then, alas,
Do I put up that womanly defence
To say I have done no harm?

Enter MURDERERS

What are these faces?
FIRST MURDERER. Where is your husband?
LADY MACDUFF. I hope, in no place so unsanctified
Where such as thou mayst find him.
FIRST MURDERER. He's a traitor.
SON. Thou liest, thou shag-ear'd villain.
FIRST MURDERER. What, you egg? [*Stabbing him*]
Young fry of treachery!
SON. He has kill'd me, mother.
Run away, I pray you. [*Dies*]

Exit LADY MACDUFF, *crying* 'Murder!'

SCENE 3

England. Before King Edward's palace

Enter MALCOLM *and* MACDUFF

MALCOLM. Let us seek out some desolate shade, and there
Weep our sad bosoms empty.
MACDUFF. Let us rather
Hold fast the mortal sword, and like good men
Bestride our down-fall'n birthdom. Each new morn
New widows howl, new orphans cry; new sorrows
Strike heaven on the face, that it resounds
As if it felt with Scotland and yell'd out
Like syllable of dolour.
MALCOLM. What I believe, I'll wail;
What know, believe; and what I can redress,
As I shall find the time to friend, I will.
What you have spoke, it may be so perchance.
This tyrant, whose sole name blisters our tongues,
Was once thought honest; you have lov'd him well;
He hath not touch'd you yet. I am young; but something
You may deserve of him through me; and wisdom
To offer up a weak, poor, innocent lamb
T' appease an angry god.
MACDUFF. I am not treacherous.
MALCOLM. But Macbeth is.
A good and virtuous nature may recoil

In an imperial charge. But I shall crave your pardon;
That which you are, my thoughts cannot transpose;
Angels are bright still, though the brightest fell.
Though all things foul would wear the brows of grace,
Yet grace must still look so.

MACDUFF. I have lost my hopes.

MALCOLM. Perchance even there where I did find my doubts.
Why in that rawness left you wife and child,
Those precious motives, those strong knots of love,
Without leave-taking? I pray you,
Let not my jealousies be your dishonours,
But mine own safeties. You may be rightly just,
Whatever I shall think.

MACDUFF. Bleed, bleed, poor country.
Great tyranny, lay thou thy basis sure,
For goodness dare not check thee. Wear thou thy wrongs.
The title is affeer'd. Fare thee well, lord.
I would not be the villain that thou think'st
For the whole space that's in the tyrant's grasp
And the rich East to boot.

MALCOLM. Be not offended.
I speak not as in absolute fear of you.
I think our country sinks beneath the yoke;
It weeps, it bleeds; and each new day a gash
Is added to her wounds. I think withal
There would be hands uplifted in my right;
And here, from gracious England, have I offer
Of goodly thousands. But, for all this,
When I shall tread upon the tyrant's head,
Or wear it on my sword, yet my poor country
Shall have more vices than it had before;
More suffer, and more sundry ways than ever,
By him that shall succeed.

MACDUFF. What should he be?

MALCOLM. It is myself I mean; in whom I know
All the particulars of vice so grafted
That, when they shall be open'd, black Macbeth
Will seem as pure as snow; and the poor state
Esteem him as a lamb, being compar'd

With my confineless harms.
MACDUFF. Not in the legions
Of horrid hell can come a devil more damn'd
In evils to top Macbeth.
MALCOLM. I grant him bloody,
Luxurious, avaricious, false, deceitful,
Sudden, malicious, smacking of every sin
That has a name; but there's no bottom, none,
In my voluptuousness. Your wives, your daughters,
Your matrons, and your maids, could not fill up
The cistern of my lust; and my desire
All continent impediments would o'erbear
That did oppose my will. Better Macbeth
Than such an one to reign.
MACDUFF. Boundless intemperance
In nature is a tyranny; it hath been
Th' untimely emptying of the happy throne
And fall of many kings. But fear not yet
To take upon you what is yours. You may
Convey your pleasures in a spacious plenty,
And yet seem cold, the time you may so hoodwink.
We have willing dames enough; there cannot be
That vulture in you to devour so many
As will to greatness dedicate themselves,
Finding it so inclin'd.
MALCOLM. With this there grows
In my most ill-compos'd affection such
A stanchless avarice that, were I King,
I should cut off the nobles for their lands,
Desire his jewels, and this other's house;
And my more-having would be as a sauce
To make me hunger more, that I should forge
Quarrels unjust against the good and loyal,
Destroying them for wealth.
MACDUFF. This avarice
Sticks deeper, grows with more pernicious root
Than summer-seeming lust; and it hath been
The sword of our slain kings. Yet do not fear;
Scotland hath foisons to fill up your will
Of your mere own. All these are portable,

With other graces weigh'd.
MALCOLM. But I have none. The king-becoming graces,
As justice, verity, temp'rance, stableness,
Bounty, perseverance, mercy, lowliness,
Devotion, patience, courage, fortitude,
I have no relish of them; but abound
In the division of each several crime,
Acting it many ways. Nay, had I pow'r, I should
Pour the sweet milk of concord into hell,
Uproar the universal peace, confound
All unity on earth.
MACDUFF. O Scotland, Scotland!
MALCOLM. If such a one be fit to govern, speak.
I am as I have spoken.
MACDUFF. Fit to govern!
No, not to live! O nation miserable,
With an untitled tyrant bloody-scept'red,
When shalt thou see thy wholesome days again,
Since that the truest issue of thy throne
By his own interdiction stands accurs'd
And does blaspheme his breed? Thy royal father
Was a most sainted king; the queen that bore thee,
Oft'ner upon her knees than on her feet,
Died every day she liv'd. Fare thee well!
These evils thou repeat'st upon thyself
Hath banish'd me from Scotland. O my breast,
Thy hope ends here!
MALCOLM. Macduff, this noble passion,
Child of integrity, hath from my soul
Wip'd the black scruples, reconcil'd my thoughts
To thy good truth and honour. Devilish Macbeth
By many of these trains hath sought to win me
Into his power; and modest wisdom plucks me
From over-credulous haste. But God above
Deal between thee and me; for even now
I put myself to thy direction, and
Unspeak mine own detraction, here abjure
The taints and blames I laid upon myself
For strangers to my nature. I am yet
Unknown to woman, never was forsworn,

Scarcely have coveted what was mine own,
At no time broke my faith, would not betray
The devil to his fellow, and delight
No less in truth than life. My first false speaking
Was this upon myself. What I am truly
Is thine and my poor country's to command:
Whither indeed, before thy here-approach,
Old Siward with ten thousand warlike men
Already at a point was setting forth.
Now we'll together; and the chance of goodness
Be like our warranted quarrel! Why are you silent?

MACDUFF. Such welcome and unwelcome things at once
'Tis hard to reconcile.

Enter a DOCTOR

MALCOLM. Well; more anon. Comes the King forth, I pray you?

DOCTOR. Ay, sir. There are a crew of wretched souls
That stay his cure. Their malady convinces
The great assay of art; but at his touch,
Such sanctity hath heaven given his hand,
They presently amend.

MALCOLM. I thank you, doctor. *Exit* DOCTOR

MACDUFF. What's the disease he means?

MALCOLM. 'Tis called the evil:
A most miraculous work in this good King;
Which often since my here-remain in England
I have seen him do. How he solicits heaven,
Himself best knows; but strangely-visited people,
All swoln and ulcerous, pitiful to the eye,
The mere despair of surgery, he cures,
Hanging a golden stamp about their necks,
Put on with holy prayers; and 'tis spoken,
To the succeeding royalty he leaves
The healing benediction. With this strange virtue,
He hath a heavenly gift of prophecy;
And sundry blessings hang about his throne
That speak him full of grace.

Enter ROSS

MACDUFF. See, who comes here?
MALCOLM. My countryman; but yet I know him not.
MACDUFF. My ever gentle cousin, welcome hither.
MALCOLM. I know him now. Good God betimes remove
The means that makes us strangers!
ROSS. Sir, amen.
MACDUFF. Stands Scotland where it did?
ROSS. Alas, poor country,
Almost afraid to know itself! It cannot
Be call'd our mother, but our grave; where nothing,
But who knows nothing, is once seen to smile;
Where sighs, and groans, and shrieks, that rent the air,
Are made, not mark'd; where violent sorrow seems
A modern ecstasy; the dead man's knell
Is there scarce ask'd for who; and good men's lives
Expire before the flowers in their caps,
Dying or ere they sicken.
MACDUFF. O, relation
Too nice, and yet too true!
MALCOLM. What's the newest grief?
ROSS. That of an hour's age doth hiss the speaker:
Each minute teems a new one.
MACDUFF. How does my wife?
ROSS. Why, well.
MACDUFF. And all my children?
ROSS. Well too.
MACDUFF. The tyrant has not batter'd at their peace?
ROSS. No; they were well at peace when I did leave 'em.
MACDUFF. Be not a niggard of your speech. How goes't?
ROSS. When I came hither to transport the tidings,
Which I have heavily borne, there ran a rumour
Of many worthy fellows that were out;
Which was to my belief witness'd the rather
For that I saw the tyrant's power afoot.
Now is the time of help; your eye in Scotland
Would create soldiers, make our women fight,
To doff their dire distresses.
MALCOLM. Be't their comfort
We are coming thither. Gracious England hath
Lent us good Siward and ten thousand men—

An older and a better soldier none
That Christendom gives out.
Ross. Would I could answer
This comfort with the like! But I have words
That would be howl'd out in the desert air,
Where hearing should not latch them.
MACDUFF. What concern they?
The general cause, or is it a fee-grief
Due to some single breast?
Ross. No mind that's honest
But in it shares some woe, though the main part
Pertains to you alone.
MACDUFF. If it be mine,
Keep it not from me; quickly let me have it.
Ross. Let not your ears despise my tongue for ever,
Which shall possess them with the heaviest sound
That ever yet they heard.
MACDUFF. Humph! I guess at it.
Ross. Your castle is surpris'd; your wife and babes
Savagely slaughter'd. To relate the manner,
Were, on the quarry of these murder'd deer,
To add the death of you.
MALCOLM. Merciful heaven!
What, man! Ne'er pull your hat upon your brows;
Give sorrow words. The grief that does not speak
Whispers the o'erfraught heart and bids it break.
MACDUFF. My children too?
Ross. Wife, children, servants, all
That could be found.
MACDUFF. And I must be from thence!
My wife kill'd too?
Ross. I have said.
MALCOLM. Be comforted.
Let's make us med'cines of our great revenge
To cure this deadly grief.
MACDUFF. He has no children. All my pretty ones?
Did you say all? O hell-kite! All?
What, all my pretty chickens and their dam
At one fell swoop?
MALCOLM. Dispute it like a man.

MACDUFF. I shall do so;
But I must also feel it as a man.
I cannot but remember such things were
That were most precious to me. Did heaven look on,
And would not take their part? Sinful Macduff,
They were all struck for thee–nought that I am;
Not for their own demerits, but for mine,
Fell slaughter on their souls. Heaven rest them now!

MALCOLM. Be this the whetstone of your sword. Let grief
Convert to anger; blunt not the heart, enrage it.

MACDUFF. O, I could play the woman with mine eyes
And braggart with my tongue! But, gentle heavens,
Cut short all intermission; front to front
Bring thou this fiend of Scotland and myself;
Within my sword's length set him; if he scape,
Heaven forgive him too!

MALCOLM. This tune goes manly.
Come, go we to the King. Our power is ready;
Our lack is nothing but our leave. Macbeth
Is ripe for shaking, and the pow'rs above
Put on their instruments. Receive what cheer you may;
The night is long that never finds the day. *Exeunt*

ACT V. SCENE 1

Dunsinane. MACBETH'S *castle*

Enter a DOCTOR OF PHYSIC *and a* WAITING-GENTLEWOMAN

DOCTOR. I have two nights watch'd with you, but can perceive no truth in your report. When was it she last walk'd?

GENTLEWOMAN. Since his Majesty went into the field, I have seen her rise from her bed, throw her nightgown upon her, unlock her closet, take forth paper, fold it, write upon't, read it, afterwards seal it, and again return to bed; yet all this while in a most fast sleep.

DOCTOR. A great perturbation in nature, to receive at once the benefit of sleep and do the effects of watching! In this slumb'ry agitation, besides her walking and other actual performances, what, at any time, have you heard her say?

GENTLEWOMAN. That, sir, which I will not report after her.

DOCTOR. You may to me; and 'tis most meet you should.

GENTLEWOMAN. Neither to you nor any one, having no witness to confirm my speech.

Enter LADY MACBETH, *with a taper*

Lo you, here she comes! This is her very guise; and, upon my life, fast asleep. Observe her; stand close.

DOCTOR. How came she by that light?

GENTLEWOMAN. Why, it stood by her. She has light by her continually; 'tis her command.

DOCTOR. You see her eyes are open.

GENTLEWOMAN. Ay, but their sense is shut.

DOCTOR. What is it she does now? Look how she rubs her hands.

GENTLEWOMAN. It is an accustomed action with her, to seem thus washing her hands; I have known her continue in this a quarter of an hour.

LADY MACBETH. Yet here's a spot.

DOCTOR. Hark, she speaks. I will set down what comes from her, to satisfy my remembrance the more strongly.

LADY MACBETH. Out, damned spot! out, I say! One, two; why then 'tis time to do't. Hell is murky. Fie, my lord, fie! a soldier, and afeard? What need we fear who knows it, when none can call our pow'r to account? Yet who would have thought the old man to have had so much blood in him?

DOCTOR. Do you mark that?

LADY MACBETH. The Thane of Fife had a wife; where is she now? What, will these hands ne'er be clean? No more o' that, my lord, no more o' that; you mar all with this starting.

DOCTOR. Go to, go to; you have known what you should not.

GENTLEWOMAN. She has spoke what she should not, I am sure of that. Heaven knows what she has known.

LADY MACBETH. Here's the smell of the blood still. All the perfumes of Arabia will not sweeten this little hand. Oh, oh, oh!

DOCTOR. What a sigh is there! The heart is sorely charg'd.

GENTLEWOMAN. I would not have such a heart in my bosom for the dignity of the whole body.

DOCTOR. Well, well, well.

GENTLEWOMAN. Pray God it be, sir.

DOCTOR. This disease is beyond my practice. Yet I have known those which have walk'd in their sleep who have died holily in their beds.

LADY MACBETH. Wash your hands, put on your nightgown, look not so pale. I tell you yet again, Banquo's buried; he cannot come out on's grave.

DOCTOR. Even so?

LADY MACBETH. To bed, to bed; there's knocking at the gate. Come, come, come, come, give me your hand. What's done cannot be undone. To bed, to bed, to bed.

Exit

DOCTOR. Will she go now to bed?

GENTLEWOMAN. Directly.

DOCTOR. Foul whisp'rings are abroad. Unnatural deeds
Do breed unnatural troubles; infected minds
To their deaf pillows will discharge their secrets.
More needs she the divine than the physician.
God, God forgive us all. Look after her;
Remove from her the means of all annoyance,
And still keep eyes upon her. So, good night.
My mind she has mated, and amaz'd my sight.
I think, but dare not speak.

GENTLEWOMAN. Good night, good doctor. *Exeunt*

SCENE 2

The country near Dunsinane

Drum and colours. Enter MENTEITH, CAITHNESS, ANGUS, LENNOX, *and soldiers*

MENTEITH. The English pow'r is near, led on by Malcolm,
His uncle Siward, and the good Macduff.
Revenges burn in them; for their dear causes
Would to the bleeding and the grim alarm

Excite the mortified man.
ANGUS. Near Birnam wood
Shall we well meet them; that way are they coming.
CAITHNESS. Who knows if Donalbain be with his brother?
LENNOX. For certain, sir, he is not; I have a file
Of all the gentry. There is Siward's son,
And many unrough youths that even now
Protest their first of manhood.
MENTEITH. What does the tyrant?
CAITHNESS. Great Dunsinane he strongly fortifies.
Some say he's mad; others, that lesser hate him,
Do call it valiant fury; but for certain
He cannot buckle his distemper'd cause
Within the belt of rule.
ANGUS. Now does he feel
His secret murders sticking on his hands;
Now minutely revolts upbraid his faith-breach;
Those he commands move only in command,
Nothing in love. Now does he feel his title
Hang loose about him, like a giant's robe
Upon a dwarfish thief.
MENTEITH. Who then shall blame
His pester'd sense to recoil and start,
When all that is within him does condemn
Itself for being there?
CAITHNESS. Well, march we on
To give obedience where 'tis truly ow'd.
Meet we the med'cine of the sickly weal;
And with him pour we in our country's purge
Each drop of us.
LENNOX. Or so much as it needs
To dew the sovereign flower and drown the weeds.
Make we our march towards Birnam. *Exeunt, marching*

SCENE 3

Dunsinane. MACBETH's *castle*

Enter MACBETH, DOCTOR, *and attendants*

MACBETH. Bring me no more reports; let them fly all.
Till Birnam wood remove to Dunsinane
I cannot taint with fear. What's the boy Malcolm?
Was he not born of woman? The spirits that know
All mortal consequences have pronounc'd me thus:
'Fear not, Macbeth; no man that's born of woman
Shall e'er have power upon thee.' Then fly, false thanes,
And mingle with the English epicures.
The mind I sway by and the heart I bear
Shall never sag with doubt nor shake with fear.

Enter SERVANT

The devil damn thee black, thou cream-fac'd loon!
Where got'st thou that goose look?
SERVANT. There is ten thousand–
MACBETH. Geese, villain?
SERVANT. Soldiers, sir.
MACBETH. Go, prick thy face, and over-red thy fear,
Thou lily-liver'd boy. What soldiers, patch?
Death of thy soul! Those linen cheeks of thine
Are counsellors to fear. What soldiers, whey-face?
SERVANT. The English force, so please you.
MACBETH. Take thy face hence. *Exit* SERVANT
Seyton!–I am sick at heart,
When I behold–Seyton, I say!–This push
Will cheer me ever, or disseat me now.
I have liv'd long enough. My way of life
Is fall'n into the sear, the yellow leaf;
And that which should accompany old age,
As honour, love, obedience, troops of friends,
I must not look to have; but, in their stead,
Curses not loud but deep, mouth-honour, breath,
Which the poor heart would fain deny, and dare not.
Seyton!

Enter SEYTON

SEYTON. What's your gracious pleasure?
MACBETH. What news more?
SEYTON. All is confirm'd, my lord, which was reported.
MACBETH. I'll fight till from my bones my flesh be hack'd.
Give me my armour.
SEYTON. 'Tis not needed yet.
MACBETH. I'll put it on.
Send out moe horses, skirr the country round;
Hang those that talk of fear. Give me mine armour.
How does your patient, doctor?
DOCTOR. Not so sick, my lord,
As she is troubled with thick-coming fancies
That keep her from her rest.
MACBETH. Cure her of that.
Canst thou not minister to a mind diseas'd,
Pluck from the memory a rooted sorrow,
Raze out the written troubles of the brain,
And with some sweet oblivious antidote
Cleanse the stuff'd bosom of that perilous stuff
Which weighs upon the heart?
DOCTOR. Therein the patient
Must minister to himself.
MACBETH. Throw physic to the dogs—I'll none of it.
Come, put mine armour on; give me my staff.
Seyton, send out. Doctor, the thanes fly from me.
Come, sir, dispatch. If thou couldst, doctor, cast
The water of my land, find her disease,
And purge it to a sound and pristine health,
I would applaud thee to the very echo,
That should applaud again.—Pull't off, I say.—
What rhubarb, senna, or what purgative drug,
Would scour these English hence? Hear'st thou of them?
DOCTOR. Ay, my good lord. Your royal preparation
Makes us hear something.
MACBETH. Bring it after me.
I will not be afraid of death and bane
Till Birnam Forest come to Dunsinane.

Exeunt all but the DOCTOR

DOCTOR. Were I from Dunsinane away and clear,
Profit again should hardly draw me here. *Exit*

SCENE 4

Before Birnam Wood

Drum and colours. Enter MALCOLM, SIWARD, MACDUFF, SIWARD'S SON, MENTEITH, CAITHNESS, ANGUS, LENNOX, ROSS, *and soldiers, marching*

MALCOLM. Cousins, I hope the days are near at hand
That chambers will be safe.
MENTEITH. We doubt it nothing.
SIWARD. What wood is this before us?
MENTEITH. The wood of Birnam.
MALCOLM. Let every soldier hew him down a bough
And bear't before him; thereby shall we shadow
The numbers of our host, and make discovery
Err in report of us.
SOLDIER. It shall be done.
SIWARD. We learn no other but the confident tyrant
Keeps still in Dunsinane, and will endure
Our setting down before't.
MALCOLM. 'Tis his main hope;
For where there is advantage to be given,
Both more and less have given him the revolt;
And none serve with him but constrained things
Whose hearts are absent too.
MACDUFF. Let our just censures
Attend the true event, and put we on
Industrious soldiership.
SIWARD. The time approaches
That will with due decision make us know
What we shall say we have, and what we owe.
Thoughts speculative their unsure hopes relate,
But certain issue strokes must arbitrate;
Towards which advance the war. *Exeunt, marching*

SCENE 5

Dunsinane. MACBETH'S *castle*

Enter MACBETH, SEYTON, *and soldiers, with drum and colours*

MACBETH. Hang out our banners on the outward walls;
The cry is still 'They come.' Our castle's strength
Will laugh a siege to scorn. Here let them lie
Till famine and the ague eat them up.
Were they not forc'd with those that should be ours,
We might have met them dareful, beard to beard,
And beat them backward home.
[*A cry within of women*]
What is that noise?
SEYTON. It is the cry of women, my good lord. *Exit*
MACBETH. I have almost forgot the taste of fears.
The time has been my senses would have cool'd
To hear a night-shriek, and my fell of hair
Would at a dismal treatise rouse and stir
As life were in't. I have supp'd full with horrors;
Direness, familiar to my slaughterous thoughts,
Cannot once start me.

Re-enter SEYTON

Wherefore was that cry?
SEYTON. The Queen, my lord, is dead.
MACBETH. She should have died hereafter;
There would have been a time for such a word.
To-morrow, and to-morrow, and to-morrow,
Creeps in this petty pace from day to day
To the last syllable of recorded time,
And all our yesterdays have lighted fools
The way to dusty death. Out, out, brief candle!
Life's but a walking shadow, a poor player,
That struts and frets his hour upon the stage,
And then is heard no more; it is a tale
Told by an idiot, full of sound and fury,
Signifying nothing.

Enter a MESSENGER

Thou com'st to use thy tongue; thy story quickly.
MESSENGER. Gracious my lord,
I should report that which I say I saw,
But know not how to do't.
MACBETH. Well, say, sir.
MESSENGER. As I did stand my watch upon the hill,
I look'd toward Birnam, and anon methought
The wood began to move.
MACBETH. Liar and slave!
MESSENGER. Let me endure your wrath, if't be not so.
Within this three mile may you see it coming;
I say, a moving grove.
MACBETH. If thou speak'st false,
Upon the next tree shalt thou hang alive,
Till famine cling thee. If thy speech be sooth,
I care not if thou dost for me as much.
I pull in resolution, and begin
To doubt th' equivocation of the fiend
That lies like truth. 'Fear not, till Birnam wood
Do come to Dunsinane.' And now a wood
Comes toward Dunsinane. Arm, arm, and out.
If this which he avouches does appear,
There is no flying hence nor tarrying here.
I gin to be aweary of the sun,
And wish th' estate o' th' world were now undone.
Ring the alarum bell. Blow wind, come wrack;
At least we'll die with harness on our back. *Exeunt*

SCENE 6

Dunsinane. Before the castle

Drum and colours. Enter MALCOLM, SIWARD, MACDUFF, *and their army with boughs*

MALCOLM. Now near enough; your leavy screens throw down,
And show like those you are. You, worthy uncle,

Shall with my cousin, your right noble son,
Lead our first battle; worthy Macduff and we
Shall take upon's what else remains to do,
According to our order.

SIWARD. Fare you well.
Do we but find the tyrant's power to-night,
Let us be beaten, if we cannot fight.

MACDUFF. Make all our trumpets speak; give them all breath,
Those clamorous harbingers of blood and death. *Exeunt*

SCENE 7

Another part of the field

Enter MACBETH

MACBETH. They have tied me to a stake; I cannot fly,
But bear-like I must fight the course. What's he
That was not born of woman? Such a one
Am I to fear, or none.

Enter young SIWARD

YOUNG SIWARD. What is thy name?

MACBETH. Thou'lt be afraid to hear it.

YOUNG SIWARD. No; though thou call'st thyself a hotter name
Than any is in hell.

MACBETH. My name's Macbeth.

YOUNG SIWARD. The devil himself could not pronounce a title
More hateful to mine ear.

MACBETH. No, nor more fearful.

YOUNG SIWARD. Thou liest, abhorred tyrant; with my sword
I'll prove the lie thou speak'st.

[*Fight, and young* SIWARD *slain*]

MACBETH. Thou wast born of woman.
But swords I smile at, weapons laugh to scorn,
Brandish'd by man that's of a woman born. *Exit*

Alarums. Enter MACDUFF

MACDUFF. That way the noise is. Tyrant, show thy face.
If thou beest slain and with no stroke of mine,
My wife and children's ghosts will haunt me still.
I cannot strike at wretched kerns whose arms
Are hir'd to bear their staves; either thou, Macbeth,
Or else my sword with an unbattered edge
I sheathe again undeeded. There thou shouldst be;
By this great clatter, one of greatest note
Seems bruited. Let me find him, Fortune,
And more I beg not. *Exit. Alarums*

Enter MALCOLM *and old* SIWARD

SIWARD. This way, my lord. The castle's gently rend'red;
The tyrant's people on both sides do fight;
The noble thanes do bravely in the war;
The day almost itself professes yours,
And little is to do.
MALCOLM. We have met with foes
That strike beside us.
SIWARD. Enter, sir, the castle. *Exeunt. Alarum*

SCENE 8

Another part of the field

Enter MACBETH

MACBETH. Why should I play the Roman fool, and die
On mine own sword? Whiles I see lives, the gashes
Do better upon them.

Enter MACDUFF

MACDUFF. Turn, hell-hound, turn.
MACBETH. Of all men else I have avoided thee.
But get thee back; my soul is too much charg'd
With blood of thine already.
MACDUFF. I have no words–
My voice is in my sword: thou bloodier villain

Than terms can give thee out. [*Fight. Alarum*]

MACBETH. Thou losest labour.
As easy mayst thou the intrenchant air
With thy keen sword impress as make me bleed.
Let fall thy blade on vulnerable crests;
I bear a charmed life, which must not yield
To one of woman born.

MACDUFF. Despair thy charm;
And let the angel whom thou still hast serv'd
Tell thee Macduff was from his mother's womb
Untimely ripp'd.

MACBETH. Accursed be that tongue that tells me so,
For it hath cow'd my better part of man;
And be these juggling fiends no more believ'd
That palter with us in a double sense,
That keep the word of promise to our ear,
And break it to our hope! I'll not fight with thee.

MACDUFF. Then yield thee, coward,
And live to be the show and gaze o' th' time.
We'll have thee, as our rarer monsters are,
Painted upon a pole, and underwrit
'Here may you see the tyrant.'

MACBETH. I will not yield,
To kiss the ground before young Malcolm's feet
And to be baited with the rabble's curse.
Though Birnam wood be come to Dunsinane,
And thou oppos'd, being of no woman born,
Yet I will try the last. Before my body
I throw my warlike shield. Lay on, Macduff;
And damn'd be him that first cries 'Hold, enough!'

Exeunt, fighting. Alarums

Retreat and flourish. Enter, with drum and colours, MALCOLM, SIWARD, ROSS, LENNOX, ANGUS, CAITHNESS, MENTEITH, *and soldiers*

MALCOLM. I would the friends we miss were safe arriv'd.

SIWARD. Some must go off; and yet, by these I see,
So great a day as this is cheaply bought.

MALCOLM. Macduff is missing, and your noble son.

ROSS. Your son, my lord, has paid a soldier's debt:

He only liv'd but till he was a man;
The which no sooner had his prowess confirm'd
In the unshrinking station where he fought,
But like a man he died.

SIWARD. Then he is dead?

ROSS. Ay, and brought off the field. Your cause of sorrow
Must not be measur'd by his worth, for then
It hath no end.

SIWARD. Had he his hurts before?

ROSS. Ay, on the front.

SIWARD. Why, then, God's soldier be he!
Had I as many sons as I have hairs,
I would not wish them to a fairer death.
And so his knell is knoll'd.

MALCOLM. He's worth more sorrow,
And that I'll spend for him.

SIWARD. He's worth no more.
They say he parted well and paid his score;
And so, God be with him! Here comes newer comfort.

Re-enter MACDUFF, *with* MACBETH'S *head*

MACDUFF. Hail, King! for so thou art. Behold where stands
Th' usurper's cursed head. The time is free.
I see thee compass'd with thy kingdom's pearl
That speak my salutation in their minds;
Whose voices I desire aloud with mine—
Hail, King of Scotland!

ALL. Hail, King of Scotland! [*Flourish*]

MALCOLM. We shall not spend a large expense of time
Before we reckon with your several loves,
And make us even with you. My Thanes and kinsmen,
Henceforth be Earls, the first that ever Scotland
In such an honour nam'd. What's more to do,
Which would be planted newly with the time—
As calling home our exil'd friends abroad
That fled the snares of watchful tyranny;
Producing forth the cruel ministers
Of this dead butcher, and his fiend-like queen,
Who, as 'tis thought, by self and violent hands
Took off her life—this, and what needful else

That calls upon us, by the grace of Grace,
We will perform in measure, time, and place.
So thanks to all at once and to each one,
Whom we invite to see us crown'd at Scone.

Flourish. Exeunt

The Tragedy of Hamlet, Prince of Denmark

HAMLET

It is unfortunate that the Elizabethan pamphleteer in his determination to display his cleverness and wit often expresses himself in terms that have sorely puzzled the scholars of later generations and that these passages now stand like conundrums that provoke speculation but defy solution. Greene's animadversions in his *Groats-worth of Witte* on the actors and on Shakespeare still provide material for argument, and the first mention of a play called *Hamlet* is embedded in an even more indecipherable passage by Greene's friend and fellow-author Nashe in a preface he wrote for Greene. In 1589 Greene published his *Menaphon*, a romance in the euphuistic vein, and for this work Nashe composed the epistle *To the Gentlemen Students of Both Universities* that stands as a kind of introduction and puff for his friend's performance. Nashe begins by comparing Greene's 'true eloquence' with that of certain 'vaine glorious Tragedians' who are betrayed into folly by 'their ideot Art-masters, that intrude themselves to our eares as the Alcumists of eloquence, who (mounted on the stage of arrogance) thinke to out-braue better pennes with the swelling bumbast of bragging blanke verse.' Amongst these writers for the stage thus censured for their bombastic style Nashe professes to discover some who are so unscholarly that they have to rely on translations when borrowing from works in any language other than their mother tongue. Having contrasted the scholarly parts and natural dexterity of Greene's mind with the ignorance and defects of these dunces Nashe again returns to elaborate his attack on the unscholarly dramatists:

> I will turne backe to my first text of Studies of delight, and talke a little in friendship with a few of our triviall translators. It is a common practise now a dayes amongst a sort of shifting companions, that runne through euery Art and thrive by none, to leaue the trade of *Nouerint*, whereto they were borne, and busie themselues with the indeuours of Art, that could scarcely Latinize their neck verse if they

should haue neede; yet English *Seneca* read by Candle-light yeelds many good sentences, as *Blood is a begger*, and so forth; and if you intreate him faire in a frostie morning, hee will affoord you whole Hamlets, I should say handfuls of Tragicall speeches. But O griefe! *Tempus edax rerum*, whats that will last alwayes? The Sea exhaled by droppes will in continuance bee drie, and *Seneca*, let blood line by line and page by page, at length must needes die to our Stage; which makes his famished followers to imitate the Kid in *Aesop*, who, enamoured with the Foxes newfangles, forsooke all hopes of life to leape into a new occupation; and these men, renouncing all possibilities of credite or estimation, to intermeddle with Italian Translations: Wherein how poorely they haue plodded, (as those that are neither prouenzall men, nor are able to distinguish of Articles) let all indifferent Gentlemen that haue trauelled in that tongue discerne by their two-pennie Pamphlets.

From this hubbub it is hard to extract any precise information; it seems clear however that among the productions of the unscholarly dramatists is a play *Hamlet*, which seems to Nashe to owe a great deal to Seneca in translation, and, further, that one of these dramatists was Kyd, for Nashe drags in the name regardless of the fact that neither Aesop nor Spenser (to whose *Shepheard's Calendar*, the May eclogue, he is referring) supplies an adequate parallel to the situation now being described. To conclude from this, as many do, that Kyd was the author of the early *Hamlet* is an assumption that the text does not justify and that later evidence makes questionable. Nashe is referring to 'a sort,' that is a group, of writers; that Kyd was one of them and a *Hamlet* one of their productions is as far as this deliberately teasing passage can by itself take us.

The question suggests itself why Nashe should so belabour the dramatists and compare the more comely style of *Menaphon* with what was reckoned the more stately style of drama, a comparison echoed in the lines prefixed to *Menaphon* by 'Thomas Brabine':

Players auant, you know not to delight;
Welcome sweete Shepheard; worth a Schollers sight.

The plausible answer is that the success of Marlowe's *Tamburlaine* had suggested to Greene that he too might try his fortune in this field, and that his first attempt had ended in failure. Greene's *Alphonsus, King of Aragon* is a poor imitation of *Tamburlaine;* that it was a failure is implied in Greene's own statement in his epistle 'To the Gentlemen Readers' prefixed to his *Perimedes the Blacksmith,* published just before *Menaphon.* In that epistle he refers to the derision directed at him by two dramatists,

> for that I could not make my verses iet upon the stage, in tragicall buskins, everie worde filling the mouth like the faburden of Bo-Bell, daring God out of heaven with that Athiest *Tamburlan* or blastpheming with the mad preest of the sun.

Instead therefore of attributing the failure of *Alphonsus* to its wretched construction and feeble verse he animadverts on his model, and as good as names its author when he adds: 'such mad and scoffing poets, that have prophetical spirits as bred of *Merlins* race, if there be any that set the end of scollarisme in an English blanck verse.'

Greene's retort to Marlowe and his fellow-authors provides the key for Nashe's subsequent strain in his epistle; and although Nashe felt justified later in declaring, 'I never abusd Marloe . . . in my life,' his references to 'ideot Art-masters,' their 'bragging blanke verse,' and their stage interests, must have been aimed, if not directly at Marlowe, at those indicated by Greene as his associates, the 'sort' Marlowe consorted with.

We know that Kyd and Marlowe were associated for a period as dramatists working for the same noble Lord and his company of actors. If this company was Lord Pembroke's, as the title-page of *Edward II,* taken in conjunction with some remarks in a letter Kyd wrote about his connection with Marlowe, suggests, we may add, again on the evidence of title-pages, Shakespeare to the group. Such a group would include all the targets that Greene and Nashe seem to be aiming at, when they talk of 'Merlin's race,' and 'the Kid in Aesop' and 'Hamlet.' Shakespeare may well have been the author of the early version of *Hamlet* that Nashe had to go somewhat out of his way to pun on. Later when Shakespeare in 1594 joined the company that was to be known as the Lord Chamberlain's men, the company introduced into their repertory three plays with titles that we recognize as Shakespearian, one of them being *Hamlet*. As the Lord Chamberlain's men are not on record as having taken over any of Kyd's work, when the companies sorted themselves out after the long and disastrous visitation of the plague from 1592 to 1594, we may, since there is no contrary evidence, assume that the early *Hamlet* was Shakespeare's own first version of the piece that we now have in its revised and final form.

The precise date by which Shakespeare had given the final form to *Hamlet* is uncertain; but it must have been before 26 July 1602 when the printer James Roberts entered it for his copy in the Stationers' Register; for this was the version that appeared, though not from Roberts's press, in a pirated edition in 1603, now known as the First Quarto of *Hamlet*. Attempts have been made to show that the piracy depends on what is still a half-revised form of the piece, but Professor Duthie's study of this bad First Quarto (1603) shows that the play the pirate or pirates had seen performed on the stage was substantially the piece preserved for us in the good Second Quarto (1605) and the First Folio texts. A date about 1600 has been proposed for the revision on the strength of a note by Gabriel Harvey in his edition of Speght's *Chaucer:*

> The Earl of Essex much commendes Albions England. . . . The younger sort takes much delight in Shakespeares Venus, and Adonis: but his Lucrece, and his tragedie of Hamlet, Prince of Denmarke, haue it in them, to please the wiser sort.

Essex was executed on 25 February 1601; Harvey's 'commends' suggest that the Earl was still alive when the note was made. As 1600 fits in well with what we can regard as a reasonable time-schedule for the plays as a whole, this date is generally accepted for the final revision of *Hamlet*.

The story of Hamlet which Shakespeare adapted for his plot comes from the *Historia Danica* of Saxo Grammaticus. Written about 1200 this history contains a wealth of story, folk-lore, tradition, and myth, the account of Amleth, prince of Jutland, being an outstanding episode yet completely in harmony with the warlike and saga-like way of life Saxo recreates for us. Challenges to mortal combat, such as that between Amleth's father and the King of Norway, are part of the routine followed by the many heroes Saxo shows us in their pursuit of fame; and the paramount duty of blood revenge is enforced again and again both by precept and example. In the story of Starkad, which rivals that of Amleth, the hero regards the man who fails to avenge his father as the most despicable and infamous of beings.

In 1576 Belleforest published a version of Saxo's story of Hamlet in the fifth volume of his *Histoires Tragiques.* As well as adding much moralizing to the story, Belleforest tries to explain more clearly to us certain of the events that mark its progress. In Saxo the jealous brother waylays and murders Amleth's father and then takes to himself his brother's widow; his excuse for this conduct is that he did it to save the queen from the hate and malice of her husband. Belleforest pauses over this incident to ask how it came about that the queen, knowing that her husband had no intention of murdering her as his assassin gave out, yet accepted the murderer as her husband. This question he answers by telling us that she had prior to her husband's murder been seduced by his brother. Shakespeare adopts this addition, but reinforces its significance by making the murder of so private a kind that the murderer has no need to accuse Hamlet's father of malice towards his wife; in Shakespeare's version, therefore, Gertrude has no need to give, as she does in Saxo and Belleforest, a tacit consent to any slander of her first husband. Belleforest also varies the detail of the temptation to which Hamlet is exposed when the fair and beautiful woman is put conveniently at his disposal. In Saxo Amleth does not hesitate to ravish the maid, though he persuades her to deny the act when she comes to be questioned later by the courtiers: in Belleforest the girl loved the prince more than herself, but the prince 'deceived the courtiers and the lady's expectation' although he affirmed the contrary in public. This detail of the girl's love Shakespeare adopts in making Ophelia in love with Hamlet, placing it in the context of the new relationship he devises for her.

In spite of a slight attempt such as this to mitigate the stark nature of the story he is telling, Belleforest's excuses and moralizings only emphasize the ideals and the customs of the age to which the original story refers us; and in Belleforest as in Saxo it is an age whose uncompromising demands on courage and family honour the original Hamlet not only meets but surpasses. For to the delight of his admirers Hamlet adds to his fearless action and ruthless spirit a wit and dexterity of mind that give his conduct a special flavour and his vengeance not only its completeness but its aesthetic appeal to those who can consider such actions as partaking of something of the nature of the fine arts.

In this story from another age Shakespeare found the material for one of the most original of his creations. Recasting the story and incorporating in his new design elements that might have seemed at first sight incompatible with the primitive features of Saxo's world, Shakespeare now makes his plot the vehicle for an infinitely more difficult theme than that so attractive to the Danish historian who could not but glory in the courage and honour of those he regarded as his countrymen. To show a man no less courageous and in every way as loyal to the honourable tradition of his ancestry as was Saxo's hero, and yet a man touched by considerations beyond the ken of his forbears, demanded what the world has recognized as one of Shakespeare's most splendid performances. That criticism has been slow to catch up with the instinctive verdict of the imagination is natural. As a philosopher has observed, the mind's way is round about and the way from the heart to the head is often a long one. It need not therefore surprise us that the enjoyment of *Hamlet* has far outrun anything that can be called criticism of the art that gives it its universal appeal.

Claudius, *King of Denmark*
Hamlet, *son to the former and nephew to the present King*
Polonius, *Lord Chamberlain*
Horatio, *friend to Hamlet*
Laertes, *son to Polonius*
Voltemand, Cornelius, Rosencrantz, Guildenstern, Osric, A Gentleman — *courtiers*
A Priest
Marcellus, Bernardo — *officers*
Francisco, *a soldier*
Reynaldo, *servant to Polonius*
Players
Two Clowns, *grave-diggers*
Fortinbras, *Prince of Norway*
A Norwegian Captain
English Ambassadors

Gertrude, *Queen of Denmark, and mother of Hamlet*
Ophelia, *daughter to Polonius*

Ghost *of Hamlet's father*

Lords, Ladies, Officers, Soldiers, Sailors, Messengers, *and* Attendants

SCENE:

Denmark

Hamlet, Prince of Denmark

ACT I. SCENE 1

Elsinore. The guard-platform of the Castle

FRANCISCO *at his post. Enter to him* BERNARDO

BERNARDO. Who's there?
FRANCISCO. Nay, answer me. Stand and unfold yourself.
BERNARDO. Long live the King!
FRANCISCO. Bernardo?
BERNARDO. He.
FRANCISCO. You come most carefully upon your hour.
BERNARDO. 'Tis now struck twelve; get thee to bed, Francisco.
FRANCISCO. For this relief much thanks. 'Tis bitter cold,
And I am sick at heart.
BERNARDO. Have you had quiet guard?
FRANCISCO. Not a mouse stirring.
BERNARDO. Well, good night.
If you do meet Horatio and Marcellus,
The rivals of my watch, bid them make haste.

Enter HORATIO *and* MARCELLUS

FRANCISCO. I think I hear them. Stand, ho! Who is there?
HORATIO. Friends to this ground.
MARCELLUS. And liegemen to the Dane.
FRANCISCO. Give you good night.
MARCELLUS. O, farewell, honest soldier!
Who hath reliev'd you?
FRANCISCO. Bernardo hath my place.
Give you good night. *Exit*
MARCELLUS. Holla, Bernardo!
BERNARDO. Say–
What, is Horatio there?
HORATIO. A piece of him.
BERNARDO. Welcome, Horatio; welcome, good Marcellus.

HORATIO. What, has this thing appear'd again to-night?
BERNARDO. I have seen nothing.
MARCELLUS. Horatio says 'tis but our fantasy,
  And will not let belief take hold of him
  Touching this dreaded sight, twice seen of us;
  Therefore I have entreated him along
  With us to watch the minutes of this night,
  That, if again this apparition come,
  He may approve our eyes and speak to it.
HORATIO. Tush, tush, 'twill not appear.
BERNARDO. Sit down awhile,
  And let us once again assail your ears,
  That are so fortified against our story,
  What we have two nights seen.
HORATIO. Well, sit we down,
  And let us hear Bernardo speak of this.
BERNARDO. Last night of all,
  When yond same star that's westward from the pole
  Had made his course t' illume that part of heaven
  Where now it burns, Marcellus and myself,
  The bell then beating one–

Enter GHOST

MARCELLUS. Peace, break thee off; look where it comes again.
BERNARDO. In the same figure, like the King that's dead.
MARCELLUS. Thou art a scholar; speak to it, Horatio.
BERNARDO. Looks 'a not like the King? Mark it, Horatio.
HORATIO. Most like. It harrows me with fear and wonder.
BERNARDO. It would be spoke to.
MARCELLUS. Question it, Horatio.
HORATIO. What art thou that usurp'st this time of night
  Together with that fair and warlike form
  In which the majesty of buried Denmark
  Did sometimes march? By heaven I charge thee, speak!
MARCELLUS. It is offended.
BERNARDO. See, it stalks away.
HORATIO. Stay! speak, speak! I charge thee, speak!

Exit GHOST

MARCELLUS. 'Tis gone, and will not answer.

BERNARDO. How now, Horatio! You tremble and look pale.
Is not this something more than fantasy?
What think you on't?
HORATIO. Before my God, I might not this believe
Without the sensible and true avouch
Of mine own eyes.
MARCELLUS. Is it not like the King?
HORATIO. As thou art to thyself:
Such was the very armour he had on
When he the ambitious Norway combated;
So frown'd he once when, in an angry parle,
He smote the sledded Polacks on the ice.
'Tis strange.
MARCELLUS. Thus twice before, and jump at this dead hour,
With martial stalk hath he gone by our watch.
HORATIO. In what particular thought to work I know not;
But, in the gross and scope of mine opinion,
This bodes some strange eruption to our state.
MARCELLUS. Good now, sit down, and tell me, he that knows,
Why this same strict and most observant watch
So nightly toils the subject of the land;
And why such daily cast of brazen cannon,
And foreign mart for implements of war;
Why such impress of shipwrights, whose sore task
Does not divide the Sunday from the week;
What might be toward, that this sweaty haste
Doth make the night joint-labourer with the day:
Who is't that can inform me?
HORATIO. That can I;
At least, the whisper goes so. Our last King,
Whose image even but now appear'd to us,
Was, as you know, by Fortinbras of Norway,
Thereto prick'd on by a most emulate pride,
Dar'd to the combat; in which our valiant Hamlet—
For so this side of our known world esteem'd him—
Did slay this Fortinbras; who, by a seal'd compact,
Well ratified by law and heraldry,
Did forfeit, with his life, all those his lands
Which he stood seiz'd of, to the conqueror;

Against the which a moiety competent
Was gaged by our King; which had return'd
To the inheritance of Fortinbras,
Had he been vanquisher; as, by the same comart
And carriage of the article design'd,
His fell to Hamlet. Now, sir, young Fortinbras,
Of unimproved mettle hot and full,
Hath in the skirts of Norway, here and there,
Shark'd up a list of lawless resolutes,
For food and diet, to some enterprise
That hath a stomach in't; which is no other,
As it doth well appear unto our state,
But to recover of us, by strong hand
And terms compulsatory, those foresaid lands
So by his father lost; and this, I take it,
Is the main motive of our preparations,
The source of this our watch, and the chief head
Of this post-haste and romage in the land.

BERNARDO. I think it be no other but e'en so.
Well may it sort, that this portentous figure
Comes armed through our watch; so like the King
That was and is the question of these wars.

HORATIO. A mote it is to trouble the mind's eye.
In the most high and palmy state of Rome,
A little ere the mightiest Julius fell,
The graves stood tenantless, and the sheeted dead
Did squeak and gibber in the Roman streets;
As, stars with trains of fire, and dews of blood,
Disasters in the sun; and the moist star
Upon whose influence Neptune's empire stands
Was sick almost to doomsday with eclipse;
And even the like precurse of fear'd events,
As harbingers preceding still the fates
And prologue to the omen coming on,
Have heaven and earth together demonstrated
Unto our climatures and countrymen.

Re-enter GHOST

But, soft, behold! Lo, where it comes again!
I'll cross it, though it blast me. Stay, illusion.

[GHOST *spreads its arms*]

If thou hast any sound or use of voice,
Speak to me.
If there be any good thing to be done,
That may to thee do ease and grace to me,
Speak to me.
If thou art privy to thy country's fate,
Which happily foreknowing may avoid,
O, speak!
Or if thou hast uphoarded in thy life
Extorted treasure in the womb of earth,
For which, they say, you spirits oft walk in death,

[*The cock crows*]

Speak of it. Stay, and speak. Stop it, Marcellus.

MARCELLUS. Shall I strike at it with my partisan?

HORATIO. Do, if it will not stand.

BERNARDO. 'Tis here!

HORATIO. 'Tis here!

MARCELLUS. 'Tis gone! *Exit* GHOST
We do it wrong, being so majestical,
To offer it the show of violence;
For it is, as the air, invulnerable,
And our vain blows malicious mockery.

BERNARDO. It was about to speak, when the cock crew.

HORATIO. And then it started like a guilty thing
Upon a fearful summons. I have heard
The cock, that is the trumpet to the morn,
Doth with his lofty and shrill-sounding throat
Awake the god of day; and at his warning,
Whether in sea or fire, in earth or air,
Th' extravagant and erring spirit hies
To his confine; and of the truth herein
This present object made probation.

MARCELLUS. It faded on the crowing of the cock.
Some say that ever 'gainst that season comes
Wherein our Saviour's birth is celebrated,
This bird of dawning singeth all night long;
And then, they say, no spirit dare stir abroad,
The nights are wholesome, then no planets strike,
No fairy takes, nor witch hath power to charm,

So hallowed and so gracious is that time.
HORATIO. So have I heard, and do in part believe it.
But look, the morn, in russet mantle clad,
Walks o'er the dew of yon high eastward hill.
Break we our watch up; and, by my advice,
Let us impart what we have seen to-night
Unto young Hamlet; for, upon my life,
This spirit, dumb to us, will speak to him.
Do you consent we shall acquaint him with it,
As needful in our loves, fitting our duty?
MARCELLUS. Let's do't, I pray; and I this morning know
Where we shall find him most convenient. *Exeunt*

SCENE 2

Elsinore. The Castle

Flourish. Enter CLAUDIUS KING OF DENMARK, GERTRUDE THE QUEEN, *and* COUNCILLORS, *including* POLONIUS, *his son* LAERTES, VOLTEMAND, CORNELIUS, *and* HAMLET

KING. Though yet of Hamlet our dear brother's death
The memory be green; and that it us befitted
To bear our hearts in grief, and our whole kingdom
To be contracted in one brow of woe;
Yet so far hath discretion fought with nature
That we with wisest sorrow think on him,
Together with remembrance of ourselves.
Therefore our sometime sister, now our queen,
Th' imperial jointress to this warlike state,
Have we, as 'twere with a defeated joy,
With an auspicious and a dropping eye,
With mirth in funeral, and with dirge in marriage,
In equal scale weighing delight and dole,
Taken to wife; nor have we herein barr'd
Your better wisdoms, which have freely gone
With this affair along. For all, our thanks.
Now follows that you know: young Fortinbras,

Holding a weak supposal of our worth,
Or thinking by our late dear brother's death
Our state to be disjoint and out of frame,
Co-leagued with this dream of his advantage—
He hath not fail'd to pester us with message
Importing the surrender of those lands
Lost by his father, with all bands of law,
To our most valiant brother. So much for him.
Now for ourself, and for this time of meeting,
Thus much the business is: we have here writ
To Norway, uncle of young Fortinbras—
Who, impotent and bed-rid, scarcely hears
Of this his nephew's purpose—to suppress
His further gait herein, in that the levies,
The lists, and full proportions, are all made
Out of his subject; and we here dispatch
You, good Cornelius, and you, Voltemand,
For bearers of this greeting to old Norway;
Giving to you no further personal power
To business with the King more than the scope
Of these delated articles allow.
Farewell; and let your haste commend your duty.

CORNELIUS.
VOLTEMAND. } In that and all things will we show our duty.

KING. We doubt it nothing; heartily farewell.

Exeunt VOLTEMAND *and* CORNELIUS

And now, Laertes, what's the news with you?
You told us of some suit; what is't, Laertes?
You cannot speak of reason to the Dane
And lose your voice. What wouldst thou beg, Laertes,
That shall not be my offer, not thy asking?
The head is not more native to the heart,
The hand more instrumental to the mouth,
Than is the throne of Denmark to thy father.
What wouldst thou have, Laertes?

LAERTES. My dread lord,
Your leave and favour to return to France;
From whence though willingly I came to Denmark
To show my duty in your coronation,
Yet now, I must confess, that duty done,

My thoughts and wishes bend again toward France,
And bow them to your gracious leave and pardon.
KING. Have you your father's leave? What says Polonius?
POLONIUS. 'A hath, my lord, wrung from me my slow leave
By laboursome petition; and at last
Upon his will I seal'd my hard consent.
I do beseech you, give him leave to go.
KING. Take thy fair hour, Laertes; time be thine,
And thy best graces spend it at thy will!
But now, my cousin Hamlet, and my son–
HAMLET. [*Aside*] A little more than kin, and less than kind.
KING. How is it that the clouds still hang on you?
HAMLET. Not so, my lord; I am too much in the sun.
QUEEN. Good Hamlet, cast thy nighted colour off,
And let thine eye look like a friend on Denmark.
Do not for ever with thy vailed lids
Seek for thy noble father in the dust.
Thou know'st 'tis common–all that lives must die,
Passing through nature to eternity.
HAMLET. Ay, madam, it is common.
QUEEN. If it be,
Why seems it so particular with thee?
HAMLET. Seems, madam! Nay, it is; I know not seems.
'Tis not alone my inky cloak, good mother,
Nor customary suits of solemn black,
Nor windy suspiration of forc'd breath,
No, nor the fruitful river in the eye,
Nor the dejected haviour of the visage,
Together with all forms, moods, shapes of grief,
That can denote me truly. These, indeed, seem;
For they are actions that a man might play;
But I have that within which passes show–
These but the trappings and the suits of woe.
KING. 'Tis sweet and commendable in your nature, Hamlet,
To give these mourning duties to your father;
But you must know your father lost a father;
That father lost, lost his; and the survivor bound,
In filial obligation, for some term
To do obsequious sorrow. But to persever
In obstinate condolement is a course

Of impious stubbornness; 'tis unmanly grief;
It shows a will most incorrect to heaven,
A heart unfortified, a mind impatient,
An understanding simple and unschool'd;
For what we know must be, and is as common
As any the most vulgar thing to sense,
Why should we in our peevish opposition
Take it to heart? Fie! 'tis a fault to heaven,
A fault against the dead, a fault to nature,
To reason most absurd; whose common theme
Is death of fathers, and who still hath cried,
From the first corse till he that died to-day,
'This must be so.' We pray you throw to earth
This unprevailing woe, and think of us
As of a father; for let the world take note
You are the most immediate to our throne;
And with no less nobility of love
Than that which dearest father bears his son
Do I impart toward you. For your intent
In going back to school in Wittenberg,
It is most retrograde to our desire;
And we beseech you bend you to remain
Here, in the cheer and comfort of our eye,
Our chiefest courtier, cousin, and our son.

QUEEN. Let not thy mother lose her prayers, Hamlet:
I pray thee stay with us; go not to Wittenberg.

HAMLET. I shall in all my best obey you, madam.

KING. Why, 'tis a loving and a fair reply.
Be as ourself in Denmark. Madam, come;
This gentle and unforc'd accord of Hamlet
Sits smiling to my heart; in grace whereof,
No jocund health that Denmark drinks to-day
But the great cannon to the clouds shall tell,
And the King's rouse the heaven shall bruit again,
Re-speaking earthly thunder. Come away.

Flourish. Exeunt all but HAMLET

HAMLET. O, that this too too solid flesh would melt,
Thaw, and resolve itself into a dew!
Or that the Everlasting had not fix'd
His canon 'gainst self-slaughter! O God! God!

How weary, stale, flat, and unprofitable,
Seem to me all the uses of this world!
Fie on't! Ah, fie! 'tis an unweeded garden,
That grows to seed; things rank and gross in nature
Possess it merely. That it should come to this!
But two months dead! Nay, not so much, not two.
So excellent a king that was to this
Hyperion to a satyr; so loving to my mother,
That he might not beteem the winds of heaven
Visit her face too roughly. Heaven and earth!
Must I remember? Why, she would hang on him
As if increase of appetite had grown
By what it fed on; and yet, within a month—
Let me not think on't. Frailty, thy name is woman!—
A little month, or ere those shoes were old
With which she followed my poor father's body,
Like Niobe, all tears—why she, even she—
O God! a beast that wants discourse of reason
Would have mourn'd longer—married with my uncle,
My father's brother; but no more like my father
Than I to Hercules. Within a month,
Ere yet the salt of most unrighteous tears
Had left the flushing in her galled eyes,
She married. O, most wicked speed, to post
With such dexterity to incestuous sheets!
It is not, nor it cannot come to good.
But break, my heart, for I must hold my tongue.

Enter HORATIO, MARCELLUS, *and* BERNARDO

HORATIO. Hail to your lordship!

HAMLET. I am glad to see you well.
Horatio—or I do forget myself.

HORATIO. The same, my lord, and your poor servant ever.

HAMLET. Sir, my good friend. I'll change that name with you.
And what make you from Wittenberg, Horatio?
Marcellus?

MARCELLUS. My good lord!

HAMLET. I am very glad to see you. [*To* BERNARDO] Good even, sir.—

But what, in faith, make you from Wittenberg?
HORATIO. A truant disposition, good my lord.
HAMLET. I would not hear your enemy say so;
Nor shall you do my ear that violence,
To make it truster of your own report
Against yourself. I know you are no truant.
But what is your affair in Elsinore?
We'll teach you to drink deep ere you depart.
HORATIO. My lord, I came to see your father's funeral.
HAMLET. I prithee do not mock me, fellow-student;
I think it was to see my mother's wedding.
HORATIO. Indeed, my lord, it followed hard upon.
HAMLET. Thrift, thrift, Horatio! The funeral bak'd-meats
Did coldly furnish forth the marriage tables.
Would I had met my dearest foe in heaven
Or ever I had seen that day, Horatio!
My father—methinks I see my father.
HORATIO. Where, my lord?
HAMLET. In my mind's eye, Horatio.
HORATIO. I saw him once; 'a was a goodly king.
HAMLET. 'A was a man, take him for all in all,
I shall not look upon his like again.
HORATIO. My lord, I think I saw him yesternight.
HAMLET. Saw who?
HORATIO. My lord, the King your father.
HAMLET. The King my father!
HORATIO. Season your admiration for a while
With an attent ear, till I may deliver,
Upon the witness of these gentlemen,
This marvel to you.
HAMLET. For God's love, let me hear.
HORATIO. Two nights together had these gentlemen,
Marcellus and Bernardo, on their watch,
In the dead waste and middle of the night,
Been thus encount'red. A figure like your father,
Armed at point exactly, cap-a-pe,
Appears before them, and with solemn march
Goes slow and stately by them; thrice he walk'd
By their oppress'd and fear-surprised eyes,
Within his truncheon's length; whilst they, distill'd

Almost to jelly with the act of fear,
Stand dumb and speak not to him. This to me
In dreadful secrecy impart they did;
And I with them the third night kept the watch;
Where, as they had delivered, both in time,
Form of the thing, each word made true and good,
The apparition comes. I knew your father;
These hands are not more like.

HAMLET. But where was this?

MARCELLUS. My lord, upon the platform where we watch.

HAMLET. Did you not speak to it?

HORATIO. My lord, I did;
But answer made it none; yet once methought
It lifted up it head and did address
Itself to motion, like as it would speak;
But even then the morning cock crew loud,
And at the sound it shrunk in haste away
And vanish'd from our sight.

HAMLET. 'Tis very strange.

HORATIO. As I do live, my honour'd lord, 'tis true;
And we did think it writ down in our duty
To let you know of it.

HAMLET. Indeed, indeed, sirs, but this troubles me.
Hold you the watch to-night?

ALL. We do, my lord.

HAMLET. Arm'd, say you?

ALL. Arm'd, my lord.

HAMLET. From top to toe?

ALL. My lord, from head to foot.

HAMLET. Then saw you not his face?

HORATIO. O yes, my lord; he wore his beaver up.

HAMLET. What, look'd he frowningly?

HORATIO. A countenance more in sorrow than in anger.

HAMLET. Pale or red?

HORATIO. Nay, very pale.

HAMLET. And fix'd his eyes upon you?

HORATIO. Most constantly.

HAMLET. I would I had been there.

HORATIO. It would have much amaz'd you.

HAMLET. Very like, very like. Stay'd it long?

HORATIO. While one with moderate haste might tell a hundred.
BOTH. Longer, longer.
HORATIO. Not when I saw't.
HAMLET. His beard was grizzl'd—no?
HORATIO. It was, as I have seen it in his life,
A sable silver'd.
HAMLET. I will watch to-night;
Perchance 'twill walk again.
HORATIO. I warr'nt it will.
HAMLET. If it assume my noble father's person,
I'll speak to it, though hell itself should gape
And bid me hold my peace. I pray you all,
If you have hitherto conceal'd this sight,
Let it be tenable in your silence still;
And whatsomever else shall hap to-night,
Give it an understanding, but no tongue;
I will requite your loves. So, fare you well—
Upon the platform, 'twixt eleven and twelve,
I'll visit you.
ALL. Our duty to your honour.
HAMLET. Your loves, as mine to you; farewell.

Exeunt all but HAMLET

My father's spirit in arms! All is not well.
I doubt some foul play. Would the night were come!
Till then sit still, my soul. Foul deeds will rise,
Though all the earth o'erwhelm them, to men's eyes. *Exit*

SCENE 3

Elsinore. The house of POLONIUS

Enter LAERTES *and* OPHELIA *his sister*

LAERTES. My necessaries are embark'd. Farewell.
And, sister, as the winds give benefit
And convoy is assistant, do not sleep,
But let me hear from you.
OPHELIA. Do you doubt that?
LAERTES. For Hamlet, and the trifling of his favour,

Hold it a fashion and a toy in blood,
A violet in the youth of primy nature,
Forward not permanent, sweet not lasting,
The perfume and suppliance of a minute;
No more.

OPHELIA. No more but so?

LAERTES. Think it no more;
For nature crescent does not grow alone
In thews and bulk, but as this temple waxes,
The inward service of the mind and soul
Grows wide withal. Perhaps he loves you now,
And now no soil nor cautel doth besmirch
The virtue of his will; but you must fear,
His greatness weigh'd, his will is not his own;
For he himself is subject to his birth:
He may not, as unvalued persons do,
Carve for himself; for on his choice depends
The sanity and health of this whole state;
And therefore must his choice be circumscrib'd
Unto the voice and yielding of that body
Whereof he is the head. Then if he says he loves you,
It fits your wisdom so far to believe it
As he in his particular act and place
May give his saying deed; which is no further
Than the main voice of Denmark goes withal.
Then weigh what loss your honour may sustain,
If with too credent ear you list his songs,
Or lose your heart, or your chaste treasure open
To his unmast'red importunity.
Fear it, Ophelia, fear it, my dear sister;
And keep you in the rear of your affection,
Out of the shot and danger of desire.
The chariest maid is prodigal enough
If she unmask her beauty to the moon.
Virtue itself scapes not calumnious strokes;
The canker galls the infants of the spring
Too oft before their buttons be disclos'd;
And in the morn and liquid dew of youth
Contagious blastments are most imminent.
Be wary, then; best safety lies in fear:

Youth to itself rebels, though none else near.
OPHELIA. I shall the effect of this good lesson keep
As watchman to my heart. But, good my brother,
Do not, as some ungracious pastors do,
Show me the steep and thorny way to heaven,
Whiles, like a puff'd and reckless libertine,
Himself the primrose path of dalliance treads
And recks not his own rede.
LAERTES. O, fear me not!

Enter POLONIUS

I stay too long. But here my father comes.
A double blessing is a double grace;
Occasion smiles upon a second leave.
POLONIUS. Yet here, Laertes! Aboard, aboard, for shame!
The wind sits in the shoulder of your sail,
And you are stay'd for. There—my blessing with thee!
And these few precepts in thy memory
Look thou character. Give thy thoughts no tongue,
Nor any unproportion'd thought his act.
Be thou familiar, but by no means vulgar.
Those friends thou hast, and their adoption tried,
Grapple them to thy soul with hoops of steel;
But do not dull thy palm with entertainment
Of each new-hatch'd, unfledg'd courage. Beware
Of entrance to a quarrel; but, being in,
Bear't that th' opposed may beware of thee.
Give every man thy ear, but few thy voice;
Take each man's censure, but reserve thy judgment.
Costly thy habit as thy purse can buy,
But not express'd in fancy; rich, not gaudy;
For the apparel oft proclaims the man;
And they in France of the best rank and station
Are of a most select and generous choice in that.
Neither a borrower nor a lender be;
For loan oft loses both itself and friend,
And borrowing dulls the edge of husbandry.
This above all—to thine own self be true,
And it must follow, as the night the day,
Thou canst not then be false to any man.

Farewell; my blessing season this in thee!

LAERTES. Most humbly do I take my leave, my lord.

POLONIUS. The time invites you; go, your servants tend.

LAERTES. Farewell, Ophelia; and remember well
What I have said to you.

OPHELIA. 'Tis in my memory lock'd,
And you yourself shall keep the key of it.

LAERTES. Farewell. *Exit*

POLONIUS. What is't, Ophelia, he hath said to you?

OPHELIA. So please you, something touching the Lord Hamlet.

POLONIUS. Marry, well bethought!
'Tis told me he hath very oft of late
Given private time to you; and you yourself
Have of your audience been most free and bounteous.
If it be so—as so 'tis put on me,
And that in way of caution—I must tell you
You do not understand yourself so clearly
As it behoves my daughter and your honour.
What is between you? Give me up the truth.

OPHELIA. He hath, my lord, of late made many tenders
Of his affection to me.

POLONIUS. Affection! Pooh! You speak like a green girl,
Unsifted in such perilous circumstance.
Do you believe his tenders, as you call them?

OPHELIA. I do not know, my lord, what I should think.

POLONIUS. Marry, I will teach you: think yourself a baby
That you have ta'en these tenders for true pay
Which are not sterling. Tender yourself more dearly;
Or—not to crack the wind of the poor phrase,
Running it thus—you'll tender me a fool.

OPHELIA. My lord, he hath importun'd me with love
In honourable fashion.

POLONIUS. Ay, fashion you may call it; go to, go to.

OPHELIA. And hath given countenance to his speech, my lord,
With almost all the holy vows of heaven.

POLONIUS. Ay, springes to catch woodcocks! I do know,
When the blood burns, how prodigal the soul
Lends the tongue vows. These blazes, daughter,

Giving more light than heat—extinct in both,
Even in their promise, as it is a-making—
You must not take for fire. From this time
Be something scanter of your maiden presence;
Set your entreatments at a higher rate
Than a command to parle. For Lord Hamlet,
Believe so much in him, that he is young,
And with a larger tether may he walk
Than may be given you. In few, Ophelia,
Do not believe his vows; for they are brokers,
Not of that dye which their investments show,
But mere implorators of unholy suits,
Breathing like sanctified and pious bonds,
The better to beguile. This is for all—
I would not, in plain terms, from this time forth
Have you so slander any moment leisure
As to give words or talk with the Lord Hamlet.
Look to't, I charge you. Come your ways.

OPHELIA. I shall obey, my lord. *Exeunt*

SCENE 4

Elsinore. The guard-platform of the Castle

Enter HAMLET, HORATIO, *and* MARCELLUS

HAMLET. The air bites shrewdly; it is very cold.

HORATIO. It is a nipping and an eager air.

HAMLET. What hour now?

HORATIO. I think it lacks of twelve.

MARCELLUS. No, it is struck.

HORATIO. Indeed? I heard it not. It then draws near the season
Wherein the spirit held his wont to walk.
[*A flourish of trumpets, and two pieces go off*]
What does this mean, my lord?

HAMLET. The King doth wake to-night and takes his rouse,
Keeps wassail, and the swagg'ring up-spring reels,
And, as he drains his draughts of Rhenish down,
The kettle-drum and trumpet thus bray out

The triumph of his pledge.

HORATIO. Is it a custom?

HAMLET. Ay, marry, is't;
But to my mind, though I am native here
And to the manner born, it is a custom
More honour'd in the breach than the observance.
This heavy-headed revel east and west
Makes us traduc'd and tax'd of other nations;
They clepe us drunkards, and with swinish phrase
Soil our addition; and, indeed, it takes
From our achievements, though perform'd at height,
The pith and marrow of our attribute.
So, oft it chances in particular men
That, for some vicious mole of nature in them,
As in their birth, wherein they are not guilty,
Since nature cannot choose his origin;
By the o'ergrowth of some complexion,
Oft breaking down the pales and forts of reason;
Or by some habit that too much o'er-leavens
The form of plausive manners—that these men,
Carrying, I say, the stamp of one defect,
Being nature's livery or fortune's star,
His virtues else, be they as pure as grace,
As infinite as man may undergo,
Shall in the general censure take corruption
From that particular fault. The dram of eale
Doth all the noble substance of a doubt
To his own scandal.

Enter GHOST

HORATIO. Look, my lord, it comes.

HAMLET. Angels and ministers of grace defend us!
Be thou a spirit of health or goblin damn'd,
Bring with thee airs from heaven or blasts from hell,
Be thy intents wicked or charitable,
Thou com'st in such a questionable shape
That I will speak to thee. I'll call thee Hamlet,
King, father, royal Dane. O, answer me!
Let me not burst in ignorance, but tell
Why thy canoniz'd bones, hearsed in death,

Have burst their cerements; why the sepulchre
Wherein we saw thee quietly enurn'd
Hath op'd his ponderous and marble jaws
To cast thee up again. What may this mean
That thou, dead corse, again in complete steel
Revisits thus the glimpses of the moon,
Making night hideous, and we fools of nature
So horridly to shake our disposition
With thoughts beyond the reaches of our souls?
Say, why is this? wherefore? What should we do?
[GHOST *beckons* HAMLET]

HORATIO. It beckons you to go away with it,
As if it some impartment did desire
To you alone.

MARCELLUS. Look with what courteous action
It waves you to a more removed ground.
But do not go with it.

HORATIO. No, by no means.

HAMLET. It will not speak; then I will follow it.

HORATIO. Do not, my lord.

HAMLET. Why, what should be the fear?
I do not set my life at a pin's fee;
And for my soul, what can it do to that,
Being a thing immortal as itself?
It waves me forth again; I'll follow it.

HORATIO. What if it tempt you toward the flood, my lord,
Or to the dreadful summit of the cliff
That beetles o'er his base into the sea,
And there assume some other horrible form,
Which might deprive your sovereignty of reason
And draw you into madness? Think of it:
The very place puts toys of desperation,
Without more motive, into every brain
That looks so many fathoms to the sea
And hears it roar beneath.

HAMLET. It waves me still.
Go on; I'll follow thee.

MARCELLUS. You shall not go, my lord.

HAMLET. Hold off your hands.

HORATIO. Be rul'd; you shall not go.

HAMLET. My fate cries out,
And makes each petty arture in this body
As hardy as the Nemean lion's nerve. [GHOST *beckons*]
Still am I call'd. Unhand me, gentlemen.
By heaven, I'll make a ghost of him that lets me.
I say, away! Go on; I'll follow thee.
Exeunt GHOST *and* HAMLET

HORATIO. He waxes desperate with imagination.
MARCELLUS. Let's follow; 'tis not fit thus to obey him.
HORATIO. Have after. To what issue will this come?
MARCELLUS. Something is rotten in the state of Denmark.
HORATIO. Heaven will direct it.
MARCELLUS. Nay, let's follow him. *Exeunt*

SCENE 5

Elsinore. The battlements of the Castle

Enter GHOST *and* HAMLET

HAMLET. Whither wilt thou lead me? Speak. I'll go no further.
GHOST. Mark me.
HAMLET. I will.
GHOST. My hour is almost come,
When I to sulph'rous and tormenting flames
Must render up myself.
HAMLET. Alas, poor ghost!
GHOST. Pity me not, but lend thy serious hearing
To what I shall unfold.
HAMLET. Speak; I am bound to hear.
GHOST. So art thou to revenge, when thou shalt hear.
HAMLET. What?
GHOST. I am thy father's spirit,
Doom'd for a certain term to walk the night,
And for the day confin'd to fast in fires,
Till the foul crimes done in my days of nature
Are burnt and purg'd away. But that I am forbid
To tell the secrets of my prison-house,
I could a tale unfold whose lightest word

Would harrow up thy soul, freeze thy young blood,
Make thy two eyes, like stars, start from their spheres,
Thy knotted and combined locks to part,
And each particular hair to stand an end,
Like quills upon the fretful porpentine.
But this eternal blazon must not be
To ears of flesh and blood. List, list, O, list!
If thou didst ever thy dear father love—

HAMLET. O God!

GHOST. Revenge his foul and most unnatural murder.

HAMLET. Murder!

GHOST. Murder most foul, as in the best it is;
But this most foul, strange, and unnatural.

HAMLET. Haste me to know't, that I, with wings as swift
As meditation or the thoughts of love,
May sweep to my revenge.

GHOST. I find thee apt;
And duller shouldst thou be than the fat weed
That roots itself in ease on Lethe wharf,
Wouldst thou not stir in this. Now, Hamlet, hear:
'Tis given out that, sleeping in my orchard,
A serpent stung me; so the whole ear of Denmark
Is by a forged process of my death
Rankly abus'd; but know, thou noble youth,
The serpent that did sting thy father's life
Now wears his crown.

HAMLET. O my prophetic soul!
My uncle!

GHOST. Ay, that incestuous, that adulterate beast,
With witchcraft of his wits, with traitorous gifts—
O wicked wit and gifts that have the power
So to seduce!—won to his shameful lust
The will of my most seeming virtuous queen.
O Hamlet, what a falling off was there,
From me, whose love was of that dignity
That it went hand in hand even with the vow
I made to her in marriage; and to decline
Upon a wretch whose natural gifts were poor
To those of mine!
But virtue, as it never will be moved,

Though lewdness court it in a shape of heaven,
So lust, though to a radiant angel link'd,
Will sate itself in a celestial bed
And prey on garbage.
But soft! methinks I scent the morning air.
Brief let me be. Sleeping within my orchard,
My custom always of the afternoon,
Upon my secure hour thy uncle stole,
With juice of cursed hebona in a vial,
And in the porches of my ears did pour
The leperous distilment; whose effect
Holds such an enmity with blood of man
That swift as quicksilver it courses through
The natural gates and alleys of the body;
And with a sudden vigour it doth posset
And curd, like eager droppings into milk,
The thin and wholesome blood. So did it mine;
And a most instant tetter bark'd about,
Most lazar-like, with vile and loathsome crust,
All my smooth body.
Thus was I, sleeping, by a brother's hand
Of life, of crown, of queen, at once dispatch'd;
Cut off even in the blossoms of my sin,
Unhous'led, disappointed, unanel'd;
No reck'ning made, but sent to my account
With all my imperfections on my head.
O, horrible! O, horrible! most horrible!
If thou hast nature in thee, bear it not;
Let not the royal bed of Denmark be
A couch for luxury and damned incest.
But, howsomever thou pursuest this act,
Taint not thy mind, nor let thy soul contrive
Against thy mother aught; leave her to heaven,
And to those thorns that in her bosom lodge
To prick and sting her. Fare thee well at once.
The glowworm shows the matin to be near,
And gins to pale his uneffectual fire.
Adieu, adieu, adieu! Remember me. *Exit*

HAMLET. O all you host of heaven! O earth! What else?
And shall I couple hell? O, fie! Hold, hold, my heart;

And you, my sinews, grow not instant old,
But bear me stiffly up. Remember thee!
Ay, thou poor ghost, whiles memory holds a seat
In this distracted globe. Remember thee!
Yea, from the table of my memory
I'll wipe away all trivial fond records,
All saws of books, all forms, all pressures past,
That youth and observation copied there,
And thy commandment all alone shall live
Within the book and volume of my brain,
Unmix'd with baser matter. Yes, by heaven!
O most pernicious woman!
O villain, villain, smiling, damned villain!
My tables—meet it is I set it down
That one may smile, and smile, and be a villain;
At least I am sure it may be so in Denmark. [*Writing*]
So, uncle, there you are. Now to my word:
It is 'Adieu, adieu! Remember me.'
I have sworn't.

HORATIO. [*Within*] My lord, my lord!

Enter HORATIO *and* MARCELLUS

MARCELLUS. Lord Hamlet!
HORATIO. Heavens secure him!
HAMLET. So be it!
MARCELLUS. Illo, ho, ho, my lord!
HAMLET. Hillo, ho, ho, boy! Come, bird, come.
MARCELLUS. How is't, my noble lord?
HORATIO. What news, my lord?
HAMLET. O, wonderful!
HORATIO. Good my lord, tell it.
HAMLET. No; you will reveal it.
HORATIO. Not I, my lord, by heaven!
MARCELLUS. Nor I, my lord.
HAMLET. How say you, then; would heart of man once think it?
But you'll be secret?
BOTH. Ay, by heaven, my lord!
HAMLET. There's never a villain dwelling in all Denmark
But he's an arrant knave.

HORATIO. There needs no ghost, my lord, come from the grave
To tell us this.
HAMLET. Why, right; you are in the right;
And so, without more circumstance at all,
I hold it fit that we shake hands and part;
You, as your business and desire shall point you—
For every man hath business and desire,
Such as it is; and for my own poor part,
Look you, I will go pray.
HORATIO. These are but wild and whirling words, my lord.
HAMLET. I am sorry they offend you, heartily;
Yes, faith, heartily.
HORATIO. There's no offence, my lord.
HAMLET. Yes, by Saint Patrick, but there is, Horatio,
And much offence too. Touching this vision here—
It is an honest ghost, that let me tell you.
For your desire to know what is between us,
O'ermaster't as you may. And now, good friends,
As you are friends, scholars, and soldiers,
Give me one poor request.
HORATIO. What is't, my lord? We will.
HAMLET. Never make known what you have seen to-night.
BOTH. My lord, we will not.
HAMLET. Nay, but swear't.
HORATIO. In faith,
My lord, not I.
MARCELLUS. Nor I, my lord, in faith.
HAMLET. Upon my sword.
MARCELLUS. We have sworn, my lord, already.
HAMLET. Indeed, upon my sword, indeed.
GHOST. [*Cries under the stage*] Swear.
HAMLET. Ha, ha, boy! say'st thou so? Art thou there, truepenny?
Come on. You hear this fellow in the cellarage:
Consent to swear.
HORATIO. Propose the oath, my lord.
HAMLET. Never to speak of this that you have seen,
Swear by my sword.
GHOST. [*Beneath*] Swear.

HAMLET. Hic et ubique? Then we'll shift our ground.
Come hither, gentlemen,
And lay your hands again upon my sword.
Swear by my sword
Never to speak of this that you have heard.
GHOST. [*Beneath*] Swear, by his sword.
HAMLET. Well said, old mole! Canst work i' th' earth so fast?
A worthy pioneer! Once more remove, good friends.
HORATIO. O day and night, but this is wondrous strange!
HAMLET. And therefore as a stranger give it welcome.
There are more things in heaven and earth, Horatio,
Than are dreamt of in your philosophy.
But come.
Here, as before, never, so help you mercy,
How strange or odd some'er I bear myself–
As I perchance hereafter shall think meet
To put an antic disposition on–
That you, at such times, seeing me, never shall,
With arms encumb'red thus, or this head-shake,
Or by pronouncing of some doubtful phrase,
As 'Well, well, we know' or 'We could, an if we would'
Or 'If we list to speak' or 'There be, an if they might'
Or such ambiguous giving out, to note
That you know aught of me–this do swear,
So grace and mercy at your most need help you.
GHOST. [*Beneath*] Swear.
HAMLET. Rest, rest, perturbed spirit! So, gentlemen,
With all my love I do commend me to you;
And what so poor a man as Hamlet is
May do t'express his love and friending to you,
God willing, shall not lack. Let us go in together;
And still your fingers on your lips, I pray.
The time is out of joint. O cursed spite,
That ever I was born to set it right!
Nay, come, let's go together. *Exeunt*

ACT II. SCENE 1

Elsinore. The house of POLONIUS

Enter POLONIUS *and* REYNALDO

POLONIUS. Give him this money and these notes, Reynaldo.
REYNALDO. I will, my lord.
POLONIUS. You shall do marvellous wisely, good Reynaldo,
Before you visit him, to make inquire
Of his behaviour.
REYNALDO. My lord, I did intend it.
POLONIUS. Marry, well said; very well said. Look you, sir,
Enquire me first what Danskers are in Paris;
And how, and who, what means, and where they keep,
What company, at what expense; and finding
By this encompassment and drift of question
That they do know my son, come you more nearer
Than your particular demands will touch it.
Take you, as 'twere, some distant knowledge of him;
As thus: 'I know his father and his friends,
And in part him.' Do you mark this, Reynaldo?
REYNALDO. Ay, very well, my lord.
POLONIUS. 'And in part him—but' you may say 'not well;
But if't be he I mean, he's very wild;
Addicted so and so'; and there put on him
What forgeries you please; marry, none so rank
As may dishonour him; take heed of that;
But, sir, such wanton, wild, and usual slips
As are companions noted and most known
To youth and liberty.
REYNALDO. As gaming, my lord.
POLONIUS. Ay, or drinking, fencing, swearing, quarrelling,
Drabbing—you may go so far.
REYNALDO. My lord, that would dishonour him.
POLONIUS. Faith, no; as you may season it in the charge.
You must not put another scandal on him,
That he is open to incontinency;
That's not my meaning. But breathe his faults so quaintly
That they may seem the taints of liberty;

The flash and outbreak of a fiery mind,
A savageness in unreclaimed blood,
Of general assault.
REYNALDO. But, my good lord—
POLONIUS. Wherefore should you do this?
REYNALDO. Ay, my lord,
I would know that.
POLONIUS. Marry, sir, here's my drift,
And I believe it is a fetch of warrant:
You laying these slight sullies on my son,
As 'twere a thing a little soil'd wi' th' working,
Mark you,
Your party in converse, him you would sound,
Having ever seen in the prenominate crimes
The youth you breathe of guilty, be assur'd
He closes with you in this consequence—
'Good sir' or so, or 'friend' or 'gentleman'
According to the phrase or the addition
Of man and country.
REYNALDO. Very good, my lord.
POLONIUS. And then, sir, does 'a this—'a does—What was I about to say? By the mass, I was about to say something; where did I leave?
REYNALDO. At 'closes in the consequence,' at 'friend or so' and 'gentleman.'
POLONIUS. At 'closes in the consequence'—ay, marry,
He closes thus: 'I know the gentleman;
I saw him yesterday, or t'other day,
Or then, or then; with such, or such; and, as you say,
There was 'a gaming; there o'ertook in's rouse;
There falling out at tennis'; or perchance
'I saw him enter such a house of sale,'
Videlicet, a brothel, or so forth. See you now
Your bait of falsehood take this carp of truth;
And thus do we of wisdom and of reach,
With windlasses and with assays of bias,
By indirections find directions out;
So, by my former lecture and advice,
Shall you my son. You have me, have you not?
REYNALDO. My lord, I have.

POLONIUS. God buy ye; fare ye well.
REYNALDO. Good my lord!
POLONIUS. Observe his inclination in yourself.
REYNALDO. I shall, my lord.
POLONIUS. And let him ply his music.
REYNALDO. Well, my lord.
POLONIUS. Farewell! *Exit* REYNALDO

Enter OPHELIA

How now, Ophelia! What's the matter?
OPHELIA. O my lord, my lord, I have been so affrighted!
POLONIUS. With what, i' th' name of God?
OPHELIA. My lord, as I was sewing in my closet,
Lord Hamlet, with his doublet all unbrac'd,
No hat upon his head, his stockings fouled,
Ungart'red and down-gyved to his ankle;
Pale as his shirt, his knees knocking each other,
And with a look so piteous in purport
As if he had been loosed out of hell
To speak of horrors—he comes before me.
POLONIUS. Mad for thy love?
OPHELIA. My lord, I do not know,
But truly I do fear it.
POLONIUS. What said he?
OPHELIA. He took me by the wrist, and held me hard;
Then goes he to the length of all his arm,
And, with his other hand thus o'er his brow,
He falls to such perusal of my face
As 'a would draw it. Long stay'd he so.
At last, a little shaking of mine arm,
And thrice his head thus waving up and down,
He rais'd a sigh so piteous and profound
As it did seem to shatter all his bulk
And end his being. That done, he lets me go,
And, with his head over his shoulder turn'd,
He seem'd to find his way without his eyes;
For out adoors he went without their helps
And to the last bended their light on me.
POLONIUS. Come, go with me. I will go seek the King.
This is the very ecstasy of love,

Whose violent property fordoes itself,
And leads the will to desperate undertakings
As oft as any passion under heaven
That does afflict our natures. I am sorry—
What, have you given him any hard words of late?

OPHELIA. No, my good lord; but, as you did command,
I did repel his letters, and denied
His access to me.

POLONIUS. That hath made him mad.
I am sorry that with better heed and judgment
I had not quoted him. I fear'd he did but trifle,
And meant to wreck thee; but beshrew my jealousy!
By heaven, it is as proper to our age
To cast beyond ourselves in our opinions
As it is common for the younger sort
To lack discretion. Come, go we to the King.
This must be known; which, being kept close, might move
More grief to hide than hate to utter love.
Come. *Exeunt*

SCENE 2

Elsinore. The Castle

Flourish. Enter KING, QUEEN, ROSENCRANTZ, GUILDENSTERN, *and attendants*

KING. Welcome, dear Rosencrantz and Guildenstern!
Moreover that we much did long to see you,
The need we have to use you did provoke
Our hasty sending. Something have you heard
Of Hamlet's transformation; so I call it,
Sith nor th' exterior nor the inward man
Resembles that it was. What it should be,
More than his father's death, that thus hath put him
So much from th' understanding of himself,
I cannot deem of. I entreat you both
That, being of so young days brought up with him,
And sith so neighboured to his youth and haviour,
That you vouchsafe your rest here in our court
Some little time; so by your companies

To draw him on to pleasures, and to gather,
So much as from occasion you may glean,
Whether aught to us unknown afflicts him thus
That, open'd, lies within our remedy.

QUEEN. Good gentlemen, he hath much talk'd of you;
And sure I am two men there is not living
To whom he more adheres. If it will please you
To show us so much gentry and good will
As to expend your time with us awhile
For the supply and profit of our hope,
Your visitation shall receive such thanks
As fits a king's remembrance.

ROSENCRANTZ. Both your Majesties
Might, by the sovereign power you have of us,
Put your dread pleasures more into command
Than to entreaty.

GUILDENSTERN. But we both obey,
And here give up ourselves, in the full bent,
To lay our service freely at your feet,
To be commanded.

KING. Thanks, Rosencrantz and gentle Guildenstern.

QUEEN. Thanks, Guildenstern and gentle Rosencrantz.
And I beseech you instantly to visit
My too much changed son. Go, some of you,
And bring these gentlemen where Hamlet is.

GUILDENSTERN. Heavens make our presence and our practices
Pleasant and helpful to him!

QUEEN. Aye amen! *Exeunt* ROSENCRANTZ, GUILDENSTERN, *and some attendants*

Enter POLONIUS

POLONIUS. Th' ambassadors from Norway, my good lord,
Are joyfully return'd.

KING. Thou still hast been the father of good news.

POLONIUS. Have I, my lord? I assure you, my good liege,
I hold my duty, as I hold my soul,
Both to my God and to my gracious King;
And I do think—or else this brain of mine
Hunts not the trail of policy so sure

As it hath us'd to do—that I have found
The very cause of Hamlet's lunacy.

KING. O, speak of that; that do I long to hear.

POLONIUS. Give first admittance to th' ambassadors;
My news shall be the fruit to that great feast.

KING. Thyself do grace to them, and bring them in.
Exit POLONIUS
He tells me, my dear Gertrude, he hath found
The head and source of all your son's distemper.

QUEEN. I doubt it is no other but the main,
His father's death and our o'erhasty marriage.

KING. Well, we shall sift him.

Re-enter POLONIUS, *with* VOLTEMAND *and* CORNELIUS

Welcome, my good friends!
Say, Voltemand, what from our brother Norway?

VOLTEMAND. Most fair return of greetings and desires.
Upon our first, he sent out to suppress
His nephew's levies; which to him appear'd
To be a preparation 'gainst the Polack;
But, better look'd into, he truly found
It was against your Highness. Whereat griev'd,
That so his sickness, age, and impotence,
Was falsely borne in hand, sends out arrests
On Fortinbras; which he, in brief, obeys;
Receives rebuke from Norway; and, in fine,
Makes vow before his uncle never more
To give th' assay of arms against your Majesty.
Whereon old Norway, overcome with joy,
Gives him threescore thousand crowns in annual fee,
And his commission to employ those soldiers,
So levied as before, against the Polack;
With an entreaty, herein further shown, [*Gives a paper*]
That it might please you to give quiet pass
Through your dominions for this enterprise,
On such regards of safety and allowance
As therein are set down.

KING. It likes us well;
And at our more considered time we'll read,
Answer, and think upon this business.

Meantime we thank you for your well-took labour.
Go to your rest; at night we'll feast together.
Most welcome home! *Exeunt* AMBASSADORS *and attendants*

POLONIUS. This business is well ended.
My liege, and madam, to expostulate
What majesty should be, what duty is,
Why day is day, night night, and time is time,
Were nothing, but to waste night, day, and time.
Therefore, since brevity is the soul of wit,
And tediousness the limbs and outward flourishes,
I will be brief. Your noble son is mad.
Mad call I it; for, to define true madness,
What is't but to be nothing else but mad?
But let that go.

QUEEN. More matter with less art.

POLONIUS. Madam, I swear I use no art at all.
That he's mad, 'tis true: 'tis true 'tis pity;
And pity 'tis 'tis true. A foolish figure!
But farewell it, for I will use no art.
Mad let us grant him, then; and now remains
That we find out the cause of this effect;
Or rather say the cause of this defect,
For this effect defective comes by cause.
Thus it remains, and the remainder thus.
Perpend.
I have a daughter–have while she is mine–
Who in her duty and obedience, mark,
Hath given me this. Now gather, and surmise. [*Reads*]

'To the celestial, and my soul's idol, the most beautified Ophelia.' That's an ill phrase, a vile phrase; 'beautified' is a vile phrase. But you shall hear. Thus: [*Reads*]

'In her excellent white bosom, these, &c.'

QUEEN. Came this from Hamlet to her?

POLONIUS. Good madam, stay awhile; I will be faithful.

[*Reads*] 'Doubt thou the stars are fire;
Doubt that the sun doth move;
Doubt truth to be a liar;
But never doubt I love.

'O dear Ophelia, I am ill at these numbers. I have not art to reckon my groans; but that I love thee best, O most best, believe it. Adieu.

'Thine evermore, most dear lady, whilst
this machine is to him,
HAMLET.'

This, in obedience, hath my daughter shown me;
And more above, hath his solicitings,
As they fell out by time, by means, and place,
All given to mine ear.

KING. But how hath she
Receiv'd his love?

POLONIUS. What do you think of me?

KING. As of a man faithful and honourable.

POLONIUS. I would fain prove so. But what might you think,
When I had seen this hot love on the wing,
As I perceiv'd it, I must tell you that,
Before my daughter told me—what might you,
Or my dear Majesty your Queen here, think,
If I had play'd the desk or table-book;
Or given my heart a winking, mute and dumb;
Or look'd upon this love with idle sight—
What might you think? No, I went round to work,
And my young mistress thus I did bespeak:
'Lord Hamlet is a prince out of thy star;
This must not be.' And then I prescripts gave her,
That she should lock herself from his resort,
Admit no messengers, receive no tokens.
Which done, she took the fruits of my advice;
And he repelled, a short tale to make,
Fell into a sadness, then into a fast,
Thence to a watch, thence into a weakness,
Thence to a lightness, and, by this declension,
Into the madness wherein now he raves
And all we mourn for.

KING. Do you think 'tis this?

QUEEN. It may be, very like.

POLONIUS. Hath there been such a time—I would fain know that—
That I have positively said ' 'Tis so,'

When it prov'd otherwise?

KING. Not that I know.

POLONIUS. Take this from this, if this be otherwise.
If circumstances lead me, I will find
Where truth is hid, though it were hid indeed
Within the centre.

KING. How may we try it further?

POLONIUS. You know sometimes he walks four hours together,
Here in the lobby.

QUEEN. So he does, indeed.

POLONIUS. At such a time I'll loose my daughter to him.
Be you and I behind an arras then;
Mark the encounter: if he love her not,
And be not from his reason fall'n thereon,
Let me be no assistant for a state,
But keep a farm and carters.

KING. We will try it.

Enter HAMLET, *reading on a book*

QUEEN. But look where sadly the poor wretch comes reading.

POLONIUS. Away, I do beseech you, both away:
I'll board him presently. O, give me leave.

Exeunt KING *and* QUEEN

How does my good Lord Hamlet?

HAMLET. Well, God-a-mercy.

POLONIUS. Do you know me, my lord?

HAMLET. Excellent well; you are a fishmonger.

POLONIUS. Not I, my lord.

HAMLET. Then I would you were so honest a man.

POLONIUS. Honest, my lord!

HAMLET. Ay, sir; to be honest, as this world goes, is to be one man pick'd out of ten thousand.

POLONIUS. That's very true, my lord.

HAMLET. For if the sun breed maggots in a dead dog, being a good kissing carrion—Have you a daughter?

POLONIUS. I have, my lord.

HAMLET. Let her not walk i' th' sun. Conception is a blessing. But as your daughter may conceive—friend, look to't.

POLONIUS. How say you by that? [*Aside*] Still harping on

my daughter. Yet he knew me not at first; 'a said I was a fishmonger. 'A is far gone, far gone. And truly in my youth I suff'red much extremity for love. Very near this. I'll speak to him again.—What do you read, my lord?

HAMLET. Words, words, words.

POLONIUS. What is the matter, my lord?

HAMLET. Between who?

POLONIUS. I mean, the matter that you read, my lord.

HAMLET. Slanders, sir; for the satirical rogue says here that old men have grey beards; that their faces are wrinkled; their eyes purging thick amber and plum-tree gum; and that they have a plentiful lack of wit, together with most weak hams—all which, sir, though I most powerfully and potently believe, yet I hold it not honesty to have it thus set down; for you yourself, sir, shall grow old as I am, if, like a crab, you could go backward.

POLONIUS. [*Aside*] Though this be madness, yet there is method in't.—Will you walk out of the air, my lord?

HAMLET. Into my grave?

POLONIUS. Indeed, that's out of the air. [*Aside*] How pregnant sometimes his replies are! a happiness that often madness hits on, which reason and sanity could not so prosperously be delivered of. I will leave him, and suddenly contrive the means of meeting between him and my daughter.—My lord. I will take my leave of you.

HAMLET. You cannot, sir, take from me anything that I will more willingly part withal—except my life, except my life, except my life.

Enter ROSENCRANTZ *and* GUILDENSTERN

POLONIUS. Fare you well, my lord.

HAMLET. These tedious old fools!

POLONIUS. You go to seek the Lord Hamlet; there he is.

ROSENCRANTZ. [*To* POLONIUS] God save you, sir!

Exit POLONIUS

GUILDENSTERN. My honour'd lord!

ROSENCRANTZ. My most dear lord!

HAMLET. My excellent good friends! How dost thou, Guildenstern? Ah, Rosencrantz! Good lads, how do you both?

ROSENCRANTZ. As the indifferent children of the earth.

GUILDENSTERN. Happy in that we are not over-happy;
On fortune's cap we are not the very button.

HAMLET. Nor the soles of her shoe?

ROSENCRANTZ. Neither, my lord.

HAMLET. Then you live about her waist, or in the middle of her favours?

GUILDENSTERN. Faith, her privates we.

HAMLET. In the secret parts of Fortune? O, most true; she is a strumpet. What news?

ROSENCRANTZ. None, my lord, but that the world's grown honest.

HAMLET. Then is doomsday near. But your news is not true. Let me question more in particular. What have you, my good friends, deserved at the hands of Fortune, that she sends you to prison hither?

GUILDENSTERN. Prison, my lord!

HAMLET. Denmark's a prison.

ROSENCRANTZ. Then is the world one.

HAMLET. A goodly one; in which there are many confines, wards, and dungeons, Denmark being one o' th' worst.

ROSENCRANTZ. We think not so, my lord.

HAMLET. Why, then, 'tis none to you; for there is nothing either good or bad, but thinking makes it so. To me it is a prison.

ROSENCRANTZ. Why, then your ambition makes it one; 'tis too narrow for your mind.

HAMLET. O God, I could be bounded in a nutshell and count myself a king of infinite space, were it not that I have bad dreams.

GUILDENSTERN. Which dreams indeed are ambition; for the very substance of the ambitious is merely the shadow of a dream.

HAMLET. A dream itself is but a shadow.

ROSENCRANTZ. Truly, and I hold ambition of so airy and light a quality that it is but a shadow's shadow.

HAMLET. Then are our beggars bodies, and our monarchs and outstretch'd heroes the beggars' shadows. Shall we to th' court? for, by my fay, I cannot reason.

BOTH. We'll wait upon you.

HAMLET. No such matter. I will not sort you with the rest

of my servants; for, to speak to you like an honest man, I am most dreadfully attended. But, in the beaten way of friendship, what make you at Elsinore?

ROSENCRANTZ. To visit you, my lord; no other occasion.

HAMLET. Beggar that I am, I am even poor in thanks; but I thank you; and sure, dear friends, my thanks are too dear a half-penny. Were you not sent for? Is it your own inclining? Is it a free visitation? Come, come, deal justly with me. Come, come; nay, speak.

GUILDENSTERN. What should we say, my lord?

HAMLET. Why any thing. But to th' purpose: you were sent for; and there is a kind of confession in your looks, which your modesties have not craft enough to colour; I know the good King and Queen have sent for you.

ROSENCRANTZ. To what end, my lord?

HAMLET. That you must teach me. But let me conjure you by the rights of our fellowship, by the consonancy of our youth, by the obligation of our ever-preserved love, and by what more dear a better proposer can charge you withal, be even and direct with me, whether you were sent for or no?

ROSENCRANTZ. [*Aside to* GUILDENSTERN] What say you?

HAMLET. [*Aside*] Nay, then, I have an eye of you.—If you love me, hold not off.

GUILDENSTERN. My lord, we were sent for.

HAMLET. I will tell you why; so shall my anticipation prevent your discovery, and your secrecy to the King and Queen moult no feather. I have of late—but wherefore I know not—lost all my mirth, forgone all custom of exercises; and indeed it goes so heavily with my disposition that this goodly frame, the earth, seems to me a sterile promontory; this most excellent canopy the air, look you, this brave o'er-hanging firmament, this majestical roof fretted with golden fire—why, it appeareth no other thing to me than a foul and pestilent congregation of vapours. What a piece of work is a man! How noble in reason! how infinite in faculties! in form and moving, how express and admirable! in action, how like an angel! in apprehension, how like a god! the beauty of the world! the paragon of animals! And yet, to me, what is this quintessence of dust? Man delights not me—no, nor woman neither, though by your smiling you seem to say so.

ROSENCRANTZ. My lord, there was no such stuff in my thoughts.

HAMLET. Why did ye laugh, then, when I said 'Man delights not me'?

ROSENCRANTZ. To think, my lord, if you delight not in man, what lenten entertainment the players shall receive from you. We coted them on the way; and hither are they coming to offer you service.

HAMLET. He that plays the king shall be welcome—his Majesty shall have tribute on me; the adventurous knight shall use his foil and target; the lover shall not sigh gratis; the humorous man shall end his part in peace; the clown shall make those laugh whose lungs are tickle a' th' sere; and the lady shall say her mind freely, or the blank verse shall halt for't. What players are they?

ROSENCRANTZ. Even those you were wont to take such delight in—the tragedians of the city.

HAMLET. How chances it they travel? Their residence, both in reputation and profit, was better both ways.

ROSENCRANTZ. I think their inhibition comes by the means of the late innovation.

HAMLET. Do they hold the same estimation they did when I was in the city? Are they so followed?

ROSENCRANTZ. No, indeed, are they not.

HAMLET. How comes it? Do they grow rusty?

ROSENCRANTZ. Nay, their endeavour keeps in the wonted pace; but there is, sir, an eyrie of children, little eyases, that cry out on the top of question, and are most tyrannically clapp'd for't. These are now the fashion, and so berattle the common stages—so they call them—that many wearing rapiers are afraid of goose quills and dare scarce come thither.

HAMLET. What, are they children? Who maintains 'em? How are they escoted? Will they pursue the quality no longer than they can sing? Will they not say afterwards, if they should grow themselves to common players—as it is most like, if their means are no better—their writers do them wrong to make them exclaim against their own succession?

ROSENCRANTZ. Faith, there has been much to-do on both sides; and the nation holds it no sin to tarre them to controversy. There was for a while no money bid for argument, unless the poet and the player went to cuffs in the question.

HAMLET. Is't possible?

GUILDENSTERN. O, there has been much throwing about of brains.

HAMLET. Do the boys carry it away?

ROSENCRANTZ. Ay, that they do, my lord—Hercules and his load too.

HAMLET. It is not very strange; for my uncle is King of Denmark, and those that would make mows at him while my father lived give twenty, forty, fifty, a hundred ducats apiece for his picture in little. 'Sblood, there is something in this more than natural, if philosophy could find it out. [*A flourish*]

GUILDENSTERN. There are the players.

HAMLET. Gentlemen, you are welcome to Elsinore. Your hands, come then; th' appurtenance of welcome is fashion and ceremony. Let me comply with you in this garb; lest my extent to the players, which, I tell you, must show fairly outwards, should more appear like entertainments than yours. You are welcome. But my uncle-father and aunt-mother are deceived.

GUILDENSTERN. In what, my dear lord?

HAMLET. I am but mad north-north-west; when the wind is southerly I know a hawk from a handsaw.

Re-enter POLONIUS

POLONIUS. Well be with you, gentlemen!

HAMLET. Hark you, Guildenstern, and you too—at each ear a hearer: that great baby you see there is not yet out of his swaddling clouts.

ROSENCRANTZ. Happily he is the second time come to them; for they say an old man is twice a child.

HAMLET. I will prophesy he comes to tell me of the players;

mark it. You say right, sir: a Monday morning; 'twas then indeed.

POLONIUS. My lord, I have news to tell you.

HAMLET. My lord, I have news to tell you. When Roscius was an actor in Rome–

POLONIUS. The actors are come hither, my lord.

HAMLET. Buzz, buzz!

POLONIUS. Upon my honour–

HAMLET. Then came each actor on his ass–

POLONIUS. The best actors in the world, either for tragedy, comedy, history, pastoral pastoral-comical, historical-pastoral, tragical-historical, tragical-comical-historical-pastoral, scene individable, or poem unlimited. Seneca cannot be too heavy nor Plautus too light. For the law of writ and the liberty, these are the only men.

HAMLET. O Jephthah, judge of Israel, what a treasure hadst thou!

POLONIUS. What a treasure had he, my lord?

HAMLET. Why–

'One fair daughter, and no more,
The which he loved passing well.'

POLONIUS. [*Aside*] Still on my daughter.

HAMLET. Am I not i' th' right, old Jephthah?

POLONIUS. If you call me Jephthah, my lord, I have a daughter that I love passing well.

HAMLET. Nay, that follows not.

POLONIUS. What follows then, my lord?

HAMLET. Why–

'As by lot, God wot'

and then, you know,

'It came to pass, as most like it was.'

The first row of the pious chanson will show you more; for look where my abridgement comes.

Enter the PLAYERS

You are welcome, masters; welcome, all.–I am glad to see thee well.–Welcome, good friends.–O, my old friend!

Why thy face is valanc'd since I saw thee last; com'st thou to beard me in Denmark?—What, my young lady and mistress! By'r lady, your ladyship is nearer to heaven than when I saw you last by the altitude of a chopine. Pray God, your voice, like a piece of uncurrent gold, be not crack'd within the ring.—Masters, you are all welcome. We'll e'en to't like French falconers, fly at anything we see. We'll have a speech straight. Come, give us a taste of your quality; come, a passionate speech.

First Player. What speech, my good lord?

Hamlet. I heard thee speak me a speech once, but it was never acted; or, if it was, not above once; for the play, I remember, pleas'd not the million; 'twas caviary to the general. But it was—as I received it, and others whose judgments in such matters cried in the top of mine—an excellent play, well digested in the scenes, set down with as much modesty as cunning. I remember one said there were no sallets in the lines to make the matter savoury, nor no matter in the phrase that might indict the author of affectation; but call'd it an honest method, as wholesome as sweet, and by very much more handsome than fine. One speech in it I chiefly lov'd: 'twas Æneas' tale to Dido; and thereabout of it especially where he speaks of Priam's slaughter. If it live in your memory, begin at this line—let me see, let me see:

'The rugged Pyrrhus, like th' Hyrcanian beast,'

'Tis not so; it begins with Pyrrhus.

'The rugged Pyrrhus, he whose sable arms,
Black as his purpose, did the night resemble
When he lay couched in the ominous horse,
Hath now this dread and black complexion smear'd
With heraldry more dismal; head to foot
Now is he total gules, horridly trick'd
With blood of fathers, mothers, daughters, sons,
Bak'd and impasted with the parching streets,
That lend a tyrannous and damned light
To their lord's murder. Roasted in wrath and fire,
And thus o'er-sized with coagulate gore,

With eyes like carbuncles, the hellish Pyrrhus
Old grandsire Priam seeks.'

So proceed you.

POLONIUS. Fore God, my lord, well spoken, with good accent and good discretion.

FIRST PLAYER. 'Anon he finds him
Striking too short at Greeks; his antique sword,
Rebellious to his arm, lies where it falls,
Repugnant to command. Unequal match'd,
Pyrrhus at Priam drives, in rage strikes wide;
But with the whiff and wind of his fell sword
Th' unnerved father falls. Then senseless Ilium,
Seeming to feel this blow, with flaming top
Stoops to his base, and with a hideous crash
Takes prisoner Pyrrhus' ear. For, lo! his sword,
Which was declining on the milky head
Of reverend Priam, seem'd i' th' air to stick.
So, as a painted tyrant, Pyrrhus stood
And, like a neutral to his will and matter,
Did nothing.
But as we often see, against some storm,
A silence in the heavens, the rack stand still,
The bold winds speechless, and the orb below
As hush as death, anon the dreadful thunder
Doth rend the region; so, after Pyrrhus' pause,
A roused vengeance sets him new a-work;
And never did the Cyclops' hammers fall
On Mars's armour, forg'd for proof eterne,
With less remorse than Pyrrhus' bleeding sword
Now falls on Priam.
Out, out, thou strumpet, Fortune! All you gods,
In general synod, take away her power;
Break all the spokes and fellies from her wheel,
And bowl the round nave down the hill of heaven,
As low as to the fiends.'

POLONIUS. This is too long.

HAMLET. It shall to the barber's, with your beard. Prithee say on. He's for a jig, or a tale of bawdry, or he sleeps. Say on; come to Hecuba.

FIRST PLAYER. 'But who, ah, who had seen the mobled queen–'

HAMLET. 'The mobled queen'?

POLONIUS. That's good; 'mobled queen' is good.

FIRST PLAYER. 'Run barefoot up and down, threat'ning the flames
With bisson rheum; a clout upon that head
Where late the diadem stood, and for a robe,
About her lank and all o'er teemed loins,
A blanket, in the alarm of fear caught up–
Who this had seen, with tongue in venom steep'd,
'Gainst Fortune's state would treason have pronounc'd.
But if the gods themselves did see her then,
When she saw Pyrrhus make malicious sport
In mincing with his sword her husband's limbs,
The instant burst of clamour that she made–
Unless things mortal move them not at all–
Would have made milch the burning eyes of heaven,
And passion in the gods.'

POLONIUS. Look whe'er he has not turn'd his colour, and has tears in 's eyes. Prithee no more.

HAMLET. 'Tis well; I'll have thee speak out the rest of this soon.–Good my lord, will you see the players well bestowed? Do you hear: let them be well used; for they are the abstract and brief chronicles of the time; after your death you were better have a bad epitaph than their ill report while you live.

POLONIUS. My lord, I will use them according to their desert.

HAMLET. God's bodykins, man, much better. Use every man after his desert, and who shall scape whipping? Use them after your own honour and dignity: the less they deserve, the more merit is in your bounty. Take them in.

POLONIUS. Come, sirs.

HAMLET. Follow him, friends. We'll hear a play to-morrow. Dost thou hear me, old friend; can you play 'The Murder of Gonzago'?

FIRST PLAYER. Ay, my lord.

HAMLET. We'll ha't to-morrow night. You could, for a need, study a speech of some dozen or sixteen lines which I would set down and insert in't, could you not?

FIRST PLAYER. Ay, my lord.

HAMLET. Very well. Follow that lord; and look you mock him not. [*Exeunt* POLONIUS *and* PLAYERS] My good friends, I'll leave you till night. You are welcome to Elsinore.

ROSENCRANTZ. Good my lord!

Exeunt ROSENCRANTZ *and* GUILDENSTERN

HAMLET. Ay, so God buy to you! Now I am alone.
O, what a rogue and peasant slave am I!
Is it not monstrous that this player here,
But in a fiction, in a dream of passion,
Could force his soul so to his own conceit
That from her working all his visage wann'd;
Tears in his eyes, distraction in's aspect,
A broken voice, and his whole function suiting
With forms to his conceit? And all for nothing!
For Hecuba!
What's Hecuba to him or he to Hecuba,
That he should weep for her? What would he do,
Had he the motive and the cue for passion
That I have? He would drown the stage with tears,
And cleave the general ear with horrid speech;
Make mad the guilty, and appal the free,
Confound the ignorant, and amaze indeed
The very faculties of eyes and ears.
Yet I,
A dull and muddy-mettl'd rascal, peak,
Like John-a-dreams, unpregnant of my cause,
And can say nothing; no, not for a king
Upon whose property and most dear life
A damn'd defeat was made. Am I a coward?
Who calls me villain, breaks my pate across,
Plucks off my beard and blows it in my face,
Tweaks me by the nose, gives me the lie i' th' throat
As deep as to the lungs? Who does me this?
Ha!

'Swounds, I should take it; for it cannot be
But I am pigeon-liver'd and lack gall
To make oppression bitter, or ere this
I should 'a fatted all the region kites
With this slave's offal. Bloody, bawdy villain!
Remorseless, treacherous, lecherous kindless villain!
O, vengeance!
Why, what an ass am I! This is most brave,
That I, the son of a dear father murder'd,
Prompted to my revenge by heaven and hell,
Must, like a whore, unpack my heart with words,
And fall a-cursing like a very drab,
A scullion! Fie upon't! foh!
About, my brains. Hum–I have heard
That guilty creatures, sitting at a play,
Have by the very cunning of the scene
Been struck so to the soul that presently
They have proclaim'd their malefactions;
For murder, though it have no tongue, will speak
With most miraculous organ. I'll have these players
Play something like the murder of my father
Before mine uncle. I'll observe his looks;
I'll tent him to the quick. If 'a do blench,
I know my course. The spirit that I have seen
May be a devil; and the devil hath power
T' assume a pleasing shape; yea and perhaps
Out of my weakness and my melancholy,
As he is very potent with such spirits,
Abuses me to damn me. I'll have grounds
More relative than this. The play's the thing
Wherein I'll catch the conscience of the King. *Exit*

ACT III. SCENE 1

Elsinore. The Castle

Enter KING, QUEEN, POLONIUS, OPHELIA, ROSENCRANTZ, *and* GUILDENSTERN

KING. And can you by no drift of conference
Get from him why he puts on this confusion,
Grating so harshly all his days of quiet
With turbulent and dangerous lunacy?
ROSENCRANTZ. He does confess he feels himself distracted,
But from what cause 'a will by no means speak.
GUILDENSTERN. Nor do we find him forward to be sounded;
But, with a crafty madness, keeps aloof
When we would bring him on to some confession
Of his true state.
QUEEN. Did he receive you well?
ROSENCRANTZ. Most like a gentleman.
GUILDENSTERN. But with much forcing of his disposition.
ROSENCRANTZ. Niggard of question; but of our demands
Most free in his reply.
QUEEN. Did you assay him
To any pastime?
ROSENCRANTZ. Madam, it so fell out that certain players
We o'er-raught on the way. Of these we told him;
And there did seem in him a kind of joy
To hear of it. They are here about the court,
And, as I think, they have already order
This night to play before him.
POLONIUS. 'Tis most true;
And he beseech'd me to entreat your Majesties
To hear and see the matter.
KING. With all my heart; and it doth much content me
To hear him so inclin'd.
Good gentlemen, give him a further edge,
And drive his purpose into these delights.
ROSENCRANTZ. We shall, my lord.
Exeunt ROSENCRANTZ *and* GUILDENSTERN
KING. Sweet Gertrude, leave us too;

For we have closely sent for Hamlet hither,
That he, as 'twere by accident, may here
Affront Ophelia.
Her father and myself—lawful espials—
Will so bestow ourselves that, seeing unseen,
We may of their encounter frankly judge,
And gather by him, as he is behav'd,
If't be th' affliction of his love or no
That thus he suffers for.

QUEEN. I shall obey you;
And for your part, Ophelia, I do wish
That your good beauties be the happy cause
Of Hamlet's wildness; so shall I hope your virtues
Will bring him to his wonted way again,
To both your honours.

OPHELIA. Madam, I wish it may. *Exit* QUEEN

POLONIUS. Ophelia, walk you here.—Gracious, so please you,
We will bestow ourselves.—Read on this book;
That show of such an exercise may colour
Your loneliness.—We are oft to blame in this:
'Tis too much prov'd, that with devotion's visage
And pious action we do sugar o'er
The devil himself.

KING [*Aside*] O, 'tis too true!
How smart a lash that speech doth give my conscience!
The harlot's cheek, beautied with plast'ring art,
Is not more ugly to the thing that helps it
Than is my deed to my most painted word.
O heavy burden!

POLONIUS. I hear him coming; let's withdraw, my lord.
Exeunt KING *and* POLONIUS

Enter HAMLET

HAMLET. To be, or not to be—that is the question;
Whether 'tis nobler in the mind to suffer
The slings and arrows of outrageous fortune,
Or to take arms against a sea of troubles,
And by opposing end them? To die, to sleep—
No more; and by a sleep to say we end
The heart-ache and the thousand natural shocks

That flesh is heir to. 'Tis a consummation
Devoutly to be wish'd. To die, to sleep;
To sleep, perchance to dream. Ay, there's the rub;
For in that sleep of death what dreams may come,
When we have shuffled off this mortal coil,
Must give us pause. There's the respect
That makes calamity of so long life;
For who would bear the whips and scorns of time,
Th' oppressor's wrong, the proud man's contumely,
The pangs of despis'd love, the law's delay,
The insolence of office, and the spurns
That patient merit of th' unworthy takes,
When he himself might his quietus make
With a bare bodkin? Who would these fardels bear,
To grunt and sweat under a weary life,
But that the dread of something after death–
The undiscover'd country, from whose bourn
No traveller returns–puzzles the will,
And makes us rather bear those ills we have
Than fly to others that we know not of?
Thus conscience does make cowards of us all;
And thus the native hue of resolution
Is sicklied o'er with the pale cast of thought,
And enterprises of great pitch and moment,
With this regard, their currents turn awry
And lose the name of action.–Soft you now!
The fair Ophelia.–Nymph, in thy orisons
Be all my sins rememb'red.

OPHELIA. Good my lord,
How does your honour for this many a day?

HAMLET. I humbly thank you; well, well, well.

OPHELIA. My lord, I have remembrances of yours
That I have longed long to re-deliver.
I pray you now receive them.

HAMLET. No, not I;
I never gave you aught.

OPHELIA. My honour'd lord, you know right well you did,
And with them words of so sweet breath compos'd
As made the things more rich; their perfume lost,
Take these again; for to the noble mind

Rich gifts wax poor when givers prove unkind.
There, my lord.

HAMLET. Ha, ha! Are you honest?

OPHELIA. My lord?

HAMLET. Are you fair?

OPHELIA. What means your lordship?

HAMLET. That if you be honest and fair, your honesty should admit no discourse to your beauty.

OPHELIA. Could beauty, my lord, have better commerce than with honesty?

HAMLET. Ay, truly; for the power of beauty will sooner transform honesty from what it is to a bawd than the force of honesty can translate beauty into his likeness. This was sometime a paradox, but now the time gives it proof. I did love you once.

OPHELIA. Indeed, my lord, you made me believe so.

HAMLET. You should not have believ'd me; for virtue cannot so inoculate our old stock but we shall relish of it. I loved you not.

OPHELIA. I was the more deceived.

HAMLET. Get thee to a nunnery. Why wouldst thou be a breeder of sinners? I am myself indifferent honest, but yet I could accuse me of such things that it were better my mother had not borne me: I am very proud, revengeful, ambitious; with more offences at my beck than I have thoughts to put them in, imagination to give them shape, or time to act them in. What should such fellows as I do crawling between earth and heaven? We are arrant knaves, all; believe none of us. Go thy ways to a nunnery. Where's your father?

OPHELIA. At home, my lord.

HAMLET. Let the doors be shut upon him, that he may play the fool nowhere but in's own house. Farewell.

OPHELIA. O, help him, you sweet heavens!

HAMLET. If thou dost marry, I'll give thee this plague for thy dowry: be thou as chaste as ice, as pure as snow, thou shalt not escape calumny. Get thee to a nunnery, go, farewell. Or, if thou wilt needs marry, marry a fool; for wise men know well enough what monsters you make of them. To a nunnery, go; and quickly too. Farewell.

OPHELIA. O heavenly powers, restore him!

HAMLET. I have heard of your paintings too, well enough; God hath given you one face, and you make yourselves another. You jig and amble, and you lisp, and nickname God's creatures, and make your wantonness your ignorance. Go to, I'll no more on't; it hath made me mad. I say we will have no moe marriage: those that are married already, all but one, shall live; the rest shall keep as they are. To a nunnery, go. *Exit*

OPHELIA. O, what a noble mind is here o'erthrown!
The courtier's, soldier's, scholar's, eye, tongue, sword;
Th' expectancy and rose of the fair state,
The glass of fashion and the mould of form,
Th' observ'd of all observers—quite, quite down!
And I, of ladies most deject and wretched,
That suck'd the honey of his music vows,
Now see that noble and most sovereign reason,
Like sweet bells jangled, out of time and harsh;
That unmatch'd form and feature of blown youth
Blasted with ecstasy. O, woe is me
T' have seen what I have seen, see what I see!

Re-enter KING *and* POLONIUS

KING. Love! His affections do not that way tend;
Nor what he spake, though it lack'd form a little,
Was not like madness. There's something in his soul
O'er which his melancholy sits on brood;
And I do doubt the hatch and the disclose
Will be some danger; which to prevent
I have in quick determination
Thus set it down: he shall with speed to England
For the demand of our neglected tribute.
Haply the seas and countries different,
With variable objects, shall expel
This something-settled matter in his heart
Whereon his brains still beating puts him thus
From fashion of himself. What think you on't?

POLONIUS. It shall do well. But yet do I believe
The origin and commencement of his grief
Sprung from neglected love. How now, Ophelia!

You need not tell us what Lord Hamlet said;
We heard it all. My lord, do as you please;
But if you hold it fit, after the play
Let his queen mother all alone entreat him
To show his grief. Let her be round with him;
And I'll be placed, so please you, in the ear
Of all their conference. If she find him not,
To England send him; or confine him where
Your wisdom best shall think.

KING. It shall be so:
Madness in great ones must not unwatch'd go. *Exeunt*

SCENE 2

Elsinore. The Castle

Enter HAMLET *and three of the* PLAYERS

HAMLET. Speak the speech, I pray you, as I pronounc'd it to you, trippingly on the tongue; but if you mouth it, as many of our players do, I had as lief the town-crier spoke my lines. Nor do not saw the air too much with your hand, thus, but use all gently; for in the very torrent, tempest, and, as I may say, whirlwind of your passion, you must acquire and beget a temperance that may give it smoothness. O, it offends me to the soul to hear a robustious periwig-pated fellow tear a passion to tatters, to very rags, to split the ears of the groundlings, who, for the most part, are capable of nothing but inexplicable dumb shows and noise. I would have such a fellow whipp'd for o'erdoing Termagant; it out-herods Herod. Pray you avoid it.

FIRST PLAYER. I warrant your honour.

HAMLET. Be not too tame neither, but let your own discretion be your tutor. Suit the action to the word, the word to the action; with this special observance, that you o'erstep not the modesty of nature; for anything so o'erdone is from the purpose of playing, whose end, both at the first and now, was and is to hold, as 'twere, the mirror up to nature; to show virtue her own feature, scorn her own image, and the very age and body of the time his form and pressure. Now, this overdone or come tardy off, though it makes the unskilful laugh, cannot but make the judicious grieve; the censure of the which one must, in your allowance, o'erweigh a whole theatre of others. O, there be players that I have seen play—and heard others praise, and that highly—not to speak it profanely, that, neither having th' accent of Christians, nor the gait of Christian, pagan, nor man, have so strutted and bellowed that I have thought some of Nature's journeymen had made men, and not made them well, they imitated humanity so abominably.

FIRST PLAYER. I hope we have reform'd that indifferently with us, sir.

HAMLET. O, reform it altogether. And let those that play your clowns speak no more than is set down for them; for there be of them that will themselves laugh, to set on some quantity of barren spectators to laugh too, though in the meantime some necessary question of the play be then to be considered. That's villainous, and shows a most pitiful ambition in the fool that uses it. Go, make you ready. *Exeunt* PLAYERS

Enter POLONIUS, ROSENCRANTZ, *and* GUILDENSTERN

How now, my lord! Will the King hear this piece of work?

POLONIUS. And the Queen too, and that presently.

HAMLET. Bid the players make haste. *Exit* POLONIUS

Will you two help to hasten them?

ROSENCRANTZ. Ay, my lord. *Exeunt they two*

HAMLET. What, ho, Horatio!

Enter HORATIO

HORATIO. Here, sweet lord, at your service.

HAMLET. Horatio, thou art e'en as just a man
As e'er my conversation cop'd withal.

HORATIO. O my dear lord!

HAMLET. Nay, do not think I flatter;
For what advancement may I hope from thee,
That no revenue hast but thy good spirits

To feed and clothe thee? Why should the poor be flatter'd?
No, let the candied tongue lick absurd pomp,
And crook the pregnant hinges of the knee
Where thrift may follow fawning. Dost thou hear?
Since my dear soul was mistress of her choice
And could of men distinguish her election,
Sh'hath seal'd thee for herself; for thou hast been
As one, in suff'ring all, that suffers nothing;
A man that Fortune's buffets and rewards
Hast ta'en with equal thanks; and blest are those
Whose blood and judgment are so well comeddled
That they are not a pipe for Fortune's finger
To sound what stop she please. Give me that man
That is not passion's slave, and I will wear him
In my heart's core, ay, in my heart of heart,
As I do thee. Something too much of this.
There is a play to-night before the King;
One scene of it comes near the circumstance
Which I have told thee of my father's death.
I prithee, when thou seest that act afoot,
Even with the very comment of thy soul
Observe my uncle. If his occulted guilt
Do not itself unkennel in one speech,
It is a damned ghost that we have seen,
And my imaginations are as foul
As Vulcan's stithy. Give him heedful note;
For I mine eyes will rivet to his face;
And, after, we will both our judgments join
In censure of his seeming.

HORATIO. Well, my lord.
If 'a steal aught the whilst this play is playing,
And scape detecting, I will pay the theft.

Enter trumpets and kettledrums. Danish march. Sound a flourish. Enter KING, QUEEN, POLONIUS, OPHELIA, ROSENCRANTZ, GUILDENSTERN, *and other* LORDS *attendant, with the guard carrying torches*

HAMLET. They are coming to the play; I must be idle.
Get you a place.

KING. How fares our cousin Hamlet?

HAMLET. Excellent, i' faith; of the chameleon's dish. I eat the air promise-cramm'd; you cannot feed capons so.

KING. I have nothing with this answer, Hamlet; these words are not mine.

HAMLET. No, nor mine now. [*To* POLONIUS] My lord, you play'd once in th' university, you say?

POLONIUS. That did I, my lord, and was accounted a good actor.

HAMLET. What did you enact?

POLONIUS. I did enact Julius Cæsar; I was kill'd i' th' Capitol; Brutus kill'd me.

HAMLET. It was a brute part of him to kill so capital a calf there. Be the players ready?

ROSENCRANTZ. Ay, my lord; they stay upon your patience.

QUEEN. Come hither, my dear Hamlet, sit by me.

HAMLET. No, good mother; here's metal more attractive.

POLONIUS. [*To the* KING] O, ho! do you mark that?

HAMLET. Lady, shall I lie in your lap? [*Lying down at* OPHELIA'S *feet*]

OPHELIA. No, my lord.

HAMLET. I mean, my head upon your lap?

OPHELIA. Ay, my lord.

HAMLET. Do you think I meant country matters?

OPHELIA. I think nothing, my lord.

HAMLET. That's a fair thought to lie between maids' legs.

OPHELIA. What is, my lord?

HAMLET. Nothing.

OPHELIA. You are merry, my lord.

HAMLET. Who, I?

OPHELIA. Ay, my lord.

HAMLET. O God, your only jig-maker! What should a man do but be merry? For look you how cheerfully my mother looks, and my father died within's two hours.

OPHELIA. Nay, 'tis twice two months, my lord.

HAMLET. So long? Nay then, let the devil wear black, for I'll have a suit of sables. O heavens! die two months ago, and not forgotten yet? Then there's hope a great man's memory may outlive his life half a year; but, by'r lady, 'a must build churches, then; or else shall 'a suffer not thinking on, with the hobby-horse, whose epitaph is 'For O, for O, the hobby-horse is forgot!'

The trumpet sounds. Hautboys play. The Dumb Show enters

Enter a KING *and a* QUEEN, *very lovingly; the* QUEEN *embracing him and he her. She kneels, and makes show of protestation unto him. He takes her up, and declines his head upon her neck. He lies him down upon a bank of flowers; she, seeing him asleep, leaves him. Anon comes in a* FELLOW, *takes off his crown, kisses it, pours poison in the sleeper's ears, and leaves him. The* QUEEN *returns; finds the* KING *dead, and makes passionate action. The* POISONER, *with some two or three* MUTES, *comes in again, seeming to condole with her. The dead body is carried away. The* POISONER *woos the* QUEEN *with gifts: she seems harsh awhile, but in the end accepts his love.* *Exeunt*

OPHELIA. What means this, my lord?

HAMLET. Marry, this is miching mallecho; it means mischief.

OPHELIA. Belike this show imports the argument of the play.

Enter PROLOGUE

HAMLET. We shall know by this fellow: the players cannot keep counsel; they'll tell all.

OPHELIA. Will 'a tell us what this show meant?

HAMLET. Ay, or any show that you will show him. Be not you asham'd to show, he'll not shame to tell you what it means.

OPHELIA. You are naught, you are naught. I'll mark the play.

PROLOGUE. *For us, and for our tragedy,*
Here stooping to your clemency,
We beg your hearing patiently. *Exit*

HAMLET. Is this a prologue, or the posy of a ring?

OPHELIA. 'Tis brief, my lord.

HAMLET. As woman's love.

Enter the Player King *and* Queen

Player King. *Full thirty times hath Phœbus' cart gone round*
Neptune's salt wash and Tellus' orbed ground,
And thirty dozen moons with borrowed sheen
About the world have times twelve thirties been,
Since love our hearts and Hymen did our hands
Unite comutual in most sacred bands.

Player Queen. *So many journeys may the sun and moon*
Make us again count o'er ere love be done!
But, woe is me, you are so sick of late,
So far from cheer and from your former state,
That I distrust you. Yet, though I distrust,
Discomfort you, my lord, it nothing must;
For women fear too much even as they love,
And women's fear and love hold quantity,
In neither aught, or in extremity.
Now, what my love is, proof hath made you know;
And as my love is siz'd, my fear is so.
Where love is great, the littlest doubts are fear;
Where little fears grow great, great love grows there.

Player King. *Faith, I must leave thee, love, and shortly too:*
My operant powers their functions leave to do;
And thou shalt live in this fair world behind,
Honour'd, belov'd; and haply one as kind
For husband shalt thou–

Player Queen. *O, confound the rest!*
Such love must needs be treason in my breast.
In second husband let me be accurst!
None wed the second but who kill'd the first.

Hamlet. That's wormwood, wormwood.

Player Queen. *The instances that second marriage move*
Are base respects of thrift, but none of love.
A second time I kill my husband dead,
When second husband kisses me in bed.

Player King. *I do believe you think what now you speak;*
But what we do determine oft we break.
Purpose is but the slave to memory,

Of violent birth, but poor validity;
Which now, the fruit unripe, sticks on the tree;
But fall unshaken when they mellow be.
Most necessary 'tis that we forget
To pay ourselves what to ourselves is debt.
What to ourselves in passion we propose,
The passion ending, doth the purpose lose.
The violence of either grief or joy
Their own enactures with themselves destroy.
Where joy most revels grief doth most lament;
Grief joys, joy grieves, on slender accident.
This world is not for aye; nor 'tis not strange
That even our loves should with our fortunes change;
For 'tis a question left us yet to prove,
Whether love lead fortune or else fortune love.
The great man down, you mark his favourite flies;
The poor advanc'd makes friends of enemies.
And hitherto doth love on fortune tend;
For who not needs shall never lack a friend,
And who in want a hollow friend doth try,
Directly seasons him his enemy.
But, orderly to end where I begun,
Our wills and fates do so contrary run
That our devices still are overthrown;
Our thoughts are ours, their ends none of our own.
So think thou wilt no second husband wed;
But die thy thoughts when thy first lord is dead.

PLAYER QUEEN. *Nor earth to me give food, nor heaven light,*
Sport and repose lock from me day and night,
To desperation turn my trust and hope,
An anchor's cheer in prison be my scope,
Each opposite that blanks the face of joy
Meet what I would have well, and it destroy,
Both here and hence pursue me lasting strife,
If, once a widow, ever I be wife!

HAMLET. If she should break it now!

PLAYER KING. *'Tis deeply sworn. Sweet, leave me here awhile;*

My spirits grow dull, and fain I would beguile
The tedious day with sleep. [*Sleeps*]

PLAYER QUEEN. *Sleep rock thy brain,*
And never come mischance between us twain! Exit

HAMLET. Madam, how like you this play?

QUEEN. The lady doth protest too much, methinks.

HAMLET. O, but she'll keep her word.

KING. Have you heard the argument? Is there no offence in't?

HAMLET. No, no; they do but jest, poison in jest; no offence i' th' world.

KING. What do you call the play?

HAMLET. 'The Mouse-trap.' Marry, how? Tropically. This play is the image of a murder done in Vienna: Gonzago is the duke's name; his wife, Baptista. You shall see anon. 'Tis a knavish piece of work; but what of that? Your Majesty, and we that have free souls, it touches us not. Let the galled jade wince, our withers are unwrung.

Enter LUCIANUS

This is one Lucianus, nephew to the King.

OPHELIA. You are as good as a chorus, my lord.

HAMLET. I could interpret between you and your love, if I could see the puppets dallying.

OPHELIA. You are keen, my lord, you are keen.

HAMLET. It would cost you a groaning to take off mine edge.

OPHELIA. Still better, and worse.

HAMLET. So you mis-take your husbands.—Begin, murderer; pox, leave thy damnable faces and begin. Come; the croaking raven doth bellow for revenge.

LUCIANUS. *Thoughts black, hands apt, drugs fit, and time agreeing;*
Confederate season, else no creature seeing;
Thou mixture rank, of midnight weeds collected,
With Hecat's ban thrice blasted, thrice infected.
Thy natural magic and dire property
On wholesome life usurps immediately.
[*Pours the poison in his ears*]

HAMLET. 'A poisons him i' th' garden for his estate. His

name's Gonzago. The story is extant, and written in very choice Italian. You shall see anon how the murderer gets the love of Gonzago's wife.

OPHELIA. The King rises.

HAMLET. What, frighted with false fire!

QUEEN. How fares my lord?

POLONIUS. Give o'er the play.

KING. Give me some light. Away!

POLONIUS. Lights, lights, lights!

Exeunt all but HAMLET *and* HORATIO

HAMLET. Why, let the strucken deer go weep,
The hart ungalled play;
For some must watch, while some must sleep;
Thus runs the world away.

Would not this, sir, and a forest of feathers—if the rest of my fortunes turn Turk with me—with two Provincial roses on my raz'd shoes, get me a fellowship in a cry of players, sir?

HORATIO. Half a share.

HAMLET. A whole one, I.

For thou dost know, O Damon dear,
This realm dismantled was
Of Jove himself; and now reigns here
A very, very—peacock.

HORATIO. You might have rhym'd.

HAMLET. O good Horatio, I'll take the ghost's word for a thousand pound. Didst perceive?

HORATIO. Very well, my lord.

HAMLET. Upon the talk of the poisoning.

HORATIO. I did very well note him.

HAMLET. Ah, ha! Come, some music. Come, the recorders.

For if the King like not the comedy,
Why, then, belike he likes it not, perdy.

Come, some music.

Re-enter ROSENCRANTZ *and* GUILDENSTERN

GUILDENSTERN. Good my lord, vouchsafe me a word with you.

HAMLET. Sir, a whole history.

GUILDENSTERN. The King, sir—

HAMLET. Ay, sir, what of him?

GUILDENSTERN. Is, in his retirement, marvellous distemp'red.

HAMLET. With drink, sir?

GUILDENSTERN. No, my lord, rather with choler.

HAMLET. Your wisdom should show itself more richer to signify this to his doctor; for for me to put him to his purgation would perhaps plunge him into far more choler.

GUILDENSTERN. Good my lord, put your discourse into some frame, and start not so wildly from my affair.

HAMLET. I am tame, sir. Pronounce.

GUILDENSTERN. The Queen, your mother, in most great affliction of spirit, hath sent me to you.

HAMLET. You are welcome.

GUILDENSTERN. Nay, good my lord, this courtesy is not of the right breed. If it shall please you to make me a wholesome answer, I will do your mother's commandment; if not, your pardon and my return shall be the end of my business.

HAMLET. Sir, I cannot.

ROSENCRANTZ. What, my lord?

HAMLET. Make you a wholesome answer; my wit's diseas'd. But, sir, such answer as I can make, you shall command: or rather, as you say, my mother. Therefore no more, but to the matter: my mother, you say—

ROSENCRANTZ. Then thus she says: your behaviour hath struck her into amazement and admiration.

HAMLET. O wonderful son, that can so stonish a mother! But is there no sequel at the heels of this mother's admiration? Impart.

ROSENCRANTZ. She desires to speak with you in her closet ere you go to bed.

HAMLET. We shall obey, were she ten times our mother. Have you any further trade with us?

ROSENCRANTZ. My lord, you once did love me.

HAMLET. And do still, by these pickers and stealers.

ROSENCRANTZ. Good my lord, what is your cause of distemper? You do surely bar the door upon your own liberty, if you deny your griefs to your friend.

HAMLET. Sir, I lack advancement.

ROSENCRANTZ. How can that be, when you have the voice of the King himself for your succession in Denmark?

HAMLET. Ay, sir, but 'While the grass grows'—the proverb is something musty.

Re-enter the PLAYERS, *with recorders*

O, the recorders! Let me see one. To withdraw with you—why do you go about to recover the wind of me, as if you would drive me into a toil?

GUILDENSTERN. O my lord, if my duty be too bold, my love is too unmannerly.

HAMLET. I do not well understand that. Will you play upon this pipe?

GUILDENSTERN. My lord, I cannot.

HAMLET. I pray you.

GUILDENSTERN. Believe me, I cannot.

HAMLET. I do beseech you.

GUILDENSTERN. I know no touch of it, my lord.

HAMLET. It is as easy as lying: govern these ventages with your fingers and thumb, give it breath with your mouth, and it will discourse most eloquent music. Look you, these are the stops.

GUILDENSTERN. But these cannot I command to any utterance of harmony; I have not the skill.

HAMLET. Why, look you now, how unworthy a thing you make of me! You would play upon me; you would seem to know my stops; you would pluck out the heart of my mystery; you would sound me from my lowest note to the top of my compass; and there is much music, excellent voice, in this little organ, yet cannot you make it speak. 'Sblood, do you think I am easier to be play'd on than a pipe? Call me what instrument you will, though you can fret me, yet you cannot play upon me.

Re-enter POLONIUS

God bless you, sir!

POLONIUS. My lord, the Queen would speak with you, and presently.

HAMLET. Do you see yonder cloud that's almost in shape of a camel?

POLONIUS. By th' mass, and 'tis like a camel indeed.
HAMLET. Methinks it is like a weasel.
POLONIUS. It is back'd like a weasel.
HAMLET. Or like a whale?
POLONIUS. Very like a whale.
HAMLET. Then I will come to my mother by and by. [*Aside*] They fool me to the top of my bent.—I will come by and by.
POLONIUS. I will say so. *Exit* POLONIUS
HAMLET. 'By and by' is easily said. Leave me, friends.
Exeunt all but HAMLET

'Tis now the very witching time of night,
When churchyards yawn, and hell itself breathes out
Contagion to this world. Now could I drink hot blood,
And do such bitter business as the day
Would quake to look on. Soft! now to my mother.
O heart, lose not thy nature; let not ever
The soul of Nero enter this firm bosom.
Let me be cruel, not unnatural:
I will speak daggers to her, but use none.
My tongue and soul in this be hypocrites—
How in my words somever she be shent,
To give them seals never, my soul, consent! *Exit*

SCENE 3

Elsinore. The Castle

Enter KING, ROSENCRANTZ, *and* GUILDENSTERN

KING. I like him not; nor stands it safe with us
To let his madness range. Therefore prepare you;
I your commission will forthwith dispatch,
And he to England shall along with you.
The terms of our estate may not endure
Hazard so near's as doth hourly grow
Out of his brows.
GUILDENSTERN. We will ourselves provide.
Most holy and religious fear it is
To keep those many many bodies safe

That live and feed upon your Majesty.
ROSENCRANTZ. The single and peculiar life is bound
With all the strength and armour of the mind
To keep itself from noyance; but much more
That spirit upon whose weal depends and rests
The lives of many. The cease of majesty
Dies not alone, but like a gulf doth draw
What's near it with it. It is a massy wheel,
Fix'd on the summit of the highest mount,
To whose huge spokes ten thousand lesser things
Are mortis'd and adjoin'd; which when it falls,
Each small annexment, petty consequence,
Attends the boist'rous ruin. Never alone
Did the king sigh, but with a general groan.
KING. Arm you, I pray you, to this speedy voyage;
For we will fetters put about this fear,
Which now goes too free-footed.
ROSENCRANTZ. We will haste us.
Exeunt ROSENCRANTZ *and* GUILDENSTERN

Enter POLONIUS

POLONIUS. My lord, he's going to his mother's closet.
Behind the arras I'll convey myself
To hear the process. I'll warrant she'll tax him home;
And, as you said, and wisely was it said,
'Tis meet that some more audience than a mother,
Since nature makes them partial, should o'erhear
The speech, of vantage. Fare you well, my liege.
I'll call upon you ere you go to bed,
And tell you what I know.
KING. Thanks, dear my lord. *Exit* POLONIUS
O, my offence is rank, it smells to heaven;
It hath the primal eldest curse upon't—
A brother's murder! Pray can I not,
Though inclination be as sharp as will.
My stronger guilt defeats my strong intent,
And, like a man to double business bound,
I stand in pause where I shall first begin,
And both neglect. What if this cursed hand
Were thicker than itself with brother's blood,

Is there not rain enough in the sweet heavens
To wash it white as snow? Whereto serves mercy
But to confront the visage of offence?
And what's in prayer but this twofold force,
To be forestalled ere we come to fall,
Or pardon'd being down? Then I'll look up;
My fault is past. But, O, what form of prayer
Can serve my turn? 'Forgive me my foul murder'!
That cannot be; since I am still possess'd
Of those effects for which I did the murder–
My crown, mine own ambition, and my queen.
May one be pardon'd and retain th' offence?
In the corrupted currents of this world
Offence's gilded hand may shove by justice;
And oft 'tis seen the wicked prize itself
Buys out the law. But 'tis not so above:
There is no shuffling; there the action lies
In his true nature; and we ourselves compell'd,
Even to the teeth and forehead of our faults,
To give in evidence. What then? What rests?
Try what repentance can. What can it not?
Yet what can it when one can not repent?
O wretched state! O bosom black as death!
O limed soul, that, struggling to be free,
Art more engag'd! Help, angels. Make assay:
Bow, stubborn knees; and, heart, with strings of steel,
Be soft as sinews of the new-born babe.
All may be well. [*Retires and kneels*]

Enter HAMLET

HAMLET. Now might I do it pat, now 'a is a-praying;
And now I'll do't–and so 'a goes to heaven,
And so am I reveng'd. That would be scann'd:
A villain kills my father; and for that,
I, his sole son, do this same villain send
To heaven.
Why, this is hire and salary, not revenge.
'A took my father grossly, full of bread,
With all his crimes broad blown, as flush as May;
And how his audit stands who knows save heaven?

But in our circumstance and course of thought
'Tis heavy with him; and am I then reveng'd
To take him in the purging of his soul,
When he is fit and season'd for his passage?
No.
Up, sword, and know thou a more horrid hent.
When he is drunk asleep, or in his rage;
Or in th' incestuous pleasure of his bed;
At game, a-swearing, or about some act
That has no relish of salvation in't—
Then trip him, that his heels may kick at heaven,
And that his soul may be as damn'd and black
As hell, whereto it goes. My mother stays.
This physic but prolongs thy sickly days. *Exit*

KING. [*Rising*] My words fly up, my thoughts remain below.
Words without thoughts never to heaven go. *Exit*

SCENE 4

The QUEEN'S *closet*

Enter QUEEN *and* POLONIUS

POLONIUS. 'A will come straight. Look you lay home to him;
Tell him his pranks have been too broad to bear with,
And that your Grace hath screen'd and stood between
Much heat and him. I'll silence me even here.
Pray you be round with him.

HAMLET. [*Within*] Mother, mother, mother!

QUEEN. I'll warrant you. Fear me not.
Withdraw, I hear him coming.

[POLONIUS *goes behind the arras*]

Enter HAMLET

HAMLET. Now, mother, what's the matter?

QUEEN. Hamlet, thou hast thy father much offended.

HAMLET. Mother, you have my father much offended.

QUEEN. Come, come, you answer with an idle tongue.

HAMLET. Go, go, you question with a wicked tongue.

QUEEN. Why, how now, Hamlet!
HAMLET. What's the matter now?
QUEEN. Have you forgot me?
HAMLET. No, by the rood, not so:
You are the Queen, your husband's brother's wife;
And—would it were not so!—you are my mother.
QUEEN. Nay then, I'll set those to you that can speak.
HAMLET. Come, come, and sit you down; you shall not budge.
You go not till I set you up a glass
Where you may see the inmost part of you.
QUEEN. What wilt thou do? Thou wilt not murder me?
Help, help, ho!
POLONIUS. [*Behind*] What, ho! help, help, help!
HAMLET. [*Draws*] How now! a rat?
Dead, for a ducat, dead!
[*Kills* POLONIUS *with a pass through the arras*]
POLONIUS. [*Behind*] O, I am slain!
QUEEN. O me, what hast thou done?
HAMLET. Nay, I know not:
Is it the King?
QUEEN. O, what a rash and bloody deed is this!
HAMLET. A bloody deed!—almost as bad, good mother,
As kill a king and marry with his brother.
QUEEN. As kill a king!
HAMLET. Ay, lady, it was my word. [*Parting the arras*]
Thou wretched, rash, intruding fool, farewell!
I took thee for thy better. Take thy fortune;
Thou find'st to be too busy is some danger.
Leave wringing of your hands. Peace; sit you down,
And let me wring your heart; for so I shall,
If it be made of penetrable stuff;
If damned custom have not braz'd it so
That it be proof and bulwark against sense.
QUEEN. What have I done that thou dar'st wag thy tongue
In noise so rude against me?
HAMLET. Such an act
That blurs the grace and blush of modesty;
Calls virtue hypocrite; takes off the rose
From the fair forehead of an innocent love,

And sets a blister there; makes marriage-vows
As false as dicers' oaths. O, such a deed
As from the body of contraction plucks
The very soul, and sweet religion makes
A rhapsody of words. Heaven's face does glow
O'er this solidity and compound mass
With heated visage, as against the doom—
Is thought-sick at the act.

QUEEN. Ay me, what act,
That roars so loud and thunders in the index?

HAMLET. Look here upon this picture and on this,
The counterfeit presentment of two brothers.
See what a grace was seated on this brow;
Hyperion's curls; the front of Jove himself;
An eye like Mars, to threaten and command;
A station like the herald Mercury
New lighted on a heaven-kissing hill—
A combination and a form indeed
Where every god did seem to set his seal,
To give the world assurance of a man.
This was your husband. Look you now what follows:
Here is your husband, like a mildew'd ear
Blasting his wholesome brother. Have you eyes?
Could you on this fair mountain leave to feed,
And batten on this moor? Ha! have you eyes?
You cannot call it love; for at your age
The heyday in the blood is tame, it's humble,
And waits upon the judgment; and what judgment
Would step from this to this? Sense, sure, you have,
Else could you not have motion; but sure that sense
Is apoplex'd; for madness would not err,
Nor sense to ecstasy was ne'er so thrall'd
But it reserv'd some quantity of choice
To serve in such a difference. What devil was't
That thus hath cozen'd you at hoodman-blind?
Eyes without feeling, feeling without sight,
Ears without hands or eyes, smelling sans all,
Or but a sickly part of one true sense
Could not so mope. O shame! where is thy blush?
Rebellious hell,

If thou canst mutine in a matron's bones,
To flaming youth let virtue be as wax
And melt in her own fire; proclaim no shame
When the compulsive ardour gives the charge,
Since frost itself as actively doth burn,
And reason panders will.

QUEEN. O Hamlet, speak no more!
Thou turn'st my eyes into my very soul;
And there I see such black and grained spots
As will not leave their tinct.

HAMLET. Nay, but to live
In the rank sweat of an enseamed bed,
Stew'd in corruption, honeying and making love
Over the nasty sty!

QUEEN. O, speak to me no more!
These words like daggers enter in my ears;
No more, sweet Hamlet.

HAMLET. A murderer and a villain!
A slave that is not twentieth part the tithe
Of your precedent lord; a vice of kings;
A cutpurse of the empire and the rule,
That from a shelf the precious diadem stole
And put it in his pocket!

QUEEN. No more!

Enter GHOST

HAMLET. A king of shreds and patches–
Save me, and hover o'er me with your wings,
You heavenly guards! What would your gracious figure?

QUEEN. Alas, he's mad!

HAMLET. Do you not come your tardy son to chide,
That, laps'd in time and passion, lets go by
Th' important acting of your dread command?
O, say!

GHOST. Do not forget; this visitation
Is but to whet thy almost blunted purpose.
But look, amazement on thy mother sits.
O, step between her and her fighting soul!
Conceit in weakest bodies strongest works.
Speak to her, Hamlet.

HAMLET. How is it with you, lady?
QUEEN. Alas, how is't with you,
That you do bend your eye on vacancy,
And with th' incorporal air do hold discourse?
Forth at your eyes your spirits wildly peep;
And, as the sleeping soldiers in th' alarm,
Your bedded hairs like life in excrements
Start up and stand an end. O gentle son,
Upon the heat and flame of thy distemper
Sprinkle cool patience! Whereon do you look?
HAMLET. On him, on him! Look you how pale he glares.
His form and cause conjoin'd, preaching to stones,
Would make them capable.—Do not look upon me,
Lest with this piteous action you convert
My stern effects; then what I have to do
Will want true colour—tears perchance for blood.
QUEEN. To whom do you speak this?
HAMLET. Do you see nothing there?
QUEEN. Nothing at all; yet all that is I see.
HAMLET. Nor did you nothing hear?
QUEEN. No, nothing but ourselves.
HAMLET. Why, look you there. Look how it steals away.
My father, in his habit as he liv'd!
Look where he goes even now out at the portal.
Exit GHOST
QUEEN. This is the very coinage of your brain.
This bodiless creation ecstasy
Is very cunning in.
HAMLET. Ecstasy!
My pulse as yours doth temperately keep time,
And makes as healthful music. It is not madness
That I have utt'red. Bring me to the test,
And I the matter will re-word which madness
Would gambol from. Mother, for love of grace,
Lay not that flattering unction to your soul,
That not your trespass but my madness speaks:
It will but skin and film the ulcerous place,
Whiles rank corruption, mining all within,
Infects unseen. Confess yourself to heaven;
Repent what's past; avoid what is to come;

And do not spread the compost on the weeds,
To make them ranker. Forgive me this my virtue;
For in the fatness of these pursy times
Virtue itself of vice must pardon beg,
Yea, curb and woo for leave to do him good.

QUEEN. O Hamlet, thou hast cleft my heart in twain.

HAMLET. O, throw away the worser part of it,
And live the purer with the other half.
Good night—but go not to my uncle's bed;
Assume a virtue, if you have it not.
That monster custom, who all sense doth eat,
Of habits devil, is angel yet in this,
That to the use of actions fair and good
He likewise gives a frock or livery
That aptly is put on. Refrain to-night;
And that shall lend a kind of easiness
To the next abstinence; the next more easy;
For use almost can change the stamp of nature,
And either curb the devil, or throw him out,
With wondrous potency. Once more, good night;
And when you are desirous to be blest,
I'll blessing beg of you. For this same lord
I do repent; but Heaven hath pleas'd it so,
To punish me with this, and this with me,
That I must be their scourge and minister.
I will bestow him, and will answer well
The death I gave him. So, again, good night.
I must be cruel only to be kind;
Thus bad begins and worse remains behind.
One word more, good lady.

QUEEN. What shall I do?

HAMLET. Not this, by no means, that I bid you do:
Let the bloat King tempt you again to bed;
Pinch wanton on your cheek; call you his mouse;
And let him, for a pair of reechy kisses,
Or paddling in your neck with his damn'd fingers,
Make you to ravel all this matter out,
That I essentially am not in madness,
But mad in craft. 'Twere good you let him know;
For who that's but a queen, fair, sober, wise,

Would from a paddock, from a bat, a gib,
Such dear concernings hide? Who would do so?
No, in despite of sense and secrecy,
Unpeg the basket on the house's top,
Let the birds fly, and, like the famous ape,
To try conclusions, in the basket creep
And break your own neck down.

QUEEN. Be thou assur'd, if words be made of breath
And breath of life, I have no life to breathe
What thou hast said to me.

HAMLET. I must to England; you know that?

QUEEN. Alack,
I had forgot. 'Tis so concluded on.

HAMLET. There's letters seal'd; and my two school-fellows,
Whom I will trust as I will adders fang'd—
They bear the mandate; they must sweep my way
And marshal me to knavery. Let it work;
For 'tis the sport to have the engineer
Hoist with his own petar; and't shall go hard
But I will delve one yard below their mines
And blow them at the moon. O, 'tis most sweet
When in one line two crafts directly meet.
This man shall set me packing.
I'll lug the guts into the neighbour room.
Mother, good night. Indeed, this counsellor
Is now most still, most secret, and most grave,
Who was in life a foolish prating knave.
Come, sir, to draw toward an end with you.
Good night, mother.

Exeunt severally; HAMLET *tugging in* POLONIUS

ACT IV. SCENE 1

Elsinore. The Castle

Enter KING, QUEEN, ROSENCRANTZ, *and* GUILDENSTERN

KING. There's matter in these sighs, these profound heaves,
You must translate; 'tis fit we understand them.

Where is your son?
QUEEN. Bestow this place on us a little while.
Exeunt ROSENCRANTZ *and* GUILDENSTERN
Ah, mine own lord, what have I seen to-night!
KING. What, Gertrude? How does Hamlet?
QUEEN. Mad as the sea and wind, when both contend
Which is the mightier. In his lawless fit,
Behind the arras hearing something stir,
Whips out his rapier, cries 'A rat, a rat!'
And in this brainish apprehension kills
The unseen good old man.
KING. O heavy deed!
It had been so with us had we been there.
His liberty is full of threats to all—
To you yourself, to us, to every one.
Alas, how shall this bloody deed be answer'd?
It will be laid to us, whose providence
Should have kept short, restrain'd, and out of haunt,
This mad young man. But so much was our love,
We would not understand what was most fit;
But, like the owner of a foul disease,
To keep it from divulging, let it feed
Even on the pith of life. Where is he gone?
QUEEN. To draw apart the body he hath kill'd;
O'er whom his very madness, like some ore
Among a mineral of metals base,
Shows itself pure: 'a weeps for what is done.
KING. O Gertrude, come away!
The sun no sooner shall the mountains touch
But we will ship him hence; and this vile deed
We must with all our majesty and skill
Both countenance and excuse. Ho, Guildenstern!

Re-enter ROSENCRANTZ *and* GUILDENSTERN

Friends, both go join you with some further aid:
Hamlet in madness hath Polonius slain,
And from his mother's closet hath he dragg'd him;
Go seek him out; speak fair, and bring the body
Into the chapel. I pray you haste in this.
Exeunt ROSENCRANTZ *and* GUILDENSTERN

Come, Gertrude, we'll call up our wisest friends
And let them know both what we mean to do
And what's untimely done; so haply slander—
Whose whisper o'er the world's diameter,
As level as the cannon to his blank,
Transports his pois'ned shot—may miss our name,
And hit the woundless air. O, come away!
My soul is full of discord and dismay. *Exeunt*

SCENE 2

Elsinore. The Castle

Enter HAMLET

HAMLET. Safely stow'd.

GENTLEMEN. [*Within*] Hamlet! Lord Hamlet!

HAMLET. But soft! What noise? Who calls on Hamlet? O, here they come!

Enter ROSENCRANTZ *and* GUILDENSTERN

ROSENCRANTZ. What have you done, my lord, with the dead body?

HAMLET. Compounded it with dust, whereto 'tis kin.

ROSENCRANTZ. Tell us where 'tis, that we may take it thence
And bear it to the chapel.

HAMLET. Do not believe it.

ROSENCRANTZ. Believe what?

HAMLET. That I can keep your counsel, and not mine own. Besides, to be demanded of a sponge—what replication should be made by the son of a king?

ROSENCRANTZ. Take you me for a sponge, my lord?

HAMLET. Ay, sir; that soaks up the King's countenance, his rewards, his authorities. But such officers do the King best service in the end: he keeps them, like an ape an apple in the corner of his jaw; first mouth'd to be last swallowed; when he needs what you have glean'd, it is but squeezing you and, sponge, you shall be dry again.

ROSENCRANTZ. I understand you not, my lord.

HAMLET. I am glad of it; a knavish speech sleeps in a foolish ear.

ROSENCRANTZ. My lord, you must tell us where the body is, and go with us to the King.

HAMLET. The body is with the King, but the King is not with the body. The King is a thing—

GUILDENSTERN. A thing, my lord!

HAMLET. Of nothing. Bring me to him. Hide fox, and all after. *Exeunt*

SCENE 3

Elsinore. The Castle

Enter KING, *attended*

KING. I have sent to seek him, and to find the body.
How dangerous is it that this man goes loose!
Yet must not we put the strong law on him:
He's lov'd of the distracted multitude,
Who like not in their judgment but their eyes;
And where 'tis so, th' offender's scourge is weigh'd,
But never the offence. To bear all smooth and even,
This sudden sending him away must seem
Deliberate pause. Diseases desperate grown
By desperate appliance are reliev'd,
Or not at all.

Enter ROSENCRANTZ

How now! what hath befall'n?

ROSENCRANTZ. Where the dead body is bestow'd, my lord,
We cannot get from him.

KING. But where is he?

ROSENCRANTZ. Without, my lord; guarded, to know your pleasure.

KING. Bring him before us.

ROSENCRANTZ. Ho, Guildenstern! bring in the lord.

Enter HAMLET *and* GUILDENSTERN

KING. Now, Hamlet, where's Polonius?

HAMLET. At supper.

KING. At supper! Where?

HAMLET. Not where he eats, but where 'a is eaten; a certain convocation of politic worms are e'en at him. Your worm is your only emperor for diet: we fat all creatures else to fat us, and we fat ourselves for maggots; your fat king and your lean beggar is but variable service—two dishes, but to one table. That's the end.

KING. Alas, alas!

HAMLET. A man may fish with the worm that hath eat of a king, and eat of the fish that hath fed of that worm.

KING. What dost thou mean by this?

HAMLET. Nothing but to show you how a king may go a progress through the guts of a beggar.

KING. Where is Polonius?

HAMLET. In heaven; send thither to see; if your messenger find him not there, seek him i' th' other place yourself. But if, indeed, you find him not within this month, you shall nose him as you go up the stairs into the lobby.

KING. [*To attendants*] Go seek him there.

HAMLET. 'A will stay till you come. *Exeunt attendants*

KING. Hamlet, this deed, for thine especial safety—
Which we do tender, as we dearly grieve
For that which thou hast done—must send thee hence
With fiery quickness. Therefore prepare thyself;
The bark is ready, and the wind at help,
Th' associates tend, and everything is bent
For England.

HAMLET. For England!

KING. Ay, Hamlet.

HAMLET. Good!

KING. So is it, if thou knew'st our purposes.

HAMLET. I see a cherub that sees them. But, come; for England! Farewell, dear mother.

KING. Thy loving father, Hamlet.

HAMLET. My mother: father and mother is man and wife; man and wife is one flesh; and so, my mother. Come, for England. *Exit*

KING. Follow him at foot; tempt him with speed aboard;
Delay it not; I'll have him hence to-night.

Away! for everything is seal'd and done
That else leans on th' affair. Pray you make haste.
Exeunt all but the KING
And, England, if my love thou hold'st at aught—
As my great power thereof may give thee sense,
Since yet thy cicatrice looks raw and red
After the Danish sword, and thy free awe
Pays homage to us—thou mayst not coldly set
Our sovereign process; which imports at full,
By letters congruing to that effect,
The present death of Hamlet. Do it, England:
For like the hectic in my blood he rages,
And thou must cure me. Till I know 'tis done,
Howe'er my haps, my joys were ne'er begun. *Exit*

SCENE 4

A plain in Denmark

Enter FORTINBRAS *with his army over the stage*

FORTINBRAS. Go, Captain, from me greet the Danish king.
Tell him that by his license Fortinbras
Craves the conveyance of a promis'd march
Over his kingdom. You know the rendezvous.
If that his Majesty would aught with us,
We shall express our duty in his eye;
And let him know so.
CAPTAIN. I will do't, my lord.
FORTINBRAS. Go softly on. *Exeunt all but the* CAPTAIN

Enter HAMLET, ROSENCRANTZ, GUILDENSTERN, *and others*

HAMLET. Good sir, whose powers are these?
CAPTAIN. They are of Norway, sir.
HAMLET. How purpos'd, sir, I pray you?
CAPTAIN. Against some part of Poland.
HAMLET. Who commands them, sir?
CAPTAIN. The nephew to old Norway, Fortinbras.
HAMLET. Goes it against the main of Poland, sir,
Or for some frontier?

CAPTAIN. Truly to speak, and with no addition,
We go to gain a little patch of ground
That hath in it no profit but the name.
To pay five ducats, five, I would not farm it;
Nor will it yield to Norway or the Pole
A ranker rate should it be sold in fee.
HAMLET. Why, then the Polack never will defend it.
CAPTAIN. Yes, it is already garrison'd.
HAMLET. Two thousand souls and twenty thousand ducats
Will not debate the question of this straw.
This is th' imposthume of much wealth and peace,
That inward breaks, and shows no cause without
Why the man dies. I humbly thank you, sir.
CAPTAIN. God buy you, sir. *Exit*
ROSENCRANTZ. Will't please you go, my lord?
HAMLET. I'll be with you straight. Go a little before.
Exeunt all but HAMLET
How all occasions do inform against me,
And spur my dull revenge! What is a man,
If his chief good and market of his time
Be but to sleep and feed? A beast, no more!
Sure he that made us with such large discourse,
Looking before and after, gave us not
That capability and godlike reason
To fust in us unus'd. Now, whether it be
Bestial oblivion, or some craven scruple
Of thinking too precisely on th' event—
A thought which, quarter'd, hath but one part wisdom
And ever three parts coward—I do not know
Why yet I live to say 'This thing's to do,'
Sith I have cause, and will, and strength, and means,
To do't. Examples gross as earth exhort me:
Witness this army, of such mass and charge,
Led by a delicate and tender prince,
Whose spirit, with divine ambition puff'd,
Makes mouths at the invisible event,
Exposing what is mortal and unsure
To all that fortune, death, and danger dare,
Even for an egg-shell. Rightly to be great
Is not to stir without great argument,

But greatly to find quarrel in a straw,
When honour's at the stake. How stand I, then,
That have a father kill'd, a mother stain'd,
Excitements of my reason and my blood,
And let all sleep, while to my shame I see
The imminent death of twenty thousand men
That, for a fantasy and trick of fame,
Go to their graves like beds, fight for a plot
Whereon the numbers cannot try the cause,
Which is not tomb enough and continent
To hide the slain? O, from this time forth,
My thoughts be bloody, or be nothing worth! *Exit*

SCENE 5

Elsinore. The Castle

Enter QUEEN, HORATIO, *and a* GENTLEMAN

QUEEN. I will not speak with her.
GENTLEMAN. She is importunate, indeed distract.
Her mood will needs be pitied.
QUEEN. What would she have?
GENTLEMAN. She speaks much of her father; says she hears
There's tricks i' th' world, and hems, and beats her heart;
Spurns enviously at straws; speaks things in doubt,
That carry but half sense. Her speech is nothing,
Yet the unshaped use of it doth move
The hearers to collection; they yawn at it,
And botch the words up fit to their own thoughts;
Which, as her winks and nods and gestures yield them,
Indeed would make one think there might be thought,
Though nothing sure, yet much unhappily.
HORATIO. 'Twere good she were spoken with; for she may strew
Dangerous conjectures in ill-breeding minds.
QUEEN. Let her come in. *Exit* GENTLEMAN
[*Aside*] To my sick soul, as sin's true nature is,
Each toy seems prologue to some great amiss.
So full of artless jealousy is guilt,

It spills itself in fearing to be spilt.

Enter Ophelia *distracted*

Ophelia. Where is the beauteous Majesty of Denmark?

Queen. How now, Ophelia!

Ophelia. [*Sings*]

How should I your true love know
From another one?
By his cockle hat and staff,
And his sandal shoon.

Queen. Alas, sweet lady, what imports this song?

Ophelia. Say you? Nay, pray you, mark. [*Sings*]

He is dead and gone, lady,
He is dead and gone;
At his head a grass-green turf,
At his heels a stone.

O, ho!

Queen. Nay, but, Ophelia—

Ophelia. Pray you, mark. [*Sings*]

White his shroud as the mountain snow—

Enter King

Queen. Alas, look here, my lord.

Ophelia. Larded with sweet flowers;
Which bewept to the grave did not go
With true-love showers.

King. How do you, pretty lady?

Ophelia. Well, God dild you! They say the owl was a baker's daughter. Lord, we know what we are, but know not what we may be. God be at your table!

King. Conceit upon her father.

Ophelia. Pray let's have no words of this; but when they ask you what it means, say you this: [*Sings*]

To-morrow is Saint Valentine's day,
All in the morning betime,
And I a maid at your window,
To be your Valentine.

Then up he rose, and donn'd his clothes,
  And dupp'd the chamber-door;
Let in the maid, that out a maid
  Never departed more.

KING. Pretty Ophelia!

OPHELIA. Indeed, la, without an oath, I'll make an end on't.

[*Sings*] By Gis and by Saint Charity,
  Alack, and fie for shame!
Young men will do't, if they come to't;
  By Cock, they are to blame.
Quoth she 'Before you tumbled me,
  You promis'd me to wed.'

He answers:

'So would I 'a done, by yonder sun,
An thou hadst not come to my bed.'

KING. How long hath she been thus?

OPHELIA. I hope all will be well. We must be patient; but I cannot choose but weep to think they would lay him i' th' cold ground. My brother shall know of it; and so I thank you for your good counsel. Come, my coach! Good night, ladies; good night, sweet ladies, good night, good night. *Exit*

KING. Follow her close; give her good watch, I pray you.
Exeunt HORATIO *and* GENTLEMAN

O, this is the poison of deep grief; it springs
All from her father's death. And now behold—
O Gertrude, Gertrude!
When sorrows come, they come not single spies,
But in battalions! First, her father slain;
Next, your son gone, and he most violent author
Of his own just remove; the people muddied,
Thick and unwholesome in their thoughts and whispers
For good Polonius' death; and we have done but greenly
In hugger-mugger to inter him; poor Ophelia
Divided from herself and her fair judgment,
Without the which we are pictures, or mere beasts;
Last, and as much containing as all these,
Her brother is in secret come from France;

Feeds on his wonder, keeps himself in clouds,
And wants not buzzers to infect his ear
With pestilent speeches of his father's death;
Wherein necessity, of matter beggar'd,
Will nothing stick our person to arraign
In ear and ear. O my dear Gertrude, this,
Like to a murd'ring piece, in many places
Gives me superfluous death. [*A noise within*]

QUEEN. Alack, what noise is this?

KING. Attend!

Enter a GENTLEMAN

Where are my Switzers? Let them guard the door.
What is the matter?

GENTLEMAN. Save yourself, my lord:
The ocean, overpeering of his list,
Eats not the flats with more impitious haste
Than young Laertes, in a riotous head,
O'erbears your officers. The rabble call him lord;
And, as the world were now but to begin,
Antiquity forgot, custom not known,
The ratifiers and props of every word,
They cry 'Choose we; Laertes shall be king.'
Caps, hands, and tongues, applaud it to the clouds,
'Laertes shall be king, Laertes king.'

QUEEN. How cheerfully on the false trail they cry!
[*Noise within*]
O, this is counter, you false Danish dogs!

KING. The doors are broke.

Enter LAERTES, *with others, in arms*

LAERTES. Where is this king?—Sirs, stand you all without.

ALL. No, let's come in.

LAERTES. I pray you give me leave.

ALL. We will, we will. *Exeunt*

LAERTES. I thank you. Keep the door.—O thou vile king,
Give me my father!

QUEEN. Calmly, good Laertes.

LAERTES. That drop of blood that's calm proclaims me bastard;

Cries cuckold to my father; brands the harlot
Even here, between the chaste unsmirched brow
Of my true mother.

KING. What is the cause, Laertes,
That thy rebellion looks so giant-like?
Let him go, Gertrude; do not fear our person:
There's such divinity doth hedge a king
That treason can but peep to what it would,
Acts little of his will. Tell me, Laertes,
Why thou art thus incens'd. Let him go, Gertrude.
Speak, man.

LAERTES. Where is my father?

KING. Dead.

QUEEN. But not by him.

KING. Let him demand his fill.

LAERTES. How came he dead? I'll not be juggled with.
To hell, allegiance! Vows, to the blackest devil!
Conscience and grace, to the profoundest pit!
I dare damnation. To this point I stand,
That both the worlds I give to negligence,
Let come what comes; only I'll be reveng'd
Most throughly for my father.

KING. Who shall stay you?

LAERTES. My will, not all the world's.
And for my means, I'll husband them so well
They shall go far with little.

KING. Good Laertes,
If you desire to know the certainty
Of your dear father, is't writ in your revenge
That, swoopstake, you will draw both friend and foe,
Winner and loser?

LAERTES. None but his enemies.

KING. Will you know them, then?

LAERTES. To his good friends thus wide I'll ope my arms
And, like the kind life-rend'ring pelican,
Repast them with my blood.

KING. Why, now you speak
Like a good child and a true gentleman.
That I am guiltless of your father's death,
And am most sensibly in grief for it,

It shall as level to your judgment 'pear
As day does to your eye.
[*A noise within:* 'Let her come in.']

LAERTES. How now! What noise is that?

Re-enter OPHELIA

O, heat dry up my brains! tears seven times salt
Burn out the sense and virtue of mine eye!
By heaven, thy madness shall be paid with weight
Till our scale turn the beam. O rose of May!
Dear maid, kind sister, sweet Ophelia!
O heavens! is't possible a young maid's wits
Should be as mortal as an old man's life?
Nature is fine in love; and where 'tis fine
It sends some precious instance of itself
After the thing it loves.

OPHELIA. [*Sings*]
They bore him barefac'd on the bier;
Hey non nonny, nonny, hey nonny;
And in his grave rain'd many a tear—

Fare you well, my dove!

LAERTES. Hadst thou thy wits, and didst persuade revenge,
It could not move thus.

OPHELIA. You must sing 'A-down, a-down,' an you call him a-down-a. O, how the wheel becomes it! It is the false steward, that stole his master's daughter.

LAERTES. This nothing's more than matter.

OPHELIA. There's rosemary, that's for remembrance; pray you, love, remember. And there is pansies, that's for thoughts.

LAERTES. A document in madness—thoughts and remembrance fitted.

OPHELIA. There's fennel for you, and columbines. There's rue for you; and here's some for me. We may call it herb of grace a Sundays. O, you must wear your rue with a difference. There's a daisy. I would give you some violets, but they wither'd all when my father died. They say 'a made a good end.

[*Sings*] For bonny sweet Robin is all my joy.

LAERTES. Thought and affliction, passion, hell itself,
She turns to favour and to prettiness.

OPHELIA. [*Sings*]

And will 'a not come again?
And will 'a not come again?
No, no, he is dead,
Go to thy death-bed,
He never will come again.

His beard was as white as snow,
All flaxen was his poll;
He is gone, he is gone,
And we cast away moan:
God-a-mercy on his soul!

And of all Christian souls, I pray God. God buy you. *Exit*

LAERTES. Do you see this, O God?

KING. Laertes, I must commune with your grief,
Or you deny me right. Go but apart,
Make choice of whom your wisest friends you will,
And they shall hear and judge 'twixt you and me.
If by direct or by collateral hand
They find us touch'd, we will our kingdom give,
Our crown, our life, and all that we call ours,
To you in satisfaction; but if not,
Be you content to lend your patience to us,
And we shall jointly labour with your soul
To give it due content.

LAERTES. Let this be so.
His means of death, his obscure funeral–
No trophy, sword, nor hatchment, o'er his bones,
No noble rite nor formal ostentation–
Cry to be heard, as 'twere from heaven to earth,
That I must call't in question.

KING. So you shall;
And where th' offence is, let the great axe fall.
I pray you go with me. *Exeunt*

SCENE 6

Elsinore. The Castle

Enter HORATIO *with an* ATTENDANT

HORATIO. What are they that would speak with me?

ATTENDANT. Sea-faring men, sir; they say they have letters for you.

HORATIO. Let them come in. *Exit* ATTENDANT
I do not know from what part of the world
I should be greeted, if not from Lord Hamlet.

Enter sailors

SAILOR. God bless you, sir.

HORATIO. Let Him bless thee too.

SAILOR. 'A shall, sir, an't please Him. There's a letter for you, sir; it came from th' ambassador that was bound for England—if your name be Horatio, as I am let to know it is.

HORATIO. [*Reads*] 'Horatio, when thou shalt have overlook'd this, give these fellows some means to the King: they have letters for him. Ere we were two days old at sea, a pirate of very warlike appointment gave us chase. Finding ourselves too slow of sail, we put on a compelled valour; and in the grapple I boarded them. On the instant they got clear of our ship; so I alone became their prisoner. They have dealt with me like thieves of mercy; but they knew what they did; I am to do a good turn for them. Let the King have the letters I have sent; and repair thou to me with as much speed as thou wouldest fly death. I have words to speak in thine ear will make thee dumb; yet are they much too light for the bore of the matter. These good fellows will bring thee where I am. Rosencrantz and Guildenstern hold their course for England; of them I have much to tell thee. Farewell.
'He that thou knowest thine, HAMLET.'

Come, I will give you way for these your letters,
And do't the speedier that you may direct me
To him from whom you brought them. *Exeunt*

SCENE 7

Elsinore. The Castle

Enter King *and* Laertes

King. Now must your conscience my acquittance seal,
And you must put me in your heart for friend,
Sith you have heard, and with a knowing ear,
That he which hath your noble father slain
Pursu'd my life.
Laertes. It well appears. But tell me
Why you proceeded not against these feats,
So crimeful and so capital in nature,
As by your safety, wisdom, all things else,
You mainly were stirr'd up.
King. O, for two special reasons,
Which may to you, perhaps, seem much unsinew'd,
But yet to me th' are strong. The Queen his mother
Lives almost by his looks; and for myself,
My virtue or my plague, be it either which—
She is so conjunctive to my life and soul
That, as the star moves not but in his sphere,
I could not but by her. The other motive,
Why to a public count I might not go,
Is the great love the general gender bear him;
Who, dipping all his faults in their affection,
Work like the spring that turneth wood to stone,
Convert his gyves to graces; so that my arrows,
Too slightly timber'd for so loud a wind,
Would have reverted to my bow again,
But not where I have aim'd them.
Laertes. And so have I a noble father lost;
A sister driven into desp'rate terms,
Whose worth, if praises may go back again,
Stood challenger on mount of all the age
For her perfections. But my revenge will come.
King. Break not your sleeps for that. You must not think
That we are made of stuff so flat and dull
That we can let our beard be shook with danger,

And think it pastime. You shortly shall hear more.
I lov'd your father, and we love our self;
And that, I hope, will teach you to imagine–

Enter a MESSENGER *with letters*

How now! What news?
MESSENGER. Letters, my lord, from Hamlet:
These to your Majesty; this to the Queen.
KING. From Hamlet! Who brought them?
MESSENGER. Sailors, my lord, they say; I saw them not.
They were given me by Claudio; he receiv'd them
Of him that brought them.
KING. Laertes, you shall hear them.
Leave us. *Exit* MESSENGER

[*Reads*] 'High and Mighty. You shall know I am set naked on your kingdom. To-morrow shall I beg leave to see your kingly eyes; when I shall, first asking your pardon thereunto, recount the occasion of my sudden and more strange return.

HAMLET.'

What should this mean? Are all the rest come back?
Or is it some abuse, and no such thing?
LAERTES. Know you the hand?
KING. 'Tis Hamlet's character. 'Naked'!
And in a postcript here, he says 'alone.'
Can you devise me?
LAERTES. I am lost in it, my lord. But let him come;
It warms the very sickness in my heart
That I shall live and tell him to his teeth
'Thus didest thou.'
KING. If it be so, Laertes–
As how should it be so, how otherwise?–
Will you be rul'd by me?
LAERTES. Ay, my lord;
So you will not o'errule me to a peace.
KING. To thine own peace. If he be now return'd,
As checking at his voyage, and that he means
No more to undertake it, I will work him
To an exploit now ripe in my device,

Under the which he shall not choose but fall;
And for his death, no wind of blame shall breathe;
But even his mother shall uncharge the practice
And call it accident.

LAERTES. My lord, I will be rul'd
The rather, if you could devise it so
That I might be the organ.

KING. It falls right.
You have been talk'd of since your travel much,
And that in Hamlet's hearing, for a quality
Wherein they say you shine. Your sum of parts
Did not together pluck such envy from him
As did that one; and that, in my regard,
Of the unworthiest siege.

LAERTES. What part is that, my lord?

KING. A very riband in the cap of youth,
Yet needful too; for youth no less becomes
The light and careless livery that it wears
Than settled age his sables and his weeds,
Importing health and graveness. Two months since
Here was a gentleman of Normandy–
I have seen myself, and serv'd against, the French,
And they can well on horseback; but this gallant
Had witchcraft in't; he grew into his seat,
And to such wondrous doing brought his horse,
As had he been incorps'd and demi-natur'd
With the brave beast. So far he topp'd my thought,
That I, in forgery of shapes and tricks,
Come short of what he did.

LAERTES. A Norman was't?

KING. A Norman.

LAERTES. Upon my life, Lamord.

KING. The very same.

LAERTES. I know him well. He is the brooch indeed
And gem of all the nation.

KING. He made confession of you;
And gave you such a masterly report
For art and exercise in your defence,
And for your rapier most especial,
That he cried out 'twould be a sight indeed

If one could match you. The scrimers of their nation
He swore had neither motion, guard, nor eye,
If you oppos'd them. Sir, this report of his
Did Hamlet so envenom with his envy
That he could nothing do but wish and beg
Your sudden coming o'er, to play with you.
Now out of this–

LAERTES. What out of this, my lord?

KING. Laertes, was your father dear to you?
Or are you like the painting of a sorrow,
A face without a heart?

LAERTES. Why ask you this?

KING. Not that I think you did not love your father;
But that I know love is begun by time,
And that I see, in passages of proof,
Time qualifies the spark and fire of it.
There lives within the very flame of love
A kind of wick or snuff that will abate it;
And nothing is at a like goodness still;
For goodness, growing to a pleurisy,
Dies in his own too much. That we would do,
We should do when we would; for this 'would' changes,
And hath abatements and delays as many
As there are tongues, are hands, are accidents;
And then this 'should' is like a spendthrift's sigh
That hurts by easing. But to the quick of th' ulcer:
Hamlet comes back; what would you undertake
To show yourself in deed your father's son
More than in words?

LAERTES. To cut his throat i' th' church.

KING. No place, indeed, should murder sanctuarize;
Revenge should have no bounds. But, good Laertes,
Will you do this? Keep close within your chamber.
Hamlet return'd shall know you are come home.
We'll put on those shall praise your excellence,
And set a double varnish on the fame
The Frenchman gave you; bring you, in fine, together,
And wager on your heads. He, being remiss,
Most generous, and free from all contriving,
Will not peruse the foils; so that with ease

Or with a little shuffling, you may choose
A sword unbated, and, in a pass of practice,
Requite him for your father.

LAERTES. I will do't;
And for that purpose I'll anoint my sword.
I bought an unction of a mountebank,
So mortal that but dip a knife in it,
Where it draws blood no cataplasm so rare,
Collected from all simples that have virtue
Under the moon, can save the thing from death
That is but scratch'd withal. I'll touch my point
With this contagion, that, if I gall him slightly,
It may be death.

KING. Let's further think of this;
Weigh what convenience both of time and means
May fit us to our shape. If this should fail,
And that our drift look through our bad performance,
'Twere better not assay'd, therefore this project
Should have a back or second, that might hold
If this did blast in proof. Soft! let me see.
We'll make a solemn wager on your cunnings—
I ha't.
When in your motion you are hot and dry—
As make your bouts more violent to that end—
And that he calls for drink, I'll have preferr'd him
A chalice for the nonce; whereon but sipping,
If he by chance escape your venom'd stuck,
Our purpose may hold there. But stay; what noise?

Enter QUEEN

QUEEN. One woe doth tread upon another's heel,
So fast they follow. Your sister's drown'd, Laertes.

LAERTES. Drown'd? O, where?

QUEEN. There is a willow grows aslant the brook
That shows his hoar leaves in the glassy stream;
Therewith fantastic garlands did she make
Of crowflowers, nettles, daisies, and long purples
That liberal shepherds give a grosser name,
But our cold maids do dead men's fingers call them.
There, on the pendent boughs her coronet weeds

Clamb'ring to hang, an envious sliver broke;
When down her weedy trophies and herself
Fell in the weeping brook. Her clothes spread wide
And, mermaid-like, awhile they bore her up;
Which time she chanted snatches of old lauds,
As one incapable of her own distress,
Or like a creature native and indued
Unto that element; but long it could not be
Till that her garments, heavy with their drink,
Pull'd the poor wretch from her melodious lay
To muddy death.

LAERTES. Alas, then she is drown'd!

QUEEN. Drown'd, drown'd.

LAERTES. Too much of water hast thou, poor Ophelia,
And therefore I forbid my tears; but yet
It is our trick; nature her custom holds,
Let shame say what it will. When these are gone,
The woman will be out. Adieu, my lord.
I have a speech o' fire that fain would blaze
But that this folly douts it. *Exit*

KING. Let's follow, Gertrude.
How much I had to do to calm his rage!
Now fear I this will give it start again;
Therefore let's follow. *Exeunt*

ACT V. SCENE 1

Elsinore. A churchyard

Enter two CLOWNS *with spades and picks*

FIRST CLOWN. Is she to be buried in Christian burial when she wilfully seeks her own salvation?

SECOND CLOWN. I tell thee she is; therefore make her grave straight. The crowner hath sat on her, and finds it Christian burial.

FIRST CLOWN. How can that be, unless she drown'd herself in her own defence?

SECOND CLOWN. Why, 'tis found so.

FIRST CLOWN. It must be 'se offendendo'; it cannot be else. For here lies the point: if I drown myself wittingly, it argues an act; and an act hath three branches–it is to act, to do, to perform; argal, she drown'd herself wittingly.

SECOND CLOWN. Nay, but hear you, Goodman Delver.

FIRST CLOWN. Give me leave. Here lies the water; good. Here stands the man; good. If the man go to this water and drown himself, it is, will he, nill he, he goes–mark you that; but if the water come to him and drown him, he drowns not himself. Argal, he that is not guilty of his own death shortens not his own life.

SECOND CLOWN. But is this law?

FIRST CLOWN. Ay, marry, is't; crowner's quest law.

SECOND CLOWN. Will you ha' the truth an't? If this had not been a gentlewoman, she should have been buried out a Christian burial.

FIRST CLOWN. Why, there thou say'st; and the more pity that great folk should have count'nance in this world to drown or hang themselves more than their even Christen. Come, my spade. There is no ancient gentlemen but gard'ners, ditchers, and grave-makers; they hold up Adam's profession.

SECOND CLOWN. Was he a gentleman?

FIRST CLOWN. 'A was the first that ever bore arms.

SECOND CLOWN. Why, he had none.

FIRST CLOWN. What, art a heathen? How dost thou understand the Scripture? The Scripture says Adam digg'd. Could he dig without arms? I'll put another question to thee. If thou answerest me not to the purpose, confess thyself–

SECOND CLOWN. Go to.

FIRST CLOWN. What is he that builds stronger than either the mason, the shipwright, or the carpenter?

SECOND CLOWN. The gallows-maker; for that frame outlives a thousand tenants.

FIRST CLOWN. I like thy wit well; in good faith the gallows does well; but how does it well? It does well to those that do ill. Now thou dost ill to say the gallows is built stronger than the church; argal, the gallows may do well to thee. To't again, come.

SECOND CLOWN. Who builds stronger than a mason, a shipwright, or a carpenter?

FIRST CLOWN. Ay, tell me that, and unyoke.

SECOND CLOWN. Marry, now I can tell.

FIRST CLOWN. To 't.

SECOND CLOWN. Mass, I cannot tell.

Enter HAMLET *and* HORATIO, *afar off*

FIRST CLOWN. Cudgel thy brains no more about it, for your dull ass will not mend his pace with beating; and when you are ask'd this question next, say 'a grave-maker': the houses he makes lasts till doomsday. Go, get thee to Yaughan; fetch me a stoup of liquor. *Exit* SECOND CLOWN

[*Digs and sings*] In youth, when I did love, did love,
Methought it was very sweet,
To contract-o-the time for-a my behove,
O, methought there-a-was nothing-a meet.

HAMLET. Has this fellow no feeling of his business, that 'a sings in grave-making?

HORATIO. Custom hath made it in him a property of easiness.

HAMLET. 'Tis e'en so; the hand of little employment hath the daintier sense.

FIRST CLOWN. [*Sings*]

But age, with his stealing steps,
Hath clawed me in his clutch,
And hath shipped me intil the land,
As if I had never been such.

[*Throws up a skull*]

HAMLET. That skull had a tongue in it, and could sing once. How the knave jowls it to the ground, as if 'twere Cain's jawbone, that did the first murder! This might be the pate of a politician, which this ass now o'erreaches; one that would circumvent God, might it not?

HORATIO. It might, my lord.

HAMLET. Or of a courtier; which could say 'Good morrow, sweet lord! How dost thou, sweet lord?' This might be my Lord Such-a-one, that praised my Lord Such-a-one's horse, when 'a meant to beg it—might it not?

HORATIO. Ay, my lord.

HAMLET. Why, e'en so; and now my Lady Worm's, chapless, and knock'd about the mazard with a sexton's spade. Here's fine revolution, an we had the trick to see't. Did these bones cost no more the breeding but to play at loggats with them? Mine ache to think on't.

FIRST CLOWN. [*Sings*]

A pick-axe and a spade, a spade,
  For and a shrouding sheet:
O, a pit of clay for to be made
  For such a guest is meet.

[*Throws up another skull*]

HAMLET. There's another. Why may not that be the skull of a lawyer? Where be his quiddities now, his quillets, his cases, his tenures, and his tricks? Why does he suffer this rude knave now to knock him about the sconce with a dirty shovel, and will not tell him of his action of battery? Hum! This fellow might be in's time a great buyer of land, with his statutes, his recognizances, his fines, his double vouchers, his recoveries. Is this the fine of his fines, and the recovery of his recoveries, to have his fine pate full of fine dirt? Will his vouchers vouch him no more of his purchases, and double ones too, than the length and breadth of a pair of indentures? The very conveyances of his lands will scarcely lie in this box; and must th' inheritor himself have no more, ha?

HORATIO. Not a jot more, my lord.

HAMLET. Is not parchment made of sheep-skins?

HORATIO. Ay, my lord, and of calves' skins too.

HAMLET. They are sheep and calves which seek out assurance in that. I will speak to this fellow. Whose grave's this, sirrah?

FIRST CLOWN. Mine, sir. [*Sings*]

O, a pit of clay for to be made
  For such a guest is meet.

HAMLET. I think it be thine indeed, for thou liest in't.

FIRST CLOWN. You lie out on't, sir, and therefore 'tis not yours. For my part, I do not lie in't, yet it is mine.

HAMLET. Thou dost lie in't, to be in't and say it is thine; 'tis for the dead, not for the quick; therefore thou liest.

FIRST CLOWN. 'Tis a quick lie, sir; 'twill away again from me to you.

HAMLET. What man dost thou dig it for?

FIRST CLOWN. For no man, sir.

HAMLET. What woman, then?

FIRST CLOWN. For none neither.

HAMLET. Who is to be buried in't?

FIRST CLOWN. One that was a woman, sir; but, rest her soul, she's dead.

HAMLET. How absolute the knave is! We must speak by the card, or equivocation will undo us. By the Lord, Horatio, this three years I have took note of it: the age is grown so picked that the toe of the peasant comes so near the heel of the courtier, he galls his kibe. How long hast thou been a grave-maker?

FIRST CLOWN. Of all the days i' th' year, I came to't that day that our last King Hamlet overcame Fortinbras.

HAMLET. How long is that since?

FIRST CLOWN. Cannot you tell that? Every fool can tell that: it was that very day that young Hamlet was born—he that is mad, and sent into England.

HAMLET. Ay, marry, why was he sent into England?

FIRST CLOWN. Why, because 'a was mad: 'a shall recover his wits there; or, if 'a do not, 'tis no great matter there.

HAMLET. Why?

FIRST CLOWN. 'Twill not be seen in him there: there the men are as mad as he.

HAMLET. How came he mad?

FIRST CLOWN. Very strangely, they say.

HAMLET. How strangely?

FIRST CLOWN. Faith, e'en with losing his wits.

HAMLET. Upon what ground?

FIRST CLOWN. Why, here in Denmark. I have been sexton here, man and boy, thirty years.

HAMLET. How long will a man lie i' th' earth ere he rot?

FIRST CLOWN. Faith, if 'a be not rotten before 'a die—as we have many pocky corses now-a-days that will scarce hold the laying in—'a will last you some eight year or nine year.

A tanner will last you nine year.

HAMLET. Why he more than another?

FIRST CLOWN. Why, sir, his hide is so tann'd with his trade that 'a will keep out water a great while; and your water is a sore decayer of your whoreson dead body. Here's a skull now; this skull has lien you i' th' earth three and twenty years.

HAMLET. Whose was it?

FIRST CLOWN. A whoreson mad fellow's it was. Whose do you think it was?

HAMLET. Nay, I know not.

FIRST CLOWN. A pestilence on him for a mad rogue! 'A poured a flagon of Rhenish on my head once. This same skull, sir, was, sir, Yorick's skull, the King's jester.

HAMLET. This?

FIRST CLOWN. E'en that.

HAMLET. Let me see. [*Takes the skull*] Alas, poor Yorick! I knew him, Horatio: a fellow of infinite jest, of most excellent fancy; he hath borne me on his back a thousand times. And now how abhorred in my imagination it is! My gorge rises at it. Here hung those lips that I have kiss'd I know not how oft. Where be your gibes now, your gambols, your songs, your flashes of merriment that were wont to set the table on a roar? Not one now to mock your own grinning–quite chap-fall'n? Now get you to my lady's chamber, and tell her, let her paint an inch thick, to this favour she must come; make her laugh at that. Prithee, Horatio, tell me one thing.

HORATIO. What's that, my lord?

HAMLET. Dost thou think Alexander look'd a this fashion i' th' earth?

HORATIO. E'en so.

HAMLET. And smelt so? Pah! [*Throws down the skull*]

HORATIO. E'en so, my lord.

HAMLET. To what base uses we may return, Horatio! Why may not imagination trace the noble dust of Alexander till 'a find it stopping a bung-hole?

HORATIO. 'Twere to consider too curiously to consider so.

HAMLET. No, faith, not a jot; but to follow him thither with modesty enough, and likelihood to lead it, as thus:

HAMLET. *Alas, poor Yorick! I knew him, Horatio: a fellow of infinite jest, of most excellent fancy; he hath borne me on his back a thousand times. . . . Where be your gibes now . . . ? Not one now to mock your own grinning—quite chap-fall'n? Now get you to my lady's chamber, and tell her, let her paint an inch thick, to this favour she must come; make her laugh at that.*

(ACT V. Scene 1)

Alexander died, Alexander was buried, Alexander returneth to dust; the dust is earth; of earth we make loam; and why of that loam whereto he was converted might they not stop a beer-barrel?

Imperious Cæsar, dead and turn'd to clay,
Might stop a hole to keep the wind away.
O, that that earth which kept the world in awe
Should patch a wall t' expel the winter's flaw!

But soft! but soft! awhile. Here comes the King.

Enter the KING, QUEEN, LAERTES, *in funeral procession after the coffin, with* PRIEST *and* LORDS *attendant*

The Queen, the courtiers. Who is this they follow?
And with such maimed rites? This doth betoken
The corse they follow did with desperate hand
Fordo it own life. 'Twas of some estate.
Couch we awhile and mark. [*Retiring with* HORATIO]

LAERTES. What ceremony else?

HAMLET. That is Laertes, a very noble youth. Mark.

LAERTES. What ceremony else?

PRIEST. Her obsequies have been as far enlarg'd
As we have warrantise. Her death was doubtful;
And, but that great command o'ersways the order,
She should in ground unsanctified have lodg'd
Till the last trumpet; for charitable prayers,
Shards, flints, and pebbles, should be thrown on her;
Yet here she is allow'd her virgin crants,
Her maiden strewments, and the bringing home
Of bell and burial.

LAERTES. Must there no more be done?

PRIEST. No more be done.
We should profane the service of the dead
To sing sage requiem and such rest to her
As to peace-parted souls.

LAERTES. Lay her i' th' earth;
And from her fair and unpolluted flesh
May violets spring! I tell thee, churlish priest,
A minist'ring angel shall my sister be
When thou liest howling.

HAMLET. What, the fair Ophelia!
QUEEN. Sweets to the sweet; farewell! [*Scattering flowers*]
I hop'd thou shouldst have been my Hamlet's wife;
I thought thy bride-bed to have deck'd, sweet maid,
And not have strew'd thy grave.
LAERTES. O, treble woe
Fall ten times treble on that cursed head
Whose wicked deed thy most ingenious sense
Depriv'd thee of! Hold off the earth awhile,
Till I have caught her once more in mine arms.
[*Leaps into the grave*]
Now pile your dust upon the quick and dead,
Till of this flat a mountain you have made
T' o'er-top old Pelion or the skyish head
Of blue Olympus.
HAMLET. [*Advancing*] What is he whose grief
Bears such an emphasis, whose phrase of sorrow
Conjures the wand'ring stars, and makes them stand
Like wonder-wounded hearers? This is I,
Hamlet the Dane. [*Leaps into the grave*]
LAERTES. The devil take thy soul! [*Grappling with him*]
HAMLET. Thou pray'st not well.
I prithee take thy fingers from my throat;
For, though I am not splenitive and rash,
Yet have I in me something dangerous,
Which let thy wiseness fear. Hold off thy hand.
KING. Pluck them asunder.
QUEEN. Hamlet! Hamlet!
ALL. Gentlemen!
HORATIO. Good my lord, be quiet. [*The attendants part them, and they come out of the grave*]
HAMLET. Why, I will fight with him upon this theme
Until my eyelids will no longer wag.
QUEEN. O my son, what theme?
HAMLET. I lov'd Ophelia: forty thousand brothers
Could not, with all their quantity of love,
Make up my sum. What wilt thou do for her?
KING. O, he is mad, Laertes.
QUEEN. For love of God, forbear him.
HAMLET. 'Swounds, show me what th'owt do:

Woo't weep, woo't fight, woo't fast, woo't tear thyself,
Woo't drink up eisel, eat a crocodile?
I'll do't. Dost come here to whine?
To outface me with leaping in her grave?
Be buried quick with her, and so will I;
And, if thou prate of mountains, let them throw
Millions of acres on us, till our ground,
Singeing his pate against the burning zone,
Make Ossa like a wart! Nay, an thou'lt mouth,
I'll rant as well as thou.

QUEEN. This is mere madness;
And thus awhile the fit will work on him;
Anon, as patient as the female dove
When that her golden couplets are disclos'd,
His silence will sit drooping.

HAMLET. Hear you, sir:
What is the reason that you use me thus?
I lov'd you ever. But it is no matter.
Let Hercules himself do what he may,
The cat will mew, and dog will have his day. *Exit*

KING. I pray thee, good Horatio, wait upon him.
Exit HORATIO
[*To* LAERTES] Strengthen your patience in our last night's speech;
We'll put the matter to the present push.—
Good Gertrude, set some watch over your son.—
This grave shall have a living monument.
An hour of quiet shortly shall we see;
Till then in patience our proceeding be. *Exeunt*

SCENE 2

Elsinore. The Castle

Enter HAMLET *and* HORATIO

HAMLET. So much for this, sir; now shall you see the other.
You do remember all the circumstance?

HORATIO. Remember it, my lord!

HAMLET. Sir, in my heart there was a kind of fighting

That would not let me sleep. Methought I lay
Worse than the mutines in the bilboes. Rashly,
And prais'd be rashness for it—let us know,
Our indiscretion sometime serves us well,
When our deep plots do pall; and that should learn us
There's a divinity that shapes our ends,
Rough-hew them how we will.

HORATIO. That is most certain.

HAMLET. Up from my cabin,
My sea-gown scarf'd about me, in the dark
Grop'd I to find out them; had my desire;
Finger'd their packet, and in fine withdrew
To mine own room again, making so bold,
My fears forgetting manners, to unseal
Their grand commission; where I found, Horatio,
Ah, royal knavery! an exact command,
Larded with many several sorts of reasons,
Importing Denmark's health and England's too,
With, ho! such bugs and goblins in my life—
That, on the supervise, no leisure bated,
No, not to stay the grinding of the axe,
My head should be struck off.

HORATIO. Is't possible?

HAMLET. Here's the commission; read it at more leisure.
But wilt thou hear now how I did proceed?

HORATIO. I beseech you.

HAMLET. Being thus benetted round with villainies—
Ere I could make a prologue to my brains,
They had begun the play—I sat me down;
Devis'd a new commission; wrote it fair.
I once did hold it, as our statists do,
A baseness to write fair, and labour'd much
How to forget that learning; but sir, now
It did me yeoman's service. Wilt thou know
Th' effect of what I wrote?

HORATIO. Ay, good my lord.

HAMLET. An earnest conjuration from the King,
As England was his faithful tributary,
As love between them like the palm might flourish,
As peace should still her wheaten garland wear

And stand a comma 'tween their amities,
And many such like as-es of great charge,
That, on the view and knowing of these contents,
Without debatement further more or less,
He should those bearers put to sudden death,
Not shriving-time allow'd.

HORATIO. How was this seal'd?

HAMLET. Why, even in that was heaven ordinant.
I had my father's signet in my purse,
Which was the model of that Danish seal;
Folded the writ up in the form of th' other;
Subscrib'd it, gave't th' impression, plac'd it safely,
The changeling never known. Now, the next day
Was our sea-fight; and what to this was sequent
Thou knowest already.

HORATIO. So Guildenstern and Rosencrantz go to't.

HAMLET. Why, man, they did make love to this employment;
They are not near my conscience; their defeat
Does by their own insinuation grow:
'Tis dangerous when the baser nature comes
Between the pass and fell incensed points
Of mighty opposites.

HORATIO. Why, what a king is this!

HAMLET. Does it not, think thee, stand me now upon—
He that hath kill'd my king and whor'd my mother;
Popp'd in between th' election and my hopes;
Thrown out his angle for my proper life,
And with such coz'nage—is't not perfect conscience
To quit him with this arm? And is't not to be damn'd
To let this canker of our nature come
In further evil?

HORATIO. It must be shortly known to him from England
What is the issue of the business there.

HAMLET. It will be short; the interim is mine.
And a man's life's no more than to say 'one.'
But I am very sorry, good Horatio,
That to Laertes I forgot myself;
For by the image of my cause I see
The portraiture of his. I'll court his favours.

But sure the bravery of his grief did put me
Into a tow'ring passion.

HORATIO. Peace; who comes here?

Enter young OSRIC

OSRIC. Your lordship is right welcome back to Denmark.

HAMLET. I humbly thank you, sir. [*Aside to* HORATIO] Dost know this water-fly?

HORATIO. [*Aside to* HAMLET] No, my good lord.

HAMLET. [*Aside to* HORATIO] Thy state is the more gracious; for 'tis a vice to know him. He hath much land, and fertile. Let a beast be lord of beasts, and his crib shall stand at the king's mess. 'Tis a chough; but, as I say, spacious in the possession of dirt.

OSRIC. Sweet lord, if your lordship were at leisure, I should impart a thing to you from his Majesty.

HAMLET. I will receive it, sir, with all diligence of spirit. Put your bonnet to his right use; 'tis for the head.

OSRIC. I thank your lordship; it is very hot.

HAMLET. No, believe me, 'tis very cold; the wind is northerly.

OSRIC. It is indifferent cold, my lord, indeed.

HAMLET. But yet methinks it is very sultry and hot for my complexion.

OSRIC. Exceedingly, my lord; it is very sultry, as 'twere—I cannot tell how. But, my lord, his Majesty bade me signify to you that 'a has laid a great wager on your head. Sir, this is the matter—

HAMLET. I beseech you, remember.

[HAMLET *moves him to put on his hat*]

OSRIC. Nay, good my lord; for my ease, in good faith. Sir, here is newly come to court Laertes; believe me, an absolute gentleman, full of most excellent differences, of very soft society and great showing. Indeed, to speak feelingly of him, he is the card or calendar of gentry, for you shall find in him the continent of what part a gentleman would see.

HAMLET. Sir, his definement suffers no perdition in you; though, I know, to divide him inventorially would dozy th' arithmetic of memory, and yet but yaw neither in respect of his quick sail. But, in the verity of extolment, I take him to be a soul of great article, and his infusion of such dearth and rareness, as to make true diction of him, his semblable is his mirror, and who else would trace him, his umbrage, nothing more.

OSRIC. Your lordship speaks most infallibly of him.

HAMLET. The concernancy, sir? Why do we wrap the gentleman in our more rawer breath?

OSRIC. Sir?

HORATIO. [*Aside to* HAMLET] Is't not possible to understand in another tongue? You will to't, sir, really.

HAMLET. What imports the nomination of this gentleman?

OSRIC. Of Laertes?

HORATIO. [*Aside*] His purse is empty already; all's golden words are spent.

HAMLET. Of him, sir.

OSRIC. I know you are not ignorant—

HAMLET. I would you did, sir; yet, in faith, if you did, it would not much approve me. Well, sir.

OSRIC. You are not ignorant of what excellence Laertes is—

HAMLET. I dare not confess that, lest I should compare with him in excellence; but to know a man well were to know himself.

OSRIC. I mean, sir, for his weapon; but in the imputation laid on him by them, in his meed he's unfellowed.

HAMLET. What's his weapon?

OSRIC. Rapier and dagger.

HAMLET. That's two of his weapons—but well.

OSRIC. The King, sir, hath wager'd with him six Barbary horses; against the which he has impon'd, as I take it, six French rapiers and poniards, with their assigns, as girdle, hangers, and so—three of the carriages, in faith, are very dear to fancy, very responsive to the hilts, most delicate carriages, and of very liberal conceit.

HAMLET. What call you the carriages?

HORATIO. [*Aside to* HAMLET] I knew you must be edified by the margent ere you had done.

OSRIC. The carriages, sir, are the hangers.

HAMLET. The phrase would be more germane to the matter if we could carry a cannon by our sides. I would it might be hangers till then. But on: six Barbary horses against six French swords, their assigns, and three liberal conceited carriages; that's the French bet against the Danish. Why is this all impon'd, as you call it?

OSRIC. The King, sir, hath laid, sir, that in a dozen passes between yourself and him he shall not exceed you three hits; he hath laid on twelve for nine, and it would come to immediate trial if your lordship would vouchsafe the answer.

HAMLET. How if I answer no?

OSRIC. I mean, my lord, the opposition of your person in trial.

HAMLET. Sir, I will walk here in the hall. If it please his Majesty, it is the breathing time of day with me; let the foils be brought, the gentleman willing, and the King hold his purpose, I will win for him an I can; if not, I will gain nothing but my shame and the odd hits.

OSRIC. Shall I redeliver you e'en so?

HAMLET. To this effect, sir, after what flourish your nature will.

OSRIC. I commend my duty to your lordship.

HAMLET. Yours, yours. [*Exit* OSRIC] He does well to commend it himself; there are no tongues else for's turn.

HORATIO. This lapwing runs away with the shell on his head.

HAMLET. 'A did comply, sir, with his dug before 'a suck'd it. Thus has he, and many more of the same bevy, that I know the drossy age dotes on, only got the tune of the time and outward habit of encounter—a kind of yesty collection, which carries them through and through the most fann'd and winnowed opinions; and do but blow them to their trial, the bubbles are out.

Enter a LORD

LORD. My lord, his Majesty commended him to you by young Osric, who brings back to him that you attend him in the hall. He sends to know if your pleasure hold to play with Laertes, or that you will take longer time.

HAMLET. I am constant to my purposes; they follow the king's pleasure: if his fitness speaks, mine is ready now—or whensoever, provided I be so able as now.

LORD. The King and Queen and all are coming down.

HAMLET. In happy time.

LORD. The Queen desires you to use some gentle entertainment to Laertes before you fall to play.

HAMLET. She well instructs me. *Exit* LORD

HORATIO. You will lose this wager, my lord.

HAMLET. I do not think so; since he went into France I have been in continual practice. I shall win at the odds. But thou wouldst not think how ill all's here about my heart; but it is no matter.

HORATIO. Nay, good my lord–

HAMLET. It is but foolery; but it is such a kind of gain-giving as would perhaps trouble a woman.

HORATIO. If your mind dislike anything, obey it. I will forestall their repair hither, and say you are not fit.

HAMLET. Not a whit, we defy augury: there is a special providence in the fall of a sparrow. If it be now, 'tis not to come; if it be not to come, it will be now; if it be not now, yet it will come–the readiness is all. Since no man owes of aught he leaves, what is't to leave betimes? Let be.

A table prepared. Trumpets, drums, and officers with cushions, foils and daggers. Enter KING, QUEEN, LAERTES, *and all the state*

KING. Come, Hamlet, come, and take this hand from me.
[*The* KING *puts* LAERTES's *hand into* HAMLET's]

HAMLET. Give me your pardon, sir. I have done you wrong;
But pardon 't, as you are a gentleman.
This presence knows,
And you must needs have heard how I am punish'd
With a sore distraction. What I have done
That might your nature, honour, and exception,
Roughly awake, I here proclaim was madness.
Was 't Hamlet wrong'd Laertes? Never Hamlet.
If Hamlet from himself be ta'en away,
And when he's not himself does wrong Laertes,
Then Hamlet does it not, Hamlet denies it.
Who does it, then? His madness. If't be so,
Hamlet is of the faction that is wrong'd;
His madness is poor Hamlet's enemy.

Sir, in this audience,
Let my disclaiming from a purpos'd evil
Free me so far in your most generous thoughts
That I have shot my arrow o'er the house
And hurt my brother.

LAERTES. I am satisfied in nature,
Whose motive in this case should stir me most
To my revenge; but in my terms of honour
I stand aloof, and will no reconcilement
Till by some elder masters of known honour
I have a voice and precedent of peace
To keep my name ungor'd—but till that time
I do receive your offer'd love like love,
And will not wrong it.

HAMLET. I embrace it freely;
And will this brother's wager frankly play.
Give us the foils. Come on.

LAERTES. Come, one for me.

HAMLET. I'll be your foil, Laertes; in mine ignorance
Your skill shall, like a star i' th' darkest night,
Stick fiery off indeed.

LAERTES. You mock me, sir.

HAMLET. No, by this hand.

KING. Give them the foils, young Osric. Cousin Hamlet,
You know the wager?

HAMLET. Very well, my lord;
Your Grace has laid the odds a' th' weaker side.

KING. I do not fear it: I have seen you both;
But since he's better'd, we have therefore odds.

LAERTES. This is too heavy; let me see another.

HAMLET. This likes me well. These foils have all a length?
[*They prepare to play*]

OSRIC. Ay, my good lord.

KING. Set me the stoups of wine upon that table.
If Hamlet give the first or second hit,
Or quit in answer of the third exchange,
Let all the battlements their ordnance fire;
The King shall drink to Hamlet's better breath,
And in the cup an union shall he throw,
Richer than that which four successive kings

In Denmark's crown have worn. Give me the cups;
And let the kettle to the trumpet speak,
The trumpet to the cannoneer without,
The cannons to the heavens, the heaven to earth,
'Now the King drinks to Hamlet.' Come, begin–
And you, the judges, bear a wary eye.

HAMLET. Come on, sir.

LAERTES. Come, my lord. [*They play*]

HAMLET. One.

LAERTES. No.

HAMLET. Judgment?

OSRIC. A hit, a very palpable hit.

LAERTES. Well, again.

KING. Stay, give me drink. Hamlet, this pearl is thine;
Here's to thy health. [*Drum, trumpets, and shot*] Give him the cup.

HAMLET. I'll play this bout first; set it by awhile.
Come. [*They play*] Another hit; what say you?

LAERTES. A touch, a touch, I do confess't.

KING. Our son shall win.

QUEEN. He's fat, and scant of breath.
Here, Hamlet, take my napkin, rub thy brows.
The Queen carouses to thy fortune, Hamlet.

HAMLET. Good madam!

KING. Gertrude, do not drink.

QUEEN. I will, my lord; I pray you pardon me.

KING. [*Aside*] It is the poison'd cup; it is too late.

HAMLET. I dare not drink yet, madam; by and by.

QUEEN. Come, let me wipe thy face.

LAERTES. My lord, I'll hit him now.

KING. I do not think't.

LAERTES. [*Aside*] And yet it is almost against my conscience.

HAMLET. Come, for the third. Laertes, you do but dally;
I pray you pass with your best violence;
I am afeard you make a wanton of me.

LAERTES. Say you so? Come on. [*They play*]

OSRIC. Nothing, neither way.

LAERTES. Have at you now!

[LAERTES *wounds* HAMLET: *then, in scuffling, they*

change rapiers, and HAMLET *wounds* LAERTES]

KING. Part them; they are incens'd.

HAMLET. Nay, come again. [*The* QUEEN *falls*]

OSRIC. Look to the Queen there, ho!

HORATIO. They bleed on both sides. How is it, my lord?

OSRIC. How is't, Laertes?

LAERTES. Why, as a woodcock, to mine own springe, Osric;
I am justly kill'd with mine own treachery.

HAMLET. How does the Queen?

KING. She swoons to see them bleed.

QUEEN. No, no, the drink, the drink! O my dear Hamlet!
The drink, the drink! I am poison'd. [*Dies*]

HAMLET. O, villainy! Ho! let the door be lock'd.
Treachery! seek it out. [LAERTES *falls*]

LAERTES. It is here, Hamlet. Hamlet, thou art slain;
No med'cine in the world can do thee good;
In thee there is not half an hour's life;
The treacherous instrument is in thy hand,
Unbated and envenom'd. The foul practice
Hath turn'd itself on me; lo, here I lie,
Never to rise again. Thy mother's poison'd.
I can no more. The King, the King's to blame.

HAMLET. The point envenom'd too!
Then, venom, to thy work. [*Stabs the* KING]

ALL. Treason! treason!

KING. O, yet defend me, friends; I am but hurt.

HAMLET. Here, thou incestuous, murd'rous, damned Dane,
Drink off this potion. Is thy union here?
Follow my mother. [KING *dies*]

LAERTES. He is justly serv'd:
It is a poison temper'd by himself.
Exchange forgiveness with me, noble Hamlet.
Mine and my father's death come not upon thee,
Nor thine on me! [*Dies*]

HAMLET. Heaven make thee free of it! I follow thee.
I am dead, Horatio. Wretched Queen, adieu!
You that look pale and tremble at this chance,
That are but mutes or audience to this act,
Had I but time, as this fell sergeant Death
Is strict in his arrest, O, I could tell you—

But let it be. Horatio, I am dead:
Thou livest; report me and my cause aright
To the unsatisfied.

HORATIO. Never believe it.
I am more an antique Roman than a Dane;
Here's yet some liquor left.

HAMLET. As th'art a man,
Give me the cup. Let go. By heaven, I'll ha't.
O God! Horatio, what a wounded name,
Things standing thus unknown, shall live behind me!
If thou didst ever hold me in thy heart,
Absent thee from felicity awhile,
And in this harsh world draw thy breath in pain,
To tell my story. [*March afar off, and shot within*] What warlike noise is this?

OSRIC. Young Fortinbras, with conquest come from Poland,
To th' ambassadors of England gives
This warlike volley.

HAMLET. O, I die, Horatio!
The potent poison quite o'er-crows my spirit.
I cannot live to hear the news from England,
But I do prophesy th' election lights
On Fortinbras; he has my dying voice.
So tell him, with th' occurrents, more and less,
Which have solicited—the rest is silence. [*Dies*]

HORATIO. Now cracks a noble heart. Good night, sweet prince,
And flights of angels sing thee to thy rest! [*March within*]
Why does the drum come hither?

Enter FORTINBRAS *and* ENGLISH AMBASSADORS, *with drum, colours, and attendants*

FORTINBRAS. Where is this sight?

HORATIO. What is it you would see?
If aught of woe or wonder, cease your search.

FORTINBRAS. This quarry cries on havoc. O proud death,
What feast is toward in thine eternal cell
That thou so many princes at a shot
So bloodily hast struck?

FIRST AMBASSADOR. The sight is dismal;

And our affairs from England come too late:
The ears are senseless that should give us hearing
To tell him his commandment is fulfill'd,
That Rosencrantz and Guildenstern are dead.
Where should we have our thanks?

HORATIO. Not from his mouth,
Had it th' ability of life to thank you:
He never gave commandment for their death.
But since, so jump upon this bloody question,
You from the Polack wars, and you from England,
Are here arrived, give order that these bodies
High on a stage be placed to the view;
And let me speak to th' yet unknowing world
How these things came about. So shall you hear
Of carnal, bloody, and unnatural acts;
Of accidental judgments, casual slaughters;
Of deaths put on by cunning and forc'd cause;
And, in this upshot, purposes mistook
Fall'n on th' inventors' heads—all this can I
Truly deliver.

FORTINBRAS. Let us haste to hear it,
And call the noblest to the audience.
For me, with sorrow I embrace my fortune;
I have some rights of memory in this kingdom,
Which now to claim my vantage doth invite me.

HORATIO. Of that I shall have also cause to speak,
And from his mouth whose voice will draw on more.
But let this same be presently perform'd,
Even while men's minds are wild, lest more mischance
On plots and errors happen.

FORTINBRAS. Let four captains
Bear Hamlet like a soldier to the stage;
For he was likely, had he been put on,
To have prov'd most royal; and for his passage
The soldier's music and the rite of war
Speak loudly for him.
Take up the bodies. Such a sight as this
Becomes the field, but here shows much amiss.
Go, bid the soldiers shoot.

Exeunt marching. A peal of ordnance shot off

The Tragedy of King Lear

KING LEAR

SHAKESPEARE read the story of Lear and his daughters in several versions, among them that given by Spenser in Canto X of the Second Book of the *Faerie Queene*. There Guyon, having reached the house of Temperance where sober Alma dwells, and found in her library books dealing with the history of Britain, learns of the British rulers beginning with Brutus, the descendant of Æneas, who first brought civilization to these parts, and ending with Gloriana the Faerie Queene herself. King Lear is the eleventh in this line. Of him Spenser says,

> Next him King Leyr in happie peace long raynd,
> But had no issue male him to succeed,
> But three faire daughters, which were well uptraind
> In all that seemed fitt for kingly seed:
> Mongst whom his realme he equally decreed
> To have divided. Tho, when feeble age
> Nigh to his utmost date he saw proceed,
> He cald his daughters, and with speeches sage
> Inquyrd, which of them most did love her parentage?

Cordelia fails to pass the test; the kingdom is parted between Gonorill and Regan;

> But without dowre the wise Cordelia
> Was sent to Aggannip of Celtica.

The thankless daughters at last cast off their father who betakes himself to Cordelia. She raises an army and restores her father to the throne; after his death she reigns long and honoured,

> Till that her sisters children, woxen strong,
> Through proud ambition against her rebeld,
> And overcommen kept in prison long,
> Till weary of that wretched life her selfe she hong.

Spenser's story with its unhappy ending is substantially that first told by Geoffrey of Monmouth about 1135 in his *Historia regum Britanniae*. This History of the Kings of Britain put Britain on a level with those countries that prided themselves on their Trojan ancestry; and, though there were even among Geoffrey's contemporaries those who felt sceptical about his story, its success was overwhelming and critical comment was drowned in popular approval. Many versions of the story and of Lear's part in it lay between Geoffrey and Shakespeare, of which it will be sufficient to name in addition to Spenser's, the account in the *Mirror for Magistrates*, and in Holinshed's *Chronicles*, all known to Shakespeare. In these, as in Geoffrey of Monmouth, the story ends with Cordelia's suicide. Shakespeare's tragic ending is not, therefore, as some have supposed, the dramatist's device to give expression to his own despair and disillusionment, but only his own treatment of the original story; the misunderstanding of Shakespeare's treatment being due to the commentators' acquaintance with another play from the same source.

The old play, as it is generally called, entitled *The True Chronicle History of King Leir and his three daughters, Gonorill, Regan, and Cordella*, was printed in 1605. Henslowe's Diary records a performance of a play called *Kinge Leare* as early as 6 April 1594. Against 14 May 1594 an entry stands in the Stationers' Register for a play of *Leire Kinge of England and his Three Daughters*, but no copy is known; and the later entry of 8 May 1605, which preceded the 1605 publication, is assumed to refer to the same work. This *King Leir* of 1605 and earlier omits the tragic conclusion completely and ends with the restoration of Leir by his daughter Cordella. The old play is one of the very few versions of Geoffrey's story that ends on this happy note; as Shakespeare was familiar with the story in its most widely known form he cannot be said to have added the tragic conclusion, for although he knew the old play he treats the source material in an entirely different key from that of *King Leir;* Shakespeare's conclusion is a development of his own conception of the familiar and unhappy tale.

To emphasize his reading of the story Shakespeare incorporated in his plot an episode from Sidney's *Arcadia*. Here too a father, the King of Paphlagonia, deceived by the son of a concubine, gives orders for the destruction of his legitimate son and heir. Leonatus the son escapes and after various wanderings returns to succour his father, by now blinded and driven out by the same villain who had plotted the death of the rightful heir. The dutiful and compassionate son with the help of friends regains the kingdom:

> In which season the blind king (having in the chief cittie of his Realme, set the crowne upon his sonne *Leonatus* head) with many tears (both of joy and sorrow) setting forth to the whole people, his owne fault and his sonnes virtue, after he had kist him, and forst his sonne to accept honour of him (as of his newe-become subject) even in a moment died, as it should seeme: his hart broken with unkindness and affliction, stretched so far beyond his limits with this excesse of comfort, as it was able no longer to keep safe his roial spirits.

This is the note on which Shakespeare concludes the story of his own Lear and of Gloster; and he added the sub-plot to secure its proper amplification.

King Lear was performed at court on 26 December 1606; in the text are found the names of evil spirits taken from Samuel Harsnett's *Declaration of Egregious Popishe Impostures* published in 1603. These dates give the limits within which Shakespeare wrote the play as we now have it.

LEAR, *King of Britain*
KING OF FRANCE
DUKE OF BURGUNDY
DUKE OF CORNWALL
DUKE OF ALBANY
EARL OF KENT
EARL OF GLOUCESTER
EDGAR, *son to Gloucester*
EDMUND, *bastard son to Gloucester*
CURAN, *a courtier*
OLD MAN, *tenant to Gloucester*
DOCTOR
FOOL
OSWALD, *steward to Goneril*
A CAPTAIN, *employed by Edmund*
GENTLEMAN *attendant on Cordelia*
A HERALD
SERVANTS *to Cornwall*

GONERIL, REGAN, CORDELIA — *daughters to Lear*

Knights *attending on Lear*, Officers, Messengers, Soldiers, *and* Attendants

SCENE:

Britain

King Lear

ACT I. SCENE 1

KING LEAR'S *palace*

Enter KENT, GLOUCESTER, *and* EDMUND

KENT. I thought the King had more affected the Duke of Albany than Cornwall.

GLOUCESTER. It did always seem so to us; but now, in the division of the kingdom, it appears not which of the Dukes he values most; for equalities are so weigh'd that curiosity in neither can make choice of either's moiety.

KENT. Is not this your son, my lord?

GLOUCESTER. His breeding, sir, hath been at my charge. I have so often blush'd to acknowledge him that now I am braz'd to't.

KENT. I cannot conceive you.

GLOUCESTER. Sir, this young fellow's mother could; whereupon she grew round-womb'd, and had indeed, sir, a son for her cradle ere she had a husband for her bed. Do you smell a fault?

KENT. I cannot wish the fault undone, the issue of it being so proper.

GLOUCESTER. But I have a son, sir, by order of law, some year elder than this, who yet is no dearer in my account. Though this knave came something saucily to the world before he was sent for, yet was his mother fair; there was good sport at his making, and the whoreson must be acknowledged.–Do you know this noble gentleman, Edmund?

EDMUND. No, my lord.

GLOUCESTER. My Lord of Kent. Remember him hereafter as my honourable friend.

EDMUND. My services to your lordship.

KENT. I must love you, and sue to know you better.

EDMUND. Sir, I shall study deserving.

GLOUCESTER. He hath been out nine years, and away he shall again. [*Sennet*] The King is coming.

Enter one bearing a coronet; then LEAR, *then the* DUKES OF ALBANY *and* CORNWALL, *next* GONERIL, REGAN, CORDELIA, *with followers*

LEAR. Attend the Lords of France and Burgundy, Gloucester.

GLOUCESTER. I shall, my liege.

Exeunt GLOUCESTER *and* EDMUND

LEAR. Meantime we shall express our darker purpose.
Give me the map there. Know that we have divided
In three our kingdom; and 'tis our fast intent
To shake all cares and business from our age,
Conferring them on younger strengths, while we
Unburden'd crawl toward death. Our son of Cornwall,
And you, our no less loving son of Albany,
We have this hour a constant will to publish
Our daughters' several dowers, that future strife
May be prevented now. The Princes, France and Burgundy,
Great rivals in our youngest daughter's love,
Long in our court have made their amorous sojourn,
And here are to be answer'd. Tell me, my daughters—
Since now we will divest us both of rule,
Interest of territory, cares of state—
Which of you shall we say doth love us most?
That we our largest bounty may extend
Where nature doth with merit challenge. Goneril,
Our eldest-born, speak first.

GONERIL. Sir, I love you more than word can wield the matter;
Dearer than eyesight, space, and liberty;
Beyond what can be valued, rich or rare;
No less than life, with grace, health, beauty, honour;
As much as child e'er lov'd, or father found;
A love that makes breath poor and speech unable:
Beyond all manner of so much I love you.

CORDELIA. [*Aside*] What shall Cordelia speak? Love, and be silent.

LEAR. Of all these bounds, even from this line to this,
With shadowy forests and with champains rich'd,
With plenteous rivers and wide-skirted meads,
We make thee lady: to thine and Albany's issues
Be this perpetual.—What says our second daughter,
Our dearest Regan, wife of Cornwall? Speak.
REGAN. I am made of that self metal as my sister,
And prize me at her worth. In my true heart
I find she names my very deed of love;
Only she comes too short, that I profess
Myself an enemy to all other joys
Which the most precious square of sense possesses,
And find I am alone felicitate
In your dear Highness' love.
CORDELIA. [*Aside*] Then poor Cordelia!
And yet not so; since I am sure my love's
More ponderous than my tongue.
LEAR. To thee and thine hereditary ever
Remain this ample third of our fair kingdom;
No less in space, validity, and pleasure,
Than that conferr'd on Goneril.—Now, our joy,
Although our last and least; to whose young love
The vines of France and milk of Burgundy
Strive to be interess'd; what can you say to draw
A third more opulent than your sisters? Speak.
CORDELIA. Nothing, my lord.
LEAR. Nothing!
CORDELIA. Nothing.
LEAR. Nothing will come of nothing. Speak again.
CORDELIA. Unhappy that I am, I cannot heave
My heart into my mouth. I love your Majesty
According to my bond; no more nor less.
LEAR. How, how, Cordelia! Mend your speech a little,
Lest you may mar your fortunes.
CORDELIA. Good my lord,
You have begot me, bred me, lov'd me; I
Return those duties back as are right fit,
Obey you, love you, and most honour you.
Why have my sisters husbands, if they say
They love you all? Haply, when I shall wed,

That lord whose hand must take my plight shall carry
Half my love with him, half my care and duty.
Sure I shall never marry like my sisters,
To love my father all.

LEAR. But goes thy heart with this?

CORDELIA. Ay, my good lord.

LEAR. So young and so untender?

CORDELIA. So young, my lord, and true.

LEAR. Let it be so! Thy truth, then, be thy dower!
For, by the sacred radiance of the sun,
The mysteries of Hecat and the night;
By all the operation of the orbs
From whom we do exist and cease to be;
Here I disclaim all my paternal care,
Propinquity and property of blood,
And as a stranger to my heart and me
Hold thee from this for ever. The barbarous Scythian,
Or he that makes his generation messes
To gorge his appetite, shall to my bosom
Be as well neighbour'd, pitied, and reliev'd,
As thou my sometime daughter.

KENT. Good my liege—

LEAR. Peace, Kent!
Come not between the dragon and his wrath.
I lov'd her most, and thought to set my rest
On her kind nursery. [*To* CORDELIA] Hence, and avoid my sight!—
So be my grave my peace as here I give
Her father's heart from her! Call France— Who stirs?
Call Burgundy. Cornwall and Albany,
With my two daughters' dowers digest this third.
Let pride, which she calls plainness, marry her.
I do invest you jointly with my power,
Pre-eminence, and all the large effects
That troop with majesty. Ourself, by monthly course,
With reservation of an hundred knights,
By you to be sustain'd, shall our abode
Make with you by due turn. Only we shall retain
The name, and all th' addition to a king:
The sway, revenue, execution of the rest,

Beloved sons, be yours; which to confirm,
This coronet part between you.

KENT. Royal Lear,
Whom I have ever honour'd as my king,
Lov'd as my father, as my master follow'd,
As my great patron thought on in my prayers—

LEAR. The bow is bent and drawn; make from the shaft.

KENT. Let it fall rather, though the fork invade
The region of my heart. Be Kent unmannerly
When Lear is mad. What wouldst thou do, old man?
Think'st thou that duty shall have dread to speak
When power to flattery bows? To plainness honour's bound
When majesty falls to folly. Reserve thy state;
And in thy best consideration check
This hideous rashness. Answer my life my judgment:
Thy youngest daughter does not love thee least;
Nor are those empty-hearted whose low sounds
Reverb no hollowness.

LEAR. Kent, on thy life, no more!

KENT. My life I never held but as a pawn
To wage against thine enemies; nor fear to lose it,
Thy safety being motive.

LEAR. Out of my sight!

KENT. See better, Lear; and let me still remain
The true blank of thine eye.

LEAR. Now by Apollo—

KENT. Now, by Apollo, King,
Thou swear'st thy gods in vain.

LEAR. O, vassal! miscreant! [*Laying his hand on his sword*]

ALBANY and CORNWALL. Dear sir, forbear.

KENT. Do;
Kill thy physician, and the fee bestow
Upon the foul disease. Revoke thy gift,
Or, whilst I can vent clamour from my throat,
I'll tell thee thou dost evil.

LEAR. Hear me, recreant;
On thine allegiance, hear me.
That thou hast sought to make us break our vows—
Which we durst never yet—and with strain'd pride

To come betwixt our sentence and our power—
Which nor our nature nor our place can bear;
Our potency made good, take thy reward.
Five days we do allot thee for provision
To shield thee from disasters of the world,
And on the sixth to turn thy hated back
Upon our kingdom; if, on the tenth day following,
Thy banish'd trunk be found in our dominions,
The moment is thy death. Away! by Jupiter,
This shall not be revok'd.

KENT. Fare thee well, King. Sith thus thou wilt appear,
Freedom lives hence, and banishment is here.
[*To* CORDELIA] The gods to their dear shelter take thee, maid,
That justly think'st, and hast most rightly said!
[*To* REGAN *and* GONERIL] And your large speeches may your deeds approve,
That good effects may spring from words of love!
Thus Kent, O princes, bids you all adieu;
He'll shape his old course in a country new. *Exit*

Flourish. Re-enter GLOUCESTER, *with* FRANCE, BURGUNDY, *and attendants*

GLOUCESTER. Here's France and Burgundy, my noble lord.

LEAR. My Lord of Burgundy,
We first address toward you, who with this king
Hath rivall'd for our daughter. What in the least
Will you require in present dower with her,
Or cease your quest of love?

BURGUNDY. Most royal Majesty,
I crave no more than hath your Highness offer'd,
Nor will you tender less.

LEAR. Right noble Burgundy,
When she was dear to us, we did hold her so;
But now her price is fallen. Sir, there she stands:
If aught within that little seeming substance,
Or all of it, with our displeasure piec'd,
And nothing more, may fitly like your Grace,
She's there, and she is yours.

BURGUNDY. I know no answer.

LEAR. Will you, with those infirmities she owes,
Unfriended, new-adopted to our hate,
Dower'd with our curse, and stranger'd with our oath,
Take her or leave her?
BURGUNDY. Pardon me, royal sir;
Election makes not up in such conditions.
LEAR. Then leave her, sir; for, by the pow'r that made me,
I tell you all her wealth. [*To* FRANCE] For you, great King,
I would not from your love make such a stray
To match you where I hate; therefore beseech you
T' avert your liking a more worthier way,
Than on a wretch whom nature is asham'd
Almost t' acknowledge hers.
FRANCE. This is most strange,
That she, whom even but now was your best object,
The argument of your praise, balm of your age,
The best, the dearest, should in this trice of time
Commit a thing so monstrous to dismantle
So many folds of favour. Sure her offence
Must be of such unnatural degree
That monsters it, or your fore-vouch'd affection
Fall into taint—which to believe of her
Must be a faith that reason without miracle
Should never plant in me.
CORDELIA. I yet beseech your Majesty—
If for I want that glib and oily art
To speak and purpose not, since what I well intend
I'll do't before I speak—that you make known
It is no vicious blot, murder, or foulness,
No unchaste action or dishonoured step,
That hath depriv'd me of your grace and favour;
But even for want of that for which I am richer—
A still-soliciting eye, and such a tongue
That I am glad I have not, though not to have it
Hath lost me in your liking.
LEAR. Better thou
Hadst not been born than not t' have pleas'd me better.
FRANCE. Is it but this? A tardiness in nature,
Which often leaves the history unspoke
That it intends to do! My Lord of Burgundy,

What say you to the lady? Love's not love
When it is mingled with regards that stands
Aloof from th' entire point. Will you have her?
She is herself a dowry.

BURGUNDY. Royal king,
Give but that portion which yourself propos'd,
And here I take Cordelia by the hand,
Duchess of Burgundy.

LEAR. Nothing! I have sworn; I am firm.

BURGUNDY. I am sorry, then, you have so lost a father
That you must lose a husband.

CORDELIA. Peace be with Burgundy!
Since that respects of fortune are his love
I shall not be his wife.

FRANCE. Fairest Cordelia, that art most rich, being poor;
Most choice, forsaken; and most lov'd, despis'd!
Thee and thy virtues here I seize upon,
Be it lawful I take up what's cast away.
Gods, gods! 'tis strange that from their cold'st neglect
My love should kindle to inflam'd respect.
Thy dow'rless daughter, King, thrown to my chance,
Is queen of us, of ours, and our fair France.
Not all the dukes of wat'rish Burgundy
Can buy this unpriz'd precious maid of me.
Bid them farewell, Cordelia, though unkind;
Thou losest here, a better where to find.

LEAR. Thou hast her, France; let her be thine; for we
Have no such daughter, nor shall ever see
That face of hers again. [*To* CORDELIA] Therefore be gone
Without our grace, our love, our benison.
Come, noble Burgundy.

Flourish. Exeunt LEAR, BURGUNDY, CORNWALL, ALBANY, GLOUCESTER, *and attendants*

FRANCE. Bid farewell to your sisters.

CORDELIA. The jewels of our father, with wash'd eyes
Cordelia leaves you. I know you what you are;
And, like a sister, am most loath to call
Your faults as they are named. Love well our father.
To your professed bosoms I commit him;

But yet, alas, stood I within his grace,
I would prefer him to a better place.
So, farewell to you both.

REGAN. Prescribe not us our duty.

GONERIL. Let your study
Be to content your lord, who hath receiv'd you
At fortune's alms. You have obedience scanted,
And well are worth the want that you have wanted.

CORDELIA. Time shall unfold what plighted cunning hides,
Who covers faults, at last with shame derides.
Well may you prosper!

FRANCE. Come, my fair Cordelia.

Exeunt FRANCE *and* CORDELIA

GONERIL. Sister, it is not little I have to say of what most nearly appertains to us both. I think our father will hence to-night.

REGAN. That's most certain, and with you; next month with us.

GONERIL. You see how full of changes his age is; the observation we have made of it hath not been little. He always lov'd our sister most; and with what poor judgment he hath now cast her off appears too grossly.

REGAN. 'Tis the infirmity of his age; yet he hath ever but slenderly known himself.

GONERIL. The best and soundest of his time hath been but rash; then must we look from his age to receive not alone the imperfections of long-engraffed condition, but therewithal the unruly waywardness that infirm and choleric years bring with them.

REGAN. Such unconstant starts are we like to have from him as this of Kent's banishment.

GONERIL. There is further compliment of leave-taking between France and him. Pray you, let us hit together; if our father carry authority with such disposition as he bears, this last surrender of his will but offend us.

REGAN. We shall further think of it.

GONERIL. We must do something, and i' th' heat. *Exeunt*

SCENE 2

GLOUCESTER'S *castle*

Enter EDMUND *with a letter*

EDMUND. Thou, Nature, art my goddess; to thy law
My services are bound. Wherefore should I
Stand in the plague of custom, and permit
The curiosity of nations to deprive me,
For that I am some twelve or fourteen moonshines
Lag of a brother? Why bastard? Wherefore base?
When my dimensions are as well compact,
My mind as generous, and my shape as true,
As honest madam's issue? Why brand they us
With base? with baseness? bastardy? base, base?
Who, in the lusty stealth of nature, take
More composition and fierce quality
Than doth, within a dull, stale, tired bed,
Go to th' creating a whole tribe of fops
Got 'tween asleep and wake? Well then,
Legitimate Edgar, I must have your land.
Our father's love is to the bastard Edmund
As to th' legitimate. Fine word 'legitimate'!
Well, my legitimate, if this letter speed,
And my invention thrive, Edmund the base
Shall top th' legitimate. I grow; I prosper.
Now, gods, stand up for bastards.

Enter GLOUCESTER

GLOUCESTER. Kent banish'd thus! and France in choler parted!
And the King gone to-night! Prescrib'd his pow'r!
Confin'd to exhibition! All this done
Upon the gad! Edmund, how now! What news?
EDMUND. So please your lordship, none.
[*Putting up the letter*]
GLOUCESTER. Why so earnestly seek you to put up that letter?
EDMUND. I know no news, my lord.
GLOUCESTER. What paper were you reading?

EDMUND. Nothing, my lord.

GLOUCESTER. No? What needed then that terrible dispatch of it into your pocket? The quality of nothing hath not such need to hide itself. Let's see. Come, if it be nothing, I shall not need spectacles.

EDMUND. I beseech you, sir, pardon me. It is a letter from my brother that I have not all o'er-read; and for so much as I have perus'd, I find it not fit for your o'er-looking.

GLOUCESTER. Give me the letter, sir.

EDMUND. I shall offend either to detain or give it. The contents, as in part I understand them, are to blame.

GLOUCESTER. Let's see, let's see.

EDMUND. I hope, for my brother's justification, he wrote this but as an essay or taste of my virtue.

GLOUCESTER. [*Reads*] 'This policy and reverence of age makes the world bitter to the best of our times; keeps our fortunes from us till our oldness cannot relish them. I begin to find an idle and fond bondage in the oppression of aged tyranny, who sways, not as it hath power, but as it is suffer'd. Come to me, that of this I may speak more. If our father would sleep till I wak'd him, you should enjoy half his revenue for ever, and live the beloved of your brother. EDGAR.'

Hum—Conspiracy! 'Sleep till I wak'd him, you should enjoy half his revenue.' My son Edgar! Had he a hand to write this? a heart and a brain to breed it in? When came this to you? Who brought it?

EDMUND. It was not brought me, my lord; there's the cunning of it. I found it thrown in at the casement of my closet.

GLOUCESTER. You know the character to be your brother's?

EDMUND. If the matter were good, my lord, I durst swear it were his; but in respect of that, I would fain think it were not.

GLOUCESTER. It is his.

EDMUND. It is his hand, my lord; but I hope his heart is not in the contents.

GLOUCESTER. Has he never before sounded you in this business?

EDMUND. Never, my lord; but I have heard him oft maintain it to be fit that, sons at perfect age and fathers declin'd, the father should be as ward to the son, and the son manage his revenue.

GLOUCESTER. O villain, villain! His very opinion in the letter! Abhorred villain! Unnatural, detested, brutish villain! Worse than brutish! Go, sirrah, seek him; I'll apprehend him. Abominable villain! Where is he?

EDMUND. I do not well know, my lord. If it shall please you to suspend your indignation against my brother till you can derive from him better testimony of his intent, you should run a certain course; where, if you violently proceed against him, mistaking his purpose, it would make a great gap in your own honour, and shake in pieces the heart of his obedience. I dare pawn down my life for him that he hath writ this to feel my affection to your honour, and to no other pretence of danger.

GLOUCESTER. Think you so?

EDMUND. If your honour judge it meet, I will place you where you shall hear us confer of this, and by an auricular assurance have your satisfaction; and that without any further delay than this very evening.

GLOUCESTER. He cannot be such a monster.

EDMUND. Nor is not, sure.

GLOUCESTER. To his father, that so tenderly and entirely loves him. Heaven and earth! Edmund, seek him out; wind me into him, I pray you. Frame the business after your own wisdom. I would unstate myself to be in a due resolution.

EDMUND. I will seek him, sir, presently; convey the business as I shall find means, and acquaint you withal.

GLOUCESTER. These late eclipses in the sun and moon portend no good to us. Though the wisdom of nature can reason it thus and thus, yet nature finds itself scourg'd by the sequent effects: love cools, friendship falls off, brothers divide; in cities, mutinies; in countries, discord; in palaces, treason; and the bond crack'd 'twixt son and father. This villain of mine comes under the prediction: there's son against father. The King falls from bias of nature: there's father against child. We have seen the best of our time:

machinations, hollowness, treachery, and all ruinous disorders, follow us disquietly to our graves. Find out this villain, Edmund; it shall lose thee nothing; do it carefully. And the noble and true-hearted Kent banish'd! His offence, honesty! 'Tis strange. *Exit*

EDMUND. This is the excellent foppery of the world, that, when we are sick in fortune, often the surfeits of our own behaviour, we make guilty of our disasters the sun, the moon, and stars; as if we were villains on necessity; fools by heavenly compulsion; knaves, thieves, and treachers, by spherical predominance; drunkards, liars, and adulterers, by an enforc'd obedience of planetary influence; and all that we are evil in, by a divine thrusting on—an admirable evasion of whoremaster man, to lay his goatish disposition on the charge of a star! My father compounded with my mother under the Dragon's tail, and my nativity was under Ursa Major, so that it follows I am rough and lecherous. Fut, I should have been that I am, had the maidenliest star in the firmament twinkled on my bastardizing. Edgar!

Enter EDGAR

Pat! He comes like the catastrophe of the old comedy. My cue is villainous melancholy, with a sigh like Tom o' Bedlam.—O, these eclipses do portend these divisions! fa, sol, la, mi.

EDGAR. How now, brother Edmund! What serious contemplation are you in?

EDMUND. I am thinking, brother, of a prediction I read this other day what should follow these eclipses.

EDGAR. Do you busy yourself with that?

EDMUND. I promise you, the effects he writes of succeed unhappily; as of unnaturalness between the child and the parent; death, dearth, dissolutions of ancient amities; divisions in state, menaces and maledictions against king and nobles; needless diffidences, banishment of friends, dissipation of cohorts, nuptial breaches, and I know not what.

EDGAR. How long have you been a sectary astronomical?

EDMUND. Come, come! When saw you my father last?

EDGAR. The night gone by.

EDMUND. Spake you with him?

EDGAR. Ay, two hours together.

EDMUND. Parted you in good terms? Found you no displeasure in him by word nor countenance?

EDGAR. None at all.

EDMUND. Bethink yourself wherein you may have offended him; and at my entreaty forbear his presence, until some little time hath qualified the heat of his displeasure, which at this instant so rageth in him that with the mischief of your person it would scarcely allay.

EDGAR. Some villain hath done me wrong.

EDMUND. That's my fear. I pray you have a continent forbearance till the speed of his rage goes slower; and, as I say, retire with me to my lodging, from whence I will fitly bring you to hear my lord speak. Pray ye go; there's my key. If you do stir abroad, go arm'd.

EDGAR. Arm'd, brother!

EDMUND. Brother, I advise you to the best. I am no honest man if there be any good meaning toward you. I have told you what I have seen and heard—but faintly; nothing like the image and horror of it. Pray you, away.

EDGAR. Shall I hear from you anon?

EDMUND. I do serve you in this business. *Exit* EDGAR
A credulous father! and a brother noble,
Whose nature is so far from doing harms
That he suspects none; on whose foolish honesty
My practices ride easy! I see the business.
Let me, if not by birth, have lands by wit:
All with me's meet that I can fashion fit. *Exit*

SCENE 3

The DUKE OF ALBANY'S *palace*

Enter GONERIL *and* OSWALD, *her steward*

GONERIL. Did my father strike my gentleman for chiding of his fool?

OSWALD. Ay, madam.

GONERIL. By day and night, he wrongs me; every hour

He flashes into one gross crime or other
That sets us all at odds. I'll not endure it.
His knights grow riotous, and himself upbraids us
On every trifle. When he returns from hunting,
I will not speak with him; say I am sick.
If you come slack of former services,
You shall do well; the fault of it I'll answer.
[*Horns within*]

OSWALD. He's coming, madam; I hear him.

GONERIL. Put on what weary negligence you please,
You and your fellows; I'd have it come to question.
If he distaste it, let him to my sister,
Whose mind and mine, I know, in that are one,
Not to be overrul'd. Idle old man,
That still would manage those authorities
That he hath given away! Now, by my life,
Old fools are babes again, and must be us'd
With checks as flatteries, when they are seen abus'd.
Remember what I have said.

OSWALD. Well, madam.

GONERIL. And let his knights have colder looks among you;
What grows of it, no matter. Advise your fellows so.
I would breed from hence occasions, and I shall,
That I may speak. I'll write straight to my sister
To hold my very course. Prepare for dinner. *Exeunt*

SCENE 4

A hall in ALBANY'S *palace*

Enter KENT, *disguised*

KENT. If but as well I other accents borrow
That can my speech defuse, my good intent
May carry through itself to that full issue
For which I raz'd my likeness. Now, banish'd Kent,
If thou canst serve where thou dost stand condemn'd,
So may it come thy master whom thou lov'st
Shall find thee full of labours.

Horns within. Enter LEAR, KNIGHTS, *and attendants*

LEAR. Let me not stay a jot for dinner; go get it ready. [*Exit an attendant*] How now! What art thou?

KENT. A man, sir.

LEAR. What dost thou profess? What wouldst thou with us?

KENT. I do profess to be no less than I seem, to serve him truly that will put me in trust, to love him that is honest, to converse with him that is wise and says little, to fear judgment, to fight when I cannot choose, and to eat no fish.

LEAR. What are thou?

KENT. A very honest-hearted fellow, and as poor as the King.

LEAR. If thou be'st as poor for a subject as he's for a king, thou art poor enough. What wouldst thou?

KENT. Service.

LEAR. Who wouldst thou serve?

KENT. You.

LEAR. Dost thou know me, fellow?

KENT. No, sir; but you have that in your countenance which I would fain call master.

LEAR. What's that?

KENT. Authority.

LEAR. What services canst thou do?

KENT. I can keep honest counsel, ride, run, mar a curious tale in telling it, and deliver a plain message bluntly. That which ordinary men are fit for, I am qualified in; and the best of me is diligence.

LEAR. How old art thou?

KENT. Not so young, sir, to love a woman for singing, nor so old to dote on her for anything: I have years on my back forty-eight.

LEAR. Follow me; thou shalt serve me. If I like thee no worse after dinner, I will not part from thee yet. Dinner, ho, dinner! Where's my knave? my fool?—Go you and call my fool hither. *Exit an attendant*

Enter OSWALD

You, you, sirrah, where's my daughter?

OSWALD. So please you— *Exit*

LEAR. What says the fellow there? Call the clotpoll back.

[*Exit a* KNIGHT] Where's my fool, ho? I think the world's asleep.

Re-enter KNIGHT

How now! Where's that mongrel?

KNIGHT. He says, my lord, your daughter is not well.

LEAR. Why came not the slave back to me when I call'd him?

KNIGHT. Sir, he answered me in the roundest manner he would not.

LEAR. He would not!

KNIGHT. My lord, I know not what the matter is; but, to my judgment, your Highness is not entertain'd with that ceremonious affection as you were wont; there's a great abatement of kindness appears as well in the general dependants as in the Duke himself also and your daughter.

LEAR. Ha! say'st thou so?

KNIGHT. I beseech you pardon me, my lord, if I be mistaken; for my duty cannot be silent when I think your Highness wrong'd.

LEAR. Thou but rememb'rest me of mine own conception. I have perceived a most faint neglect of late, which I have rather blamed as mine own jealous curiosity than as a very pretence and purpose of unkindness. I will look further into't. But where's my fool? I have not seen him this two days.

KNIGHT. Since my young lady's going into France, sir, the fool hath much pined away.

LEAR. No more of that; I have noted it well. Go you and tell my daughter I would speak with her. [*Exit an attendant.*] Go you, call hither my fool.

Exit another attendant

Re-enter OSWALD

O, you sir, you! Come you hither, sir. Who am I, sir?

OSWALD. My lady's father.

LEAR. 'My lady's father'! my lord's knave! you whoreson dog! you slave! you cur!

OSWALD. I am none of these, my lord; I beseech your pardon.

LEAR. Do you bandy looks with me, you rascal!

[*Striking him*]

OSWALD. I'll not be strucken, my lord.

KENT. Nor tripp'd neither, you base football player.

[*Tripping up his heels*]

LEAR. I thank thee, fellow; thou serv'st me, and I'll love thee.

KENT. Come, sir, arise, away! I'll teach you differences. Away, away! If you will measure your lubber's length again, tarry; but away! Go to! Have you wisdom? So.

[*Pushes* OSWALD *out*]

LEAR. Now, my friendly knave, I thank thee; there's earnest of thy service. [*Giving* KENT *money*]

Enter FOOL

FOOL. Let me hire him too; here's my coxcomb.

[*Offering* KENT *his cap*]

LEAR. How now, my pretty knave! How dost thou?

FOOL. Sirrah, you were best take my coxcomb.

KENT. Why, fool?

FOOL. Why? For taking one's part that's out of favour. Nay, an thou canst not smile as the wind sits, thou'lt catch cold shortly. There, take my coxcomb. Why, this fellow has banish'd two on's daughters, and did the third a blessing against his will; if thou follow him, thou must needs wear my coxcomb.—How now, nuncle! Would I had two coxcombs and two daughters!

LEAR. Why, my boy?

FOOL. If I gave them all my living, I'd keep my coxcombs myself. There's mine; beg another of thy daughters.

LEAR. Take heed, sirrah—the whip.

FOOL. Truth's a dog must to kennel; he must be whipp'd out, when Lady the brach may stand by th' fire and stink.

LEAR. A pestilent gall to me!

FOOL. Sirrah, I'll teach thee a speech.

LEAR. Do.

FOOL. Mark it, nuncle:

Have more than thou showest,
Speak less than thou knowest,
Lend less than thou owest,

Ride more than thou goest,
Learn more than thou trowest,
Set less than thou throwest;
Leave thy drink and thy whore,
And keep in-a-door,
And thou shalt have more
Than two tens to a score.

KENT. This is nothing, fool.

FOOL. Then 'tis like the breath of an unfee'd lawyer—you gave me nothing for't. Can you make no use of nothing, nuncle?

LEAR. Why, no, boy; nothing can be made out of nothing.

FOOL. [*To* KENT] Prithee tell him, so much the rent of his land comes to; he will not believe a fool.

LEAR. A bitter fool!

FOOL. Dost thou know the difference, my boy, between a bitter fool and a sweet one?

LEAR. No, lad; teach me.

FOOL. That lord that counsell'd thee
To give away thy land,
Come place him here by me—
Do thou for him stand.
The sweet and bitter fool
Will presently appear;
The one in motley here,
The other found out there.

LEAR. Dost thou call me fool, boy?

FOOL. All thy other titles thou hast given away; that thou wast born with.

KENT. This is not altogether fool, my lord.

FOOL. No, faith, lords and great men will not let me; if I had a monopoly out, they would have part on't. And ladies too—they will not let me have all the fool to myself; they'll be snatching. Nuncle, give me an egg, and I'll give thee two crowns.

LEAR. What two crowns shall they be?

FOOL. Why, after I have cut the egg i' th' middle and eat up the meat, the two crowns of the egg. When thou clovest thy crown i' th' middle, and gav'st away both parts, thou bor'st thine ass on thy back o'er the dirt. Thou hadst little wit in thy bald crown when thou gav'st thy golden one away. If I speak like myself in this, let him be whipp'd that first finds it so. [*Sings*]

Fools had ne'er less grace in a year;
For wise men are grown foppish,
And know not how their wits to wear,
Their manners are so apish.

LEAR. When were you wont to be so full of songs, sirrah?

FOOL. I have us'd it, nuncle, e'er since thou mad'st thy daughters thy mothers; for when thou gav'st them the rod, and put'st down thine own breeches, [*Sings*]

Then they for sudden joy did weep,
And I for sorrow sung,
That such a king should play bo-peep
And go the fools among.

Prithee, nuncle, keep a schoolmaster that can teach thy fool to lie. I would fain learn to lie.

LEAR. An you lie, sirrah, we'll have you whipp'd.

FOOL. I marvel what kin thou and thy daughters are. They'll have me whipp'd for speaking true: thou'lt have me whipp'd for lying; and sometimes I am whipp'd for holding my peace. I had rather be any kind o' thing than a fool; and yet I would not be thee, nuncle; thou hast pared thy wit o' both sides, and left nothing i' th' middle. Here comes one o' th' parings.

Enter GONERIL

LEAR. How now, daughter! What makes that frontlet on? You are too much of late i' th' frown.

FOOL. Thou wast a pretty fellow when thou hadst no need to care for her frowning; now thou art an O without a figure. I am better than thou art now: I am a fool, thou art nothing. [*To* GONERIL] Yes, forsooth, I will hold my tongue; so your face bids me, though you say nothing. Mum, mum!

He that keeps nor crust nor crumb,
Weary of all, shall want some.

[*Pointing to* LEAR] That's a sheal'd peascod.

GONERIL. Not only, sir, this your all-licens'd fool,
But other of your insolent retinue
Do hourly carp and quarrel, breaking forth
In rank and not-to-be-endured riots. Sir,
I had thought, by making this well known unto you,
To have found a safe redress; but now grow fearful,
By what yourself too late have spoke and done,
That you protect this course, and put it on
By your allowance; which if you should, the fault
Would not scape censure, nor the redresses sleep,
Which, in the tender of a wholesome weal,
Might in their working do you that offence
Which else were shame, that then necessity
Will call discreet proceeding.

FOOL. For, you know, nuncle,
The hedge-sparrow fed the cuckoo so long
That it had it head bit off by it young.
So, out went the candle, and we were left darkling.

LEAR. Are you our daughter?

GONERIL. I would you would make use of your good wisdom,
Whereof I know you are fraught, and put away
These dispositions which of late transport you
From what you rightly are.

FOOL. May not an ass know when the cart draws the horse?
Whoop, Jug! I love thee.

LEAR. Does any here know me? This is not Lear.
Does Lear walk thus? speak thus? Where are his eyes?
Either his notion weakens, or his discernings
Are lethargied.—Ha! waking? 'Tis not so.—
Who is it that can tell me who I am?

FOOL. Lear's shadow.

LEAR. I would learn that; for, by the marks of sovereignty, knowledge, and reason, I should be false persuaded I had daughters.

FOOL. Which they will make an obedient father.

LEAR. Your name, fair gentlewoman?

GONERIL. This admiration, sir, is much o' th' savour
Of other your new pranks. I do beseech you
To understand my purposes aright.

As you are old and reverend, should be wise.
Here do you keep a hundred knights and squires;
Men so disorder'd, so debosh'd and bold,
That this our court, infected with their manners,
Shows like a riotous inn. Epicurism and lust
Makes it more like a tavern or a brothel
Than a grac'd palace. The shame itself doth speak
For instant remedy. Be then desir'd
By her that else will take the thing she begs
A little to disquantity your train;
And the remainders that shall still depend
To be such men as may besort your age,
Which know themselves and you.

LEAR. Darkness and devils!
Saddle my horses; call my train together.
Degenerate bastard! I'll not trouble thee;
Yet have I left a daughter.

GONERIL. You strike my people; and your disorder'd rabble
Make servants of their betters.

Enter ALBANY

LEAR. Woe that too late repents!—O, sir, are you come?
Is it your will? Speak, sir.—Prepare my horses.
Ingratitude, thou marble-hearted fiend,
More hideous when thou show'st thee in a child
Than the sea-monster!

ALBANY. Pray, sir, be patient.

LEAR. [*To* GONERIL]Detested kite! thou liest:
My train are men of choice and rarest parts,
That all particulars of duty know;
And in the most exact regard support
The worships of their name.—O most small fault,
How ugly didst thou in Cordelia show!
Which, like an engine, wrench'd my frame of nature
From the fix'd place; drew from my heart all love
And added to the gall. O Lear, Lear, Lear!
Beat at this gate that let thy folly in [*Striking his head*]
And thy dear judgment out! Go, go, my people.
Exeunt KENT *and* KNIGHTS

ALBANY. My lord, I am guiltless, as I am ignorant

Of what hath moved you.
LEAR. It may be so, my lord.
Hear, Nature, hear; dear goddess, hear.
Suspend thy purpose, if thou didst intend
To make this creature fruitful.
Into her womb convey sterility;
Dry up in her the organs of increase;
And from her derogate body never spring
A babe to honour her! If she must teem,
Create her child of spleen, that it may live
And be a thwart disnatur'd torment to her.
Let it stamp wrinkles in her brow of youth,
With cadent tears fret channels in her cheeks,
Turn all her mother's pains and benefits
To laughter and contempt, that she may feel
How sharper than a serpent's tooth it is
To have a thankless child. Away, away! *Exit*
ALBANY. Now, gods that we adore, whereof comes this?
GONERIL. Never afflict yourself to know more of it;
But let his disposition have that scope
As dotage gives it.

Re-enter LEAR

LEAR. What, fifty of my followers at a clap!
Within a fortnight!
ALBANY. What's the matter, sir?
LEAR. I'll tell thee. [*To* GONERIL] Life and death! I am asham'd
That thou hast power to shake my manhood thus;
That these hot tears, which break from me perforce,
Should make thee worth them. Blasts and fogs upon thee!
Th' untented woundings of a father's curse
Pierce every sense about thee!—Old fond eyes,
Beweep this cause again, I'll pluck ye out,
And cast you, with the waters that you loose,
To temper clay. Ha! Is't come to this?
Let it be so. I have another daughter,
Who, I am sure, is kind and comfortable.
When she shall hear this of thee, with her nails
She'll flay thy wolfish visage. Thou shalt find

That I'll resume the shape which thou dost think
I have cast off for ever. *Exit* LEAR

GONERIL. Do you mark that?

ALBANY. I cannot be so partial, Goneril,
To the great love I bear you—

GONERIL. Pray you, content.—What, Oswald, ho!
[*To the* FOOL] You, sir, more knave than fool, after your master.

FOOL. Nuncle Lear, nuncle Lear, tarry—take the fool with thee.

A fox, when one has caught her,
And such a daughter,
Should sure to the slaughter,
If my cap would buy a halter.
So the fool follows after. *Exit*

GONERIL. This man hath had good counsel. A hundred knights!
'Tis politic and safe to let him keep
At point a hundred knights—yes, that on every dream,
Each buzz, each fancy, each complaint, dislike,
He may enguard his dotage with their pow'rs,
And hold our lives in mercy. Oswald, I say!

ALBANY. Well, you may fear too far.

GONERIL. Safer than trust too far.
Let me still take away the harms I fear,
Not fear still to be taken. I know his heart.
What he hath utter'd I have writ my sister.
If she sustain him and his hundred knights,
When I have show'd th' unfitness—

Re-enter OSWALD

How now, Oswald!
What, have you writ that letter to my sister?

OSWALD. Ay, madam.

GONERIL. Take you some company, and away to horse;
Inform her full of my particular fear,
And thereto add such reasons of your own
As may compact it more. Get you gone;
And hasten your return. [*Exit* OSWALD] No, no, my lord,
This milky gentleness and course of yours,

Though I condemn not, yet, under pardon,
You are much more ataxt for want of wisdom
Than prais'd for harmful mildness.

ALBANY. How far your eyes may pierce I cannot tell.
Striving to better, oft we mar what's well.

GONERIL. Nay, then–

ALBANY. Well, well; th' event. *Exeunt*

SCENE 5

Court before the DUKE OF ALBANY'S *palace*

Enter LEAR, KENT, *and* FOOL

LEAR. Go you before to Gloucester with these letters. Acquaint my daughter no further with anything you know than comes from her demand out of the letter. If your diligence be not speedy, I shall be there afore you.

KENT. I will not sleep, my lord, till I have delivered your letter. *Exit*

FOOL. If a man's brains were in's heels, were't not in danger of kibes?

LEAR. Ay, boy.

FOOL. Then, I prithee, be merry; thy wit shall not go slip-shod.

LEAR. Ha, ha, ha!

FOOL. Shalt see thy other daughter will use thee kindly; for though she's as like this as a crab's like an apple, yet I can tell what I can tell.

LEAR. What canst tell, boy?

FOOL. She will taste as like this as a crab does to a crab. Thou canst tell why one's nose stands i' th' middle on's face?

LEAR. No.

FOOL. Why to keep one's eyes of either side's nose, that what a man cannot smell out, he may spy into.

LEAR. I did her wrong.

FOOL. Canst tell how an oyster makes his shell?

LEAR. No.

FOOL. Nor I neither; but I can tell why a snail has a house.

LEAR. Why?

FOOL. Why, to put's head in; not to give it away to his daughters, and leave his horns without a case.

LEAR. I will forget my nature. So kind a father!—Be my horses ready?

FOOL. Thy asses are gone about 'em. The reason why the seven stars are no moe than seven is a pretty reason.

LEAR. Because they are not eight?

FOOL. Yes, indeed. Thou wouldst make a good fool.

LEAR. To take't again perforce! Monster ingratitude!

FOOL. If thou wert my fool, nuncle, I'd have thee beaten for being old before thy time.

LEAR. How's that?

FOOL. Thou shouldst not have been old till thou hadst been wise.

LEAR. O, let me not be mad, not mad, sweet heaven!
Keep me in temper; I would not be mad!

Enter GENTLEMAN

How now! are the horses ready?

GENTLEMAN. Ready, my lord.

LEAR. Come, boy.

FOOL. She that's a maid now, and laughs at my departure,
Shall not be a maid long, unless things be cut shorter.

Exeunt

ACT II. SCENE 1

A court-yard in the EARL OF GLOUCESTER'S *castle*

Enter EDMUND *and* CURAN, *meeting*

EDMUND. Save thee, Curan.

CURAN. And you, sir. I have been with your father, and given him notice that the Duke of Cornwall and Regan his Duchess will be here with him this night.

EDMUND. How comes that?

CURAN. Nay, I know not. You have heard of the news abroad; I mean the whisper'd one, for they are yet but ear-bussing arguments?

EDMUND. Not I. Pray you, what are they?

CURAN. Have you heard of no likely wars toward 'twixt the Dukes of Cornwall and Albany?

EDMUND. Not a word.

CURAN. You may do, then, in time. Fare you well, sir. *Exit*

EDMUND. The Duke be here to-night? The better! best!
This weaves itself perforce into my business.
My father hath set guard to take my brother;
And I have one thing, of a queasy question,
Which I must act. Briefness and fortune work!
Brother, a word! Descend. Brother, I say!

Enter EDGAR

My father watches. O sir, fly this place;
Intelligence is given where you are hid;
You have now the good advantage of the night.
Have you not spoken 'gainst the Duke of Cornwall?
He's coming hither, now, i' th' night, i' th' haste,
And Regan with him. Have you nothing said
Upon his party 'gainst the Duke of Albany?
Advise yourself.

EDGAR. I am sure on't, not a word.

EDMUND. I hear my father coming. Pardon me,
In cunning I must draw my sword upon you.
Draw; seem to defend yourself; now quit you well.—
Yield; come before my father. Light, ho, here!—
Fly, brother.—Torches, torches!—So, farewell. *Exit* EDGAR
Some blood drawn on me would beget opinion
[*Wounds his arm*]
Of my more fierce endeavour. I have seen drunkards
Do more than this in sport.—Father, father!
Stop, stop! No help?

Enter GLOUCESTER, *and servants with torches*

GLOUCESTER. Now, Edmund, where's the villain?

EDMUND. Here stood he in the dark, his sharp sword out,
Mumbling of wicked charms, conjuring the moon
To stand's auspicious mistress.

GLOUCESTER. But where is he?

EDMUND. Look, sir, I bleed.

GLOUCESTER. Where is the villain, Edmund?
EDMUND. Fled this way, sir. When by no means he could—
GLOUCESTER. Pursue him, ho! Go after. [*Exeunt servants*]—
By no means what?
EDMUND. Persuade me to the murder of your lordship;
But that I told him the revenging gods
'Gainst parricides did all their thunders bend;
Spoke with how manifold and strong a bond
The child was bound to th' father. Sir, in fine,
Seeing how loathly opposite I stood
To his unnatural purpose, in fell motion,
With his prepared sword, he charges home
My unprovided body, latch'd mine arm;
But when he saw my best alarum'd spirits,
Bold in the quarrel's right, rous'd to th' encounter,
Or whether gasted by the noise I made,
Full suddenly he fled.
GLOUCESTER. Let him fly far.
Not in this land shall he remain uncaught;
And found—dispatch. The noble Duke my master,
My worthy arch and patron, comes to-night;
By his authority I will proclaim it,
That he which finds him shall deserve our thanks,
Bringing the murderous coward to the stake;
He that conceals him, death.
EDMUND. When I dissuaded him from his intent,
And found him pight to do it, with curst speech
I threaten'd to discover him; he replied,
'Thou unpossessing bastard! dost thou think,
If I would stand against thee, would the reposure
Of any trust, virtue, or worth, in thee
Make thy words faith'd? No. What I should deny—
As this I would; ay, though thou didst produce
My very character—I'd turn it all
To thy suggestion, plot, and damned practice;
And thou must make a dullard of the world,
If they not thought the profits of my death
Were very pregnant and potential spurs
To make thee seek it.'
GLOUCESTER. O strong and fast'ned villain!

Would he deny his letter?—I never got him.
[*Tucket within*]
Hark, the Duke's trumpets! I know not why he comes.
All ports I'll bar; the villain shall not scape;
The Duke must grant me that. Besides, his picture
I will send far and near, that all the kingdom
May have due note of him; and of my land,
Loyal and natural boy, I'll work the means
To make thee capable.

Enter CORNWALL, REGAN, *and attendants*

CORNWALL. How now, my noble friend! since I came hither,
Which I can call but now, I have heard strange news.
REGAN. If it be true, all vengeance comes too short
Which can pursue th' offender. How dost, my lord?
GLOUCESTER. O, madam, my old heart is crack'd, it's crack'd!
REGAN. What, did my father's godson seek your life?
He whom my father nam'd? your Edgar?
GLOUCESTER. O lady, lady, shame would have it hid!
REGAN. Was he not companion with the riotous knights
That tend upon my father?
GLOUCESTER. I know not, madam. 'Tis too bad, too bad.
EDMUND. Yes, madam, he was of that consort.
REGAN. No marvel, then, though he were ill affected.
'Tis they have put him on the old man's death,
To have th' expense and waste of his revenues.
I have this present evening from my sister
Been well inform'd of them; and with such cautions
That, if they come to sojourn at my house,
I'll not be there.
CORNWALL. Nor I, assure thee, Regan.
Edmund, I hear that you have shown your father
A child-like office.
EDMUND. It was my duty, sir.
GLOUCESTER. He did bewray his practice, and receiv'd
This hurt you see, striving to apprehend him.
CORNWALL. Is he pursued?
GLOUCESTER. Ay, my good lord.
CORNWALL. If he be taken, he shall never more

Be fear'd of doing harm. Make your own purpose,
How in my strength you please. For you, Edmund,
Whose virtue and obedience doth this instant
So much commend itself, you shall be ours.
Natures of such deep trust we shall much need;
You we first seize on.

EDMUND. I shall serve you, sir,
Truly, however else.

GLOUCESTER. For him I thank your Grace.

CORNWALL. You know not why we came to visit you—

REGAN. Thus out of season, threading dark-ey'd night:
Occasions, noble Gloucester, of some poise,
Wherein we must have use of your advice.
Our father he hath writ, so hath our sister,
Of differences, which I best thought it fit
To answer from our home; the several messengers
From hence attend dispatch. Our good old friend,
Lay comforts to your bosom, and bestow
Your needful counsel to our businesses,
Which craves the instant use.

GLOUCESTER. I serve you, madam.
Your Graces are right welcome. *Exeunt*

SCENE 2

Before GLOUCESTER'S *castle*

Enter KENT *and* OSWALD *severally*

OSWALD. Good dawning to thee, friend. Art of this house?

KENT. Ay.

OSWALD. Where may we set our horses?

KENT. I' th' mire.

OSWALD. Prithee, if thou lov'st me, tell me.

KENT. I love thee not.

OSWALD. Why then, I care not for thee.

KENT. If I had thee in Lipsbury pinfold, I would make thee care for me.

OSWALD. Why dost thou use me thus? I know thee not.

KENT. Fellow, I know thee.

OSWALD. What dost thou know me for?

KENT. A knave, a rascal, an eater of broken meats; a base, proud, shallow, beggarly, three-suited, hundred-pound, filthy, worsted-stocking knave; a lily-liver'd, action-taking, whoreson, glass-gazing, superserviceable, finical rogue; one-trunk-inheriting slave; one that wouldst be a bawd in way of good service, and art nothing but the composition of a knave, beggar, coward, pander, and the son and heir of a mongrel bitch; one whom I will beat into clamorous whining, if thou deny'st the least syllable of thy addition.

OSWALD. Why, what a monstrous fellow art thou, thus to rail on one that is neither known of thee nor knows thee?

KENT. What a brazen-fac'd varlet art thou, to deny thou knowest me! Is it two days since I tripp'd up thy heels and beat thee before the King? Draw, you rogue; for, though it be night, yet the moon shines; I'll make a sop o' th' moonshine of you; you whoreson cullionly barber-monger, draw. [*Drawing his sword*]

OSWALD. Away! I have nothing to do with thee.

KENT. Draw, you rascal. You come with letters against the King, and take Vanity the puppet's part against the royalty of her father. Draw, you rogue, or I'll so carbonado your shanks. Draw, you rascal; come your ways.

OSWALD. Help, ho! murder! help.

KENT. Strike, you slave; stand, rogue, stand; you neat slave, strike. [*Beating him*]

OSWALD. Help, ho! murder! murder!

Enter EDMUND *with his rapier drawn*, GLOUCESTER, CORNWALL, REGAN, *and servants*

EDMUND. How now! What's the matter? Part!

KENT. With you, goodman boy, an you please. Come, I'll flesh ye; come on, young master.

GLOUCESTER. Weapons! arms! What's the matter here?

CORNWALL. Keep peace, upon your lives;
He dies that strikes again. What is the matter?

REGAN. The messengers from our sister and the King.

CORNWALL. What is your difference? Speak.

OSWALD. I am scarce in breath, my lord.

KENT. No marvel, you have so bestirr'd your valour. You

cowardly rascal, nature disclaims in thee: a tailor made thee.

CORNWALL. Thou art a strange fellow. A tailor make a man?

KENT. Ay, a tailor, sir. A stone-cutter or a painter could not have made him so ill, though they had been but two years o' th' trade.

CORNWALL. Speak yet, how grew your quarrel?

OSWALD. This ancient ruffian, sir, whose life I have spar'd at suit of his grey beard–

KENT. Thou whoreson zed! thou unnecessary letter! My lord, if you will give me leave, I will tread this unbolted villain into mortar, and daub the wall of a jakes with him. –Spare my grey beard, you wagtail?

CORNWALL. Peace, sirrah!
You beastly knave, know you no reverence?

KENT. Yes, sir; but anger hath a privilege.

CORNWALL. Why art thou angry?

KENT. That such a slave as this should wear a sword,
Who wears no honesty. Such smiling rogues as these,
Like rats, oft bite the holy cords a-twain
Which are too intrinse t' unloose; smooth every passion
That in the natures of their lords rebel;
Bring oil to fire, snow to their colder moods;
Renege, affirm, and turn their halcyon beaks
With every gale and vary of their masters,
Knowing nought, like dogs, but following.
A plague upon your epileptic visage!
Smile you my speeches, as I were a fool?
Goose, if I had you upon Sarum plain,
I'd drive ye cackling home to Camelot.

CORNWALL. What, art thou mad, old fellow?

GLOUCESTER. How fell you out? Say that.

KENT. No contraries hold more antipathy
Than I and such a knave.

CORNWALL. Why dost thou call him knave? What is his fault?

KENT. His countenance likes me not.

CORNWALL. No more, perchance, does mine, nor his, nor hers.

KENT. Sir, 'tis my occupation to be plain:

I have seen better faces in my time
Than stands on any shoulder that I see
Before me at this instant.

CORNWALL. This is some fellow
Who, having been prais'd for bluntness, doth affect
A saucy roughness, and constrains the garb
Quite from his nature. He cannot flatter, he,
An honest mind and plain—he must speak truth.
An they will take it, so; if not, he's plain.
These kind of knaves I know, which in this plainness
Harbour more craft and more corrupter ends
Than twenty silly ducking observants
That stretch their duties nicely.

KENT. Sir, in good faith, in sincere verity,
Under th' allowance of your great aspect,
Whose influence, like the wreath of radiant fire
On flickering Phœbus' front—

CORNWALL. What mean'st by this?

KENT. To go out of my dialect, which you discommend so much. I know, sir, I am no flatterer. He that beguil'd you in a plain accent was a plain knave; which, for my part, I will not be, though I should win your displeasure to entreat me to't.

CORNWALL. What was th' offence you gave him?

OSWALD. I never gave him any.
It pleas'd the King his master very late
To strike at me, upon his misconstruction;
When he, compact, and flattering his displeasure,
Tripp'd me behind; being down, insulted, rail'd,
And put upon him such a deal of man
That worthied him, got praises of the King
For him attempting who was self-subdu'd;
And in the fleshment of this dread exploit,
Drew on me here again.

KENT. None of these rogues and cowards
But Ajax is their fool.

CORNWALL. Fetch forth the stocks.
You stubborn ancient knave, you reverend braggart,
We'll teach you.

KENT. Sir, I am too old to learn.

Call not your stocks for me; I serve the King,
On whose employment I was sent to you.
You shall do small respect, show too bold malice
Against the grace and person of my master,
Stocking his messenger.

CORNWALL. Fetch forth the stocks. As I have life and honour,
There shall he sit till noon.

REGAN. Till noon! Till night, my lord; and all night too.

KENT. Why, madam, if I were your father's dog,
You should not use me so.

REGAN. Sir, being his knave, I will.

CORNWALL. This is a fellow of the self-same colour
Our sister speaks of. Come, bring away the stocks.
[*Stocks brought out*]

GLOUCESTER. Let me beseech your Grace not to do so.
His fault is much, and the good King his master
Will check him for't; your purpos'd low correction
Is such as basest and contemned'st wretches
For pilf'rings and most common trespasses
Are punish'd with. The King must take it ill
That he, so slightly valued in his messenger,
Should have him thus restrained.

CORNWALL. I'll answer that.

REGAN. My sister may receive it much more worse
To have her gentleman abus'd, assaulted,
For following her affairs. Put in his legs.
[KENT *is put in the stocks*]
Come, my good lord, away.
Exeunt all but GLOUCESTER *and* KENT

GLOUCESTER. I am sorry for thee, friend; 'tis the Duke's pleasure
Whose disposition, all the world well knows,
Will not be rubb'd nor stopp'd. I'll entreat for thee.

KENT. Pray, do not, sir. I have watch'd and travell'd hard;
Some time I shall sleep out, the rest I'll whistle.
A good man's fortune may grow out at heels.
Give you good morrow!

GLOUCESTER. The Duke's to blame in this;
'Twill be ill taken. *Exit*

KENT. Good King, that must approve the common saw,
Thou out of heaven's benediction com'st
To the warm sun!
Approach, thou beacon to this under globe,
That by thy comfortable beams I may
Peruse this letter. Nothing almost sees miracles
But misery. I know 'tis from Cordelia,
Who hath most fortunately been inform'd
Of my obscured course. [*Reads*] '–and shall find time
From this enormous state–seeking to give
Losses their remedies.' All weary and o'er-watch'd,
Take vantage, heavy eyes, not to behold
This shameful lodging.
Fortune, good night; smile once more; turn thy wheel.
[*He sleeps*]

SCENE 3

The open country

Enter EDGAR

EDGAR. I heard myself proclaim'd,
And by the happy hollow of a tree
Escap'd the hunt. No port is free; no place
That guard and most unusual vigilance
Does not attend my taking. Whiles I may scape
I will preserve myself; and am bethought
To take the basest and most poorest shape
That ever penury in contempt of man
Brought near to beast. My face I'll grime with filth,
Blanket my loins, elf all my hairs in knots,
And with presented nakedness outface
The winds and persecutions of the sky.
The country gives me proof and precedent
Of Bedlam beggars, who, with roaring voices,
Strike in their numb'd and mortified bare arms
Pins, wooden pricks, nails, sprigs of rosemary;
And with this horrible object, from low farms,
Poor pelting villages, sheep-cotes, and mills,

Sometimes with lunatic bans, sometime with prayers,
Enforce their charity. Poor Turlygod! poor Tom!
That's something yet. Edgar I nothing am. *Exit*

SCENE 4

Before GLOUCESTER'S *castle*

Enter LEAR, FOOL *and* GENTLEMAN, *to* KENT *in the stocks*

LEAR. 'Tis strange that they should so depart from home,
And not send back my messenger.
GENTLEMAN. As I learn'd,
The night before there was no purpose in them
Of this remove.
KENT. Hail to thee, noble master!
LEAR. Ha!
Mak'st thou this shame thy pastime?
KENT. No, my lord.
FOOL. Ha, ha! he wears cruel garters. Horses are tied by the heads, dogs and bears by th' neck, monkeys by th' loins, and men by th' legs. When a man's over-lusty at legs, then he wears wooden netherstocks.
LEAR. What's he that hath so much thy place mistook
To set thee here?
KENT. It is both he and she,
Your son and daughter.
LEAR. No.
KENT. Yes.
LEAR. No, I say.
KENT. I say, yea.
LEAR. No, no; they would not.
KENT. Yes, they have.
LEAR. By Jupiter, I swear, no.
KENT. By Juno, I swear, ay.
LEAR. They durst not do't;
They could not, would not do't; 'tis worse than murder
To do upon respect such violent outrage.
Resolve me with all modest haste which way

Thou might'st deserve or they impose this usage,
Coming from us.

KENT. My lord, when at their home
I did commend your Highness' letters to them
Ere I was risen from the place that show'd
My duty kneeling, came there a reeking post,
Stew'd in his haste, half breathless, panting forth
From Goneril his mistress salutations;
Deliver'd letters, spite of intermission,
Which presently they read; on whose contents
They summon'd up their meiny, straight took horse,
Commanded me to follow and attend
The leisure of their answer, gave me cold looks;
And meeting here the other messenger,
Whose welcome I perceiv'd had poison'd mine,
Being the very fellow which of late
Display'd so saucily against your Highness,
Having more man than wit about me, drew.
He rais'd the house with loud and coward cries.
Your son and daughter found this trespass worth
The shame which here it suffers.

FOOL. Winter's not gone yet, if the wild geese fly that way.

Fathers that wear rags
Do make their children blind;
But fathers that bear bags
Shall see their children kind.
Fortune, that arrant whore,
Ne'er turns the key to th' poor.

But, for all this, thou shalt have as many dolours for thy daughters as thou canst tell in a year.

LEAR. O, how this mother swells up toward my heart!
Hysterica passio—down, thou climbing sorrow,
Thy element's below. Where is this daughter?

KENT. With the earl, sir, here within.

LEAR. Follow me not; stay here. *Exit*

GENTLEMAN. Made you no more offence but what you speak of?

KENT. None.
How chance the King comes with so small a number?

FOOL. An thou hadst been set i' th' stocks for that question, thou'dst well deserv'd it.

KENT. Why, fool?

FOOL. We'll set thee to school to an ant, to teach thee there's no labouring i' th' winter. All that follow their noses are led by their eyes but blind men; and there's not a nose among twenty but can smell him that's stinking. Let go thy hold when a great wheel runs down a hill, lest it break thy neck with following; but the great one that goes upward, let him draw thee after. When a wise man gives thee better counsel, give me mine again. I would have none but knaves follow it, since a fool gives it.

That sir which serves and seeks for gain,
And follows but for form,
Will pack when it begins to rain,
And leave thee in the storm.

But I will tarry; the fool will stay
And let the wise man fly.
The knave turns fool that runs away;
The fool no knave, perdy.

KENT. Where learn'd you this, fool?

FOOL. Not i' th' stocks, fool.

Re-enter LEAR *and* GLOUCESTER

LEAR. Deny to speak with me! They are sick! They are weary!
They have travell'd all the night! Mere fetches;
The images of revolt and flying off.
Fetch me a better answer.

GLOUCESTER. My dear lord,
You know the fiery quality of the Duke;
How unremovable and fix'd he is
In his own course.

LEAR. Vengeance! plague! death! confusion!
Fiery? What quality? Why Gloucester, Gloucester,
I'd speak with the Duke of Cornwall and his wife.

GLOUCESTER. Well, my good lord, I have inform'd them so.

LEAR. Inform'd them! Dost thou understand me, man?

GLOUCESTER. Ay, my good lord.

LEAR. The King would speak with Cornwall; the dear father

Would with his daughter speak; commands their service.
Are they inform'd of this? My breath and blood!
Fiery? the fiery Duke? Tell the hot Duke that–
No, but not yet. May be he is not well.
Infirmity doth still neglect all office
Whereto our health is bound; we are not ourselves
When nature, being oppress'd, commands the mind
To suffer with the body. I'll forbear;
And am fallen out with my more headier will
To take the indispos'd and sickly fit
For the sound man. Death on my state! Wherefore
Should he sit here? This act persuades me
That this remotion of the Duke and her
Is practice only. Give me my servant forth.
Go tell the Duke and's wife I'd speak with them–
Now, presently. Bid them come forth and hear me,
Or at their chamber door I'll beat the drum
Till it cry sleep to death.

GLOUCESTER. I would have all well betwixt you. *Exit*

LEAR. O me, my heart, my rising heart! But, down.

FOOL. Cry to it, nuncle, as the cockney did to the eels when she put 'em i' th' paste alive; she knapp'd 'em o' th' coxcombs with a stick, and cried 'Down, wantons, down.' 'Twas her brother that, in pure kindness to his horse, butter'd his hay.

Enter CORNWALL, REGAN, GOUCESTER, *and servants*

LEAR. Good morrow to you both.

CORNWALL. Hail to your Grace! [KENT *here set at liberty*]

REGAN. I am glad to see your Highness.

LEAR. Regan, I think you are; I know what reason
I have to think so. If thou shouldst not be glad,
I would divorce me from thy mother's tomb,
Sepulchring an adultress. [*To* KENT] O, are you free?
Some other time for that.–Beloved Regan,
Thy sister's naught. O Regan, she hath tied
Sharp-tooth'd unkindness, like a vulture, here.
[*Points to his heart*]
I can scarce speak to thee; thou'lt not believe
With how deprav'd a quality–O Regan!

REGAN. I pray you, sir, take patience. I have hope
You less know how to value her desert
Than she to scant her duty.
LEAR. Say, how is that?
REGAN. I cannot think my sister in the least
Would fail her obligation. If, sir, perchance
She have restrain'd the riots of your followers,
'Tis on such ground, and to such wholesome end,
As clears her from all blame.
LEAR. My curses on her!
REGAN. O, sir, you are old;
Nature in you stands on the very verge
Of her confine. You should be rul'd and led
By some discretion that discerns your state
Better than you yourself. Therefore I pray you
That to our sister you do make return;
Say you have wrong'd her, sir.
LEAR. Ask her forgiveness?
Do you but mark how this becomes the house:
'Dear daughter, I confess that I am old; [*Kneeling*]
Age is unnecessary; on my knees I beg
That you'll vouchsafe me raiment, bed, and food.'
REGAN. Good sir, no more; these are unsightly tricks.
Return you to my sister.
LEAR. [*Rising*] Never, Regan.
She hath abated me of half my train;
Look'd black upon me; struck me with her tongue,
Most serpent-like, upon the very heart.
All the stor'd vengeances of heaven fall
On her ingrateful top! Strike her young bones,
You taking airs, with lameness.
CORNWALL. Fie, sir, fie!
LEAR. You nimble lightnings, dart your blinding flames
Into her scornful eyes. Infect her beauty,
You fen-suck'd fogs, drawn by the pow'rful sun
To fall and blast her pride.
REGAN. O the blest gods!
So will you wish on me when the rash mood is on.
LEAR. No, Regan, thou shalt never have my curse:
Thy tender-hefted nature shall not give

Thee o'er to harshness. Her eyes are fierce, but thine
Do comfort and not burn. 'Tis not in thee
To grudge my pleasures, to cut off my train,
To bandy hasty words, to scant my sizes,
And, in conclusion, to oppose the bolt
Against my coming in; thou better know'st
The offices of nature, bond of childhood,
Effects of courtesy, dues of gratitude;
Thy half o' th' kingdom hast thou not forgot,
Wherein I thee endow'd.

REGAN. Good sir, to th' purpose.

LEAR. Who put my man i' th' stocks? [*Tucket within*]

CORNWALL. What trumpet's that?

REGAN. I know't—my sister's. This approves her letter,
That she would soon be here.

Enter OSWALD

Is your lady come?

LEAR. This is a slave whose easy-borrow'd pride
Dwells in the fickle grace of her he follows.
Out, varlet, from my sight!

CORNWALL. What means your Grace?

Enter GONERIL

LEAR. Who stock'd my servant? Regan, I have good hope
Thou didst not know on't.—Who comes here? O heavens,
If you do love old men, if your sweet sway
Allow obedience, if you yourselves are old,
Make it your cause; send down, and take my part.
[*To* GONERIL] Art not asham'd to look upon this beard?—
O Regan, will you take her by the hand?

GONERIL. Why not by th' hand, sir? How have I offended?
All's not offence that indiscretion finds,
And dotage terms so.

LEAR. O sides, you are too tough!
Will you yet hold?—How came my man i' th' stocks?

CORNWALL. I set him there, sir; but his own disorders
Deserv'd much less advancement.

LEAR. You! did you?

REGAN. I pray you, father, being weak, seem so.

If, till the expiration of your month,
You will return and sojourn with my sister,
Dismissing half your train, come then to me.
I am now from home, and out of that provision
Which shall be needful for your entertainment.

LEAR. Return to her, and fifty men dismiss'd?
No, rather I abjure all roofs, and choose
To wage against the enmity o' th' air,
To be a comrade with the wolf and owl—
Necessity's sharp pinch! Return with her?
Why, the hot-blooded France, that dowerless took
Our youngest born—I could as well be brought
To knee this throne, and, squire-like, pension beg
To keep base life afoot. Return with her?
Persuade me rather to be slave and sumpter
To this detested groom. [*Pointing to* OSWALD]

GONERIL. At your choice, sir.

LEAR. I prithee, daughter, do not make me mad.
I will not trouble thee, my child; farewell.
We'll no more meet, no more see one another.
But yet thou art my flesh, my blood, my daughter;
Or rather a disease that's in my flesh,
Which I must needs call mine; thou art a boil,
A plague-sore, or embossed carbuncle
In my corrupted blood. But I'll not chide thee;
Let shame come when it will, I do not call it;
I do not bid the Thunder-bearer shoot,
Nor tell tales of thee to high-judging Jove.
Mend when thou canst; be better at thy leisure;
I can be patient; I can stay with Regan,
I and my hundred knights.

REGAN. Not altogether so.
I look'd not for you yet, nor am provided
For your fit welcome. Give ear, sir, to my sister;
For those that mingle reason with your passion
Must be content to think you old, and so—
But she knows what she does.

LEAR. Is this well spoken?

REGAN. I dare avouch it, sir. What, fifty followers?
Is it not well? What should you need of more?

Yea, or so many, sith that both charge and danger
Speak 'gainst so great a number? How in one house
Should many people under two commands
Hold amity? 'Tis hard; almost impossible.

GONERIL. Why might not you, my lord, receive attendance
From those that she calls servants, or from mine?

REGAN. Why not, my lord? If then they chanc'd to slack ye,
We could control them. If you will come to me—
For now I spy a danger—I entreat you
To bring but five and twenty. To no more
Will I give place or notice.

LEAR. I gave you all.

REGAN. And in good time you gave it.

LEAR. Made you my guardians, my depositaries;
But kept a reservation to be followed
With such a number. What, must I come to you
With five and twenty, Regan? Said you so?

REGAN. And speak't again, my lord. No more with me.

LEAR. Those wicked creatures yet do look well-favour'd
When others are more wicked; not being the worst
Stands in some rank of praise. [*To* GONERIL] I'll go with thee.
Thy fifty yet doth double five and twenty,
And thou art twice her love.

GONERIL. Hear me, my lord:
What need you five and twenty, ten, or five,
To follow in a house where twice so many
Have a command to tend you?

REGAN. What need one?

LEAR. O, reason not the need! Our basest beggars
Are in the poorest thing superfluous.
Allow not nature more than nature needs,
Man's life is cheap as beast's. Thou art a lady;
If only to go warm were gorgeous,
Why, nature needs not what thou gorgeous wear'st,
Which scarcely keeps thee warm. But, for true need—
You heavens, give me that patience, patience I need.
You see me here, you gods, a poor old man,
As full of grief as age; wretched in both.
If it be you that stirs these daughters' hearts

Against their father, fool me not so much
To bear it tamely; touch me with noble anger,
And let not women's weapons, water-drops,
Stain my man's cheeks! No, you unnatural hags,
I will have such revenges on you both
That all the world shall—I will do such things—
What they are yet I know not; but they shall be
The terrors of the earth. You think I'll weep.
No, I'll not weep. [*Storm and tempest*]
I have full cause of weeping; but this heart
Shall break into a hundred thousand flaws
Or ere I'll weep. O fool, I shall go mad!

Exeunt LEAR, GLOUCESTER, KENT, *and* FOOL

CORNWALL. Let us withdraw; 'twill be a storm.
REGAN. This house is little: the old man and's people
Cannot be well bestow'd.
GONERIL. 'Tis his own blame; hath put himself from rest,
And must needs taste his folly.
REGAN. For his particular, I'll receive him gladly,
But not one follower.
GONERIL. So am I purpos'd.
Where is my Lord of Gloucester?
CORNWALL. Followed the old man forth.

Re-enter GLOUCESTER

He is return'd.
GLOUCESTER. The King is in high rage.
CORNWALL. Whither is he going?
GLOUCESTER. He calls to horse; but will I know not whither.
CORNWALL. 'Tis best to give him way; he leads himself.
GONERIL. My lord, entreat him by no means to stay.
GLOUCESTER. Alack, the night comes on, and the high winds
Do sorely ruffle; for many miles about
There's scarce a bush.
REGAN. O sir, to wilful men
The injuries that they themselves procure
Must be their schoolmasters. Shut up your doors.
He is attended with a desperate train;
And what they may incense him to, being apt
To have his ear abus'd, wisdom bids fear.

ACT II. SCENE 4

CORNWALL. Shut up your doors, my lord; 'tis a wild night.
My Regan counsels well. Come out o' th' storm. *Exeunt*

ACT III. SCENE 1

A heath

Storm still. Enter KENT *and a* GENTLEMAN, *severally*

KENT. Who's there, besides foul weather?
GENTLEMAN. One minded like the weather, most unquietly.
KENT. I know you. Where's the King?
GENTLEMAN. Contending with the fretful elements;
Bids the wind blow the earth into the sea,
Or swell the curled waters 'bove the main,
That things might change or cease; tears his white hair,
Which the impetuous blasts, with eyeless rage,
Catch in their fury, and make nothing of;
Strives in his little world of man to outscorn
The to-and-fro conflicting wind and rain.
This night, wherein the cub-drawn bear would couch,
The lion and the belly-pinched wolf
Keep their fur dry, unbonneted he runs,
And bids what will take all.
KENT. But who is with him?
GENTLEMAN. None but the fool; who labours to out-jest
His heart-struck injuries.
KENT. Sir, I do know you,
And dare, upon the warrant of my note,
Commend a dear thing to you. There is division,
Although as yet the face of it be cover'd
With mutual cunning, 'twixt Albany and Cornwall;
Who have–as who have not that their great stars
Thron'd and set high?–servants, who seem no less,
Which are to France the spies and speculations
Intelligent of our state. What hath been seen,
Either in snuffs and packings of the Dukes;
Or the hard rein which both of them hath borne

Against the old kind King; or something deeper,
Whereof perchance these are but furnishings—
But true it is from France there comes a power
Into this scatter'd kingdom, who already,
Wise in our negligence, have secret feet
In some of our best ports, and are at point
To show their open banner. Now to you:
If on my credit you dare build so far
To make your speed to Dover, you shall find
Some that will thank you making just report
Of how unnatural and bemadding sorrow
The King hath cause to plain.
I am a gentleman of blood and breeding;
And from some knowledge and assurance offer
This office to you.

GENTLEMAN. I will talk further with you.

KENT. No, do not.
For confirmation that I am much more
Than my out-wall, open this purse and take
What it contains. If you shall see Cordelia,
As fear not but you shall, show her this ring;
And she will tell you who your fellow is
That yet you do not know. Fie on this storm!
I will go seek the King.

GENTLEMAN. Give me your hand. Have you no more to say?

KENT. Few words, but, to effect, more than all yet;
That when we have found the King—in which your pain
That way, I'll this—he that first lights on him
Holla the other. *Exeunt severally*

SCENE 2

Another part of the heath

Storm still. Enter LEAR *and* FOOL

LEAR. Blow, winds, and crack your cheeks; rage, blow.
You cataracts and hurricanoes, spout
Till you have drench'd our steeples, drown'd the cocks.
You sulph'rous and thought-executing fires,

Vaunt-couriers of oak-cleaving thunderbolts,
Singe my white head. And thou, all-shaking thunder
Strike flat the thick rotundity o' th' world;
Crack nature's moulds, all germens spill at once,
That makes ingrateful man.

FOOL. O nuncle, court holy water in a dry house is better than this rain-water out o' door. Good nuncle, in; ask thy daughters' blessing. Here's a night pities neither wise men nor fools.

LEAR. Rumble thy bellyful. Spit, fire; spout, rain.
Nor rain, wind, thunder, fire, are my daughters.
I tax not you, you elements, with unkindness;
I never gave you kingdom, call'd you children;
You owe me no subscription. Then let fall
Your horrible pleasure. Here I stand, your slave,
A poor, infirm, weak and despis'd old man;
But yet I call you servile ministers
That will with two pernicious daughters join
Your high-engender'd battles 'gainst a head
So old and white as this. O, ho! 'tis foul!

FOOL. He that has a house to put's head in has a good head-piece.

The cod-piece that will house
  Before the head has any,
The head and he shall louse;
  So beggars marry many.

The man that makes his toe
  What he his heart should make
Shall of a corn cry woe,
  And turn his sleep to wake.

For there was never yet fair woman but she made mouths in a glass.

Enter KENT

LEAR. No, I will be the pattern of all patience;
I will say nothing.

KENT. Who's there?

FOOL. Marry, here's grace and a cod-piece; that's a wise man and a fool.

KENT. Alas, sir, are you here? Things that love night
Love not such nights as these; the wrathful skies
Gallow the very wanderers of the dark
And make them keep their caves. Since I was man
Such sheets of fire, such bursts of horrid thunder,
Such groans of roaring wind and rain, I never
Remember to have heard. Man's nature cannot carry
Th' affliction nor the fear.

LEAR. Let the great gods,
That keep this dreadful pudder o'er our heads,
Find out their enemies now. Tremble, thou wretch,
That hast within thee undivulged crimes
Unwhipp'd of justice. Hide thee, thou bloody hand;
Thou perjur'd, and thou simular man of virtue
That art incestuous; caitiff, to pieces shake,
That under covert and convenient seeming
Hast practis'd on man's life. Close pent-up guilts,
Rive your concealing continents, and cry
These dreadful summoners grace. I am a man
More sinn'd against than sinning.

KENT. Alack, bare-headed!
Gracious my lord, hard by here is a hovel;
Some friendship will it lend you 'gainst the tempest.
Repose you there, while I to this hard house—
More harder than the stones whereof 'tis rais'd;
Which even but now, demanding after you,
Denied me to come in—return, and force
Their scanted courtesy.

LEAR. My wits begin to turn.
Come on, my boy. How dost, my boy? Art cold?
I am cold myself. Where is this straw, my fellow?
The art of our necessities is strange
That can make vile things precious. Come, your hovel.
Poor fool and knave, I have one part in my heart
That's sorry yet for thee.

FOOL. [*Sings*]

He that has and a little tiny wit
With heigh-ho, the wind and the rain—
Must make content with his fortunes fit,
Though the rain it raineth every day.

LEAR. True, my good boy. Come, bring us to this hovel.

Exeunt LEAR *and* KENT

FOOL. This is a brave night to cool a courtezan. I'll speak a prophecy ere I go.

When priests are more in word than matter;
When brewers mar their malt with water;
When nobles are their tailors' tutors;
No heretics burn'd, but wenches' suitors;
When every case in law is right;
No squire in debt, nor no poor knight;
When slanders do not live in tongues;
Nor cutpurses come not to throngs;
When usurers tell their gold i' th' field;
And bawds and whores do churches build–
Then shall the realm of Albion
Come to great confusion.
Then comes the time, who lives to see't,
That going shall be us'd with feet.

This prophecy Merlin shall make, for I live before his time. *Exit*

SCENE 3

GLOUCESTER'S *castle*

Enter GLOUCESTER *and* EDMUND

GLOUCESTER. Alack, alack, Edmund, I like not this unnatural dealing. When I desired their leave that I might pity him, they took from me the use of mine own house, charg'd me, on pain of perpetual displeasure, neither to speak of him, entreat for him, or any way sustain him.

EDMUND. Most savage and unnatural!

GLOUCESTER. Go to; say you nothing. There is division between the Dukes; and a worse matter than that. I have received a letter this night–'tis dangerous to be spoken; I have lock'd the letter in my closet. These injuries the King now bears will be revenged home; there is part of a power already footed. We must incline to the King. I will look him, and privily relieve him. Go you and maintain talk with the Duke, that my charity be not of him perceived; if he ask for me, I am ill, and gone to bed. If I die for it, as no less is threatened me, the King my old master must be relieved. There is strange things toward, Edmund; pray you be careful. *Exit*

EDMUND. This courtesy, forbid thee, shall the Duke
Instantly know, and of that letter too.
This seems a fair deserving, and must draw me
That which my father loses—no less than all.
The younger rises, when the old doth fall. *Exit*

SCENE 4

Before a hovel on the heath

Storm still. Enter LEAR, KENT, *and* FOOL

KENT. Here is the place, my lord; good my lord, enter.
The tyranny of the open night's too rough
For nature to endure.
LEAR. Let me alone.
KENT. Good my lord, enter here.
LEAR. Wilt break my heart?
KENT. I had rather break mine own. Good my lord, enter.
LEAR. Thou think'st 'tis much that this contentious storm
Invades us to the skin; so 'tis to thee,
But where the greater malady is fix'd,
The lesser is scarce felt. Thou'dst shun a bear;
But if thy flight lay toward the roaring sea,
Thou'dst meet the bear i' th' mouth. When the mind's free
The body's delicate; this tempest in my mind
Doth from my senses take all feeling else,
Save what beats there. Filial ingratitude!
Is it not as this mouth should tear this hand
For lifting food to't? But I will punish home.
No, I will weep no more. In such a night,
To shut me out! Pour on; I will endure.
In such a night as this! O Regan, Goneril!
Your old kind father, whose frank heart gave all!
O, that way madness lies; let me shun that;

No more of that.

KENT. Good my lord, enter here.

LEAR. Prithee go in thyself; seek thine own ease.
This tempest will not give me leave to ponder
On things would hurt me more. But I'll go in.
[*To the* FOOL] In, boy; go first.—You houseless poverty—
Nay, get thee in. I'll pray, and then I'll sleep. *Exit* FOOL
Poor naked wretches, wheresoe'er you are,
That bide the pelting of this pitiless storm,
How shall your houseless heads and unfed sides,
Your loop'd and window'd raggedness, defend you
From seasons such as these? O, I have ta'en
Too little care of this! Take physic, pomp;
Expose thyself to feel what wretches feel,
That thou mayst shake the superflux to them,
And show the heavens more just.

EDGAR. [*Within*] Fathom and half, fathom and half! Poor Tom!

Enter FOOL *from the hovel*

FOOL. Come not in here, nuncle, here's a spirit. Help me, help me!

KENT. Give me thy hand. Who's there?

FOOL. A spirit, a spirit. He says his name's poor Tom.

KENT. What art thou that dost grumble there i' th' straw? Come forth.

Enter EDGAR, *disguised as a madman*

EDGAR. Away! the foul fiend follows me.
Through the sharp hawthorn blows the cold wind
Humh! go to thy cold bed and warm thee.

LEAR. Didst thou give all to thy daughters? And art thou come to this?

EDGAR. Who gives anything to poor Tom? whom the foul fiend hath led through fire and through flame, through ford and whirlpool, o'er bog and quagmire; that hath laid knives under his pillow and halters in his pew, set ratsbane by his porridge; made him proud of heart, to ride on a bay trotting-horse over four-inched bridges, to course his own shadow for a traitor. Bless thy five wits! Tom's a-cold.

O, do de, do de, do de. Bless thee from whirlwinds, star-blasting, and taking! Do poor Tom some charity, whom the foul fiend vexes. There could I have him now—and there—and there again—and there. [*Storm still*]

LEAR. What, has his daughters brought him to this pass?
Could'st thou save nothing? Would'st thou give 'em all?

FOOL. Nay, he reserv'd a blanket, else we had been all sham'd.

LEAR. Now all the plagues that in the pendulous air
Hang fated o'er men's faults light on thy daughters!

KENT. He hath no daughters, sir.

LEAR. Death, traitor! Nothing could have subdu'd nature
To such a lowness but his unkind daughters.
Is it the fashion that discarded fathers
Should have thus little mercy on their flesh?
Judicious punishment! 'twas this flesh begot
Those pelican daughters.

EDGAR. Pillicock sat on Pillicock-hill.
Alow, alow, loo, loo!

FOOL. This cold night will turn us all to fools and madmen.

EDGAR. Take heed o' th' foul fiend; obey thy parents; keep thy words justly; swear not; commit not with man's sworn spouse; set not thy sweet heart on proud array. Tom's a-cold.

LEAR. What hast thou been?

EDGAR. A serving-man, proud in heart and mind; that curl'd my hair; wore gloves in my cap; serv'd the lust of my mistress' heart, and did the act of darkness with her; swore as many oaths as I spake words, and broke them in the sweet face of heaven; one that slept in the contriving of lust, and wak'd to do it. Wine lov'd I deeply, dice dearly; and in woman out-paramour'd the Turk. False of heart, light of ear, bloody of hand; hog in sloth, fox in stealth, wolf in greediness, dog in madness, lion in prey. Let not the creaking of shoes nor the rustling of silks betray thy poor heart to woman. Keep thy foot out of brothels, thy hand out of plackets, thy pen from lenders' books, and defy the foul fiend.
Still through the hawthorn blows the cold wind.
Says suum, mun, nonny.

Dolphin my boy, boy, sessa! let him trot by.

[Storm still]

LEAR. Why, thou wert better in a grave than to answer with thy uncover'd body this extremity of the skies. Is man no more than this? Consider him well. Thou ow'st the worm no silk, the beast no hide, the sheep no wool, the cat no perfume. Ha! here's three on's are sophisticated! Thou art the thing itself: unaccommodated man is no more but such a poor, bare, forked animal as thou art. Off, off, you lendings! Come, unbutton here.

[Tearing off his clothes]

Enter GLOUCESTER *with a torch*

FOOL. Prithee, nuncle, be contented; 'tis a naughty night to swim in. Now a little fire in a wild field were like an old lecher's heart—a small spark, all the rest on's body cold. Look, here comes a walking fire.

EDGAR. This is the foul fiend Flibbertigibbet; he begins at curfew, and walks till the first cock; he gives the web and the pin, squenes the eye, and makes the hare-lip; mildews the white wheat, and hurts the poor creature of earth.

Swithold footed thrice the 'old;
He met the nightmare and her ninefold;
Bid her alight
And her troth plight,
And aroint thee, witch, aroint thee!

KENT. How fares your Grace?

LEAR. What's he?

KENT. Who's there? What is't you seek?

GLOUCESTER. What are you there? Your names?

EDGAR. Poor Tom; that eats the swimming frog, the toad, the tadpole, the wall-newt, and the water; that in the fury of his heart, when the foul fiend rages, eats cowdung for sallets, swallows the old rat and the ditch-dog, drinks the green mantle of the standing pool; who is whipp'd from tithing to tithing, and stock-punish'd, and imprison'd; who hath had three suits to his back, six shirts to his body—

Horse to ride, and weapon to wear;
But mice and rats, and such small deer,

Have been Tom's food for seven long year.
Beware my follower. Peace, Smulkin; peace, thou fiend!

GLOUCESTER. What, hath your Grace no better company?

EDGAR. The prince of darkness is a gentleman; Modo he's call'd, and Mahu.

GLOUCESTER. Our flesh and blood, my lord, is grown so vile
That it doth hate what gets it.

EDGAR. Poor Tom's a-cold.

GLOUCESTER. Go in with me: my duty cannot suffer
T' obey in all your daughters' hard commands.
Though their injunction be to bar my doors,
And let this tyrannous night take hold upon you,
Yet have I ventur'd to come seek you out,
And bring you where both fire and food is ready.

LEAR. First let me talk with this philosopher.
What is the cause of thunder?

KENT. Good my lord, take his offer; go into th' house.

LEAR. I'll talk a word with this same learned Theban.
What is your study?

EDGAR. How to prevent the fiend and to kill vermin.

LEAR. Let me ask you one word in private.

KENT. Importune him once more to go, my lord;
His wits begin t' unsettle. [*Storm still*]

GLOUCESTER. Canst thou blame him?
His daughters seek his death. Ah, that good Kent!–
He said it would be thus–poor, banish'd man!
Thou sayest the King grows mad; I'll tell thee, friend,
I am almost mad myself. I had a son,
Now outlaw'd from my blood; he sought my life
But lately, very late. I lov'd him, friend–
No father his son dearer. True to tell thee,
The grief hath craz'd my wits. What a night's this!
I do beseech your Grace–

LEAR. O, cry you mercy, sir.
Noble philosopher, your company.

EDGAR. Tom's a-cold.

GLOUCESTER. In, fellow, there, into th' hovel; keep thee warm.

LEAR. Come, let's in all.

KENT. This way, my lord.

LEAR. With him;
I will keep still with my philosopher.

KENT. Good my lord, soothe him; let him take the fellow.

GLOUCESTER. Take him you on.

KENT. Sirrah, come on; go along with us.

LEAR. Come, good Athenian.

GLOUCESTER. No words, no words! Hush.

EDGAR. Child Rowland to the dark tower came,
His word was still 'Fie, foh, and fum,
I smell the blood of a British man.' *Exeunt*

SCENE 5

GLOUCESTER'S *castle*

Enter CORNWALL *and* EDMUND

CORNWALL. I will have my revenge ere I depart his house.

EDMUND. How, my lord, I may be censured, that nature thus gives way to loyalty, something fears me to think of.

CORNWALL. I now perceive it was not altogether your brother's evil disposition made him seek his death; but a provoking merit, set a-work by a reprovable badness in himself.

EDMUND. How malicious is my fortune, that I must repent to be just! This is the letter he spoke of, which approves him an intelligent party to the advantages of France. O heavens! that this treason were not, or not I the detector!

CORNWALL. Go with me to the Duchess.

EDMUND. If the matter of this paper be certain, you have mighty business in hand.

CORNWALL. True or false, it hath made thee Earl of Gloucester. Seek out where thy father is, that he may be ready for our apprehension.

EDMUND. [*Aside*] If I find him comforting the King, it will stuff his suspicion more fully.–I will persever in my course of loyalty, though the conflict be sore between that and my blood.

CORNWALL. I will lay trust upon thee; and thou shalt find a dearer father in my love. *Exeunt*

SCENE 6

An outhouse of GLOUCESTER'S *castle*

Enter KENT *and* GLOUCESTER

GLOUCESTER. Here is better than the open air; take it thankfully. I will piece out the comfort with what addition I can. I will not be long from you.

KENT. All the pow'r of his wits have given way to his impatience. The gods reward your kindness!

Exit GLOUCESTER

Enter LEAR, EDGAR, *and* FOOL

EDGAR. Frateretto calls me, and tells me Nero is an angler in the lake of darkness. Pray, innocent, and beware the foul fiend.

FOOL. Prithee, nuncle, tell me whether a madman be a gentleman or a yeoman?

LEAR. A king, a king!

FOOL. No; he's a yeoman that has a gentleman to his son; for he's a mad yeoman that sees his son a gentleman before him.

LEAR. To have a thousand with red burning spits
Come hizzing in upon 'em–

EDGAR. The foul fiend bites my back.

FOOL. He's mad that trusts in the tameness of a wolf, a horse's health, a boy's love, or a whore's oath.

LEAR. It shall be done; I will arraign them straight.
[*To* EDGAR] Come, sit thou here, most learned justicer.
[*To the* FOOL] Thou, sapient sir, sit here.–Now, you she-foxes!

EDGAR. Look where he stands and glares!
Want'st thou eyes at trial, madam?
Come o'er the bourn, Bessy, to me.

FOOL. Her boat hath a leak,
And she must not speak,
Why she dares not come over to thee.

EDGAR. The foul fiend haunts poor Tom in the voice of a nightingale. Hoppedance cries in Tom's belly for two white herring. Croak not, black angel; I have no food for thee.

KENT. How do you, sir? Stand you not so amaz'd.
Will you lie down and rest upon the cushions?

LEAR. I'll see their trial first. Bring in their evidence.
[*To* EDGAR] Thou robed man of justice, take thy place.
[*To the* FOOL] And thou, his yoke-fellow of equity,
Bench by his side. [*To* KENT] You are o' th' commission,
Sit you too.

EDGAR. Let us deal justly.

Sleepest or wakest thou, jolly shepherd?
Thy sheep be in the corn;
And for one blast of thy minikin mouth,
Thy sheep shall take no harm.

Pur! the cat is grey.

LEAR. Arraign her first; 'tis Goneril. I here take my oath before this honourable assembly she kick'd the poor King her father.

FOOL. Come hither, mistress. Is your name Goneril?

LEAR. She cannot deny it.

FOOL. Cry you mercy, I took you for a joint-stool.

LEAR. And here's another, whose warp'd looks proclaim
What store her heart is made on. Stop her there!
Arms, arms, sword, fire! Corruption in the place!
False justicer, why hast thou let her scape?

EDGAR. Bless thy five wits!

KENT. O pity! Sir, where is the patience now
That you so oft have boasted to retain?

EDGAR. [*Aside*] My tears begin to take his part so much
They mar my counterfeiting.

LEAR. The little dogs and all,
Tray, Blanch, and Sweetheart, see, they bark at me.

EDGAR. Tom will throw his head at them.
Avaunt, you curs!

Be thy mouth or black or white,
Tooth that poisons if it bite;
Mastiff, greyhound, mongrel grim,
Hound or spaniel, brach or lym,
Or bobtail tike or trundle-tail—
Tom will make him weep and wail;

For, with throwing thus my head,
Dogs leapt the hatch, and all are fled.

Do, de, de, de. Sessa! Come, march to wakes and fairs and market towns. Poor Tom, thy horn is dry.

LEAR. Then let them anatomize Regan; see what breeds about her heart. Is there any cause in nature that make these hard hearts? [*To* EDGAR] You, sir, I entertain for one of my hundred; only I do not like the fashion of your garments. You will say they are Persian, but let them be chang'd.

KENT. Now, good my lord, lie here and rest awhile.

LEAR. Make no noise, make no noise; draw the curtains. So, so. We'll go to supper i' th' morning.

FOOL. And I'll go to bed at noon.

Re-enter GLOUCESTER

GLOUCESTER. Come hither, friend. Where is the King my master?

KENT. Here, sir: but trouble him not—his wits are gone.

GLOUCESTER. Good friend, I prithee, take him in thy arms;
I have o'erheard a plot of death upon him.
There is a litter ready; lay him in't
And drive toward Dover, friend, where thou shalt meet
Both welcome and protection. Take up thy master;
If thou shouldst dally half an hour, his life,
With thine, and all that offer to defend him,
Stand in assured loss. Take up, take up;
And follow me, that will to some provision
Give thee quick conduct.

KENT. Oppressed nature sleeps.
This rest might yet have balm'd thy broken sinews,
Which, if convenience will not allow,
Stand in hard cure. [*To the* FOOL] Come, help to bear thy master;
Thou must not stay behind.

GLOUCESTER. Come, come, away. *Exeunt all but* EDGAR

EDGAR. When we our betters see bearing our woes,
We scarcely think our miseries our foes.
Who alone suffers suffers most i' th' mind,
Leaving free things and happy shows behind;

But then the mind much sufferance doth o'erskip
When grief hath mates, and bearing fellowship.
How light and portable my pain seems now,
When that which makes me bend makes the King bow—
He childed as I father'd! Tom, away!
Mark the high noises; and thyself bewray,
When false opinion, whose wrong thoughts defile thee,
In thy just proof repeals and reconciles thee.
What will hap more to-night, safe scape the King!
Lurk, lurk. *Exit*

SCENE 7

GLOUCESTER'S *castle*

Enter CORNWALL, REGAN, GONERIL, EDMUND, *and servants*

CORNWALL. [*To* GONERIL] Post speedily to my lord your husband; show him this letter. The army of France is landed.—Seek out the traitor Gloucester.

Exeunt some of the servants

REGAN. Hang him instantly.

GONERIL. Pluck out his eyes.

CORNWALL. Leave him to my displeasure. Edmund, keep you our sister company. The revenges we are bound to take upon your traitorous father are not fit for your beholding. Advise the Duke, where you are going, to a most festinate preparation; we are bound to the like. Our posts shall be swift and intelligent betwixt us. Farewell, dear sister; farewell, my Lord of Gloucester.

Enter OSWALD

How now! where's the King?

OSWALD. My Lord of Gloucester hath convey'd him hence.
Some five or six and thirty of his knights,
Hot questrists after him, met him at gate;
Who, with some other of the lord's dependants,
Are gone with him toward Dover, where they boast
To have well-armed friends.

CORNWALL. Get horses for your mistress.

GONERIL. Farewell, sweet lord, and sister.

CORNWALL. Edmund, farewell.

Exeunt GONERIL, EDMUND, *and* OSWALD

Go seek the traitor Gloucester,
Pinion him like a thief, bring him before us.

Exeunt other servants

Though well we may not pass upon his life
Without the form of justice, yet our power
Shall do a court'sy to our wrath, which men
May blame, but not control.

Enter GLOUCESTER, *brought in by two or three*

Who's there? the traitor?

REGAN. Ingrateful fox! 'tis he.

CORNWALL. Bind fast his corky arms.

GLOUCESTER. What means your Graces? Good my friends, consider
You are my guests; do me no foul play, friends.

CORNWALL. Bind him, I say. [*Servants bind him*]

REGAN. Hard, hard. O filthy traitor!

GLOUCESTER. Unmerciful lady as you are, I'm none.

CORNWALL. To this chair bind him. Villain, thou shalt find—

[REGAN *plucks his beard*]

GLOUCESTER. By the kind gods, 'tis most ignobly done
To pluck me by the beard.

REGAN. So white, and such a traitor!

GLOUCESTER. Naughty lady,
These hairs which thou dost ravish from my chin
Will quicken and accuse thee. I am your host.
With robbers' hands my hospitable favours
You should not ruffle thus. What will you do?

CORNWALL. Come, sir, what letters had you late from France?

REGAN. Be simple-answer'd, for we know the truth.

CORNWALL. And what confederacy have you with the traitors
Late footed in the kingdom?

REGAN. To whose hands you have sent the lunatic King:
Speak.

GLOUCESTER. I have a letter guessingly set down,

Which came from one that's of a neutral heart,
And not from one oppos'd.

CORNWALL. Cunning.

REGAN. And false.

CORNWALL. Where hast thou sent the King?

GLOUCESTER. To Dover.

REGAN. Wherefore to Dover? Wast thou not charg'd at peril—

CORNWALL. Wherefore to Dover? Let him first answer that.

GLOUCESTER. I am tied to the stake, and I must stand the course.

REGAN. Wherefore to Dover?

GLOUCESTER. Because I would not see thy cruel nails
Pluck out his poor old eyes; nor thy fierce sister
In his anointed flesh rash boarish fangs.
The sea, with such a storm as his bare head
In hell-black night endur'd, would have buoy'd up
And quench'd the stelled fires.
Yet, poor old heart, he holp the heavens to rain.
If wolves had at thy gate howl'd that dern time,
Thou shouldst have said 'Good porter, turn the key.'
All cruels else subscribe, but I shall see
The winged vengeance overtake such children.

CORNWALL. See't shalt thou never. Fellows, hold the chair.
Upon these eyes of thine I'll set my foot.

GLOUCESTER. He that will think to live till he be old,
Give me some help!—O cruel! O you gods!

REGAN. One side will mock another; th' other too.

CORNWALL. If you see vengeance—

FIRST SERVANT. Hold your hand, my lord.
I have serv'd you ever since I was a child;
But better service have I never done you,
Than now to bid you hold.

REGAN. How now, you dog!

FIRST SERVANT. If you did wear a beard upon your chin
I'd shake it on this quarrel. What do you mean?

CORNWALL. My villain! [*They draw and fight*]

FIRST SERVANT. Nay, then come on, and take the chance of anger. [CORNWALL *is wounded*]

REGAN. Give me thy sword. A peasant stand up thus!

[*She takes a sword and stabs him from behind*]

FIRST SERVANT. O, I am slain! My lord, you have one eye left
To see some mischief on him. O! [*Dies*]

CORNWALL. Lest it see more, prevent it. Out, vile jelly!
Where is thy lustre now?

GLOUCESTER. All dark and comfortless! Where's my son Edmund?
Edmund, enkindle all the sparks of nature
To quit this horrid act.

REGAN. Out, treacherous villain!
Thou call'st on him that hates thee. It was he
That made the overture of thy treasons to us;
Who is too good to pity thee.

GLOUCESTER. O my follies! Then Edgar was abus'd.
Kind gods, forgive me that, and prosper him.

REGAN. Go thrust him out at gates and let him smell
His way to Dover. [GLOUCESTER *led out*]
How is't my lord? How look you?

CORNWALL. I have receiv'd a hurt. Follow me, lady.
Turn out that eyeless villain; throw this slave
Upon the dunghill. Regan, I bleed apace.
Untimely comes this hurt. Give me your arm.

Exit CORNWALL, *led by* REGAN

SECOND SERVANT. I'll never care what wickedness I do,
If this man come to good.

THIRD SERVANT. If she live long,
And in the end meet the old course of death,
Women will all turn monsters.

SECOND SERVANT. Let's follow the old Earl and get the Bedlam
To lead him where he would. His roguish madness
Allows itself to anything.

THIRD SERVANT. Go thou. I'll fetch some flax and whites of eggs
To apply to his bleeding face. Now heaven help him!

Exeunt

ACT IV. SCENE 1

The Heath

Enter EDGAR

EDGAR. Yet better thus and known to be contemn'd,
Than still contemn'd and flatter'd. To be worst,
The lowest and most dejected thing of fortune,
Stands still in esperance, lives not in fear.
The lamentable change is from the best;
The worst returns to laughter. Welcome, then,
Thou unsubstantial air that I embrace!
The wretch that thou hast blown unto the worst
Owes nothing to thy blasts.

Enter GLOUCESTER, *led by an* OLD MAN

But who comes here?
My father, poorly led? World, world, O world!
But that thy strange mutations make us hate thee,
Life would not yield to age.

OLD MAN. O my good lord, I have been your tenant, and your father's tenant, these fourscore years.

GLOUCESTER. Away, get thee away; good friend, be gone.
Thy comforts can do me no good at all;
Thee they may hurt.

OLD MAN. You cannot see your way.

GLOUCESTER. I have no way, and therefore want no eyes;
I stumbled when I saw: full oft 'tis seen
Our means secure us, and our mere defects
Prove our commodities. O dear son Edgar,
The food of thy abused father's wrath!
Might I but live to see thee in my touch,
I'd say I had eyes again!

OLD MAN. How now! Who's there?

EDGAR. [*Aside*] O gods! Who is't can say 'I am at the worst'?
I am worse than e'er I was.

OLD MAN. 'Tis poor mad Tom.

EDGAR. [*Aside*] And worse I may be yet. The worst is not
So long as we can say 'This is the worst.'

OLD MAN. Fellow, where goest?

GLOUCESTER. Is it a beggar-man?

OLD MAN. Madman and beggar too.

GLOUCESTER. He has some reason, else he could not beg.
I' th' last night's storm I such a fellow saw;
Which made me think a man a worm. My son
Came then into my mind; and yet my mind
Was then scarce friends with him. I have heard more since.
As flies to wanton boys are we to th' gods—
They kill us for their sport.

EDGAR. [*Aside*] How should this be?
Bad is the trade that must play fool to sorrow,
Ang'ring itself and others.—Bless thee, master!

GLOUCESTER. Is that the naked fellow?

OLD MAN. Ay, my lord.

GLOUCESTER. Then, prithee, get thee away. If for my sake
Thou wilt o'ertake us hence a mile or twain
I' th' way toward Dover, do it for ancient love;
And bring some covering for this naked soul,
Which I'll entreat to lead me.

OLD MAN. Alack, sir, he is mad.

GLOUCESTER. 'Tis the times' plague when madmen lead the blind.
Do as I bid thee, or rather do thy pleasure;
Above the rest, be gone.

OLD MAN. I'll bring him the best 'parel that I have,
Come on't what will. *Exit*

GLOUCESTER. Sirrah, naked fellow!

EDGAR. Poor Tom's a-cold. [*Aside*] I cannot daub it further.

GLOUCESTER. Come hither, fellow.

EDGAR. [*Aside*] And yet I must.—Bless thy sweet eyes, they bleed.

GLOUCESTER. Know'st thou the way to Dover?

EDGAR. Both stile and gate, horse-way and footpath. Poor Tom hath been scar'd out of his good wits. Bless thee, good man's son, from the foul fiend! Five fiends have been in poor Tom at once: of lust, as Obidicut; Hobbididence, prince of dumbness; Mahu, of stealing; Modo, of murder; Flibbertigibbet, of mopping and mowing, who since possesses chambermaids and waiting-women. So, bless thee, master!

GLOUCESTER. Here, take this purse, thou whom the heavens' plagues
Have humbled to all strokes. That I am wretched
Makes thee the happier. Heavens, deal so still!
Let the superfluous and lust-dieted man
That slaves your ordinance, that will not see
Because he does not feel, feel your power quickly;
So distribution should undo excess,
And each man have enough. Dost thou know Dover?

EDGAR. Ay, master.

GLOUCESTER. There is a cliff whose high and bending head
Looks fearfully in the confined deep:
Bring me but to the very brim of it
And I'll repair the misery thou dost bear
With something rich about me. From that place
I shall no leading need.

EDGAR. Give me thy arm;
Poor Tom shall lead thee. *Exeunt*

SCENE 2

Before the DUKE OF ALBANY'S *palace*

Enter GONERIL *and* EDMUND

GONERIL. Welcome, my lord. I marvel our mild husband
Not met us on the way.

Enter OSWALD

Now, where's your master?

OSWALD. Madam, within, but never man so chang'd.
I told him of the army that was landed;
He smil'd at it. I told him you were coming;
His answer was 'The worse.' Of Gloucester's treachery,
And of the loyal service of his son,
When I inform'd him, then he call'd me sot,
And told me I had turn'd the wrong side out.
What most he should dislike seems pleasant to him;

What like, offensive.

GONERIL. [*To* EDMUND] Then shall you go no further.
It is the cowish terror of his spirit
That dares not undertake; he'll not feel wrongs
Which tie him to an answer. Our wishes on the way
May prove effects. Back, Edmund, to my brother;
Hasten his musters and conduct his pow'rs.
I must change arms at home, and give the distaff
Into my husband's hands. This trusty servant
Shall pass between us. Ere long you are like to hear,
If you dare venture in your own behalf,
A mistress's command. Wear this; spare speech.
[*Giving a favour*]
Decline your head; this kiss, if it durst speak,
Would stretch thy spirits up into the air.
Conceive, and fare thee well.

EDMUND. Yours in the ranks of death.

GONERIL. My most dear Gloucester. *Exit* EDMUND
O, the difference of man and man!
To thee a woman's services are due.
My fool usurps my body.

OSWALD. Madam, here comes my lord. *Exit*

Enter ALBANY

GONERIL. I have been worth the whistle.

ALBANY. O Goneril!
You are not worth the dust which the rude wind
Blows in your face. I fear your disposition:
That nature which contemns it origin
Cannot be border'd certain in itself;
She that herself will sliver and disbranch
From her material sap perforce must wither
And come to deadly use.

GONERIL. No more; the text is foolish.

ALBANY. Wisdom and goodness to the vile seem vile;
Filths savour but themselves. What have you done?
Tigers, not daughters, what have you perform'd?
A father, and a gracious aged man,
Whose reverence even the head-lugg'd bear would lick,
Most barbarous, most degenerate, have you madded.

Could my good brother suffer you to do it?
A man, a Prince, by him so benefited!
If that the heavens do not their visible spirits
Send quickly down to tame these vile offences,
It will come
Humanity must perforce prey on itself,
Like monsters of the deep.

GONERIL. Milk-liver'd man!
That bear'st a cheek for blows, a head for wrongs;
Who hast not in thy brows an eye discerning
Thine honour from thy suffering; that not know'st
Fools do those villains pity who are punish'd
Ere they have done their mischief. Where's thy drum?
France spreads his banners in our noiseless land,
With plumed helm thy state begins to threat,
Whilst thou, a moral fool, sits still, and cries
'Alack, why does he so?'

ALBANY. See thyself, devil!
Proper deformity shows not in the fiend
So horrid as in woman.

GONERIL. O vain fool!

ALBANY. Thou changed and self-cover'd thing, for shame!
Be-monster not thy feature. Were't my fitness
To let these hands obey my blood,
They are apt enough to dislocate and tear
Thy flesh and bones. Howe'er thou art a fiend,
A woman's shape doth shield thee.

GONERIL. Marry, your manhood—mew!

Enter a MESSENGER

ALBANY. What news?

MESSENGER. O, my good lord, the Duke of Cornwall's dead,
Slain by his servant, going to put out
The other eye of Gloucester.

ALBANY. Gloucester's eyes!

MESSENGER. A servant that he bred, thrill'd with remorse,
Oppos'd against the act, bending his sword
To his great master; who, thereat enrag'd,
Flew on him, and amongst them fell'd him dead;
But not without that harmful stroke which since

Hath pluck'd him after.

ALBANY. This shows you are above,
You justicers, that these our nether crimes
So speedily can venge! But, O poor Gloucester!
Lost he his other eye?

MESSENGER. Both, both, my lord.
This letter, madam, craves a speedy answer;
'Tis from your sister.

GONERIL. [*Aside*] One way I like this well;
But being widow, and my Gloucester with her,
May all the building in my fancy pluck
Upon my hateful life. Another way
The news is not so tart.—I'll read, and answer. *Exit*

ALBANY. Where was his son, when they did take his eyes?

MESSENGER. Come with my lady hither.

ALBANY. He is not here.

MESSENGER. No, my good lord; I met him back again.

ALBANY. Knows he the wickedness?

MESSENGER. Ay, my good lord; 'twas he inform'd against him
And quit the house on purpose that their punishment
Might have the freer course.

ALBANY. Gloucester, I live
To thank thee for the love thou show'dst the King,
And to revenge thine eyes. Come hither, friend:
Tell me what more thou know'st. *Exeunt*

SCENE 3

The French camp near Dover

Enter KENT *and a* GENTLEMAN

KENT. Why the King of France is so suddenly gone back know you no reason?

GENTLEMAN. Something he left imperfect in the state, which since his coming forth is thought of, which imports to the kingdom so much fear and danger that his personal return was most required and necessary.

KENT. Who hath he left behind him general?

GENTLEMAN. The Marshal of France, Monsieur La Far.

KENT. Did your letters pierce the Queen to any demonstration of grief?

GENTLEMAN. Ay, sir; she took them, read them in my presence,
And now and then an ample tear trill'd down
Her delicate cheek. It seem'd she was a queen
Over her passion, who, most rebel-like,
Sought to be king o'er her.

KENT. O, then it mov'd her.

GENTLEMAN. Not to a rage; patience and sorrow strove
Who should express her goodliest. You have seen
Sunshine and rain at once: her smiles and tears
Were like a better way. Those happy smilets
That play'd on her ripe lip seem'd not to know
What guests were in her eyes, which parted thence
As pearls from diamonds dropp'd. In brief,
Sorrow would be a rarity most beloved
If all could so become it.

KENT. Made she no verbal question?

GENTLEMAN. Faith, once or twice she heav'd the name of father
Pantingly forth, as if it press'd her heart;
Cried 'Sisters! sisters! Shame of ladies! Sisters!
Kent! father! sisters! What i' th' storm? i' th' night?
Let pity not be believ'd!' There she shook
The holy water from her heavenly eyes,
And clamour moisten'd; then away she started
To deal with grief alone.

KENT. It is the stars,
The stars above us, govern our conditions,
Else one self mate and make could not beget
Such different issues. You spoke not with her since?

GENTLEMAN. No.

KENT. Was this before the King return'd?

GENTLEMAN. No, since.

KENT. Well, sir, the poor distressed Lear's i' th' town;
Who sometime in his better tune remembers
What we are come about, and by no means
Will yield to see his daughter.

GENTLEMAN. Why, good sir?

KENT. A sovereign shame so elbows him; his own unkindness,
That stripp'd her from his benediction, turn'd her
To foreign casualties, gave her dear rights
To his dog-hearted daughters—these things sting
His mind so venomously that burning shame
Detains him from Cordelia.

GENTLEMAN. Alack, poor gentleman!

KENT. Of Albany's and Cornwall's powers you heard not?

GENTLEMAN. 'Tis so; they are afoot.

KENT. Well, sir, I'll bring you to our master Lear,
And leave you to attend him. Some dear cause
Will in concealment wrap me up awhile;
When I am known aright, you shall not grieve
Lending me this acquaintance. I pray you go
Along with me. *Exeunt*

SCENE 4

The French camp. A tent

Enter with drum and colours, CORDELIA, DOCTOR, *and soldiers*

CORDELIA. Alack, 'tis he! Why, he was met even now
As mad as the vex'd sea, singing aloud,
Crown'd with rank fumiter and furrow weeds,
With hardocks, hemlock, nettles, cuckoo-flow'rs,
Darnel, and all the idle weeds that grow
In our sustaining corn. A century send forth;
Search every acre in the high-grown field,
And bring him to our eye. *Exit an* OFFICER
What can man's wisdom,
In the restoring his bereaved sense?
He that helps him, take all my outward worth.

DOCTOR. There is means, madam.
Our foster-nurse of nature is repose,
The which he lacks; that to provoke in him
Are many simples operative, whose power

Will close the eye of anguish.
CORDELIA. All blest secrets,
All you unpublish'd virtues of the earth,
Spring with my tears; be aidant and remediate,
In the good man's distress. Seek, seek for him;
Lest his ungovern'd rage dissolve the life
That wants the means to lead it.

Enter a MESSENGER

MESSENGER. News, madam:
The British pow'rs are marching hitherward.
CORDELIA. 'Tis known before; our preparation stands
In expectation of them. O dear father!
It is thy business that I go about;
Therefore great France
My mourning and importun'd tears hath pitied.
No blown ambition doth our arms incite,
But love, dear love, and our ag'd father's right.
Soon may I hear and see him! *Exeunt*

SCENE 5

GLOUCESTER'S *castle*

Enter REGAN *and* OSWALD

REGAN. But are my brother's pow'rs set forth?
OSWALD. Ay, madam.
REGAN. Himself in person there?
OSWALD. Madam, with much ado.
Your sister is the better soldier.
REGAN. Lord Edmund spake not with your lord at home?
OSWALD. No, madam.
REGAN. What might import my sister's letter to him?
OSWALD. I know not, lady.
REGAN. Faith, he is posted hence on serious matter.
It was great ignorance, Gloucester's eyes being out,
To let him live; where he arrives he moves
All hearts against us. Edmund, I think, is gone
In pity of his misery, to dispatch
His nighted life; moreover, to descry

The strength o' th' enemy.

OSWALD. I must needs after him, madam, with my letter.

REGAN. Our troops set forth to-morrow: stay with us;
The ways are dangerous.

OSWALD. I may not, madam:
My lady charg'd my duty in this business.

REGAN. Why should she write to Edmund? Might not you
Transport her purposes by word? Belike
Some things—I know not what. I'll love thee much—
Let me unseal the letter.

OSWALD. Madam, I had rather—

REGAN. I know your lady does not love her husband;
I am sure of that; and at her late being here
She gave strange œillades and most speaking looks
To noble Edmund. I know you are of her bosom.

OSWALD. I, madam?

REGAN. I speak in understanding; y'are, I know't.
Therefore I do advise you take this note.
My lord is dead; Edmund and I have talk'd;
And more convenient is he for my hand
Than for your lady's. You may gather more.
If you do find him, pray you give him this;
And when your mistress hears thus much from you,
I pray desire her call her wisdom to her.
So fare you well.
If you do chance to hear of that blind traitor,
Preferment falls on him that cuts him off.

OSWALD. Would I could meet him, madam! I should show
What party I do follow.

REGAN. Fare thee well. *Exeunt*

SCENE 6

The country near Dover

Enter GLOUCESTER, *and* EDGAR *dressed like a peasant*

GLOUCESTER. When shall I come to th' top of that same hill?

EDGAR. You do climb up it now; look how we labour.

GLOUCESTER. Methinks the ground is even.

EDGAR. Horrible steep.
Hark, do you hear the sea?
GLOUCESTER. No, truly.
EDGAR. Why then, your other senses grow imperfect
By your eyes' anguish.
GLOUCESTER. So may it be indeed.
Methinks thy voice is alter'd, and thou speak'st
In better phrase and matter than thou didst.
EDGAR. Y'are much deceiv'd: in nothing am I chang'd
But in my garments.
GLOUCESTER. Methinks y'are better spoken.
EDGAR. Come on, sir; here's the place. Stand still. How fearful
And dizzy 'tis to cast one's eyes so low!
The crows and choughs that wing the midway air
Show scarce so gross as beetles. Half-way down
Hangs one that gathers samphire—dreadful trade!
Methinks he seems no bigger than his head.
The fishermen that walk upon the beach
Appear like mice; and yond tall anchoring bark
Diminish'd to her cock; her cock, a buoy
Almost too small for sight. The murmuring surge
That on th' unnumb'red idle pebble chafes
Cannot be heard so high. I'll look no more;
Lest my brain turn, and the deficient sight
Topple down headlong.
GLOUCESTER. Set me where you stand.
EDGAR. Give me your hand. You are now within a foot
Of th' extreme verge. For all beneath the moon
Would I not leap upright.
GLOUCESTER. Let go my hand.
Here, friend, 's another purse; in it a jewel
Well worth a poor man's taking. Fairies and gods
Prosper it with thee! Go thou further off;
Bid me farewell, and let me hear thee going.
EDGAR. Now fare ye well, good sir.
GLOUCESTER. With all my heart.
EDGAR. Why I do trifle thus with his despair
Is done to cure it.
GLOUCESTER. [*Kneeling*] O you mighty gods!

This world I do renounce, and in your sights
Shake patiently my great affliction off.
If I could bear it longer, and not fall
To quarrel with your great opposeless wills,
My snuff and loathed part of nature should
Burn itself out. If Edgar live, O, bless him!
[*Rising*] Now, fellow, fare thee well.

EDGAR. Gone, sir; farewell,
[GLOUCESTER *casts himself down*]
And yet I know not how conceit may rob
The treasury of life, when life itself
Yields to the theft. Had he been where he thought,
By this had thought been past.—Alive or dead?
Ho, you sir! friend! Hear you, sir! Speak!—
Thus might he pass indeed. Yet he revives—
What are you, sir?

GLOUCESTER. Away, and let me die.

EDGAR. Hadst thou been aught but gossamer, feathers, air,
So many fathom down precipitating,
Thou'dst shiver'd like an egg; but thou dost breathe,
Hast heavy substance, bleed'st not, speak'st, art sound.
Ten masts at each make not the altitude
Which thou hast perpendicularly fell.
Thy life's a miracle. Speak yet again.

GLOUCESTER. But have I fall'n, or no?

EDGAR. From the dread summit of this chalky bourn.
Look up a-height; the shrill-gorg'd lark so far
Cannot be seen or heard. Do but look up.

GLOUCESTER. Alack, I have no eyes.
Is wretchedness depriv'd that benefit,
To end itself by death? 'Twas yet some comfort,
When misery could beguile the tyrant's rage
And frustrate his proud will.

EDGAR. Give me your arm.
Up—so. How is't? Feel you your legs? You stand.

GLOUCESTER. Too well, too well.

EDGAR. This is above all strangeness.
Upon the crown o' th' cliff what thing was that
Which parted from you?

GLOUCESTER. A poor unfortunate beggar.

EDGAR. As I stood here below, methought his eyes
Were two full moons; he had a thousand noses,
Horns whelk'd and waved like the enridged sea.
It was some fiend; therefore, thou happy father,
Think that the clearest gods, who make them honours
Of men's impossibilities, have preserved thee.

GLOUCESTER. I do remember now. Henceforth I'll bear
Affliction till it do cry out itself
'Enough, enough' and die. That thing you speak of
I took it for a man; often 'twould say,
'The fiend, the fiend.' He led me to that place.

EDGAR. Bear free and patient thoughts.

Enter LEAR, *fantastically dressed with weeds*

But who comes here?
The safer sense will ne'er accommodate
His master thus.

LEAR. No, they cannot touch me for coining; I am the King himself.

EDGAR. O thou side-piercing sight!

LEAR. Nature's above art in that respect. There's your press-money. That fellow handles his bow like a crow-keeper; draw me a clothier's yard. Look, look, a mouse! Peace, peace; this piece of toasted cheese will do't. There's my gauntlet; I'll prove it on a giant. Bring up the brown bills. O, well flown, bird! i' the clout, i' the clout–hewgh! Give the word.

EDGAR. Sweet marjoram.

LEAR. Pass.

GLOUCESTER. I know that voice.

LEAR. Ha! Goneril, with a white beard! They flatter'd me like a dog, and told me I had white hairs in my beard ere the black ones were there. To say 'ay' and 'no' to everything that I said! 'Ay' and 'no' too was no good divinity. When the rain came to wet me once, and the wind to make me chatter; when the thunder would not peace at my bidding; there I found 'em, there I smelt 'em out. Go to, they are not men o' their words. They told me I was everything; 'tis a lie–I am not ague-proof.

GLOUCESTER. The trick of that voice I do well remember.

Is't not the King?

LEAR. Ay, every inch a king.
When I do stare, see how the subject quakes.
I pardon that man's life. What was thy cause?
Adultery?
Thou shalt not die. Die for adultery? No.
The wren goes to't, and the small gilded fly
Does lecher in my sight.
Let copulation thrive; for Gloucester's bastard son
Was kinder to his father than my daughters
Got 'tween the lawful sheets.
To't, luxury, pell-mell, for I lack soldiers.
Behold yond simp'ring dame
Whose face between her forks presages snow,
That minces virtue and does shake the head
To hear of pleasure's name—
The fitchew nor the soiled horse goes to't
With a more riotous appetite.
Down from the waist they are centaurs,
Though women all above;
But to the girdle do the gods inherit,
Beneath is all the fiends';
There's hell, there's darkness, there is the sulphurous pit—
Burning, scalding, stench, consumption.
Fie, fie, fie! pah, pah! Give me an ounce of civet, good apothecary, to sweeten my imagination. There's money for thee.

GLOUCESTER. O, let me kiss that hand!

LEAR. Let me wipe it first; it smells of mortality.

GLOUCESTER. O ruin'd piece of nature! This great world
Shall so wear out to nought. Dost thou know me?

LEAR. I remember thine eyes well enough. Dost thou squiny at me? No, do thy worst, blind Cupid; I'll not love. Read thou this challenge; mark but the penning of it.

GLOUCESTER. Were all thy letters suns, I could not see one.

EDGAR. [*Aside*] I would not take this from report. It is,
And my heart breaks at it.

LEAR. Read.

GLOUCESTER. What, with the case of eyes?

LEAR. O, ho, are you there with me? No eyes in your head

nor no money in your purse? Your eyes are in a heavy case, your purse in a light; yet you see how this world goes.

GLOUCESTER. I see it feelingly.

LEAR. What, art mad? A man may see how this world goes with no eyes. Look with thine ears. See how yond justice rails upon yond simple thief. Hark, in thine ear: change places and, handy-dandy, which is the justice, which is the thief? Thou hast seen a farmer's dog bark at a beggar?

GLOUCESTER. Ay, sir.

LEAR. And the creature run from the cur?
There thou mightst behold the great image of authority: a dog's obey'd in office.
Thou rascal beadle, hold thy bloody hand.
Why dost thou lash that whore? Strip thy own back;
Thou hotly lusts to use her in that kind
For which thou whip'st her. The usurer hangs the cozener.
Through tatter'd clothes small vices do appear;
Robes and furr'd gowns hide all. Plate sin with gold,
And the strong lance of justice hurtless breaks;
Arm it in rags, a pigmy's straw does pierce it.
None does offend, none–I say none; I'll able 'em.
Take that of me, my friend, who have the power
To seal th' accuser's lips. Get thee glass eyes,
And, like a scurvy politician, seem
To see the things thou dost not. Now, now, now, now!
Pull off my boots. Harder, harder–so.

EDGAR. O, matter and impertinency mix'd!
Reason in madness!

LEAR. If thou wilt weep my fortunes, take my eyes.
I know thee well enough; thy name is Gloucester.
Thou must be patient; we came crying hither.
Thou know'st the first time that we smell the air
We wawl and cry. I will preach to thee. Mark.

GLOUCESTER. Alack, alack the day!

LEAR. When we are born, we cry that we are come
To this great stage of fools. This a good block!
It were a delicate stratagem to shoe
A troop of horse with felt; I'll put't in proof;

And when I have stol'n upon these son-in-laws,
Then kill, kill, kill, kill, kill, kill!

Enter a GENTLEMAN, *with attendants*

GENTLEMAN. O, here he is: lay hand upon him.—Sir,
Your most dear daughter—
LEAR. No rescue? What, a prisoner? I am even
The natural fool of fortune. Use me well;
You shall have ransom. Let me have surgeons;
I am cut to th' brains.
GENTLEMAN. You shall have any thing.
LEAR. No seconds? All myself?
Why, this would make a man a man of salt,
To use his eyes for garden water-pots,
Ay, and laying Autumn's dust.
GENTLEMAN. Good sir—
LEAR. I will die bravely, like a smug bridegroom. What!
I will be jovial. Come, come; I am a king,
My masters, know you that.
GENTLEMAN. You are a royal one, and we obey you.
LEAR. Then there's life in't. Nay, an you get it, you shall get it by running. Sa, sa, sa, sa.

Exit running; attendants follow

GENTLEMAN. A sight most pitiful in the meanest wretch,
Past speaking of in a king! Thou hast one daughter
Who redeems nature from the general curse
Which twain have brought her to.
EDGAR. Hail, gentle sir.
GENTLEMAN. Sir, speed you; what's your will?
EDGAR. Do you hear aught, sir, of a battle toward?
GENTLEMAN. Most sure and vulgar; every one hears that
Which can distinguish sound.
EDGAR. But, by your favour,
How near's the other army?
GENTLEMAN. Near and on speedy foot; the main descry
Stands on the hourly thought.
EDGAR. I thank you, sir; that's all.
GENTLEMAN. Though that the Queen on special cause is here,
Her army is mov'd on.

EDGAR. I thank you, sir. *Exit* GENTLEMAN

GLOUCESTER. You ever-gentle gods, take my breath from me;
Let not my worser spirit tempt me again
To die before you please.

EDGAR. Well pray you, father.

GLOUCESTER. Now, good sir, what are you?

EDGAR. A most poor man, made tame to fortune's blows,
Who, by the art of known and feeling sorrows,
Am pregnant to good pity. Give me your hand;
I'll lead you to some biding.

GLOUCESTER. Hearty thanks;
The bounty and the benison of heaven
To boot, and boot!

Enter OSWALD

OSWALD. A proclaim'd prize! Most happy!
That eyeless head of thine was first fram'd flesh
To raise my fortunes. Thou old unhappy traitor,
Briefly thyself remember. The sword is out
That must destroy thee.

GLOUCESTER. Now let thy friendly hand
Put strength enough to't. [EDGAR *interposes*]

OSWALD. Wherefore, bold peasant,
Dar'st thou support a publish'd traitor? Hence;
Lest that th' infection of his fortune take
Like hold on thee. Let go his arm.

EDGAR. Chill not let go, zir, without vurther 'casion.

OSWALD. Let go, slave, or thou diest.

EDGAR. Good gentleman, go your gait, and let poor volk pass. An chud ha' bin zwagger'd out of my life, 'twould not ha' bin zo long as 'tis by a vortnight. Nay, come not near th' old man; keep out, che vor ye, or Ice try whether your costard or my ballow be the harder. Chill be plain with you.

OSWALD. Out, dunghill!

EDGAR. Chill pick your teeth, zir. Come; no matter vor your foins. [*They fight*]

OSWALD. Slave, thou hast slain me. Villain, take my purse;
If ever thou wilt thrive, bury my body,

And give the letters which thou find'st about me
To Edmund Earl of Gloucester. Seek him out
Upon the English party. O, untimely death!
Death! [*He dies*]

EDGAR. I know thee well; a serviceable villain,
As duteous to the vices of thy mistress
As badness would desire.

GLOUCESTER. What, is he dead?

EDGAR. Sit you down, father; rest you.
Let's see these pockets; the letters that he speaks of
May be my friends. He's dead; I am only sorry
He had no other death's-man. Let us see.
Leave, gentle wax; and, manners, blame us not:
To know our enemies' minds we'd rip their hearts;
Their papers is more lawful.
[*Reads*] 'Let our reciprocal vows be rememb'red. You have many opportunities to cut him off; if your will want not, time and place will be fruitfully offer'd. There is nothing done if he return the conqueror; then am I the prisoner, and his bed my gaol; from the loathed warmth whereof deliver me, and supply the place for your labour.

'Your (wife, so I would say) affectionate servant,
'GONERIL.'

O indistinguish'd space of woman's will!
A plot upon her virtuous husband's life;
And the exchange my brother! Here, in the sands
Thee I'll rake up, the post unsanctified
Of murderous lechers; and in the mature time
With this ungracious paper strike the sight
Of the death-practis'd duke. For him 'tis well
That of thy death and business I can tell.

GLOUCESTER. The King is mad; how stiff is my vile sense,
That I stand up, and have ingenious feeling
Of my huge sorrows! Better I were distract;
So should my thoughts be sever'd from my griefs,
And woes by wrong imaginations lose
The knowledge of themselves. [*Drum afar off*]

EDGAR. Give me your hand.
Far off methinks I hear the beaten drum.
Come, father, I'll bestow you with a friend. *Exeunt*

SCENE 7

A tent in the French camp

Music. Enter Cordelia, Kent, Doctor, *and* Gentleman

Cordelia. O thou good Kent, how shall I live and work
To match thy goodness? My life will be too short,
And every measure fail me.

Kent. To be acknowledg'd, madam, is o'erpaid.
All my reports go with the modest truth;
Nor more nor clipp'd, but so.

Cordelia. Be better suited.
These weeds are memories of those worser hours;
I prithee put them off.

Kent. Pardon, dear madam;
Yet to be known shortens my made intent:
My boon I make it that you know me not
Till time and I think meet.

Cordelia. Then be't so, my good lord. [*To the* Doctor]
How does the King?

Doctor. Madam, sleeps still.

Cordelia. O you kind gods,
Cure this great breach in his abused nature!
Th' untun'd and jarring senses, O, wind up
Of this child-changed father!

Doctor. So please your Majesty
That we may wake the King; he hath slept long.

Cordelia. Be govern'd by your knowledge, and proceed
I' th' sway of your own will. [*To the* Gentleman] Is he array'd?

Gentleman. Ay, madam; in the heaviness of sleep
We put fresh garments on him.

Doctor. Be by, good madam, when we do awake him;
I doubt not of his temperance.

Cordelia. Very well.

Doctor. Please you, draw near. Louder the music there!

[*He draws the curtains and discovers* Lear *asleep in bed*]

CORDELIA. O my dear father! Restoration hang
  Thy medicine on my lips, and let this kiss
  Repair those violent harms that my two sisters
  Have in thy reverence made.
KENT. Kind and dear princess!
CORDELIA. Had you not been their father, these white flakes
  Did challenge pity of them. Was this a face
  To be oppos'd against the warring winds?
  To stand against the deep dread bolted thunder?
  In the most terrible and nimble stroke
  Of quick cross lightning? to watch—poor perdu!—
  With this thin helm? Mine enemy's dog,
  Though he had bit me, should have stood that night
  Against my fire; and wast thou fain, poor father,
  To hovel thee with swine and rogues forlorn,
  In short and musty straw? Alack, alack!
  'Tis wonder that thy life and wits at once
  Had not concluded all.—He wakes; speak to him.
DOCTOR. Madam, do you; 'tis fittest.
CORDELIA. How does my royal lord? How fares your Majesty?
LEAR. You do me wrong to take me out o' th' grave.
  Thou art a soul in bliss; but I am bound
  Upon a wheel of fire, that mine own tears
  Do scald like molten lead.
CORDELIA. Sir, do you know me?
LEAR. You are a spirit, I know. Where did you die?
CORDELIA. Still, still far wide!
DOCTOR. He's scarce awake; let him alone awhile.
LEAR. Where have I been? Where am I? Fair daylight?
  I am mightily abus'd. I should e'en die with pity
  To see another thus. I know not what to say.
  I will not swear these are my hands. Let's see.
  I feel this pin prick. Would I were assur'd
  Of my condition!
CORDELIA. O, look upon me, sir,
  And hold your hands in benediction o'er me.
  No, sir, you must not kneel.
LEAR. Pray, do not mock me:
  I am a very foolish fond old man,

Fourscore and upward, not an hour more nor less;
And, to deal plainly,
I fear I am not in my perfect mind.
Methinks I should know you, and know this man;
Yet I am doubtful; for I am mainly ignorant
What place this is; and all the skill I have
Remembers not these garments; nor I know not
Where I did lodge last night. Do not laugh at me;
For, as I am a man, I think this lady
To be my child Cordelia.

CORDELIA. And so I am, I am.

LEAR. Be your tears wet? Yes, faith. I pray weep not;
If you have poison for me I will drink it.
I know you do not love me; for your sisters
Have, as I do remember, done me wrong:
You have some cause, they have not.

CORDELIA. No cause, no cause.

LEAR. Am I in France?

KENT. In your own kingdom, sir.

LEAR. Do not abuse me.

DOCTOR. Be comforted, good madam. The great rage,
You see, is kill'd in him; and yet it is danger
To make him even o'er the time he has lost.
Desire him to go in; trouble him no more
Till further settling.

CORDELIA. Will't please your Highness walk?

LEAR. You must bear with me.
Pray you now, forget and forgive; I am old and foolish.

Exeunt all but KENT *and* GENTLEMAN

GENTLEMAN. Holds it true, sir, that the Duke of Cornwall was so slain?

KENT. Most certain, sir.

GENTLEMAN. Who is conductor of his people?

KENT. As 'tis said, the bastard son of Gloucester.

GENTLEMAN. They say Edgar, his banish'd son, is with the Earl of Kent in Germany.

KENT. Report is changeable. 'Tis time to look about; the powers of the kingdom approach apace.

GENTLEMAN. The arbitrement is like to be bloody. Fare you well, sir. *Exit*

KENT. *My* point and period will be throughly wrought,
Or well or ill, as this day's battle's fought. *Exit*

ACT V. SCENE 1

The British camp near Dover

Enter, with drum and colours, EDMUND, REGAN, GENTLEMAN, *and soldiers*

EDMUND. Know of the Duke if his last purpose hold,
Or whether since he is advis'd by aught
To change the course. He's full of alteration
And self-reproving—bring his constant pleasure.
Exit an OFFICER

REGAN. Our sister's man is certainly miscarried.

EDMUND. 'Tis to be doubted, madam.

REGAN. Now, sweet lord,
You know the goodness I intend upon you.
Tell me—but truly—but then speak the truth—
Do you not love my sister?

EDMUND. In honour'd love.

REGAN. But have you never found my brother's way
To the forfended place?

EDMUND. That thought abuses you.

REGAN. I am doubtful that you have been conjunct
And bosom'd with her, as far as we call hers.

EDMUND. No, by mine honour, madam.

REGAN. I never shall endure her. Dear my lord,
Be not familiar with her.

EDMUND. Fear me not.
She and the Duke her husband!

Enter, with drum and colours, ALBANY, GONERIL, *and soldiers*

GONERIL. [*Aside*] I had rather lose the battle than that sister
Should loosen him and me.

ALBANY. Our very loving sister, well be-met.
Sir, this I heard: the King is come to his daughter
With others whom the rigour of our state

Forc'd to cry out. Where I could not be honest
I never yet was valiant. For this business,
It touches us as France invades our land,
Not bolds the King, with others whom, I fear,
Most just and heavy causes make oppose.

EDMUND. Sir, you speak nobly.

REGAN. Why is this reason'd?

GONERIL. Combine together 'gainst the enemy;
For these domestic-door particulars
Are not the question here.

ALBANY. Let's then determine
With th' ancient of war on our proceeding.

EDMUND. I shall attend you presently at your tent.

REGAN. Sister, you'll go with us?

GONERIL. No.

REGAN. 'Tis most convenient; pray you go with us.

GONERIL. [*Aside*] O, ho, I know the riddle.—I will go.

As they are going out, enter EDGAR, *disguised*

EDGAR. If e'er your Grace had speech with man so poor,
Hear me one word.

ALBANY. I'll overtake you.—Speak.
Exeunt all but ALBANY *and* EDGAR

EDGAR. Before you fight the battle, ope this letter.
If you have victory, let the trumpet sound
For him that brought it; wretched though I seem
I can produce a champion that will prove
What is avouched there. If you miscarry,
Your business of the world hath so an end,
And machination ceases. Fortune love you!

ALBANY. Stay till I have read the letter.

EDGAR. I was forbid it.
When time shall serve, let but the herald cry,
And I'll appear again.

ALBANY. Why, fare thee well. I will o'erlook thy paper.
Exit EDGAR

Re-enter EDMUND

EDMUND. The enemy's in view; draw up your powers.
Here is the guess of their true strength and forces

By diligent discovery; but your haste
Is now urg'd on you.

ALBANY. We will greet the time. *Exit*

EDMUND. To both these sisters have I sworn my love;
Each jealous of the other, as the stung
Are of the adder. Which of them shall I take?
Both? one? or neither? Neither can be enjoy'd,
If both remain alive: to take the widow,
Exasperates, makes mad her sister Goneril;
And hardly shall I carry out my side,
Her husband being alive. Now then, we'll use
His countenance for the battle; which being done,
Let her who would be rid of him devise
His speedy taking off. As for the mercy
Which he intends to Lear and to Cordelia–
The battle done, and they within our power,
Shall never see his pardon; for my state
Stands on me to defend, not to debate. *Exit*

SCENE 2

A field between the two camps

Alarum within. Enter, with drum and colours, the powers of France over the stage, CORDELIA *with her* FATHER *in her hand, and exeunt*

Enter EDGAR *and* GLOUCESTER

EDGAR. Here, father, take the shadow of this tree
For your good host; pray that the right may thrive.
If ever I return to you again
I'll bring you comfort.

GLOUCESTER. Grace go with you, sir! *Exit* EDGAR

Alarum and retreat within. Re-enter EDGAR

EDGAR. Away, old man; give me thy hand; away!
King Lear hath lost, he and his daughter ta'en.
Give me thy hand; come on.

GLOUCESTER. No further, sir; a man may rot even here.

EDGAR. What, in ill thoughts again? Men must endure

Their going hence, even as their coming hither:
Ripeness is all. Come on.
GLOUCESTER. And that's true too. *Exeunt*

SCENE 3

The British camp near Dover

Enter, in conquest, with drum and colours, EDMUND;
LEAR *and* CORDELIA *prisoners; soldiers,* CAPTAIN

EDMUND. Some officers take them away. Good guard,
Until their greater pleasures first be known
That are to censure them.
CORDELIA. We are not the first
Who with best meaning have incurr'd the worst.
For thee, oppressed King, am I cast down;
Myself could else out-frown false Fortune's frown.
Shall we not see these daughters and these sisters?
LEAR. No, no, no, no! Come, let's away to prison.
We two alone will sing like birds i' th' cage;
When thou dost ask me blessing, I'll kneel down
And ask of thee forgiveness; so we'll live,
And pray, and sing, and tell old tales, and laugh
At gilded butterflies, and hear poor rogues
Talk of court news; and we'll talk with them too–
Who loses and who wins; who's in, who's out–
And take upon's the mystery of things
As if we were God's spies; and we'll wear out
In a wall'd prison packs and sects of great ones
That ebb and flow by th' moon.
EDMUND. Take them away.
LEAR. Upon such sacrifices, my Cordelia,
The gods themselves throw incense. Have I caught thee?
He that parts us shall bring a brand from heaven
And fire us hence like foxes. Wipe thine eyes;
The good years shall devour them, flesh and fell,
Ere they shall make us weep. We'll see 'em starv'd first.
Come. *Exeunt* LEAR *and* CORDELIA, *guarded*
EDMUND. Come hither, Captain; hark.

[*Giving a paper*] Take thou this note; go follow them to prison.
One step I have advanc'd thee; if thou dost
As this instructs thee, thou dost make thy way
To noble fortunes. Know thou this, that men
Are as the time is; to be tender-minded
Does not become a sword. Thy great employment
Will not bear question; either say thou'lt do't,
Or thrive by other means.

CAPTAIN. I'll do't, my lord.

EDMUND. About it; and write happy when th' hast done.
Mark—I say, instantly; and carry it so
As I have set it down.

CAPTAIN. I cannot draw a cart nor eat dried oats;
If it be man's work, I'll do't. *Exit*

Flourish. Enter ALBANY, GONERIL, REGAN, *and soldiers*

ALBANY. Sir, you have show'd to-day your valiant strain,
And fortune led you well. You have the captives
Who were the opposites of this day's strife;
I do require them of you, so to use them
As we shall find their merits and our safety
May equally determine.

EDMUND. Sir, I thought it fit
To send the old and miserable King
To some retention and appointed guard;
Whose age has charms in it, whose title more,
To pluck the common bosom on his side,
And turn our impress'd lances in our eyes
Which do command them. With him I sent the Queen,
My reason all the same; and they are ready
To-morrow, or at further space, t' appear
Where you shall hold your session. At this time
We sweat and bleed; the friend hath lost his friend
And the best quarrels, in the heat, are curs'd
By those that feel their sharpness.
The question of Cordelia and her father
Requires a fitter place.

ALBANY. Sir, by your patience,
I hold you but a subject of this war,

Not as a brother.

REGAN. That's as we list to grace him.
Methinks our pleasure might have been demanded
Ere you had spoke so far. He led our powers,
Bore the commission of my place and person,
The which immediacy may well stand up
And call itself your brother.

GONERIL. Not so hot.
In his own grace he doth exalt himself,
More than in your addition.

REGAN. In my rights,
By me invested, he compeers the best.

ALBANY. That were the most, if he should husband you.

REGAN. Jesters do oft prove prophets.

GONERIL. Holla, holla!
That eye that told you so look'd but asquint.

REGAN. Lady, I am not well; else I should answer
From a full-flowing stomach. General,
Take thou my soldiers, prisoners, patrimony;
Dispose of them, of me; the walls is thine.
Witness the world that I create thee here
My lord and master.

GONERIL. Mean you to enjoy him?

ALBANY. The let-alone lies not in your good will.

EDMUND. Nor in thine, lord.

ALBANY. Half-blooded fellow, yes.

REGAN. [*To* EDMUND] Let the drum strike, and prove my title thine.

ALBANY. Stay yet; hear reason. Edmund, I arrest thee
On capital treason; and, in thy attaint,
[*Pointing to* GONERIL]
This gilded serpent. For your claim, fair sister,
I bar it in the interest of my wife;
'Tis she is sub-contracted to this lord,
And I, her husband, contradict your banns.
If you will marry, make your loves to me—
My lady is bespoke.

GONERIL. An interlude!

ALBANY. Thou art arm'd, Gloster. Let the trumpet sound.
If none appear to prove upon thy person

Thy heinous, manifest, and many treasons,
There is my pledge; [*Throwing down a glove*]
I'll make it on thy heart,
Ere I taste bread, thou art in nothing less
Than I have here proclaim'd thee.

REGAN. Sick, O, sick!

GONERIL. [*Aside*] If not, I'll ne'er trust medicine.

EDMUND. There's my exchange. [*Throwing down a glove*]
What in the world he is
That names me traitor, villain-like he lies.
Call by thy trumpet: he that dares approach,
On him, on you, who not, I will maintain
My truth and honour firmly.

ALBANY. A herald, ho!

EDMUND. A herald, ho, a herald!

ALBANY. Trust to thy single virtue; for thy soldiers,
All levied in my name, have in my name
Took their discharge.

REGAN. My sickness grows upon me.

ALBANY. She is not well; convey her to my tent.

Exit REGAN, *led*

Enter a HERALD

Come hither, herald. Let the trumpet sound,
And read out this.

HERALD. [*Reads*] 'If any man of quality or degree within the lists of the army will maintain upon Edmund, supposed Earl of Gloucester, that he is a manifold traitor, let him appear by the third sound of the trumpet. He is bold in his defence.'

Sound, trumpet. [*First trumpet*]

HERALD. Again! [*Second trumpet*]

HERALD. Again! [*Third trumpet*]

[*Trumpet answers within*]

Enter EDGAR, *armed, at the third sound, a trumpet before him*

ALBANY. Ask him his purposes, why he appears
Upon this call o' th' trumpet.

HERALD. What are you?

Your name, your quality, and why you answer
This present summons?

EDGAR. Know, my name is lost,
By treason's tooth bare-gnawn and canker-bit;
Yet am I noble as the adversary
I come to cope.

ALBANY. Which is that adversary?

EDGAR. What's he that speaks for Edmund Earl of Gloucester?

EDMUND. Himself. What say'st thou to him?

EDGAR. Draw thy sword,
That, if my speech offend a noble heart,
Thy arm may do thee justice; here is mine.
Behold, it is the privilege of mine honours,
My oath, and my profession. I protest—
Maugre thy strength, youth, place, and eminence,
Despite thy victor sword and fire-new fortune,
Thy valour and thy heart—thou art a traitor;
False to thy gods, thy brother, and thy father;
Conspirant 'gainst this high illustrious prince;
And, from th' extremest upward of thy head
To the descent and dust below thy foot,
A most toad-spotted traitor. Say thou 'No,'
This sword, this arm, and my best spirits, are bent
To prove upon thy heart, whereto I speak,
Thou liest.

EDMUND. In wisdom I should ask thy name;
But, since thy outside looks so fair and warlike,
And that thy tongue some say of breeding breathes,
What safe and nicely I might well delay
By rule of knighthood, I disdain and spurn.
Back do I toss these treasons to thy head;
With the hell-hated lie o'erwhelm thy heart;
Which—for they yet glance by and scarcely bruise—
This sword of mine shall give them instant way
Where they shall rest for ever. Trumpets, speak.

[*Alarums. They fight.* EDMUND *falls*]

ALBANY. Save him, save him!

GONERIL. This is practice, Gloucester.
By th' law of war thou wast not bound to answer
An unknown opposite; thou art not vanquish'd,

But cozen'd and beguil'd.

ALBANY. Shut your mouth, dame,
Or with this paper shall I stopple it. Hold, sir.
Thou worse than any name, read thine own evil.
No tearing, lady; I perceive you know it.

GONERIL. Say, if I do–the laws are mine, not thine.
Who can arraign me for't?

ALBANY. Most monstrous! O
Know'st thou this paper?

GONERIL. Ask me not what I know. *Exit*

ALBANY. Go after her. She's desperate; govern her.
Exit an OFFICER

EDMUND. What you have charg'd me with, that have I done,
And more, much more; the time will bring it out.
'Tis past, and so am I. But what art thou
That hast this fortune on me? If thou'rt noble,
I do forgive thee.

EDGAR. Let's exchange charity.
I am no less in blood than thou art, Edmund;
If more, the more th' hast wrong'd me.
My name is Edgar, and thy father's son.
The gods are just, and of our pleasant vices
Make instruments to plague us:
The dark and vicious place where thee he got
Cost him his eyes.

EDMUND. Th' hast spoken right, 'tis true;
The wheel is come full circle; I am here.

ALBANY. Methought thy very gait did prophesy
A royal nobleness. I must embrace thee.
Let sorrow split my heart if ever I
Did hate thee or thy father!

EDGAR. Worthy prince, I know't.

ALBANY. Where have you hid yourself?
How have you known the miseries of your father?

EDGAR. By nursing them, my lord. List a brief tale;
And when 'tis told, O that my heart would burst!
The bloody proclamation to escape
That follow'd me so near–O our lives' sweetness,
That we the pain of death would hourly die
Rather than die at once!–taught me to shift

Into a madman's rags, t' assume a semblance
That very dogs disdain'd; and in this habit
Met I my father with his bleeding rings,
Their precious stones new lost; became his guide,
Led him, begg'd for him, sav'd him from despair;
Never—O fault!—reveal'd myself unto him
Until some half-hour past, when I was arm'd;
Not sure, though hoping, of this good success,
I ask'd his blessing, and from first to last
Told him my pilgrimage. But his flaw'd heart—
Alack, too weak the conflict to support!—
'Twixt two extremes of passion, joy and grief,
Burst smilingly.

EDMUND. This speech of yours hath mov'd me,
And shall perchance do good; but speak you on;
You look as you had something more to say.

ALBANY. If there be more, more woeful, hold it in;
For I am almost ready to dissolve,
Hearing of this.

EDGAR. This would have seem'd a period
To such as love not sorrow; but another,
To amplify too much, would make much more,
And top extremity.
Whilst I was big in clamour, came there in a man
Who, having seen me in my worst estate,
Shunn'd my abhorr'd society; but then, finding
Who 'twas that so endur'd, with his strong arms
He fastened on my neck and bellowed out
As he'd burst heaven; threw him on my father;
Told the most piteous tale of Lear and him
That ever ear receiv'd; which in recounting
His grief grew puissant, and the strings of life
Began to crack. Twice then the trumpets sounded
And there I left him tranc'd.

ALBANY. But who was this?

EDGAR. Kent, sir, the banish'd Kent, who in disguise
Follow'd his enemy King, and did him service
Improper for a slave.

Enter a GENTLEMAN *with a bloody knife*

GENTLEMAN. Help, help, O, help!
EDGAR. What kind of help?
ALBANY. Speak, man.
EDGAR. What means this bloody knife?
GENTLEMAN. 'Tis hot, it smokes;
It came even from the heart of—O, she's dead!
ALBANY. Who dead? Speak, man.
GENTLEMAN. Your lady, sir, your lady! and her sister
By her is poison'd; she confesses it.
EDMUND. I was contracted to them both. All three
Now marry in an instant.
EDGAR. Here comes Kent.

Enter KENT

ALBANY. Produce the bodies, be they alive or dead.
Exit GENTLEMAN
This judgment of the heavens, that makes us tremble,
Touches us not with pity. O, is this he?
The time will not allow the compliment
Which very manners urges.
KENT. I am come
To bid my King and master aye good night.
Is he not here?
ALBANY. Great thing of us forgot!
Speak, Edmund, where's the King? and where's Cordelia?
[*The bodies of* GONERIL *and* REGAN *are brought in*]
See'st thou this object, Kent?
KENT. Alack, why thus?
EDMUND. Yet Edmund was belov'd.
The one the other poison'd for my sake,
And after slew herself.
ALBANY. Even so. Cover their faces.
EDMUND. I pant for life. Some good I mean to do,
Despite of mine own nature. Quickly send—
Be brief in it—to th' castle; for my writ
Is on the life of Lear and on Cordelia.
Nay, send in time.
ALBANY. Run, run, O, run!
EDGAR. To who, my lord? Who has the office? Send
Thy token of reprieve.

EDMUND. Well thought on. Take my sword;
Give it the Captain.
ALBANY. Haste thee, for thy life. *Exit* EDGAR
EDMUND. He hath commission from thy wife and me
To hang Cordelia in the prison, and
To lay the blame upon her own despair,
That she fordid herself.
ALBANY. The gods defend her! Bear him hence awhile.
[EDMUND *is borne off*]

Enter LEAR, *with* CORDELIA *dead in his arms;* EDGAR, CAPTAIN, *and others following*

LEAR. Howl, howl, howl, howl! O, you are men of stones!
Had I your tongues and eyes, I'd use them so
That heaven's vault should crack. She's gone for ever.
I know when one is dead and when one lives;
She's dead as earth. Lend me a looking-glass;
If that her breath will mist or stain the stone,
Why, then she lives.
KENT. Is this the promis'd end?
EDGAR. Or image of that horror?
ALBANY. Fall and cease!
LEAR. This feather stirs; she lives. If it be so,
It is a chance which does redeem all sorrows
That ever I have felt.
KENT. O my good master! [*Kneeling*]
LEAR. Prithee away.
EDGAR. 'Tis noble Kent, your friend.
LEAR. A plague upon you, murderers, traitors all!
I might have sav'd her; now she's gone for ever.
Cordelia, Cordelia! stay a little. Ha!
What is't thou say'st? Her voice was ever soft,
Gentle, and low—an excellent thing in woman.
I kill'd the slave that was a-hanging thee.
CAPTAIN. 'Tis true, my lords, he did.
LEAR. Did I not, fellow?
I have seen the day, with my good biting falchion,
I would have made them skip: I am old now,
And these same crosses spoil me. Who are you?
Mine eyes are not o' th' best. I'll tell you straight.

KENT. If fortune brag of two she lov'd and hated,
  One of them we behold.
LEAR. This is a dull sight. Are you not Kent?
KENT. The same–
  Your servant Kent. Where is your servant Caius?
LEAR. He's a good fellow, I can tell you that;
  He'll strike, and quickly too. He's dead and rotten.
KENT. No, my good lord; I am the very man–
LEAR. I'll see that straight.
KENT. That from your first of difference and decay
  Have follow'd your sad steps.
LEAR. You are welcome hither.
KENT. Nor no man else! All's cheerless, dark, and deadly.
  Your eldest daughters have fordone themselves
  And desperately are dead.
LEAR. Ay, so I think.
ALBANY. He knows not what he says; and vain is it
  That we present us to him.
EDGAR. Very bootless.

Enter a MESSENGER

MESSENGER. Edmund is dead, my lord.
ALBANY. That's but a trifle here.
  You lords and noble friends, know our intent.
  What comfort to this great decay may come
  Shall be applied. For us, we will resign
  During the life of this old Majesty,
  To him our absolute power. [*To* EDGAR *and* KENT] You
    to your rights;
  With boot, and such addition as your honours
  Have more than merited. All friends shall taste
  The wages of their virtue, and all foes
  The cup of their deservings. O, see, see!
LEAR. And my poor fool is hang'd! No, no, no life!
  Why should a dog, a horse, a rat have life,
  And thou no breath at all? Thou'lt come no more,
  Never, never, never, never, never.
  Pray you undo this button. Thank you, sir.
  Do you see this? Look on her. Look, her lips.
  Look there, look there! [*He dies*]

LEAR. *Howl, howl, howl, howl! O, you are men of stones!*
Had I your tongues and eyes, I'd use them so
That heaven's vault should crack. She's gone for ever. . . .
Why should a dog, a horse, a rat have life,
And thou no breath at all? Thou'lt come no more,
Never, never, never, never, never.

(ACT V. Scene 3)

EDGAR. He faints. My lord, my lord!
KENT. Break, heart; I prithee break.
EDGAR. Look up, my lord.
KENT. Vex not his ghost. O, let him pass! He hates him
That would upon the rack of this tough world
Stretch him out longer.
EDGAR. He is gone indeed.
KENT. The wonder is he hath endur'd so long:
He but usurp'd his life.
ALBANY. Bear them from hence. Our present business
Is general woe. [*To* KENT *and* EDGAR] Friends of my soul, you twain
Rule in this realm and the gor'd state sustain.
KENT. I have a journey, sir, shortly to go.
My master calls me; I must not say no.
EDGAR. The weight of this sad time we must obey;
Speak what we feel, not what we ought to say.
The oldest hath borne most; we that are young
Shall never see so much nor live so long.

Exeunt with a dead march

The Tragedy of
Othello, the Moor of Venice

OTHELLO

How shakespeare hit upon the name Othello no one knows; for so far it has not been discovered in any document or printed work. Its very sound however carries with it something of the sense in which Shakespeare wished us to see the heroic character of the man.

In the Italian story, which Shakespeare found in Cinthio's *Hecatommithi* and from which he took the raw material for his plot, the only character given a name is Disdemona, her husband being always referred to as the Moor. How Cinthio envisaged his Moor is not clear, for only at one place does the Italian tell us of his colour: where the Ensign enforces his assertions that Disdemona loves the Captain by saying, 'your blackness already displeases her.' Shakespeare would have had to be more definite than this, since he was presenting his Moor on the stage; but in spite of the many references to Othello's colour and features commentators still argue about Shakespeare's intention.

There are two Moors in earlier plays by Shakespeare, Aaron in *Titus Andronicus* and the Prince of Morocco in *Merchant of Venice*. The first, Aaron, seems to have been presented on the stage as a Negro, for apart from such references as that to his 'fleece of woolly hair,' we have in the Peacham drawing [*Shakespeare Survey*, 1948] what is perhaps an early illustration of how he figured on the stage; if so, he was clearly made up as a Negro. E. K. Chambers, who was one of the first to emphasize the importance of this drawing, went so far as to say that this drawing should 'inform students of *Othello* as well as of *Titus*, that to the Elizabethan mind a Moor was not tawny but dead black.' He had, in his enthusiasm for his discovery, forgotten the stage direction in the first quarto (1600) of the *Merchant of Venice*, 'Enter *Morochus* a tawnie Moore all in white.' This is among other things a costume direction; it indicates the kind of robes to be worn by the Prince and his entourage; it also shows that the writer understood perfectly the difference between the black and the tawny Moor. As Dowden pointed out this distinction was accepted generally in the days of King James; 'For they make the river Senega to divide and bound the Moors, so that on the south side they are black, on the other only tawny.' The distinction must have been equally familiar to the Elizabethans, as a recent acquisition by the Shakespeare Institute at Stratford-upon-Avon makes evident.

On 8 August 1600 there arrived at Dover an embassy from Muley Hamet, King of Barbary, headed by Abd el-Ouahed. The ambassador and his party remained in England for some six months, attracting a good deal of comment and causing not a little embarrassment in official circles. The story of their stay is told, and the portrait painted of the ambassador in 1600 illustrated, in *Shakespeare Survey*, 1958. As Mr. Bernard Harris says there: 'Through all the ambiguity of terminology and stage tradition the portrait of the Moorish ambassador reminds us of the common acquaintance of the Elizabethans with real, as distinct from fictional, Moors.' The hand that penned the stage direction about the 'tawny Moore' belonged to someone who was aware of the distinction between real and fictional Moors.

The embassy, though it accomplished little, helped to expedite the exchange of prisoners between England and Barbary, for an order followed by the Privy Council deporting 'negars and blackamoores'; many of these Moorish captives must have been tawny. Elizabethan terminology may be ambiguous but it is obvious that the educated public could distinguish quite clearly between a Berber and a Negro.

The portrait of the Moorish ambassador and the story of his embassy, when added to the evidence provided by the stage direction from *Merchant of Venice*, while they do not settle for us the particular choice of make-up Shakespeare decided on for his Othello, show that the question about his race is still an open one.

For answering this question Mr. Bernard Harris provides two suggestions. Emphasizing the deep difference between the Londoners and their visitors he says: 'To Elizabethan Londoners the appearance and conduct of the Moors was a spectacle and an outrage.' To present Othello as a Moor rather than a Negro would not then have destroyed for Londoners the sense of incompatibility that Shakespeare required as one element in the attitude of a contemporary audience to the marriage of the Moor and the Venetian lady. So imperfect were the sympathies between the Londoners and the Moors that Mr. Bernard Harris adds: 'Cinthio's is not the whole tale after all; the fundamental dramatic contrast of racial difference is Shakespeare's first departure from his source.' But this contrast was the very point of Cinthio's story, as Professor Dover Wilson has emphasized by drawing attention to Cinthio's introductory discourse to the tales; for the story Shakespeare drew on was to illustrate the dangers of a marriage between those of different race and with a different manner of life. These, however, were the very circumstances that Shakespeare saw would provide the ideal foundation for a drama that would show how these differences so far from being impediments to the marriage of true minds were elements whose fusion would demonstrate the great triumph of love. This triumph Shakespeare shows us in Desdemona's dying words and in the manner of Othello's death. Shakespeare does not allow the attitude adopted by Cinthio's Disdemona, who regards her unhappiness as a warning against a marriage such as hers, to point the moral of Desdemona's fate; for her marriage is one that conquers all that the wickedness of the world and the ignorance of man can do against it.

Shakespeare arranges his time scheme so that we see both the monstrous nature of the slander to which Desdemona is subjected and the peculiarity of the circumstances that gave it plausibility. In art the impression is the fact and Shakespeare has enforced the impression with a dramatic tact that matches his imaginative understanding.

Duke of Venice
Brabantio, *a Senator, father to Desdemona*
Other Senators
Gratiano, *brother to Brabantio* } *two noble Venetians*
Lodovico, *kinsman to Brabantio* }
Othello, *the Moor, in the service of Venice*
Cassio, *his honourable Lieutenant*
Iago, *his Ancient, a villain*
Roderigo, *a gulled Venetian gentleman*
Montano, *Governor of Cyprus, before Othello*
Clown, *servant to Othello*

Desdemona, *daughter to Brabantio, and wife to Othello*
Emilia, *wife to Iago*
Bianca, *a courtezan, in love with Cassio*

Gentlemen of Cyprus, Sailors, Officers, Messengers, Musicians, Herald, Attendants, *&c.*

SCENE:

Venice; Cyprus

Othello, the Moor of Venice

ACT I. SCENE 1

Venice. A street

Enter Roderigo *and* Iago

Roderigo. Tush, never tell me; I take it much unkindly
That you, Iago, who has had my purse
As if the strings were thine, shouldst know of this.
Iago. 'Sblood, but you will not hear me.
If ever I did dream of such a matter,
Abhor me.
Roderigo. Thou told'st me thou didst hold him in thy hate.
Iago. Despise me if I do not. Three great ones of the city,
In personal suit to make me his lieutenant,
Off-capp'd to him; and, by the faith of man,
I know my price, I am worth no worse a place.
But he, as loving his own pride and purposes,
Evades them with a bombast circumstance
Horribly stuff'd with epithets of war;
And, in conclusion,
Nonsuits my mediators; 'For, certes,' says he,
'I have already chose my officer.'
And what was he?
Forsooth, a great arithmetician,
One Michael Cassio, a Florentine,
A fellow almost damn'd in a fair wife,
That never set a squadron in the field,
Nor the division of a battle knows
More than a spinster; unless the bookish theoric,
Wherein the toged consuls can propose
As masterly as he—mere prattle, without practice,
Is all his soldiership. But he, sir, had the election;
And I, of whom his eyes had seen the proof
At Rhodes, at Cyprus, and on other grounds,
Christian and heathen, must be be-lee'd and calm'd

By debitor and creditor—this counter-caster,
He, in good time, must his lieutenant be,
And I, God bless the mark! his Moorship's ancient.

RODERIGO. By heaven, I rather would have been his hangman!

IAGO. Why, there's no remedy; 'tis the curse of service:
Preferment goes by letter and affection,
Not by the old gradation, where each second
Stood heir to the first. Now, sir, be judge yourself
Whether I in any just term am affin'd
To love the Moor.

RODERIGO. I would not follow him, then.

IAGO. O, sir, content you.
I follow him to serve my turn upon him:
We cannot all be masters, nor all masters
Cannot be truly follow'd. You shall mark
Many a duteous and knee-crooking knave
That, doting on his own obsequious bondage,
Wears out his time, much like his master's ass,
For nought but provender; and when he's old, cashier'd.
Whip me such honest knaves. Others there are
Who, trimm'd in forms and visages of duty,
Keep yet their hearts attending on themselves;
And, throwing but shows of service on their lords,
Do well thrive by 'em and, when they have lin'd their coats,
Do themselves homage—these fellows have some soul;
And such a one do I profess myself.
For, sir,
It is as sure as you are Roderigo,
Were I the Moor, I would not be Iago.
In following him I follow but myself—
Heaven is my judge, not I for love and duty,
But seeming so for my peculiar end.
For when my outward action doth demonstrate
The native act and figure of my heart
In compliment extern, 'tis not long after
But I will wear my heart upon my sleeve
For daws to peck at: I am not what I am.

RODERIGO. What a full fortune does the thick-lips owe,

If he can carry't thus!
IAGO. Call up her father.
Rouse him, make after him, poison his delight,
Proclaim him in the streets; incense her kinsmen,
And, though he in a fertile climate dwell,
Plague him with flies; though that his joy be joy,
Yet throw such changes of vexation on't
As it may lose some colour.
RODERIGO. Here is her father's house. I'll call aloud.
IAGO. Do, with like timorous accent and dire yell
As when, by night and negligence, the fire
Is spied in populous cities.
RODERIGO. What, ho, Brabantio! Signior Brabantio, ho!
IAGO. Awake! What, ho, Brabantio! Thieves, thieves, thieves!
Look to your house, your daughter, and your bags.
Thieves! thieves!

BRABANTIO *appears above at a window*

BRABANTIO. What is the reason of this terrible summons?
What is the matter there?
RODERIGO. Signior, is all your family within?
IAGO. Are your doors lock'd?
BRABANTIO. Why, wherefore ask you this?
IAGO. Zounds, sir, you're robb'd; for shame, put on your gown;
Your heart is burst; you have lost half your soul.
Even now, now, very now, an old black ram
Is tupping your white ewe. Arise, arise;
Awake the snorting citizens with the bell,
Or else the devil will make a grandsire of you.
Arise, I say.
BRABANTIO. What, have you lost your wits?
RODERIGO. Most reverend signior, do you know my voice?
BRABANTIO. Not I; what are you?
RODERIGO. My name is Roderigo.
BRABANTIO. The worser welcome!
I have charg'd thee not to haunt about my doors;
In honest plainness thou hast heard me say
My daughter is not for thee; and now, in madness,
Being full of supper and distempering draughts,

Upon malicious bravery dost thou come
To start my quiet.

RODERIGO. Sir, sir, sir—

BRABANTIO. But thou must needs be sure
My spirit and my place have in their power
To make this bitter to thee.

RODERIGO. Patience, good sir.

BRABANTIO. What tell'st thou me of robbing? This is Venice;
My house is not a grange.

RODERIGO. Most grave Brabantio,
In simple and pure soul I come to you.

IAGO. Zounds, sir, you are one of those that will not serve God if the devil bid you. Because we come to do you service, and you think we are ruffians, you'll have your daughter cover'd with a Barbary horse; you'll have your nephews neigh to you; you'll have coursers for cousins and gennets for germans.

BRABANTIO. What profane wretch art thou?

IAGO. I am one, sir, that comes to tell you your daughter and the Moor are now making the beast with two backs.

BRABANTIO. Thou art a villain.

IAGO. You are—a Senator.

BRABANTIO. This thou shalt answer; I know thee, Roderigo.

RODERIGO. Sir, I will answer anything. But I beseech you,
If't be your pleasure and most wise consent—
As partly I find it is—that your fair daughter,
At this odd-even and dull watch o' th' night,
Transported with no worse nor better guard
But with a knave of common hire, a gondolier,
To the gross clasps of a lascivious Moor—
If this be known to you, and your allowance,
We then have done you bold and saucy wrongs;
But if you know not this, my manners tell me
We have your wrong rebuke. Do not believe
That, from the sense of all civility,
I thus would play and trifle with your reverence.
Your daughter, if you have not given her leave,
I say again, hath made a gross revolt;
Tying her duty, beauty, wit, and fortunes,
In an extravagant and wheeling stranger

Of here and everywhere. Straight satisfy yourself.
If she be in her chamber or your house,
Let loose on me the justice of the state
For thus deluding you.

BRABANTIO. Strike on the tinder, ho!
Give me a taper; call up all my people.
This accident is not unlike my dream.
Belief of it oppresses me already.
Light, I say; light! *Exit from above*

IAGO. Farewell; for I must leave you.
It seems not meet nor wholesome to my place
To be producted—as if I stay I shall—
Against the Moor; for I do know the state,
However this may gall him with some check,
Cannot with safety cast him; for he's embark'd
With such loud reason to the Cyprus wars,
Which even now stands in act, that, for their souls,
Another of his fathom they have none
To lead their business; in which regard,
Though I do hate him as I do hell pains,
Yet, for necessity of present life,
I must show out a flag and sign of love,
Which is indeed but sign. That you shall surely find him,
Lead to the Sagittary the raised search;
And there will I be with him. So, farewell. *Exit*

Enter below, BRABANTIO, *in his night gown, and servants with torches*

BRABANTIO. It is too true an evil. Gone she is;
And what's to come of my despised time
Is nought but bitterness. Now, Roderigo,
Where didst thou see her?—O unhappy girl!—
With the Moor, say'st thou?—Who would be a father?—
How didst thou know 'twas she?—O, thou deceivest me
Past thought!—What said she to you?—Get moe tapers;
Raise all my kindred.—Are they married, think you?

RODERIGO. Truly, I think they are.

BRABANTIO. O heaven! How got she out? O treason of the blood!
Fathers, from hence trust not your daughters' minds

By what you see them act. Is there not charms
By which the property of youth and maidhood
May be abus'd? Have you not read, Roderigo,
Of some such thing?

RODERIGO. Yes, sir, I have indeed.

BRABANTIO. Call up my brother.—O that you had had her!—
Some one way, some another.—Do you know
Where we may apprehend her and the Moor?

RODERIGO. I think I can discover him, if you please
To get good guard, and go along with me.

BRABANTIO. Pray lead me on. At every house I'll call;
I may command at most.—Get weapons, ho!
And raise some special officers of night.—
On, good Roderigo; I'll deserve your pains. *Exeunt*

SCENE 2

Venice. Another street

Enter OTHELLO, IAGO, *and attendants with torches*

IAGO. Though in the trade of war I have slain men,
Yet do I hold it very stuff o' th' conscience
To do no contriv'd murder. I lack iniquity
Sometime to do me service. Nine or ten times
I had thought to have yerk'd him here under the ribs.

OTHELLO. 'Tis better as it is.

IAGO. Nay, but he prated,
And spoke such scurvy and provoking terms
Against your honour
That, with the little godliness I have,
I did full hard forbear him. But I pray, sir,
Are you fast married? For be assur'd of this,
That the magnifico is much beloved,
And hath in his effect a voice potential
As double as the Duke's. He will divorce you,
Or put upon you what restraint and grievance
That law, with all his might to enforce it on,
Will give him cable.

OTHELLO. Let him do his spite.

My services which I have done the signiory
Shall out-tongue his complaints. 'Tis yet to know—
Which, when I know that boasting is an honour,
I shall promulgate—I fetch my life and being
From men of royal siege; and my demerits
May speak unbonneted to as proud a fortune
As this that I have reach'd. For know, Iago,
But that I love the gentle Desdemona,
I would not my unhoused free condition
Put into circumscription and confine
For the seas' worth.

Enter CASSIO *and* OFFICERS *with torches*

But look what lights come yonder.
IAGO. Those are the raised father and his friends.
You were best go in.
OTHELLO. Not I; I must be found.
My parts, my title, and my perfect soul
Shall manifest me rightly. Is it they?
IAGO. By Janus, I think no.
OTHELLO. The servants of the Duke and my lieutenant—
The goodness of the night upon you, friends!
What is the news?
CASSIO. The Duke does greet you, General;
And he requires your haste-post-haste appearance
Even on the instant.
OTHELLO. What is the matter, think you?
CASSIO. Something from Cyprus, as I may divine.
It is a business of some heat: the galleys
Have sent a dozen sequent messengers
This very night at one another's heels;
And many of the consuls, rais'd and met,
Are at the Duke's already. You have been hotly call'd for;
When, being not at your lodging to be found,
The Senate hath sent about three several quests
To search you out.
OTHELLO. 'Tis well I am found by you.
I will but spend a word here in the house,
And go with you. *Exit*
CASSIO. Ancient, what makes he here?

IAGO. Faith, he to-night hath boarded a land carrack.
If it prove lawful prize, he's made for ever.
CASSIO. I do not understand.
IAGO. He's married.
CASSIO. To who?

Re-enter OTHELLO

IAGO. Marry, to—Come, Captain, will you go?
OTHELLO. Have with you.

Enter BRABANTIO, RODERIGO, *and* OFFICERS *with torches and weapons*

CASSIO. Here comes another troop to seek for you.
IAGO. It is Brabantio. General, be advis'd;
He comes to bad intent.
OTHELLO. Holla! stand there.
RODERIGO. Signior, it is the Moor.
BRABANTIO. Down with him, thief.

[*They draw on both sides*]

IAGO. You, Roderigo; come, sir, I am for you.
OTHELLO. Keep up your bright swords, for the dew will rust them.
Good signior, you shall more command with years
Than with your weapons.
BRABANTIO. O thou foul thief, where hast thou stow'd my daughter?
Damn'd as thou art, thou hast enchanted her;
For I'll refer me to all things of sense,
If she in chains of magic were not bound,
Whether a maid so tender, fair, and happy,
So opposite to marriage that she shunn'd
The wealthy curled darlings of our nation,
Would ever have, to incur a general mock,
Run from her guardage to the sooty bosom
Of such a thing as thou—to fear, not to delight.
Judge me the world, if 'tis not gross in sense
That thou hast practis'd on her with foul charms,
Abus'd her delicate youth with drugs or minerals
That weakens motion. I'll have't disputed on;
'Tis probable, and palpable to thinking.

I therefore apprehend and do attach thee
For an abuser of the world, a practiser
Of arts inhibited and out of warrant.
Lay hold upon him. If he do resist,
Subdue him at his peril.

OTHELLO. Hold your hands,
Both you of my inclining and the rest.
Were it my cue to fight, I should have known it
Without a prompter. Where will you that I go
To answer this your charge?

BRABANTIO. To prison; till fit time
Of law and course of direct session
Call thee to answer.

OTHELLO. What if I do obey?
How may the Duke be therewith satisfied,
Whose messengers are here about my side,
Upon some present business of the state,
To bring me to him.

FIRST OFFICER. 'Tis true, most worthy signior;
The Duke's in council, and your noble self,
I am sure, is sent for.

BRABANTIO. How! The Duke in council!
In this time of the night! Bring him away.
Mine's not an idle cause. The Duke himself,
Or any of my brothers of the state,
Cannot but feel this wrong as 'twere their own;
For if such actions may have passage free,
Bond-slaves and pagans shall our statesmen be. *Exeunt*

SCENE 3

Venice. A council-chamber

Enter DUKE *and* SENATORS, *set at a table with lights; and attendants*

DUKE. There is no composition in these news
That gives them credit.

FIRST SENATOR. Indeed, they are disproportion'd;
My letters say a hundred and seven galleys.

DUKE. And mine a hundred and forty.
SECOND SENATOR. And mine two hundred.
But though they jump not on a just account–
As in these cases, where the aim reports,
'Tis oft with difference–yet do they all confirm
A Turkish fleet, and bearing up to Cyprus.
DUKE. Nay, it is possible enough to judgment.
I do not so secure me in the error
But the main article I do approve
In fearful sense.
SAILOR. [*Within*] What, ho! what, ho! what, ho!

Enter SAILOR

OFFICER. A messenger from the galleys.
DUKE. Now, what's the business?
SAILOR. The Turkish preparation makes for Rhodes;
So was I bid report here to the state
By Signior Angelo.
DUKE. How say you by this change?
FIRST SENATOR. This cannot be,
By no assay of reason. 'Tis a pageant
To keep us in false gaze. When we consider
The importancy of Cyprus to the Turk,
And let ourselves again but understand
That as it more concerns the Turk than Rhodes,
So may he with more facile question bear it,
For that it stands not in such warlike brace,
But altogether lacks th' abilities
That Rhodes is dress'd in–if we make thought of this,
We must not think the Turk is so unskilful
To leave that latest which concerns him first,
Neglecting an attempt of ease and gain
To wake and wage a danger profitless.
DUKE. Nay, in all confidence, he's not for Rhodes.
OFFICER. Here is more news.

Enter a MESSENGER

MESSENGER. The Ottomites, reverend and gracious,
Steering with due course toward the isle of Rhodes,
Have there injointed them with an after fleet.

FIRST SENATOR. Ay, so I thought. How many, as you guess?
MESSENGER. Of thirty sail; and now they do restem
Their backward course, bearing with frank appearance
Their purposes toward Cyprus. Signior Montano,
Your trusty and most valiant servitor,
With his free duty recommends you thus,
And prays you to believe him.
DUKE. 'Tis certain, then, for Cyprus.
Marcus Lucchese, is not he in town?
FIRST SENATOR. He's now in Florence.
DUKE. Write from us: wish him post-post-haste dispatch.

Enter BRABANTIO, OTHELLO, IAGO, RODERIGO, *and* OFFICERS

FIRST SENATOR. Here comes Brabantio and the valiant Moor.
DUKE. Valiant Othello, we must straight employ you
Against the general enemy Ottoman.
[*To* BRABANTIO] I did not see you; welcome, gentle signior;
We lack'd your counsel and your help to-night.
BRABANTIO. So did I yours. Good your Grace, pardon me:
Neither my place, nor aught I heard of business,
Hath rais'd me from my bed; nor doth the general care
Take hold on me; for my particular grief
Is of so flood-gate and o'erbearing nature
That it engluts and swallows other sorrows,
And it is still itself.
DUKE. Why, what's the matter?
BRABANTIO. My daughter! O, my daughter!
ALL. Dead?
BRABANTIO. Ay, to me.
She is abus'd, stol'n from me, and corrupted,
By spells and medicines bought of mountebanks;
For nature so preposterously to err,
Being not deficient, blind, or lame of sense,
Sans witchcraft could not.
DUKE. Whoe'er he be that in this foul proceeding
Hath thus beguil'd your daughter of herself,
And you of her, the bloody book of law
You shall yourself read in the bitter letter

After your own sense; yea, though our proper son
Stood in your action.

BRABANTIO. Humbly I thank your Grace.
Here is the man—this Moor whom now, it seems,
Your special mandate for the state affairs
Hath hither brought.

ALL. We are very sorry for't.

DUKE. [*To* OTHELLO] What, in your own part, can you say to this?

BRABANTIO. Nothing, but this is so.

OTHELLO. Most potent, grave, and reverend signiors,
My very noble and approv'd good masters:
That I have ta'en away this old man's daughter,
It is most true; true, I have married her—
The very head and front of my offending
Hath this extent, no more. Rude am I in my speech,
And little blest with the soft phrase of peace;
For since these arms of mine had seven years' pith,
Till now some nine moons wasted, they have us'd
Their dearest action in the tented field;
And little of this great world can I speak
More than pertains to feats of broil and battle;
And therefore little shall I grace my cause
In speaking for myself. Yet, by your gracious patience,
I will a round unvarnish'd tale deliver
Of my whole course of love—what drugs, what charms,
What conjuration, and what mighty magic,
For such proceedings am I charg'd withal,
I won his daughter.

BRABANTIO. A maiden never bold,
Of spirit so still and quiet that her motion
Blush'd at herself; and she—in spite of nature,
Of years, of country, credit, every thing—
To fall in love with what she fear'd to look on!
It is a judgment maim'd and most imperfect
That will confess perfection so could err
Against all rules of nature, and must be driven
To find out practices of cunning hell,
Why this should be. I therefore vouch again
That with some mixtures powerful o'er the blood,

Or with some dram conjur'd to this effect,
He wrought upon her.

DUKE. To vouch this is no proof—
Without more wider and more overt test
Than these thin habits and poor likelihoods
Of modern seeming do prefer against him.

FIRST SENATOR. But, Othello, speak.
Did you by indirect and forced courses
Subdue and poison this young maid's affections?
Or came it by request, and such fair question
As soul to soul affordeth?

OTHELLO. I do beseech you,
Send for the lady to the Sagittary,
And let her speak of me before her father.
If you do find me foul in her report,
The trust, the office, I do hold of you
Not only take away, but let your sentence
Even fall upon my life.

DUKE. Fetch Desdemona hither.

OTHELLO. Ancient, conduct them; you best know the place.
Exeunt IAGO *and attendants*
And, till she come, as faithful as to heaven
I do confess the vices of my blood,
So justly to your grave ears I'll present
How I did thrive in this fair lady's love,
And she in mine.

DUKE. Say it, Othello.

OTHELLO. Her father lov'd me, oft invited me;
Still questioned me the story of my life
From year to year—the battles, sieges, fortunes,
That I have pass'd.
I ran it through, even from my boyish days
To th' very moment that he bade me tell it;
Wherein I spake of most disastrous chances,
Of moving accidents by flood and field;
Of hairbreadth scapes i' th' imminent deadly breach;
Of being taken by the insolent foe
And sold to slavery; of my redemption thence,
And portance in my travel's history;
Wherein of antres vast and deserts idle,

Rough quarries, rocks, and hills whose heads touch heaven,
It was my hint to speak—such was the process;
And of the Cannibals that each other eat,
The Anthropophagi, and men whose heads
Do grow beneath their shoulders. This to hear
Would Desdemona seriously incline;
But still the house affairs would draw her thence;
Which ever as she could with haste dispatch,
She'd come again, and with a greedy ear
Devour up my discourse. Which I observing,
Took once a pliant hour, and found good means
To draw from her a prayer of earnest heart
That I would all my pilgrimage dilate,
Whereof by parcels she had something heard,
But not intentively. I did consent,
And often did beguile her of her tears,
When I did speak of some distressful stroke
That my youth suffered. My story being done,
She gave me for my pains a world of sighs;
She swore, in faith, 'twas strange, 'twas passing strange;
'Twas pitiful, 'twas wondrous pitiful.
She wish'd she had not heard it; yet she wish'd
That heaven had made her such a man. She thank'd me;
And bade me, if I had a friend that lov'd her,
I should but teach him how to tell my story,
And that would woo her. Upon this hint I spake;
She lov'd me for the dangers I had pass'd;
And I lov'd her that she did pity them.
This only is the witchcraft I have us'd.
Here comes the lady; let her witness it.

Enter DESDEMONA, IAGO, *and attendants*

DUKE. I think this tale would win my daughter too.
Good Brabantio,
Take up this mangled matter at the best.
Men do their broken weapons rather use
Than their bare hands.

BRABANTIO. I pray you hear her speak.

If she confess that she was half the wooer,
Destruction on my head if my bad blame
Light on the man! Come hither, gentle mistress.
Do you perceive in all this noble company
Where most you owe obedience?

DESDEMONA. My noble father,
I do perceive here a divided duty:
To you I am bound for life and education;
My life and education both do learn me
How to respect you; you are the lord of duty—
I am hitherto your daughter; but here's my husband,
And so much duty as my mother show'd
To you, preferring you before her father,
So much I challenge that I may profess
Due to the Moor, my lord.

BRABANTIO. God bu'y, I ha done.
Please it your Grace, on to the state affairs—
I had rather to adopt a child than get it.
Come hither, Moor:
I here do give thee that with all my heart
Which, but thou hast already, with all my heart
I would keep from thee. For your sake, jewel,
I am glad at soul I have no other child;
For thy escape would teach me tyranny,
To hang clogs on them. I have done, my lord.

DUKE. Let me speak like yourself, and lay a sentence
Which, as a grise or step, may help these lovers
Into your favour.
When remedies are past, the griefs are ended
By seeing the worst, which late on hopes depended.
To mourn a mischief that is past and gone
Is the next way to draw new mischief on.
What cannot be preserv'd when fortune takes,
Patience her injury a mockery makes.
The robb'd that smiles steals something from the thief;
He robs himself that spends a bootless grief.

BRABANTIO. So let the Turk of Cyprus us beguile:
We lose it not so long as we can smile.
He bears the sentence well that nothing bears
But the free comfort which from thence he hears;

But he bears both the sentence and the sorrow
That to pay grief must of poor patience borrow.
These sentences, to sugar or to gall,
Being strong on both sides, are equivocal.
But words are words: I never yet did hear
That the bruis'd heart was pierced through the ear.
I humbly beseech you proceed to th' affairs of state.

DUKE. The Turk with a most mighty preparation makes for Cyprus. Othello, the fortitude of the place is best known to you; and though we have there a substitute of most allowed sufficiency, yet opinion, a sovereign mistress of effects, throws a more safer voice on you. You must therefore be content to slubber the gloss of your new fortunes with this more stubborn and boisterous expedition.

OTHELLO. The tyrant custom, most grave senators,
Hath made the flinty and steel couch of war
My thrice-driven bed of down. I do agnize
A natural and prompt alacrity
I find in hardness; and would undertake
This present wars against the Ottomites.
Most humbly, therefore, bending to your state,
I crave fit disposition for my wife;
Due reference of place and exhibition;
With such accommodation and besort
As levels with her breeding.

DUKE. If you please,
Be't at her father's.

BRABANTIO. I'll not have it so.

OTHELLO. Nor I.

DESDEMONA. Nor I. I would not there reside,
To put my father in impatient thoughts
By being in his eye. Most gracious Duke,
To my unfolding lend your prosperous ear,
And let me find a charter in your voice
T' assist my simpleness.

DUKE. What would you, Desdemona?

DESDEMONA. That I did love the Moor to live with him,
My downright violence and storm of fortunes
May trumpet to the world. My heart's subdu'd
Even to the very quality of my lord:

I saw Othello's visage in his mind;
And to his honours and his valiant parts
Did I my soul and fortunes consecrate.
So that, dear lords, if I be left behind,
A moth of peace, and he go to the war,
The rites for why I love him are bereft me,
And I a heavy interim shall support
By his dear absence. Let me go with him.

OTHELLO. Let her have your voice.
Vouch with me, heaven, I therefore beg it not
To please the palate of my appetite;
Nor to comply with heat—the young affects
In me defunct—and proper satisfaction;
But to be free and bounteous to her mind.
And heaven defend your good souls that you think
I will your serious and great business scant
For she is with me. No, when light-wing'd toys
Of feather'd Cupid seel with wanton dullness
My speculative and offic'd instruments,
That my disports corrupt and taint my business,
Let huswives make a skillet of my helm,
And all indign and base adversities
Make head against my estimation!

DUKE. Be it as you shall privately determine,
Either for her stay or going. Th' affair cries haste,
And speed must answer it. You must away to-night.

DESDEMONA. To-night, my lord!

DUKE. This night.

OTHELLO. With all my heart.

DUKE. At nine i' th' morning here we'll meet again.
Othello, leave some officer behind,
And he shall our commission bring to you;
With such things else of quality and respect
As doth import you.

OTHELLO. So please your Grace, my ancient;
A man he is of honesty and trust.
To his conveyance I assign my wife,
With what else needful your good Grace shall think
To be sent after me.

DUKE. Let it be so.

Good night to every one. [*To* BRABANTIO] And, noble signior,
If virtue no delighted beauty lack,
Your son-in-law is far more fair than black.

FIRST SENATOR. Adieu, brave Moor; use Desdemona well.

BRABANTIO. Look to her, Moor, if thou hast eyes to see:
She has deceiv'd her father, and may thee.

Exeunt DUKE, SENATORS, OFFICERS, *&c.*

OTHELLO. My life upon her faith!—Honest Iago,
My Desdemona must I leave to thee.
I prithee let thy wife attend on her;
And bring them after in the best advantage.
Come, Desdemona, I have but an hour
Of love, of worldly matter and direction,
To spend with thee. We must obey the time.

Exeunt OTHELLO *and* DESDEMONA

RODERIGO. Iago!

IAGO. What say'st thou, noble heart?

RODERIGO. What will I do, thinkest thou?

IAGO. Why, go to bed and sleep.

RODERIGO. I will incontinently drown myself.

IAGO. Well, if thou dost, I shall never love thee after it. Why, thou silly gentleman!

RODERIGO. It is silliness to live when to live is torment; and then have we a prescription to die when death is our physician.

IAGO. O villainous! I ha look'd upon the world for four times seven years; and since I could distinguish betwixt a benefit and an injury, I never found a man that knew how to love himself. Ere I would say I would drown myself for the love of a guinea-hen, I would change my humanity with a baboon.

RODERIGO. What should I do? I confess it is my shame to be so fond, but it is not in my virtue to amend it.

IAGO. Virtue? A fig! 'Tis in ourselves that we are thus or thus. Our bodies are our gardens to the which our wills are gardeners; so that if we will plant nettles or sow lettuce, set hyssop and weed up thyme, supply it with one gender of herbs or distract it with many, either to have it sterile with idleness or manur'd with industry—why, the power and corrigible authority of this lies in our wills. If the balance of our lives had not one scale of reason to poise another of sensuality, the blood and baseness of our natures would conduct us to most preposterous conclusions. But we have reason to cool our raging motions, our carnal stings, our unbitted lusts; whereof I take this that you call love to be a sect or scion.

RODERIGO. It cannot be.

IAGO. It is merely a lust of the blood and a permission of the will. Come, be a man. Drown thyself? Drown cats and blind puppies! I have profess'd me thy friend, and I confess me knit to thy deserving with cables of perdurable toughness. I could never better stead thee than now. Put money in thy purse; follow thou the wars; defeat thy favour with an usurp'd beard. I say, put money in thy purse. It cannot be long that Desdemona should continue her love to the Moor—put money in thy purse—nor he his to her: it was a violent commencement in her, and thou shalt see an answerable sequestration—put but money in thy purse. These Moors are changeable in their wills—fill thy purse with money. The food that to him now is as luscious as locusts shall be to him shortly as acerbe as the coloquintida. She must change for youth; when she is sated with his body, she will find the error of her choice. Therefore put money in thy purse. If thou wilt needs damn thyself, do it a more delicate way than drowning. Make all the money thou canst. If sanctimony and a frail vow betwixt an erring barbarian and a supersubtle Venetian be not too hard for my wits and all the tribe of hell, thou shalt enjoy her; therefore make money. A pox a drowning thyself! 'Tis clean out of the way. Seek thou rather to be hang'd in compassing thy joy than to be drown'd and go without her.

RODERIGO. Wilt thou be fast to my hopes, if I depend on the issue?

IAGO. Thou art sure of me—go make money. I have told thee often, and I retell thee again and again I hate the Moor. My cause is hearted: thine hath no less reason. Let us be conjunctive in our revenge against him. If thou canst cuckold him, thou dost thyself a pleasure, me a sport.

There are many events in the womb of time which will be delivered. Traverse; go; provide thy money. We will have more of this to-morrow. Adieu.

RODERIGO. Where shall we meet i' th' morning?

IAGO. At my lodging.

RODERIGO. I'll be with thee betimes.

IAGO. Go to; farewell. Do you hear, Roderigo?

RODERIGO. What say you?

IAGO. No more of drowning, do you hear?

RODERIGO. I am chang'd.

IAGO. Go to; farewell. Put money enough in your purse.

RODERIGO. I'll sell all my land. *Exit* RODERIGO

IAGO. Thus do I ever make my fool my purse;
For I mine own gain'd knowledge should profane
If I would time expend with such a snipe
But for my sport and profit. I hate the Moor;
And it is thought abroad that 'twixt my sheets
'Has done my office. I know not if't be true;
Yet I, for mere suspicion in that kind,
Will do as if for surety. He holds me well;
The better shall my purpose work on him.
Cassio's a proper man. Let me see now:
To get his place, and to plume up my will
In double knavery. How, how? Let's see:
After some time to abuse Othello's ear
That he is too familiar with his wife.
He hath a person and a smooth dispose
To be suspected–fram'd to make women false.
The Moor is of a free and open nature
That thinks men honest that but seem to be so;
And will as tenderly be led by th' nose
As asses are.
I ha't–it is engender'd. Hell and night
Must bring this monstrous birth to the world's light. *Exit*

ACT II. SCENE 1

Cyprus. A sea-port

Enter MONTANO, *Governor of Cyprus, with two other* GENTLEMEN

MONTANO. What from the cape can you discern at sea?
FIRST GENTLEMAN. Nothing at all; it is a high-wrought flood.
I cannot 'twixt the heaven and the main
Descry a sail.
MONTANO. Methinks the wind hath spoke aloud at land;
A fuller blast ne'er shook our battlements.
If it ha ruffian'd so upon the sea,
What ribs of oak, when mountains melt on them,
Can hold the mortise? What shall we hear of this?
SECOND GENTLEMAN. A segregation of the Turkish fleet.
For do but stand upon the banning shore,
The chidden billow seems to pelt the clouds;
The wind-shak'd surge, with high and monstrous mane,
Seems to cast water on the burning Bear,
And quench the guards of th' ever-fired pole.
I never did like molestation view
On the enchafed flood.
MONTANO. If that the Turkish fleet
Be not enshelter'd and embay'd, they are drown'd:
It is impossible they bear it out.

Enter a third GENTLEMAN

THIRD GENTLEMAN. News, lads! Your wars are done.
The desperate tempest hath so bang'd the Turk
That their designment halts. A noble ship of Venice
Hath seen a grievous wreck and sufferance
On most part of their fleet.
MONTANO. How! Is this true?
THIRD GENTLEMAN. The ship is here put in,
A Veronesa; Michael Cassio,
Lieutenant to the warlike Moor Othello,
Is come ashore: the Moor himself at sea,
And is in full commission here for Cyprus.

MONTANO. I am glad on't; 'tis a worthy governor.

THIRD GENTLEMAN. But this same Cassio, though he speak of comfort
Touching the Turkish loss, yet he looks sadly
And prays the Moor be safe; for they were parted
With foul and violent tempest.

MONTANO. Pray heaven he be;
For I have serv'd him, and the man commands
Like a full soldier. Let's to the sea-side, ho!
As well to see the vessel that's come in
As to throw out our eyes for brave Othello,
Even till we make the main and th' aerial blue
An indistinct regard.

THIRD GENTLEMAN. Come, let's do so;
For every minute is expectancy
Of more arrivance.

Enter CASSIO

CASSIO. Thanks you, the valiant of this war-like isle,
That so approve the Moor. O, let the heavens
Give him defence against their elements,
For I have lost him on a dangerous sea!

MONTANO. Is he well shipp'd?

CASSIO. His bark is stoutly timber'd, and his pilot
Of very expert and approv'd allowance;
Therefore my hopes, not surfeited to death,
Stand in bold cure. [*Within:* 'A sail, a sail, a sail!']

Enter a MESSENGER

CASSIO. What noise?

MESSENGER. The town is empty; on the brow o' th' sea
Stand ranks of people, and they cry 'A sail!'

CASSIO. My hopes do shape him for the Governor. [*A shot*]

SECOND GENTLEMAN. They do discharge the shot of courtesy:
Our friend at least.

CASSIO. I pray you, sir, go forth,
And give us truth who 'tis that is arriv'd.

SECOND GENTLEMAN. I shall. *Exit*

MONTANO. But, good Lieutenant, is your general wiv'd?

CASSIO. Most fortunately: he hath achiev'd a maid
That paragons description and wild fame;
One that excels the quirks of blazoning pens,
And in th' essential vesture of creation
Does tire the ingener.

Re-enter second GENTLEMAN

Now, who has put in?
SECOND GENTLEMAN. 'Tis one Iago, ancient to the General.
CASSIO. 'Has had most favourable and happy speed.
Tempests themselves, high seas, and howling winds,
The gutter'd rocks, and congregated sands,
Traitors ensteep'd to enclog the guiltless keel,
As having sense of beauty, do omit
Their mortal natures, letting go safely by
The divine Desdemona.
MONTANO. What is she?
CASSIO. She that I spake of—our great Captain's Captain,
Left in the conduct of the bold Iago;
Whose footing here anticipates our thoughts
A se'nnight's speed. Great Jove, Othello guard,
And swell his sail with thine own powerful breath,
That he may bless this bay with his tall ship,
Make love's quick pants in Desdemona's arms,
Give renew'd fire to our extincted spirits,
And bring all Cyprus comfort!

Enter DESDEMONA, IAGO, EMILIA, RODERIGO, *and attendants*

O, behold,
The riches of the ship is come ashore!
Ye men of Cyprus, let her have your knees.
Hail to thee, lady! and the grace of heaven,
Before, behind thee, and on every hand,
Enwheel thee round!
DESDEMONA. I thank you, valiant Cassio.
What tidings can you tell me of my lord?
CASSIO. He is not yet arriv'd; nor know I aught
But that he's well, and will be shortly here.
DESDEMONA. O, but I fear! How lost you company?
CASSIO. The great contention of the sea and skies

Parted our fellowship. [*Within:* 'A sail, a sail!']
But hark–'A sail!' [*A shot*]

SECOND GENTLEMAN. They give their greeting to the citadel:
This likewise is a friend.

CASSIO. So speaks this voice.
See for the news. *Exit* GENTLEMAN
Good ancient, you are welcome. [*To* EMILIA] Welcome, mistress.
Let it not gall your patience, good Iago,
That I extend my manners; 'tis my breeding
That gives me this bold show of courtesy. [*Kissing her*]

IAGO. Sir, would she give you so much of her lips
As of her tongue she oft bestows on me,
You'd have enough.

DESDEMONA. Alas, she has no speech!

IAGO. I know too much.
I find it aye when I ha list to sleep.
Marry, before your ladyship, I grant,
She puts her tongue a little in her heart
And chides with thinking.

EMILIA. You ha little cause to say so.

IAGO. Come on, come on; you are pictures out a-doors, bells in your parlours, wildcats in your kitchens, saints in your injuries, devils being offended, players in your huswifery, and huswives in your beds.

DESDEMONA. O, fie upon thee, slanderer!

IAGO. Nay, it is true, or else I am a Turk:
You rise to play, and go to bed to work.

EMILIA. You shall not write my praise.

IAGO. No, let me not.

DESDEMONA. What wouldst write of me if thou shouldst praise me?

IAGO. O gentle lady, do not put me to't;
For I am nothing if not critical.

DESDEMONA. Come on, assay.–There's one gone to the harbour?

IAGO. Ay, madam.

DESDEMONA. I am not merry; but I do beguile
The thing I am by seeming otherwise.
Come, how wouldst thou praise me?

IAGO. I am about it; but, indeed, my invention comes from my pate as birdlime does from frieze—it plucks out brains and all. But my Muse labours, and thus she is deliver'd:
If she be fair and wise—fairness and wit,
The one's for use, the other useth it.

DESDEMONA. Well prais'd. How if she be black and witty?

IAGO. If she be black, and thereto have a wit,
She'll find a white that shall her blackness hit.

DESDEMONA. Worse and worse!

EMILIA. How if fair and foolish?

IAGO. She never yet was foolish that was fair;
For even her folly help'd her to an heir.

DESDEMONA. These are old fond paradoxes to makes fools laugh i' th' alehouse. What miserable praise hast thou for her that's foul and foolish?

IAGO. There's none so foul, and foolish thereunto,
But does foul pranks which fair and wise ones do.

DESDEMONA. O heavy ignorance! that praises the worst best. But what praise couldst thou bestow on a deserving woman indeed—one that, in the authority of her merits, did justly put on the vouch of very malice itself?

IAGO. She that was ever fair, and never proud;
Had tongue at will, and yet was never loud;
Never lack'd gold, and yet went never gay;
Fled from her wish, and yet said 'Now I may';
She that, being ang'red, her revenge being nigh,
Bade her wrong stay and her displeasure fly;
She that in wisdom never was so frail
To change the cod's head for the salmon's tail;
She that could think, and ne'er disclose her mind;
See suitors following, and not look behind:
She was a wight, if ever such wight were—

DESDEMONA. To do what?

IAGO. To suckle fools and chronicle small beer.

DESDEMONA. O most lame and impotent conclusion! Do not learn of him, Emilia, though he be thy husband. How say you, Cassio? Is he not a most profane and liberal counsellor?

CASSIO. He speaks home, madam. You may relish him more in the soldier than in the scholar.

IAGO. [*Aside*] He takes her by the palm. Ay, well said, whisper. With as little a web as this will I ensnare as great a fly as Cassio. Ay, smile upon her, do; I will gyve thee in thine own courtship. You say true; 'tis so, indeed. If such tricks as these strip you out of your lieutenantry, it had been better you had not kiss'd your three fingers so oft, which now again you are most apt to play the sir in. Very good; well kissed! and excellent courtesy! 'Tis so indeed. Yet again your fingers to your lips? Would they were clyster-pipes for your sake! [*Trumpet within*] The Moor! I know his trumpet.

CASSIO. 'Tis truly so.

DESDEMONA. Let's meet him, and receive him.

CASSIO. Lo, where he comes!

Enter OTHELLO *and attendants*

OTHELLO. O my fair warrior!

DESDEMONA. My dear Othello!

OTHELLO. It gives me wonder great as my content
To see you here before me. O my soul's joy!
If after every tempest come such calms,
May the winds blow till they have waken'd death,
And let the labouring bark climb hills of seas
Olympus-high and duck again as low
As hell's from heaven. If it were now to die,
'Twere now to be most happy; for I fear
My soul hath her content so absolute
That not another comfort like to this
Succeeds in unknown fate.

DESDEMONA. The heavens forbid
But that our loves and comforts should increase
Even as our days do grow!

OTHELLO. Amen to that, sweet powers!
I cannot speak enough of this content;
It stops me here; it is too much of joy.
And this, and this, the greatest discords be [*They kiss*]
That e'er our hearts shall make!

IAGO. [*Aside*] O, you are well tun'd now!
But I'll set down the pegs that make this music,
As honest as I am.

OTHELLO. Come, let us to the castle.
News, friends: our wars are done; the Turks are drown'd.
How do our old acquaintance of the isle?
Honey, you shall be well desir'd in Cyprus;
I have found great love amongst them. O my sweet,
I prattle out of fashion, and I dote
In mine own comforts. I prithee, good Iago,
Go to the bay, and disembark my coffers;
Bring thou the Master to the citadel;
He is a good one, and his worthiness
Does challenge much respect. Come, Desdemona,
Once more well met at Cyprus.

Exeunt all but IAGO *and* RODERIGO

IAGO. [*To one leaving*] Do thou meet me presently at the harbour. [*To* RODERIGO] Come hither. If thou be'st valiant —as they say base men being in love have then a nobility in their natures more than is native to them—list me. The Lieutenant to-night watches on the court of guard. First, I must tell thee this: Desdemona is directly in love with him.

RODERIGO. With him! Why, 'tis not possible.

IAGO. Lay thy finger thus, and let thy soul be instructed. Mark me with what violence she first lov'd the Moor, but for bragging and telling her fantastical lies. To love him still for prating?—let not thy discreet heart think it. Her eye must be fed; and what delight shall she have to look on the devil? When the blood is made dull with the act of sport, there should be—again to inflame it, and to give satiety a fresh appetite—loveliness in favour, sympathy in years, manners, and beauties—all which the Moor is defective in. Now for want of these requir'd conveniences, her delicate tenderness will find itself abus'd, begin to heave the gorge, disrelish and abhor the Moor; very nature will instruct her in it, and compel her to some second choice. Now, sir, this granted—as it is a most pregnant and unforc'd position—who stands so eminent in the degree of this fortune as Cassio does? A knave very voluble; no further conscionable than in putting on the mere form of civil and humane seeming, for the better compassing of his salt and most hidden loose affection? Why, none; why, none. A slipper and subtle knave; a finder-out of occasion; that has an eye can stamp and counterfeit advantages, though true advantage never present itself; a devilish knave! Besides, the knave is handsome, young, and hath all those requisites in him that folly and green minds look after; a pestilent complete knave, and the woman hath found him already.

RODERIGO. I cannot believe that in her; she's full of most blest condition.

IAGO. Blest fig's end! The wine she drinks is made of grapes. If she had been blest, she would never have lov'd the Moor. Blest pudding! Didst thou not see her paddle with the palm of his hand? Didst not mark that?

RODERIGO. Yes, that I did; but that was but courtesy.

IAGO. Lechery, by this hand; an index and obscure prologue to the history of lust and foul thoughts. They met so near with their lips that their breaths embrac'd together. Villainous thoughts, Roderigo! When these mutualities so marshal the way, hard at hand comes the master and main exercise, th' incorporate conclusion. Pish! But, sir, be you rul'd by me; I have brought you from Venice. Watch you to-night; for your command, I'll lay't upon you. Cassio knows you not; I'll not be far from you. Do you find some occasion to anger Cassio, either by speaking too loud, or tainting his discipline, or from what other course you please, which the time shall more favourably minister.

RODERIGO. Well.

IAGO. Sir, he's rash, and very sudden in choler, and haply with his truncheon may strike at you; provoke him that he may; for even out of that will I cause these of Cyprus to mutiny, whose qualification shall come into no true taste again but by the displanting of Cassio. So shall you have a shorter journey to your desires by the means I shall then have to prefer them; and the impediment most profitably remov'd, without the which there were no expectation of our prosperity.

RODERIGO. I will do this, if you can bring it to any opportunity.

IAGO. I warrant thee. Meet me by and by at the citadel. I must fetch his necessaries ashore. Farewell.

RODERIGO. Adieu. *Exit*

IAGO. That Cassio loves her, I do well believe it;
That she loves him, 'tis apt and of great credit.
The Moor, howbeit that I endure him not,
Is of a constant, loving, noble nature;
And I dare think he'll prove to Desdemona
A most dear husband. Now I do love her too;
Not out of absolute lust, though peradventure
I stand accountant for as great a sin,
But partly led to diet my revenge,
For that I do suspect the lustful Moor
Hath leap'd into my seat; the thought whereof
Doth like a poisonous mineral gnaw my inwards;
And nothing can nor shall content my soul
Till I am even'd with him, wife for wife;
Or failing so, yet that I put the Moor
At least into a jealousy so strong
That judgment cannot cure. Which thing to do,
If this poor trash of Venice, whom I trash
For his quick hunting, stand the putting on,
I'll have our Michael Cassio on the hip,
Abuse him to the Moor in the rank garb—
For I fear Cassio with my night-cap too;
Make the Moor thank me, love me, and reward me,
For making him egregiously an ass,
And practising upon his peace and quiet
Even to madness. 'Tis here, but yet confus'd:
Knavery's plain face is never seen till us'd. *Exit*

SCENE 2

Cyprus. A street

Enter OTHELLO'S HERALD *with a proclamation; people following*

HERALD. It is Othello's pleasure, our noble and valiant general, that, upon certain tidings now arriv'd, importing the mere perdition of the Turkish fleet, every man put himself into triumph; some to dance, some to make bonfires, each man to what sport and revels his addiction leads him; for, besides these beneficial news, it is the celebration of his nuptial. So much was his pleasure should be proclaimed. All offices are open; and there is full liberty of feasting from this present hour of five till the bell have told eleven. Heaven bless the isle of Cyprus and our noble general Othello! *Exeunt*

SCENE 3

Cyprus. The citadel

Enter OTHELLO, DESDEMONA, CASSIO, *and attendants*

OTHELLO. Good Michael, look you to the guard to-night.
Let's teach ourselves that honourable stop,
Not to outsport discretion.

CASSIO. Iago hath direction what to do;
But, notwithstanding, with my personal eye
Will I look to't.

OTHELLO. Iago is most honest.
Michael, good night. To-morrow with your earliest
Let me have speech with you. [*To* DESDEMONA] Come, my dear love,
The purchase made, the fruits are to ensue;
That profit's yet to come 'twixt me and you.–
Good night. *Exeunt* OTHELLO, DESDEMONA, *and attendants*

Enter IAGO

CASSIO. Welcome, Iago; we must to the watch.

IAGO. Not this hour, Lieutenant; 'tis not yet ten a clock. Our general cast us thus early for the love of his Desdemona; who let us not therefore blame. He hath not yet made wanton the night with her; and she is sport for Jove.

CASSIO. She is a most exquisite lady.

IAGO. And, I'll warrant her, full of game.

CASSIO. Indeed, she is a most fresh and delicate creature.

IAGO. What an eye she has! Methinks it sounds a parley to provocation.

CASSIO. An inviting eye; and yet methinks right modest.

IAGO. And when she speaks, is it not an alarm to love?

CASSIO. She is indeed perfection.

IAGO. Well, happiness to their sheets! Come, Lieutenant, I have a stoup of wine; and here without are a brace of Cyprus gallants that would fain have a measure to the health of the black Othello.

CASSIO. Not to-night, good Iago. I have very poor and unhappy brains for drinking; I could well wish courtesy would invent some other custom of entertainment.

IAGO. O, they are our friends—but one cup; I'll drink for you.

CASSIO. I have drunk but one cup to-night, and that was craftily qualified too, and behold what innovation it makes here. I am unfortunate in the infirmity, and dare not task my weakness with any more.

IAGO. What, man! 'Tis a night of revels. The gallants desire it.

CASSIO. Where are they?

IAGO. Here at the door; I pray you call them in.

CASSIO. I'll do't; but it dislikes me. *Exit*

IAGO. If I can fasten but one cup upon him,
With that which he hath drunk to-night already,
He'll be as full of quarrel and offence
As my young mistress' dog. Now my sick fool Roderigo,
Whom love hath turn'd almost the wrong side outward,
To Desdemona hath to-night carous'd
Potations pottle deep; and he's to watch.
Three else of Cyprus—noble swelling spirits,
That hold their honours in a wary distance,
The very elements of this warlike isle—
Have I to-night fluster'd with flowing cups,
And they watch too. Now, 'mongst this flock of drunkards
Am I to put our Cassio in some action
That may offend the isle—but here they come.

Re-enter CASSIO *with* MONTANO, *and* GENTLEMEN, *followed by servant with wine*

If consequence do but approve my dream,
My boat sails freely, both with wind and stream.

CASSIO. Fore God, they have given me a rouse already.

MONTANO. Good faith, a little one; not past a pint, as I am a soldier.

IAGO. Some wine, ho! [*Sings*]

And let me the canakin clink, clink;
And let me the canakin clink.
A soldier's a man;
O, man's life's but a span;
Why, then, let a soldier drink—

Some wine, boys.

CASSIO. Fore God, an excellent song!

IAGO. I learn'd it in England, where indeed they are most potent in potting: your Dane, your German, and your swag-bellied Hollander—Drink, ho!—are nothing to your English.

CASSIO. Is your Englishman so expert in his drinking?

IAGO. Why, he drinks you with facility your Dane dead drunk; he sweats not to overthrow your Almain; he gives your Hollander a vomit ere the next pottle can be fill'd.

CASSIO. To the health of our General!

MONTANO. I am for it, Lieutenant; and I'll do you justice.

IAGO. O sweet England! [*Sings*]

King Stephen was and a worthy peer,
His breeches cost him but a crown;
He held 'em sixpence all too dear,
With that he call'd the tailor lown.

He was a wight of high renown,
And thou art but of low degree.
'Tis pride that pulls the country down;
Then take thy auld cloak about thee—

Some wine, ho!

CASSIO. Fore God, this is a more exquisite song than the other.

IAGO. Will you hear't again?

CASSIO. No; for I hold him to be unworthy of his place that does those things. Well, God's above all; and there be souls must be saved, and there be souls must not be saved.

IAGO. It's true, good Lieutenant.

CASSIO. For mine own part—no offence to the General, nor

any man of quality—I hope to be saved.

IAGO. And so do I too, Lieutenant.

CASSIO. Ay, but, by your leave, not before me; the Lieutenant is to be saved before the Ancient. Let's have no more of this; let's to our affairs. God forgive us our sins. Gentlemen, let's look to our business. Do not think, gentlemen, I am drunk. This is my ancient; this is my right hand, and this is my left hand. I am not drunk now; I can stand well enough, and I speak well enough.

ALL. Excellent well.

CASSIO. Why, very well, then. You must not think, then, that I am drunk. *Exit*

MONTANO. To the platform, masters; come, let's set the watch.

IAGO. You see this fellow that is gone before:
He is a soldier fit to stand by Cæsar
And give direction; and do but see his vice;
'Tis to his virtue a just equinox,
The one as long as th' other. 'Tis pity of him.
I fear the trust Othello puts him in,
On some odd time of his infirmity,
Will shake this island.

MONTANO. But is he often thus?

IAGO. 'Tis evermore the prologue to his sleep:
He'll watch the horologe a double set,
If drink rock not his cradle.

MONTANO. It were well
The General were put in mind of it.
Perhaps he sees it not, or his good nature
Prizes the virtue that appears in Cassio,
And looks not on his evils. Is not this true?

Enter RODERIGO

IAGO. [*Aside to him*] How, now, Roderigo!
I pray you, after the Lieutenant; go. *Exit* RODERIGO

MONTANO. And 'tis great pity that the noble Moor
Should hazard such a place as his own second
With one of an ingraft infirmity:
It were an honest action to say
So to the Moor.

IAGO. Not I, for this fair island;
I do love Cassio well; and would do much
To cure him of this evil. [*Within:* 'Help, help!']
But hark, what noise?

Re-enter CASSIO, *driving in* RODERIGO

CASSIO. Zounds, you rogue, you rascal!

MONTANO. What's the matter, Lieutenant?

CASSIO. A knave teach me my duty! But I'll beat the knave into a twiggen bottle.

RODERIGO. Beat me!

CASSIO. Dost thou prate, rogue? [*Strikes him*]

MONTANO. Nay, good Lieutenant; I pray you, sir, hold your hand.

CASSIO. Let me go, sir, or I'll knock you o'er the mazard.

MONTANO. Come, come, you're drunk.

CASSIO. Drunk! [*They fight*]

IAGO. [*Aside to* RODERIGO] Away, I say!
Go out and cry a mutiny. *Exit* RODERIGO
Nay, good Lieutenant. God's will, gentlemen!
Help, ho!–Lieutenant–sir–Montano–sir–
Help, masters! Here's a goodly watch indeed!
[*A bell rung*]
Who's that which rings the bell? Diablo, ho!
The town will rise. God's will, Lieutenant, hold.
You'll be asham'd for ever.

Re-enter OTHELLO *and* GENTLEMEN, *with weapons*

OTHELLO. What is the matter here?

MONTANO. Zounds, I bleed still; I am hurt to the death–He dies.

OTHELLO. Hold, for your lives!

IAGO. Hold, ho! Lieutenant–sir–Montano–gentlemen–
Have you forgot all sense of place and duty?
Hold! The General speaks to you; hold, hold, for shame!

OTHELLO. Why, how now, ho! From whence ariseth this?
Are we turn'd Turks, and to ourselves do that
Which Heaven hath forbid the Ottomites?
For Christian shame, put by this barbarous brawl.
He that stirs next to carve for his own rage

Holds his soul light: he dies upon his motion.
Silence that dreadful bell; it frights the isle
From her propriety. What's the matter, masters?
Honest Iago, that looks dead with grieving,
Speak. Who began this? On thy love, I charge thee.

IAGO. I do not know. Friends all but now, even now,
In quarter, and in terms, like bride and groom
Divesting them for bed; and then, but now,
As if some planet had unwitted men,
Swords out, and tilting one at other's breast
In opposition bloody. I cannot speak
Any beginning to this peevish odds;
And would in action glorious I had lost
These legs that brought me to a part of it!

OTHELLO. How comes it, Michael, you are thus forgot?

CASSIO. I pray you, pardon me; I cannot speak.

OTHELLO. Worthy Montano, you were wont be civil;
The gravity and stillness of your youth
The world hath noted, and your name is great
In mouths of wisest censure—what's the matter
That you unlace your reputation thus,
And spend your rich opinion for the name
Of a night-brawler? Give me answer to't.

MONTANO. Worthy Othello, I am hurt to danger;
Your officer Iago can inform you,
While I spare speech, which something now offends me,
Of all that I do know; nor know I aught
By me that's said or done amiss this night,
Unless self-charity be sometimes a vice,
And to defend ourselves it be a sin
When violence assails us.

OTHELLO. Now, by heaven,
My blood begins my safer guides to rule;
And passion, having my best judgment collied,
Assays to lead the way. Zounds, if I stir
Or do but lift this arm, the best of you
Shall sink in my rebuke. Give me to know
How this foul rout began, who set it on;
And he that is approv'd in this offence,
Though he had twinn'd with me, both at a birth,

Shall lose me. What! in a town of war,
Yet wild, the people's hearts brim full of fear,
To manage private and domestic quarrel,
In night, and on the court and guard of safety!
'Tis monstrous. Iago, who began't?

MONTANO. If partially affin'd, or leagu'd in office,
Thou dost deliver more or less than truth,
Thou art no soldier.

IAGO. Touch me not so near;
I had rather ha this tongue cut from my mouth
Than it should do offence to Michael Cassio;
Yet, I persuade myself, to speak the truth
Shall nothing wrong him. This it is, General.
Montano and myself being in speech,
There comes a fellow crying out for help,
And Cassio following him with determin'd sword
To execute upon him. Sir, this gentleman
Steps in to Cassio and entreats his pause;
Myself the crying fellow did pursue,
Lest by his clamour, as it so fell out,
The town might fall in fright; he, swift of foot,
Outran my purpose, and I return'd the rather
For that I heard the clink and fall of swords,
And Cassio high in oath; which till to-night
I ne'er might see before. When I came back,
For this was brief, I found them close together
At blow and thrust, even as again they were
When you yourself did part them.
More of this matter can I not report;
But men are men; the best sometimes forget.
Though Cassio did some little wrong to him,
As men in rage strike those that wish them best,
Yet surely Cassio, I believe, receiv'd
From him that fled some strange indignity
Which patience could not pass.

OTHELLO. I know, Iago,
Thy honesty and love doth mince this matter,
Making it light to Cassio. Cassio, I love thee;
But never more be officer of mine.

Re-enter DESDEMONA, *attended*

Look if my gentle love be not rais'd up.
I'll make thee an example.

DESDEMONA. What is the matter, dear?

OTHELLO. All's well now, sweeting;
Come away to bed. [*To* MONTANO] Sir, for your hurts,
Myself will be your surgeon. Lead him off. [*He is led off*]
Iago, look with care about the town,
And silence those whom this vile brawl distracted.
Come, Desdemona; 'tis the soldiers' life
To have their balmy slumbers wak'd with strife.

Exeunt all but IAGO *and* CASSIO

IAGO. What, are you hurt, Lieutenant?

CASSIO. Ay, past all surgery.

IAGO. Marry, God forbid!

CASSIO. Reputation, reputation, reputation! O, I have lost my reputation! I have lost the immortal part of myself, and what remains is bestial. My reputation, Iago, my reputation!

IAGO. As I am an honest man, I had thought you had receiv'd some bodily wound; there is more sense in that than in reputation. Reputation is an idle and most false imposition; oft got without merit, and lost without deserving. You have lost no reputation at all, unless you repute yourself such a loser. What, man! there are more ways to recover the General again; you are but now cast in his mood, punishment more in policy than in malice; even so as one would beat his offenceless dog to affright an imperious lion. Sue to him again, and he's yours.

CASSIO. I will rather sue to be despis'd than to deceive so good a commander with so slight, so drunken, and so indiscreet an officer. Drunk! And speak parrot! And squabble, swagger, swear! And discourse fustian with one's own shadow! O thou invisible spirit of wine, if thou hast no name to be known by, let us call thee devil!

IAGO. What was he that you follow'd with your sword? What had he done to you?

CASSIO. I know not.

IAGO. Is't possible?

CASSIO. I remember a mass of things, but nothing distinctly; a quarrel, but nothing wherefore. O God, that men should put an enemy in their mouths to steal away their brains! That we should with joy, pleasance, revel and applause, transform ourselves into beasts!

IAGO. Why, but you are now well enough. How come you thus recovered?

CASSIO. It hath pleas'd the devil drunkenness to give place to the devil wrath. One unperfectness shows me another, to make me frankly despise myself.

IAGO. Come, you are too severe a moraller. As the time, the place, and the condition of this country stands, I could heartily wish this had not so befall'n; but since it is as it is, mend it for your own good.

CASSIO. I will ask him for my place again: he shall tell me I am a drunkard. Had I as many mouths as Hydra, such an answer would stop them all. To be now a sensible man, by and by a fool, and presently a beast! O strange! Every inordinate cup is unblest, and the ingredience is a devil.

IAGO. Come, come, good wine is a good familiar creature if it be well us'd; exclaim no more against it. And, good Lieutenant, I think you think I love you.

CASSIO. I have well approv'd it, sir. I drunk!

IAGO. You or any man living may be drunk at a time, man. I'll tell you what you shall do. Our General's wife is now the General–I may say so in this respect, for that he hath devoted and given up himself to the contemplation, mark, and denotement, of her parts and graces–confess yourself freely to her; importune her help to put you in your place again: she is of so free, so kind, so apt, so blessed a disposition, she holds it a vice in her goodness not to do more than she is requested. This broken joint between you and her husband entreat her to splinter; and, my fortunes against any lay worth naming, this crack of your love shall grow stronger than it was before.

CASSIO. You advise me well.

IAGO. I protest, in the sincerity of love and honest kindness.

CASSIO. I think it freely; and betimes in the morning I will beseech the virtuous Desdemona to undertake for me. I am desperate of my fortunes if they check me here.

IAGO. You are in the right. Good night, Lieutenant; I must to the watch.

CASSIO. Good night, honest Iago. *Exit*

IAGO. And what's he, then, that says I play the villain?
When this advice is free I give and honest,
Probal to thinking, and indeed the course
To win the Moor again? For 'tis most easy
The inclining Desdemona to subdue
In any honest suit: she's fram'd as fruitful
As the free elements. And then for her
To win the Moor—were't to renounce his baptism,
All seals and symbols of redeemed sin—
His soul is so enfetter'd to her love
That she may make, unmake, do what she list,
Even as her appetite shall play the god
With his weak function. How am I, then, a villain
To counsel Cassio to this parallel course,
Directly to his good? Divinity of hell!
When devils will their blackest sins put on,
They do suggest at first with heavenly shows,
As I do now; for whiles this honest fool
Plies Desdemona to repair his fortunes,
And she for him pleads strongly to the Moor,
I'll pour this pestilence into his ear—
That she repeals him for her body's lust;
And by how much she strives to do him good
She shall undo her credit with the Moor.
So will I turn her virtue into pitch;
And out of her own goodness make the net
That shall enmesh them all.

Enter RODERIGO

How now, Roderigo!

RODERIGO. I do follow here in the chase, not like a hound that hunts, but one that fills up the cry. My money is almost spent; I have been to-night exceedingly well cudgell'd; and I think the issue will be—I shall have so much experience for my pains as that comes to; and so, with no money at all, and a little more wit, return again to Venice.

IAGO. How poor are they that have not patience!
What wound did ever heal but by degrees?
Thou know'st we work by wit, and not by witchcraft;

And wit depends on dilatory time.
Does't not go well? Cassio hath beaten thee,
And thou, by that small hurt, hast cashier'd Cassio.
Though other things grow fair against the sun,
Yet fruits that blossom first will first be ripe.
Content thyself awhile. By th' mass, 'tis morning!
Pleasure and action make the hours seem short.
Retire thee; go where thou art billeted.
Away, I say; thou shalt know more hereafter.
Nay, get thee gone. *Exit* RODERIGO
Two things are to be done:
My wife must move for Cassio to her mistress;
I'll set her on;
Myself awhile to draw the Moor apart
And bring him jump when he may Cassio find
Soliciting his wife. Ay, that's the way;
Dull not device by coldness and delay. *Exit*

ACT III. SCENE 1

Cyprus. Before the citadel

Enter CASSIO, *with* MUSICIANS

CASSIO. Masters, play here; I will content your pains.
Something that's brief; and bid 'Good morrow, General.' [*Music*]

Enter CLOWN

CLOWN. Why masters, ha your instruments been in Naples, that they speak i' th' nose thus?

FIRST MUSICIAN. How, sir, how?

CLOWN. Are these, I pray, call'd wind instruments?

FIRST MUSICIAN. Ay, marry, are they, sir.

CLOWN. O, thereby hangs a tail.

FIRST MUSICIAN. Whereby hangs a tale, sir?

CLOWN. Marry, sir, by many a wind instrument that I know. But, masters, here's money for you; and the General so likes your music that he desires you, of all loves, to make no more noise with it.

FIRST MUSICIAN. Well, sir, we will not.

CLOWN. If you have any music that may not be heard, to't again; but, as they say, to hear music the General does not greatly care.

FIRST MUSICIAN. We have none such, sir.

CLOWN. Then put up your pipes in your bag, for I'll away. Go; vanish into air; away. *Exeunt* MUSICIANS

CASSIO. Dost thou hear, my honest friend?

CLOWN. No, I hear not your honest friend; I hear you.

CASSIO. Prithee keep up thy quillets. There's a poor piece of gold for thee. If the gentlewoman that attends the General's wife be stirring, tell her there's one Cassio entreats her a little favour of speech. Wilt thou do this?

CLOWN. She is stirring, sir; if she will stir hither, I shall seem to notify unto her.

CASSIO. Do, good my friend. *Exit* CLOWN

Enter IAGO

In happy time, Iago.

IAGO. You have not been abed, then?

CASSIO. Why, no; the day had broke before we parted.
I have made bold, Iago,
To send in to your wife: my suit to her
Is that she will to virtuous Desdemona
Procure me some access.

IAGO. I'll send her to you presently;
And I'll devise a mean to draw the Moor
Out of the way, that your converse and business
May be more free.

CASSIO. I humbly thank you for't. [*Exit* IAGO] I never knew
A Florentine more kind and honest.

Enter EMILIA

EMILIA. Good morrow, good Lieutenant. I am sorry
For your displeasure; but all will sure be well.
The General and his wife are talking of it;
And she speaks for you stoutly: the Moor replies
That he you hurt is of great fame in Cyprus
And great affinity, and that in wholesome wisdom
He might not but refuse you; but he protests he loves you

And needs no other suitor but his likings
To take the safest occasion by the front
To bring you in again.

CASSIO. Yet, I beseech you,
If you think fit, or that it may be done,
Give me advantage of some brief discourse
With Desdemona alone.

EMILIA. Pray you come in.
I will bestow you where you shall have time
To speak your bosom freely.

CASSIO. I am much bound to you. *Exeunt*

SCENE 2

Cyprus. The citadel

Enter OTHELLO, IAGO, *and* GENTLEMEN

OTHELLO. These letters give, Iago, to the pilot;
And by him do my duties to the Senate.
That done, I will be walking on the works;
Repair there to me.

IAGO. Well, my good lord, I'll do't.

OTHELLO. This fortification, gentlemen–shall we see't?

GENTLEMEN. We'll wait upon your lordship. *Exeunt*

SCENE 3

Cyprus. The garden of the citadel

Enter DESDEMONA, CASSIO, *and* EMILIA

DESDEMONA. Be thou assur'd, good Cassio, I will do
All my abilities in thy behalf.

EMILIA. Good madam, do. I warrant it grieves my husband
As if the case were his.

DESDEMONA. O, that's an honest fellow. Do not doubt, Cassio,
But I will have my lord and you again
As friendly as you were.

CASSIO. Bounteous madam,
Whatever shall become of Michael Cassio,
He's never any thing but your true servant.
DESDEMONA. I know't—I thank you. You do love my lord;
You have known him long; and be you well assur'd
He shall in strangeness stand no farther off
Than in a politic distance.
CASSIO. Ay, but, lady,
That policy may either last so long,
Or feed upon such nice and waterish diet,
Or breed itself so out of circumstances,
That, I being absent, and my place supplied,
My general will forget my love and service.
DESDEMONA. Do not doubt that; before Emilia here
I give thee warrant of thy place. Assure thee,
If I do vow a friendship, I'll perform it
To the last article. My lord shall never rest;
I'll watch him tame, and talk him out of patience;
His bed shall seem a school, his board a shrift;
I'll intermingle everything he does
With Cassio's suit. Therefore be merry, Cassio;
For thy solicitor shall rather die
Than give thy cause away.

Enter OTHELLO *and* IAGO

EMILIA. Madam, here comes my lord.
CASSIO. Madam, I'll take my leave.
DESDEMONA. Why, stay, and hear me speak.
CASSIO. Madam, not now. I am very ill at ease,
Unfit for mine own purposes.
DESDEMONA. Well, do your discretion. *Exit* CASSIO
IAGO. Ha! I like not that.
OTHELLO. What dost thou say?
IAGO. Nothing, my lord; or if—I know not what.
OTHELLO. Was not that Cassio parted from my wife?
IAGO. Cassio, my lord! No, sure, I cannot think it,
That he would sneak away so guilty-like,
Seeing your coming.
OTHELLO. I do believe 'twas he.
DESDEMONA. How now, my lord!

I have been talking with a suitor here,
A man that languishes in your displeasure.
OTHELLO. Who is't you mean?
DESDEMONA. Why, your lieutenant, Cassio. Good my lord,
If I have any grace or power to move you,
His present reconciliation take;
For if he be not one that truly loves you,
That errs in ignorance, and not in cunning,
I have no judgment in an honest face.
I prithee call him back.
OTHELLO. Went he hence now?
DESDEMONA. Yes, faith; so humbled
That he hath left part of his grief with me
To suffer with him. Good love, call him back.
OTHELLO. Not now, sweet Desdemona; some other time.
DESDEMONA. But shall't be shortly?
OTHELLO. The sooner, sweet, for you.
DESDEMONA. Shall't be to-night at supper?
OTHELLO. No, not to-night.
DESDEMONA. To-morrow dinner, then?
OTHELLO. I shall not dine at home;
I meet the captains at the citadel.
DESDEMONA. Why, then, to-morrow night, or Tuesday morn,
On Tuesday noon or night, on Wednesday morn.
I prithee name the time; but let it not
Exceed three days. I'faith, he's penitent;
And yet his trespass, in our common reason—
Save that, they say, the wars must make example
Out of her best—is not almost a fault
T' incur a private check. When shall he come?
Tell me, Othello—I wonder in my soul
What you would ask me that I should deny,
Or stand so mamm'ring on. What! Michael Cassio,
That came a-wooing with you, and so many a time,
When I have spoke of you dispraisingly,
Hath ta'en your part—to have so much to do
To bring him in! By'r Lady, I could do much—
OTHELLO. Prithee, no more; let him come when he will;
I will deny thee nothing.
DESDEMONA. Why, this is not a boon;

'Tis as I should entreat you wear your gloves,
Or feed on nourishing dishes, or keep you warm,
Or sue to you to do a peculiar profit
To your own person. Nay, when I have a suit
Wherein I mean to touch your love indeed,
It shall be full of poise and difficult weight,
And fearful to be granted.

OTHELLO. I will deny thee nothing.
Whereon I do beseech thee grant me this,
To leave me but a little to myself.

DESDEMONA. Shall I deny you? No; farewell, my lord.

OTHELLO. Farewell, my Desdemona. I'll come to thee straight.

DESDEMONA. Emilia, come.—Be as your fancies teach you;
Whate'er you be, I am obedient.

Exeunt DESDEMONA *and* EMILIA

OTHELLO. Excellent wretch! Perdition catch my soul
But I do love thee; and when I love thee not
Chaos is come again.

IAGO. My noble lord!

OTHELLO. What dost thou say, Iago?

IAGO. Did Michael Cassio, when you woo'd my lady,
Know of your love?

OTHELLO. He did, from first to last. Why dost thou ask?

IAGO. But for a satisfaction of my thought—
No further harm.

OTHELLO. Why of thy thought, Iago?

IAGO. I did not think he had been acquainted with her.

OTHELLO. O, yes; and went between us very often.

IAGO. Indeed!

OTHELLO. Indeed? Ay, indeed. Discern'st thou aught in that?
Is he not honest?

IAGO. Honest, my lord?

OTHELLO. Honest? Ay, honest.

IAGO. My lord, for aught I know.

OTHELLO. What dost thou think?

IAGO. Think, my lord?

OTHELLO. Think, my lord! By heaven, he echoes me,
As if there were some monster in his thought
Too hideous to be shown. Thou dost mean something:

I heard thee say but now thou lik'st not that,
When Cassio left my wife. What didst not like?
And when I told thee he was of my counsel
In my whole course of wooing, thou criedst 'Indeed!'
And didst contract and purse thy brow together,
As if thou then hadst shut up in thy brain
Some horrible conceit. If thou dost love me,
Show me thy thought.

IAGO. My lord, you know I love you.

OTHELLO. I think thou dost;
And for I know thou art full of love and honesty,
And weigh'st thy words before thou giv'st them breath,
Therefore these stops of thine affright me the more;
For such things in a false disloyal knave
Are tricks of custom; but in a man that's just
They are close delations, working from the heart
That passion cannot rule.

IAGO. For Michael Cassio,
I dare presume I think that he is honest.

OTHELLO. I think so too.

IAGO. Men should be that they seem;
Or those that be not, would they might seem none!

OTHELLO. Certain, men should be what they seem.

IAGO. Why then, I think Cassio's an honest man.

OTHELLO. Nay, yet there's more in this.
I prithee speak to me as to thy thinkings,
As thou dost ruminate; and give thy worst of thoughts
The worst of words.

IAGO. Good my lord, pardon me.
Though I am bound to every act of duty,
I am not bound to that all slaves are free to—
Utter my thoughts. Why, say they are vile and false,
As where's that palace whereinto foul things
Sometimes intrude not? Who has that breast so pure
But some uncleanly apprehensions
Keep leets and law-days, and in sessions sit
With meditations lawful?

OTHELLO. Thou dost conspire against thy friend, Iago,
If thou but think'st him wrong'd, and mak'st his ear
A stranger to thy thoughts.

IAGO. I do beseech you,
Though I perchance am vicious in my guess,
As, I confess, it is my nature's plague
To spy into abuses, and oft my jealousy
Shapes faults that are not—that your wisdom
From one that so imperfectly conjects,
Would take no notice; nor build yourself a trouble
Out of his scattering and unsure observance.
It were not for your quiet nor your good,
Nor for my manhood, honesty, or wisdom,
To let you know my thoughts.

OTHELLO. Zounds! What dost thou mean?

IAGO. Good name in man and woman, dear my lord,
Is the immediate jewel of their souls:
Who steals my purse steals trash; 'tis something, nothing;
'Twas mine, 'tis his, and has been slave to thousands;
But he that filches from me my good name
Robs me of that which not enriches him
And makes me poor indeed.

OTHELLO. By heaven, I'll know thy thoughts.

IAGO. You cannot, if my heart were in your hand;
Nor shall not, whilst 'tis in my custody.

OTHELLO. Ha!

IAGO. O, beware, my lord, of jealousy;
It is the green-ey'd monster which doth mock
The meat it feeds on. That cuckold lives in bliss
Who, certain of his fate, loves not his wronger;
But, O, what damned minutes tells he o'er
Who dotes, yet doubts, suspects, yet strongly loves!

OTHELLO. O misery!

IAGO. Poor and content is rich, and rich enough;
But riches fineless is as poor as winter
To him that ever fears he shall be poor.
Good God, the souls of all my tribe defend
From jealousy!

OTHELLO. Why, why is this?
Think'st thou I'd make a life of jealousy,
To follow still the changes of the moon
With fresh suspicions? No; to be once in doubt
Is once to be resolv'd. Exchange me for a goat

When I shall turn the business of my soul
To such exsufflicate and blown surmises
Matching thy inference. 'Tis not to make me jealous
To say my wife is fair, feeds well, loves company,
Is free of speech, sings, plays, and dances well;
Where virtue is, these are more virtuous.
Nor from mine own weak merits will I draw
The smallest fear or doubt of her revolt;
For she had eyes, and chose me. No, Iago;
I'll see before I doubt; when I doubt, prove;
And, on the proof, there is no more but this—
Away at once with love or jealousy!

IAGO. I am glad of this; for now I shall have reason
To show the love and duty that I bear you
With franker spirit. Therefore, as I am bound,
Receive it from me. I speak not yet of proof.
Look to your wife; observe her well with Cassio;
Wear your eyes thus, not jealous nor secure.
I would not have your free and noble nature
Out of self-bounty be abus'd; look to't.
I know our country disposition well:
In Venice they do let God see the pranks
They dare not show their husbands; their best conscience
Is not to leave't undone, but keep't unknown.

OTHELLO. Dost thou say so?

IAGO. She did deceive her father, marrying you;
And when she seem'd to shake and fear your looks,
She lov'd them most.

OTHELLO. And so she did.

IAGO. Why, go to then!
She that, so young, could give out such a seeming,
To seel her father's eyes up close as oak—
He thought 'twas witchcraft. But I am much to blame;
I humbly do beseech you of your pardon
For too much loving you.

OTHELLO. I am bound to thee for ever.

IAGO. I see this hath a little dash'd your spirits.

OTHELLO. Not a jot, not a jot.

IAGO. I'faith, I fear it has.
I hope you will consider what is spoke

Comes from my love; but I do see you are mov'd.
I am to pray you not to strain my speech
To grosser issues nor to larger reach
Than to suspicion.

OTHELLO. I will not.

IAGO. Should you do so, my lord,
My speech should fall into such vile success
Which my thoughts aim'd not. Cassio's my worthy friend–
My lord, I see you are mov'd.

OTHELLO. No, not much mov'd.
I do not think but Desdemona's honest.

IAGO. Long live she so! and long live you to think so!

OTHELLO. And yet, how nature erring from itself–

IAGO. Ay, there's the point: as–to be bold with you–
Not to affect many proposed matches
Of her own clime, complexion, and degree,
Whereto we see in all things nature tends–
Foh! one may smell in such a will most rank,
Foul disproportion, thoughts unnatural.
But pardon me–I do not in position
Distinctly speak of her; though I may fear
Her will, recoiling to her better judgment,
May fall to match you with her country forms,
And happily repent.

OTHELLO. Farewell, farewell.
If more thou dost perceive, let me know more;
Set on thy wife to observe. Leave me, Iago.

IAGO. My lord, I take my leave. [*Going*]

OTHELLO. Why did I marry? This honest creature doubtless
Sees and knows more–much more than he unfolds.

IAGO. [*Returning*] My lord, I would I might entreat your honour
To scan this thing no further; leave it to time.
Although 'tis fit that Cassio have his place,
For, sure, he fills it up with great ability,
Yet if you please to hold him off awhile,
You shall by that perceive him and his means.
Note if your lady strain his entertainment
With any strong or vehement importunity;

Much will be seen in that. In the mean time
Let me be thought too busy in my fears—
As worthy cause I have to fear I am—
And hold her free, I do beseech your honour.
OTHELLO. Fear not my government.
IAGO. I once more take my leave. *Exit*
OTHELLO. This fellow's of exceeding honesty,
And knows all qualities, with a learned spirit,
Of human dealing. If I do prove her haggard,
Though that her jesses were my dear heart-strings,
I'd whistle her off and let her down the wind
To prey at fortune. Haply, for I am black
And have not those soft parts of conversation
That chamberers have, or for I am declin'd
Into the vale of years—yet that's not much—
She's gone; I am abus'd; and my relief
Must be to loathe her. O curse of marriage,
That we can call these delicate creatures ours,
And not their appetites! I had rather be a toad,
And live upon the vapour of a dungeon,
Than keep a corner in the thing I love
For others' uses. Yet 'tis the plague of great ones;
Prerogativ'd are they less than the base;
'Tis destiny unshunnable, like death:
Even then this forked plague is fated to us
When we do quicken. Look where she comes.

Re-enter DESDEMONA *and* EMILIA

If she be false, O, then heaven mocks itself!
I'll not believe it.
DESDEMONA. How now, my dear Othello?
Your dinner, and the generous islanders
By you invited, do attend your presence.
OTHELLO. I am to blame.
DESDEMONA. Why do you speak so faintly?
Are you not well?
OTHELLO. I have a pain upon my forehead here.
DESDEMONA. Faith, that's with watching; 'twill away again.
Let me but bind it hard, within this hour
It will be well.

[*He puts the handkerchief from him, and she drops it*]

OTHELLO. Your napkin is too little.
Let it alone. Come, I'll go in with you.

DESDEMONA. I am very sorry that you are not well.

Exeunt OTHELLO *and* DESDEMONA

EMILIA. I am glad I have found this napkin.
This was her first remembrance from the Moor.
My wayward husband hath a hundred times
Woo'd me to steal it; but she so loves the token—
For he conjur'd her she should ever keep it—
That she reserves it evermore about her
To kiss and talk to. I'll ha the work ta'en out,
And give't Iago. What he'll do with it
Heaven knows, not I;
I nothing but to please his fantasy.

Re-enter IAGO

IAGO. How now! What do you here alone?

EMILIA. Do not you chide; I have a thing for you.

IAGO. You have a thing for me?
It is a common thing!

EMILIA. Ha!

IAGO. To have a foolish wife.

EMILIA. O, is that all? What will you give me now
For that same handkerchief?

IAGO. What handkerchief?

EMILIA. What handkerchief!
Why that the Moor first gave to Desdemona;
That which so often you did bid me steal.

IAGO. Hast stole it from her?

EMILIA. No, faith; she let it drop by negligence,
And to the advantage, I, being here, took't up.
Look, here it is.

IAGO. A good wench! Give it me.

EMILIA. What will you do with't, that you have been so earnest
To have me filch it?

IAGO. Why, what's that to you? [*Snatching it*]

EMILIA. If it be not for some purpose of import,
Give me't again. Poor lady, she'll run mad

When she shall lack it.
IAGO. Be not acknown on't; I have use for it.
Go, leave me. *Exit* EMILIA
I will in Cassio's lodging lose this napkin,
And let him find it. Trifles light as air
Are to the jealous confirmations strong
As proofs of holy writ; this may do something.
The Moor already changes with my poison.
Dangerous conceits are in their natures poisons
Which at the first are scarce found to distaste
But, with a little act upon the blood,
Burn like the mines of sulphur.

Re-enter OTHELLO

I did say so.
Look where he comes! Not poppy, nor mandragora,
Nor all the drowsy syrups of the world,
Shall ever medicine thee to that sweet sleep
Which thou owed'st yesterday.
OTHELLO. Ha! Ha! false to me, to me?
IAGO. Why, how now, General? No more of that.
OTHELLO. Avaunt! be gone! Thou hast set me on the rack.
I swear 'tis better to be much abus'd
Than but to know't a little.
IAGO. How now, my lord!
OTHELLO. What sense had I in her stol'n hours of lust?
I saw't not, thought it not, it harm'd not me.
I slept the next night well, fed well, was free and merry;
I found not Cassio's kisses on her lips.
He that is robb'd, not wanting what is stol'n,
Let him not know't, and he's not robb'd at all.
IAGO. I am sorry to hear this.
OTHELLO. I had been happy if the general camp,
Pioneers and all, had tasted her sweet body,
So I had nothing known. O, now for ever.
Farewell the tranquil mind! farewell content!
Farewell the plumed troops, and the big wars
That makes ambition virtue! O, farewell!
Farewell the neighing steed and the shrill trump,
The spirit-stirring drum, th' ear-piercing fife,

The royal banner, and all quality,
Pride, pomp, and circumstance, of glorious war!
And O ye mortal engines whose rude throats
Th' immortal Jove's dread clamours counterfeit,
Farewell! Othello's occupation's gone.
IAGO. Is't possible, my lord?
OTHELLO. Villain, be sure thou prove my love a whore—
[*Taking him by the throat*]
Be sure of it; give me the ocular proof;
Or, by the worth of man's eternal soul,
Thou hadst been better have been born a dog
Than answer my wak'd wrath.
IAGO. Is't come to this?
OTHELLO. Make me to see't; or, at the least, so prove it
That the probation bear no hinge nor loop
To hang a doubt on; or woe upon thy life!
IAGO. My noble lord—
OTHELLO. If thou dost slander her and torture me,
Never pray more; abandon all remorse;
On horror's head horrors accumulate;
Do deeds to make heaven weep, all earth amaz'd;
For nothing canst thou to damnation add
Greater than that.
IAGO. O grace! O heaven forgive me!
Are you a man? Have you a soul or sense?—
God buy you; take mine office. O wretched fool,
That liv'st to make thine honesty a vice!
O monstrous world! Take note, take note, O world,
To be direct and honest is not safe.
I thank you for this profit; and from hence
I'll love no friend, sith love breeds such offence.
OTHELLO. Nay, stay. Thou shouldst be honest.
IAGO. I should be wise; for honesty's a fool,
And loses that it works for.
OTHELLO. By the world,
I think my wife be honest, and think she is not;
I think that thou art just, and think thou art not.
I'll have some proof. Her name, that was as fresh
As Dian's visage, is now begrim'd and black
As mine own face. If there be cords or knives,

Poison, or fire, or suffocating streams,
I'll not endure it. Would I were satisfied!
IAGO. I see, sir, you are eaten up with passion;
I do repent me that I put it to you.
You would be satisfied?
OTHELLO. Would! Nay, and I will.
IAGO. And may; but how—how satisfied, my lord?
Would you, the supervisor, grossly gape on—
Behold her topp'd?
OTHELLO. Death and damnation! O!
IAGO. It were a tedious difficulty, I think,
To bring them to that prospect. Damn them, then,
If ever mortal eyes do see them bolster
More than their own! What then? How then?
What shall I say? Where's satisfaction?
It is impossible you should see this,
Were they as prime as goats, as hot as monkeys,
As salt as wolves in pride, and fools as gross
As ignorance made drunk. But yet, I say,
If imputation and strong circumstances
Which lead directly to the door of truth
Will give you satisfaction, you might have't.
OTHELLO. Give me a living reason she's disloyal.
IAGO. I do not like the office;
But, sith I am enter'd in this cause so far,
Prick'd to't by foolish honesty and love,
I will go on. I lay with Cassio lately,
And, being troubled with a raging tooth,
I could not sleep.
There are a kind of men so loose of soul
That in their sleeps will mutter their affairs:
One of this kind is Cassio.
In sleep I heard him say 'Sweet Desdemona,
Let us be wary, let us hide our loves,'
And then, sir, would he gripe and wring my hand,
Cry 'O sweet creature!' then kiss me hard,
As if he pluck'd up kisses by the roots,
That grew upon my lips—then laid his leg
Over my thigh—and sigh'd, and kiss'd, and then
Cried 'Cursed fate that gave thee to the Moor!'

OTHELLO. O monstrous! monstrous!
IAGO. Nay, this was but his dream.
OTHELLO. But this denoted a foregone conclusion.
IAGO. 'Tis a shrewd doubt, though it be but a dream,
And this may help to thicken other proofs
That do demonstrate thinly.
OTHELLO. I'll tear her all to pieces.
IAGO. Nay, but be wise; yet we see nothing done;
She may be honest yet. Tell me but this:
Have you not sometimes seen a handkerchief
Spotted with strawberries in your wife's hand?
OTHELLO. I gave her such a one; 'twas my first gift.
IAGO. I know not that; but such a handkerchief—
I am sure it was your wife's—did I to-day
See Cassio wipe his beard with.
OTHELLO. If it be that—
IAGO. If it be that, or any that was hers,
It speaks against her with the other proofs.
OTHELLO. O that the slave had forty thousand lives!
One is too poor, too weak for my revenge.
Now do I see 'tis true. Look here, Iago—
All my fond love thus do I blow to heaven.
'Tis gone.
Arise, black vengeance, from the hollow hell.
Yield up, O love, thy crown and hearted throne
To tyrannous hate! Swell, bosom, with thy fraught,
For 'tis of aspics' tongues.
IAGO. Yet be content.
OTHELLO. O, blood, blood, blood!
IAGO. Patience, I say; your mind perhaps may change.
OTHELLO. Never, Iago. Like to the Pontic sea,
Whose icy current and compulsive course
Ne'er feels retiring ebb, but keeps due on
To the Propontic and the Hellespont;
Even so my bloody thoughts, with violent pace,
Shall ne'er look back, ne'er ebb to humble love,
Till that a capable and wide revenge
Swallow them up. [*He kneels*] Now, by yond marble heaven,
In the due reverence of a sacred vow

I here engage my words.

IAGO. [*Kneeling*] Do not rise yet.
Witness, you ever-burning lights above,
You elements that clip us round about,
Witness that here Iago doth give up
The execution of his wit, hands, heart,
To wrong'd Othello's service! Let him command,
And to obey shall be in me remorse,
What bloody business ever. [*They rise*]

OTHELLO. I greet thy love,
Not with vain thanks, but with acceptance bounteous,
And will upon the instant put thee to't.
Within these three days let me hear thee say
That Cassio's not alive.

IAGO. My friend is dead;
'Tis done at your request. But let her live.

OTHELLO. Damn her, lewd minx! O, damn her, damn her!
Come, go with me apart; I will withdraw
To furnish me with some swift means of death
For the fair devil. Now art thou my lieutenant.

IAGO. I am your own for ever. *Exeunt*

SCENE 4

Cyprus. Before the citadel

Enter DESDEMONA, EMILIA, *and* CLOWN

DESDEMONA. Do you know, sirrah, where the Lieutenant Cassio lies?

CLOWN. I dare not say he lies anywhere.

DESDEMONA. Why, man?

CLOWN. He's a soldier; and for one to say a soldier lies, 'tis stabbing.

DESDEMONA. Go to. Where lodges he?

CLOWN. To tell you where he lodges is to tell you where I lie.

DESDEMONA. Can anything be made of this?

CLOWN. I know not where he lodges; and for me to devise a lodging, and say he lies here or he lies there, were to lie in mine own throat.

DESDEMONA. Can you inquire him out, and be edified by report?

CLOWN. I will catechize the world for him; that is, make questions, and by them answer.

DESDEMONA. Seek him; bid him come hither: tell him I have mov'd my lord on his behalf, and hope all will be well.

CLOWN. To do this is within the compass of man's wit; and therefore I will attempt the doing it. *Exit*

DESDEMONA. Where should I lose the handkerchief, Emilia?

EMILIA. I know not, madam.

DESDEMONA. Believe me, I had rather lose my purse
Full of crusadoes; and but my noble Moor
Is true of mind, and made of no such baseness
As jealous creatures are, it were enough
To put him to ill thinking.

EMILIA. Is he not jealous?

DESDEMONA. Who, he? I think the sun where he was born
Drew all such humours from him.

Enter OTHELLO

EMILIA. Look where he comes.

DESDEMONA. I will not leave him now till Cassio
Be call'd to him. How is't with you, my lord?

OTHELLO. Well, my good lady. [*Aside*] O, hardness to dissemble!—
How do you, Desdemona?

DESDEMONA. Well, my good lord.

OTHELLO. Give me your hand. This hand is moist, my lady.

DESDEMONA. It yet hath felt no age nor known no sorrow.

OTHELLO. This argues fruitfulness and liberal heart:
Hot, hot, and moist. This hand of yours requires
A sequester from liberty, fasting and prayer,
Much castigation, exercise devout;
For here's a young and sweating devil here
That commonly rebels. 'Tis a good hand,
A frank one.

DESDEMONA. You may indeed say so;
For 'twas that hand that gave away my heart.

OTHELLO. A liberal hand. The hearts of old gave hands;
But our new heraldry is hands, not hearts.

DESDEMONA. I cannot speak of this. Come now, your promise.
OTHELLO. What promise, chuck?
DESDEMONA. I have sent to bid Cassio come speak with you.
OTHELLO. I have a salt and sorry rheum offends me;
  Lend me thy handkerchief.
DESDEMONA. Here, my lord.
OTHELLO. That which I gave you.
DESDEMONA. I have it not about me.
OTHELLO. Not?
DESDEMONA. No, faith, my lord.
OTHELLO. That's a fault. That handkerchief
  Did an Egyptian to my mother give.
  She was a charmer, and could almost read
  The thoughts of people; she told her, while she kept it,
  'Twould make her amiable, and subdue my father
  Entirely to her love; but if she lost it,
  Or made a gift of it, my father's eye
  Should hold her loathely, and his spirits should hunt
  After new fancies. She, dying, gave it me,
  And bid me, when my fate would have me wive,
  To give it her. I did so; and take heed on't;
  Make it a darling like your precious eye;
  To lose't or give't away were such perdition
  As nothing else could match.
DESDEMONA. Is't possible?
OTHELLO. 'Tis true. There's magic in the web of it.
  A sibyl that had numb'red in the world
  The sun to course two hundred compasses
  In her prophetic fury sew'd the work;
  The worms were hallowed that did breed the silk;
  And it was dy'd in mummy which the skilful
  Conserv'd of maidens' hearts.
DESDEMONA. I'faith! Is't true?
OTHELLO. Most veritable; therefore look to't well.
DESDEMONA. Then would to God that I had never seen't!
OTHELLO. Ha! Wherefore?
DESDEMONA. Why do you speak so startingly and rash?
OTHELLO. Is't lost? Is't gone? Speak. Is't out o' th' way?
DESDEMONA. Heaven bless us!
OTHELLO. Say you?

DESDEMONA. It is not lost; but what an if it were?
OTHELLO. How!
DESDEMONA. I say it is not lost.
OTHELLO. Fetch't, let me see't.
DESDEMONA. Why, so I can, sir, but I will not now.
This is a trick to put me from my suit:
Pray you let Cassio be receiv'd again.
OTHELLO. Fetch me the handkerchief: my mind misgives.
DESDEMONA. Come, come;
You'll never meet a more sufficient man.
OTHELLO. The handkerchief!
DESDEMONA. I pray talk me of Cassio.
OTHELLO. The handkerchief!
DESDEMONA. A man that all his time
Hath founded his good fortunes on your love,
Shar'd dangers with you—
OTHELLO. The handkerchief!
DESDEMONA. I'faith, you are to blame.
OTHELLO. Zounds! *Exit*
EMILIA. Is not this man jealous?
DESDEMONA. I ne'er saw this before.
Sure there's some wonder in this handkerchief;
I am most unhappy in the loss of it.
EMILIA. 'Tis not a year or two shows us a man.
They are all but stomachs, and we all but food;
They eat us hungerly, and when they are full,
They belch us.

Enter CASSIO *and* IAGO

Look you, Cassio and my husband.
IAGO. There is no other way; 'tis she must do't.
And, lo, the happiness! Go and importune her.
DESDEMONA. How now, good Cassio, what's the news with you?
CASSIO. Madam, my former suit. I do beseech you
That by your virtuous means I may again
Exist, and be a member of his love
Whom I, with all the office of my heart,
Entirely honour. I would not be delay'd.
If my offence be of such mortal kind

That nor my service past, nor present sorrows,
Nor purpos'd merit in futurity,
Can ransom me into his love again,
But to know so must be my benefit;
So shall I clothe me in a forc'd content,
And shut myself up in some other course,
To fortune's alms.

DESDEMONA. Alas, thrice-gentle Cassio!
My advocation is not now in tune;
My lord is not my lord; nor should I know him,
Were he in favour as in humour alter'd.
So help me every spirit sanctified,
As I have spoken for you all my best,
And stood within the blank of his displeasure
For my free speech! you must awhile be patient.
What I can do I will; and more I will
Than for myself I dare; let that suffice you.

IAGO. Is my lord angry?

EMILIA. He went hence but now,
And certainly in strange unquietness.

IAGO. Can he be angry? I have seen the cannon
When it hath blown his ranks into the air,
And, like the devil, from his very arm
Puff'd his own brother—and is he angry?
Something of moment, then. I will go meet him.
There's matter in't indeed, if he be angry.

DESDEMONA. I prithee do so. *Exit* IAGO
Something sure of state
Either from Venice, or some unhatch'd practice
Made demonstrable here in Cyprus to him,
Hath puddled his clear spirit; and in such cases
Men's natures wrangle with inferior things,
Though great ones are their object. 'Tis even so;
For let our finger ache, and it endues
Our other healthful members even to a sense
Of pain. Nay, we must think, men are not gods,
Nor of them look for such observancy
As fits the bridal. Beshrew me much, Emilia,
I was—unhandsome warrior as I am—
Arraigning his unkindness with my soul;

But now I find I had suborn'd the witness,
And he's indicted falsely.

EMILIA. Pray heaven it be state matters, as you think,
And no conception nor no jealous toy
Concerning you.

DESDEMONA. Alas the day, I never gave him cause!

EMILIA. But jealous souls will not be answer'd so;
They are not ever jealous for the cause,
But jealous for they are jealous. 'Tis a monster
Begot upon it self, born on it self.

DESDEMONA. Heaven keep that monster from Othello's mind!

EMILIA. Lady, amen.

DESDEMONA. I will go seek him. Cassio, walk hereabout.
If I do find him fit, I'll move your suit,
And seek to effect it to my uttermost.

CASSIO. I humbly thank your ladyship.

Exeunt DESDEMONA *and* EMILIA

Enter BIANCA

BIANCA. Save you, friend Cassio!

CASSIO. What make you from home?
How is it with you, my most fair Bianca?
I' faith, sweet love, I was coming to your house.

BIANCA. And I was going to your lodging, Cassio.
What, keep a week away? seven days and nights?
Eightscore eight hours? and lovers' absent hours,
More tedious than the dial eight score times?
O weary reckoning!

CASSIO. Pardon me, Bianca.
I have this while with leaden thoughts been press'd;
But I shall in a more continuate time
Strike off this score of absence. Sweet Bianca,
[*Giving her* DESDEMONA's *handkerchief*]
Take me this work out.

BIANCA. O Cassio, whence came this?
This is some token from a newer friend:
To the felt absence now I feel a cause.
Is't come to this? Well, well.

CASSIO. Go to, woman!
Throw your vile guesses in the devil's teeth,

From whence you have them. You are jealous now
That this is from some mistress, some remembrance.
No, by my faith, Bianca.
BIANCA. Why, whose is it?
CASSIO. I know not neither; I found it in my chamber.
I like the work well; ere it be demanded–
As like enough it will–I would have it copied.
Take it, and do't; and leave me for this time.
BIANCA. Leave you! Wherefore?
CASSIO. I do attend here on the General;
And think it no addition, nor my wish,
To have him see me woman'd.
BIANCA. Why, I pray you?
CASSIO. Not that I love you not.
BIANCA. But that you do not love me.
I pray you bring me on the way a little;
And say if I shall see you soon at night.
CASSIO. 'Tis but a little way that I can bring you,
For I attend here; but I'll see you soon.
BIANCA. 'Tis very good; I must be circumstanc'd. *Exeunt*

ACT IV. SCENE 1

Cyprus. Before the citadel

Enter OTHELLO *and* IAGO

IAGO. Will you think so?
OTHELLO. Think so, Iago?
IAGO. What,
To kiss in private?
OTHELLO. An unauthoriz'd kiss.
IAGO. Or to be naked with her friend abed
An hour or more, not meaning any harm?
OTHELLO. Naked abed, Iago, and not mean harm!
It is hypocrisy against the devil.
They that mean virtuously and yet do so,
The devil their virtue tempts, and they tempt heaven.
IAGO. So they do nothing, 'tis a venial slip;

But if I give my wife a handkerchief—
OTHELLO. What then?
IAGO. Why, then 'tis hers, my lord; and, being hers,
She may, I think, bestow't on any man.
OTHELLO. She is protectress of her honour too:
May she give that?
IAGO. Her honour is an essence that's not seen;
They have it very oft that have it not.
But, for the handkerchief—
OTHELLO. By heaven, I would most gladly have forgot it.
Thou said'st—O, it comes o'er my memory
As doth the raven o'er the infected house,
Boding to all—he had my handkerchief.
IAGO. Ay, what of that?
OTHELLO. That's not so good now.
IAGO. What
If I had said I had seen him do you wrong?
Or heard him say—as knaves be such abroad,
Who having, by their own importunate suit,
Or voluntary dotage of some mistress,
Convinced or supplied them, cannot choose
But they must blab—
OTHELLO. Hath he said anything?
IAGO. He hath, my lord; but be you well assur'd,
No more than he'll unswear.
OTHELLO. What hath he said?
IAGO. Faith, that he did—I know not what he did.
OTHELLO. What? what?
IAGO. Lie—
OTHELLO. With her?
IAGO. With her, on her; what you will.
OTHELLO. Lie with her—lie on her? We say lie on her when they belie her. Lie with her. Zounds, that's fulsome. Handkerchief—confessions—handkerchief! To confess, and be hang'd for his labour—first, to be hang'd, and then to confess. I tremble at it. Nature would not invest herself in such shadowing passion without some instruction. It is not words that shakes me thus—pish!—noses, ears, and lips. Is't possible? Confess! Handkerchief! O devil!
[*Falls in a trance*]

IAGO. Work on,
My medicine, work. Thus credulous fools are caught;
And many worthy and chaste dames even thus,
All guiltless, meet reproach. What, ho! my lord!
My lord, I say! Othello!

Enter CASSIO

How now, Cassio!
CASSIO. What's the matter?
IAGO. My lord is fall'n into an epilepsy.
This is his second fit; he had one yesterday.
CASSIO. Rub him about the temples.
IAGO. No, forbear.
The lethargy must have his quiet course;
If not, he foams at mouth, and by and by
Breaks out to savage madness. Look, he stirs.
Do you withdraw yourself a little while;
He will recover straight; when he is gone,
I would on great occasion speak with you. *Exit* CASSIO
How is it, General? Have you not hurt your head?
OTHELLO. Dost thou mock me?
IAGO. I mock you? No, by heaven!
Would you would bear your fortune like a man!
OTHELLO. A horned man's a monster and a beast.
IAGO. There's many a beast then in a populous city,
And many a civil monster.
OTHELLO. Did he confess it?
IAGO. Good sir, be a man;
Think every bearded fellow that's but yok'd
May draw with you; there's millions now alive
That nightly lie in those unproper beds
Which they dare swear peculiar: your case is better.
O, 'tis the spite of hell, the fiend's arch-mock,
To lip a wanton in a secure couch,
And to suppose her chaste! No, let me know;
And knowing what I am, I know what she shall be.
OTHELLO. O, thou art wise; 'tis certain.
IAGO. Stand you awhile apart.
Confine yourself but in a patient list.
Whilst you were here o'erwhelmed with your grief—

A passion most unsuiting such a man—
Cassio came hither; I shifted him away,
And laid good 'scuse upon your ecstasy;
Bade him anon return, and here speak with me;
The which he promis'd. Do but encave yourself,
And mark the fleers, the gibes, and notable scorns,
That dwell in every region of his face;
For I will make him tell the tale anew—
Where, how, how oft, how long ago, and when,
He hath, and is again to cope your wife.
I say, but mark his gesture. Marry, patience;
Or I shall say you are all in all in spleen,
And nothing of a man.

OTHELLO. Dost thou hear, Iago?
I will be found most cunning in my patience;
But—dost thou hear?—most bloody.

IAGO. That's not amiss;
But yet keep time in all. Will you withdraw?
[OTHELLO *withdraws*]
Now will I question Cassio of Bianca,
A huswife that by selling her desires
Buys herself bread and clothes; it is a creature
That dotes on Cassio, as 'tis the strumpet's plague
To beguile many and be beguil'd by one.
He, when he hears of her, cannot restrain
From the excess of laughter.

Re-enter CASSIO

Here he comes.
As he shall smile Othello shall go mad;
And his unbookish jealousy must construe
Poor Cassio's smiles, gestures, and light behaviours,
Quite in the wrong. How do you now, Lieutenant?

CASSIO. The worser that you give me the addition
Whose want even kills me.

IAGO. Ply Desdemona well, and you are sure on't.
Now, if this suit lay in Bianca's dower,
How quickly should you speed!

CASSIO. Alas, poor caitiff!

OTHELLO. Look how he laughs already!

IAGO. I never knew a woman love man so.

CASSIO. Alas, poor rogue! I think, i' faith, she loves me.

OTHELLO. Now he denies it faintly, and laughs it out.

IAGO. Do you hear, Cassio?

OTHELLO. Now he importunes him
To tell it o'er. Go to; well said, well said.

IAGO. She gives it out that you shall marry her.
Do you intend it?

CASSIO. Ha, ha, ha!

OTHELLO. Do you triumph, Roman? Do you triumph?

CASSIO. I marry her! What, a customer! I prithee bear some charity to my wit; do not think it so unwholesome. Ha, ha, ha!

OTHELLO. So, so, so, so—they laugh that wins.

IAGO. Faith, the cry goes that you marry her.

CASSIO. Prithee say true.

IAGO. I am a very villain else.

OTHELLO. Ha you scor'd me? Well.

CASSIO. This is the monkey's own giving out: she is persuaded I will marry her, out of her own love and flattery, not out of my promise.

OTHELLO. Iago beckons me; now he begins the story.

CASSIO. She was here even now; she haunts me in every place. I was t'other day talking on the sea-bank with certain Venetians, and thither comes the bauble—by this hand, she falls me thus about my neck.

OTHELLO. Crying 'O dear Cassio!' as it were: his gesture imports it.

CASSIO. So hangs, and lolls, and weeps upon me; so hales, and pulls me. Ha, ha, ha!

OTHELLO. Now he tells how she pluck'd him to my chamber. O, I see that nose of yours, but not that dog I shall throw't to.

CASSIO. Well, I must leave her company.

Enter BIANCA

IAGO. Before me! Look where she comes.

CASSIO. 'Tis such another fitchew! marry, a perfum'd one. What do you mean by this haunting of me?

BIANCA. Let the devil and his dam haunt you. What did you mean by that same handkerchief you gave me even now?

I was a fine fool to take it. I must take out the whole work—a likely piece of work that you should find it in your chamber and know not who left it there! This is some minx's token, and I must take out the work? There—give it your hobby-horse. Wheresoever you had it, I'll take out no work on't.

CASSIO. How now, my sweet Bianca! how now! how now!

OTHELLO. By heaven, that should be my handkerchief!

BIANCA. An you'll come to supper to-night, you may; an you will not, come when you are next prepar'd for. *Exit*

IAGO. After her, after her.

CASSIO. Faith, I must; she'll rail i' th' street else.

IAGO. Will you sup there?

CASSIO. Faith, I intend so.

IAGO. Well, I may chance to see you; for I would very fain speak with you.

CASSIO. Prithee come; will you?

IAGO. Go to; say no more. *Exit* CASSIO

OTHELLO. [*Coming forward*] How shall I murder him, Iago?

IAGO. Did you perceive how he laugh'd at his vice?

OTHELLO. O Iago!

IAGO. And did you see the handkerchief?

OTHELLO. Was that mine?

IAGO. Yours, by this hand. And to see how he prizes the foolish woman your wife! She gave it him, and he hath giv'n it his whore.

OTHELLO. I would have him nine years a-killing. A fine woman! a fair woman! a sweet woman!

IAGO. Nay, you must forget that.

OTHELLO. Ay, let her rot, and perish, and be damn'd to-night; for she shall not live. No, my heart is turn'd to stone; I strike it, and it hurts my hand. O, the world hath not a sweeter creature; she might lie by an emperor's side and command him tasks.

IAGO. Nay, that's not your way.

OTHELLO. Hang her! I do but say what she is: so delicate with her needle, an admirable musician—O, she will sing the savageness out of a bear!—of so high and plenteous wit and invention.

IAGO. She's the worse for all this.

OTHELLO. O, a thousand, a thousand times—and then of so gentle a condition.

IAGO. Ay, too gentle.

OTHELLO. Nay, that's certain. But yet the pity of it, Iago! O, Iago, the pity of it, Iago!

IAGO. If you be so fond over her iniquity, give her patent to offend; for, if it touch not you, it comes near nobody.

OTHELLO. I will chop her into messes. Cuckold me!

IAGO. O, 'tis foul in her.

OTHELLO. With mine officer!

IAGO. That's fouler.

OTHELLO. Get me some poison, Iago—this night. I'll not expostulate with her, lest her body and beauty unprovide my mind again—this night, Iago.

IAGO. Do it not with poison; strangle her in her bed, even the bed she hath contaminated.

OTHELLO. Good, good; the justice of it pleases; very good.

IAGO. And for Cassio—let me be his undertaker. You shall hear more by midnight.

OTHELLO. Excellent good. [*A trumpet*]
What trumpet is that same?

IAGO. I warrant, something from Venice.

Enter LODOVICO, DESDEMONA, *and attendants*

'Tis Lodovico—this comes from the Duke.
See, your wife's with him.

LODOVICO. God save thee, worthy General!

OTHELLO. With all my heart, sir.

LODOVICO. The Duke and Senators of Venice greet you.
[*Gives him a packet*]

OTHELLO. I kiss the instrument of their pleasures.
[*Opens the packet and reads*]

DESDEMONA. And what's the news, good cousin Lodovico?

IAGO. I am very glad to see you, signior;
Welcome to Cyprus.

LODOVICO. I thank you. How does Lieutenant Cassio?

IAGO. Lives, sir.

DESDEMONA. Cousin, there's fall'n between him and my lord
An unkind breach; but you shall make all well.

OTHELLO. Are you sure of that?
DESDEMONA. My lord?
OTHELLO. [*Reads*] 'This fail you not to do as you will'—
LODOVICO. He did not call; he's busy in the paper.
Is there division 'twixt thy lord and Cassio?
DESDEMONA. A most unhappy one. I would do much
T' atone them, for the love I bear to Cassio.
OTHELLO. Fire and brimstone!
DESDEMONA. My lord?
OTHELLO. Are you wise?
DESDEMONA. What, is he angry?
LODOVICO. May be the letter mov'd him;
For, as I think, they do command him home,
Deputing Cassio in his government.
DESDEMONA. By my troth, I am glad on't.
OTHELLO. Indeed!
DESDEMONA. My lord?
OTHELLO. I am glad to see you mad.
DESDEMONA. Why, sweet Othello?
OTHELLO. Devil! [*Striking her*]
DESDEMONA. I have not deserv'd this.
LODOVICO. My lord, this would not be believ'd in Venice,
Though I should swear I saw't. 'Tis very much.
Make her amends; she weeps.
OTHELLO. O devil, devil!
If that the earth could teem with woman's tears,
Each drop she falls would prove a crocodile.
Out of my sight!
DESDEMONA. I will not stay to offend you. [*Going*]
LODOVICO. Truly, an obedient lady.
I do beseech your lordship, call her back.
OTHELLO. Mistress!
DESDEMONA. My lord?
OTHELLO. What would you with her, sir?
LODOVICO. Who, I, my lord?
OTHELLO. Ay; you did wish that I would make her turn.
Sir, she can turn, and turn, and yet go on,
And turn again; and she can weep, sir, weep;
And she's obedient, as you say, obedient,
Very obedient.—Proceed you in your tears.—

Concerning this, sir,—O, well-painted passion!—
I am commanded home.—Get you away;
I'll send for you anon.—Sir, I obey the mandate,
And will return to Venice.—Hence, avaunt!

Exit DESDEMONA

Cassio shall have my place. And, sir, to-night,
I do entreat that we may sup together.
You are welcome, sir, to Cyprus.—Goats and monkeys!

Exit

LODOVICO. Is this the noble Moor whom our full Senate
Call all in all sufficient? Is this the nature
Whom passion could not shake, whose solid virtue
The shot of accident nor dart of chance
Could neither graze nor pierce?

IAGO. He is much chang'd.

LODOVICO. Are his wits safe? Is he not light of brain?

IAGO. He's that he is. I may not breathe my censure.
What he might be, if what he might he is not,
I would to heaven he were!

LODOVICO. What, strike his wife!

IAGO. Faith, that was not so well; yet would I knew
That stroke would prove the worst!

LODOVICO. Is it his use?
Or did the letters work upon his blood,
And new-create this fault?

IAGO. Alas, alas!
It is not honesty in me to speak
What I have seen and known. You shall observe him;
And his own courses will denote him so
That I may save my speech. Do but go after,
And mark how he continues.

LODOVICO. I am sorry that I am deceiv'd in him. *Exeunt*

SCENE 2

Cyprus. The citadel

Enter OTHELLO *and* EMILIA

OTHELLO. You have seen nothing, then?

EMILIA. Nor ever heard, nor ever did suspect.
OTHELLO. Yes, you have seen Cassio and she together.
EMILIA. But then I saw no harm, and then I heard
  Each syllable that breath made up between them.
OTHELLO. What, did they never whisper?
EMILIA. Never, my lord.
OTHELLO. Nor send you out o' th' way?
EMILIA. Never.
OTHELLO. To fetch her fan, her gloves, her mask, nor nothing?
EMILIA. Never, my lord.
OTHELLO. That's strange.
EMILIA. I durst, my lord, to wager she is honest,
  Lay down my soul at stake. If you think other,
  Remove your thought—it doth abuse your bosom.
  If any wretch have put this in your head,
  Let heaven requite it with the serpent's curse;
  For if she be not honest, chaste, and true,
  There's no man happy; the purest of their wives
  Is foul as slander.
OTHELLO. Bid her come hither. Go. *Exit* EMILIA
  She says enough; yet she's a simple bawd
  That cannot say as much. This is a subtle whore,
  A closet-lock-and-key of villainous secrets;
  And yet she'll kneel and pray; I have seen her do't.

Re-enter EMILIA *with* DESDEMONA

DESDEMONA. My lord, what is your will?
OTHELLO. Pray you, chuck, come hither.
DESDEMONA. What is your pleasure?
OTHELLO. Let me see your eyes; look in my face.
DESDEMONA. What horrible fancy's this?
OTHELLO. [*To* EMILIA] Some of your function, mistress:
  Leave procreants alone, and shut the door;
  Cough, or cry hem, if any body come.
  Your mystery, your mystery; nay, dispatch. *Exit* EMILIA
DESDEMONA. Upon my knees, what doth your speech import?
  I understand a fury in your words,
  But not the words.
OTHELLO. Why, what art thou?

DESDEMONA. Your wife, my lord; your true and loyal wife.

OTHELLO. Come, swear it, damn thyself; lest, being like one of heaven, the devils themselves should fear to seize thee; therefore be double-damn'd—swear thou art honest.

DESDEMONA. Heaven doth truly know it.

OTHELLO. Heaven truly knows that thou art false as hell.

DESDEMONA. To whom, my lord? With whom? How am I false?

OTHELLO. Ah, Desdemona! away! away! away!

DESDEMONA. Alas the heavy day! Why do you weep?
Am I the motive of these tears, my lord?
If haply you my father do suspect
An instrument of this your calling back,
Lay not your blame on me; if you have lost him,
Why, I have lost him too.

OTHELLO. Had it pleas'd heaven
To try me with affliction; had they rain'd
All kind of sores and shames on my bare head,
Steep'd me in poverty to the very lips,
Given to captivity me and my utmost hopes,
I should have found in some place of my soul
A drop of patience; but, alas, to make me
The fixed figure for the time of scorn
To point his slow unmoving finger at!—O, O!
Yet could I bear that too; well, very well;
But there, where I have garner'd up my heart,
Where either I must live or bear no life,
The fountain from the which my current runs,
Or else dries up—to be discarded thence!
Or keep it as a cistern for foul toads
To knot and gender in! Turn thy complexion there,
Patience, thou young and rose-lipp'd cherubin—
Ay, here, look grim as hell.

DESDEMONA. I hope my noble lord esteems me honest.

OTHELLO. O, ay; as summer flies are in the shambles,
That quicken even with blowing. O thou weed
Who art so lovely fair and smell'st so sweet
That the sense aches at thee!
Would thou had'st never been born!

DESDEMONA. Alas, what ignorant sin have I committed?

OTHELLO. Was this fair paper, this most goodly book,
Made to write 'whore' upon? What committed!
Committed! O thou public commoner!
I should make very forges of my cheeks
That would to cinders burn up modesty,
Did I but speak thy deeds. What committed!
Heaven stops the nose at it, and the moon winks;
The bawdy wind, that kisses all it meets,
Is hush'd within the hollow mine of earth
And will not hear it. What committed!
Impudent strumpet!

DESDEMONA. By heaven, you do me wrong.

OTHELLO. Are not you a strumpet?

DESDEMONA. No, as I am a Christian.
If to preserve this vessel for my lord
From any other foul unlawful touch
Be not to be a strumpet, I am none.

OTHELLO. What, not a whore?

DESDEMONA. No, as I shall be sav'd.

OTHELLO. Is't possible?

DESDEMONA. O, heaven forgive us!

OTHELLO. I cry you mercy, then.
I took you for that cunning whore of Venice
That married with Othello.—You, mistress,
That have the office opposite to Saint Peter
And keeps the gate of hell!

Re-enter EMILIA

You, you, ay you!
We ha done our course; there's money for your pains.
I pray you turn the key, and keep our counsel. *Exit*

EMILIA. Alas, what does this gentleman conceive?
How do you, madam? How do you, my good lady?

DESDEMONA. Faith, half asleep.

EMILIA. Good madam, what's the matter with my lord?

DESDEMONA. With who?

EMILIA. Why, with my lord, madam.

DESDEMONA. Who is thy lord?

EMILIA. He that is yours, sweet lady.

DESDEMONA. I have none. Do not talk to me, Emilia;

I cannot weep, nor answers have I none
But what should go by water. Prithee, to-night
Lay on my bed my wedding sheets—remember;
And call thy husband hither.

EMILIA. Here's a change indeed! *Exit*

DESDEMONA. 'Tis meet I should be us'd so, very meet.
How have I been behav'd, that he might stick
The small'st opinion on my great'st abuse?

Re-enter EMILIA *with* IAGO

IAGO. What is your pleasure, madam? How is't with you?

DESDEMONA. I cannot tell. Those that do teach young babes
Do it with gentle means and easy tasks.
He might have chid me so; for, in good faith,
I am a child to chiding.

IAGO. What is the matter, lady?

EMILIA. Alas, Iago, my lord hath so bewhor'd her,
Thrown such despite and heavy terms upon her
That true hearts cannot bear it.

DESDEMONA. Am I that name, Iago?

IAGO. What name, fair lady?

DESDEMONA. Such as she says my lord did say I was.

EMILIA. He call'd her whore. A beggar in his drink
Could not have laid such terms upon his callat.

IAGO. Why did he so?

DESDEMONA. I do not know; I am sure I am none such.

IAGO. Do not weep, do not weep. Alas, the day!

EMILIA. Hath she forsook so many noble matches,
Her father, and her country, and her friends,
To be call'd whore? Would it not make one weep?

DESDEMONA. It is my wretched fortune.

IAGO. Beshrew him for't!
How comes this trick upon him?

DESDEMONA. Nay, heaven doth know.

EMILIA. I will be hang'd if some eternal villain,
Some busy and insinuating rogue,
Some cogging, cozening slave, to get some office,
Have not devis'd this slander; I'll be hang'd else.

IAGO. Fie, there is no such man; it is impossible.

DESDEMONA. If any such there be, heaven pardon him!

EMILIA. A halter pardon him! and hell gnaw his bones!
Why should he call her whore? Who keeps her company?
What place, what time, what form, what likelihood?
The Moor's abus'd by some outrageous knave,
Some base notorious knave, some scurvy fellow.
O heaven, that such companions thou'dst unfold,
And put in every honest hand a whip
To lash the rascals naked through the world
Even from the east to the west!

IAGO. Speak within door.

EMILIA. O, fie upon them! Some such squire he was
That turn'd your wit the seamy side without
And made you to suspect me with the Moor.

IAGO. You are a fool; go to.

DESDEMONA. O God! Iago,
What shall I do to win my lord again?
Good friend, go to him; for, by this light of heaven,
I know not how I lost him. Here I kneel.
If e'er my will did trespass 'gainst his love,
Either in discourse of thought or actual deed,
Or that mine eyes, mine ears, or any sense,
Delighted them in any other form,
Or that I do not yet, and ever did,
And ever will—though he do shake me off
To beggarly divorcement—love him dearly,
Comfort forswear me! Unkindness may do much;
And his unkindness may defeat my life,
But never taint my love. I cannot say 'whore';
It does abhor me now I speak the word;
To do the act that might the addition earn,
Not the world's mass of vanity could make me.

IAGO. I pray you be content; 'tis but his humour.
The business of the state does him offence,
And he does chide with you.

DESDEMONA. If 'twere no other!

IAGO. It is but so, I warrant. [*Trumpets within*]
Hark how these instruments summon you to supper.
The messengers of Venice stay the meat.
Go in, and weep not; all things shall be well.

Exeunt DESDEMONA *and* EMILIA

Enter Roderigo

How now, Roderigo!

Roderigo. I do not find that thou deal'st justly with me.

Iago. What in the contrary?

Roderigo. Every day thou daff'st me with some device, Iago; and rather, as it seems to me now, keep'st from me all conveniency than suppliest me with the least advantage of hope. I will, indeed, no longer endure it; nor am I yet persuaded to put up in peace what already I have foolishly suffer'd.

Iago. Will you hear me, Roderigo?

Roderigo. Faith, I have heard too much; for your words and performances are no kin together.

Iago. You charge me most unjustly.

Roderigo. With nought but truth. I have wasted myself out of my means. The jewels you have had from me to deliver to Desdemona would half have corrupted a votarist. You have told me she hath receiv'd them, and return'd me expectations and comforts of sudden respect and acquaintance; but I find none.

Iago. Well; go to; very well.

Roderigo. Very well! go to! I cannot go to, man, nor 'tis not very well; by this hand, I say 'tis very scurvy, and begin to find myself fopt in it.

Iago. Very well.

Roderigo. I tell you 'tis not very well. I will make myself known to Desdemona. If she will return me my jewels, I will give over my suit and repent my unlawful solicitation; if not, assure yourself I will seek satisfaction of you.

Iago. You have said now.

Roderigo. Ay, and said nothing but what I protest intendment of doing.

Iago. Why, now I see there's mettle in thee; and even from this instant do build on thee a better opinion than ever before. Give me thy hand, Roderigo. Thou hast taken against me a most just exception; but yet, I protest, I have dealt most directly in thy affair.

Roderigo. It hath not appear'd.

Iago. I grant, indeed, it hath not appear'd; and your suspicion is not without wit and judgment. But, Roderigo, if thou hast that in thee indeed, which I have greater reason to believe now than ever—I mean purpose, courage, and valour—this night show it; if thou the next night following enjoy not Desdemona, take me from this world with treachery, and devise engines for my life.

RODERIGO. Well, what is it? Is it within reason and compass?

IAGO. Sir, there is especial commission come from Venice to depute Cassio in Othello's place.

RODERIGO. Is that true? Why, then Othello and Desdemona return again to Venice.

IAGO. O, no; he goes into Mauritania, and taketh away with him the fair Desdemona, unless his abode be linger'd here by some accident; wherein none can be so determinate as the removing of Cassio.

RODERIGO. How do you mean removing of him?

IAGO. Why, by making him uncapable of Othello's place—knocking out his brains.

RODERIGO. And that you would have me to do?

IAGO. Ay, an if you dare do yourself a profit and right. He sups to-night with a harlotry, and thither will I go to him—he knows not yet of his honourable fortune. If you will watch his going thence, which I will fashion to fall out between twelve and one, you may take him at your pleasure. I will be near to second your attempt, and he shall fall between us. Come, stand not amaz'd at it, but go along with me; I will show you such a necessity in his death that you shall think yourself bound to put it on him. It is now high supper-time, and the night grows to waste. About it.

RODERIGO. I will hear further reason for this.

IAGO. And you shall be satisfied. *Exeunt*

SCENE 3

Cyprus. The citadel

Enter OTHELLO, DESDEMONA, LODOVICO, EMILIA, *and attendants*

LODOVICO. I do beseech you, sir, trouble yourself no further.

OTHELLO. O, pardon me; 'twill do me good to walk.

LODOVICO. Madam, good night; I humbly thank your ladyship.

DESDEMONA. Your honour is most welcome.

OTHELLO. Will you walk, sir? O, Desdemona!

DESDEMONA. My lord?

OTHELLO. Get you to bed on th' instant; I will be return'd forthwith. Dispatch your attendant there. Look't be done.

DESDEMONA. I will, my lord.

Exeunt OTHELLO, LODOVICO, *and attendants*

EMILIA. How goes it now? He looks gentler than he did.

DESDEMONA. He says he will return incontinent.
He hath commanded me to go to bed,
And bade me to dismiss you.

EMILIA. Dismiss me!

DESDEMONA. It was his bidding; therefore, good Emilia,
Give me my nightly wearing, and adieu.
We must not now displease him.

EMILIA. I would you had never seen him.

DESDEMONA. So would not I: my love doth so approve him
That even his stubbornness, his checks, his frowns—
Prithee unpin me—have grace and favour in them.

EMILIA. I have laid those sheets you bade me on the bed.

DESDEMONA. All's one. Good faith, how foolish are our minds!
If I do die before thee, prithee shroud me
In one of these same sheets.

EMILIA. Come, come, you talk.

DESDEMONA. My mother had a maid call'd Barbary:
She was in love; and he she lov'd prov'd mad,
And did forsake her. She had a song of 'willow';
An old thing 'twas, but it express'd her fortune,
And she died singing it. That song to-night
Will not go from my mind; I have much to do
But to go hang my head all at one side
And sing it like poor Barbary. Prithee dispatch.

EMILIA. Shall I go fetch your night-gown?

DESDEMONA. No, unpin me here.
This Lodovico is a proper man.

EMILIA. A very handsome man.

DESDEMONA. He speaks well.

EMILIA. I know a lady in Venice would have walk'd barefoot to Palestine for a touch of his nether lip.

DESDEMONA. [*Sings*]

The poor soul sat sighing by a sycamore tree,
  Sing all a green willow;
Her hand on her bosom, her head on her knee.
  Sing willow, willow, willow.
The fresh streams ran by her, and murmur'd her moans;
  Sing willow, willow, willow;
Her salt tears fell from her and soft'ned the stones;
  Sing willow—

Lay by these—
  willow, willow.—

Prithee, hie thee; he'll come anon.—

  Sing all a green willow must be my garland.
Let nobody blame him; his scorn I approve—

Nay, that's not next. Hark! who is't that knocks?

EMILIA. It is the wind.

DESDEMONA. [*Sings*]

I call'd my love false love; but what said he then?
  Sing willow, willow, willow:
If I court moe women, you'll couch with moe men—

So, get thee gone; good night. Mine eyes do itch;
Doth that bode weeping?

EMILIA. 'Tis neither here nor there.

DESDEMONA. I have heard it said so. O, these men, these men!
Dost thou in conscience think—tell me, Emilia—
That there be women do abuse their husbands
In such gross kind?

EMILIA. There be some such, no question.

DESDEMONA. Wouldst thou do such a deed for all the world?

EMILIA. Why, would not you?

DESDEMONA. No, by this heavenly light!

EMILIA. Nor I neither by this heavenly light; I might do't as well i' th' dark.

DESDEMONA. Wouldst thou do such a deed for all the world?

EMILIA. The world's a huge thing.

It is a great price for a small vice.

DESDEMONA. Good troth, I think thou wouldst not.

EMILIA. By my troth, I think I should; and undo't when I had done it. Marry, I would not do such a thing for a joint-ring, nor for measures of lawn, nor for gowns, petticoats, nor caps, nor any petty exhibition; but for all the whole world—ud's pity, who would not make her husband cuckold to make him a monarch? I should venture purgatory for't.

DESDEMONA. Beshrew me, if I would do such a wrong for the whole world.

EMILIA. Why, the wrong is but a wrong i' th' world; and having the world for your labour, 'tis a wrong in your own world, and you might quickly make it right.

DESDEMONA. I do not think there is any such woman.

EMILIA. Yes, a dozen; and as many to th' vantage as would store the world they play'd for.
But I do think it is their husbands' faults
If wives do fall. Say that they slack their duties,
And pour our treasures into foreign laps;
Or else break out in peevish jealousies,
Throwing restraint upon us; or say they strike us,
Or scant our former having in despite;
Why, we have galls; and though we have some grace,
Yet have we some revenge. Let husbands know
Their wives have sense like them; they see and smell,
And have their palates both for sweet and sour
As husbands have. What is it that they do
When they change us for others? Is it sport?
I think it is. And doth affection breed it?
I think it doth. Is't frailty that thus errs?
It is so too. And have not we affections,
Desires for sport, and frailty, as men have?
Then let them use us well; else let them know
The ills we do their ills instruct us so.

DESDEMONA. Good night, good night. God me such uses send,
Not to pick bad from bad, but by bad mend! *Exeunt*

ACT V. SCENE 1

Cyprus. A street

Enter IAGO *and* RODERIGO

IAGO. Here, stand behind this bulk; straight will he come.
Wear thy good rapier bare, and put it home.
Quick, quick; fear nothing; I'll be at thy elbow.
It makes us or it mars us; think on that,
And fix most firm thy resolution.

RODERIGO. Be near at hand; I may miscarry in't.

IAGO. Here, at thy hand. Be bold, and take thy stand.
[*Withdraws*]

RODERIGO. I have no great devotion to the deed;
And yet he hath given me satisfying reasons—
'Tis but a man gone. Forth, my sword; he dies.

IAGO. I have rubb'd this young quat almost to the sense,
And he grows angry. Now, whether he kill Cassio
Or Cassio him, or each do kill the other,
Every way makes my gain. Live Roderigo,
He calls me to a restitution large
Of gold and jewels that I bobb'd from him
As gifts to Desdemona;
It must not be. If Cassio do remain,
He hath a daily beauty in his life
That makes me ugly; and besides, the Moor
May unfold me to him; there stand I in much peril.
No, he must die. Be't so. I hear him coming.

Enter CASSIO

RODERIGO. I know his gait, 'tis he. Villain, thou diest!
[*Thrusts at* CASSIO]

CASSIO. That thrust had been mine enemy indeed
But that my coat is better than thou know'st.
I will make proof of thine.
[*Draws, and wounds* RODERIGO]

RODERIGO. O, I am slain!
[IAGO *stabs* CASSIO *from behind in the leg, and exit*]

CASSIO. I am maim'd for ever. Help, ho! murder! murder!
[*Falls*]

Enter OTHELLO *at a distance*

OTHELLO. The voice of Cassio. Iago keeps his word.
RODERIGO. O, villain that I am!
OTHELLO. It is even so.
CASSIO. O, help, ho! light! a surgeon!
OTHELLO. 'Tis he. O brave Iago, honest and just,
That hast such noble sense of thy friend's wrong!
Thou teachest me—minion, your dear lies dead,
And your unblest fate hies. Strumpet, I come.
Forth of my heart those charms, thine eyes, are blotted;
Thy bed, lust-stain'd, shall with lust's blood be spotted.
Exit

Enter LODOVICO *and* GRATIANO *at a distance*

CASSIO. What, ho! No watch? No passage? Murder! murder!
GRATIANO. 'Tis some mischance; the voice is very direful.
CASSIO. O, help!
LODOVICO. Hark!
RODERIGO. O wretched villain!
LODOVICO. Two or three groan. 'Tis heavy night;
These may be counterfeits; let's think't unsafe
To come in to the cry without more help.
RODERIGO. Nobody come? Then shall I bleed to death.

Re-enter IAGO *with a light*

LODOVICO. Hark!
GRATIANO. Here's one comes in his shirt, with light and weapons.
IAGO. Who's there? Whose noise is this that cries on murder?
LODOVICO. We do not know.
IAGO. Did not you hear a cry?
CASSIO. Here, here! For heaven's sake, help me!
IAGO. What's the matter?
GRATIANO. This is Othello's ancient, as I take it.
LODOVICO. The same indeed; a very valiant fellow.
IAGO. What are you here that cry so grievously?
CASSIO. Iago? O, I am spoil'd, undone by villains!
Give me some help.
IAGO. O me, Lieutenant! What villains have done this?
CASSIO. I think that one of them is hereabout,

And cannot make away.
IAGO. O treacherous villains!—
[*To* LODOVICO *and* GRATIANO] What are you there? Come in, and give some help.
RODERIGO. O, help me there!
CASSIO. That's one of them.
IAGO. O murd'rous slave! O villain! [*Stabs* RODERIGO]
RODERIGO. O damn'd Iago! O inhuman dog!
IAGO. Kill men i' th' dark! Where be these bloody thieves?
How silent is this town! Ho! murder! murder!
What may you be? Are you of good or evil?
LODOVICO. As you shall prove us, praise us.
IAGO. Signior Lodovico?
LODOVICO. He, sir.
IAGO. I cry you mercy. Here's Cassio hurt by villains.
GRATIANO. Cassio!
IAGO. How is't, brother?
CASSIO. My leg is cut in two.
IAGO. Marry, heaven forbid!
Light, gentlemen. I'll bind it with my shirt.

Enter BIANCA

BIANCA. What is the matter, ho? Who is't that cried?
IAGO. Who is't that cried!
BIANCA. O my dear Cassio!
My sweet Cassio! O Cassio, Cassio, Cassio!
IAGO. O notable strumpet! Cassio, may you suspect
Who they should be that have thus mangled you?
CASSIO. No.
GRATIANO. I am sorry to find you thus; I have been to seek you.
IAGO. Lend me a garter. So.
O, for a chair, to bear him easily hence!
BIANCA. Alas, he faints! O Cassio, Cassio, Cassio!
IAGO. Gentlemen all, I do suspect this trash
To be a party in this injury.
Patience awhile, good Cassio. Come, come;
Lend me a light. Know we this face or no?
Alas, my friend and my dear countryman
Roderigo? No—yes, sure; O heaven! Roderigo.

GRATIANO. What, of Venice?
IAGO. Even he, sir; did you know him?
GRATIANO. Know him! Ay.
IAGO. Signior Gratiano? I cry your gentle pardon;
These bloody accidents must excuse my manners,
That so neglected you.
GRATIANO. I am glad to see you.
IAGO. How do you, Cassio?—O, a chair, a chair!
GRATIANO. Roderigo!
IAGO. He, he, 'tis he. [*A chair brought in*] O, that's well said; the chair.
Some good man bear him carefully from hence;
I'll fetch the General's surgeon. [*To* BIANCA] For you, mistress,
Save you your labour.—He that lies slain here, Cassio,
Was my dear friend. What malice was between you?
CASSIO. None in the world; nor do I know the man.
IAGO. [*To* BIANCA] What, look you pale?—O, bear him out o' th' air. [CASSIO *and* RODERIGO *are borne off*]
Stay you, good gentlemen.—Look you pale, mistress?—
Do you perceive the gastness of her eye?—
Nay, an you stare, we shall hear more anon.—
Behold her well; I pray you look upon her.
Do you see, gentlemen? Nay, guiltiness will speak
Though tongues were out of use.

Enter EMILIA

EMILIA. 'Las, what's the matter? What's the matter, husband?
IAGO. Cassio hath here been set on in the dark
By Roderigo and fellows that are 'scap'd.
He's almost slain, and Roderigo quite dead.
EMILIA. Alas, good gentleman! Alas, good Cassio!
IAGO. This is the fruits of whoring. Prithee, Emilia,
Go know of Cassio where he supp'd to-night.—
What, do you shake at that?
BIANCA. He supp'd at my house; but I therefore shake not.
IAGO. O, did he so? I charge you go with me.
EMILIA. Fie, fie upon thee, strumpet!
BIANCA. I am no strumpet, but of life as honest
As you that thus abuse me.

EMILIA. As I! Foh! Fie upon thee!
IAGO. Kind gentlemen, let's go see poor Cassio dress'd.—
Come, mistress, you must tell's another tale.
Emilia, run you to the citadel,
And tell my lord and lady what hath happ'd.
Will you go on afore? [*Aside*] This is the night
That either makes me or fordoes me quite. *Exeunt*

SCENE 2

Cyprus. The citadel

DESDEMONA *in her bed. Enter* OTHELLO *with a light*

OTHELLO. It is the cause, it is the cause, my soul—
Let me not name it to you, you chaste stars—
It is the cause. Yet I'll not shed her blood,
Nor scar that whiter skin of hers than snow,
And smooth as monumental alabaster.
Yet she must die, else she'll betray more men.
Put out the light, and then put out the light.
If I quench thee, thou flaming minister,
I can again thy former light restore,
Should I repent me; but once put out thy light,
Thou cunning'st pattern of excelling nature,
I know not where is that Promethean heat
That can thy light relume. When I have pluck'd thy rose,
I cannot give it vital growth again;
It needs must wither. I'll smell thee on the tree.
[*Kissing her*]
O balmy breath, that dost almost persuade
Justice to break her sword! One more, one more.
Be thus when thou art dead, and I will kill thee,
And love thee after. One more, and that's the last:
So sweet was ne'er so fatal. I must weep,
But they are cruel tears. This sorrow's heavenly;
It strikes where it doth love. She wakes.
DESDEMONA. Who's there? Othello?
OTHELLO. Ay, Desdemona.
DESDEMONA. Will you come to bed, my lord?

OTHELLO. *Put out the light, and then put out the light.*
If I quench thee, thou flaming minister,
I can again thy former light restore,
Should I repent me; but once put out thy light,
Thou cunning'st pattern of excelling nature,
I know not where is that Promethean heat
That can thy light relume.

(ACT V. Scene 2)

OTHELLO. Have you pray'd to-night, Desdemona?
DESDEMONA. Ay, my lord.
OTHELLO. If you bethink yourself of any crime
 Unreconcil'd as yet to heaven and grace,
 Solicit for it straight.
DESDEMONA. Alack, my lord,
 What may you mean by that?
OTHELLO. Well, do it, and be brief; I will walk by.
 I would not kill thy unprepared spirit;
 No, heaven forfend!—I would not kill thy soul.
DESDEMONA. Talk you of killing?
OTHELLO. Ay, I do.
DESDEMONA. Then heaven
 Have mercy on me!
OTHELLO. Amen, with all my heart!
DESDEMONA. If you say so, I hope you will not kill me.
OTHELLO. Humh!
DESDEMONA. And yet I fear you; for you're fatal then
 When your eyes roll so. Why I should fear I know not,
 Since guiltiness I know not; but yet I feel I fear.
OTHELLO. Think on thy sins.
DESDEMONA. They are loves I bear to you.
OTHELLO. Ay, and for that thou diest.
DESDEMONA. That death's unnatural that kills for loving.
 Alas, why gnaw you so your nether lip?
 Some bloody passion shakes your very frame.
 These are portents; but yet I hope, I hope,
 They do not point on me.
OTHELLO. Peace, and be still.
DESDEMONA. I will so. What's the matter?
OTHELLO. That handkerchief which I so lov'd and gave thee
 Thou gav'st to Cassio.
DESDEMONA. No, by my life and soul!
 Send for the man and ask him.
OTHELLO. Sweet soul, take heed,
 Take heed of perjury; thou art on thy death-bed.
DESDEMONA. Ay, but not yet to die.
OTHELLO. Yes, presently.
 Therefore confess thee freely of thy sin;
 For to deny each article with oath

Cannot remove nor choke the strong conception
That I do groan withal. Thou art to die.

DESDEMONA. Then, Lord have mercy on me!

OTHELLO. I say, amen.

DESDEMONA. And have you mercy too! I never did
Offend you in my life; never lov'd Cassio
But with such general warranty of heaven
As I might love. I never gave him token.

OTHELLO. By heaven, I saw my handkerchief in's hand.
O perjur'd woman! thou dost stone my heart,
And mak'st me call what I intend to do
A murder, which I thought a sacrifice.
I saw the handkerchief.

DESDEMONA. He found it, then;
I never gave it him. Send for him hither;
Let him confess a truth.

OTHELLO. He hath confess'd.

DESDEMONA. What, my lord?

OTHELLO. That he hath–ud's death!–us'd thee.

DESDEMONA. How? unlawfully?

OTHELLO. Ay.

DESDEMONA. He will not say so.

OTHELLO. No, his mouth is stopp'd;
Honest Iago hath ta'en order for't.

DESDEMONA. O, my fear interprets! What, is he dead?

OTHELLO. Had all his hairs been lives, my great revenge
Had stomach for them all.

DESDEMONA. Alas, he is betray'd, and I undone!

OTHELLO. Out, strumpet! Weep'st thou for him to my face?

DESDEMONA. O, banish me, my lord, but kill me not!

OTHELLO. Down, strumpet.

DESDEMONA. Kill me to-morrow; let me live to-night.

OTHELLO. Nay, an you strive–

DESDEMONA. But half an hour!

OTHELLO. Being done, there is no pause.

DESDEMONA. But while I say one prayer!

OTHELLO. It is too late. [*Smothers her*]

DESDEMONA. O Lord, Lord, Lord!

EMILIA. [*Within*] My lord, my lord! what, ho! my lord, my lord!

OTHELLO. What voice is this? Not dead? not yet quite dead?
I that am cruel am yet merciful;
I would not have thee linger in thy pain.
So, so.
EMILIA. [*Within*] What, ho! my lord, my lord!
OTHELLO. Who's there?
EMILIA. [*Within*] O, good my lord, I'd speak a word with you!
OTHELLO. Yes—'tis Emilia—by and by. She's dead.
'Tis like she comes to speak of Cassio's death;
The noise was high. Ha! no more moving?
Still as the grave. Shall she come in? Were't good?
I think she stirs again. No. What's the best?
If she come in she'll sure speak to my wife.
My wife! my wife! what wife? I have no wife.
O insupportable! O heavy hour!
Methinks it should be now a huge eclipse
Of sun and moon, and that th' affrighted globe
Did yawn at alteration.
EMILIA. [*Within*] I do beseech you that I may speak with you. O, good my lord!
OTHELLO. I had forgot thee: O, come in, Emilia.
Soft, by and by. Let me the curtains draw.
Where art thou? [*Unlocks the door*]

Enter EMILIA

What's the matter with thee now?
EMILIA. O, my good lord, yonder's foul murders done!
OTHELLO. What, now?
EMILIA. But now, my lord.
OTHELLO. It is the very error of the moon;
She comes more nearer earth than she was wont,
And makes men mad.
EMILIA. Cassio, my lord, hath kill'd a young Venetian
Call'd Roderigo.
OTHELLO. Roderigo kill'd!
And Cassio kill'd!
EMILIA. No, Cassio is not kill'd.
OTHELLO. Not Cassio kill'd! Then murder's out of tune,

And sweet revenge grows harsh.
DESDEMONA. O, falsely, falsely murder'd!
EMILIA. O Lord, what cry is that?
OTHELLO. That! what?
EMILIA. Out and alas! that was my lady's voice.
Help! help, ho! help! O lady, speak again!
Sweet Desdemona! O sweet mistress, speak!
DESDEMONA. A guiltless death I die.
EMILIA. O, who hath done this deed?
DESDEMONA. Nobody. I myself. Farewell.
Commend me to my kind lord. O, farewell! [*She dies*]
OTHELLO. Why, how should she be murd'red?
EMILIA. Alas, who knows?
OTHELLO. You heard her say herself it was not I.
EMILIA. She said so. I must needs report a truth.
OTHELLO. She's like a liar gone to burning hell:
'Twas I that kill'd her.
EMILIA. O, the more angel she,
And you the blacker devil!
OTHELLO. She turn'd to folly, and she was a whore.
EMILIA. Thou dost belie her, and thou art a devil.
OTHELLO. She was false as water.
EMILIA. Thou art rash as fire to say
That she was false. O, she was heavenly true!
OTHELLO. Cassio did top her; ask thy husband else.
O, I were damn'd beneath all depth in hell
But that I did proceed upon just grounds
To this extremity. Thy husband knew it all.
EMILIA. My husband!
OTHELLO. Thy husband.
EMILIA. That she was false to wedlock?
OTHELLO. Ay, with Cassio. Nay, had she been true,
If heaven would make me such another world
Of one entire and perfect chrysolite,
I'd not have sold her for it.
EMILIA. My husband!
OTHELLO. Ay, 'twas he that told me on her first.
An honest man he is, and hates the slime
That sticks on filthy deeds.
EMILIA. My husband!

OTHELLO. What needs this iterance, woman? I say thy husband.

EMILIA. O mistress, villainy hath made mocks with love!
My husband say that she was false!

OTHELLO. He, woman;
I say thy husband; dost understand the word?
My friend, thy husband—honest, honest Iago.

EMILIA. If he say so, may his pernicious soul
Rot half a grain a day! He lies to th' heart.
She was too fond of her most filthy bargain.

OTHELLO. Ha!

EMILIA. Do thy worst:
This deed of thine is no more worthy heaven
Than thou wast worthy her.

OTHELLO. Peace, you were best.

EMILIA. Thou hast not half that power to do me harm
As I have to be hurt. O gull! O dolt!
As ignorant as dirt! Thou hast done a deed—
I care not for thy sword; I'll make thee known,
Though I lost twenty lives. Help! help, ho! help!
The Moor hath kill'd my mistress! Murder! murder!

Enter MONTANO, GRATIANO, IAGO, *and others*

MONTANO. What is the matter? How now, General!

EMILIA. O, are you come, Iago? You have done well,
That men must lay their murders on your neck.

GRATIANO. What is the matter?

EMILIA. Disprove this villain, if thou be'st a man:
He says thou told'st him that his wife was false.
I know thou didst not; thou'rt not such a villain.
Speak, for my heart is full.

IAGO. I told him what I thought, and told no more
Than what he found himself was apt and true.

EMILIA. But did you ever tell him she was false?

IAGO. I did.

EMILIA. You told a lie—an odious, damned lie.
Upon my soul, a lie—a wicked lie.
She false with Cassio! Did you say with Cassio?

IAGO. With Cassio, mistress. Go to, charm your tongue.

EMILIA. I will not charm my tongue; I am bound to speak:

My mistress here lies murdered in her bed.
ALL. O heavens forfend!
EMILIA. And your reports have set the murder on.
OTHELLO. Nay, stare not, masters: it is true, indeed.
GRATIANO. 'Tis a strange truth.
MONTANO. O monstrous act!
EMILIA. Villainy, villainy, villainy!
I think upon't. I think–I smell't. O villainy!
I thought so then. I'll kill myself for grief.
O villainy, villainy!
IAGO. What, are you mad? I charge you get you home.
EMILIA. Good gentlemen, let me have leave to speak.
'Tis proper I obey him, but not now.
Perchance, Iago, I will ne'er go home.
OTHELLO. O! O! O! [*Falls on the bed*]
EMILIA. Nay, lay thee down and roar;
For thou hast kill'd the sweetest innocent
That e'er did lift up eye.
OTHELLO. [*Rising*] O, she was foul!
I scarce did know you, uncle. There lies your niece,
Whose breath indeed these hands have newly stopp'd.
I know this act shows horrible and grim.
GRATIANO. Poor Desdemona! I am glad thy father's dead.
Thy match was mortal to him, and pure grief
Shore his old thread atwain. Did he live now,
This sight would make him do a desperate turn,
Yea, curse his better angel from his side,
And fall to reprobance.
OTHELLO. 'Tis pitiful; but yet Iago knows
That she with Cassio hath the act of shame
A thousand times committed; Cassio confess'd it;
And she did gratify his amorous works
With that recognizance and pledge of love
Which I first gave her; I saw it in his hand.
It was a handkerchief, an antique token
My father gave my mother.
EMILIA. O God! O heavenly God!
IAGO. Zounds, hold your peace.
EMILIA. 'Twill out, 'twill out. I, peace!
No, I will speak as liberal as the north.

Let heaven and men and devils, let them all,
All, all, cry shame against me, yet I'll speak.

IAGO. Be wise, and get you home.

EMILIA. I will not. [IAGO *offers to stab his wife*]

GRATIANO. Fie! your sword upon a woman?

EMILIA. O thou dull Moor! That handkerchief thou speak'st of
I found by fortune, and did give my husband;
For often with a solemn earnestness–
More than indeed belong'd to such a trifle–
He begg'd of me to steal it.

IAGO. Villainous whore!

EMILIA. She give it Cassio! No, alas, I found it,
And I did give't my husband.

IAGO. Filth, thou liest.

EMILIA. By heaven, I do not, I do not, gentlemen.
O murderous coxcomb! What should such a fool
Do with so good a wife?

[*The Moor runs at* IAGO; MONTANO *and others disarm the Moor.* IAGO *kills his wife and escapes*]

OTHELLO. Are there no stones in heaven but what serves for the thunder? Precious villain!

GRATIANO. The woman falls; sure he hath kill'd his wife.

EMILIA. Ay, ay. O, lay me by my mistress' side.

GRATIANO. He's gone, but his wife's kill'd.

MONTANO. 'Tis a notorious villain. Take you this weapon,
Which I have here recover'd from the Moor.
Come, guard the door without; let him not pass,
But kill him rather. I'll after that same villain,
For 'tis a damned slave.

Exeunt MONTANO, GRATIANO, *and others*

OTHELLO. I am not valiant neither–
But every puny whipster gets my sword.
But why should honour outlive honesty?
Let it go all.

EMILIA. What did thy song bode, lady?
Hark, canst thou hear me? I will play the swan,
And die in music. [*Sings*] Willow, willow, willow.–
Moor, she was chaste; she lov'd thee, cruel Moor;
So come my soul to bliss, as I speak true;

So speaking as I think, alas, I die. [*She dies*]

OTHELLO. I have another weapon in this chamber;
It was a sword of Spain, the ice-brook's temper.
O, here it is. Uncle, I must come forth.

GRATIANO. [*Within*] If thou attempt it, it will cost thee dear;
Thou hast no weapon, and perforce must suffer.

OTHELLO. Look in upon me, then, and speak with me,
Or, naked as I am, I will assault thee.

Re-enter GRATIANO

GRATIANO. What is the matter?

OTHELLO. Behold, I have a weapon;
A better never did itself sustain
Upon a soldier's thigh. I have seen the day
That with this little arm and this good sword
I have made my way through more impediments
Than twenty times your stop. But, O vain boast!
Who can control his fate? 'Tis not so now.
Be not afraid though you do see me weapon'd;
Here is my journey's end, here is my butt,
And very sea-mark of my utmost sail.
Do you go back dismay'd? 'Tis a lost fear;
Man but a rush against Othello's breast,
And he retires. Where should Othello go?
Now, how dost thou look now? O ill-starr'd wench!
Pale as thy smock! When we shall meet at compt,
This look of thine will hurl my soul from heaven,
And fiends will snatch at it. Cold, cold, my girl!
Even like thy chastity. O cursed, cursed slave!
Whip me, ye devils,
From the possession of this heavenly sight.
Blow me about in winds, roast me in sulphur,
Wash me in steep-down gulfs of liquid fire.
O Desdemona! Dead! Desdemona! Dead! O! O!

Enter LODOVICO, MONTANO, CASSIO *carried in a chair, and* OFFICERS, *with* IAGO *prisoner*

LODOVICO. Where is this rash and most unfortunate man?

OTHELLO. That's he that was Othello—here I am.

LODOVICO. Where is that viper? Bring the villain forth.
OTHELLO. I look down towards his feet—but that's a fable.
If that thou be'st a devil, I cannot kill thee. [*Wounds* IAGO]
LODOVICO. Wrench his sword from him.
IAGO. I bleed, sir; but not kill'd.
OTHELLO. I am not sorry neither: I'd have thee live;
For, in my sense, 'tis happiness to die.
LODOVICO. O thou Othello, that was once so good,
Fall'n in the practice of a damned slave,
What shall be said to thee?
OTHELLO. Why, any thing:
An honourable murderer, if you will;
For nought I did in hate, but all in honour.
LODOVICO. This wretch hath part confess'd his villainy.
Did you and he consent in Cassio's death?
OTHELLO. Ay.
CASSIO. Dear General, I never gave you cause.
OTHELLO. I do believe it, and I ask your pardon.
Will you, I pray, demand that demi-devil
Why he hath thus ensnar'd my soul and body?
IAGO. Demand me nothing. What you know, you know.
From this time forth I never will speak word.
LODOVICO. What, not to pray?
GRATIANO. Torments will ope your lips.
OTHELLO. Well, thou dost best.
LODOVICO. Sir, you shall understand what hath befall'n,
Which, as I think, you know not. Here is a letter
Found in the pocket of the slain Roderigo;
And here another: the one of them imports
The death of Cassio to be undertook
By Roderigo.
OTHELLO. O villain!
CASSIO. Most heathenish and most gross!
LODOVICO. Now here's another discontented paper,
Found in his pocket too; and this, it seems,
Roderigo meant t' have sent this damned villain;
But that, belike, Iago in the nick
Came in and satisfied him.
OTHELLO. O thou pernicious caitiff!
How came you, Cassio, by that handkerchief

That was my wife's?

CASSIO. I found it in my chamber;
And he himself confess'd it even now
That there he dropp'd it for a special purpose
Which wrought to his desire.

OTHELLO. O fool! fool! fool!

CASSIO. There is besides in Roderigo's letter,
How he upbraids Iago that he made him
Brave me upon the watch; whereon it came
That I was cast; and even but now he spake,
After long seeming dead, Iago hurt him,
Iago set him on.

LODOVICO. You must forsake this room and go with us.
Your power and your command is taken off,
And Cassio rules in Cyprus. For this slave,
If there be any cunning cruelty
That can torment him much and hold him long,
It shall be his. You shall close prisoner rest
Till that the nature of your fault be known
To the Venetian state. Come, bring away.

OTHELLO. Soft you; a word or two before you go.
I have done the state some service, and they know't—
No more of that. I pray you, in your letters,
When you shall these unlucky deeds relate,
Speak of me as I am; nothing extenuate,
Nor set down aught in malice. Then must you speak
Of one that lov'd not wisely, but too well;
Of one not easily jealous, but, being wrought,
Perplexed in the extreme; of one whose hand,
Like the base Indian, threw a pearl away
Richer than all his tribe; of one whose subdu'd eyes,
Albeit unused to the melting mood,
Drops tears as fast as the Arabian trees
Their med'cinable gum. Set you down this:
And say besides that in Aleppo once,
Where a malignant and a turban'd Turk
Beat a Venetian and traduc'd the state,
I took by th' throat the circumcised dog,
And smote him—thus. [*He stabs himself*]

LODOVICO. O bloody period!

GRATIANO. All that is spoke is marr'd.
OTHELLO. I kiss'd thee ere I kill'd thee. No way but this–
Killing my self, to die upon a kiss.
[*Falls on the bed and dies*]
CASSIO. This did I fear, but thought he had no weapon;
For he was great of heart.
LODOVICO. [*To* IAGO] O Spartan dog,
More fell than anguish, hunger, or the sea!
Look on the tragic loading of this bed.
This is thy work.–The object poisons sight;
Let it be hid. Gratiano, keep the house,
And seize upon the fortunes of the Moor,
For they succeed on you. To you, Lord Governor
Remains the censure of this hellish villain;
The time, the place, the torture–O, enforce it!
Myself will straight aboard; and to the state
This heavy act with heavy heart relate. *Exeunt*

The Tragedy of
Antony and Cleopatra

ANTONY AND CLEOPATRA

This is the play which most clearly shows how the critic must insist that Shakespeare's stage-craft be judged not by the material demands of the modern stage that aims at realism of setting and place but by the conditions governing the treatment of Shakespeare's unlocalized stage. A play with some forty-two scenes, some of them running only to two, four, or six lines, with regular changes of place, cannot be produced in its original form in a style that aims at the realistic representation of background. Yet the play reads without our losing our sense of the continuity of the action; now we are in Egypt, now in Rome, but the relation of scene to scene is never in doubt. Granville-Barker has very cleverly emphasized this aspect of the plotting by two quotations from Dr. Johnson. Johnson recognized the continuity of interest when he said:

> This play keeps curiosity always busy, and the passions always interested. The continual hurry of the action, the variety of incidents, and the quick succession of one personage to another, call the mind forward without intermission from the first Act to the last.

Yet, as Granville-Barker notes, having praised the sustained interest of the piece Johnson thinks of the way he imagines a play should be put together to satisfy a scholarly scrutiny and concludes:

> The events, of which the principals are described according to history, are produced without any art of connection or care of disposition.

Shakespeare, it would seem, had flung together some episodes from the story of Antony, and by a happy chance they so fitted together that the mind passes without intermission from one to the other. Those who fancy chance is so accommodating should, as one critic has said, try their own luck at this game in the hope they may pull from fortune's wheel so interesting and sustained a plot.

The continuity that Johnson emphasizes was lost on the

stage of his day as it must be on any realistic stage. Shakespeare took no care to dispose things to fit such a stage; the art of connection demanded by that stage was different in form at least from that required at the Globe in Shakespeare's day. Unfortunately the belief that the world is getting better and better has persuaded some to believe that Shakespeare's stage must be inferior to that of yesterday, and that this inferiority helps to explain the clumsiness of such a play as *Antony and Cleopatra* and the impossibility of adapting it as a whole to the picture stage. It is allowed that the Greek theatre has its right to its own peculiarities, for it is protected by the distance the language places between it and modern comprehension; the Age of Elizabeth and James, however, seems to come very close to us especially in a modernized text, and one is apt to forget that the Acts and Scenes of such an edition do not correspond precisely to what the Acts and Scenes of a modern piece stand for. Putting aside Act-division in Shakespeare for the moment, we may say that within the Act there was no break between scene and scene. Shakespeare's stage allowed of the same fluidity that is found in reading. Characters come and go without any shifting of scenery; what they say shows us where they are or how what they speak and do is related to what has gone before. The spectator's interest is carried on from episode to episode just as in reading, for what we are interested in is how events translate themselves in terms of the characters' emotions and purposes; we do not need to see the battle at Actium, for what happened there and its consequences for the actors are brought home to us by the words of those who are watching it. In their fears and horror is mirrored for us the defeat of Antony.

The conflict in Johnson's thoughts about the play has been echoed by many commentators. Dowden felt that *Antony and Cleopatra* could not be said to be well constructed, yet after explaining why this judgment seems reasonable he concludes, 'None the less the final impression is one of unity—and that impression is ineffaceable.' It is difficult to see what more one can ask from a play than this unity and power of impression; and this quarrel with a masterpiece that achieves its end by means we disapprove of is seen as a failure of our historical sense once we relate the play to 'the theatre of its nativity.'

It has been pointed out by Bradley and others that the first half of *Antony and Cleopatra* is, compared with *Julius Cæsar* or *Macbeth*, superficially lacking in drama. The opening conversation between the Roman officers is not followed as in *Julius Cæsar* by any public commotion; we have no fighting as in *Romeo and Juliet* or *Coriolanus*, only conversations between various parties and what may seem courtly or imperial junketings. Yet Shakespeare creates a sense of opposition and tension that is none the less powerful and ominous because to the casual eye the surface of affairs seems to run smoothly and well. At the very moment when Menas thinks Antony and Octavius are 'for ever knit together' Enobarbus can say 'the band that seems to tie their friendship together will be the very strangler of their amity.' Rome and Egypt stand for two different and indeed opposite views of life. The tension shows in the opening scene in the conversation of the soldiers and the feelings attending the departure of Antony to the West; and, in the Roman scenes that follow, Shakespeare, although he establishes for us Antony's competence and power when he cares to assume the part of the Roman soldier and politician, reveals the side to which Antony's inclinations draw him. Antony does not bear himself as one broken down by debauchery and incapable of anything more than lechery in idleness; he turns to Cleopatra not in his decay but at the very time when he has vindicated his position as one of the rulers of the world. Yet so clearly has Shakespeare established the incompatibility of the two ways of life that Actium seems the inevitable sequel to the smooth but deadly drift of Antony's inclinations.

The duel between Antony and Octavius repeats in a more spacious theatre that between Richard and Bolingbroke. Richard throws away a kingdom, while Antony squanders an empire, and as Antony has the capacity for rule and affairs that Richard had not, the Roman's conduct might be judged the more heinous, especially when such an aggravation as his liaison with Cleopatra is put in the balance. Yet two considerations throw out the parallel between Richard and Antony. Richard is a king of England and it is not merely what he does but its effect as well that interests the dramatist and the spectators; Richard has a task against which he cannot alto-

gether escape measurement. No such national feelings obscure or distort the sense of what Antony is; and now Cleopatra need not be cited against him. Rather she becomes a witness to his pre-eminence, and the more remarkable she is in herself the more convincing her testimony. Unlike the English king, Antony had a positive rather than a negative attitude to the circumstances in which he found himself. He chose one way in preference to another, although capable of either part. His choice makes clear to us the man he was and that with all his faults he had the greatness without which there could have been no tragedy.

MARK ANTONY OCTAVIUS CÆSAR M. AEMILIUS LEPIDUS	*Triumvirs*
SEXTUS POMPEIUS	
DOMITIUS ENOBARBUS VENTIDIUS EROS SCARUS DERCETAS DEMETRIUS PHILO	*friends to Antony*
MÆCENAS AGRIPPA DOLABELLA PROCULEIUS THYREUS GALLUS	*friends to Cæsar*
MENAS MENECRATES VARRIUS	*friends to Pompey*

TAURUS, *Lieutenant-General to Cæsar*
CANIDIUS, *Lieutenant-General to Antony*
SILIUS, *an Officer in Ventidius's army*
EUPHRONIUS, *an Ambassador from Antony to Cæsar*

ALEXAS MARDIAN SELEUCUS DIOMEDES	*attendants on Cleopatra*

A SOOTHSAYER
A CLOWN

CLEOPATRA, *Queen of Egypt*
OCTAVIA, *sister to Cæsar and wife to Antony*

CHARMIAN IRAS	*ladies attending on Cleopatra*

Officers, Soldiers, Messengers, *and* Attendants

SCENE:
The Roman Empire

Antony and Cleopatra

ACT I. SCENE 1

Alexandria. CLEOPATRA'S *palace*

Enter DEMETRIUS *and* PHILO

PHILO. Nay, but this dotage of our general's
O'erflows the measure. Those his goodly eyes,
That o'er the files and musters of the war
Have glow'd like plated Mars, now bend, now turn,
The office and devotion of their view
Upon a tawny front. His captain's heart,
Which in the scuffles of great fights hath burst
The buckles on his breast, reneges all temper,
And is become the bellows and the fan
To cool a gipsy's lust.

Flourish. Enter ANTONY, CLEOPATRA, *her* LADIES, *the train, with eunuchs fanning her*

Look where they come!
Take but good note, and you shall see in him
The triple pillar of the world transform'd
Into a strumpet's fool. Behold and see.
CLEOPATRA. If it be love indeed, tell me how much.
ANTONY. There's beggary in the love that can be reckon'd.
CLEOPATRA. I'll set a bourn how far to be belov'd.
ANTONY. Then must thou needs find out new heaven, new earth.

Enter a MESSENGER

MESSENGER. News, my good lord, from Rome.
ANTONY. Grates me the sum.
CLEOPATRA. Nay, hear them, Antony.
Fulvia perchance is angry; or who knows
If the scarce-bearded Cæsar have not sent
His pow'rful mandate to you: 'Do this or this;

Take in that kingdom and enfranchise that;
Perform't, or else we damn thee.'

ANTONY. How, my love?

CLEOPATRA. Perchance? Nay, and most like,
You must not stay here longer; your dismission
Is come from Cæsar; therefore hear it, Antony.
Where's Fulvia's process? Cæsar's I would say? Both?
Call in the messengers. As I am Egypt's Queen,
Thou blushest, Antony, and that blood of thine
Is Cæsar's homager. Else so thy cheek pays shame
When shrill-tongu'd Fulvia scolds. The messengers!

ANTONY. Let Rome in Tiber melt, and the wide arch
Of the rang'd empire fall! Here is my space.
Kingdoms are clay; our dungy earth alike
Feeds beast as man. The nobleness of life
Is to do thus [*embracing*], when such a mutual pair
And such a twain can do't, in which I bind,
On pain of punishment, the world to weet
We stand up peerless.

CLEOPATRA. Excellent falsehood!
Why did he marry Fulvia, and not love her?
I'll seem the fool I am not. Antony
Will be himself.

ANTONY. But stirr'd by Cleopatra.
Now for the love of Love and her soft hours,
Let's not confound the time with conference harsh;
There's not a minute of our lives should stretch
Without some pleasure now. What sport to-night?

CLEOPATRA. Hear the ambassadors.

ANTONY. Fie, wrangling queen!
Whom everything becomes—to chide, to laugh,
To weep; whose every passion fully strives
To make itself in thee fair and admir'd.
No messenger but thine, and all alone
To-night we'll wander through the streets and note
The qualities of people. Come, my queen;
Last night you did desire it. Speak not to us.

Exeunt ANTONY *and* CLEOPATRA, *with the train*

DEMETRIUS. Is Cæsar with Antonius priz'd so slight?

PHILO. Sir, sometimes when he is not Antony,

He comes too short of that great property
Which still should go with Antony.

DEMETRIUS. I am full sorry
That he approves the common liar, who
Thus speaks of him at Rome; but I will hope
Of better deeds to-morrow. Rest you happy! *Exeunt*

SCENE 2

Alexandria. CLEOPATRA'S *palace*

Enter CHARMIAN, IRAS, ALEXAS, *and a* SOOTHSAYER

CHARMIAN. Lord Alexas, sweet Alexas, most anything Alexas, almost most absolute Alexas, where's the soothsayer that you prais'd so to th' Queen? O that I knew this husband, which you say must charge his horns with garlands!

ALEXAS. Soothsayer!

SOOTHSAYER. Your will?

CHARMIAN. Is this the man? Is't you, sir, that know things?

SOOTHSAYER. In nature's infinite book of secrecy
A little I can read.

ALEXAS. Show him your hand.

Enter ENOBARBUS

ENOBARBUS. Bring in the banquet quickly; wine enough
Cleopatra's health to drink.

CHARMIAN. Good, sir, give me good fortune.

SOOTHSAYER. I make not, but foresee.

CHARMIAN. Pray, then, foresee me one.

SOOTHSAYER. You shall be yet far fairer than you are.

CHARMIAN. He means in flesh.

IRAS. No, you shall paint when you are old.

CHARMIAN. Wrinkles forbid!

ALEXAS. Vex not his prescience; be attentive.

CHARMIAN. Hush!

SOOTHSAYER. You shall be more beloving than beloved.

CHARMIAN. I had rather heat my liver with drinking.

ALEXAS. Nay, hear him.

CHARMIAN. Good now, some excellent fortune! Let me be married to three kings in a forenoon, and widow them all. Let me have a child at fifty, to whom Herod of Jewry may do homage. Find me to marry me with Octavius Cæsar, and companion me with my mistress.

SOOTHSAYER. You shall outlive the lady whom you serve.

CHARMIAN. O, excellent! I love long life better than figs.

SOOTHSAYER. You have seen and prov'd a fairer former fortune
Than that which is to approach.

CHARMIAN. Then belike my children shall have no names. Prithee, how many boys and wenches must I have?

SOOTHSAYER. If every of your wishes had a womb,
And fertile every wish, a million.

CHARMIAN. Out, fool! I forgive thee for a witch.

ALEXAS. You think none but your sheets are privy to your wishes.

CHARMIAN. Nay, come, tell Iras hers.

ALEXAS. We'll know all our fortunes.

ENOBARBUS. Mine, and most of our fortunes, to-night, shall be—drunk to bed.

IRAS. There's a palm presages chastity, if nothing else.

CHARMIAN. E'en as the o'erflowing Nilus presageth famine.

IRAS. Go, you wild bedfellow, you cannot soothsay.

CHARMIAN. Nay, if an oily palm be not a fruitful prognostication, I cannot scratch mine ear. Prithee, tell her but a worky-day fortune.

SOOTHSAYER. Your fortunes are alike.

IRAS. But how, but how? Give me particulars.

SOOTHSAYER. I have said.

IRAS. Am I not an inch of fortune better than she?

CHARMIAN. Well, if you were but an inch of fortune better than I, where would you choose it?

IRAS. Not in my husband's nose.

CHARMIAN. Our worser thoughts heavens mend! Alexas—come, his fortune, his fortune! O, let him marry a woman that cannot go, sweet Isis, I beseech thee! And let her die too, and give him a worse! And let worse follow worse, till the worst of all follow him laughing to his grave, fiftyfold a cuckold! Good Isis, hear me this prayer, though thou deny me a matter of more weight; good Isis, I beseech thee!

IRAS. Amen. Dear goddess, hear that prayer of the people! For, as it is a heartbreaking to see a handsome man loose-wiv'd, so it is a deadly sorrow to behold a foul knave uncuckolded. Therefore, dear Isis, keep decorum, and fortune him accordingly!

CHARMIAN. Amen.

ALEXAS. Lo now, if it lay in their hands to make me a cuckold, they would make themselves whores but they'ld do't!

Enter CLEOPATRA

ENOBARBUS. Hush! Here comes Antony.

CHARMIAN. Not he; the Queen.

CLEOPATRA. Saw you my lord?

ENOBARBUS. No, lady.

CLEOPATRA. Was he not here?

CHARMIAN. No, madam.

CLEOPATRA. He was dispos'd to mirth; but on the sudden
A Roman thought hath struck him. Enobarbus!

ENOBARBUS. Madam?

CLEOPATRA. Seek him, and bring him hither. Where's Alexas?

ALEXAS. Here, at your service. My lord approaches.

Enter ANTONY, *with a* MESSENGER *and attendants*

CLEOPATRA. We will not look upon him. Go with us.

Exeunt CLEOPATRA, ENOBARBUS, *and the rest*

MESSENGER. Fulvia thy wife first came into the field.

ANTONY. Against my brother Lucius?

MESSENGER. Ay.
But soon that war had end, and the time's state
Made friends of them, jointing their force 'gainst Cæsar,
Whose better issue in the war from Italy
Upon the first encounter drave them.

ANTONY. Well, what worst?

MESSENGER. The nature of bad news infects the teller.

ANTONY. When it concerns the fool or coward. On!
Things that are past are done with me. 'Tis thus:

Who tells me true, though in his tale lie death,
I hear him as he flatter'd.

MESSENGER. Labienus–
This is stiff news–hath with his Parthian force
Extended Asia from Euphrates,
His conquering banner shook from Syria
To Lydia and to Ionia,
Whilst–

ANTONY. Antony, thou wouldst say.

MESSENGER. O, my lord!

ANTONY. Speak to me home; mince not the general tongue;
Name Cleopatra as she is call'd in Rome.
Rail thou in Fulvia's phrase, and taunt my faults
With such full licence as both truth and malice
Have power to utter. O, then we bring forth weeds
When our quick minds lie still, and our ills told us
Is as our earing. Fare thee well awhile.

MESSENGER. At your noble pleasure. *Exit*

ANTONY. From Sicyon, ho, the news! Speak there!

FIRST ATTENDANT. The man from Sicyon–is there such an one?

SECOND ATTENDANT. He stays upon your will.

ANTONY. Let him appear.
These strong Egyptian fetters I must break,
Or lose myself in dotage.

Enter another MESSENGER *with a letter*

What are you?

SECOND MESSENGER. Fulvia thy wife is dead.

ANTONY. Where died she?

SECOND MESSENGER. In Sicyon.
Her length of sickness, with what else more serious
Importeth thee to know, this bears. [*Gives the letter*]

ANTONY. Forbear me. *Exit* MESSENGER
There's a great spirit gone! Thus did I desire it.
What our contempts doth often hurl from us
We wish it ours again; the present pleasure,
By revolution low'ring, does become
The opposite of itself. She's good, being gone;
The hand could pluck her back that shov'd her on.

I must from this enchanting queen break off.
Ten thousand harms, more than the ills I know,
My idleness doth hatch. How now, Enobarbus!

Re-enter ENOBARBUS

ENOBARBUS. What's your pleasure, sir?

ANTONY. I must with haste from hence.

ENOBARBUS. Why, then we kill all our women. We see how mortal an unkindness is to them; if they suffer our departure, death's the word.

ANTONY. I must be gone.

ENOBARBUS. Under a compelling occasion, let women die. It were pity to cast them away for nothing, though between them and a great cause they should be esteemed nothing. Cleopatra, catching but the least noise of this, dies instantly; I have seen her die twenty times upon far poorer moment. I do think there is mettle in death, which commits some loving act upon her, she hath such a celerity in dying.

ANTONY. She is cunning past man's thought.

ENOBARBUS. Alack, sir, no! Her passions are made of nothing but the finest part of pure love. We cannot call her winds and waters sighs and tears; they are greater storms and tempests than almanacs can report. This cannot be cunning in her; if it be, she makes a show'r of rain as well as Jove.

ANTONY. Would I had never seen her!

ENOBARBUS. O sir, you had then left unseen a wonderful piece of work, which not to have been blest withal would have discredited your travel.

ANTONY. Fulvia is dead.

ENOBARBUS. Sir?

ANTONY. Fulvia is dead.

ENOBARBUS. Fulvia?

ANTONY. Dead.

ENOBARBUS. Why, sir, give the gods a thankful sacrifice. When it pleaseth their deities to take the wife of a man from him, it shows to man the tailors of the earth; comforting therein that when old robes are worn out there are members to make new. If there were no more women but Fulvia, then had you indeed a cut, and the case to be lamented. This grief is crown'd with consolation: your old smock brings forth a new petticoat; and indeed the tears live in an onion that should water this sorrow.

ANTONY. The business she hath broached in the state
Cannot endure my absence.

ENOBARBUS. And the business you have broach'd here cannot be without you; especially that of Cleopatra's, which wholly depends on your abode.

ANTONY. No more light answers. Let our officers
Have notice what we purpose. I shall break
The cause of our expedience to the Queen,
And get her leave to part. For not alone
The death of Fulvia, with more urgent touches,
Do strongly speak to us; but the letters too
Of many our contriving friends in Rome
Petition us at home. Sextus Pompeius
Hath given the dare to Cæsar, and commands
The empire of the sea; our slippery people,
Whose love is never link'd to the deserver
Till his deserts are past, begin to throw
Pompey the Great and all his dignities
Upon his son; who, high in name and power,
Higher than both in blood and life, stands up
For the main soldier; whose quality, going on,
The sides o' th' world may danger. Much is breeding
Which, like the courser's hair, hath yet but life
And not a serpent's poison. Say our pleasure,
To such whose place is under us, requires
Our quick remove from hence.

ENOBARBUS. I shall do't. *Exeunt*

SCENE 3

Alexandria. CLEOPATRA's *palace*

Enter CLEOPATRA, CHARMIAN, IRAS, *and* ALEXAS

CLEOPATRA. Where is he?

CHARMIAN. I did not see him since.

CLEOPATRA. See where he is, who's with him, what he does.
I did not send you. If you find him sad,
Say I am dancing; if in mirth, report
That I am sudden sick. Quick, and return. *Exit* ALEXAS

CHARMIAN. Madam, methinks, if you did love him dearly,
You do not hold the method to enforce
The like from him.

CLEOPATRA. What should I do I do not?

CHARMIAN. In each thing give him way; cross him in nothing.

CLEOPATRA. Thou teachest like a fool—the way to lose him.

CHARMIAN. Tempt him not so too far; I wish, forbear;
In time we hate that which we often fear.

Enter ANTONY

But here comes Antony.

CLEOPATRA. I am sick and sullen.

ANTONY. I am sorry to give breathing to my purpose—

CLEOPATRA. Help me away, dear Charmian; I shall fall.
It cannot be thus long; the sides of nature
Will not sustain it.

ANTONY. Now, my dearest queen—

CLEOPATRA. Pray you, stand farther from me.

ANTONY. What's the matter?

CLEOPATRA. I know by that same eye there's some good news.
What says the married woman? You may go.
Would she had never given you leave to come!
Let her not say 'tis I that keep you here—
I have no power upon you; hers you are.

ANTONY. The gods best know—

CLEOPATRA. O, never was there queen
So mightily betray'd! Yet at the first
I saw the treasons planted.

ANTONY. Cleopatra—

CLEOPATRA. Why should I think you can be mine and true,
Though you in swearing shake the throned gods,
Who have been false to Fulvia? Riotous madness,
To be entangled with those mouth-made vows,
Which break themselves in swearing!

ANTONY. Most sweet queen–
CLEOPATRA. Nay, pray you seek no colour for your going,
But bid farewell, and go. When you sued staying,
Then was the time for words. No going then!
Eternity was in our lips and eyes,
Bliss in our brows' bent, none our parts so poor
But was a race of heaven. They are so still,
Or thou, the greatest soldier of the world,
Art turn'd the greatest liar.
ANTONY. How now, lady!
CLEOPATRA. I would I had thy inches. Thou shouldst know
There were a heart in Egypt.
ANTONY. Hear me, queen:
The strong necessity of time commands
Our services awhile; but my full heart
Remains in use with you. Our Italy
Shines o'er with civil swords: Sextus Pompeius
Makes his approaches to the port of Rome;
Equality of two domestic powers
Breed scrupulous faction; the hated, grown to strength,
Are newly grown to love. The condemn'd Pompey,
Rich in his father's honour, creeps apace
Into the hearts of such as have not thrived
Upon the present state, whose numbers threaten;
And quietness, grown sick of rest, would purge
By any desperate change. My more particular,
And that which most with you should safe my going,
Is Fulvia's death.
CLEOPATRA. Though age from folly could not give me freedom,
It does from childishness. Can Fulvia die?
ANTONY. She's dead, my Queen.
Look here, and at thy sovereign leisure read
The garboils she awak'd. At the last, best.
See when and where she died.
CLEOPATRA. O most false love!
Where be the sacred vials thou shouldst fill
With sorrowful water? Now I see, I see,
In Fulvia's death how mine receiv'd shall be.
ANTONY. Quarrel no more, but be prepar'd to know

The purposes I bear; which are, or cease,
As you shall give th' advice. By the fire
That quickens Nilus' slime, I go from hence
Thy soldier, servant, making peace or war
As thou affects.

CLEOPATRA. Cut my lace, Charmian, come!
But let it be; I am quickly ill and well—
So Antony loves.

ANTONY. My precious queen, forbear,
And give true evidence to his love, which stands
An honourable trial.

CLEOPATRA. So Fulvia told me.
I prithee turn aside and weep for her;
Then bid adieu to me, and say the tears
Belong to Egypt. Good now, play one scene
Of excellent dissembling, and let it look
Like perfect honour.

ANTONY. You'll heat my blood; no more.

CLEOPATRA. You can do better yet; but this is meetly.

ANTONY. Now, by my sword—

CLEOPATRA. And target. Still he mends;
But this is not the best. Look, prithee, Charmian,
How this Herculean Roman does become
The carriage of his chafe.

ANTONY. I'll leave you, lady.

CLEOPATRA. Courteous lord, one word.
Sir, you and I must part—but that's not it.
Sir, you and I have lov'd—but there's not it.
That you know well. Something it is I would—
O, my oblivion is a very Antony,
And I am all forgotten!

ANTONY. But that your royalty
Holds idleness your subject, I should take you
For idleness itself.

CLEOPATRA. 'Tis sweating labour
To bear such idleness so near the heart
As Cleopatra this. But, sir, forgive me;
Since my becomings kill me when they do not
Eye well to you. Your honour calls you hence;
Therefore be deaf to my unpitied folly,

And all the gods go with you! Upon your sword
Sit laurel victory, and smooth success
Be strew'd before your feet!

ANTONY. Let us go. Come.
Our separation so abides and flies
That thou, residing here, goes yet with me,
And I, hence fleeting, here remain with thee.
Away! *Exeunt*

SCENE 4

Rome. CÆSAR'S *house*

Enter OCTAVIUS CÆSAR, *reading a letter;*
LEPIDUS, *and their train*

CÆSAR. You may see, Lepidus, and henceforth know,
It is not Cæsar's natural vice to hate
Our great competitor. From Alexandria
This is the news: he fishes, drinks, and wastes
The lamps of night in revel; is not more manlike
Than Cleopatra, nor the queen of Ptolemy
More womanly than he; hardly gave audience, or
Vouchsaf'd to think he had partners. You shall find there
A man who is the abstract of all faults
That all men follow.

LEPIDUS. I must not think there are
Evils enow to darken all his goodness.
His faults, in him, seem as the spots of heaven,
More fiery by night's blackness; hereditary
Rather than purchas'd; what he cannot change
Than what he chooses.

CÆSAR. You are too indulgent. Let's grant it is not
Amiss to tumble on the bed of Ptolemy,
To give a kingdom for a mirth, to sit
And keep the turn of tippling with a slave,
To reel the streets at noon, and stand the buffet
With knaves that smell of sweat. Say this becomes him—
As his composure must be rare indeed
Whom these things cannot blemish—yet must Antony
No way excuse his foils when we do bear

So great weight in his lightness. If he fill'd
His vacancy with his voluptuousness,
Full surfeits and the dryness of his bones
Call on him for't! But to confound such time
That drums him from his sport and speaks as loud
As his own state and ours–'tis to be chid
As we rate boys who, being mature in knowledge,
Pawn their experience to their present pleasure,
And so rebel to judgment.

Enter a MESSENGER

LEPIDUS. Here's more news.
MESSENGER. Thy biddings have been done; and every hour,
Most noble Cæsar, shalt thou have report
How 'tis abroad. Pompey is strong at sea,
And it appears he is belov'd of those
That only have fear'd Cæsar. To the ports
The discontents repair, and men's reports
Give him much wrong'd.
CÆSAR. I should have known no less.
It hath been taught us from the primal state
That he which is was wish'd until he were;
And the ebb'd man, ne'er lov'd till ne'er worth love,
Comes dear'd by being lack'd. This common body,
Like to a vagabond flag upon the stream,
Goes to and back, lackeying the varying tide,
To rot itself with motion.
MESSENGER. Cæsar, I bring thee word
Menecrates and Menas, famous pirates,
Make the sea serve them, which they ear and wound
With keels of every kind. Many hot inroads
They make in Italy; the borders maritime
Lack blood to think on't, and flush youth revolt.
No vessel can peep forth but 'tis as soon
Taken as seen; for Pompey's name strikes more
Than could his war resisted.
CÆSAR. Antony,
Leave thy lascivious wassails. When thou once
Was beaten from Modena, where thou slew'st
Hirtius and Pansa, consuls, at thy heel

Did famine follow; whom thou fought'st against,
Though daintily brought up, with patience more
Than savages could suffer. Thou didst drink
The stale of horses and the gilded puddle
Which beasts would cough at. Thy palate then did deign
The roughest berry on the rudest hedge;
Yea, like the stag when snow the pasture sheets,
The barks of trees thou brows'd. On the Alps
It is reported thou didst eat strange flesh,
Which some did die to look on. And all this–
It wounds thine honour that I speak it now–
Was borne so like a soldier that thy cheek
So much as lank'd not.

LEPIDUS. 'Tis pity of him.

CÆSAR. Let his shames quickly
Drive him to Rome. 'Tis time we twain
Did show ourselves i' th' field; and to that end
Assemble we immediate council. Pompey
Thrives in our idleness.

LEPIDUS. To-morrow, Cæsar,
I shall be furnish'd to inform you rightly
Both what by sea and land I can be able
To front this present time.

CÆSAR. Till which encounter
It is my business too. Farewell.

LEPIDUS. Farewell, my lord. What you shall know meantime
Of stirs abroad, I shall beseech you, sir,
To let me be partaker.

CÆSAR. Doubt not, sir;
I knew it for my bond. *Exeunt*

SCENE 5

Alexandria. CLEOPATRA'S *palace*

Enter CLEOPATRA, CHARMIAN, IRAS, *and* MARDIAN

CLEOPATRA. Charmian!

CHARMIAN. Madam?

CLEOPATRA. Ha, ha!

Give me to drink mandragora.
CHARMIAN. Why, madam?
CLEOPATRA. That I might sleep out this great gap of time
My Antony is away.
CHARMIAN. You think of him too much.
CLEOPATRA. O, 'tis treason!
CHARMIAN. Madam, I trust, not so.
CLEOPATRA. Thou, eunuch Mardian!
MARDIAN. What's your Highness' pleasure?
CLEOPATRA. Not now to hear thee sing; I take no pleasure
In aught an eunuch has. 'Tis well for thee
That, being unseminar'd, thy freer thoughts
May not fly forth of Egypt. Hast thou affections?
MARDIAN. Yes, gracious madam.
CLEOPATRA. Indeed?
MARDIAN. Not in deed, madam; for I can do nothing
But what indeed is honest to be done.
Yet have I fierce affections, and think
What Venus did with Mars.
CLEOPATRA. O Charmian,
Where think'st thou he is now? Stands he or sits he?
Or does he walk? or is he on his horse?
O happy horse, to bear the weight of Antony!
Do bravely, horse; for wot'st thou whom thou mov'st?
The demi-Atlas of this earth, the arm
And burgonet of men. He's speaking now,
Or murmuring 'Where's my serpent of old Nile?'
For so he calls me. Now I feed myself
With most delicious poison. Think on me,
That am with Phœbus' amorous pinches black,
And wrinkled deep in time? Broad-fronted Cæsar,
When thou wast here above the ground, I was
A morsel for a monarch; and great Pompey
Would stand and make his eyes grow in my brow;
There would he anchor his aspect and die
With looking on his life.

Enter ALEXAS

ALEXAS. Sovereign of Egypt, hail!
CLEOPATRA. How much unlike art thou Mark Antony!

Yet, coming from him, that great med'cine hath
With his tinct gilded thee.
How goes it with my brave Mark Antony?

ALEXAS. Last thing he did, dear Queen,
He kiss'd—the last of many doubled kisses—
This orient pearl. His speech sticks in my heart.

CLEOPATRA. Mine ear must pluck it thence.

ALEXAS. 'Good friend,' quoth he
'Say the firm Roman to great Egypt sends
This treasure of an oyster; at whose foot,
To mend the petty present, I will piece
Her opulent throne with kingdoms. All the East,
Say thou, shall call her mistress.' So he nodded,
And soberly did mount an arm-gaunt steed,
Who neigh'd so high that what I would have spoke
Was beastly dumb'd by him.

CLEOPATRA. What, was he sad or merry?

ALEXAS. Like to the time o' th' year between the extremes
Of hot and cold; he was nor sad nor merry.

CLEOPATRA. O well-divided disposition! Note him,
Note him, good Charmian; 'tis the man; but note him!
He was not sad, for he would shine on those
That make their looks by his; he was not merry,
Which seem'd to tell them his remembrance lay
In Egypt with his joy; but between both.
O heavenly mingle! Be'st thou sad or merry,
The violence of either thee becomes,
So does it no man else. Met'st thou my posts?

ALEXAS. Ay, madam, twenty several messengers.
Why do you send so thick?

CLEOPATRA. Who's born that day
When I forget to send to Antony
Shall die a beggar. Ink and paper, Charmian.
Welcome, my good Alexas. Did I, Charmian,
Ever love Cæsar so?

CHARMIAN. O that brave Cæsar!

CLEOPATRA. Be chok'd with such another emphasis!
Say 'the brave Antony.'

CHARMIAN. The valiant Cæsar!

CLEOPATRA. By Isis, I will give thee bloody teeth

If thou with Cæsar paragon again
My man of men.

CHARMIAN. By your most gracious pardon,
I sing but after you.

CLEOPATRA. My salad days,
When I was green in judgment, cold in blood,
To say as I said then. But come, away!
Get me ink and paper.
He shall have every day a several greeting,
Or I'll unpeople Egypt. *Exeunt*

ACT II. SCENE 1

Messina. POMPEY'S *house*

Enter POMPEY, MENECRATES, *and* MENAS, *in warlike manner*

POMPEY. If the great gods be just, they shall assist
The deeds of justest men.

MENECRATES. Know, worthy Pompey,
That what they do delay they not deny.

POMPEY. Whiles we are suitors to their throne, decays
The thing we sue for.

MENECRATES. We, ignorant of ourselves,
Beg often our own harms, which the wise pow'rs
Deny us for our good; so find we profit
By losing of our prayers.

POMPEY. I shall do well.
The people love me, and the sea is mine;
My powers are crescent, and my auguring hope
Says it will come to th' full. Mark Antony
In Egypt sits at dinner, and will make
No wars without doors. Cæsar gets money where
He loses hearts. Lepidus flatters both,
Of both is flatter'd; but he neither loves,
Nor either cares for him.

MENAS. Cæsar and Lepidus
Are in the field. A mighty strength they carry.

POMPEY. Where have you this? 'Tis false.
MENAS. From Silvius, sir.
POMPEY. He dreams. I know they are in Rome together,
Looking for Antony. But all the charms of love,
Salt Cleopatra, soften thy wan'd lip!
Let witchcraft join with beauty, lust with both;
Tie up the libertine in a field of feasts,
Keep his brain fuming. Epicurean cooks
Sharpen with cloyless sauce his appetite,
That sleep and feeding may prorogue his honour
Even till a Lethe'd dullness–

Enter VARRIUS

How now, Varrius!
VARRIUS. This is most certain that I shall deliver:
Mark Antony is every hour in Rome
Expected. Since he went from Egypt 'tis
A space for farther travel.
POMPEY. I could have given less matter
A better ear. Menas, I did not think
This amorous surfeiter would have donn'd his helm
For such a petty war; his soldiership
Is twice the other twain. But let us rear
The higher our opinion, that our stirring
Can from the lap of Egypt's widow pluck
The ne'er-lust-wearied Antony.
MENAS. I cannot hope
Cæsar and Antony shall well greet together.
His wife that's dead did trespasses to Cæsar;
His brother warr'd upon him; although, I think,
Not mov'd by Antony.
POMPEY. I know not, Menas,
How lesser enmities may give way to greater.
Were't not that we stand up against them all,
'Twere pregnant they should square between themselves;
For they have entertained cause enough
To draw their swords. But how the fear of us
May cement their divisions, and bind up
The petty difference we yet not know.
Be't as our gods will have't! It only stands

Our lives upon to use our strongest hands.
Come, Menas. *Exeunt*

SCENE 2

Rome. The house of LEPIDUS

Enter ENOBARBUS *and* LEPIDUS

LEPIDUS. Good Enobarbus, 'tis a worthy deed,
And shall become you well, to entreat your captain
To soft and gentle speech.
ENOBARBUS. I shall entreat him
To answer like himself. If Cæsar move him,
Let Antony look over Cæsar's head
And speak as loud as Mars. By Jupiter,
Were I the wearer of Antonius' beard,
I would not shave't to-day.
LEPIDUS. 'Tis not a time
For private stomaching.
ENOBARBUS. Every time
Serves for the matter that is then born in't.
LEPIDUS. But small to greater matters must give way.
ENOBARBUS. Not if the small come first.
LEPIDUS. Your speech is passion;
But pray you stir no embers up. Here comes
The noble Antony.

Enter ANTONY *and* VENTIDIUS

ENOBARBUS. And yonder, Cæsar.

Enter CÆSAR, MÆCENAS, *and* AGRIPPA

ANTONY. If we compose well here, to Parthia.
Hark, Ventidius.
CÆSAR. I do not know, Mæcenas. Ask Agrippa.
LEPIDUS. Noble friends,
That which combin'd us was most great, and let not
A leaner action rend us. What's amiss,
May it be gently heard. When we debate
Our trivial difference loud, we do commit

Murder in healing wounds. Then, noble partners,
The rather for I earnestly beseech,
Touch you the sourest points with sweetest terms,
Nor curstness grow to th' matter.

ANTONY. 'Tis spoken well.
Were we before our armies, and to fight,
I should do thus. [*Flourish*]

CÆSAR. Welcome to Rome.

ANTONY. Thank you.

CÆSAR. Sit.

ANTONY. Sit, sir.

CÆSAR. Nay, then. [*They sit*]

ANTONY. I learn you take things ill which are not so,
Or being, concern you not.

CÆSAR. I must be laugh'd at
If, or for nothing or a little, I
Should say myself offended, and with you
Chiefly i' the world; more laugh'd at that I should
Once name you derogately when to sound your name
It not concern'd me.

ANTONY. My being in Egypt, Cæsar,
What was't to you?

CÆSAR. No more than my residing here at Rome
Might be to you in Egypt. Yet, if you there
Did practise on my state, your being in Egypt
Might be my question.

ANTONY. How intend you–practis'd?

CÆSAR. You may be pleas'd to catch at mine intent
By what did here befall me. Your wife and brother
Made wars upon me, and their contestation
Was theme for you; you were the word of war.

ANTONY. You do mistake your business; my brother never
Did urge me in his act. I did inquire it,
And have my learning from some true reports
That drew their swords with you. Did he not rather
Discredit my authority with yours,
And make the wars alike against my stomach,
Having alike your cause? Of this my letters
Before did satisfy you. If you'll patch a quarrel,
As matter whole you have not to make it with,

It must not be with this.
CÆSAR. You praise yourself
By laying defects of judgment to me; but
You patch'd up your excuses.
ANTONY. Not so, not so;
I know you could not lack, I am certain on't,
Very necessity of this thought, that I,
Your partner in the cause 'gainst which he fought,
Could not with graceful eyes attend those wars
Which fronted mine own peace. As for my wife,
I would you had her spirit in such another!
The third o' th' world is yours, which with a snaffle
You may pace easy, but not such a wife.
ENOBARBUS. Would we had all such wives, that the men might go to wars with the women!
ANTONY. So much uncurbable, her garboils, Cæsar,
Made out of her impatience—which not wanted
Shrewdness of policy too—I grieving grant
Did you too much disquiet. For that you must
But say I could not help it.
CÆSAR. I wrote to you
When rioting in Alexandria; you
Did pocket up my letters, and with taunts
Did gibe my missive out of audience.
ANTONY. Sir,
He fell upon me ere admitted. Then
Three kings I had newly feasted, and did want
Of what I was i' th' morning; but next day
I told him of myself, which was as much
As to have ask'd him pardon. Let this fellow
Be nothing of our strife; if we contend,
Out of our question wipe him.
CÆSAR. You have broken
The article of your oath, which you shall never
Have tongue to charge me with.
LEPIDUS. Soft, Cæsar!
ANTONY. No;
Lepidus, let him speak.
The honour is sacred which he talks on now,
Supposing that I lack'd it. But on, Cæsar:

The article of my oath—

CÆSAR. To lend me arms and aid when I requir'd them,
The which you both denied.

ANTONY. Neglected, rather;
And then when poisoned hours had bound me up
From mine own knowledge. As nearly as I may,
I'll play the penitent to you; but mine honesty
Shall not make poor my greatness, nor my power
Work without it. Truth is, that Fulvia,
To have me out of Egypt, made wars here;
For which myself, the ignorant motive, do
So far ask pardon as befits mine honour
To stoop in such a case.

LEPIDUS. 'Tis noble spoken.

MÆCENAS. If it might please you to enforce no further
The griefs between ye—to forget them quite
Were to remember that the present need
Speaks to atone you.

LEPIDUS. Worthily spoken, Mæcenas.

ENOBARBUS. Or, if you borrow one another's love for the instant, you may, when you hear no more words of Pompey, return it again. You shall have time to wrangle in when you have nothing else to do.

ANTONY. Thou art a soldier only. Speak no more.

ENOBARBUS. That truth should be silent I had almost forgot.

ANTONY. You wrong this presence; therefore speak no more.

ENOBARBUS. Go to, then—your considerate stone!

CÆSAR. I do not much dislike the matter, but
The manner of his speech; for't cannot be
We shall remain in friendship, our conditions
So diff'ring in their acts. Yet if I knew
What hoop should hold us stanch, from edge to edge
O' th' world, I would pursue it.

AGRIPPA. Give me leave, Cæsar.

CÆSAR. Speak, Agrippa.

AGRIPPA. Thou hast a sister by the mother's side,
Admir'd Octavia. Great Mark Antony
Is now a widower.

CÆSAR. Say not so, Agrippa.
If Cleopatra heard you, your reproof

Were well deserv'd of rashness.
ANTONY. I am not married, Cæsar. Let me hear
Agrippa further speak.
AGRIPPA. To hold you in perpetual amity,
To make you brothers, and to knit your hearts
With an unslipping knot, take Antony
Octavia to his wife; whose beauty claims
No worse a husband than the best of men;
Whose virtue and whose general graces speak
That which none else can utter. By this marriage
All little jealousies, which now seem great,
And all great fears, which now import their dangers,
Would then be nothing. Truths would be tales,
Where now half tales be truths. Her love to both
Would each to other, and all loves to both,
Draw after her. Pardon what I have spoke;
For 'tis a studied, not a present thought,
By duty ruminated.
ANTONY. Will Cæsar speak?
CÆSAR. Not till he hears how Antony is touch'd
With what is spoke already.
ANTONY. What power is in Agrippa,
If I would say 'Agrippa, be it so,'
To make this good?
CÆSAR. The power of Cæsar, and
His power unto Octavia.
ANTONY. May I never
To this good purpose, that so fairly shows,
Dream of impediment! Let me have thy hand.
Further this act of grace; and from this hour
The heart of brothers govern in our loves
And sway our great designs!
CÆSAR. There is my hand.
A sister I bequeath you, whom no brother
Did ever love so dearly. Let her live
To join our kingdoms and our hearts; and never
Fly off our loves again!
LEPIDUS. Happily, amen!
ANTONY. I did not think to draw my sword 'gainst Pompey;
For he hath laid strange courtesies and great

Of late upon me. I must thank him only,
Lest my remembrance suffer ill report;
At heel of that, defy him.

LEPIDUS. Time calls upon's.
Of us must Pompey presently be sought,
Or else he seeks out us.

ANTONY. Where lies he?

CÆSAR. About the Mount Misenum.

ANTONY. What is his strength by land?

CÆSAR. Great and increasing; but by sea
He is an absolute master.

ANTONY. So is the fame.
Would we had spoke together! Haste we for it.
Yet, ere we put ourselves in arms, dispatch we
The business we have talk'd of.

CÆSAR. With most gladness;
And do invite you to my sister's view,
Whither straight I'll lead you.

ANTONY. Let us, Lepidus,
Not lack your company.

LEPIDUS. Noble Antony,
Not sickness should detain me. [*Flourish*]

Exeunt all but ENOBARBUS, AGRIPPA, MÆCENAS

MÆCENAS. Welcome from Egypt, sir.

ENOBARBUS. Half the heart of Cæsar, worthy Mæcenas! My honourable friend, Agrippa!

AGRIPPA. Good Enobarbus!

MÆCENAS. We have cause to be glad that matters are so well digested. You stay'd well by't in Egypt.

ENOBARBUS. Ay, sir; we did sleep day out of countenance and made the night light with drinking.

MÆCENAS. Eight wild boars roasted whole at a breakfast, and but twelve persons there. Is this true?

ENOBARBUS. This was but as a fly by an eagle. We had much more monstrous matter of feast, which worthily deserved noting.

MÆCENAS. She's a most triumphant lady, if report be square to her.

ENOBARBUS. When she first met Mark Antony she purs'd up his heart, upon the river of Cydnus.

AGRIPPA. There she appear'd indeed! Or my reporter devis'd well for her.

ENOBARBUS. I will tell you.
The barge she sat in, like a burnish'd throne,
Burn'd on the water. The poop was beaten gold;
Purple the sails, and so perfumed that
The winds were love-sick with them; the oars were silver,
Which to the tune of flutes kept stroke, and made
The water which they beat to follow faster,
As amorous of their strokes. For her own person,
It beggar'd all description. She did lie
In her pavilion, cloth-of-gold, of tissue,
O'erpicturing that Venus where we see
The fancy out-work nature. On each side her
Stood pretty dimpled boys, like smiling Cupids,
With divers-colour'd fans, whose wind did seem
To glow the delicate cheeks which they did cool,
And what they undid did.

AGRIPPA. O, rare for Antony!

ENOBARBUS. Her gentlewomen, like the Nereides,
So many mermaids, tended her i' th' eyes,
And made their bends adornings. At the helm
A seeming mermaid steers. The silken tackle
Swell with the touches of those flower-soft hands
That yarely frame the office. From the barge
A strange invisible perfume hits the sense
Of the adjacent wharfs. The city cast
Her people out upon her; and Antony,
Enthron'd i' th' market-place, did sit alone,
Whistling to th' air; which, but for vacancy,
Had gone to gaze on Cleopatra too,
And made a gap in nature.

AGRIPPA. Rare Egyptian!

ENOBARBUS. Upon her landing, Antony sent to her,
Invited her to supper. She replied
It should be better he became her guest;
Which she entreated. Our courteous Antony,
Whom ne'er the word of 'No' woman heard speak,
Being barber'd ten times o'er, goes to the feast,
And for his ordinary pays his heart

For what his eyes eat only.
AGRIPPA. Royal wench!
She made great Cæsar lay his sword to bed.
He ploughed her, and she cropp'd.
ENOBARBUS. I saw her once
Hop forty paces through the public street;
And, having lost her breath, she spoke, and panted,
That she did make defect perfection,
And, breathless, pow'r breathe forth.
MÆCENAS. Now Antony must leave her utterly.
ENOBARBUS. Never! He will not.
Age cannot wither her, nor custom stale
Her infinite variety. Other women cloy
The appetites they feed, but she makes hungry
Where most she satisfies; for vilest things
Become themselves in her, that the holy priests
Bless her when she is riggish.
MÆCENAS. If beauty, wisdom, modesty, can settle
The heart of Antony, Octavia is
A blessed lottery to him.
AGRIPPA. Let us go.
Good Enobarbus, make yourself my guest
Whilst you abide here.
ENOBARBUS. Humbly, sir, I thank you. *Exeunt*

SCENE 3

Rome. CÆSAR'S *house*

Enter ANTONY, CÆSAR, OCTAVIA *between them*

ANTONY. The world and my great office will sometimes
Divide me from your bosom.
OCTAVIA. All which time
Before the gods my knee shall bow my prayers
To them for you.
ANTONY. Good night, sir. My Octavia,
Read not my blemishes in the world's report.
I have not kept my square; but that to come

Shall all be done by th' rule. Good night, dear lady.

OCTAVIA. Good night, sir.

CÆSAR. Good night. *Exeunt* CÆSAR *and* OCTAVIA

Enter SOOTHSAYER

ANTONY. Now, sirrah, you do wish yourself in Egypt?

SOOTHSAYER. Would I had never come from thence, nor you thither!

ANTONY. If you can—your reason.

SOOTHSAYER. I see it in my motion, have it not in my tongue; but yet hie you to Egypt again.

ANTONY. Say to me,
Whose fortunes shall rise higher, Cæsar's or mine?

SOOTHSAYER. Cæsar's.
Therefore, O Antony, stay not by his side.
Thy dæmon, that thy spirit which keeps thee, is
Noble, courageous, high, unmatchable,
Where Cæsar's is not; but near him thy angel
Becomes a fear, as being o'erpow'r'd. Therefore
Make space enough between you.

ANTONY. Speak this no more.

SOOTHSAYER. To none but thee; no more but when to thee.
If thou dost play with him at any game,
Thou art sure to lose; and of that natural luck
He beats thee 'gainst the odds. Thy lustre thickens
When he shines by. I say again, thy spirit
Is all afraid to govern thee near him;
But, he away, 'tis noble.

ANTONY. Get thee gone.
Say to Ventidius I would speak with him.

Exit SOOTHSAYER

He shall to Parthia.—Be it art or hap,
He hath spoken true. The very dice obey him;
And in our sports my better cunning faints
Under his chance. If we draw lots, he speeds;
His cocks do win the battle still of mine,
When it is all to nought, and his quails ever
Beat mine, inhoop'd, at odds. I will to Egypt;
And though I make this marriage for my peace,
I' th' East my pleasure lies.

Enter VENTIDIUS

O, come, Ventidius,
You must to Parthia. Your commission's ready;
Follow me and receive't. *Exeunt*

SCENE 4

Rome. A street

Enter LEPIDUS, MÆCENAS, *and* AGRIPPA

LEPIDUS. Trouble yourselves no further. Pray you hasten
Your generals after.
AGRIPPA. Sir, Mark Antony
Will e'en but kiss Octavia, and we'll follow.
LEPIDUS. Till I shall see you in your soldier's dress,
Which will become you both, farewell.
MÆCENAS. We shall,
As I conceive the journey, be at th' Mount
Before you, Lepidus.
LEPIDUS. Your way is shorter;
My purposes do draw me much about.
You'll win two days upon me.
BOTH. Sir, good success!
LEPIDUS. Farewell. *Exeunt*

SCENE 5

Alexandria. CLEOPATRA'S *palace*

Enter CLEOPATRA, CHARMIAN, IRAS, *and* ALEXAS

CLEOPATRA. Give me some music–music, moody food
Of us that trade in love.
ALL. The music, ho!

Enter MARDIAN *the eunuch*

CLEOPATRA. Let it alone! Let's to billiards. Come, Charmian.
CHARMIAN. My arm is sore; best play with Mardian.
CLEOPATRA. As well a woman with an eunuch play'd

As with a woman. Come, you'll play with me, sir?
MARDIAN. As well as I can, madam.
CLEOPATRA. And when good will is show'd, though't come too short,
The actor may plead pardon. I'll none now.
Give me mine angle—we'll to th' river. There,
My music playing far off, I will betray
Tawny-finn'd fishes; my bended hook shall pierce
Their slimy jaws; and as I draw them up
I'll think them every one an Antony,
And say 'Ah ha! Y'are caught.'
CHARMIAN. 'Twas merry when
You wager'd on your angling; when your diver
Did hang a salt fish on his hook, which he
With fervency drew up.
CLEOPATRA. That time? O times
I laughed him out of patience; and that night
I laugh'd him into patience; and next morn,
Ere the ninth hour, I drunk him to his bed,
Then put my tires and mantles on him, whilst
I wore his sword Philippan.

Enter a MESSENGER

O! from Italy?
Ram thou thy fruitful tidings in mine ears,
That long time have been barren.
MESSENGER. Madam, madam—
CLEOPATRA. Antony's dead! If thou say so, villain,
Thou kill'st thy mistress; but well and free,
If thou so yield him, there is gold, and here
My bluest veins to kiss—a hand that kings
Have lipp'd, and trembled kissing.
MESSENGER. First, madam, he is well.
CLEOPATRA. Why, there's more gold.
But, sirrah, mark, we use
To say the dead are well. Bring it to that,
The gold I give thee will I melt and pour
Down thy ill-uttering throat.
MESSENGER. Good madam, hear me.
CLEOPATRA. Well, go to, I will.

But there's no goodness in thy face. If Antony
Be free and healthful—why so tart a favour
To trumpet such good tidings? If not well,
Thou shouldst come like a Fury crown'd with snakes,
Not like a formal man.

MESSENGER. Will't please you hear me?

CLEOPATRA. I have a mind to strike thee ere thou speak'st.
Yet, if thou say Antony lives, is well,
Or friends with Cæsar, or not captive to him,
I'll set thee in a shower of gold, and hail
Rich pearls upon thee.

MESSENGER. Madam, he's well.

CLEOPATRA. Well said.

MESSENGER. And friends with Cæsar.

CLEOPATRA. Th'art an honest man.

MESSENGER. Cæsar and he are greater friends than ever.

CLEOPATRA. Make thee a fortune from me.

MESSENGER. But yet, madam—

CLEOPATRA. I do not like 'but yet.' It does allay
The good precedence; fie upon 'but yet'!
'But yet' is as a gaoler to bring forth
Some monstrous malefactor. Prithee, friend,
Pour out the pack of matter to mine ear,
The good and bad together. He's friends with Cæsar;
In state of health, thou say'st; and, thou say'st, free.

MESSENGER. Free, madam! No; I made no such report.
He's bound unto Octavia.

CLEOPATRA. For what good turn?

MESSENGER. For the best turn i' th' bed.

CLEOPATRA. I am pale, Charmian.

MESSENGER. Madam, he's married to Octavia.

CLEOPATRA. The most infectious pestilence upon thee!
[*Strikes him down*]

MESSENGER. Good madam, patience.

CLEOPATRA. What say you? Hence, [*Strikes him*]
Horrible villain! or I'll spurn thine eyes
Like balls before me; I'll unhair thy head;
[*She hales him up and down*]
Thou shalt be whipp'd with wire and stew'd in brine,
Smarting in ling'ring pickle.

MESSENGER. Gracious madam,
I that do bring the news made not the match.
CLEOPATRA. Say 'tis not so, a province I will give thee,
And make thy fortunes proud. The blow thou hadst
Shall make thy peace for moving me to rage;
And I will boot thee with what gift beside
Thy modesty can beg.
MESSENGER. He's married, madam.
CLEOPATRA. Rogue, thou hast liv'd too long. [*Draws a knife*]
MESSENGER. Nay, then I'll run.
What mean you, madam? I have made no fault. *Exit*
CHARMIAN. Good madam, keep yourself within yourself:
The man is innocent.
CLEOPATRA. Some innocents scape not the thunderbolt.
Melt Egypt into Nile! and kindly creatures
Turn all to serpents! Call the slave again.
Though I am mad, I will not bite him. Call!
CHARMIAN. He is afear'd to come.
CLEOPATRA. I will not hurt him.
These hands do lack nobility, that they strike
A meaner than myself; since I myself
Have given myself the cause.

Enter the MESSENGER *again*

Come hither, sir.
Though it be honest, it is never good
To bring bad news. Give to a gracious message
An host of tongues; but let ill tidings tell
Themselves when they be felt.
MESSENGER. I have done my duty.
CLEOPATRA. Is he married?
I cannot hate thee worser than I do
If thou again say 'Yes.'
MESSENGER. He's married, madam.
CLEOPATRA. The gods confound thee! Dost thou hold there still?
MESSENGER. Should I lie, madam?
CLEOPATRA. O, I would thou didst,
So half my Egypt were submerg'd and made
A cistern for scal'd snakes! Go, get thee hence.

Hadst thou Narcissus in thy face, to me
Thou wouldst appear most ugly. He is married?

MESSENGER. I crave your Highness' pardon.

CLEOPATRA. He is married?

MESSENGER. Take no offence that I would not offend you;
To punish me for what you make me do
Seems much unequal. He's married to Octavia.

CLEOPATRA. O, that his fault should make a knave of thee
That art not what th'art sure of! Get thee hence.
The merchandise which thou hast brought from Rome
Are all too dear for me. Lie they upon thy hand,
And be undone by 'em! *Exit* MESSENGER

CHARMIAN. Good your Highness, patience.

CLEOPATRA. In praising Antony I have disprais'd Cæsar.

CHARMIAN. Many times, madam.

CLEOPATRA. I am paid for't now. Lead me from hence,
I faint. O Iras, Charmian! 'Tis no matter.
Go to the fellow, good Alexas; bid him
Report the feature of Octavia, her years,
Her inclination; let him not leave out
The colour of her hair. Bring me word quickly.
Exit ALEXAS
Let him for ever go–let him not, Charmian–
Though he be painted one way like a Gorgon,
The other way's a Mars. [*To* MARDIAN]
Bid you Alexas
Bring me word how tall she is.–Pity me, Charmian,
But do not speak to me. Lead me to my chamber. *Exeunt*

SCENE 6

Near Misenum

Flourish. Enter POMPEY *and* MENAS *at one door, with drum and trumpet; at another*, CÆSAR, ANTONY, LEPIDUS, ENOBARBUS, MÆCENAS, AGRIPPA, *with soldiers marching*

POMPEY. Your hostages I have, so have you mine;
And we shall talk before we fight.

CÆSAR. Most meet
That first we come to words; and therefore have we
Our written purposes before us sent;
Which if thou hast considered, let us know
If 'twill tie up thy discontented sword
And carry back to Sicily much tall youth
That else must perish here.
POMPEY. To you all three,
The senators alone of this great world,
Chief factors for the gods: I do not know
Wherefore my father should revengers want,
Having a son and friends, since Julius Cæsar,
Who at Philippi the good Brutus ghosted,
There saw you labouring for him. What was't
That mov'd pale Cassius to conspire? and what
Made the all-honour'd honest Roman, Brutus,
With the arm'd rest, courtiers of beauteous freedom,
To drench the Capitol, but that they would
Have one man but a man? And that is it
Hath made me rig my navy, at whose burden
The anger'd ocean foams; with which I meant
To scourge th' ingratitude that despiteful Rome
Cast on my noble father.
CÆSAR. Take your time.
ANTONY. Thou canst not fear us, Pompey, with thy sails;
We'll speak with thee at sea; at land thou know'st
How much we do o'er-count thee.
POMPEY. At land, indeed,
Thou dost o'er-count me of my father's house.
But since the cuckoo builds not for himself,
Remain in't as thou mayst.
LEPIDUS. Be pleas'd to tell us—
For this is from the present—how you take
The offers we have sent you.
CÆSAR. There's the point.
ANTONY. Which do not be entreated to, but weigh
What it is worth embrac'd.
CÆSAR. And what may follow,
To try a larger fortune.
POMPEY. You have made me offer

Of Sicily, Sardinia; and I must
Rid all the sea of pirates; then to send
Measures of wheat to Rome; this 'greed upon,
To part with unhack'd edges and bear back
Our targes undinted.

ALL. That's our offer.

POMPEY. Know, then,
I came before you here a man prepar'd
To take this offer; but Mark Antony
Put me to some impatience. Though I lose
The praise of it by telling, you must know,
When Cæsar and your brother were at blows,
Your mother came to Sicily and did find
Her welcome friendly.

ANTONY. I have heard it, Pompey,
And am well studied for a liberal thanks
Which I do owe you.

POMPEY. Let me have your hand.
I did not think, sir, to have met you here.

ANTONY. The beds i' th' East are soft; and thanks to you,
That call'd me timelier than my purpose hither;
For I have gained by't.

CÆSAR. Since I saw you last
There is a change upon you.

POMPEY. Well, I know not
What counts harsh fortune casts upon my face;
But in my bosom shall she never come
To make my heart her vassal.

LEPIDUS. Well met here.

POMPEY. I hope so, Lepidus. Thus we are agreed.
I crave our composition may be written,
And seal'd between us.

CÆSAR. That's the next to do.

POMPEY. We'll feast each other ere we part, and let's
Draw lots who shall begin.

ANTONY. That will I, Pompey.

POMPEY. No, Antony, take the lot;
But, first or last, your fine Egyptian cookery
Shall have the fame. I have heard that Julius Cæsar
Grew fat with feasting there.

ANTONY. You have heard much.

POMPEY. I have fair meanings, sir.

ANTONY. And fair words to them.

POMPEY. Then so much have I heard;
And I have heard Apollodorus carried—

ENOBARBUS. No more of that! He did so.

POMPEY. What, I pray you?

ENOBARBUS. A certain queen to Cæsar in a mattress.

POMPEY. I know thee now. How far'st thou, soldier?

ENOBARBUS. Well;
And well am like to do, for I perceive
Four feasts are toward.

POMPEY. Let me shake thy hand.
I never hated thee; I have seen thee fight,
When I have envied thy behaviour.

ENOBARBUS. Sir,
I never lov'd you much; but I ha' prais'd ye
When you have well deserv'd ten times as much
As I have said you did.

POMPEY. Enjoy thy plainness;
It nothing ill becomes thee.
Aboard my galley I invite you all.
Will you lead, lords?

ALL. Show's the way, sir.

POMPEY. Come. *Exeunt all but* ENOBARBUS *and* MENAS

MENAS. [*Aside*] Thy father, Pompey, would ne'er have made this treaty.—You and I have known, sir.

ENOBARBUS. At sea, I think.

MENAS. We have, sir.

ENOBARBUS. You have done well by water.

MENAS. And you by land.

ENOBARBUS. I will praise any man that will praise me; though it cannot be denied what I have done by land.

MENAS. Nor what I have done by water.

ENOBARBUS. Yes, something you can deny for your own safety: you have been a great thief by sea.

MENAS. And you by land.

ENOBARBUS. There I deny my land service. But give me your hand, Menas; if our eyes had authority, here they might take two thieves kissing.

MENAS. All men's faces are true, whatsome'er their hands are.

ENOBARBUS. But there is never a fair woman has a true face.

MENAS. No slander: they steal hearts.

ENOBARBUS. We came hither to fight with you.

MENAS. For my part, I am sorry it is turn'd to a drinking. Pompey doth this day laugh away his fortune.

ENOBARBUS. If he do, sure he cannot weep't back again.

MENAS. Y'have said, sir. We look'd not for Mark Antony here. Pray you, is he married to Cleopatra?

ENOBARBUS. Cæsar's sister is call'd Octavia.

MENAS. True, sir; she was the wife of Caius Marcellus.

ENOBARBUS. But she is now the wife of Marcus Antonius.

MENAS. Pray ye, sir?

ENOBARBUS. 'Tis true.

MENAS. Then is Cæsar and he for ever knit together.

ENOBARBUS. If I were bound to divine of this unity, I would not prophesy so.

MENAS. I think the policy of that purpose made more in the marriage than the love of the parties.

ENOBARBUS. I think so too. But you shall find the band that seems to tie their friendship together will be the very strangler of their amity: Octavia is of a holy, cold, and still conversation.

MENAS. Who would not have his wife so?

ENOBARBUS. Not he that himself is not so; which is Mark Antony. He will to his Egyptian dish again; then shall the sighs of Octavia blow the fire up in Cæsar, and, as I said before, that which is the strength of their amity shall prove the immediate author of their variance. Antony will use his affection where it is; he married but his occasion here.

MENAS. And thus it may be. Come, sir, will you aboard? I have a health for you.

ENOBARBUS. I shall take it, sir. We have us'd our throats in Egypt.

MENAS. Come, let's away. *Exeunt*

SCENE 7

On board POMPEY'S *galley, off Misenum*

Music plays. Enter two or three SERVANTS *with a banquet*

FIRST SERVANT. Here they'll be, man. Some o' their plants are ill-rooted already; the least wind i' th' world will blow them down.

SECOND SERVANT. Lepidus is high-colour'd.

FIRST SERVANT. They have made him drink alms-drink.

SECOND SERVANT. As they pinch one another by the disposition, he cries out 'No more!'; reconciles them to his entreaty and himself to th' drink.

FIRST SERVANT. But it raises the greater war between him and his discretion.

SECOND SERVANT. Why, this it is to have a name in great men's fellowship. I had as lief have a reed that will do me no service as a partizan I could not heave.

FIRST SERVANT. To be call'd into a huge sphere, and not to be seen to move in't, are the holes where eyes should be, which pitifully disaster the cheeks.

A sennet sounded. Enter CÆSAR, ANTONY, LEPIDUS, POMPEY, AGRIPPA, MÆCENAS, ENOBARBUS, MENAS, *with other* CAPTAINS

ANTONY. [*To* CÆSAR] Thus do they, sir: they take the flow o' th' Nile
By certain scales i' th' pyramid; they know
By th' height, the lowness, or the mean, if dearth
Or foison follow. The higher Nilus swells
The more it promises; as it ebbs, the seedsman
Upon the slime and ooze scatters his grain,
And shortly comes to harvest.

LEPIDUS. Y'have strange serpents there.

ANTONY. Ay, Lepidus.

LEPIDUS. Your serpent of Egypt is bred now of your mud by the operation of your sun; so is your crocodile.

ANTONY. They are so.

POMPEY. Sit—and some wine! A health to Lepidus!

LEPIDUS. I am not so well as I should be, but I'll ne'er out.

ENOBARBUS. Not till you have slept. I fear me you'll be in till then.

LEPIDUS. Nay, certainly, I have heard the Ptolemies' pyramises are very goodly things. Without contradiction I have heard that.

MENAS. [*Aside to* POMPEY] Pompey, a word.

POMPEY. [*Aside to* MENAS] Say in mine ear; what is't?

MENAS. [*Aside to* POMPEY] Forsake thy seat, I do beseech thee, Captain,
And hear me speak a word.

POMPEY. [*Whispers in's ear*] Forbear me till anon–
This wine for Lepidus!

LEPIDUS. What manner o' thing is your crocodile?

ANTONY. It is shap'd, sir, like itself, and it is as broad as it hath breadth; it is just so high as it is, and moves with it own organs. It lives by that which nourisheth it, and the elements once out of it, it transmigrates.

LEPIDUS. What colour is it of?

ANTONY. Of it own colour too.

LEPIDUS. 'Tis a strange serpent.

ANTONY. 'Tis so. And the tears of it are wet.

CÆSAR. Will this description satisfy him?

ANTONY. With the health that Pompey gives him, else he is a very epicure.

POMPEY. [*Aside to* MENAS] Go, hang, sir, hang! Tell me of that! Away!
Do as I bid you.–Where's this cup I call'd for?

MENAS. [*Aside to* POMPEY] If for the sake of merit thou wilt hear me,
Rise from thy stool.

POMPEY. [*Aside to* MENAS] I think th'art mad. [*Rises and walks aside*] The matter?

MENAS. I have ever held my cap off to thy fortunes.

POMPEY. Thou hast serv'd me with much faith. What's else to say?–
Be jolly, lords.

ANTONY. These quicksands, Lepidus,
Keep off them, for you sink.

MENAS. Wilt thou be lord of all the world?

POMPEY. What say'st thou?
MENAS. Wilt thou be lord of the whole world? That's twice.
POMPEY. How should that be?
MENAS. But entertain it,
And though you think me poor, I am the man
Will give thee all the world.
POMPEY. Hast thou drunk well?
MENAS. No, Pompey, I have kept me from the cup.
Thou art, if thou dar'st be, the earthly Jove;
Whate'er the ocean pales or sky inclips
Is thine, if thou wilt ha't.
POMPEY. Show me which way.
MENAS. These three world-sharers, these competitors,
Are in thy vessel. Let me cut the cable;
And when we are put off, fall to their throats.
All there is thine.
POMPEY. Ah, this thou shouldst have done,
And not have spoke on't. In me 'tis villainy:
In thee't had been good service. Thou must know
'Tis not my profit that does lead mine honour:
Mine honour, it. Repent that e'er thy tongue
Hath so betray'd thine act. Being done unknown,
I should have found it afterwards well done,
But must condemn it now. Desist, and drink.
MENAS. [*Aside*] For this,
I'll never follow thy pall'd fortunes more.
Who seeks, and will not take when once 'tis offer'd,
Shall never find it more.
POMPEY. This health to Lepidus!
ANTONY. Bear him ashore. I'll pledge it for him, Pompey.
ENOBARBUS. Here's to thee, Menas!
MENAS. Enobarbus, welcome!
POMPEY. Fill till the cup be hid.
ENOBARBUS. There's a strong fellow, Menas.
[*Pointing to the servant who carries off* LEPIDUS]
MENAS. Why?
ENOBARBUS. 'A bears the third part of the world, man; see'st not?
MENAS. The third part, then, is drunk. Would it were all,

That it might go on wheels!
ENOBARBUS. Drink thou; increase the reels.
MENAS. Come.
POMPEY. This is not yet an Alexandrian feast.
ANTONY. It ripens towards it. Strike the vessels, ho!
Here's to Cæsar!
CÆSAR. I could well forbear't.
It's monstrous labour when I wash my brain
And it grows fouler.
ANTONY. Be a child o' th' time.
CÆSAR. Possess it, I'll make answer.
But I had rather fast from all four days
Than drink so much in one.
ENOBARBUS. [*To* ANTONY] Ha, my brave emperor!
Shall we dance now the Egyptian Bacchanals
And celebrate our drink?
POMPEY. Let's ha't, good soldier.
ANTONY. Come, let's all take hands,
Till that the conquering wine hath steep'd our sense
In soft and delicate Lethe.
ENOBARBUS. All take hands.
Make battery to our ears with the loud music,
The while I'll place you; then the boy shall sing;
The holding every man shall bear as loud
As his strong sides can volley.
[*Music plays.* ENOBARBUS *places them hand in hand*]

THE SONG

Come, thou monarch of the vine,
Plumpy Bacchus with pink eyne!
In thy fats our cares be drown'd,
With thy grapes our hairs be crown'd.
Cup us till the world go round,
Cup us till the world go round!

CÆSAR. What would you more? Pompey, good night. Good brother,
Let me request you off; our graver business
Frowns at this levity. Gentle lords, let's part;
You see we have burnt our cheeks. Strong Enobarb

Is weaker than the wine, and mine own tongue
Splits what it speaks. The wild disguise hath almost
Antick'd us all. What needs more words? Good night.
Good Antony, your hand.

POMPEY. I'll try you on the shore.

ANTONY. And shall, sir. Give's your hand.

POMPEY. O Antony,
You have my father's house—but what? We are friends.
Come, down into the boat.

ENOBARBUS. Take heed you fall not.

Exeunt all but ENOBARBUS *and* MENAS

Menas, I'll not on shore.

MENAS. No, to my cabin.
These drums! these trumpets, flutes! what!
Let Neptune hear we bid a loud farewell
To these great fellows. Sound and be hang'd, sound out!

[*Sound a flourish, with drums*]

ENOBARBUS. Hoo! says 'a. There's my cap.

MENAS. Hoo! Noble Captain, come. *Exeunt*

ACT III. SCENE 1

A plain in Syria

Enter VENTIDIUS, *as it were in triumph, with* SILIUS *and other Romans,* OFFICERS *and soldiers; the dead body of* PACORUS *borne before him*

VENTIDIUS. Now, darting Parthia, art thou struck, and now
Pleas'd fortune does of Marcus Crassus' death
Make me revenger. Bear the King's son's body
Before our army. Thy Pacorus, Orodes,
Pays this for Marcus Crassus.

SILIUS. Noble Ventidius,
Whilst yet with Parthian blood thy sword is warm
The fugitive Parthians follow; spur through Media,
Mesopotamia, and the shelters whither
The routed fly. So thy grand captain, Antony,
Shall set thee on triumphant chariots and

Put garlands on thy head.
VENTIDIUS. O Silius, Silius,
I have done enough. A lower place, note well,
May make too great an act; for learn this, Silius:
Better to leave undone than by our deed
Acquire too high a fame when him we serve's away.
Cæsar and Antony have ever won
More in their officer, than person. Sossius,
One of my place in Syria, his lieutenant,
For quick accumulation of renown,
Which he achiev'd by th' minute, lost his favour.
Who does i' th' wars more than his captain can
Becomes his captain's captain; and ambition,
The soldier's virtue, rather makes choice of loss
Than gain which darkens him.
I could do more to do Antonius good,
But 'twould offend him; and in his offence
Should my performance perish.
SILIUS. Thou hast, Ventidius, that
Without the which a soldier and his sword
Grants scarce distinction. Thou wilt write to Antony?
VENTIDIUS. I'll humbly signify what in his name,
That magical word of war, we have effected;
How, with his banners, and his well-paid ranks,
The ne'er-yet-beaten horse of Parthia
We have jaded out o' th' field.
SILIUS. Where is he now?
VENTIDIUS. He purposeth to Athens; whither, with what haste
The weight we must convey with's will permit,
We shall appear before him.—On, there; pass along.

Exeunt

SCENE 2

Rome. CÆSAR'S *house*

Enter AGRIPPA *at one door*, ENOBARBUS *at another*

AGRIPPA. What, are the brothers parted?
ENOBARBUS. They have dispatch'd with Pompey; he is gone;

The other three are sealing. Octavia weeps
To part from Rome; Cæsar is sad; and Lepidus,
Since Pompey's feast, as Menas says, is troubled
With the green sickness.

AGRIPPA. 'Tis a noble Lepidus.

ENOBARBUS. A very fine one. O, how he loves Cæsar!

AGRIPPA. Nay, but how dearly he adores Mark Antony!

ENOBARBUS. Cæsar? Why he's the Jupiter of men.

AGRIPPA. What's Antony? The god of Jupiter.

ENOBARBUS. Spake you of Cæsar? How! the nonpareil!

AGRIPPA. O, Antony! O thou Arabian bird!

ENOBARBUS. Would you praise Cæsar, say 'Cæsar'—go no further.

AGRIPPA. Indeed, he plied them both with excellent praises.

ENOBARBUS. But he loves Cæsar best. Yet he loves Antony.
Hoo! hearts, tongues, figures, scribes, bards, poets, cannot
Think, speak, cast, write, sing, number—hoo!—
His love to Antony. But as for Cæsar,
Kneel down, kneel down, and wonder.

AGRIPPA. Both he loves.

ENOBARBUS. They are his shards, and he their beetle. [*Trumpets within*] So—
This is to horse. Adieu, noble Agrippa.

AGRIPPA. Good fortune, worthy soldier, and farewell.

Enter CÆSAR, ANTONY, LEPIDUS, *and* OCTAVIA

ANTONY. No further, sir.

CÆSAR. You take from me a great part of myself;
Use me well in't. Sister, prove such a wife
As my thoughts make thee, and as my farthest band
Shall pass on thy approof. Most noble Antony,
Let not the piece of virtue which is set
Betwixt us as the cement of our love
To keep it builded be the ram to batter
The fortress of it; for better might we
Have lov'd without this mean, if on both parts
This be not cherish'd.

ANTONY. Make me not offended
In your distrust.

CÆSAR. I have said.

ANTONY. You shall not find,
Though you be therein curious, the least cause
For what you seem to fear. So the gods keep you,
And make the hearts of Romans serve your ends!
We will here part.

CÆSAR. Farewell, my dearest sister, fare thee well.
The elements be kind to thee and make
Thy spirits all of comfort! Fare thee well.

OCTAVIA. My noble brother!

ANTONY. The April's in her eyes. It is love's spring,
And these the showers to bring it on. Be cheerful.

OCTAVIA. Sir, look well to my husband's house; and—

CÆSAR. What, Octavia?

OCTAVIA. I'll tell you in your ear.

ANTONY. Her tongue will not obey her heart, nor can
Her heart inform her tongue—the swan's down feather,
That stands upon the swell at the full of tide,
And neither way inclines.

ENOBARBUS. [*Aside to* AGRIPPA] Will Cæsar weep?

AGRIPPA. [*Aside to* ENOBARBUS] He has a cloud in's face.

ENOBARBUS. [*Aside to* AGRIPPA] He were the worse for that, were he a horse;
So is he, being a man.

AGRIPPA. [*Aside to* ENOBARBUS] Why, Enobarbus,
When Antony found Julius Cæsar dead,
He cried almost to roaring; and he wept
When at Philippi he found Brutus slain.

ENOBARBUS. [*Aside to* AGRIPPA] That year, indeed, he was troubled with a rheum;
What willingly he did confound he wail'd,
Believe't—till I weep too.

CÆSAR. No, sweet Octavia,
You shall hear from me still; the time shall not
Out-go my thinking on you.

ANTONY. Come, sir, come;
I'll wrestle with you in my strength of love.
Look, here I have you; thus I let you go,
And give you to the gods.

CÆSAR. Adieu; be happy!

LEPIDUS. Let all the number of the stars give light

To thy fair way!
CÆSAR. Farewell, farewell! [*Kisses* OCTAVIA]
ANTONY. Farewell! *Trumpets sound. Exeunt*

SCENE 3

Alexandria. CLEOPATRA'S *palace*

Enter CLEOPATRA, CHARMIAN, IRAS, *and* ALEXAS

CLEOPATRA. Where is the fellow?
ALEXAS. Half afeard to come.
CLEOPATRA. Go to, go to.

Enter the MESSENGER *as before*

Come hither, sir.
ALEXAS. Good Majesty,
Herod of Jewry dare not look upon you
But when you are well pleas'd.
CLEOPATRA. That Herod's head
I'll have. But how, when Antony is gone,
Through whom I might command it? Come thou near.
MESSENGER. Most gracious Majesty!
CLEOPATRA. Didst thou behold Octavia?
MESSENGER. Ay, dread Queen.
CLEOPATRA. Where?
MESSENGER. Madam, in Rome
I look'd her in the face, and saw her led
Between her brother and Mark Antony.
CLEOPATRA. Is she as tall as me?
MESSENGER. She is not, madam.
CLEOPATRA. Didst hear her speak? Is she shrill-tongu'd or low?
MESSENGER. Madam, I heard her speak: she is low-voic'd.
CLEOPATRA. That's not so good. He cannot like her long.
CHARMIAN. Like her? O Isis! 'tis impossible.
CLEOPATRA. I think so, Charmian. Dull of tongue and dwarfish!
What majesty is in her gait? Remember,

If e'er thou look'dst on majesty.
MESSENGER. She creeps.
Her motion and her station are as one;
She shows a body rather than a life,
A statue than a breather.
CLEOPATRA. Is this certain?
MESSENGER. Or I have no observance.
CHARMIAN. Three in Egypt
Cannot make better note.
CLEOPATRA. He's very knowing;
I do perceive't. There's nothing in her yet.
The fellow has good judgment.
CHARMIAN. Excellent.
CLEOPATRA. Guess at her years, I prithee.
MESSENGER. Madam,
She was a widow.
CLEOPATRA. Widow? Charmian, hark!
MESSENGER. And I do think she's thirty.
CLEOPATRA. Bear'st thou her face in mind? Is't long or round?
MESSENGER. Round even to faultiness.
CLEOPATRA. For the most part, too, they are foolish that are so.
Her hair, what colour?
MESSENGER. Brown, madam; and her forehead
As low as she would wish it.
CLEOPATRA. There's gold for thee.
Thou must not take my former sharpness ill.
I will employ thee back again; I find thee
Most fit for business. Go make thee ready;
Our letters are prepar'd. *Exeunt* MESSENGER
CHARMIAN. A proper man.
CLEOPATRA. Indeed, he is so. I repent me much
That so I harried him. Why, methinks, by him,
This creature's no such thing.
CHARMIAN. Nothing, madam.
CLEOPATRA. The man hath seen some majesty, and should know.
CHARMIAN. Hath he seen majesty? Isis else defend,
And serving you so long!

CLEOPATRA. I have one thing more to ask him yet, good Charmian.
But 'tis no matter; thou shalt bring him to me
Where I will write. All may be well enough.

CHARMIAN. I warrant you, madam. *Exeunt*

SCENE 4

Athens. ANTONY'S *house*

Enter ANTONY *and* OCTAVIA

ANTONY. Nay, nay, Octavia, not only that—
That were excusable, that and thousands more
Of semblable import—but he hath wag'd
New wars 'gainst Pompey; made his will, and read it
To public ear;
Spoke scantly of me; when perforce he could not
But pay me terms of honour, cold and sickly
He vented them, most narrow measure lent me;
When the best hint was given him, he not took't,
Or did it from his teeth.

OCTAVIA. O my good lord,
Believe not all; or if you must believe,
Stomach not all. A more unhappy lady,
If this division chance, ne'er stood between,
Praying for both parts.
The good gods will mock me presently
When I shall pray 'O, bless my lord and husband!'
Undo that prayer by crying out as loud
'O, bless my brother!' Husband win, win brother,
Prays, and destroys the prayer; no mid-way
'Twixt these extremes at all.

ANTONY. Gentle Octavia,
Let your best love draw to that point which seeks
Best to preserve it. If I lose mine honour,
I lose myself; better I were not yours
Than yours so branchless. But, as you requested,
Yourself shall go between's. The meantime, lady,
I'll raise the preparation of a war

Shall stain your brother. Make your soonest haste;
So your desires are yours.

OCTAVIA. Thanks to my lord.
The Jove of power make me, most weak, most weak,
Your reconciler! Wars 'twixt you twain would be
As if the world should cleave, and that slain men
Should solder up the rift.

ANTONY. When it appears to you where this begins,
Turn your displeasure that way, for our faults
Can never be so equal that your love
Can equally move with them. Provide your going;
Choose your own company, and command what cost
Your heart has mind to. *Exeunt*

SCENE 5

Athens. ANTONY's *house*

Enter ENOBARBUS *and* EROS, *meeting*

ENOBARBUS. How now, friend Eros!

EROS. There's strange news come, sir.

ENOBARBUS. What, man?

EROS. Cæsar and Lepidus have made wars upon Pompey.

ENOBARBUS. This is old. What is the success?

EROS. Cæsar, having made use of him in the wars 'gainst Pompey, presently denied him rivality, would not let him partake in the glory of the action; and not resting here, accuses him of letters he had formerly wrote to Pompey; upon his own appeal, seizes him. So the poor third is up, till death enlarge his confine.

ENOBARBUS. Then, world, thou hast a pair of chaps—no more;
And throw between them all the food thou hast,
They'll grind the one the other. Where's Antony?

EROS. He's walking in the garden—thus, and spurns
The rush that lies before him; cries 'Fool Lepidus!'
And threats the throat of that his officer
That murd'red Pompey.

ENOBARBUS. Our great navy's rigg'd.

EROS. For Italy and Cæsar. More, Domitius:
My lord desires you presently; my news
I might have told hereafter.
ENOBARBUS. 'Twill be naught;
But let it be. Bring me to Antony.
EROS. Come, sir. *Exeunt*

SCENE 6

Rome. CÆSAR'S *house*

Enter CÆSAR, AGRIPPA, *and* MÆCENAS

CÆSAR. Contemning Rome, he has done all this and more
In Alexandria. Here's the manner of't:
I' th' market-place, on a tribunal silver'd,
Cleopatra and himself in chairs of gold
Were publicly enthron'd; at the feet sat
Cæsarion, whom they call my father's son,
And all the unlawful issue that their lust
Since then hath made between them. Unto her
He gave the stablishment of Egypt; made her
Of lower Syria, Cyprus, Lydia,
Absolute queen.
MÆCENAS. This in the public eye?
CÆSAR. I' th' common show-place, where they exercise.
His sons he there proclaim'd the kings of kings:
Great Media, Parthia, and Armenia,
He gave to Alexander; to Ptolemy he assign'd
Syria, Cilicia, and Phœnicia. She
In th' habiliments of the goddess Isis
That day appear'd; and oft before gave audience,
As 'tis reported, so.
MÆCENAS. Let Rome be thus
Inform'd.
AGRIPPA. Who, queasy with his insolence
Already, will their good thoughts call from him.
CÆSAR. The people knows it, and have now receiv'd
His accusations.
AGRIPPA. Who does he accuse?
CÆSAR. Cæsar; and that, having in Sicily

Sextus Pompeius spoil'd, we had not rated him
His part o' th' isle. Then does he say he lent me
Some shipping, unrestor'd. Lastly, he frets
That Lepidus of the triumvirate
Should be depos'd; and, being, that we detain
All his revenue.

AGRIPPA. Sir, this should be answer'd.

CÆSAR. 'Tis done already, and messenger gone.
I have told him Lepidus was grown too cruel,
That he his high authority abus'd,
And did deserve his change. For what I have conquer'd
I grant him part; but then, in his Armenia
And other of his conquer'd kingdoms, I
Demand the like.

MÆCENAS. He'll never yield to that.

CÆSAR. Nor must not then be yielded to in this.

Enter OCTAVIA, *with her train*

OCTAVIA. Hail, Cæsar, and my lord! hail, most dear Cæsar!

CÆSAR. That ever I should call thee cast-away!

OCTAVIA. You have not call'd me so, nor have you cause.

CÆSAR. Why have you stol'n upon us thus? You come not
Like Cæsar's sister. The wife of Antony
Should have an army for an usher, and
The neighs of horse to tell of her approach
Long ere she did appear. The trees by th' way
Should have borne men, and expectation fainted,
Longing for what it had not. Nay, the dust
Should have ascended to the roof of heaven,
Rais'd by your populous troops. But you are come
A market-maid to Rome, and have prevented
The ostentation of our love, which left unshown
Is often left unlov'd. We should have met you
By sea and land, supplying every stage
With an augmented greeting.

OCTAVIA. Good my lord,
To come thus was I not constrain'd, but did it
On my free will. My lord, Mark Antony,
Hearing that you prepar'd for war, acquainted
My grieved ear withal; whereon I begg'd

His pardon for return.
CÆSAR. Which soon he granted,
Being an obstruct 'tween his lust and him.
OCTAVIA. Do not say so, my lord.
CÆSAR. I have eyes upon him,
And his affairs come to me on the wind.
Where is he now?
OCTAVIA. My lord, in Athens.
CÆSAR. No, my most wronged sister: Cleopatra
Hath nodded him to her. He hath given his empire
Up to a whore, who now are levying
The kings o' th' earth for war. He hath assembled
Bocchus, the king of Libya; Archelaus
Of Cappadocia; Philadelphos, king
Of Paphlagonia; the Thracian king, Adallas;
King Manchus of Arabia; King of Pont;
Herod of Jewry; Mithridates, king
Of Comagene; Polemon and Amyntas,
The kings of Mede and Lycaonia, with a
More larger list of sceptres.
OCTAVIA. Ay me most wretched,
That have my heart parted betwixt two friends,
That does afflict each other!
CÆSAR. Welcome hither.
Your letters did withhold our breaking forth,
Till we perceiv'd both how you were wrong led
And we in negligent danger. Cheer your heart;
Be you not troubled with the time, which drives
O'er your content these strong necessities,
But let determin'd things to destiny
Hold unbewail'd their way. Welcome to Rome;
Nothing more dear to me. You are abus'd
Beyond the mark of thought, and the high gods,
To do you justice, make their ministers
Of us and those that love you. Best of comfort,
And ever welcome to us.
AGRIPPA. Welcome, lady.
MÆCENAS. Welcome, dear madam.
Each heart in Rome does love and pity you;
Only th' adulterous Antony, most large

In his abominations, turns you off,
And gives his potent regiment to a trull
That noises it against us.

OCTAVIA. Is it so, sir?

CÆSAR. Most certain. Sister, welcome. Pray you
Be ever known to patience. My dear'st sister! *Exeunt*

SCENE 7

ANTONY'S *camp near Actium*

Enter CLEOPATRA *and* ENOBARBUS

CLEOPATRA. I will be even with thee, doubt it not.

ENOBARBUS. But why, why, why?

CLEOPATRA. Thou hast forspoke my being in these wars,
And say'st it is not fit.

ENOBARBUS. Well, is it, is it?

CLEOPATRA. Is't not denounc'd against us? Why should not we
Be there in person?

ENOBARBUS. [*Aside*] Well, I could reply:
If we should serve with horse and mares together
The horse were merely lost; the mares would bear
A soldier and his horse.

CLEOPATRA. What is't you say?

ENOBARBUS. Your presence needs must puzzle Antony;
Take from his heart, take from his brain, from 's time,
What should not then be spar'd. He is already
Traduc'd for levity; and 'tis said in Rome
That Photinus an eunuch and your maids
Manage this war.

CLEOPATRA. Sink Rome, and their tongues rot
That speak against us! A charge we bear i' th' war,
And, as the president of my kingdom, will
Appear there for a man. Speak not against it;
I will not stay behind.

Enter ANTONY *and* CANIDIUS

ENOBARBUS. Nay, I have done.

Here comes the Emperor.
ANTONY. Is it not strange, Canidius,
That from Tarentum and Brundusium
He could so quickly cut the Ionian sea,
And take in Toryne?—You have heard on't, sweet?
CLEOPATRA. Celerity is never more admir'd
Than by the negligent.
ANTONY. A good rebuke,
Which might have well becom'd the best of men
To taunt at slackness. Canidius, we
Will fight with him by sea.
CLEOPATRA. By sea! What else?
CANIDIUS. Why will my lord do so?
ANTONY. For that he dares us to't.
ENOBARBUS. So hath my lord dar'd him to single fight.
CANIDIUS. Ay, and to wage this battle at Pharsalia,
Where Cæsar fought with Pompey. But these offers,
Which serve not for his vantage, he shakes off;
And so should you.
ENOBARBUS. Your ships are not well mann'd;
Your mariners are muleteers, reapers, people
Ingross'd by swift impress. In Cæsar's fleet
Are those that often have 'gainst Pompey fought;
Their ships are yare; yours heavy. No disgrace
Shall fall you for refusing him at sea,
Being prepar'd for land.
ANTONY. By sea, by sea.
ENOBARBUS. Most worthy sir, you therein throw away
The absolute soldiership you have by land;
Distract your army, which doth most consist
Of war-mark'd footmen; leave unexecuted
Your own renowned knowledge; quite forgo
The way which promises assurance; and
Give up yourself merely to chance and hazard
From firm security.
ANTONY. I'll fight at sea.
CLEOPATRA. I have sixty sails, Cæsar none better.
ANTONY. Our overplus of shipping will we burn,
And, with the rest full-mann'd, from th' head of Actium
Beat th' approaching Cæsar. But if we fail,

We then can do't at land.

Enter a MESSENGER

Thy business?

MESSENGER. The news is true, my lord: he is descried;
Cæsar has taken Toryne.

ANTONY. Can he be there in person? 'Tis impossible—
Strange that his power should be. Canidius,
Our nineteen legions thou shalt hold by land,
And our twelve thousand horse. We'll to our ship.
Away, my Thetis!

Enter a SOLDIER

How now, worthy soldier?

SOLDIER. O noble Emperor, do not fight by sea;
Trust not to rotten planks. Do you misdoubt
This sword and these my wounds? Let th' Egyptians
And the Phœnicians go a-ducking; we
Have us'd to conquer standing on the earth
And fighting foot to foot.

ANTONY. Well, well—away.

Exeunt ANTONY, CLEOPATRA, *and* ENOBARBUS

SOLDIER. By Hercules, I think I am i' th' right.

CANIDIUS. Soldier, thou art; but his whole action grows
Not in the power on't. So our leader's led,
And we are women's men.

SOLDIER. You keep by land
The legions and the horse whole, do you not?

CANIDIUS. Marcus Octavius, Marcus Justeius,
Publicola, and Cælius are for sea;
But we keep whole by land. This speed of Cæsar's
Carries beyond belief.

SOLDIER. While he was yet in Rome,
His power went out in such distractions as
Beguil'd all spies.

CANIDIUS. Who's his lieutenant, hear you?

SOLDIER. They say one Taurus.

CANIDIUS. Well I know the man.

Enter a MESSENGER

ACT III. SCENE 7

MESSENGER. The Emperor calls Canidius.
CANIDIUS. With news the time's with labour and throes forth
Each minute some. *Exeunt*

SCENE 8

A plain near Actium

Enter CÆSAR, *with his army, marching*

CÆSAR. Taurus!
TAURUS. My lord?
CÆSAR. Strike not by land; keep whole; provoke not battle
Till we have done at sea. Do not exceed
The prescript of this scroll. Our fortune lies
Upon this jump. *Exeunt*

SCENE 9

Another part of the plain

Enter ANTONY *and* ENOBARBUS

ANTONY. Set we our squadrons on yon side o' th' hill,
In eye of Cæsar's battle; from which place
We may the number of the ships behold,
And so proceed accordingly. *Exeunt*

SCENE 10

Another part of the plain

CANIDIUS *marcheth with his land army one way over the stage, and* TAURUS, *the Lieutenant of* CÆSAR, *the other way. After their going in is heard the noise of a sea-fight*

Alarum. Enter ENOBARBUS

ENOBARBUS. Naught, naught, all naught! I can behold no longer.

Th' Antoniad, the Egyptian admiral,
With all their sixty, fly and turn the rudder.
To see't mine eyes are blasted.

Enter SCARUS

SCARUS. Gods and goddesses,
All the whole synod of them!
ENOBARBUS. What's thy passion?
SCARUS. The greater cantle of the world is lost
With very ignorance; we have kiss'd away
Kingdoms and provinces.
ENOBARBUS. How appears the fight?
SCARUS. On our side like the token'd pestilence,
Where death is sure. Yon ribaudred nag of Egypt—
Whom leprosy o'ertake!—i' th' midst o' th' fight,
When vantage like a pair of twins appear'd,
Both as the same, or rather ours the elder—
The breese upon her, like a cow in June—
Hoists sails and flies.
ENOBARBUS. That I beheld;
Mine eyes did sicken at the sight and could not
Endure a further view.
SCARUS. She once being loof'd,
The noble ruin of her magic, Antony,
Claps on his sea-wing, and, like a doting mallard,
Leaving the fight in height, flies after her.
I never saw an action of such shame;
Experience, manhood, honour, ne'er before
Did violate so itself.
ENOBARBUS. Alack, alack!

Enter CANIDIUS

CANIDIUS. Our fortune on the sea is out of breath,
And sinks most lamentably. Had our general
Been what he knew himself, it had gone well.
O, he has given example for our flight
Most grossly by his own!
ENOBARBUS. Ay, are you thereabouts?
Why then, good night indeed.

CANIDIUS. Toward Peloponnesus are they fled.
SCARUS. 'Tis easy to't; and there I will attend
What further comes.
CANIDIUS. To Cæsar will I render
My legions and my horse; six kings already
Show me the way of yielding.
ENOBARBUS. I'll yet follow
The wounded chance of Antony, though my reason
Sits in the wind against me. *Exeunt*

SCENE 11

Alexandria. CLEOPATRA'S *palace*

Enter ANTONY *with attendants*

ANTONY. Hark! the land bids me tread no more upon't;
It is asham'd to bear me. Friends, come hither.
I am so lated in the world that I
Have lost my way for ever. I have a ship
Laden with gold; take that; divide it. Fly,
And make your peace with Cæsar.
ALL. Fly? Not we!
ANTONY. I have fled myself, and have instructed cowards
To run and show their shoulders. Friends, be gone;
I have myself resolv'd upon a course
Which has no need of you; be gone.
My treasure's in the harbour, take it. O,
I follow'd that I blush to look upon.
My very hairs do mutiny; for the white
Reprove the brown for rashness, and they them
For fear and doting. Friends, be gone; you shall
Have letters from me to some friends that will
Sweep your way for you. Pray you look not sad,
Nor make replies of loathness; take the hint
Which my despair proclaims. Let that be left
Which leaves itself. To the sea-side straight way.
I will possess you of that ship and treasure.
Leave me, I pray, a little; pray you now;

Nay, do so, for indeed I have lost command;
Therefore I pray you. I'll see you by and by. [*Sits down*]

Enter CLEOPATRA, *led by* CHARMIAN *and* IRAS, EROS *following*

EROS. Nay, gentle madam, to him! Comfort him.
IRAS. Do, most dear Queen.
CHARMIAN. Do? Why, what else?
CLEOPATRA. Let me sit down. O Juno!
ANTONY. No, no, no, no, no.
EROS. See you here, sir?
ANTONY. O, fie, fie, fie!
CHARMIAN. Madam!
IRAS. Madam, O good Empress!
EROS. Sir, sir!
ANTONY. Yes, my lord, yes. He at Philippi kept
His sword e'en like a dancer, while I struck
The lean and wrinkled Cassius; and 'twas I
That the mad Brutus ended; he alone
Dealt on lieutenantry, and no practice had
In the brave squares of war. Yet now—no matter.
CLEOPATRA. Ah, stand by!
EROS. The Queen, my lord, the Queen!
IRAS. Go to him, madam, speak to him.
He is unqualitied with very shame.
CLEOPATRA. Well then, sustain me. O!
EROS. Most noble sir, arise; the Queen approaches.
Her head's declin'd, and death will seize her but
Your comfort makes the rescue.
ANTONY. I have offended reputation—
A most unnoble swerving.
EROS. Sir, the Queen.
ANTONY. O, whither hast thou led me, Egypt? See
How I convey my shame out of thine eyes
By looking back what I have left behind
'Stroy'd in dishonour.
CLEOPATRA. O my lord, my lord,
Forgive my fearful sails! I little thought
You would have followed.
ANTONY. Egypt, thou knew'st too well

My heart was to thy rudder tied by th' strings,
And thou shouldst tow me after. O'er my spirit
Thy full supremacy thou knew'st, and that
Thy beck might from the bidding of the gods
Command me.

CLEOPATRA. O, my pardon!

ANTONY. Now I must
To the young man send humble treaties, dodge
And palter in the shifts of lowness, who
With half the bulk o' th' world play'd as I pleas'd,
Making and marring fortunes. You did know
How much you were my conqueror, and that
My sword, made weak by my affection, would
Obey it on all cause.

CLEOPATRA. Pardon, pardon!

ANTONY. Fall not a tear, I say; one of them rates
All that is won and lost. Give me a kiss;
Even this repays me.
We sent our schoolmaster; is 'a come back?
Love, I am full of lead. Some wine,
Within there, and our viands! Fortune knows
We scorn her most when most she offers blows. *Exeunt*

SCENE 12

CÆSAR'S *camp in Egypt*

Enter CÆSAR, AGRIPPA, DOLABELLA, THYREUS, *with others*

CÆSAR. Let him appear that's come from Antony.
Know you him?

DOLABELLA. Cæsar, 'tis his schoolmaster:
An argument that he is pluck'd, when hither
He sends so poor a pinion of his wing,
Which had superfluous kings for messengers
Not many moons gone by.

Enter EUPHRONIUS, *Ambassador from* ANTONY

CÆSAR. Approach, and speak.

EUPHRONIUS. Such as I am, I come from Antony.

I was of late as petty to his ends
As is the morn-dew on the myrtle leaf
To his grand sea.
CÆSAR. Be't so. Declare thine office.
EUPHRONIUS. Lord of his fortunes he salutes thee, and
Requires to live in Egypt; which not granted,
He lessens his requests and to thee sues
To let him breathe between the heavens and earth,
A private man in Athens. This for him.
Next, Cleopatra does confess thy greatness,
Submits her to thy might, and of thee craves
The circle of the Ptolemies for her heirs,
Now hazarded to thy grace.
CÆSAR. For Antony,
I have no ears to his request. The Queen
Of audience nor desire shall fail, so she
From Egypt drive her all-disgraced friend,
Or take his life there. This if she perform,
She shall not sue unheard. So to them both.
EUPHRONIUS. Fortune pursue thee!
CÆSAR. Bring him through the bands. *Exit* EUPHRONIUS
[*To* THYREUS] To try thy eloquence, now 'tis time. Dispatch;
From Antony win Cleopatra. Promise,
And in our name, what she requires; add more,
From thine invention, offers. Women are not
In their best fortunes strong; but want will perjure
The ne'er-touch'd vestal. Try thy cunning, Thyreus;
Make thine own edict for thy pains, which we
Will answer as a law.
THYREUS. Cæsar, I go.
CÆSAR. Observe how Antony becomes his flaw,
And what thou think'st his very action speaks
In every power that moves.
THYREUS. Cæsar, I shall. *Exeunt*

SCENE 13

Alexandria. CLEOPATRA'S *palace*

Enter CLEOPATRA, ENOBARBUS, CHARMIAN, *and* IRAS

CLEOPATRA. What shall we do, Enobarbus?
ENOBARBUS. Think, and die.
CLEOPATRA. Is Antony or we in fault for this?
ENOBARBUS. Antony only, that would make his will
Lord of his reason. What though you fled
From that great face of war, whose several ranges
Frighted each other? Why should he follow?
The itch of his affection should not then
Have nick'd his captainship, at such a point,
When half to half the world oppos'd, he being
The mered question. 'Twas a shame no less
Than was his loss, to course your flying flags
And leave his navy gazing.
CLEOPATRA. Prithee, peace.

Enter EUPHRONIUS, *the Ambassador; with* ANTONY

ANTONY. Is that his answer?
EUPHRONIUS. Ay, my lord.
ANTONY. The Queen shall then have courtesy, so she
Will yield us up.
EUPHRONIUS. He says so.
ANTONY. Let her know't.
To the boy Cæsar send this grizzled head,
And he will fill thy wishes to the brim
With principalities.
CLEOPATRA. That head, my lord?
ANTONY. To him again. Tell him he wears the rose
Of youth upon him; from which the world should note
Something particular. His coin, ships, legions,
May be a coward's whose ministers would prevail
Under the service of a child as soon
As i' th' command of Cæsar. I dare him therefore
To lay his gay comparisons apart,
And answer me declin'd, sword against sword,

Ourselves alone. I'll write it. Follow me.
Exeunt ANTONY *and* EUPHRONIUS

EUPHRONIUS. [*Aside*] Yes, like enough high-battled Cæsar will
Unstate his happiness, and be stag'd to th' show
Against a sworder! I see men's judgments are
A parcel of their fortunes, and things outward
Do draw the inward quality after them,
To suffer all alike. That he should dream,
Knowing all measures, the full Cæsar will
Answer his emptiness! Cæsar, thou hast subdu'd
His judgment too.

Enter a SERVANT

SERVANT. A messenger from Cæsar.

CLEOPATRA. What, no more ceremony? See, my women!
Against the blown rose may they stop their nose
That kneel'd unto the buds. Admit him, sir. *Exit* SERVANT

ENOBARBUS. [*Aside*] Mine honesty and I begin to square.
The loyalty well held to fools does make
Our faith mere folly. Yet he that can endure
To follow with allegiance a fall'n lord
Does conquer him that did his master conquer,
And earns a place i' th' story.

Enter THYREUS

CLEOPATRA. Cæsar's will?

THYREUS. Hear it apart.

CLEOPATRA. None but friends: say boldly.

THYREUS. So, haply, are they friends to Antony.

ENOBARBUS. He needs as many, sir, as Cæsar has,
Or needs not us. If Cæsar please, our master
Will leap to be his friend. For us, you know
Whose he is we are, and that is Cæsar's.

THYREUS. So.
Thus then, thou most renown'd: Cæsar entreats
Not to consider in what case thou stand'st
Further than he is Cæsar.

CLEOPATRA. Go on. Right royal!

THYREUS. He knows that you embrace not Antony

As you did love, but as you fear'd him.

CLEOPATRA. O!

THYREUS. The scars upon your honour, therefore, he
Does pity, as constrained blemishes,
Not as deserv'd.

CLEOPATRA. He is a god, and knows
What is most right. Mine honour was not yielded,
But conquer'd merely.

ENOBARBUS. [*Aside*] To be sure of that,
I will ask Antony. Sir, sir, thou art so leaky
That we must leave thee to thy sinking, for
Thy dearest quit thee. *Exit*

THYREUS. Shall I say to Cæsar
What you require of him? For he partly begs
To be desir'd to give. It much would please him
That of his fortunes you should make a staff
To lean upon. But it would warm his spirits
To hear from me you had left Antony,
And put yourself under his shroud,
The universal landlord.

CLEOPATRA. What's your name?

THYREUS. My name is Thyreus.

CLEOPATRA. Most kind messenger,
Say to great Cæsar this: in deputation
I kiss his conqu'ring hand. Tell him I am prompt
To lay my crown at 's feet, and there to kneel.
Tell him from his all-obeying breath I hear
The doom of Egypt.

THYREUS. 'Tis your noblest course.
Wisdom and fortune combating together,
If that the former dare but what it can,
No chance may shake it. Give me grace to lay
My duty on your hand.

CLEOPATRA. Your Cæsar's father oft,
When he hath mus'd of taking kingdoms in,
Bestow'd his lips on that unworthy place,
As it rain'd kisses.

Re-enter ANTONY *and* ENOBARBUS

ANTONY. Favours, by Jove that thunders!

What art thou, fellow?

THYREUS. One that but performs
The bidding of the fullest man, and worthiest
To have command obey'd.

ENOBARBUS. [*Aside*] You will be whipt.

ANTONY. Approach there.—Ah, you kite!—Now, gods and devils!
Authority melts from me. Of late, when I cried 'Ho!'
Like boys unto a muss, kings would start forth
And cry 'Your will?' Have you no ears? I am
Antony yet.

Enter servants

Take hence this Jack and whip him.

ENOBARBUS. 'Tis better playing with a lion's whelp
Than with an old one dying.

ANTONY. Moon and stars!
Whip him. Were't twenty of the greatest tributaries
That do acknowledge Cæsar, should I find them
So saucy with the hand of she here—what's her name
Since she was Cleopatra? Whip him, fellows,
Till like a boy you see him cringe his face,
And whine aloud for mercy. Take him hence.

THYREUS. Mark Antony—

ANTONY. Tug him away. Being whipt,
Bring him again: the Jack of Cæsar's shall
Bear us an errand to him. *Exeunt servants with* THYREUS
You were half blasted ere I knew you. Ha!
Have I my pillow left unpress'd in Rome,
Forborne the getting of a lawful race,
And by a gem of women, to be abus'd
By one that looks on feeders?

CLEOPATRA. Good my lord—

ANTONY. You have been a boggler ever.
But when we in our viciousness grow hard—
O misery on't!—the wise gods seel our eyes,
In our own filth drop our clear judgments, make us
Adore our errors, laugh at's while we strut
To our confusion.

CLEOPATRA. O, is't come to this?

ANTONY. I found you as a morsel cold upon
Dead Cæsar's trencher. Nay, you were a fragment
Of Cneius Pompey's, besides what hotter hours,
Unregist'red in vulgar fame, you have
Luxuriously pick'd out; for I am sure,
Though you can guess what temperance should be,
You know not what it is.
CLEOPATRA. Wherefore is this?
ANTONY. To let a fellow that will take rewards,
And say 'God quit you!' be familiar with
My playfellow, your hand, this kingly seal
And plighter of high hearts! O that I were
Upon the hill of Basan to outroar
The horned herd! For I have savage cause,
And to proclaim it civilly were like
A halter'd neck which does the hangman thank
For being yare about him.

Re-enter a SERVANT *with* THYREUS

Is he whipt?
SERVANT. Soundly, my lord.
ANTONY. Cried he? and begg'd 'a pardon?
SERVANT. He did ask favour.
ANTONY. If that thy father live, let him repent
Thou wast not made his daughter; and be thou sorry
To follow Cæsar in his triumph, since
Thou hast been whipt for following him. Henceforth
The white hand of a lady fever thee!
Shake thou to look on't. Get thee back to Cæsar;
Tell him thy entertainment; look thou say
He makes me angry with him; for he seems
Proud and disdainful, harping on what I am,
Not what he knew I was. He makes me angry;
And at this time most easy 'tis to do't,
When my good stars, that were my former guides,
Have empty left their orbs and shot their fires
Into th' abysm of hell. If he mislike
My speech and what is done, tell him he has
Hipparchus, my enfranched bondman, whom
He may at pleasure whip or hang or torture,

As he shall like, to quit me. Urge it thou.
Hence with thy stripes, be gone. *Exit* THYREUS

CLEOPATRA. Have you done yet?

ANTONY. Alack, our terrene moon
Is now eclips'd, and it portends alone
The fall of Antony.

CLEOPATRA. I must stay his time.

ANTONY. To flatter Cæsar, would you mingle eyes
With one that ties his points?

CLEOPATRA. Not know me yet?

ANTONY. Cold-hearted toward me?

CLEOPATRA. Ah, dear, if I be so,
From my cold heart let heaven engender hail,
And poison it in the source, and the first stone
Drop in my neck; as it determines, so
Dissolve my life! The next Cæsarion smite!
Till by degrees the memory of my womb,
Together with my brave Egyptians all,
By the discandying of this pelleted storm,
Lie graveless, till the flies and gnats of Nile
Have buried them for prey.

ANTONY. I am satisfied.
Cæsar sits down in Alexandria, where
I will oppose his fate. Our force by land
Hath nobly held; our sever'd navy too
Have knit again, and fleet, threat'ning most sea-like.
Where hast thou been, my heart? Dost thou hear, lady?
If from the field I shall return once more
To kiss these lips, I will appear in blood.
I and my sword will earn our chronicle.
There's hope in't yet.

CLEOPATRA. That's my brave lord!

ANTONY. I will be treble-sinew'd, hearted, breath'd,
And fight maliciously. For when mine hours
Were nice and lucky, men did ransom lives
Of me for jests; but now I'll set my teeth,
And send to darkness all that stop me. Come,
Let's have one other gaudy night. Call to me
All my sad captains; fill our bowls once more;
Let's mock the midnight bell.

CLEOPATRA. It is my birthday.
I had thought t'have held it poor; but since my lord
Is Antony again, I will be Cleopatra.
ANTONY. We will yet do well.
CLEOPATRA. Call all his noble captains to my lord.
ANTONY. Do so, we'll speak to them; and to-night I'll force
The wine peep through their scars. Come on, my queen,
There's sap in't yet. The next time I do fight
I'll make death love me; for I will contend
Even with his pestilent scythe. *Exeunt all but* ENOBARBUS
ENOBARBUS. Now he'll outstare the lightning. To be furious
Is to be frighted out of fear, and in that mood
The dove will peck the estridge; and I see still
A diminution in our captain's brain
Restores his heart. When valour preys on reason,
It eats the sword it fights with. I will seek
Some way to leave him. *Exit*

ACT IV. SCENE 1

CÆSAR'S *camp before Alexandria*

Enter CÆSAR, AGRIPPA, *and* MÆCENAS, *with his army;*
CÆSAR *reading a letter*

CÆSAR. He calls me boy, and chides as he had power
To beat me out of Egypt. My messenger
He hath whipt with rods; dares me to personal combat,
Cæsar to Antony. Let the old ruffian know
I have many other ways to die, meantime
Laugh at his challenge.
MÆCENAS. Cæsar must think
When one so great begins to rage, he's hunted
Even to falling. Give him no breath, but now
Make boot of his distraction. Never anger
Made good guard for itself.
CÆSAR. Let our best heads
Know that to-morrow the last of many battles
We mean to fight. Within our files there are

Of those that serv'd Mark Antony but late
Enough to fetch him in. See it done;
And feast the army; we have store to do't,
And they have earn'd the waste. Poor Antony! *Exeunt*

SCENE 2

Alexandria. CLEOPATRA'S *palace*

Enter ANTONY, CLEOPATRA, ENOBARBUS, CHARMIAN, IRAS, ALEXAS, *with others*

ANTONY. He will not fight with me, Domitius?
ENOBARBUS. No.
ANTONY. Why should he not?
ENOBARBUS. He thinks, being twenty times of better fortune,
He is twenty men to one.
ANTONY. To-morrow, soldier,
By sea and land I'll fight. Or I will live,
Or bathe my dying honour in the blood
Shall make it live again. Woo't thou fight well?
ENOBARBUS. I'll strike, and cry 'Take all.'
ANTONY. Well said; come on.
Call forth my household servants; let's to-night
Be bounteous at our meal.

Enter three or four servitors

Give me thy hand,
Thou has been rightly honest. So hast thou;
Thou, and thou, and thou. You have serv'd me well,
And kings have been your fellows.
CLEOPATRA. [*Aside to* ENOBARBUS] What means this?
ENOBARBUS. [*Aside to* CLEOPATRA] 'Tis one of those odd tricks which sorrow shoots
Out of the mind.
ANTONY. And thou art honest too.
I wish I could be made so many men,
And all of you clapp'd up together in
An Antony, that I might do you service
So good as you have done.

SERVANT. The gods forbid!
ANTONY. Well, my good fellows, wait on me to-night.
  Scant not my cups, and make as much of me
  As when mine empire was your fellow too,
  And suffer'd my command.
CLEOPATRA. [*Aside to* ENOBARBUS] What does he mean?
ENOBARBUS. [*Aside to* CLEOPATRA] To make his followers
    weep.
ANTONY. Tend me to-night;
  May be it is the period of your duty.
  Haply you shall not see me more; or if,
  A mangled shadow. Perchance to-morrow
  You'll serve another master. I look on you
  As one that takes his leave. Mine honest friends,
  I turn you not away; but, like a master
  Married to your good service, stay till death.
  Tend me to-night two hours, I ask no more,
  And the gods yield you for't!
ENOBARBUS. What mean you, sir,
  To give them this discomfort? Look, they weep;
  And I, an ass, am onion-ey'd. For shame!
  Transform us not to women.
ANTONY. Ho, ho, ho!
  Now the witch take me if I meant it thus!
  Grace grow where those drops fall! My hearty friends,
  You take me in too dolorous a sense;
  For I spake to you for your comfort, did desire you
  To burn this night with torches. Know, my hearts,
  I hope well of to-morrow, and will lead you
  Where rather I'll expect victorious life
  Than death and honour. Let's to supper, come,
  And drown consideration. *Exeunt*

SCENE 3

Alexandria. Before CLEOPATRA'*s palace*

Enter a company of soldiers

FIRST SOLDIER. Brother, good night. To-morrow is the day.

SECOND SOLDIER. It will determine one way. Fare you well.
Heard you of nothing strange about the streets?

FIRST SOLDIER. Nothing. What news?

SECOND SOLDIER. Belike 'tis but a rumour. Good night to you.

FIRST SOLDIER. Well, sir, good night.

[*They meet other soldiers*]

SECOND SOLDIER. Soldiers, have careful watch.

FIRST SOLDIER. And you. Good night, good night.

[*The two companies separate and place themselves in every corner of the stage*]

SECOND SOLDIER. Here we. And if to-morrow
Our navy thrive, I have an absolute hope
Our landmen will stand up.

THIRD SOLDIER. 'Tis a brave army,
And full of purpose.

[*Music of the hautboys is under the stage*]

SECOND SOLDIER. Peace, what noise?

THIRD SOLDIER. List, list!

SECOND SOLDIER. Hark!

THIRD SOLDIER. Music i' th' air.

FOURTH SOLDIER. Under the earth.

THIRD SOLDIER. It signs well, does it not?

FOURTH SOLDIER. No.

THIRD SOLDIER. Peace, I say!
What should this mean?

SECOND SOLDIER. 'Tis the god Hercules, whom Antony lov'd,
Now leaves him.

THIRD SOLDIER. Walk; let's see if other watchmen
Do hear what we do.

SECOND SOLDIER. How now, masters!

SOLDIERS. [*Speaking together*] How now!
How now! Do you hear this?

FIRST SOLDIER. Ay; is't not strange?

THIRD SOLDIER. Do you hear, masters? Do you hear?

FIRST SOLDIER. Follow the noise so far as we have quarter;
Let's see how it will give off.

SOLDIERS. Content. 'Tis strange. *Exeunt*

SCENE 4

Alexandria. CLEOPATRA'S *palace*

Enter ANTONY *and* CLEOPATRA, CHARMIAN, IRAS, *with others*

ANTONY. Eros! mine armour, Eros!
CLEOPATRA. Sleep a little.
ANTONY. No, my chuck. Eros! Come, mine armour, Eros!

Enter EROS *with armour*

Come, good fellow, put mine iron on.
If fortune be not ours to-day, it is
Because we brave her. Come.
CLEOPATRA. Nay, I'll help too.
What's this for?
ANTONY. Ah, let be, let be! Thou art
The armourer of my heart. False, false; this, this.
CLEOPATRA. Sooth, la, I'll help. Thus it must be.
ANTONY. Well, well;
We shall thrive now. Seest thou, my good fellow?
Go put on thy defences.
EROS. Briefly, sir.
CLEOPATRA. Is not this buckled well?
ANTONY. Rarely, rarely!
He that unbuckles this, till we do please
To daff't for our repose, shall hear a storm.
Thou fumblest, Eros, and my queen's a squire
More tight at this than thou. Dispatch. O love,
That thou couldst see my wars to-day, and knew'st
The royal occupation! Thou shouldst see
A workman in't.

Enter an armed SOLDIER

Good-morrow to thee. Welcome.
Thou look'st like him that knows a warlike charge.
To business that we love we rise betime,
And go to't with delight.
SOLDIER. A thousand, sir,

Early though't be, have on their riveted trim,
And at the port expect you.
[*Shout. Flourish of trumpets within*]

Enter CAPTAINS *and soldiers*

CAPTAIN. The morn is fair. Good morrow, General.
ALL. Good morrow, General.
ANTONY. 'Tis well blown, lads.
This morning, like the spirit of a youth
That means to be of note, begins betimes.
So, so. Come, give me that. This way. Well said.
Fare thee well, dame, whate'er becomes of me.
This is a soldier's kiss. Rebukeable,
And worthy shameful check it were, to stand
On more mechanic compliment; I'll leave thee
Now like a man of steel. You that will fight,
Follow me close; I'll bring you to't. Adieu.
Exeunt ANTONY, EROS, CAPTAINS *and soldiers*
CHARMIAN. Please you retire to your chamber?
CLEOPATRA. Lead me.
He goes forth gallantly. That he and Cæsar might
Determine this great war in single fight!
Then, Antony—but now. Well, on. *Exeunt*

SCENE 5

Alexandria. ANTONY'S *camp*

Trumpets sound. Enter ANTONY *and* EROS, *a* SOLDIER *meeting them*

SOLDIER. The gods make this a happy day to Antony!
ANTONY. Would thou and those thy scars had once prevail'd
To make me fight at land!
SOLDIER. Hadst thou done so,
The kings that have revolted, and the soldier
That has this morning left thee, would have still
Followed thy heels.
ANTONY. Who's gone this morning?
SOLDIER. Who?

One ever near thee. Call for Enobarbus,
He shall not hear thee; or from Cæsar's camp
Say 'I am none of thine.'

ANTONY. What say'st thou?

SOLDIER. Sir,
He is with Cæsar.

EROS. Sir, his chests and treasure
He has not with him.

ANTONY. Is he gone?

SOLDIER. Most certain.

ANTONY. Go, Eros, send his treasure after; do it;
Detain no jot, I charge thee. Write to him–
I will subscribe–gentle adieus and greetings;
Say that I wish he never find more cause
To change a master. O, my fortunes have
Corrupted honest men! Dispatch. Enobarbus! *Exeunt*

SCENE 6

Alexandria. CÆSAR'S *camp*

Flourish. Enter AGRIPPA, CÆSAR, *with* DOLABELLA *and* ENOBARBUS

CÆSAR. Go forth, Agrippa, and begin the fight.
Our will is Antony be took alive;
Make it so known.

AGRIPPA. Cæsar, I shall. *Exit*

CÆSAR. The time of universal peace is near.
Prove this a prosp'rous day, the three-nook'd world
Shall bear the olive freely.

Enter a MESSENGER

MESSENGER. Antony
Is come into the field.

CÆSAR. Go charge Agrippa
Plant those that have revolted in the vant,
That Antony may seem to spend his fury
Upon himself. *Exeunt all but* ENOBARBUS

ENOBARBUS. Alexas did revolt and went to Jewry on

Affairs of Antony; there did dissuade
Great Herod to incline himself to Cæsar
And leave his master Antony. For this pains
Cæsar hath hang'd him. Canidius and the rest
That fell away have entertainment, but
No honourable trust. I have done ill,
Of which I do accuse myself so sorely
That I will joy no more.

Enter a SOLDIER *of* CÆSAR'S

SOLDIER. Enobarbus, Antony
Hath after thee sent all thy treasure, with
His bounty overplus. The messenger
Came on my guard, and at thy tent is now
Unloading of his mules.

ENOBARBUS. I give it you.

SOLDIER. Mock not, Enobarbus.
I tell you true. Best you saf'd the bringer
Out of the host. I must attend mine office,
Or would have done't myself. Your emperor
Continues still a Jove. *Exit*

ENOBARBUS. I am alone the villain of the earth,
And feel I am so most. O Antony,
Thou mine of bounty, how wouldst thou have paid
My better service, when my turpitude
Thou dost so crown with gold! This blows my heart.
If swift thought break it not, a swifter mean
Shall outstrike thought; but thought will do't, I feel.
I fight against thee? No! I will go seek
Some ditch wherein to die; the foul'st best fits
My latter part of life. *Exit*

SCENE 7

Field of battle between the camps

Alarum. Drums and trumpets. Enter AGRIPPA *and others*

AGRIPPA. Retire. We have engag'd ourselves too far.

Cæsar himself has work, and our oppression
Exceeds what we expected. *Exeunt*

Alarums. Enter Antony, *and* Scarus *wounded*

Scarus. O my brave Emperor, this is fought indeed!
Had we done so at first, we had droven them home
With clouts about their heads.
Antony. Thou bleed'st apace.
Scarus. I had a wound here that was like a T,
But now 'tis made an H.
Antony. They do retire.
Scarus. We'll beat 'em into bench-holes. I have yet
Room for six scotches more.

Enter Eros

Eros. They are beaten, sir, and our advantage serves
For a fair victory.
Scarus. Let us score their backs
And snatch 'em up, as we take hares, behind.
'Tis sport to maul a runner.
Antony. I will reward thee
Once for thy sprightly comfort, and tenfold
For thy good valour. Come thee on.
Scarus. I'll halt after. *Exeunt*

SCENE 8

Under the walls of Alexandria

Alarum. Enter Antony, *again in a march;* Scarus *with others*

Antony. We have beat him to his camp. Run one before
And let the Queen know of our gests. To-morrow,
Before the sun shall see's, we'll spill the blood
That has to-day escap'd. I thank you all;
For doughty-handed are you, and have fought
Not as you serv'd the cause, but as't had been
Each man's like mine; you have shown all Hectors.
Enter the city, clip your wives, your friends,

Tell them your feats; whilst they with joyful tears
Wash the congealment from your wounds and kiss
The honour'd gashes whole.

Enter CLEOPATRA, *attended*

[*To* SCARUS] Give me thy hand–
To this great fairy I'll commend thy acts,
Make her thanks bless thee. O thou day o' th' world,
Chain mine arm'd neck. Leap thou, attire and all,
Through proof of harness to my heart, and there
Ride on the pants triumphing.

CLEOPATRA. Lord of lords!
O infinite virtue, com'st thou smiling from
The world's great snare uncaught?

ANTONY. Mine nightingale,
We have beat them to their beds. What, girl! though grey
Do something mingle with our younger brown, yet ha' we
A brain that nourishes our nerves, and can
Get goal for goal of youth. Behold this man;
Commend unto his lips thy favouring hand–
Kiss it, my warrior–he hath fought to-day
As if a god in hate of mankind had
Destroyed in such a shape.

CLEOPATRA. I'll give thee, friend,
An armour all of gold; it was a king's.

ANTONY. He has deserv'd it, were it carbuncled
Like holy Phœbus' car. Give me thy hand.
Through Alexandria make a jolly march;
Bear our hack'd targets like the men that owe them.
Had our great palace the capacity
To camp this host, we all would sup together,
And drink carouses to the next day's fate,
Which promises royal peril. Trumpeters,
With brazen din blast you the city's ear;
Make mingle with our rattling tabourines,
That heaven and earth may strike their sounds together
Applauding our approach. *Exeunt*

SCENE 9

CÆSAR's *camp*

Enter a CENTURION *and his company;* ENOBARBUS *follows*

CENTURION. If we be not reliev'd within this hour,
We must return to th' court of guard. The night
Is shiny, and they say we shall embattle
By th' second hour i' th' morn.
FIRST WATCH. This last day was
A shrewd one to's.
ENOBARBUS. O, bear me witness, night–
SECOND WATCH. What man is this?
FIRST WATCH. Stand close and list him.
ENOBARBUS. Be witness to me, O thou blessed moon,
When men revolted shall upon record
Bear hateful memory, poor Enobarbus did
Before thy face repent!
CENTURION. Enobarbus?
SECOND WATCH. Peace!
Hark further.
ENOBARBUS. O sovereign mistress of true melancholy,
The poisonous damp of night disponge upon me,
That life, a very rebel to my will,
May hang no longer on me. Throw my heart
Against the flint and hardness of my fault,
Which, being dried with grief, will break to powder,
And finish all foul thoughts. O Antony,
Nobler than my revolt is infamous,
Forgive me in thine own particular,
But let the world rank me in register
A master-leaver and a fugitive!
O Antony! O Antony! [*Dies*]
FIRST WATCH. Let's speak to him.
CENTURION. Let's hear him, for the things he speaks
May concern Cæsar.
SECOND WATCH. Let's do so. But he sleeps.
CENTURION. Swoons rather; for so bad a prayer as his
Was never yet for sleep.

FIRST WATCH. Go we to him.
SECOND WATCH. Awake, sir, awake; speak to us.
FIRST WATCH. Hear you, sir?
CENTURION. The hand of death hath raught him.
  [*Drums afar off*] Hark! the drums
  Demurely wake the sleepers. Let us bear him
  To th' court of guard; he is of note. Our hour
  Is fully out.
SECOND WATCH. Come on, then;
  He may recover yet. *Exeunt with the body*

SCENE 10

Between the two camps

Enter ANTONY *and* SCARUS, *with their army*

ANTONY. Their preparation is to-day by sea;
  We please them not by land.
SCARUS. For both, my lord.
ANTONY. I would they'd fight i' th' fire or i' th' air;
  We'd fight there too. But this it is, our foot
  Upon the hills adjoining to the city
  Shall stay with us–Order for sea is given;
  They have put forth the haven–
  Where their appointment we may best discover
  And look on their endeavour. *Exeunt*

SCENE 11

Between the camps

Enter CÆSAR *and his army*

CÆSAR. But being charg'd, we will be still by land,
  Which, as I take't, we shall; for his best force
  Is forth to man his galleys. To the vales,
  And hold our best advantage. *Exeunt*

SCENE 12

A hill near Alexandria

Enter ANTONY *and* SCARUS

ANTONY. Yet they are not join'd. Where yond pine does stand
I shall discover all. I'll bring thee word
Straight how 'tis like to go. *Exit*
SCARUS. Swallows have built
In Cleopatra's sails their nests. The augurers
Say they know not, they cannot tell; look grimly,
And dare not speak their knowledge. Antony
Is valiant and dejected; and by starts
His fretted fortunes give him hope and fear
Of what he has and has not.
[*Alarum afar off, as at a sea-fight*]

Re-enter ANTONY

ANTONY. All is lost!
This foul Egyptian hath betrayed me.
My fleet hath yielded to the foe, and yonder
They cast their caps up and carouse together
Like friends long lost. Triple-turn'd whore! 'tis thou
Hast sold me to this novice; and my heart
Makes only wars on thee. Bid them all fly;
For when I am reveng'd upon my charm,
I have done all. Bid them all fly; begone. *Exit* SCARUS
O sun, thy uprise shall I see no more!
Fortune and Antony part here; even here
Do we shake hands. All come to this? The hearts
That spaniel'd me at heels, to whom I gave
Their wishes, do discandy, melt their sweets
On blossoming Cæsar; and this pine is bark'd
That overtopp'd them all. Betray'd I am.
O this false soul of Egypt! this grave charm—
Whose eye beck'd forth my wars and call'd them home,
Whose bosom was my crownet, my chief end—
Like a right gypsy hath at fast and loose

Beguil'd me to the very heart of loss.
What, Eros, Eros!

Enter CLEOPATRA

Ah, thou spell! Avaunt!
CLEOPATRA. Why is my lord enrag'd against his love?
ANTONY. Vanish, or I shall give thee thy deserving
And blemish Cæsar's triumph. Let him take thee
And hoist thee up to the shouting plebeians;
Follow his chariot, like the greatest spot
Of all thy sex; most monster-like, be shown
For poor'st diminutives, for doits, and let
Patient Octavia plough thy visage up
With her prepared nails. *Exit* CLEOPATRA
'Tis well th'art gone,
If it be well to live; but better 'twere
Thou fell'st into my fury, for one death
Might have prevented many. Eros, ho!
The shirt of Nessus is upon me; teach me,
Alcides, thou mine ancestor, thy rage;
Let me lodge Lichas on the horns o' th' moon,
And with those hands that grasp'd the heaviest club
Subdue my worthiest self. The witch shall die.
To the young Roman boy she hath sold me, and I fall
Under this plot. She dies for't. Eros, ho! *Exit*

SCENE 13

Alexandria. CLEOPATRA'S *palace*

Enter CLEOPATRA, CHARMIAN, IRAS, *and* MARDIAN

CLEOPATRA. Help me, my women. O, he is more mad
Than Telamon for his shield; the boar of Thessaly
Was never so emboss'd.
CHARMIAN. To th' monument!
There lock yourself, and send him word you are dead.
The soul and body rive not more in parting
Than greatness going off.
CLEOPATRA. To th' monument!

Mardian, go tell him I have slain myself;
Say that the last I spoke was 'Antony'
And word it, prithee, piteously. Hence, Mardian,
And bring me how he takes my death. To th' monument!
Exeunt

SCENE 14

CLEOPATRA'S *palace*

Enter ANTONY *and* EROS

ANTONY. Eros, thou yet behold'st me?
EROS. Ay, noble lord.
ANTONY. Sometime we see a cloud that's dragonish;
A vapour sometime like a bear or lion,
A tower'd citadel, a pendent rock,
A forked mountain, or blue promontory
With trees upon't that nod unto the world
And mock our eyes with air. Thou hast seen these signs;
They are black vesper's pageants.
EROS. Ay, my lord.
ANTONY. That which is now a horse, even with a thought
The rack dislimns, and makes it indistinct,
As water is in water.
EROS. It does, my lord.
ANTONY. My good knave Eros, now thy captain is
Even such a body. Here I am Antony;
Yet cannot hold this visible shape, my knave.
I made these wars for Egypt; and the Queen—
Whose heart I thought I had, for she had mine,
Which, whilst it was mine, had annex'd unto't
A million moe, now lost—she, Eros, has
Pack'd cards with Cæsar, and false-play'd my glory
Unto an enemy's triumph.
Nay, weep not, gentle Eros; there is left us
Ourselves to end ourselves.

Enter MARDIAN

O, thy vile lady!
She has robb'd me of my sword.

MARDIAN. No, Antony;
My mistress lov'd thee, and her fortunes mingled
With thine entirely.
ANTONY. Hence, saucy eunuch; peace!
She hath betray'd me, and shall die the death.
MARDIAN. Death of one person can be paid but once,
And that she has discharg'd. What thou wouldst do
Is done unto thy hand. The last she spake
Was 'Antony! most noble Antony!'
Then in the midst a tearing groan did break
The name of Antony; it was divided
Between her heart and lips. She rend'red life,
Thy name so buried in her.
ANTONY. Dead then?
MARDIAN. Dead.
ANTONY. Unarm, Eros; the long day's task is done,
And we must sleep. That thou depart'st hence safe
Does pay thy labour richly. Go. *Exit* MARDIAN
Off, pluck off!
The sevenfold shield of Ajax cannot keep
The battery from my heart. O, cleave, my sides!
Heart, once be stronger than thy continent,
Crack thy frail case. Apace, Eros, apace.–
No more a soldier. Bruised pieces, go;
You have been nobly borne.–From me awhile. *Exit* EROS
I will o'ertake thee, Cleopatra, and
Weep for my pardon. So it must be, for now
All length is torture. Since the torch is out,
Lie down, and stray no farther. Now all labour
Mars what it does; yea, very force entangles
Itself with strength. Seal then, and all is done.
Eros!–I come, my queen.–Eros!–Stay for me;
Where souls do couch on flowers, we'll hand in hand,
And with our sprightly port make the ghosts gaze.
Dido and her Æneas shall want troops,
And all the haunt be ours.–Come, Eros, Eros!

Re-enter EROS

EROS. What would my lord?
ANTONY. Since Cleopatra died,

I have liv'd in such dishonour that the gods
Detest my baseness. I, that with my sword
Quarter'd the world, and o'er green Neptune's back
With ships made cities, condemn myself to lack
The courage of a woman; less noble mind
Than she which by her death our Cæsar tells
'I am conqueror of myself.' Thou art sworn, Eros,
That, when the exigent should come—which now
Is come indeed—when I should see behind me
Th' inevitable prosecution of
Disgrace and horror, that, on my command,
Thou then wouldst kill me. Do't; the time is come.
Thou strik'st not me; 'tis Cæsar thou defeat'st.
Put colour in thy cheek.

EROS. The gods withhold me!
Shall I do that which all the Parthian darts,
Though enemy, lost aim and could not?

ANTONY. Eros,
Wouldst thou be window'd in great Rome and see
Thy master thus with pleach'd arms, bending down
His corrigible neck, his face subdu'd
To penetrative shame, whilst the wheel'd seat
Of fortunate Cæsar, drawn before him, branded
His baseness that ensued?

EROS. I would not see't.

ANTONY. Come, then; for with a wound I must be cur'd.
Draw that thy honest sword, which thou hast worn
Most useful for thy country.

EROS. O, sir, pardon me!

ANTONY. When I did make thee free, swor'st thou not then
To do this when I bade thee? Do it at once,
Or thy precedent services are all
But accidents unpurpos'd. Draw, and come.

EROS. Turn from me then that noble countenance,
Wherein the worship of the whole world lies.

ANTONY. Lo thee! [*Turning from him*]

EROS. My sword is drawn.

ANTONY. Then let it do at once
The thing why thou hast drawn it.

EROS. My dear master,

My captain and my emperor, let me say,
Before I strike this bloody stroke, farewell.

ANTONY. 'Tis said, man; and farewell.

EROS. Farewell, great chief. Shall I strike now?

ANTONY. Now, Eros.

EROS. Why, there then! Thus do I escape the sorrow
Of Antony's death. [*Kills himself*]

ANTONY. Thrice nobler than myself!
Thou teachest me, O valiant Eros, what
I should, and thou couldst not. My queen and Eros
Have, by their brave instruction, got upon me
A nobleness in record. But I will be
A bridegroom in my death, and run into't
As to a lover's bed. Come, then; and, Eros,
Thy master dies thy scholar. To do thus
[*Falling on his sword*]
I learn'd of thee. How? not dead? not dead?—
The guard, ho! O, dispatch me!

Enter DERCETAS *and a guard*

FIRST GUARD. What's the noise?

ANTONY. I have done my work ill, friends. O, make an end
Of what I have begun.

SECOND GUARD. The star is fall'n.

FIRST GUARD. And time is at his period.

ALL. Alas, and woe!

ANTONY. Let him that loves me, strike me dead.

FIRST GUARD. Not I.

SECOND GUARD. Nor I.

THIRD GUARD. Nor any one. *Exeunt guard*

DERCETAS. Thy death and fortunes bid thy followers fly.
This sword but shown to Cæsar, with this tidings,
Shall enter me with him.

Enter DIOMEDES

DIOMEDES. Where's Antony?

DERCETAS. There, Diomed, there.

DIOMEDES. Lives he?
Wilt thou not answer, man? *Exit* DERCETAS

ANTONY. Art thou there, Diomed? Draw thy sword and give me

Sufficing strokes for death.

DIOMEDES. Most absolute lord,
My mistress Cleopatra sent me to thee.

ANTONY. When did she send thee?

DIOMEDES. Now, my lord.

ANTONY. Where is she?

DIOMEDES. Lock'd in her monument. She had a prophesying fear
Of what hath come to pass; for when she saw—
Which never shall be found—you did suspect
She had dispos'd with Cæsar, and that your rage
Would not be purg'd, she sent you word she was dead;
But fearing since how it might work, hath sent
Me to proclaim the truth; and I am come,
I dread, too late.

ANTONY. Too late, good Diomed. Call my guard, I prithee.

DIOMEDES. What, ho! the Emperor's guard! The guard, what ho!
Come, your lord calls!

Enter four or five of the guard of ANTONY

ANTONY. Bear me, good friends, where Cleopatra bides;
'Tis the last service that I shall command you.

FIRST GUARD. Woe, woe are we, sir, you may not live to wear
All your true followers out.

ALL. Most heavy day!

ANTONY. Nay, good my fellows, do not please sharp fate
To grace it with your sorrows. Bid that welcome
Which comes to punish us, and we punish it,
Seeming to bear it lightly. Take me up.
I have led you oft; carry me now, good friends,
And have my thanks for all. *Exeunt, bearing* ANTONY

SCENE 15

Alexandria. A monument

Enter Cleopatra *and her maids aloft, with* Charmian *and* Iras

Cleopatra. O Charmian, I will never go from hence!
Charmian. Be comforted, dear madam.
Cleopatra. No, I will not.
All strange and terrible events are welcome,
But comforts we despise; our size of sorrow,
Proportion'd to our cause, must be as great
As that which makes it.

Enter Diomedes, *below*

How now! Is he dead?
Diomedes. His death's upon him, but not dead.
Look out o' th' other side your monument;
His guard have brought him thither.

Enter, below, Antony, *borne by the guard*

Cleopatra. O sun,
Burn the great sphere thou mov'st in! Darkling stand
The varying shore o' th' world. O Antony,
Antony, Antony! Help, Charmian; help, Iras, help;
Help, friends below! Let's draw him hither.
Antony. Peace!
Not Cæsar's valour hath o'erthrown Antony,
But Antony's hath triumph'd on itself.
Cleopatra. So it should be, that none but Antony
Should conquer Antony; but woe 'tis so!
Antony. I am dying, Egypt, dying; only
I here importune death awhile, until
Of many thousand kisses the poor last
I lay upon thy lips.
Cleopatra. I dare not, dear.
Dear my lord, pardon! I dare not,
Lest I be taken. Not th' imperious show
Of the full-fortun'd Cæsar ever shall

Be brooch'd with me. If knife, drugs, serpents, have
Edge, sting, or operation, I am safe.
Your wife Octavia, with her modest eyes
And still conclusion, shall acquire no honour
Demuring upon me. But come, come, Antony—
Help me, my women—we must draw thee up;
Assist, good friends.

ANTONY. O, quick, or I am gone.

CLEOPATRA. Here's sport indeed! How heavy weighs my lord!
Our strength is all gone into heaviness;
That makes the weight. Had I great Juno's power,
The strong-wing'd Mercury should fetch thee up,
And set thee by Jove's side. Yet come a little.
Wishers were ever fools. O come, come, come,

[*They heave* ANTONY *aloft to* CLEOPATRA]

And welcome, welcome! Die where thou hast liv'd.
Quicken with kissing. Had my lips that power,
Thus would I wear them out.

ALL. A heavy sight!

ANTONY. I am dying, Egypt, dying.
Give me some wine, and let me speak a little.

CLEOPATRA. No, let me speak; and let me rail so high
That the false huswife Fortune break her wheel,
Provok'd by my offence.

ANTONY. One word, sweet queen:
Of Cæsar seek your honour, with your safety. O!

CLEOPATRA. They do not go together.

ANTONY. Gentle, hear me:
None about Cæsar trust but Proculeius.

CLEOPATRA. My resolution and my hands I'll trust;
None about Cæsar.

ANTONY. The miserable change now at my end
Lament nor sorrow at; but please your thoughts
In feeding them with those my former fortunes
Wherein I liv'd the greatest prince o' th' world,
The noblest; and do now not basely die,
Not cowardly put off my helmet to
My countryman—a Roman by a Roman
Valiantly vanquish'd. Now my spirit is going

I can no more.
CLEOPATRA. Noblest of men, woo't die?
Hast thou no care of me? Shall I abide
In this dull world, which in thy absence is
No better than a sty? O, see, my women, [*Antony dies*]
The crown o' th' earth doth melt. My lord!
O, wither'd is the garland of the war,
The soldier's pole is fall'n! Young boys and girls
Are level now with men. The odds is gone,
And there is nothing left remarkable
Beneath the visiting moon. [*Swoons*]
CHARMIAN. O, quietness, lady!
IRAS. She's dead too, our sovereign.
CHARMIAN. Lady!
IRAS. Madam!
CHARMIAN. O madam, madam, madam!
IRAS. Royal Egypt, Empress!
CHARMIAN. Peace, peace, Iras!
CLEOPATRA. No more but e'en a woman, and commanded
By such poor passion as the maid that milks
And does the meanest chares. It were for me
To throw my sceptre at the injurious gods;
To tell them that this world did equal theirs
Till they had stol'n our jewel. All's but nought;
Patience is sottish, and impatience does
Become a dog that's mad. Then is it sin
To rush into the secret house of death
Ere death dare come to us? How do you, women?
What, what! good cheer! Why, how now, Charmian!
My noble girls! Ah, women, women, look,
Our lamp is spent, it's out! Good sirs, take heart.
We'll bury him; and then, what's brave, what's noble,
Let's do it after the high Roman fashion,
And make death proud to take us. Come, away;
This case of that huge spirit now is cold.
Ah, women, women! Come; we have no friend
But resolution and the briefest end.
Exeunt; those above bearing off ANTONY'S *body*

ACT V. SCENE 1

Alexandria. CÆSAR'S *camp*

Enter CÆSAR, AGRIPPA, DOLABELLA, MÆCENAS, GALLUS, PROCULEIUS, *and others, his Council of War*

CÆSAR. Go to him, Dolabella, bid him yield;
Being so frustrate, tell him he mocks
The pauses that he makes.
DOLABELLA. Cæsar, I shall. *Exit*

Enter DERCETAS *with the sword of* ANTONY

CÆSAR. Wherefore is that? And what art thou that dar'st
Appear thus to us?
DERCETAS. I am call'd Dercetas;
Mark Antony I serv'd, who best was worthy
Best to be serv'd. Whilst he stood up and spoke,
He was my master, and I wore my life
To spend upon his haters. If thou please
To take me to thee, as I was to him
I'll be to Cæsar; if thou pleasest not,
I yield thee up my life.
CÆSAR. What is't thou say'st?
DERCETAS. I say, O Cæsar, Antony is dead.
CÆSAR. The breaking of so great a thing should make
A greater crack. The round world
Should have shook lions into civil streets,
And citizens to their dens. The death of Antony
Is not a single doom; in the name lay
A moiety of the world.
DERCETAS. He is dead, Cæsar,
Not by a public minister of justice,
Nor by a hired knife; but that self hand
Which writ his honour in the acts it did
Hath, with the courage which the heart did lend it,
Splitted the heart. This is his sword;
I robb'd his wound of it; behold it stain'd
With his most noble blood.
CÆSAR. Look you sad, friends?
The gods rebuke me, but it is tidings

To wash the eyes of kings.
AGRIPPA. And strange it is
That nature must compel us to lament
Our most persisted deeds.
MÆCENAS. His taints and honours
Wag'd equal with him.
AGRIPPA. A rarer spirit never
Did steer humanity. But you gods will give us
Some faults to make us men. Cæsar is touch'd.
MÆCENAS. When such a spacious mirror's set before him,
He needs must see himself.
CÆSAR. O Antony,
I have follow'd thee to this! But we do lance
Diseases in our bodies. I must perforce
Have shown to thee such a declining day
Or look on thine; we could not stall together
In the whole world. But yet let me lament,
With tears as sovereign as the blood of hearts,
That thou, my brother, my competitor
In top of all design, my mate in empire,
Friend and companion in the front of war,
The arm of mine own body, and the heart
Where mine his thoughts did kindle—that our stars,
Unreconciliable, should divide
Our equalness to this. Hear me, good friends—

Enter an EGYPTIAN

But I will tell you at some meeter season.
The business of this man looks out of him;
We'll hear him what he says. Whence are you?
EGYPTIAN. A poor Egyptian, yet the Queen, my mistress,
Confin'd in all she has, her monument,
Of thy intents desires instruction,
That she preparedly may frame herself
To th' way she's forc'd to.
CÆSAR. Bid her have good heart.
She soon shall know of us, by some of ours,
How honourable and how kindly we
Determine for her; for Cæsar cannot learn
To be ungentle.

EGYPTIAN. So the gods preserve thee! *Exit*

CÆSAR. Come hither, Proculeius. Go and say
We purpose her no shame. Give her what comforts
The quality of her passion shall require,
Lest, in her greatness, by some mortal stroke
She do defeat us; for her life in Rome
Would be eternal in our triumph. Go,
And with your speediest bring us what she says,
And how you find her.

PROCULEIUS. Cæsar, I shall. *Exit*

CÆSAR. Gallus, go you along. *Exit* GALLUS
Where's Dolabella, to second Proculeius?

ALL. Dolabella!

CÆSAR. Let him alone, for I remember now
How he's employ'd; he shall in time be ready.
Go with me to my tent, where you shall see
How hardly I was drawn into this war,
How calm and gentle I proceeded still
In all my writings. Go with me, and see
What I can show in this. *Exeunt*

SCENE 2

Alexandria. The monument

Enter CLEOPATRA, CHARMIAN, IRAS, *and* MARDIAN

CLEOPATRA. My desolation does begin to make
A better life. 'Tis paltry to be Cæsar:
Not being Fortune, he's but Fortune's knave,
A minister of her will; and it is great
To do that thing that ends all other deeds,
Which shackles accidents and bolts up change,
Which sleeps, and never palates more the dug,
The beggar's nurse and Cæsar's.

Enter, to the gates of the monument, PROCULEIUS, GALLUS, *and soldiers*

PROCULEIUS. Cæsar sends greetings to the Queen of Egypt,
And bids thee study on what fair demands

Thou mean'st to have him grant thee.
CLEOPATRA. What's thy name?
PROCULEIUS. My name is Proculeius.
CLEOPATRA. Antony
Did tell me of you, bade me trust you; but
I do not greatly care to be deceiv'd,
That have no use for trusting. If your master
Would have a queen his beggar, you must tell him
That majesty, to keep decorum, must
No less beg than a kingdom. If he please
To give me conquer'd Egypt for my son,
He gives me so much of mine own as I
Will kneel to him with thanks.
PROCULEIUS. Be of good cheer;
Y'are fall'n into a princely hand; fear nothing.
Make your full reference freely to my lord,
Who is so full of grace that it flows over
On all that need. Let me report to him
Your sweet dependency, and you shall find
A conqueror that will pray in aid for kindness
Where he for grace is kneel'd to.
CLEOPATRA. Pray you tell him
I am his fortune's vassal and I send him
The greatness he has got. I hourly learn
A doctrine of obedience, and would gladly
Look him i' th' face.
PROCULEIUS. This I'll report, dear lady.
Have comfort, for I know your plight is pitied
Of him that caus'd it.
GALLUS. You see how easily she may be surpris'd.

Here PROCULEIUS *and two of the guard ascend the monument by a ladder placed against a window, and come behind* CLEOPATRA. *Some of the guard unbar and open the gates*

Guard her till Cæsar come. *Exit*
IRAS. Royal Queen!
CHARMIAN. O Cleopatra! thou art taken, Queen!
CLEOPATRA. Quick, quick, good hands. [*Drawing a dagger*]
PROCULEIUS. Hold, worthy lady, hold, [*Disarms her*]

Do not yourself such wrong, who are in this
Reliev'd, but not betray'd.

CLEOPATRA. What, of death too,
That rids our dogs of languish?

PROCULEIUS. Cleopatra,
Do not abuse my master's bounty by
Th' undoing of yourself. Let the world see
His nobleness well acted, which your death
Will never let come forth.

CLEOPATRA. Where art thou, death?
Come hither, come! Come, come, and take a queen
Worth many babes and beggars!

PROCULEIUS. O, temperance, lady!

CLEOPATRA. Sir, I will eat no meat; I'll not drink, sir;
If idle talk will once be necessary,
I'll not sleep neither. This mortal house I'll ruin,
Do Cæsar what he can. Know, sir, that I
Will not wait pinion'd at your master's court,
Nor once be chastis'd with the sober eye
Of dull Octavia. Shall they hoist me up,
And show me to the shouting varletry
Of censuring Rome? Rather a ditch in Egypt
Be gentle grave unto me! Rather on Nilus' mud
Lay me stark-nak'd, and let the water-flies
Blow me into abhorring! Rather make
My country's high pyramides my gibbet,
And hang me up in chains!

PROCULEIUS. You do extend
These thoughts of horror further than you shall
Find cause in Cæsar.

Enter DOLABELLA

DOLABELLA. Proculeius,
What thou hast done thy master Cæsar knows,
And he hath sent for thee. For the Queen,
I'll take her to my guard.

PROCULEIUS. So, Dolabella,
It shall content me best. Be gentle to her.
[*To* CLEOPATRA] To Cæsar I will speak what you shall please,

If you'll employ me to him.

CLEOPATRA. Say I would die.

Exeunt PROCULEIUS *and soldiers*

DOLABELLA. Most noble Empress, you have heard of me?

CLEOPATRA. I cannot tell.

DOLABELLA. Assuredly you know me.

CLEOPATRA. No matter, sir, what I have heard or known.
You laugh when boys or women tell their dreams;
Is't not your trick?

DOLABELLA. I understand not, madam.

CLEOPATRA. I dreamt there was an Emperor Antony–
O, such another sleep, that I might see
But such another man!

DOLABELLA. If it might please ye–

CLEOPATRA. His face was as the heav'ns, and therein stuck
A sun and moon, which kept their course and lighted
The little O, the earth.

DOLABELLA. Most sovereign creature–

CLEOPATRA. His legs bestrid the ocean; his rear'd arm
Crested the world. His voice was propertied
As all the tuned spheres, and that to friends;
But when he meant to quail and shake the orb,
He was as rattling thunder. For his bounty,
There was no winter in't; an autumn 'twas
That grew the more by reaping. His delights
Were dolphin-like: they show'd his back above
The element they liv'd in. In his livery
Walk'd crowns and crownets; realms and islands were
As plates dropp'd from his pocket.

DOLABELLA. Cleopatra–

CLEOPATRA. Think you there was or might be such a man
As this I dreamt of?

DOLABELLA. Gentle madam, no.

CLEOPATRA. You lie, up to the hearing of the gods.
But if there be nor ever were one such,
It's past the size of dreaming. Nature wants stuff
To vie strange forms with fancy; yet t' imagine
An Antony were nature's piece 'gainst fancy,
Condemning shadows quite.

DOLABELLA. Hear me, good madam.

CLEOPATRA. *My resolution's plac'd, and I have nothing*
Of woman in me. Now from head to foot
I am marble-constant; now the fleeting moon
No planet is of mine. . . .
Give me my robe, put on my crown; I have
Immortal longings in me. Now no more
The juice of Egypt's grape shall moist this lip.
(ACT V. Scene 2)

Your loss is, as yourself, great; and you bear it
As answering to the weight. Would I might never
O'ertake pursu'd success, but I do feel,
By the rebound of yours, a grief that smites
My very heart at root.

CLEOPATRA. I thank you, sir.
Know you what Cæsar means to do with me?

DOLABELLA. I am loath to tell you what I would you knew.

CLEOPATRA. Nay, pray you, sir.

DOLABELLA. Though he be honourable–

CLEOPATRA. He'll lead me, then, in triumph?

DOLABELLA. Madam, he will. I know't. [*Flourish*]
[*Within:* 'Make way there–Cæsar!']

Enter CÆSAR; GALLUS, PROCULEIUS, MÆCENAS, SELEUCUS, *and others of his train*

CÆSAR. Which is the Queen of Egypt?

DOLABELLA. It is the Emperor, madam. [CLEOPATRA *kneels*]

CÆSAR. Arise, you shall not kneel.
I pray you, rise; rise, Egypt.

CLEOPATRA. Sir, the gods
Will have it thus; my master and my lord
I must obey.

CÆSAR. Take to you no hard thoughts.
The record of what injuries you did us,
Though written in our flesh, we shall remember
As things but done by chance.

CLEOPATRA. Sole sir o' th' world,
I cannot project mine own cause so well
To make it clear, but do confess I have
Been laden with like frailties which before
Have often sham'd our sex.

CÆSAR. Cleopatra, know
We will extenuate rather than enforce.
If you apply yourself to our intents–
Which towards you are most gentle–you shall find
A benefit in this change; but if you seek
To lay on me a cruelty by taking
Antony's course, you shall bereave yourself

Of my good purposes, and put your children
To that destruction which I'll guard them from,
If thereon you rely. I'll take my leave.

CLEOPATRA. And may, through all the world. 'Tis yours, and we,
Your scutcheons and your signs of conquest, shall
Hang in what place you please. Here, my good lord.

CÆSAR. You shall advise me in all for Cleopatra.

CLEOPATRA. This is the brief of money, plate, and jewels,
I am possess'd of. 'Tis exactly valued,
Not petty things admitted. Where's Seleucus?

SELEUCUS. Here, madam.

CLEOPATRA. This is my treasurer; let him speak, my lord,
Upon his peril, that I have reserv'd
To myself nothing. Speak the truth, Seleucus.

SELEUCUS. Madam,
I had rather seal my lips than to my peril
Speak that which is not.

CLEOPATRA. What have I kept back?

SELEUCUS. Enough to purchase what you have made known.

CÆSAR. Nay, blush not, Cleopatra; I approve
Your wisdom in the deed.

CLEOPATRA. See, Cæsar! O, behold,
How pomp is followed! Mine will now be yours;
And, should we shift estates, yours would be mine.
The ingratitude of this Seleucus does
Even make me wild. O slave, of no more trust
Than love that's hir'd! What, goest thou back? Thou shalt
Go back, I warrant thee; but I'll catch thine eyes
Though they had wings. Slave, soulless villain, dog!
O rarely base!

CÆSAR. Good Queen, let us entreat you.

CLEOPATRA. O Cæsar, what a wounding shame is this,
That thou vouchsafing here to visit me,
Doing the honour of thy lordliness
To one so meek, that mine own servant should
Parcel the sum of my disgraces by
Addition of his envy! Say, good Cæsar,
That I some lady trifles have reserv'd,

Immoment toys, things of such dignity
As we greet modern friends withal; and say
Some nobler token I have kept apart
For Livia and Octavia, to induce
Their mediation—must I be unfolded
With one that I have bred? The gods! It smites me
Beneath the fall I have. [*To* SELEUCUS] Prithee go hence;
Or I shall show the cinders of my spirits
Through th' ashes of my chance. Wert thou a man,
Thou wouldst have mercy on me.

CÆSAR. Forbear, Seleucus. *Exit* SELEUCUS

CLEOPATRA. Be it known that we, the greatest, are misthought
For things that others do; and when we fall
We answer others' merits in our name,
Are therefore to be pitied.

CÆSAR. Cleopatra,
Not what you have reserv'd, nor what acknowledg'd,
Put we i' th' roll of conquest. Still be't yours,
Bestow it at your pleasure; and believe
Cæsar's no merchant, to make prize with you
Of things that merchants sold. Therefore be cheer'd;
Make not your thoughts your prisons. No, dear Queen;
For we intend so to dispose you as
Yourself shall give us counsel. Feed and sleep.
Our care and pity is so much upon you
That we remain your friend; and so, adieu.

CLEOPATRA. My master and my lord!

CÆSAR. Not so. Adieu.

Flourish. Exeunt CÆSAR *and his train*

CLEOPATRA. He words me, girls, he words me, that I should not
Be noble to myself. But hark thee, Charmian!

[*Whispers* CHARMIAN]

IRAS. Finish, good lady; the bright day is done,
And we are for the dark.

CLEOPATRA. Hie thee again.
I have spoke already, and it is provided;
Go put it to the haste.

CHARMIAN. Madam, I will.

Re-enter DOLABELLA

DOLABELLA. Where's the Queen?
CHARMIAN. Behold, sir. *Exit*
CLEOPATRA. Dolabella!
DOLABELLA. Madam, as thereto sworn by your command,
Which my love makes religion to obey,
I tell you this: Cæsar through Syria
Intends his journey, and within three days
You with your children will he send before.
Make your best use of this; I have perform'd
Your pleasure and my promise.
CLEOPATRA. Dolabella,
I shall remain your debtor.
DOLABELLA. I your servant.
Adieu, good Queen; I must attend on Cæsar.
CLEOPATRA. Farewell, and thanks. *Exit* DOLABELLA
Now, Iras, what think'st thou?
Thou an Egyptian puppet shall be shown
In Rome as well as I. Mechanic slaves,
With greasy aprons, rules, and hammers, shall
Uplift us to the view; in their thick breaths,
Rank of gross diet, shall we be enclouded,
And forc'd to drink their vapour.
IRAS. The gods forbid!
CLEOPATRA. Nay, 'tis most certain, Iras. Saucy lictors
Will catch at us like strumpets, and scald rhymers
Ballad us out o' tune; the quick comedians
Extemporally will stage us, and present
Our Alexandrian revels; Antony
Shall be brought drunken forth, and I shall see
Some squeaking Cleopatra boy my greatness
I' th' posture of a whore.
IRAS. O the good gods!
CLEOPATRA. Nay, that's certain.
IRAS. I'll never see't, for I am sure mine nails
Are stronger than mine eyes.
CLEOPATRA. Why, that's the way
To fool their preparation and to conquer
Their most absurd intents.

Enter CHARMIAN

Now, Charmian!
Show me, my women, like a queen. Go fetch
My best attires. I am again for Cydnus,
To meet Mark Antony. Sirrah, Iras, go.
Now, noble Charmian, we'll dispatch indeed;
And when thou hast done this chare, I'll give thee leave
To play till doomsday. Bring our crown and all.
Exit IRAS. *A noise within*
Wherefore's this noise?

Enter a GUARDSMAN

GUARDSMAN. Here is a rural fellow
That will not be denied your Highness' presence.
He brings you figs.

CLEOPATRA. Let him come in. *Exit* GUARDSMAN
What poor an instrument
May do a noble deed! He brings me liberty.
My resolution's plac'd, and I have nothing
Of woman in me. Now from head to foot
I am marble-constant; now the fleeting moon
No planet is of mine.

Re-enter GUARDSMAN *and* CLOWN, *with a basket*

GUARDSMAN. This is the man.

CLEOPATRA. Avoid, and leave him. *Exit* GUARDSMAN
Hast thou the pretty worm of Nilus there
That kills and pains not?

CLOWN. Truly, I have him. But I would not be the party that should desire you to touch him, for his biting is immortal; those that do die of it do seldom or never recover.

CLEOPATRA. Remember'st thou any that have died on't?

CLOWN. Very many, men and women too. I heard of one of them no longer than yesterday: a very honest woman, but something given to lie, as a woman should not do but in the way of honesty; how she died of the biting of it, what pain she felt—truly she makes a very good report o' th' worm. But he that will believe all that they say shall never be saved by half that they do. But this is most falliable, the worm's an odd worm.

CLEOPATRA. Get thee hence; farewell.

CLOWN. I wish you all joy of the worm.

[*Sets down the basket*]

CLEOPATRA. Farewell.

CLOWN. You must think this, look you, that the worm will do his kind.

CLEOPATRA. Ay, ay; farewell.

CLOWN. Look you, the worm is not to be trusted but in the keeping of wise people; for indeed there is no goodness in the worm.

CLEOPATRA. Take thou no care; it shall be heeded.

CLOWN. Very good. Give it nothing, I pray you, for it is not worth the feeding.

CLEOPATRA. Will it eat me?

CLOWN. You must not think I am so simple but I know the devil himself will not eat a woman. I know that a woman is a dish for the gods, if the devil dress her not. But truly, these same whoreson devils do the gods great harm in their women, for in every ten that they make the devils mar five.

CLEOPATRA. Well, get thee gone; farewell.

CLOWN. Yes, forsooth. I wish you joy o' th' worm. *Exit*

Re-enter IRAS, *with a robe, crown, &c.*

CLEOPATRA. Give me my robe, put on my crown; I have
Immortal longings in me. Now no more
The juice of Egypt's grape shall moist this lip.
Yare, yare, good Iras; quick. Methinks I hear
Antony call. I see him rouse himself
To praise my noble act. I hear him mock
The luck of Cæsar, which the gods give men
To excuse their after wrath. Husband, I come.
Now to that name my courage prove my title!
I am fire and air; my other elements
I give to baser life. So, have you done?
Come then, and take the last warmth of my lips.
Farewell, kind Charmian. Iras, long farewell.

[*Kisses them.* IRAS *falls and dies*]

Have I the aspic in my lips? Dost fall?
If thus thou and nature can so gently part,

The stroke of death is as a lover's pinch,
Which hurts and is desir'd. Dost thou lie still?
If thou vanishest, thou tell'st the world
It is not worth leave-taking.

CHARMIAN. Dissolve, thick cloud, and rain, that I may say
The gods themselves do weep.

CLEOPATRA. This proves me base.
If she first meet the curled Antony,
He'll make demand of her, and spend that kiss
Which is my heaven to have. Come, thou mortal wretch,
[*To an asp, which she applies to her breast*]
With thy sharp teeth this knot intrinsicate
Of life at once untie. Poor venomous fool,
Be angry and dispatch. O couldst thou speak,
That I might hear thee call great Cæsar ass
Unpolicied!

CHARMIAN. O Eastern star!

CLEOPATRA. Peace, peace!
Dost thou not see my baby at my breast
That sucks the nurse asleep?

CHARMIAN. O, break! O, break!

CLEOPATRA. As sweet as balm, as soft as air, as gentle—
O Antony! Nay, I will take thee too:
[*Applying another asp to her arm*]
What should I stay— [*Dies*]

CHARMIAN. In this vile world? So, fare thee well.
Now boast thee, death, in thy possession lies
A lass unparallel'd. Downy windows, close;
And golden Phœbus never be beheld
Of eyes again so royal! Your crown's awry;
I'll mend it and then play—

Enter the guard, rushing in

FIRST GUARD. Where's the Queen?

CHARMIAN. Speak softly, wake her not.

FIRST GUARD. Cæsar hath sent—

CHARMIAN. Too slow a messenger. [*Applies an asp*]
O, come apace, dispatch. I partly feel thee.

FIRST GUARD. Approach, ho! All's not well: Cæsar's beguil'd.

SECOND GUARD. There's Dolabella sent from Cæsar; call him.

FIRST GUARD. What work is here! Charmian, is this well done?

CHARMIAN. It is well done, and fitting for a princess
Descended of so many royal kings.
Ah, soldier! [CHARMIAN *dies*]

Re-enter DOLABELLA

DOLABELLA. How goes it here?

SECOND GUARD. All dead.

DOLABELLA. Cæsar, thy thoughts
Touch their effects in this. Thyself art coming
To see perform'd the dreaded act which thou
So sought'st to hinder.
[*Within:* 'A way there, a way for Cæsar!']

Re-enter CÆSAR *and all his train*

DOLABELLA. O sir, you are too sure an augurer:
That you did fear is done.

CÆSAR. Bravest at the last,
She levell'd at our purposes, and being royal,
Took her own way. The manner of their deaths?
I do not see them bleed.

DOLABELLA. Who was last with them?

FIRST GUARD. A simple countryman that brought her figs.
This was his basket.

CÆSAR. Poison'd then.

FIRST GUARD. O Cæsar,
This Charmian liv'd but now; she stood and spake.
I found her trimming up the diadem
On her dead mistress. Tremblingly she stood,
And on the sudden dropp'd.

CÆSAR. O noble weakness!
If they had swallow'd poison 'twould appear
By external swelling; but she looks like sleep,
As she would catch another Antony
In her strong toil of grace.

DOLABELLA. Here on her breast
There is a vent of blood, and something blown;
The like is on her arm.

FIRST GUARD. This is an aspic's trail; and these fig-leaves

Have slime upon them, such as th' aspic leaves
Upon the caves of Nile.

CÆSAR. Most probable
That so she died; for her physician tells me
She hath pursu'd conclusions infinite
Of easy ways to die. Take up her bed,
And bear her women from the monument.
She shall be buried by her Antony;
No grave upon the earth shall clip in it
A pair so famous. High events as these
Strike those that make them; and their story is
No less in pity than his glory which
Brought them to be lamented. Our army shall
In solemn show attend this funeral,
And then to Rome. Come, Dolabella, see
High order in this great solemnity. *Exeunt*

Cymbeline

CYMBELINE

CYMBELINE stands in the First Folio last among the tragedies, but in spite of this and the title that names it *The Tragedy of Cymbeline* it belongs to a group of plays that come in date of composition after the tragedies and that may contain violent or unhappy deaths without, however, failing to provide for the characters with whom the spectators are most concerned a happy ending. The Queen and Cloten her son are both dead before the last act of *Cymbeline* closes, but this does not detract from the happiness of the others, for even the King himself may be excused for finding in the recovery of his lost sons and missing daughter a happiness that gives him no leisure to brood on the loss of a homicidal-minded spouse.

It is inevitable that comparisons between these later plays and the tragedies should raise a number of questions that can be answered in a reasonable way only by looking at Shakespeare's plays from a position that allows us to see them as episodes in his whole career as a dramatist. Why should Shakespeare, having shown in *Othello* his powers of construction and concentration, choose in *Cymbeline* so apparently rambling and episodic a manner of plotting? The suggestion that this change merely reflects a decline in his powers seems unlikely, if only because we cannot trace the progress of any such decay. His last tragedy, *Coriolanus,* does not lack firmness of outline or any of the old authority; his next works are in an entirely different vein. This change is clearly deliberate. Some critics have felt it necessary to provide some explanation other than a change of direction in the dramatist's interests, or at least to insist that this change of interest was consequent on physical and mental collapse. It is clear however that many of the features that distinguish *Cymbeline* from the tragedies are either deliberate or to be explained by a mental condition that would be quite incompatible with other aspects of the work. Shakespeare knew as well as we know, Granville-Barker points out, that in the Rome of Augustus no one could have found Frenchmen, Dutchmen, and Spaniards, discussing the rival merits of their mistresses, or the villain of the piece wagering ten thousand ducats. Shakespeare had already shown his audiences a very different picture of the Rome of Augustus. Neither *Julius Cæsar* nor *Coriolanus* offers an antiquarian's reconstruction of Rome, but what we have there is something quite different from Philario's supper party. Either the nervous breakdown we hear about from the commentators had razed from Shakespeare's mind his earlier reading in Plutarch and elsewhere, or Shakespeare was now engaged on a type of plot that not merely permitted but accommodated such unhistorical detail.

Shakespeare has put together features from many different sources. Into the story of Cymbeline, which he adapted from Holinshed, who tells of that king's relations with the Emperor Augustus, we find inserted an Italian tale of intrigue from the *Decameron.* Boccaccio tells how a Genoese merchant laid a wager on his wife's chastity, and, being persuaded that he has lost, gives orders for his wife's death. She escapes in man's attire and takes service with the Sultan, discovers and unmasks her calumniator, and is reconciled to her husband. As in Shakespeare, the villain is carried in a chest into the lady's bedchamber, and in the night steals a girdle and other of her belongings as well as noting the mole on her left breast. His fate however is harder than Iachimo's, for the Sultan has him anointed with honey and left bound to a stake till he is eaten alive by wasps and hornets. The English version of the story, *Frederick of Jennen,* does not contain this detail which Shakespeare used not in *Cymbeline,* but in *The Winter's Tale,* as a comic stroke by Autolycus, in the threat to the clown in Act IV, Scene 4:

> He has a son—who shall be flay'd alive; then 'nointed over with honey, set on the head of a wasp's nest . . .

Shakespeare must therefore have used Boccaccio, whatever other versions he consulted, and this need cause no surprise as it is clear from *Othello* and elsewhere that he had recourse to Italian *novelle* for material.

In this intrigue part of his plot Shakespeare incorporates the familiar motif of the sleep that resembles death, a useful device that permits of the transition in the narrative required by the plot. Shakespeare, in describing the stand made by Belarius, Guiderius, and Arviragus, in Act V, Scene 2, had recourse to the account in Holinshed of the exploit of a husbandman Hay and his two sons who secured for the Scots at the battle of Loncart with the Danes in A.D. 976 the victory in what looked like the face of defeat.

It was this amalgam of history and folk-motif, and bourgeois intrigue, that so taxed Dr. Johnson's sense of decorum that he declared:

> To remark the folly of the fiction, the absurdity of the conduct, the confusion of the names and manners of different times, and the impossibility of the events in any system of life, were to waste criticism upon unresisting imbecility, upon faults too evident for detection, and too gross for aggravation.

We cannot suppose that Shakespeare was unaware of the medley he had concocted, and that no system of life in the sense of a historical period could be cited to justify his liberties. That apart, however, there is little one can regard as out of place in a romantic adventure of this time. Sleeping-potions are part of the machinery of such a genre and bandits may live on the fringes of elegant society.

Johnson's criticism, however, has suggested to many commentators that the play is not wholly Shakespeare's. Some have gone very far in their assignments to other hands; but by considering what a very judicious adherent to the general feeling that the play is not wholly by Shakespeare has to say on this topic we may realize the critical difficulties this view in its turn raises. 'A fair amount of the play—both of its design and execution—is pretty certainly not Shakespeare's,' summarizes Granville-Barker's impression. Yet when he comes to discuss the detail of the plot and the way the pieces dovetail together his analysis contradicts his general impression. With such various individuals or groups as the stolen princes, Iachimo, Posthumus, to work into the story, Shakespeare cannot keep them all continuously before us, nor does he wish to do so, for Imogen is the real protagonist of the play; she provides the continuity. To let Posthumus slip from the current of the story and then to reintroduce him again as in the play seems to Granville-Barker the surest evidence of an alien hand, although the actual writing in this section is, he admits, not un-Shakespearean. Yet Shakespeare in emphasizing the repentance of Posthumus before he regains his lost happiness prepares him for the final discovery very much as he prepares Leontes for the statue scene in *The Winter's Tale.* It cannot be claimed that the treatment of these two penitents differs so markedly in style and feeling that we must assign the passages to different hands.

The real difficulty that the introduction of hands other than Shakespeare's into the discussion raises is best seen, however, when Granville-Barker comes to analyse the last scene. As he admits,

> The finer phases of the play's construction are to be seen in the swift forwarding of the first part of the story, in the subtle composition of Iachimo's three scenes . . . and in the elaboration of the finale. . . . This last has not lacked praise.

And he quotes Barrett Wendell's observations on the complexity and fullness of the material to be resolved. It is difficult to believe that the composer of this finale, who cannot have been anyone but Shakespeare, was piecing together fragments casually introduced by other hands. There is a contrivance about it all that makes it difficult to believe that what went before could come from any mind other than that which so effectively ran them together at the conclusion.

CYMBELINE, *King of Britain*
CLOTEN, *son to the Queen by a former husband*
POSTHUMUS LEONATUS, *a gentleman, husband to Imogen*
BELARIUS, *a banished lord, disguised under the name of* MORGAN
GUIDERIUS, ARVIRAGUS — *sons to Cymbeline, disguised under the names of* POLYDORE *and* CADWAL, *supposed sons to Belarius*
PHILARIO, *friend to Posthumus* — *Italians*
IACHIMO, *friend to Philario* — *Italians*
A FRENCH GENTLEMAN, *friend to Philario*
CAIUS LUCIUS, *General of the Roman Forces*
A ROMAN CAPTAIN
TWO BRITISH CAPTAINS
PISANIO, *servant to Posthumus*
CORNELIUS, *a physician*
TWO LORDS *of Cymbeline's court*
TWO GENTLEMEN *of the same*
TWO GAOLERS

QUEEN, *wife to Cymbeline*
IMOGEN, *daughter to Cymbeline by a former queen*
HELEN, *a lady attending on Imogen*

Apparitions

Lords, Ladies, Roman Senators, Tribunes, a Soothsayer, a Dutch Gentleman, a Spanish Gentleman, Musicians, Officers, Captains, Soldiers, Messengers, *and* Attendants

SCENE:

Britain; Italy

Cymbeline

ACT I. SCENE 1

Britain. The garden of CYMBELINE'S *palace*

FIRST GENTLEMAN. You do not meet a man but frowns; our bloods
No more obey the heavens than our courtiers
Still seem as does the King's.

SECOND GENTLEMAN. But what's the matter?

FIRST GENTLEMAN. His daughter, and the heir of's kingdom, whom
He purpos'd to his wife's sole son—a widow
That late he married—hath referr'd herself
Unto a poor but worthy gentleman. She's wedded;
Her husband banish'd; she imprison'd. All
Is outward sorrow, though I think the King
Be touch'd at very heart.

SECOND GENTLEMAN. None but the King?

FIRST GENTLEMAN. He that hath lost her too. So is the Queen,
That most desir'd the match. But not a courtier,
Although they wear their faces to the bent
Of the King's looks, hath a heart that is not
Glad at the thing they scowl at.

SECOND GENTLEMAN. And why so?

FIRST GENTLEMAN. He that hath miss'd the Princess is a thing
Too bad for bad report; and he that hath her—
I mean that married her, alack, good man!
And therefore banish'd—is a creature such
As, to seek through the regions of the earth
For one his like, there would be something failing
In him that should compare. I do not think
So fair an outward and such stuff within
Endows a man but he.

SECOND GENTLEMAN. You speak him far.
FIRST GENTLEMAN. I do extend him, sir, within himself;
Crush him together rather than unfold
His measure duly.
SECOND GENTLEMAN. What's his name and birth?
FIRST GENTLEMAN. I cannot delve him to the root; his father
Was call'd Sicilius, who did join his honour
Against the Romans with Cassibelan,
But had his titles by Tenantius, whom
He serv'd with glory and admir'd success,
So gain'd the sur-addition Leonatus;
And had, besides this gentleman in question,
Two other sons, who, in the wars o' th' time,
Died with their swords in hand; for which their father,
Then old and fond of issue, took such sorrow
That he quit being; and his gentle lady,
Big of this gentleman, our theme, deceas'd
As he was born. The King he takes the babe
To his protection, calls him Posthumus Leonatus,
Breeds him and makes him of his bed-chamber,
Puts to him all the learnings that his time
Could make him the receiver of; which he took,
As we do air, fast as 'twas minist'red,
And in's spring became a harvest, liv'd in court—
Which rare it is to do—most prais'd, most lov'd,
A sample to the youngest; to th' more mature
A glass that feated them; and to the graver
A child that guided dotards. To his mistress,
For whom he now is banish'd—her own price
Proclaims how she esteem'd him and his virtue;
By her election may be truly read
What kind of man he is.
SECOND GENTLEMAN. I honour him
Even out of your report. But pray you tell me,
Is she sole child to th' King?
FIRST GENTLEMAN. His only child.
He had two sons—if this be worth your hearing,
Mark it—the eldest of them at three years old,
I' th' swathing clothes the other, from their nursery

Were stol'n; and to this hour no guess in knowledge
Which way they went.

SECOND GENTLEMAN. How long is this ago?

FIRST GENTLEMAN. Some twenty years.

SECOND GENTLEMAN. That a king's children should be so convey'd,
So slackly guarded, and the search so slow
That could not trace them!

FIRST GENTLEMAN. Howsoe'er 'tis strange,
Or that the negligence may well be laugh'd at,
Yet is it true, sir.

SECOND GENTLEMAN. I do well believe you.

FIRST GENTLEMAN. We must forbear; here comes the gentleman,
The Queen, and Princess. *Exeunt*

Enter the QUEEN, POSTHUMUS, *and* IMOGEN

QUEEN. No, be assur'd you shall not find me, daughter,
After the slander of most stepmothers,
Evil-ey'd unto you. You're my prisoner, but
Your gaoler shall deliver you the keys
That lock up your restraint. For you, Posthumus,
So soon as I can win th' offended King,
I will be known your advocate. Marry, yet
The fire of rage is in him, and 'twere good
You lean'd unto his sentence with what patience
Your wisdom may inform you.

POSTHUMUS. Please your Highness,
I will from hence to-day.

QUEEN. You know the peril.
I'll fetch a turn about the garden, pitying
The pangs of barr'd affections, though the King
Hath charg'd you should not speak together. *Exit*

IMOGEN. O dissembling courtesy! How fine this tyrant
Can tickle where she wounds! My dearest husband,
I something fear my father's wrath, but nothing–
Always reserv'd my holy duty–what
His rage can do on me. You must be gone;
And I shall here abide the hourly shot
Of angry eyes, not comforted to live

But that there is this jewel in the world
That I may see again.

POSTHUMUS. My queen! my mistress!
O lady, weep no more, lest I give cause
To be suspected of more tenderness
Than doth become a man. I will remain
The loyal'st husband that did e'er plight troth;
My residence in Rome at one Philario's,
Who to my father was a friend, to me
Known but by letter; thither write, my queen,
And with mine eyes I'll drink the words you send,
Though ink be made of gall.

Re-enter QUEEN

QUEEN. Be brief, I pray you.
If the King come, I shall incur I know not
How much of his displeasure. [*Aside*] Yet I'll move him
To walk this way. I never do him wrong
But he does buy my injuries, to be friends;
Pays dear for my offences. *Exit*

POSTHUMUS. Should we be taking leave
As long a term as yet we have to live,
The loathness to depart would grow. Adieu!

IMOGEN. Nay, stay a little.
Were you but riding forth to air yourself,
Such parting were too petty. Look here, love:
This diamond was my mother's; take it, heart;
But keep it till you woo another wife,
When Imogen is dead.

POSTHUMUS. How, how? Another?
You gentle gods, give me but this I have,
And sear up my embracements from a next
With bonds of death! Remain, remain thou here
[*Puts on the ring*]
While sense can keep it on. And, sweetest, fairest,
As I my poor self did exchange for you,
To your so infinite loss, so in our trifles
I still win of you. For my sake wear this;
It is a manacle of love; I'll place it
Upon this fairest prisoner. [*Puts a bracelet on her arm*]

IMOGEN. O the gods!
  When shall we see again?

Enter CYMBELINE *and* LORDS

POSTHUMUS. Alack, the King!
CYMBELINE. Thou basest thing, avoid; hence from my sight
  If after this command thou fraught the court
  With thy unworthiness, thou diest. Away!
  Thou'rt poison to my blood.
POSTHUMUS. The gods protect you,
  And bless the good remainders of the court!
  I am gone. *Exit*
IMOGEN. There cannot be a pinch in death
  More sharp than this is.
CYMBELINE. O disloyal thing,
  That shouldst repair my youth, thou heap'st
  A year's age on me!
IMOGEN. I beseech you, sir,
  Harm not yourself with your vexation.
  I am senseless of your wrath; a touch more rare
  Subdues all pangs, all fears.
CYMBELINE. Past grace? obedience?
IMOGEN. Past hope, and in despair; that way past grace.
CYMBELINE. That mightst have had the sole son of my queen!
IMOGEN. O blessed that I might not! I chose an eagle,
  And did avoid a puttock.
CYMBELINE. Thou took'st a beggar, wouldst have made my throne
  A seat for baseness.
IMOGEN. No; I rather added
  A lustre to it.
CYMBELINE. O thou vile one!
IMOGEN. Sir,
  It is your fault that I have lov'd Posthumus.
  You bred him as my playfellow, and he is
  A man worth any woman; overbuys me
  Almost the sum he pays.
CYMBELINE. What, art thou mad?
IMOGEN. Almost, sir. Heaven restore me! Would I were

A neat-herd's daughter, and my Leonatus
Our neighbour shepherd's son!

Re-enter QUEEN

CYMBELINE. Thou foolish thing!
[*To the* QUEEN] They were again together. You have done
Not after our command. Away with her,
And pen her up.
QUEEN. Beseech your patience.—Peace,
Dear lady daughter, peace!—Sweet sovereign,
Leave us to ourselves, and make yourself some comfort
Out of your best advice.
CYMBELINE. Nay, let her languish
A drop of blood a day and, being aged,
Die of this folly. *Exit, with* LORDS

Enter PISANIO

QUEEN. Fie! you must give way.
Here is your servant. How now, sir! What news?
PISANIO. My lord your son drew on my master.
QUEEN. Ha!
No harm, I trust, is done?
PISANIO. There might have been,
But that my master rather play'd than fought,
And had no help of anger; they were parted
By gentlemen at hand.
QUEEN. I am very glad on't.
IMOGEN. Your son's my father's friend; he takes his part
To draw upon an exile! O brave sir!
I would they were in Afric both together;
Myself by with a needle, that I might prick
The goer-back. Why came you from your master?
PISANIO. On his command. He would not suffer me
To bring him to the haven; left these notes
Of what commands I should be subject to,
When't pleas'd you to employ me.
QUEEN. This hath been
Your faithful servant. I dare lay mine honour
He will remain so.
PISANIO. I humbly thank your Highness.

QUEEN. Pray walk awhile.

IMOGEN. About some half-hour hence,
Pray you speak with me. You shall at least
Go see my lord aboard. For this time leave me. *Exeunt*

SCENE 2

Britain. A public place

Enter CLOTEN *and two* LORDS

FIRST LORD. Sir, I would advise you to shift a shirt; the violence of action hath made you reek as a sacrifice. Where air comes out, air comes in; there's none abroad so wholesome as that you vent.

CLOTEN. If my shirt were bloody, then to shift it. Have I hurt him?

SECOND LORD. [*Aside*] No, faith; not so much as his patience.

FIRST LORD. Hurt him! His body's a passable carcass if he be not hurt. It is a throughfare for steel if it be not hurt.

SECOND LORD. [*Aside*] His steel was in debt; it went o' th' back side the town.

CLOTEN. The villain would not stand me.

SECOND LORD. [*Aside*] No; but he fled forward still, toward your face.

FIRST LORD. Stand you? You have land enough of your own; but he added to your having, gave you some ground.

SECOND LORD. [*Aside*] As many inches as you have oceans. Puppies!

CLOTEN. I would they had not come between us.

SECOND LORD. [*Aside*] So would I, till you had measur'd how long a fool you were upon the ground.

CLOTEN. And that she should love this fellow, and refuse me!

SECOND LORD. [*Aside*] If it be a sin to make a true election, she is damn'd.

FIRST LORD. Sir, as I told you always, her beauty and her brain go not together; she's a good sign, but I have seen small reflection of her wit.

SECOND LORD. [*Aside*] She shines not upon fools, lest the reflection should hurt her.

CLOTEN. Come, I'll to my chamber. Would there had been some hurt done!

SECOND LORD. [*Aside*] I wish not so; unless it had been the fall of an ass, which is no great hurt.

CLOTEN. You'll go with us?

FIRST LORD. I'll attend your lordship.

CLOTEN. Nay, come, let's go together.

SECOND LORD. Well, my lord. *Exeunt*

SCENE 3

Britain. CYMBELINE'S *palace*

Enter IMOGEN *and* PISANIO

IMOGEN. I would thou grew'st unto the shores o' th' haven,
And questioned'st every sail; if he should write,
And I not have it, 'twere a paper lost,
As offer'd mercy is. What was the last
That he spake to thee?

PISANIO. It was: his queen, his queen!

IMOGEN. Then wav'd his handkerchief?

PISANIO. And kiss'd it, madam.

IMOGEN. Senseless linen, happier therein than I!
And that was all?

PISANIO. No, madam; for so long
As he could make me with his eye, or care
Distinguish him from others, he did keep
The deck, with glove, or hat, or handkerchief,
Still waving, as the fits and stirs of's mind
Could best express how slow his soul sail'd on,
How swift his ship.

IMOGEN. Thou shouldst have made him
As little as a crow, or less, ere left
To after-eye him.

PISANIO. Madam, so I did.

IMOGEN. I would have broke mine eyestrings, crack'd them but

To look upon him, till the diminution
Of space had pointed him sharp as my needle;
Nay, followed him till he had melted from
The smallness of a gnat to air, and then
Have turn'd mine eye and wept. But, good Pisanio,
When shall we hear from him?

PISANIO. Be assur'd, madam,
With his next vantage.

IMOGEN. I did not take my leave of him, but had
Most pretty things to say. Ere I could tell him
How I would think on him at certain hours
Such thoughts and such; or I could make him swear
The shes of Italy should not betray
Mine interest and his honour; or have charg'd him,
At the sixth hour of morn, at noon, at midnight,
T' encounter me with orisons, for then
I am in heaven for him; or ere I could
Give him that parting kiss which I had set
Betwixt two charming words, comes in my father,
And like the tyrannous breathing of the north
Shakes all our buds from growing.

Enter a LADY

LADY. The Queen, madam,
Desires your Highness' company.

IMOGEN. Those things I bid you do, get them dispatch'd.
I will attend the Queen.

PISANIO. Madam, I shall. *Exeunt*

SCENE 4

Rome. PHILARIO'S *house*

Enter PHILARIO, IACHIMO, *a* FRENCHMAN, *a* DUTCHMAN, *and a* SPANIARD

IACHIMO. Believe it, sir, I have seen him in Britain. He was then of a crescent note, expected to prove so worthy as since he hath been allowed the name of. But I could then have look'd on him without the help of admiration, though the catalogue of his endowments had been tabled by his side, and I to peruse him by items.

PHILARIO. You speak of him when he was less furnish'd than now he is with that which makes him both without and within.

FRENCHMAN. I have seen him in France; we had very many there could behold the sun with as firm eyes as he.

IACHIMO. This matter of marrying his king's daughter, wherein he must be weighed rather by her value than his own, words him, I doubt not, a great deal from the matter.

FRENCHMAN. And then his banishment.

IACHIMO. Ay, and the approbation of those that weep this lamentable divorce under her colours are wonderfully to extend him, be it but to fortify her judgment, which else an easy battery might lay flat, for taking a beggar, without less quality. But how comes it he is to sojourn with you? How creeps acquaintance?

PHILARIO. His father and I were soldiers together, to whom I have been often bound for no less than my life.

Enter POSTHUMUS

Here comes the Briton. Let him be so entertained amongst you as suits with gentlemen of your knowing to a stranger of his quality. I beseech you all be better known to this gentleman, whom I commend to you as a noble friend of mine. How worthy he is I will leave to appear hereafter, rather than story him in his own hearing.

FRENCHMAN. Sir, we have known together in Orleans.

POSTHUMUS. Since when I have been debtor to you for courtesies, which I will be ever to pay and yet pay still.

FRENCHMAN. Sir, you o'errate my poor kindness. I was glad I did atone my countryman and you; it had been pity you should have been put together with so mortal a purpose as then each bore, upon importance of so slight and trivial a nature.

POSTHUMUS. By your pardon, sir. I was then a young traveller; rather shunn'd to go even with what I heard than in my every action to be guided by others' experiences; but upon my mended judgment—if I offend not to say it is mended—my quarrel was not altogether slight.

FRENCHMAN. Faith, yes, to be put to the arbitrement of swords, and by such two that would by all likelihood have confounded one the other or have fall'n both.

IACHIMO. Can we, with manners, ask what was the difference?

FRENCHMAN. Safely, I think. 'Twas a contention in public, which may, without contradiction, suffer the report. It was much like an argument that fell out last night, where each of us fell in praise of our country mistresses; this gentleman at that time vouching—and upon warrant of bloody affirmation—his to be more fair, virtuous, wise, chaste, constant, qualified, and less attemptable, than any the rarest of our ladies in France.

IACHIMO. That lady is not now living, or this gentleman's opinion, by this, worn out.

POSTHUMUS. She holds her virtue still, and I my mind.

IACHIMO. You must not so far prefer her fore ours of Italy.

POSTHUMUS. Being so far provok'd as I was in France, I would abate her nothing, though I profess myself her adorer, not her friend.

IACHIMO. As fair and as good—a kind of hand-in-hand comparison—had been something too fair and too good for any lady in Britain. If she went before others I have seen as that diamond of yours outlustres many I have beheld, I could not but believe she excelled many; but I have not seen the most precious diamond that is, nor you the lady.

POSTHUMUS. I prais'd her as I rated her. So do I my stone.

IACHIMO. What do you esteem it at?

POSTHUMUS. More than the world enjoys.

IACHIMO. Either your unparagon'd mistress is dead, or she's outpriz'd by a trifle.

POSTHUMUS. You are mistaken: the one may be sold or given, if there were wealth enough for the purchase or merit for the gift; the other is not a thing for sale, and only the gift of the gods.

IACHIMO. Which the gods have given you?

POSTHUMUS. Which by their graces I will keep.

IACHIMO. You may wear her in title yours; but you know strange fowl light upon neighbouring ponds. Your ring may be stol'n too. So your brace of unprizable estimations, the one is but frail and the other casual; a cunning thief, or a that-way-accomplish'd courtier, would hazard the winning both of first and last.

POSTHUMUS. Your Italy contains none so accomplish'd a courtier to convince the honour of my mistress, if in the holding or loss of that you term her frail. I do nothing doubt you have store of thieves; notwithstanding, I fear not my ring.

PHILARIO. Let us leave here, gentlemen.

POSTHUMUS. Sir, with all my heart. This worthy signior, I thank him, makes no stranger of me; we are familiar at first.

IACHIMO. With five times so much conversation I should get ground of your fair mistress; make her go back even to the yielding, had I admittance and opportunity to friend.

POSTHUMUS. No, no.

IACHIMO. I dare thereupon pawn the moiety of my estate to your ring, which, in my opinion, o'ervalues it something. But I make my wager rather against your confidence than her reputation; and, to bar your offence herein too, I durst attempt it against any lady in the world.

POSTHUMUS. You are a great deal abus'd in too bold a persuasion, and I doubt not you sustain what y'are worthy of by your attempt.

IACHIMO. What's that?

POSTHUMUS. A repulse; though your attempt, as you call it, deserve more—a punishment too.

PHILARIO. Gentlemen, enough of this. It came in too suddenly; let it die as it was born, and I pray you be better acquainted.

IACHIMO. Would I had put my estate and my neighbour's on th' approbation of what I have spoke!

POSTHUMUS. What lady would you choose to assail?

IACHIMO. Yours, whom in constancy you think stands so safe. I will lay you ten thousand ducats to your ring that, commend me to the court where your lady is, with no more advantage than the opportunity of a second conference, and I will bring from thence that honour of hers which you imagine so reserv'd.

POSTHUMUS. I will wage against your gold, gold to it. My ring I hold dear as my finger; 'tis part of it.

IACHIMO. You are a friend, and therein the wiser. If you buy ladies' flesh at a million a dram, you cannot preserve it from tainting. But I see you have some religion in you, that you fear.

POSTHUMUS. This is but a custom in your tongue; you bear a graver purpose, I hope.

IACHIMO. I am the master of my speeches, and would undergo what's spoken, I swear.

POSTHUMUS. Will you? I shall but lend my diamond till your return. Let there be covenants drawn between's. My mistress exceeds in goodness the hugeness of your unworthy thinking. I dare you to this match: here's my ring.

PHILARIO. I will have it no lay.

IACHIMO. By the gods, it is one. If I bring you no sufficient testimony that I have enjoy'd the dearest bodily part of your mistress, my ten thousand ducats are yours; so is your diamond too. If I come off, and leave her in such honour as you have trust in, she your jewel, this your jewel, and my gold are yours—provided I have your commendation for my more free entertainment.

POSTHUMUS. I embrace these conditions; let us have articles betwixt us. Only, thus far you shall answer: if you make your voyage upon her, and give me directly to understand you have prevail'd, I am no further your enemy—she is not worth our debate; if she remain unseduc'd, you not making it appear otherwise, for your ill opinion and th' assault you have made to her chastity you shall answer me with your sword.

IACHIMO. Your hand—a covenant! We will have these things set down by lawful counsel, and straight away for Britain, lest the bargain should catch cold and starve. I will fetch my gold and have our two wagers recorded.

POSTHUMUS. Agreed. *Exeunt* POSTHUMUS *and* IACHIMO

FRENCHMAN. Will this hold, think you?

PHILARIO. Signior Iachimo will not from it. Pray let us follow 'em. *Exeunt*

SCENE 5

Britain. CYMBELINE'S *palace*

Enter QUEEN, LADIES, *and* CORNELIUS

QUEEN. Whiles yet the dew's on ground, gather those flowers;
Make haste; who has the note of them?
LADY. I, madam.
QUEEN. Dispatch. *Exeunt* LADIES
Now, Master Doctor, have you brought those drugs?
CORNELIUS. Pleaseth your Highness, ay. Here they are, madam. [*Presenting a box*]
But I beseech your Grace, without offence—
My conscience bids me ask—wherefore you have
Commanded of me these most poisonous compounds
Which are the movers of a languishing death,
But, though slow, deadly?
QUEEN. I wonder, Doctor,
Thou ask'st me such a question. Have I not been
Thy pupil long? Hast thou not learn'd me how
To make perfumes? distil? preserve? yea, so
That our great king himself doth woo me oft
For my confections? Having thus far proceeded—
Unless thou think'st me devilish—is't not meet
That I did amplify my judgment in
Other conclusions? I will try the forces
Of these thy compounds on such creatures as
We count not worth the hanging—but none human—
To try the vigour of them, and apply
Allayments to their act, and by them gather
Their several virtues and effects.
CORNELIUS. Your Highness
Shall from this practice but make hard your heart;
Besides, the seeing these effects will be
Both noisome and infectious.
QUEEN. O, content thee.

Enter PISANIO

[*Aside*] Here comes a flattering rascal; upon him
Will I first work. He's for his master,

An enemy to my son.—How now, Pisanio!
Doctor, your service for this time is ended;
Take your own way.

CORNELIUS. [*Aside*] I do suspect you, madam;
But you shall do no harm.

QUEEN. [*To* PISANIO] Hark thee, a word.

CORNELIUS. [*Aside*] I do not like her. She doth think she has
Strange ling'ring poisons. I do know her spirit,
And will not trust one of her malice with
A drug of such damn'd nature. Those she has
Will stupefy and dull the sense awhile,
Which first perchance she'll prove on cats and dogs,
Then afterward up higher; but there is
No danger in what show of death it makes,
More than the locking up the spirits a time,
To be more fresh, reviving. She is fool'd
With a most false effect; and I the truer
So to be false with her.

QUEEN. No further service, Doctor,
Until I send for thee.

CORNELIUS. I humbly take my leave. *Exit*

QUEEN. Weeps she still, say'st thou? Dost thou think in time
She will not quench, and let instructions enter
Where folly now possesses? Do thou work.
When thou shalt bring me word she loves my son,
I'll tell thee on the instant thou art then
As great as is thy master; greater, for
His fortunes all lie speechless, and his name
Is at last gasp. Return he cannot, nor
Continue where he is. To shift his being
Is to exchange one misery with another,
And every day that comes comes to decay
A day's work in him. What shalt thou expect
To be depender on a thing that leans,
Who cannot be new built, nor has no friends
So much as but to prop him?

[*The* QUEEN *drops the box.* PISANIO *takes it up*]

Thou tak'st up
Thou know'st not what; but take it for thy labour.
It is a thing I made, which hath the King

Five times redeem'd from death. I do not know
What is more cordial. Nay, I prithee take it;
It is an earnest of a further good
That I mean to thee. Tell thy mistress how
The case stands with her; do't as from thyself.
Think what a chance thou changest on; but think
Thou hast thy mistress still; to boot, my son,
Who shall take notice of thee. I'll move the King
To any shape of thy preferment, such
As thou'lt desire; and then myself, I chiefly,
That set thee on to this desert, am bound
To load thy merit richly. Call my women.
Think on my words. *Exit* PISANIO
A sly and constant knave,
Not to be shak'd; the agent for his master,
And the remembrancer of her to hold
The hand-fast to her lord. I have given him that
Which, if he take, shall quite unpeople her
Of leigers for her sweet; and which she after,
Except she bend her humour, shall be assur'd
To taste of too.

Re-enter PISANIO *and* LADIES

So, so. Well done, well done.
The violets, cowslips, and the primroses,
Bear to my closet. Fare thee well, Pisanio;
Think on my words. *Exeunt* QUEEN *and* LADIES

PISANIO. And shall do.
But when to my good lord I prove untrue
I'll choke myself—there's all I'll do for you. *Exit*

SCENE 6

Britain. The palace

Enter IMOGEN *alone*

IMOGEN. A father cruel and a step-dame false;
A foolish suitor to a wedded lady
That hath her husband banish'd. O, that husband!

My supreme crown of grief! and those repeated
Vexations of it! Had I been thief-stol'n,
As my two brothers, happy! but most miserable
Is the desire that's glorious. Blessed be those,
How mean soe'er, that have their honest wills,
Which seasons comfort. Who may this be? Fie!

Enter PISANIO *and* IACHIMO

PISANIO. Madam, a noble gentleman of Rome
Comes from my lord with letters.
IACHIMO. Change you, madam?
The worthy Leonatus is in safety,
And greets your Highness dearly. [*Presents a letter*]
IMOGEN. Thanks, good sir.
You're kindly welcome.
IACHIMO. [*Aside*] All of her that is out of door most rich!
If she be furnish'd with a mind so rare,
She is alone th' Arabian bird, and I
Have lost the wager. Boldness be my friend!
Arm me, audacity, from head to foot!
Or, like the Parthian, I shall flying fight;
Rather, directly fly.
IMOGEN. [*Reads*] 'He is one of the noblest note, to whose kindnesses I am most infinitely tied. Reflect upon him accordingly, as you value your trust. LEONATUS.'
So far I read aloud;
But even the very middle of my heart
Is warm'd by th' rest and takes it thankfully.
You are as welcome, worthy sir, as I
Have words to bid you; and shall find it so
In all that I can do.
IACHIMO. Thanks, fairest lady.
What, are men mad? Hath nature given them eyes
To see this vaulted arch and the rich crop
Of sea and land, which can distinguish 'twixt
The fiery orbs above and the twinn'd stones
Upon the number'd beach, and can we not
Partition make with spectacles so precious
'Twixt fair and foul?
IMOGEN. What makes your admiration?

IACHIMO. It cannot be i' th' eye, for apes and monkeys,
'Twixt two such shes, would chatter this way and
Contemn with mows the other; nor i' th' judgment,
For idiots in this case of favour would
Be wisely definite; nor i' th' appetite;
Sluttery, to such neat excellence oppos'd,
Should make desire vomit emptiness,
Not so allur'd to feed.
IMOGEN. What is the matter, trow?
IACHIMO. The cloyed will–
That satiate yet unsatisfied desire, that tub
Both fill'd and running–ravening first the lamb,
Longs after for the garbage.
IMOGEN. What, dear sir,
Thus raps you? Are you well?
IACHIMO. Thanks, madam; well.–Beseech you, sir,
Desire my man's abode where I did leave him.
He's strange and peevish.
PISANIO. I was going, sir,
To give him welcome. *Exit*
IMOGEN. Continues well my lord? His health beseech you?
IACHIMO. Well, madam.
IMOGEN. Is he dispos'd to mirth? I hope he is.
IACHIMO. Exceeding pleasant; none a stranger there
So merry and so gamesome. He is call'd
The Britain reveller.
IMOGEN. When he was here
He did incline to sadness, and oft-times
Not knowing why.
IACHIMO. I never saw him sad.
There is a Frenchman his companion, one
An eminent monsieur that, it seems, much loves
A Gallian girl at home. He furnaces
The thick sighs from him; whiles the jolly Briton–
Your lord, I mean–laughs from's free lungs, cries 'O,
Can my sides hold, to think that man–who knows
By history, report, or his own proof,
What woman is, yea, what she cannot choose
But must be–will's free hours languish for
Assured bondage?'

IMOGEN. Will my lord say so?
IACHIMO. Ay, madam, with his eyes in flood with laughter.
It is a recreation to be by
And hear him mock the Frenchman. But heavens know
Some men are much to blame.
IMOGEN. Not he, I hope.
IACHIMO. Not he; but yet heaven's bounty towards him might
Be us'd more thankfully. In himself, 'tis much;
In you, which I account his, beyond all talents.
Whilst I am bound to wonder, I am bound
To pity too.
IMOGEN. What do you pity, sir?
IACHIMO. Two creatures heartily.
IMOGEN. Am I one, sir?
You look on me: what wreck discern you in me
Deserves your pity?
IACHIMO. Lamentable! What,
To hide me from the radiant sun and solace
I' th' dungeon by a snuff?
IMOGEN. I pray you, sir,
Deliver with more openness your answers
To my demands. Why do you pity me?
IACHIMO. That others do,
I was about to say, enjoy your—But
It is an office of the gods to venge it,
Not mine to speak on't.
IMOGEN. You do seem to know
Something of me, or what concerns me; pray you—
Since doubting things go ill often hurts more
Than to be sure they do; for certainties
Either are past remedies, or, timely knowing,
The remedy then born—discover to me
What both you spur and stop.
IACHIMO. Had I this cheek
To bathe my lips upon; this hand, whose touch,
Whose every touch, would force the feeler's soul
To th' oath of loyalty; this object, which
Takes prisoner the wild motion of mine eye,
Fixing it only here; should I, damn'd then,

Slaver with lips as common as the stairs
That mount the Capitol; join gripes with hands
Made hard with hourly falsehood–falsehood as
With labour; then by-peeping in an eye
Base and illustrious as the smoky light
That's fed with stinking tallow–it were fit
That all the plagues of hell should at one time
Encounter such revolt.

IMOGEN. My lord, I fear,
Has forgot Britain.

IACHIMO. And himself. Not I
Inclin'd to this intelligence pronounce
The beggary of his change; but 'tis your graces
That from my mutest conscience to my tongue
Charms this report out.

IMOGEN. Let me hear no more.

IACHIMO. O dearest soul, your cause doth strike my heart
With pity that doth make me sick! A lady
So fair, and fasten'd to an empery,
Would make the great'st king double, to be partner'd
With tomboys hir'd with that self exhibition
Which your own coffers yield! with diseas'd ventures
That play with all infirmities for gold
Which rottenness can lend nature! such boil'd stuff
As well might poison poison! Be reveng'd;
Or she that bore you was no queen, and you
Recoil from your great stock.

IMOGEN. Reveng'd?
How should I be reveng'd? If this be true–
As I have such a heart that both mine ears
Must not in haste abuse–if it be true,
How should I be reveng'd?

IACHIMO. Should he make me
Live like Diana's priest betwixt cold sheets,
Whiles he is vaulting variable ramps,
In your despite, upon your purse? Revenge it.
I dedicate myself to your sweet pleasure,
More noble than that runagate to your bed,
And will continue fast to your affection,
Still close as sure.

IMOGEN. What ho, Pisanio!
IACHIMO. Let me my service tender on your lips.
IMOGEN. Away! I do condemn mine ears that have
So long attended thee. If thou wert honourable,
Thou wouldst have told this tale for virtue, not
For such an end thou seek'st, as base as strange.
Thou wrong'st a gentleman who is as far
From thy report as thou from honour; and
Solicits here a lady that disdains
Thee and the devil alike.—What ho, Pisanio!—
The King my father shall be made acquainted
Of thy assault. If he shall think it fit
A saucy stranger in his court to mart
As in a Romish stew, and to expound
His beastly mind to us, he hath a court
He little cares for, and a daughter who
He not respects at all.—What ho, Pisanio!
IACHIMO. O happy Leonatus! I may say
The credit that thy lady hath of thee
Deserves thy trust, and thy most perfect goodness
Her assur'd credit. Blessed live you long,
A lady to the worthiest sir that ever
Country call'd his! and you his mistress, only
For the most worthiest fit! Give me your pardon.
I have spoke this to know if your affiance
Were deeply rooted, and shall make your lord
That which he is new o'er; and he is one
The truest manner'd, such a holy witch
That he enchants societies into him,
Half all men's hearts are his.
IMOGEN. You make amends.
IACHIMO. He sits 'mongst men like a descended god:
He hath a kind of honour sets him off
More than a mortal seeming. Be not angry,
Most mighty Princess, that I have adventur'd
To try your taking of a false report, which hath
Honour'd with confirmation your great judgment
In the election of a sir so rare,
Which you know cannot err. The love I bear him
Made me to fan you thus; but the gods made you,

Unlike all others, chaffless. Pray your pardon.
IMOGEN. All's well, sir; take my pow'r i' th' court for yours.
IACHIMO. My humble thanks. I had almost forgot
T' entreat your Grace but in a small request,
And yet of moment too, for it concerns
Your lord; myself and other noble friends
Are partners in the business.
IMOGEN. Pray what is't?
IACHIMO. Some dozen Romans of us, and your lord—
The best feather of our wing—have mingled sums
To buy a present for the Emperor;
Which I, the factor for the rest, have done
In France. 'Tis plate of rare device, and jewels
Of rich and exquisite form, their values great;
And I am something curious, being strange,
To have them in safe stowage. May it please you
To take them in protection?
IMOGEN. Willingly;
And pawn mine honour for their safety. Since
My lord hath interest in them, I will keep them
In my bedchamber.
IACHIMO. They are in a trunk,
Attended by my men. I will make bold
To send them to you only for this night;
I must aboard to-morrow.
IMOGEN. O, no, no.
IACHIMO. Yes, I beseech; or I shall short my word
By length'ning my return. From Gallia
I cross'd the seas on purpose and on promise
To see your Grace.
IMOGEN. I thank you for your pains.
But not away to-morrow!
IACHIMO. O, I must, madam.
Therefore I shall beseech you, if you please
To greet your lord with writing, do't to-night.
I have outstood my time, which is material
To th' tender of our present.
IMOGEN. I will write.
Send your trunk to me; it shall safe be kept
And truly yielded you. You're very welcome. *Exeunt*

ACT II. SCENE 1

Britain. Before CYMBELINE'S *palace*

Enter CLOTEN *and the two* LORDS

CLOTEN. Was there ever man had such luck! When I kiss'd the jack, upon an up-cast to be hit away! I had a hundred pound on't; and then a whoreson jackanapes must take me up for swearing, as if I borrowed mine oaths of him, and might not spend them at my pleasure.

FIRST LORD. What got he by that? You have broke his pate with your bowl.

SECOND LORD. [*Aside*] If his wit had been like him that broke it, it would have run all out.

CLOTEN. When a gentleman is dispos'd to swear, it is not for any standers-by to curtail his oaths. Ha?

SECOND LORD. No, my lord; [*Aside*] nor crop the ears of them.

CLOTEN. Whoreson dog! I give him satisfaction? Would he had been one of my rank!

SECOND LORD. [*Aside*] To have smell'd like a fool.

CLOTEN. I am not vex'd more at anything in th' earth. A pox on't! I had rather not be so noble as I am; they dare not fight with me, because of the Queen my mother. Every jackslave hath his bellyful of fighting, and I must go up and down like a cock that nobody can match.

SECOND LORD. [*Aside*] You are cock and capon too; and you crow, cock, with your comb on.

CLOTEN. Sayest thou?

SECOND LORD. It is not fit your lordship should undertake every companion that you give offence to.

CLOTEN. No, I know that; but it is fit I should commit offence to my inferiors.

SECOND LORD. Ay, it is fit for your lordship only.

CLOTEN. Why, so I say.

FIRST LORD. Did you hear of a stranger that's come to court to-night?

CLOTEN. A stranger, and I not known on't?

SECOND LORD. [*Aside*] He's a strange fellow himself, and knows it not.

FIRST LORD. There's an Italian come, and, 'tis thought, one of Leonatus' friends.

CLOTEN. Leonatus? A banish'd rascal; and he's another, whatsoever he be. Who told you of this stranger?

FIRST LORD. One of your lordship's pages.

CLOTEN. Is it fit I went to look upon him? Is there no derogation in't?

SECOND LORD. You cannot derogate, my lord.

CLOTEN. Not easily, I think.

SECOND LORD. [*Aside*] You are a fool granted; therefore your issues, being foolish, do not derogate.

CLOTEN. Come, I'll go see this Italian. What I have lost to-day at bowls I'll win to-night of him. Come, go.

SECOND LORD. I'll attend your lordship.

Exeunt CLOTEN *and* FIRST LORD

That such a crafty devil as is his mother
Should yield the world this ass! A woman that
Bears all down with her brain; and this her son
Cannot take two from twenty, for his heart,
And leave eighteen. Alas, poor princess,
Thou divine Imogen, what thou endur'st,
Betwixt a father by thy step-dame govern'd,
A mother hourly coining plots, a wooer
More hateful than the foul expulsion is
Of thy dear husband, than that horrid act
Of the divorce he'd make! The heavens hold firm
The walls of thy dear honour, keep unshak'd
That temple, thy fair mind, that thou mayst stand
T' enjoy thy banish'd lord and this great land! *Exit*

SCENE 2

Britain. IMOGEN'S *bedchamber in* CYMBELINE'S *palace; a trunk in one corner*

Enter IMOGEN *in her bed, and a* LADY *attending*

IMOGEN. Who's there? My woman? Helen?

LADY. Please you, madam.

IMOGEN. What hour is it?

LADY. Almost midnight, madam.
IMOGEN. I have read three hours then. Mine eyes are weak;
Fold down the leaf where I have left. To bed.
Take not away the taper, leave it burning;
And if thou canst awake by four o' th' clock,
I prithee call me. Sleep hath seiz'd me wholly. *Exit* LADY
To your protection I commend me, gods.
From fairies and the tempters of the night
Guard me, beseech ye!
[*Sleeps.* IACHIMO *comes from the trunk*]
IACHIMO. The crickets sing, and man's o'er-labour'd sense
Repairs itself by rest. Our Tarquin thus
Did softly press the rushes ere he waken'd
The chastity he wounded. Cytherea,
How bravely thou becom'st thy bed! fresh lily,
And whiter than the sheets! That I might touch!
But kiss; one kiss! Rubies unparagon'd,
How dearly they do't! 'Tis her breathing that
Perfumes the chamber thus. The flame o' th' taper
Bows toward her and would under-peep her lids
To see th' enclosed lights, now canopied
Under these windows white and azure, lac'd
With blue of heaven's own tinct. But my design
To note the chamber. I will write all down:
Such and such pictures; there the window; such
Th' adornment of her bed; the arras, figures–
Why, such and such; and the contents o' th' story.
Ah, but some natural notes about her body
Above ten thousand meaner movables
Would testify, t' enrich mine inventory.
O sleep, thou ape of death, lie dull upon her!
And be her sense but as a monument,
Thus in a chapel lying! Come off, come off;
[*Taking off her bracelet*]
As slippery as the Gordian knot was hard!
'Tis mine; and this will witness outwardly,
As strongly as the conscience does within,
To th' madding of her lord. On her left breast
A mole cinque-spotted, like the crimson drops
I' th' bottom of a cowslip. Here's a voucher

Stronger than ever law could make; this secret
Will force him think I have pick'd the lock and ta'en
The treasure of her honour. No more. To what end?
Why should I write this down that's riveted,
Screw'd to my memory? She hath been reading late
The tale of Tereus; here the leaf's turn'd down
Where Philomel gave up. I have enough.
To th' trunk again, and shut the spring of it.
Swift, swift, you dragons of the night, that dawning
May bare the raven's eye! I lodge in fear;
Though this a heavenly angel, hell is here. [*Clock strikes*]
One, two, three. Time, time! *Exit into the trunk*

SCENE 3

CYMBELINE'S *palace. An ante-chamber adjoining* IMOGEN'S *apartments*

Enter CLOTEN *and* LORDS

FIRST LORD. Your lordship is the most patient man in loss, the most coldest that ever turn'd up ace.

CLOTEN. It would make any man cold to lose.

FIRST LORD. But not every man patient after the noble temper of your lordship. You are most hot and furious when you win.

CLOTEN. Winning will put any man into courage. If I could get this foolish Imogen, I should have gold enough. It's almost morning, is't not?

FIRST LORD. Day, my lord.

CLOTEN. I would this music would come. I am advised to give her music a mornings; they say it will penetrate.

Enter musicians

Come on, tune. If you can penetrate her with your fingering, so. We'll try with tongue too. If none will do, let her remain; but I'll never give o'er. First, a very excellent good-conceited thing; after, a wonderful sweet air, with admirable rich words to it—and then let her consider.

SONG

Hark, hark! the lark at heaven's gate sings,
And Phœbus 'gins arise,
His steeds to water at those springs
On chalic'd flow'rs that lies;
And winking Mary-buds begin
To ope their golden eyes.
With everything that pretty bin,
My lady sweet, arise;
Arise, arise!

So, get you gone. If this penetrate, I will consider your music the better; if it do not, it is a vice in her ears which horsehairs and calves' guts, nor the voice of unpaved eunuch to boot, can never amend. *Exeunt musicians*

Enter CYMBELINE *and* QUEEN

SECOND LORD. Here comes the King.

CLOTEN. I am glad I was up so late, for that's the reason I was up so early. He cannot choose but take this service I have done fatherly.–Good morrow to your Majesty and to my gracious mother.

CYMBELINE. Attend you here the door of our stern daughter?
Will she not forth?

CLOTEN. I have assail'd her with musics, but she vouchsafes no notice.

CYMBELINE. The exile of her minion is too new;
She hath not yet forgot him; some more time
Must wear the print of his remembrance out,
And then she's yours.

QUEEN. You are most bound to th' King,
Who lets go by no vantages that may
Prefer you to his daughter. Frame yourself
To orderly soliciting, and be friended
With aptness of the season; make denials
Increase your services; so seem as if
You were inspir'd to do those duties which
You tender to her; that you in all obey her,
Save when command to your dismission tends,
And therein you are senseless.

CLOTEN. Senseless? Not so.

Enter a MESSENGER

MESSENGER. So like you, sir, ambassadors from Rome;
The one is Caius Lucius.
CYMBELINE. A worthy fellow,
Albeit he comes on angry purpose now;
But that's no fault of his. We must receive him
According to the honour of his sender;
And towards himself, his goodness forespent on us,
We must extend our notice. Our dear son,
When you have given good morning to your mistress,
Attend the Queen and us; we shall have need
T' employ you towards this Roman. Come, our queen.
Exeunt all but CLOTEN
CLOTEN. If she be up, I'll speak with her; if not,
Let her lie still and dream. By your leave, ho! [*Knocks*]
I know her women are about her; what
If I do line one of their hands? 'Tis gold
Which buys admittance; oft it doth—yea, and makes
Diana's rangers false themselves, yield up
Their deer to th' stand o' th' stealer; and 'tis gold
Which makes the true man kill'd and saves the thief;
Nay, sometime hangs both thief and true man. What
Can it not do and undo? I will make
One of her women lawyer to me, for
I yet not understand the case myself.
By your leave. [*Knocks*]

Enter a LADY

LADY. Who's there that knocks?
CLOTEN. A gentleman.
LADY. No more?
CLOTEN. Yes, and a gentlewoman's son.
LADY. That's more
Than some whose tailors are as dear as yours
Can justly boast of. What's your lordship's pleasure?
CLOTEN. Your lady's person; is she ready?
LADY. Ay,
To keep her chamber.
CLOTEN. There is gold for you; sell me your good report.

LADY. How? My good name? or to report of you
What I shall think is good? The Princess!

Enter IMOGEN

CLOTEN. Good morrow, fairest sister. Your sweet hand.
Exit LADY

IMOGEN. Good morrow, sir. You lay out too much pains
For purchasing but trouble. The thanks I give
Is telling you that I am poor of thanks,
And scarce can spare them.

CLOTEN. Still I swear I love you.

IMOGEN. If you but said so, 'twere as deep with me.
If you swear still, your recompense is still
That I regard it not.

CLOTEN. This is no answer.

IMOGEN. But that you shall not say I yield, being silent,
I would not speak. I pray you spare me. Faith,
I shall unfold equal discourtesy
To your best kindness; one of your great knowing
Should learn, being taught, forbearance.

CLOTEN. To leave you in your madness 'twere my sin;
I will not.

IMOGEN. Fools are not mad folks.

CLOTEN. Do you call me fool?

IMOGEN. As I am mad, I do;
If you'll be patient, I'll no more be mad;
That cures us both. I am much sorry, sir,
You put me to forget a lady's manners
By being so verbal; and learn now, for all,
That I, which know my heart, do here pronounce,
By th' very truth of it, I care not for you,
And am so near the lack of charity
To accuse myself I hate you; which I had rather
You felt than make't my boast.

CLOTEN. You sin against
Obedience, which you owe your father. For
The contract you pretend with that base wretch,
One bred of alms and foster'd with cold dishes,
With scraps o' th' court—it is no contract, none.
And though it be allowed in meaner parties—

Yet who than he more mean?—to knit their souls—
On whom there is no more dependency
But brats and beggary—in self-figur'd knot,
Yet you are curb'd from that enlargement by
The consequence o' th' crown, and must not foil
The precious note of it with a base slave,
A hilding for a livery, a squire's cloth,
A pantler—not so eminent!

IMOGEN. Profane fellow!
Wert thou the son of Jupiter, and no more
But what thou art besides, thou wert too base
To be his groom. Thou wert dignified enough,
Even to the point of envy, if 'twere made
Comparative for your virtues to be styl'd
The under-hangman of his kingdom, and hated
For being preferr'd so well.

CLOTEN. The south fog rot him!

IMOGEN. He never can meet more mischance than come
To be but nam'd of thee. His mean'st garment
That ever hath but clipp'd his body is dearer
In my respect than all the hairs above thee,
Were they all made such men. How now, Pisanio!

Enter PISANIO

CLOTEN. 'His garments'! Now the devil—

IMOGEN. To Dorothy my woman hie thee presently.

CLOTEN. 'His garment'!

IMOGEN. I am sprited with a fool;
Frighted, and ang'red worse. Go bid my woman
Search for a jewel that too casually
Hath left mine arm. It was thy master's; shrew me,
If I would lose it for a revenue
Of any king's in Europe! I do think
I saw't this morning; confident I am
Last night 'twas on mine arm; I kiss'd it.
I hope it be not gone to tell my lord
That I kiss aught but he.

PISANIO. 'Twill not be lost.

IMOGEN. I hope so. Go and search. *Exit* PISANIO

CLOTEN. You have abus'd me.

'His meanest garment'!
IMOGEN. Ay, I said so, sir.
If you will make 't an action, call witness to 't.
CLOTEN. I will inform your father.
IMOGEN. Your mother too.
She's my good lady and will conceive, I hope,
But the worst of me. So I leave you, sir,
To th' worst of discontent. *Exit*
CLOTEN. I'll be reveng'd.
'His mean'st garment'! Well. *Exit*

SCENE 4

Rome. PHILARIO'S *house*

Enter POSTHUMUS *and* PHILARIO

POSTHUMUS. Fear it not, sir; I would I were so sure
To win the King as I am bold her honour
Will remain hers.
PHILARIO. What means do you make to him?
POSTHUMUS. Not any; but abide the change of time,
Quake in the present winter's state, and wish
That warmer days would come. In these fear'd hopes
I barely gratify your love; they failing,
I must die much your debtor.
PHILARIO. Your very goodness and your company
O'erpays all I can do. By this your king
Hath heard of great Augustus. Caius Lucius
Will do's commission throughly; and I think
He'll grant the tribute, send th' arrearages,
Or look upon our Romans, whose remembrance
Is yet fresh in their grief.
POSTHUMUS. I do believe
Statist though I am none, nor like to be,
That this will prove a war; and you shall hear
The legions now in Gallia sooner landed
In our not-fearing Britain than have tidings
Of any penny tribute paid. Our countrymen
Are men more order'd than when Julius Cæsar

Smil'd at their lack of skill, but found their courage
Worthy his frowning at. Their discipline,
Now mingled with their courages, will make known
To their approvers they are people such
That mend upon the world.

Enter IACHIMO

PHILARIO. See! Iachimo!
POSTHUMUS. The swiftest harts have posted you by land,
And winds of all the corners kiss'd your sails,
To make your vessel nimble.
PHILARIO. Welcome, sir.
POSTHUMUS. I hope the briefness of your answer made
The speediness of your return.
IACHIMO. Your lady
Is one of the fairest that I have look'd upon.
POSTHUMUS. And therewithal the best; or let her beauty
Look through a casement to allure false hearts,
And be false with them.
IACHIMO. Here are letters for you.
POSTHUMUS. Their tenour good, I trust.
IACHIMO. 'Tis very like.
PHILARIO. Was Caius Lucius in the Britain court
When you were there?
IACHIMO. He was expected then,
But not approach'd.
POSTHUMUS. All is well yet.
Sparkles this stone as it was wont, or is't not
Too dull for your good wearing?
IACHIMO. If I have lost it,
I should have lost the worth of it in gold.
I'll make a journey twice as far t' enjoy
A second night of such sweet shortness which
Was mine in Britain; for the ring is won.
POSTHUMUS. The stone's too hard to come by.
IACHIMO. Not a whit,
Your lady being so easy.
POSTHUMUS. Make not, sir,
Your loss your sport. I hope you know that we
Must not continue friends.

IACHIMO. Good sir, we must,
If you keep covenant. Had I not brought
The knowledge of your mistress home, I grant
We were to question farther; but I now
Profess myself the winner of her honour,
Together with your ring; and not the wronger
Of her or you, having proceeded but
By both your wills.
POSTHUMUS. If you can make't apparent
That you have tasted her in bed, my hand
And ring is yours. If not, the foul opinion
You had of her pure honour gains or loses
Your sword or mine, or masterless leaves both
To who shall find them.
IACHIMO. Sir, my circumstances,
Being so near the truth as I will make them,
Must first induce you to believe—whose strength
I will confirm with oath; which I doubt not
You'll give me leave to spare when you shall find
You need it not.
POSTHUMUS. Proceed.
IACHIMO. First, her bedchamber,
Where I confess I slept not, but profess
Had that was well worth watching—it was hang'd
With tapestry of silk and silver; the story,
Proud Cleopatra when she met her Roman
And Cydnus swell'd above the banks, or for
The press of boats or pride. A piece of work
So bravely done, so rich, that it did strive
In workmanship and value; which I wonder'd
Could be so rarely and exactly wrought,
Since the true life on't was—
POSTHUMUS. This is true;
And this you might have heard of here, by me
Or by some other.
IACHIMO. More particulars
Must justify my knowledge.
POSTHUMUS. So they must,
Or do your honour injury.
IACHIMO. The chimney

Is south the chamber, and the chimneypiece
Chaste Dian bathing. Never saw I figures
So likely to report themselves. The cutter
Was as another nature, dumb; outwent her,
Motion and breath left out.

POSTHUMUS. This is a thing
Which you might from relation likewise reap,
Being, as it is, much spoke of.

IACHIMO. The roof o' th' chamber
With golden cherubins is fretted; her andirons–
I had forgot them–were two winking Cupids
Of silver, each on one foot standing, nicely
Depending on their brands.

POSTHUMUS. This is her honour!
Let it be granted you have seen all this, and praise
Be given to your remembrance; the description
Of what is in her chamber nothing saves
The wager you have laid.

IACHIMO. Then, if you can, [*Shows the bracelet*]
Be pale. I beg but leave to air this jewel. See!
And now 'tis up again. It must be married
To that your diamond; I'll keep them.

POSTHUMUS. Jove!
Once more let me behold it. Is it that
Which I left with her?

IACHIMO. Sir–I thank her–that.
She stripp'd it from her arm; I see her yet;
Her pretty action did outsell her gift,
And yet enrich'd it too. She gave it me, and said
She priz'd it once.

POSTHUMUS. May be she pluck'd it off
To send it me.

IACHIMO. She writes so to you, doth she?

POSTHUMUS. O, no, no, no! 'tis true. Here, take this too;
[*Gives the ring*]
It is a basilisk unto mine eye,
Kills me to look on't. Let there be no honour
Where there is beauty; truth where semblance; love
Where there's another man. The vows of women
Of no more bondage be to where they are made

Than they are to their virtues, which is nothing.
O, above measure false!

PHILARIO. Have patience, sir,
And take your ring again; 'tis not yet won.
It may be probable she lost it, or
Who knows if one her women, being corrupted
Hath stol'n it from her?

POSTHUMUS. Very true;
And so I hope he came by't. Back my ring.
Render to me some corporal sign about her,
More evident than this; for this was stol'n.

IACHIMO. By Jupiter, I had it from her arm!

POSTHUMUS. Hark you, he swears; by Jupiter he swears.
'Tis true–nay, keep the ring, 'tis true. I am sure
She would not lose it. Her attendants are
All sworn and honourable–they induc'd to steal it!
And by a stranger! No, he hath enjoy'd her.
The cognizance of her incontinency
Is this: she hath bought the name of whore thus dearly.
There, take thy hire; and all the fiends of hell
Divide themselves between you!

PHILARIO. Sir, be patient;
This is not strong enough to be believ'd
Of one persuaded well of.

POSTHUMUS. Never talk on't;
She hath been colted by him.

IACHIMO. If you seek
For further satisfying, under her breast–
Worthy the pressing–lies a mole, right proud
Of that most delicate lodging. By my life,
I kiss'd it; and it gave me present hunger
To feed again, though full. You do remember
This stain upon her?

POSTHUMUS. Ay, and it doth confirm
Another stain, as big as hell can hold,
Were there no more but it.

IACHIMO. Will you hear more?

POSTHUMUS. Spare your arithmetic; never count the turns.
Once, and a million!

IACHIMO. I'll be sworn–

POSTHUMUS. No swearing.
If you will swear you have not done't, you lie;
And I will kill thee if thou dost deny
Thou'st made me cuckold.
IACHIMO. I'll deny nothing.
POSTHUMUS. O that I had her here to tear her limb-meal!
I will go there and do't, i' th' court, before
Her father. I'll do something— *Exit*
PHILARIO. Quite besides
The government of patience! You have won.
Let's follow him and pervert the present wrath
He hath against himself.
IACHIMO. With all my heart. *Exeunt*

SCENE 5

Rome. Another room in PHILARIO'S *house*

Enter POSTHUMUS

POSTHUMUS. Is there no way for men to be, but women
Must be half-workers? We are all bastards,
And that most venerable man which I
Did call my father was I know not where
When I was stamp'd. Some coiner with his tools
Made me a counterfeit; yet my mother seem'd
The Dian of that time. So doth my wife
The nonpareil of this. O, vengeance, vengeance!
Me of my lawful pleasure she restrain'd,
And pray'd me oft forbearance; did it with
A pudency so rosy, the sweet view on't
Might well have warm'd old Saturn; that I thought her
As chaste as unsunn'd snow. O, all the devils!
This yellow Iachimo in an hour—was't not?
Or less!—at first? Perchance he spoke not, but,
Like a full-acorn'd boar, a German one,
Cried 'O!' and mounted; found no opposition
But what he look'd for should oppose and she
Should from encounter guard. Could I find out
The woman's part in me! For there's no motion

That tends to vice in man but I affirm
It is the woman's part. Be it lying, note it,
The woman's; flattering, hers; deceiving, hers;
Lust and rank thoughts, hers, hers; revenges, hers;
Ambitions, covetings, change of prides, disdain,
Nice longing, slanders, mutability,
All faults that man may name, nay, that hell knows,
Why, hers, in part or all; but rather all;
For even to vice
They are not constant, but are changing still
One vice but of a minute old for one
Not half so old as that. I'll write against them,
Detest them, curse them. Yet 'tis greater skill
In a true hate to pray they have their will:
The very devils cannot plague them better. *Exit*

ACT III. SCENE 1

Britain. A hall in CYMBELINE'S *palace*

Enter in state, CYMBELINE, QUEEN, CLOTEN, *and* LORDS *at one door, and at another* CAIUS LUCIUS *and attendants*

CYMBELINE. Now say, what would Augustus Cæsar with us?
LUCIUS. When Julius Cæsar—whose remembrance yet
Lives in men's eyes, and will to ears and tongues
Be theme and hearing ever—was in this Britain,
And conquer'd it, Cassibelan, thine uncle,
Famous in Cæsar's praises no whit less
Than in his feats deserving it, for him
And his succession granted Rome a tribute,
Yearly three thousand pounds, which by thee lately
Is left untender'd.
QUEEN. And, to kill the marvel,
Shall be so ever.
CLOTEN. There be many Cæsars
Ere such another Julius. Britain is
A world by itself, and we will nothing pay
For wearing our own noses.

QUEEN. That opportunity,
Which then they had to take from 's, to resume
We have again. Remember, sir, my liege,
The kings your ancestors, together with
The natural bravery of your isle, which stands
As Neptune's park, ribb'd and pal'd in
With rocks unscalable and roaring waters,
With sands that will not bear your enemies' boats
But suck them up to th' top-mast. A kind of conquest
Cæsar made here; but made not here his brag
Of 'came, and saw, and overcame.' With shame–
The first that ever touch'd him–he was carried
From off our coast, twice beaten; and his shipping–
Poor ignorant baubles!–on our terrible seas,
Like egg-shells mov'd upon their surges, crack'd
As easily 'gainst our rocks; for joy whereof
The fam'd Cassibelan, who was once at point–
O, giglot fortune!–to master Cæsar's sword,
Made Lud's Town with rejoicing fires bright
And Britons strut with courage.

CLOTEN. Come, there's no more tribute to be paid. Our kingdom is stronger than it was at that time; and, as I said, there is no moe such Cæsars. Other of them may have crook'd noses; but to owe such straight arms, none.

CYMBELINE. Son, let your mother end.

CLOTEN. We have yet many among us can gripe as hard as Cassibelan. I do not say I am one; but I have a hand. Why tribute? Why should we pay tribute? If Cæsar can hide the sun from us with a blanket, or put the moon in his pocket, we will pay him tribute for light; else, sir, no more tribute, pray you now.

CYMBELINE. You must know,
Till the injurious Romans did extort
This tribute from us, we were free. Cæsar's ambition–
Which swell'd so much that it did almost stretch
The sides o' th' world–against all colour here
Did put the yoke upon's; which to shake off
Becomes a warlike people, whom we reckon
Ourselves to be.

CLOTEN. We do.

CYMBELINE. Say then to Cæsar,
Our ancestor was that Mulmutius which
Ordain'd our laws—whose use the sword of Cæsar
Hath too much mangled; whose repair and franchise
Shall, by the power we hold, be our good deed,
Though Rome be therefore angry. Mulmutius made our laws,
Who was the first of Britain which did put
His brows within a golden crown, and call'd
Himself a king.

LUCIUS. I am sorry, Cymbeline,
That I am to pronounce Augustus Cæsar—
Cæsar, that hath moe kings his servants than
Thyself domestic officers—thine enemy.
Receive it from me, then: war and confusion
In Cæsar's name pronounce I 'gainst thee; look
For fury not to be resisted. Thus defied,
I thank thee for myself.

CYMBELINE. Thou art welcome, Caius.
Thy Cæsar knighted me; my youth I spent
Much under him; of him I gather'd honour,
Which he to seek of me again, perforce,
Behoves me keep at utterance. I am perfect
That the Pannonians and Dalmatians for
Their liberties are now in arms, a precedent
Which not to read would show the Britons cold;
So Cæsar shall not find them.

LUCIUS. Let proof speak.

CLOTEN. His majesty bids you welcome. Make pastime with us a day or two, or longer. If you seek us afterwards in other terms, you shall find us in our salt-water girdle. If you beat us out of it, it is yours; if you fall in the adventure, our crows shall fare the better for you; and there's an end.

LUCIUS. So, sir.

CYMBELINE. I know your master's pleasure, and he mine;
All the remain is, welcome. *Exeunt*

SCENE 2

Britain. Another room in CYMBELINE'S *palace*

Enter PISANIO *reading of a letter*

PISANIO. How? of adultery? Wherefore write you not
What monsters her accuse? Leonatus!
O master, what a strange infection
Is fall'n into thy ear! What false Italian–
As poisonous-tongu'd as handed–hath prevail'd
On thy too ready hearing? Disloyal? No.
She's punish'd for her truth, and undergoes,
More goddess-like than wife-like, such assaults
As would take in some virtue. O my master!
Thy mind to her is now as low as were
Thy fortunes. How? that I should murder her?
Upon the love, and truth, and vows, which I
Have made to thy command? I, her? Her blood?
If it be so to do good service, never
Let me be counted serviceable. How look I
That I should seem to lack humanity
So much as this fact comes to? [*Reads*] 'Do't. The letter
That I have sent her, by her own command
Shall give thee opportunity.' O damn'd paper,
Black as the ink that's on thee! Senseless bauble,
Art thou a fedary for this act, and look'st
So virgin-like without? Lo, here she comes.

Enter IMOGEN

I am ignorant in what I am commanded.
IMOGEN. How now, Pisanio!
PISANIO. Madam, here is a letter from my lord.
IMOGEN. Who? thy lord? That is my lord–Leonatus?
O, learn'd indeed were that astronomer
That knew the stars as I his characters–
He'd lay the future open. You good gods,
Let what is here contain'd relish of love,
Of my lord's health, of his content; yet not
That we two are asunder–let that grieve him!

Some griefs are med'cinable; that is one of them,
For it doth physic love—of his content,
All but in that. Good wax, thy leave. Blest be
You bees that make these locks of counsel! Lovers
And men in dangerous bonds pray not alike;
Though forfeiters you cast in prison, yet
You clasp young Cupid's tables. Good news, gods!

[*Reads*]

'Justice and your father's wrath, should he take me in his dominion, could not be so cruel to me as you, O the dearest of creatures, would even renew me with your eyes. Take notice that I am in Cambria, at Milford Haven. What your own love will out of this advise you, follow. So he wishes you all happiness that remains loyal to his vow, and your increasing in love

LEONATUS POSTHUMUS.'

O for a horse with wings! Hear'st thou, Pisanio?
He is at Milford Haven. Read, and tell me
How far 'tis thither. If one of mean affairs
May plod it in a week, why may not I
Glide thither in a day? Then, true Pisanio—
Who long'st like me to see thy lord, who long'st—
O, let me 'bate!—but not like me, yet long'st,
But in a fainter kind—O, not like me,
For mine's beyond beyond!—say, and speak thick—
Love's counsellor should fill the bores of hearing
To th' smothering of the sense—how far it is
To this same blessed Milford. And by th' way
Tell me how Wales was made so happy as
T' inherit such a haven. But first of all,
How we may steal from hence; and for the gap
That we shall make in time from our hence-going
And our return, to excuse. But first, how get hence.
Why should excuse be born or ere begot?
We'll talk of that hereafter. Prithee speak,
How many score of miles may we well ride
'Twixt hour and hour?

PISANIO. One score 'twixt sun and sun,
Madam, 's enough for you, and too much too.

IMOGEN. Why, one that rode to's execution, man,
Could never go so slow. I have heard of riding wagers
Where horses have been nimbler than the sands
That run i' th' clock's behalf. But this is fool'ry.
Go bid my woman feign a sickness; say
She'll home to her father; and provide me presently
A riding suit, no costlier than would fit
A franklin's huswife.
PISANIO. Madam, you're best consider.
IMOGEN. I see before me, man. Nor here, nor here,
Nor what ensues, but have a fog in them
That I cannot look through. Away, I prithee;
Do as I bid thee. There's no more to say;
Accessible is none but Milford way. *Exeunt*

SCENE 3

Wales. A mountainous country with a cave

Enter from the cave BELARIUS, GUIDERIUS, *and* ARVIRAGUS

BELARIUS. A goodly day not to keep house with such
Whose roof's as low as ours! Stoop, boys; this gate
Instructs you how t' adore the heavens, and bows you
To a morning's holy office. The gates of monarchs
Are arch'd so high that giants may jet through
And keep their impious turbans on without
Good morrow to the sun. Hail, thou fair heaven!
We house i' th' rock, yet use thee not so hardly
As prouder livers do.
GUIDERIUS. Hail, heaven!
ARVIRAGUS. Hail, heaven!
BELARIUS. Now for our mountain sport. Up to yond hill,
Your legs are young; I'll tread these flats. Consider,
When you above perceive me like a crow,
That it is place which lessens and sets off;
And you may then revolve what tales I have told you
Of courts, of princes, of the tricks in war.
This service is not service so being done,

But being so allow'd. To apprehend thus
Draws us a profit from all things we see,
And often to our comfort shall we find
The sharded beetle in a safer hold
Than is the full-wing'd eagle. O, this life
Is nobler than attending for a check,
Richer than doing nothing for a bribe,
Prouder than rustling in unpaid-for silk:
Such gain the cap of him that makes him fine,
Yet keeps his book uncross'd. No life to ours!

GUIDERIUS. Out of your proof you speak. We, poor unfledg'd,
Have never wing'd from view o' th' nest, nor know not
What air's from home. Haply this life is best,
If quiet life be best; sweeter to you
That have a sharper known; well corresponding
With your stiff age. But unto us it is
A cell of ignorance, travelling abed,
A prison for a debtor that not dares
To stride a limit.

ARVIRAGUS. What should we speak of
When we are old as you? When we shall hear
The rain and wind beat dark December, how,
In this our pinching cave, shall we discourse
The freezing hours away? We have seen nothing;
We are beastly: subtle as the fox for prey,
Like warlike as the wolf for what we eat.
Our valour is to chase what flies; our cage
We make a choir, as doth the prison'd bird,
And sing our bondage freely.

BELARIUS. How you speak!
Did you but know the city's usuries,
And felt them knowingly—the art o' th' court,
As hard to leave as keep, whose top to climb
Is certain falling, or so slipp'ry that
The fear's as bad as falling; the toil o' th' war,
A pain that only seems to seek out danger
I' th' name of fame and honour, which dies i' th' search,
And hath as oft a sland'rous epitaph
As record of fair act; nay, many times,

Doth ill deserve by doing well; what's worse–
Must curtsy at the censure. O, boys, this story
The world may read in me; my body's mark'd
With Roman swords, and my report was once
First with the best of note. Cymbeline lov'd me;
And when a soldier was the theme, my name
Was not far off. Then was I as a tree
Whose boughs did bend with fruit; but in one night
A storm, or robbery, call it what you will,
Shook down my mellow hangings, nay, my leaves,
And left me bare to weather.

GUIDERIUS. Uncertain favour!

BELARIUS. My fault being nothing–as I have told you oft–
But that two villains, whose false oaths prevail'd
Before my perfect honour, swore to Cymbeline
I was confederate with the Romans. So
Follow'd my banishment, and this twenty years
This rock and these demesnes have been my world,
Where I have liv'd at honest freedom, paid
More pious debts to heaven than in all
The fore-end of my time. But up to th' mountains!
This is not hunters' language. He that strikes
The venison first shall be the lord o' th' feast;
To him the other two shall minister;
And we will fear no poison, which attends
In place of greater state. I'll meet you in the valleys.

Exeunt GUIDERIUS *and* ARVIRAGUS

How hard it is to hide the sparks of nature!
These boys know little they are sons to th' King,
Nor Cymbeline dreams that they are alive.
They think they are mine; and though train'd up thus meanly
I' th' cave wherein they bow, their thoughts do hit
The roofs of palaces, and nature prompts them
In simple and low things to prince it much
Beyond the trick of others. This Polydore,
The heir of Cymbeline and Britain, who
The King his father call'd Guiderius–Jove!
When on my three-foot stool I sit and tell
The warlike feats I have done, his spirits fly out

Into my story; say 'Thus mine enemy fell,
And thus I set my foot on's neck'; even then
The princely blood flows in his cheek, he sweats,
Strains his young nerves, and puts himself in posture
That acts my words. The younger brother, Cadwal,
Once Arviragus, in as like a figure
Strikes life into my speech, and shows much more
His own conceiving. Hark, the game is rous'd!
O Cymbeline, heaven and my conscience knows
Thou didst unjustly banish me! Whereon,
At three and two years old, I stole these babes,
Thinking to bar thee of succession as
Thou refts me of my lands. Euriphile,
Thou wast their nurse; they took thee for their mother,
And every day do honour to her grave.
Myself, Belarius, that am Morgan call'd,
They take for natural father. The game is up. *Exit*

SCENE 4

Wales, near Milford Haven

Enter PISANIO *and* IMOGEN

IMOGEN. Thou told'st me, when we came from horse, the place
Was near at hand. Ne'er long'd my mother so
To see me first as I have now. Pisanio! Man!
Where is Posthumus? What is in thy mind
That makes thee stare thus? Wherefore breaks that sigh
From th' inward of thee? One but painted thus
Would be interpreted a thing perplex'd
Beyond self-explication. Put thyself
Into a haviour of less fear, ere wildness
Vanquish my staider senses. What's the matter?
Why tender'st thou that paper to me with
A look untender! If't be summer news,
Smile to't before; if winterly, thou need'st
But keep that count'nance still. My husband's hand?
That drug-damn'd Italy hath out-craftied him,

And he's at some hard point. Speak, man; thy tongue
May take off some extremity, which to read
Would be even mortal to me.

PISANIO. Please you read,
And you shall find me, wretched man, a thing
The most disdain'd of fortune.

IMOGEN. [*Reads*] 'Thy mistress, Pisanio, hath play'd the strumpet in my bed, the testimonies whereof lie bleeding in me. I speak not out of weak surmises, but from proof as strong as my grief and as certain as I expect my revenge. That part thou, Pisanio, must act for me, if thy faith be not tainted with the breach of hers. Let thine own hands take away her life; I shall give thee opportunity at Milford Haven; she hath my letter for the purpose; where, if thou fear to strike, and to make me certain it is done, thou art the pander to her dishonour, and equally to me disloyal.'

PISANIO. What shall I need to draw my sword? The paper
Hath cut her throat already. No, 'tis slander,
Whose edge is sharper than the sword, whose tongue
Outvenoms all the worms of Nile, whose breath
Rides on the posting winds and doth belie
All corners of the world. Kings, queens, and states,
Maids, matrons, nay, the secrets of the grave,
This viperous slander enters. What cheer, madam?

IMOGEN. False to his bed? What is it to be false?
To lie in watch there, and to think on him?
To weep twixt clock and clock? If sleep charge nature,
To break it with a fearful dream of him,
And cry myself awake? That's false to's bed,
Is it?

PISANIO. Alas, good lady!

IMOGEN. I false! Thy conscience witness! Iachimo,
Thou didst accuse him of incontinency;
Thou then look'dst like a villain; now, methinks,
Thy favour's good enough. Some jay of Italy,
Whose mother was her painting, hath betray'd him.
Poor I am stale, a garment out of fashion,
And for I am richer than to hang by th' walls
I must be ripp'd. To pieces with me! O,

Men's vows are women's traitors! All good seeming,
By thy revolt, O husband, shall be thought
Put on for villainy; not born where't grows,
But worn a bait for ladies.

PISANIO. Good madam, hear me.

IMOGEN. True honest men being heard, like false Æneas,
Were, in his time, thought false; and Sinon's weeping
Did scandal many a holy tear, took pity
From most true wretchedness. So thou, Posthumus,
Wilt lay the leaven on all proper men:
Goodly and gallant shall be false and perjur'd
From thy great fail. Come, fellow, be thou honest;
Do thou thy master's bidding; when thou seest him,
A little witness my obedience. Look!
I draw the sword myself; take it, and hit
The innocent mansion of my love, my heart.
Fear not; 'tis empty of all things but grief;
Thy master is not there, who was indeed
The riches of it. Do his bidding; strike.
Thou mayst be valiant in a better cause,
But now thou seem'st a coward.

PISANIO. Hence, vile instrument!
Thou shalt not damn my hand.

IMOGEN. Why, I must die;
And if I do not by thy hand, thou art
No servant of thy master's. Against self-slaughter
There is a prohibition so divine
That cravens my weak hand. Come, here's my heart–
Something's afore't. Soft, soft! we'll no defence!–
Obedient as the scabbard. What is here?
The scriptures of the loyal Leonatus
All turn'd to heresy? Away, away,
Corrupters of my faith! you shall no more
Be stomachers to my heart. Thus may poor fools
Believe false teachers; though those that are betray'd
Do feel the treason sharply, yet the traitor
Stands in worse case of woe. And thou, Posthumus,
That didst set up my disobedience 'gainst the King
My father, and make me put into contempt the suits
Of princely fellows, shalt hereafter find

It is no act of common passage but
A strain of rareness; and I grieve myself
To think, when thou shalt be disedg'd by her
That now thou tirest on, how thy memory
Will then be pang'd by me. Prithee dispatch.
The lamp entreats the butcher. Where's thy knife?
Thou art too slow to do thy master's bidding,
When I desire it too.

PISANIO. O gracious lady,
Since I receiv'd command to do this business
I have not slept one wink.

IMOGEN. Do't, and to bed then.

PISANIO. I'll wake mine eyeballs first.

IMOGEN. Wherefore then
Didst undertake it? Why hast thou abus'd
So many miles with a pretence? This place?
Mine action and thine own? our horses' labour?
The time inviting thee? the perturb'd court,
For my being absent?—whereunto I never
Purpose return. Why hast thou gone so far
To be unbent when thou hast ta'en thy stand,
Th' elected deer before thee?

PISANIO. But to win time
To lose so bad employment, in the which
I have consider'd of a course. Good lady,
Hear me with patience.

IMOGEN. Talk thy tongue weary—speak.
I have heard I am a strumpet, and mine ear,
Therein false struck, can take no greater wound,
Nor tent to bottom that. But speak.

PISANIO. Then, madam,
I thought you would not back again.

IMOGEN. Most like—
Bringing me here to kill me.

PISANIO. Not so, neither;
But if I were as wise as honest, then
My purpose would prove well. It cannot be
But that my master is abus'd. Some villain,
Ay, and singular in his art, hath done you both
This cursed injury.

IMOGEN. Some Roman courtezan!
PISANIO. No, on my life!
I'll give but notice you are dead, and send him
Some bloody sign of it, for 'tis commanded
I should do so. You shall be miss'd at court,
And that will well confirm it.
IMOGEN. Why, good fellow,
What shall I do the while? where bide? how live?
Or in my life what comfort, when I am
Dead to my husband?
PISANIO. If you'll back to th' court–
IMOGEN. No court, no father, nor no more ado
With that harsh, noble, simple nothing–
That Cloten, whose love-suit hath been to me
As fearful as a siege.
PISANIO. If not at court,
Then not in Britain must you bide.
IMOGEN. Where then?
Hath Britain all the sun that shines? Day, night,
Are they not but in Britain? I' th' world's volume
Our Britain seems as of it, but not in't;
In a great pool a swan's nest. Prithee think
There's livers out of Britain.
PISANIO. I am most glad
You think of other place. Th' ambassador,
Lucius the Roman, comes to Milford Haven
To-morrow. Now, if you could wear a mind
Dark as your fortune is, and but disguise
That which t' appear itself must not yet be
But by self-danger, you should tread a course
Pretty and full of view; yea, happily, near
The residence of Posthumus; so nigh, at least,
That though his actions were not visible, yet
Report should render him hourly to your ear
As truly as he moves.
IMOGEN. O! for such means,
Though peril to my modesty, not death on't,
I would adventure.
PISANIO. Well then, here's the point:
You must forget to be a woman; change

Command into obedience; fear and niceness–
The handmaids of all women, or, more truly,
Woman it pretty self–into a waggish courage;
Ready in gibes, quick-answer'd, saucy, and
As quarrelous as the weasel. Nay, you must
Forget that rarest treasure of your cheek,
Exposing it–but, O, the harder heart!
Alack, no remedy!–to the greedy touch
Of common-kissing Titan, and forget
Your laboursome and dainty trims wherein
You made great Juno angry.

IMOGEN. Nay, be brief;
I see into thy end, and am almost
A man already.

PISANIO. First, make yourself but like one.
Fore-thinking this, I have already fit–
'Tis in my cloak-bag–doublet, hat, hose, all
That answer to them. Would you, in their serving,
And with what imitation you can borrow
From youth of such a season, fore noble Lucius
Present yourself, desire his service, tell him
Wherein you're happy–which will make him know
If that his head have ear in music; doubtless
With joy he will embrace you; for he's honourable,
And, doubling that, most holy. Your means abroad–
You have me, rich; and I will never fail
Beginning nor supplyment.

IMOGEN. Thou art all the comfort
The gods will diet me with. Prithee away!
There's more to be consider'd; but we'll even
All that good time will give us. This attempt
I am soldier to, and will abide it with
A prince's courage. Away, I prithee.

PISANIO. Well, madam, we must take a short farewell,
Lest, being miss'd, I be suspected of
Your carriage from the court. My noble mistress,
Here is a box; I had it from the Queen.
What's in't is precious. If you are sick at sea
Or stomach-qualm'd at land, a dram of this
Will drive away distemper. To some shade,

And fit you to your manhood. May the gods
Direct you to the best!
IMOGEN. Amen. I thank thee. *Exeunt severally*

SCENE 5

Britain. CYMBELINE'S *palace*

Enter CYMBELINE, QUEEN, CLOTEN, LUCIUS, *and* LORDS

CYMBELINE. Thus far; and so farewell.
LUCIUS. Thanks, royal sir.
My emperor hath wrote; I must from hence,
And am right sorry that I must report ye
My master's enemy.
CYMBELINE. Our subjects, sir,
Will not endure his yoke; and for ourself
To show less sovereignty than they, must needs
Appear unkinglike.
LUCIUS. So, sir. I desire of you
A conduct overland to Milford Haven.
Madam, all joy befall your Grace, and you!
CYMBELINE. My lords, you are appointed for that office;
The due of honour in no point omit.
So farewell, noble Lucius.
LUCIUS. Your hand, my lord.
CLOTEN. Receive it friendly; but from this time forth
I wear it as your enemy.
LUCIUS. Sir, the event
Is yet to name the winner. Fare you well.
CYMBELINE. Leave not the worthy Lucius, good my lords,
Till he have cross'd the Severn. Happiness!
Exeunt LUCIUS *and* LORDS
QUEEN. He goes hence frowning; but it honours us
That we have given him cause.
CLOTEN. 'Tis all the better;
Your valiant Britons have their wishes in it.
CYMBELINE. Lucius hath wrote already to the Emperor
How it goes here. It fits us therefore ripely
Our chariots and our horsemen be in readiness.

The pow'rs that he already hath in Gallia
Will soon be drawn to head, from whence he moves
His war for Britain.

QUEEN. 'Tis not sleepy business,
But must be look'd to speedily and strongly.

CYMBELINE. Our expectation that it would be thus
Hath made us forward. But, my gentle queen,
Where is our daughter? She hath not appear'd
Before the Roman, nor to us hath tender'd
The duty of the day. She looks us like
A thing more made of malice than of duty;
We have noted it. Call her before us, for
We have been too slight in sufferance. *Exit a* MESSENGER

QUEEN. Royal sir,
Since the exile of Posthumus, most retir'd
Hath her life been; the cure whereof, my lord,
'Tis time must do. Beseech your Majesty,
Forbear sharp speeches to her; she's a lady
So tender of rebukes that words are strokes,
And strokes death to her.

Re-enter MESSENGER

CYMBELINE. Where is she, sir? How
Can her contempt be answer'd?

MESSENGER. Please you, sir,
Her chambers are all lock'd, and there's no answer
That will be given to th' loud of noise we make.

QUEEN. My lord, when last I went to visit her,
She pray'd me to excuse her keeping close;
Whereto constrain'd by her infirmity
She should that duty leave unpaid to you
Which daily she was bound to proffer. This
She wish'd me to make known; but our great court
Made me to blame in memory.

CYMBELINE. Her doors lock'd?
Not seen of late? Grant, heavens, that which I fear
Prove false! *Exit*

QUEEN. Son, I say, follow the King.

CLOTEN. That man of hers, Pisanio, her old servant,
I have not seen these two days.

QUEEN. Go, look after. *Exit* CLOTEN
Pisanio, thou that stand'st so for Posthumus!
He hath a drug of mine. I pray his absence
Proceed by swallowing that; for he believes
It is a thing most precious. But for her,
Where is she gone? Haply despair hath seiz'd her;
Or, wing'd with fervour of her love, she's flown
To her desir'd Posthumus. Gone she is
To death or to dishonour, and my end
Can make good use of either. She being down,
I have the placing of the British crown.

Re-enter CLOTEN

How now, my son?
CLOTEN. 'Tis certain she is fled.
Go in and cheer the King. He rages; none
Dare come about him.
QUEEN. All the better. May
This night forestall him of the coming day! *Exit*
CLOTEN. I love and hate her; for she's fair and royal,
And that she hath all courtly parts more exquisite
Than lady, ladies, woman. From every one
The best she hath, and she, of all compounded,
Outsells them all. I love her therefore; but
Disdaining me and throwing favours on
The low Posthumus slanders so her judgment
That what's else rare is chok'd; and in that point
I will conclude to hate her, nay, indeed,
To be reveng'd upon her. For when fools
Shall–

Enter PISANIO

Who is here? What, are you packing, sirrah?
Come hither. Ah, you precious pander! Villain,
Where is thy lady? In a word, or else
Thou art straightway with the fiends.
PISANIO. O good my lord!
CLOTEN. Where is thy lady? or, by Jupiter–
I will not ask again. Close villain,
I'll have this secret from thy heart, or rip
Thy heart to find it. Is she with Posthumus?

From whose so many weights of baseness cannot
A dram of worth be drawn.

PISANIO. Alas, my lord,
How can she be with him? When was she miss'd?
He is in Rome.

CLOTEN. Where is she, sir? Come nearer.
No farther halting! Satisfy me home
What is become of her.

PISANIO. O my all-worthy lord!

CLOTEN. All-worthy villain!
Discover where thy mistress is at once,
At the next word. No more of 'worthy lord'!
Speak, or thy silence on the instant is
Thy condemnation and thy death.

PISANIO. Then, sir,
This paper is the history of my knowledge
Touching her flight. [*Presenting a letter*]

CLOTEN. Let's see't. I will pursue her
Even to Augustus' throne.

PISANIO. [*Aside*] Or this or perish.
She's far enough; and what he learns by this
May prove his travel, not her danger.

CLOTEN. Humh!

PISANIO. [*Aside*] I'll write to my lord she's dead. O Imogen,
Safe mayst thou wander, safe return again!

CLOTEN. Sirrah, is this letter true?

PISANIO. Sir, as I think.

CLOTEN. It is Posthumus' hand; I know't. Sirrah, if thou wouldst not be a villain, but do me true service, undergo those employments wherein I should have cause to use thee with a serious industry—that is, what villainy soe'er I bid thee do, to perform it directly and truly—I would think thee an honest man; thou shouldst neither want my means for thy relief nor my voice for thy preferment.

PISANIO. Well, my good lord.

CLOTEN. Wilt thou serve me? For since patiently and constantly thou hast stuck to the bare fortune of that beggar Posthumus, thou canst not, in the course of gratitude, but be a diligent follower of mine. Wilt thou serve me?

PISANIO. Sir, I will.

CLOTEN. Give me thy hand; here's my purse. Hast any of thy late master's garments in thy possession?

PISANIO. I have, my lord, at my lodging, the same suit he wore when he took leave of my lady and mistress.

CLOTEN. The first service thou dost me, fetch that suit hither. Let it be thy first service; go.

PISANIO. I shall, my lord. *Exit*

CLOTEN. Meet thee at Milford Haven! I forgot to ask him one thing; I'll remember't anon. Even there, thou villain Posthumus, will I kill thee. I would these garments were come. She said upon a time—the bitterness of it I now belch from my heart—that she held the very garment of Posthumus in more respect than my noble and natural person, together with the adornment of my qualities. With that suit upon my back will I ravish her; first kill him, and in her eyes. There shall she see my valour, which will then be a torment to her contempt. He on the ground, my speech of insultment ended on his dead body, and when my lust hath dined—which, as I say, to vex her I will execute in the clothes that she so prais'd—to the court I'll knock her back, foot her home again. She hath despis'd me rejoicingly, and I'll be merry in my revenge.

Re-enter PISANIO, *with the clothes*

Be those the garments?

PISANIO. Ay, my noble lord.

CLOTEN. How long is't since she went to Milford Haven?

PISANIO. She can scarce be there yet.

CLOTEN. Bring this apparel to my chamber; that is the second thing that I have commanded thee. The third is that thou wilt be a voluntary mute to my design. Be but duteous and true, preferment shall tender itself to thee. My revenge is now at Milford, would I had wings to follow it! Come, and be true. *Exit*

PISANIO. Thou bid'st me to my loss; for true to thee
Were to prove false, which I will never be,
To him that is most true. To Milford go,
And find not her whom thou pursuest. Flow, flow,
You heavenly blessings, on her! This fool's speed
Be cross'd with slowness! Labour be his meed! *Exit*

SCENE 6

Wales. Before the cave of BELARIUS

Enter IMOGEN *alone, in boy's clothes*

IMOGEN. I see a man's life is a tedious one.
I have tir'd myself, and for two nights together
Have made the ground my bed. I should be sick
But that my resolution helps me. Milford,
When from the mountain-top Pisanio show'd thee,
Thou wast within a ken. O Jove! I think
Foundations fly the wretched; such, I mean,
Where they should be reliev'd. Two beggars told me
I could not miss my way. Will poor folks lie,
That have afflictions on them, knowing 'tis
A punishment or trial? Yes; no wonder,
When rich ones scarce tell true. To lapse in fulness
Is sorer than to lie for need; and falsehood
Is worse in kings than beggars. My dear lord!
Thou art one o' th' false ones. Now I think on thee
My hunger's gone; but even before, I was
At point to sink for food. But what is this?
Here is a path to't; 'tis some savage hold.
I were best not call; I dare not call. Yet famine,
Ere clean it o'erthrow nature, makes it valiant.
Plenty and peace breeds cowards; hardness ever
Of hardiness is mother. Ho! who's here?
If anything that's civil, speak; if savage,
Take or lend. Ho! No answer? Then I'll enter.
Best draw my sword; and if mine enemy
But fear the sword, like me, he'll scarcely look on't.
Such a foe, good heavens! *Exit into the cave*

Enter BELARIUS, GUIDERIUS, *and* ARVIRAGUS

BELARIUS. You, Polydore, have prov'd best woodman and
Are master of the feast. Cadwal and I
Will play the cook and servant; 'tis our match.
The sweat of industry would dry and die
But for the end it works to. Come, our stomachs

Will make what's homely savoury; weariness
Can snore upon the flint, when resty sloth
Finds the down pillow hard. Now, peace be here,
Poor house, that keep'st thyself!

GUIDERIUS. I am thoroughly weary.

ARVIRAGUS. I am weak with toil, yet strong in appetite.

GUIDERIUS. There is cold meat i' th' cave; we'll browse on that
Whilst what we have kill'd be cook'd.

BELARIUS. [*Looking into the cave*] Stay, come not in.
But that it eats our victuals, I should think
Here were a fairy.

GUIDERIUS. What's the matter, sir?

BELARIUS. By Jupiter, an angel! or, if not,
An earthly paragon! Behold divineness
No elder than a boy!

Re-enter IMOGEN

IMOGEN. Good masters, harm me not.
Before I enter'd here I call'd, and thought
To have begg'd or bought what I have took. Good troth,
I have stol'n nought; nor would not though I had found
Gold strew'd i' th' floor. Here's money for my meat.
I would have left it on the board, so soon
As I had made my meal, and parted
With pray'rs for the provider.

GUIDERIUS. Money, youth?

ARVIRAGUS. All gold and silver rather turn to dirt,
As 'tis no better reckon'd but of those
Who worship dirty gods.

IMOGEN. I see you're angry.
Know, if you kill me for my fault, I should
Have died had I not made it.

BELARIUS. Whither bound?

IMOGEN. To Milford Haven.

BELARIUS. What's your name?

IMOGEN. Fidele, sir. I have a kinsman who
Is bound for Italy; he embark'd at Milford;
To whom being going, almost spent with hunger,
I am fall'n in this offence.

BELARIUS. Prithee, fair youth,
Think us no churls, nor measure our good minds
By this rude place we live in. Well encounter'd!
'Tis almost night; you shall have better cheer
Ere you depart, and thanks to stay and eat it.
Boys, bid him welcome.
GUIDERIUS. Were you a woman, youth,
I should woo hard but be your groom. In honesty
I bid for you as I'd buy.
ARVIRAGUS. I'll make't my comfort
He is a man. I'll love him as my brother;
And such a welcome as I'd give to him
After long absence, such is yours. Most welcome!
Be sprightly, for you fall 'mongst friends.
IMOGEN. 'Mongst friends,
If brothers. [*Aside*] Would it had been so that they
Had been my father's sons! Then had my prize
Been less, and so more equal ballasting
To thee, Posthumus.
BELARIUS. He wrings at some distress.
GUIDERIUS. Would I could free't!
ARVIRAGUS. Or I, whate'er it be,
What pain it cost, what danger! Gods!
BELARIUS. [*Whispering*] Hark, boys.
IMOGEN. [*Aside*] Great men,
That had a court no bigger than this cave,
That did attend themselves, and had the virtue
Which their own conscience seal'd them, laying by
That nothing-gift of differing multitudes,
Could not out-peer these twain. Pardon me, gods!
I'd change my sex to be companion with them,
Since Leonatus' false.
BELARIUS. It shall be so.
Boys, we'll go dress our hunt. Fair youth, come in.
Discourse is heavy, fasting; when we have supp'd,
We'll mannerly demand thee of thy story,
So far as thou wilt speak it.
GUIDERIUS. Pray draw near.
ARVIRAGUS. The night to th' owl and morn to th' lark less welcome.

IMOGEN. Thanks, sir.
ARVIRAGUS. I pray draw near. *Exeunt*

SCENE 7

Rome. A public place

Enter two ROMAN SENATORS *and* TRIBUNES

FIRST SENATOR. This is the tenour of the Emperor's writ:
That since the common men are now in action
'Gainst the Pannonians and Dalmatians,
And that the legions now in Gallia are
Full weak to undertake our wars against
The fall'n-off Britons, that we do incite
The gentry to this business. He creates
Lucius proconsul; and to you, the tribunes,
For this immediate levy, he commands
His absolute commission. Long live Cæsar!
TRIBUNE. Is Lucius general of the forces?
SECOND SENATOR. Ay.
TRIBUNE. Remaining now in Gallia?
FIRST SENATOR. With those legions
Which I have spoke of, whereunto your levy
Must be supplyant. The words of your commission
Will tie you to the numbers and the time
Of their dispatch.
TRIBUNE. We will discharge our duty. *Exeunt*

ACT IV. SCENE 1

Wales. Near the cave of BELARIUS

Enter CLOTEN *alone*

CLOTEN. I am near to th' place where they should meet, if Pisanio have mapp'd it truly. How fit his garments serve me! Why should his mistress, who was made by him that made the tailor, not be fit too? The rather—saving reverence of the word–for 'tis said a woman's fitness comes by fits. Therein I must play the workman. I dare speak it to myself, for it is not vain-glory for a man and his glass to confer in his own chamber–I mean, the lines of my body are as well drawn as his; no less young, more strong, not beneath him in fortunes, beyond him in the advantage of the time, above him in birth, alike conversant in general services, and more remarkable in single oppositions. Yet this imperceiverant thing loves him in my despite. What mortality is! Posthumus, thy head, which now is growing upon thy shoulders, shall within this hour be off; thy mistress enforced; thy garments cut to pieces before her face; and all this done, spurn her home to her father, who may, haply, be a little angry for my so rough usage; but my mother, having power of his testiness, shall turn all into my commendations. My horse is tied up safe. Out, sword, and to a sore purpose! Fortune, put them into my hand. This is the very description of their meeting-place; and the fellow dares not deceive me. *Exit*

SCENE 2

Wales. Before the cave of BELARIUS

Enter, from the cave, BELARIUS, GUIDERIUS, ARVIRAGUS, *and* IMOGEN

BELARIUS. [*To* IMOGEN] You are not well. Remain here in the cave;
We'll come to you after hunting.
ARVIRAGUS. [*To* IMOGEN] Brother, stay here.
Are we not brothers?
IMOGEN. So man and man should be;
But clay and clay differs in dignity,
Whose dust is both alike. I am very sick.
GUIDERIUS. Go you to hunting; I'll abide with him.
IMOGEN. So sick I am not, yet I am not well;
But not so citizen a wanton as
To seem to die ere sick. So please you, leave me;
Stick to your journal course. The breach of custom

Is breach of all. I am ill, but your being by me
Cannot amend me; society is no comfort
To one not sociable. I am not very sick,
Since I can reason of it. Pray you trust me here.
I'll rob none but myself; and let me die,
Stealing so poorly.

GUIDERIUS. I love thee; I have spoke it.
How much the quantity, the weight as much
As I do love my father.

BELARIUS. What? how? how?

ARVIRAGUS. If it be sin to say so, sir, I yoke me
In my good brother's fault. I know not why
I love this youth, and I have heard you say
Love's reason's without reason. The bier at door,
And a demand who is't shall die, I'd say
'My father, not this youth.'

BELARIUS. [*Aside*] O noble strain!
O worthiness of nature! breed of greatness!
Cowards father cowards and base things sire base.
Nature hath meal and bran, contempt and grace.
I'm not their father; yet who this should be
Doth miracle itself, lov'd before me.–
'Tis the ninth hour o' th' morn.

ARVIRAGUS. Brother, farewell.

IMOGEN. I wish ye sport.

ARVIRAGUS. Your health. [*To* BELARIUS] So please you, sir.

IMOGEN. [*Aside*] These are kind creatures. Gods, what lies I have heard!
Our courtiers say all's savage but at court.
Experience, O, thou disprov'st report!
Th' imperious seas breed monsters; for the dish,
Poor tributary rivers as sweet fish.
I am sick still; heart-sick. Pisanio,
I'll now taste of thy drug. [*Swallows some*]

GUIDERIUS. I could not stir him.
He said he was gentle, but unfortunate;
Dishonestly afflicted, but yet honest.

ARVIRAGUS. Thus did he answer me; yet said hereafter
I might know more.

BELARIUS. To th' field, to th' field!

We'll leave you for this time. Go in and rest.
ARVIRAGUS. We'll not be long away.
BELARIUS. Pray be not sick,
For you must be our huswife.
IMOGEN. Well, or ill,
I am bound to you.
BELARIUS. And shalt be ever. *Exit* IMOGEN *into the cave*
This youth, howe'er distress'd, appears he hath had
Good ancestors.
ARVIRAGUS. How angel-like he sings!
GUIDERIUS. But his neat cookery! He cut our roots in characters,
And sauc'd our broths as Juno had been sick,
And he her dieter.
ARVIRAGUS. Nobly he yokes
A smiling with a sigh, as if the sigh
Was that it was for not being such a smile;
The smile mocking the sigh that it would fly
From so divine a temple to commix
With winds that sailors rail at.
GUIDERIUS. I do note
That grief and patience, rooted in him both,
Mingle their spurs together.
ARVIRAGUS. Grow patience!
And let the stinking elder, grief, untwine
His perishing root with the increasing vine!
BELARIUS. It is great morning. Come, away! Who's there?

Enter CLOTEN

CLOTEN. I cannot find those runagates; that villain
Hath mock'd me. I am faint.
BELARIUS. Those runagates?
Means he not us? I partly know him; 'tis
Cloten, the son o' th' Queen. I fear some ambush.
I saw him not these many years, and yet
I know 'tis he. We are held as outlaws. Hence!
GUIDERIUS. He is but one; you and my brother search
What companies are near. Pray you away;
Let me alone with him. *Exeunt* BELARIUS *and* ARVIRAGUS
CLOTEN. Soft! What are you

That fly me thus? Some villain mountaineers?
I have heard of such. What slave art thou?

GUIDERIUS. A thing
More slavish did I ne'er than answering
'A slave' without a knock.

CLOTEN. Thou art a robber,
A law-breaker, a villain. Yield thee, thief.

GUIDERIUS. To who? To thee? What art thou? Have not I
An arm as big as thine, a heart as big?
Thy words, I grant, are bigger, for I wear not
My dagger in my mouth. Say what thou art;
Why I should yield to thee.

CLOTEN. Thou villain base,
Know'st me not by my clothes?

GUIDERIUS. No, nor thy tailor, rascal,
Who is thy grandfather; he made those clothes,
Which, as it seems, make thee.

CLOTEN. Thou precious varlet,
My tailor made them not.

GUIDERIUS. Hence, then, and thank
The man that gave them thee. Thou art some fool;
I am loath to beat thee.

CLOTEN. Thou injurious thief,
Hear but my name, and tremble.

GUIDERIUS. What's thy name?

CLOTEN. Cloten, thou villain.

GUIDERIUS. Cloten, thou double villain, be thy name,
I cannot tremble at it. Were it toad, or adder, spider,
'Twould move me sooner.

CLOTEN. To thy further fear,
Nay, to thy mere confusion, thou shalt know
I am son to th' Queen.

GUIDERIUS. I'm sorry for't; not seeming
So worthy as thy birth.

CLOTEN. Art not afeard?

GUIDERIUS. Those that I reverence, those I fear—the wise:
At fools I laugh, not fear them.

CLOTEN. Die the death.
When I have slain thee with my proper hand,
I'll follow those that even now fled hence,

And on the gates of Lud's Town set your heads.
Yield, rustic mountaineer. *Exeunt, fighting*

Re-enter BELARIUS *and* ARVIRAGUS

BELARIUS. No company's abroad.
ARVIRAGUS. None in the world; you did mistake him, sure.
BELARIUS. I cannot tell; long is it since I saw him,
But time hath nothing blurr'd those lines of favour
Which then he wore; the snatches in his voice,
And burst of speaking, were as his. I am absolute
'Twas very Cloten.
ARVIRAGUS. In this place we left them.
I wish my brother make good time with him,
You say he is so fell.
BELARIUS. Being scarce made up,
I mean to man, he had not apprehension
Or roaring terrors; for defect of judgment
Is oft the cease of fear.

Re-enter GUIDERIUS *with* CLOTEN'S *head*

But, see, thy brother.
GUIDERIUS. This Cloten was a fool, an empty purse;
There was no money in't. Not Hercules
Could have knock'd out his brains, for he had none;
Yet I not doing this, the fool had borne
My head as I do his.
BELARIUS. What hast thou done?
GUIDERIUS. I am perfect what: cut off one Cloten's head,
Son to the Queen, after his own report;
Who call'd me traitor, mountaineer, and swore
With his own single hand he'd take us in,
Displace our heads where—thank the gods!—they grow,
And set them on Lud's Town.
BELARIUS. We are all undone.
GUIDERIUS. Why, worthy father, what have we to lose
But that he swore to take, our lives? The law
Protects not us; then why should we be tender
To let an arrogant piece of flesh threat us,
Play judge and executioner all himself,
For we do fear the law? What company

Discover you abroad?

BELARIUS. No single soul
Can we set eye on, but in all safe reason
He must have some attendants. Though his humour
Was nothing but mutation—ay, and that
From one bad thing to worse—not frenzy, not
Absolute madness could so far have rav'd,
To bring him here alone. Although perhaps
It may be heard at court that such as we
Cave here, hunt here, are outlaws, and in time
May make some stronger head—the which he hearing,
As it is like him, might break out and swear
He'd fetch us in; yet is't not probable
To come alone, either he so undertaking
Or they so suffering. Then on good ground we fear,
If we do fear this body hath a tail
More perilous than the head.

ARVIRAGUS. Let ordinance
Come as the gods foresay it. Howsoe'er,
My brother hath done well.

BELARIUS. I had no mind
To hunt this day; the boy Fidele's sickness
Did make my way long forth.

GUIDERIUS. With his own sword,
Which he did wave against my throat, I have ta'en
His head from him. I'll throw't into the creek
Behind our rock, and let it to the sea
And tell the fishes he's the Queen's son, Cloten.
That's all I reck. *Exit*

BELARIUS. I fear 'twill be reveng'd.
Would, Polydore, thou hadst not done't! though valour
Becomes thee well enough.

ARVIRAGUS. Would I had done't,
So the revenge alone pursu'd me! Polydore,
I love thee brotherly, but envy much
Thou hast robb'd me of this deed. I would revenges,
That possible strength might meet, would seek us through,
And put us to our answer.

BELARIUS. Well, 'tis done.
We'll hunt no more to-day, nor seek for danger

Where there's no profit. I prithee to our rock.
You and Fidele play the cooks; I'll stay
Till hasty Polydore return, and bring him
To dinner presently.

ARVIRAGUS. Poor sick Fidele!
I'll willingly to him; to gain his colour
I'd let a parish of such Cloten's blood,
And praise myself for charity. *Exit*

BELARIUS. O thou goddess,
Thou divine Nature, thou thyself thou blazon'st
In these two princely boys! They are as gentle
As zephyrs blowing below the violet,
Not wagging his sweet head; and yet as rough,
Their royal blood enchaf'd, as the rud'st wind
That by the top doth take the mountain pine
And make him stoop to th' vale. 'Tis wonder
That an invisible instinct should frame them
To royalty unlearn'd, honour untaught,
Civility not seen from other, valour
That wildly grows in them, but yields a crop
As if it had been sow'd. Yet still it's strange
What Cloten's being here to us portends,
Or what his death will bring us.

Re-enter GUIDERIUS

GUIDERIUS. Where's my brother?
I have sent Cloten's clotpoll down the stream,
In embassy to his mother; his body's hostage
For his return. [*Solemn music*]

BELARIUS. My ingenious instrument!
Hark, Polydore, it sounds. But what occasion
Hath Cadwal now to give it motion? Hark!

GUIDERIUS. Is he at home?

BELARIUS. He went hence even now.

GUIDERIUS. What does he mean? Since death of my dear'st mother
It did not speak before. All solemn things
Should answer solemn accidents. The matter?
Triumphs for nothing and lamenting toys
Is jollity for apes and grief for boys.

ARVIRAGUS. *The bird is dead*
That we have made so much on. I had rather
Have skipp'd from sixteen years of age to sixty,
To have turn'd my leaping time into a crutch,
Than have seen this.
GUIDERIUS. *O sweetest, fairest lily!*
My brother wears thee not the one half so well
As when thou grew'st thyself.
(ACT IV. Scene 2)

Is Cadwal mad?

Re-enter ARVIRAGUS, *with* IMOGEN *as dead, bearing her in his arms*

BELARIUS. Look, here he comes,
And brings the dire occasion in his arms
Of what we blame him for!
ARVIRAGUS. The bird is dead
That we have made so much on. I had rather
Have skipp'd from sixteen years of age to sixty,
To have turn'd my leaping time into a crutch,
Than have seen this.
GUIDERIUS. O sweetest, fairest lily!
My brother wears thee not the one half so well
As when thou grew'st thyself.
BELARIUS. O melancholy!
Who ever yet could sound thy bottom? find
The ooze to show what coast thy sluggish crare
Might'st easiliest harbour in? Thou blessed thing!
Jove knows what man thou mightst have made; but I,
Thou diedst, a most rare boy, of melancholy.
How found you him?
ARVIRAGUS. Stark, as you see;
Thus smiling, as some fly had tickled slumber,
Not as death's dart, being laugh'd at; his right cheek
Reposing on a cushion.
GUIDERIUS. Where?
ARVIRAGUS. O' th' floor;
His arms thus leagu'd. I thought he slept, and put
My clouted brogues from off my feet, whose rudeness
Answer'd my steps too loud.
GUIDERIUS. Why, he but sleeps.
If he be gone he'll make his grave a bed;
With female fairies will his tomb be haunted,
And worms will not come to thee.
ARVIRAGUS. With fairest flowers,
Whilst summer lasts and I live here, Fidele,
I'll sweeten thy sad grave. Thou shalt not lack
The flower that's like thy face, pale primrose; nor
The azur'd hare-bell, like thy veins; no, nor

The leaf of eglantine, whom not to slander,
Out-sweet'ned not thy breath. The ruddock would,
With charitable bill—O bill, sore shaming
Those rich-left heirs that let their fathers lie
Without a monument!—bring thee all this;
Yea, and furr'd moss besides, when flow'rs are none,
To winter-ground thy corse—

GUIDERIUS. Prithee have done,
And do not play in wench-like words with that
Which is so serious. Let us bury him,
And not protract with admiration what
Is now due debt. To th' grave.

ARVIRAGUS. Say, where shall's lay him?

GUIDERIUS. By good Euriphile, our mother.

ARVIRAGUS. Be't so;
And let us, Polydore, though now our voices
Have got the mannish crack, sing him to th' ground,
As once to our mother; use like note and words,
Save that Euriphile must be Fidele.

GUIDERIUS. Cadwal,
I cannot sing. I'll weep, and word it with thee;
For notes of sorrow out of tune are worse
Than priests and fanes that lie.

ARVIRAGUS. We'll speak it, then.

BELARIUS. Great griefs, I see, med'cine the less, for Cloten
Is quite forgot. He was a queen's son, boys;
And though he came our enemy, remember
He was paid for that. Though mean and mighty rotting
Together have one dust, yet reverence—
That angel of the world—doth make distinction
Of place 'tween high and low. Our foe was princely;
And though you took his life, as being our foe,
Yet bury him as a prince.

GUIDERIUS. Pray you fetch him hither.
Thersites' body is as good as Ajax',
When neither are alive.

ARVIRAGUS. If you'll go fetch him,
We'll say our song the whilst. Brother, begin.

Exit BELARIUS

GUIDERIUS. Nay, Cadwal, we must lay his head to th' East;

My father hath a reason for't.

ARVIRAGUS. 'Tis true.

GUIDERIUS. Come on, then, and remove him.

ARVIRAGUS. So. Begin.

SONG

GUIDERIUS. Fear no more the heat o' th' sun
Nor the furious winter's rages;
Thou thy worldly task hast done,
Home art gone, and ta'en thy wages.
Golden lads and girls all must,
As chimney-sweepers, come to dust.

ARVIRAGUS. Fear no more the frown o' th' great;
Thou art past the tyrant's stroke.
Care no more to clothe and eat;
To thee the reed is as the oak.
The sceptre, learning, physic, must
All follow this and come to dust.

GUIDERIUS. Fear no more the lightning flash,
ARVIRAGUS. Nor th' all-dreaded thunder-stone;
GUIDERIUS. Fear not slander, censure rash;
ARVIRAGUS. Thou hast finish'd joy and moan.
BOTH. All lovers young, all lovers must
Consign to thee and come to dust.

GUIDERIUS. No exorciser harm thee!
ARVIRAGUS. Nor no witchcraft charm thee!
GUIDERIUS. Ghost unlaid forbear thee!
ARVIRAGUS. Nothing ill come near thee!
BOTH. Quiet consummation have,
And renowned be thy grave!

Re-enter BELARIUS *with the body of* CLOTEN

GUIDERIUS. We have done our obsequies. Come, lay him down.

BELARIUS. Here's a few flowers; but 'bout midnight, more.
The herbs that have on them cold dew o' th' night
Are strewings fit'st for graves. Upon their faces.
You were as flow'rs, now wither'd. Even so
These herblets shall which we upon you strew.

Come on, away. Apart upon our knees.
The ground that gave them first has them again.
Their pleasures here are past, so is their pain.

Exeunt all but IMOGEN

IMOGEN. [*Awaking*] Yes, sir, to Milford Haven. Which is the way?
I thank you. By yond bush? Pray, how far thither?
'Ods pittikins! can it be six mile yet?
I have gone all night. Faith, I'll lie down and sleep.
But, soft! no bedfellow. O gods and goddesses!

[*Seeing the body*]

These flow'rs are like the pleasures of the world;
This bloody man, the care on't. I hope I dream;
For so I thought I was a cave-keeper,
And cook to honest creatures. But 'tis not so;
'Twas but a bolt of nothing, shot at nothing,
Which the brain makes of fumes. Our very eyes
Are sometimes, like our judgments, blind. Good faith,
I tremble still with fear; but if there be
Yet left in heaven as small a drop of pity
As a wren's eye, fear'd gods, a part of it!
The dream's here still. Even when I wake it is
Without me, as within me; not imagin'd, felt.
A headless man? The garments of Posthumus?
I know the shape of's leg; this is his hand,
His foot Mercurial, his Martial thigh,
The brawns of Hercules; but his Jovial face—
Murder in heaven! How! 'Tis gone. Pisanio,
All curses madded Hecuba gave the Greeks,
And mine to boot, be darted on thee! Thou,
Conspir'd with that irregulous devil, Cloten,
Hath here cut off my lord. To write and read
Be henceforth treacherous! Damn'd Pisanio
Hath with his forged letters—damn'd Pisanio—
From this most bravest vessel of the world
Struck the main-top. O Posthumus! alas,
Where is thy head? Where's that? Ay me! where's that?
Pisanio might have kill'd thee at the heart,
And left this head on. How should this be? Pisanio?
'Tis he and Cloten; malice and lucre in them

Have laid this woe here. O, 'tis pregnant, pregnant!
The drug he gave me, which he said was precious
And cordial to me, have I not found it
Murd'rous to th' senses? That confirms it home.
This is Pisanio's deed, and Cloten. O!
Give colour to my pale cheek with thy blood,
That we the horrider may seem to those
Which chance to find us. O, my lord, my lord!
[*Falls fainting on the body*]

Enter LUCIUS, CAPTAINS, *and a* SOOTHSAYER

CAPTAIN. To them the legions garrison'd in Gallia,
After your will, have cross'd the sea, attending
You here at Milford Haven; with your ships,
They are in readiness.
LUCIUS. But what from Rome?
CAPTAIN. The Senate hath stirr'd up the confiners
And gentlemen of Italy, most willing spirits,
That promise noble service; and they come
Under the conduct of bold Iachimo,
Sienna's brother.
LUCIUS. When expect you them?
CAPTAIN. With the next benefit o' th' wind.
LUCIUS. This forwardness
Makes our hopes fair. Command our present numbers
Be muster'd; bid the captains look to't. Now, sir,
What have you dream'd of late of this war's purpose?
SOOTHSAYER. Last night the very gods show'd me a vision—
I fast and pray'd for their intelligence—thus:
I saw Jove's bird, the Roman eagle, wing'd
From the spongy south to this part of the west,
There vanish'd in the sunbeams; which portends,
Unless my sins abuse my divination,
Success to th' Roman host.
LUCIUS. Dream often so,
And never false. Soft, ho! what trunk is here
Without his top? The ruin speaks that sometime
It was a worthy building. How? a page?
Or dead or sleeping on him? But dead, rather;
For nature doth abhor to make his bed

With the defunct, or sleep upon the dead.
Let's see the boy's face.

CAPTAIN. He's alive, my lord.

LUCIUS. He'll then instruct us of this body. Young one,
Inform us of thy fortunes; for it seems
They crave to be demanded. Who is this
Thou mak'st thy bloody pillow? Or who was he
That, otherwise than noble nature did,
Hath alter'd that good picture? What's thy interest
In this sad wreck? How came't? Who is't? What art thou?

IMOGEN. I am nothing; or if not,
Nothing to be were better. This was my master,
A very valiant Briton and a good,
That here by mountaineers lies slain. Alas!
There is no more such masters. I may wander
From east to occident; cry out for service;
Try many, all good; serve truly; never
Find such another master.

LUCIUS. 'Lack, good youth!
Thou mov'st no less with thy complaining than
Thy master in bleeding. Say his name, good friend.

IMOGEN. Richard du Champ. [*Aside*] If I do lie, and do
No harm by it, though the gods hear, I hope
They'll pardon it.—Say you, sir?

LUCIUS. Thy name?

IMOGEN. Fidele, sir.

LUCIUS. Thou dost approve thyself the very same;
Thy name well fits thy faith, thy faith thy name.
Wilt take thy chance with me? I will not say
Thou shalt be so well master'd; but, be sure,
No less belov'd. The Roman Emperor's letters,
Sent by a consul to me, should not sooner
Than thine own worth prefer thee. Go with me.

IMOGEN. I'll follow, sir. But first, an't please the gods,
I'll hide my master from the flies, as deep
As these poor pickaxes can dig; and when
With wild wood-leaves and weeds I ha' strew'd his grave,
And on it said a century of prayers,
Such as I can, twice o'er, I'll weep and sigh;

And leaving so his service, follow you,
So please you entertain me.

LUCIUS. Ay, good youth;
And rather father thee than master thee.
My friends,
The boy hath taught us manly duties; let us
Find out the prettiest daisied plot we can,
And make him with our pikes and partisans
A grave. Come, arm him. Boy, he is preferr'd
By thee to us; and he shall be interr'd
As soldiers can. Be cheerful; wipe thine eyes.
Some falls are means the happier to arise. *Exeunt*

SCENE 3

Britain. CYMBELINE'S *palace*

Enter CYMBELINE, LORDS, PISANIO, *and attendants*

CYMBELINE. Again! and bring me word how 'tis with her.
Exit an attendant
A fever with the absence of her son;
A madness, of which her life's in danger. Heavens,
How deeply you at once do touch me! Imogen,
The great part of my comfort, gone; my queen
Upon a desperate bed, and in a time
When fearful wars point at me; her son gone,
So needful for this present. It strikes me past
The hope of comfort. But for thee, fellow,
Who needs must know of her departure and
Dost seem so ignorant, we'll enforce it from thee
By a sharp torture.

PISANIO. Sir, my life is yours;
I humbly set it at your will; but for my mistress,
I nothing know where she remains, why gone,
Nor when she purposes return. Beseech your Highness,
Hold me your loyal servant.

LORD. Good my liege,
The day that she was missing he was here.
I dare be bound he's true and shall perform

All parts of his subjection loyally. For Cloten,
There wants no diligence in seeking him,
And will no doubt be found.

CYMBELINE. The time is troublesome.
[*To* PISANIO] We'll slip you for a season; but our jealousy
Does yet depend.

LORD. So please your Majesty,
The Roman legions, all from Gallia drawn,
Are landed on your coast, with a supply
Of Roman gentlemen by the Senate sent.

CYMBELINE. Now for the counsel of my son and queen!
I am amaz'd with matter.

LORD. Good my liege,
Your preparation can affront no less
Than what you hear of. Come more, for more you're ready.
The want is but to put those pow'rs in motion
That long to move.

CYMBELINE. I thank you. Let's withdraw,
And meet the time as it seeks us. We fear not
What can from Italy annoy us; but
We grieve at chances here. Away! *Exeunt all but* PISANIO

PISANIO. I heard no letter from my master since
I wrote him Imogen was slain. 'Tis strange.
Nor hear I from my mistress, who did promise
To yield me often tidings. Neither know I
What is betid to Cloten, but remain
Perplex'd in all. The heavens still must work.
Wherein I am false I am honest; not true, to be true.
These present wars shall find I love my country,
Even to the note o' th' King, or I'll fall in them.
All other doubts, by time let them be clear'd:
Fortune brings in some boats that are not steer'd. *Exit*

SCENE 4

Wales. Before the cave of BELARIUS

Enter BELARIUS, GUIDERIUS, *and* ARVIRAGUS

GUIDERIUS. The noise is round about us.
BELARIUS. Let us from it.
ARVIRAGUS. What pleasure, sir, find we in life, to lock it
From action and adventure?
GUIDERIUS. Nay, what hope
Have we in hiding us? This way the Romans
Must or for Britons slay us, or receive us
For barbarous and unnatural revolts
During their use, and slay us after.
BELARIUS. Sons,
We'll higher to the mountains; there secure us.
To the King's party there's no going. Newness
Of Cloten's death—we being not known, not muster'd
Among the bands—may drive us to a render
Where we have liv'd, and so extort from's that
Which we have done, whose answer would be death,
Drawn on with torture.
GUIDERIUS. This is, sir, a doubt
In such a time nothing becoming you
Nor satisfying us.
ARVIRAGUS. It is not likely
That when they hear the Roman horses neigh,
Behold their quarter'd fires, have both their eyes
And ears so cloy'd importantly as now,
That they will waste their time upon our note,
To know from whence we are.
BELARIUS. O, I am known
Of many in the army. Many years,
Though Cloten then but young, you see, not wore him
From my remembrance. And, besides, the King
Hath not deserv'd my service nor your loves,
Who find in my exile the want of breeding,
The certainty of this hard life; aye hopeless
To have the courtesy your cradle promis'd,

But to be still hot summer's tanlings and
The shrinking slaves of winter.

GUIDERIUS. Than be so,
Better to cease to be. Pray, sir, to th' army.
I and my brother are not known; yourself
So out of thought, and thereto so o'ergrown,
Cannot be questioned.

ARVIRAGUS. By this sun that shines,
I'll thither. What thing is't that I never
Did see man die! scarce ever look'd on blood
But that of coward hares, hot goats, and venison!
Never bestrid a horse, save one that had
A rider like myself, who ne'er wore rowel
Nor iron on his heel! I am asham'd
To look upon the holy sun, to have
The benefit of his blest beams, remaining
So long a poor unknown.

GUIDERIUS. By heavens, I'll go!
If you will bless me, sir, and give me leave,
I'll take the better care; but if you will not,
The hazard therefore due fall on me by
The hands of Romans!

ARVIRAGUS. So say I. Amen.

BELARIUS. No reason I, since of your lives you set
So slight a valuation, should reserve
My crack'd one to more care. Have with you, boys!
If in your country wars you chance to die,
That is my bed too, lads, and there I'll lie.
Lead, lead. [*Aside*] The time seems long; their blood thinks scorn
Till it fly out and show them princes born. *Exeunt*

ACT V. SCENE 1

Britain. The Roman camp

Enter POSTHUMUS *alone, with a bloody handkerchief*

POSTHUMUS. Yea, bloody cloth, I'll keep thee; for I wish'd
Thou shouldst be colour'd thus. You married ones,
If each of you should take this course, how many
Must murder wives much better than themselves
For wrying but a little! O Pisanio!
Every good servant does not all commands;
No bond but to do just ones. Gods! if you
Should have ta'en vengeance on my faults, I never
Had liv'd to put on this; so had you saved
The noble Imogen to repent, and struck
Me, wretch more worth your vengeance. But alack,
You snatch some hence for little faults; that's love,
To have them fall no more. You some permit
To second ills with ills, each elder worse,
And make them dread it, to the doer's thrift.
But Imogen is your own. Do your best wills,
And make me blest to obey. I am brought hither
Among th' Italian gentry, and to fight
Against my lady's kingdom. 'Tis enough
That, Britain, I have kill'd thy mistress; peace!
I'll give no wound to thee. Therefore, good heavens,
Hear patiently my purpose. I'll disrobe me
Of these Italian weeds, and suit myself
As does a Britain peasant. So I'll fight
Against the part I come with; so I'll die
For thee, O Imogen, even for whom my life
Is every breath a death. And thus unknown,
Pitied nor hated, to the face of peril
Myself I'll dedicate. Let me make men know
More valour in me than my habits show.
Gods, put the strength o' th' Leonati in me!
To shame the guise o' th' world, I will begin
The fashion—less without and more within. *Exit*

SCENE 2

Britain. A field of battle between the British and Roman camps

Enter LUCIUS, IACHIMO, *and the Roman army at one door, and the British army at another,* LEONATUS POSTHUMUS *following like a poor soldier. They march over and go out. Alarums. Then enter again, in skirmish,* IACHIMO *and* POSTHUMUS. *He vanquisheth and disarmeth* IACHIMO, *and then leaves him*

IACHIMO. The heaviness and guilt within my bosom
Takes off my manhood. I have belied a lady,
The Princess of this country, and the air on't
Revengingly enfeebles me; or could this carl,
A very drudge of nature's, have subdu'd me
In my profession? Knighthoods and honours borne
As I wear mine are titles but of scorn.
If that thy gentry, Britain, go before
This lout as he exceeds our lords, the odds
Is that we scarce are men, and you are gods. *Exit*

The battle continues; the BRITONS *fly;* CYMBELINE *is taken. Then enter to his rescue* BELARIUS, GUIDERIUS, *and* ARVIRAGUS

BELARIUS. Stand, stand! We have th' advantage of the ground;
The lane is guarded; nothing routs us but
The villainy of our fears.
GUIDERIUS AND ARVIRAGUS. Stand, stand, and fight!

Re-enter POSTHUMUS, *and seconds the Britons; they rescue* CYMBELINE, *and exeunt. Then re-enter* LUCIUS *and* IACHIMO, *with* IMOGEN

LUCIUS. Away, boy, from the troops, and save thyself;
For friends kill friends, and the disorder's such
As war were hoodwink'd.
IACHIMO. 'Tis their fresh supplies.

LUCIUS. It is a day turn'd strangely. Or betimes
Let's reinforce or fly. *Exeunt*

SCENE 3

Another part of the field

Enter POSTHUMUS *and a Britain* LORD

LORD. Cam'st thou from where they made the stand?
POSTHUMUS. I did:
Though you, it seems, come from the fliers.
LORD. I did.
POSTHUMUS. No blame be to you, sir, for all was lost,
But that the heavens fought. The King himself
Of his wings destitute, the army broken,
And but the backs of Britons seen, all flying,
Through a strait lane—the enemy, full-hearted,
Lolling the tongue with slaught'ring, having work
More plentiful than tools to do't, struck down
Some mortally, some slightly touch'd, some falling
Merely through fear, that the strait pass was damm'd
With dead men hurt behind, and cowards living
To die with length'ned shame.
LORD. Where was this lane?
POSTHUMUS. Close by the battle, ditch'd, and wall'd with turf,
Which gave advantage to an ancient soldier—
An honest one, I warrant, who deserv'd
So long a breeding as his white beard came to,
In doing this for's country. Athwart the lane
He, with two striplings—lads more like to run
The country base than to commit such slaughter;
With faces fit for masks, or rather fairer
Than those for preservation cas'd or shame—
Made good the passage, cried to those that fled
'Our Britain's harts die flying, not our men.
To darkness fleet souls that fly backwards! Stand;
Or we are Romans and will give you that,
Like beasts, which you shun beastly, and may save

But to look back in frown. Stand, stand!' These three,
Three thousand confident, in act as many—
For three performers are the file when all
The rest do nothing—with this word 'Stand, stand!'
Accommodated by the place, more charming
With their own nobleness, which could have turn'd
A distaff to a lance, gilded pale looks,
Part shame, part spirit renew'd; that some turn'd coward
But by example—O, a sin in war
Damn'd in the first beginners!—gan to look
The way that they did and to grin like lions
Upon the pikes o' th' hunters. Then began
A stop i' th' chaser, a retire; anon
A rout, confusion thick. Forthwith they fly,
Chickens, the way which they stoop'd eagles; slaves,
The strides they victors made; and now our cowards,
Like fragments in hard voyages, became
The life o' th' need. Having found the back-door open
Of the unguarded hearts, heavens, how they wound!
Some slain before, some dying, some their friends
O'erborne i' th' former wave. Ten chas'd by one
Are now each one the slaughterman of twenty.
Those that would die or ere resist are grown
The mortal bugs o' th' field.

LORD. This was strange chance:
A narrow lane, an old man, and two boys.

POSTHUMUS. Nay, do not wonder at it; you are made
Rather to wonder at the things you hear
Than to work any. Will you rhyme upon't,
And vent it for a mock'ry? Here is one:
'Two boys, an old man (twice a boy), a lane,
Preserv'd the Britons, was the Romans' bane.'

LORD. Nay, be not angry, sir.

POSTHUMUS. 'Lack, to what end?
Who dares not stand his foe I'll be his friend;
For if he'll do as he is made to do,
I know he'll quickly fly my friendship too.
You have put me into rhyme.

LORD. Farewell; you're angry. *Exit*

POSTHUMUS. Still going? This is a lord! O noble misery,

To be i' th' field and ask 'What news?' of me!
To-day how many would have given their honours
To have sav'd their carcasses! took heel to do't,
And yet died too! I, in mine own woe charm'd,
Could not find death where I did hear him groan,
Nor feel him where he struck. Being an ugly monster,
'Tis strange he hides him in fresh cups, soft beds,
Sweet words; or hath moe ministers than we
That draw his knives i' th' war. Well, I will find him;
For being now a favourer to the Briton,
No more a Briton, I have resum'd again
The part I came in. Fight I will no more,
But yield me to the veriest hind that shall
Once touch my shoulder. Great the slaughter is
Here made by th' Roman; great the answer be
Britons must take. For me, my ransom's death;
On either side I come to spend my breath,
Which neither here I'll keep nor bear again,
But end it by some means for Imogen.

Enter two BRITISH CAPTAINS *and soldiers*

FIRST CAPTAIN. Great Jupiter be prais'd! Lucius is taken.
'Tis thought the old man and his sons were angels.
SECOND CAPTAIN. There was a fourth man, in a silly habit,
That gave th' affront with them.
FIRST CAPTAIN. So 'tis reported;
But none of 'em can be found. Stand! who's there?
POSTHUMUS. A Roman,
Who had not now been drooping here if seconds
Had answer'd him.
SECOND CAPTAIN. Lay hands on him; a dog!
A leg of Rome shall not return to tell
What crows have peck'd them here. He brags his service,
As if he were of note. Bring him to th' King.

Enter CYMBELINE, BELARIUS, GUIDERIUS, ARVIRAGUS, PISANIO, *and Roman captives. The* CAPTAINS *present* POSTHUMUS *to* CYMBELINE, *who delivers him over to a gaoler. Exeunt omnes*

SCENE 4

Britain. A prison

Enter POSTHUMUS *and two* GAOLERS

FIRST GAOLER. You shall not now be stol'n, you have locks upon you;
So graze as you find pasture.
SECOND GAOLER. Ay, or a stomach. *Exeunt* GAOLERS
POSTHUMUS. Most welcome, bondage! for thou art a way,
I think, to liberty. Yet am I better
Than one that's sick o' th' gout, since he had rather
Groan so in perpetuity than be cur'd
By th' sure physician death, who is the key
T' unbar these locks. My conscience, thou art fetter'd
More than my shanks and wrists; you good gods, give me
The penitent instrument to pick that bolt,
Then, free for ever! Is't enough I am sorry?
So children temporal fathers do appease;
Gods are more full of mercy. Must I repent,
I cannot do it better than in gyves,
Desir'd more than constrain'd. To satisfy,
If of my freedom 'tis the main part, take
No stricter render of me than my all.
I know you are more clement than vile men,
Who of their broken debtors take a third,
A sixth, a tenth, letting them thrive again
On their abatement; that's not my desire.
For Imogen's dear life take mine; and though
'Tis not so dear, yet 'tis a life; you coin'd it.
'Tween man and man they weigh not every stamp;
Though light, take pieces for the figure's sake;
You rather mine, being yours. And so, great pow'rs,
If you will take this audit, take this life,
And cancel these cold bonds. O Imogen!
I'll speak to thee in silence. [*Sleeps*]

Solemn music. Enter, as in an apparition, SICILIUS LEONATUS, *father to* POSTHUMUS, *an old man at-*

tired like a warrior; leading in his hand an ancient matron, his Wife, *and mother to* Posthumus, *with music before them. Then, after other music, follows the two young* Leonati, *brothers to* Posthumus, *with wounds, as they died in the wars. They circle* Posthumus *round as he lies sleeping*

Sicilius. No more, thou thunder-master, show
Thy spite on mortal flies.
With Mars fall out, with Juno chide,
That thy adulteries
Rates and revenges.
Hath my poor boy done aught but well,
Whose face I never saw?
I died whilst in the womb he stay'd
Attending nature's law;
Whose father then, as men report
Thou orphans' father art,
Thou shouldst have been, and shielded him
From this earth-vexing smart.

Mother. Lucina lent not me her aid,
But took me in my throes,
That from me was Posthumus ripp'd,
Came crying 'mongst his foes,
A thing of pity.

Sicilius. Great Nature like his ancestry
Moulded the stuff so fair
That he deserv'd the praise o' th' world
As great Sicilius' heir.

First Brother. When once he was mature for man,
In Britain where was he
That could stand up his parallel,
Or fruitful object be
In eye of Imogen, that best
Could deem his dignity?

Mother. With marriage wherefore was he mock'd,
To be exil'd and thrown
From Leonati seat and cast

From her his dearest one,
Sweet Imogen?

SICILIUS. Why did you suffer Iachimo,
Slight thing of Italy,
To taint his nobler heart and brain
With needless jealousy,
And to become the geck and scorn
O' th' other's villainy?

SECOND BROTHER. For this from stiller seats we came,
Our parents and us twain,
That, striking in our country's cause,
Fell bravely and were slain,
Our fealty and Tenantius' right
With honour to maintain.

FIRST BROTHER. Like hardiment Posthumus hath
To Cymbeline perform'd.
Then, Jupiter, thou king of gods,
Why hast thou thus adjourn'd
The graces for his merits due,
Being all to dolours turn'd?

SICILIUS. Thy crystal window ope; look out;
No longer exercise
Upon a valiant race thy harsh
And potent injuries.

MOTHER. Since, Jupiter, our son is good,
Take off his miseries.

SICILIUS. Peep through thy marble mansion. Help!
Or we poor ghosts will cry
To th' shining synod of the rest
Against thy deity.

BROTHERS. Help, Jupiter! or we appeal,
And from thy justice fly.

JUPITER *descends in thunder and lightning, sitting upon an eagle. He throws a thunderbolt. The* GHOSTS *fall on their knees*

JUPITER. No more, you petty spirits of region low,
Offend our hearing; hush! How dare you ghosts
Accuse the Thunderer whose bolt, you know,
Sky-planted, batters all rebelling coasts?
Poor shadows of Elysium, hence, and rest
Upon your never-withering banks of flow'rs.
Be not with mortal accidents opprest:
No care of yours it is; you know 'tis ours.
Whom best I love I cross; to make my gift,
The more delay'd, delighted. Be content;
Your low-laid son our godhead will uplift;
His comforts thrive, his trials well are spent.
Our Jovial star reign'd at his birth, and in
Our temple was he married. Rise, and fade!
He shall be lord of Lady Imogen,
And happier much by his affliction made.
This tablet lay upon his breast, wherein
Our pleasure his full fortune doth confine;
And so, away; no farther with your din
Express impatience, lest you stir up mine.
Mount, eagle, to my palace crystalline. [*Ascends*]
SICILIUS. He came in thunder; his celestial breath
Was sulphurous to smell; the holy eagle
Stoop'd, as to foot us. His ascension is
More sweet than our blest fields. His royal bird
Prunes the immortal wing, and cloys his beak,
As when his god is pleas'd.
ALL. Thanks, Jupiter!
SICILIUS. The marble pavement closes, he is enter'd
His radiant roof. Away! and, to be blest,
Let us with care perform his great behest. [GHOSTS *vanish*]

POSTHUMUS. [*Waking*] Sleep, thou has been a grandsire and begot
A father to me; and thou hast created
A mother and two brothers. But, O scorn,
Gone! They went hence so soon as they were born.
And so I am awake. Poor wretches, that depend
On greatness' favour, dream as I have done;
Wake and find nothing. But, alas, I swerve;

Many dream not to find, neither deserve,
And yet are steep'd in favours; so am I,
That have this golden chance, and know not why.
What fairies haunt this ground? A book? O rare one!
Be not, as is our fangled world, a garment
Nobler than that it covers. Let thy effects
So follow to be most unlike our courtiers,
As good as promise.

[*Reads*] 'When as a lion's whelp shall, to himself unknown, without seeking find, and be embrac'd by a piece of tender air; and when from a stately cedar shall be lopp'd branches which, being dead many years, shall after revive, be jointed to the old stock, and freshly grow; then shall Posthumus end his miseries, Britain be fortunate and flourish in peace and plenty.'

'Tis still a dream, or else such stuff as madmen
Tongue, and brain not; either both or nothing,
Or senseless speaking, or a speaking such
As sense cannot untie. Be what it is,
The action of my life is like it, which
I'll keep, if but for sympathy.

Re-enter GAOLER

GAOLER. Come, sir, are you ready for death?

POSTHUMUS. Over-roasted rather; ready long ago.

GAOLER. Hanging is the word, sir; if you be ready for that, you are well cook'd.

POSTHUMUS. So, if I prove a good repast to the spectators, the dish pays the shot.

GAOLER. A heavy reckoning for you, sir. But the comfort is, you shall be called to no more payments, fear no more tavern bills, which are often the sadness of parting, as the procuring of mirth. You come in faint for want of meat, depart reeling with too much drink; sorry that you have paid too much, and sorry that you are paid too much; purse and brain both empty; the brain the heavier for being too light, the purse too light, being drawn of heaviness. O, of this contradiction you shall now be quit. O, the charity of a penny cord! It sums up thousands in a trice. You have no true debitor and creditor but it; of what's past, is, and to come, the discharge. Your neck, sir, is pen, book, and counters; so the acquittance follows.

POSTHUMUS. I am merrier to die than thou art to live.

GAOLER. Indeed, sir, he that sleeps feels not the toothache. But a man that were to sleep your sleep, and a hangman to help him to bed, I think he would change places with his officer; for look you, sir, you know not which way you shall go.

POSTHUMUS. Yes indeed do I, fellow.

GAOLER. Your death has eyes in's head, then; I have not seen him so pictur'd. You must either be directed by some that take upon them to know, or to take upon yourself that which I am sure you do not know, or jump the after-inquiry on your own peril. And how you shall speed in your journey's end, I think you'll never return to tell one.

POSTHUMUS. I tell thee, fellow, there are none want eyes to direct them the way I am going, but such as wink and will not use them.

GAOLER. What an infinite mock is this, that a man should have the best use of eyes to see the way of blindness! I am sure hanging's the way of winking.

Enter a MESSENGER

MESSENGER. Knock off his manacles; bring your prisoner to the King.

POSTHUMUS. Thou bring'st good news: I am call'd to be made free.

GAOLER. I'll be hang'd then.

POSTHUMUS. Thou shalt be then freer than a gaoler; no bolts for the dead. *Exeunt* POSTHUMUS *and* MESSENGER

GAOLER. Unless a man would marry a gallows and beget young gibbets, I never saw one so prone. Yet, on my conscience, there are verier knaves desire to live, for all he be a Roman; and there be some of them too that die against their wills; so should I, if I were one. I would we were all of one mind, and one mind good. O, there were desolation of gaolers and gallowses! I speak against my present profit, but my wish hath a preferment in't. *Exit*

SCENE 5

Britain. CYMBELINE'S *tent*

Enter CYMBELINE, BELARIUS, GUIDERIUS, ARVIRAGUS, PISANIO, LORDS, OFFICERS, *and attendants*

CYMBELINE. Stand by my side, you whom the gods have made
Preservers of my throne. Woe is my heart
That the poor soldier that so richly fought,
Whose rags sham'd gilded arms, whose naked breast
Stepp'd before targes of proof, cannot be found.
He shall be happy that can find him, if
Our grace can make him so.
BELARIUS. I never saw
Such noble fury in so poor a thing;
Such precious deeds in one that promis'd nought
But beggary and poor looks.
CYMBELINE. No tidings of him?
PISANIO. He hath been search'd among the dead and living,
But no trace of him.
CYMBELINE. To my grief, I am
The heir of his reward; [*To* BELARIUS, GUIDERIUS, *and* ARVIRAGUS] which I will add
To you, the liver, heart, and brain, of Britain,
By whom I grant she lives. 'Tis now the time
To ask of whence you are. Report it.
BELARIUS. Sir,
In Cambria are we born, and gentlemen;
Further to boast were neither true nor modest,
Unless I add we are honest.
CYMBELINE. Bow your knees.
Arise my knights o' th' battle; I create you
Companions to our person, and will fit you
With dignities becoming your estates.

Enter CORNELIUS *and* LADIES

There's business in these faces. Why so sadly
Greet you our victory? You look like Romans,

And not o' th' court of Britain.
CORNELIUS. Hail, great King!
To sour your happiness I must report
The Queen is dead.
CYMBELINE. Who worse than a physician
Would this report become? But I consider
By med'cine life may be prolong'd, yet death
Will seize the doctor too. How ended she?
CORNELIUS. With horror, madly dying, like her life;
Which, being cruel to the world, concluded
Most cruel to herself. What she confess'd
I will report, so please you; these her women
Can trip me if I err, who with wet cheeks
Were present when she finish'd.
CYMBELINE. Prithee say.
CORNELIUS. First, she confess'd she never lov'd you; only
Affected greatness got by you, not you;
Married your royalty, was wife to your place;
Abhorr'd your person.
CYMBELINE. She alone knew this;
And but she spoke it dying, I would not
Believe her lips in opening it. Proceed.
CORNELIUS. Your daughter, whom she bore in hand to love
With such integrity, she did confess
Was as a scorpion to her sight; whose life,
But that her flight prevented it, she had
Ta'en off by poison.
CYMBELINE. O most delicate fiend!
Who is't can read a woman? Is there more?
CORNELIUS. More, sir, and worse. She did confess she had
For you a mortal mineral, which, being took,
Should by the minute feed on life, and ling'ring,
By inches waste you. In which time she purpos'd,
By watching, weeping, tendance, kissing, to
O'ercome you with her show; and in time,
When she had fitted you with her craft, to work
Her son into th' adoption of the crown;
But failing of her end by his strange absence,
Grew shameless-desperate, open'd, in despite
Of heaven and men, her purposes, repented

The evils she hatch'd were not effected; so,
Despairing, died.

CYMBELINE. Heard you all this, her women?

LADY. We did, so please your Highness.

CYMBELINE. Mine eyes
Were not in fault, for she was beautiful;
Mine ears, that heard her flattery; nor my heart
That thought her like her seeming. It had been vicious
To have mistrusted her; yet, O my daughter!
That it was folly in me thou mayst say,
And prove it in thy feeling. Heaven mend all!

Enter LUCIUS, IACHIMO, *the* SOOTHSAYER, *and other Roman prisoners, guarded;* POSTHUMUS *behind, and* IMOGEN

Thou com'st not, Caius, now for tribute; that
The Britons have raz'd out, though with the loss
Of many a bold one, whose kinsmen have made suit
That their good souls may be appeas'd with slaughter
Of you their captives, which ourself have granted;
So think of your estate.

LUCIUS. Consider, sir, the chance of war. The day
Was yours by accident; had it gone with us,
We should not, when the blood was cool, have threaten'd
Our prisoners with the sword. But since the gods
Will have it thus, that nothing but our lives
May be call'd ransom, let it come. Sufficeth
A Roman with a Roman's heart can suffer.
Augustus lives to think on't; and so much
For my peculiar care. This one thing only
I will entreat: my boy, a Briton born,
Let him be ransom'd. Never master had
A page so kind, so duteous, diligent,
So tender over his occasions, true,
So feat, so nurse-like; let his virtue join
With my request, which I'll make bold your Highness
Cannot deny; he hath done no Briton harm
Though he have serv'd a Roman. Save him, sir,
And spare no blood beside.

CYMBELINE. I have surely seen him;

His favour is familiar to me. Boy,
Thou hast look'd thyself into my grace,
And art mine own. I know not why, wherefore
To say 'Live, boy.' Ne'er thank thy master. Live;
And ask of Cymbeline what boon thou wilt,
Fitting my bounty and thy state, I'll give it;
Yea, though thou do demand a prisoner,
The noblest ta'en.

IMOGEN. I humbly thank your Highness.

LUCIUS. I do not bid thee beg my life, good lad,
And yet I know thou wilt.

IMOGEN. No, no! Alack,
There's other work in hand. I see a thing
Bitter to me as death; your life, good master,
Must shuffle for itself.

LUCIUS. The boy disdains me,
He leaves me, scorns me. Briefly die their joys
That place them on the truth of girls and boys.
Why stands he so perplex'd?

CYMBELINE. What wouldst thou, boy?
I love thee more and more; think more and more
What's best to ask. Know'st him thou look'st on? Speak,
Wilt have him live? Is he thy kin? thy friend?

IMOGEN. He is a Roman, no more kin to me
Than I to your Highness; who, being born your vassal,
Am something nearer.

CYMBELINE. Wherefore ey'st him so?

IMOGEN. I'll tell you, sir, in private, if you please
To give me hearing.

CYMBELINE. Ay, with all my heart,
And lend my best attention. What's thy name?

IMOGEN. Fidele, sir.

CYMBELINE. Thou'rt my good youth, my page;
I'll be thy master. Walk with me; speak freely.

[CYMBELINE *and* IMOGEN *converse apart*]

BELARIUS. Is not this boy reviv'd from death?

ARVIRAGUS. One sand another
Not more resembles—that sweet rosy lad
Who died and was Fidele. What think you?

GUIDERIUS. The same dead thing alive.

BELARIUS. Peace, peace! see further. He eyes us not; forbear.
Creatures may be alike; were't he, I am sure
He would have spoke to us.
GUIDERIUS. But we saw him dead.
BELARIUS. Be silent; let's see further.
PISANIO. [*Aside*] It is my mistress.
Since she is living, let the time run on
To good or bad. [CYMBELINE *and* IMOGEN *advance*]
CYMBELINE. Come, stand thou by our side;
Make thy demand aloud. [*To* IACHIMO] Sir, step you forth;
Give answer to this boy, and do it freely,
Or, by our greatness and the grace of it,
Which is our honour, bitter torture shall
Winnow the truth from falsehood. On, speak to him.
IMOGEN. My boon is that this gentleman may render
Of whom he had this ring.
POSTHUMUS. [*Aside*] What's that to him?
CYMBELINE. That diamond upon your finger, say
How came it yours?
IACHIMO. Thou'lt torture me to leave unspoken that
Which to be spoke would torture thee.
CYMBELINE. How? me?
IACHIMO. I am glad to be constrain'd to utter that
Which torments me to conceal. By villainy
I got this ring; 'twas Leonatus' jewel,
Whom thou didst banish; and—which more may grieve thee,
As it doth me—a nobler sir ne'er liv'd
'Twixt sky and ground. Wilt thou hear more, my lord?
CYMBELINE. All that belongs to this.
IACHIMO. That paragon, thy daughter,
For whom my heart drops blood and my false spirits
Quail to remember—Give me leave, I faint.
CYMBELINE. My daughter? What of her? Renew thy strength;
I had rather thou shouldst live while nature will
Than die ere I hear more. Strive, man, and speak.
IACHIMO. Upon a time—unhappy was the clock
That struck the hour!—it was in Rome—accurs'd

The mansion where!—'twas at a feast—O, would
Our viands had been poison'd, or at least
Those which I heav'd to head!—the good Posthumus—
What should I say? he was too good to be
Where ill men were, and was the best of all
Amongst the rar'st of good ones—sitting sadly
Hearing us praise our loves of Italy
For beauty that made barren the swell'd boast
Of him that best could speak; for feature, laming
The shrine of Venus or straight-pight Minerva,
Postures beyond brief nature; for condition,
A shop of all the qualities that man
Loves woman for; besides that hook of wiving,
Fairness which strikes the eye—

CYMBELINE. I stand on fire.
Come to the matter.

IACHIMO. All too soon I shall,
Unless thou wouldst grieve quickly. This Posthumus,
Most like a noble lord in love and one
That had a royal lover, took his hint;
And not dispraising whom we prais'd—therein
He was as calm as virtue—he began
His mistress' picture; which by his tongue being made,
And then a mind put in't, either our brags
Were crack'd of kitchen trulls, or his description
Prov'd us unspeaking sots.

CYMBELINE. Nay, nay, to th' purpose.

IACHIMO. Your daughter's chastity—there it begins.
He spake of her as Dian had hot dreams
And she alone were cold; whereat I, wretch,
Made scruple of his praise, and wager'd with him
Pieces of gold 'gainst this which then he wore
Upon his honour'd finger, to attain
In suit the place of's bed, and win this ring
By hers and mine adultery. He, true knight,
No lesser of her honour confident
Than I did truly find her, stakes this ring;
And would so, had it been a carbuncle
Of Phœbus' wheel; and might so safely, had it
Been all the worth of's car. Away to Britain

Post I in this design. Well may you, sir,
Remember me at court, where I was taught
Of your chaste daughter the wide difference
'Twixt amorous and villainous. Being thus quench'd
Of hope, not longing, mine Italian brain
Gan in your duller Britain operate
Most vilely; for my vantage, excellent;
And, to be brief, my practice so prevail'd
That I return'd with simular proof enough
To make the noble Leonatus mad,
By wounding his belief in her renown
With tokens thus and thus; averring notes
Of chamber-hanging, pictures, this her bracelet–
O cunning, how I got it!–nay, some marks
Of secret on her person, that he could not
But think her bond of chastity quite crack'd,
I having ta'en the forfeit. Whereupon–
Methinks I see him now–

POSTHUMUS. [*Coming forward*] Ay, so thou dost,
Italian fiend! Ay me, most credulous fool,
Egregious murderer, thief, anything
That's due to all the villains past, in being,
To come! O, give me cord, or knife, or poison,
Some upright justicer! Thou, King, send out
For torturers ingenious. It is I
That all th' abhorred things o' th' earth amend
By being worse than they. I am Posthumus,
That kill'd thy daughter; villain-like, I lie–
That caus'd a lesser villain than myself,
A sacrilegious thief, to do't. The temple
Of virtue was she; yea, and she herself.
Spit, and throw stones, cast mire upon me, set
The dogs o' th' street to bay me. Every villain
Be call'd Posthumus Leonatus, and
Be villainy less than 'twas! O Imogen!
My queen, my life, my wife! O Imogen,
Imogen, Imogen!

IMOGEN. Peace, my lord. Hear, hear!

POSTHUMUS. Shall's have a play of this? Thou scornful page,
There lies thy part. [*Strikes her. She falls*]

PISANIO. O gentlemen, help!
  Mine and your mistress! O, my lord Posthumus!
  You ne'er kill'd Imogen till now. Help, help!
  Mine honour'd lady!
CYMBELINE. Does the world go round?
POSTHUMUS. How comes these staggers on me?
PISANIO. Wake, my mistress!
CYMBELINE. If this be so, the gods do mean to strike me
  To death with mortal joy.
PISANIO. How fares my mistress?
IMOGEN. O, get thee from my sight;
  Thou gav'st me poison. Dangerous fellow, hence!
  Breathe not where princes are.
CYMBELINE. The tune of Imogen!
PISANIO. Lady,
  The gods throw stones of sulphur on me, if
  That box I gave you was not thought by me
  A precious thing! I had it from the Queen.
CYMBELINE. New matter still?
IMOGEN. It poison'd me.
CORNELIUS. O gods!
  I left out one thing which the Queen confess'd,
  Which must approve thee honest. 'If Pisanio
  Have' said she 'given his mistress that confection
  Which I gave him for cordial, she is serv'd
  As I would serve a rat.'
CYMBELINE. What's this, Cornelius?
CORNELIUS. The Queen, sir, very oft importun'd me
  To temper poisons for her; still pretending
  The satisfaction of her knowledge only
  In killing creatures vile, as cats and dogs,
  Of no esteem. I, dreading that her purpose
  Was of more danger, did compound for her
  A certain stuff, which, being ta'en would cease
  The present pow'r of life, but in short time
  All offices of nature should again
  Do their due functions. Have you ta'en of it?
IMOGEN. Most like I did, for I was dead.
BELARIUS. My boys,
  There was our error.

GUIDERIUS. This is sure Fidele.
IMOGEN. Why did you throw your wedded lady from you?
  Think that you are upon a rock, and now
  Throw me again. [*Embracing him*]
POSTHUMUS. Hang there like fruit, my soul,
  Till the tree die!
CYMBELINE. How now, my flesh? my child?
  What, mak'st thou me a dullard in this act?
  Wilt thou not speak to me?
IMOGEN. [*Kneeling*] Your blessing, sir.
BELARIUS. [*To* GUIDERIUS *and* ARVIRAGUS] Though you did love this youth, I blame ye not;
  You had a motive for't.
CYMBELINE. My tears that fall
  Prove holy water on thee! Imogen,
  Thy mother's dead.
IMOGEN. I am sorry for't, my lord.
CYMBELINE. O, she was naught, and long of her it was
  That we meet here so strangely; but her son
  Is gone, we know not how nor where.
PISANIO. My lord,
  Now fear is from me, I'll speak troth. Lord Cloten,
  Upon my lady's missing, came to me
  With his sword drawn, foam'd at the mouth, and swore,
  If I discover'd not which way she was gone,
  It was my instant death. By accident
  I had a feigned letter of my master's
  Then in my pocket, which directed him
  To seek her on the mountains near to Milford;
  Where, in a frenzy, in my master's garments,
  Which he enforc'd from me, away he posts
  With unchaste purpose, and with oath to violate
  My lady's honour. What became of him
  I further know not.
GUIDERIUS. Let me end the story:
  I slew him there.
CYMBELINE. Marry, the gods forfend!
  I would not thy good deeds should from my lips
  Pluck a hard sentence. Prithee, valiant youth,
  Deny't again.

GUIDERIUS. I have spoke it, and I did it.
CYMBELINE. He was a prince.
GUIDERIUS. A most incivil one. The wrongs he did me
Were nothing prince-like; for he did provoke me
With language that would make me spurn the sea,
If it could so roar to me. I cut off's head,
And am right glad he is not standing here
To tell this tale of mine.
CYMBELINE. I am sorry for thee.
By thine own tongue thou art condemn'd, and must
Endure our law. Thou'rt dead.
IMOGEN. That headless man
I thought had been my lord.
CYMBELINE. Bind the offender,
And take him from our presence.
BELARIUS. Stay, sir King.
This man is better than the man he slew,
As well descended as thyself, and hath
More of thee merited than a band of Clotens
Had ever scar for. [*To the guard*] Let his arms alone;
They were not born for bondage.
CYMBELINE. Why, old soldier,
Wilt thou undo the worth thou art unpaid for
By tasting of our wrath? How of descent
As good as we?
ARVIRAGUS. In that he spake too far.
CYMBELINE. And thou shalt die for't.
BELARIUS. We will die all three;
But I will prove that two on's are as good
As I have given out him. My sons, I must
For mine own part unfold a dangerous speech,
Though haply well for you.
ARVIRAGUS. Your danger's ours.
GUIDERIUS. And our good his.
BELARIUS. Have at it then by leave!
Thou hadst, great King, a subject who
Was call'd Belarius.
CYMBELINE. What of him? He is
A banish'd traitor.
BELARIUS. He it is that hath

Assum'd this age; indeed a banish'd man;
I know not how a traitor.

CYMBELINE. Take him hence,
The whole world shall not save him.

BELARIUS. Not too hot.
First pay me for the nursing of thy sons,
And let it be confiscate all, so soon
As I have receiv'd it.

CYMBELINE. Nursing of my sons?

BELARIUS. I am too blunt and saucy: here's my knee.
Ere I arise I will prefer my sons;
Then spare not the old father. Mighty sir,
These two young gentlemen that call me father,
And think they are my sons, are none of mine;
They are the issue of your loins, my liege,
And blood of your begetting.

CYMBELINE. How? my issue?

BELARIUS. So sure as you your father's. I, old Morgan,
Am that Belarius whom you sometime banish'd.
Your pleasure was my mere offence, my punishment
Itself, and all my treason; that I suffer'd
Was all the harm I did. These gentle princes—
For such and so they are—these twenty years
Have I train'd up; those arts they have as I
Could put into them. My breeding was, sir, as
Your Highness knows. Their nurse, Euriphile,
Whom for the theft I wedded, stole these children
Upon my banishment; I mov'd her to't,
Having receiv'd the punishment before
For that which I did then. Beaten for loyalty
Excited me to treason. Their dear loss,
The more of you 'twas felt, the more it shap'd
Unto my end of stealing them. But, gracious sir,
Here are your sons again, and I must lose
Two of the sweet'st companions in the world.
The benediction of these covering heavens
Fall on their heads like dew! for they are worthy
To inlay heaven with stars.

CYMBELINE. Thou weep'st and speak'st.
The service that you three have done is more

Unlike than this thou tell'st. I lost my children.
If these be they, I know not how to wish
A pair of worthier sons.

BELARIUS. Be pleas'd awhile.
This gentleman, whom I call Polydore,
Most worthy prince, as yours, is true Guiderius;
This gentleman, my Cadwal, Arviragus,
Your younger princely son; he, sir, was lapp'd
In a most curious mantle, wrought by th' hand
Of his queen mother, which for more probation
I can with ease produce.

CYMBELINE. Guiderius had
Upon his neck a mole, a sanguine star;
It was a mark of wonder.

BELARIUS. This is he,
Who hath upon him still that natural stamp.
It was wise nature's end in the donation,
To be his evidence now.

CYMBELINE. O, what am I?
A mother to the birth of three? Ne'er mother
Rejoic'd deliverance more. Blest pray you be,
That, after this strange starting from your orbs,
You may reign in them now! O Imogen,
Thou hast lost by this a kingdom.

IMOGEN. No, my lord;
I have got two worlds by't. O my gentle brothers,
Have we thus met? O, never say hereafter
But I am truest speaker! You call'd me brother,
When I was but your sister: I you brothers,
When we were so indeed.

CYMBELINE. Did you e'er meet?

ARVIRAGUS. Ay, my good lord.

GUIDERIUS. And at first meeting lov'd,
Continu'd so until we thought he died.

CORNELIUS. By the Queen's dram she swallow'd.

CYMBELINE. O rare instinct!
When shall I hear all through? This fierce abridgment
Hath to it circumstantial branches, which
Distinction should be rich in. Where? how liv'd you?
And when came you to serve our Roman captive?

How parted with your brothers? how first met them?
Why fled you from the court? and whither? These,
And your three motives to the battle, with
I know not how much more, should be demanded,
And all the other by-dependances,
From chance to chance; but nor the time nor place
Will serve our long interrogatories. See,
Posthumus anchors upon Imogen;
And she, like harmless lightning, throws her eye
On him, her brothers, me, her master, hitting
Each object with a joy; the counterchange
Is severally in all. Let's quit this ground,
And smoke the temple with our sacrifices.
[*To* BELARIUS] Thou art my brother; so we'll hold thee ever.

IMOGEN. You are my father too, and did relieve me
To see this gracious season.

CYMBELINE. All o'erjoy'd
Save these in bonds. Let them be joyful too,
For they shall taste our comfort.

IMOGEN. My good master,
I will yet do you service.

LUCIUS. Happy be you!

CYMBELINE. The forlorn soldier, that so nobly fought,
He would have well becom'd this place and grac'd
The thankings of a king.

POSTHUMUS. I am, sir,
The soldier that did company these three
In poor beseeming; 'twas a fitment for
The purpose I then follow'd. That I was he,
Speak, Iachimo. I had you down, and might
Have made you finish.

IACHIMO. [*Kneeling*] I am down again;
But now my heavy conscience sinks my knee,
As then your force did. Take that life, beseech you,
Which I so often owe; but your ring first,
And here the bracelet of the truest princess
That ever swore her faith.

POSTHUMUS. Kneel not to me.
The pow'r that I have on you is to spare you;

The malice towards you to forgive you. Live,
And deal with others better.

CYMBELINE. Nobly doom'd!
We'll learn our freeness of a son-in-law;
Pardon's the word to all.

ARVIRAGUS. You holp us, sir,
As you did mean indeed to be our brother;
Joy'd are we that you are.

POSTHUMUS. Your servant, Princes. Good my lord of Rome,
Call forth your soothsayer. As I slept, methought
Great Jupiter, upon his eagle back'd,
Appear'd to me, with other spritely shows
Of mine own kindred. When I wak'd, I found
This label on my bosom; whose containing
Is so from sense in hardness that I can
Make no collection of it. Let him show
His skill in the construction.

LUCIUS. Philarmonus!

SOOTHSAYER. Here, my good lord.

LUCIUS. Read, and declare the meaning.

SOOTHSAYER. [*Reads*] 'When as a lion's whelp shall, to himself unknown, without seeking find, and be embrac'd by a piece of tender air; and when from a stately cedar shall be lopp'd branches which, being dead many years, shall after revive, be jointed to the old stock, and freshly grow; then shall Posthumus end his miseries, Britain be fortunate and flourish in peace and plenty.'

Thou, Leonatus, art the lion's whelp;
The fit and apt construction of thy name,
Being Leo-natus, doth import so much.
[*To* CYMBELINE] The piece of tender air, thy virtuous daughter,
Which we call 'mollis aer,' and 'mollis aer'
We term it 'mulier'; which 'mulier' I divine
Is this most constant wife, who even now
Answering the letter of the oracle,
Unknown to you, unsought, were clipp'd about
With this most tender air.

CYMBELINE. This hath some seeming.

SOOTHSAYER. The lofty cedar, royal Cymbeline,
Personates thee; and thy lopp'd branches point
Thy two sons forth, who, by Belarius stol'n,
For many years thought dead, are now reviv'd,
To the majestic cedar join'd, whose issue
Promises Britain peace and plenty.
CYMBELINE. Well,
My peace we will begin. And, Caius Lucius,
Although the victor, we submit to Cæsar
And to the Roman empire, promising
To pay our wonted tribute, from the which
We were dissuaded by our wicked queen,
Whom heavens in justice, both on her and hers,
Have laid most heavy hand.
SOOTHSAYER. The fingers of the pow'rs above do tune
The harmony of this peace. The vision
Which I made known to Lucius ere the stroke
Of yet this scarce-cold battle, at this instant
Is full accomplish'd; for the Roman eagle,
From south to west on wing soaring aloft,
Lessen'd herself and in the beams o' th' sun
So vanish'd; which foreshow'd our princely eagle,
Th' imperial Cæsar, should again unite
His favour with the radiant Cymbeline,
Which shines here in the west.
CYMBELINE. Laud we the gods;
And let our crooked smokes climb to their nostrils
From our bless'd altars. Publish we this peace
To all our subjects. Set we forward; let
A Roman and a British ensign wave
Friendly together. So through Lud's Town march;
And in the temple of great Jupiter
Our peace we'll ratify; seal it with feasts.
Set on there! Never was a war did cease,
Ere bloody hands were wash'd, with such a peace. *Exeunt*

Pericles,
Prince of Tyre

PERICLES, PRINCE OF TYRE

HEMINGE and Condell did not include *Pericles* in their collected edition of the plays. Only in the second issue of the Third Folio was it added to the others. Six others were added with it at that time: *The London Prodigal*, *The History of Thomas Lord Cromwell*, *Sir John Oldcastle*, *The Puritan Widow*, *A Yorkshire Tragedy*, *The Tragedy of Locrine*. None of these six has any claim to be Shakespeare's, so that *Pericles* comes into the Folio canon in bad company. Its merits are in certain places, however, so conspicuous that there can be little doubt that Shakespeare contributed a considerable part of the piece.

That Heminge and Condell omitted *Pericles* from the First Folio because it was only in part by Shakespeare is a conjecture supported by other external evidence about its printing. On 20 May 1608 the publisher Edward Blount entered *Pericles* and *Antony and Cleopatra* in the Stationers' Register as his copy. As Blount was the stationer to whom Heminge and Condell entrusted the sixteen plays for entry in the Stationers' Register immediately before their publication in the First Folio, there can hardly have been any difficulty in including *Pericles* had the editors so desired, for the right of publication was safely in the hands of Blount, their agent, thanks to his entry of 20 May. It is true that in spite of Blount's entry an edition, not sponsored by Blount, and with a very unsatisfactory text, appeared in quarto in 1609. This pirated version might be regarded as an obstacle to Blount's own printing of the piece, for the state of the law governing printing in Elizabethan and Jacobean times made such anomalies possible, were it not that Jaggard included it in the 1619 volume of plays he attributed to Shakespeare; as Jaggard was the printer of the First Folio, both the printer and his colleague the publisher Blount had such a claim on *Pericles* that its omission from the First Folio cannot be attributed to any difficulty about printing rights. Its omission was therefore in no way forced on the editors, and although the quarto edition attributed the piece to Shakespeare, Heminge and Condell would know the authorship of a play performed by their company, as *Pericles* was, and if they knew that Shakespeare had no more than a share, however extensive, in it, this would explain their leaving it aside. Unfortunately when the stationers added it to the Third Folio in 1664 they had no good version at their disposal and merely reprinted a reprint of the faulty edition of 1609.

The assumption that *Pericles* was omitted from the First Folio because of its divided authorship is also supported by the very clear division of the play into two parts. The first two acts are on the whole poor stuff; while suddenly with the opening of the third act the voice of Shakespeare is unmistakable; from there to the end Shakespeare was clearly in charge. As the version of the play that has come down to us is a most imperfect one, it has been suggested that the differences between the first and second parts of the piece might be explained by the different quality not of the original text but of those who reported it. This, however, would not explain those differences between the parts that underlie the vocabulary and versification; and were this suggestion accepted and the play attributed wholly to Shakespeare, we should then be confronted with the difficulty of explaining its omission from the First Folio. The differences between the two parts are so obvious at different levels as to make the attribution of the play to two authors the simplest solution, and one that agrees entirely with the external evidence from publication.

That Shakespeare was responsible for the second part of the play finds confirmation not merely in the style and vocabulary but in the general tone and treatment of a theme he keeps handling and rehandling in his final period. Marina and her fortunes correspond to Perdita and Miranda and their loss or banishment and restoration. The theme had so strong a hold on his imagination that he was able to adapt what must be judged the not very promising story of *Pericles* to his purpose. *The Winter's Tale* may be said to contain a number of violent episodes, for it was no part of Shakespeare's plan to minimize the unpleasant features of the world in which his heroines had to find their happiness, but the Pericles story has some specially unpleasant features, as Chaucer had in earlier times protested. That the play is not wholly Shakespeare's allows us to conjecture that he did not himself turn of his own accord to the wonderfully popular, in spite of the features Chaucer comments on, story of the Prince of Tyre, but that examining in his professional capacity as the company's senior dramatist a play submitted for inspection or even perhaps a yet unfinished piece, he saw the advantage of grafting a conception of his own on to what was a pretty rude stock. The result was completely successful as a popular attraction. Numerous contemporary references attest its drawing power. One of the most interesting occurs in Ben Jonson's Ode beginning,

> Come leave the loathed stage
> And the more loathsome age;
> Where pride and impudence, in faction knit,
> Usurp the chair of wit!

This Ode he wrote after the failure of his comedy *The New Inn* in his own defence; asking himself what the age finds to its taste, Jonson continues,

> No doubt some mouldy tale,
> Like Pericles, and stale
> As the shrieve's crusts, and nasty as his fish—

Another tribute hard on the heels of its earlier production must be noticed. In 1608 George Wilkins published *The Painfull Adventures of Pericles Prince of Tyre* which he offers to the reader as 'The True History of the Play of *Pericles*' as acted by the King's men. It has been suggested that Wilkins was also the author of part of the play; yet his procedure in adapting the play to his prose version, as well as his manner, does not seem that of one as familiar with the original as its part author would be. The play draws on two main sources, Gower's version of the Apollonius of Tyre story in his *Confessio Amantis*, and Laurence Twine's *Patterne of Paynfull Adventures*. Wilkins does not seem to know Gower at first hand, while he supplements freely from Twine.

It must be recognized that while the presence of Shakespeare's hand in a considerable part of the play seems beyond all question, we can only guess at the particular circumstances in which he contributed to such a piece, although the demands

of the Jacobean theatre must often have prompted a ready and skilful pen to fill out or adjust some production to an acceptable shape. We have Jonson's word that a second pen had a good share in his *Sejanus;* we can only guess that the happy genius who helped Jonson out was Shakespeare, for the borrowed matter Jonson replaced later with his own. In *Pericles* we have an instance, doubtless, where Shakespeare transformed a piece; but who the other author was, and the details generally of the collaboration, careful examination by scholars has so far failed to establish with certainty. What has been achieved, however, by this study in the interpretation of the play is important and indeed decisive. Dryden could say

> *Shakespear's* own Muse her *Pericles* first bore;
> The Prince of *Tyre* was elder than the *Moore.*

Later criticism has shown that *Pericles,* though a far less closely knit drama, comes after not before *Othello;* yet at the same time the placing of *Pericles* with *The Winter's Tale, Cymbeline,* and *The Tempest* emphasizes the peculiar nature of the interests Shakespeare now had in mind and assists in the interpretation without which neither *Pericles* nor its companions can be fairly judged.

GOWER, *as Chorus*

ANTIOCHUS, *King of Antioch*
PERICLES, *Prince of Tyre*
HELICANUS } *two lords of Tyre*
ESCANES }
SIMONIDES, *King of Pentapolis*
CLEON, *Governor of Tharsus*
LYSIMACHUS, *Governor of Mytilene*
CERIMON, *a lord of Ephesus*
THALIARD, *a lord of Antioch*
PHILEMON, *servant to Cerimon*
LEONINE, *servant to Dionyza*
MARSHAL
A PANDER
BOULT, *his servant*

THE DAUGHTER *of Antiochus*
DIONYZA, *wife to Cleon*
THAISA, *daughter to Simonides*
MARINA, *daughter to Pericles and Thaisa*
LYCHORIDA, *nurse to Marina*
A BAWD

DIANA

Lords, Ladies, Knights, Gentlemen, Sailors, Pirates, Fishermen, *and* Messengers

SCENE:

Dispersedly in various countries

Pericles, Prince of Tyre

ACT I

Antioch. Before the palace

Enter GOWER

To sing a song that old was sung,
From ashes ancient Gower is come,
Assuming man's infirmities,
To glad your ear and please your eyes.
It hath been sung at festivals,
On ember-eves and holy-ales;
And lords and ladies in their lives
Have read it for restoratives.
The purchase is to make men glorious;
Et bonum quo antiquius, eo melius.
If you, born in those latter times,
When wit's more ripe, accept my rhymes,
And that to hear an old man sing
May to your wishes pleasure bring,
I life would wish, and that I might
Waste it for you, like taper-light.
This Antioch, then, Antiochus the Great
Built up, this city, for his chiefest seat;
The fairest in all Syria—
I tell you what mine authors say.
This king unto him took a fere,
Who died and left a female heir,
So buxom, blithe, and full of face,
As heaven had lent her all his grace;
With whom the father liking took,
And her to incest did provoke.
Bad child! Worse father! To entice his own
To evil should be done by none.
But custom what they did begin
Was with long use account no sin.

The beauty of this sinful dame
Made many princes thither frame
To seek her as a bed-fellow,
In marriage-pleasures play-fellow;
Which to prevent he made a law–
To keep her still, and men in awe–
That whoso ask'd her for his wife,
His riddle told not, lost his life.
So for her many a wight did die,
As yon grim looks do testify.
What now ensues to the judgment of your eye
I give, my cause who best can justify. *Exit*

SCENE 1

Antioch. The palace

Enter ANTIOCHUS, PRINCE PERICLES, *and followers*

ANTIOCHUS. Young Prince of Tyre, you have at large received
The danger of the task you undertake.
PERICLES. I have, Antiochus, and, with a soul
Embold'ned with the glory of her praise,
Think death no hazard in this enterprise.
ANTIOCHUS. Bring in our daughter, clothed like a bride
For the embracements even of Jove himself; [*Music*]
At whose conception, till Lucina reigned,
Nature this dowry gave to glad her presence:
The senate-house of planets all did sit,
To knit in her their best perfections.

Enter the DAUGHTER *of* ANTIOCHUS

PERICLES. See where she comes, apparell'd like the spring,
Graces her subjects, and her thoughts the king
Of every virtue gives renown to men.
Her face the book of praises, where is read
Nothing but curious pleasures, as from thence
Sorrow were ever raz'd, and testy wrath
Could never be her mild companion.

You gods that made me man, and sway in love,
That have inflam'd desire in my breast
To taste the fruit of yon celestial tree,
Or die in the adventure, be my helps,
As I am son and servant to your will,
To compass such a boundless happiness!

ANTIOCHUS. Prince Pericles—

PERICLES. That would be son to great Antiochus.

ANTIOCHUS. Before thee stands this fair Hesperides,
With golden fruit, but dangerous to be touch'd;
For death-like dragons here affright thee hard.
Her face, like heaven, enticeth thee to view
Her countless glory, which desert must gain;
And which, without desert, because thine eye
Presumes to reach, all the whole heap must die.
Yon sometimes famous princes, like thyself,
Drawn by report, advent'rous by desire,
Tell thee, with speechless tongues and semblance pale,
That, without covering, save yon field of stars,
Here they stand martyrs, slain in Cupid's wars;
And with dead cheeks advise thee to desist
For going on death's net, whom none resist.

PERICLES. Antiochus, I thank thee, who hath taught
My frail mortality to know itself,
And by those fearful objects to prepare
This body, like to them, to what I must;
For death remembered should be like a mirror,
Who tells us life's but breath, to trust it error.
I'll make my will then, and, as sick men do,
Who know the world, see heaven, but, feeling woe,
Gripe not at earthly joys as erst they did;
So I bequeath a happy peace to you
And all good men, as every prince should do;
My riches to the earth from whence they came;
[*To the* PRINCESS] But my unspotted fire of love to you.
Thus ready for the way of life or death,
I wait the sharpest blow, Antiochus.

ANTIOCHUS. Scorning advice, read the conclusion then:
Which read and not expounded, 'tis decreed,
As these before thee, thou thyself shalt bleed.

DAUGHTER. Of all 'say'd yet, mayst thou prove prosperous!
Of all 'say'd yet, I wish thee happiness!
PERICLES. Like a bold champion I assume the lists
Nor ask advice of any other thought
But faithfulness and courage. [*Reads*]

THE RIDDLE

I am no viper, yet I feed
On mother's flesh which did me breed.
I sought a husband, in which labour
I found that kindness in a father.
He's father, son, and husband mild;
I mother, wife, and yet his child.
How they may be, and yet in two,
As you will live, resolve it you.

[*Aside*] Sharp physic is the last. But, O you powers
That give heaven countless eyes to view men's acts,
Why cloud they not their sights perpetually,
If this be true, which makes me pale to read it?
Fair glass of light, I lov'd you, and could still,
Were not this glorious casket stor'd with ill.
But I must tell you now my thoughts revolt;
For he's no man on whom perfections wait
That, knowing sin within, will touch the gate.
You are a fair viol, and your sense the strings;
Who, finger'd to make man his lawful music,
Would draw heaven down, and all the gods, to hearken;
But, being play'd upon before your time,
Hell only danceth at so harsh a chime.
Good sooth, I care not for you.
ANTIOCHUS. Prince Pericles, touch not, upon thy life,
For that's an article within our law
As dangerous as the rest. Your time's expir'd:
Either expound now, or receive your sentence.
PERICLES. Great King,
Few love to hear the sins they love to act;
'Twould braid yourself too near for me to tell it.
Who has a book of all that monarchs do,
He's more secure to keep it shut than shown;

For vice repeated is like the wand'ring wind,
Blows dust in others' eyes, to spread itself;
And yet the end of all is bought thus dear,
The breath is gone, and the sore eyes see clear
To stop the air would hurt them. The blind mole casts
Copp'd hills towards heaven, to tell the earth is throng'd
By man's oppression, and the poor worm doth die for't.
Kings are earth's gods; in vice their law's their will;
And if Jove stray, who dares say Jove doth ill?
It is enough you know; and it is fit,
What being more known grows worse, to smother it.
All love the womb that their first being bred;
Then give my tongue like leave to love my head.

ANTIOCHUS. [*Aside*] Heaven, that I had thy head! He has found the meaning.
But I will gloze with him.—Young Prince of Tyre,
Though by the tenour of our strict edict,
Your exposition misinterpreting,
We might proceed to cancel of your days;
Yet hope, succeeding from so fair a tree
As your fair self, doth tune us otherwise.
Forty days longer we do respite you;
If by which time our secret be undone,
This mercy shows we'll joy in such a son;
And until then your entertain shall be
As doth befit our honour and your worth.

Exeunt all but PERICLES

PERICLES. How courtesy would seem to cover sin,
When what is done is like an hypocrite,
The which is good in nothing but in sight!
If it be true that I interpret false,
Then were it certain you were not so bad
As with foul incest to abuse your soul;
Where now you're both a father and a son
By your untimely claspings with your child—
Which pleasure fits a husband, not a father—
And she an eater of her mother's flesh
By the defiling of her parent's bed;
And both like serpents are, who, though they feed
On sweetest flowers, yet they poison breed.

Antioch, farewell! for wisdom sees those men
Blush not in actions blacker than the night
Will shun no course to keep them from the light.
One sin I know another doth provoke:
Murder's as near to lust as flame to smoke.
Poison and treason are the hands of sin,
Ay, and the targets to put off the shame.
Then, lest my life be cropp'd to keep you clear,
By flight I'll shun the danger which I fear. *Exit*

Re-enter ANTIOCHUS

ANTIOCHUS. He hath found the meaning,
For which we mean to have his head.
He must not live to trumpet forth my infamy,
Nor tell the world Antiochus doth sin
In such a loathed manner;
And therefore instantly this prince must die;
For by his fall my honour must keep high.
Who attends us there?

Enter THALIARD

THALIARD. Doth your Highness call?
ANTIOCHUS. Thaliard, you are of our chamber, and our mind partakes
Her private actions to your secrecy;
And for your faithfulness we will advance you.
Thaliard, behold here's poison and here's gold;
We hate the Prince of Tyre, and thou must kill him.
It fits thee not to ask the reason why,
Because we bid it. Say, is it done?
THALIARD. My lord,
'Tis done.
ANTIOCHUS. Enough.

Enter a MESSENGER

Let your breath cool yourself, telling your haste.
MESSENGER. My lord, Prince Pericles is fled. *Exit*
ANTIOCHUS. As thou wilt live, fly after; and like an arrow shot from a well-experienc'd archer hits the mark his eye

doth level at, so thou never return unless thou say Prince Pericles is dead.

THALIARD. My lord, if I can get him within my pistol's length I'll make him sure enough. So, farewell to your Highness.

ANTIOCHUS. Thaliard, adieu! [*Exit* THALIARD] Till Pericles be dead
My heart can lend no succour to my head. *Exit*

SCENE 2

Tyre. The palace

Enter PERICLES *with his* LORDS

PERICLES. Let none disturb us. *Exeunt* LORDS
Why should this change of thoughts,
The sad companion, dull-ey'd melancholy,
Be my so us'd a guest as not an hour
In the day's glorious walk, or peaceful night,
The tomb where grief should sleep, can breed me quiet?
Here pleasures court mine eyes, and mine eyes shun them,
And danger, which I fear'd, is at Antioch,
Whose arm seems far too short to hit me here.
Yet neither pleasure's art can joy my spirits,
Nor yet the other's distance comfort me.
Then it is thus: the passions of the mind,
That have their first conception by misdread,
Have after-nourishment and life by care;
And what was first but fear what might be done
Grows elder now, and cares it be not done.
And so with me. The great Antiochus—
'Gainst whom I am too little to contend,
Since he's so great can make his will his act—
Will think me speaking, though I swear to silence;
Nor boots it me to say I honour him,
If he suspect I may dishonour him;
And what may make him blush in being known,
He'll stop the course by which it might be known.
With hostile forces he'll o'erspread the land,

And with th' ostent of war will look so huge
Amazement shall drive courage from the state;
Our men be vanquish'd ere they do resist,
And subjects punish'd that ne'er thought offence;
Which care of them, not pity of myself—
Who am no more but as the tops of trees
Which fence the roots they grow by and defend them—
Makes both my body pine and soul to languish,
And punish that before that he would punish.

Enter HELICANUS *and all the* LORDS

FIRST LORD. Joy and all comfort in your sacred breast!
SECOND LORD. And keep your mind till you return to us,
Peaceful and comfortable!
HELICANUS. Peace, peace, and give experience tongue.
They do abuse the king that flatter him,
For flattery is the bellows blows up sin;
The thing the which is flattered but a spark,
To which that blast gives heat and stronger glowing;
Whereas reproof, obedient, and in order,
Fits kings as they are men, for they may err.
When Signior Sooth here does proclaim a peace,
He flatters you, makes war upon your life.
Prince, pardon me, or strike me if you please;
I cannot be much lower than my knees. [*Kneels*]
PERICLES. All leave us else; but let your cares o'erlook
What shipping and what lading's in our haven,
And then return to us. [*Exeunt* LORDS] Helicanus, thou
Hast moved us. What seest thou in our looks?
HELICANUS. An angry brow, dread lord.
PERICLES. If there be such a dart in princes' frowns,
How durst thy tongue move anger to our face?
HELICANUS. How dare the plants look up to heaven, from whence
They have their nourishment?
PERICLES. Thou know'st I have power
To take thy life from thee.
HELICANUS. I have ground the axe myself;
Do but you strike the blow.
PERICLES. Rise, pr'ythee, rise.

Sit down. Thou art no flatterer.
I thank thee for't; and heaven forbid
That kings should let their ears hear their faults chid!
Fit counsellor and servant for a prince,
Who by thy wisdom mak'st a prince thy servant,
What wouldst thou have me do?

HELICANUS. To bear with patience
Such griefs as you yourself do lay upon yourself.

PERICLES. Thou speak'st like a physician, Helicanus,
That ministers a potion unto me
That thou wouldst tremble to receive thyself.
Attend me, then: I went to Antioch,
Where, as thou know'st, against the face of death,
I sought the purchase of a glorious beauty,
From whence an issue I might propagate
Are arms to princes and bring joys to subjects.
Her face was to mine eye beyond all wonder;
The rest—hark in thine ear—as black as incest;
Which by my knowledge found, the sinful father
Seem'd not to strike, but smooth. But thou know'st this,
'Tis time to fear when tyrants seem to kiss.
Which fear so grew in me I hither fled
Under the covering of a careful night,
Who seem'd my good protector; and, being here,
Bethought me what was past, what might succeed.
I knew him tyrannous; and tyrants' fears
Decrease not, but grow faster than the years;
And should he doubt it, as no doubt he doth,
That I should open to the list'ning air
How many worthy princes' bloods were shed
To keep his bed of blackness unlaid ope,
To lop that doubt, he'll fill this land with arms,
And make pretence of wrong that I have done him;
When all, for mine, if I may call offence,
Must feel war's blow, who spares not innocence;
Which love to all, of which thyself art one,
Who now reprov'dst me for't—

HELICANUS. Alas, sir!

PERICLES. Drew sleep out of mine eyes, blood from my cheeks,

Musings into my mind, with thousand doubts
How I might stop this tempest ere it came;
And, finding little comfort to relieve them,
I thought it princely charity to grieve them.

HELICANUS. Well, my lord, since you have given me leave to speak,
Freely will I speak. Antiochus you fear,
And justly too, I think, you fear the tyrant,
Who either by public war or private treason
Will take away your life.
Therefore, my lord, go travel for a while
Till that his rage and anger be forgot,
Or till the Destinies do cut his thread of life.
Your rule direct to any; if to me,
Day serves not light more faithful than I'll be.

PERICLES. I do not doubt thy faith;
But should he wrong my liberties in my absence?

HELICANUS. We'll mingle our bloods together in the earth,
From whence we had our being and our birth.

PERICLES. Tyre, I now look from thee then, and to Tharsus
Intend my travel, where I'll hear from thee;
And by whose letters I'll dispose myself.
The care I had and have of subjects' good
On thee I lay, whose wisdom's strength can bear it.
I'll take thy word for faith, not ask thine oath:
Who shuns not to break one will sure crack both.
But in our orbs we'll live so round and safe
That time of both this truth shall ne'er convince,
Thou show'dst a subject's shine, I a true prince. *Exeunt*

SCENE 3

Tyre. The palace

Enter THALIARD

THALIARD. So, this is Tyre, and this the court. Here must I kill King Pericles; and if I do it not, I am sure to be hang'd at home. 'Tis dangerous. Well, I perceive he was a wise fellow and had good discretion that, being bid to ask what he would of the king, desired he might know none of his secrets. Now do I see he had some reason for't; for if a king bid a man be a villain, he's bound by the indenture of his oath to be one. Husht! here comes the lords of Tyre.

Enter HELICANUS, ESCANES, *with other* LORDS

HELICANUS. You shall not need, my fellow peers of Tyre,
Further to question me of your King's departure:
His seal'd commission, left in trust with me,
Does speak sufficiently he's gone to travel.

THALIARD. [*Aside*] How! the King gone!

HELICANUS. If further yet you will be satisfied
Why, as it were unlicens'd of your loves,
He would depart, I'll give some light unto you.
Being at Antioch–

THALIARD. [*Aside*] What from Antioch?

HELICANUS. Royal Antiochus, on what cause I know not,
Took some displeasure at him; at least he judg'd so;
And doubting lest that he had err'd or sinn'd,
To show his sorrow, he'd correct himself;
So puts himself unto the shipman's toil,
With whom each minute threatens life or death.

THALIARD. [*Aside*] Well, I perceive
I shall not be hang'd now although I would;
But since he's gone, the King's seas must please
He scap'd the land to perish at the seas.
I'll present myself.–Peace to the Lords of Tyre!

HELICANUS. Lord Thaliard from Antiochus is welcome.

THALIARD. From him I come
With message unto princely Pericles;
But since my landing I have understood
Your lord has betook himself to unknown travels,
Now message must return from whence it came.

HELICANUS. We have no reason to desire it,
Commended to our master, not to us;
Yet, ere you shall depart, this we desire–
As friends to Antioch, we may feast in Tyre. *Exeunt*

SCENE 4

Tharsus. The Governor's house

Enter CLEON *the Governor of Tharsus, with* DIONYZA *his wife, and others*

CLEON. My Dionyza, shall we rest us here,
And by relating tales of others' griefs
See if 'twill teach us to forget our own?
DIONYZA. That were to blow at fire in hope to quench it;
For who digs hills because they do aspire
Throws down one mountain to cast up a higher.
O my distressed lord, even such our griefs are!
Here they are but felt and seen with mischief's eyes,
But like to groves, being topp'd, they higher rise.
CLEON. O Dionyza,
Who wanteth food, and will not say he wants it,
Or can conceal his hunger till he famish?
Our tongues and sorrows to sound deep
Our woes into the air; our eyes to weep?
Till tongues fetch breath that may proclaim them louder;
That, if heaven slumber while their creatures want,
They may awake their helps to comfort them.
I'll then discourse our woes, felt several years,
And, wanting breath to speak, help me with tears.
DIONYZA. I'll do my best, sir.
CLEON. This Tharsus, o'er which I have the government,
A city on whom plenty held full hand,
For Riches strew'd herself even in her streets;
Whose towers bore heads so high they kiss'd the clouds,
And strangers ne'er beheld but wond'red at;
Whose men and dames so jetted and adorn'd,
Like one another's glass to trim them by;
Their tables were stor'd full, to glad the sight,
And not so much to feed on as delight;
All poverty was scorn'd, and pride so great
The name of help grew odious to repeat.
DIONYZA. O, 'tis too true!
CLEON. But see what heaven can do! By this our change

These mouths who but of late earth, sea, and air,
Were all too little to content and please,
Although they gave their creatures in abundance,
As houses are defil'd for want of use,
They are now starv'd for want of exercise.
Those palates who, not yet two summers younger,
Must have inventions to delight the taste,
Would now be glad of bread, and beg for it.
Those mothers who to nouzle up their babes
Thought nought too curious are ready now
To eat those little darlings whom they lov'd.
So sharp are hunger's teeth that man and wife
Draw lots who first shall die to lengthen life.
Here stands a lord, and there a lady weeping;
Here many sink, yet those which see them fall
Have scarce strength left to give them burial.
Is not this true?

DIONYZA. Our cheeks and hollow eyes do witness it.

CLEON. O, let those cities that of Plenty's cup
And her prosperities so largely taste,
With their superfluous riots, hear these tears!
The misery of Tharsus may be theirs.

Enter a LORD

LORD. Where's the Lord Governor?

CLEON. Here.
Speak out thy sorrows which thou bring'st in haste,
For comfort is too far for us to expect.

LORD. We have descried, upon our neighbouring shore,
A portly sail of ships make hitherward.

CLEON. I thought as much.
One sorrow never comes but brings an heir
That may succeed as his inheritor;
And so in ours: some neighbouring nation,
Taking advantage of our misery,
Hath stuff'd the hollow vessels with their power,
To beat us down, the which are down already;
And make a conquest of unhappy me,
Whereas no glory's got to overcome.

LORD. That's the least fear; for by the semblance

Of their white flags display'd, they bring us peace,
And come to us as favourers, not as foes.

CLEON. Thou speak'st like him's untutor'd to repeat:
Who makes the fairest show means most deceit.
But bring they what they will and what they can,
What need we fear?
Our ground's the lowest, and we are halfway there.
Go tell their general we attend him here,
To know for what he comes, and whence he comes,
And what he craves.

LORD. I go, my lord. *Exit*

CLEON. Welcome is peace, if he on peace consist;
If wars, we are unable to resist.

Enter PERICLES, *with attendants*

PERICLES. Lord Governor, for so we hear you are,
Let not our ships and number of our men
Be like a beacon fir'd t'amaze your eyes.
We have heard your miseries as far as Tyre,
And seen the desolation of your streets;
Nor come we to add sorrow to your tears,
But to relieve them of their heavy load;
And these our ships, you happily may think
Are like the Troyan horse war stuff'd within
With bloody veins, expecting overthrow,
Are stor'd with corn to make your needy bread,
And give them life whom hunger starv'd half dead.

ALL. The gods of Greece protect you!
And we'll pray for you. [*They kneel*]

PERICLES. Arise, I pray you, rise.
We do not look for reverence, but for love,
And harbourage for ourself, our ships, and men.

CLEON. The which when any shall not gratify,
Or pay you with unthankfulness in thought,
Be it our wives, our children, or ourselves,
The curse of heaven and men succeed their evils!
Till when–the which I hope shall ne'er be seen–
Your Grace is welcome to our town and us.

PERICLES. Which welcome we'll accept; feast here awhile,
Until our stars that frown lend us a smile. *Exeunt*

ACT II

Enter GOWER

GOWER. Here have you seen a mighty king
His child I wis to incest bring;
A better prince and benign lord,
That will prove awful both in deed and word.
Be quiet then, as men should be,
Till he hath pass'd necessity.
I'll show you those in troubles reign,
Losing a mite, a mountain gain.
The good in conversation,
To whom I give my benison,
Is still at Tharsus, where each man
Thinks all is writ he spoken can;
And, to remember what he does,
Build his statue to make him glorious.
But tidings to the contrary
Are brought your eyes. What need speak I?

DUMB SHOW

Enter, at one door, PERICLES, *talking with* CLEON; *all the train with them. Enter, at another door, a* GENTLEMAN *with a letter to* PERICLES; PERICLES *shows the letter to* CLEON. PERICLES *gives the messenger a reward, and knights him. Exit* PERICLES *at one door and* CLEON *at another*

Good Helicane, that stay'd at home,
Not to eat honey like a drone
From others' labours; for though he strive
To killen bad, keep good alive;
And, to fulfil his prince' desire,
Sends word of all that haps in Tyre:
How Thaliard came full bent with sin
And had intent to murder him;
And that in Tharsus was not best
Longer for him to make his rest.
He, doing so, put forth to seas,
Where when men been, there's seldom ease;

For now the wind begins to blow;
Thunder above and deeps below
Makes such unquiet that the ship
Should house him safe is wreck'd and split;
And he, good prince, having all lost,
By waves from coast to coast is toss'd.
All perishen of man, of pelf,
Ne aught escapen but himself;
Till fortune, tir'd with doing bad,
Threw him ashore, to give him glad.
And here he comes. What shall be next,
Pardon old Gower–this longs the text. *Exit*

SCENE 1

Pentapolis. An open place by the seaside

Enter PERICLES, *wet*

PERICLES. Yet cease your ire, you angry stars of heaven!
Wind, rain, and thunder, remember earthly man
Is but a substance that must yield to you;
And I, as fits my nature, do obey you.
Alas, the sea hath cast me on the rocks,
Wash'd me from shore to shore, and left me breath
Nothing to think on but ensuing death.
Let it suffice the greatness of your powers
To have bereft a prince of all his fortunes;
And having thrown him from your wat'ry grave,
Here to have death in peace is all he'll crave.

Enter three FISHERMEN

FIRST FISHERMAN. What, ho, Pilch!

SECOND FISHERMAN. Ha, come and bring away the nets.

FIRST FISHERMAN. What, Patchbreech, I say!

THIRD FISHERMAN. What say you, master?

FIRST FISHERMAN. Look how thou stirr'st now. Come away, or I'll fetch thee with a wanion.

THIRD FISHERMAN. Faith, master, I am thinking of the poor men that were cast away before us even now.

FIRST FISHERMAN. Alas, poor souls! It grieved my heart to hear what pitiful cries they made to us to help them, when, well-a-day, we could scarce help ourselves.

THIRD FISHERMAN. Nay, master, said not I as much when I saw the porpas how he bounc'd and tumbled? They say they're half fish, half flesh. A plague on them! They ne'er come but I look to be wash'd. Master, I marvel how the fishes live in the sea.

FIRST FISHERMAN. Why, as men do a-land—the great ones eat up the little ones. I can compare our rich misers to nothing so fitly as to a whale: 'a plays and tumbles, driving the poor fry before him, and at last devours them all at a mouthful. Such whales have I heard on a' th' land, who never leave gaping till they've swallow'd the whole parish, church, steeple, bells, and all.

PERICLES. [*Aside*] A pretty moral.

THIRD FISHERMAN. But, master, if I had been the sexton, I would have been that day in the belfry.

SECOND FISHERMAN. Why, man?

THIRD FISHERMAN. Because he should have swallowed me too; and when I had been in his belly I would have kept such a jangling of the bells that he should never have left till he cast bells, steeple, church, and parish up again. But if the good King Simonides were of my mind—

PERICLES. [*Aside*] Simonides!

THIRD FISHERMAN. We would purge the land of these drones that rob the bee of her honey.

PERICLES. [*Aside*] How from the finny subject of the sea
These fishers tell the infirmities of men,
And from their wat'ry empire recollect
All that may men approve or men detect!—
Peace be at your labour, honest fishermen!

SECOND FISHERMAN. Honest—good fellow! What's that? If it be a day fits you, scratch't out of the calendar, and nobody look after it.

PERICLES. May see the sea hath cast upon your coast—

SECOND FISHERMAN. What a drunken knave was the sea to cast thee in our way!

PERICLES. A man whom both the waters and the wind
In that vast tennis-court hath made the ball

For them to play upon entreats you pity him;
He asks of you that never us'd to beg.

FIRST FISHERMAN. No, friend, cannot you beg? Here's them in our country of Greece gets more with begging than we can do with working.

SECOND FISHERMAN. Canst thou catch any fishes, then?

PERICLES. I never practis'd it.

SECOND FISHERMAN. Nay, then thou wilt starve, sure; for here's nothing to be got now-a-days unless thou canst fish for't.

PERICLES. What I have been I have forgot to know;
But what I am want teaches me to think on:
A man throng'd up with cold; my veins are chill,
And have no more of life than may suffice
To give my tongue that heat to ask your help;
Which if you shall refuse, when I am dead,
For that I am a man, pray see me buried.

FIRST FISHERMAN. Die quoth-a? Now gods forbid't! And I have a gown here! Come, put it on; keep thee warm. Now, afore me, a handsome fellow! Come, thou shalt go home, and we'll have flesh for holidays, fish for fasting days, and moreo'er puddings and flapjacks; and thou shalt be welcome.

PERICLES. I thank you, sir.

SECOND FISHERMAN. Hark you, my friend; you said you could not beg.

PERICLES. I did but crave.

SECOND FISHERMAN. But crave! Then I'll turn craver too, and so I shall scape whipping.

PERICLES. Why, are all your beggars whipp'd, then?

SECOND FISHERMAN. O, not all, my friend, not all! For if all your beggars were whipp'd, I would wish no better office than to be beadle. But, master, I'll go draw up the net.

Exit with THIRD FISHERMAN

PERICLES. [*Aside*] How well this honest mirth becomes their labour!

FIRST FISHERMAN. Hark you, sir; do you know where ye are?

PERICLES. Not well.

FIRST FISHERMAN. Why, I'll tell you: this is call'd Pentapolis, and our king the good Simonides.

PERICLES. The good Simonides, do you call him?

FIRST FISHERMAN. Ay, sir; and he deserves so to be call'd for his peaceable reign and good government.

PERICLES. He is a happy king, since he gains from his subjects the name of good by his government. How far is his court distant from this shore?

FIRST FISHERMAN. Marry, sir, half a day's journey; and I'll tell you, he hath a fair daughter, and to-morrow is her birthday, and there are princes and knights come from all parts of the world to joust and tourney for her love.

PERICLES. Were my fortunes equal to my desires, I could wish to make one there.

FIRST FISHERMAN. O sir, things must be as they may; and what a man cannot get he may lawfully deal for—his wife's soul.

Re-enter SECOND *and* THIRD FISHERMEN, *drawing up a net*

SECOND FISHERMAN. Help, master, help! Here's a fish hangs in the net like a poor man's right in the law; 'twill hardly come out. Ha! Bots on't! 'Tis come at last, and 'tis turn'd to a rusty armour.

PERICLES. An armour, friends! I pray you let me see it.
Thanks, Fortune, yet, that after all my crosses
Thou givest me somewhat to repair myself;
And though it was mine own, part of my heritage
Which my dead father did bequeath to me,
With this strict charge, even as he left his life:
'Keep it, my Pericles. It hath been a shield
'Twixt me and death'; and pointed to this brace
'For that it sav'd me, keep it. In like necessity—
The which the gods protect thee from!—may't defend thee!'
It kept where I kept, I so dearly lov'd it;
Till the rough seas, that spare not any man,
Took it in rage, though calm'd have given't again—
I thank thee for't. My shipwreck now's no ill,
Since I have here my father's gift in his will.

FIRST FISHERMAN. What mean you, sir?

PERICLES. To beg of you, kind friends, this coat of worth

For it was sometime target to a king;
I know it by this mark. He lov'd me dearly,
And for his sake I wish the having of it;
And that you'd guide me to your sovereign's court,
Where with it I may appear a gentleman;
And if that ever my low fortune's better,
I'll pay your bounties; till then rest your debtor.

FIRST FISHERMAN. Why, wilt thou tourney for the lady?

PERICLES. I'll show the virtue I have borne in arms.

FIRST FISHERMAN. Why, do 'e take it, and the gods give thee good on't!

SECOND FISHERMAN. Ay, but hark you, my friend; 'twas we that made up this garment through the rough seams of the waters; there are certain condolements, certain vails. I hope, sir, if you thrive, you'll remember from whence you had them.

PERICLES. Believe't, I will.
By your furtherance I am cloth'd in steel;
And spite of all the rupture of the sea
This jewel holds his building on my arm.
Unto thy value I will mount myself
Upon a courser whose delightful steps
Shall make the gazer joy to see him tread.
Only, my friend, I yet am unprovided
Of a pair of bases.

SECOND FISHERMAN. We'll sure provide. Thou shalt have my best gown to make thee a pair; and I'll bring thee to the court myself.

PERICLES. Then honour be but a goal to my will;
This day I'll rise, or else add ill to ill. *Exeunt*

SCENE 2

Pentapolis. A public way or platform leading to the lists. A pavilion by the side of it for the reception of the KING, PRINCESS, LORDS, *&c.*

Enter SIMONIDES, THAISA, LORDS, *and attendants*

SIMONIDES. Are the knights ready to begin the triumph?

FIRST LORD. They are, my liege;
And stay your coming to present themselves.
SIMONIDES. Return them we are ready; and our daughter here,
In honour of whose birth these triumphs are,
Sits here like beauty's child, whom nature gat
For men to see, and seeing wonder at. *Exit a* LORD
THAISA. It pleaseth you, my royal father, to express
My commendations great, whose merit's less.
SIMONIDES. It's fit it should be so; for princes are
A model which heaven makes like to itself:
As jewels lose their glory if neglected,
So princes their renowns if not respected.
'Tis now your honour, daughter, to entertain
The labour of each knight in his device.
THAISA. Which, to preserve mine honour, I'll perform.

Enter a KNIGHT; *he passes over, and his* SQUIRE *presents his shield to the* PRINCESS

SIMONIDES. Who is the first that doth prefer himself?
THAISA. A knight of Sparta, my renowned father;
And the device he bears upon his shield
Is a black Ethiope reaching at the sun;
The word, 'Lux tua vita mihi.'
SIMONIDES. He loves you well that holds his life of you.

The SECOND KNIGHT *passes by*

Who is the second that presents himself?
THAISA. A prince of Macedon, my royal father;
And the device he bears upon his shield
Is an arm'd knight that's conquer'd by a lady;
The motto thus, in Spanish, 'Piu por dulzura que por fuerza.'

The THIRD KNIGHT *passes by*

SIMONIDES. And what's the third?
THAISA. The third of Antioch
And his device a wreath of chivalry;
The word, 'Me pompæ provexit apex.'

The FOURTH KNIGHT *passes by*

SIMONIDES. What is the fourth?
THAISA. A burning torch that's turned upside down;
The word, 'Quod me alit, me extinguit.'
SIMONIDES. Which shows that beauty hath his power and will,
Which can as well inflame as it can kill.

The FIFTH KNIGHT *passes by*

THAISA. The fifth, an hand environed with clouds,
Holding out gold that's by the touchstone tried;
The motto thus, 'Sic spectanda fides.'

PERICLES *as* SIXTH KNIGHT *passes by*

SIMONIDES. And what's the sixth and last, the which the knight himself
With such a graceful courtesy deliver'd?
THAISA. He seems to be a stranger; but his present is
A withered branch, that's only green at top;
The motto, 'In hac spe vivo.'
SIMONIDES. A pretty moral;
From the dejected state wherein he is,
He hopes by you his fortunes yet may flourish.
FIRST LORD. He had need mean better than his outward show
Can any way speak in his just commend;
For by his rusty outside he appears
To have practis'd more the whipstock than the lance.
SECOND LORD. He well may be a stranger, for he comes
To an honour'd triumph strangely furnished.
THIRD LORD. And on set purpose let his armour rust
Until this day, to scour it in the dust.
SIMONIDES. Opinion's but a fool, that makes us scan
The outward habit by the inward man.
But stay, the knights are coming. We will withdraw
Into the gallery. *Exeunt*
[*Great shouts within, and all cry* 'The mean knight!']

SCENE 3

Pentapolis. A hall of state. A banquet prepared

Enter KING SIMONIDES, THAISA, LADIES, MARSHAL, LORDS, KNIGHTS, *from tilting, and attendants*

SIMONIDES. Knights!
To say you're welcome were superfluous.
To place upon the volume of your deeds,
As in a title-page, your worth in arms
Were more than you expect, or more than's fit,
Since every worth in show commends itself.
Prepare for mirth, for mirth becomes a feast;
You are princes and my guests.

THAISA. But you my knight and guest;
To whom this wreath of victory I give,
And crown you king of this day's happiness.

PERICLES. 'Tis more by fortune, lady, than my merit.

SIMONIDES. Call it by what you will, the day is yours;
And here I hope is none that envies it.
In framing an artist, art hath thus decreed,
To make some good, but others to exceed;
And you are her labour'd scholar. Come, queen o' th' feast—
For, daughter, so you are—here take your place.
Marshal the rest as they deserve their grace.

KNIGHTS. We are honour'd much by good Simonides.

SIMONIDES. Your presence glads our days. Honour we love;
For who hates honour hates the gods above.

MARSHAL. Sir, yonder is your place.

PERICLES. Some other is more fit.

FIRST KNIGHT. Contend not, sir; for we are gentlemen
That neither in our hearts nor outward eyes
Envy the great nor shall the low despise.

PERICLES. You are right courteous knights.

SIMONIDES. Sit, sir, sit.
[*Aside*] By Jove, I wonder, that is king of thoughts,
These cates resist me, she but thought upon.

THAISA. [*Aside*] By Juno, that is queen of marriage,

All viands that I eat do seem unsavoury,
Wishing him my meat.—Sure he's a gallant gentleman.
SIMONIDES. He's but a country gentleman;
Has done no more than other knights have done;
Has broken a staff or so; so let it pass.
THAISA. [*Aside*] To me he seems like diamond to glass.
PERICLES. [*Aside*] Yon king's to me like to my father's picture,
Which tells me in that glory once he was;
Had princes sit like stars about his throne,
And he the sun, for them to reverence;
None that beheld him but, like lesser lights,
Did vail their crowns to his supremacy:
Where now his son's like a glowworm in the night,
The which hath fire in darkness, none in light.
Whereby I see that Time's the king of men;
He's both their parent, and he is their grave,
And gives them what he will, not what they crave.
SIMONIDES. What, are you merry, Knights?
FIRST KNIGHT. Who can be other in this royal presence?
SIMONIDES. Here, with a cup that's stor'd unto the brim—
As you do love, fill to your mistress' lips—
We drink this health to you.
KNIGHTS. We thank your Grace.
SIMONIDES. Yet pause awhile.
Yon knight doth sit too melancholy,
As if the entertainment in our court
Had not a show might countervail his worth.
Note it not you, Thaisa?
THAISA. What is't
To me, my father?
SIMONIDES. O, attend, my daughter:
Princes, in this, should live like gods above,
Who freely give to every one that comes
To honour them;
And princes not doing so are like to gnats,
Which make a sound, but kill'd are wond'red at.
Therefore to make his entertain more sweet,
Here, say we drink this standing-bowl of wine to him.
THAISA. Alas, my father, it befits not me

Unto a stranger knight to be so bold:
He may my proffer take for an offence,
Since men take women's gifts for impudence.

SIMONIDES. How!
Do as I bid you, or you'll move me else.

THAISA. [*Aside*] Now, by the gods, he could not please me better.

SIMONIDES. And furthermore tell him we desire to know of him
Of whence he is, his name and parentage.

THAISA. The King my father, sir, has drunk to you.

PERICLES. I thank him.

THAISA. Wishing it so much blood unto your life.

PERICLES. I thank both him and you, and pledge him freely.

THAISA. And further he desires to know of you
Of whence you are, your name and parentage.

PERICLES. A gentleman of Tyre—my name, Pericles;
My education been in arts and arms;
Who, looking for adventures in the world,
Was by the rough seas reft of ships and men,
And after shipwreck driven upon this shore.

THAISA. He thanks your Grace; names himself Pericles,
A gentleman of Tyre,
Who only by misfortune of the seas,
Bereft of ships and men, cast on this shore.

SIMONIDES. Now, by the gods, I pity his misfortune,
And will awake him from his melancholy.
Come, gentlemen, we sit too long on trifles
And waste the time which looks for other revels.
Even in your armours, as you are address'd,
Will very well become a soldier's dance.
I will not have excuse, with saying this
Loud music is too harsh for ladies' heads,
Since they love men in arms as well as beds. [*They dance*]
So, this was well ask'd, 'twas so well perform'd.
Come, sir;
Here is a lady that wants breathing too;
And I have heard you knights of Tyre
Are excellent in making ladies trip;
And that their measures are as excellent.

PERICLES. In those that practise them they are, my lord.
SIMONIDES. O, that's as much as you would be denied
Of your fair courtesy. [*The* KNIGHTS *and* LADIES *dance*]
Unclasp, unclasp.
Thanks, gentlemen, to all; all have done well,
[*To* PERICLES] But you the best.—Pages and lights, to conduct
These knights unto their several lodgings!—Yours, sir,
We have given order to be next our own.
PERICLES. I am at your Grace's pleasure.
SIMONIDES. Princes, it is too late to talk of love,
And that's the mark I know you level at.
Therefore each one betake him to his rest;
To-morrow all for speeding do their best. *Exeunt*

SCENE 4

Tyre. The Governor's house

Enter HELICANUS *and* ESCANES

HELICANUS. No, Escanes; know this of me—
Antiochus from incest liv'd not free;
For which, the most high gods not minding longer
To withhold the vengeance that they had in store,
Due to this heinous capital offence,
Even in the height and pride of all his glory,
When he was seated in a chariot
Of an inestimable value, and his daughter with him,
A fire from heaven came and shrivell'd up
Their bodies, even to loathing; for they so stunk
That all those eyes ador'd them ere their fall
Scorn now their hand should give them burial.
ESCANES. 'Twas very strange.
HELICANUS. And yet but justice: for though
This king were great, his greatness was no guard
To bar heaven's shaft, but sin had his reward.
ESCANES. 'Tis very true.

Enter two or three LORDS

FIRST LORD. See, not a man in private conference
  Or council has respect with him but he.
SECOND LORD. It shall no longer grieve without reproof.
THIRD LORD. And curs'd be he that will not second it!
FIRST LORD. Follow me, then. Lord Helicane, a word.
HELICANUS. With me? and welcome. Happy day, my lords.
FIRST LORD. Know that our griefs are risen to the top,
  And now at length they overflow their banks.
HELICANUS. Your griefs! for what? Wrong not your prince you love.
FIRST LORD. Wrong not yourself, then, noble Helicane;
  But if the prince do live, let us salute him,
  Or know what ground's made happy by his breath.
  If in the world he live, we'll seek him out;
  If in his grave he rest, we'll find him there;
  And be resolv'd he lives to govern us,
  Or, dead, give's cause to mourn his funeral,
  And leave us to our free election.
SECOND LORD. Whose death's indeed the strongest in our censure;
  And knowing this kingdom, if without a head,
  Like goodly buildings left without a roof,
  Soon fall to ruin, your noble self,
  That best know how to rule and how to reign,
  We thus submit unto—our sovereign.
ALL. Live, noble Helicane!
HELICANUS. By honour's cause, forbear your suffrages.
  If that you love Prince Pericles, forbear.
  Take I your wish, I leap into the seas,
  Where's hourly trouble for a minute's ease.
  A twelvemonth longer let me entreat you
  To forbear the absence of your king;
  If in which time expir'd he not return,
  I shall with aged patience bear your yoke.
  But if I cannot win you to this love,
  Go search like nobles, like noble subjects,
  And in your search spend your adventurous worth;
  Whom if you find, and win unto return,
  You shall like diamonds sit about his crown.
FIRST LORD. To wisdom he's a fool that will not yield;

And since Lord Helicane enjoineth us,
We with our travels will endeavour it.

HELICANUS. Then you love us, we you, and we'll clasp hands:
When peers thus knit, a kingdom ever stands. *Exeunt*

SCENE 5

Pentapolis. The palace

Enter SIMONIDES, *reading of a letter, at one door. The* KNIGHTS *meet him*

FIRST KNIGHT. Good morrow to the good Simonides.

SIMONIDES. Knights, from my daughter this I let you know,
That for this twelvemonth she'll not undertake
A married life.
Her reason to herself is only known,
Which from her by no means can I get.

SECOND KNIGHT. May we not get access to her, my lord?

SIMONIDES. Faith, by no means; she hath so strictly tied her
To her chamber that it is impossible.
One twelve moons more she'll wear Diana's livery.
This by the eye of Cynthia hath she vow'd,
And on her virgin honour will not break it.

THIRD KNIGHT. Loath to bid farewell, we take our leaves.

Exeunt KNIGHTS

SIMONIDES. So,
They are well dispatch'd. Now to my daughter's letter.
She tells me here she'll wed the stranger knight,
Or never more to view nor day nor light.
'Tis well, mistress; your choice agrees with mine;
I like that well. Nay, how absolute she's in't,
Not minding whether I dislike or no!
Well, I do commend her choice;
And will no longer have it be delay'd.
Soft! here he comes: I must dissemble it.

Enter PERICLES

PERICLES. All fortune to the good Simonides!

SIMONIDES. To you as much, sir! I am beholding to you
For your sweet music this last night. I do
Protest my ears were never better fed
With such delightful pleasing harmony.
PERICLES. It is your Grace's pleasure to commend;
Not my desert.
SIMONIDES. Sir, you are music's master.
PERICLES. The worst of all her scholars, my good lord.
SIMONIDES. Let me ask you one thing:
What do you think of my daughter, sir?
PERICLES. A most virtuous princess.
SIMONIDES. And she is fair too, is she not?
PERICLES. As a fair day in summer—wondrous fair.
SIMONIDES. Sir, my daughter thinks very well of you;
Ay, so well that you must be her master,
And she will be your scholar; therefore look to it.
PERICLES. I am unworthy for her schoolmaster.
SIMONIDES. She thinks not so; peruse this writing else.
PERICLES. [*Aside*] What's here?
A letter, that she loves the knight of Tyre.
'Tis the king's subtlety to have my life.—
O, seek not to entrap me, gracious lord,
A stranger and distressed gentleman,
That never aim'd so high to love your daughter,
But bent all offices to honour her!
SIMONIDES. Thou hast bewitch'd my daughter, and thou art
A villain.
PERICLES. By the gods, I have not.
Never did thought of mine levy offence;
Nor never did my actions yet commence
A deed might gain her love or your displeasure.
SIMONIDES. Traitor, thou liest.
PERICLES. Traitor!
SIMONIDES. Ay, traitor.
PERICLES. Even in his throat—unless it be the King—
That calls me traitor I return the lie.
SIMONIDES. [*Aside*] Now, by the gods, I do applaud his courage.
PERICLES. My actions are as noble as my thoughts,
That never relish'd of a base descent.

I came unto your court for honour's cause,
And not to be a rebel to her state;
And he that otherwise accounts of me,
This sword shall prove he's honour's enemy.
SIMONIDES. No?
Here comes my daughter, she can witness it.

Enter THAISA

PERICLES. Then, as you are as virtuous as fair,
Resolve your angry father if my tongue
Did e'er solicit, or my hand subscribe
To any syllable that made love to you.
THAISA. Why, sir, say if you had,
Who takes offence at that would make me glad?
SIMONIDES. Yea, mistress, are you so peremptory?
[*Aside*] I am glad on't with all my heart.–
I'll tame you; I'll bring you in subjection.
Will you, not having my consent,
Bestow your love and your affections
Upon a stranger?–[*Aside*] who, for aught I know,
May be, nor can I think the contrary,
As great in blood as I myself.–
Therefore, hear you, mistress: either frame
Your will to mine–and you, sir, hear you,
Either be rul'd by me–or I will make you–
Man and wife.
Nay, come, your hands and lips must seal it too;
And being join'd, I'll thus your hopes destroy,
And for further grief–God give you joy!
What, are you both pleas'd?
THAISA. Yes, if you love me, sir.
PERICLES. Even as my life my blood that fosters it.
SIMONIDES. What, are you both agreed?
BOTH. Yes, if't please your Majesty.
SIMONIDES. It pleaseth me so well that I will see you wed;
And then, with what haste you can, get you to bed.

Exeunt

ACT III

Enter GOWER

GOWER. Now sleep yslaked hath the rout;
No din but snores the house about,
Made louder by the o'er-fed breast
Of this most pompous marriage feast.
The cat, with eyne of burning coal,
Now couches fore the mouse's hole;
And crickets sing at the oven's mouth,
Aye the blither for their drouth.
Hymen hath brought the bride to bed,
Where, by the loss of maidenhead,
A babe is moulded. Be attent,
And time that is so briefly spent
With your fine fancies quaintly eche.
What's dumb in show I'll plain with speech.

DUMB SHOW

Enter PERICLES *and* SIMONIDES *at one door, with attendants; a* MESSENGER *meets them, kneels, and gives* PERICLES *a letter.* PERICLES *shows it* SIMONIDES; *the* LORDS *kneel to* PERICLES. *Then enter* THAISA, *with child, with* LYCHORIDA, *a nurse. The* KING *shows her the letter; she rejoices. She and* PERICLES *take leave of her father, and depart with* LYCHORIDA *and their attendants. Then exeunt* SIMONIDES *and the rest*

By many a dern and painful perch
Of Pericles the careful search,
By the four opposing coigns
Which the world together joins,
Is made with all due diligence
That horse and sail and high expense
Can stead the quest. At last from Tyre—
Fame answering the most strange inquire—
To the court of King Simonides
Are letters brought, the tenour these:
Antiochus and his daughter dead,

The men of Tyrus on the head
Of Helicanus would set on
The crown of Tyre, but he will none.
The mutiny he there hastes t' oppress;
Says to 'em, if King Pericles
Come not home in twice six moons,
He, obedient to their dooms,
Will take the crown. The sum of this,
Brought hither to Pentapolis,
Y-ravished the regions round,
And every one with claps can sound
'Our heir-apparent is a king!
Who dream'd, who thought of such a thing?'
Brief, he must hence depart to Tyre.
His queen with child makes her desire–
Which who shall cross?–along to go.
Omit we all their dole and woe.
Lychorida, her nurse, she takes,
And so to sea. Their vessel shakes
On Neptune's billow; half the flood
Hath their keel cut: but fortune's mood
Varies again; the grizzled north
Disgorges such a tempest forth
That, as a duck for life that dives,
So up and down the poor ship drives.
The lady shrieks, and, well-a-near,
Does fall in travail with her fear;
And what ensues in this fell storm
Shall for itself itself perform.
I nill relate, action may
Conveniently the rest convey;
Which might not what by me is told.
In your imagination hold
This stage the ship, upon whose deck
The sea-toss'd Pericles appears to speak. *Exit*

SCENE 1

Enter PERICLES, *a-shipboard*

PERICLES. Thou god of this great vast, rebuke these surges,
Which wash both heaven and hell; and thou that hast
Upon the winds command, bind them in brass,
Having call'd them from the deep! O, still
Thy deaf'ning dreadful thunders; gently quench
Thy nimble sulphurous flashes!—O, how, Lychorida,
How does my queen?—Thou stormest venomously;
Wilt thou spit all thyself? The seaman's whistle
Is as a whisper in the ears of death,
Unheard.—Lychorida!—Lucina, O
Divinest patroness, and midwife gentle
To those that cry by night, convey thy deity
Aboard our dancing boat; make swift the pangs
Of my queen's travails!

Enter LYCHORIDA, *with an* INFANT

Now, Lychorida!

LYCHORIDA. Here is a thing too young for such a place,
Who, if it had conceit, would die, as I
Am like to do. Take in your arms this piece
Of your dead queen.

PERICLES. How, how, Lychorida?

LYCHORIDA. Patience, good sir; do not assist the storm.
Here's all that is left living of your queen—
A little daughter. For the sake of it,
Be manly, and take comfort.

PERICLES. O you gods!
Why do you make us love your goodly gifts,
And snatch them straight away? We here below
Recall not what we give, and therein may
Use honour with you.

LYCHORIDA. Patience, good sir, even for this charge.

PERICLES. Now, mild may be thy life!
For a more blusterous birth had never babe;
Quiet and gentle thy conditions! for
Thou art the rudeliest welcome to this world

That ever was prince's child. Happy what follows!
Thou hast as chiding a nativity
As fire, air, water, earth, and heaven, can make,
To herald thee from the womb.
Even at the first thy loss is more than can
Thy portage quit with all thou canst find here.
Now the good gods throw their best eyes upon't!

Enter two SAILORS

FIRST SAILOR. What courage, sir? God save you!

PERICLES. Courage enough: I do not fear the flaw;
It hath done to me the worst. Yet, for the love
Of this poor infant, this fresh-new seafarer,
I would it would be quiet.

FIRST SAILOR. Slack the bolins there.—Thou wilt not, wilt thou? Blow, and split thyself.

SECOND SAILOR. But sea-room, an the brine and cloudy billow kiss the moon, I care not.

FIRST SAILOR. Sir, your queen must overboard: the sea works high, the wind is loud, and will not lie till the ship be clear'd of the dead.

PERICLES. That's your superstition.

FIRST SAILOR. Pardon us, sir; with us at sea it hath been still observed, and we are strong in custom. Therefore briefly yield 'er; for she must overboard straight.

PERICLES. As you think meet. Most wretched queen!

LYCHORIDA. Here she lies, sir.

PERICLES. A terrible childbed hast thou had, my dear;
No light, no fire. Th' unfriendly elements
Forgot thee utterly; nor have I time
To give thee hallow'd to thy grave, but straight
Must cast thee, scarcely coffin'd, in the ooze;
Where, for a monument upon thy bones,
And aye-remaining lamps, the belching whale
And humming water must o'erwhelm thy corpse,
Lying with simple shells. O Lychorida,
Bid Nestor bring me spices, ink and paper,
My casket and my jewels; and bid Nicander
Bring me the satin coffer. Lay the babe
Upon the pillow. Hie thee, whiles I say

A priestly farewell to her. Suddenly, woman.

Exit LYCHORIDA

SECOND SAILOR. Sir, we have a chest beneath the hatches, caulk'd and bitumed ready.

PERICLES. I thank thee. Mariner, say what coast is this?

SECOND SAILOR. We are near Tharsus.

PERICLES. Thither, gentle mariner,
Alter thy course for Tyre. When canst thou reach it?

SECOND SAILOR. By break of day, if the wind cease.

PERICLES. O, make for Tharsus!
There will I visit Cleon, for the babe
Cannot hold out to Tyrus; there I'll leave it
At careful nursing. Go thy ways, good mariner:
I'll bring the body presently. *Exeunt*

SCENE 2

Ephesus. CERIMON'S *house*

Enter CERIMON, *with a* SERVANT, *and some persons who have been shipwrecked*

CERIMON. Philemon, ho!

Enter PHILEMON

PHILEMON. Doth my lord call?

CERIMON. Get fire and meat for these poor men.
'T 'as been a turbulent and stormy night.

SERVANT. I have been in many; but such a night as this,
Till now, I ne'er endured.

CERIMON. Your master will be dead ere you return;
There's nothing can be minist'red to nature
That can recover him. [*To* PHILEMON] Give this to the 'pothecary,
And tell me how it works. *Exeunt all but* CERIMON

Enter two GENTLEMEN

FIRST GENTLEMAN. Good morrow.

SECOND GENTLEMAN. Good morrow to your lordship.

CERIMON. Gentlemen, why do you stir so early?

FIRST GENTLEMAN. Sir,

Our lodgings, standing bleak upon the sea,
Shook as the earth did quake;
The very principals did seem to rend,
And all to topple. Pure surprise and fear
Made me to quit the house.

SECOND GENTLEMAN. That is the cause we trouble you so early;
'Tis not our husbandry.

CERIMON. O, you say well.

FIRST GENTLEMAN. But I much marvel that your lordship, having
Rich tire about you, should at these early hours
Shake off the golden slumber of repose.
'Tis most strange
Nature should be so conversant with pain,
Being thereto not compell'd.

CERIMON. I hold it ever
Virtue and cunning were endowments greater
Than nobleness and riches: careless heirs
May the two latter darken and expend;
But immortality attends the former,
Making a man a god. 'Tis known I ever
Have studied physic, through which secret art,
By turning o'er authorities, I have,
Together with my practice, made familiar
To me and to my aid the blest infusions
That dwell in vegetives, in metals, stones;
And I can speak of the disturbances
That nature works, and of her cures; which doth give me
A more content in course of true delight
Than to be thirsty after tottering honour,
Or tie my treasure up in silken bags,
To please the fool and death.

SECOND GENTLEMAN. Your honour has through Ephesus pour'd forth
Your charity, and hundreds call themselves
Your creatures, who by you have been restor'd:
And not your knowledge, your personal pain, but even
Your purse, still open, hath built Lord Cerimon
Such strong renown as time shall never raze.

ACT III. SCENE 2

Enter two or three servants with a chest

FIRST SERVANT. So, lift there.

CERIMON. What's that?

FIRST SERVANT. Sir, even now did the sea toss up upon our shore this chest. 'Tis of some wreck.

CERIMON. Set't down, let's look upon't.

SECOND GENTLEMAN. 'Tis like a coffin, sir.

CERIMON. Whate'er it be,
'Tis wondrous heavy. Wrench it open straight.
If the sea's stomach be o'ercharg'd with gold,
'Tis a good constraint of fortune it belches upon us.

SECOND GENTLEMAN. 'Tis so, my lord.

CERIMON. How close 'tis caulk'd and bitumed!
Did the sea cast it up?

FIRST SERVANT. I never saw so huge a billow, sir, as toss'd it upon shore.

CERIMON. Wrench it open. Soft! It smells most sweetly in my sense.

SECOND GENTLEMAN. A delicate odour.

CERIMON. As ever hit my nostril. So, up with it.
O you most potent gods! What's here? A corse!

FIRST GENTLEMAN. Most strange!

CERIMON. Shrouded in cloth of state; balm'd and entreasur'd with full bags of spices. A passport too. Apollo, perfect me in the characters! [*Reads from a scroll*]

Here I give to understand–
If e'er this coffin drives a-land–
I, King Pericles, have lost
This queen, worth all our mundane cost.
Who finds her, give her burying;
She was the daughter of a king.
Besides this treasure for a fee,
The gods requite his charity!

If thou livest, Pericles, thou hast a heart
That ever cracks for woe! This chanc'd to-night.

SECOND GENTLEMAN. Most likely, sir.

CERIMON. Nay, certainly to-night;
For look how fresh she looks! They were too rough

That threw her in the sea. Make a fire within.
Fetch hither all my boxes in my closet. *Exit a* SERVANT
Death may usurp on nature many hours,
And yet the fire of life kindle again
The o'erpress'd spirits. I heard of an Egyptian
That had nine hours lien dead,
Who was by good appliance recovered.

Re-enter a servant, with boxes, napkins, and fire

Well said, well said! The fire and cloths.
The rough and woeful music that we have,
Cause it to sound, beseech you.
The vial once more. How thou stirr'st, thou block!
The music there! I pray you give her air.
Gentlemen,
This queen will live; nature awakes; a warmth
Breathes out of her. She hath not been entranc'd
Above five hours. See how she gins to blow
Into life's flower again!

FIRST GENTLEMAN. The heavens,
Through you, increase our wonder, and set up
Your fame for ever.

CERIMON. She is alive. Behold,
Her eyelids, cases to those heavenly jewels
Which Pericles hath lost, begin to part
Their fringes of bright gold; the diamonds
Of a most praised water do appear,
To make the world twice rich. Live, and make
Us weep to hear your fate, fair creature,
Rare as you seem to be. [*She moves*]

THAISA. O dear Diana, where am I?
Where's my lord? What world is this?

SECOND GENTLEMAN. Is not this strange?

FIRST GENTLEMAN. Most rare.

CERIMON. Hush, my gentle neighbours!
Lend me your hands: to the next chamber bear her;
Get linen. Now this matter must be look'd to,
For her relapse is mortal.
Come, come; and Æsculapius guide us!
Exeunt, carrying her away

SCENE 3

Tharsus. CLEON'S *house*

Enter PERICLES, CLEON, DIONYZA, *and* LYCHORIDA *with* MARINA *in her arms*

PERICLES. Most honour'd Cleon, I must needs be gone;
My twelve months are expir'd, and Tyrus stands
In a litigious peace. You and your lady
Take from my heart all thankfulness! The gods
Make up the rest upon you!
CLEON. Your shafts of fortune, though they hurt you mortally,
Yet glance full wand'ringly on us.
DIONYZA. O your sweet queen!
That the strict Fates had pleas'd you had brought her hither,
To have bless'd mine eyes with her!
PERICLES. We cannot but obey
The powers above us. Could I rage and roar
As doth the sea she lies in, yet the end
Must be as 'tis. My gentle babe Marina, whom,
For she was born at sea, I have nam'd so, here
I charge your charity withal, leaving her
The infant of your care; beseeching you
To give her princely training, that she may
Be manner'd as she is born.
CLEON. Fear not, my lord, but think
Your grace, that fed my country with your corn,
For which the people's prayers still fall upon you,
Must in your child be thought on. If neglection
Should therein make me vile, the common body,
By you reliev'd, would force me to my duty.
But if to that my nature need a spur,
The gods revenge it upon me and mine
To the end of generation!
PERICLES. I believe you;
Your honour and your goodness teach me to't
Without your vows. Till she be married, madam,

Marina. *I will rob Tellus of her weed,*
To strew thy green with flowers. The yellows, blues,
The purple violets, and marigolds,
Shall as a carpet hang upon thy grave
While summer days do last.

(Act IV. Scene 1)

By bright Diana, whom we honour all,
Unscissor'd shall this hair of mine remain,
Though I show ill in't. So I take my leave.
Good madam, make me blessed in your care
In bringing up my child.

DIONYZA. I have one myself,
Who shall not be more dear to my respect
Than yours, my lord.

PERICLES. Madam, my thanks and prayers.

CLEON. We'll bring your Grace e'en to the edge o' th' shore,
Then give you up to the mask'd Neptune and
The gentlest winds of heaven.

PERICLES. I will embrace
Your offer. Come, dearest madam. O, no tears,
Lychorida, no tears.
Look to your little mistress, on whose grace
You may depend hereafter. Come, my lord. *Exeunt*

SCENE 4

Ephesus. CERIMON'S *house*

Enter CERIMON *and* THAISA

CERIMON. Madam, this letter, and some certain jewels,
Lay with you in your coffer; which are
At your command. Know you the character?

THAISA. It is my lord's.
That I was shipp'd at sea I well remember,
Even on my eaning time; but whether there
Delivered, by the holy gods,
I cannot rightly say. But since King Pericles,
My wedded lord, I ne'er shall see again,
A vestal livery will I take me to,
And never more have joy.

CERIMON. Madam, if this you purpose as ye speak,
Diana's temple is not distant far,
Where you may abide till your date expire.
Moreover, if you please, a niece of mine

Shall there attend you.

THAISA. My recompense is thanks, that's all;
Yet my good will is great, though the gift small. *Exeunt*

ACT IV

Enter GOWER

GOWER. Imagine Pericles arriv'd at Tyre,
Welcom'd and settled to his own desire.
His woeful queen we leave at Ephesus,
Unto Diana there a votaress.
Now to Marina bend your mind,
Whom our fast-growing scene must find
At Tharsus, and by Cleon train'd
In music, letters; who hath gain'd
Of education all the grace,
Which makes her both the heart and place
Of general wonder. But, alack,
That monster Envy, oft the wrack
Of earned praise, Marina's life
Seeks to take off by treason's knife.
And in this kind hath our Cleon
One daughter, and a wench full grown,
Even ripe for marriage-rite; this maid
Hight Philoten; and it is said
For certain in our story, she
Would ever with Marina be.
Be't when she weav'd the sleided silk
With fingers long, small, white as milk;
Or when she would with sharp needle wound
The cambric, which she made more sound
By hurting it; or when to th' lute
She sung, and made the night-bird mute,
That still records with moan; or when
She would with rich and constant pen
Vail to her mistress Dian; still
This Philoten contends in skill

With absolute Marina. So
The dove of Paphos might with the crow
Vie feathers white. Marina gets
All praises, which are paid as debts,
And not as given. This so darks
In Philoten all graceful marks
That Cleon's wife, with envy rare,
A present murderer does prepare
For good Marina, that her daughter
Might stand peerless by this slaughter.
The sooner her vile thoughts to stead,
Lychorida, our nurse, is dead;
And cursed Dionyza hath
The pregnant instrument of wrath
Prest for this blow. The unborn event
I do commend to your content;
Only I carry winged time
Post on the lame feet of my rhyme;
Which never could I so convey
Unless your thoughts went on my way.
Dionyza does appear,
With Leonine, a murderer. *Exit*

SCENE 1

Tharsus. An open place near the seashore

Enter DIONYZA *and* LEONINE

DIONYZA. Thy oath remember; thou hast sworn to do't.
'Tis but a blow, which never shall be known.
Thou canst not do a thing in the world so soon
To yield thee so much profit. Let not conscience,
Which is but cold, inflaming love in thy bosom,
Inflame too nicely; nor let pity, which
Even women have cast off, melt thee, but be
A soldier to thy purpose.
LEONINE. I will do't; but yet she is a goodly creature.
DIONYZA. The fitter, then, the gods should have her.
Here she comes weeping for her only mistress' death.

Thou art resolv'd?
LEONINE. I am resolv'd.

Enter MARINA *with a basket of flowers*

MARINA. No, I will rob Tellus of her weed,
To strew thy green with flowers. The yellows, blues,
The purple violets, and marigolds,
Shall as a carpet hang upon thy grave
While summer days do last. Ay me! poor maid,
Born in a tempest, when my mother died,
This world to me is like a lasting storm,
Whirring me from my friends.
DIONYZA. How now, Marina! Why do you keep alone?
How chance my daughter is not with you? Do not
Consume your blood with sorrowing; you have
A nurse of me. Lord, how your favour's chang'd
With this unprofitable woe! Come,
Give me your flowers. On the sea margent
Walk with Leonine; the air is quick there,
And it pierces and sharpens the stomach. Come,
Leonine, take her by the arm, walk with her.
MARINA. No, I pray you;
I'll not bereave you of your servant.
DIONYZA. Come, come;
I love the king your father, and yourself,
With more than foreign heart. We every day
Expect him here. When he shall come, and find
Our paragon to all reports thus blasted,
He will repent the breadth of his great voyage;
Blame both my lord and me that we have taken
No care to your best courses. Go, I pray you,
Walk, and be cheerful once again; reserve
That excellent complexion which did steal
The eyes of young and old. Care not for me;
I can go home alone.
MARINA. Well, I will go;
But yet I have no desire to it.
DIONYZA. Come, come, I know 'tis good for you.
Walk half an hour, Leonine, at the least.
Remember what I have said.

LEONINE. I warrant you, madam.
DIONYZA. I'll leave you, my sweet lady, for a while.
Pray walk softly; do not heat your blood.
What! I must have a care of you.
MARINA. My thanks, sweet madam. *Exit* DIONYZA
Is this wind westerly that blows?
LEONINE. South-west.
MARINA. When I was born the wind was north.
LEONINE. Was't so?
MARINA. My father, as nurse says, did never fear,
But cried 'Good seamen!' to the sailors, galling
His kingly hands hauling ropes;
And, clasping to the mast, endur'd a sea
That almost burst the deck.
LEONINE. When was this?
MARINA. When I was born.
Never was waves nor wind more violent;
And from the ladder-tackle washes off
A canvas-climber. 'Ha!' says one 'wilt out?'
And with a dropping industry they skip
From stern to stern; the boatswain whistles, and
The master calls, and trebles their confusion.
LEONINE. Come, say your prayers.
MARINA. What mean you?
LEONINE. If you require a little space for prayer,
I grant it. Pray; but be not tedious, for
The gods are quick of ear, and I am sworn
To do my work with haste.
MARINA. Why will you kill me?
LEONINE. To satisfy my lady.
MARINA. Why would she have me kill'd?
Now, as I can remember, by my troth,
I never did her hurt in all my life.
I never spake bad word, nor did ill turn
To any living creature. Believe me, la,
I never kill'd a mouse, nor hurt a fly;
I trod upon a worm against my will,
But I wept for it. How have I offended,
Wherein my death might yield her any profit,
Or my life imply her any danger?

LEONINE. My commission
Is not to reason of the deed, but do't.

MARINA. You will not do't for all the world, I hope.
You are well-favour'd, and your looks foreshow
You have a gentle heart. I saw you lately
When you caught hurt in parting two that fought.
Good sooth, it show'd well in you. Do so now:
Your lady seeks my life; come you between,
And save poor me, the weaker.

LEONINE. I am sworn,
And will dispatch. [*Seizes her*]

Enter PIRATES

FIRST PIRATE. Hold, villain! [LEONINE *runs away*]

SECOND PIRATE. A prize! a prize!

THIRD PIRATE. Half part, mates, half part!
Come, let's have her aboard suddenly.
Exeunt PIRATES *with* MARINA

Re-enter LEONINE

LEONINE. These roguing thieves serve the great pirate Valdes,
And they have seiz'd Marina. Let her go;
There's no hope she will return. I'll swear she's dead
And thrown into the sea. But I'll see further.
Perhaps they will but please themselves upon her,
Not carry her aboard. If she remain,
Whom they have ravish'd must by me be slain. *Exit*

SCENE 2

Mytilene. A brothel

Enter PANDER, BAWD, *and* BOULT

PANDER. Boult!

BOULT. Sir?

PANDER. Search the market narrowly. Mytilene is full of gallants. We lost too much money this mart by being too wenchless.

BAWD. We were never so much out of creatures. We have but poor three, and they can do no more than they can do; and they with continual action are even as good as rotten.

PANDER. Therefore let's have fresh ones, whate'er we pay for them. If there be not a conscience to be us'd in every trade, we shall never prosper.

BAWD. Thou say'st true; 'tis not our bringing up of poor bastards—as, I think, I have brought up some eleven—

BOULT. Ay, to eleven; and brought them down again. But shall I search the market?

BAWD. What else, man? The stuff we have, a strong wind will blow it to pieces, they are so pitifully sodden.

PANDER. Thou sayest true; they are too unwholesome, o' conscience. The poor Transylvanian is dead that lay with the little baggage.

BOULT. Ay, she quickly poop'd him; she made him roast meat for worms. But I'll go search the market. *Exit*

PANDER. Three or four thousand chequins were as pretty a proportion to live quietly, and so give over.

BAWD. Why to give over, I pray you? Is it a shame to get when we are old?

PANDER. O, our credit comes not in like the commodity, nor the commodity wages not with the danger; therefore, if in our youths we could pick up some prety estate, 'twere not amiss to keep our door hatch'd. Besides, the sore terms we stand upon with the gods will be strong with us for giving o'er.

BAWD. Come, other sorts offend as well as we.

PANDER. As well as we! Ay, and better too; we offend worse. Neither is our profession any trade; it's no calling. But here comes Boult.

Re-enter BOULT, *with the* PIRATES *and* MARINA

BOULT. [*To* MARINA] Come your ways.—My masters, you say she's a virgin?

FIRST PIRATE. O, sir, we doubt it not.

BOULT. Master, I have gone through for this piece you see. If you like her, so; if not, I have lost my earnest.

BAWD. Boult, has she any qualities?

BOULT. She has a good face, speaks well, and has excellent good clothes; there's no further necessity of qualities can make her be refus'd.

BAWD. What's her price, Boult?

BOULT. I cannot be bated one doit of a thousand pieces.

PANDER. Well, follow me, my master; you shall have your money presently. Wife, take her in; instruct her what she has to do, that she may not be raw in her entertainment.

Exeunt PANDER *and* PIRATES

BAWD. Boult, take you the marks of her—the colour of her hair, complexion, height, her age, with warrant of her virginity, and cry 'He that will give most shall have her first.' Such a maidenhead were no cheap thing, if men were as they have been. Get this done as I command you.

BOULT. Performance shall follow. *Exit*

MARINA. Alack that Leonine was so slack, so slow!
He should have struck, not spoke; or that these pirates,
Not enough barbarous, had not o'erboard thrown me
For to seek my mother!

BAWD. Why lament you, pretty one?

MARINA. That I am pretty.

BAWD. Come, the gods have done their part in you.

MARINA. I accuse them not.

BAWD. You are light into my hands, where you are like to live.

MARINA. The more my fault
To scape his hands where I was like to die.

BAWD. Ay, and you shall live in pleasure.

MARINA. No.

BAWD. Yes, indeed shall you, and taste gentlemen of all fashions. You shall fare well; you shall have the difference of all complexions. What! do you stop your ears?

MARINA. Are you a woman?

BAWD. What would you have me be, an I be not a woman?

MARINA. An honest woman, or not a woman.

BAWD. Marry, whip thee, gosling! I think I shall have something to do with you. Come, you're a young foolish sapling, and must be bow'd as I would have you.

MARINA. The gods defend me!

BAWD. If it please the gods to defend you by men, then men

must comfort you, men must feed you, men must stir you up. Boult's return'd.

Re-enter BOULT

Now, sir, hast thou cried her through the market?

BOULT. I have cried her almost to the number of her hairs; I have drawn her picture with my voice.

BAWD. And I prithee tell me how dost thou find the inclination of the people, especially of the younger sort?

BOULT. Faith, they listened to me as they would have hearkened to their father's testament. There was a Spaniard's mouth so wat'red that he went to bed to her very description.

BAWD. We shall have him here to-morrow with his best ruff on.

BOULT. To-night, to-night. But, mistress, do you know the French knight that cowers i' th' hams?

BAWD. Who? Monsieur Veroles?

BOULT. Ay, he; he offered to cut a caper at the proclamation; but he made a groan at it, and swore he would see her to-morrow.

BAWD. Well, well; as for him, he brought his disease hither: here he does but repair it. I know he will come in our shadow to scatter his crowns in the sun.

BOULT. Well, if we had of every nation a traveller, we should lodge them with this sign.

BAWD. [*To* MARINA] Pray you, come hither awhile. You have fortunes coming upon you. Mark me: you must seem to do that fearfully which you commit willingly; to despise profit where you have most gain. To weep that you live as ye do makes pity in your lovers; seldom but that pity begets you a good opinion, and that opinion a mere profit.

MARINA. I understand you not.

BOULT. O, take her home, mistress, take her home. These blushes of hers must be quench'd with some present practice.

BAWD. Thou sayest true, i' faith, so they must; for your bride goes to that with shame which is her way to go with warrant.

BOULT. Faith, some do, and some do not. But, mistress, if I have bargain'd for the joint—

BAWD. Thou mayest cut a morsel off the spit.

BOULT. I may so.

BAWD. Who should deny it? Come, young one, I like the manner of your garments well.

BOULT. Ay, by my faith, they shall not be chang'd yet.

BAWD. Boult, spend thou that in the town; report what a sojourner we have; you'll lose nothing by custom. When nature fram'd this piece she meant thee a good turn; therefore say what a paragon she is, and thou hast the harvest out of thine own report.

BOULT. I warrant you, mistress, thunder shall not so awake the beds of eels as my giving out her beauty stir up the lewdly inclined. I'll bring home some to-night.

BAWD. Come your ways; follow me.

MARINA. If fires be hot, knives sharp, or water deep,
Untied I still my virgin knot will keep.
Diana aid my purpose!

BAWD. What have we to do with Diana? Pray you, will you go with us? *Exeunt*

SCENE 3

Tharsus. CLEON'S *house*

Enter CLEON *and* DIONYZA

DIONYZA. Why are you foolish? Can it be undone?

CLEON. O Dionyza, such a piece of slaughter
The sun and moon ne'er look'd upon!

DIONYZA. I think
You'll turn a child again.

CLEON. Were I chief lord of all this spacious world,
I'd give it to undo the deed. O lady,
Much less in blood than virtue, yet a princess
To equal any single crown o' th' earth
I' th' justice of compare! O villain Leonine!
Whom thou hast pois'ned too.
If thou hadst drunk to him, 't had been a kindness

Becoming well thy fact. What canst thou say
When noble Pericles shall demand his child?

DIONYZA. That she is dead. Nurses are not the Fates,
To foster it, nor ever to preserve.
She died at night; I'll say so. Who can cross it?
Unless you play the pious innocent,
And for an honest attribute cry out
'She died by foul play.'

CLEON. O, go to. Well, well.
Of all the faults beneath the heavens the gods
Do like this worst.

DIONYZA. Be one of those that thinks
The petty wrens of Tharsus will fly hence,
And open this to Pericles. I do shame
To think of what a noble strain you are,
And of how coward a spirit.

CLEON. To such proceeding
Who ever but his approbation added,
Though not his prime consent, he did not flow
From honourable sources.

DIONYZA. Be it so, then.
Yet none does know, but you, how she came dead,
Nor none can know, Leonine being gone.
She did distain my child, and stood between
Her and her fortunes. None would look on her,
But cast their gazes on Marina's face;
Whilst ours was blurted at, and held a mawkin,
Not worth the time of day. It pierc'd me thorough;
And though you call my course unnatural,
You not your child well loving, yet I find
It greets me as an enterprise of kindness
Perform'd to your sole daughter.

CLEON. Heavens forgive it!

DIONYZA. And as for Pericles,
What should he say? We wept after her hearse,
And yet we mourn; her monument
Is almost finish'd, and her epitaphs
In glittering golden characters express
A general praise to her, and care in us
At whose expense 'tis done.

CLEON. Thou art like the harpy,
Which, to betray, dost, with thine angel's face,
Seize with thine eagle's talons.
DIONYZA. You are like one that superstitiously
Doth swear to the gods that winter kills the flies;
But yet I know you'll do as I advise. *Exeunt*

SCENE 4

Before MARINA'S *monument at Tharsus*

Enter GOWER

GOWER. Thus time we waste, and longest leagues make short;
Sail seas in cockles, have an wish but for't;
Making, to take our imagination,
From bourn to bourn, region to region.
By you being pardon'd, we commit no crime
To use one language in each several clime
Where our scenes seem to live. I do beseech you
To learn of me, who stand i' th' gaps to teach you
The stages of our story. Pericles
Is now again thwarting the wayward seas,
Attended on by many a lord and knight,
To see his daughter, all his life's delight.
Old Helicanus goes along. Behind
Is left to govern it, you bear in mind,
Old Escanes, whom Helicanus late
Advanc'd in time to great and high estate.
Well-sailing ships and bounteous winds have brought
This king to Tharsus—think this pilot thought;
So with his steerage shall your thoughts grow on—
To fetch his daughter home, who first is gone.
Like motes and shadows see them move awhile;
Your ears unto your eyes I'll reconcile.

DUMB SHOW

Enter PERICLES, *at one door, with all his train:* CLEON *and* DIONYZA *at the other.* CLEON *shows* PERICLES *the tomb of* MARINA, *whereat* PERICLES *makes lamentation, puts on sackcloth, and in a mighty passion departs. Then exeunt* CLEON *and* DIONYZA

See how belief may suffer by foul show!
This borrowed passion stands for true old woe;
And Pericles, in sorrow all devour'd,
With sighs shot through and biggest tears o'ershower'd,
Leaves Tharsus, and again embarks. He swears
Never to wash his face nor cut his hairs;
He puts on sackcloth, and to sea. He bears
A tempest which his mortal vessel tears,
And yet he rides it out. Now please you wit
The epitaph is for Marina writ
By wicked Dionyza. [*Reads the inscription on* MARINA'S *monument*]

'The fairest, sweetest, and best lies here,
Who withered in her spring of year.
She was of Tyrus the King's daughter,
On whom foul death hath made this slaughter;
Marina was she call'd; and at her birth,
Thetis, being proud, swallowed some part o' th' earth;
Therefore the earth, fearing to be o'er-flowed,
Hath Thetis' birth-child on the heavens bestowed;
Wherefore she does–and swears she'll never stint–
Make raging battery upon shores of flint.'

No visor does become black villainy
So well as soft and tender flattery.
Let Pericles believe his daughter's dead,
And bear his courses to be ordered
By Lady Fortune; while our scene must play
His daughter's woe and heavy well-a-day
In her unholy service. Patience, then,
And think you now are all in Mytilen. *Exit*

SCENE 5

Mytilene. A street before the brothel

Enter, from the brothel, two GENTLEMEN

FIRST GENTLEMAN. Did you ever hear the like?

SECOND GENTLEMAN. No, nor never shall do in such a place as this, she being once gone.

FIRST GENTLEMAN. But to have divinity preach'd there! Did you ever dream of such a thing?

SECOND GENTLEMAN. No, no. Come, I am for no more bawdy-houses. Shall's go hear the vestals sing?

FIRST GENTLEMAN. I'll do anything now that is virtuous; but I am out of the road of rutting for ever. *Exeunt*

SCENE 6

Mytilene. A room in the brothel

Enter PANDER, BAWD, *and* BOULT

PANDER. Well, I had rather than twice the worth of her she had ne'er come here.

BAWD. Fie, fie, upon her! She's able to freeze the god Priapus, and undo a whole generation. We must either get her ravished or be rid of her. When she should do for clients her fitment, and do me the kindness of our profession, she has me her quirks, her reasons, her master-reasons, her prayers, her knees; that she would make a puritan of the devil, if he should cheapen a kiss of her.

BOULT. Faith, I must ravish her, or she'll disfurnish us of all our cavalleria and make our swearers priests.

PANDER. Now the pox upon her green-sickness for me!

BAWD. Faith, there's no way to be rid on't but by the way to the pox. Here comes the Lord Lysimachus disguised.

BOULT. We should have both lord and lown, if the peevish baggage would but give way to customers.

Enter LYSIMACHUS

LYSIMACHUS. How now! How a dozen of virginities?

BAWD. Now, the gods to bless your Honour!

BOULT. I am glad to see your Honour in good health.

LYSIMACHUS. You may so; 'tis the better for you that your resorters stand upon sound legs. How now! Wholesome iniquity have you, that a man may deal withal and defy the surgeon?

BAWD. We have here one, sir, if she would—but there never came her like in Mytilene.

LYSIMACHUS. If she'd do the deed of darkness, thou wouldst say.

BAWD. Your Honour knows what 'tis to say well enough.

LYSIMACHUS. Well, call forth, call forth.

BOULT. For flesh and blood, sir, white and red, you shall see a rose; and she were a rose indeed, if she had but—

LYSIMACHUS. What, prithee?

BOULT. O, sir, I can be modest.

LYSIMACHUS. That dignifies the renown of a bawd no less than it gives a good report to a number to be chaste.

Exit BOULT

BAWD. Here comes that which grows to the stalk—never plucked yet, I can assure you.

Re-enter BOULT *with* MARINA

Is she not a fair creature?

LYSIMACHUS. Faith, she would serve after a long voyage at sea. Well, there's for you. Leave us.

BAWD. I beseech your Honour, give me leave: a word, and I'll have done presently.

LYSIMACHUS. I beseech you, do.

BAWD. [*Aside to* MARINA] First, I would have you note this is an honourable man.

MARINA. I desire to find him so, that I may worthily note him.

BAWD. Next, he's the governor of this country, and a man whom I am bound to.

MARINA. If he govern the country, you are bound to him indeed; but how honourable he is in that I know not.

BAWD. Pray you, without any more virginal fencing, will you use him kindly? He will line your apron with gold.

MARINA. What he will do graciously I will thankfully receive.

LYSIMACHUS. Ha' you done?

BAWD. My lord, she's not pac'd yet; you must take some pains to work her to your manage. Come, we will leave his Honour and her together. Go thy ways.

Exeunt BAWD, PANDER, *and* BOULT

LYSIMACHUS. Now, pretty one, how long have you been at this trade?

MARINA. What trade, sir?

LYSIMACHUS. Why, I cannot name't but I shall offend.

MARINA. I cannot be offended with my trade. Please you to name it.

LYSIMACHUS. How long have you been of this profession?

MARINA. E'er since I can remember.

LYSIMACHUS. Did you go to't so young? Were you a gamester at five or at seven?

MARINA. Earlier too, sir, if now I be one.

LYSIMACHUS. Why, the house you dwell in proclaims you to be a creature of sale.

MARINA. Do you know this house to be a place of such resort, and will come into't? I hear say you're of honourable parts, and are the governor of this place.

LYSIMACHUS. Why, hath your principal made known unto you who I am?

MARINA. Who is my principal?

LYSIMACHUS. Why, your herb-woman; she that sets seeds and roots of shame and iniquity. O, you have heard something of my power, and so stand aloof for more serious wooing. But I protest to thee, pretty one, my authority shall not see thee, or else look friendly upon thee. Come, bring me to some private place. Come, come.

MARINA. If you were born to honour, show it now;
If put upon you, make the judgment good
That thought you worthy of it.

LYSIMACHUS. How's this? how's this? Some more; be sage.

MARINA. For me,
That am a maid, though most ungentle fortune
Have plac'd me in this sty, where, since I came,
Diseases have been sold dearer than physic—

That the gods
Would set me free from this unhallowed place,
Though they did change me to the meanest bird
That flies i' th' purer air!

LYSIMACHUS. I did not think
Thou couldst have spoke so well; ne'er dreamt thou couldst.
Had I brought hither a corrupted mind,
Thy speech had altered it. Hold, here's gold for thee:
Persever in that clear way thou goest,
And the gods strengthen thee!

MARINA. The good gods preserve you!

LYSIMACHUS. For me, be you thoughten
That I came with no ill intent; for to me
The very doors and windows savour vilely.
Fare thee well. Thou art a piece of virtue, and
I doubt not but thy training hath been noble.
Hold, here's more gold for thee.
A curse upon him, die he like a thief,
That robs thee of thy goodness! If thou dost
Hear from me, it shall be for thy good.

Re-enter BOULT

BOULT. I beseech your Honour, one piece for me.

LYSIMACHUS. Avaunt, thou damned doorkeeper!
Your house, but for this virgin that doth prop it,
Would sink and overwhelm you. Away! *Exit*

BOULT. How's this? We must take another course with you. If your peevish chastity, which is not worth a breakfast in the cheapest country under the cope, shall undo a whole household, let me be gelded like a spaniel. Come your ways.

MARINA. Whither would you have me?

BOULT. I must have your maidenhead taken off, or the common hangman shall execute it. Come your ways. We'll have no more gentlemen driven away. Come your ways, I say.

Re-enter BAWD

BAWD. How now! What's the matter?

BOULT. Worse and worse, mistress; she has here spoken holy words to the Lord Lysimachus.

BAWD. O abominable!

BOULT. She makes our profession as it were to stink afore the face of the gods.

BAWD. Marry, hang her up for ever!

BOULT. The nobleman would have dealt with her like a nobleman, and she sent him away as cold as a snowball; saying his prayers too.

BAWD. Boult, take her away; use her at thy pleasure. Crack the glass of her virginity, and make the rest malleable.

BOULT. An if she were a thornier piece of ground than she is, she shall be ploughed.

MARINA. Hark, hark, you gods!

BAWD. She conjures. Away with her. Would she had never come within my doors! Marry, hang you! She's born to undo us. Will you not go the way of womenkind? Marry, come up, my dish of chastity with rosemary and bays!

Exit

BOULT. Come, mistress; come your ways with me.

MARINA. Whither wilt thou have me?

BOULT. To take from you the jewel you hold so dear.

MARINA. Prithee tell me one thing first.

BOULT. Come now, your one thing.

MARINA. What canst thou wish thine enemy to be?

BOULT. Why, I could wish him to be my master, or, rather, my mistress.

MARINA. Neither of these are so bad as thou art,
Since they do better thee in their command.
Thou hold'st a place for which the pained'st fiend
Of hell would not in reputation change;
Thou art the damned doorkeeper to every
Coistrel that comes inquiring for his Tib;
To the choleric fisting of every rogue
Thy ear is liable; thy food is such
As hath been belch'd on by infected lungs.

BOULT. What would you have me do? Go to the wars, would you, where a man may serve seven years for the loss of a leg, and have not money enough in the end to buy him a wooden one?

MARINA. Do anything but this thou doest. Empty
Old receptacles, or common shores, of filth;
Serve by indenture to the common hangman.
Any of these ways are yet better than this;
For what thou professest, a baboon, could he speak,
Would own a name too dear. That the gods
Would safely deliver me from this place!
Here, here's gold for thee.
If that thy master would gain by me,
Proclaim that I can sing, weave, sew, and dance,
With other virtues which I'll keep from boast;
And I will undertake all these to teach.
I doubt not but this populous city will
Yield many scholars.

BOULT. But can you teach all this you speak of?

MARINA. Prove that I cannot, take me home again
And prostitute me to the basest groom
That doth frequent your house.

BOULT. Well, I will see what I can do for thee. If I can place thee, I will.

MARINA. But amongst honest women?

BOULT. Faith, my acquaintance lies little amongst them. But since my master and mistress have bought you, there's no going but by their consent. Therefore I will make them acquainted with your purpose, and I doubt not but I shall find them tractable enough. Come, I'll do for thee what I can; come your ways. *Exeunt*

ACT V

Enter GOWER

GOWER. Marina thus the brothel scapes and chances
Into an honest house, our story says.
She sings like one immortal, and she dances
As goddess-like to her admired lays;
Deep clerks she dumbs; and with her needle composes
Nature's own shape of bud, bird, branch, or berry,

That even her art sisters the natural roses;
Her inkle, silk, twin with the rubied cherry;
That pupils lacks she none of noble race,
Who pour their bounty on her; and her gain
She gives the cursed bawd. Here we her place;
And to her father turn our thoughts again,
Where we left him on the sea. We there him lost;
Whence, driven before the winds, he is arriv'd
Here where his daughter dwells; and on this coast
Suppose him now at anchor. The city striv'd
God Neptune's annual feast to keep; from whence
Lysimachus our Tyrian ship espies,
His banners sable, trimm'd with rich expense;
And to him in his barge with fervour hies.
In your supposing once more put your sight.
Of heavy Pericles, think this his bark;
Where what is done in action, more, if might,
Shall be discover'd; please you sit and hark. *Exit*

SCENE 1

On board PERICLES' *ship, off Mytilene. A pavilion on deck with a curtain before it;* PERICLES *within it, reclining on a couch. A barge lying beside the Tyrian vessel*

Enter two SAILORS, *one belonging to the Tyrian vessel, the other to the barge; to them* HELICANUS

TYRIAN SAILOR. [*To the* SAILOR *of Mytilene*] Where is Lord Helicanus? He can resolve you.
O, here he is.
Sir, there is a barge put off from Mytilene,
And in it is Lysimachus the Governor,
Who craves to come aboard. What is your will?
HELICANUS. That he have his. Call up some gentlemen.
TYRIAN SAILOR. Ho, gentlemen! my lord calls.

Enter two or three GENTLEMEN

FIRST GENTLEMAN. Doth your lordship call?

HELICANUS. Gentlemen, there is some of worth would come aboard;
I pray greet him fairly.

The GENTLEMEN *and the two* SAILORS *descend, and go on board the barge. Enter, from thence,* LYSIMACHUS *and* LORDS, *with the* GENTLEMEN *and the two* SAILORS

TYRIAN SAILOR. Sir,
This is the man that can, in aught you would,
Resolve you.
LYSIMACHUS. Hail, reverend sir! The gods preserve you!
HELICANUS. And you, sir, to outlive the age I am,
And die as I would do.
LYSIMACHUS. You wish me well.
Being on shore, honouring of Neptune's triumphs,
Seeing this goodly vessel ride before us,
I made to it, to know of whence you are.
HELICANUS. First, what is your place?
LYSIMACHUS. I am the Governor
Of this place you lie before.
HELICANUS. Sir,
Our vessel is of Tyre, in it the King;
A man who for this three months hath not spoken
To any one, nor taken sustenance
But to prorogue his grief.
LYSIMACHUS. Upon what ground is his distemperature?
HELICANUS. 'Twould be too tedious to repeat;
But the main grief springs from the loss
Of a beloved daughter and a wife.
LYSIMACHUS. May we not see him?
HELICANUS. You may;
But bootless is your sight—he will not speak
To any.
LYSIMACHUS. Yet let me obtain my wish.
HELICANUS. Behold him. [PERICLES *discovered*] This was a goodly person
Till the disaster that, one mortal night,
Drove him to this.
LYSIMACHUS. Sir King, all hail! The gods preserve you!

Hail, royal sir!

HELICANUS. It is in vain; he will not speak to you.

FIRST LORD. Sir, we have a maid in Mytilene, I durst wager,
Would win some words of him.

LYSIMACHUS. 'Tis well bethought.
She, questionless, with her sweet harmony
And other chosen attractions, would allure,
And make a batt'ry through his deafen'd parts,
Which now are midway stopp'd.
She is all happy as the fairest of all,
And, with her fellow maids, is now upon
The leafy shelter that abuts against
The island's side.

[*He whispers* FIRST LORD, *who goes off in the barge of* LYSIMACHUS]

HELICANUS. Sure, all's effectless; yet nothing we'll omit
That bears recovery's name. But, since your kindness
We have stretch'd thus far, let us beseech you
That for our gold we may provision have,
Wherein we are not destitute for want,
But weary for the staleness.

LYSIMACHUS. O sir, a courtesy
Which if we should deny, the most just gods
For every graff would send a caterpillar,
And so inflict our province. Yet once more
Let me entreat to know at large the cause
Of your king's sorrow.

HELICANUS. Sit, sir, I will recount it to you.
But, see, I am prevented.

Re-enter, from the barge, FIRST LORD,
with MARINA *and another girl*

LYSIMACHUS. O, here is
The lady that I sent for. Welcome, fair one!
Is't not a goodly presence?

HELICANUS. She's a gallant lady.

LYSIMACHUS. She's such a one that, were I well assur'd
Came of gentle kind and noble stock,
I'd wish no better choice, and think me rarely wed.
Fair one, all goodness that consists in bounty

Expect even here, where is a kingly patient.
If that thy prosperous and artificial feat
Can draw him but to answer thee in aught,
Thy sacred physic shall receive such pay
As thy desires can wish.

MARINA. Sir, I will use
My utmost skill in his recovery,
Provided
That none but I and my companion maid
Be suffered to come near him.

LYSIMACHUS. Come, let us leave her;
And the gods make her prosperous! [MARINA *sings*]

LYSIMACHUS. Mark'd he your music?

MARINA. No, nor look'd on us.

LYSIMACHUS. See, she will speak to him.

MARINA. Hail sir! my lord, lend ear.

PERICLES. Hum, ha!

MARINA. I am a maid,
My lord, that ne'er before invited eyes,
But have been gaz'd on like a comet. She speaks,
My lord, that, may be, hath endur'd a grief
Might equal yours, if both were justly weigh'd.
Though wayward fortune did malign my state,
My derivation was from ancestors
Who stood equivalent with mighty kings;
But time hath rooted out my parentage,
And to the world and awkward casualties
Bound me in servitude. [*Aside*] I will desist;
But there is something glows upon my cheek,
And whispers in mine ear 'Go not till he speak.'

PERICLES. My fortunes–parentage–good parentage–
To equal mine!–was it not thus? What say you?

MARINA. I said, my lord, if you did know my parentage
You would not do me violence.

PERICLES. I do think so. Pray you turn your eyes upon me.
You are like something that–What countrywoman?
Here of these shores?

MARINA. No, nor of any shores.
Yet I was mortally brought forth, and am
No other than I appear.

PERICLES. I am great with woe, and shall deliver weeping.
My dearest wife was like this maid, and such a one
My daughter might have been: my queen's square brows
Her stature to an inch; as wand-like straight;
As silver-voic'd; her eyes as jewel-like,
And cas'd as richly; in pace another Juno;
Who starves the ears she feeds, and makes them hungry
The more she gives them speech. Where do you live?
MARINA. Where I am but a stranger. From the deck
You may discern the place.
PERICLES. Where were you bred?
And how achiev'd you these endowments, which
You make more rich to owe?
MARINA. If I should tell my history, it would seem
Like lies, disdain'd in the reporting.
PERICLES. Prithee speak.
Falseness cannot come from thee; for thou lookest
Modest as Justice, and thou seem'st a palace
For the crown'd Truth to dwell in. I will believe thee,
And make my senses credit thy relation
To points that seem impossible; for thou lookest
Like one I lov'd indeed. What were thy friends?
Didst thou not say, when I did push thee back—
Which was when I perceiv'd thee—that thou cam'st
From good descending?
MARINA. So indeed I did.
PERICLES. Report thy parentage. I think thou said'st
Thou hadst been toss'd from wrong to injury,
And that thou thought'st thy griefs might equal mine,
If both were opened.
MARINA. Some such thing
I said, and said no more but what my thoughts
Did warrant me was likely.
PERICLES. Tell thy story;
If thine consider'd prove the thousand part
Of my endurance, thou art a man, and I
Have suffered like a girl. Yet thou dost look
Like Patience gazing on kings' graves, and smiling
Extremity out of act. What were thy friends?
How lost thou them? Thy name, my most kind virgin?

Recount, I do beseech thee. Come, sit by me.
MARINA. My name is Marina.
PERICLES. O, I am mock'd,
And thou by some incensed god sent hither
To make the world to laugh at me.
MARINA. Patience, good sir,
Or here I'll cease.
PERICLES. Nay, I'll be patient.
Thou little know'st how thou dost startle me
To call thyself Marina.
MARINA. The name
Was given me by one that had some power,
My father, and a king.
PERICLES. How! a king's daughter?
And call'd Marina?
MARINA. You said you would believe me;
But, not to be a troubler of your peace,
I will end here.
PERICLES. But are you flesh and blood?
Have you a working pulse, and are no fairy?
Motion! Well; speak on. Where were you born?
And wherefore call'd Marina?
MARINA. Call'd Marina
For I was born at sea.
PERICLES. At sea! what mother?
MARINA. My mother was the daughter of a king;
Who died the minute I was born,
As my good nurse Lychorida hath oft
Delivered weeping.
PERICLES. O, stop there a little!
[*Aside*] This is the rarest dream that e'er dull sleep
Did mock sad fools withal. This cannot be:
My daughter's buried.—Well, where were you bred?
I'll hear you more, to th' bottom of your story,
And never interrupt you.
MARINA. You scorn; believe me, 'twere best I did give o'er.
PERICLES. I will believe you by the syllable
Of what you shall deliver. Yet give me leave—
How came you in these parts? where were you bred?
MARINA. The King my father did in Tharsus leave me;

Till cruel Cleon, with his wicked wife,
Did seek to murder me; and having woo'd
A villain to attempt it, who having drawn to do't,
A crew of pirates came and rescued me;
Brought me to Mytilene. But, good sir,
Whither will you have me? Why do you weep? It may be
You think me an impostor. No, good faith;
I am the daughter to King Pericles,
If good King Pericles be.

PERICLES. Ho, Helicanus!

HELICANUS. Calls my lord?

PERICLES. Thou art a grave and noble counsellor,
Most wise in general. Tell me, if thou canst,
What this maid is, or what is like to be,
That thus hath made me weep?

HELICANUS. I know not; but
Here is the regent, sir, of Mytilene
Speaks nobly of her.

LYSIMACHUS. She never would tell
Her parentage; being demanded that,
She would sit still and weep.

PERICLES. O Helicanus, strike me, honour'd sir;
Give me a gash, put me to present pain,
Lest this great sea of joys rushing upon me
O'erbear the shores of my mortality,
And drown me with their sweetness. O, come hither,
Thou that beget'st him that did thee beget;
Thou that wast born at sea, buried at Tharsus,
And found at sea again! O Helicanus,
Down on thy knees, thank the holy gods as loud
As thunder threatens us. This is Marina.
What was thy mother's name? Tell me but that,
For truth can never be confirm'd enough,
Though doubts did ever sleep.

MARINA. First, sir, I pray,
What is your title?

PERICLES. I am Pericles of Tyre; but tell me now
My drown'd queen's name, as in the rest you said
Thou hast been godlike perfect,

The heir of kingdoms and another life
To Pericles thy father.

MARINA. Is it no more to be your daughter than
To say my mother's name was Thaisa?
Thaisa was my mother, who did end
The minute I began.

PERICLES. Now blessing on thee! Rise; thou art my child.
Give me fresh garments. Mine own, Helicanus–
She is not dead at Tharsus, as she should have been
By savage Cleon. She shall tell thee all;
When thou shalt kneel, and justify in knowledge
She is thy very princess. Who is this?

HELICANUS. Sir, 'tis the Governor of Mytilene,
Who, hearing of your melancholy state,
Did come to see you.

PERICLES. I embrace you.
Give me my robes. I am wild in my beholding.
O heavens bless my girl! But hark, what music?
Tell Helicanus, my Marina, tell him
O'er, point by point, for yet he seems to doubt,
How sure you are my daughter. But, what music?

HELICANUS. My lord, I hear none.

PERICLES. None?
The music of the spheres! List, my Marina.

LYSIMACHUS. It is not good to cross him; give him way.

PERICLES. Rarest sounds! Do ye not hear?

LYSIMACHUS. My lord, I hear. [*Music*]

PERICLES. Most heavenly music!
It nips me unto list'ning, and thick slumber
Hangs upon mine eyes: let me rest. [*Sleeps*]

LYSIMACHUS. A pillow for his head.
So, leave him all. Well, my companion-friends,
If this but answer to my just belief,
I'll well remember you. *Exeunt all but* PERICLES

DIANA *appears to* PERICLES *as in a vision*

DIANA. My temple stands in Ephesus. Hie thee thither,
And do upon mine altar sacrifice.
There, when my maiden priests are met together,
Before the people all,

Reveal how thou at sea didst lose thy wife.
To mourn thy crosses, with thy daughter's, call,
And give them repetition to the life.
Or perform my bidding or thou liv'st in woe;
Do it, and happy—by my silver bow!
Awake and tell thy dream. [*Disappears*]

PERICLES. Celestial Dian, goddess argentine,
I will obey thee. Helicanus!

Re-enter HELICANUS, LYSIMACHUS, MARINA, *&c.*

HELICANUS. Sir?

PERICLES. My purpose was for Tharsus, there to strike
The inhospitable Cleon; but I am
For other service first: toward Ephesus
Turn our blown sails; eftsoons I'll tell thee why.
[*To* LYSIMACHUS] Shall we refresh us, sir, upon your shore,
And give you gold for such provision
As our intents will need?

LYSIMACHUS. Sir,
With all my heart; and when you come ashore
I have another suit.

PERICLES. You shall prevail,
Were it to woo my daughter; for it seems
You have been noble towards her.

LYSIMACHUS. Sir, lend me your arm.

PERICLES. Come, my Marina. *Exeunt*

SCENE 2

Ephesus. Before the Temple of Diana

Enter GOWER

GOWER. Now our sands are almost run;
More a little, and then dumb.
This, my last boon, give me,
For such kindness must relieve me—
That you aptly will suppose
What pageantry, what feats, what shows,

What minstrelsy, and pretty din,
The regent made in Mytilen
To greet the King. So he thrived,
That he is promis'd to be wived
To fair Marina; but in no wise
Till he had done his sacrifice,
As Dian bade; whereto being bound,
The interim, pray you, all confound.
In feather'd briefness sails are fill'd,
And wishes fall out as they're will'd.
At Ephesus the temple see,
Our king, and all his company.
That he can hither come so soon,
Is by your fancies' thankful boon. *Exit*

SCENE 3

Ephesus. The Temple of Diana; THAISA *standing near the altar as High Priestess; a number of virgins on each side;* CERIMON *and other inhabitants of Ephesus attending*

Enter PERICLES, *with his train;* LYSIMACHUS, HELICANUS, MARINA, *and a* LADY

PERICLES. Hail, Dian! to perform thy just command,
I here confess myself the King of Tyre;
Who, frighted from my country, did wed
At Pentapolis the fair Thaisa.
At sea in childbed died she, but brought forth
A maid-child, call'd Marina; who, O goddess,
Wears yet thy silver livery. She at Tharsus
Was nurs'd with Cleon; who at fourteen years
He sought to murder; but her better stars
Brought her to Mytilene; 'gainst whose shore
Riding, her fortunes brought the maid aboard us,
Where, by her own most clear remembrance, she
Made known herself my daughter.
THAISA. Voice and favour!
You are, you are–O royal Pericles! [*Swoons*]

PERICLES. What means the nun? She dies! Help, gentlemen!
CERIMON. Noble sir,
If you have told Diana's altar true,
This is your wife.
PERICLES. Reverend appearer, no;
I threw her o'erboard with these very arms.
CERIMON. Upon this coast, I warrant you.
PERICLES. 'Tis most certain.
CERIMON. Look to the lady. O, she's but overjoy'd.
Early in blustering morn this lady was
Thrown upon this shore. I op'd the coffin,
Found there rich jewels; recover'd her, and plac'd her
Here in Diana's temple.
PERICLES. May we see them?
CERIMON. Great sir, they shall be brought you to my house,
Whither I invite you. Look, Thaisa is
Recovered.
THAISA. O, let me look!
If he be none of mine, my sanctity
Will to my sense bend no licentious ear,
But curb it, spite of seeing. O, my lord,
Are you not Pericles? Like him you spake,
Like him you are. Did you not name a tempest,
A birth and death?
PERICLES. The voice of dead Thaisa!
THAISA. That Thaisa am I, supposed dead
And drown'd.
PERICLES. Immortal Dian!
THAISA. Now I know you better.
When we with tears parted Pentapolis,
The King my father gave you such a ring. [*Shows a ring*]
PERICLES. This, this! No more, you gods! your present kindness
Makes my past miseries sports. You shall do well
That on the touching of her lips I may
Melt and no more be seen. O, come, be buried
A second time within these arms!
MARINA. My heart
Leaps to be gone into my mother's bosom.
[*Kneels to* THAISA]

PERICLES. Look who kneels here! Flesh of thy flesh, Thaisa;
Thy burden at the sea, and call'd Marina,
For she was yielded there.
THAISA. Blest and mine own!
HELICANUS. Hail, madam, and my queen!
THAISA. I know you not.
PERICLES. You have heard me say, when I did fly from Tyre,
I left behind an ancient substitute.
Can you remember what I call'd the man?
I have nam'd him oft.
THAISA. 'Twas Helicanus then.
PERICLES. Still confirmation.
Embrace him, dear Thaisa; this is he.
Now do I long to hear how you were found;
How possibly preserv'd; and who to thank,
Besides the gods, for this great miracle.
THAISA. Lord Cerimon, my lord—this man
Through whom the gods have shown their power—that can
From first to last resolve you.
PERICLES. Reverend sir,
The gods can have no mortal officer
More like a god than you. Will you deliver
How this dead queen re-lives?
CERIMON. I will, my lord.
Beseech you, first, go with me to my house,
Where shall be shown you all was found with her;
How she came plac'd here in the temple;
No needful thing omitted.
PERICLES. Pure Dian, bless thee for thy vision! I
Will offer night-oblations to thee. Thaisa,
This Prince, the fair-betrothed of your daughter,
Shall marry her at Pentapolis. And now,
This ornament
Makes me look dismal will I clip to form;
And what this fourteen years no razor touch'd,
To grace thy marriage-day I'll beautify.
THAISA. Lord Cerimon hath letters of good credit, sir,
My father's dead.

PERICLES. Heavens make a star of him! Yet there, my queen,
We'll celebrate their nuptials, and ourselves
Will in that kingdom spend our following days.
Our son and daughter shall in Tyrus reign.
Lord Cerimon, we do our longing stay
To hear the rest untold. Sir, lead's the way. *Exeunt*

Enter GOWER

GOWER. In Antiochus and his daughter you have heard
Of monstrous lust the due and just reward:
In Pericles, his queen, and daughter, seen,
Although assail'd with fortune fierce and keen,
Virtue preserv'd from fell destruction's blast,
Led on by heaven, and crown'd with joy at last.
In Helicanus may you well descry
A figure of truth, of faith, of loyalty;
In reverend Cerimon there well appears
The worth that learned charity aye wears.
For wicked Cleon and his wife, when fame
Had spread their cursed deed, and honour'd name
Of Pericles, to rage the city turn,
That him and his they in his palace burn;
The gods for murder seemed so content
To punish—although not done, but meant.
So, on your patience evermore attending,
New joy wait on you! Here our play has ending. *Exit*

Glossary

GLOSSARY

A, contraction for *of* or *on*.

'A, weak form of *he*, e.g., *Ham.*, 2.i, *There was 'a gaming.*

Abate, beat down, humble; *most abated captives*, *Cor.*, 3.iii; deprive, *Lear*, 2.iv; *abate her nothing*, in no way lower my estimate of her, *Cym.*, 1.iv.

Abatement, reduction, qualification, *Ham.*, 4.vii; reduced condition, *Cym.*, 5.iv.

Abhor, *how abhorred*, how disgusting, *Ham.*, 5.i; *It does abhor me*, horrify and disgust, *Oth.*, 4.ii.

Abhorring, *beneath abhorring*, too shameful to imagine, *Cor.*, 1.i; *Blow me into abhorring*, reduce to object of loathing, *Ant. & Cleo.*, 5.ii.

Abide, remain for short time, *Mac.*, 3.i; *abide this deed*, face the consequences of, *Jul. Caes.*, 3.i.

Ability, individual power, *Cor.*, 2.i; *abilities*, means of defence, *Oth.*, 1.iii.

Abject, *to the abject rear*, even to the least thrustful, *Troil. & Cres.*, 3.iii; *abjectly*, low in estimation, *Titus*, 2.iii.

Abjure, solemnly renounce, *Lear*, 2.iv; *here abjure the taints and blames*, solemnly assert one's innocence of, *Mac.*, 4.iii.

Able, vigorous, good, *Timon*, 2.i; *be able*, be of strength in resources, *Ant. & Cleo.*, 1.iv; *verb*, answer for, *Lear*, 4.vi.

Abode, *desire my man's abode*, my servant's remaining, *Cym.*, 1.vi.

Abomination, inhuman act, *Ant. & Cleo.*, 3.vi.

About, *about it*, set about it, *Oth.*, 4.ii.

Abram, auburn, *Cor.*, 2.iii.

Abridge, shorten, *Jul. Caes.*, 3.i.

Abridgement, the players who cut short Hamlet's talk, *Ham.*, 2.ii; summary, short account, *Cym.*, 5.v.

Abroach, *to set abroach*, reopen, start again, *Rom. & Jul.*, 1.i.

Abruption, abrupt breaking off, *Troil. & Cres.*, 3.ii.

Absence, euphemism for death, *Mac.*, 3.i.

Absent, *lovers' absent hours*, hours when they are apart, *Oth.*, 3.iv.

Absolute, unqualified, *Mac.*, 4.iii; uncompromising, *Cor.*, 3.ii; *his absolute 'shall'*, where 'shall' instead of 'will' implies authority and command, *Cor.*, 3.i; *absolute queen*, in no way vassal to Rome, *Ant. & Cleo.*, 3.vi; *absolute hope*, a feeling of certainty, *Ant. & Cleo.*, 4.iii; *absolute soldiership*, superiority in generalship, *Ant. & Cleo.*, 3.vii; used humorously in *Ant. & Cleo.*, 1.ii.

Abstract, summary, condensed account, *Ham.*, 2.ii; *abstract of all faults*, as if he had picked out the faults of men and compressed them into his own way of life, *Ant. & Cleo.*, 1.iv.

Absurd, *to reason most absurd*, utterly deaf to reason, *Ham.*, 1.ii.

Abuse, *verb*, disfigure, *Rom. & Jul.*, 4.i; deceive, *Mac.*, 2.i; etc.; misrepresent, *Oth.*, 2.i; insult, *Cym.*, 2.iii; *noun*, deception, *Ham.*, 4.vii; corruption, *Jul. Caes.*, 2.i; *self-abuse*, self-deception, *Mac.*, 3.iv.

Accent, tone of voice, *Oth.*, 1.i; expression, *Lear*, 2.ii; *new tuners of accents*, those who affect a new fashion in speech, *Rom. & Jul.*, 2.iv.

Accepted, *most accepted pain*, labour freely rewarded, *Troil. & Cres.*, 3.iii.

Accessible, clearly approachable, *Cym.*, 3.ii.

Accident, event, *Rom. & Jul.*, 5.ii; unexpected happening, *Oth.*, 4.ii; *moving accident*, exciting happening, *Oth.*, 1.iii.

Accidental, *accidental evils*, not touching the essence of our being, *Jul. Caes.*, 4.iii.

Accite, summon, *Titus*, 1.i.

Accommodate, dress up, *Lear*, 4.vi; *unaccommodated man*, man naked or deprived of the clothing of civilization, *Lear*, 3.iv.

Accord, a fitting of action to the spoken word, *Titus*, 5.ii; *Jove's accord*, heaven willing, *Troil. & Cres.*, 1.iii; consent, *Ham.*, 1.ii.

Accountant, liable to answer for, *Oth.*, 2.i.

Ace, single spot on dice (with pun on 'ass'), *Cym.*, 2.iii.

Acerbe, bitter, *Oth.*, 1.iii.

GLOSSARY

ACHERON, one of the five rivers of the lower world, but called a lake in *Titus*, 5.iii; stands for hell itself in *Mac.*, 3.v.

ACHIEVEMENT, possession, love gratified, *Troil. & Cres.*, 1.iii; notable act, *Ham.*, 1.iv.

ACKNOWN, *be not acknown on't*, don't admit knowledge of this, *Oth.*, 3.iii.

ACQUITTANCE, discharge of a debt, *Cym.*, 5.iv.

ACROSS, *arms across*, arms folded, *Jul. Caes.*, 2.i.

ACT, action, *Ham.*, 1.ii; *Cym.*, 5.iii; *native act*, habitual action, *Oth.*, 1.i.

ACTAEON, Theban prince who came on Diana bathing and was transformed to a stag, *Titus*, 2.iii.

ACTION-TAKING, seeking redress in law rather than by his own hand, *Lear*, 2.ii.

ACTIVE, physical, *Troil. & Cres.*, 2.iii.

ACTUAL, *actual performances*, physical acts, *Mac.*, 5.i; *actual deed*, physical act, *Oth.*, 4.ii.

ADAMANT, lode-stone, *Troil. & Cres.*, 3.ii.

ADDICTION, natural inclination, *Oth.*, 2.ii.

ADDITION, dignities that go with a title or office, *Lear*, 1.i; description of title acquired by habits or service, *Troil. & Cres.*, 2.iii and 3.ii.

ADDRESS, *address'd*, clothed, *Per.*, 2.iii; *address in*, present in form or shape, *Troil. & Cres.*, 5.x; make ready, *Troil. & Cres.*, 4.iv.

ADHERE, agree, *Mac.*, 1.vii; feel friendly toward, *Ham.*, 2.ii.

ADMIRAL, flagship, *Ant. & Cleo.*, 3.x.

ADMIRATION, assumption of doubt and wonder, *Lear*, 1.iv; wonder, astonishment, *Ham.*, 1.ii.

ADMIRED, *admir'd disorder*, Macbeth's agitation that astonished his guests and gave rise to wonder, *Mac.*, 3.iv.

ADMIT, choose as suitable, *Titus*, 1.i.

ADOPTION, *their adoption tried*, the quality of the friendship being proved by experience, *Ham.*, 1.iii; *the adoption of the crown*, being chosen as the king's heir, *Cym.*, 5.v.

ADVERTISE, inform, *Troil. & Cres.*, 2.ii.

ADVICE, consideration, *Cym.*, 1.i; *file our engines with advice*, perfect our devices with her counsel, *Titus*, 2.i.

ADVISE, take thought about it, *Rom. & Jul.*, 3.v.

ÆDILE, Roman official responsible for public order and public works, *Cor.*, 3.i.

AERIAL, *th'aerial blue*, the blue of the sky, *Oth.*, 2.i.

AERY, nest and young of eagles, applied to the young actors of the boys' companies, *Ham.*, 2.ii.

AFFECT, aspire to, *Cor.*, 3.iii and 4.vi; desire, *Titus*, 2.i; incline to, *Oth.*, 3.iii.

AFFECTION, inclination, of a bad kind in *Troil. & Cres.*, 2.ii; affectation (of style), *Ham.*, 2.ii.

AFFEER'D, *the title is affeer'd*, (tyranny) is confirmed in its title, *Mac.*, 4.iii.

AFFIANCE, trust, *Cym.*, 1.vi.

AFFIN'D, related, *Troil. & Cres.*, 1.iii; *partially affin'd*, so akin to him as to misrepresent things in his favour, *Oth.*, 2.iii.

AFFINITY, *of great affinity*, with powerful family connection, *Oth.*, 3.i.

AFFIRMATION, *of bloody affirmation*, to support an assertion with one's blood (as in a duel), *Cym.*, 1.iv.

AFFRONT, meet face to face, *Ham.*, 3.i; meet as in battle, *Cym.*, 4.iii; *be affronted*, be confronted, paired with, *Troil. & Cres.*, 3.ii.

AFFY, trust, *Titus*, 1.i.

AGAINST, *against thou shalt awake*, in time for the necessary action on your waking, *Rom. & Jul.*, 4.i.

AGATE-STONE, the stone in a ring on which a figure was cut, *Rom. & Jul.*, 1.iv.

AGNIZE, admit, acknowledge, *Oth.*, 1.iii.

AIM, conjecture, *Jul. Caes.*, 1.ii; *Oth.*, 1.iii.

ALCIDES, Hercules, *Titus*, 4.ii; *Ant. & Cleo.*, 4.xii.

ALL, *all myself*, only myself, *Lear*, 4.vi.

ALLAY, weaken, detract from, *Ant. & Cleo.*, 2.v; dilute, *Cor.*, 2.i.

ALLAYMENT, dilution in metaphorical sense, *Troil. & Cres.*, 4.iv; antidote, *Cym.*, 1.v.

ALLOW, sanction, prescribe, *Lear*, 2.iv.

ALLOWANCE, approval, judgment, *Ham.*, 3.ii; *Troil. & Cres.*, 1.iii; *of very expert and approved allowance*, of acknowledged competence, *Oth.*, 2.i.

ALLOW'D, licensed to have, invested by authority with, *Timon*, 5.i.

ALMANAC, calendar, but such compilations contained prognostications of various sorts, *Ant. & Cleo.*, 1.ii.

ALMS, *at fortune's alms*, as an act of charity, *Lear*, 1.i; *to fortune's alms*, taking what fortune chooses to give, *Oth.*, 3.iv.

Amain, strongly, *Troil. & Cres.*, 5.viii.
Amazedly, astonished and perplexed, *Mac.*, 4.i.
Amazement, wonder and astonishment, *Ham.*, 3.iv; astonishment that paralyses, *Per.*, 1.ii.
An, shortened form of 'and' = if; *what an if*, although, *Titus*, 4.iv.
Anchises, father of Aeneas, *Troil. & Cres.*, 4.i.
Anchor, anchorite, hermit, *Ham.*, 3.ii.
Ancient, (corrupt form of 'ensign') standard-bearer, *Oth.*, 1.i.
Angle, hook, fishing-tackle, used metaphorically in *Ham.*, 5.ii.
Annoy, injure, *Jul. Caes.*, 1.iii; *Cym.*, 4.iii; annoyance, injury, *Mac.*, 5.i.
Anthropophagi, cannibals, *Oth.*, 1.iii.
Antic, *antic disposition*, fantastic mode of behaviour, *Ham.*, 1.v; *antic round*, fantastic dance, *Mac.*, 4.i; *antic face*, mask, *Rom. & Jul.*, 1.v; as *noun* in *Troil. & Cres.*, 5.iii.
Anticipation, *my anticipation prevent your discovery*, my forecast save you (by coming before) the confession you would have to make, *Ham.*, 2.ii.
Anticked, *antick'd us all*, turned us all into fools, *Ant. & Cleo.*, 2.vii.
Antre, cave, *Oth.*, 1.iii.
Apoplex'd, paralysed, *Ham.*, 3.iv.
Appetite, desire, his choice of particular enemies for slaughter, *Troil. & Cres.*, 5.v; desire, caprice, *Oth.*, 2.iii.
Appliance, remedy (from medicine), *Ham.*, 4.iii; *Per.*, 3.ii.
Apply, illustrate, *Troil. & Cres.*, 1.iii; *apply for*, interpret as, *Jul. Caes.*, 2.ii.
Appointment, equipment, *Troil. & Cres.*, 4.v; armament, dispositions for battles, *Ant. & Cleo.*, 4.x.
Apprehension, insight of highest kind, *Ham.*, 2.ii; *the apprehension of his present portance*, the perception of his conduct and bearing, *Cor.*, 2.iii.
Apprehensive, with mental powers, *Jul. Caes.*, 3.i.
Approof, *on thy approof*, your conduct will provide the proof of my praise, *Ant. & Cleo.*, 3.ii.
Appurtenance, what goes with, a feature of, *Ham.*, 2.ii.
Aqua Vitae, whisky or strong spirit, *Rom. & Jul.*, 3.ii.
Aquilon, north wind, *Troil. & Cres.*, 4.v.
Arabian, *Arabian bird*, the phoenix, so the sole specimen of his kind, *Ant. & Cleo.*, 3.ii; *Cym.*, 1.vi.
Arch, *arch and patron*, chief, first in rank, *Lear*, 2.i; *arch-mock*, most spiteful jest, *Oth.*, 4.i.
Argal, corrupt form of *ergo*, therefore, *Ham.*, 5.i.
Argentine, shining like silver, *Per.*, 5.i.
Argue, is evidence of, *Timon*, 5.ii.
Argument, matter of concern, *Mac.*, 2.iii; *great argument*, weighty cause, *Ham.*, 4.iv; plot of play, *Ham.*, 3.ii; the contents (as of a book), *Timon*, 2.ii; evidence, *Ant. & Cleo.*, 3.xii.
Argus, hundred-eyed monster, *Troil. & Cres.*, 1.ii.
Ariachne, Arachne, changed to a spider, for her pride in her weaving, by Athene, *Troil. & Cres.*, 5.ii.
Aries, the Ram, the first sign of the zodiac, *Titus*, 4.iii.
Arm-gaunt, *arm-gaunt steed*, of doubtful meaning, sometimes explained as horse become lean with service in armour, *Ant. & Cleo.*, 1.v.
Aroint, *aroint thee*, begone, *Mac.*, 1.iii; *Lear*, 3.iv.
Arraign, *arraigning his unkindness*, charging him with unkindness, *Oth.*, 3.iv.
Arrant, out-and-out, complete, *Lear*, 2.iv; *arrant thief*, here the moon is likened to the roving (errant) thief, the out-and-out robber, *Timon*, 4.iii; so *arrant knave*, complete rascal, *Ham.*, 1.v.
Arras, tapestry hangings along wall of room, *Ham.*, 2.ii.
Arrearages, the arrears of tribute, *Cym.*, 2.iv.
Art, learning, discipline (as contrasted with 'nature'), *Jul. Caes.*, 4.iii (*also see* **Arts**).
Article, stipulation in agreement, *Cor.*, 2.iii; *of great article*, great importance, *Ham.*, 5.ii.
Articulate, make treaty or agreement, *Cor.*, 1.ix.
Artificial, *artificial strife*, art's struggle to overgo nature, *Timon*, 1.i; *artificial* [*stone*], the philosopher's stone that was supposed to change metals to gold, *Timon*, 2.ii; *artificial feat*, the operation of your art (skill), *Per.*, 5.i.
Artist, a skilful practitioner in arms, *Per.*, 2.iii; *the artist and unread*, the learned or skilful as opposed to the uninstructed, *Troil. & Cres.*, 1.iii.
Arts, training in manners and knowledge, *Cym.*, 5.v.
As-es, *see* **Charge**.
Ash, spear of ash-wood, *Cor.*, 4.v.

ASHAM'D, disgraced, *Oth.*, 2.iii.

ASPECT, *ill aspects of planets*, the baleful look of planets in positions harmful to man, *Troil. & Cres.*, 1.iii; *anchor his aspect*, fix his gaze, *Ant. & Cleo.*, 1.v; satirically in *Lear*, 2.ii.

ASPIC, the deadly asp, *Ant. & Cleo.*, 5.ii; *aspics' tongues*, the stings of snakes, *Oth.*, 3.iii.

ASPIRATION, desire of eminence, *Troil. & Cres.*, 4.v.

ASPIRE, ascend to, *Rom. & Jul.*, 3.i; attain, *Titus*, 1.i.

ASSAIL'D, wooed, *Cym.*, 2.iii.

ASSAULT, *of general assault*, a fault besetting many men, *Ham.*, 2.i.

ASSAY, try, *Ham.*, 4.vii; etc.; *convinces the great assay of art*, defeats the greatest effort of medical skill, *Mac.*, 4.iii; *noun*, test, *Oth.*, 1.iii.

ASSIGN, entrust, *Oth.*, 1.iii.

ASSIGNS, the accompanying equipment, as girdle and hangers, *Ham.*, 5.ii.

ASSISTANCE, *affecting one sole throne without assistance*, aiming at rule without associates, *Cor.*, 4.vi.

ASSUBJUGATE, lower, treat as inferior, *Troil. & Cres.*, 2.iii.

ASSUME, *assume the lists*, take up the challenge of the riddle, like a champion entering to fight at a tournament, *Per.*, 1.i.

ASSURANCE, legal security, then security simply, *Ham.*, 5.i; certainty of victory, *Ant. & Cleo.*, 3.vii.

ASTONISH, terrify, *Jul. Caes.*, 1.iii.

ASTRAEA, goddess of Justice, *Titus*, 4.iii.

ASTRONOMER, astrologer, *Troil. & Cres.*, 5.i; *Cym.*, 3.ii; *sectary astronomical*, a devotee of astrology, *Lear*, 1.ii.

ATE, goddess of discord, *Jul. Caes.*, 3.i.

ATHWART, across, *Rom. & Jul.*, 1.iv; *Cym.*, 5.iii.

ATONE, be at one, agree, *Cor.*, 4.vi; reconcile, *Timon*, 5.iv; bring together in friendship, *Oth.*, 4.i; *Ant. & Cleo.*, 2.ii.

ATTACH, arrest, *Cor.*, 3.i; *Oth.*, 1.ii; *attach'd*, affected, *Troil. & Cres.*, 5.ii.

ATTACHMENT, *attachment to thy senses*, sleep, the arrest of the senses, *Troil. & Cres.*, 4.ii.

ATTAINT, fault, *Troil. & Cres.*, 1.ii; *attainted*, charged with or guilty of wrongdoing; *in thine attaint*, as a partner in the treason, *Lear*, 5.iii.

ATTEMPT, try to capture, *Timon*, 1.i; *attempt of war*, enterprise, *Mac.*, 3.vi; *for him attempting who was self-subdued*, for attacking a man who was down by accident, *Lear*, 2.ii; *an attempt of ease and gain*, an enterprise easy and sure of success, *Oth.*, 1.iii.

ATTEMPTABLE, *less attemptable than any*, more armed against seduction, *Cym.*, 1.iv.

ATTEND, dance attendance, *Timon*, 1.i; *Cym.*, 3.iii; await, *Cor.*, 1.i; give heed to, *Cym.*, 1.vi; be present at as participant, *Ant. & Cleo.*, 2.ii; *attended*, waited on by servants, *Ham.*, 2.ii.

ATTENT, attentive, *Per.*, 3.*Prol.*

ATTEST, call as witness, *Troil. & Cres.*, 2.ii; testimony, *Troil. & Cres.*, 5.ii.

ATTRIBUTE, *for an honest attribute*, to get credit for honesty, *Per.*, 4.iii; *attributes*, the qualities referred to as hers, *Troil. & Cres.*, 3.i; reputation, *Ham.*, 1.iv.

ATTRIBUTIVE, *attributive to what infectiously itself affects*, credits the idol with the qualities it foolishly confers on it, *Troil. & Cres.*, 2.ii.

AUDIBLE, capable of hearing, *Cor.*, 4.v.

AUDIENCE, hearing and attention, *Ham.*, 1.iii; *did gibe my missive out of audience*, mocked my messenger out of a hearing, *Ant. & Cleo.*, 2.ii.

AUDIT, reckoning, *Cym.*, 5.iv; *make my audit up*, submit the true account, *Cor.*, 1.i; account with heaven, *Ham.*, 3.iii.

AUGER, tool for boring small holes, so *auger's bore*, smallest space, *Cor.*, 4.vi; *auger-hole*, where the danger could lurk unseen, *Mac.*, 2.iii.

AUGUR, the diviner or his divination, *Mac.*, 3.iv; *augurer* in *Cor.*, 2.i; *augury* in *Ham.*, 5.ii; *my auguring hope*, my hope that divines the future, *Ant. & Cleo.*, 2.i.

AULD, old, *Oth.*, 2.iii.

AURICULAR, *auricular assurance*, satisfaction by hearing for yourself, *Lear*, 1.ii.

AUSPICIOUS, favourable, helping, *Lear*, 2.i.

AUTHENTIC, *authentic place*, place of authority, *Troil. & Cres.*, 1.iii.

AUTHORITY, those of rank, *Cor.*, 1.i; *authority of manners*, the rule governing one's manner to one's superior, *Timon*, 2.ii; *authorities*, writings of the masters of medicine, *Per.*, 3.ii.

AUTHORIZ'D, *authoriz'd by her grandam*, repeated as vouched for by her grandmother, *Mac.*, 3.iv.

AVAUNT, begone, *Mac.*, 3.iv; *Ant. & Cleo.*, 4.xii.

AVOID, depart, *Ant. & Cleo.*, 5.ii; desert, *Troil. & Cres.*, 2.ii; *avoid the house*, leave the house, *Cor.*, 4.v.

AVOUCH, assert, *Mac.*, 5.v; *Lear*, 5.i; *my will avouch it*, my will take the responsibility of the deed, *Mac.*, 3.i; *noun*, testimony, *Ham.*, 1.i.

AWFUL, commanding fear and respect, *Per.*, 2.*Prol.*

AWKWARD, *awkward casualties*, thwarting accidents, *Per.*, 5.i.

BACCHANAL, dance, *Ant. & Cleo.*, 2.vii, in honor of the wine-god, Bacchus, *Ant. & Cleo.*, 2.viii.

BACK, *steel to the very back*, like a good sword of steel all through, not merely edged with steel, *Titus*, 4.iii; something in support, *Ham.*, 4.vii.

BACKSIDE, the unfrequented side, such as a debtor anxious to escape arrest might use, *Cym.*, 1.ii.

BACKWARDLY, contrarily, *Timon*, 3.iii.

BADGE, *badg'd with blood*, as retainers wore a badge to indicate the lord they served, so the murderers, according to Macbeth, wore the mark of their service, *Mac.*, 2.iii.

BAGGAGE, a worthless woman, *Rom. & Jul.*, 3.v; wench, *Per.*, 4.ii.

BAIL, person providing security for the appearance of an accused, *Titus*, 2.iii.

BAIT, set upon, *Cor.*, 4.ii; (as a bear by dogs), *Mac.*, 5.viii; *Jul. Caes.*, 4.iii.

BALD, with hat removed, *Cor.*, 4.v.

BALE, *one side must have bale*, one must come off worst, *Cor.*, 1.i; *baleful*, harmful, *Titus*, 2.iii.

BALL, *two-fold balls*, golden orbs, symbols of the ruler as sovereign of England and Scotland, *Mac.*, 4.i.

BALLASTING, *more equal ballasting*, more equal in rank, *Cym.*, 3.vi.

BALLOW, cudgel, *Lear*, 4.vi.

BALMY, fragrant, *Oth.*, 5.ii.

BAN, curse, *Ham.*, 3.ii.

BANDY, exchange (as a ball is hit to and fro), *Lear*, 1.iv; hit to and fro as in a ball-game, *Rom. & Jul.*, 2.v; so to quarrel or fight, *Rom. & Jul.*, 3.i.

BANE, destruction, *Troil. & Cres.*, 4.iii; *Titus*, 5.iii.

BANNING, *banning shore*, prohibiting the advance of the sea, *Oth.*, 2.i.

BANNS, official notice of marriage, *Lear*, 5.iii.

BANQUET, a light repast of fruit, wine, sweets, served some time after supper, *Rom. & Jul.*, 1.v.

BAR, shut out, ward off, *Per.*, 2.iv; *barred*, shut out, dispensed with, *Ham.*, 1.ii; *purpose so barr'd*, carefully directed action thus held up, *Cor.*, 3.i.

BARBER-MONGER, one always at the barber, thus conceited, effeminate, *Lear*, 2.ii.

BARE, needy, *Rom. & Jul.*, 5.i.

BARK, *bark about*, to cover as with bark, *Ham.*, 1.v.

BASAN, a land noted for its cattle (Psalms xxii. 12) and hills, *Ant. & Cleo.*, 3.xiii.

BASE, course, as at game of prisoners' base, *Cym.*, 5.iii.

BASES, cloth extensions to knee, worn by mounted knights, *Per.*, 2.i.

BASILISK, the fabled cockatrice that kills with its look, *Cym.*, 2.iv.

BASIS, *on Pompey's basis*, pedestal of Pompey's statue, *Jul. Caes.*, 3.i.

BASTE, *bastes his arrogance with his own seam*, as the cook pours hot fat over the roast on the spit, *Troil. & Cres.*, 2.ii.

BATE, reduce, impugn, *Timon*, 3.iii; beat or flutter like a bird's wings, *Rom. & Jul.*, 3.ii; *be bated*, be reduced (in price), *Per.*, 4.ii.

BATTEN, feed like an animal, *Ham.*, 3.iv; *Cor.*, 4.v.

BATTERY, *action of battery*, to charge an assailant with assault and battery, *Ham.*, 5.i.

BATTLE, *our first battle*, the vanguard, *Mac.*, 5.vi.

BAUBLE, the fool's staff terminating in a carved head, *Titus*, 5.i; so something trifling, of no account, *Troil. & Cres.*, 1.iii; used of ships worthless in stormy seas, *Cym.*, 3.i.

BAY, (1) reddish brown, *Timon*, 1.ii; *Lear*, 3.iv; (2) bark, *Cym.*, 5.v; *bay at him*, as a dog might bark after him, *Troil. & Cres.*, 2.iii; *make a bay*, let the hounds gather and bark; *at bay*, when the hunted animal has to turn on its pursuers; so, in extremity, *Titus*, 4.ii.

BEACON, *beacon to this under globe*, the moon, *Lear*, 2.ii.

BEAGLE, kind of dog; can be used of women as term of commendation or scorn; so, scornfully in *Timon*, 4.iii.

BEAM, spear, *Troil. & Cres.*, 5.v.

BEAR, (1) manage, direct, *Cor.*, 1.i; obtain, win, *Oth.*, 1.iii; *bear Caesar hard*, feel enmity towards, *Jul. Caes.*, 2.i; *bear in hand*, delude, practise on, *Ham.*, 2.ii; pretend, *Cym.*, 5.v; (2) *the burning bear*, constellation of the Great Bear, *Oth.*, 2.i.

BEARD, face defiantly (with pun on 'beard' on chin), *Ham.*, 2.ii.

BEARER, owner, *Troil. & Cres.*, 3.iii; sufferer, *Timon*, 5.iv; *bearing*, conduct, *Cor.*, 2.iii.

BEAVER, the part of the helmet that was drawn down to cover the face, *Ham.*, 1.ii.

BECK, gesture of summons, beckoning, *Ham.*, 3.i; *Ant. & Cleo.*, 3.xi; *verb* in *Ant. & Cleo.*, 4.xii.

BECOME, *become as new into the world*, having to make a fresh start among strangers, *Troil. & Cres.*, 3.iii; *what becomed love I might*, with the modesty the circumstances prescribed, *Rom. & Jul.*, 4.ii; *becomes his flow*, conducts himself in his misfortune, *Ant. & Cleo.*, 3.xii; *Cym.*, 5.v.

BECOMINGS, graces, *Ant. & Cleo.*, 1.iii.

BEDLAM, the asylum in London was the hospital of Saint Mary of Bethlehem, shortened to *Bedlam*, which could be used of the institution or those afflicted with madness; *Tom o' Bedlam*, the name of a Bedlam beggar, a vagrant half-wit, *Lear*, 1.ii and 2.iii.

BED-WORK, soft, easy work contrasted with the rigours of the battle-field, *Troil. & Cres.*, 1.iii.

BEEF-WITTED, brainless as an ox, *Troil. & Cres.*, 2.i.

BEETLE, *bettle-brows*, the mask he is about to don with its projecting eye-brows, *Rom. & Jul.*, 1.iv; *beetles o'er*, overhangs, *Ham.*, 1.iv.

BEGGAR, cheapen utterly, *Troil. & Cres.*, 2.ii; *of matter beggar'd*, lacking good cause, *Ham.*, 4.v.

BEGGARY, *beggary of his change*, the lowness of his new life, *Cym.*, 1.vi.

BEGOT, born, *Rom. & Jul.*, 1.iv.

BEGUILE, cheat, *Ham.*, 1.iii; *beguile thy sorrow*, forget it by diverting the mind, *Titus*, 4.i; *beguile the thing I am*, disguise or direct my anxiety by an assumption of mirth, *Oth.*, 2.i.

BEHALF, *in* or *on his behalf*, in his interest, for his benefit, *Timon*, 3.i; *Oth.*, 3.iv; *sands that run i' the clock's behalf*, in an hour-glass that serves as a clock, *Cym.*, 3.ii.

BEHAVED, *as he is behaved*, from the way he conducts himself, *Ham.*, 3.i.

BEHAVIOUR, *light behaviour*, jesting manner, *Oth.*, 4.i.

BEHEST, command, *Cym.*, 5.iv.

BEHIND, yet to come, *Mac.*, 1.iii.

BEHOLD, sight, *Cor.*, 1.iii; *wild in my beholding*, disordered in my appearance, *Per.*, 5.i; *beholding to you*, indebted to you, *Per.*, 2.v.

BEHOVE, is fitting for, *Ham.*, 1.iii; *behoveful*, needful, *Rom. & Jul.*, 4.iii.

BELDAM, hag, *Mac.*, 3.v.

BE-LEE'D, cut off from the wind, so held up (in my progress to promotion), *Oth.*, 1.i.

BELIE, fill with lies, *Cym.*, 3.iv; slander, *Oth.*, 4.i.

BELIKE, probably, *Ham.*, 3.ii; *Lear*, 4.v.

BE-MONSTER, assume an inhuman shape or appearance, *Lear*, 4.ii.

BENCH, seat of authority, or those who sit on it, *Cor.*, 3.i, where a *graver bench* refers to the senate as a whole; so *bencher*, senator, *Cor.*, 2.i.

BEND, *noun*, glance, *Jul. Caes.*, 1.ii; *made their bends adornings*, added a beauty to the tableau by their graceful service, *Ant. & Cleo.*, 2.ii; *verb*, turn, incline, *Ham.*, 1.ii; direct, *Lear*, 2.i.

BENEDICTION, blessing, *Lear*, 2.ii.

BENEFICIAL, good, *Oth.*, 2.ii.

BENISON, blessing, *Mac.*, 2.iv; *Lear*, 1.i.

BENT, from archery, so *top of my bent*, to the fullest extent of my humour, *Ham.*, 3.ii; *the attentive bent*, ready to listen, *Troil. & Cres.*, 1.iii; *thy bent of love*, the aim of your love, *Rom. & Jul.*, 2.ii; *to the bent of*, according to the humour or inclination of, *Cym.*, 1.i; *bent with sin*, determined on evil, *Per.*, 2.*Chor.*

BERAY, befoul, *Titus*, 2.iii.

BEREAVE, deprive or injure, *Lear*, 4.iv.

BESEECH, *ungain'd beseech*, the lover as long as he is unaccepted must continue to beg, *Troil. & Cres.*, 1.ii.

BESEEMING, appearance, *Cym.*, 5.v.

BESHREW, (imprecation) plague on someone or something or other, *Rom. & Jul.*, 5.ii; *Oth.*, 4.ii.

BESIDE, *foes that strike beside us*, on our side (for part of the enemy came over to them) *Mac.*, 5.vii; *spare no blood beside*, spare no one else, *Cym.*, 5.v.

BESORT, *may besort your age*, may be like you in age and gravity, *Lear*, 1.iv; *noun*, *accommodation and besort*, suitable provision, *Oth.*, 1.iii.

Bespeak, address, *Ham.*, 2.ii.

Bespoke, engaged to be married (used ironically, as her husband is speaking), *Lear*, 5.iii.

Best, *as in the best it is*, as it is even at the best, *Ham.*, 1.v; *good as the best*, the plan couldn't be improved on, *Timon*, 5.i; *the best*, the leading men, *Cor.*, 1.ix; *at the best*, make the best of what may seem an unfortunate event, *Oth.*, 1.iii; *to the best*, for the best, *Lear*, 1.ii.

Bestow, place, *Oth.*, 3.i; dispose of, *Ant. & Cleo.*, 5.ii; give, *Lear*, 2.i; lodge, accommodate, *Ham.*, 2.ii; *Lear*, 2.iv; live, reside, *Mac.*, 3.ii; *bestow thy time*, enter my service, spend your days with, *Jul. Caes.*, 5.v; *bestow her funeral*, give her burial, *Titus*, 4.ii; *bestow your sued-for tongues*, present your much sought votes without being asked, *Cor.*, 2.iii; *their bestowing*, their functions, *Troil. & Cres.*, 3.ii; *evilly bestow'd*, expended on evil men, *Timon*, 4.iii.

Beteem, allow, *Ham.*, 1.ii.

Bethink, *bethink yourself*, call to mind, *Oth.*, 5.ii; *Lear*, 1.ii; *am bethought to*, purpose to, have a plan to, *Lear*, 2.iii.

Betide, befall, *Titus*, 4.ii; *betid to*, happened to, *Cym.*, 4.iii.

Betime, early, *Ham.*, 4.v; *Ant. & Cleo.*, 4.iv.

Betoken, signify, *Ham.*, 5.i.

Betray, deceive, *Oth.*, 5.ii; *Titus*, 5.ii; reveal, *Ant. & Cleo.*, 2.vii; *Titus*, 4.ii; *betray's in deepest consequence*, mislead us in the later and important business, *Mac.*, 1.iii.

Better, *our better mirth*, our mirth that will be all the better for the absence of a gloomy companion, *Cor.*, 1.iii; *better phrase*, more educated idiom, *Lear*, 4.vi; *verb, better'd*, rated as better, *Ham.*, 5.ii; *better thee*, have the advantage of you, *Per.*, 4.vi.

Bevy, collection, *Ham.*, 5.ii.

Bewray, reveal, discover, *Titus*, 2.iv; etc.

Beyond, *to cast beyond ourselves*, go too far (in our fears or suspicions), *Ham.*, 2.i; *beyond beyond*, infinite, *Cym.*, 3.ii.

Bias, the curved course given by the shape of the ball used in the ancient game of bowls, so *bias of nature*, the conduct prescribed by our humanity, *Lear*, 1.ii; *assays of bias*, approaches that are indirect; *sphered bias cheek*, swollen like the specially curved side of the bowl that gives the oblique course to it, *Troil. & Cres.*, 4.v; so used of oblique ways or thoughts that are censurable or unfortunate, *Troil. & Cres.*, 1.iii and 4.v.

Biding, dwelling, refuge, *Lear*, 4.vi.

Bifold, twofold, *Troil. & Cres.*, 5.ii.

Big, full to overflowing, *Jul. Caes.*, 3.i; *big compare*, proud comparisons, *Troil. & Cres.*, 3.ii; valiant, stout, *Cor.*, 3.ii; *a heart as big*, proud and courageous, *Cym.*, 4.ii; so *bigger*, more boastful, *Cym.*, 4.ii; *the big wars*, the pride, pomp and circumstance of battle, *Oth.*, 3.iii; *big in clamour*, loud in lamentation (or perhaps filled with lament), *Lear*, 5.iii.

Bilboes, *mutines in the bilboes*, mutineers in irons or fetters (Bilbao in Spain giving its name to iron and steel work), *Ham.*, 5.ii.

Bill, a weapon like a pole-axe, *Rom. & Jul.*, 1.i; *the brown bills*, the regiment so armed, the weapon being browned against rust, *Lear*, 4.vi.

Bill, list, catalogue, *Mac.*, 3.i.

Birth-child, *Thetis' birth-child*, Marina having been born at sea, the element of Thetis, *Per.*, 4.iv.

Bisson, *your bisson conspectuities*, your almost blind sights, *Cor.*, 2.i; *bisson rheum*, blinding tears, *Ham.*, 2.ii.

Bite, *bite my thumb at*, an insulting gesture, *Rom. & Jul.*, 1.i; *bite thee by the ear*, a gesture of friendly admiration, *Rom. & Jul.*, 2.iv; *bite our tongues*, keep silence, *Titus*, 3.i.

Bitumed, *caulk'd and bitumed*, the seams made tight with oakum and melted pitch, *Per.*, 3.i.

Black-corner'd, concealing, *Timon*, 5.i.

Blade, sword; *a good blade*, a good swordsman, *Rom. & Jul.*, 2.iv.

Blame, fault, *Lear*, 2.iv.

Blank, (1) white spot in the centre of target, so target of any sort, *Ham.*, 4.i; *Lear*, 1.i; *within the blank of his displeasure*, in the line of fire, directly exposed to his anger, *Oth.*, 3.iv; (2) a document to be filled in as the holder decides, so *a blank to danger*, where danger may fill in consequences unguessed at by the man who gives it the opportunity, *Troil. & Cres.*, 3.iii; *lots to blanks*, all the money (in lottery) to nothing (blanks being losing tickets), *Cor.*, 5.ii.

Blast, to cause to sicken, *Ham.*, 1.i;

blast in proof, fail in execution (the metaphor perhaps taken from testing of cannon), *Ham.*, 4.vii; *half blasted*, partly withered, not young, *Ant. & Cleo.*, 3.xiii; split with noise, *Ant. & Cleo.*, 4.vii; *contagious blastments*, infectious contacts that spread destruction, *Ham.*, 1.iii.

BLAZE, proclaim to the world, *Rom. & Jul.*, 3.iii.

BLAZON, *noun, this eternal blazon*, this proclamation of the secrets of eternity, *Ham.*, 1.v; *verb*, describe (borrowed from heraldry and its description of arms), *Rom. & Jul.*, 2.vi; proclaim, *Titus*, 4.iv; *blazoning pens*, writers attempting to describe perfection, *Oth.*, 2.i; *thyself thou blazon'st*, reveal yourself, *Cym.*, 4.ii.

BLEARED, *bleared sights*, the dim-sighted, *Cor.*, 2.i.

BLEEDING, *dismiss the controversy bleeding*, leave it still unsettled, *Cor.*, 2.i.

BLENCH, flinch, *Ham.*, 2.ii; *Troil. & Cres.*, 1.i and 2.ii.

BLEST, *blest infusions*, with healing power, *Per.*, 3.ii.

BLIND, *blind fortune*, pure chance (not his skill or valour), *Cor.*, 5.vi.

BLOAT, bloated, self-indulgent, *Ham.*, 3.iv.

BLOCK, wood on which hats were moulded, so *a good block*, a well-fashioned hat, *Lear*, 4.vi.

BLOOD, passion, feeling, *Lear*, 4.ii; contrasted with 'judgement' in *Ham.*, 3.ii; *in blood*, in condition (the term is transferred from the chase where a deer could be said to be 'in blood'), *Cor.*, 4.v; *worst in blood to run*, in the worst condition for useful exertion, *Cor.*, 1.i; *the near in blood*, the nearer in kinship, *Mac.*, 2.iii; *of blood*, of royal descent, *Troil. & Cres.*, 3.iii; *young bloods*, the physical make-up of the young, *Jul. Caes.*, 4.iii; *the blood and baseness of our natures*, its carnal tendencies, *Oth.*, 1.iii; temperament, nature generally, *Cym.*, 1.i.

BLOOD-BOLTER'D, with the hair matted with blood, *Mac.*, 4.i.

BLOSSOM, a child showing the beauty and promise of infancy, *Titus*, 4.ii; *in the blossoms of my sin*, in full flourish, *Ham.*, 1.v; *blossoming Caesar*, coming to the height of prosperity and success, *Ant. & Cleo.*, 4.xii.

BLOWN, *blown tide*, swollen tide, *Cor.*, 5.iv; *blown ambition*, puffed-up, swollen, *Lear*, 4.iv; *blown sails*, swollen by the winds, *Per.*, 5.i; *blows my heart*, bursts it with shame, *Ant. & Cleo.*, 4.vi; *that quicken even with blowing*, fly-blown meat being fouled by eggs and maggots of flies, *Oth.*, 4.ii.

BLOWSE, (usually = a ruddy fat-faced wench), a term of endearment in *Titus*, 4.ii.

BLUNT, brusque, rude, *Cym.*, 5.v; without affectation, *Jul. Caes.*, 3.ii; *Lear*, 1.iv; devoid of courtesy, *Lear*, 2.ii.

BLUR, *blurr'd those lines of favour*, made his features unrecognizable, *Cym.*, 4.ii.

BLURT, *blurt at*, make mouths at, show contempt for, *Per.*, 4.iii.

BLUSTEROUS, *blusterous birth*, being born in a storm, *Per.*, 3.i.

BOB, (1) thump, *Troil. & Cres.*, 2.i; (2) cheat, *Troil. & Cres.*, 3.i; swindle, *Oth.*, 5.i.

BODE, foretell (generally evil), *Troil. & Cres.*, 5.ii; portend, *Ham.*, 1.i; *boding to all*, ominous, *Oth.*, 4.i.

BODEMENTS, prophecies, *Troil. & Cres.*, 5.iii; *Mac.*, 4.i.

BODKIN, dagger, *Ham.*, 3.i.

BODY, *this common body*, the populace, *Cor.*, 1.iv; etc.

BODYKINS, *God's bodykins*, God's dear body, *Ham.*, 2.ii.

BOGGLER, a disloyal capricious wanton, *Ant. & Cleo.*, 3.xiii.

BOIL, *boil'd stuff*, diseased flesh (venereal disease was treated by sweating the patient in a tub), *Cym.*, 1.vi.

BOLD, confident, *Titus*, 5.i; *Cym.*, 2.iv; *too bold upon your rest*, too venturesome in disturbing your repose, *Jul. Caes.*, 2.i; *bold cure*, confident of cure, *Oth.*, 2.i; *verb*, *as France invades our land not bolds the king*, not because France comforts the king but because France invades our land, *Lear*, 5.i.

BOLIN, bowline, rope from sail to bow, *Per.*, 3.i.

BOLT, fetter, *Ant. & Cleo.*, 5.ii; *bolting*, the sifting the flour from the bran, *Troil. & Cres.*, 1.i; *bolted language*, refined, specially polite speech, *Cor.*, 3.i.

BOMBAST, cotton stuffing for garments, so inflated language; *a bombast circumstance*, inflated and roundabout speech, *Oth.*, 1.i.

BOND, obligation, duty, *Ant. & Cleo.*, 1.iv; *that great bond*, the terms in which Banquo and Fleance live (as the ancestors of kings), so their very lives, *Mac.*, 3.ii.

Bondage, firm attachment, loyalty, *Cym.*, 2.iv; bound like a malefactor, *Cym.*, 5.v.

Bone, *her young bones*, her child, *Lear*, 2.iv.

Bonjour, greeting, *Titus*, 1.i.

Bonnet, covering for the head, regularly worn indoors, removed in the presence of superiors, *Ham.*, 5.ii; or as an act of courtesy, *Cor.*, 3.ii; or duplicity, *bonneted into their estimation*, by doffing the bonnet as to superiors, *Cor.*, 2.ii.

Book, a written document, *Cym.*, 5.iv; account, history, *Per.*, 1.i; *a prayer without book*, so as to repeat it by heart, *Troil. & Cres.*, 2.i; *you kiss by the book*, more by art than by nature, *Rom. & Jul.*, 1.v.

Boot, something extra, over and above, *Troil. & Cres.*, 4.v; *to boot*, added to the bargain, *Mac.*, 4.iii; *make boot of*, take advantage of, *Ant. & Cleo.*, 4.i; *verb*, profit, avail, *Titus*, 5.iii; *Per.*, 1.ii; add by way of an extra, *Ant. & Cleo.*, 2.v.

Bootless, unavailing, *Titus*, 3.i; *very bootless*, utterly useless, *Lear*, 5.iii.

Border, *border'd certain*, surely confined within the bounds of humane conduct, *Lear*, 4.ii.

Bore, calibre of gun, so used of size or importance of a subject, *Ham.*, 4.vi; *bores of hearing*, the ears, *Cym.*, 3.ii.

Boreas, north wind, *Troil. & Cres.*, 1.iii.

Borrow, *borrow'd likeness*, assumed likeness, *Rom. & Jul.*, 4.i; *borrow'd grave*, supposed burial, *Rom. & Jul.*, 5.iii; *borrow'd motion*, false show of feeling, *Per.*, 4.iv.

Bosom, *bosom multiplied*, the bosom of the many-headed multitude, *Cor.*, 3.i; *in their bosoms*, in their secrets, *Jul. Caes.*, 5.i; *bosom's lord*, Love, *Rom. & Jul.*, 5.i; *our bosom interest*, our affectionate concern for, *Mac.*, 1.ii; *common bosom*, affections of the people, *Lear*, 5.iii; *of her bosom*, in her confidence, *Lear*, 4.v; thoughts, mind, *Oth.*, 3.i; *Lear*, 2.i; *verb*, *bosom'd with*, most intimate with, *Lear*, 5.i.

Botch, clumsy patch of work, *Mac.*, 3.i; *verb*, patch, *Timon*, 4.iii; patch together in clumsy way, *Ham.*, 4.v; *botcher*, patcher of old clothes or material, *Cor.*, 2.i.

Bots, a disease of horses; used as an oath, *Per.*, 2.i.

Bound, ready, *Ham.*, 1.v; confined, *Ham.*, 2.ii; *are bound to the like*, also intend to do so, *Lear*, 3.vii.

Bourn, brook, *Lear*, 3.vi; limit, boundary, *Ham.*, 3.i; *Ant. & Cleo.*, 1.i; *this chalky bourn*, the cliffs of Dover, *Lear*, 4.vi.

Bout, spell of fencing, *Ham.*, 4.vii; of dancing, *Rom. & Jul.*, 1.v.

Bow, bend, *Per.*, 4.ii; *Ant. & Cleo.*, 2.iii; *bow'd his nature*, submitted it to the requirements of the occasion, *Cor.*, 5.vi.

Boy, *boy my greatness*, act the part of Queen (boys taking the female parts in the Elizabethan and Jacobean theatre), *Ant. & Cleo.*, 5.ii.

Brace, (1) pair, *Cor.*, 2.i; *Oth.*, 2.iii; (2) armour for the arms, usually, but the whole suit in *Per.*, 2.i; *stands not in such warlike brace*, so armed for war, *Oth.*, 1.iii.

Brach, a bitch hound, *Lear*, 1.iv.

Brag, speak with proper pride, *Rom. & Jul.*, 1.v; *brags his service*, boasts of his actions, *Cym.*, 5.iii.

Braid, upbraid, censure, *Per.*, 1.i.

Brain, *throwing about of brains*, exchange of satirical hits, *Ham.*, 2.ii; *tongue and brain not*, utter without understanding it, *Cym.*, 5.iv.

Brainish, *brainish apprehension*, misapprehension of disordered mind, *Ham.*, 4.i.

Brainsickly, in disordered or insane fashion, *Mac.*, 2.ii.

Bran, husks of grain; *meal and bran*, the flour and the husks, so the qualities of men, *Cym.*, 4.ii.

Branch, division, *Ham.*, 5.i; *two branches*, her arms, *Titus*, 2.iv; *circumstantial branches*, detailed parts, *Cym.*, 5.v.

Branchless, stripped of honour, *Ant. & Cleo.*, 3.iv.

Brand, mark of infamy, *Cor.*, 3.i; *depending on their brands*, Cupids leaning on their torches, *Cym.*, 2.iv.

Brass, used to indicate something enduring in nature, *walls of beaten brass*, *Jul. Caes.*, 1.iii.

Brave, *adj.*, splendidly arrayed, *Troil. & Cres.*, *Prol.*; excellent, *Troil. & Cres.*, 1.ii; *brave night*, fine night (used ironically), *Lear*, 3.ii; *a piece of work so bravely done*, so splendidly wrought, *Cym.*, 2.iv; *verb*, make a show, swagger, *Titus*, 4.i; provoke, threaten, *Oth.*, 5.ii; defy, *Ant. & Cleo.*, 4.iv; *noun*, challenge, defiance, *Troil. & Cres.*, 4.v.

Bravery, ostentatious display, *Ham.*,

5.ii; *fearful bravery*, making a show that conceals their fears, though it might inspire fear in the ignorant, *Jul. Caes.*, 5.i; bravado, *Oth.*, 1.i; *natural bravery of the isle*, defiant or challenging features and position, *Cym.*, 3.i.

BRAWN, arm, *Cor.*, 4.v; *the brawns of Hercules*, arms like Hercules, *Cym.*, 4.ii.

BRAZE, plated it as with brass, *Ham.*, 3.iv; *brazed to it*, hardened to it, indifferent, *Lear*, 1.i; *brazen-faced*, shameless, *Lear*, 2.ii.

BREACH, gap created in defences, *Rom. & Jul.*, 1.iv; *a custom more honour'd in the breach than the observance*, a custom better neglected or broken with than followed, *Ham.*, 1.iv; *deadly breach*, where fighting would be most fierce, *Oth.*, 1.iii; a gap in friendship, *Oth.*, 4.i; *nuptial breaches*, divorces, *Lear*, 1.ii.

BREADTH, extent, *Per.*, 4.i.

BREAK, break off, *Titus*, 5.iii; wound (by blow on head), *Ham.*, 2.ii; interrupt, *Ant. & Cleo.*, 4.xiv; communicate, disclose, *Ant. & Cleo.*, 1.ii; *break themselves*, perjure themselves (i.e., the speaker), *Ant. & Cleo.*, 1.iii; *broken debtors*, bankrupts, *Cym.*, 5.iv; *break this enterprise*, propose such a scheme, *Mac.*, 1.vii; *broken music*, music in parts, *Troil. & Cres.*, 3.i; *broke*, ruined, *Timon*, 4.ii; *almost broke my heart*, nearly died, *Titus*, 5.i.

BREATH, exercise, walk, *Troil. & Cres.*, 2.iii and 4.v.

BREATHE, speak of, *Ham.*, 2.i; *breathed*, trained, long practised in, *Timon*, 1.i; fit physically, *Ant. & Cleo.*, 3.xi.

BREATHER, a human being, *Ant. & Cleo.*, 3.iii.

BREATHING, exercise, *Per.*, 2.iii; *give breathing to*, express in words, *Ant. & Cleo.*, 1.iii; *breathing time of day*, for exercise and recreation, *Ham.*, 5.ii.

BREECH'D, covered, *Mac.*, 2.iii.

BREED, *blaspheme his breed*, shames his ancestors, *Mac.*, 4.iii; kind, *Ham.*, 3.ii; *breed of greatness*, noble strain, race, *Cym.*, 4.ii; *verb*, maintained, *Lear*, 4.ii; *bred of alms*, brought up on charity, *Cym.*, 2.iii; *bred out into*, degenerated into, *Timon*, 1.i.

BREESE, BREEZE, gadfly, *Troil. & Cres.*, 1.iii; *Ant. & Cleo.*, 3.x.

BRIAREUS, giant with a hundred hands, *Troil. & Cres.*, 1.ii.

BRIEF, mortal, *Cym.*, 5.v; *noun*, inventory, *Ant. & Cleo.*, 5.ii.

BRIEFLY, very recently, *Cor.*, 1.vi; quickly, *Cym.*, 5.v; *Ant. & Cleo.*, 4.iv.

BRIEFNESS, speed, *Lear*, 2.i.

BRINDED, brindled, *Mac.*, 4.i.

BROACH, spit, take up on the point, *Titus*, 4.ii; tap (as a cask), *Timon*, 2.ii; set afoot, begin, *Titus*, 2.i; *the business she hath broached*, the trouble she has started, *Ant. & Cleo.*, 1.ii.

BROAD, open and unrestrained, *Ham.*, 3.iv; haughty, contemptuous, *Troil. & Cres.*, 1.iii.

BROGUE, rustic shoe, *Cym.*, 4.ii.

BROKE, BROKEN, *see* BREAK.

BROKER, go-between, *Ham.*, 1.iii.

BROOCHED, adorned (in his triumph), *Ant. & Cleo.*, 4.xv.

BROOD, *on brood*, as if hatching some scheme, *Ham.*, 3.i.

BROOK, allow, endure, *Jul. Caes.*, 1.ii.

BRUIT, report, *Timon*, 5.i; *bruited*, announced, by the noise that heralds him, *Mac.*, 5.vii; *bruit again*, echo, *Ham.*, 1.ii.

BUDGE, retreat, withdraw, *Cor.*, 1.vi; *budger*, shirker, *Cor.*, 1.viii.

BUG, an object that inspires terror, *Ham.*, 5.ii; *the mortal bugs*, the deadly terrors, *Cym.*, 5.iii.

BUGBEAR, a goblin or imaginary terror, *Troil. & Cres.*, 4.ii.

BUILDING, place, *Per.*, 2.i.

BULK, wooden projection in front of shop, *Cor.*, 2.i; *Oth.*, 5.i.

BULL, *the Bull*, the constellation Taurus, *Titus*, 4.iii; *bull-bearing Milo*, strong man and Olympic victor, *Troil. & Cres.*, 2.iii.

BURDEN, *of importless burden*, irrelevant discourse, *Troil. & Cres.*, 1.iii.

BURGONET, helmet, *Ant. & Cleo.*, 1.v.

BURN, *burn daylight*, waste time, *Rom. & Jul.*, 1.iv.

BUSS, kiss, *Cor.*, 3.ii. [*Oth.*, 5.ii.

BUTT, target at archery, so aim, goal,

BUTTON, *butcher of a silk button*, like the fencer who prided himself on being able to hit his opponent even on any button, *Rom. & Jul.*, 2.iv.

BUXOM, comely, *Per.*, 1.*Prol.*

BUY, *buy out*, bribe, *Ham.*, 3.iii; ransom, redeem, *Timon*, 3.v; *does buy my injuries*, pays for them like benefits, *Cym.*, 1.i.

BY-DEPENDANCES, accompanying detail, *Cym.*, 5.v.

CABLE, *give him cable*, give him rope or scope, *Oth.*, 1.ii.

GLOSSARY

Cadent, falling, *Lear*, 1.iv.

Caduceus, *serpentine craft of thy caduceus*, the winged staff of Mercury was entwined by two snakes, *Troil. & Cres.*, 2.iii.

Caitiff, villain, *Oth.*, 5.ii; wretch (in a pitiful sense), *Oth.*, 4.i.

Calamity, misery, *Ham.*, 3.i; *Cor.*, 1.i. [*Jul. Caes.*, 1.iii.

Calculate, forecast like astrologers,

Calendar, *calendar of gentry*, as sure a guide to polite conduct as the calendar is of times and seasons, *Ham.*, 5.ii.

Call, *call upon*, request, *Timon*, 2.ii; invoke, *Rom. & Jul.*, 2.ii; *call up*, summon, *Ham.*, 4.i; *call on him*, call him to account, *Ant. & Cleo.*, 1.iv.

Callet, a trull, *Oth.*, 4.ii.

Calumniate, slander, *Troil. & Cres.*, 5.ii; so *calumniating time* in 3.iii; *calumnious strokes*, slanders, *Ham.*, 1.iii.

Can, (1) *can well on horseback*, are skilled horsemen, *Ham.*, 4.vii; know, *Cym.*, 4.ii; (2) = gan, began, *Per.*, 3.*Prol.*

Cancel, terminate, have done with, *Mac.*, 3.ii; etc.; *noun*, destruction, *Per.*, 1.i.

Cancer, the Crab, the sign of the zodiac the sun enters at midsummer, *Troil. & Cres.*, 2.iii.

Candidatus, a candidate (for those seeking office presented themselves wearing white), *Titus*, 1.i.

Candle, *night's candles*, the stars, *Rom. & Jul.*, 3.v.

Candy, *candied with frost*, white as if sugared, *Timon*, 4.iii.

Canker, canker-worm, *Ham.*, 1.iii; *Rom. & Jul.*, 2.iii; *canker'd country*, corrupt country, *Cor.*, 4.v; in two senses, rusty and inveterate, *Rom. & Jul.*, 1.i; *canker-bit*, eaten into by the worm, *Lear*, 5.iii.

Canon, church law, *Timon*, 4.iii; *Ham.*, 1.ii (here generally taken as referring to the sixth commandment); so any rule, such as that governing use of 'shall' and 'will', *Cor.*, 3.i.

Canonize, place among the famous heroes, *Troil. & Cres.*, 2.ii; *canoniz'd bones*, buried according to rites of church, *Ham.*, 1.iv.

Canopy, cover over bed on posts, *Rom. & Jul.*, 5.iii; sky, *Cor.*, 4.v; *verb*, cover, shade, *Cym.*, 2.ii.

Cantle, a segment cut from a sphere, *Ant. & Cleo.*, 3.x.

Canvas-climber, sailor aloft to trim sails, *Per.*, 4.i.

Cap, *take my cap, Jupiter*, throwing it up for joy, *Cor.*, 2.i; *Ham.*, 4.v; the cap was removed as a mark of respect, *Cor.*, 2.i; *throw their caps at*, give up for lost, *Timon*, 3.iv; *cap-and-knee slaves*, saluting and bowing rascals, *Timon*, 3.vi; reference to fool's cap in *Timon*, 4.iii; *gain the cap*, get a respectful salutation, *Cym.*, 3.iii; *held my cap oft to thy fortunes*, served you loyally, *Ant. & Cleo.*, 2.vii; *wore gloves in my cap*, a lady's glove as a love-token, *Lear*, 3.iv.

Capable, able to respond, *Ham.*, 3.iv; intelligent, *Troil. & Cres.*, 3.iii; capacious, *Oth.*, 3.iii; able to inherit, *Lear*, 2.i.

Cap-a-pe, from head to foot, *Ham.*, 1.ii.

Caparison, merely the trappings, *Cor.*, 1.ix.

Capital, punishable by death, *Cor.*, 3.iii; fatal, *Cor.*, 5.iii; *so capital a calf*, such a big ass (with pun on Capitol), *Ham.*, 3.ii.

Capitol, the fortress and sanctuary of Rome, *Ham.*, 3.ii.

Capitulate, come to terms, *Cor.*, 5.iii.

Capocchia, simpleton, *Troil. & Cres.*, 4.ii.

Car, chariot, *Titus*, 5.ii; etc.

Carbonado, score across like piece of meat for broiling, *Lear*, 2.ii.

Carbuncle, a gem of deep red colour, *Ham.*, 2.ii; *Cym.*, 5.v; tumour, *Lear*, 2.iv; *carbuncled*, decorated with carbuncles, *Ant. & Cleo.*, 4.viii.

Card, playing-card, *Titus*, 5.i; card of the mariner's compass, *Ham.*, 5.i.

Care, *call our cares fears*, represent the benefits conferred on the people as acts of fear not of statesmanship, *Cor.*, 3.i; desire, *Rom. & Jul.*, 3.v; *verb*, feel other than indifferent, *Lear*, 2.ii.

Careful, concerned, *Titus*, 4.iv.

Careless, *careless force and forceless care*, powerfully and fearlessly, *Troil. & Cres.*, 5.v; *careless livery*, costume in keeping with care-free youth, *Ham.*, 4.vii; *careless trifle*, not worth one's care, *Mac.*, 1.vi.

Carelessness, *noble carelessness*, the indifference of a noble mind, *Cor.*, 2.ii.

Carl, churl, *Cym.*, 5.ii.

Carper, critic, despiser of society, *Timon*, 4.iii.

Carrack, a galleon, *Oth.*, 1.ii (where marriage to an heiress is likened to the capture of a ship with rich cargo).

CARRIAGE, social behaviour, *Timon*, 3.ii; conduct of an affair, *Troil. & Cres.*, 2.iii; tenor, import, *Ham.*, 1.i; conveyance, *Cym.*, 3.iv; *the carriage of his chafe*, his deportment in anger, *Ant. & Cleo.*, 1.iii; *carriages*, the supports of the swords, *Ham.*, 5.ii.

CARRION, flesh, dead and corrupting as in the dog, alive but liable to corruption as in Ophelia, *Ham.*, 2.ii.

CARRY, capture, *Cor.*, 4.vii; *carries it away*, gets the best of it, gets away with his swagger, *Rom. & Jul.*, 3.i; *if he can carry't thus*, if he succeeds in spite of the opposition, *Oth.*, 1.i; *carry it so*, execute the deed thus, *Lear*, 5.iii; endure, *Lear*, 3.ii; *carry out my side*, execute my plan, *Lear*, 5.i.

CARVE, *carve for himself*, act merely on his own taste or inclination, *Ham.*, 1.iii; *carve for his own rage*, satisfy his desire to attack his enemy, *Oth.*, 2.iii.

CASE, *case of favour*, choice between two faces, *Cym.*, 1.vi; the circumstances in which he needs an advocate, *Cym.*, 2.iii; *the casing air*, the air that embraces everything, *Mac.*, 3.iv.

CASHIER, dismiss, *Oth.*, 1.i; bring about the dismissal, *Oth.*, 2.iii.

CASQUE, helmet, so standing for the soldier's life, *Cor.*, 4.vii.

CAST, throw as in wrestling, *Mac.*, 2.iii; *cast the gorge at*, revolt in disgust from, *Timon*, 4.iii; *cast upon*, confer, *Cor.*, 2.i; *cast the water*, make a diagnosis of the country's trouble, *Mac.*, 5.iii; remove him from command, *Oth.*, 1.i; *cast in his mood*, dismissed in a burst of displeasure, *Oth.*, 2.iii; *cast on*, directed against, *Ant. & Cleo.*, 2.vi; reckon, *Ant. & Cleo.*, 3.ii.

CASTIGATE, mortify, *Timon*, 4.iii.

CASTIGATION, self-discipline, *Oth.*, 3.iv.

CASUAL, accidental, *Ham.*, 5.ii; subject to accident, *Cym.*, 1.iv; *casually*, *Cym.*, 2.iii.

CASUALTY, *foreign casualties*, the chances of life in a strange country, *Lear*, 4.iii; *awkward casualties*, adverse chances, *Per.*, 5.i.

CAT, the civet-cat, *Lear*, 3.iv.

CATAPLASM, plaster, poultice, *Ham.*, 4.vii.

CATASTROPHE, *like the catastrophe of the old comedy*, like the concluding event that, however improbably, rounds off the plays of long ago, *Lear*, 1.ii.

CATLINGS, catgut for fiddle-strings, *Troil. & Cres.*, 3.iii.

CAUDLE, qualify as one would a cordial or refreshing drink, *Timon*, 4.iii.

CAULK, make seams (of ship, barrel) water-tight, *Per.*, 3.i.

CAUSE, debate, matter of dispute, *Troil. & Cres.*, 5.ii; unfortunate affair, *Cor.*, 3.i; *the first and second cause*, part of the ritual of duelling, causes for taking up a quarrel, *Rom. & Jul.*, 2.iv; affair, *Oth.*, 3.iii; charge, *Lear*, 4.vi; *it is the cause*, the nature of the charge, the peculiar form of guilt, *Oth.*, 5.ii.

CAUTEL, deceit, *Ham.*, 1.iii.

CAUTELOUS, *swear priests and cowards and men cautelous*, take an oath from deceitful men, *Jul. Caes.*, 2.i; *cautelous baits*, crafty traps, *Cor.*, 4.i.

CAUTERIZE, burn, *Timon*, 5.i.

CAUTION, warning, *Cor.*, 2.ii; *Mac.*, 4.i. [*Ham.*, 2.ii.

CAVIARY, caviar, an acquired taste,

CEASE, *noun*, death, decease, *Ham.*, 3.iii; *verb*, come to an end altogether, *Mac.*, 4.ii; *be not ceased*, do not be put off, *Timon*, 2.i.

CELEBRATE, make a ceremony of, *Ant. & Cleo.*, 2.vii; used of religious or solemn rite, *Ham.*, 1.i.

CENSOR, Roman magistrate who supervised public morals and public buildings, *Cor.*, 2.iii.

CENSURE, opinion, *Ham.*, 1.iii; sentence, *Cor.*, 3.iii; *mouths of wisest censure*, men of soundest judgement, *Oth.*, 2.iii; condemnation, *Oth.*, 5.ii; blame, *Lear*, 1.iv; reproof, *Cym.*, 3.iii; *verb*, pronounce sentence, *Lear*, 5.iii; judge, *Cor.*, 2.i; *Jul. Caes.*, 3.ii.

CENTRE, *this centre*, the earth, on the Ptolemaic system the centre of the universe, *Troil. & Cres.*, 1.iii; the centre of the earth, and so of the whole universe, *Ham.*, 2.ii.

CENTURY, division of Roman army, about a hundred strong, *Cor.*, 1.vii; a company of a hundred soldiers, *Lear*, 4.iv.

CERBERUS, the dog of Hades, *Troil. & Cres.*, 2.i.

CEREMONY, *deck'd with ceremonies*, with ceremonial hangings, *Jul. Caes.*, 1.i; omen obtained from some rite, *Jul. Caes.*, 2.ii.

CHAFE, anger, *Ant. & Cleo.*, 1.iii; *the chafed boar*, enraged, *Titus*, 4.ii; *flies each bound it chafes*, sweeps away from the bank it washes, *Timon.* 1.i.

CHAFFLESS, without chaff, so without worthless elements of character, *Cym.*, 1.vi.

CHAIR, orator's seat, *Cor.*, 4.vii; *public chair*, rostrum, *Jul. Caes.*, 3.ii; throne, *Ant. & Cleo.*, 3.vi; sedan-chair, *Oth.*, 5.i.

CHALICE, cup, so *chalic'd flowers*, shaped like cups, *Cym.*, 2.iii.

CHALLENGE, claim, *Rom. & Jul.*, 3.v; accuse, *Titus*, 1.i; blame, *Mac.*, 3.iv; claim deservedly, *Oth.*, 2.i; deserve, *Lear*, 1.i.

CHAMBERER, a frequenter of ladies' chambers rather than the field of battle, *Oth.*, 3.iii.

CHAMBER-HANGING, tapestry, *Cym.*, 5.v.

CHAMELEON, *chameleon's dish*, the air, on which it was supposed to feed, *Ham.*, 3.ii.

CHAMPAIN, open country, *Lear*, 1.i.

CHAMPION, *champion me to the utterance*, challenge me to a duel to the death, *Mac.*, 3.i.

CHANCE, misfortune, disaster, *Mac.*, 2.iii; accident, *Ham.*, 4.vii; *common chances*, ordinary ill-luck, *Cor.*, 4.i; opportunity, *Cor.*, 4.vii; *from chance to chance*, from one event to another, *Cym.*, 5.v; so *disastrous chances*, *Oth.*, 1.iii; *what a chance*, what an opportunity for advancement, *Cym.*, 1.v; fortune, *Cym.*, 5.iv; luck, *Ant. & Cleo.*, 2.iii; *verb, chance it as it may*, let it happen as it will, *Timon*, 5.i; *how chance?* how comes it about? *Lear*, 2.iv.

CHANGE, exchange, *Troil. & Cres.*, 3.iii; *change of honours*, fresh honours, *Cor.*, 2.i; change of conduct, *Jul. Caes.*, 4.ii; capricious change of mind, *Lear*, 1.i; political change, *Ant. & Cleo.*, 1.iii; change of affection, *Cym.*, 1.vi; change of countenance, blush, *Cym.*, 1.vi; *verb*, change countenance, *Jul. Caes.*, 3.i; exchange, *Oth.*, 1.iii; *changing*, fickle, *Titus*, 1.i.

CHANSON, *pious chanson*, scriptural ballad, *Ham.*, 2.ii.

CHAOS, anarchy, *Troil. & Cres.*, 1.iii; *chaos is come again*, the end of the world will have come, *Oth.*, 3.iii.

CHAP, jaw, *Mac.*, 1.ii; *Ant. & Cleo.*, 3.v; *chaps of age*, wrinkles, *Titus*, 5.iii; *chapless*, with lower jaw missing, *Ham.*, 5.i; *chap-fall'n*, with previous meaning, and additional sense of mirthless (crestfallen), *Ham.*, 5.i.

CHAPMAN, merchant, *Troil. & Cres.*, [4.i.

CHARACTER, the inscription on the tomb, *Timon*, 5.iii; handwriting, *Ham.*, 4.vi; etc.; figures, *Troil. & Cres.*, 1.iii; face, countenance, *Cor.*, 2.i; *in the character*, in his true character, *Cor.*, 5.iv; *verb*, engrave on your memory, *Ham.*, 1.iii.

CHARACTERLESS, *mighty states characterless are grated to dusty nothing*, leaving no memory behind, *Troil. & Cres.*, 3.ii.

CHARACTERY, *all the charactery of my sad brows*, the meaning of my troubled look, *Jul. Caes.*, 2.i.

CHARE, chore, routine tasks about the house, *Ant. & Cleo.*, 4.xv.

CHARGE, military command, *Ant. & Cleo.*, 4.iv; *not nice but full of charge*, not trivial but important, *Rom. & Jul.*, 5.ii; *as-es of great charge*, 'as' clauses on weighty topics (with pun on 'ass'), *Ham.*, 5.ii; *answering us with our own charge*, returning to us merely the cost of the expedition, *Cor.*, 5.vi; *I'll nothing do on charge*, at the command of an enemy, *Troil. & Cres.*, 4.iv; *verb*, overburden, *Mac.*, 5.i; weigh down, overcome, *Cym.*, 3.iv; *charge my fantasy*, afflict my imagination, *Jul. Caes.*, 3.iii.

CHARM, silence, *Oth.*, 5.ii; *my charm*, witch who has beguiled him, *Ant. & Cleo.*, 4.xii; *charmer*, sorceress, *Oth.*, 3.iv; *I charm you that*, I conjure you that, *Jul. Caes.*, 2.i; *a charmed life*, protected by spells, *Mac.*, 5.viii.

CHARON, the ferryman who rowed the shades across the Styx to Hades, *Troil. & Cres.*, 3.ii.

CHARTER, privilege, *Cor.*, 1.ix; public rights established by law, *Cor.*, 2.iii; *a charter in your voice*, your support of the right I now plead for, *Oth.*, 1.iii.

CHARY, circumspect, shy, *Ham.*, 1.iii.

CHASE, reserve for hunting, *Titus*, 2.iii; race, *Jul. Caes.*, 1.ii; hunt, *Oth.*, 2.iii.

CHAT, *while she chats him*, talks about him (Coriolanus), *Cor.*, 2.i.

CHAUDRON, entrails, *Mac.*, 4.i.

CHE = I, *che vor ye*, I warrant you, *Lear*, 4.vi. Shakespeare here used a Somerset dialect adapted for stage purposes, where *chill* = I will, *chud* = I would, and where initial *f* and *s* are voiced to *v* and *z*, as in *vortnight* and *zir*.

CHEAPEN, *cheapen a kiss,* bargain for a kiss, *Per.,* 4.vi.

CHEATER, officer of the Exchequer, then of swindler generally, *Titus,* 5.i.

CHECK, hold back, *Oth.,* 2.iii; reprove, *Lear,* 2.ii; *check my courage,* bridle my disposition, *Cor.,* 3.iii; rebuke, *Jul. Caes.,* 4.iii; *checking at his voyage,* abandoning it for some other plan (the term is borrowed from falconry: a hawk checks when it turns from the quarry to follow some other bird), *Ham.,* 4.vii.

CHECKER, to pattern like a chessboard with different colours, *Rom. & Jul.,* 2.iii.

CHEER, *change of cheer,* change of look, countenance, *Titus,* 1.i; cheerfulness, *Ham.,* 3.ii; *royal cheer,* the choicest food, *Timon,* 3.vi; *give the cheer,* give the welcome to the feast, *Mac.,* 3.iv; *verb,* encourage, *Timon,* 1.ii.

CHEQUIN, gold coin, Italian or Turkish, *Per.,* 4.ii.

CHERISH, *cherish factions,* promote strife, *Timon,* 3.v.

CHERUB, *a cherub that sees them,* the cherubim having special powers of vision, *Ham.,* 4.iii.

CHEVERIL, very flexible leather, *Rom. & Jul.,* 2.iv.

CHIDE, quarrel, *Cym.,* 5.iv; *as chiding a nativity,* as stormy a birth, *Per.,* 3.i; *chiding fortune,* the storm, *Troil. & Cres.,* 1.iii.

CHILD, daughter, *Lear,* 4.vii; candidate for knighthood, *Child Rowland, Lear,* 3.iv; *childed,* having children, *Lear,* 3.vi; *child-changed,* reduced to misery by his children's treatment, *Lear,* 4.vii.

CHIMNEY, fire-place, *Cym.,* 2.iv.

CHINKS, money, *Rom. & Jul.,* 1.v.

CHIVALRY, knighthood and its ideals, *Troil. & Cres.,* 1.ii.

CHOICE, *most choice forsaken,* specially worthy of being chosen, *Lear,* 1.i.

CHOKE, *choke the air with dust,* fill it to the point of suffocation, *Timon,* 5.ii; *choke their art,* render their skill helpless, *Mac.,* 1.ii.

CHOLER, bile, *Ham.,* 3.ii; this was one of the four humours and in excess gave rise to anger, so with play on words in *Rom. & Jul.,* 1.i; *choleric,* easily angered, *Lear,* 1.i.

CHOOSE, *he cannot choose,* he cannot do otherwise (than do well), *Cor.,* 4.iii; *Ham.,* 4.vii; *when I cannot choose,* have no alternative, *Lear,* 1.iv.

CHOPINE, a type of shoe fashionable in Venice, with high cork heel and sole, *Ham.,* 2.ii.

CHORUS, the speaker who, as in *Henry V* or *Pericles,* explains and comments on the action, *Ham.,* 3.ii.

CHOUGH, crow or jackdaw, *Mac.,* 3.iv; *Lear,* 4.vi.

CHRISTEN, *see* EVEN.

CHURCH, *to church to-morrow,* to have the marriage, *Rom. & Jul.,* 4.ii.

CHURL, miser, niggard, *Rom. & Jul.,* 5.iii; *churlish,* rude, rough, *Troil. & Cres.,* 1.ii; uncharitable, *Ham.,* 5.i.

CICATRICE, scar, *Cor.,* 2.i; used of memory of a defeat, *Ham.,* 4.iii.

CIMMERIAN, the Cimmerians in the Odyssey dwelt in the land of darkness, so used of the Moor, *Titus,* 2.iii.

CINQUE-SPOTTED, with five spots, *Cym.,* 2.ii.

CIRCLE, *the wheel is come full circle,* the wheel of Fortune has completed its turn, *Lear,* 5.iii; crown, *Ant. & Cleo.,* 3.xii.

CIRCUMSTANCE, affair, *Ham.,* 1.iii; *comes near the circumstance,* much resembles in detail, *Ham.,* 3.ii; the detail, *Rom. & Jul.,* 2.v; *drift of circumstance,* roundabout means, *Ham.,* 3.i; argument, going round the points, *Troil. & Cres.,* 3.iii; further ceremony, *Ham.,* 1.v; *breed itself so out of circumstance,* continue because of new conditions, *Oth.,* 3.iii; *strong circumstances,* strong circumstantial evidence, *Oth.,* 3.iii; *pride, pomp, and circumstance,* ceremony, trappings, *Oth.,* 3.iii; *bombast circumstance,* made much of some detail and so a long-winded roundabout story, *Oth.,* 1.i; *be circumstanced,* submit to the conditions of the occasion, *Oth.,* 3.iv.

CIRCUMSTANTIAL, *circumstantial branches,* detail of time, place, etc., that emerges from the story, *Cym.,* 5.v.

CIRCUMVENT, cheat, overreach, *Ham.,* 5.i.

CIRCUMVENTION, strategy, *Troil. & Cres.,* 2.iii; information that gave the means of defeating the enemy's plan, *Cor.,* 1.ii.

CITIZEN, *so citizen a wanton,* so effeminate because of city-breeding, *Cym.,* 4.ii.

CIVET, a musky perfume from civet-cat, *Lear,* 4.vi.

CIVIL, *civil blood*, the blood of the citizens, *Rom. & Jul.*, 1.*Prol.*; *civil streets*, the ways of orderly society, *Ant. & Cleo.*, 5.i; civilized and with the appropriate feelings, *Cym.*, 3.vi; *civil swords*, used in civil war, *Ant. & Cleo.*, 1.iii; polite, *Oth.*, 2.i.

CIVILITY, humane manners, *Cym.*, 4.ii.

CLAP, applause, *Per.*, 3.*Prol.*; *at a clap*, at a blow, *Lear*, 1.iv.

CLAPPER-CLAW, exchange blows, *Troil. & Cres.*, 5.iv.

CLASP, hold shut, *Cym.*, 3.ii; embrace, *Oth.*, 1.i.

CLAY, often used to convey idea of mortality, as *kingdoms are clay*, *Ant. & Cleo.*, 1.i; and *Cym.*, 4.ii, where the differences in living creatures are contrasted with the uniformity of their dust.

CLEANLY, cleverly, *Titus*, 2.i.

CLEAR, serene, *Mac.*, 1.v; pure, *Timon*, 4.iii; *clearest*, glorious, *Lear*, 4.vi; without fault or blemish, *Ant. & Cleo.*, 5.ii; free from reproach, apparently innocent, *Per.*, 1.i; *verb*, pay a debt, redeem, *Timon*, 2.ii.

CLEARNESS, alibi, no taint of suspicion, *Mac.*, 3.i.

CLEAVE, (1) adhere, hold, *Mac.*, 1.iii and 2.i; (2) split, *Timon*, 3.iv; etc.

CLEPE, call, *Ham.*, 1.iv.

CLERK, scholar, *Per.*, 5. *Prol.*

CLIMATE, region, *Jul. Caes.*. 1.iii; *Oth.*, 1.i; so *climature*, *Ham.*, 1.i.

CLIMB, reach, *Timon*, 1.i.

CLING, waste, shrivel, *Mac.*, 5.v.

CLIP, cut, omit, *Lear*, 4.vii; embrace, hold, *Ant. & Cleo.*, 5.ii; *Oth.*, 3.iii.

CLOAK-BAG, portmanteau, *Cym.*, 3.iv.

CLOCK, *'twixt clock and clock*, between the striking of one hour and the next, *Cym.*, 3.iv.

CLOG, *to hang clogs on them*, to impose restrictions (as one restricts an animal's movements by fastening some weight to it), *Oth.*, 1.iii.

CLOISTERED, *cloister'd flight*, within the narrow limits, between buildings, *Mac.*, 3.ii.

CLOSE, *noun*, enclosure, *Timon*, 5.i; *adj.*, secret, *Ham.*, 2.i; etc., in prison, *Oth.*, 5.ii; inward and involuntary, *Oth.*, 3.iii; *verb*, join, *Mac.*, 3.ii; *closes with you in this consequence*, he agrees with you in the account he follows on with, *Ham.*, 2.i.

CLOSELY, secretly, *Rom. & Jul.*, 5.iii.

CLOSET, room, study, *Jul. Caes.*, 2.i; a desk or private repository, *Mac.*, 5.i; private room, press or lock-up in a room, so *a closet lock and key of villainous secrets*, one who keeps undivulged the secrets she knows, *Oth.*, 4.ii; *closet-war*, conducted from the safety of headquarters, *Troil. & Cres.*, 1.iii.

CLOSURE, end, *Titus*, 5.iii.

CLOTH, *painted cloths*, cloth or canvas on which were painted figures and mottoes, a cheap substitute for tapestry, *Troil. & Cres.*, 5.x; *a squire's cloth*, a livery suitable for a squire, *Cym.*, 2.iii.

CLOTHIER, *draw me a clothier's yard*, draw the arrow, which was a clothier's yard in length, to the head, *Lear*, 4.vi.

CLOUD, *cloud in's face*, darken'd as with a cloud of grief, then turned by Enobarbus into the term as used of horses, a dark spot on the face, *Ant. & Cleo.*, 3.ii.

CLOUT, the centre of the target, *Lear*, 4.vi.

CLOUTED, *clouted brogues*, shoes studded with nails, *Cym.*, 4.ii.

CLOY, (1) claw, *Cym.*, 5.iv; (2) fill to overflowing, *Cym.*, 4.iv; *cloyless*, that prevents satiety, *Ant. & Cleo.*, 2.i.

CLUTCH, grasp, *Ham.*, 5.i.

CLYSTER-PIPE, syringe, *Oth.*, 2.i.

CO-ACT, act together, *Troil. & Cres.*, 5.ii.

COAL, *carry coals*, do the dirty work, so suffer insults, *Rom. & Jul.*, 1.i.

COASTING, *a coasting welcome*, the manner in which they invite attentions, *Troil. & Cres.*, 4.v.

COAT, suit of armor, *Per.*, 2.i; *lined their coats*, made a substantial fortune, *Oth.*, 1.i.

COBLOAF, a little loaf with a round head, *Troil. & Cres.*, 2.i.

COCK, the weather-cock on the steeple, *Lear*, 3.ii.

COCK-A-HOOP, *set cock-a-hoop*, set all in disorder, *Rom. & Jul.*, 1.v.

COCKATRICE, the deadly basilisk, a fabled serpent that kills with its glance, *Rom. & Jul.*, 3.ii.

COCKLE, (1) *the cockle of rebellion*, the weed that spoils the field of society, *Cor.*, 3.i; (2) the cockle-shell; *cockle hat*, hat with shell attached, the badge of a pilgrim, the cockle-shell indicating that the pilgrimage was to the shrine of St. James of Compostela in Spain, *Ham.*, 4.v.

COCKNEY, indicates stupidity or inefficiency in some way, here perhaps a city woman unaccustomed to eel-pie, *Lear*, 2.iv.

COCYTUS, one of the five rivers of the infernal regions, *Titus*, 2.iii.

CODDING, lecherous, *Titus*, 5.i.

COFFIN, pie-crust, *Titus*, 5.ii.

COG, cheat, *Oth.*, 4.ii; *cogging Greeks*, lying Greeks; *cog their hearts from them*, win their hearts by lying words, *Cor.*, 3.ii.

COGNITION, knowledge, *Troil. & Cres.*, 5.ii.

COGNIZANCE, the badge by which a chief and his retainers were known, so a token of remembrance, *Jul. Caes.*, 2.ii; *the cognizance of her incontinency*, the bracelet, *Cym.*, 2.iv.

COIGN, corner-stone, *Cor.*, 5.iv; *Per.*, 3.*Prol.*; *coign of vantage*, corner convenient for bird to build in, *Mac.*, 1.vi.

COIL, much ado, *Timon*, 1.ii; *mortal coil*, turmoil of life, *Ham.*, 3.i.

COISTREL, low knave, *Per.*, 4.vi.

COLD, cool, phlegmatic, and, in following line, gloomy, disappointed, *Cym.*, 2.iii; chilling, *Lear*, 1.i; *cold blood*, in moments of deliberation, unmoved by passion, *Timon*, 3.v; chaste, *Ham.*, 4.vii; *coldly*, used punningly in *Ham.*, 1.ii; with indifference, *Ham.*, 4.iii; chastely, *Troil. & Cres.*, 1.iii.

COLDNESS, lack of zeal, *Oth.*, 2.iii.

COLLATERAL, *by collateral hand*, the hand of an accessory his own or another's, so indirectly, *Ham.*, 4.v.

COLLECTION, *move the hearers to collection*, encourage the hearers to try to make sense of, or deductions from, the utterances, *Ham.*, 4.v; *no collection of it*, no interpretation of it, *Cym.*, 5.v.

COLLIED, darkened, *Oth.*, 2.iii.

COLMEKILL, Iona (the cell of Columba), *Mac.*, 2.iv; *Saint Colme's inch*, St. Columba's isle, Inchcolm in the Firth of Forth, *Mac.*, 1.ii.

COLOQUINTIDA, colocynth, a bitter purge, *Oth.*, 1.iii.

COLOSSUS, gigantic statue of Apollo in Rhodes harbour, one of the seven wonders of the world, *Jul. Caes.*, 1.ii; so *colossus-wise* in *Troil. & Cres.*, 5.v.

COLOUR, justification (with play on usual meaning), *Ham.*, 3.iv; excuse, *Jul. Caes.*, 2.i; *verb*, *colour your loneliness*, provide a reason (though a false one) for your being alone, *Ham.*, 3.i; *under her colours*, those who take her side in the trouble, *Cym.*, 1.iv; *against all colour*, without any show of justice, *Cym.*, 3.i; *a fellow of the self-same colour*, a rascal of the same sort as, *Lear*, 2.ii; *seek no colour*, offer no excuse, *Ant. & Cleo.*, 1.iii; *verb*, dye, *Cym.*, 5.i.

COMART, bargain, agreement, *Ham.*, 1.i.

COME, *am I come near ye now?* do I touch on a tender spot?; *lack humanity so much as this fact comes to*, so inhuman as to be capable of this deed, *Cym.*, 3.ii; *come forth*, appear (as on the stage of the world), *Ant. & Cleo.*, 5.ii.

COMEDDLE, mingle, *Ham.*, 3.ii.

COMFORT, joy, *Cor.*, 5.iii; aid, assistance, *Lear*, 4.i; encouragement, *Oth.*, 4.ii; *verb*, aid, assist, *Titus*, 2.iii; bring relief to, *Lear*, 3.v.

COMFORTABLE, ready to help and bring comfort, *Timon*, 4.iii; cheerful, *Cor.*, 1.iii; one who will aid and comfort, *Lear*, 1.iv; of good comfort, in good spirits, *Per.*, 1.ii.

COMFORTLESS, giving no help or comfort, *Titus*, 3.i; providing no help, *Lear*, 3.vii.

COMMEND, commendation, *Per.*, 2.ii; *verb*, deliver, *Lear*, 2.iv; mention as worthy, *Ant. & Cleo.*, 4.viii.

COMMENT, *the very comment of thy soul*, with a keenness of observation that penetrates to the very being, *Ham.*, 3.ii.

COMMERCE, intercourse, *Ham.*, 3.i.

COMMISSION, warrant (the whole passage is in legal terms), *Rom. & Jul.*, 4.i; *Ant. & Cleo.*, 2.iii; *join'd in commission*, become a colleague in the command, *Cor.*, 4.vii; mandate, *Oth.*, 4.ii; *bore the commission of my place and person*, had warrant to act as if he were of my rank and my very self, *Lear*, 5.iii; *o' the commission*, one of those entrusted with a task, *Lear*, 3.vi.

COMMIT, commit adultery, *Lear*, 3.iv; so *committed*, *Oth.*, 4.ii.

COMMODIOUS, accommodating, *Troil. & Cres.*, 5.ii.

COMMODITY, profitable quality, advantage, *Lear*, 4.i; merchandise, *Per.*, 4.ii; profit, *Per.*, 4.ii.

COMMON, *the noble and the common*, the nobles and the plebeians, *Cor.*, 3.i; *the common enemy of man*, which all have in common, the devil, *Mac.*, 3.i.

COMMONER, prostitute, *Oth.*, 4.ii.

COMMON-KISSING, kissing everyone, *Cym.*, 3.iv.

COMPACT, agreement, *Ham.*, 1.i; *adj.*, (1) composed of, *Titus*, 5.iii; *well compact*, well made, *Lear*, 1.ii; (2) *compact and flattering his displeasure*, leagued with him, having an understanding with him, *Lear*, 2.ii.

COMPANION, fellow (used contemptuously) *Cor.*, 5.ii; *companion me with my mistress*, make me the equal in rank, *Ant. & Cleo.*, 1.ii.

COMPANIONSHIP, an equal place, *Cor.*, 3.ii; *all of companionship*, all in a body, *Timon*, 1.i.

COMPARATIVE, *made comparative for your virtues*, made a measure of your respective merits, *Cym.*, 2.iii.

COMPARE, *there would be something failing in him that should compare*, some lack of judgement in the man who thought he had found the equal of Posthumus, *Cym.*, 1.i.

COMPARISON, *his gay comparison*, what makes him compare so advantageously in external resources (some editors read *caparisons*), *Ant. & Cleo.*, 3.xiii.

COMPASS, course, *Jul. Caes.*, 5.iii; the range of a musical instrument, so of a man's nature, *Ham.*, 3.ii; bounds, *Rom. & Jul.*, 4.i; yearly circuit, *Oth.*, 3.iv; scope, reach, *Oth.*, 3.iv; *within reason and compass*, reasonably possible, *Oth.*, 1.iii; *verb, compass'd window*, round, as a bay-window, *Troil. & Cres.*, 1.ii; *compassing*, embracing, winning, *Oth.*, 1.iii.

COMPEER, equal, *Lear*, 5.iii.

COMPELLED, *a compelled valour*, forced by circumstances to show fight, *Ham.*, 4.vi.

COMPETENCY, *that natural competency*, the sufficiency required by the nature, *Cor.*, 1.i.

COMPETITOR, associate, *Ant. & Cleo.*, 1.iv; 2.vii; and 5.i.

COMPLAIN, lament, *Cym.*, 4.ii.

COMPLAINT, a lament (the idea of accusation is often included), *Lear*, 1.iv.

COMPLETE, *complete man*, fully accomplished, *Troil. & Cres.*, 3.iii; *complete knave*, fully equipped for knavery, *Oth.*, 2.i.

COMPLEXION, temperament, supposed to be determined by combination of the four humours; accordingly a man might be sanguine, phlegmatic, choleric, or melancholy; one of these too strongly developed would produce unbalanced conduct, *Ham.*, 1.iv; *Per.*, 4.ii; appearance, *Jul. Caes.*, 1.iii.

COMPLIMENT, ceremony, *Rom. & Jul.*, 2.ii; *Lear*, 1.i; formality, *Rom. & Jul.*, 2.iv; *in compliment extern*, in outward behaviour; *Oth.*, 1.i; *mechanic compliment*, vulgar show, *Ant. & Cleo.*, 4.iv.

COMPLIMENTAL, courteous, *Troil. & Cres.*, 3.i.

COMPLY, *comply with*, satisfy, *Oth.*, 1.iii; *comply with you in this garb*, observe the fashion and ceremony appropriate to welcome, *Ham.*, 2.ii.

COMPOSE, come to terms, make a treaty, *Ant. & Cleo.*, 2.ii.

COMPOSITION, treaty, *Ant. & Cleo.*, 2.vi; compounding, *Lear*, 2.ii; *no composition in these news*, no consistency in the reports, *Oth.*, 1.iii; *our swifter composition*, our coming to terms of peace more quickly, *Cor.*, 3.i.

COMPOST, COMPOSTURE, manure, *Ham.*, 3.iv; *Timon*, 4.iii.

COMPOSURE, nature, temperament, *Troil. & Cres.*, 2.iii; *Ant. & Cleo.*, 1.iv; combination, *Troil. & Cres.*, 2.iii.

COMPOUND, agree, *Cor.*, 5.vi.

COMPT, the reckoning, so Day of Judgement, *Oth.*, 5.ii; *in compt*, as a trust, to be accounted for, *Mac.*, 1.vi; *have the dates in compt*, so as to reckon the interest, *Timon*, 2.i.

CON, get by heart, *Troil. & Cres.*, 2.i; *thanks I must you con*, feel thanks to, *Timon*, 4.iii.

CONCEAL, *my conceal'd lady*, secret wife, *Rom. & Jul.*, 3.iii.

CONCEIT, idea, *Oth.*, 3.iii; the faculty of mind, *Per.*, 3.i; *conceit upon her father*, obsessed with her father's death, *Ham.*, 4.v; *whose conceit lies in his hamstring*, no brains and all swagger, *Troil. & Cres.*, 1.iii; apprehensions of the mind, *Ham.*, 3.iv; *of very liberal conceit*, of elaborate or fanciful design, *Ham.*, 5.ii; *verb*, conceive, *Jul. Caes.*, 1.iii.

CONCEIVE, *conceived to scope*, designed well for its theme, *Timon*, 1.i; form in the mind and in the womb, *Lear*, 1.i.

CONCEPTION, idea, plan, *Troil. & Cres.*, 1.iii; intelligence (with pun on pregnancy), *Ham.*, 2.ii; belief, *Oth.*, 5.ii.

CONCERNANCY, meaning, import, *Ham.*, 5.ii; *dear concernings*, matters of such personal interest, *Ham.*, 3.iv.

CONCLUSION, experiment, *Ant. & Cleo.*, 5.ii; *Cym.*, 1.v; *still conclu-*

sion, quiet judgement, *Ant. & Cleo.*, 4.xv; riddle, *Per.*, 1.i; *to try conclusions*, to make the experiment, *Ham.*, 3.iv.

CONCUPY, lust, *Troil. & Cres.*, 5.ii.

CONDEMN, *condemning shadows*, as things inferior to the reality, *Ant. & Cleo.*, 5.ii; sentence, *Lear*, 1.iv.

CONDITION, *all conditions*, all classes of men, *Timon*, 1.i; medium (painting), *Timon*, 1.i; character, *Timon*, 4.iii; *imperfections of long-engraffed condition*, faults long associated with his nature, *Lear*, 1.i; *full of most blest condition*, a nature entirely virtuous, *Oth.*, 2.i.

CONDOLEMENT, grieving, *Ham.*, 1.ii; payment in compensation, *Per.*, 2.i.

CONDUCE, take place, *Troil. & Cres.*, 5.ii.

CONDUCT, guide, escort, *Rom. & Jul.*, 5.iii; *Cym.*, 3.v; command, leadership, *Titus*, 4.iv; *Cym.*, 4.ii; guidance, *Lear*, 3.vi.

CONDUIT, figure on a fountain from which water issues, *Titus*, 2.iv.

CONEY, rabbit, *Cor.*, 4.v.

CONFECTION, drug, so at times poison, *Cym.*, 1.v. and 5.v.

CONFECTIONARY, place for sweets, so for indulgence, *Timon*, 4.iii.

CONFEDERACY, league, alliance, *Lear*, 3.vii.

CONFEDERATE, associated with, *Cym.*, 3.iii; *confederate in the fact*, united in doing the deed, *Titus*, 4.i; *confederate season*, opportunity as it were a partner in the deed, *Ham.*, 3.ii.

CONFIDENT, strongly trusting, *Titus*, 1.i; trustful, *Cym.*, 5.v; *three thousand confident*, as determined as if they were three thousand, *Cym.*, 5.iii.

CONFINE, prison, cell, *Ham.*, 2.ii; *Ant. & Cleo.*, 3.v; walls, *Rom. & Jul.*, 3.i; region, *Jul. Caes.*, 3.i; *the very verge of her confine*, on the boundary of the land of the living, *Lear*, 2.iv; *confineless*, boundless, *Mac.*, 4.iii.

CONFINER, inhabitant, *Cym.*, 4.ii.

CONFIRM, be sure of, trust, *Timon*, 1.ii.

CONFOUND, destroy, *Timon*, 4.iii; *Ant. & Cleo.*, 3.ii; consume, *Cor.*, 1.vi; waste, *Ant. & Cleo.*, 1.i.

CONJECTURAL, *conjectural marriages*, marriages they guess will take place, *Cor.*, 1.i.

CONJUNCT, intimately associated, [*Lear*, 2.ii.

CONJUNCTIVE, closely joined, *Ham.*, 4.ii; *Oth.*, 1.iii.

CONJURATION, exhortation, *Ham.*, 5.ii; incantation, *Oth.*, 1.iii.

CONJURE, call as by magic, *Timon*, 1.i; call on with magic spells, *Lear*, 2.i; *conjured to this effect*, rendered efficacious by magic, *Oth.*, 1.iii.

CONSCIENCE, knowledge of moral issues, *Ham.*, 3.i; conviction, *Timon*, 2.ii; knowledge, inmost thoughts, *Cym.*, 1.vi; regard for right and wrong, *Oth.*, 3.iii.

CONSCIONABLE, conscientious, *Oth.*, 2.i.

CONSENT, *consent of*, agreement about, *Cor.*, 2.iii; *verb*, agree, *Troil. & Cres.*, 4.v; *consent in*, together plan, *Oth.*, 5.ii.

CONSEQUENCE, *in this consequence*, as follows, *Ham.*, 2.i; *mortal consequences*, future events, *Mac.*, 5.iii; the sequel, what follows, *Oth.*, 2.iii; *the consequence of the crown*, the royal succession, *Cym.*, 2.iii.

CONSERVE, to prepare (of a drug), *Oth.*, 3.iv.

CONSIDER, reward, *Cym.*, 2.iii; *considerate*, thoughtful, *Ant. & Cleo.*, 2.ii; *consideration*, speculation, *Ant. & Cleo.*, 4.ii.

CONSIGN, subscribe to, accept the same terms as, *Cym.*, 4.ii; mark with a seal, agree; so *consign'd kisses*, seals of love added as confirmation, *Troil. & Cres.*, 4.iv.

CONSORT, associate with, *Rom. & Jul.*, 3.i (with pun on 'consort', music in harmony, in next line); company, used in deprecatory sense, *Lear*, 2.i.

CONSPECTUITIES, *see* BISSON.

CONSTANTLY, assuredly, *Troil. & Cres.*, 4.i; faithfully, *Cym.*, 3.v.

CONSTRAIN, *constrains the garb from his nature*, forces his manner of address to assume a form very different from his true nature, *Lear*, 2.ii.

CONSTRINGE, draw together, *Troil. & Cres.*, 5.ii.

CONSUMMATION, death, final settlement, *Ham.*, 3.i; *Cym.*, 4.ii.

CONTAINING, contents, *Cym.*, 5.v.

CONTENT, please, *Titus*, 5.ii; reward, *Oth.*, 3.i; *noun*, *my heart's content*, both its contents and its contentment suggested, *Troil. & Cres.*, 1.ii; *lends content*, harmonizes in making a beautiful whole, *Rom. & Jul.*, 1.iii.

CONTINENT, that which contains, *Ham.*, 4.iv; so breast or body in *Ant. & Cleo.*, 4.xii; *Lear*, 3.ii; a summary, embodiment, *Ham.*, 5.ii; *adj.*, restricting, *Mac.*, 4.iii; restraining, *Lear*, 1.ii.

CONTINUATE, lasting, *Timon*, 1.i; *more continuate time*, less interrupted, *Oth.*, 3.iv.

CONTRACT, *contracted to them both*, to both given promise of marriage, *Lear*, 5.iii.

CONTRACTION, the contract of marriage, the most solemn form of agreement, *Ham.*, 3.iv.

CONTRIVE, plan, *Troil. & Cres.*, 1.iii; *contriving*, underhand dealing, *Ham.*, 4.vii; *contriving friends*, friends involved in the political plots, *Ant. & Cleo.*, 1.ii; *contriver*, plotter, *Jul. Caes.*, 2.i.

CONTROL, overpower, *Cor.*, 3.i; thwart, *Titus*, 1.i; master, *Oth.*, 5.ii; hinder, prevent, *Lear*, 3.vii; *controller*, critic, *Titus*, 2.iii; *controlment*, restraint, *Titus*, 2.i.

CONTROVERSY, *hearts of controversy*, as contending with one another or with the stream, *Jul. Caes.*, 1.ii.

CONTUMELY, contempt, *Ham.*, 3.i.

CONVENIENCE, favorable circumstances, *Lear*, 3.vi; *required conveniences*, necessary aids, *Oth.*, 2.i; conveniency, opportunity, *Oth.*, 4.ii.

CONVENIENT, suitable, fitting, *Lear*, 4.v; *convenient seeming*, appearance of decency, *Lear*, 3.ii.

CONVENT, summon, *Cor.*, 2.ii.

CONVERSANT, experienced, *Cym.*, 4.i.

CONVERSATION, deportment, *Oth.*, 3.ii; *Ant. & Cleo.*, 2.vi.

CONVERSE, associate, *Lear*, 1.iv.

CONVEY, manage secretly, *Lear*, 1.ii; steal away, *Cym.*, 1.i; *convey your pleasures*, enjoy them secretly, *Mac.*, 4.iii.

CONVEYANCE, deed by which property is transferred, *Ham.*, 5.i; veins, *Cor.*, 5.i.

CONVINCE, prove guilty, *Troil. & Cres.*, 2.ii; overcome, *Mac.*, 1.vii; etc.

CONVIVE, feast, *Troil. & Cres.*, 4.v.

CONVOCATION, assembly, *Ham.*, 4.iii.

COPE, (1) encounter, *Troil. & Cres.*, 1.ii; etc.; (2) sky, *Per.*, 4.vi.

COPPED, peaked, *Per.*, 1.i.

COPY, *nature's copy's not eterne*, nature hasn't given them a perpetual lease of life (copy = copyhold tenure) but only at its will, or (copy = a cast from a mould) can be broken or destroyed, *Mac.*, 3.ii; pattern, example, *Timon*, 3.iii.

CORDIAL, comforting, reviving, *Cym.*, 4.ii.

CORE, core of a boil, *Troil. & Cres.*, 2.i.

CORINTH, slang for house of ill fame, *Timon*, 2.ii.

CO-RIVAL, try to match, *Troil. & Cres.*, 1.iii.

CORMORANT, voracious (like the bird), greedy, *Cor.*, 1.i.

CORPORAL, material, *Mac.*, 1.iii; bodily, *Cym.*, 2.iv.

CORRIGIBLE, *the corrigible authority*, the power to correct, *Oth.*, 1.iii; submissive to correction, *Ant. & Cleo.*, 4.xiv.

COSTARD, large apple, so the head, *Lear*, 4.vi.

COTE, pass, *Ham.*, 2.ii.

COT-QUEAN, a man meddling with house affairs, *Rom. & Jul.*, 4.iv.

COUCH, to hide, *Ham.*, 5.i; conceal, *Troil. & Cres.*, 1.i; remain in its den, *Lear*, 3.i; *noun, couchings*, servile gestures, *Jul. Caes.*, 3.i.

COUNTENANCE, favour, sanction, *Jul. Caes.*, 1.iii; authority, *Lear*, 5.i; demeanour, *Lear*, 1.ii; *verb*, provide a suitable audience for such an event, *Mac.*, 2.iii.

COUNTER, hunting counter is when the hound follows the trail backwards, *Ham.*, 4.v.

COUNTER-CASTER, arithmetician (used scoffingly), *Oth.*, 1.i.

COUNTERCHANGE, *the counterchange is severally in all*, all have exchanged looks, individually and collectively, *Cym.*, 5.v.

COUNTERFEIT, portrait, then, with double significance, to make a portrait and to act the cheat, *Timon*, 5.i; false coin, *Troil. & Cres.*, 2.iii; so a bastard, *Cym.*, 2.v; mere deceit, *Oth.*, 5.i; portrait, *Ham.*, 3.iv.

COUNTERVAIL, equal, *Rom. & Jul.*, 2.vi; *Per.*, 2.iii.

COUPLETS, her newly-hatched pair (for the pigeon lays only two eggs for a sitting), *Ham.*, 5.i.

COURAGE, young blood, *Ham.*, 1.iii.

COURSE, revolution (as of sun), *Troil. & Cres.*, 4.i; beaten way, habit, *Ham.*, 3.iii; a bout in a fight, *Cor.*, 1.v; as in bear-baiting, *Mac.*, 5.vii; routine, *Lear*, 3.vii; habits, *Oth.*, 4.i; career, way of life, *Oth.*, 3.iv; *by monthly course*, every month alternately, *Lear*, 1.i; *your journal course*, your daily routine, *Cym.*, 5.ii; the attack (as of dogs at bear-baiting), *Lear*, 3.vii; *verb*, run, *Oth.*, 3.iv; hunt, *Lear*, 3.iv; pursue, *Mac.*, 1.vi.

COURSER, *the courser's hair*, a horse's hair placed in water was supposed to become a living creature, *Ant. & Cleo.*, 1.ii.

COURTESY, bow, curtsy, *Jul. Caes.*, 3.i; *Troil. & Cres.*, 2.iii; *the courtesy your cradle promised*, the rank and kind of life natural in the station of life in which you were born, *Cym.*, 4.iv.

COURT HOLY WATER, flattery, soothing but empty words, *Lear*, 3.ii.

COURTSHIP, condition appropriate to courtier, *Rom. & Jul.*, 3.iii; manners acceptable at a court, *Oth.*, 2.i.

COUSIN, nephew, *Ham.*, 3.ii; and of relationships generally; *cousin-german*, first cousin, *Troil. & Cres.*, 4.v.

COVERT, hidden, secret, *Jul. Caes.*, 4.i; *Lear*, 3.ii.

COXCOMB, fool's cap, *Lear*, 1.iv; head, *Lear*, 2.iv.

COY, disdain, *Cor.*, 5.i.

COZEN, COZENER, cheat, *Oth.*, 4.ii; *Lear*, 4.vi.

COZENAGE, deceit, *Ham.*, 5.ii.

CRAB, crabapple, *Lear*, 1.v.

CRACK, a little rascal, *Cor.*, 1.iii; change of voice between youth and manhood, *Cym.*, 4.ii; *verb*, give out in boasting voice, *Cym.*, 5.v; *cracked within the ring*, a coin in which a crack extended within the ring round the sovereign's head was not current, so punning on ring = sound of voice, *Ham.*, 2.ii.

CRANK, winding passage, *Cor.*, 1.i.

CRANTS, a garland (hung up in church for one who died young), *Ham.*, 5.i.

CRARE, a small trading vessel, *Cym.*, 4.ii.

CRAZE, damage, crack, *Lear*, 3.iv.

CRAZED, deranged, half-mad, *Mac.*, 3.i.

CREATURE, dependent, *Timon*, 1.i; *your creatures*, those who owe their lives to your skill, *Per.*, 3.ii.

CREDENCE, trust, *Troil. & Cres.*, 5.ii; *credent*, trusting, *Ham.*, 1.iii.

CREDIT, the trust placed in a man, *Jul. Caes.*, 3.i; *my credit*, your faith in me, *Lear*, 3.i; *gives them credit*, makes them credible, *Oth.*, 1.iii.

CRESCENT, growing, *Ant. & Cleo.*, 2.i; *nature crescent*, man's being as it grows, *Ham.*, 1.iii.

CREST, helmet, *Mac.*, 5.viii; horse's crest (or that of other animal), applied figuratively as in *Jul. Caes.*, 4.ii; *his rear'd arm crested the world*, was raised above (like the arm that formed a crest to some heraldic coats), *Ant. & Cleo.*, 5.ii.

CROSS, cross the ghost's path, stop it, *Ham.*, 1.i; contradict, *Jul. Caes.*, 1.ii; *adj.*, perverse, *Rom. & Jul.*, 4.iii; *noun*, a coin stamped with a cross, so *when all's spent he'ld be cross'd then, an he could*, be in possession of money (with play on the earlier idea of being thwarted), *Timon*, 1.ii.

CROTCHET, (1) note in music, (2) rudeness, so punningly in *Rom. & Jul.*, 4.v.

CROW-KEEPER, boy bearing bow to scare away crows, *Rom. & Jul.*, 1.iv; *Lear*, 4.vi.

CROWNER, coroner, *Ham.*, 5.i.

CRUEL, *cruel garters* (with pun on crewel-worsted), *Lear*, 2.iv.

CRUSADE, Portuguese coin, stamped with a cross, *Oth.*, 2.iv.

CRY, public applause, *Troil. & Cres.*, 3.iii; pack, *Cor.*, 3.iii; *cry of players*, company of actors, *Ham.*, 3.ii, *fill up the cry*, just one of the pack (used of hounds), *Oth.*, 2.iii; report, rumour, *Oth.*, 4.i.

CUNNING, skill, *Ham.*, 4.vii; *Ant. & Cleo.*, 2.iii; profession, *Timon*, 4.iii; *in cunning*, deliberately, knowingly, *Oth.*, 3.iii; learning, knowledge, *Per.*, 3.ii.

CURIOSITY, fastidiousness, *Timon*, 4.iii; minute examination, *Lear*, 1.i; *curiosity of nations*, the scruples nations show in the laws about bastards, *Lear*, 1.ii.

CURIOUS, anxious, particular, *Cym.*, 1.vi; fastidious, critical, *Rom. & Jul.*, 1.iv; *Ant. & Cleo.*, 3.ii; *curious mantle*, skilfully made, *Cym.*, 5.v; *too curious dreg*, dreg causing disquiet, *Troil. & Cres.*, 3.ii; *too curiously*, over-ingeniously, *Ham.*, 5.i.

CYNIC, of school of Diogenes, who was surly even with kings, so rude fellow, *Jul. Caes.*, 4.iii.

DAFF, put off, *Ant. & Cleo.*, 4.iv; thrust aside, *Oth.*, 4.ii.

DAINTY, *daintier-sense*, delicate feeling (more shrinking, unprofessional), *Ham.*, 5.i; *she that makes dainty*, shrinks away from, *Rom. & Jul.*, 1.v.

DAISY, emblem of dissembling, *Ham.*, 4.v.

DALLY, delay, trifle the time away, *Lear*, 3.vi.

DAMASK, the rose colour of the complexion, *Cor.*, 2.i.

DAMN, mark for death, *Jul. Caes.*, 4.i; condemn, *Ant. & Cleo.*, 1.i.

DAMP, mist drawn from the ground, *Ant. & Cleo.*, 4.ix.

DANCING-RAPIER, worn as ornament only, *Titus*, 2.i.

DANGER, harm, *Rom. & Jul.*, 5.iii; *Jul. Caes.*, 2.i; *verb*, endanger, *Ant. & Cleo.*, 1.ii; *not what is dangerous present*, not only what is now threatening, *Cor.*, 3.ii.

DANSKER, a Dane (the form, not found elsewhere in English, is adopted from the Danish), *Ham.*, 2.i.

DAPHNE, nymph changed to a laurel tree as she fled from Apollo, *Troil. & Cres.*, 1.i.

DARDAN, (1) Trojan, and (2) gate of Troy, *Troil. & Cres.*, 1.*Prol.*

DARE, (1) have courage to, and (2) challenge, *Rom. & Jul.*, 2.iv; to venture in assertion, *I dare vouch*, *Cor.*, 3.i; *all that fortune, death and danger dare*, may offer (as if in challenge), *Ham.*, 4.iv; *given the dare*, defied, *Ant. & Cleo.*, 1.ii; *I durst to*, I venture to, *Oth.*, 4.ii.

DAREFUL, defiant, *Mac.*, 5.v.

DARK, *our darker purpose*, our more secret intention, *Lear*, 1.i; *verb*, obscure, *Per.*, 4.*Prol.*

DARKEN, obscure his fame, *Cor.*, 2.i, *gain which darkens him*, success which brings envy and detraction, *Ant. & Cleo.*, 3.i.

DARKLING, in the dark, *Ant. & Cleo.*, 4.xv; *Lear*, 1.iv.

DARKNESS, realm of darkness, death, *Cym.*, 5.iii; *act of darkness*, fornication, *Lear*, 3.iv; *instruments of darkness*, agents of hell, *Mac.*, 1.iii.

DARNEL, a weed, tares, *Lear*, 4.iv.

DARTING, *darting Parthia* (the Parthian cavalry's favourite manoeuvre was to retreat discharging their arrows on the advancing enemy), *Ant. & Cleo.*, 3.i.

DASH, depress, *Oth.*, 3.iii.

DATE, *his fracted dates*, broken promises to pay on a certain day, *Timon*, 2.i; so *date-broke bonds*, *Timon*, 2.ii; *the date is out*, the fashion is over for, *Rom. & Jul.*, 1.iv; *short date of breath*, the little of life left, *Rom. & Jul.*, 5.iii; *dateless*, for all eternity, *Rom. & Jul.*, 5.iii.

DAUB, cover, plaster, *Lear*, 2.ii; cover with a disguise, *Lear*, 4.i.

DAW, jackdaw, used of a foolish chatterbox, *Cor.*, 4.v; *Oth.*, 1.i.

DAY, *take no longer days*, be quick about it, *Titus*, 4.ii; *time of day*, greeting, *Per.*, 4.iii; *the duty of the day*, morning salutation, *Cym.*, 3.v; light, so *day o' the world*, *Ant. & Cleo.*, 4.viii.

DAYLIGHT, *burn daylight*, waste time, *Rom. & Jul.*, 1.iv.

DAZZLE, fail to see clearly, owing to age, *Titus*, 3.ii.

DEAD, pale as death, *Oth.*, 2.iii; like death, *Lear*, 5.iii.

DEADLY, *deadly deed*, homicide, *Titus*, 5.iii; *deadly*, fatally, *Troil. & Cres.*, 5.v; *deadly-standing*, glaring (of eye), *Titus*, 2.iii.

DEAL, *some deal*, somewhat, *Titus*, 3.i; *deal of man*, show of manhood, *Lear*, 2.ii; *verb*, *dealt on lieutenantry*, acted through his officers, *Ant. & Cleo.*, 3.xi; *deal with*, treat according to desert, *Titus*, 5.ii; *deal double with*, deceive, *Rom. & Jul.*, 2.iv; hand over, *Timon*, 1.ii.

DEAR, (1) important, *Lear*, 3.i; *your dear*, your lover, *Oth.*, 5.i; *our dear'st repute*, what is reckon'd our best, *Troil. & Cres.*, 1.iii; *dear man*, man of worth, honour (with other meanings of *dear*), *Troil. & Cres.*, 5.iii; earnest, *Troil. & Cres.*, 5.iii; *dearest foe* (as touching us nearly), *Ham.*, 1.ii; (2) grievous, *Timon*, 5.i; *Oth.*, 1.iii.

DEARLY, (1) richly, finely, *Cym.*, 2.ii; lovingly, *Cym.*, 1.vi; *how dearly ever parted*, however finely gifted, *Troil. & Cres.*, 3.iii; (2) deeply, *Ham.*, 4.iii.

DEARTH, scarcity (so expensive), *Ham.*, 5.ii.

DEATH-MARK'D, fated to lead to death, *Rom. & Jul.*, 1.*Prol.*

DEATH-PRACTISED, *the death-practised duke*, the duke against whose life a plot was made, *Lear*, 4.vi.

DEATH-TOKEN, like the plague-spots that indicate death, *Troil. & Cres.*, 2.iii.

DEBATE, quarrel, *Cym.*, 1.iv; *verb*, dispute, quarrel, *Ant. & Cleo.*, 2.ii; settle by combat, *Ham.*, 4.iv; discuss, *Titus*, 5.iii.

DEBATEMENT, consideration, *Ham.*, 5.ii.

DEBILE, feeble, *Cor.*, 1.ix.

DEBITOR, *debitor and creditor*, accountant, *Cym.*, 5.iv; *Oth.*, 1.i.

DEBONAIR, gracious, gentle, *Troil. & Cres.*, 1.iii.

DEBOSH'D, debauch'd, *Lear*, 1.iv.

DECAY, destroy, *Cym.*, 1.v; perish, *Ant. & Cleo.*, 2.i.

DECEPTIOUS, delusive, *Troil. & Cres.*, 5.ii.

DECIMATION, execution of every tenth man as a punishment on body as a whole, *Timon*, 5.iv.

Decipher, detect, *Titus*, 4.ii.

Declare, interpret, make clear, *Cym.*, 5.v.

Decline, go through subject part by part as one would set out the inflexions of a noun in Latin, *Troil. & Cres.*, 2.iii; sink, move down, either in physical or moral sense, *Ham.*, 1.v; *fathers declin'd*, enfeebled by age, *Lear*, 1.ii; *Oth.*, 3.iii; fallen in fortune, *Ant. & Cleo.*, 3.xiii.

Decree, decision, *Rom. & Jul.*, 3.v.

Dedicate, offer up, *Mac.*, 4.iii; *a dedicated beggar to the air*, given up to a homeless life, *Timon*, 4.ii; commit oneself to, *Cym.*, 5.i.

Deed, *my very deed of love*, my love as it indeed is, *Lear*, 1.i; *the deed of saying*, the keeping of a promise, *Timon*, 5.i; a written document in legal form (Juliet plays on this meaning and that of *deed* = act), *Rom. & Jul.*, 4.i; *deed-achieving honour*, honour gained by deeds, *Cor.*, 2.i; *deedless in his tongue*, never boasting, *Troil. & Cres.*, 4.v.

Deem, thought, *Troil. & Cres.*, 4.iv; judge, *Cym.*, 5.iv.

Deep, *in deepest consequence*, in matters of the greatest importance that follow, *Mac.*, 1.iii; used of a heavy debt, *Timon*, 3.iv; of a carefully conceived scheme, *Ham.*, 5.ii; *deeply sworn*, solemnly, *Ham.*, 3.ii; completely, *Titus*, 4.i; *deeper read*, more learned, *Titus*, 4.i; *as deep with me*, as inward or heartfelt, *Cym.*, 2.iii; *deep clerks*, learned scholars, *Per.*, 5.*Prol.*

Deer, beasts, *Lear*, 3.iv.

Defeat, destruction, *Ham.*, 2.ii and 5.ii; *verb*, ruin, destroy, *Oth.*, 4.ii; disappoint, *Ant. & Cleo.*, 4.xiv; *defeat thy favour*, do away with your unsoldierly looks, *Oth.*, 1.iii.

Defect, *our will became the servant to defect*, circumstances prevented our being as hospitable as we wished, *Mac.*, 2.i.

Defective, wanting, lacking, *Oth.*, 2.i; *defective for requital*, deficient in means to make fitting recompense, *Cor.*, 2.ii.

Defence, skill in fence, *Ham.*, 4.vii; means of defence, *Rom. & Jul.*, 3.iii; *defences*, armour, equipment, *Ant. & Cleo.*, 4.iv.

Defend, forbid, *Oth.*, 1.iii; *Isis else defend*, Isis forbid that it should be otherwise! *Ant. & Cleo.*, 3.iii.

Deficient, the deficient sight, vision failing, *Lear*, 4.vi.

Definement, description, *Ham.*, 5.ii.

Definite, without hesitation, *Cym.*, 1.vi.

Defuse, confuse others about my identity, disguise, *Lear*, 1.iv.

Defy, challenge, *Ant. & Cleo.*, 2.ii.

Degree, step, stage, *Cor.*, 2.ii; rank, distinction, *Troil. & Cres.*, 1.iii; the principle of order by which persons (or objects) stand in proper relation to one another, *Troil. & Cres.*, 1.iii; *the sweet degrees*, the pleasant stages of a well-provided-for life, *Timon*, 4.iii; *so eminent in the degree of this fortune*, so high on the steps that lead to this good fortune, *Oth.*, 2.i.

Deign, not disdain to eat, *Ant. & Cleo.*, 1.iv.

Deject, cast down, *Troil. & Cres.*, 2.ii; *Ham.*, 3.i.

Delate, set out in full, *Ham.*, 1.ii.

Delation, *close delations*, secret and instinctive accusations, *Oth.*, 3.iii.

Delicate, pleasant, *Mac.*, 1.vi; skilfully wrought, *Ham.*, 5.ii; delightful, *Ant. & Cleo.*, 2.vii; exquisite, *Cym.*, 2.iv; skilful, *Oth.*, 4.i; ingenious, *Lear*, 4.vi.

Delighted, giving delight, *Oth.*, 1.iii; delightful, *Cym.*, 5.iv.

Delivered, brought forward, *Oth.*, 1.iii.

Demand, question, *Ham.*, 2.i; *Lear*, 1.v.

Demerit, fault, sin, *Mac.*, 4.iii; merit, *Cor.*, 1.i; desert, whether good or bad, *Oth.*, 1.ii.

Demesne, estate, *Rom. & Jul.*, 3.v; region, *Cym.*, 3.iii.

Demi-Atlas, Atlas carried the earth on his shoulders; Antony now shared the task, so Cleopatra suggests, with Augustus, *Ant. & Cleo.*, 1.v.

Demi-natur'd, like a Centaur: half man, half horse, *Ham.*, 4.vii.

Demon, guardian spirit, genius, *Ant. & Cleo.*, 2.iii.

Demonstrable, apparent, *Oth.*, 3.iv.

Den, *see* God.

Denote, indicate, *Ham.*, 1.ii; *Oth.*, 3.iii.

Depart, separate, *Timon*, 1.i; *Cym.*, 1.i.

Depend, impend, *Rom. & Jul.*, 3.i; *Cym.*, 4.iii; lean, *Cym.*, 2.iv; remain as dependents, retainers, *Lear*, 1.iv; *depending*, impending, *Troil. & Cres.*, 2.iii.

Dependency, responsibility in social world, *Cym.*, 2.iii.

Depravation, detraction, censure, *Troil. & Cres.*, 5.ii.

Deprive, disinherit, *Lear*, 1.ii.

Deputation, office of deputy; *topless deputation*, Agamemnon as Jove's deputy having no superior on earth, *Troil. & Cres.*, 1.ii; *in deputation*, through his deputy, *Ant. & Cleo.*, 3.xii.

Depute, appoint as representative, *Oth.*, 4.i.

Derive, *derive this*, show how you deduce this, *Troil. & Cres.*, 2.iii.

Dern, wild, dark, *Lear*, 3.vii; *Per.*, 3.*Prol.*

Derogate, lose dignity, *Cym.*, 2.i; a few lines later the meaning is shifted to 'degenerate,' as in *Lear*, 1.iv.

Descending, *good descending*, noble parentage, *Per.*, 5.i.

Descry, *the main descry stands on the hourly thought*, the main body may be reported as in sight almost immediately, *Lear*, 4.vi.

Desert, *to this desert*, to this act that deserves well, *Cym.*, 1.v.

Deserving, *a fair deserving*, a good chance to seem entitled to reward, *Lear*, 3.iii; *without deserving*, through no fault, *Oth.*, 2.iii.

Design, scheme, enterprise, *Mac.*, 2.i; *Ant. & Cleo.*, 2.ii; *in top of all design*, in the greatest enterprises, *Ant. & Cleo.*, 5.i; *verb, the article design'd*, the clause of the agreement as drawn up, *Ham.*, 1.i.

Designment, enterprise, *Oth.*, 2.i; *Cor.*, 5.vi.

Desire, request, *Troil. & Cres.*, 4.v; bid, instruct, *Cym.*, 1.vi; *well desired*, warmly welcome, *Oth.*, 2.i.

Desperate, hopeless, *Oth.*, 2.iii; reckless, *Oth.*, 5.ii; *Ant. & Cleo.*, 1.iii; *desperately*, hopeless and reckless, *Lear*, 5.iii.

Desperation, *toys of desperation*, impulses to self-destruction, *Ham.*, 1.iv.

Despised, *despised time*, my old age now made hateful to me, *Oth.*, 1.i.

Despite, scorn, *Oth.*, 4.ii; *in despite*, in spite of all opposition (as if the tomb satisfied with its contents would reject any further prey), *Rom. & Jul.*, 5.iii; spitefully, *Oth.*, 4.iii; *in your despite*, in contempt of you, *Cym.*, 1.vi.

Despiteful, malicious and ungrateful, *Ant. & Cleo.*, 2.vi.

Destinies, the three Fates, goddesses who spin and cut the thread of life, *Per.*, 1.ii.

Detect, inform against, *Titus*, 2.iv; regard as evil, *Per.*, 2.i; *detecting*, detection, *Ham.*, 3.ii; *detector*, revealer, informer, *Lear*, 3.v.

Determinate, final, decisive, *Oth.*, 4.iii.

Determination, decision, *Troil. & Cres.*, 2.ii; resolution, *Ham.*, 3.i.

Determine, end, *Cor.*, 3.iii.

Device, a fanciful entertainment, a masque, *Timon*, 1.ii; design, *Cym.*, 1.vi; emblem or motto on a shield, *Per.*, 2.ii.

Devise, imagine, *Ant. & Cleo.*, 2.ii.

Dexter, right, *Troil. & Cres.*, 4.v.

Dial, clock, *Rom. & Jul.*, 2.iv.

Dialogue, converse, *Timon*, 2.ii.

Dich, do it, *Timon*, 1.ii.

Dido, queen of Carthage, in love with Aeneas. In Virgil she rejects his advances when he visits the underworld; *Ant. & Cleo.*, 4.xiv; *Ham.*, 2.ii.

Die, *the spotted die*, dice, *Timon*, 5.iv.

Diet, diet prescribed by physician, *Timon*, 4.iii; sustenance, *Oth.*, 3.iii. (as if prescribed for an invalid); *dieted to my request*, in the humour (after dining well) to grant the request, *Cor.*, 5.i.

Dieter, one administering a prescribed diet, *Cym.*, 4.ii.

Difference, disagreement, *Cym.*, 1.iv; change of condition, *Lear*, 5.iii; in a family coat-of-arms certain small differences indicated the seniority in the family of the individual member displaying the coat (Ophelia in using the term indicates the difference between her plight and that of the queen), *Ham.*, 4.v; *full of most excellent differences*, an affected use of the heraldic term to indicate merits peculiar to an individual, *Ham.*, 5.ii; *passions of some difference*, conflicting emotions, *Jul. Caes.*, 1.ii; *differency*, difference, *Cor.*, 5.iv.

Differing, *that nothing-gift of differing multitudes*, the worthless approval of the changeable many, *Cym.*, 3.vi.

Difficult, *difficult weight*, difficult to estimate, or handle, *Oth.*, 3.iii.

Diffidence, mistrust among groups, *Lear*, 1.ii.

Digest, relish, *Cor.*, 3.i; arrange, settle, *Ham.*, 2.ii; *Ant. & Cleo.*, 2.ii; incorporate, *Lear*, 1.i.

Dignity, worth, *Cym.*, 5.iv.

Digress, deviate, *Rom. & Jul.*, 3.iii; transgress, *Titus*, 5.iii.

Dilate, narrate in full, *Oth.*, 1.iii; *dilated parts*, widely extended regions, so ample gifts of mind and body, *Troil. & Cres.*, 2.iii.

Diligent, attentive, *Timon*, 3.iv; *diligent discovery*, active reconnaissance, *Lear*, 5.i.
Dimension, *my dimensions*, bodily shape, *Lear*, 1.ii.
Diminutive, small in size and worth, *Troil. & Cres.*, 5.i; *for poor'st diminutive, for doits*, for paltry payments (*doits* most editors read for Folio *dolts;* those who retain *dolts* read *fore* (before) in place of *for*, and interpret: before the poorest sort and dolts), *Ant. & Cleo.*, 4.xii.
Dint, impression, *Jul. Caes.*, 3.ii.
Direction, the disposition of affairs or soldiers, *Oth.*, 1.iii and 2.iii; *by indirections find directions out*, come at truth by a roundabout way, *Ham.*, 2.i.
Directitude (servant's coinage; Malone would read 'discreditude'), *Cor.*, 4.v.
Directive, subject to direction, *Troil. & Cres.*, 1.iii.
Directly, by evidence leading straight to the conclusion, *Cym.*, 1.iv.
Disappointed, without the necessary equipment, so unprepared, *Ham.*, 1.v.
Disaster, an unfavourable aspect of star or planet, *Ham.*, 1.i; unlucky, harmful circumstances, *Lear*, 1.i; *verb* (used with terms of astronomy), ruin, *Ant. & Cleo.*, 2.vii.
Disbench, make rise from seat, *Cor.*, 2.ii.
Discandy, lose firmness, *Ant. & Cleo.*, 4.xii.
Discernings, power of discerning, *Lear*, 1.iv.
Discharge, perform a part, *Cor.*, 3.ii; *noun*, payment, *Cym.*, 5.iv.
Discipline, instruction, *Troil. & Cres.*, 2.iii; *verb*, chastise, *Cor.*, 2.i.
Disclaim, *disclaims in*, disowns, *Lear*, 2.ii.
Disclaiming, disavowal, *Ham.*, 5.ii.
Discomfort, discourage, *Troil. & Cres.*, 5.x; *Jul. Caes.*, 5.iii.
Discontents, malcontents, those who feel hostile to the established order, *Ant. & Cleo.*, 1.iv.
Discourse, thought (where reason seems at odds with reality), *Troil. & Cres.*, 5.ii; conversation, *Ham.*, 3.i; *discourse of reason*, the process or faculty of reasoning, *Ham.*, 1.ii; *Troil. & Cres.*, 2.ii; *discourse of thought*, in meditation, *Oth.*, 4.ii; *verb*, tell over, *Per.*, 1.iv.
Discover, reveal, *Rom. & Jul.*, 3.i; reconnoitre, *Timon*, 5.ii; recognize, *Jul. Caes.*, 2.i; expose, *Lear*, 2.i; spy, *Cym.*, 4.ii.
Discovery, disclosure, *Ham.*, 2.ii; exposure, *Timon*, 5.i; report of a scout, *Mac.*, 5.iv; reconnaissance, *Lear*, 5.i.
Discretion, judgement, *Troil. & Cres.*, 1.ii.
Disguise, intoxication, *Ant. & Cleo.*, 2.vii.
Dishonour'd, dishonorable, *Lear*, 1.i; *dishonour'd rub*, obstacle to honourable recognition, *Cor.*, 3.i.
Dislike, dissension, *Lear*, 1.iv; *verb*, displease, *Oth.*, 2.iii.
Dislimn, *the rack dislimns*, the cloud loses the shape fancy gives it, *Ant. & Cleo.*, 4.xiv.
Dismal, boding disaster (from *dies mali* of medieval calendar), *Ham.*, 2.ii; etc.
Disme, tenth man, *Troil. & Cres.*, 2.ii.
Dismission, rejection, *Cym.*, 2.iii.
Disnatured, unnatural, *Lear*, 1.iv.
Disorb'd, driven from its sphere (of a star), *Troil. & Cres.*, 2.ii.
Disorder'd, disorderly, *Lear*, 1.iv.
Dispatch, dismissal, *Cor.*, 5.iii; management, *Mac.*, 1.v; finish of business, *Cor.*, 1.i; *attend dispatch*, ready waiting to be sent with messages, *Lear*, 2.i; *verb*, hasten, so *post-post-haste dispatch*, with the utmost haste, *Oth.*, 1.iii; deprive, *Ham.*, 1.v; settle business with, *Ant. & Cleo.*, 3.ii; settle with life, kill oneself, *Ant. & Cleo.*, 5.ii; kill, *Lear*, 2.i; *well dispatch'd*, happily parted with, *Per.*, 2.v.
Dispose, temper, natural inclination, *Troil. & Cres.*, 2.iii; *a smooth dispose*, an agreeable manner of address, *Oth.*, 1.iii; *verb*, place, *Troil. & Cres.*, 4.v; *dispose myself*, order my proceedings, *Per.*, 1.ii; *disposed with*, come to terms with, *Ant. & Cleo.*, 4.xiv; *dispose you*, arrange for you, *Ant. & Cleo.*, 5.ii.
Disposition, mood, form of behaving, *Ham.*, 1.v; arrangements, *Oth.*, 1.iii; *dispositions*, humours, caprice, *Lear*, 1.ii.
Disproperty, take away, *Cor.*, 2.i.
Disproportion'd, inconsistent, contradictory, *Oth.*, 1.iii.
Dissipation, *dissipation of cohorts*, disbanding of regiments, *Lear*, 1.ii.
Dissolution, destruction, *Lear*, 1.ii.
Dissolve, destroy, *Lear*, 4.iv.
Distain, sully, overshadow, *Troil. & Cres.*, 1.iii; *Per.*, 4.iii.
Distance, space between combatants in fencing, *Rom. & Jul.*, 2.iv; *bloody distance*, mortal enmity,

Mac., 3.i; *that hold their honours in a wary distance*, like fencers they keep dishonour at a proper distance, ready to deal with a false move, *Oth.*, 2.iii.

DISTASTE, make unpalatable, *Troil. & Cres.*, 4.iv; detract from, *Troil. & Cres.*, 2.ii; be unpalatable, *Oth.*, 3.iii; dislike, *Lear*, 1.iii; *distasteful*, malevolent, disapproving, *Timon*, 2.ii.

DISTEMPER, disturbed or diseased condition of mind or body (due to excess of some humour), *Ham.*, 2.ii; *distempered*, in disturbed state, *Ham.*, 3.ii; *distempering draughts*, excess of drink, *Oth.*, 1.i.

DISTEMPERATURE, bodily or mental trouble, *Rom. & Jul.*, 2.iii; disturbance of mind, *Per.*, 5.i.

DISTINCTION, discrimination, *Troil. & Cres.*, 3.ii and 1.iii.

DISTINCTLY, separately, according to their formations and not confusedly, *Cor.*, 4.iii; explicitly, directly, *Oth.*, 3.iii.

DISTRACT, beside one's self, desperate and confused, *Ham.*, 4.v; *verb, distract your army*, divide (perhaps 'confuse'), *Ant. & Cleo.*, 3.vii; divide, parcel it out, *Oth.*, 1.iii; *this distracted globe*, this perturbed head, *Ham.*, 1.v; *distracted multitude*, confused commoners, *Ham.*, 4.iii.

DISTRACTION, despair, *Ham.*, 2.ii; perturbation of mind, *Ham.*, 5.ii; *distractions*, detachments, divisions, *Ant. & Cleo.*, 3.vii; confusion, *Ant. & Cleo.*, 4.i.

DIVIDANT, *scarce is dividant*, hardly to be separated, distinguished, *Timon*, 4.iii.

DIVISION, the dividing up of a melody into shorter notes, so producing a variation; hence applied to long vocal runs, and so applicable to lark's song, *Rom. & Jul.*, 3.v; hence variation in *Mac.*, 4.iii; *the division of a battle*, the right ordering of his troops, *Oth.*, 1.i.

DOCTRINE, instruction, *Rom. & Jul.*, 1.i; lesson, *Ant. & Cleo.*, 5.ii.

DOCUMENT, *a document in madness*, instruction even from one distracted, *Ham.*, 4.v.

DOG, R is the dog's letter, like its snarl, *Rom. & Jul.*, 2.iv.

DOIT, a Dutch coin of small value, *Cor.*, 4.iv; for use in *Ant. & Cleo.*, 4.xii, *see* DIMINUTIVE.

DOLE, grief, *Ham.*, 1.ii; *Per.*, 3.*Prol.*

DOLLAR, Spanish dollars and German thalers were current in Shakespeare's day, *Mac.*, 1.ii.

DOLOURS, sorrows (with play on 'dollars'), *Lear*, 2.iv.

DOMESTIC, *malice domestic*, internal plotting, *Mac.*, 3.ii; *domestic powers*, forces of the same country, *Ant. & Cleo.*, 1.iii; *domestic-door particulars*, family quarrels, *Lear*, 5.i.

DOOM, *day of doom*, day of death, *Titus*, 2.iii; *crack of doom*, the trumpet blast that will announce the Day of Judgement, *Mac.*, 4.i; *verb*, pass sentence, *Rom. & Jul.*, 3.i; *verb*, judge, *Cym.*, 5.v.

DOOMSDAY, day of death, *Rom. & Jul.*, 5.iii; Day of Judgement (which is to be preceded by darkness), *Ham.*, 1.i; *Ant. & Cleo.*, 5.ii.

DOOR, *speak within door*, speak quietly (don't be heard in the street), *Oth.*, 4.ii.

DOTANT, dotard, *Cor.*, 5.ii.

DOTE, behave foolishly, *Troil. & Cres.*, 2.ii; be foolishly fond or enamoured, *Troil. & Cres.*, 5.iv; *Lear*, 1.iv.

DOUBLE, *deal double*, deceive, *Rom. & Jul.*, 2.iv; *double vouchers*, a legal process in which two witnesses were called to vouch a title, *Ham.*, 5.i.

DOUBLET, man's close-fitting coat, *Jul. Caes.*, 1.ii; *Cym.*, 3.iv.

DOUBT, suspect, *Ham.*, 1.ii; fear, *Cor.*, 3.i; etc.

DOUBTFUL, apprehensive, *Mac.*, 3.ii; *I am doubtful*, I suspect, *Lear*, 5.i.

DOUT, extinguish, *Ham.*, 4.vii.

DOWN-GYVED, hanging down, like fetters on his ankles, *Ham.*, 2.i.

DRACHMA, Greek silver coin, *Jul. Caes.*, 3.ii.

DRAGON, *the dragon's tail*, the moon's descending node, where it cuts the plane of the ecliptic; astrologers, when they had to allow for it in any horoscope, regarded its effects as specially malignant, *Lear*, 1.ii. [potion, *Oth.*, 1.iii.

DRAM, poison, *Rom. & Jul.*, 3.v;

DRAUGHT, cesspool, *Timon*, 5.i.

DRAW, assemble, *Jul. Caes.*, 1.iii; *draw me*, win for me (as in a lottery), *Lear*, 3.iii.

DRAWER, tapster, *Rom. & Jul.*, 1.iii.

DREADFUL, *dreadful bell*, alarm bell, so spreading fear, *Oth.*, 2.iii.

DRESS, make ready, *Troil. & Cres.*, 1.iii.

DRIFT, scheme, *Rom. & Jul.*, 4.i; argument, *Troil. & Cres.*, 3.iii.

DRINK, carousing, *Timon*, 3.v; *Ant. & Cleo.*, 2.vii; *verb*, *I drunk him to his bed*, I was still sober while he, drinking equally with me, was so drunk that he was put to bed, *Ant. & Cleo.*, 2.v.

DRIVE, attack, *Titus*, 2.iii.

DROPPING, tearful, downcast, *Ham.*, 1.ii; *dropping industry*, dripping wet as they work, *Per.*, 4.i.

DROUTH, thirst, *Per.*, 3.*Prol.*

DRUG, poison, harmful potion, *Ham.*, 3.ii; *Oth.*, 1.ii; *drug-damn'd Italy*, detested for the use there of poison, *Cym.*, 3.iv.

DRY-BEAT, beat severely, *Rom. & Jul.*, 3.i.

DUCAT, gold coin of about ten shillings value, Italian silver coin, *Ham.*, 3.iv; *Cym.*, 1.iv.

DUDGEON, kind of wood used in dagger-hilts, so hilt itself, *Mac.*, 2.i.

DUE, debt, *Timon*, 2.ii.

DUMB, *dumb shows*, showing action without accompaniment of words, *Titus*, 3.i; *verb*, strike dumb, *Per.*, 5.*Prol.*

DUMP, melancholy tune, *Rom. & Jul.*, 4.v.

DUN, in *Rom. & Jul.*, 1.iv, various meanings are played on: the colour dun, and dun as a name for a horse; as well perhaps as 'done.'

DUP, open, *Ham.*, 4.v.

DURST, *see* DARE.

DUTEOUS, servile, *Oth.*, 1.i.

DUTY, obedience, *Lear*, 4.v; *at duty*, at command, *Timon*, 4.iii.

DWELL, *dwell on form*, observe the conventions prescribed by society, *Rom. & Jul.*, 2.ii.

EACH, *ten masts at each*, one above the other, *Lear*, 4.vi.

EAGER, sharp, *Ham.*, 1.iv; acid, *Ham.*, 1.v.

EAGLE, *Jove's bird, the Roman eagle*, the eagle was the most important standard of a Roman legion, the bird an emblem of Jove, *Cym.*, 4.ii and 5.v.

EALE, (perhaps) evil, *Ham.*, 1.iv.

EAN, give birth to, *Per.*, 3.iv.

EAR, plough, *Ant. & Cleo.*, 1.iv; *ear-bussing arguments*, the lips kissing the listener's ear, so whispered news, *Lear*, 2.i.

EARN, yearn, *Jul. Caes.*, 2.ii; *earn our chronicle*, deserve our place in story, *Ant. & Cleo.*, 3.xiii.

EARNEST, token payment as pledge of some bargain or service, *Timon*, 4.iii; etc.

EARTH, *the hopeful lady of my earth*, (in the literal sense) only heir (but with more intimate significance), *Rom. & Jul.*, 2.ii.

EASES, means of alleviating pain, *Troil. & Cres.*, 5.x.

EASILY, in comfort, *Oth.*, 5.i.

EASY, compliant, *Cym.*, 2.iv; *easy price*, at a cheap rate, *Titus*, 3.i; *easy groans*, not caused by any great effort, *Cor.*, 5.ii; *an easy battery might lay flat*, which criticism would find an easy target, *Cym.*, 1.iv; *easy-borrowed pride*, not native pride but vanity that comes easily to one in such employment, *Lear*, 2.iv.

EAT, *eat the air, promise-crammed*, entertained with words only, *Ham.*, 3.ii; *what a number of men eat Timon*, prey on him, abuse his generosity, *Timon*, 1.ii; *one man eats into another's pride*, takes advantage of the proud man's neglect of his reputation to increase their own, *Troil. & Cres.*, 3.iii; *eats the sword*, turns it against itself, *Ant. & Cleo.*, 3.xiii.

EBB, *ebb of your estate*, decay of your fortune, *Timon*, 2.ii; *his ebbs, his flows*, his caprice, *Troil. & Cres.*, 2.iii; *the ebb'd man*, from whom success has withdrawn, *Ant. & Cleo.*, 1.iv; *ne'er feels retiring ebb*, the current runs one way only, *Oth.*, 3.iii.

ECHE, to piece out, *Per.*, 3.*Prol.*

ECSTASY, frenzy, *Titus*, 4.i; *a modern ecstasy*, common everyday disturbance of mind, *Mac.*, 4.iii; fit of madness, *Ham.*, 3.iv; swoon, *Oth.*, 4.i; *ecstasy of love*, love putting him beside himself, *Ham.*, 2.i; so *blasted with ecstasy*, *Ham.*, 3.i.

EDGE, sword, *Cor.*, 5.vi; *edge of all extremity*, to the death, *Troil. & Cres.*, 4.v; *give him a further edge*, sharpen his inclination, *Ham.*, 3.i; *edge of husbandry*, urge to live within one's income, *Ham.*, 1.iii.

EDIFY, instruct, *Oth.*, 3.iv; *edified by the margent*, instructed as by an editorial note (in the margin of the text), *Ham.*, 5.ii; *edifies another*, satisfies another, to whom she reveals her real meaning, *Troil. & Cres.*, 5.iii.

EFFECT, *effects of watching*, acts of one awake, *Mac.*, 5.i; *my stern effects*, deadly purpose, *Ham.*, 3.iv; *possess'd of those effects*, in possession of the gain obtained by his act, *Ham.*, 3.iii; *thy thoughts touch their effects*, your fears are realized, *Ant. & Cleo.*, 5.ii; *to effect*, to the purpose, *Lear*, 3.i; *Oth.*, 1.iii; *the large effects*, the pomp and circumstance, *Lear*, 1.i; *verb*, give effect to, *Troil. & Cres.*, 5.x.

EFFECTLESS, vain, *Per.*, 5.i; *effectless use*, to no profitable end, *Titus*, 3.i.

EFTSOONS, soon, *Per.*, 5.i.

EGAL, *the extent of egal justice*, the exercise of impartial justice, *Titus*, 4.iv.

EGREGIOUS, out of the ordinary, monstrous, *Cym.*, 5.v; *egregiously*, to an unusual degree, *Oth.*, 2.i.

EISEL, vinegar, *Ham.*, 5.i.

ELD, old men, *Troil. & Cres.*, 2.ii; *elders*, senators, *Cor.*, 1.i; *the primal eldest curse*, the curse of Cain, *Ham.*, 3.iii.

ELECTED, *the elected deer*, the victim singled out, *Cym.*, 3.iv.

ELECTION, choice, *Ham.*, 3.ii.

ELEMENTS, the four elements, earth, air, fire, and water, were the constituent parts of everything, so in *Ant. & Cleo.*, 5.ii; *the two moist elements*, sea and sky; *the elements so mixed in him*, his nature was so happily compounded, *Jul. Caes.*, 5.v; *you elements*, as manifested in storm, etc., *Lear*, 3.ii; the conditions in which some being or essence finds its natural habitation, *Ant. & Cleo.*, 5.ii; *Lear*, 2.iv.

ELF, tangle, *Lear*, 2.iii; *elf-locks*, tangles in the hair, the knotting blamed on the fairies, *Rom. & Jul.*, 1.iv.

ELL, forty-five inches, *Rom. & Jul.*, 2.iv.

'EM, unstressed form of *hem*, since replaced by *them*.

EMBARQUEMENTS, embargo, hindrance, *Cor.*, 1.x.

EMBATTLE, form line of battle, *Ant. & Cleo.*, 4.ix.

EMBAY'D, anchored in some safe bay, *Oth.*, 2.i.

EMBER-EVES, evenings before ember-days, *Per.*, 1.*Prol.*

EMBOSS, foam at the mouth as from exertion, *Ant. & Cleo.*, 4.xiii; so *embossed froth*, *Timon*, 5.i.

EMBRACE, welcome as a friend or retainer, *Cor.*, 4.vii and 3.iv; cherish, favour, *Timon*, 1.i; welcome, *Troil. & Cres.*, 4.i; suffer, *Mac.*, 3.i; submit to, endure, *Lear*, 4.i; *embrace your offer*, accept with gratitude, *Per.*, 3.iii.

EMBRASURE, embrace, *Troil. & Cres.*, 4.iv.

EMINENCE, advantage, *Troil. & Cres.*, 2.iii; *present him eminence*, do him special honour (as chief guest), *Mac.*, 3.ii.

EMINENT, *not so eminent*, not even of that rank, *Cym.*, 2.iii.

EMPERY, title and authority of emperor, *Titus*, 1.i; *fasten'd to an empery*, married to one who ruled an empire, *Cym.*, 1.vi.

EMPHASIS, vehement expression or display, *Ham.*, 5.i; *such another emphasis*, strong expression of admiration, *Ant. & Cleo.*, 1.v.

EMPIRICUTIC, empirical, mere quackery, *Cor.*, 2.i.

EMPLOYMENT, service, *Ham.*, 5.ii.

EMPOISON, poison, destroy, *Cor.*, 5.vi.

EMULATE, envious, ambitious, *Ham.*, 1.i.

EMULATION, rivalry, *Cor.*, 1.x; envy, contention, *Jul. Caes.*, 2.iii; faction, *Troil. & Cres.*, 2.ii.

EMULOUS, honourably ambitious, *Troil. & Cres.*, 4.i; envious, *Troil. & Cres.*, 2.iii.

ENACTS, *close enacts*, secret workings, *Titus*, 4.ii.

ENACTURE, enactment, *Ham.*, 3.ii.

ENCAVE, conceal, *Oth.*, 4.i.

ENCHAFED, *enchafed flood*, the furious sea, *Oth.*, 2.i; angered, roused, *Cym.*, 4.ii.

ENCHANTING, bewitching, as having more than natural powers, *Ant. & Cleo.*, 1.ii.

ENCLOG, hinder, *Oth.*, 2.i.

ENCOMPASSMENT, talking round the matter, *Ham.*, 2.i.

ENCOUNTER, *outward habit of encounter*, fashionable tricks of behaviour in society, *Ham.*, 5.ii; *verb*, befall, *Cym.*, 1.vi.

ENCOUNTERER, a forward person, *Troil. & Cres.*, 4.v.

ENCUMBER'D, folded, *Ham.*, 1.v.

END, *an end*, on end, *Ham.*, 1.v; *for an end*, to settle the matter, *Cor.*, 2.i; *the promis'd end*, the end of the world, *Lear*, 5.iii; *verb*, kill, *Ant. & Cleo.*, 4.xiv; *to spend the time to end it*, treat it as a pastime, without thought of gain, *Cor.*, 2.ii; *which he did end all his*, which he garnered as his own (the crop others had helped to sow and reap), *Cor.*, 5.vi.

END-ALL, the end of the matter, without consequences, *Mac.*, 1.vii.

ENDEARED, bound by gratitude, *Timon*, 3.ii.

ENDOW, bestow, *Lear*, 2.iv; furnish, *Cym.*, 1.i; have as dowry, *Timon*, 1.i.
ENDUE, furnish, *Cor.*, 2.ii; infect, *Oth.*, 3.iv.
ENDURANCE, suffering, *Per.*, 5.i.
ENDURE, continue, *Cor.*, 1.vi.
ENEMY, *common enemy of man*, the devil, *Mac.*, 3.i.
ENFORCE, violate, ravish, *Titus*, 5.iii; *Cym.*, 4.i; stress, emphasize, *Cor.*, 2.iii; *Jul. Caes.*, 3.ii; charge, *Cor.*, 3.iii; urge on, *Cor.*, 3.iii; *much enforced*, forcibly struck, *Jul. Caes.*, 4.iii; *enforce their charity*, importune, *Lear*, 2.iii.
ENFORCEDLY, forced by circumstance, *Timon*, 4.iii.
ENFRANCHED, freed from bondage, *Ant. & Cleo.*, 3.xiii.
ENFRANCHISE, deliver, *Titus*, 4.ii; free, *Timon*, 1.i; free from subjection, *Ant. & Cleo.*, 1.i.
ENFRANCHISEMENT, repeal from exile, *Jul. Caes.*, 3.i.
ENGAGE, *all engag'd*, pawned, given as security for debt, *Timon*, 2.ii; pledge, *Jul. Caes.*, 2.i; *Oth.*, 3.iii; give one's word, promise, *Troil. & Cres.*, 5.iii; enlist, *Troil. & Cres.*, 2.ii; entangle, *Ham.*, 3.ii; *engaged ourselves*, ventured, *Ant. & Cleo.*, 4.vii.
ENGAGEMENTS, the affairs to which he is pledged, *Jul. Caes.*, 2.i.
ENGINE, *engines*, plots, *Titus*, 2.i; *engine of her thoughts*, her tongue, *Titus*, 3.i; battering-ram, *Troil. & Cres.*, 1.iii; *the fatal engine*, the Trojan Horse, *Titus*, 5.iii; *engines for my life*, schemes against my life, *Oth.*, 4.ii; some mechanical contrivance, *Lear*, 1.iv.
ENGINEER, sapper, responsible for mines and explosives, *Troil. & Cres.*, 2.iii; *Ham.*, 3.iv.
ENGINER, inventor, *Oth.*, 2.i.
ENGLUT, swallow, *Timon*, 2.ii; *Oth.*, 1.iii.
ENGRAFFED, ENGRAFTED, *imperfections of long-engraffed condition*, faults of character deeply rooted, *Lear*, 1.i; *engraft infirmity*, habitual weakness, *Oth.*, 2.iii; *engrafted love*, firmly attached devotion, *Jul. Caes.*, 2.i.
ENGROSS, collect, *Ant. & Cleo.*, 3.vii; *engrossing death*, death that takes complete and sole possession, *Rom. & Jul.*, 5.iii.
ENJOY, possess, *Cym.*, 1.iv; *enjoy thy plainness*, still possess your blunt speech, *Ant. & Cleo.*, 2.vi.
ENKINDLE, *enkindle all the sparks of nature*, act as becomes a son, *Lear*, 3.vii; *enkindle you unto*, fire you to hope for, *Mac.*, 1.iii.
ENLARD, fatten, *Troil. & Cres.*, 2.iii.
ENLARGE, give free or extended expression to, *Jul. Caes.*, 4.ii; *obsequies . . . as far enlarged*, the service as complete as, *Ham.*, 5.i; *enlarge his confine*, set him free, *Ant. & Cleo.*, 3.v.
ENLARGEMENT, freedom of choice, *Cym.*, 2.iii.
ENORMITY, excessive quality, *Cor.*, 2.i.
ENORMOUS, abnormal, monstrous, *Lear*, 2.ii.
ENOW, enough, *Mac.*, 2.ii; *Ant. & Cleo.*, 1.iv.
ENRAPT, in transport, inspired, *Troil. & Cres.*, 5.iii.
ENSEAMED, greasy, *Ham.*, 3.iv.
ENSEAR, dry up, *Timon*, 4.iii.
ENTER, *enter me with*, gain me favourable reception by, *Ant. & Cleo.*, 4.xiv; *enter'd in our counsels*, have intelligence of our plans, *Cor.*, 1.ii.
ENTERTAIN, give hospitable reception, *Timon*, 5.iii; *Cancer . . . entertaining great Hyperion*, when the sun is in Cancer (midsummer), *Troil. & Cres.*, 2.iii; receive into service, *Jul. Caes.*, 5.v; etc.; receive, *Timon*, 1.ii; *entertain'd me with my own device*, performed my mask to my great satisfaction, *Timon*, 1.ii; think of, *Rom. & Jul.*, 3.i; treat, attend to, *Lear*, 1.iv; accept a suggestion, *Ant. & Cleo.*, 2.vii.
ENTERTAINMENT, hospitable, friendly attention; service, *Timon*, 1.i; reception, *Cor.*, 4.v; courtesy, *Ham.*, 5.ii; *your commendation for my more free entertainment*, your letter of introduction that will ensure a cordial reception, *Cym.*, 1.iv; employment in someone's service, *Ant. & Cleo.*, 4.vi.
ENTIRE, flawless, *Cor.*, 1.iv; whole, complete, *Jul. Caes.*, 1.iii; *aloof from the entire point*, missing the whole point, *Lear*, 1.i; *of one entire and perfect chrysolite*, wholly of flawless chrysolite, *Oth.*, 5.ii.
ENTRANC'D, unconscious, *Per.*, 3.ii.
ENTREASUR'D, stored as if a treasure-house, *Per.*, 3.ii.
ENTREAT, *entreat an hour to serve*, find a suitable occasion, *Mac.*, 2.1; invite, *Troil. & Cres.*, 4.v; *at entreats*, to entreaty, *Titus*, 1.i.

Entreatments, familiar intercourse (the original idea is negotiation after a truce), *Ham.*, 1.iii.

Envenom, poison, *Ham.*, 4.vii.

Envious, inspired by personal malice, *Jul. Caes.*, 2.i; malicious, *Ham.*, 4.vii.

Envy, ill-will, *Cor.*, 3.iii; malice, *Jul. Caes.*, 2.i; *Ant. & Cleo.*, 5.ii; *verb, envied against*, shown ill-will towards, *Cor.*, 3.iii; *rather than envy you*, rather than as malice towards you, *Cor.*, 3.iii; grudge, but in honourable way, *Cym.*, 4.ii.

Enwheel, encompass, *Oth.*, 2.i.

Epicure, hardened toper, *Ant. & Cleo.*, 2.vii; *English epicures*, the luxurious English (as contrasted with the plain-living Scots), *Mac.*, 5.iii; *epicurean cooks*, cooks fit to serve a sybarite, *Ant. & Cleo.*, 2.i; *epicurism*, riotous living, *Lear*, 1.iv.

Epicurus, Athenian philosopher (341–270 B.C.); *I held Epicurus strong*, I accepted as true the doctrines of Epicurus, who regarded as mere superstition the attention to omens, etc., *Jul. Caes.*, 5.i.

Epileptic, grinning (for Oswald is trying to put a smiling face on it), *Lear*, 2.ii.

Epithet, *epithets of war*, martial expressions, *Oth.*, 1.i.

Epitome, *epitome of yours*, yourself in little, *Cor.*, 5.iii.

Equal, of same rank and financial standing, *Timon*, 1.i; *equalness*, partnership, *Ant. & Cleo.*, 5.i.

Equality, *equalities are so weighted*, the shares are so equally balanced, *Lear*, 1.i; *equality of two domestic powers*, two factions in the state of equal strength, *Ant. & Cleo.*, 1.iii.

Equinox, equal length of day and night, *Oth.*, 2.iii.

Equivalent, equal in power and dignity, *Per.*, 5.i.

Equivocal, ambiguous, *Oth.*, 1.iii.

Equivocate, to use, with intent to mislead, a form of words that admits of two interpretations, *Mac.*, 2.iii; *the equivocation of the fiend that lies like truth*, the devil being through the Witches' prophecies the great equivocator, *Mac.*, 5.v.

Erebus, hell, *Jul. Caes.*, 2.i.

Errant, Erring, wandering, *Ham.*, 1.i; etc.

Error, deliberate untruth, *Troil. & Cres.*, 5.iv; *error of the moon*, deviation from normal course, *Oth.*, 5.ii.

Erst, formerly, *Titus*, 4.i; *Per.*, 1.i.

Escape, escapade, transgression, *Titus*, 4.ii; *Oth.*, 1.iii.

Escoted, *how are they escoted?* who pays for their maintenance? *Ham.*, 2.ii. (*cf. scot-free*, pay one's *shot*).

Especial, *thine especial safety*, individual, *Ham.*, 4.iii; *especially*, in particular, exclusively, *Cor.*, 1.i.

Esperance, hope, *Troil. & Cres.*, 5.ii; *Lear*, 4.i.

Espial, spy, *Ham.*, 3.i.

Essay, trial, *Lear*, 1.ii.

Essence, quality, characteristic, *Oth.*, 4.i.

Essential, *the essential vesture of creation*, the actual endowments devised for her by her Creator, *Oth.*, 2.i.

Essentially, fundamentally, in fact, *Ham.*, 3.iv.

Establish, *establish our estate upon*, settle the succession on, *Mac.*, 1.iv.

Estate, state, condition, *Rom. & Jul.*, 3.iii; *Lear*, 5.iii; unhappy position, *Cym.*, 5.v; fortune, *Per.*, 4.ii; *th' estate o' th' world*, the ordered existence, *Mac.*, 5.v; rank, *Ham.*, 5.i; *the terms of our estate*, the conditions required for our rule as king, *Ham.*, 3.iii.

Esteem, opinion, *Mac.*, 1.vii; popular estimation, *Troil. & Cres.*, 3.iii; value, *Cym.*, 5.v and 1.vi; regard, *Mac.*, 4.iii.

Estimate, price, *Timon*, 1.i; worth, reputation, *Cor.*, 3.iii.

Estimation, something regarded as of value, *Troil. & Cres.*, 2.ii; reputation, *Ham.*, 2.ii; *Oth.*, 1.iii; *your brace of unprizeable estimations*, these two things that you regard as beyond all price, *Cym.*, 1.iv.

Estridge, ostrich, *Ant. & Cleo.*, 3.xiii.

Eternal, unchanging, *Troil. & Cres.*, 5.ii; *this eternal blazon*, this proclamation of the state of eternity, *Ham.*, 1.v; *eternal devil*, the very devil (used to mark extreme abhorrence), *Jul. Caes.*, 1.ii; *would be eternal*, would make ever memorable, *Ant. & Cleo.*, 5.i; *eternal villain* (used intensively), *Oth.*, 4.ii.

Eterne, *in them nature's copy's not eterne*, they have not a perpetual possession of life, but only a tenure that may be terminated, *Mac.*, 3.ii; *proof eterne*, to be forever impenetrable, *Ham.*, 2.ii.

Even, *even and direct*, straightforward, *Ham.*, 2.ii; *the even virtue of our enterprise*, the honourable nature of the attempt, *Jul. Caes.*, 2.i; *even with you*, our debt to you paid, *Mac.*, 5.viii; *even Christen*, fellow Christian, *Ham.*, 5.i; *adverb*, precisely, *Ham.*, 1.ii; *even to the state's best health*, (emphatic use) to the extent of services in saving the state, *Timon*, 2.ii; *to make him even o'er*, to make him clear about, *Lear*, 4.vii; *we'll even all*, to be equal to all, *Cym.*, 3.iv; *even'd with him*, to be quits with him, *Oth.*, 2.i; *to go even*, act in accord with, *Cym.*, 1.iv.

EVENT, enterprise, consequence, *Ham.*, 4.iv (where *invisible* means not to be foreseen); outcome, *Troil. & Cres.*, 2.ii; the sequel, what's to come (will decide between us), *Lear*, 1.iv; the issue, *Cym.*, 3.v.

EVER, for ever, *Mac.*, 5.iii; *Timon*, 1.i; *or ever*, before ever, *Ham.*, 1.ii.

EVERLASTING, *the Everlasting*, God, *Ham.*, 1.ii.

EVIDENCE, *their evidence*, the evidence against them, *Lear*, 3.vi.

EVIDENT, certain, inevitable, *Cor.*, 4.vii and 5.iii; acceptable as proof, *Cym.*, 2.iv.

EVIL, misfortune, *Oth.*, 1.i; *purposed evil*, deliberate wrong-doing, *Ham.*, 5.ii; *the evil*, scrofula (supposed to be cured by the king's touch, so the king's evil), *Mac.*, 4.iii; disease, *Cor.*, 1.i; *accidental evils*, misfortunes incident to life, so to be regarded by a Stoic as not touching the soul, *Jul. Caes.*, 4.iii; *adj.*, *planets evil*, threatening misfortune, *Troil. & Cres.*, 1.iii.

EVIL-EY'D, maliciously disposed, *Cym.*, 1.i.

EXACT, *of grace exact*, perfect in every way, *Troil. & Cres.*, 1.iii; precise, *Timon*, 2.ii; *in the most exact regard*, with the strictest attention, *Lear*, 1.iv; *exactly*, properly, *Ham.*, 1.ii; *exactly wrought*, so true to nature, *Cym.*, 2.iv.

EXALT, *exalt himself*, achieve rank and status, *Lear*, 5.iii; *exalted banks*, high banks, *Jul. Caes.*, 1.i.

EXAMPLE, *much example for't*, many previous instances, *Timon*, 1.ii; *example you with*, give you precedent for, *Timon*, 4.iii.

EXCEED, excel, *Per.*, 2.iii; *exceeding*, outstanding, *Oth.*, 3.iii.

EXCELLENT, notable (used to emphasize the extent of the folly or untruth), *Titus*, 2.iii; etc.; *excellently*, highly, *Troil. & Cres.*, 4.i.

EXCEPT, *is it excepted?* does the bond expressly make this reservation? *Jul. Caes.*, 2.i.

EXCEPTION, objection, resentment, *Ham.*, 5.ii; disapproval, *Oth.*, 4.ii.

EXCEPTLESS, that makes no exception, *Timon*, 4.iii.

EXCHANGE, fencing-bout, *Ham.*, 5.ii; the acceptance given to the challenge, *Lear*, 5.iii.

EXCITE, rouse, *Mac.*, 5.ii; provoke, *Cym.*, 5.v; *excitements to the field*, exhortations to battle, *Troil. & Cres.*, 1.iii; *Ham.*, 4.iv.

EXCLAIM, outcry, *Troil. & Cres.*, 5.iii; *verb*, *exclaim against*, miscall, *Ham.*, 2.ii; denounce, *Oth.*, 2.iii.

EXCREMENTS, nails, hair, what grows out of the body, *Ham.*, 3.iv.

EXCUSE, pardon, *Cor.*, 1.iii.

EXECUTION, performance, application, *Troil. & Cres.*, 1.iii; slaughter, *Troil. & Cres.*, 5.v; administration, *Lear*, 1.i; *the execution of his wit*, what his mind can do, *Oth.*, 3.iii.

EXECUTE, perform, inflict, *Titus*, 2.iii; *execute upon him*, attack him, *Oth.*, 2.iii.

EXEMPT, *from wealth exempt*, free from, denied riches, *Timon*, 4.ii.

EXERCISE, exertion, *Cor.*, 1.v; sport, *Troil. & Cres.*, 4.iv; act of devotion (reading a prayer-book), *Ham.*, 3.i; practice, *Ham.*, 4.vii; bodily act, *Oth.*, 2.i; religious act, *Oth.*, 3.iv; *verb*, perform, inflict, *Cym.*, 5.iv.

EXHALATIONS, meteors (supposedly *exhaled*, drawn out of bodies as a vapour by the sun), *Jul. Caes.*, 2.i; *Rom. & Jul.*, 3.v.

EXHAUST, draw forth, *Timon*, 4.iii.

EXHIBITION, cash allowance, *Oth.*, 1.iii; *confined to exhibition*, depending entirely on an allowance, *Lear*, 1.ii; *Cym.*, 1.vi.

EXIGENT, crisis, *Jul. Caes.*, 5.i; emergency, fatal moment, *Ant. & Cleo.*, 4.xiv.

EXORCIST, one with power to call up spirits, conjurer, *Jul. Caes.*, 2.i; *Cym.*, 4.ii.

EXPECT, await, *Ant. & Cleo.*, 4.iv; *Per.*, 1.iv; *noun*, expectation, *Troil. & Cres.*, 1.iii.

EXPECTANCE, speculation, *Troil. & Cres.*, 4.v.

EXPECTANCY, the hope, *Ham.*, 3.i; expectation, *Oth.*, 2.i.

EXPECTATION, waiting, *Jul. Caes.*, 1.i; readiness, *Lear*, 4.iv.

EXPECTERS, those waiting to see the outcome, *Troil. & Cres.*, 4.v.

Expedience, hasty enterprise, *Ant. & Cleo.*, 1.ii.

Expense, squandering, *Lear*, 2.i.

Expire, bring to an end, *Rom. & Jul.*, 1.iv.

Expostulate, discuss, *Ham.*, 2.ii; *Oth.*, 4.i; *expostulation*, converse, *Troil. & Cres.*, 4.iv.

Exposture, exposure, *Cor.*, 4.i.

Exposure, exposed position, *Troil. & Cres.*, 1.iii.

Express, manifest, *Lear*, 4.iii; *in form and moving how express and admirable*, as a child may be called the express image of his father, so Hamlet regards man's form as the image of some perfect model (*cf.* his description of his father, 3.iv), *Ham.*, 2.ii; *expressly*, clearly, *Troil. & Cres.*, 3.iii.

Expressure, expression, *Troil. & Cres.*, 3.iii.

Exsufflicate, *exsufflicate and blown*, (perhaps) puffy and fly-blown, *Oth.*, 3.iii.

Extant, present, *Troil. & Cres.*, 4.v.

Extend, magnify his virtues, *Cym.*, 1.iv; take possession of (legal metaphor), *Ant. & Cleo.*, 1.ii; display, *Oth.*, 2.i; *extend him within himself*, enlarge on his merits only within the bounds of truth, *Cym.*, 1.i; amplify, *Troil. & Cres.*, 3.iii.

Extent, *my extent to the players*, the courtesy I show the actors, *Ham.*, 2.ii.

Extenuate, *his glory not extenuated*, his glory not lessened in any way, *Jul. Caes.*, 3.ii.

Extern, *compliment extern*, outward deportment, *Oth.*, 1.i.

Extravagant, wandering, *Ham.*, 1.i; *Oth.*, 1.i.

Extremes, terrible dilemma, *Rom. & Jul.*, 4.i; wild suggestions, *Titus*, 3.i.

Extremity, deadliness, *Cym.*, 3.iv; *extremities*, extreme courses, *Jul. Caes.*, 2.i.

Eyas, a nestling (used of young hawks taken from the nest for training), so *little eyases*, the boys in the children's company in training as actors, *Ham.*, 2.ii.

Eye, *eye well to you*, appear good in your eyes, *Ant. & Cleo.*, 1.iii.

Eyrie, nest or brood of eagle or hawk, so used of the child-actors, *Ham.*, 2.ii.

Fable, a fiction, *Oth.*, 5.ii.

Face, *that great face of war*, its dangerous look, *Ant. & Cleo.*, 3.xiii; so *face of peril*, *Cym.*, 5.i; so of open recognition or avowal, *Lear*, 3.i.

Fact, something done, usually evil deed, *Mac.*, 3.ii; so *confederate in the fact*, *Titus*, 4.i; *to lack humanity so much as this fact comes to*, to be inhuman enough to commit such a crime, *Cym.*, 3.ii.

Faction, (1) party strife: *cherish factions*, encourage dissension, *Timon*, 3.v; *equality of two domestic powers breed scrupulous faction*, with opposite parties in the state equal, they quarrel over trifles, *Ant. & Cleo.*, 1.iii; (2) alliance: *their fraction is more our wish than their faction*, *Troil. & Cres.*, 2.iii; *the faction*, the conspirators, *Jul. Caes.*, 2.i; *the faction of fools*, company, *Troil. & Cres.*, 2.i.

Factionary, *factionary on the party of your general*, active in support of, *Cor.*, 5.ii.

Factious, *be factious*, join the party, *Jul. Caes.*, 1.iii.

Factor, substitute, deputy, *Ant. & Cleo.*, 2.vi; agent, *Cym.*, 1.vi.

Faculty, ability, power, *Ham.*, 2.ii; *preformed faculties*, their powers and functions as formed by nature, *Jul. Caes.*, 1.iii; *the very faculties of eyes and ears*, *Ham.*, 2.ii; powers and privileges, *Mac.*, 1.vii.

Fail, fault, *Timon*, 5.i; failure in truth and honesty, *Cym.*, 3.iv; *verb*, withhold, *Mac.*, 3.vi; omit, come short in, *Lear*, 2.iv; *Cym.*, 3.iv.

Fain, glad; but, often, willing only because there was no other resource, *Lear*, 4.vii; *adv.*, gladly, *Rom. & Jul.*, 3.ii; *Oth.*, 4.i.

Faint, feeble, *Troil. & Cres.*, 1.iii; *a most faint neglect*, lack of active and ready service, *Lear*, 1.iv; *verb*, lose heart, *Troil. & Cres.*, 2.ii.

Faintly, almost inaudible, *Cor.*, 5.i; (of a description) only hinting at the truth, *Lear*, 1.ii; without conviction, *Oth.*, 4.i.

Fair, *revolted fair*, unfaithful woman, *Troil. & Cres.*, 5.ii.

Fairly, in becoming fashion, *Timon*, 1.ii; courteously, *Ham.*, 2.ii; completely, *Rom. & Jul.*, 2.iv; with proper respect, *Per.*, 5.i; auspiciously, *Ant. & Cleo.*, 2.ii.

Fairness, beauty, *Cym.*, 5.v; *Oth.*, 2.i; *to the fairness of my power*, as well as I can, *Cor.*, 1.ix.

Fairy, enchantress, *Ant. & Cleo.*, [4.iii.

FAITH'D, credited, *Lear*, 2.i.

FAITHFULLY, earnestly, *Timon*, 3.ii.

FAITHFULNESS, true love, *Per.*, 1.i.

FALCHION, sword, *Lear*, 5.iii.

FALCON, *the falcon as the tercel*, the female hawk as the male hawk, *Troil. & Cres.*, 3.ii; *Mac.*, 2.iv.

FALCONER, *French falconers*, the French were masters in falconry, but perhaps indiscriminate in their choice of prey, *Ham.*, 2.ii.

FALL, *at fall*, in low water, short of cash, *Timon*, 2.ii; *verb*, befall, *Jul. Caes.*, 5.i; *Ant. & Cleo.*, 3.vii; *fall away*, desert, *Ant. & Cleo.*, 4.vi; *it falls right*, luckily you can have your wish, *Ham.*, 4.vii; *falling-off*, abandonment, *Ham.*, 1.v; *falling-from*, desertion, *Timon*, 4.iii; *fall'n-off Britons*, revolted Britons, *Cym.*, 3.vii.

FALLING-SICKNESS, epilepsy, *Jul. Caes.*, 1.ii.

FALSE, out of tune, *Jul. Caes.*, 4.iii; imaginary, *Mac.*, 2.i; *false fire*, powder without shot, blank discharge, *Ham.*, 3.ii; *verb*, *false themselves*, turn traitor, *Cym.*, 2.iii; *adv.*, *false struck*, perfidiously, *Cym.*, 3.iv; *adj.*, *be false with*, commit adultery with, *Cym.*, 2.iv.

FALSE-FAC'D, hypocritical, *Cor.*, 1.x.

FALSEHOOD, faithlessness, *Troil. & Cres.*, 4.ii; dishonesty, *Timon*, 2.ii; *excellent falsehood*, deceit, *Ant. & Cleo.*, 1.i.

FALSELY, perfidiously, *Cor.*, 3.i; wrongly, *Oth.*, 5.ii.

FALSENESS, untruth, *Per.*, 5.i.

FAME, reputation, *Troil. & Cres.*, 1.iii; rumour, report, *Titus*, 2.i; etc.; *the fame*, the prize, *Ant. & Cleo.*, 2.vi; renown, *Cym.*, 3.iii; *fam'd*, made famous, *Jul. Caes.*, 1.ii.

FAMILIAR, domestic, friendly, *Troil. & Cres.*, 3.iii; friendly, *Ham.*, 1.iii; intimate, *Troil. & Cres.*, 5.ii; obvious, *Troil. & Cres.*, 3.iii; homely, serviceable, *Oth.*, 2.iii; known, *Cym.*, 5.v; acquainted, *Cym.*, 1.iv.

FAMINE, starvation, *Mac.*, 5.v; *Cym.*, 3.vi.

FAMISH, *a single famish'd kiss*, a single kiss to one longing for more, *Troil. & Cres.*, 4.iv; die, *Timon*, 2.ii.

FAMOUS, notorious, *Ant. & Cleo.*, 1.iv.

FAN, test (from the winnowing-fan that removes the chaff), *Cym.*, 1.vi.

FANCY, *not express'd in fancy*, not revealing an eccentric taste, *Ham.*, 1.iii; *dear to fancy*, pleasing to our sense of the fashionable, *Ham.*, 5.ii; *after new fancies*, after new loves, *Oth.*, 3.iv; imagination, *Ant. & Cleo.*, 2.ii; *verb*, love, *Troil. & Cres.*, 5.ii.

FANE, temple, *Cor.*, 1.x; *Cym.*, 4.ii.

FANG, seize, *Timon*, 4.iii; *adders fang'd*, with teeth, *Ham.*, 3.iv.

FANGLED, *our fangled world*, given over to show and appearance, *Cym.*, 5.iv.

FANTASTIC, incredible, *Troil. & Cres.*, 5.v.

FANTASTICAL, imaginary, *Mac.*, 1.iii; prodigious, *Oth.*, 2.i.

FANTASTICO, one ostentatiously out of the ordinary, *Rom. & Jul.*, 2.iv.

FANTASY, hallucination, *Ham.*, 1.i; *Rom. & Jul.*, 1.iv; *fantasies*, disturbing fancies, *Jul. Caes.*, 2.i; notion, *Ham.*, 4.iv; whim, *Oth.*, 3.iii.

FAR, *you speak him far*, you praise him highly, *Cym.*, 1.i.

FARDEL, burden, *Ham.*, 3.i.

FARE, to be in a way of life (the following line plays on the meaning of 'feeding'), *Ham.*, 3.ii; both meanings–feed, be in luck–in *Cym.*, 3.i.

FARM, lease, rent, *Ham.*, 4.iv.

FARROW, *her nine farrow*, her litter of nine, *Mac.*, 4.i.

FASHION, the creation of a season only, *Ham.*, 1.iii; *out of fashion*, unbecomingly, *Oth.*, 2.i; *of all fashions*, of all kinds, *Per.*, 4.ii; *verb*, *fashion in*, work in, *Troil. & Cres.*, 4.iv; shape, *Jul. Caes.*, 2.i; mould to a purpose, persuade, *Jul. Caes.*, 2.i; arrange, *Oth.*, 4.iii; *fashion fit*, contrive to my own advantage, *Lear*, 1.ii.

FASHION-MONGER, one who apes what he thinks the new modes, *Rom. & Jul.*, 2.iv.

FAST, sound (of sleep) *Mac.*, 5.i; *Rom. & Jul.*, 4.v; firm, fixed, *Lear*, 1.i; unwavering as a support, *Oth.*, 1.iii.

FASTEN, *fasten upon*, thrust upon, pass off upon, *Oth.*, 2.iii; *fasten'd villain*, confirmed, hardened villain, *Lear*, 2.i.

FAT, *he's fat and scant of breath*, refers not to the corpulence of the actor but to the sweat caused by his exertion, *Ham.*, 5.ii; *noun*, vat, *Ant. & Cleo.*, 2.vii.

FATAL, ominous, *Jul. Caes.*, 5.i; or indicating what is the decree of fate, *Mac.*, 2.i.

FATE, *oppose his fate*, bar the path

on which fate leads him, *Ant. & Cleo.*, 3.xiii; *the Fates*, the Goddesses of Destiny, *Per.*, 4.iii; *verb*, *hang fated o'er men's faults*, are the inevitable punishment of faults, *Lear*, 3.iv; predestined, *Oth.*, 3.iii.

FATHOM, measure of six feet, from original meaning of outstretched arms; *a waist most fathomless*, not to be embraced, *Troil. & Cres.*, 2.ii; *another of his fathom*, grasp, *Oth.*, 1.i.

FATIGATE, tired, *Cor.*, 2.ii.

FAULT, misfortune, *Per.*, 4.ii; *for fault of*, for want of, *Rom. & Jul.*, 2.iv.

FAVOUR, *leave and favour*, gracious permission, *Ham.*, 1.ii; *under favour*, with permission, *Timon*, 3.v; charm, *Ham.*, 4.v; *Cym.*, 1.vi; appearance, countenance, *Jul. Caes.*, 1.ii; pardon, mercy, *Mac.*, 1.iii; *Ant. & Cleo.*, 3.xiii; *my hospitable favours*, the features of your host, *Lear*, 3.vii; *verb*, express approval, *Ant. & Cleo.*, 4.viii.

FAVOURABLY, advantageously, *Oth.*, 2.i.

FAWN, friendly gesture, *Cor.*, 3.ii; of a dog, *Cor.*, 1.vi; *Timon*, 3.iv.

FAY, faith, *Ham.*, 2.ii.

FEALTY, loyalty, *Titus*, 1.i; *Cym.*, 5.iv.

FEAR, *no fear in him*, no cause for fear from him, *Jul. Caes.*, 2.i; so *Ham.*, 3.iii; *put thyself into a haviour of less fear*, do not behave in a manner that so gives cause for fear, *Cym.*, 3.iv; *verb*, *as fearing thee*, as doubting thee, *Troil. & Cres.*, 4.iv; *fears me*, gives me cause for apprehension, *Lear*, 3.v; frighten, *Ant. & Cleo.*, 2.vi; *as fear not but you shall*, as you certainly will, *Lear*, 3.i; *fear'd hopes*, hopes not free from fear, *Cym.*, 2.iv.

FEARFUL, causing fear, *Jul. Caes.*, 1.iii; apprehensive, *Rom. & Jul.*, 3.iii; dreadful, *Oth.*, 3.iii; filled with fear, *Lear*, 1.iv; *fearfully*, threateningly, *Rom. & Jul.*, 5.iii; menacingly, *Lear*, 4.ii.

FEARFULNESS, awe, *Jul. Caes.*, 1.i.

FEAST, keep holiday, *Per.*, 1.iv; *Oth.*, 2.ii; *when you did feast*, invite others to your feasts, *Timon*, 4.iii.

FEASTING, *feasting presence*, chamber set out for banquet, *Rom. & Jul.*, 5.iii.

FEAST-WON, gained by entertainment, *Timon*, 2.ii.

FEAT, exhibition of various skills, *Per.*, 5.ii; *a glass that feated them*, a mirror, an example by which they could see how to improve their fashion and form, *Cym.*, 1.i; *adj.*, dextrous, neat, *Cym.*, 5.v.

FEATHER, sort, *Timon*, 1.i; *forest of feathers*, feathers being worn on hats, *Ham.*, 3.ii; *the best feather of our wing*, chief among us, *Cym.*, 1.vi; *feather'd*, winged, *Oth.*, 1.iii; *Per.*, 5.ii.

FEATURE, form, *Lear*, 4.ii; general appearance, *Ham.*, 3.i; etc.

FEDARY, accomplice, *Cym.*, 3.ii.

FEE, remuneration, *Lear*, 1.i; *sold in fee*, sold with absolute and perpetual possession, *Ham.*, 4.iv; *fee simple*, the most complete and absolute form of tenure or possession, *Rom. & Jul.*, 3.i.

FEED, pasture, fodder, *Titus*, 4.iv.

FEEDER, parasite, *Timon*, 2.ii; servant, *Ant. & Cleo.*, 3.xiii.

FEE-FARM, tenure like *fee simple* (*q.v.*) but with a rent; *a kiss in fee-farm*, a kiss without restriction, *Troil. & Cres.*, 3.ii.

FEE-GRIEF, grief private to some individual, *Mac.*, 4.iii.

FEEL, test, *Lear*, 1.ii; *to the felt absence now I feel a cause*, I now understand the cause of your absence which has so affected me, *Oth.*, 3.iv.

FEELER, *the feeler's soul*, the soul of the person affected by the touch, *Cym.*, 1.vi.

FEELING, heartfelt, *Rom. & Jul.*, 3.v; *Lear*, 4.vi.

FEELINGLY, adequately, *Ham.*, 5.ii; *I see it feelingly*, I understand it not by my senses but by my inward sorrow, *Lear*, 4.vi.

FEIGN, imagine (as in a poem); also, later, with play on the meaning 'to deceive,' *Timon*, 1.i.

FELICITATE, made happy, *Lear*, 1.i.

FELL, *noun*, skin, *Lear*, 5.iii; *my fell of hair*, the covering of hair on my skin, *Mac.*, 5.v; *adj.*, cruel, *Oth.*, 5.ii; deadly, *Cym.*, 4.ii; *fell as death*, savage, implacable, *Troil. & Cres.*, 4.v; *Ham.*, 5.ii; *verb*, strike down, *Lear*, 4.ii; hew down, overthrow, *Timon*, 4.iii.

FELLOW, equal, *Jul. Caes.*, 3.1 and 5.iii; comrade, *Timon*, 4.ii; *noble fellow*, of Coriolanus himself, *Cor.*, 1.iv; *princely fellows*, her equals in rank, *Cym.*, fellow-servant, *Lear*, 1.iii; *these great fellows*, the triumvirs and allies, *Ant. & Cleo.*, 2.vii; also a term used in addressing servants.

FELLOWSHIP, partnership, *Ham.*, 3.ii; alliance, *Timon*, 5.ii; friendship, *Ham.*, 2.ii; convoy of ships, *Oth.*, 2.i; *to have a name in great men's fellowship*, to associate with the great without the qualification of greatness, *Ant. & Cleo.*, 2.vii.

FELLIES, the curved pieces of outer circle of wheel receiving the spokes, *Ham.*, 2.ii.

FENNEL, in the language of flowers represented dissembling and flattery, so given to King Claudius, *Ham.*, 4.v.

FENNY, bred in marshes, *Mac.*, 4.i.

FEN-SUCK'D, *fen-suck'd fogs*, fogs drawn up from the marshes, *Lear*, 2.iv.

FERE, spouse, *Titus*, 4.i; *Per.*, 1.*Prol.*

FERVENCY, eagerness, *Ant. & Cleo.*, 2.v.

FESTINATE, speedy, *Lear*, 3.vii.

FETCH, device, stratagem, *Ham.*, 2.i; *fetches*, tricks, pretexts, *Lear*, 2.iv; *verb*, *fetch my life and being*, am descended from, *Oth.*, 1.ii; *fetch a turn*, walk a little, *Cym.*, 1.i; *fetch in*, to capture, *Ant. & Cleo.*, 4.i; *fetch thee with a wanion*, deal you a blow, *Per.*, 2.i.

FETTLE, make ready, *Rom. & Jul.*, 3.v.

FEVER, to put in a fever, *Ant. & Cleo.*, 3.xiii.

FICTION, feigning, *Timon*, 5.i.

FIDDLESTICK, rapier, *Rom. & Jul.*, 3.i.

FIDIUSED, formed in jest from 'Aufidius,' *Cor.*, 2.i.

FIELD, place suitable for duelling, *Rom. & Jul.*, 3.i; *our fielded friends*, our friends drawn up for battle, *Cor.*, 1.iv.

FIERCE, intense, *Timon*, 4.ii; terrible, *Ham.*, 1.i; fiery, ardent, *Troil. & Cres.*, 1.i; *Lear.*, 1.ii; *fierce abridgement*, impetuous summary, *Cym.*, 5.v.

FIGURE, *the baby figure . . . of things to come at large*, the shape and nature of the full consequences of what seems trivial, *Troil. & Cres.*, 1.iii; form, *Ham.*, 1.i; figure of speech, *Ham.*, 2.ii; figure on dial of clock, *Oth.*, 4.ii; *in as like a figure*, as if acting a similar part, *Cym.*, 3.iv; *figure of truth*, embodiment of truth, *Per.*, 5.iii; *figure of my heart*, character, *Oth.*, 1.i; *figures*, ideas, fancies, *Jul. Caes.*, 2.i; written characters, *Timon*, 5.iii; carven images, *Cym.*, 2.iv.

FILE, effective strength of a fighting-force, *Cym.*, 5.ii; *the valued file*, the list setting out what is specially valued in each breed, *Mac.*, 3.i; *the common file*, the rank and file, *Cor.*, 1.vi; *the right-hand file*, the patricians, *Cor.*, 2.i; *files*, ranks, numbers, *Timon*, 5.ii; *Ant. & Cleo.*, 1.i; *verb*, (1) perfect (as if finishing with a file): *she will file our engines with advice*, perfect our plots, *Titus*, 2.i; (2) defile, *Mac.*, 3.i.

FILLS, shafts or thills of a cart, *Troil. & Cres.*, 3.ii; *verb*, *fills up the cry*, like a hound that merely runs with the pack, *Oth.*, 2.iii.

FILLET, slice, *Mac.*, 4.i.

FILM, gossamer, *Rom. & Jul.*, 1.iv; *verb*, cover with thin skin, *Ham.*, 3.iv.

FILTHY, *filthy witness*, blood, *Mac.*, 2.ii.

FIND, experience, *Cor.*, 5.iii; discover, *Titus*, 4.ii; understand, *Cor.*, 3.iii; *find him not*, fails to penetrate his secret, *Ham.*, 3.i; *the woman hath found him already*, has seen his true nature, *Oth.*, 2.i; *find me to*, discover (from a study of my hand) that, *Ant. & Cleo.*, 1.ii.

FINE, various meanings played on in *Ham.*, 5.i: a legal device (*fine and recovery*) for converting an entailed holding into a fee-simple (*q.v.*); the end; and (*adj.*) clever, astute (used ironically); *more handsome than fine*, admirable rather than appealing by mere cleverness, *Ham.*, 2.ii; *in fine*, finally, *Lear*, 2.i; *a fine fool*, an egregious ass, *Oth.*, 4.i.

FINELESS, endless, *Oth.*, 3.iii.

FINENESS, purity (of a metal), *Troil. & Cres.*, 1.iii; ingenuity, subtlety, *Troil. & Cres.*, 1.iii.

FINGER, play on an instrument, *Cym.*, 2.iii; *Per.*, 1.i; *finger'd their packet*, abstracted their instructions, *Ham.*, 5.ii.

FINISH, die, *Ant. & Cleo.*, 5.ii; *Cym.*, 5.v.

FIRE, *fire us hence like foxes*, as foxes are smoked out of their holes, *Lear*, 5.iii; *stand on fire*, burn with impatience, *Cym.*, 5.v.

FIRE-NEW, *fire-new fortune*, brand-new honours, *Lear*, 5.iii.

FIRM, constant, *Ant. & Cleo.*, 1.v.

FIRST, *protest their first of manhood*, have their first chance to show they are men, *Mac.*, 5.ii; *upon our first*, at once, without further question, *Ham.*, 2.ii; *familiar at first,* intimate at our first meeting, *Cym.,* 1.iv.

FIRSTLINGS, the early outcome, *Troil. & Cres.,* 1.*Prol.; Mac.,* 4.i.

FISTING, abuse, rough usage, *Per.,* 4.vi.

FIT, (1) well-fitting (of garments), *Cym.,* 4.i; *I have already fit,* ready, *Cym.,* 3.iv; *all with me's meet that I can fashion fit,* all is fair to me that I can turn to my own advantage, *Lear,* 1.ii; *must make content with his fortunes fit,* find his content in whatever fortune does for him, *Lear,* 3.ii; *verb,* be suitable, in place, *Rom. & Jul.,* 1.v; *Titus,* 3.i; (2) *in his lawless fit,* in one of his recurring attacks of madness, *Ham.,* 4.i; *the fits o' the season,* the outrages that keep happening in these times, *Mac.,* 4.ii; the recurring divisions of a song or poem, *Troil. & Cres.,* 3.i; *if it be a day fits you,* if your fit of lunacy recurs on a particular day, *Per.,* 2.i.

FITCHEW, polecat, *Troil. & Cres.,* 5.i; *Lear,* 4.vi; wench, *Oth.,* 4.i.

FITFUL, *life's fitful fever,* marked by periodic attacks, *Mac.,* 3.ii.

FITLY, opportunely, *Timon,* 3.iv; *may fitly like your grace,* may please your grace sufficiently, *Lear,* 1.i; *I will fitly bring you to hear,* at a suitable moment, *Lear,* 1.ii.

FITMENT, *'twas a fitment for the purpose I then follow'd,* equipment, designed for my purpose, *Cym.,* 5.v; *do her fitment,* what is appropriate, proper in the circumstances, *Per.,* 4.vi.

FITNESS, convenience, inclination, *Ham.,* 5.ii; the most effective opportunity, *Troil. & Cres.,* 1.iii; *a woman's fitness comes by fits,* a woman's inclination is variable, *Cym.,* 4.i; were't my fitness to, did my humanity permit, *Lear,* 4.ii.

FIVE-FINGER-TIED, (perhaps) by giving her hand (as in marriage), *Troil. & Cres.,* 5.ii.

FIX'D, certain, *Timon,* 1.i.

FLAKE, lock of hair, *Lear,* 4.vii.

FLAMEN, priest in ancient Rome, *Cor.,* 2.i.

FLAPJACK, pancake, *Per.,* 2.i.

FLATTERY, delusion, *Titus,* 3.i; *sweet flattery,* pleasing delusion, *Oth.,* 4.i.

FLAW, break in fortunes, *Ant. & Cleo.,* 3.xii; *winter's flaw,* the gusts of winter, *Ham.,* 5.i; *Cor.,* 5.iii; sudden bursts of feeling, *Mac.,* 3.iv.

FLECKEL'D, dappled, *Rom. & Jul.,* 2.iii.

FLEER, sneer, *Rom. & Jul.,* 1.v; etc.

FLEET, to be afloat, *Ant. & Cleo.,* 3.xiii; *the fleeting moon,* inconstant, *Ant. & Cleo.,* 5.ii.

FLESH, *get thyself in flesh,* into a healthy condition, *Rom. & Jul.,* 5.i; *in flesh,* in body, the physical man, *Cor.,* 2.ii; *he means in flesh,* in physical attractions (then taken up as meaning in complexion), *Ant. & Cleo.,* 1.ii; *verb, I'll flesh you,* to give him his first taste of fighting (the adaptation of a term from hunting), with the further suggestion of giving him a taste of the sword, *Lear,* 2.ii.

FLESHMENT, *in the fleshment of this dread exploit,* in the eagerness for combat provoked by this earlier initiation, *Lear,* 2.ii.

FLEXURE, bending, *Troil. & Cres.,* 2.iii.

FLIBBERTIGIBBET, one of the devils in Harsnett's *Declaration of Egregious Popish Impostures* (1603), *Lear,* 3.iv and 4.i. From the same *Declaration* Shakespeare took Smulkin, Modo, Mahu, Obidicut, and Hobbididence.

FLIGHTY, *the flighty purpose,* the purpose swift to leave performance behind, *Mac.,* 4.i.

FLING, *flung in rage from,* abandoned in his fury, *Timon,* 4.ii; *flung out,* kicked out, defied control, *Mac.,* 2.iv.

FLIRT-GILL, woman of light behaviour (*gill* from *Gillian*), *Rom. & Jul.,* 2.iv.

FLOOD, *the great flood,* Deucalion's flood, *Jul. Caes.,* 1.ii (*cf. Cor.,* 2.i); *at the flood,* full tide, *Jul. Caes.,* 4.iii; *Troil. & Cres.,* 1.iii.

FLOOD-GATE, impetuous (like water pouring through a sluice), *Oth.,* 1.iii.

FLOURISH, embellishment, *Ham.,* 2.ii; *verb, trumpets flourish,* sound a fanfare, *Titus,* 4.ii; triumph, *Jul. Caes.,* 3.ii.

FLOUT, mock, *Troil. & Cres.,* 4.ii; insult, *Mac.,* 1.ii.

FLOW, *set mine eyes at flow,* wept, *Timon,* 2.ii; *Timon,* 5.iv; *the flow o' the Nile,* height of the river, *Ant. & Cleo.,* 2.vii; *verb,* circulate in full measure, *Timon,* 1.ii; come by descent, *Per.,* 4.iii; *ebb and flow,* to fall and rise as the tide, *Lear,* 5.iii; *ebb and flow,* of tears, *Rom. & Jul.,* 3.v; *flow to great dis-*

traction, a madness comes over you, *Troil. & Cres.*, 5.ii; *the numbers that Petrarch flowed in*, the verses that Petrarch abounded in, *Rom. & Jul.*, 2.iv.

FLOWER, beauty, *Per.*, 3.ii.

FLUSH, lusty, *Ant. & Cleo.*, 1.iv; *the time is flush*, fully come, *Timon*, 5.iv; *as flush as May*, in full flower, *Ham.*, 3.iii.

FLUSHING, redness, *Ham.*, 1.ii.

FLUSTER, heat with wine, *Oth.*, 2.iii.

FLY, *fly at anything*, let the hawk fly at any game, *Ham.*, 2.ii; *fly an ordinary pitch* (from falconry, *pitch* being the highest point of the hawk's flight), conduct himself more like an ordinary citizen, *Jul. Caes.*, 1.i; *fly out of itself*, abandon its true nature, *Cor.*, 1.x; *flying off*, desertion, *Lear*, 2.iv; *fly off*, separate, *Ant. & Cleo.*, 2.ii.

FOAL, give birth to offspring, *Timon*, 2.i.

FOB, *fob off our disgrace*, pass off our distress lightly, *Cor.*, 1.i; *fopt in it*, duped in this matter, *Oth.*, 4.ii.

FOIL, (1) the setting for a jewel, so what sets someone off to advantage, *Ham.*, 5.ii; (2) rapier, *Ham.*, 2.ii; (3) disgrace, *Ant. & Cleo.*, 1.iv; (4) *verb* (from wrestling), throw, defeat, *Cor.*, 1.ix.

FOIN, thrust in fencing, *Lear*, 4.vi.

FOISON, good harvest, *Ant. & Cleo.*, 2.vii; *foisons*, resources, *Mac.*, 4.iii.

FOLLOW, pursue in hostile manner, *Cor.*, 4.v; *Ant. & Cleo.*, 5.i; *following her affairs*, attending to, in performance of her business, *Lear*, 2.ii; *follows but for form*, serves only in show, *Lear*, 2.iv.

FOLLOWER, the various meanings—servant or retainer, pursuer or enemy, one who walks behind another—are played on in *Rom. & Jul.*, 3.i.

FOLLY, wantonness, *Troil. & Cres.*, 5.ii; *Oth.*, 2.i.

FOND, foolish, *Timon*, 1.ii; *fond bondage*, endured only by the foolish, *Lear*, 1.ii; doting, *Oth.*, 4.i; silly, *Oth.*, 2.i; eager, *Cor.*, 5.iii; desirous, *Cym.*, 1.i.

FOOL, *full dish of fool*, dish with whipped cream (with play on usual meaning), *Troil. & Cres.*, 5.i; *verb*, make ridiculous or foolish, *Ant. & Cleo.*, 5.ii; *Lear*, 2.iv.

FOOT, *follow him at foot*, closely, at his heels, *Ham.*, 4.iii; *on foot*, standing, *Troil. & Cres.*, 1.iii; *upon the foot of motion*, to express itself, *Mac.*, 2.iii; *at whose foot*, immediately after which, *Ant. & Cleo.*, 1.v; *verb*, seize with talons, *Cym.*, 5.iv; *a power already footed*, a force already landed, *Lear*, 3.iii.

FOOTING, landing, *Oth.*, 2.i.

FOPPERY, folly, *Lear*, 1.ii.

FOPPISH, foolish, *Lear*, 1.iv.

FOPT, *see* FOB.

FOR, *for why*, because, *Titus*, 3.i; *I forgive thee for a witch*, being as you are a witch, sorcerer, *Ant. & Cleo.*, 1.ii; *stands up for the main soldier*, has claims to be the chief soldier of the age, *Ant. & Cleo.*, 1.ii; *advise thee to desist for going on death's net*, for fear of going, *Per.*, 1.i.

FORBEAR, leave alone, *Ham.*, 5.i; *Cym.*, 4.ii; show patience, *Rom. & Jul.*, 5.iii; *forbear his presence*, avoid meeting him, *Lear*, 1.ii; *forbear me*, withdraw, *Ant. & Cleo.*, 1.ii and 5.ii; leave uninjured, *Oth.*, 1.ii; withdraw, *Per.*, 2.iv; endure, *Per.*, 2.iv.

FORBEARANCE, restraint, *Cym.*, 2.iii.

FORBID, *a man forbid*, under the witch's ban, as if under a curse, *Mac.*, 1.iii; *the heavens forbid but that our loves and comfort should increase*, may the heavens avert that they should not, *Oth.*, 2.i.

FORCE, compulsion, *Timon*, 5.ii; *forces*, operative power, *Cym.*, 1.iv; *verb*, *forced affection*, constrained adherence, *Jul. Caes.*, 4.iii; reinforce, *Mac.*, 5.v; constrain, *Ham.*, 3.i; ravish, *Titus*, 4.i; urge, *Cor.*, 3.ii; stuff, *Troil. & Cres.*, 2.iii and 5.i; compel, *Lear*, 3.ii; *indirect and forced courses*, dishonest and violent (as with poison) means, *Oth.*, 1.iii.

FORDO, destroy, *Ham.*, 5.i; kill, *Lear*, 5.ii; ruin, *Oth.*, 5.i.

FORE, before: (in time) *Cor.*, 4.vii; (in place) *Troil. & Cres.*, 1.iii; *Per.*, 3.*Prol.*; (of rank or estimation) *Cym.*, 1.iv.

FORE-ADVISED, previously instructed, *Cor.*, 2.iii.

FORE-END, earlier part, *Cym.*, 3.iii.

FOREGONE, *a foregone conclusion*, a previous act (of which the dream was an echo), *Oth.*, 3.iii (the expression bears a different sense in modern usage).

FOREHAND, the mainstay, *Troil. & Cres.*, 1.iii.

FOREIGN, not of the household; *with more than foreign heart*, not like a stranger, *Per.*, 4.i; so *foreign laps*, *Oth.*, 4.iii.

Forerun, anticipate, *Rom. & Jul.*, 5.i.

Foresay, decree, predetermine, *Cym.*, 4.ii.

Foresee, provide for, *Timon*, 4.iii.

Forespent, formerly bestowed, *Cym.*, 2.iii.

Forestall, *forestalled*, prevented, *Ham.*, 3.iii; *forestall prescience*, discount all foresight, *Troil. & Cres.*, 1.iii; *this night forestall him of the coming day*, rid himself of the anger we should expect to-morrow, *Cym.*, 3.v.

Forfeit, what is lost by some failure of duty, *Cym.*, 5.v; *the forfeit of the peace*, penalty for breach of peace, *Rom. & Jul.*, 1.i; *forfeits*, those whose lives he could have taken, *Troil. & Cres.*, 4.v.

Forfeiters, those failing to keep some bond, *Cym.*, 3.ii.

Forfend, prohibit, *Titus*, 1.i; avert, forbid, *Oth.*, 5.ii; *forfended*, forbidden, *Lear*, 5.i.

Forgery, *in forgery of*, in imagining, *Ham.*, 4.vii.

Forget, forget oneself, *Oth.*, 2.iii.

Forgetful, inconsiderate, *Jul. Caes.*, 4.iii; *forgetfulness*, neglect, ingratitude, *Timon*, 5.i.

Fork, arrowhead, *Lear*, 1.i.

Forlorn, bare, abandoned, *Titus*, 2.iii; lost, *Cym.*, 5.v; outcast, *Lear*, 4.vii.

Form, behaviour, *Jul. Caes.*, 1.ii; established custom, *Timon*, 3.v.

Formal, normal, *Ant. & Cleo.*, 2.v; *formal ostentation*, the ceremony proper to the occasion, *Ham.*, 4.v; *formal constancy*, the self-possession the part requires before the public (as contrasted with their private feelings), *Jul. Caes.*, 2.i.

Former, foremost, *Jul. Caes.*, 5.i.

Forsake, renounce, *Timon*, 3.vi; refuse, *Oth.*, 4.ii.

Forsooth, in truth, *Titus*, 4.iv; *Lear*, 1.iv; used ironically in *Troil. & Cres.*, 1.iii; *Oth.*, 1.i.

Forswear, to swear to renounce; so *comfort forswear me*, *Oth.*, 4.ii; *forsworn to grant*, denied on oath that I would grant, *Cor.*, 5.iii; *forsworn to love*, *Rom. & Jul.*, 1.i; abandon, *Timon*, 4.iii; *Rom. & Jul.*, 1.v.

Forth, *forth on*, forward without impediment, *Timon*, 1.i; henceforward, *Jul. Caes.*, 4.iii; in the field, on service from home, *Cor.*, 1.iii; out, *Titus*, 5.iii; *did make my way long forth*, my excursion seem long, *Cym.*, 4.ii; elsewhere, at sea, *Ant. & Cleo.*, 4.xi.

Forthright, *the direct forthright*, the straight path ahead, *Troil. & Cres.*, 3.iii.

Fortitude, strength (offensive or defensive), *Oth.*, 1.iii.

Fortune, the goddess, with her wheel, *Ant. & Cleo.*, 4.xv; called *strumpet* because she gives her favours to men capriciously and deserts them shamelessly, *Ham.*, 2.ii; her indifference to merit portrayed by the Poet, *Timon*, 1.i; *daily fortune*, continual success, *Cor.*, 4.vii; *to prey at fortune*, at random, at whatever chance offers, *Oth.*, 3.iii; success, *Lear*, 5.iii; *fortunes*, chances, *Cor.*, 4.v; possessions, *Oth.*, 5.ii; *verb*, arrange someone's future career, *Ant. & Cleo.*, 1.ii.

Forward, ready, willing, *Ham.*, 3.i; zealous, *Titus*, 1.i; stirring, early at the task, *Cym.*, 3.v.

Fosset-seller, seller of taps for wine-casks, *Cor.*, 2.i.

Foster, feed, *Titus*, 2.iii; *Cym.*, 2.iii.

Foul, ugly, ill-favoured, *Oth.*, 2.i; *Ant. & Cleo.*, 1.ii; stormy, *Oth.*, 2.i; *foulest wares*, of poorest quality, *Troil. & Cres.*, 1.iii; wicked, *Ham.*, 1.i; *verb*, soil, *Ham.*, 2.i.

Foulness, wickedness, *Lear*, 1.i.

Found, build on, *Oth.*, 3.iv; *founded*, firmly established, *Mac.*, 3.iv.

Foundations, plays on the meanings: a place like a town fixed on its foundations, and a charitable establishment, *Cym.*, 3.vi.

Foxship, cunning and ingratitude, *Cor.*, 4.ii.

Fracted, broken, *Timon*, 2.i.

Fraction, breach of friendship, *Troil. & Cres.*, 2.iii; *fractions*, broken pieces, *Troil. & Cres.*, 5.ii; casual remarks, *Timon*, 2.ii.

Fragment, odd pittance, *Timon*, 4.iii; *a fragment of Cneius Pompey's*, what is left after his enjoyment of her, *Ant. & Cleo.*, 3.xiii; *fragments*, applied contemptuously to the plebeians, *Cor.*, 1.i; *Troil. & Cres.*, 5.i; *fragments in hard voyages*, at first despised, then of consequence, *Cym.*, 5.iii.

Frame, wooden erection, *Ham.*, 5.i; type, *Timon*, 1.i; *into some frame*, into some order or relevance, *Ham.*, 3.ii; *frame of things*, the ordered structure of the universe, *Mac.*, 3.ii; *frame of nature*, the fabric of my being, *Lear*, 1.iv; *verb*, arrange, *Cor.*, 5.iii; fashion, *Timon*, 5.i; perform, *Ant. & Cleo.*, 2.ii; *thither frame*, direct their steps there, *Per.*, 1.*Prol.*

FRANCHISE, liberties, rights, *Cor.*, 4.vi; *whose repair and franchise* (of laws), renewal and free use, *Cym.*, 3.i; *franchis'd*, free to do the right, *Mac.*, 2.i.

FRANK, free, generous, *Cor.*, 3.i; *Lear*, 3.iv; honest, willing, *Rom. & Jul.*, 2.ii; honest, free, *Oth.*, 3.iv.

FRANKLIN, a freeholder, but not of aristocratic family, *Cym.*, 3.ii.

FRANKLY, without restraint or reservation, *Oth.*, 2.iii; *Troil. & Cres.*, 5.viii; freely, *Timon*, 2.ii; fully and freely, *Ham.*, 3.i; fairly, *Ham.*, 5.ii.

FRAUGHT, *noun*, burden, *Oth.*, 3.iii; *verb*, burden, *Cym.*, 1.i; stored, *Lear*, 1.iv; loaded, *Troil. & Cres.*, 1.*Prol.*; *fraughtage*, cargo, *Troil. & Cres.*, 1.*Prol.*

FRAY, to fright, *Troil. & Cres.*, 3.ii.

FREE, honourable, *Troil. & Cres.*, 1.iii; *Oth.*, 3.iii; guiltless, *Ham.*, 2.ii; innocent, *Oth.*, 3.iii; cheerful, *Lear*, 4.vi; *Oth.*, 3.ii; *with his free duty*, devoted in service, *Oth.*, 1.iii; *free awe*, awe not due to present subjection but to the memory of past defeat, *Ham.*, 4.iii; *verb*, exonerate, *Cor.*, 4.vii; banish, *Mac.*, 3.vi; remove, *Cym.*, 3.vi.

FREEDOMS, rights, *Cor.*, 2.i.

FREE-HEARTED, generous, *Timon*, 3.i.

FREELY, readily, *Mac.*, 1.vii; in freedom, *Ant. & Cleo.*, 4.vi.

FREENESS, generosity, *Cym.*, 5.v.

FRESH, refreshing, *Cym.*, 5.iii; *fresh-new*, inexperienced, *Per.*, 3.i.

FRET, (1) two meanings, the stops on the finger-board of a guitar and the action of annoying someone, are played on in *Ham.*, 3.ii; (2) to chequer, *Jul. Caes.*, 2.i; decorate a roof with variegated patterns and colours, *Ham.*, 2.ii; *fretted fortune*, combines both meanings, chequered and decayed, *Ant. & Cleo.*, 4.xii.

FRIEND, paramour, *Oth.*, 4.i; *though I profess myself her adorer, not her friend*, speaking not merely as her lover (who might exaggerate) but her adorer, *Cym.*, 1.iv; *verb*, assist, *Cym.*, 2.iii.

FRIENDSHIP, good service, *Timon*, 4.iii; *Lear*, 3.ii.

FRIEZE, coarse woollen cloth, *Oth.*, 2.i.

FROM, *from the present*, beside the matter at issue, *Ant. & Cleo.*, 2.vi.

FRONT, forehead, forelock, *Oth.*, 3.i; *Ant. & Cleo.*, 1.i; line of battle; *smiling fronts*, victorious ranks and the further idea of smiling faces, *Cor.*, 1.vi; *front of war*, front rank, *Ant. & Cleo.*, *verb*, stand in front of, *Troil. & Cres.*, 4.v; face, oppose, *Cor.*, 5.ii; *Ant. & Cleo.*, 2.ii.

FRONTIER, fortress or town on frontier, *Ham.*, 4.iv.

FRONTLET, a band round forehead, and so used of frown in *Lear*, 1.iv.

FROSTY, *frosty signs*, grey hairs, *Titus*, 5.iii.

FRUIT, dessert, *Ham.*, 2.ii; offspring, *Titus*, 5.i; consequence, *Oth.*, 5.i.

FRUITFUL, abundant, *Timon*, 5.i; teeming, *Ham.*, 1.ii; *fruitful as the free elements*, a generosity like the elements at the disposal of all, *Oth.*, 2.iii; *fruitful prognostication*, sign of fertility, *Ant. & Cleo.*, 1.ii; *fruitfully*, abundantly, *Lear*, 4.vi.

FRUSH, to batter, *Troil. & Cres.*, 5.vi.

FRUSTRATE, ineffectual, *Ant. & Cleo.*, 5.i.

FULFILL, carry out, *Ham.*, 5.ii; *fulfilling bolts*, adequately, fitting the corresponding parts, *Troil. & Cres.*, 1.*Prol.*

FULL, complete, *Oth.*, 2.i; *full voice*, unanimously, *Cor.*, 3.iii; *fullest man*, exceeding others in qualities of man, *Ant. & Cleo.*, 3.xiii; *adv.*, often for emphasis.

FULL-ACORN'D, full of acorns, *Cym.*, 2.v.

FULL-FLOWING, *full-flowing stomach*, the full tide of anger, *Lear*, 5.iii.

FULNESS, prosperity, wealth, *Cym.*, 3.vi.

FULSOME, disgusting, *Oth.*, 4.i.

FUMING, fuddled with wine, *Ant. & Cleo.*, 2.i.

FUNCTION, the operation of the mind, *Mac.*, 1.iii; power of body and mind, *Oth.*, 2.iii.

FUNERAL, proper burial, *Titus*, 1.i; obsequies, *Jul. Caes.*, 5.iii.

FURNACE, *verb*, give off as a furnace does, *Cym.*, 1.vi.

FURNISH, dress, *Rom. & Jul.*, 4.ii; supply, *Ham.*, 1.ii; *Ant. & Cleo.*, 1.iv.

FURNISHINGS, what shows outward, *Lear*, 3.i.

FURTHER, *no further*, no more concern, *Cor.*, 2.iii; *Cor.*, 3.iii; *hark further*, listen longer, *Ant. & Cleo.*, 4.ix; *adj.*, *at further space*, some time later, *Lear.*, 5.iii; *verb*, help forward, *Ant. & Cleo.*, 2.ii; *furtherance*, help, *Per.*, 2.i.

FURY, one of the three goddesses of vengeance, *Titus*, 5.ii; *Ant. & Cleo.*, 2.v; *prophetic fury*, inspired rapture, *Oth.*, 3.iv.

FUST, grow musty, *Ham.*, 4.iv; *fusty*, mouldy, *Troil. & Cres.*, 2.i.

FUSTIAN, rubbish (fustian being a coarse cloth), *Oth.*, 2.iii.

GAD, sharp-pointed iron or steel instrument, *Titus*, 4.i; *upon the gad*, on the spur of the moment, *Lear*, 1.ii.

GAGE, to stake, pledge, *Ham.*, 1.i; *gaging me to keep an oath*, holding me pledged to, *Troil. & Cres.*, 5.i.

GAIN, acquire, *Per.*, 4.*Prol; gain the cap*, obtain the respectful salutation, *Cym.*, 3.iii; restore, *Cym.*, 4.ii; *gains or loses your sword or mine*, the result of one or other proving victor in the duel, *Cym.*, 2.iv.

GAIN-GIVING, misgiving, *Ham.*, 5.ii.

GAINSAY, forbid, *Troil. & Cres.*, 4.v.

'GAINST, *ever 'gainst that season comes*, always just before that time, *Ham.*, 1.i.

GAIT, *stay not here thy gait*, walk on, *Timon*, 5.iv; progress, proceedings, *Ham.*, 1.ii; *go your gait*, go your own way, *Lear*, 4.vi; *what majesty is in her gait?* her deportment generally, *Ant. & Cleo.*, 3.iii.

GALEN, court-physician to Marcus Aurelius, second century A.D.; his writings cover wide field of medicine and were authoritative in Shakespeare's day, *Cor.*, 2.i (here the reference is anachronistic).

GALL, *noun, they have galls*, they have courage (gall providing, it was thought, the power of resentment, anger, or offensive action), *Troil. & Cres.*, 1.iii; *Oth.*, 4.iii; *pigeon-liver'd and lack gall*, the pigeon being supposed to secrete no gall, so lacking in spirit to resent wrong, *Ham.*, 2.ii; *verb*, wound, *Titus*, 4.iii; *Ham.*, 4.vii; *galled jade*, horse whose skin is rubbed into sore spot, *Ham.*, 3.ii; *galls his kibe*, hurts by treading on sore on his heel, *Ham.*, 5.i; *galled eyes*, inflamed by tears, *Ham.*, 1.ii; *galling*, injuring by friction, *Per.*, 4.i.

GALLANTRY, the chivalry, the chief warriors, *Troil. & Cres.*, 3.i.

GALLIA, France, *Cym.*, 1.vi; *Gallian*, French, *Cym.*, 1.vi.

GALLOW, terrify, *Lear*, 3.ii.

GALLOWGLASSES, heavy-armed footmen from Ireland or isles of Scotland, *Mac.*, 1.ii.

GAME, amorous play, *Oth.*, 2.iii; *daughters of the game*, lascivious wenches, *Troil. & Cres.*, 4.v.

GAMESTER, prostitute, *Per.*, 4.vi.

GAN, began.

GAPE, desire strongly, *Rom. & Jul.*, 2. *Chor.;* threaten, *Ham.*, 1.ii.

GARB, manner (not dress), *Ham.*, 2.ii; *the same austerity and garb*, with the same severe style, *Cor.*, 4.vii; *doth affect a saucy roughness, and constrains the garb quite from his nature*, pretending to be blunt he is merely impertinent, so distorting the real nature of the manner he assumes, *Lear*, 2.ii; *abuse him in the rank garb*, slander him in a vile way, *Oth.*, 2.i.

GARBOILS, disturbances, troubles, *Ant. & Cleo.*, 1.iii.

GARLAND, the prize of victory, *Cor.*, 2.ii; *him that was your garland*, whom you regarded as worthy of favour, *Cor.*, 1.i; *the garland of the war*, the first of soldiers, *Ant. & Cleo.*, 4.xv.

GASTED, frightened, *Lear*, 2.i.

GASTNESS, look of fear, *Oth.*, 5.i.

GATHER, infer from information available, *Ham.*, 2.ii; *you may gather more*, form a conclusion from the hints given, *Lear*, 4.v.

GAUDY, festive, *Ant. & Cleo.*, 3.xiii.

GAWD, (1) toy, bauble, *Troil. & Cres.*, 3.iii; (2) *nicely gawded cheeks*, delicate complexions, *Cor.*, 2.i.

GEAR, appliance, *Rom. & Jul.*, 5.i; *Troil. & Cres.*, 3.ii; business, affair, *Troil. & Cres.*, 1.i; *Rom. & Jul.*, 2.iv.

GECK, gull, fool, *Cym.*, 5.iv.

GENDER, sort, race, kind, *Oth.*, 1.iii; *the general gender*, the ordinary man, *Ham.*, 4.vii; *verb*, beget, *Oth.*, 4.ii.

GENERAL, concerning all; *in general name*, the challenge being not to any individual but open to all, *Troil. & Cres.*, 1.iii; *my general and exceptless rashness*, applying to all without exception, *Timon*, 4.iii; *the general sex*, women considered collectively, *Troil. & Cres.*, 5.ii; *the general ear*, the public ear, *Ham.*, 2.ii; *noun, the horse in general*, the whole of the cavalry, *Jul. Caes.*, 4.ii; *the general*, the whole body, *Troil. & Cres.*, 1.iii; *Ham.*, 2.ii; *severals and generals of grace exact*, the precise qualities belonging to individuals and to the whole, *Troil. & Cres.*, 1.iii; *general warranty*, the permission given to all, *Oth.*, 5.ii; *the general dependants*, the servants as a body, *Lear*, 1.iv; *the general camp*, the whole camp, *Oth.*, 3.iii; *general graces*, all-over merit, *Ant. & Cleo.*, 2.ii; *general services*, engagements in which armies take part, *Cym.*, 4.i; *noun, most wise in general*, in all respects, *Per.*, 5.i.

GENERALLY, without exception, universally, *Timon*, 2.ii.

GENERATION, procreation, *Troil. & Cres.*, 3.i; *a generation of vipers*, offspring of, *Troil. & Cres.*, 3.i; breed, *Timon*, 1.i; *makes his generation messes*, eats his offspring, *Lear*, 1.i.

GENEROSITY, those of noble birth, *Cor.*, 1.i.

GENEROUS, with the instincts of a gentleman, man of good birth, *Ham.*, 1.iii; *the generous islanders*, men of rank in the island, *Oth.*, 3.iii.

GENIUS, guardian spirit, controlling the lower powers, so the higher or reasoning part of man's nature, *Jul. Caes.*, 2.1; *Mac.*, 3.i.

GENNET, horse of Spanish breed, *Oth.*, 1.i.

GENTLE, well-born, *Cym.*, 4.ii; *of a gentle kind*, of a good family, *Per.*, 5.i; *gentle senses*, the senses gratified and so made gentle by the atmosphere, *Mac.*, 1.vi.

GENTLENESS, courteous service, *Titus*, 1.i.

GENTRY, good birth, men of rank, *Cor.*, 3.i; etc.; courtesy, *Ham.*, 2.ii.

GERMAN, GERMANE, akin, *Timon*, 4.iii; relevant, *Ham.*, 5.ii; *germans*, close kin, *Oth.*, 1.i.

GERMENS, seeds of life, *Mac.*, 4.i; *Oth.*, 1.i.

GESTS, deeds, achievements, *Ant. & Cleo.*, 4.iii.

GET, make money, *Per.*, 4.ii.

GHASTLY, pale as ghosts with fear, *Jul. Caes.*, 1.iii.

GHOST, corpse, *Ham.*, 1.iv; *verb*, haunt, *Ant. & Cleo.*, 2.vi.

GHOSTLY, spiritual, *Rom. & Jul.*, 2.ii.

GIB, tom-cat, *Ham.*, 3.iv.

GIGLOT, strumpet, *Cym.*, 3.i.

GILD, make like gold, *Ant. & Cleo.*, 1.v; smear (with 'golden' blood, and with reference to guilt), *Mac.*, 2.ii; *Offence's gilded hand*, with gold as bribe (as well perhaps with blood), *Ham.*, 3.iii.

GILT, *in thy gilt*, prosperity and show, *Timon*, 4.iii.

GIN, begin.

GIPSY, *Cleopatra, a gipsy*, as gipsies were thought to come from Egypt, *Rom. & Jul.*, 2.iv; Cleopatra is given their dark complexion, *Ant. & Cleo.*, 1.i.

GIRD, to taunt, *Cor.*, 1.i.

GIS, *by Gis*, by Jesus, *Ham.*, 4.v.

GIVE, describe, *Cor.*, 1.ix; represent, report, *Ant. & Cleo.*, 1.iv; *my mind gave me*, I suspected, *Cor.*, 4.v; *give you the minstrel*, call you a common fiddler, *Rom. & Jul.*, 4.v; *Mac.*, 1.iii; yield (to tears), *Timon*, 4.iii.

GIVING OUT, assertion, *Ham.*, 1.v; report, *Oth.*, 4.i.

GLAD, good luck, gladness, *Per.*, 2.*Prol.*

GLASS, *glasses of my sight*, eyes, *Cor.*, 3.ii; magic mirror, *Mac.*, 4.i; *glass-fac'd flatterer*, reflecting another's moods and fortune like a mirror, *Timon*, 1.i; *fair glass of light*, reflection of beauty, *Per.*, 1.i; *glass eyes*, spectacles, *Lear*, 4.vi; *glass-gazing*, vain, *Lear*, 2.ii.

GLAZE, glare, *Jul. Caes.*, 1.iii.

GLEAN, find, infer, *Ham.*, 2.ii.

GLEEK, a jibe, *Rom. & Jul.*, 4.v.

GLOBE, head, *Ham.*, 1.v.

GLORIOUS, *the desire that's glorious*, set on fame or excellence, *Cym.*, 1.vi; *Per.*, 1.*Prol.*

GLOSS, *to set a gloss on*, to hide under a show of goodness, *Timon*, 1.ii.

GLOVE, *throw my glove to Death*, as a challenge, in token of his opinion, *Troil. & Cres.*, 4.iv; *Timon*, 5.iv.

GLOW, flush, *Ant. & Cleo.*, 2.ii; shine, *Ant. & Cleo.*, 1.i.

GLOZE, interpret, expound, *Troil. & Cres.*, 2.ii; cover with fair words her intention, *Titus*, 4.iv; talk beside the point, speciously, *Per.*, 1.i.

GO, used as a rebuke, *Rom. & Jul.*, 1.v; *goes withal*, agrees with, *Ham.*, 1.iii; *go great with*, become pregnant with, *Timon*, 4.iii; *there it goes*, well done! *Titus*, 4.iii; walk, *Lear*, 1.iv; accord, *Lear*, 1.i; *to go even with what I heard*, to give what I heard the weight my own judgement indicated, *Cym.*, 1.iv; *gone through for*, made a bargain for, *Per.*, 4.ii.

GOAL, *get goal for goal of youth*, prove a match for, *Ant. & Cleo.*, 4.viii.

GOATISH, lustful, *Lear*, 1.ii.

GOD, *God ye good den*, God give ye good even, *Rom. & Jul.*, 2.iv; so *God gi' go' den* in *Rom. & Jul.*,

1.ii; and *God-i-goden* in 3.v; *God-den*, *Cor.*, 2.i; *by God's lid*, by God's eyelid, *Troil. & Cres.*, 1.ii; *God 'ield us*, God (yield) repay, reward us, *Mac.*, 1.vi; so *God dild you*, *Ham.*, 4.v; *the gods yield you for't*, repay you, *Ant. & Cleo.*, 4.iii; *verb*, *godded me*, idolized me, *Cor.*, 5.iii.

GOD-A-MERCY, God have mercy, *Ham.*, 4.v; thank you (confused with *gramercy*), *Ham.*, 2.ii.

GODLIKE, divinely, *Per.*, 5.i.

GOLDEN, wealthy, *Timon*, 4.iii; precious, *Troil. & Cres.*, 1.ii; *golden lads and girls*, fortunate and fair, *Cym.*, 4.ii.

GOOD, *were as good*, might as well, *Titus*, 4.iii; *Troil. & Cres.*, 2.i; wealthy, *Cor.*, 1.i; *make good*, hold, defend, *Cor.*, 1.v; fulfill, *Timon*, 1.ii; assert, maintain, *Lear*, 1.i; confirm, *Ant. & Cleo.*, 2.ii; *as good as*, not better than, *Per.*, 4.ii; *the good years shall devour them*, (cf. *Mer. Wives Win.*, 1.iv, where it is used as an exclamation) used here to denote some undefined malefic power, *Lear*, 5.iii.

GOOD-CONCEITED, ingeniously conceived, *Cym.*, 2.iii.

GOODMAN, prefixed to occupation, *goodman delver* in *Ham.*, 5.i; *goodman boy*, used sarcastically, *Rom. & Jul.*, 1.v; expressing contempt, *Lear*, 2.ii.

GOODNESS, success, *Mac.*, 4.iii.

GOOSE, tailor's iron, the handle's shape giving it goose-like form, *Mac.*, 2.iii.

GORGE, what has been swallowed, so *cast the gorge at*, vomit because of, *Timon*, 4.iii; *heave the gorge*, vomit, reject, *Oth.*, 2.i; *my gorge rises*, I sicken, feel disgust, *Ham.*, 5.i; *verb*, feed greedily, *Jul. Caes.*, 5.i; glut, *Lear*, 1.i.

GORGET, armour for the throat, *Troil. & Cres.*, 1.ii.

GORGON, of three fabulous women with snakes for hair; Medusa was the mortal one, her look turning beholders to stone, *Mac.*, 2.iii; *Ant. & Cleo.*, 2.v.

GOSPEL, *so gospell'd*, so Christian as to love your enemy, *Mac.*, 3.i.

GOSSIP, one associated with parents at a baptism; at the feast there would be much talking, so a tattling woman, *Rom. & Jul.*, 3.v; so *a long tongu'd babbling gossip*, *Titus*, 4.ii.

GOUT, *gouts of blood*, heavy drops, *Mac.*, 2.i.

GOVERN, direct, carry through, *Titus*, 5.ii; manipulate, *Ham.*, 3.ii; prevail, *Ant. & Cleo.*, 2.ii.

GOVERNMENT, control, *Rom. & Jul.*, 4.i; discretion, *Oth.*, 3.iii; command, *Oth.*, 4.i.

GRACE, *a Grace*, one of the beautiful daughters of Zeus, *Per.*, 1.i; mercy, *Lear*, 3.ii; blessedness, happiness, *Cym.*, 1.i; *in grace whereof*, in honour of, *Ham.*, 1.ii; so *do grace* in *Ham.*, 2.ii; *do grace to me*, guide me to an act acceptable to heaven, *Ham.*, 1.i; *the powerful grace that lies in flowers*, beneficent power, *Rom. & Jul.*, 2.iii; *grace and rude will*, the selfish and harmful opposed to the unselfish and helpful instincts or properties, *Rom. & Jul.*, 2.iii; virtues, *Mac.*, 4.iii; used in addressing persons of high rank, punningly in *Troil. & Cres.*, 3.i; *verb*, honour and favour, *Cor.*, 5.iii; etc.; *a graced palace*, dignified, honourable, *Lear*, 1.iv.

GRACEFUL, favourable, *Ant. & Cleo.*, 2.ii.

GRACIOUS, regarded with favour, *Titus*, 1.i; *gracious silence*, beautiful, loving beyond words, *Cor.*, 2.i; blest, *Ham.*, 1.i; kind, *Lear*, 4.ii.

GRACIOUSLY, piously, *Titus*, 1.i; virtuously, charitably, *Per.*, 4.vi.

GRADATION, *by the old gradation*, the former system of promotion, *Oth.*, 1.i.

GRAFF, shoot, *Per.*, 5.i.

GRAFTED, rooted, incorporated, *Mac.*, 4.iii; *will not be grafted to your relish*, natures too base to have any conception of nobler ideals, *Cor.*, 2.i.

GRAIN, a fast scarlet dye from cochineal, so any fast dye; *grained spots*, indelible stains, *Ham.*, 3.iv.

GRAMERCY, corruption of Old French *grant merci:* great thanks, *Timon*, 2.ii.

GRAND, principal, chief, *Ant. & Cleo.*, 3.i; *grand sea*, ocean, *Ant. & Cleo.*, 3.xii.

GRANGE, house in the country, so isolated, *Oth.*, 1.i.

GRANT, allow, *Ant. & Cleo.*, 3.i; *a fool granted*, an allowed fool, *Cym.*, 2.i.

GRASP, embraces, *Troil. & Cres.*, 4.ii.

GRATE, wear away, *Troil. & Cres.*, 3.ii; disturb, fret, *Ham.*, 3.i; annoy, *Ant. & Cleo.*, 1.i. [etc.

GRATIFY, reward, requite, *Cor.*, 2.ii;

GRATULATE, greet, *Timon*, 1.ii; welcome with joy, *Titus*, 1.i.

GRAVE, *verb*, bury, *Timon*, 4.iii; *adj.*, deadly, *Ant. & Cleo.*, 4.xii.
GRAVEL, stones in the bladder, *Troil. & Cres.*, 5.i.
GRAYMALKIN, a familiar spirit in the shape of a cat, *Mac.*, 1.i.
GREAT, *great morning*, broad day, *Troil. & Cres.*, 4.iii; *Cym.*, 4.ii; *great with*, pregnant with, *Timon*, 4.iii.
'GREE, agree, *Ant. & Cleo.*, 2.vi.
GREENLY, without judgement, *Ham.*, 4.v.
GREEN SICKNESS, form of anaemia associated with love-lorn girls, *Ant. & Cleo.*, 3.ii; *Per.*, 4.vi.
GREET, meet as friends, *Ant. & Cleo.*, 2.i; gratify, *Per.*, 4.iii; *greet the time*, at once meet the danger of the moment, *Lear*, 5.i.
GRIEF, grievance, *Jul. Caes.*, 1.iii; etc.; pain, *Rom. & Jul.*, 1.i.
GRIEF-SHOT, sorrow-stricken, *Cor.*, 5.i.
GRIEVANCE, cause of grief, *Rom. & Jul.*, 1.i; annoyance, distress, *Oth.*, 1.ii.
GRIEVE, be a grievance, *Per.*, 2.iv; regret, *Lear*, 4.iii.
GRIEVOUSLY, heavily, at a great cost, *Jul. Caes.*, 3.ii; distressfully, *Oth.*, 5.i.
GRIPE, *noun or verb*, grasp; *verb*, seize so as to hurt, so *griping grief*, *Rom. & Jul.*, 4.v.
GRISE, degree, step, *Oth.*, 1.iii; *grise of fortune*, social position, rank, *Timon*, 4.iii.
GRIZZLED, greyish, *Ham.*, 1.ii; *Ant. & Cleo.*, 3.xiii; snowy, *Per.*, 3.*Prol.*
GROSS, large and not to be missed, *Ham.*, 4.iv; *gross and scope of my opinion*, the general drift of my thought, *Ham.*, 1.i; *gross in sense*, obvious to the intelligence, *Oth.*, 1.ii.
GROSSLY, unprepared spiritually, *Ham.*, 3.iii; stupidly, dully, *Oth.*, 3.iii; shamefully, *Ant. & Cleo.*, 3.x; evidently, *Lear*, 1.i.
GROSSNESS, great bulk, *Troil. & Cres.*, 1.iii.
GROUND, motive, cause, *Titus*, 2.i; in music the bass that supports the descant, *Titus*, 2.i; *get ground of*, secure an advantage over, *Cym.*, 1.iv; *grounds*, evidence, *Ham.*, 2.ii.
GROW, *a great way growing on the south*, a good deal farther south, *Jul. Caes.*, 2.i; *policy grows into an ill opinion*, politic management becomes discredited, *Troil. & Cres.*, 5.iv; *nor curstness grow to the matter*, do not allow bad feeling to become incorporated with the business, *Ant. & Cleo.*, 2.ii; *his whole action grows not in the power on't*, his plan doesn't spring from its strength to ensure victory, *Ant. & Cleo.*, 3.vii.
GUARD, *upon my brother's guard*, protected by my brother, *Cor.*, 1.x; *to my guard*, into my custody, *Ant. & Cleo.*, 5.ii; *the guards of th' ever-fired pole*, the two stars of Ursa Minor which protect the pole-star from the Great Bear (Ursa Major), *Oth.*, 2.i.
GUARDAGE, protected condition, *Oth.*, 1.ii.
GUARDANT, *a Jack guardant*, an officious sentinel, *Cor.*, 5.ii.
GUISE, custom, fashion, *Timon*, 4.iii; etc.
GULES, heraldic term for red, *Ham.*, 2.ii.
GULF, gullet, *Mac.*, 4.i.
GULL, unfledged bird (as well as a fool), *Timon*, 2.i.
GUST, outburst, *Timon*, 3.v.
GUTTER'D, channelled by the sea, *Oth.*, 2.i.
GYVE, fetter, entangle, *Oth.*, 2.i; *gyves*, fetters, *Ham.*, 4.vii.

HA, have.
HABIT, dress, deportment, *Timon*, 4.iii; *Ham.*, 3.iv; tendency in conduct or action, *Ham.*, 1.iv; appearance, *Per.*, 2.ii; *these thin habits*, flimsy dressing for your suspicion, *Oth.*, 1.iii; *habited*, dressed, *Titus*, 2.iii.
HABITMENTS, dress, *Ant. & Cleo.*, 3.vi.
HAGGARD, wild hawk, so applied to unchaste woman, *Oth.*, 3.iii.
HAIR, *merry against the hair*, contrary to the disposition of things, *Troil. & Cres.*, 1.ii; *the courser's hair*, horsehair placed in water was supposed to become an eel, *Ant. & Cleo.*, 1.ii.
HALCYON, kingfisher; *turn their halcyon beaks with every gale*, a dead kingfisher when hung up was supposed to act as a weather-cock, *Lear*, 2.ii.
HALF-BLOODED, bastard, of good blood on only one side, *Lear*, 5.iii.
HALF-CAPS, distant, uncordial salutations, *Timon*, 2.ii.
HALL, *a hall!* call to clear the floor for dancing, *Rom. & Jul.*, 1.v.
HALT, *the blank verse shall halt for't*, the regularity of the verse must give way, its feet must suffer derangement, *Ham.*, 2.ii; *no further*

halting, hesitation, paltering, *Cym.*, 3.v.

HAM, knee, *Ham.*, 2.ii; crook of the knee, *Per.*, 4.ii.

HAND, *hot at hand*, at the start, *Jul. Caes.*, 4.ii; *out of hand*, at once, extempore, *Titus*, 5.ii; *borne in hand*, deceived by apparent good-will, *Mac.*, 3.i; *Ham.*, 2.ii; *made fair hands*, made a pretty mess of the business, *Cor.*, 4.vi; *that will to hand*, that will be put in action, *Mac.*, 3.iv; *whom she bore in hand to love*, merely professed to love, *Cym.*, 5.v; *done unto thy hand*, already done, *Ant. & Cleo.*, 4.xiv; *on whom plenty held full hand*, where plenty reigned, *Per.*, 1.iv.

HAND-FAST, marriage-bond, *Cym.*, 1.v.

HAND-IN-HAND, *a kind of hand-in-hand comparison*, the objects compared being treated as equal, *Cym.*, 1.iv.

HANDSAW, hernshaw, heron (there are other explanations), *Ham.*, 2.ii.

HANDSOME, *more handsome than fine*, splendid in general conception and not contrived by laborious accumulation of parts, *Ham.*, 2.ii.

HANDY-DANDY, which hand will you take?—formula in choosing-game, *Lear*, 4.vi.

HANGER, straps holding the scabbard to the belt, *Ham.*, 5.ii.

HANGINGS, the fruit, the honours already mentioned, *Cym.*, 3.iii.

HAP, *dear hap*, good fortune, *Rom. & Jul.*, 2.ii; *howe'er my haps*, in whatever a way my fortunes go, *Ham.*, 4.iii.

HAPLY, HAPPILY, perhaps; *thy country's fate, which happily foreknowing may avoid*, dangers which perhaps the ghost's revelation might enable them to nullify, *Ham.*, 1.i; *haply amplified*, perhaps exaggerated, *Cor.*, 5.ii; *happily repent*, perhaps rue her bargain, *Oth.*, 3.iii.

HAPPINESS, *a happiness*, a fitness, propriety, *Ham.*, 2.ii; used as a greeting at parting, *Cym.*, 3.v.

HAPPY, successful, fortunate, *Cor.*, 4.vii; *Lear*, 4.vi; *not so happy, yet much happier*, not so fortunate, but more blest, *Mac.*, 1.iii; *in happy time*, most opportunely, *Ham.*, 5.ii; *happy verse*, felicitous, *Timon*, 1.i; favourable, convenient, *Lear*, 2.iii; gifted, accomplished, *Cym.*, 3.iv.

HARBINGER, an officer who went ahead to arrange accommodation for king, *Mac.*, 1.iv; forerunner, *Ham.*, 1.i.

HARBOUR, lodging, *Timon*, 5.iv.

HARD, hardened, confirmed, *Timon*, 4.iii; *Ant. & Cleo.*, 3.xiii; *hard point*, critical situation, *Cym.*, 3.iv; *bears me hard*, regards me with dislike, *Jul. Caes.*, 1.ii; *and't shall go hard but*, it's as good as certain, *Ham.*, 3.iv; *adv.*, *hard upon*, immediately after, *Ham.*, 1.ii; *hard at hand*, almost immediately, *Oth.*, 2.i; *full hard forbear him*, with great difficulty refrain from attacking him, *Oth.*, 1.ii.

HARDIMENT, bold action, *Troil. & Cres.*, 4.v; brave service, *Cym.*, 5.iv.

HARDINESS, courage, *Cym.*, 3.vi.

HARDLY, with difficulty, *Cor.*, 5.ii; etc.; unfeelingly, *Cym.*, 3.iii.

HARDNESS, *so from sense in hardness*, so difficult to make sense of, *Cym.*, 5.v; hardship, *Oth.*, 1.iii; *Cym.*, 3.vi.

HARDOCKS, some variety of dock-weed, *Lear*, 4.iv.

HARLOT, of men as of women, unprincipled, *Cor.*, 3.ii; baggage, *Rom. & Jul.*, 4.ii.

HARLOTRY, harlot, *Oth.*, 4.iii.

HARMONY, music, *Ham.*, 3.ii; *Per.*, 5.i.

HARNESS, armour, *Troil. & Cres.*, 5.iii; *through proof of harness*, through the armour's proved strength, *Ant. & Cleo.*, 4.viii; *harness'd*, armed, *Troil. & Cres.*, 1.ii.

HARP, keep coming over, *Ant. & Cleo.*, 3.xiii; *Ham.*, 2.ii; *harp'd my fear aright*, struck the very note of my fear, *Mac.*, 4.i.

HARPY, fabulous vulture with face and breasts of a woman, *Per.*, 4.iii.

HARROW, devastate, *Cor.*, 5.iii; afflict, *Ham.*, 1.i.

HARSH, rough, *Troil. & Cres.*, 1.i; *harshly*, violently, *Ham.*, 3.i.

HASTE, *take his haste*, hasten, *Timon*, 5.i; *haste me to know't*, tell me of it quickly, *Ham.*, 1.v; *put it to the haste*, do it quickly, *Ant. & Cleo.*, 5.ii.

HATCH, (1) half-door, *Lear*, 3.vi; *hatched*, closed, *Per.*, 4.ii; (2) *hatch'd in silver*, grey-haired, *Troil. & Cres.*, 1.iii.

HATCHMENT, tablet displaying coat of arms of deceased, *Ham.*, 4.v.

HATE, object of hate, *Cor.*, 1.i.

HATEFUL, full of hate, *Troil. & Cres.*, 4.i.

HAUNT, *out of haunt*, away from society, *Ham.*, 4.i; *all the haunt be ours,* the throng will follow us, *Ant. & Cleo.*, 4.xiv.

HAVE, *have after,* let us follow, *Ham.*, 1.iv; *have at you,* I attack you, *Rom. & Jul.*, 4.v; *have with you,* lead the way, *Cor.*, 2.i; *Oth.*, 1.ii; *have at it,* I shall begin, *Cym.*, 5.v.

HAVING, possession material or spiritual, *Troil. & Cres.*, 3.iii; *Per.*, 2.i; material assets, *Timon,* 2.ii; allowance, *Oth.*, 4.iii.

HAVIOUR, conduct, *Rom. & Jul.*, 2.ii; appearance, *Ham.*, 1.ii; bearing, *Cym.*, 3.iv.

HAVOC, order for general slaughter, *Jul. Caes.*, 3.i; *cries on havoc* (*Ham.*, 5.ii), *see* QUARRY.

HAWK'D AT, attacked as by a hawk, *Mac.*, 2.iv.

HAY, *the hay* (from *habet* = he has it), a hit in fencing, *Rom. & Jul.*, 2.iv.

HAZARD, *put in hazard,* risked, *Cor.*, 2.iii; *hazard such a place with one of,* take a chance about the efficiency of the appointment in selecting such a man. *Oth.*, 2.iii; *the circle of the Ptolemies now hazarded to thy grace,* the disposal of the crown of Egypt lost by us to you in the chance of war depends on your favour and generosity, *Ant. & Cleo.*, 3.xii.

HE, *death to any he,* person, *Rom. & Jul.*, 5.i; *he as he,* the one as the other, *Troil. & Cres.*, 4.i.

HEAD, *in a riotous head,* along with a turbulent mob, *Ham.*, 4.v; *made a head for,* brought an army against, *Cor.*, 2.ii; *make head,* collect an army, *Jul. Caes.*, 4.i; source, fountainhead, *Ham.*, 1.i; *drawn to head,* mobilized, *Cym.*, 3.v; *the very head and front of my offending hath this extent,* bring together and set out all the ways I have offended and the total will come to no more than this, *Oth.*, 1.iii; *heave to head,* to eat, *Cym.*, 5.v.

HEALTH, personal safety, *Jul. Caes.*, 4.iii; public safety, *Timon,* 2.ii; *spirit of health,* a good spirit, *Ham.*, 1.iv; well-being, *Titus,* 4.iv; in drinking, a toast, *Ham.*, 1.ii.

HEAR, *we'll hear ourselves again,* talk together again, *Mac.*, 3.iv; *he hears no music,* no music in himself, no delight in that elsewhere, *Jul. Caes.*, 1.ii; *I heard no letter from my master,* received no word, *Cym.*, 4.iii; *hear these tears,* be moved by such miseries, *Per.*, 1.iv.

HEARSED, buried, *Ham.*, 1.iv.

HEART, for emphasis, as *heart of heart* in *Ham.*, 3.ii; *from heart of very heart* in *Troil. & Cres.*, 4.v; *the very heart of loss,* beyond all hope of recovery, *Ant. & Cleo.*, 4.xii.

HEART-BLOOD, *heart-blood of beauty,* beauty in its finest state (the servant's fun), *Troil. & Cres.*, 3.i.

HEARTED, planted deep in my heart, *Oth.*, 1.iii; *hearted throne,* throne in the heart, *Oth.*, 3.iii.

HEARTLESS, *heartless hinds,* spiritless menials, *Rom. & Jul.*, 1.i.

HEART'S EASE, a popular Elizabethan tune, *Rom. & Jul.*, 4.v.

HEART-STRUCK, inflicted on the heart, *Lear,* 3.i.

HEARTY, kind-hearted, *Ant. & Cleo.*, 4.ii.

HEAT, *i' th' heat,* immediately, *Lear,* 1.i; *business of some heat,* urgent matter, *Oth.*, 1.ii; *verb, heat my blood,* anger me, *Ant. & Cleo.*, 1.iii; *heated visage,* with indignation, *Ham.*, 3.iv.

HEAVE, *heaving spleens,* pugnacious promptings, *Troil. & Cres.*, 2.ii; *heave the gorge,* sicken with disgust, *Oth.*, 2.i.

HEAVILY, depressingly, *Ham.*, 2.ii.

HEAVINESS, oppression, *Cym.*, 5.ii.

HEAVY, *goes heavy with him,* sudden death having prevented confession of his sins, *Ham.*, 3.iii; heinous, *Ham.*, 4.i; *discourse is heavy, fasting,* talk is tedious and irksome to the hungry man, *Cym.*, 3.vi; *heavy terms,* abusive names, *Oth.*, 4.ii; *heavy causes,* just and good reason, *Lear,* 5.i; *heavy ignorance aloft to fly,* dullness, stupidity, *Oth.*, 2.i; dark, *Oth.*, 5.i.

HEAVY-HEADED, drunken, *Ham.*, 1.iv.

HEBONA, the Folio reads *hebenon,* by some taken for henbane or for yew; *hebona* is supposed to refer to ebony and its sap regarded as the poison referred to, *Ham.*, 1.v.

HECATE, divinity of classical antiquity, associated with ghost world and later with witches, *Mac.*, 2.i; etc.

HECTIC, consumptive fever, *Ham.*, 4.iii.

HEDGE, *hedge aside,* off the main road, *Troil. & Cres.*, 3.iii; *hedge us out,* divert us, to put us off, *Troil. & Cres.*, 3.i.

HEDGE-PIG, hedgehog, *Mac.*, 4.i.

HEEL, dance, *Troil. & Cres.*, 4.iv; *out at heels,* depressed, out of luck, *Lear,* 2.ii.

HEIGHT, dignity, *Titus*, 4.ii; *perform'd at height*, in an outstanding manner, *Ham.*, 1.iv; *the fight in height*, at its most critical phase, *Ant. & Cleo.*, 3.x.

HEIGHTEN, raise to authority, *Cor.*, 5.vi.

HELL-HATED, as hateful as hell, *Lear*, [5.iii.

HELP, *at help*, favourable, *Ham.*, 4.iii; *helps*, assistants, *Cor.*, 2.i; helpers, *Per.*, 1.i; *verb*, cure, *Lear*, 4.iv; *the thing that helps it*, the paint (compared with which the skin beneath is ugly), *Ham.*, 3.i; *be holp*, be cured, *Rom. & Jul.*, 1.ii.

HENCE, from the present time, *Jul. Caes.*, 2.i; *here and hence*, in this world and the next, *Ham.*, 3.ii; *messengers from hence*, messengers to go from this place, *Lear*, 2.i.

HENT, sometimes taken to mean 'grasp'; but in *Oth.*, 1.iii *hent* (Q_1) means 'occasion' or 'opportunity'; *Ham.*, 3.iii.

HER, represents at times old form of 'their'; as *the wars must make examples out of her best*, *Oth.*, 3.iii.

HERALD, an officer concerned with the ceremonies proper to chivalry, intercourse between belligerents, order of precedence, armorial bearings, conduct of funerals, proclamations, etc.; so of Mercury the messenger of the gods, *Ham.*, 3.iv; messenger, *Jul. Caes.*, 1.iii; *verb*, usher, *Mac.*, 1.iii; *Per.*, 3.i.

HERALDRY, the code administered by the heralds, especially concerning the right to armorial bearings, formalities of individual combat, state ceremonies, *Ham.*, 1.i and 2.ii; *our new heraldry*, our new code (here of conduct), *Oth.*, 3.iv.

HERB OF GRACE, rue, associated with repentance, *Ham.*, 4.v.

HERE, at this point, *Cor.*, 3.ii; in this world, *Rom. & Jul.*, 3.v; *Mac.*, 1.vii; (used as noun) *thou losest here*, the life you lead here, this particular set, *Lear*, 1.i.

HERE-APPROACH, arrival, *Mac.*, 4.iii.

HEREDITARY, what comes to them in due season, *Timon*, 2.ii.

HERMIT, beadsman, remembering in prayer the merits of the donor, *Mac.*, 1.vi; *Titus*, 3.ii.

HEROD, presented in the mystery plays as a ranting tyrant; *out-herods Herod*, goes beyond in absurdity the old ranting style, *Ham.*, 3.ii; *Herod of Jewry*, the suggestion here is that even such a tyrant (his character in the miracle plays) couldn't face Cleopatra in her rage, *Ant. & Cleo.*, 3.iii.

HESPERIDES, three nymphs who with an unsleeping dragon guarded the golden apples in their far western garden; used of the daughter of Antiochus to indicate the danger attending her wooing, *Per.*, 1.i.

HEW, *hew to't*, achieve it, *Timon*, 5.iv.

HEWGH, imitate the sound of an arrow, *Lear*, 4.vi.

HEYDAY, ardour, *Ham.*, 3.iv; *heyday*, see HOY-DAY.

HIDE, protect, *Cym.*, 4.ii; *hide thee from prevention*, protect you from detection, *Jul. Caes.*, 2.i; *hide fox*, from game of hide-and-seek, *Ham.*, 4.ii; *till the cup be hid*, brimming, *Ant. & Cleo.*, 2.vii.

HIDEOUS, revolting, *Lear*, 1.i.

HIE, hasten, *Cor.*, 1.ii.

HIGH, above the ordinary, *Troil. & Cres.*, 1.iii; *high supper-time*, more than time for supper, *Oth.*, 4.ii; *high order*, special arrangements, *Ant. & Cleo.*, 5.ii; *high-battled*, in high command, *Ant. & Cleo.*, 3.xiii; *high-engender'd*, begun in the heavens, *Lear*, 3.ii; *high-judging*, judging in heaven, supreme judge, *Lear*, 2.iv; *high-lone*, all by herself, *Rom. & Jul.*, 1.iii; *high-sighted*, looking down from despotic height, *Jul. Caes.*, 2.i; *high-vic'd*, wickedness ascending to heaven, *Timon*, 4.iii.

HIGHT, called, named, *Per.*, 4.*Prol.*

HILDING, baggage, *Rom. & Jul.*, 2.iv; menial, *Cym.*, 2.iii.

HIND, female deer, *Jul. Caes.*, 1.iii; menial, *Rom. & Jul.*, 1.i; the most ordinary man, *Cym.*, 5.iii.

HINT, occasion, *Cor.*, 3.iii; *it was my hint to speak*, I had occasion to relate, *Oth.*, 1.iii; *upon this hint I spake* (*hint* does not mean as today 'suggestion'; Othello is not informing the senate that Desdemona made him an overt invitation), I took advantage of this opportunity, *Oth.*, 1.iii; *when the best hint was given him*, when the occasion was most favourable, *Ant. & Cleo.*, 3.iv.

HIP, fruit of dog-rose, *Timon*, 4.iii; *on the hip*, at a disadvantage (term from wrestling), *Oth.*, 2.i.

HIS, its; *Mars his gauntlet*, for Mars's, *Troil. & Cres.*, 4.v.

HISTORY, type of play, *Ham.*, 2.ii; story, *Oth.*, 1.iii; account, *Cym.*, 3.v; *Lear*, 1.i.

HIT, *hit your thoughts*, coincide with, *Mac.*, 3.vi; *hits right*, proves a happy coincidence, *Timon*, 3.i; *let's hit together*, agree to act together, *Lear*, 1.i.

HOAR, grey, *Ham.*, 4.vii; *hoar leprosy*, white leprosy, *Timon*, 4.iii; mouldy, *Rom. & Jul.*, 2.iv; *verb*, smite with leprosy, *Timon*, 4.iii.

HOBBIDIDENCE, *see* FLIBBERTIGIBBET.

HOBBY-HORSE, 'the figure of a horse' fastened round the waist of a morris dancer; the antics of this particular character in the dance gave offence to the Puritans, and the part fell into disuse, *Ham.*, 3.ii; trull, *Oth.*, 4.i.

HOLD, *hold up Adam's profession*, maintain, *Ham.*, 5.i; endure, *Cor.*, 3.ii; value, *Ham.*, 4.iii and 2.ii; *hold rumour from what we fear*, credit rumour because of our fears, *Mac.*, 4.ii; remain constant, *Jul. Caes.*, 1.ii; *holds idleness your subject*, makes trifling serve you as a subject might, *Ant. & Cleo.*, 1.iii; *I hold it*, I am convinced now as always, *Per.*, 3.ii; *hold there still*, continue to affirm something, *Ant. & Cleo.*, 2.v; *noun*, *take hold of me*, arrest my attention, *Oth.*, 1.iii; fastness, *Cym.*, 3.vi.

HOLD-DOOR, *hold-door trade*, that of pimps and panders, *Troil. & Cres.*, 5.x.

HOLDING, burden of a song, *Ant. & Cleo.*, 2.vii.

HOLIDAM, an oath on holy relics, reduced later to a mere asseveration, *Rom. & Jul.*, 1.iii.

HOLLOWNESS, *reverbs no hollowness*, does not sound as empty vessels do, loud with insincerity, *Lear*, 1.i.

HOLP, *see* HELP.

HOLY-ALES, (suggestion for holy dayes (Q_1), to rhyme with festivales), church-ales or festivals, *Per.*, 1.*Prol.*

HOLY-WATER, *court holy-water*, flattery, specious promises, *Lear*, 3.ii.

HOMAGER, vassal, *Ant. & Cleo.*, 1.i.

HOME, *speak him home*, do justice in words to his merits, *Cor.*, 2.ii; *draw home enough*, draw the bow fully, *Titus*, 4.iii; *charges home*, attempts a fatal thrust, *Lear*, 2.i; *revenged home*, thoroughly repaid, in full measure, *Lear*, 3.iii; *he speaks home*, home truths, bluntly, *Oth.*, 2.i; *take her home*, where she may learn, *Per.*, 4.ii.

HONEST, honourable in thought and act; *general honest thought*, unselfish interest in general good, *Jul. Caes.*, 5.v; chaste, *Timon*, 4.iii; *Oth.*, 3.iii; truthful, *Oth.*, 3.iii.

HONEST-NATURED, used ironically in *Timon*, 5.i.

HONESTY, *honesty to honesty engaged*, mutual faith in our honourable intentions, *Jul. Caes.*, 2.i; decorum, *Ham.*, 2.ii; chastity, *Ham.*, 3.i; *Ant. & Cleo.*, 5.ii; generosity, *Timon*, 3.i; *why should honour outlive honesty?* why should the respect and formal honour man showed me survive my loss of honourable character? *Oth.*, 5.ii; proper in a subordinate, *Oth.*, 4.i.

HONEY-STALKS, clover stalks, *Titus*, 4.iv.

HONOURABLE, dignified, *Oth.*, 4.iii; *an honourable trial*, the trial of its honourable nature, *Ant. & Cleo.*, 1.iii.

HONOURABLY, with becoming ceremony, *Titus*, 4.iv.

HONOURED, *the honour'd number*, the patricians, *Cor.*, 3.i; *more honour'd*, *see* BREACH; *honour'd finger*, that of a gentleman, *Cym.*, 5.v; *an honour'd triumph*, a royal entertainment, *Per.*, 2.ii; honourable, *Ant. & Cleo.*, 4.viii; *Lear*, 5.i.

HOOD, to blindfold a hawk till the game is sighted, *Rom. & Jul.*, 3.ii.

HOODMAN-BLIND, blindman's buff, *Ham.*, 3.iv.

HOODWINK'D, blindfolded, *Rom. & Jul.*, 1.iv; *Cym.*, 5.ii.

HOPE, expectation, *Jul. Caes.*, 3.i; the object of hope (as was Hector's son), *Titus*, 4.i; *the worst, which late on hopes depended*, the misfortune which hitherto could be estimated only by your fears (*hope* being expectation of any kind, even fear), *Oth.*, 1.iii; *verb*, *if I hope well*, if my hopes are realized, *Timon*, 4.iii; expect, suppose, *Ant. & Cleo.*, 2.i.

HOPEFUL, *our hopeful booty*, those we hope to victimize, *Titus*, 2.iii.

HOPELESS, *pawn his fortunes to hopeless restitution*, even if he knew his pledge (his fortunes) was never to be restored to him, *Cor.*, 3.i.

HORN, the horn carried by beggars sounded to attract the charitable and used to hold what was given them to drink, *Lear*, 3.vi; *horns*, of the cuckold, *Troil. & Cres.*, 4.v; *Ant. & Cleo.*, 1.ii; *verb*, to deceive a husband, so *horning*, giving your husband's head horns, (with reference to Actaeon's fate), *Titus*, 2.iii.

HOROLOGE, clock, *Oth.*, 2.iii.
HORRIDLY, horribly, *Ham.*, 1.iv.
HORS'D, mounted, *Cor.*, 2.i.
HORSE-DRENCH, medicine for horses, *Cor.*, 2.i.
HORSEHAIRS, for the fiddle-bow, *Cym.*, 2.iii.
HOSE, doublet and hose were main items in male attire, hose covering the legs, *Cym.*, 3.iv; *French hose*, a tight-fitting sort of breeches, *Mac.*, 2.iii.
HOT, *a hot friend*, devoted, ardent, *Jul. Caes.*, 4.ii; *hot wine*, of good alcoholic strength, *Cor.*, 2.i; impetuous, *Ant. & Cleo.*, 1.iv; *hotly*, urgently, *Oth.*, 1.ii.
HOUSE, *so good a house*, so hospitable, *Timon*, 3.i; *keep his house*, stay at home, *Timon*, 3.iii; *becomes the house*, does credit to a well-governed family, *Lear*, 2.iv; *not to keep house*, not to stay indoors, *Cym.*, 3.iii and 3.vi, where *keep'st thyself* means that he thought it empty.
HOUSEKEEPER, watch-dog, *Mac.*, 3.i; *manifest house-keepers*, notorious stay-at-homes, *Cor.*, 1.iii.
HOW, what price? *Troil. & Cres.*, 4.ii; *Per.*, 4.vi; *how say you by?* what do you think of? *Ham.*, 2.ii; *Oth.*, 1.iii; *how say'st thou?* what do you make of the fact? *Mac.*, 3.iv.
HOWBEIT, nevertheless, *Cor.*, 1.ix; *howbeit that*, although, *Oth.*, 2.i.
HOWE'ER, HOWEVER, although, notwithstanding, *Troil. & Cres.*, 1.iii; etc.
HOWLET, owl, *Mac.*, 4.i.
HOWSOE'ER, HOWSOEVER, in any event, *Timon*, 4.iii; whatever the outcome, *Troil. & Cres.*, 3.iii; *Cym.*, 4.ii; *howsoe'er 'tis strange*, notwithstanding the remarkable nature of the fact, *Cym.*, 1.i.
HOWSOMEVER, in whatever manner, *Ham.*, 1.v.
HOY-DAY, HEY-DAY, expressing surprise and contempt, *Troil. & Cres.*, 5.i; *Timon*, 1.ii.
HUGGER-MUGGER, without ceremony and ostentation due to deceased's rank, *Ham.*, 4.v.
HULK, large cargo vessel, *Troil. & Cres.*, 2.iii.
HUMAN, HUMANE, (always *humane* in early editions), *the milk of human kindness*, belonging to the species, *Mac.*, 1.v; *thy human sons*, mankind as a whole, *Timon*, 4.iii; *the humane way*, the way proper for men of good-will, civilized, *Cor.*, 3.i; *civil and humane seeming*, good-breeding, *Oth.*, 2.i.
HUMANITY, human qualities, *Oth.*, 1.iii; *Ant. & Cleo.*, 5.i; *they imitated humanity*, the idea of man as they presented it, *Ham.*, 3.ii; *opposite to humanity*, enemy of civility and manners, *Timon*, 1.i.
HUMBLED, contrite, *Oth.*, 3.iii.
HUMOROUS, moist, *Rom. & Jul.*, 2.i; whimsical, *Cor.*, 2.i; *humorous predominance*, whatever humour (*q.v.*) prevails with him at the moment, *Troil. & Cres.*, 2.iii; *the humourous man*, the actor who plays characters dominated by one of the humours, *Ham.*, 2.ii.
HUMOUR. There were four humours: blood, phlegm, choler, melancholy. As one or other of these fluids predominated in the system, so the man's temperament and complexion varied: *a man into whom nature hath so crowded humours*, the mixture, however, not being completely satisfactory, *Troil. & Cres.*, 1.ii; *the humours of the dank morning*, the moisture and mist, *Jul. Caes.*, 2.i; *his humour was nothing but mutation*, his outstanding characteristic was desire for constant novelty, change of interest, *Cym.*, 4.ii; *the sun drew all such humours from him*, follies such as jealousy, *Oth.*, 3.iv.
HUNGERLY, eagerly, *Timon*, 1.i.
HUNGRY, barren, *Cor.*, 5.iii.
HUNT, the game, *Cym.*, 3.vi.
HUNTS-UP, morning song originally (as in *Titus*, 2.ii; *the hunt is up*), a hunting-song, *Rom. & Jul.*, 3.v.
HURLY-BURLY, confusion and noise, *Mac.*, 1.i.
HURRICANO, waterspout, *Troil. & Cres.*, 5.ii; *Lear*, 3.ii.
HURRY, tumult, *Cor.*, 4.vi.
HURTLE, resound, *Jul. Caes.*, 2.ii.
HUSBAND, marry, *Lear*, 5.iii.
HUSBANDRY, economical management, *Mac.*, 2.i; *Ham.*, 1.iii; diligence as shown by early rising, *Per.*, 3.ii; *as there were husbandry in war*, requiring early rising like domestic economy, *Troil. & Cres.*, 1.ii.
HYDRA, many-headed monster in form of a snake, killed by Hercules, *Oth.*, 2.iii.
HYMEN, whose presence was invoked at Greek marriages, so regarded as god of marriage; the torch was one of his symbols, *Ham.*, 3.ii; *Per.*, 3.*Prol.*

Hymenaeus, alternative form of Hymen (*q.v.*), so *readiness for Hymenaeus*, ready for marriage ceremony, *Titus*, 1.i.

Hyperbole, gross exaggeration, *Troil. & Cres.*, 1.iii.

Hyperbolical, *acclamations hyperbolical*, extravagant approval, *Cor.*, 1.ix.

Hyperion, the god of the sun, *Ham.*, 3.iv.

Hyrcan, Hyrcanian; Hyrcania on the south-east shore of the Caspian was regarded as a wild country and the home of savage beasts; *Mac.*, 3.iv; *Hyrcanian beast*, the tiger; *Ham.*, 2.ii.

Hysterica passio, hysteria, *Lear*, 2.iv.

Ice-brook, *the ice-brook's temper*, tempered in ice-cold water, the blades of Toledo being famous for their quality, *Oth.*, 5.ii.

Ides, in March, the fifteenth day, *Jul. Caes.*, 1.ii.

Idiot, *Mars his idiot*, his licensed fool, *Troil. & Cres.*, 2.i.

Idle, useless, *Lear*, 4.iv; barren, lifeless, *Oth.*, 1.iii; trifling, *Timon*, 1.ii; *Oth.*, 1.ii; *verb*, float at random, *Rom. & Jul.*, 2.vi.

Ignominy, Ignomy, disgrace, *Titus*, 4.ii.

Ignorant, *this ignorant present*, as not knowing the future, *Mac.*, 1.v; *your ignorant election*, foolish, *Cor.*, 2.ii; *ignorant in what I am commanded*, unskilled in the business, *Cym.*, 3.ii; *ignorant sin*, fault committed in ignorance, *Oth.*, 4.ii.

Ilion, Ilium, the citadel of Troy, *Troil. & Cres.*, 2.ii.

Ill, sin, *Cym.*, 5.i; crime, *Titus*, 5.i; *ills*, trials of life, *Ham.*, 3.i; *adj.*, of evil intent, *Jul. Caes.*, 4.iii; unskilled, *Ham.*, 2.ii.

Ill-favour'd, ugly, *Titus*, 3.ii.

Illness, wickedness or ruthlessness (that may go with ambition), *Mac.*, 1.v.

Ill-temper'd, *blood ill-temper'd*, recalls the notion of the humours being badly mixed, so producing mental disturbance, *Jul. Caes.*, 4.iii.

Illustrious, lacking lustre, *Cym.*, 1.vi.

Image, likeness, *Ham.*, 1.i. and 5.ii; imitation, *Ham.*, 3.ii; a mental picture, *Mac.*, 1.iii; sign, *Lear*, 2.iv; type, *Lear*, 4.vi.

Imaginary, *the imaginary relish*, the very idea of it, *Troil. & Cres.*, 3.ii.

Imagination, *he waxes desperate with imagination*, frantic in his delusion, *Ham.*, 1.iv; *wrong imaginations*, delusions, *Lear*, 4.vi.

Imagin'd, *imagin'd happiness*, inward joy, *Rom. & Jul.*, 2.vi.

Imbecility, weakness, *Troil. & Cres.*, 1.iii.

Immaterial, slight, worthless, *Troil. & Cres.*, 5.i.

Immediacy, *the which immediacy*, as my direct representative, *Lear*, 5.iii.

Immediate, *the most immediate to our throne*, the next in rank to the king, so probable heir, *Ham.*, 1.ii; *the immediate jewel of their souls*, next their very heart, *Oth.*, 3.iii; *the immediate author*, the direct cause, *Ant. & Cleo.*, 2.vi.

Imminence, *dare all imminence*, defy every threat (even of impending death), *Troil. & Cres.*, 5.x.

Immoment, of no importance, *Ant. & Cleo.*, 5.ii.

Immure, wall, *Troil. & Cres.*, *Prol.*

Impair, inadequate, *Troil. & Cres.*, 4.v.

Impart, express, *Ham.*, 1.ii; *impartment*, communication, *Ham.*, 1.iv.

Impasted, made into a paste, *Ham.*, 2.ii.

Imperceiverant, lacking in discernment, *Cym.*, 4.i.

Imperious, imperial, *Troil. & Cres.*, 4.v; *Ham.*, 5.i; *imperious show*, the emperor's triumph, *Ant. & Cleo.*, 4.xv.

Impertinency, *matter and impertinency*, sense and incoherence, *Lear*, 4.vi.

Impitious, impetuous, remorseless, *Ham.*, 4.v.

Imploratators, solicitors, *Ham.*, 1.iii.

Imply, *imply her*, have as a consequence for her, *Per.*, 4.i.

Impone, to stake, *Ham.*, 5.ii.

Import, *of dear import*, great importance, *Rom. & Jul.*, 5.iii; *verb*, *imports at full*, carries clear instruction for, *Ham.*, 4.iii; concern, *Ham.*, 5.ii; be of importance to, *Troil. & Cres.*, 4.ii; etc.; involve, *Lear*, 4.iii; carry as consequence, *Ant. & Cleo.*, 2.ii; signify, *Oth.*, 4.i; have as purport, *Oth.*, 5.ii.

Importance, *importance of so slight and trivial a nature*, a matter of no importance, *Cym.*, 1.iv.

Importancy, value, *Oth.*, 1.iii.

Important, *the important acting of*, the urgent performance of, *Ham.*, 3.iv; *importantly*, with urgent business, *Cym.*, 4.iv.

Importunacy, importunity, *Timon*, 2.ii.

Importune, beg a respite, *Ant. & Cleo.*, 4.xv; *importun'd*, importunate, *Lear*, 4.iv.

Imposition, injunction, task, *Troil. & Cres.*, 3.ii; *an idle and most false imposition*, the public imposing on or giving a man his reputation thoughtlessly, *Oth.*, 2.iii.

Imposthume, abscess, *Ham.*, 4.iv.

Impress, conscription, forced service, *Ham.*, 1.i; *Ant. & Cleo.*, 3.vii; *under an impress*, under compulsion (with play on imprint of the blow), *Troil. & Cres.*, 2.i; *verb*, compel into service, *Mac.*, 4.i; *our impress'd lances*, those enlisted in our forces, *Lear*, 5.iii.

Impressure, impression (made as a token or evidence of), *Troil. & Cres.*, 4.v.

Imputation, reputation, *Troil. & Cres.*, 1.iii; *Ham.*, 5.ii; *imputation and strong circumstance*, probability founded on circumstantial evidence, *Oth.*, 3.iii.

In, *to be in*, drunk, *Ant. & Cleo.*, 2.vii.

In-a-door, at home, within doors, *Lear*, 1.iv.

Incapable, unable to realize, *Ham.*, 4.vii; *incapable of help*, beyond help, *Cor.*, 4.vi.

Incarnadine, to dye red, *Mac.*, 2.ii.

Incense, provoke, *Jul. Caes.*, 1.iii; incite, *Lear*, 2.iv.

Inch, *Saint Colme's inch*, St. Columba's isle (in the Forth, Inchcolm), *Mac.*, 1.ii.

Incident, of common occurrence, *Timon*, 5.i.

Incivil, rude, *Cym.*, 5.v.

Inclination, temper, character, *Ant. & Cleo.*, 2.v; *observe his inclination in yourself*, study his behaviour with your own eyes, *Ham.*, 2.i.

Incline, favour, *Cor.*, 2.iii; side with, *Lear*, 3.iii; bend her ear, *Oth.*, 1.iii; have a disposition towards, *Cym.*, 1.vi.

Inclining, *noun*, inclination, freewill, *Ham.*, 2.ii; *you of my inclining*, my party, *Oth.*, 1.ii.

Inclips, embraces, *Ant. & Cleo.*, 2.vii.

Include, *includes itself in power*, comes to power in the end, *Troil. & Cres.*, 1.iii.

Incontinent, Incontinently, at once, *Oth.*, 1.iii and 4.iii.

Incorporal, without form or body, *Ham.*, 3.iv.

Incorporate, forming one body, *Cor.*, 1.i; *Oth.*, 2.i; *one incorporate to*, a member of (the conspiracy), *Jul. Caes.*, 1.iii.

Incorps'd, made one body, *Ham.*, 4.vii.

Incorrect, unchastened, *Ham.*, 1.ii.

Increase, offspring, *Cor.*, 3.iii.

Indenture, agreement, *Per.*, 1.iii; *a pair of indentures*, duplicate agreement torn zigzag-wise, each party holding one copy, *Ham.*, 5.i.

Index, table of contents, so indication of what is to follow, *Ham.*, 3.iv; etc.

India, used as a type of infinite riches, *Troil. & Cres.*, 1.i.

Indict, accuse, *Ham.*, 2.ii; *Oth.*, 3.iv.

Indifferent, not bad (in mock modesty), *Timon*, 1.i; *indifferent honest*, fairly honest, *Ham.*, 3.i.

Indifferently, fairly well, *Ham.*, 3.ii; impartially, *Jul. Caes.*, 1.ii; *Titus*, 1.i.

Indign, disgraceful, *Oth.*, 1.iii.

Indirect, unlawful, *Oth.*, 1.iii; *indirection*, dishonest means, *Jul. Caes.*, 4.iii; *indirections*, roundabout ways, *Ham.*, 2.i.

Indisposition, disinclination (to see to business), *Timon*, 2.ii.

Indistinguishable, *indistinguishable cur*, a mongrel, not truebred, *Troil. & Cres.*, 5.i.

Individable, observing the unities of time and place, *Ham.*, 2.ii.

Indrench'd, immersed, *Troil. & Cres.*, 1.i.

Indued, having acquired qualities adapted to environment, *Ham.*, 4.vii.

Industrious, well-directed, *Mac.*, 5.iv.

Infected, soured by misfortune, *Timon*, 4.iii; made untrustworthy, *Cor.*, 5.vi; plague-stricken, *Oth.*, 4.i.

Infectiously, *what infectiously itself affects*, an object to which the worshipper is drawn only by his mistaken sense of value, *Troil. & Cres.*, 2.ii.

Infer, allege, *Timon*, 3.v.

Inference, train of thought, *Oth.*, 3.iii.

Infirmity, human weakness, fault, *Per.*, 2.i; *a man of their infirmity*, a man human like them, *Cor.*, 3.i; disease, *Mac.*, 3.iv.

Influence, the power that was supposed to flow from the celestial bodies, *Ham.*, 1.i; etc.

Inform, assume body and form, *Mac.*, 2.i; inspire, *Cor.*, 5.iii; give instruction, *Mac.*, 1.v; instruct, *Ant. & Cleo.*, 3.ii; *Cym.*, 1.i.

Infuse, inspire, *Jul. Caes.*, 1.iii.

Infusion, nature, *Ham.*, 5.ii.

INFUSIONS, medicinal qualities, *Per.*, 3.ii.
INGENIOUS, *ingenious sense*, sensibility of mind, *Ham.*, 5.i; *ingenious feeling*, full consciousness, *Lear*, 4.vi.
INGENIOUSLY, ingenuously, frankly, *Timon*, 2.ii.
INGRAFT, firmly implanted, *Oth.*, 2.iii.
INGREDIENCE, ingredient, *Oth.*, 2.iii; ingredients, *Mac.*, 1.vii.
INHABIT, live, exist, *Mac.*, 3.iv.
INHERENT, not to be removed, *Cor.*, 3.ii.
INHERIT, possess and enjoy, *Cor.*, 2.i; *Rom. & Jul.*, 1.ii; possess, govern, *Lear*, 4.vi; *Cym.*, 3.ii.
INHERITANCE, possession, *Ham.*, 1.i.
INHERITOR, owner, *Ham.*, 5.i.
INHIBITED, prohibited, *Oth.*, 1.ii.
INHIBITION, what denies them their residence in the city, *Ham.*, 2.ii.
INHOOP'D, in the small circular arena confining the fighting birds, *Ant. & Cleo.*, 2.iii.
INITIATE, *initiate fear*, the beginner's fears, *Mac.*, 3.iv.
INJOINT, combine, *Oth.*, 1.iii.
INJURIOUS, slanderous, *Cor.*, 3.iii; insultingly harmful, *Troil. & Cres.*, 4.iv; insulting, *Cym.*, 4.ii; malicious, *Ant. & Cleo.*, 4.xv.
INJURY, *his injury*, the wrong done to him, *Cor.*, 5.i.
INKLE, tape, or linen yarn from which it is made, *Per.*, 5.*Prol.*
INNOCENT, fool, *Lear*, 3.vi; *Per.*, 4.iii.
INNOVATION, the new fashion in theatre-going, *Ham.*, 2.ii; disturbance, *Oth.*, 2.iii.
INOCULATE, to engraft, and so change the quality, *Ham.*, 3.i.
INQUIRE, search, *Per.*, 3.*Prol.*; *inquire him out*, ask where he stays, *Oth.*, 3.iv.
INSANE, causing insanity to the eater, *Mac.*, 1.iii.
INSCULPTURE, carved inscription, *Timon*, 5.iv.
INSINUATE, flatter, fawn, *Titus*, 4.ii; wheedle, *Oth.*, 4.ii; *the insinuating nod*, of assumed good fellowship, *Cor.*, 2.iii.
INSINUATION, sycophantic intrusion, *Ham.*, 5.ii.
INSISTURE, (doubtful, perhaps) constancy, *Troil. & Cres.*. 1.iii.
INSTANCE, motive, inducement, *Ham.*, 3.ii; cause, *Troil. & Cres.*, 1.iii; proof, *Troil. & Cres.*, 5.ii; pattern, samples, *Ham.*, 4.v; *what instance for it?* authority, *Troil. & Cres.*, 5.x.
INSTANT, *in the instant*, immediately, *Rom. & Jul.*, 1.i; *Ham.*, 4.vi; *adj.*, *the instant way*, the path now ahead, *Troil. & Cres.*, 3.iii; *the instant army*, the force at present available, *Cor.*, 5.i; *adv.*, immediately, *Ham.*, 1.v.
INSTRUCTION, *without some instruction*, without there being good grounds for it, *Oth.*, 4.i.
INSTRUMENT, agent, *Oth.*, 4.ii; document, *Oth.*, 4.i.
INSULT, triumph, exult, *Titus*, 3.ii; *Lear*, 2.ii.
INSULTMENT, *speech of insultment*, expression of victor's triumph and contempt, *Cym.*, 3.v.
INSUPPRESSIVE, not to be suppressed, *Jul. Caes.*, 2.i.
INTELLIGENCE, secret, inspired communication, *Cym.*, 4.ii.
INTELLIGENT, *intelligent of our state*, conveying information about our government, *Lear*, 3.i; informative, *Lear*, 3.vii.
INTEND, *intend my travel*, propose to travel, *Per.*, 1.ii; *how intend you—practis'd?* what do you imply by 'practis'd'?, *Ant. & Cleo.*, 2.ii; *intending other serious matters*, pretending to have other serious business, *Timon*, 2.ii.
INTENT, meaning, *Ant. & Cleo.*, 2.ii.
INTENTIVELY, with complete attention, *Oth.*, 1.iii.
INTERCEPT, to interrupt, *Titus*, 2.ii and 3.i.
INTERDICTION, *his own interdiction*, his self-condemnation (excluding him as unworthy), *Mac.*, 4.iii.
INTERESS'D, entitled, *Lear*, 1.i.
INTEREST, *our bosom interest*, personal trust (in his loyalty), *Mac.*, 1.ii; *interest of territory*, possession and rule of territory, *Lear*, 1.i.
INTERIM, *by interims*, at intervals, *Cor.*, 1.vi.
INTERJOIN, *interjoin their issues*, make common cause (hardly, let their children intermarry), *Cor.*, 4.iv.
INTERLUDE, a kind of brief play, usually comic; so applied to farcical episode, *Lear*, 5.iii.
INTERMISSION, delay, *Mac.*, 4.iii; *spite of intermission*, though it meant delay in other business, *Lear*, 2.iv.
INTERMIT, postpone, *Jul. Caes.*, 1.i.
INTERROGATORIES, questions, *Cym.*, 5.v.
INTIL, into, *Ham.*, 5.i.
INTO, unto, *Troil. & Cres.*, 3.iii; towards, *Cym.*, 1.vi.
INTRENCHANT, invulnerable, *Mac.*, 5.viii.

INTRINSE, intricate, *Lear*, 2.ii; *Ant. & Cleo.*, 5.ii.

INVENTION, deliberate falsehood, *Cor.*, 3.ii; *Mac.*, 3.i.

INVENTORIALLY, item by item, *Ham.*, 5.ii.

INVESTMENTS, dress, garments, *Ham.*, 1.iii.

INVISIBLE, pervasive, *Ant. & Cleo.*, 2.ii; hidden, *Cym.*, 4.ii.

IRIS, goddess of the rainbow, *Troil. & Cres.*, 1.iii.

IRREGULOUS, lawless, *Cym.*, 4.ii.

ISIS, national Egyptian deity, wife of Osiris and mother of Horus, *Ant. & Cleo.*, 1.ii.

ISSUE, deed, *Jul. Caes.*, 3.i; decision, *Mac.*, 5.iv; children, descendants, *Mac.*, 3.i; act, *Cym.*, 2.i; consequence, *Oth.*, 3.iii; *better issue*, better fortune, *Ant. & Cleo.*, 1.ii.

IT, the common form of the genitive of *it* was *his*, but the form *it* is sometimes found, as, *fordo it own life*, *Ham.*, 5.i; *it had it head bit off*, *Lear*, 1.iv.

ITERANCE, repetition, *Oth.*, 5.ii.

ITERATION, repeated citations, repetition of tags, *Troil. & Cres.*, 3.ii.

IWIS, certainly, in truth, *Per.*, 2.*Prol.*

JACK, knave, *Rom. & Jul.*, 2.iv; *a Jack guardant*, a knavish sentry, *Cor.*, 5.ii; *minute-jack*, the figure for striking bell on clock, so time-server, *Timon*, 3.vi; *this Jack of Caesar's*, menial, *Ant. & Cleo.*, 3.xiii; *Jack-slave*, common fellow, *Cym.*, 2.i; *jacks*, used in bowls as aiming-mark, *Cym.*, 2.i.

JACKANAPES, ape, but used of interfering fellow, *Cym.*, 2.i.

JADE, poor type of horse, *Ham.*, 3.ii; *verb*, drive to exhaustion, reduce to sorry condition, *Ant. & Cleo.*, 3.i.

JAKES, a privy, *Lear*, 2.ii.

JANUS, Roman god represented with two faces, one looking forward, the other backward; used in *Oth.*, 1.ii, because Iago comes to a conclusion the opposite of his earlier opinion.

JAUNCE, trail about, *Rom. & Jul.*, 2.v; *noun*, going to and from, *Rom. & Jul.*, 2.v.

JAY, showy female, *Cym.*, 3.iv.

JEALOUS, suspicious, *Oth.*, 3.iv; apprehensive, *Lear*, 5.i; *jealous on me*, suspicious of me, doubtful of my honesty, *Jul. Caes.*, 1.ii; *nothing jealous*, in no way doubtful, *Jul. Caes.*, 1.ii.

JEALOUS-HOOD, suspicious and officious female, *Rom. & Jul.*, 4.iv.

JEALOUSY, *artless jealousy*, ill-concealed apprehension, *Ham.*, 4.v; *jealousies*, suspicions, *Mac.*, 4.iii.

JENNET, small Spanish horse, *Oth.*, 1.i.

JESSES, fastenings on legs of hawks, *Oth.*, 3.iii.

JET, encroach, *Titus*, 2.i; swagger, *Cym.*, 3.iii.

JIG, plays were followed by a dance and singing presenting some comic turn, *Ham.*, 2.ii; *verb*, move in affected manner, *Ham.*, 3.i.

JIG-MAKER, composer of farcical dance pieces, *Ham.*, 3.ii.

JOHN-A-DREAMS, mooning fellow, *Ham.*, 2.ii.

JOINTRESS, dowager, entitled to estate reserved for her, *Ham.*, 1.ii.

JOINT-RING, ring with separable halves, *Oth.*, 4.iii.

JOINT-STOOL, JOIN-STOOL, carefully wrought stool, *Rom. & Jul.*, 1.v; *Lear*, 3.vi.

JOURNAL, daily, *Cym.*, 4.ii.

JOVIAL, those born under Jupiter (Jove) were supposed to have his easy, convivial temperament and characteristic features, *Mac.*, 3.ii; etc.

JOWL, cast down, *Ham.*, 5.i.

JUDICIOUS, judicial, *Cor.*, 5.vi; fitting the crime, *Lear*, 3.iv.

JUG, Joan, *Lear*, 1.iv.

JUMP, venture, *Ant. & Cleo.*, 3.viii; *adv.*, precisely, *Ham.*, 1.i; *Oth.*, 2.iii; *verb*, risk, *Cym.*, 5.iv; *jump the life to come*, take a chance about future life, *Mac.*, 1.vii; *jump a body with a dangerous physic*, take the risk of administering a dangerous drug, *Cor.*, 3.i.

JUST, loyal, *Jul. Caes.*, 3.ii; exact, *Titus*, 5.iii; *Rom. & Jul.*, 3.ii; *in thy just proof*, on the evidence of your honesty, innocence, *Lear*, 3.vi; *just report*, true report, *Lear*, 3.i; *a just equinox*, when night and day are exactly equal; so vice and virtue balance exactly, *Oth.*, 2.iii.

JUSTICE, *do you justice*, keep level with you in drinking, *Oth.*, 2.iii.

JUSTICER, judge, *Lear*, 3.vi; *Cym.*, 5.v.

JUSTIFY, *justify in knowledge*, acknowledge, *Per.*, 5.i.

JUTTY, projecting feature, *Mac.*, 1.vi.

KAM, *clean kam*, quite crooked, so beside the point, *Cor.*, 3.i.

KEEP, inhabit, *Rom. & Jul.*, 3.ii; lodge, resort, *Ham.*, 2.i; *thy spirit which keeps thee*, dwells with thee as guardian, *Ant. & Cleo.*, 2.iii; *it kept where I kept*, remained always with me, *Per.*, 2.i.

KEN, recognize (even at a distance), *Troil. & Cres.*, 4.v; *within a ken*, within sight (a *ken* being reckoned at 20 miles or so), *Cym.*, 3.vi.

KERCHIEF, woman's head-covering worn by men in illness, *Jul. Caes.*, 2.i.

KERN, lightly armed Irish soldier, *Mac.*, 1.ii.

KETTLE, kettle-drum, *Ham.*, 5.ii.

KIBE, chilblain, often on the heel, *Ham.*, 5.i; *Lear*, 1.v.

KILLEN, old form of infinitive of 'kill,' *Per.*, 2.*Prol.*

KIN, *one touch of nature makes the whole world kin*, one characteristic or weakness is common to human kind, *Troil. & Cres.*, 3.iii.

KIND, human, *Timon*, 2.ii; in keeping with humane existence (the ladies being not merely a beautiful but social addition to the banquet), *Timon*, 1.ii; *noun, from quality and kind*, acting contrary to their nature, *Jul. Caes.*, 1.iii; *by kind*, by the nature of the place, *Titus*, 2.i; *the worm will do its kind*, the serpent will act according to its nature, *Ant. & Cleo.*, 5.ii; *in that kind*, in the very manner, *Lear*, 4.vi.

KINDLESS, inhuman, *Ham.*, 2.ii.

KINDLY, exactly, *Rom. & Jul.*, 2.iv; *kindly creature*, the kind of harmless useful creatures supported by the law, *Ant. & Cleo.*, 2.v; *adv.*, after their nature, i.e., heartlessly, *Lear*, 1.v.

KINGDOM, world, *Jul. Caes.*, 2.i; *kingdom'd Achilles*, the little kingdom that is Achilles (being divided against himself), *Troil. & Cres.*, 2.iii.

KISS, *kiss the mistress*, to touch the jack at bowls, so of the lady, *Troil. & Cres.*, 3.ii; *kissed the jack*, touched the jack at bowls, *Cym.*, 2.i.

KITE, foul bird of prey, used of person, *Lear*, 1.iv; *region kites*, the birds of the air, the kite being voracious and ready to prey on garbage, *Ham.*, 2.ii.

KNAP, rap, hit, *Lear*, 2.iv.

KNAVE, often used affectionately of servant as in *Jul. Caes.*, 4.iii; plebeian, *Cor.*, 2.i; young fellow, *Lear*, 1.i; a servant, *Lear*, 1.iv; *Ant. & Cleo.*, 5.ii.

KNEE, *your knee*, kneel down, *Cor.*, 5.iii; *here's my knee*, that is, he kneels, *Cym.*, 5.v; *knee-crooking knave*, obsequious fellow, *Oth.*, 1.i; *verb*, kneel before, *Lear*, 2.iv.

KNIT, unite, *Per.*, 1.i and 2.iv; *sleep that knits up the ravell'd sleave of care*, straightens out the tangled troubles of waking life, *Mac.*, 2.ii; *the amity that wisdom knits not*, friendship not cemented by sound sense, *Troil. & Cres.*, 2.iii.

KNOT, intertwine, *Oth.*, 4.ii; *sorrow-wreathen knot*, arms folded in despair, *Titus*, 3.ii; *the knot of us*, firmly united company, *Jul. Caes.*, 3.i.

KNOTTED, gnarled and tough, *Troil. & Cres.*, 1.iii; *Jul. Caes.*, 1.iii.

KNOW OF, learn from, *Lear*, 5.i.

KNOWING, breeding, *Cym.*, 1.iv and 2.iii; *in my knowing*, to my knowledge, *Timon*, 3.ii; *former knowings*, previous experience, *Mac.*, 2.iv.

KNOWINGLY, by experience, *Cym.*, 3.iii.

KNOWLEDGE, acquaintance, *Ham.*, 2.i; the facts as known to the messenger, *Mac.*, 1.ii; *mine own knowledge of myself*, sense of responsibility, *Ant. & Cleo.*, 2.ii.

LABEL, slip bearing a seal attached to a deed or document, *Rom. & Jul.*, 4.i; document, *Cym.*, 5.v.

LABOUR, diligence in duty, *Ham.*, 2.ii; *verb*, endeavour, *Timon*, 1.i; exert oneself, *Lear*, 4.vi; *labour'd scholar*, on whom much labour has been bestowed, so highly finished, *Per.*, 2.iii; suffer pangs of childbirth, *Oth.*, 2.i; *labouring breath*, the idea of labour in childbirth associated with excited breathing, *Troil. & Cres.*, 4.iv; *labouring for nine*, almost nine o'clock (so used because nine was the number of young expected of some creatures), *Timon*, 3.iv.

LABOURSOME, laborious, *Ham.*, 1.ii; elaborate, so demanding much attention, *Cym.*, 3.iv.

LACK, miss, *Oth.*, 3.iii; *by being lack'd*, when his absence becomes felt, *Ant. & Cleo.*, 1.iv; *it lacks of twelve*, not quite midnight, *Ham.*, 1.iv; be wanting, *Ham.*, 1.v; *when I am lack'd*, when I am needed and missed, *Cor.*, 4.i; *noun, our lack*, all that is wanting to our expedition, *Mac.*, 4.iii.

LACKEY, follow in servile fashion, *Ant. & Cleo.*, 1.iv.

LADING, cargo, *Titus*, 1.i.

LADY, the leading female part, *Ham.*, 2.ii; mistress, *Lear*, 1.i.

LAG, *the common lag*, the vulgar herd that came after the senators,

Timon, 3.vi; *lag of*, later than, *Lear*, 1.ii.

LAME, to make rivals appear lame and imperfect, *Cym.*, 5.v.

LAMMAS-TIDE, 1st August, *Rom. & Jul.*, 1.iii; *Lammas Eve*, the day before, *Rom. & Jul.*, 1.iii.

LAND-FISH, an unnatural creature, *Troil. & Cres.*, 3.iii.

LANGUISH, afflicting symptoms, *Rom. & Jul.*, 1.ii; lingering disease, *Ant. & Cleo.*, 5.ii.

LANGUOR, affliction, *Titus*, 3.i.

LANK, become shrunken, *Ant. & Cleo.*, 1.iv.

LANTERN, turret light with numerous windows, *Rom. & Jul.*, 5.iii.

LAP, wrap, *Cym.*, 5.v; *lapp'd in proof*, clad in armour, *Mac.*, 1.ii.

LAPSE, *to lapse in fulness*, to sin or lie when prosperous (and so not constrained by poverty), *Cym.*, 3.vi; *would without lapsing*, without falling into absurdity or untruth, *Cor.*, 5.ii.

LARD, fatten, *Timon*, 4.iii; enrich, decorate, *Ham.*, 4.v.

LARGE, *large in mirth*, free in enjoyment, *Mac.*, 3.iv; *things to come at large*, things that will come in the natural course to gigantic size, *Troil. & Cres.*, 1.iii; *largest bounty*, most valuable, *Lear*, 1.i; *large speeches*, great in promise and protestation, *Lear*, 1.i; *most large in his abominations*, unrestrained in his immoral acts, *Ant. & Cleo.*, 3.vi.

LARGE-HANDED, rapacious, *Timon*, 4.i.

'LARUM, sounds of war, *Cor.*, 1.iv; sounds of warlike acclamation, *Titus*, 1.i.

LAST, farewell, *Timon*, 3.vi; *try the last*, fight it out to the end (or perhaps put to the test the truth of Macduff's being of no woman born), *Mac.*, 5.viii; *in the last*, at last, *Cor.*, 5.vi; *at the last*, at the very end, *Ant. & Cleo.*, 5.ii.

LATCH, catch, *Mac.*, 4.iii; *Lear*, 2.i.

LATE, recent; *of late*, till a short time ago, *Ant. & Cleo.*, 3.xii; *latest*, the last, the remainder, *Timon*, 4.ii.

LATED, belated, *Mac.*, 3.iii; *Ant. & Cleo.*, 3.xi.

LATH, sword (applied in derision), *Titus*, 2.i; *bow of lath*, so imitation one, *Rom. & Jul.*, 1.iv.

LAUD, (1) hymn, psalm, *Ham.*, 4.vii; (2) praise, commendation, *Troil. & Cres.*, 3.iii.

LAUGHTER, object of laughter, *Jul. Caes.*, 4.iii. [*Mac.*, 3.ii.

LAVE, wash to keep untarnished,

LAVISH, unrestrained, aggressive, *Mac.*, 1.ii.

LAVOLT, dance, *Troil. & Cres.*, 4.iv.

LAW-DAY, a meeting of a court, *Oth.*, 3.iii.

LAY, *noun*, stake, wager, *Oth.*, 2.iii; *Cym.*, 1.iv; *verb*, bury, *Cym.*, 4.ii; wager, *Ham.*, 5.ii; *lay for hearts*, captivate, win supporters, *Timon*, 3.v; *lay home to*, rate roundly, *Ham.*, 3.iv; *laying on*, hard hitting, *Troil. & Cres.*, 1.ii.

LAZAR, leper, *Troil. & Cres.*, 2.iii.

LEAD, in invitations to withdraw, as *will you lead*, *Ant. & Cleo.*, 2.vi; *Cym.*, 4.iv.

LEADEN, *leaden mace*, producing heaviness and sleep, *Jul. Caes.*, 4.iii.

LEADING, command, direction, *Cor.*, 4.v.

LEADS, roofs, *Cor.*, 2.i.

LEAGUE, friendship, *Titus*, 5.iii.

LEAGU'D, folded, *Cym.*, 4.ii; *leagu'd in office*, because of professional loyalty, *Oth.*, 2.iii.

LEAN, bare, *Titus*, 2.iii; *a leaner action*, a less important matter, *Ant. & Cleo.*, 2.ii; *verb*, be on point of collapse, *Cym.*, 1.v; incline, submit, *Timon*, 3.iv; *Cym.*, 1.i; *leans on the affair*, depends upon the scheme, *Ham.*, 4.iii.

LEARN, teach; *learn me*, inform me of, *Troil. & Cres.*, 2.i.

LEARNED, instructed, *Cor.*, 3.i; experienced, *Oth.*, 3.iii.

LEARNING, accomplishment, *Ham.*, 5.ii; instruction, *Cym.*, 1.i; information, *Ant. & Cleo.*, 2.ii.

LEASE, *live the lease of nature*, live to die a natural death, *Mac.*, 4.i.

LEASING, *stamp'd the leasing*, passed falsehood under the stamp of truth, *Cor.*, 5.ii.

LEAST, *spoke the least*, underestimated if anything, *Timon*, 5.ii; *in the least*, at the lowest, *Lear*, 1.i.

LEAVE, *leave of means*, as resources permitted, *Timon*, 2.ii; *under leave*, by permission, *Jul. Caes.*, 3.ii; *give leave*, please withdraw, *Rom. & Jul.*, 1.iii; formal permission to depart, *Mac.*, 4.iii; *verb*, *left your voices*, given your vote, *Cor.*, 2.iii; deserted, *Cor.*, 1.iv; omit, *Troil. & Cres.*, 3.iii; desist, drop the subject, *Cym.*, 1.iv; leave off, *Cym.*, 2.ii.

LEECH, physician, *Timon*, 5.iv.

LEER, complexion, *Titus*, 4.ii.

LEET, court held by a lord of a manor, *Oth.*, 3.iii.

LEGS, bowings in salutation, *Cor.*, 2.i; *Timon*, 1.ii.

LEIGER, ambassador, representative, agent, *Cym.*, 1.v.

LEISURE, delay, *Ham.*, 5.ii; opportunity, *Timon*, 2.ii; *trust by leisure*, not trust for long enough, *Titus*, 1.i.

LEND, bestow on, *Lear*, 4.iii.

LENDINGS, clothes (provided by art not nature), *Lear*, 3.iv.

LENGTH, *all length*, any further extension of life, *Ant. & Cleo.*, 4.xiv.

LENGTHEN, *lengthening my return*, postponing the date of my return, *Cym.*, 1.vi.

LENTEN, scanty, *Ham.*, 2.ii; *Lenten pie*, pie without meat, *Rom. & Jul.*, 2.iv (perhaps here a game-pie made against Lent and eaten bit by bit during the period and so apt to go stale).

LEPEROUS, causing skin-condition like leprosy, *Ham.*, 1.v.

LESS (sometimes used in negative or quasi-negative expressions where meaning is 'more'), *Cor.*, 1.iv; *Cym.*, 1.iv; so *lesser*, *Troil. & Cres.*, 1.i.

LESSON'D, taught, *Cor.*, 2.iii; *Titus*, 5.ii.

LET, (1) hinder, *Ham.*, 1.iv; *let their ears hear their faults hid*, prevent their ears' hearing their faults, *Per.*, 1.ii; (2) *let to know*, informed, *Ham.*, 4.vi; *let out*, lent, *Timon*, 3.v.

LET-ALONE, prohibition, *Lear*, 5.iii.

LETHARGIED, dulled, *Lear*, 1.iv.

LETHARGY, unconscious fit, *Oth.*, 4.i.

LETHE, (1) the river of oblivion, *Ham.*, 1.v; the waters of Lethe produced forgetfulness, so wine relieves the mind of care and substitutes a happy oblivion, *Ant. & Cleo.*, 2.vii; so *Lethe'd dulness*, 2.i; (2) blood of slain animal, *Jul. Caes.*, 3.i.

LETTER, literal meaning, *Oth.*, 1.iii; *Cym.*, 5.v; *I heard no letter*, not a jot, *Cym.*, 4.iii; *by letter*, by influence (as in letters of recommendation), *Oth.*, 1.i.

LEVEL, *noun*, aim, *Rom. & Jul.*, 3.iii; *adj.*, *as level as the cannon to his blank*, as sure of aim as the cannon, *Ham.*, 4.i; straight, *Timon*, 4.iii; *verb*, guess, *Ant. & Cleo.*, 5.ii; *levels with her breeding*, is adequate for one of her station, *Oth.*, 1.iii; *no levell'd malice*, no direct censure of any particular individual, *Timon*, 1.i.

LEVY, *levy offence*, (as in 'levy war') bring together for offensive action, *Per.*, 2.v.

LEWD, lustful, *Oth.*, 3.iii.

LIABLE, subject, exposed to, *Jul. Caes.*, 2.ii; etc.

LIBERAL, free in talk, *Ham.*, 4.viii; licentious, *Oth.*, 2.i; full and grateful, *Ant. & Cleo.*, 2.vi; *of very liberal conceit*, of a design worthy of a gentleman, *Ham.*, 5.ii; *adv.*, freely, *Oth.*, 5.ii.

LIBERTY, licence, *Timon*, 4.i; *Ham.*, 2.i; *the liberty*, freedom from the unities of time and place, *Ham.*, 2.ii; *liberties*, royal rights, domains, *Per.*, 1.ii.

LICENCE, permission, *Ham.*, 4.iv; *Ant. & Cleo.*, 1.ii.

LICENTIOUS, regardless of right and wrong, *Timon*, 5.iv.

LICTORS, officers attending on Roman magistrates, *Ant. & Cleo.*, 5.ii.

LID, eyelid, *Troil. & Cres.*, 1.ii.

LIE, lodge, *Cor.*, 1.ix; *Oth.*, 3.iv; adopt a defensive attitude, *Troil. & Cres.*, 1.ii; rest, *Per.*, 3.i.

LIEUTENANTRY, *dealt on lieutenantry*, directed but did not participate in the fighting, *Ant. & Cleo.*, 3.xi.

LIFE, nature, as imitated by art, *Tim.*, 1.i; animated being, *Ant. & Cleo.*, 3.iii; *the true life on't*, its fidelity to nature, *Cym.*, 2.iv; *to the life*, in accordance with the facts, *Per.*, 5.i; *lives*, living enemies, *Mac.*, 5.viii.

LIFE-ENDURING, self-sacrificing (as the pelican was supposed to feed its young with its blood), *Ham.*, 4.v.

LIFTER, thief, *Troil. & Cres.*, 1.ii; etc.

LIGHT, frivolous, *Ham.*, 2.ii and 4.vii; venial, *Oth.*, 2.iii; cheap, *Oth.*, 2.iii; light-headed, *Cym.*, 5.iv; *light of ear*, a ready ear for wickedness, *Lear*, 3.iv; *verb*, fall on, *Ham.*, 5.ii; descend, *Oth.*, 1.iii; *you are light into my hands*, you have fallen into my keeping, *Per.*, 4.ii.

LIGHTNESS, instability of mind, *Ham.*, 2.ii. [*& Jul.*, 5.iii.

LIGHTNING, lightening of spirit, *Rom.*

LIKE, likely; *adv.*, equally, *Cym.*, 3.iii; *noun*, *every like is not the same*, things that look alike are not necessarily of the same kind, *Jul. Caes.*, 2.ii; *verb*, please, *Ham.*, 5.ii; *Lear*, 1.i; in ceremonious forms of address as, *so like you, sir*, may you be pleased to see, *Cym.*, 2.iii.

LIKELIHOODS, *poor likelihoods of modern seeming*, weak grounds of proof from common misrepresentations, *Oth.*, 1.iii.

LILY-LIVER'D, cowardly, *Mac.*, 5.iii; *Lear*, 2.ii.

LIMBEC, a retort, alembic, *Mac.*, 1.vii.
LIMB-MEAL, limb from limb, *Cym.*, 2.iv.
LIMBO, the just who died before the coming of Christ inhabited Limbo; but the name is used of hell itself in *Titus*, 3.i.
LIME, bird-lime, *Mac.*, 4.ii; *limed soul*, caught by sin as the bird by lime, *Ham.*, 3.iii.
LIMEKILNS, centres of burning sensation, *Troil. & Cres.*, 5.i.
LIMITATION, appointed time, *Cor.*, 2.iii.
LIMITED, *limited professions*, making respectable professions, *Timon*, 4.iii; *limited service*, prescribed duty, *Mac.*, 2.iii.
LINE, strengthen, *Mac.*, 1.iii; *lined their coats*, enriched themselves, *Oth.*, 1.i; *Per.*, 4.vi; *noun*, *lines of favour*, the contours of his face, *Cym.*, 4.ii.
LINEN, *linen cheeks*, white, *Mac.*, 5.iii.
LINGER, delay, *Oth.*, 4.ii; *lingering by inches*, operating imperceptibly, *Cym.*, 5.v.
LION-SICK, with pride, *Troil. & Cres.*, 2.iii.
LIP, *make a lip at*, show contempt towards, *Cor.*, 2.i.
LIQUORISH, spirituous, *Timon*, 4.iii.
LIST, *noun*, (1) boundary, *Ham.*, 4.v; *in a patient list*, within the limits of self-control, *Oth.*, 4.i; arena, place of contest, *Mac.*, 3.i; *Per.*, 1.i; (2) muster, *Ham.*, 1.i; *Ant. & Cleo.*, 3.vi; (3) inclination, *Oth.*, 2.i.
LIST, *verb*, (1) desire, *Oth.*, 2.iii; (2) listen, harken, *Lear*, 5.iii.
LITIGIOUS, precarious, *Per.*, 3.iii.
LITTER, give birth, used contemptuously of human beings, *Cor.*, 3.i.
LITTLE, *in little*, in miniature, *Ham.*, 2.ii.
LIVELY, living, *Titus*, 3.i; *lively warrant*, authority from life itself, *Titus*, 5.iii; lifelike, *Timon*, 1.i and 5.i.
LIVER, (1) the organ associated with love, passion, and courage, *Troil. & Cres.*, 2.ii; (2) a live person, *Cym.*, 3.iv.
LIVERY, retainer's uniform, so *nature's livery*, the qualities and form we get from nature, *Ham.*, 1.iv.
LIVING, possession, means of livelihood, *Lear*, 1.iv.
LOAD, reward, *Cym.*, 1.v.
LOATHLY, in abhorrence, *Oth.*, 3.iv; *loathly opposite*, utterly opposed, *Lear*, 2.i.
LOATHNESS, reluctance, *Ant. & Cleo.*, 3.xi; *Cym.*, 1.i.
LOCKRAM, linen of coarse kind, *Cor.*, 2.i.
LOCUSTS, suggested perhaps by the biblical diet (*Matthew* 3.4) of locusts and wild honey; some take it as the fruit of the carob tree, *Oth.*, 1.iii.
LODGE, to flatten crops, *Mac.*, 4.i.
LODGING, *shameful lodging*, the stocks, *Lear*, 2.ii.
LOGGATS, small logs of wood for throwing at a mark, *Ham.*, 5.i.
LONG, (1) *think long*, eagerly anticipate, *Rom. & Jul.*, 4.v; (2) *long of*, because of, *Cor.*, 5.iv; *Cym.*, 5.v; (3) *this longs the text*, belongs to the play, not to Gower, *Per.*, 2.*Prol.*
'LONG, belong, *Cor.*, 5.iii.
LONG-ENGRAFFED, firmly embedded, *Lear*, 1.i.
'LOO, cry to urge on dogs, *Troil. & Cres.*, 5.vii.
LOOF'D, a technical term from sailing, but in *Ant. & Cleo.*, 3.x, means moved away from the battle.
LOOK, *look you out*, find an occasion to, *Timon*, 3.ii; expect, *Mac.*, 5.iii; *look up*, take courage, *Ham.*, 3.iii; *look upon*, to look as a mere spectator, *Troil. & Cres.*, 5.vi; *look through*, discover itself, *Ham.*, 4.vii; *look it be done*, see that it is done, *Oth.*, 4.iii.
LOOP, hook, *Oth.*, 3.iii.
LOOP'D, full of holes, *Lear*, 3.iv.
LOOSE, casual, *Troil. & Cres.*, 3.iii; perfunctory, *Troil. & Cres.*, 4.iv; wanton, *Titus*, 2.i; *Oth.*, 2.i; undisciplined, *Oth.*, 3.iii; separate, *Lear*, 5.i; *verb*, unclasp hands, *Titus*, 2.iii; unleash, *Ham.*, 2.ii; release an arrow, *Titus*, 4.iii.
LOOSE-WIVED, married to a wanton, *Ant. & Cleo.*, 1.ii.
LOSE, destroy, *Ham.*, 3.ii; *lose your voice*, speak in vain, without response, *Ham.*, 1.ii; *lose thee nothing*, prove not unprofitable to you, *Lear*, 1.ii; *lost me in your liking*, deprived me of, *Lear*, 1.i; *loses your sword*, leaves it without a master, *Cym.*, 2.iv; *a lost fear*, needless, *Oth.*, 5.ii.
LOSS, destruction, *Lear*, 3.vi; *the heart of loss*, complete ruin, *Ant. & Cleo.*, 4.xii.
LOTS, winning numbers in lottery, so *lots to blanks*, all the world to nothing, *Cor.*, 5.ii.
LOTTERY, prize, *Ant. & Cleo.*, 2.ii; *by lottery*, by chance (just as the

tyrant in his caprice decrees), *Jul. Caes.*, 2.i; *put to lottery*, to be settled by drawing lots, *Troil. & Cres.*, 2.i.

LOUD, stormy, *Ham.*, 4.vii; emphatic, *Oth.*, 1.i.

LOUSE, become lousy, *Lear*, 3.ii.

LOVE, *of all loves*, form of entreaty, *Oth.*, 3.i.

LOVE-DAY, day of reconciliation, *Titus*, 1.i.

LOW, humbler, *Cym.*, 3.iii; *so low with him*, so lacking in financial resources, *Timon*, 3.vi.

LOWN, rascal, *Oth.*, 2.iii; *lord and lown*, high and low, *Per.*, 4.vi.

LOWNESS, degradation, *Lear*, 3.iv; *Ant. & Cleo.*, 3.xi.

LUCRE, gain, greed of, *Cym.*, 4.ii.

LUD'S TOWN, London (the name of the mythical king Lud is preserved in Ludgate), *Cym.*, 3.i.

LUNES, lunatic behaviour, *Troil. & Cres.*, 2.iii.

LUPERCAL, *feast of Lupercal*, feast in honour of Pan, the Lupercal being the cave where it was supposed Romulus and Remus were suckled by a wolf, *Jul. Caes.*, 1.i.

LURCH, *lurch'd all swords of the garland*, gained all the honour (a card term indicating a clean sweep of the stakes), *Cor.*, 2.ii.

LUST, *I'll answer to my lust*, I'll answer in deeds (not merely words) for my desires, *Troil. & Cres.*, 4.iv; *lust-dieted*, surfeited, *Lear*, 4.ii.

LUSTIHOOD, manly vigour, *Troil. & Cres.*, 2.ii.

LUSTY, merry, *Rom. & Jul.*, 1.iv; vigorous, *Jul. Caes.*, 1.ii.

LUXURIOUS, lascivious, *Mac.*, 4.iii; *luxuriously*, lasciviously, *Ant. & Cleo.*, 3.xiii.

LUXURY, lust, *Ham.*, 1.v.

LYCURGUS, regarded as founder of Spartan laws, so ideal type of magistrate, *Cor.*, 2.i.

LYM, bloodhound, *Lear*, 3.vi.

MACE, staff of sheriff's officer laid on shoulder of person to be arrested. Morpheus, the god of sleep, is described as having one of lead, *Jul. Caes.*, 4.iii.

MACHINE, the mechanism of the bodily frame, *Ham.*, 2.ii.

MACULATION, stain, impurity, *Troil. & Cres.*, 4.iv.

MADE-UP, *a made-up villain*, a complete villain, *Timon*, 5.i.

MAGGOT-PIE, magpie, *Mac.*, 2.ii.

MAGNIFICO, title given to Venetian grandees, *Oth.*, 1.ii.

MAHU, a devil, *Lear*, 3.iv.

MAIL, a piece of mail-armour, *Troil. & Cres.*, 3.iii; *mail'd*, gauntleted, *Cor.*, 1.iii.

MAIM, *maims of shame*, shameful wounds, *Cor.*, 4.v.

MAIN, sea, *Oth.*, 2.i; the mainland, *Lear*, 3.i; *the main soldier*, the most distinguished, *Ant. & Cleo.*, 1.ii; *the main of Poland*, the chief part of Poland, *Ham.*, 4.iv; *main opinion*, strong belief, *Jul. Caes.*, 2.i; *the main voice*, powerful authority, *Ham.*, 1.iii.

MAINLY, *so mainly as*, so much as, *Troil. & Cres.*, 4.iv; *mainly ignorant*, absolutely ignorant, *Lear*, 4.vii.

MAKE, (1) *make strong party*, gather a force of friends, *Cor.*, 3.ii; *what make you?* what business brings you? *Ham.*, 1.ii; *Oth.*, 3.iv; *I'll not meddle nor make no farther*, have no part in the affair, *Troil. & Cres.*, 1.i; *make against me*, seem to inculpate me, *Rom. & Jul.*, 5.iii; *make good time with*, prove successful against, *Cym.*, 4.ii; *makes me*, brings me success, *Oth.*, 5.i and 1.ii; *makes not up*, makes not its choice, *Lear*, 1.i; *from your love make such a stray*, wander from the way to your love, *Lear*, 1.i.

MAKE, (2) *mate and make*, husband and wife, *Lear*, 4.iii.

MALICE, a malicious act, *Cor.*, 2.ii.

MALICIOUSLY, without remorse, *Ant. & Cleo.*, 3.xiii.

MALIGN, envy, *Cor.*, 1.i; regard with envy, *Per.*, 5.i.

MALKIN, slattern, *Cor.*, 2.i; *Per.*, 4.iii.

MALLECHO, *miching mallecho*, crafty or skulking crime, *Ham.*, 3.ii.

MAMMERING, hesitating, *Oth.*, 3.iii.

MAMMET, puppet, *Rom. & Jul.*, 3.v.

MAMMOCK, to tear in pieces, *Cor.*, 1.iii.

MAN, *man but a rush against*, direct, manage (as a weapon) a bulrush against, *Oth.*, 5.ii.

MANAGE, direction, *Troil. & Cres.*, 3.iii; *Per.*, 4.vi; conduct, *Rom. & Jul.*, 3.i; *verb*, wield, *Rom. & Jul.*, 1.i; exercise, *Lear*, 1.iii; conduct, carry on, *Oth.*, 2.iii.

MANDRAGORA, mandrake (*q.v.*); a narcotic was made from the plant, *Oth.*, 3.iii; *Ant. & Cleo.*, 1.v.

MANDRAKE, plant with forked root recalling human shape; supposed to shriek when torn from earth and deprive hearer of reason, *Rom. & Jul.*, 4.iii.

MAN-ENTER, *his pupil age man-enter'd thus*, thus in his youth initiated into manhood, *Cor.*, 2.ii.

MANKIND, *are you mankind?* are you in your senses? *Cor.*, 4.ii.

MANNER, *to the manner born*, familiar from birth with the usage, *Ham.*, 1.iv.

MANNER'D, educated in deportment, [*Per.*, 3.iii.

MANSIONRY, *does approve by his lov'd mansionry*, shows by the way his kind love to nest here, *Mac.*, 1.vi.

MANTLE, to cover as with a mantle, *Cor.*, 1.vi; scum, *Lear*, 3.iv.

MANY, *many my near occasions*, my many important affairs, *Timon*, 3.vi; *the many*, the plebeians, *Cor.*, 3.i; *many our contriving friends*, many friends plotting on our behalf, *Ant. & Cleo.*, 1.ii.

MAP, *map of woe*, embodiment, picture, of woe, *Titus*, 3.ii.

MAPPERY, studying maps at headquarters, not face to face with the enemy, *Troil. & Cres.*, 1.iii.

MARBLE, *marble heaven*, bright and variegated like marble (or eternal), *Oth.*, 3.iii; *marble-hearted*, hardhearted, *Lear*, 1.iv; *marble-constant*, firm of purpose, *Ant. & Cleo.*, 5.ii.

MARBLED, *marbled mansions all above*, heaven, *Timon*, 4.iii.

MARCHPANE, marzipan, *Rom. & Jul.*, 1.v.

MARGENT, margin of a text (where an explanatory note would appear), *Ham.*, 5.ii; *Rom. & Jul.*, 1.iii.

MARK, *God save (or bless) the mark!* to avert evil omen, then to qualify scornfully or apologetically some remark, *Rom. & Jul.*, 3.ii; *Oth.*, 1.i; *beyond the mark of others*, beyond the power or reach, *Cor.*, 2.ii; *Ant. & Cleo.*, 3.vi; notice, *Oth.*, 2.iii.

MARKET, *market of his time*, the way he spends his time, *Ham.*, 4.iv.

MARKMAN, marksman, *Rom. & Jul.*, 1.i.

MARRY, from Mary, to express surprise, affirmation, etc., *Rom. & Jul.*, 4.v; *Ham.*, 3.ii; indeed, to be sure, *Cym.*, 1.i; scornfully, in *Lear*, 4.ii.

MART, *verb*, dispose of for gain, *Jul. Caes.*, 4.iii; traffic, *Cym.*, 1.vi; *noun*, market-gathering, *Per.*, 4.ii; *foreign mart*, purchase abroad, *Ham.*, 1.i.

MARTIAL, like that of Mars, the god of war, *Cym.*, 4.ii.

MARTLET, house martin, swallow, *Mac.*, 1.vi.

MARTYR, to injure, mutilate, *Titus*, 3.i; *Rom. & Jul.*, 4.v; *her martyr'd signs*, the signs forced on her by her mutilations, *Titus*, 3.ii.

MARVEL, astonishment, *Cym.*, 3.i.

MARY-BUDS, buds of marigold, *Cym.*, 2.iii.

MAST, acorns, food for swine, *Timon*, 4.iii.

MASTER, *adj.*, same as 'main' in *master and main*, *Oth.*, 2.i; *Per.*, 4.vi.

MASTERLY, *a masterly report*, a report of the mastery shown by the subject of the report, *Ham.*, 4.vii.

MASTIC, *mastic jaws*, like a mastiff's, *Troil. & Cres.*, 1.iii.

MATCH, *cry a match*, claim a win, *Rom. & Jul.*, 2.iv; wager, *Cym.*, 1.iv; bargain, *Cym.*, 3.vi; *Troil. & Cres.*, 4.v; *a match, sir*, the bargain is made, *Cor.*, 2.iii; *verb*, show equal skill, *Ham.*, 4.vii; meet in combat, *Cym.*, 2.i.

MATE, to confound, *Mac.*, 5.i.

MATERIAL, important, *Mac.*, 3.i; *Cym.*, 1.vi; *material sap*, the sap that provides the growth and substance, *Lear*, 4.ii.

MATTER, meaning, sense, *Ham.*, 2.ii; *Lear*, 4.vi; *it's no matter for that*, of no importance, *Cor.*, 4.v; *matter in't*, the business is serious, *Oth.*, 3.iv.

MAUGRE, in spite of, *Titus*, 4.ii; *Lear*, [5.iii.

MAZARD, head, *Ham.*, 5.i; *Oth.*, 2.iii.

MEAN, method, device, *Rom. & Jul.*, 3.iii; *Ant. & Cleo.*, 4.vi; means of approach to, *Ham.*, 4.vi; *this mean*, this that stands between us as a link, *Ant. & Cleo.*, 3.ii; opportunity, *Oth.*, 3.i; *what means do you make?* what efforts do you make to placate the king? *Cym.*, 2.iv.

MEASLES, scurvy complaint or fellow, *Cor.*, 3.i.

MEASURE, judgement, *Troil. & Cres.*, 1.iii; *with measure*, adequately, *Cor.*, 2.ii; a draught of wine, *Mac.*, 3.iv; a dance, *Rom. & Jul.*, 1.iv; glass, health, *Oth.*, 2.iii; *verb*, *measure your lubber's length*, lie stretched on the ground, *Lear*, 1.iv.

MECHANIC, workman, *Cor.*, 5.iii; *adj.*, engaged in manual work, *Ant. & Cleo.*, 5.ii; vulgar, *Ant. & Cleo.*, 4.iv; *being mechanical*, of the working class, *Jul. Caes.*, 1.i.

MED'CINABLE, healing, *Troil. & Cres.*, 1.iii; *Oth.*, 5.ii; having a medicinal effect (figuratively), *Cym.*, 3.ii.

MEDIATOR, one who pleads for another, *Oth.*, 1.i.

MEDICINE, poison, *Lear*, 5.iii; slander (as if a poison), *Oth.*, 4.i; love-philtre, *Oth.*, 1.iii; *that great medicine*, the elixir of the alchemist that would turn common objects to gold, *Ant. & Cleo.*, 1.v; *verb*, restore, *Oth.*, 3.iii; cure, *Cym.*, 4.ii.

MEDLAR, fruit like apple, eaten when almost rotten (with pun on 'meddler'), *Timon*, 4.iii.

MEED, reward, merit, *Cor.*, 2.ii; etc.

MEEK, gentle, courteous, *Jul. Caes.*, 3.i.

MEET, *meet with this time's guise*, accord with present manners, *Timon*, 4.iii.

MEETLY, not bad, *Ant. & Cleo.*, 1.iii.

MEINY, household retainers, *Lear*, 2.iv.

MELTING, *the melting mood*, tearfulness, *Oth.*, 5.ii.

MEMBER, *a member of his love*, a person loved by him, *Oth.*, 3.iv.

MEMORIAL, *memorial kisses*, kisses of remembrance, *Troil. & Cres.*, 5.ii.

MEMORIZE, *memorize another Golgotha*, make the place of battle as famous for the traces of death as was Golgotha, *Mac.*, 1.ii.

MEMORY, *rights of memory*, known and just claim to succeed as king, *Ham.*, 5.ii; memorial, *Cor.*, 4.v; *memory of my womb*, children, *Ant. & Cleo.*, 3.xiii; *memories*, reminders, *Lear*, 4.vii.

MEND, improve, dignify, *Timon*, 1.i; heal the wound, *Cor.*, 3.ii; *Timon*, 5.i; behave better, *Cor.*, 1.iv; make more valuable, atone for its imperfection, *Ant. & Cleo.*, 1.v; put right again, *Oth.*, 2.iii; adjust, *Ant. & Cleo.*, 5.ii; *people such that mend upon the world*, grow better with time, *Cym.*, 2.iv; *mend my soul*, in exclamations as in *Rom. & Jul.*, 1.v; *Cym.*, 5.v; *mends*, the remedy, *Troil. & Cres.*, 1.i.

MERCURIAL, swift, like that of Mercury, the messenger of the Gods, *Cym.*, 4.ii.

MERCY, *by mercy*, in all fairness, *Timon*, 3.v; *at mercy*, at the mercy of the enemy, *Cor.*, 1.x; *in mercy*, at his mercy, *Lear*, 1.iv; *cry you mercy*, beg your pardon, *Rom. & Jul.*, 4.v; (jocularly in *Lear*, 3.vi).

MERE, complete, *Mac.*, 4.iii; etc.; *your pleasure was my mere offence*, my only offence was your caprice, *Cym.*, 5.v.

MERED, *he being the mered question*, he alone being on trial (not Cleopatra), *Ant. & Cleo.*, 3.xiii.

MERELY, completely, *Ant. & Cleo.*, 3.vii; *Ham.*, 1.ii; *merely awry*, entirely beside the point, *Cor.*, 3.i.

MERIT, *others' merits*, others' deservings, good or bad, *Ant. & Cleo.*, 5.ii; *a provoking merit*, a lack of merit prompting hostile reaction, *Lear*, 3.v; *for the sake of merit*, because of my faithful service, *Ant. & Cleo.*, 2.vii.

MERRY, *merry with me*, mocking me, *Timon*, 3.ii.

MESH, mix salt and water in brewing, used figuratively, in *Titus*, 3.ii.

MESS, banquet, *Timon*, 4.iii; *the king's mess*, the king's table, *Ham.*, 5.ii; *makes his generation messes*, makes his children his food, *Lear*, 1.i; portions, as if of food, *Oth.*, 4.i.

METAPHYSICAL, supernatural, *Mac.*, 1.v.

METEOR, *some meteor that the sun exhales*, the sun was supposed to draw up vapours and ignite them to make meteors, *Rom. & Jul.*, 3.v.

METTLE, spirit, *Oth.*, 4.ii; *undaunted mettle*, courageous nature, *Mac.*, 1.vii; *Jul. Caes.*, 2.i; *quick mettle*, of agile mind, *Jul. Caes.*, 1.i.

MICHING, skulking, *Ham.*, 3.ii.

MICKLE, great, *Rom. & Jul.*, 2.iii.

MICROCOSM, man regarded as the universe in little, *Cor.*, 2.i.

MILCH, weep, *Ham.*, 2.ii.

MILD, *her mild companion*, companion of her mildness, serenity, *Per.*, 1.i; serene, *Per.*, 3.i.

MILK-LIVER'D, cowardly, without spirit, *Lear*, 4.ii.

MILKY, cowardly, *Timon*, 3.i; ineffective, soft-hearted, *Lear*, 1.iv; *milky head*, grey-haired, *Ham.*, 2.ii.

MINCE, make light of, *Oth.*, 2.iii; *Ant. & Cleo.*, 1.ii; *minces virtue*, poses as virtuous in an affected manner, *Lear*, 4.vi.

MIND, remind, *Cor.*, 5.i; *too much minded by herself alone*, too inclined to brooding in solitude, *Rom. & Jul.*, 4.i.

MINERAL, mine, *Ham.*, 4.i; love-philtre, *Oth.*, 1.ii; poison, *Oth.*, 2.i; *Cym.*, 5.v.

MINGLE, mixture, *Ant. & Cleo.*, 1.v; *verb*, *mingle eyes*, exchange friendly and knowing looks, *Ant. & Cleo.*, 3.xiii; subscribe together, *Cym.*, 1.vi.

MINIKIN, delicate, youthful, *Lear*, 3.vi.

MINION, favourite, *Timon*, 4.iii; ideal specimen, *Mac.*, 2.iv; wilful hussy. *Rom. & Jul.*, 3.v; shameless woman, *Oth.*, 5.i.

MINIM, very short note, *Rom. & Jul.*, 2.iv.

MINISTER, agent, *Ham.*, 1.iv; agent of retribution, *Ham.*, 3.iv; *Ant. & Cleo.*, 3.vi; servant, *Oth.*, 5.ii; *verb*, doctor, heal, *Mac.*, 5.iii; serve, *Cor.*, 1.i; *Cym.*, 3.iii; impart, *Cym.*, 1.i; administer (of a drug), *Rom. & Jul.*, 4.iii; *Per.*, 3.ii.

MINUTE-JACKS, time-servers, *Timon*, 3.vi.

MINUTELY, happening every minute, *Mac.*, 5.ii.

MIRABLE, wonderful, admirable, *Troil. & Cres.*, 4.v.

MIRACLE, *doth miracle itself*, be incomprehensible, *Cym.*, 4.ii.

MIRE, to sink as in mud, *Timon*, 4.iii.

MIRTH, object of ridicule, *Jul. Caes.*, 4.iii; a jest, *Ant. & Cleo.*, 1.iv.

MISADVENTURED, unfortunate, *Rom. & Jul.*, 1.*Prol.*

MISANTHROPOS, hater of mankind, *Timon*, 4.iii.

MISCARRY, come to harm, *Lear*, 5.i.

MISCHIEF, destruction, *Jul. Caes.*, 3.ii; misfortune, *Oth.*, 1.iii; harm, *Lear*, 1.ii; *nature's mischief*, the evil tendencies in human nature, or nature generally, *Mac.*, 1.v; *verb*, harm, *Timon*, 4.iii.

MISDOUBT, mistrust, *Ant. & Cleo.*, 3.vii.

MISDREAD, fear of evil, *Per.*, 1.ii.

MISERY, *than misery itself would give*, than poverty would have available for giving, *Cor.*, 2.ii; *noble misery*, shameful state for one of rank, *Cym.*, 5.iii.

MISGIVE, have suspicions, *Oth.*, 3.iv.

MISPRIZE, despise, *Troil. & Cres.*, 4.v.

MISSION, armed intervention, *Troil. & Cres.*, 3.iii.

MISSIVE, messenger, *Mac.*, 1.v; *Ant. & Cleo.*, 2.ii.

MISTAKE, *purposes mistook*, schemes ill-conceived, *Ham.*, 5.ii; *you mistake my fortunes*, you misjudge my position, *Timon*, 2.ii; *thy place mistook*, failed to honour your office as king's messenger, *Lear*, 2.iv; misunderstand, misrepresent, *Ant. & Cleo.*, 2.ii; *mis-take your husbands* (with pun on 'must take' of marriage), marry into misery, *Ham.*, 3.ii.

MISTEMPER'D, tempered for evil ends (with pun on *ill-tempered*), *Rom. & Jul.*, 1.i.

MISTHOUGHT, thought ill of, *Ant. & Cleo.*, 5.ii.

MISTRESS, the jack at bowls, *Troil. & Cres.*, 3.ii.

MO, MOE, more, *Ant. & Cleo.*, 4.xiv; *Look, moe!* more visitors, *Timon*, 1.i.

MOAN, lamentation, *Troil. & Cres.*, 2.ii; *finished joy and moan*, joy and sorrow, *Cym.*, 4.ii.

MOBLED, muffled, *Ham.*, 2.ii.

MOCK, *mock their charge*, treat their duty as a jest, *Mac.*, 2.ii; deceive, *Titus*, 1.i; *he mocks the pauses that he makes*, his delay in surrendering is ridiculous, *Ant. & Cleo.*, 5.i; cheat, *Cym.*, 4.ii.

MOCKERY, *malicious mockery*, futile as far as inflicting injury, *Ham.*, 1.i.

MODERN, everyday; *a modern ecstasy*, common, everyday excitement, *Mac.*, 4.iii; *likelihoods of modern seeming*, grounds of probability that are no more than everyday happenings without significance, *Oth.*, 1.iii; *modern friends*, mere acquaintances, *Ant. & Cleo.*, 5.ii.

MODEST, *modest doubt*, reasonable thought for the future, *Troil. & Cres.*, 2.ii; *the modest truth*, the very opposite of exaggeration, *Lear*, 4.vii; *modest haste*, briefly, yet keeping to the facts, *Lear*, 2.iv.

MODESTY, *cold modesty*, no exaggeration, *Jul. Caes.*, 3.i; in natural manner, *Ham.*, 2.ii.

MODICUM, small quantity, *Troil. & Cres.*, 2.i.

MOIETY, *moiety competent*, equal stake, share, *Ham.*, 1.i; *a moiety of the world*, half the world, *Ant. & Cleo.*, 5.i; share, *Lear*, 1.i.

MOIST, *moist star*, the moon, *Ham.*, 1.i.

MOLESTATION, turmoil, *Oth.*, 2.i.

MOMENT, *on the moment*, immediately, *Timon*, 1.i; *upon far poorer moment*, for a much less important cause, *Ant. & Cleo.*, 1.ii.

MONSTER, *that monsters it*, that makes it seem so unnatural and huge, *Lear*, 1.i.

MONSTER'D, grossly exaggerated, *Cor.*, 2.ii.

MONSTROUS, unnatural, *Timon*, 4.ii; *Per.*, 5.iii.

MONSTRUOSITY, unnatural feature, *Troil. & Cres.*, 3.ii.

MONUMENT, memorial, *Timon*, 4.iii; tomb, *Rom. & Jul.*, 3.v; etc.; effigy, *Cym.*, 2.ii.

MONUMENTAL, *in monumental mockery*, a memorial or relic of forgotten times, *Troil. & Cres.*, 3.iii; *monumental alabaster*, alabaster being favourite material for effigies on tombs, *Oth.*, 5.ii.

MOOD, anger, *Rom. & Jul.*, 3.i; displeasure, *Oth.*, 2.iii.

Moon, month, *Ham.*, 3.ii; *till now some nine moons wasted*, until some nine months ago, *Oth.*, 1.iii; symbol of Diana, goddess of chastity, *Cor.*, 5.iii.

Moonshine, *twelve or fourteen moonshines lag of a brother*, twelve or so months younger than my brother, *Lear*, 1.ii; *a sop o' the moonshine*, let the moonshine into him with his sword, *Lear*, 2.ii.

Mop, grimace; *mopping and mowing*, making faces, like the waiting-women moved by the devil Flibbertigibbet, *Lear*, 4.i.

Mope, act without full use of one's wits, *Ham.*, 3.iv.

Moral, hidden meaning, allegorical, *Timon*, 1.i; *adj.*, moralizing, *Lear*, 4.ii.

Moraler, one who expounds moral principles, *Oth.*, 2.iii.

Mortal, *mortal coil*, the troubles of human existence, and the mortality that encloses man, *Ham.*, 3.i; *more than a mortal seeming*, more than the air of a mere human being, *Cym.*, 1.vi.

Mortality, human existence, *Mac.*, 2.iii; death, *Lear*, 4.vi; *the shores of my mortality*, the bounds of my life, *Per.*, 5.i.

Mortally, *mortally brought forth*, of human parents, *Per.*, 5.i; in deadly fashion, *Per.*, 3.iii.

Mortify, numb, render insensible, *Lear*, 2.iii; *Jul. Caes.*, 2.i.

Mortise, *hold the mortise*, hold together at the joints, *Oth.*, 2.i; *mortised*, jointed (as with mortise and tenon), *Ham.*, 3.iii.

Moth, a parasite, *Oth.*, 1.iii; *fill Ithaca full of moths*, parasites (the suitors of Penelope), also moths that infest wool, etc., *Cor.*, 1.iii.

Mother, hysteria, *Lear*, 2.iv; *whose mother was her painting*, a creature of rouge and paint, *Cym.*, 3.iv.

Motion, life, *Rom. & Jul.*, 3.ii; *upon the foot of motion*, ready to manifest itself, *Mac.*, 2.iii; exertion, *Ham.*, 4.vii; promotion, *Jul. Caes.*, 2.i; appeal, proposal, *Cor.*, 2.ii; the action of the virginal, *Cym.*, 4.ii; desire, *Oth.*, 1.iii; sense, intelligence, *Oth.*, 1.ii; mental sight, intuition, *Ant. & Cleo.*, 2.iii.

Motive, instigator, *Timon*, 5.iv; organ, limb, *Troil. & Cres.*, 4.v; cause, *Ant. & Cleo.*, 2.ii; *Oth.*, 4.ii.

Motley, the long coat worn by professional fools, woven of green and yellow threads, *Lear*, 1.iv.

Mould, shape, earth-born, *Cor.*, 3.ii; *the mould of form*, model of behaviour, *Ham.*, 3.i.

Moult, lose, *Ham.*, 2.ii.

Mountant, rising, *Timon*, 4.iii.

Mountebank, *mountebank their loves*, gain their loves by my glib talk, *Cor.*, 3.ii.

Mouse-hunt, woman-hunter, *Rom. & Jul.*, 4.iv.

Mouth, *spend his mouth*, give words not deeds, *Troil. & Cres.*, 5.i; *mouth-friends*, in profession only, *Timon*, 3.vi; *mouths of wisest censure*, the judgements of the wise, *Oth.*, 2.iii; *mouth-made vows*, promise without performance, *Ant. & Cleo.*, 1.iii.

Move, anger, *Jul. Caes.*, 4.iii; persuade, *Rom. & Jul.*, 3.iv; prompt, *Ham.*, 3.ii; undertake, *Timon*, 5.ii; *moved my lord*, made representations to my lord, *Oth.*, 3.iv; *move your suit*, plead your case, *Oth.*, 3.iv; *moving accidents*, exciting events, *Oth.*, 1.iii.

Mover, remover of plunder, so (ironically) active being, *Cor.*, 1.v; cause, *Cym.*, 1.v.

Mow, grimace, *Cym.*, 1.vi; *Ham.*, 2.ii.

Much, very, *Oth.*, 1.i; *'tis very much*, serious indeed, *Oth.*, 4.i.

Muddy-mettled, dull-spirited, *Ham.*, 2.ii.

Muffled, blindfolded, *Rom. & Jul.*, 1.i.

Mull'd, blunted, *Cor.*, 4.v.

Multipotent, almighty, *Troil. & Cres.*, 4.v.

Multitudinous, *the multitudinous tongue*, belonging to the multitude, *Cor.*, 3.i; *multitudinous seas*, vast with innumerable waves, *Mac.*, 2.ii.

Mummy, preparation of dead bodies, supposedly magical, *Mac.*, 4.i; *Oth.*, 3.iv.

Muniments, instruments of war, *Cor.*, 1.i.

Murdering-piece, cannon firing case-shot, *Ham.*, 4.v.

Music, band of musicians, *Rom. & Jul.*, 4.iv; *Cym.*, 2.iii.

Muss, a scramble of articles thrown to a group, *Ant. & Cleo.*, 3.xiii.

Mutation, capricious change, *Cym.*, 4.ii.

Mute, actor with no speaking part, *Ham.*, 5.ii; dumb servant, *Cym.*, 3.v.

Mutine, mutineer, *Ham.*, 5.ii.

Mutiny, strife, *Rom. & Jul.*, 1.*Prol.*; *verb*, break into strife, *Oth.*, 2.i; quarrel, *Ant. & Cleo.*, 3.xi.

Mutual, common, *Titus*, 5.iii; *mutual cunning*, cunning on both sides, each deceiving the other, *Lear*, 3.i;

a *mutual pair*, united in feeling, each an echo to other's love, *Ant. & Cleo.*, 1.i; *mutually*, jointly, *Cor.*, 1.i.

Mutualities, exchange of intimacies between pair, *Oth.*, 2.i.

Myrmidon, *the great Myrmidon*, Achilles, *Troil. & Cres.*, 1.iii.

Mystery, trade, *Timon*, 4.iii; *Oth.*, 4.ii; *the mysteries of Hecat*, the secret rites of the queen of Hades, and goddess of magic, *Lear*, 1.i.

Nag, *ribaudred nag*, lewd jade, *Ant. & Cleo.*, 3.x.

Naked, unarmed, *Cor.*, 1.x; *Oth.*, 5.ii; unprovided, *Ham.*, 4.vii; undisguised, *Timon*, 5.i.

Nakedness, unfurnished, unprovided, *Timon*, 4.i.

Name, honourable reputation, *Cym.*, 1.iv; *the whole name*, the whole glory, *Cor.*, 2.i; *the second name*, second in reputation as a soldier, *Cor.*, 4.vi; *our general name*, womanhood, or humanity generally, *Titus*, 2.iii; *verb*, *name the word of hands*, utter the word 'hands,' *Titus*, 3.ii.

Napkin, handkerchief, *Jul. Caes.*, 3.ii; etc.

Naples, associated at the time with venereal disease, *Oth.*, 3.i.

Napless, threadbare, *Cor.*, 2.i.

Narcissus, cited as a type of beauty, *Ant. & Cleo.*, 2.v.

Narrow, *narrow measure*, grudging praise, *Ant. & Cleo.*, 3.iv; *narrowly*, thoroughly, *Per.*, 4.i.

Native, motive, *Cor.*, 3.i; *adj.*, related, *Ham.*, 1.ii; by right of birth or status, *Timon*, 4.iii; natural, normal, *Oth.*, 2.i; *Rom. & Jul.*, 4.i; characteristic of my true nature, *Oth.*, 1.i; *the native hue of resolution*, the complexion naturally associated with resolute men, *Ham.*, 3.i.

Nativity, birth, with reference to the circumstances, planetary, etc., affecting the child's destiny, *Lear*, 1.ii; *Per.*, 3.i.

Natural, related by blood, *Timon*, 4.iii; *the natural touch*, the common characteristic in nature that makes parents (birds and beasts) protect their young, *Mac.*, 4.ii; *natural in thine art*, a wonderful imitator of nature, *Timon*, 5.i; *natural father*, real father, *Cym.*, 3.iii; *natural boy*, though illegitimate he seems to behave like a true son, *Lear*, 2.i; not artificial, *Per.*, 5.*Prol.*

Nature, *one touch of nature makes the whole world kin*, humanity has one common characteristic, *Troil. & Cres.*, 3.iii; *nature's mischief*, the cruel deeds prompted by our nature, or the calamities that come on human kind, *Mac.*, 1.v; *nature's copy*, the tenure (copyhold being terminable) on which we hold our life, *Mac.*, 3.ii; *nature's livery or fortune's star*, the distinction between nature and fortune is explained in *As You Like It* (1.ii): 'Fortune reigns in the gifts of the world, not in the lineaments of Nature,' *Ham.*, 1.iv; *the wisdom of nature*, scientific explanation, *Lear*, 1.ii; *falls from the bias of nature*, acts contrary to humane feeling, *Lear*, 1.ii; *where nature doth with merit challenge*, where the claim of merit is added to that of nature (she being his child), *Lear*, 1.i.

Naught, ruin, *Ant. & Cleo.*, 3.x; *adj.*, worthless, wicked, *Lear*, 2.iv; naughty, lewd, *Ham.*, 1.iv.

Naughtily, lewdly, *Troil. & Cres.*, 4.ii.

Naughty, good for nothing, wicked, *Troil. & Cres.*, 4.ii; *Lear*, 3.vii; bad, *Lear*, 3.iv.

Nave, navel, *Mac.*, 1.ii; hub of wheel, *Ham.*, 2.ii.

Navel, centre, *Cor.*, 3.i.

Navigation, shipping, *Mac.*, 4.i.

Ne, nor, *Per.*, 2.*Prol.*

Neapolitan, *Neapolitan bone-ache*, venereal disease, *Troil. & Cres.*, 2.iii.

Near, *near occasions*, important private affairs, *Timon*, 3.vi; *my near'st of life*, what is most vital and innermost to my being, *Mac.*, 3.i; *adv.*, intimately, *Timon*, 1.ii; *so near*, as in my honour as a soldier, that being nearest my heart, *Oth.*, 2.iii.

Nearly, with certain reserves, *Ant. & Cleo.*, 2.ii; intimately, *Lear*, 1.i.

Neat, *you neat slave*, you dandified rascal, *Lear*, 2.ii.

Neat-herd, cowherd, *Cym.*, 1.i.

Necessary, inevitable, *Ham.*, 3.ii; useful, *Cor.*, 2.i.

Necessity, *the art of our necessities is strange*, our poverty and distress have a strange power of making precious what seems common to the well-off, *Lear*, 3.ii.

Neck, *upon their first lord's neck*, by means of his ruin, *Timon*, 4.iii; *on your neck*, to your charge, *Oth.*, 5.ii.

Need, *for a need*, if urgently required, *Ham.*, 2.ii; *verb, what needs this iterance?* what necessity is there for this repetition? *Oth.*, 5.ii.

NEEDLY, of necessity, *Rom. & Jul.*, 3.ii.

NEEDY, *such a needy time,* a time destitute of joy, *Rom. & Jul.*, 3.v; *your needy bread,* the bread necessary for your sustenance, *Per.*, 1.iv.

NEGLECTION, neglect, *Troil. & Cres.*, 1.iii; *Per.*, 3.iii.

NEGLIGENCE, *give to negligence,* regard with indifference, treat with no regard, *Ham.*, 4.v.

NEGLIGENT, *and we in negligent danger,* in danger if we neglected to take action, *Ant. & Cleo.*, 3.vi.

NEIGHBOUR'D, intimate, *Ham.*, 2.ii; *Lear*, 1.i.

NEIGHBOURHOOD, social harmony such as should exist among neighbours, *Timon*, 4.i.

NEMEAN, *the Nemean lion,* the capture of its skin was one of the labours of Hercules, *Ham.*, 1.iv.

NEPHEW, cousin, *Troil. & Cres.*, 1.ii; *grandson, Oth.*, 1.i.

NEPTUNE, *the mask'd Neptune,* calm seas, *Per.*, 3.iii.

NEREIDES, daughters of Nereus, sea-nymphs, fifty in number, *Ant. & Cleo.*, 2.ii.

NERVE, sinew, *Ham.*, 1.v; etc.; *nervy,* powerful, *Cor.*, 2.i.

NESSUS, the centaur killed by Hercules; a shirt dipped in the centaur's blood, given to the hero's wife Deianira as a love-charm and given by her in good faith to retain her husband's love, burnt into the flesh of Hercules and drove him to death, *Ant. & Cleo.*, 4.xii.

NETHER, done here below, *Lear*, 4.ii.

NEW, *shall make your lord that which he is new o'er,* shall now go back from my false description to give a true account of him as he is, *Cym.*, 1.vi.

NICE, precise, *Troil. & Cres.*, 4.v; too detailed, *Mac.*, 4.iii; petty, *Rom. & Jul.*, 3.i; *Jul. Caes.*, 4.iii; *mine hours were nice and lucky,* so permitting the gratification of caprice, *Ant. & Cleo.*, 3.xiii; *nice-preserved,* coyly guarded, *Titus*, 2.iii.

NICELY, gracefully, *Cym.*, 2.iv; punctiliously, *Lear*, 2.ii and 5.iii; *nicely-gauded,* delicately coloured, *Cor.*, 2.i.

NICENESS, demure, reserved, *Cym.*, 3.iv.

NICK, *in the nick,* at the critical moment, *Oth.*, 5.ii.

NICKNAME, deliberately misapply names, *Ham.*, 3.i.

NIGGARD, pay only in part, *Jul. Caes.*, 4.iii.

NIGHT-BIRD, nightingale, *Per.*, 4.*Prol.*

NIGHTED, *nighted colour,* mourning in looks and dress, *Ham.*, 1.ii; *his nighted life,* darkened by blindness and misery, *Lear*, 4.v.

NIGHTGOWN, dressing-gown, *Mac.*, 2.ii; *Oth.*, 4.iii.

NIGHTLY, *adj.*, active at night, *Titus*, 2.iii; *adv.*, by night, *Rom. & Jul.*, 4.i.

NILL, will not, *Ham.*, 5.i; *Per.* 3.*Prol.*

NIMBLE-PINION'D, swift-winged, *Rom. & Jul.*, 2.v.

NINE-FOLD, the nine foals that go with the night-mare, *Lear*, 3.iv.

NIOBE, wife of Amphion, King of Thebes; her seven sons and seven daughters were slain by Apollo and Diana, *Ham.*, 1.ii.

NIP, grip the attention, *Per.*, 5.i.

NOBLE, *against all noble sufferance,* beyond the endurance of the nobility, *Cor.*, 3.i; *the noble,* the senate, *Cor.*, 3.i.

NOBLENESS, rank, dignity, *Mac.*, 1.iv; aristocratic birth, *Per.*, 3.ii.

NOISE, rumour, *Troil. & Cres.*, 1.ii; *Timon*, 4.iii; music, *Mac.*, 4.i; *Ant. & Cleo.*, 4.iii; *noises it against us,* raises disturbance against us, *Ant. & Cleo.*, 3.vi.

NOMINATION, the mentioning by name, *Ham.*, 5.ii.

NONCE, *for the nonce,* for this occasion, *Ham.*, 4.vii.

NONE, *none our parts,* none of our features, *Ant. & Cleo.*, 1.iii.

NONPAREIL, one without equal, *Mac.*, 3.iv; etc.

NONSUIT, to dismiss, *Oth.*, 1.i.

NORTH, north wind, *Oth.*, 5.ii.

NOSE-PAINTING, making the nose red by drinking, *Mac.*, 2.iii.

NOT, not only, *Cor.*, 3.ii; *Per.*, 3.ii.

NOTE, mark, *Cym.*, 2.ii; *my wind-pipe's dangerous notes,* indications of its vulnerable spots, *Timon*, 1.ii; *of dreadful note,* remarkable for its horror, *Mac.*, 3.ii; *without note,* without attracting attention, *Cor.*, 1.ix; *the note of judgement,* the judgement of the wise, *Troil. & Cres.*, 2.iii; *warrant of my note,* my confidence that comes from my knowledge of you, *Lear*, 3.i; *even to the note o' the king,* so that the king shall have knowledge of it, *Cym.*, 4.iii; *verb,* stigmatize as a thief, *Jul. Caes.*, 4.iii; indicate,

Ham., 1.v; *she's noted*, goes to that tune (marked as a lewd woman), *Troil. & Cres.*, 4.ii.

NOTHING-GIFT, worthless gift, *Cym.*, 3.vi.

NOTICE, observation, *Cor.*, 2.iii; information, *Oth.*, 3.iii.

NOTION, understanding, *Mac.*, 3.i; *Lear*, 1.iv.

NOUZLE, rear, *Per.*, 1.iv.

NOYANCE, harm, *Ham.*, 3.iii.

NUMBER, multitude, *Jul. Caes.*, 3.ii; *the honour'd number*, the patricians, *Cor.*, 3.i; *numbers*, verses, *Ham.*, 2.ii; *Rom. & Jul.*, 2.iv; *verb*, put into verse, *Ant. & Cleo.*, 3.ii.

NUNCLE, from 'mine uncle'; customary address of a fool to his master, *Lear*, 1.iv.

NURSERY, care, *Lear*, 1.i; *a nursery of like evil*, a crop of troubles, *Troil. & Cres.*, 1.iii.

O, *an O without a figure*, nothing, *Lear*, 1.iv; the earth, *Ant. & Cleo.*, 5.ii.

O', for *on* or *of*.

OAKEN, *oaken garland*, garland of oak leaves, the reward for saving the life of a fellow-citizen, *Cor.*, 2.i.

OATHABLE, recognized as fit to be sworn on oath in law-court, *Timon*, 4.iii.

OBJECT, something presented to the sight, *Ham.*, 1.i; appearance, *Cor.*, 1.i; what the mind is directed at, *Oth.*, 3.iv; *Lear*, 1.i.

OBLIQUE, crooked, dishonest, *Timon*, 4.iii; *oblique memorial*, the horns of the bull being used as a sign for the cuckold, *Troil. & Cres.*, 5.i.

OBLIVIOUS, causing forgetfulness, *Mac.*, 5.iii.

OBSCURE, *obscure plot*, dark spot, *Titus*, 2.iii; *obscure bird*, bird of darkness, the owl, *Mac.*, 2.iii; *obscure funeral*, humble, private, *Ham.*, 4.v; *obscure prologue*, indicating the sequel, though not explicitly, *Oth.*, 2.i; *verb*, *obscured course*, disguised, *Lear*, 2.ii.

OBSEQUIES, funeral rites, *Ham.*, 5.i; acts in memory of the dead, *Rom. & Jul.*, 5.iii.

OBSEQUIOUS, *obsequious tears*, showing respect for the dead, *Titus*, 5.iii; *Ham.*, 1.ii; *obsequious bondage*, used cynically by Iago, who regards dutiful service as folly, *Oth.*, 1.i.

OBSERVANCE, rule, *Timon*, 4.i; care, *Ham.*, 3.ii; respect, reverence, *Troil. & Cres.*, 1.iii; perception, *Ant. & Cleo.*, 3.ii.

OBSERVANCY, care and attention, *Oth.*, 3.iv.

OBSERVANT, careful, *Ham.*, 1.i; *noun*, flunkey, *Lear*, 2.ii.

OBSERVATION, attention, heed, *Ham.*, 1.v; experience, *Lear*, 1.i.

OBSERVE, humour, please, *Jul. Caes.*, 4.iii; *in an observing kind*, in a humble or respectful manner, *Troil. & Cres.*, 2.iii; *the observed of all observers*, the most regarded of all the courtiers, *Ham.*, 3.i.

OBSTRUCT, hindrance, *Ant. & Cleo.*, 3.vi.

OCCASION, *occasions*, needs, *Timon*, 2.ii; *Cym.*, 5.v; *he married but his occasion*, for political convenience, *Ant. & Cleo.*, 2.vi.

OCCULTED, hidden, *Ham.*, 3.ii.

OCCUPATION, handicraft, *Cor.*, 4.i; *the voice of occupation*, the vote, wishes of artisans, *Cor.*, 4.vi; *Jul. Caes.*, 1.ii; *royal occupation*, soldiering, *Ant. & Cleo.*, 4.iv.

OCCURRENTS, happenings, *Ham.*, 5.ii.

OD, used in oaths for God; *Od's pittikins*, God's pity, *Cym.*, 4.iv.

ODD, *odd with*, at strife with, *Troil. & Cres.*, 4.v; *the odd hits*, the extra hits that would mean defeat, *Ham.*, 5.ii.

ODD-EVEN, of night, between midnight and one, but perhaps later, *Oth.*, 1.i.

ODDLY, unfairly, *Troil. & Cres.*, 1.iii.

ODDS, *no odds*, no difference, *Timon*, 1.ii; *at the odds*, with the handicap I'm allowed, *Ham.*, 5.ii; *the odds of multitude*, superior numbers, *Troil. & Cres.*, 5.iv; strife, *Timon*, 4.iii; *Oth.*, 2.iii.

OEILLADES, amorous looks, *Lear*, 4.v.

O'ERCOME, overgrown, *Titus*, 2.iii.

O'ERFRAUGHT, over-burdened, *Mac.*, 4.iii.

O'ERGROWN, advanced in years, *Cym.*, 4.iv.

O'ERLEAP, pass over, omit, *Cor.*, 2.ii; *o'erleaps itself*, overshoots the target, overreaches itself, *Mac.*, 1.vii.

O'ER-RAUGHT, overtook, *Ham.*, 3.i.

O'ER-REACH, have the better of, *Ham.*, 5.i.

O'ERSHOOT, *o'ershot myself*, gone beyond discretion, *Jul. Caes.*, 3.ii.

O'ER-SIZED, smeared over, *Ham.*, 2.ii.

O'ERSKIP, disregard, *Lear*, 3.vi.

O'ERSWAY, *great command o'ersways the order*, royal command puts aside the customary rule, *Ham.*, 5.i.

O'ER-TEEMED, exhausted by many births, *Ham.*, 2.ii.

O'ER-WRESTED, *o'er-wrested seeming*, exaggerated imitation, *Troil. & Cres.*, 1.iii.

Off, *that's off*, beside the point, *Cor.*, 2.ii.

Offence, harm, *Jul. Caes.*, 4.iii; *sick offence*, a cause of thought-sickness, *Jul. Caes.*, 2.i; the ill-gotten gain, *Ham.*, 3.iii; injury, *Oth.*, 2.iii; displeasure, *Ant. & Cleo.*, 3.i; *Cym.*, 1.iv.

Offend, do harm, *Titus*, 3.i; go against, *Timon*, 5.iv; afflict, *Oth.*, 3.iv; *Cym.*, 5.iv; wrong, *Oth.*, 5.ii; *offended reputation*, wounded my honour, *Ant. & Cleo.*, 3.xi; *offended in*, displeased by, *Ant. & Cleo.*, 3.ii.

Offer, attempt, *Troil. & Cres.*, 2.iii.

Office, *the insolence of office*, of those in official positions, *Ham.*, 3.i; *offices of man*, the various compartments of his body, *Cor.*, 1.i; *the office and devotion*, devoted attention, *Ant. & Cleo.*, 1.i; *office of my heart*, devotion, *Oth.*, 3.iv; the kitchen, etc., in a great house, *Mac.*, 2.i; *Oth.*, 2.ii; *verb*, prevent, *Cor.*, 5.ii; *my speculative and offic'd instruments*, eyes, mental as well as of body, *Oth.*, 1.iii.

Officer, agent, *Ham.*, 4.ii; *Per.*, 5.iii; hangman, *Cym.*, 5.iv; servant, *Mac.*, 1.vii.

Officious, willing and energetic, *Titus*, 5.ii.

Old, hardened in some practice, *Troil. & Cres.*, 1.ii; *Rom. & Jul.*, 3.iii; *have old turning the key*, have lots of key-turning, *Mac.*, 2.iii; *old course*, his aged steps, *Lear*, 1.i; *old course of death*, customary, *Lear*, 3.vii; as expression of loving familiarity, *old Nile*, *Ant. & Cleo.*, i.v; *adv.*, in olden days, *Per.*, 1.*Prol.*

'Old, wold, moor land, *Lear*, 3.iv.

Omen, the fateful event that the omen had foretold, *Ham.*, 1.i.

Ominous, fatal, *Ham.*, 2.ii. [2.i.

Omit, neglect, *Cor.*, 3.i; forgo, *Oth.*,

On, sometimes used where modern usage employs another preposition.

Once, to sum up, once for all, *Cor.*, 2.iii; *Oth.*, 3.iii; one day, *Jul. Caes.*, 4.ii; once when, *Cor.*, 2.iii; at any time, *Ant. & Cleo.*, 5.ii.

One-trunk-inheriting, possessing no more than the goods that would fill only a chest, *Lear*, 2.ii.

Open, generous, *Troil. & Cres.*, 4.v; manifest, *Jul. Caes.*, 4.i; *the open night*, night in the open, out of doors, *Lear*, 3.iv; *open banner*, their allegiance openly declared, *Lear*, 3.i; *verb*, disclose, *Mac.*, 4.iii; etc.

Operant, potent, *Timon*, 4.iii; vital, *Ham.*, 3.ii.

Operation, activity; *Troil. & Cres.*, 3.iii; effect, potency, *Ant. & Cleo.*, 4.xv.

Opinion, favourable opinion of oneself, so sometimes arrogance, sometimes self-confidence, *Troil. & Cres.*, 1.iii; etc.; unfavourable judgement, *Oth.*, 4.ii.

Oppose, *my doors opposed against my passage*, blocked by duns, *Timon*, 3.iv; *thou oppos'd*, with you as adversary, *Mac.*, 5.viii; *oppose his foe*, fight with, *Timon*, 3.v; *oppos'd against*, exposed to, *Lear*, 4.vii; *oppose the bolt against*, bar the door against, *Lear*, 2.iv.

Opposite, adversary, *Ham.*, 5.ii; enemy, *Lear*, 5.iii; *adj.*, opposed to, *Oth.*, 1.ii; hostile, *Timon*, 1.i.

Opposition, *the opposition of your person*, your presence as one of the contestants, *Ham.*, 5.ii; *single oppositions*, duels, single combats, *Cym.*, 4.i.

Oppress, injure, *Timon*, 4.iii; overwhelm, tax beyond capacity, *Timon*, 2.ii; overwhelm with fear, *Ham.*, 1.ii; suppress, *Per.*, 3.*Prol.*; distress, *Lear*, 5.iii.

Oppression, distress, *Rom. & Jul.*, 1.i.

Oppugnancy, conflict, *Troil. & Cres.*, 1.iii.

Or, before, *Ham.*, 1.ii; *Cym.*, 2.iv.

Orb, the sphere in which a planet was thought to move, *Rom. & Jul.*, 2.ii; *Ant. & Cleo.*, 5.ii; the earth, *Ham.*, 2.ii; the moon, *Timon*, 4.iii; sphere of action, *Per.*, 1.ii; *operation of the orbs*, influence of the planets, *Lear*, 1.i.

Orbed, spherical, *Ham.*, 3.ii.

Ordain, intend, design, *Rom. & Jul.*, 4.v; institute, *Cym.*, 3.i.

Order, *the order*, custom, established rule, *Ham.*, 5.i; dispositions for battle, *Mac.*, 5.vi; *order of his funeral*, the ceremonies, *Jul. Caes.*, 3.i; *order of law*, in a legitimate way, *Lear*, 1.i; due ceremony, *Ant. & Cleo.*, 5.ii; *take order for*, arrange for, *Oth.*, 5.ii; *verb*, govern, *Titus*, 5.iii; *order'd*, disciplined, *Cym.*, 2.iv.

Ordinance, established natures, *Jul. Caes.*, 1.iii; rank, *Cor.*, 3.ii; *that slaves your ordinance*, who converts to his own selfish desires the mercies God provides for man, *Lear*, 4.i; the dispensation of the gods, *Cym.*, 4.ii.

Ordinant, preordaining, *Ham.*, 5.ii.

ORDINARY, meal to be had at a recognized price in a tavern or inn; applied ironically in *Ant. & Cleo.*, 2.ii.

ORGILLOUS, proud, *Troil. & Cres.*, 1. *Prol.*

ORIENT, *orient pearl*, as the finest pearls came from the East, Ceylon, etc., *Ant. & Cleo.*, 1.v.

ORIFEX, opening, *Troil. & Cres.*, 5.ii.

ORISON, prayer, *Ham.*, 3.i; *Cym.*, 1.iii.

ORT, scrap of food, *Troil. & Cres.*, 5.ii; *Timon*, 4.iii.

OSTENT, display, *Per.*, 1.ii.

OSTENTATION, display of zeal, *Cor.*, 1.vi; manifestation, *Ant. & Cleo.*, 3.vi; *formal ostentation*, due ceremony, *Ham.*, 1.vi.

OTHER, sometimes used as plural; *adv.*, otherwise, *Cor.*, 4.vi; *Oth.*, 4.ii.

OTTOMITE, Turk, *Oth.*, 1.iii.

OUT, in revolt and in arms, *Mac.*, 4.iii; completely, *Cor.*, 4.v; at a loss, *Cor.*, 5.iii; angry with, at odds with, *Jul. Caes.*, 1.i (with pun on *out* as indicating a hole in his shoe); abroad on service, *Lear*, 1.i; *prep.*, out of, *Cor.*, 5.ii.

OUT-CRAFTY, to defeat by guile, treachery, *Cym.*, 3.iv.

OUTFACE, to defy, *Lear*, 2.iii.

OUT-GO, out-run, exhaust, *Ant. & Cleo.*, 3.ii; *outgo*, go beyond, exceed, *Timon*, 1.i.

OUT-HEROD, *it out-herods Herod*, to rant even more outrageously than was customary in the part of Herod in the old mystery plays, *Ham.*, 3.ii.

OUTLIVE, live without apprehension, unaffected by, *Timon*, 4.iii.

OUT-PARAMOUR, *out-paramour'd the Turk*, more mistresses than the Turk wives and concubines, *Lear*, 3.iv.

OUT-PEER, surpass, *Cym.*, 3.vi.

OUTRAGE, public outcry, *Rom. & Jul.*, 5.iii.

OUTSTAND, overstay, *Cym.*, 1.vi.

OUTSTRETCH, *outstretch'd his span*, measured out his span of life, *Timon*, 5.iii; *outstretch'd heroes*, elongated like a shadow, the hero being extended by ambition, and ambition a shadow, *Ham.*, 2.ii.

OUT-WALL, exterior, *Lear*, 3.i.

OVER-, *see also* O'ER-.

OVERBULK, outgrow and smother, *Troil. & Cres.*, 1.iii.

OVERBUY, outweigh in worth, *Cym.*, 1.i.

OVERCOME, pass over, visit, *Mac.*, 3.iv.

OVERHOLD, *overhold his price*, require too high a price for his service, *Troil. & Cres.*, 2.iii.

OVERT, objective, verifiable, *Oth.*, 1.iii.

OVERTURE, proposal, *Cor.*, 1.ix; disclosure, *Lear*, 3.vii.

OVERWHELMING, overhanging, *Rom. & Jul.*, 5.i.

OWE, possess, obtain, own, *Mac.*, 1.iii; etc.

OYES, (*French*, oyez), the call of the public crier for attention, *Troil. & Cres.*, 4.v.

PACE, control, as in horsemanship, *Ant. & Cleo.*, 2.ii; train, *Per.*, 4.vi.

PACK, *verb*, plot, *Titus*, 4.ii; *Lear*, 3.i; *noun*, a gang, conspiring to some end, *Lear*, 5.iii.

PAGE, to serve as a personal attendant, *Timon*, 4.iii.

PAGEANT, (the wagon on which a scene in the miracle plays was staged at the various stations appointed for performance), so of show or spectacle, sometimes with idea of unreality or deception, *Ant. & Cleo.*, 4.xiv; *Oth.*, 1.iii; *verb*, imitate, present as a dramatic show, *Troil. & Cres.*, 1.iii.

PAINFUL, *by many a painful perch*, laborious journey (*see* PERCH), *Per.*, 3.*Prol.*

PAINTED, specious, false, *Ham.*, 3.i; *painted cloths*, canvas hangings painted with figures and moral sentences were a cheap substitute for figured tapestries, *Troil. & Cres.*, 5.x.

PALATE, to taste, *Ant. & Cleo.*, 5.ii; *the great'st taste most palates theirs*, the taste of the majority will be what pleases the plebeians, *Cor.*, 3.i.

PALE, palisade, *Ham.*, 1.iv; *Troil. & Cres.*, 2.iii; *verb*, (1) enclose, *Ant. & Cleo.*, 2.vii; *Cym.*, 3.i; (2) dim, *Ham.*, 1.v.

PALL, (1) wrap as in a mantle, *Mac.*, 1.v; (2) fail, *Ham.*, 5.ii; *pall'd*, drooping, *Ant. & Cleo.*, 2.vii.

PALLIAMENT, a robe, *Titus*, 1.i.

PALMY, flourishing, victorious, *Ham.*, 1.i.

PALTER, double-dealing, in speech or word, *Jul. Caes.*, 2.i; *verb*, dodge, cheat, *Ant. & Cleo.*, 3.xi.

PANG'D, tormented, *Cym.*, 3.iv.

PARADOX, *old fond paradoxes*, views contrary to received opinion, inspired by drink rather than wisdom, *Oth.*, 2.i.

PARAGON, to compare with an idea,

Ant. & Cleo., 1.v; to provide a model for, *Oth.*, 2.i.

PARALLEL, *as near as the extremest ends of parallels*, that don't meet, *Troil. & Cres.*, 1.iii.

PARCEL, portion, detachment, *Cor.*, 1.ii; etc.; *verb*, add to the items, *Ant. & Cleo.*, 5.ii.

PARD, panther, leopard, *Troil. & Cres.*, 3.ii.

PARDON, permission, *Ham.*, 4.vii; *Ant. & Cleo.*, 3.vi; *verb, pardon that man's life*, remit the death-penalty, *Lear*, 4.vi; *these pardon me's*, those affecting fashionable form of manners, *Rom. & Jul.*, 2.iv.

'PAREL, apparel, *Lear*, 4.i.

PARLE, exchange of terms, dispute, *Titus*, 5.iii; *Ham.*, 1.i.

PARLEY, *sound a parley*, give sign of willingness to come together, *Oth.*, 2.iii.

PART, accomplishment, endowment, *Ham.*, 4.vii; *how dearly ever parted*, however gifted, *Troil. & Cres.*, 3.iii.

PARTAKE, to impart, *Per.*, 1.i.

PARTIALLY, *partially affined*, constrained by undue favour (owing to friendship, etc.), *Oth.*, 2.iii.

PARTICIPATE, participating, *Cor.*, 1.i.

PARTICULAR, individual, *Troil. & Cres.*, 1.ii and iii; *Ham.*, 1.ii; *my particular fear*, my own cause for apprehension, *Lear*, 1.iv; *my particular grief*, private, personal, *Oth.*, 1.iii; *something particular*, an individual exploit, *Ant. & Cleo.*, 3.xiii; *noun, by particulars*, one by one, *Cor.*, 2.iii; *in a most dear particular*, as an individual, as a personal friend, *Cor.*, 5.i; *his particular*, his private interest, *Timon*, 4.iii; *for his particular*, for him as an individual, *Lear*, 2.iv; *my more particular*, my own especial reason, *Ant. & Cleo.*, 1.iii; *forgive me in thine own particular*, for your part, as the individual I have wronged, *Ant. & Cleo.*, 4.ix.

PARTICULARLY, *halts not particularly*, does not concentrate on any individual, *Timon*, 1.i.

PARTISAN, long-handled spear and axe, *Ham.*, 1.i; *Ant. & Cleo.*, 2.vii.

PARTY, cause, interest; *upon his party*, on his side, *Lear*, 2.i; *an intelligent party*, a confederate of the enemy, giving them information, *Lear*, 3.v; *parties*, accomplices, *Cor.*, 5.vi.

PASH, to bash, *Troil. & Cres.*, 2.iii.

PASS, *a pass of practice*, a treacherous thrust, *Ham.*, 4.vii; *verb*, (1) exceed description, *Troil. & Cres.*, 1.ii; *he passes*, he surpasses his fellows, *Timon*, 1.i; (2) undergo, experience, *Oth.*, 1.iii; *pass upon*, pass sentence on, *Lear*, 3.vii.

PASSABLE, affording free passage, *Cym.*, 1.ii.

PASSADO, lunge in fencing, *Rom. & Jul.*, 2.iv.

PASSAGE, death, *Ham.*, 5.ii; course, *Rom. & Jul.*, 1.*Prol.*; *passages of proof*, evidence of experience, *Ham.*, 4.vii; *no passage?* are there no passers-by? *Oth.*, 5.i; occurrence, *Cym.*, 3.iv.

PASSING, exceedingly, *Ham.*, 2.ii; *Oth.*, 1.iii.

PASSION, emotion, *Ham.*, 2.i; *Lear*, 5.iii; compassion, *Titus*, 1.i; mental disorder, *Mac.*, 3.iv; outburst of passion in speech, *Troil. & Cres.*, 5.ii; suffering, unhappiness, *Ant. & Cleo.*, 5.i.

PASSIONATE, to give expression to passion, *Titus*, 3.ii.

PASTRY, room for baking, *Rom. & Jul.*, 4.iv.

PATCH, (1) fool, *Mac.*, 5.iii; (2) *patch a quarrel*, find excuse of any kind for a quarrel, *Ant. & Cleo.*, 2.ii.

PATCHERY, knavery, *Timon*, 5.i.

PATENT, privilege, *Oth.*, 4.i.

PATH, to go one's way, *Jul. Caes.*, 2.i.

PATIENCE, *patience perforce*, patience under compulsion, *Rom. & Jul.*, 1.v; permission, pleasure, *Ham.*, 3.ii; *Lear*, 5.iii.

PAUSE, *deliberate pause*, carefully considered, *Ham.*, 4.iii.

PAUSER, *the pauser reason*, reason which makes one hesitate, *Mac.*, 2.iii.

PAVEMENT, the sky, the floor of heaven (the trapdoor of the 'heavens'), *Cym.*, 5.iv.

PAVILION, tent, *Troil. & Cres.*, 1.iii; awning, *Ant. & Cleo.*, 2.ii.

PAWN, forfeit, *Ant. & Cleo.*, 1.iv; wager, *Cym.*, 1.iv; *noun*, pledge, *Lear*, 1.i.

PEAK, droop, *Mac.*, 1.iii; mope, *Ham.*, 2.ii.

PECULIAR, individual, *Ham.*, 3.iii; private, reserved for an individual, *Oth.*, 4.i; *my peculiar care*, my concern for myself, *Cym.*, 5.v.

PELICAN, supposed to feed her young with her own blood, *Ham.*, 4.v; *Lear*, 3.iv.

PELION, mountain; in their attempt to scale Olympus the giants heaped Ossa on Pelion, *Ham.*, 5.i.

PELLET, form into pellets, *Ant. & Cleo.*, 3.xiii.

PELTING, paltry, *Troil. & Cres.*, 4.v; *Lear*, 2.iii.
PENDULOUS, overhanging, *Lear*, 3.iv.
PENETRATIVE, deepest, *Ant. & Cleo.*, 4.xiv.
PENTECOST, Whit Sunday, seventh Sunday after Easter, *Rom. & Jul.*, 1.v.
PENT-HOUSE, *pent-house lid*, eyelid, *Mac.*, 1.iii.
PERCH, measure of length, *Per.*, 3.*Prol.*
PERDITION, self-destruction, *Troil. & Cres.*, 5.ii.
PERDU, a soldier on a post or task of special danger, so as good as lost, *Lear*, 4.vii.
PERDURABLE, lasting, *Oth.*, 1.iii.
PERDY, by God, in truth, certainly, *Ham.*, 3.ii; *Lear*, 2.iv.
PEREMPTORY, determined, *Cor.*, 3.i; *Per.*, 2.v.
PERFECT, reliable, *Mac.*, 1.v; satisfied, *Timon*, 1.ii; unqualified, *Troil. & Cres.*, 4.iv; fully informed, sure, *Cym.*, 3.i; *perfect age*, manhood, *Lear*, 1.ii; *perfect soul*, clear conscience, *Oth.*, 1.ii; *verb*, instruct, *Per.*, 3.ii.
PERFECTION, performance, *Troil. & Cres.*, 3.ii; type of performance, *Timon*, 3.vi.
PERFORCE, under compulsion, *Rom. & Jul.*, 1.v.
PERFUMES, *their diseased perfumes*, their harlots, *Timon*, 4.iii.
PERIOD, conclusion, end of sentence, *Oth.*, 5.ii; *verb*, come to an end, *Timon*, 1.i.
PERIWIG-PATED, actors wore wigs; the suggestion here is that there wasn't much sense beneath the wig, *Ham.*, 3.ii.
PERJURE, corrupt, *Ant. & Cleo.*, 3.xii.
PERPEND, consider, *Ham.*, 2.ii.
PERSIAN, rich and ornate, *Lear*, 3.vi.
PERSISTED, persisted in, steadily pursued, *Ant. & Cleo.*, 5.i.
PERSISTIVE, persevering, *Troil. & Cres.*, 1.iii.
PERSON, *a proper man of person*, a fine figure of a man, *Troil. & Cres.*, 1.ii; appearance, *Ham.*, 1.ii; a handsome exterior, *Oth.*, 1.iii.
PERSONATE, represent, *Timon*, 1.i; *Cym.*, 5.v.
PERSPICUOUS, apparent, *Troil. & Cres.*, 1.iii.
PERSUADE, false persuaded, wrongly convinced, *Lear*, 1.iv.
PERSUASION, belief based on some circumstance, *Timon*, 3.vi; opinion, *Cym.*, 1.iv.
PERUSE, inspect, *Ham.*, 4.vii; *Cym.*, 1.ii.
PERVERT, turn aside, divert, *Cym.*, 2.iv.
PETAR, a bomb or charge for blowing in gates, *Ham.*, 3.iv.
PETITIONARY, suppliant, *Cor.*, 5.ii.
PEW, balcony (outside window, perhaps), *Lear*, 3.iv.
PHANTASMA, nightmare, *Jul. Caes.*, 2.i.
PHEEZE, frighten, do away with, *Troil. & Cres.*, 2.iii.
PHILIPPAN, which he carried at Philippi, *Ant. & Cleo.*, 2.v.
PHILOMEL, Pandion, King of Attica, had two daughters, Philomel and Procne; Procne was married to Tereus, who ravished Philomel and cut out her tongue to conceal his crime; in revenge Procne feasted Tereus on their son Itylus. In the fable they are all transformed into birds, Philomel into the nightingale, *Titus*, 2.iv.
PHILOSOPHER, the philosopher's stone to turn all metals into gold was the dream of the alchemists, *Timon*, 2.ii.
PHOENIX, fabulous Arabian bird; beyond compare, as only one of its kind existed at any time, *Timon*, 2.i.
PHYSIC, to cure, banish, *Mac.*, 2.iii; keep in health, vigour, *Cym.*, 3.ii.
PHYSICAL, beneficial, as blood-letting was regarded as a cure of many troubles, *Cor.*, 1.v; *Jul. Caes.*, 2.i.
PIA MATER, used of the brain, *Troil. & Cres.*, 2.i.
PICK, throw, *Cor.*, 1.i.
PICKERS, hands, *Ham.*, 3.ii.
PIECE, cask of wine; *flat tamed piece*, applied to woman, *Troil. & Cres.*, 4.i; *verb*, make up the sum, *Cor.*, 2.iii; complete by addition, *Ant. & Cleo.*, 1.iv.
PIGEON-LIVER'D, the liver, the supposed seat of emotions, being thought to be missing in the pigeon, there would be no flow of gall and so no courageous reaction, *Ham.*, 2.ii.
PIGHT, pitched, *Troil. & Cres.*, 5.x; fixed, determined, *Lear*, 2.i.
PILCHER, scabbard, *Rom. & Jul.*, 3.i.
PILL, plunder, *Timon*, 4.i.
PIN, peg or stud in centre of target, *Rom. & Jul.*, 2.iv; *the web and the pin*, cataract, *Lear*, 3.iv.
PINION, feather, *Ant. & Cleo.*, 3.xii.
PIONEER, miner, sapper, *Ham.*, 1.v.
PITCH, height to which hawk soars before swooping, *Jul. Caes.*, 1.i; *Ham.*, 3.i.
PITIFULLY, compassionately, *Timon*, 3.v; contemptibly, *Ant. & Cleo.*, 2.vii.

PITTIKINS, *'Ods pittikins*, corruption of 'God's pity,' *Cym.*, 4.ii.

PLACE, pitch to which hawk soars, *Mac.*, 2.iv; rank, *Troil. & Cres.*, 2.iii; accommodation, *Oth.*, 1.iii.

PLACKET, petticoat, *Lear*, 3.iv, so a woman, *Troil. & Cres.*, 2.iii.

PLAGUE, *plague of custom*, the disabilities the common law imposes on me, *Lear*, 1.ii.

PLAIN, (1) explain, *Per.*, 3.*Prol.;* (2) complain, *Lear*, 3.i.

PLANETARY, *planetary influence*, the force that was supposed to flow down from the planets and affect human affairs, *Lear*, 1.ii.

PLANT, sole of the foot, also vegetable, *Ant. & Cleo.*, 2.vii.

PLANTAGE, plants (with reference to the effect of the moon on their growth), *Troil. & Cres.*, 3.ii.

PLATE, *plates*, coins, *Ant. & Cleo.*, 5.ii; *plated Mars*, Mars in armour, *Ant. & Cleo.*, 1.i.

PLAUSIVE, *plausive manners*, mannerly behaviour, *Ham.*, 1.iv.

PLEACH'D, folded, *Ant. & Cleo.*, 4.xiv.

PLEASANCE, pleasure, *Oth.*, 2.iii.

PLEASANT, facetious, *Troil. & Cres.*, 3.i; mirthful, *Cym.*, 1.vi; *pleasantly*, in sport, *Troil. & Cres.*, 4.v.

PLEASURE, *speaks your pleasure*, is more than kind, *Timon*, 3.i.

PLEDGE, toast, *Ham.*, 1.iv; *Ant. & Cleo.*, 2.vii.

PLEURISY, excess, *Ham.*, 4.vii.

PLIANT, suitable, *Oth.*, 1.iii.

PLIGHTED, concealed in the folds of hypocrisy, *Lear*, 1.i.

PLUCK, pull down, *Lear*, 4.ii.

PLUME, *plume up my will*, add another feather to my cap, *Oth.*, 1.iii.

POINT, *at point*, in readiness, just about to, *Cor.*, 3.i; etc.; *at ample point*, in fullest measure, *Troil. & Cres.*, 3.iii; *at point exactly*, completely, *Ham.*, 1.ii; *at a point*, fully prepared, *Mac.*, 4.iii.

POINTS, (1) orders, *Cor.*, 4.vi; (2) laces attaching hose to doublet, *Ant. & Cleo.*, 3.xiii.

POISE, weight, momentum, *Troil. & Cres.*, 1.iii; importance, *Lear*, 2.i; *verb*, weigh, compare, *Rom. & Jul.*, 1.ii; counterbalance, *Oth.*, 1.iii.

POISON, destroy, *Cor.*, 5.ii; cause to sicken, *Oth.*, 5.ii.

POLACK, Polish nation, *Ham.*, 2.ii.

POLE, pole-star, *Oth.*, 2.i.

POLICY, established regime, *Lear*, 1.ii.

POLITIC, cunning, time-serving, *Timon*, 3.iii; *convocation of politic worms*, come together for their own gain, *Ham.*, 4.iii; *a politic distance*, a reserve made necessary by the state of public feeling, *Oth.*, 3.iii.

POLITICIAN, schemer, *Ham.*, 5.i; time-server and self-seeker, *Lear*, 4.vi.

POLL, head, *Ham.*, 4.v; *the greater poll*, the greater number, *Cor.*, 3.i.

POLL'D, *leave his passage poll'd*, leave a track marked by his destruction, *Cor.*, 4.v.

POMP, procession, *Timon*, 1.ii.

PONTIC SEA, Black Sea, *Oth.*, 3.iii.

POOP, to cause to founder, *Per.*, 4.ii.

POOR-JOHN, salted hake, poor stuff, *Rom. & Jul.*, 1.i.

POP'RIN PEAR, a variety of pear, named from Poperinghe, *Rom. & Jul.*, 2.i.

POPULAR, plebeian, *Cor.*, 2.i.

PORPENTINE, porcupine, *Ham.*, 1.v.

PORRIDGE, pottage or soup, *Troil. & Cres.*, 1.ii; *Lear*, 3.iv.

PORT, (1) gate, *Troil. & Cres.*, 4.iv; *Ant. & Cleo.*, 4.iv; (2) demeanour, bearing, *Ant. & Cleo.*, 4.xiv.

PORTABLE, endurable, *Mac.*, 4.iii; *Lear*, 3.vi.

PORTAGE, the profit the sailor could make on what he was permitted to trade on his own, apart from the owner's cargo; so the loss the child has sustained by her mother's death is greater than any gain her subsequent voyage through life will produce, *Per.* 3.i.

PORTANCE, bearing, conduct, *Cor.*, 2.iii; *Per.*, 1.iv.

PORTLY, well-behaved, *Rom. & Jul.*, 1.v; *a portly sail of ship*, an imposing fleet, *Per.*, 1.iv.

POSITION, assertion, *Troil. & Cres.*, 3.iii; *in position*, in the assertion I now make, *Oth.*, 3.ii.

POSSESS, inform, *Troil. & Cres.*, 4.iv; *Ant. & Cleo.*, 3.x; rule (like an evil spirit), *Cym.*, 1.iv.

POSSET, hot milk curdled with wine, etc., *Mac.*, 2.ii; *verb*, curdle, *Ham.*, 1.v.

POSSIBILITY, *with possibility*, within reason, *Titus*, 3.i.

POST, messenger, *Mac.*, 1.iii; *Lear*, 2.iv; *took post*, made haste, *Rom. & Jul.*, 5.i; *adv.*, speedily, *Per.*, 4.*Prol.;* *post-post-haste*, with extra speed, *Oth.*, 1.iii; *in post*, with post-horses, speedily, *Rom. & Jul.*, 5.iii; *post-haste*, pressure of work, *Ham.*, 1.i; *verb*, convey quickly, deliver immediately, *Troil. & Cres.*, 1.iii; *Cym.*, 2.iv.

POSTER, *posters of the sea and land*,

travellers who cover sea or land with speed of supernatural beings, *Mac.*, 1.iii.

POSY, *posy of a ring*, motto engraved on finger-ring, *Ham.*, 3.ii.

POTATO, Spanish or sweet potato, *Troil. & Cres.*, 5.ii.

POTCH, thrust, stab, *Cor.*, 1.x.

POTENTIAL, influential, *Oth.*, 1.ii.

POTTING, drinking, boozing, *Oth.*, 2.iii.

POTTLE, a large (two-quart) tankard, *Oth.*, 2.iii.

POUND, shut up like animals in a pound, *Cor.*, 1.iv.

POWER, army, *Mac.*, 4.iii.

PRACTICE, treachery, *Cor.*, 4.i; trickery, *Lear*, 5.iii; *my practices*, my treacherous designs, *Lear*, 1.ii.

PRACTISE, employ foul trickery, *Oth.*, 1.ii; so *practiser*, *Oth.*, 1.ii.

PRAETOR, judicial functionary of senior rank, *Jul. Caes.*, 2.iv.

PRAISE, merit, *Troil. & Cres.*, 2.ii; *book of praises*, virtues, *Per.*, 1.i; *verb*, prize, *Per.*, 3.ii; value, *Troil. & Cres.*, 3.ii.

PRAY, *pray in aid*, legal expression for asking help from someone with interest in one's case; so treat you as an ally not as conquered enemy, *Ant. & Cleo.*, 5.ii.

PRECEDENCE, *the good precedence*, what was said before, *Ant. & Cleo.*, 2.v.

PRECEDENT, done before, *Ant. & Cleo.*, 4.xiv; *precedent passions*, passions experienced at earlier stage in life, *Timon*, 1.i.

PRECIOUS, *spectacles so precious*, eyes so sensitive, *Cym.*, 1.vi; ironically in *Oth.*, 5.ii.

PRECIPITATING, falling headlong, *Lear*, 4.vi.

PRECIPITATION, extent of the fall from the height, *Cor.*, 3.ii.

PRECURSE, foreshadowing, *Ham.*, 1.i.

PREDOMINANCE, *humorous predominance*, inflated egotism and sense of superiority, *Troil. & Cres.*, 2.iii; *spherical predominance*, the compulsion exercised by some ruling planet or planets, *Lear*, 1.ii.

PREFER, offer, *Ham.*, 4.vii; present, recommend, *Jul. Caes.*, 5.v; *Per.*, 2.ii; *prefer him to a better place*, offer him a more hospitable home, *Lear*, 1.i; introduce, recommend, *Cym.*, 2.iii; further, promote, *Oth.*, 2.i.

PREFORMED, *preformed faculties*, inherited characteristics, *Jul. Caes.*, 1.iii.

PREGNANT, significant, *Ham.*, 2.ii; ready, *Ham.*, 3.ii; *Lear*, 2.i; manifest, *Oth.*, 2.i; *pregnant they should*, reasonable to suppose that they would, *Ant. & Cleo.*, 2.i; *pregnantly*, quickly and clearly, *Timon*, 1.i.

PRENOMINATE, *adj.*, before-named, *Ham.*, 2.i; *verb*, name in advance, *Troil. & Cres.*, 4.v.

PRE-ORDINANCE, established rule, *Jul. Caes.*, 3.i.

PREPARATION, army, *Cor.*, 1.ii; armament, *Oth.*, 1.iii.

PRESCIENCE, foresight, *Troil. & Cres.*, 1.iii; *his prescience*, a mock title for the soothsayer (on the model of 'his reverence'), *Ant. & Cleo.*, 1.ii.

PRESCRIPT, instructions, orders, *Ant. & Cleo.*, 3.viii; *Ham.*, 2.ii.

PRESENCE, assembly, *Ham.*, 5.ii; *Ant. & Cleo.*, 2.ii; *feasting presence*, state-room set out for banquet, *Rom. & Jul.*, 5.iii.

PRESENT, immediately, *Ham.*, 4.iii; immediate, urgent, *Timon*, 2.ii; *Oth.*, 1.ii; *noun*, the proposal before us, *Cor.*, 1.vi; *this ignorant present*, the present time, the future still unknown, *Mac.*, 1.v; *from the present*, away from the point, not relevant to the matter in hand, *Ant. & Cleo.*, 2.vi; *verb*, relate, *Oth.*, 1.iii.

PRESENTLY, immediately, *Cor.*, 5.vi.

PRESENTMENT, *counterfeit presentment*, portrait, *Ham.*, 3.iv; dedication of work to a patron, *Timon*, 1.i.

PRESS, with reference to the pressing to death with weights of accused persons who would not plead, *Troil. & Cres.*, 3.ii.

PRESS-MONEY, paid to the recruit as an earnest of his enlistment, *Lear*, 4.vi.

PRESSURE, impression (as if stamped in wax), *Ham.*, 3.ii.

PREST, ready, *Per.*, 4.*Prol.*

PRETENCE, intention, design, *Cor.*, 1.ii; *Lear*, 1.ii.

PRETEND, profess, *Titus*, 1.i; *what good could they pretend?* what gain for themselves were they planning?

PREVENT, *prevent your discovery*, forestall your confession, *Ham.*, 2.ii.

PREVENTION, precaution, *Troil. & Cres.*, 1.iii.

PRICK, mark against hour on dial of clock, *Rom. & Jul.*, 2.iv; *verb*, mark on list, *Jul. Caes.*, 4.i.

PRICK-SONG, song set out in notation, *Rom. & Jul.*, 2.iv.

PRIDE, *pride of place*, the highest point the hawk attains before swooping on prey, *Mac.*, 2.iv.

PRIMITIVE, archetypal, *Troil. & Cres.*, 5.i.

PRIMOGENITY, legal right of elder, *Troil. & Cres.*, 1.iii.

PRIMY, *primy nature*, nature in early promise, *Ham.*, 1.iii.

PRINCIPAL, main rafter, *Per.*, 3.ii.

PRINCOX, forward fellow, *Rom. & Jul.*, 1.v.

PRIZE, value, *Cym.*, 3.vi.

PRIZER, one who values something, *Troil. & Cres.*, 2.ii.

PROBAL, such as commends itself to thought, *Oth.*, 2.iii.

PROCEED, with reference to those who proceed to a degree at a university, *Timon*, 4.iii; come from, be caused, *Cym.*, 3.v.

PROCESS, mandate, *Ham.*, 4.iii; *process of your speech*, drift of your narrative, *Troil. & Cres.*, 4.i; account, *Ham.*, 1.v; course of law, *Cor.*, 3.i; summons, command, *Ant. & Cleo.*, 1.i; the sequence of adventures (or, the manner of wooing), *Oth.*, 1.iii.

PROCNE, *see* PHILOMEL.

PROCURE, cause, *Lear*, 2.iv.

PRODIGIOUS, unnatural, ominous, *Troil. & Cres.*, 5.i.

PRODUCTED, produced, *Oth.*, 1.i.

PROFESS, *profess myself to*, make maudlin gestures of friendship to, *Jul. Caes.*, 1.ii; adopt a pose or habit, *Troil. & Cres.*, 3.iii; *What dost thou profess?* What is your trade or skill? *Lear*, 1.iv; avow one's code of duty (the sense into which Kent turns Lear's question), *Lear*, 1.iv; *professed bosoms*, full of protestations, *Lear*, 1.i.

PROFIT, lesson, instruction, *Oth.*, 3.ii.

PROFOUND, distended, on the point of falling, *Mac.*, 3.v.

PROGENY, race, *Cor.*, 1.viii.

PROGNOSTICATION, *a fruitful prognostication*, a sure sign of fertility, *Ant. & Cleo.*, 1.ii.

PROGRESS, state journey of a king, *Ham.*, 4.iii.

PROJECT, to set forth, state, *Ant. & Cleo.*, 5.ii.

PROMETHEAN, *Promethean heat*, the fire from heaven (the demigod Prometheus stole fire from the gods to give to men), *Oth.*, 5.ii.

PROMISE, assure, *Lear*, 1.ii; *I promise you*, I may tell you, *Timon*, 1.ii.

PROMPT, naturally inclined, *Troil. & Cres.*, 4.iv; ready, *Ant. & Cleo.*, 3.xiii; *verb*, suggest, *Cor.*, 3.ii; instruct, warn, *Timon*, 2.ii.

PRONE, ready and eager, *Cym.*, 5.iv.

PROOF, *adj.*, impenetrable, *Cor.*, 1.iv; *noun*, *for proof eterne*, to stand the test for ever, *Ham.*, 2.ii; *lapp'd in proof*, in armour, *Mac.*, 1.ii; *rough in proof*, when experienced, *Rom. & Jul.*, 1.i; *targes of proof*, strong shields, *Cym.*, 5.v; *in thy just proof*, proof that you are honest, *Lear*, 3.vi; experience, *Cym.*, 1.vi.

PROPEND, *I propend to you in resolution to*, I incline to share your determination to, *Troil. & Cres.*, 2.ii.

PROPENSION, inclination, *Troil. & Cres.*, 2.ii.

PROPER, *my proper life*, my own life, *Ham.*, 5.ii; *our proper son*, our own son, *Oth.*, 1.iii; *proper deformity . . . in the fiend*, naturally associated with the devil, *Lear*, 4.ii; *proper man*, handsome, manly, *Jul. Caes.*, 1.i; *Oth.*, 1.iii.

PROPERLY, as my personal affair, *Cor.*, 5.ii.

PROPERTIED, had the quality, *Ant. & Cleo.*, 5.ii.

PROPERTY, *a property of easiness*, a habit that comes easily to him, *Ham.*, 5.i; *as a property*, merely an instrumental member, *Jul. Caes.*, 4.i; *great property*, characteristic magnanimity, *Ant. & Cleo.*, 1.i; *property of blood*, identity of blood, consanguinity, *Lear*, 1.i; *verb*, appropriate, *Timon*, 1.i.

PROPONTIC, Sea of Marmora, *Oth.*, 3.iii.

PROPORTION, proper relative value, *Mac.*, 1.iv; portion, fortune, *Per.*, 4.ii; *the past proportion*, the greatness beyond reckoning, *Troil. & Cres.*, 2.ii.

PROPOSE, discourse, *Oth.*, 1.i; *proposed for the deserver*, promised as a reward, *Troil. & Cres.*, 3.ii.

PROPOSITION, promise, *Troil. & Cres.*, 1.iii.

PROPRIETY, condition proper to a community, *Oth.*, 2.iii.

PROPUGNATION, defence, *Troil. & Cres.*, 2.ii.

PROROGUE, postpone, *Rom. & Jul.*, 2.ii and 4.i; *prorogue his honour*, delay the action demanded by honour, *Ant. & Cleo.*, 2.i; protract, *Per.*, 5.i.

PROSECUTION, *the inevitable prosecution*, the pursuit one cannot escape, *Ant. & Cleo.*, 4.xiv.

PROSPECT, *to that prospect*, to that revelation of their conduct, *Oth.*, 3.iii.

PROTEST, *full of protest*, with many

vows, *Troil. & Cres.*, 3.ii; *verb*, proclaim, vow, *Ham.*, 3.ii; assert, *Oth.*, 4.ii; *protest their first manhood*, proclaim they are entering on manhood, *Mac.*, 4.ii.

PROTESTER, one professing friendship, *Jul. Caes.*, 1.ii.

PROTRACT, postpone, *Cym.*, 4.ii.

PROTRACTIVE, sustained and delaying, *Troil. & Cres.*, 1.iii.

PROVAND, fodder, *Cor.*, 2.i.

PROVE, find by experience, *Ham.*, 3.i and ii; experience, *Ant. & Cleo.*, 1.ii.

PROVERB'D, provided with a proverb that justifies my action, *Rom. & Jul.*, 1.iv.

PROVIDE, to make preparation, *Ham.*, 3.iii; *provide your going*, make the necessary preparations for your journey, *Ant. & Cleo.*, 3.iv; *provided for*, murdered, *Mac.*, 1.v.

PROVIDENCE, foresight, *Troil. & Cres.*, 3.iii.

PROVINCIAL ROSES, rosettes on shoes (roses of Provence, the double damask rose; Provins near Paris was also famous for roses and was sometimes confused with the province), *Ham.*, 3.ii.

PROVOKE, cause, prompt, *Ham.*, 2.ii; produce, *Lear*, 4.iv.

PRUNE, *prunes the immortal wing*, preens its heavenly plumage, *Cym.*, 5.iv.

PSALTERY, stringed instrument, *Cor.*, 5.iv.

PUBLISH'D, proclaimed, *Lear*, 4.vi.

PUDDER, commotion, *Lear*, 3.ii.

PUDENCY, modesty, *Cym.*, 2.v.

PUISSANT, powerful, *Jul. Caes.*, 3.i; *Lear*, 5.iii.

PULPIT, *common pulpits*, the rostra in the Forum, *Jul. Caes.*, 3.i.

PUN, to pound, *Troil. & Cres.*, 2.i.

PUNTO REVERSO, thrust in fencing, *Rom. & Jul.*, 2.iv.

PURBLIND, blind, *Troil. & Cres.*, 1.ii.

PURCHASE, profit, *Per.*, 1.*Prol.*; *verb*, *hereditary rather than purchas'd*, inherited, not deliberately adopted, *Ant. & Cleo.*, 1.iv; *true purchasing*, gained by merit, *Cor.*, 2.i; strive, *Timon*, 3.ii.

PURGATION, purge as if with medicine, and clear from guilt, *Ham.*, 3.ii.

PURGE, the medicine to purge the evil, the force going to drive out Macbeth, *Mac.*, 5.ii.

PURGERS, physicians of the public weal, *Jul. Caes.*, 2.i.

PURPOSE, effect, *Troil. & Cres.*, 1.iii; proposal, *Ant. & Cleo.*, 2.vi; *this war's purpose*, the campaign, *Cym.*, 4.ii.

PURVEYOR, officer who went ahead to see to food and lodging, *Mac.*, 1.vi.

PUSH, critical action, *Mac.*, 5.iii; *put to the present push*, put into immediate action, *Ham.*, 5.i.

PUT, assert, *Timon*, 5.i; *put to their books*, mortgaged, *Timon*, 1.ii; *put you to't*, test you thoroughly, *Cor.*, 1.i; compel, *Cym.*, 2.iii; *put by*, desist from, *Oth.*, 2.iii; *put on*, stake, *Cym.*, 1.iv; incite, urge, *Lear*, 2.i; *put me to't*, drive me to a task (of plain speaking), *Oth.*, 2.i.

PUTTOCK, bird of prey, kite, *Troil. & Cres.*, 5.i; *Cym.*, 1.i.

QUAIL, courtesan, *Troil. & Cres.*, 5.i; *verb*, terrify, *Ant. & Cleo.*, 5.ii.

QUAINTLY, skilfully, ingeniously, *Ham.*, 2.i; *quaintly eche*, eke out imaginatively the brief doings on the stage, *Per.*, 3.*Prol.*

QUAK'D, *gladly quak'd*, trembling with admiration, *Cor.*, 1.ix.

QUALIFICATION, disturbed condition (the peace of mind of the islanders having been qualified by threats of violence), *Oth.*, 2.i.

QUALIFY, cool, *Troil. & Cres.*, 2.ii; dim, reduce, *Ham.*, 4.vii; modify, *Lear*, 1.ii; *craftily qualified*, the spirit diluted, skilfully mixed to neutralize intoxicant, *Oth.*, 2.iii.

QUALITY, good parts, natural and acquired excellence, *Troil. & Cres.*, 4.iv; accomplishment, *Ham.*, 4.vii; *pursue the quality*, continue in the profession of acting, *Ham.*, 2.ii; occasion, *Troil. & Cres.*, 4.i; rank, *Cym.*, 1.iv; profession, *Oth.*, 1.iii; nature, character, *Lear*, 2.iv; *qualities*, attractions, *Per.*, 4.ii.

QUANTITY, *hold quantity*, are proportionate, weigh alike, *Ham.*, 3.ii.

QUARREL, cause for war, *Cor.*, 4.v; occasion of fighting, *Lear*, 5.iii; pugnacity, *Oth.*, 2.iii; *Rome's great quarrel*, her imperial cause, *Titus*, 3.i; *damned quarrel*, rebellion, *Mac.*, 1.ii.

QUARRELOUS, quarrelsome, *Cym.*, 3.iv.

QUARRY, the heap of game killed in the hunt, so of human bodies, *Mac.*, 4.iii; *Cor.*, 1.i; *this quarry cries on havoc*, the bodies proclaim a merciless slaughter, *Ham.*, 5.ii.

QUARTER, the area over which the guard extends, *Ant. & Cleo.*, 4.iii;

in quarter, in good comradeship, *Oth.*, 2.iii; *pass his quarter*, break the bounds fixed for the army's use, *Timon*, 5.iv.

QUARTER'D, slaughtered, *Cor.*, 1.i; *their quarter'd fires*, the camp-fires in the area occupied by the enemy, *Cym.*, 4.iv.

QUAT, pimple, *Oth.*, 5.i.

QUEASY, disgusted with, *Ant. & Cleo.*, 3.vi; *of a queasy question*, of a hazardous kind, *Lear*, 2.i.

QUELL, murder, *Mac.*, 1.vii.

QUENCH, slacken in ardour, *Cym.*, 1.v.

QUEST, legal enquiry, *Ham.*, 5.i; search-party, *Oth.*, 1.ii.

QUESTION, *call hers in question more*, make me dwell all the more intently on her beauty (while I am trying to forget), *Rom. & Jul.*, 1.i; business, conversation, *Oth.*, 1.iii; *Troil. & Cres.*, 4.i; talk, *Ham.*, 3.i; *the question of his death*, the rights and wrongs of his assassination, *Jul. Caes.*, 3.ii; discussion, *Lear*, 1.ii; *made she no verbal question?* did she not speak? *Lear*, 4.iii; *with more facile question bear it*, capture it in an easier encounter, *Oth.*, 1.iii; *verb*, examine in detail, *Jul. Caes.*, 4.iii; *question farther*, fight a duel over the business, *Cym.*, 2.iv.

QUESTIONABLE, that may be spoken to, interrogated, *Ham.*, 1.iv.

QUESTRISTS, seekers, *Lear*, 3.vii.

QUICK, fresh, *Per.*, 4.i; *quick-answer'd*, sharp in reply, *Cym.*, 3.iv.

QUICKEN, revive, *Ant. & Cleo.*, 4.xv.

QUIDDITIES, subtle distinctions, *Ham.*, 5.i.

QUIETUS, final settlement of an account, discharge, *Ham.*, 3.i.

QUILLETS, quibbles, *Ham.*, 5.i; *keep up thy quillets*, spare your quibbles, *Oth.*, 3.i.

QUINTESSENCE, *quintessence of dust*, the animating principle of no more than dust, *Ham.*, 2.ii.

QUIRE, be attuned with, *Cor.*, 3.ii; place for singers, *Cym.*, 3.iii.

QUIRKS, caprices, *Per.*, 4.vi; ingenious turns of expression, *Oth.*, 2.i.

QUIT, free from a vexation, *Timon*, 4.iii; repay, settle a score, *Ham.*, 5.ii; *to be full quit*, to be fully revenged on, *Cor.*, 4.v; free, *Cym.*, 5.iv; avenge, requite, *Lear*, 3.vii; repay, *Per.*, 3.i; conduct oneself, *Lear*, 2.i.

QUITTANCE, *all use of quittance*, what custom prescribes in the way of acknowledgement or repayment, *Timon*, 1.i.

QUOTE, observe, *Ham.*, 2.i; *Rom. & Jul.*, 1.iv.

QUOTH'A, said he (usually with sarcastic implication), *Rom. & Jul.*, 2.iv; *Per.*, 2.i.

RACE, *a race of heaven*, of heavenly kind, *Ant. & Cleo.*, 1.iii.

RACK, driven clouds in upper air, *Ham.*, 2.ii; *Ant. & Cleo.*, 4.xiv.

RAG, beggarly fellow, *Timon*, 4.iii.

RAGE, riot, burn, *Ham.*, 4.iii; act madly, *Ant. & Cleo.*, 4.i; *raging motions*, vehement impulses, *Oth.*, 1.iii.

RAKE, famished and lean person, *Cor.*, 1.i.

RAMP, a wanton, *Cym.*, 1.vi.

RAMPIRE, *rampir'd gates*, barricaded, *Timon*, 5.iv.

RANCOUR, *put rancours in the vessel of my peace*, put evil in my soul like poison in a vial, *Mac.*, 3.i.

RANGE, stand in order, *Cor.*, 3.i; *whose several ranges*, whose respective ranks, *Ant. & Cleo.*, 3.xiii.

RANGER, *Diana's rangers*, the virgins who made up Diana's troop of hunters, *Cym.*, 2.iii.

RANK, swollen with pride, *Troil. & Cres.*, 1.iii; *a ranker rate*, a greater price, *Ham.*, 4.iv; of a person in morbid condition requiring to be bled, *Jul. Caes.*, 3.i; foul in speech, *Troil. & Cres.*, 1.iii; foul-smelling (with pun on 'social position'), *Cym.*, 2.i; *Ant. & Cleo.*, 5.ii; unchaste, *Cym.*, 2.v; *in the rank garb*, in lascivious style, or as one lascivious in manner, *Oth.*, 2.i; *adv.*, *how rank soever rounded in by danger*, overmuch, *Troil. & Cres.*, 1.iii; *rankly absurd*, grossly deceived, *Ham.*, 1.v.

RANSACK, *the ransack'd queen*, carried off unlawfully, *Troil. & Cres.*, 2.ii.

RANSOM, atonement, *Cym.*, 5.iii.

RAP, *what thus raps you?* puts you beside yourself, *Cym.*, 1.vi.

RAPTURE, robbery, *Per.*, 2.i; a fit, seizure, *Cor.*, 2.i.

RARENESS, rarity, *Ham.*, 5.ii.

RASCAL, a lean and worthless deer, so a worthless fellow, *Cor.*, 1.i; *adj.*, worthless, *Jul. Caes.*, 4.iii.

RASH, stick, *Lear*, 3.vii; urgent, *Troil. & Cres.*, 4.ii; *rashly*, on the spur of the moment, *Ham.*, 5.ii.

RATE, assign (a share), *Ant. & Cleo.*, 3.vi.

RATHER, *the rather*, the more quickly, *Mac.*, 1.vii.

RAUGHT, taken hold of, *Ant. & Cleo.*, 4.ix.

RAVEL, *the ravell'd sleave of care*, the tangled and anxious thoughts, *Mac.*, 2.ii; *ravel out*, make plain, disentangle, *Ham.*, 3.iv.

RAVEN, RAVIN, devour, *Mac.*, 2.iv; *Cym.*, 1.vi; *ravin'd*, ravenous, *Mac.*, 4.i.

RAVISH, carry away unlawfully, *Troil. & Cres.*, 1.*Prol.*; tear away, *Lear*, 3.vii; *with ravishing strides*, stepping as one who wishes to surprise and rape, here to kill, *Mac.*, 2.i.

RAW, inflamed, *Troil. & Cres.*, 5.i; crude, unpolished (of discourse), *Ham.*, 5.ii; untaught, unskilled, *Per.*, 4.ii; *in that rawness*, in that unprotected state, *Mac.*, 4.iii.

RAZE, *raze out*, obliterate, *Mac.*, 5.iii.

REACH, practical ability, *Ham.*, 2.i.

REAR-WARD, sequel, a blow following upon another, *Rom. & Jul.*, 3.ii.

REASON, justice, *Titus*, 1.i; *verb*, plead, *Cor.*, 5.iii; discourse, *Cym.*, 4.ii; argue, *Lear*, 2.iv.

REAVE, deprive, *Cym.*, 3.iii.

REBECK, three-stringed fiddle, used as musician's name in *Rom. & Jul.*, 4.v.

REBOUND, *by the rebound of yours*, echoing yours, *Ant. & Cleo.*, 5.ii.

REBUKE, master, cow, *Mac.*, 3.i; check, *Per.*, 3.i.

RECEIPT, receptacle, *Mac.*, 1.vii; takings, what is received, *Cor.*, 1.i.

RECEIVE, perceive, judge, *Ham.*, 2.ii; hear, *Per.*, 1.i.

RECK, heed, *Ham.*, 1.iii; care for, *Cym.*, 4.ii.

RECKLESS, neglectful, *Cor.*, 3.i.

RECKONING, *of honourable reckoning*, much esteemed, *Rom. & Jul.*, 1.ii.

RECOGNIZANCE, legal bond, defining a debt, *Ham.*, 5.i; so a pledge, token, *Oth.*, 5.ii.

RECOIL, become corrupt, degenerate, *Mac.*, 4.iii; shrink, *Mac.*, 5.ii; show yourself unworthy, *Cym.*, 1.vi.

RECOLLECT, observe in the specimens they catch, *Per.*, 2.i.

RECOMMEND, *we recommend to you our purposes to them*, we commit to you the announcement to the people of our intentions, *Cor.*, 2.ii; inform, *Oth.*, 1.iii.

RECONCILE, recall to favour, *Lear*, 3.vi.

RECONCILIATION, *his present reconciliation take*, be reconciled with him now, *Oth.*, 3.iii.

RECORD, *manifold record*, common experience, *Timon*, 1.i; memories, *Ham.*, 1.v; *verb*, witness, *Timon*, 4.ii; sing, relate in song, *Per.*, 4.*Prol.*

RECORDATION, a recording, *Troil. & Cres.*, 5.ii.

RECORDER, a kind of flageolet, *Ham.*, [3.ii.

RECOURSE, flow, *Troil. & Cres.*, 5.iii.

RECOVER, reconcile, *Oth.*, 2.iii; *recover the wind of me*, to get to the windward of the game so that it may make off down wind into the net, *Ham.*, 3.ii.

RECOVERABLE, that can be traced again, *Timon*, 3.iv.

RECOVERY, legal process to break an entail, *Ham.*, 5.i.

RECREANT, traitor, *Cor.*, 5.iii; *Lear*, 1.i.

RECREATE, disport, refresh, *Jul. Caes.*, 3.ii.

RECTORSHIP, rule, *Cor.*, 2.iii.

REDE, counsel, *Ham.*, 1.iii.

REDEEM, rescue, liberate, *Rom. & Jul.*, 4.iii; exonerate, *Timon*, 4.iii.

REDELIVER, to report, *Ham.*, 5.ii.

REECHY, dirty, *Cor.*, 2.i.

REEKY, stinking, *Rom. & Jul.*, 4.i.

REEL, *reel the streets*, stagger in drunken fashion through the streets, *Ant. & Cleo.*, 1.iv; *reels*, revelry, *Ant. & Cleo.*, 2.vii.

REFER, *refer me*, appeal, *Oth.*, 1.ii; *hath referr'd herself*, married, *Cym.*, 1.i.

REFERENCE, appointment, *Oth.*, 1.iii; *make your full reference*, entrust yourself completely, *Ant. & Cleo.*, 5.ii.

REFLECT, shine, *Titus*, 1.i; *reflect upon him*, regard him, *Cym.*, 1.vi.

REFLECTION, shining, brightness, *Cym.*, 1.ii; *whence the sun gives his reflection*, the East, *Mac.*, 1.ii.

REFUGE, resource, *Cor.*, 5.iii; *Timon*, 3.iii.

REFUSE, disown, *Rom. & Jul.*, 2.ii; *Troil. & Cres.*, 4.v; reject, *Oth.*, 3.i; decline to encounter, *Ant. & Cleo.*, 3.vii.

REGARD, heed, *Timon*, 1.ii; *good regard*, sound considerations, *Jul. Caes.*, 3.i; *with this regard*, because of this consideration, *Ham.*, 3.i; *an indistinct regard*, a prospect in which sky and sea are indistinguishably blended, *Oth.*, 2.i; *exact regard*, special care, *Lear*, 1.iv; *regards*, considerations, *Lear*, 1.i; *in which regard*, by reason of this, *Oth.*, 1.i; *verb*, honour, *Cor.*, 5.vi; *Jul. Caes.*, 5.iii.

REGARDFULLY, *voiced so regardfully*, spoke of so highly, *Timon*, 4.iii.

REGIMENT, rule, sway, *Ant. & Cleo.*, 3.vi.

Region, the heavens, *Ham.*, 2.ii; *region kites*, of the air, *Ham.*, 2.ii; *region low*, the lowest of the strata of the atmosphere, its inhabitants' low rank, *Cym.*, 5.iv.

Register, *in register*, in the chronicle of actions, *Ant. & Cleo.*, 4.ix.

Rein, *the hard rein*, the severe treatment, *Lear*, 3.i.

Rejoice, to feel joy at, *Cym.*, 5.v; *rejoicing fires*, bonfires, *Cym.*, 3.i.

Rejoindure, union, *Troil. & Cres.*, 4.iv.

Relations, *understood relations*, combinations rightly interpreted, *Mac.*, 3.iv.

Relative, relevant, *Ham.*, 2.ii.

Religion, feeling for the truth, respect, *Cym.*, 1.iv; a supreme form of devotion, *Ant. & Cleo.*, 5.ii.

Relish, *relish'd of*, tainted with, *Per.*, 2.v.

Relume, rekindle, *Oth.*, 5.ii.

Remain, *the remain*, what is left to do, *Cym.*, 3.i; *here-remain*, residence, *Mac.*, 4.iii; *verb*, *let her remain*, leave her alone, *Cym.*, 2.iii; dwell, *Cym.*, 4.iii; make remain, stay, *Cor.*, 1.iv.

Remainder, remains of his fortune, *Timon*, 4.iii; left-over, *Troil. & Cres.*, 2.ii; those who remain, *Cym.*, 1.i.

Remediate, remedial, *Lear*, 4.iv.

Remember, polite request to person, to put on a hat as in *Ham.*, 5.ii; *be you remembered*, bear in mind, *Titus*, 4.iii; *briefly thyself remember*, recall and repent your sins quickly, *Lear*, 4.vi; remind, *Lear*, 1.iv.

Remembrance, reputation, *Ant. & Cleo.*, 2.ii; memory, *Cym.*, 2.iv; *commend to your remembrances*, favourable regard, *Cor.*, 2.iii; *Mac.*, 3.ii.

Remembrancer, one who reminds someone, *Mac.*, 3.iv; *Cym.*, 1.v.

Remorse, pity, *Lear*, 4.ii; *shall be in me remorse*, the deed, however bloody, will seem to me like a compassionate act, *Oth.*, 3.iii.

Remotion, flight, change of place, *Timon*, 4.iii; removal, journeying, *Lear*, 2.iv.

Remove, the raising of the siege, *Cor.*, 1.ii; banishment, departure, *Ham.*, 4.v; *verb*, kill, *Oth.*, 4.iii.

Removed, *removed ground*, a secluded spot, *Ham.*, 1.iv.

Render, admission, statement, *Timon*, 5.i; *Cym.*, 4.iv; the rendering of an account, *Cym.*, 5.iv; *verb*, describe, *Cym.*, 3.iv.

Renege, deny, *Lear*, 2.ii; renounce, *Ant. & Cleo.*, 1.i.

Repair, renew, *Cym.*, 2.ii; *their repair hither*, their coming, *Ham.*, 5.ii.

Repeal, recall to favour, *Oth.*, 2.iii; recall the sentence of banishment, *Lear*, 3.vi; *freedom of repeal*, unconditional permission to return, *Jul. Caes.*, 3.i.

Repetition, recital, *Cor.*, 1.i; *Per.*, 5.i.

Replication, echo, *Jul. Caes.*, 1.i; reply, *Ham.*, 4.ii.

Report, *perfectest report*, sure testimony, *Mac.*, 1.v; *true reports*, trustworthy witnesses, *Ant. & Cleo.*, 2.ii; *verb*, *report themselves*, speak for themselves, *Cym.*, 2.iv; *where the aim reports*, where the purpose makes itself clear, *Oth.*, 1.iii.

Reporter, informant, *Ant. & Cleo.*, 2.ii.

Reposure, reposal, *Lear*, 2.i.

Reproachful, abusive, *Titus*, 1.i.

Reprobance, damnation, *Oth.*, 5.ii.

Reproof, *the reproof of chance*, the defiance of circumstances, *Troil. & Cres.*, 1.iii; punishment, *Timon*, 5.iv; *your reproof were well deserved of rashness*, you would deserve the reproach of rashness, *Ant. & Cleo.*, 2.ii.

Repugnancy, opposition, *Timon*, 3.v.

Repugnant, refractory, *Ham.*, 2.ii.

Repured, freed from all impurities, *Troil. & Cres.*, 3.ii.

Require, ask, request, *Cor.*, 2.ii; etc.

Rescue, forcible intervention, release of arrested individual, *Cor.*, 3.i.

Reservation, *making but reservation of yourselves*, thinking only of your own interests, *Cor.*, 3.iii.

Reserve, preserve, *Titus*, 1.i; keep in one's own possession, *Lear*, 1.i; guard carefully, *Cym.*, 4.iv; *always reserved my holy duty*, so far as I may say it without breach of duty, *Cym.*, 1.i.

Resist, prove distasteful to, repel, *Per.*, 2.iii.

Resolutes, bold fellows, *Ham.*, 1.i.

Resolution, certainty about the matter, *Lear*, 1.ii.

Resolve, dissolve, *Timon*, 4.iii; *be resolved how*, be satisfied how, *Jul. Caes.*, 3.i; *stand resolv'd*, resolute to endure, *Titus*, 1.i; *resolve yourselves apart*, make up your minds among yourselves by yourselves, *Mac.*, 3.i; solve a riddle, *Per.*, 1.i; explain to, *Lear*, 2.iv.

Resort, *her resort*, permission to visit

her, *Timon*, 1.i; *his resort*, his visiting her, *Ham.*, 2.ii. [*Per.*, 4.vi.

Resorters, frequenters, customers,

Respect, *in respect of his*, in comparison with his affluence, *Timon*, 3.ii; *show more respect*, more realistic attitude, less wilfulness, *Cor.*, 3.i; the consideration, the thought, *Ham.*, 3.i; rank, *Jul. Caes.*, 1.ii; *Oth.*, 1.iii; reputation, *Jul. Caes.*, 5.v; too much weighing of pro and con, *Troil. & Cres.*, 2.ii; *in my respect*, in my eyes, *Cym.*, 2.iii; *Per.*, 3.iii; *respects of fortune*, considerations of money and rank, *Lear*, 1.i; *upon respect*, on the king's messenger entitled to privilege and respect, *Lear*, 2.iv; *verb, not respected for*, no longer considered as, *Cor.*, 3.i; esteem, *Per.*, 2.ii.

Respective, *respective lenity*, the forbearance he has exercised because of the family connection between Tybalt and Juliet, *Rom. & Jul.*, 3.i.

Respectively, for your own sake, personally, *Timon*, 3.i.

Responsive, *very responsive to*, in good keeping with, *Ham.*, 5.ii.

Rest, (1) in the card game of primero, the stake on which the game turned, so *to set up one's rest* is to stake, hazard, determine; with play on other meanings of *rest*, *Rom. & Jul.*, 4.v; etc.; (2) repose, so *full of rest*, vigour, *Jul. Caes.*, 4.iii; abode, stay, *Per.*, 2.*Prol.; verb, what rests?* what can I do now? *Ham.*, 3.iii.

Restem, sail back again, *Oth.*, 1.iii.

Restrain, *restraining aid*, withholding help, *Timon*, 5.i.

Resty, sluggish, *Troil. & Cres.*, 1.iii; *resty sloth*, indolence, *Cym.*, 3.vi.

Retention, detention, *Lear*, 5.iii.

Retentive, confining, *Jul. Caes.*, 1.iii.

Retrograde, contrary, *Ham.*, 1.ii.

Reverb, reverberate, *Lear*, 1.i.

Reverence, *settlest admired reverence in a slave*, enable baseness to appear worthy of respect, *Timon*, 5.i; *saving reverence*, apologetic phrase, introducing indecent suggestions in *Cym.*, 4.i.

Reversion, *no perfection in reversion shall have a praise in present*, give no praise now to merit that may be hoped for or expected in the future, *Troil. & Cres.*, 3.ii.

Revolt, rebel, *Cym.*, 4.iv; desertion, *Ant. & Cleo.*, 4.ix; disobedient act, *Oth.*, 1.i; *give him the revolt*, rebel against him, *Mac.*, 5.iv; *revolted fair*, unfaithful woman, *Troil. & Cres.*, 5.ii.

Revolution, time having changed the relative position of things, *Ham.*, 5.i; *by revolution*, in course of time, *Ant. & Cleo.*, 1.ii.

Rhapsody, meaningless farrago, *Ham.*, 3.iv.

Rhenish, Rhine wine, *Ham.*, 1.iv.

Rheum, watering at the eyes, *Ant. & Cleo.*, 3.ii; *bisson rheum*, blinding tears, *Ham.*, 2.ii; *rheumy*, dank, causing rheum in men, *Jul. Caes.*, 2.i. [3.x.

Ribaudred, wanton, *Ant. & Cleo.*,

Rich, *rich beholding*, looks of admiration, *Troil. & Cres.*, 3.iii; delightful, *Troil. & Cres.*, 1.iii; *your rich opinion*, the high opinion people have of you, *Oth.*, 2.iii; *richly*, splendidly, *Cym.*, 5.v; *verb*, enriched, *Lear*, 1.i. [5.i.

Rid, *rid me*, make away with, *Timon*,

Riggish, wanton, *Ant. & Cleo.*, 2.ii.

Right, *do me right*, give me my due, justice, *Titus*, 1.i; authority, *Cor.*, 3.iii; *adv.*, exactly, *Troil. & Cres.*, 1.iii. [cians, *Cor.*, 2.i.

Right-hand, *right-hand file*, patri-

Ring, *cracked within the ring*, of a boy's voice; the simile refers to coin which was uncurrent if a crack at the edge extended within the ring round the royal effigy; the 'ring' of the voice must also be intact, *Ham.*, 2.ii.

Riotous, full of drunkards, *Lear*, 1.iv; unrestrained, *Ant. & Cleo.*, 1.iii; *riotous feeders*, revellers, topers, and gluttons, *Timon*, 2.ii.

Ripely, at once, the time being ripe, *Cym.*, 3.v.

Rival, partner, *Ham.*, 1.i.

Rivality, partnership, equality, *Ant. & Cleo.*, 3.v.

Rive, split, *Troil. & Cres.*, 1.i; *Lear*, 3.ii; rend, *Ant. & Cleo.*, 4.xiii.

Rivelled, wrinkled, *Troil. & Cres.*, 5.i. [*Cleo.*, 4.iv.

Rivet, *riveted trim*, armour, *Ant. &*

Road, inroad, *Cor.*, 3.i.

Rogue, vagrant, *Lear*, 4.vii; term of affection, *Oth.*, 4.i.

Roguing, roaming, *Per.*, 4.i; *his roguish madness*, being a half-wit and a vagrant, *Lear*, 3.vii. [2.ii.

Roisting, uproarious, *Troil. & Cres.*,

Romage, turmoil, *Ham.*, 1.i.

Ronyon, scabby creature, *Mac.*, 1.iii.

Rood, cross, *Ham.*, 3.iv.

Roof, *thin roofs*, bald heads, *Timon*, 4.iii; *roof'd*, under one roof, gathered together, *Mac.*, 3.iv.

Rooky, *rooky wood*, rookery, *Mac.*, 3.ii. [*Rom. & Jul.*, 2.iv.

Ropery, knavery, loose behaviour,

Roscius, most famous of Roman actors, friend of Cicero, *Ham.*, 2.ii.

Rose, *cakes of roses*, cakes of rose-petals, used as perfume, *Rom. & Jul.*, 5.i.

Roted, learnt by rote, *Cor.*, 3.ii.

Rother, ox, *Timon*, 4.iii.

Round, plain-spoken, *Ham.*, 3.i; honest, straightforward, *Oth.*, 1.iii; *in the roundest manner*, in the plainest way, without observing ceremony, *Lear*, 1.iv; *round and safe*, unblemished and trustworthy, *Per.*, 1.ii; *adv.*, directly, *Ham.*, 2.ii; *noun*, *the golden round*, the crown, *Mac.*, 1.v; rung of ladder, *Jul. Caes.*, 2.i.

Rouse, bumper, *Ham.*, 1.ii; *Oth.*, 2.iii; carousal, *Ham.*, 1.iv.

Row, stanza, *Ham.*, 2.ii.

Royal, *royal hope*, the prospect of being king, *Mac.*, 1.iii; *royal knavery*, the wickedness of a king, *Ham.*, 5.ii; *royal peril*, war being for Antony 'a royal occupation,' fit for kings and heroes, *Ant. & Cleo.*, 4.viii.

Royalty, *royalty of nature*, noble character, *Mac.*, 3.i; princely bearing and behaviour, *Cym.*, 4.ii.

Rub, in bowling, something that deflects the bowl from the course it runs, so of an obstacle of a hidden kind, *Cor.*, 3.i; so unevenness (of execution), *Mac.*, 3.i; *verb, rub on and kiss the mistress:* as *mistress* in bowls meant the *jack*, and *kiss* is also a term in the game, the pun is a triple one, *Troil. & Cres.*, 3.ii; *will not be rubb'd nor stopp'd*, diverted by any opposition, *Lear*, 2.ii.

Ruddock, robin, *Cym.*, 4.ii.

Rude, uncivilized, *Jul. Caes.*, 3.ii.

Rudeness, rusticity, clumsiness, *Jul. Caes.*, 1.ii; *Cym.*, 4.ii.

Rue, pity, *Titus*, 1.i.

Ruffle, swagger, *Titus*, 1.i; bluster, [*Lear*, 2.iv.

Ruinate, subvert, *Titus*, 5.iii.

Ruinous, enfeebled, *Timon*, 4.iii.

Rule, integrity, *Troil. & Cres.*, 5.ii.

Rumour, *a rumour like a fray*, the noise of a distant disturbance, *Jul. Caes.*, 2.iv.

Rumourer, spreader of reports, *Cor.*, [4.vi.

Rump-fed, fat-rumped, *Mac.*, 1.iii.

Runagate, vagabond, *Rom. & Jul.*, 3.v; fugitive, *Cym.*, 4.ii.

Rush, rushes were spread as a covering for the floor, *Cym.*, 2.ii; *Rom. & Jul.*, 1.iv; emblem of a harmless weapon, *Oth.*, 5.ii; *verb*, thrust, *Rom. & Jul.*, 3.iii.

Ruthful, pitiable, *Troil. & Cres.*, 5.iii; *Titus*, 5.i.

'S, *suffix*, us (for 'we'), *where shall's lay him?*, *Cym.*, 4.ii; *within's*, within this, *Ham.*, 3.ii; *prefix*, God's.

Sable, black, *Ham.*, 2.ii.

Sables, *suit of sables*, richly trimmed or lined with sable fur, *Ham.*, 3.ii and 4.vii.

Sackbut, kind of trombone, *Cor.*, [5.iv.

Sacred, of royal persons, so *sacred breast*, royal breast, *Per.*, 1.ii; *sacred aunt*, *Troil. & Cres.*, 4.v; so sarcastically in *our empress with her sacred wit*, *Titus*, 2.i.

Sacrificial, as if devotional, *Timon*, [1.i.

Sad, grave, serious, *Jul. Caes.*, 1.ii; *sadly*, in earnest, *Rom. & Jul.*, 1.i; *in sadness*, in all seriousness, *Rom. & Jul.*, 1.i.

Safe, sane; *the safer sense*, a sound mind, *Lear*, 4.vi; *Oth.*, 4.i; *a safer judgement*, more sane, considered, *Cor.*, 2.iii; *verb*, provide safe-conduct, *Ant. & Cleo.*, 4.vii; render safe, *Ant. & Cleo.*, 1.iii; *adv.*, *safe toward*, well designed for, *Mac.*, 1.iv.

Safety, safe custody, *Rom. & Jul.*, 5.iii; *in safety*, well, *Cym.*, 1.vi; *safeties*, means of safety, *Mac.*, 4.iii.

Sage, solemn, *Ham.*, 5.i.

Sagittary, the Centaur whom medieval romances represent fighting as an archer for the Trojans, *Troil. & Cres.*, 5.v; the sign of a house, *Oth.*, 1.i.

Salad, *my salad days*, my early, green, inexperienced years, *Ant. & Cleo.*, 1.v.

Sallet, salad, so tasty, spicy additions, *Ham.*, 2.ii.

Salt, used of tears, *Cor.*, 5.vi; *a man of salt*, reduced to tears, *Lear*, 4.vi; *adj.*, lewd, *Oth.*, 2.i; lascivious, *Ant. & Cleo.*, 2.i; *salt hours*, lecherous, *Timon*, 4.iii.

Samphire, sea-fennel, for which Dover cliffs were famous, *Lear*, 4.vi.

Sample, an example, *Cym.*, 1.i.

Sampler, piece of needle-work, sample of proficiency, *Titus*, 2.iv.

Sanctify, *sanctifies himself with's hands*, touches his hand with the reverence of a devotee, *Cor.*, 4.v.

Sanctimony, *sanctimony and a frail vow*, (in the circumstances) an outward show of piety and faith, *Oth.*, 1.iii; *sanctimonies*, holy things, *Troil. & Cres.*, 5.ii.

Sanctuarize, protect, give sanctuary to, *Ham.*, 4.vii.

Sands, of the hour-glass, *Cym.*, 3.ii.

Sanguine, red, *Cym.*, 5.v; with reference to youthful faces, *Titus*, 4.ii.

Sans, without; *sans all*, without the other senses, *Ham.*, 3.iv. [5.i.

Sarcenet, fine silk, *Troil. & Cres.*,

Sarum, Salisbury, *Lear*, 2.ii.

Saturn, the cold planet supposed to inspire moroseness and hate, *Titus*, 2.iii; *Cym.*, 2.v.

Saucy, sharp, tormenting, *Mac.*, 3.iv; lascivious, *Cym.*, 1.vi.

Save, in greetings; *save thee*, God save thee, *Timon*, 4.iii; *Lear*, 2.i; *saved my longing*, spared me the impatience of my desire to see you, *Timon*, 1.i.

Savour, smell, *Per.*, 4.vi; *filths savour but themselves*, the wicked have a taste only for their own kind of vileness, *Lear*, 4.ii.

Say, flavour, touch, *Lear*, 5.ii; *verb*, assay, attempt, *Per.*, 1.i; *say you?* what do you say? *Ham.*, 4.v; *Oth.*, 3.iv; *there thou say'st*, you speak truly on that point, *Ham.*, 5.i; *you've said*, you speak truly, *Ant. & Cleo.*, 2.vi. [*Oth.*, 1.i.

'Sblood, God's blood, *Ham.*, 2.ii;

Scaffoldage, the stage, the boards, *Troil. & Cres.*, 1.iii.

Scald, scalding the feathers off poultry is used to suggest the sweating-tub is being prepared for the diseases of madam's customers, *Timon*, 2.ii.

Scale, weigh, compare, *Cor.*, 2.iii; *scales*, graduated markings, *Ant. & Cleo.*, 2.vii.

Scandal, defame, *Cor.*, 3.i; bring scandal on, *Cym.*, 3.iv.

Scant, *scants us with*, puts us off with, *Troil. & Cres.*, 1.iii; *scant my sizes*, reduce my allowances, *Lear*, 2.iv; withhold, *Lear*, 1.i; *scantly*, grudgingly, deprecatingly, *Ant. & Cleo.*, 3.iv. [1.iii.

Scantling, sample, *Troil. & Cres.*,

Scarf, wrap round as with a scarf, *Ham.*, 5.ii; *scarf up*, blindfold, *Mac.*, 3.ii.

Scatter, *this scatter'd kingdom*, disunited realm, *Lear*, 3.i; *scattering*, random, *Oth.*, 3.iii.

Scene, place represented by the stage, *Troil. & Cres.*, 1.*Prol.*; *scene individable*, unity of place (contrasted with *poem unlimited*, where we might be now in Rome, now in Egypt), *Ham.*, 2.ii.

Schedule, document, *Jul. Caes.*, 3.i.

Scion, twig, for grafting, *Oth.*, 1.iii.

Sconce, head, *Ham.*, 5.i. [*mon*, 1.i.

Scope, *to scope*, to the purpose, *Ti-*

Score, notch (with swords), *Ant. & Cleo.*, 4.vii; *score up against*, score off a person, *Oth.*, 4.i.

Scorn, derision, *Titus*, 3.i; object of mockery, *Titus*, 1.i; *Cym.*, 5.v; a scoff, *Oth.*, 4.i.

Scotch, cut, wound, *Mac.*, 3.ii; etc.

Scrimer, fencer, *Ham.*, 4.vii.

Scriptures, writings, *Cym.*, 3.iv.

Scrowl, scrawl, *Titus*, 2.iv.

Scruple, third of a dram, *Troil. & Cres.*, 4.i; *not making any scruple of*, not finding the least cause for offence or distaste in, *Troil. & Cres.*, 4.i; *made scruple of*, to doubt, question, *Cym.*, 5.v.

Scrupulous, *scrupulous faction*, bickering about trifles, *Ant. & Cleo.*, 1.iii.

Scull, *scaled sculls*, shoal of fish, *Troil. & Cres.*, 5.v.

'Sdeath, God's death, *Cor.*, 1.i.

Seal, confirm, sanction, *Cor.*, 2.iii; *Cym.*, 3.vi; finish, complete (like putting a seal to a document), *Ant. & Cleo.*, 4.xiv; *give them seals*, confirm his words with deeds, *Ham.*, 3.ii. [2.iii.

Seam, grease, fat, *Troil. & Cres.*,

Sear, withered state, *Mac.*, 5.iii; *sear-up*, render lifeless, wrap as in death, *Cym.*, 1.i.

Search, of a wound, to probe, *Titus*, 2.iii; search-party, *Oth.*, 1.i.

Searchers, officers that reported on the causes of deaths and kept watch for cases of plague, *Rom. & Jul.*, 5.ii. [*Jul.*, 5.iii.

Sea-sick, tired of the sea, *Rom. &*

Season, what preserves or keeps fresh, *Mac.*, 3.iv; *the fits o' th' season*, the critical, hectic conditions of our time, *Mac.*, 4.ii; *of such a season*, of about your own age, *Cym.*, 3.iv; *verb*, temper, moderate, *Ham.*, 1.ii; *all season'd office*, rendered palatable by custom, *Cor.*, 3.iii; *seasons him his enemy*, matures, ripens him into an enemy, *Ham.*, 3.ii; *seasons comfort*, brings out the full flavour of happiness, *Cym.*, 1.vi.

Seat, situation, *Mac.*, 1.vi; abode, *Cym.*, 5.iv.

Second, supporter, *Cor.*, 1.iv; *Lear*, 4.vi; *your condemned seconds*, your confounded meddlesome support, *Cor.*, 1.viii; *adj.*, *second voice*, voice of a deputy, *Troil. & Cres.*, 2.iii; *verb*, follow up, *Cym.*, 5.i; *the report is seconded*, is confirmed, supported, *Cor.*, 4.vi.

Sect, (1) a party, *Timon*, 3.v; *Lear*, 5.iii; (2) a cutting twig for grafting, *Oth.*, 1.iii.

SECTARY, *sectary astronomical*, a devotee of astrology, *Lear*, 1.ii.

SECURE, free from all suspicion or fear, *Ham.*, 1.v; *Oth.*, 4.i; *verb*, render careless, deprive of circumspection, *Lear*, 4.i; *secure thy heart*, be easy in mind, *Timon*, 2.ii; guard, *Ham.*, 1.v; *adv.*, *securely done*, confidently, *Troil. & Cres.*, 4.v.

SECURITY, heedless confidence, *Mac.*, 3.v.

SEE, meet, see each other, *Cym.*, 1.i; *Troil. & Cres.*, 4.iv; *see him out*, make sure he goes, *Cor.*, 3.iii; *see to*, arrange, *Ant. & Cleo.*, 5.ii.

SEEDED, mature, but ready to multiply itself, *Troil. & Cres.*, 1.iii.

SEEK, reclaim, *Cym.*, 3.i; *seeking*, petition, *Cor.*, 1.i.

SEEL, from falconry, where it refers to the closing of the hawk's eyes in early training, so to blind, *Mac.*, 3.ii; close up, *Oth.*, 3.iii; *Ant. & Cleo.*, 3.xiii.

SEEMING, appearance, outward bearing, *Ham.*, 3.ii; imitation, impersonation, *Troil. & Cres.*, 1.iii; hypocrisy, disguise, *Lear*, 3.ii; *modern seeming*, commonplace, everyday appearances, *Oth.*, 1.iii; deceptive bearing, *Oth.*, 3.iii; *this hath some seeming*, probability, *Cym.*, 5.v.

SEETHE, boil, *Timon*, 4.iii; *my business seethes*, is at boiling point, urgent, *Troil. & Cres.*, 3.i; *sodden*, diseased, *Per.*, 4.ii; *sodden business*, with reference to the sweating-tub and venereal disease, *Troil. & Cres.*, 3.i.

SEGREGATION, dispersal, *Oth.*, 2.i.

SEIZED OF, possessed of, *Ham.*, 1.i.

SEIZURE, grasp, *Troil. & Cres.*, 1.i.

SELD, seldom, *Troil. & Cres.*, 4.v; *seld-shown*, seldom seen, *Cor.*, 2.i.

SELF, *by self and violent hands*, by her own hands, *Mac.*, 5.viii; *self-blood*, very same blood, *Titus*, 4.ii; *self-breath*, his own voice, *Troil. & Cres.*, 2.iii; *self-comparisons*, acts comparable, matching his opponent's, *Mac.*, 1.ii; *self-affected*, loving himself, *Troil. & Cres.*, 2.iii; *one self mate and make*, the very same husband and wife, *Lear*, 4.iii; *that self exhibition*, that very money, *Cym.*, 1.vi; *self-bounty*, your own generosity, *Oth.*, 3.iii; *self-explication*, the ability to express one's condition, *Cym.*, 3.iv; *self-cover'd*, covered with deformity of your own choice, *Lear*, 4.ii.

SEMBLABLE, similar, *Ant. & Cleo.*, 3.iv; *his semblable*, anyone who is as he is a man, *Timon*, 4.iii.

SEMBLANCE, outward attraction, *Cym.*, 2.iv.

SEND, *has only sent his present occasion now*, to notify you of his immediate necessity, *Timon*, 3.ii; *I send him the greatness he has got*, I acknowledge by my message his sovereignty, *Ant. & Cleo.*, 5.ii.

SENECA, Roman philosopher and tragic poet, 4 B.C.–65 A.D.; the nine tragedies attributed to his pen were regarded in Shakespeare's day as models for those who aimed at a classical decorum, *Ham.*, 2.ii.

SE'NNIGHT, a week, *Oth.*, 2.i; etc.

SENSE, feeling, sensation, perception; these meanings are played on in turn in *Ham.*, 3.iv; one's senses or being, *Troil. & Cres.*, 3.ii; vital powers, *Cym.*, 2.ii.

SENSELESS, deaf, *Cym.*, 2.iii.

SENSIBLE, confirmed by one's senses, *Ham.*, 1.i; capable of sensation, *Cor.*, 1.iii; *sensible to feeling as to sight*, capable of being apprehended by touch as well as visible, *Mac.*, 2.i.

SENSIBLY, feelingly, *Ham.*, 4.v; *who sensibly outdares*, who, though a creature endowed with feeling and exposed to pain, etc., yet ventures, *Cor.*, 1.iv; *sensibly fed of that self-blood*, nourished by the same blood, *Titus*, 4.ii.

SEQUENCE, one after the other, *Titus*, 4.i.

SEQUESTER, separate, *Troil. & Cres.*, 3.iii; separation, *Oth.*, 3.iv.

SEQUESTRATION, separation, parting, *Oth.*, 1.iii.

SERE, *tickle o' th' sere*, easily set off (like a gun with a low trigger pressure, the sere being part of the trigger mechanism), *Ham.*, 2.ii (*see also* SEAR).

SERGEANT, sheriff's officer, *Ham.*, 5.ii.

SERPIGO, eruption of the skin, *Troil. & Cres.*, 2.iii.

SERVICE, *variable service*, different courses, *Ham.*, 4.iii.

SERVICEABLE, *a serviceable villain*, a useful tool in crime, *Lear*, 4.vi.

SESSA, an interjection expressing complacency, *Lear*, 3.iv.

SET, hand or game at cards, *Titus*, 5.i; the group of the twelve figures on the clock, *Oth.*, 2.iii; *verb*, stake, *Troil. & Cres.*, 1.*Prol.*, etc.; estimate, *Ham.*, 4.iii; *set down before*, besiege; *set only to himself*, intent only on his own thoughts, *Timon*, 5.i; *set down the pegs*, slacken the strings, untune, *Oth.*, 2.i; *set my rest* (*see* Rest), *Lear*, 1.i.

Settle, *settlest . . . reverence*, *see* Reverence; *till further settling*, till his mind is more composed, *Lear*, 4.vii.

Several, *severals*, individual gifts, *Troil. & Cres.*, 1.iii; *severally*, each one on his own particular mission, *Timon*, 2.ii; *severally entreat him*, let individuals in turn entertain him, *Troil. & Cres.*, 4.v; *severally in all*, all rejoice, each in his own particular way, *Cym.*, 5.v.

Sewer, supervises arrangement and service of meal, *Mac.*, 1.vii.

Sex, *general sex*, all womankind, *Troil. & Cres.*, 5.ii. [2.iii.

'Sfoot, God's foot, *Troil. & Cres.*,

Shadowing, *shadowing passion*, like an eclipse (this time, of the mind), portending something, *Oth.*, 4.i.

Shag-ear'd, with hair hanging over the ears, like a shag-dog, *Mac.*, 4.ii.

Shall, *his absolute 'shall,'* expressing determination and purpose, in place of 'will' of conditional futurity, *Cor.*, 3.i. [3.ii; *Cym.*, 3.iii.

Shard-borne, sharded, winged, *Mac.*,

Shards, bits of broken pottery, *Ham.*, 5.i; wings, *Ant. & Cleo.*, 2.i.

Share, *to share from*, to take as his share, *Troil. & Cres.*, 1.iii.

Shark up, gather wherever he could find them, eagerly and without distinction, as the greedy shark feeds, *Ham.*, 1.i.

Sharp, excite, *Ant. & Cleo.*, 2.i.

Sharpen, make keen, eager, lead on, *Troil. & Cres.*, 5.ii.

She, woman, *Cym.*, 1.iii.

Sheal'd, shelled; *sheal'd peascod*, empty, the peas having been extracted, *Lear*, 1.iv.

Sheet, cover as with a sheet, *Ant. & Cleo.*, 1.iv; *sheeted*, in shrouds, *Ham.*, 1.i.

Shent, reprove, abuse, *Ham.*, 3.ii.

Shield, *God shield*, God forbid that, *Rom. & Jul.*, 4.i.

Shift, expedient, *Titus*, 4.i; *verb*, exchange, *Ant. & Cleo.*, 5.ii; change (of clothing), *Cym.*, 1.ii; move, *Oth.*, 4.i; *shift away*, steal away, *Mac.*, 2.iii.

Shirt, *a shirt and a smock*, a man and a woman, *Rom. & Jul.*, 2.iv.

Shive, slice, *Titus*, 2.i.

Shore, *the varying shore o' th' world*, where fortune ebbs and flows as on the sea-shore, *Ant. & Cleo.*, 4.xv; *common shores*, drains, *Per.*, 4.vi.

Short, *keep short*, on short tether, close control, *Ham.*, 4.i; *short my word*, fail to keep my promise, *Cym.*, 1.vi.

Shorten, *shorten'd in our aim*, fail to reach our target or original objectives, *Cor.*, 1.ii; *shortens my made intent*, would anticipate and spoil my plan, *Lear*, 4.vii.

Shot, the reckoning, *Cym.*, 5.iv.

Shough, shaggy dog, *Mac.*, 3.i.

Shrew, *shrew me*, beshrew me, blame on me, *Cym.*, 2.iii.

Shrewd, vexatious, *Ant. & Cleo.*, 4.ix; *shrewdly*, keenly, *Ham.*, 1.iv.

Shrift, confessional, or penance demanded for absolution, *Oth.*, 3.iii.

Shrill-gorg'd, shrill-throated, *Lear*, 4.vi.

Shrine, image, *Cym.*, 5.v; the image of the saint, *Rom. & Jul.*, 1.v.

Shroud, protection, *Ant. & Cleo.*, 3.xiii.

Shunless, *which he painted with shunless destiny*, as crosses were marked on the doors of plague-stricken houses, so he marked with blood the gate of the doomed city, *Cor.*, 2.ii.

Shut up, ended the day, *Mac.*, 2.i.

Sibyl, the Cumaean Sibyl in Virgil's *Aeneid* writes her prophecies on leaves, which, if the shrine is disturbed, are scattered by the wind and become confused and unintelligible; that is why Titus wishes to substitute a leaf of brass, *Titus*, 4.i.

Sick, disordered, *Troil. & Cres.*, 1.ii; *Ant. & Cleo.*, 1.iii; infected with envy, *Troil. & Cres.*, 1.iii; *sickly*, weakly, with little force, *Ant. & Cleo.*, 3.iv.

Sickens, *his destruction sickens*, confusion become worse confounded, *Mac.*, 4.i.

Sickness, misery, impatience, *Ham.*, 4.vii; disorder, *Timon*, 5.i.

Side, *side factious*, to take sides with one or other party, *Cor.*, 1.i.

Side-piercing, harrowing, heartrending, *Lear*, 4.vi. [1.ii.

Siege, rank, class, *Ham.*, 4.vii; *Oth.*,

Sieve, receptacle for scraps, *Troil. & Cres.*, 2.ii. [*Troil. & Cres.*, 3.ii.

Sight, second sight, foreknowledge,

Sightless, invisible, *Mac.*, 1.v.

Sign, outward appearance, *Cym.*, 1.ii; *verb*, signify, bode, *Ant. & Cleo.*, 4.iii; *sign'd in thy spoil*, bearing the marks of your fate, *Jul. Caes.*, 3.i.

Signiory, the governing body of Venice, *Oth.*, 1.ii.

Silly, *in a silly habit*, poorly, humbly dressed, *Cym.*, 5.iii.

SIMPLE, medicinal herb, *Lear*, 4.iv; so ingredient that could be element in a compound, *Rom. & Jul.*, 5.i; *simple-answer'd*, truthful, without evasions, *Lear*, 3.vii; *simpleness*, innocent of the arts of persuasion, plain integrity of purpose, *Oth.*, 1.iii.

SIMPLICITY, name given by worldlings to 'simple truth,' *Troil. & Cres.*, 4.iv.

SIMULAR, *simular man of virtue*, hypocrite, *Lear*, 3.ii; *simular proof*, fabricated evidence, *Cym.*, 5.v.

SINEW, nerve, *Lear*, 3.vi.

SINGLE, insignificant, *Cor.*, 2.i; feeble, *Mac.*, 1.iii; individual, *Lear*, 5.iii; *a single doom*, the fall of one man only, *Ant. & Cleo.*, 5.i; *verb*, pick out as if hunting, *Titus*, 2.i; *singly*, uniquely, *Timon*, 4.iii.

SINGLE-SOLED, thin, having as it were only one thickness of leather, *Rom. & Jul.*, 2.iv.

SINGULARITY, peculiar and characteristic position he has adopted, *Cor.*, 1.i.

SINISTER, left, *Troil. & Cres.*, 4.v.

SINON, the Greek whose tearful lies moved the Trojans to admit the fatal horse, *Cym.*, 3.iv; *Titus*, 5.iii.

SIR, *sole sir*, sovereign, *Ant. & Cleo.*, 5.ii; gentleman, *Cym.*, 1.vi; *sir-reverence*, save your reverence, with due respect or apology, *Rom. & Jul.*, 1.iv.

SISTER, be akin to, *Per.*, 5.*Prol.*

SIT, sit discussing, *Per.*, 2.iii; *sit down*, besiege, *Ant. & Cleo.*, 5.xiii; *Cor.*, 4.vii; *the crowner hath sat on her*, the coroner has held his inquest on her death, *Ham.*, 5.i.

SITH, SITHENCE, since, *Ham.*, 2.ii; *Cor.*, 3.i.

SIZE, *as my love is siz'd*, according to the greatness of my love, *Ham.*, 3.ii; *noun*, allowance, *Lear*, 2.iv; share, dimension, *Ant. & Cleo.*, 4.xv.

SKAINS-MATES, carriers of daggers, ruffians, companions of loose women, *Rom. & Jul.*, 2.iv.

SKILL, mind, memory, *Lear*, 4.vii; cunning, policy, *Cym.*, 2.v.

SKILLET, saucepan, *Oth.*, 1.iii.

SKIPPING, flighty, ill-disciplined, *Mac.*, 1.ii.

SKIRR, sour, *Mac.*, 5.iii.

SKYISH, touching the sky, *Ham.*, 5.i.

SLAB, thick, glutinous, *Mac.*, 4.i.

SLACK, *come slack of*, fail to come up to the standard of, *Lear*, 1.iii; *verb*, neglect, *Lear*, 2.iv.

SLANDER, reproach of cowardice, *Rom. & Jul.*, 3.i; *no slander*, that's true, *Ant. & Cleo.*, 2.vi; *verb*, waste, *Ham.*, 1.iii; discredit, *Cym.*, 3.v.

SLAVE, *slaves your ordinance*, misuses the dispensations of God, *Lear*, 4.ii.

SLEAVE, *ravell'd sleave*, tangled mass (as of silk), *Mac.*, 2.ii.

SLEDDED, *sledded Polacks*, the Poles using sledges, *Ham.*, 1.i.

SLEID, SLEIDED SILK, raw silk, *Troil. & Cres.*, 5.i; *Per.*, 4.*Prol.*

SLEIGHT, cunning, *Mac.*, 3.v.

SLIGHT, irresponsible, *Oth.*, 2.iii; *too slight in sufferance*, too patient, forbearing, *Cym.*, 3.v; *slightness*, frivolity, caprice, *Cor.*, 3.i.

SLIP, a counterfeit coin, with pun on 'slip' = escape, desertion, *Rom. & Jul.*, 2.iv (*cf. Troil. & Cres.*, 2.iii); scion, dependant, *Titus*, 5.i; *verb*, free, *Jul. Caes.*, 3.i; *Cym.*, 4.iii.

SLIPPER, slippery, cunning, *Oth.*, 2.i.

SLIPPERY, fickle, inconstant, *Ant. & Cleo.*, 1.ii.

SLIPSHOD, in slippers, *Lear*, 1.v.

SLIVER, a small branch that is broken off, *Ham.*, 4.vii; tear off, *Lear*, 4.ii.

SLOP, loose breeches, *Rom. & Jul.*, 2.iv.

SLUBBER, spoil, sully, *Oth.*, 1.iii.

SLUTTISH, wanton, *Troil. & Cres.*, 4.v.

SMALL, *small beer*, weak beer, so the trivialities of daily life, *Oth.*, 2.i; slender, *Per.*, 4.*Prol.*

SMATCH, smack, taste, *Jul. Caes.*, 5.v.

SMATTER, chatter, *Rom. & Jul.*, 3.v.

SMILE, *smile you my speeches*, mock at my remarks, *Lear*, 2.ii.

SMOCK, woman's undergarment, so a woman, *Rom. & Jul.*, 2.iv.

SMOKE, *smoke for it*, get it hot, *Titus*, 4.ii.

SMOOTH, flatter, *Titus*, 4.iv; *Timon*, 4.iii; speak in friendly way, *Per.*, 1.ii; humour, *Lear*, 2.ii; *smooth thy name*, say it lovingly, and as the name of a man of honour, *Rom. & Jul.*, 3.ii.

SMUG, spruce, *Lear*, 4.vi.

SMULKIN, a fiend, *Lear*, 3.iv.

SNATCH, a quick bit of poaching, *Titus*, 2.i; fragment, *Ham.*, 4.vii; *snatches in his voice*, staccato style of utterance, *Cym.*, 4.ii.

SNIPE, fool, *Oth.*, 1.iii.

SNUFF, (1) charred wick, *Ham.*, 4.vii; so of some worn-out or inferior person, *Cym.*, 1.vi; *my snuff*, the useless end of my life, *Lear*, 4.vi; (2) huff, offence-taking, *Lear*, 3.i.

SOD, SODDEN, *see* SEETHE.

SOFT, go softly, carefully, pause, *Titus*, 4.ii; stop, *Ant. & Cleo.*, 2.ii.

SOHO, cry on sighting the hare on her form (hence 'No hare, sir'), *Rom. & Jul.*, 2.iv.

SOIL, *soil our addition*, blacken the good name our merits have gained for us, *Ham.*, 1.iv; *soiled horse*, stall-fed with green food, *Lear*, 4.vi; *noun*, blemish, *Ham.*, 1.iii.

SOILURE, stain on her character, debasement, *Troil. & Cres.*, 4.i.

SOLE, *affecting one sole throne*, aiming at absolute rule, *Cor.*, 4.vi; *whose sole name*, whose mere name, *Mac.*, 4.iii.

SOLELY, *solely sovereign sway*, absolute sovereign power, *Mac.*, 1.v; absolutely, *Cor.*, 4.vii.

SOLEMN, *a solemn hunting*, a festive and courtly meet for hunting, *Titus*, 2.i.

SOLEMNITY, festivity, *Rom. & Jul.*, 1.v; ceremony, *Ant. & Cleo.*, 5.ii.

SOLICIT, urge, bring something about, *Ham.*, 5.ii; pray to heaven, *Oth.*, 5.ii; *soliciting*, incitement, *Mac.*, 1.iii; *orderly soliciting*, businesslike wooing, *Cym.*, 2.iii.

SOLICITATION, illicit courtship, *Oth.*, 4.ii.

SOLIDARE, small coin, *Timon*, 3.i.

SOLON, *Solon's happiness*, death; Solon having warned Croesus that no one should be counted happy till he was dead, *Titus*, 1.i.

SOMETIME, on a certain occasion, *Cor.*, 1.ix; formerly, *Ham.*, 3.i; *Cym.*, 5.v; *adj.*, former, *Lear*, 1.i.

SOON, *soon at night*, sometime tonight, *Rom. & Jul.*, 2.v; towards evening, *Oth.*, 3.iv; *soonest*, quickest, *Ant. & Cleo.*, 3.v.

SOOTH, truth, *Mac.*, 5.v; flattery; personified, *Signior Sooth*, *Per.*, 1.ii.

SOP, something steeped in liquor, *Troil. & Cres.*, 1.iii; *sop o' th' moonshine of you*, steep you in moonshine by stabbing you in many places and so letting it in, *Lear*, 2.ii.

SOPHISTICATED, not '*the thing itself*,' contaminated, disguised by clothes, *Lear*, 3.iv.

SORROWED, full of sorrow and regret, *Timon*, 5.i.

SORROW-WREATHEN KNOT, folded arms, *Titus*, 3.ii.

SORRY, troublesome, *Oth.*, 3.iv.

SORT, (1) *draw the sort*, draw the lot, *Troil. & Cres.*, 1.iii; (2) manner, *Cor.*, 1.iii; *in sort*, in some degree only, *Jul. Caes.*, 2.i; *verb*, *sort you with*, associate you with, *Ham.*, 2.ii; choose, *Rom. & Jul.*, 4.ii; suit, be in keeping with something, *Troil. & Cres.*, 1.i; *well may it sort*, be in keeping with the time, *Ham.*, 1.i.

SOVEREIGN, supreme in power and efficacy, *Cor.*, 2.i; *opinion, a sovereign mistress of effects*, confidence is the supreme agent in securing success, *Oth.*, 1.iii.

SOVEREIGNTY, *sovereignty of nature*, a power inherent in the creature's very nature, *Cor.*, 4.vii; *deprive your sovereignty of reason*, dethrone your reason that exercises a sovereign control over your conduct, *Ham.*, 1.iv.

SOWL, to drag by the ear, *Cor.*, 4.v.

SPACE, interval of time, *Lear*, 5.iii.

SPANIEL, follow, fawn, *Ant. & Cleo.*, 4.xii.

SPARE, forbear, *Cor.*, 1.i; *spare me*, save me having to speak my mind, *Cym.*, 2.iii.

SPARTAN, fierce, relentless, *Oth.*, 5.ii.

SPEAK, begin the battle, *Cor.*, 1.iv; proclaim, manifest, *Timon*, 1.i; give the order for action, *Ham.*, 5.ii; reveal, *Ant. & Cleo.*, 3.xii; indicate, *Cym.*, 4.ii; *Per.*, 1.iii; *speak him far*, praise him highly, *Cym.*, 1.i; *speak with thee at sea*, fight you on the sea, *Ant. & Cleo.*, 2.vi; *speak him home*, do justice to his conduct in my words, *Cor.*, 2.ii.

SPECIAL, *a special party*, a representative with a specially particular duty, *Titus*, 1.i.

SPECIALTY, *the specialty of rule*, the rights recognized as peculiar to authority, *Troil. & Cres.*, 1.iii.

SPECTACLES, eyes, *Cym.*, 1.vi.

SPECTATORSHIP, *in spectatorship*, in the viewing, *Cor.*, 5.ii.

SPECULATION, sight as possessed by normal human beings, *Mac.*, 3.iv; *speculations*, scouts, *Lear*, 3.i.

SPECULATIVE, with power of vision, *Oth.*, 1.iii; *thoughts speculative*, fancies that picture a happy outcome, *Mac.*, 5.iv.

SPEED, *the speed of him*, outstripped him, *Mac.*, 1.v; *be my speed*, my help, *Rom. & Jul.*, 5.iii; *a se'ennight's speed*, a week before they were expected, *Oth.*, 2.i; fortune, success (with quibble on 'speed' = swiftness), *Cym.*, 3.v; *verb*, fare for good or ill, *Cym.*, 5.iv; succeed, *Lear*, 1.ii; *speed how it will*, whatever the result, *Cor.*, 5.i; prosper, *Timon*, 3.ii; *I am sped*, finished, done for, *Rom. & Jul.*, 3.i.

SPEKEN, (archaic form), to speak, *Per.*, 2.*Prol.*

SPEND, forfeit, exchange, *Oth.*, 2.iii;

spend his mouth, be vocal enough, *Troil. & Cres.*, 5.i; *spent*, eaten, *Rom. & Jul.*, 2.iv.

SPERR, bar the gates, *Troil. & Cres.*, 1.*Prol.*

SPHERE, in the Ptolemaic system the sun, moon, and planets were carried by hollow crystalline spheres concentric with the earth, *Ant. & Cleo.*, 4.xv; *Ham.*, 1.v; *in his sphere*, in its orbit, *Ham.*, 4.vii; *this sphere*, the earth, *Timon*, 1.i; *the tuned spheres*, the spheres were thought to give out a heavenly music as they revolved, *Ant. & Cleo.*, 5.ii; *Per.*, 5.i; worldly place and duty, *Ant. & Cleo.*, 2.vii.

SPHERED, set in its sphere, *Troil. & Cres.*, 1.iii; rounded, *Troil. & Cres.*, 4.v.

SPHERICAL, *spherical predominance*, the influence of the planets, *Lear*, 1.ii. [*Lear*, 3.ii.

SPILL, destroy, betray, *Ham.*, 4.v;

SPILTH, extravagant flow, *Timon*, 2.ii.

SPIRIT, courage, *Cor.*, 1.iv; *Cym.*, 5.iii; disposition, *Timon*, 5.iv; *spirit of sense*, the utmost fineness of sensibility, *Troil & Cres.*, 1.i; soul, mind, *Ham.*, 3.iv; life, *Ant. & Cleo.*, 4.xv; inclination, *Cym.*, 1.v; power, *Oth.*, 2.iii; *master spirits*, the elite, *Jul. Caes.*, 3.i.

SPITAL-HOUSE, hospital, *Timon*, 4.iii.

SPITE, injury, *Rom. & Jul.*, 4.i; contempt, *Rom. & Jul.*, 1.i; *Troil. & Cres.*, 5.v; insult, *Oth.*, 4.i.

SPLEEN, *the weakest spleen*, the coldest-hearted (the spleen being the organ regarded as the seat of the passions and emotions), *Troil. & Cres.*, 2.ii; *child of spleen*, of disobedient temper, *Lear*, 1.iv; of ungovernable passion, *Oth.*, 4.i; irascibility, *Rom. & Jul.*, 3.i; *Jul. Caes.*, 4.iii; so *splenitive*, *Ham.*, 5.i.

SPLENITIVE, *see* SPLEEN.

SPLINTER, join with splints, mend, *Oth.*, 2.iii.

SPLIT, mangle, stutter, *Ant. & Cleo.*, 2.vii; *I shall split all in pleasure of my spleen*, burst with laughing, *Troil. & Cres.*, 1.iii.

SPOIL, booty, conquest, *Titus*, 1.i; *Cor.*, 3.iii; *commit to the wanton spoil*, to the ravagement, *Cor.*, 2.i; *perpetual spoil*, bearing the marks of your murder (like the huntsman that has cut from the quarry the reward for the hounds), *Jul. Caes.*, 3.i.

SPONGY, soaked in drink, *Mac.*, 1.vii; moist, wet, *Cym.*, 4.ii.

SPORT, theatrical entertainment, *Jul. Caes.*, 3.i; amorous dalliance, *Titus*, 2.iii; *Oth.*, 2.i.

SPOT, *a fine spot*, a good pattern in embroidery, *Cor.*, 1.iii; disgrace, *Ant. & Cleo.*, 4.xii; *verb*, *spotted with*, having as a pattern, *Oth.*, 3.iii; *spotted die*, dice, *Timon*, 5.iv.

SPRING, source (here the East), *Mac.*, 1.ii. [2.iii.

SPIRITED, haunted, disturbed, *Cym.*,

SPRITELY, ghostly, *Cym.*, 5.v.

SPY, *the perfect spy o' th' time*, the information for the right timing of the deed, *Mac.*, 3.i.

SQUARE, *not kept my square*, not observed the proper limit of conduct, *Ant. & Cleo.*, 2.iii; *the most precious square of sense*, the utmost sensibility, *Lear*, 1.i; *in the brave squares of war*, among the front-line formations, *Ant. & Cleo.*, 3.xi; *adj.*, proper, fitting, *Timon*, 5.iv; *square brows*, high forehead, *Per.*, 5.i; *if report be square to her*, accurate in its report of her, *Ant. & Cleo.*, 2.ii; *verb*, estimate, judge, *Troil. & Cres.*, 5.ii; quarrel, *Titus*, 2.i; *Ant. & Cleo.*, 2.i.

SQUENE, squint, *Lear*, 3.iv. [4.vi.

SQUINY, squint, look askance, *Lear*,

SQUIRE-LIKE, like one of the attendants, *Lear*, 2.iv. [*& Cleo.*, 3.vi.

STABLISHMENT, possession, rule, *Ant.*

STAGE, platform, *Ham.*, 5.ii; exhibit in public, *Ant. & Cleo.*, 3.xiii.

STAGGER, perplexity, giddiness, *Cym.*, 5.v.

STAIN, eclipse, *Ant. & Cleo.*, 3.v.

STALE, laughing-stock, *Titus*, 1.i; to make common, *Troil. & Cres.*, 2.iii.

STALL, *stall together*, rest at peace with one another, *Ant. & Cleo.*, 5.i.

STAMP, coin, *Mac.*, 4.iii; with effigy stamped on it, *Cym.*, 5.iv; *verb*, coin, turn to advantage, *Oth.*, 2.i; *stamp'd the leasing*, put the stamp of currency (as on a coin) on the untruth, *Cor.*, 5.ii.

STANCH, satiate, *Titus*, 3.i; firm, watertight, *Ant. & Cleo.*, 2.ii; *stanchless*, insatiable, *Mac.*, 4.iii.

STAND, the butt past which the deer is driven within range of the hunter, *Cym.*, 2.ii; *verb*, *stands our lives upon to*, it is a matter of life and death to us to, *Ant. & Cleo.*, 2.i; *the main descry stands on the hourly thought*, the appearance of the main body is expected hourly, *Lear*, 4.vi; *stand me now upon*, be my duty, *Ham.*, 5.ii; *stand on haste*, am all impatience, *Rom. & Jul.*, 2.iii.

STAR, *out of thy star*, out of thy social sphere, *Ham.*, 2.ii; *star-cross'd*, ill-fated, *Rom. & Jul.*, 1.*Prol.; our Jovial star*, those born under Jupiter were supposed to be fortunate and happy, *Cym.*, 5.iv; *the seven stars*, the Pleiades, *Lear*, 1.iv.

STAR-BLASTING, being blighted by the influence of a malignant star (e.g., lunatic under the influence of the moon), *Lear*, 3.iv.

STARE, stand on end, *Jul. Caes.*, 4.iii.

START, caprice, *Lear*, 1.i; *startingly*, abruptly, wildly, *Oth.*, 3.iv.

STARVE, paralyse, *Timon*, 1.i.

STATE, rank, *Mac.*, 4.ii; *state of man*, comparing man to the body politic, *Jul. Caes.*, 2.i; seat of dignity, *Mac.*, 3.iv; court, *Jul. Caes.*, 1.ii; noble company, *Troil. & Cres.*, 2.iii; council, *Troil. & Cres.*, 2.iii; *my state*, my place among the factions, *Lear*, 5.i; *states*, persons of rank, nobles, *Cym.*, 3.iv.

STATION, bearing, figure, *Ham.*, 3.iv; *Ant. & Cleo.*, 3.iii.

STATIST, statesman, *Ham.*, 5.ii; *Cym.*, 2.iv.

STATUTE, mortgage, *Ham.*, 5.i.

STAY, *stay the siege*, await the siege, endure, *Rom. & Jul.*, 1.i; *to stay the providence of some high powers*, to await the dispensation of the powers above, *Jul. Caes.*, 5.i.

STEAD, help, *Rom. & Jul.*, 2.iii; profit, *Oth.*, 1.iii.

STEEPY, precipitous, *Timon*, 1.i.

STEERAGE, direction, *Rom. & Jul.*, 1.iv; course steered by ship, *Per.*, 4.*Prol.*

STEW, brothel, *Cym.*, 1.vi.

STICKING-PLACE, to gain the right tension, as in a stringed instrument, *Mac.*, 1.vii.

STICKLER-LIKE, like an umpire, *Troil. & Cres.*, 5.viii.

STILL, always, *Rom. & Jul.*, 5.iii; *Ham.*, 2.ii; continually, *Oth.*, 1.iii; *still-soliciting*, always looking for advantage to self, *Lear*, 1.i.

STINT, cause to cease, *Timon*, 5.iv; cease, *Rom. & Jul.*, 1.iii; *Per.*, 4.iv.

STITHY, forge, *Ham.*, 3.ii; *stithied*, forged on the anvil, *Troil. & Cres.*, 4.v.

STOCCATA, thrust in fencing, *alla stoccata carries it away*, the rapier-man wins the day, *Rom. & Jul.*, 3.i.

STOCK-PUNISHED, by being put in the stocks, *Lear*, 3.iv.

STOMACH, seat of emotions; anger, *Lear*, 5.iii; *enterprise that hath a stomach in't*, that calls for courage, guts, *Ham.*, 1.i; *ease their stomachs*, their resentment, *Titus*, 3.i; *verb*, *stomach not all*, do not take offence at everything, *Ant. & Cleo.*, 3.iv; *private stomaching*, personal quarrels, *Ant. & Cleo.*, 2.ii.

STOMACHER, ornamental covering of the breast, worn by women, *Cym.*, 3.iv.

STONE, *artificial one*, the alchemist's stone that was thought to change base metal to gold, *Timon*, 2.ii; used of dumbness: *your considerate stone*, dumb though thoughtful, *Ant. & Cleo.*, 2.ii; polished crystal as mirror, *Lear*, 5.iii; *verb*, harden, *Oth.*, 5.ii.

STONISH, astonish, amaze, *Ham.*, 3.ii.

STOOP, in falconry, to swoop on the prey, used of the eagle, *Cym.*, 5.iv.

STOP, check, *Cym.*, 5.iii.

STORE, *sacred storehouse*, burial place, *Mac.*, 2.iv; *in store*, entombed, *Titus*, 1.i; *what store*, what kind of process, type of thought, *Lear*, 3.vi; *verb*, people, *Oth.*, 4.iii.

STORY, praise, commend, *Cym.*, 1.iv.

STOUP, a tankard, *Ham.*, 5.i; *Oth.*, 2.iii.

STOUT, strong, *Timon*, 4.iii; proud, *Cor.*, 3.ii; determined, *Mac.*, 1.iii; *adv.*, strongly, *Oth.*, 2.i.

STOUTNESS, obstinacy, *Cor.*, 3.ii; pride, *Cor.*, 5.vi.

STRAIGHT, immediately, *Ham.*, 2.ii; *Ant. & Cleo.*, 4.xii.

STRAIGHT-PIGHT, erect, *Cym.*, 5.v.

STRAIN, (1) race, stock, *Timon*, 1.i; etc.; character, quality, *Cym.*, 3.iv; (2) tendency, *Timon*, 4.iii; visitation, impulse, *Troil. & Cres.*, 2.ii; *make no strain but*, make no difficulty in thinking that, *Troil. & Cres.*, 1.iii; a time, *Jul. Caes.*, 4.iii; *verb*, use to the utmost, *Timon*, 5.i; *straining harsh discords*, uttering a discordant strain, *Rom. & Jul.*, 3.v; *strain my speech*, stretch out what I have said, *Oth.*, 3.iii; *strain his entertainment*, exert herself unduly for his restoration to office, *Oth.*, 3.iii.

STRAIT, narrow passage, *Troil. & Cres.*, 3.iii; *adj.*, strict, *Timon*, 1.i; narrow, *Cym.*, 5.iii.

STRANGE, ignorant, *Timon*, 4.iii; *a strange soul*, just arrived and so ignorant, *Troil. & Cres.*, 3.ii; distant, reserved, *Rom. & Jul.*, 2.ii; notable, *Ham.*, 1.v; unusual, exceptional, *Titus*, 2.i; *Ant. & Cleo.*, 2.ii; foreign, unfamiliar with the customs of the country, *Cym.*, 1.vi.

STRANGELY, *in a reserved manner*, as if you were a foreigner and had no knowledge of him, *Troil. &*

Cres., 3.iii; *strangely-visited*, sorely afflicted, *Mac.*, 4.iii.

STRANGER'D *with our oath*, disowned as a daughter by my vow, *Lear*, 1.i.

STRANGLE, blanket, suppress, *Mac.*, 2.iv.

STRAY, lapse, turning aside, *Lear*, 1.i.

STRENGTH, armed followers, *Titus*, 1.i; force, army, *Titus*, 1.i; *Ant. & Cleo.*, 2.i; authority, *Lear*, 2.i; *a proof of strength she could not publish more*, she could not give a stronger proof, *Troil. & Cres.*, 5.ii.

STRETCH, *our means stretch'd*, most economically employed, *Jul. Caes.*, 4.i; *stretch their duties*, to perform in an officious manner, *Lear*, 2.ii.

STRICT, *too strict a paradox*, what is too clearly a paradox, an absurd position, *Timon*, 3.v.

STRIDE, *stride a limit*, pass beyond a restricted area, *Cym.*, 3.iii.

STRIKE, blast, infect, *Ham.*, 1.i; *Lear*, 2.iv; *strike the vessels*, broach the casks of wine, *Ant. & Cleo.*, 2.vii.

STUBBORN, *stubborn critics*, natural faultfinders, *Troil. & Cres.*, 5.ii; harsh, *Oth.*, 1.iii.

STUCK, thrust, *Ham.*, 4.vii.

STUDIED, *studied in his death*, as if rehearsed well in the part he had to play, *Mac.*, 1.iv; *well studied for*, thoroughly prepared, *Ant. & Cleo.*, 2.vi.

SUB-CONTRACTED, a sub-contract is consequent on a contract and affects some part of the whole; the lady's liaison is here treated ironically as affecting a detail in the contract of marriage, *Lear*, 5.iii.

SUBDUE, degrade, disgrace, *Cor.*, 1.i.

SUBDUEMENTS, opportunities to slay the vanquished, *Troil. & Cres.*, 4.v.

SUBJECT, *subject of the land*, the people, *Ham.*, 1.i; *a subject of this war*, one under authority, *Lear*, 5.iii; *the finny subject of the sea*, fishes, *Per.*, 2.i.

SUBSCRIBE, sign, *Ham.*, 5.ii; *subscribe his thought*, acknowledge the truth of his opinion, *Troil. & Cres.*, 2.iii; *subscribe to*, agree to, obey, *Titus*, 4.ii; put one's signature to a document, *Ant. & Cleo.*, 4.vi; *all cruels else subscribe*, let all other cruelties pass as forgivable, *Lear*, 3.vii.

SUBSCRIPTION, submission, obedience, *Lear*, 3.ii.

SUBTLETY, stratagem, *Per.*, 2.v.

SUBURBS, going with 'harlot,' as the brothels were in the suburbs, *Jul. Caes.*, 2.i.

SUCCEED, follow, *Lear*, 1.ii; *Per.*, 1.iv; devolve on, pass legally to, *Oth.*, 5.ii.

SUCCESS, outcome, result, *Troil. & Cres.*, 1.iii; *Ant. & Cleo.*, 3.v.

SUCCESSANTLY, in turn, following another, *Titus*, 4.iv.

SUCCESSION, *to the succession of new days*, from day to day, *Timon*, 2.ii; *their own succession*, their own future occupation, *Ham.*, 2.ii; *his succession*, those who followed him on the throne, *Cym.*, 3.i.

SUCCESSIVE TITLE, title by lineal descent to succeed to the throne, *Titus*, 1.i.

SUDDEN, immediate, *Ham.*, 5.ii; *Oth.*, 4.ii; speedy, *Jul. Caes.*, 3.i; hasty, ill-considered, *Cor.*, 2.iii; *Oth.*, 2.i.

SUDDENLY, *suddenly contrive*, arrange what will seem unprepared and prove a surprise, *Ham.*, 2.ii.

SUFFER, endure, *Per.*, 5.i; submit, *Oth.*, 5.ii; deteriorate, *Ant. & Cleo.*, 3.xiii; *discerning thine honour from thy suffering*, distinguishing what honour must reject from what should be endured, *Lear*, 4.ii; *suffering souls*, submissive, enduring tamely, *Jul. Caes.*, 2.i; *suffer'd*, been underestimated, *Timon*, 1.i.

SUFFERANCE, suffering, endurance (of another's action), *Troil. & Cres.*, 2.i; *against all noble sufferance*, contrary to what the nobility can permit or endure, *Cor.*, 3.i; forbearance, *Cym.*, 3.v; distress, *Lear*, 3.vi; damage, *Oth.*, 2.i.

SUFFICIENT, fit, able, *Oth.*, 3.iv.

SUGGEST, prompt the people to believe, *Cor.*, 2.i; tempt, *Oth.*, 2.iii.

SUGGESTION, prompting, temptation, *Lear*, 2.i; *Mac.*, 1.iii.

SUIT, dress, *Lear*, 4.vii; *suited*, dressed, and in keeping with the occasion, *Troil. & Cres.*, 1.*Prol.*

SULLY, blemish, fault, *Ham.*, 2.i.

SULPHUR, lightning, *Cor.*, 5.iii; *stones of sulphur*, thunderbolt, ball of lightning, *Cym.*, 5.v.

SULPHUROUS, of lightning, *Lear*, 3.ii; of hell-fire, *Lear*, 4.vi.

SUM, import, what it adds up to, *Ant. & Cleo.*, 1.i.

SUMMER-SEEMING, ephemeral, appearing only in one season of life, *Mac.*, 4.iii.

SUMMONER, officer of ecclesiastical court who summons offenders, *Lear*, 3.ii.

SUPERFLUOUS, *superfluous kings*, a superfluity of kings, *Ant. & Cleo.*, 3.xii; *superfluous riots*, revelling in luxury, *Per.*, 1.iv.

SUPERFLUX, superfluity, *Lear*, 3.iv.

Superscription, address, *Timon*, 2.ii.
Superserviceable, over-officious, *Lear*, 2.ii. [*Ham.*, 2.ii.
Supervise, *on the supervise*, at sight,
Supervisor, spectator, *Oth.*, 3.iii.
Supply, reinforcement, *Cym.*, 5.ii; gratify, *Oth.*, 4.i; *my place supplied*, filled, *Oth.*, 3.iii.
Supplyant, auxiliary, *Cym.*, 3.vii.
Supplyment, continuance of supply, *Cym.*, 3.iv.
Supposing, imagination, *Per.*, 5.*Prol.*
Sur-addition, additional name, in honour of his valour, *Cym.*, 1.i.
Sure, *make him sure enough*, kill him, *Per.*, 1.i; infallible, *Cym.*, 5.iv.
Surety, *do as if for surety*, act as if it were true, *Oth.*, 1.iii. [5.ii.
Surpriz'd, captured, *Ant. & Cleo.*,
Surveying, *surveying vantage*, seeing an opportunity, *Mac.*, 1.ii.
Suspect, suspicion, *Timon*, 4.iii.
Suspicion, *to answer their suspicion*, to answer the crime of which they are suspected, *Titus*, 2.iii; *his suspicion*, the suspicion entertained about him, *Lear*, 3.v.
Suspiration, breathing, *Ham.*, 1.ii.
Swarth, with black complexion, *Titus*, 2.iii.
Swashing, slashing, *Rom. & Jul.*, 1.i.
Swath, swaddling-band, the bandages put round a new-born infant, *Timon*, 4.iii.
Sway, control, *Troil. & Cres.*, 2.ii; rule, *Lear*, 1.i; *verb*, *the mind I sway by*, the mind that controls my actions, *Mac.*, 5.iii.
Swear, invoke, *Lear*, 1.i; *swears and lies*, swears an oath of loyalty and breaks it, *Mac.*, 4.ii.
Sweat, take the cure for venereal disease, *Troil. & Cres.*, 5.x.
Sweet, perfumed, *Titus*, 2.iv.
Sweeting, sweet kind of apple, *Rom. & Jul.*, 2.iv.
Swelling, stately, *Mac.*, 1.iii.
Swelter'd, exuded like sweat, *Mac.*, 4.i. [1.iii.
Swinge, momentum, *Troil. & Cres.*,
Swithold, Saint Vitalis, invoked as a protection against nightmare, *Lear*, 3.iv.
Swits, switch, *Rom. & Jul.*, 2.iv.
Switzers, Swiss bodyguard, *Ham.*, 4.v.
Swoopstake, taking all the stakes, so making no reservations, *Ham.*, 5.v.
Sword, as the hilt forms a cross with the blade and grip, oaths could be sworn on it, *Ham.*, 1.v.
Sworder, gladiator, *Ant. & Cleo.*, 3.xiii.
Swound, swoon, *Rom. & Jul.*, 3.ii.
'Swounds, God's wounds, *Ham.*, 2.ii.
Sympathy, correspondence, *Titus*, 3.i; harmony, *Oth.*, 2.i; *for sympathy*, because of the correspondence, *Cym.*, 5.iv.

Table, *my tables*, memorandum book, *Ham.*, 1.v; so metaphorically of the mind, *the tables of their thoughts*, *Troil. & Cres.*, 4.v; *Ham.*, 1.v; *table-book*, notebook, *Ham.*, 2.ii; *Cupid's tables*, love-letters, *Cym.*, 3.ii; *tabled*, set down in writing, *Cym.*, 1.iv.
Tackled, *tackled stair*, rope ladder, *Rom. & Jul.*, 2.iv.
Taint, disgrace, defeat, *Troil. & Cres.*, 1.iii; fault, *Ant. & Cleo.*, 5.i; *fall'n into taint*, become corrupted, *Lear*, 1.i; *verb*, infect, corrupt, *Troil. & Cres.*, 3.iii; *Cym.*, 3.iv; defile, *Ham.*, 1.v; become infected, *Mac.*, 5.iii; injure, *Oth.*, 1.iii; disparage, *Oth.*, 2.i; *tainting*, corruption, *Cym.*, 1.iv.
Tag, rabble, *Cor.*, 3.i; *tag-rag people*, rabble, *Jul. Caes.*, 1.ii.
Take, bewitch, *Ham.*, 1.i; strike, kill, *Troil. & Cres.*, 5.v; *take upon oneself*, profess, pretend, *Troil. & Cres.*, 1.ii; *Lear*, 5.iii; assume, *Ham.*, 2.i; *take't of my soul*, let me tell you on my word, *Timon*, 2.iv; recognize as, identify, *Titus*, 5.ii; have recourse to, *Per.*, 4.iv; *the witch take me*, cast evil spell on me, *Ant. & Cleo.*, 4.ii; *taking airs*, infectious, harmful, *Lear*, 2.iv; *I'll have the work ta'en out*, I shall have the pattern copied, *Oth.*, 3.iii; learn, *Lear*, 4.vi; *take me up for*, rebuke, *Cym.*, 2.i.
Taking-off, murder, *Mac.*, 1.vii; *Lear*, 5.i. [price, *Cym.*, 1.vi.
Talent, *beyond all talents*, beyond
Tall, *a very tall man*, a stout fellow, *Rom. & Jul.*, 2.iv; of ship, large, *Lear*, 4.vi; *tall youth*, good fighting-men, *Ant. & Cleo.*, 2.vi.
Tamed, broached (used of a cask), *Troil. & Cres.*, 4.i.
Tanling, one so exposed as to be tanned by the sun, *Cym.*, 4.iv.
Targe, shield, *Cym.*, 5.v.
Target, small shield, *Ham.*, 2.ii; *Ant. & Cleo.*, 1.iii.
Tarpeian, *the rock Tarpeian*, from which traitors were cast down, *Cor.*, 3.i; so *the steep Tarpeian death*, *Cor.*, 3.iii.
Tarre, *to tarre them to*, to incite them to quarrel, *Ham.*, 2.ii.
Tart, unpleasant, *Lear*, 4.ii; sour-looking, *Ant. & Cleo.*, 2.v.
Tartar, *Tartar's bow*, the shape of bow given to Cupid was supposed

to be that of the Tartar's weapon, *Rom. & Jul.*, 1.iv.

TASSEL-GENTLE, tercel male hawk, *Rom. & Jul.*, 2.ii.

TASTE, trial, specimen, *Cor.*, 3.i; *in some taste*, in some measure, *Jul. Caes.*, 4.i; *whose qualification shall come into no true taste again*, the mutinous spirit will not be qualified or diluted to something that has a taste agreeable with health and peace, *Oth.*, 2.i; *verb*, put to the proof, *Troil. & Cres.*, 3.ii; experience, test, *Lear*, 2.iv.

TAX, censure, satire, *Timon*, 1.i; *verb*, censure, *Ham.*, 1.iv.

TEEN, sorrow, *Rom. & Jul.*, 1.iii.

TELAMON, Ajax, son of Telamon, was competitor with Ulysses for the arms of Achilles; he lost his reason when they were given to Ulysses, *Ant. & Cleo.*, 4.xiii.

TELL, count, *Ham.*, 1.ii; *Oth.*, 3.iii; count out (money), *Timon*, 3.iv; know, so *canst thou tell?* contemptuous expression, *Titus*, 1.i; solve a riddle, *Per.*, 1.*Prol.*

TELLUS, the earth (Tellus was an earth-goddess), *Ham.*, 3.ii; *Per.*, 4.i.

TEMPER, quality, character, *Mac.*, 3.i; *in temper*, in equable state of mind, *Lear*, 1.v; *verb*, mix, compound, *Ham.*, 5.ii; *Cym.*, 5.v; add fluid to make mixture, *Titus*, 5.ii; persuade to a certain action, *Titus*, 4.iv; moisten to workable condition, *Lear*, 1.iv.

TEMPERANCE, moderation, *Cor.*, 3.iii; normal condition, sanity, *Lear*, 4.vii; chastity, *Ant. & Cleo.*, 3.xiii.

TENABLE, *tenable in your silence*, kept as a secret, *Ham.*, 1.ii.

TEND, be in attendance, *Ham.*, 4.iii; wait upon, serve, *Troil. & Cres.*, 2.iii; etc.

TENDANCE, those waiting to pay court, *Timon*, 1.i; care, attention, *Cym.*, 5.v.

TENDER, offer, *Rom. & Jul.*, 3.iv; regard, care, *Lear*, 1.iv; *verb*, (1) offer, *Timon*, 1.i; *Cym.*, 3.v; (2) value, *Rom. & Jul.*, 3.i.

TENDER-HEFTED, sensitive (though the exact meaning is doubtful), *Lear*, 2.iv.

TENT, a probe, *Troil. & Cres.*, 2.ii; (with pun), 5.i; *verb*, search, probe, *Ham.*, 2.ii; *Cym.*, 3.iv; cleanse, so as to heal, *Cor.*, 3.i.

TENTH, *the destin'd tenth*, every tenth man being doomed to death, *Timon*, 5.iv.

TERCEL, male goshawk, *Troil. & Cres.*, 3.ii.

TEREUS, *see* PHILOMEL.

TERMAGANT, a ranting part in the Mystery cycles, thought to be a Mohammedan deity, *Ham.*, 3.ii.

TERRENE, earthly, *Ant. & Cleo.*, 3.xiii.

TEST, evidence, *Oth.*, 1.iii.

THANE, Scots title (the thanes become earls in last scene), *Mac.*, 5.viii.

THANKFUL, worthy of thanks, *Per.*, 5.ii.

THEORIC, theory, *Oth.*, 1.i.

THERE, *are you there with me?* is that your meaning? *Lear*, 4.vi; so *are you thereabouts? Ant. & Cleo.*, 3.x.

THERETO, in addition, *Cym.*, 4.iv; so *thereunto*, *Oth.*, 2.i.

THESSALY, *the boar of Thessaly*, the boar sent by Artemis to ravage Thessaly, killed in the Calydonian hunt by Meleager, *Ant. & Cleo.*, 4.xiii.

THETIS, a sea-nymph and mother of Achilles; used for the sea by confusion with Tethys, wife of Oceanus, *Troil. & Cres.*, 1.iii; *Per.*, 4.iv; used of Cleopatra as partner of Antony who hoped to rule the sea, *Ant. & Cleo.*, 3.vii.

THEWS, sinews, strength, *Ham.*, 1.iii.

THICK, of sight, dim, *Jul. Caes.*, 5.iii; *speak thick*, fast, *Cym.*, 3.ii; *thicken*, grow dim, *Mac.*, 3.ii; etc.

THINK, brood, meditate, *Ant. & Cleo.*, 3.xiii; *does it not, think thee*, in your opinion, *Ham.*, 5.ii; *always thought*, keeping clearly in mind, *Mac.*, 3.i; *or else shall he suffer not thinking on*, or else he will be forgotten, *Ham.*, 3.ii.

THIS, sometimes for 'this is,' *Lear*, 4.vi.

THOROUGH, through, *Timon*, 4.iii; *Per.*, 4.iii.

THOUGHT, anxious consideration, *Ham.*, 3.i; *take thought*, surrender to melancholy thoughts, *Jul. Caes.*, 2.i.

THOUGHTEN, *be you thoughten*, think, *Per.*, 4.vi.

THOUGHT-EXECUTING, rapid as thought, *Lear*, 3.ii.

THOUGHT-SICK, deeply grieved, sunk in gloom, *Ham.*, 3.iv.

THRACIAN, *the Thracian poet*, Orpheus, whose music tamed even Cerberus, *Titus*, 2.iv; *the Thracian tyrant*, Polymnestor, who murdered Polydorus, Priam's youngest son; Hecuba in revenge killed his sons and had him blinded, *Titus*, 1.i.

THREE-NOOK'D, three-cornered, *Ant. & Cleo.*, 4.vi.

THREE-SUITED, a servant's allowance of livery, *Lear*, 2.ii.

THRIFT, worldly profit, gain, *Ham.*, 3.ii; *Cym.*, 5.i.

THRIFTY, *a thrifty shoeing-horn*, a useful but subservient hanger-on, *Troil. & Cres.*, 5.i.
THRONG'D, oppressed, *Per.*, 1.i.
THROUGH, THROUGHLY, thoroughly, *Troil. & Cres.*, 2.iii; etc.; (so as to find the opponent), *Cym.*, 4.ii.
THROW, *tumbled past the throw*, overshot the mark, *Cor.*, 5.ii.
THUNDER-BEARER, THUNDER-DARTER, THUNDERER, Jove, *Troil. & Cres.*, 2.iii; etc. [*Caes.*, 1.iii; *Cym.*, 4.ii.
THUNDERSTONE, thunderbolt, *Jul.*
THWART, not straight, off the line, *Troil. & Cres.*, 1.iii; perverse, *Lear*, 1.iv; *thwarting the wayward seas*, crossing, *Per.*, 4.iv.
TIB, slang term for woman, *Per.*, 4.vi.
TICE, entice, *Titus*, 2.iii.
TICKLE, *tickle o' th' sere*, easily set off (*see* SERE), *Ham.*, 2.ii.
TICKLISH, one inclined for dalliance, *Troil. & Cres.*, 4.v.
TIGHT, deft, *Ant. & Cleo.*, 4.iv.
TIKE, cur, *Lear*, 3.vi.
TIME, *at more time*, at more leisure, *Mac.*, 1.iii; life, *Timon*, 3.v; *Oth.*, 1.i; so *thy long-experienced time*, *Rom. & Jul.*, 4.i; the future, *Cor.*, 5.iii; time of life, age, *Cym.*, 1.i; lifetime, *Lear*, 1.i; present state of things, *Ant. & Cleo.*, 3.vi; *time of scorn*, scornful world, *Oth.*, 4.ii.
TIMELESS, untimely, *Rom. & Jul.*, 5.iii. [earlier, *Ant. & Cleo.*, 2.vi.
TIMELY, early, *Mac.*, 1.iii; *timelier*,
TIME-PLEASERS, seekers of popularity for their own ends, *Cor.*, 3.i.
TINCT, colour, *Ham.*, 3.iv; *Cym.*, 2.ii; the grand elixir of the alchemists that was to turn base metal into gold, so used of the value conferred on Antony's messenger, *Ant. & Cleo.*, 1.v.
TINCTURES, *tinctures, stains, relics*, on handkerchiefs dipped in the blood and kept as relics, *Jul. Caes.*, 2.ii.
TIRE, (1) *rich tire about you*, living in opulence, *Per.*, 3.ii; head-dress, *Ant. & Cleo.*, 2.v; (2) embrace lustfully, *Cym.*, 3.iv; (from falconry) prey, feed voraciously; so of thoughts, considering deeply, *Timon*, 3.vi. [*& Cres.*, 5.iii.
TISICK, a consumptive cough, *Troil.*
TISSUE, fabric woven of gold thread and silk, *Ant. & Cleo.*, 2.ii.
TITHE, tenth, *Troil. & Cres.*, 2.ii; *a tithed death*, death of every tenth man, *Timon*, 5.iv. [*& Jul.*, 1.iv.
TITHE-PIG, pig given as tithe, *Rom.*
TITHING, a locality (originally containing some ten families, or the tenth of a hundred), *Lear*, 3.iv.
TITLES, possessions generally, *Mac.*, 4.ii.
TOAD-SPOTTED, the toad was regarded as venomous; so *toad-spotted traitor*, as marked all over by infamy as the toad is covered by its venomous spots, *Lear*, 5.iii.
TOAST, a piece of toast steeped in wine, so plunged into the sea, *Troil. & Cres.*, 1.iii.
TO-BLESS, bless entirely, *Per.*, 4.vi.
TOFORE, previously, *Titus*, 3.i.
TOGE, toga, gown, so *wolvish toge*, as it was felt as a dishonest disguise, *Cor.*, 2.iii; *toged*, gowned, *Oth.*, 1.i.
TOIL, (1) net, snare, *Ham.*, 3.ii; (2) cause to toil, *Ham.*, 1.i.
TOKEN, *token'd pestilence*, the spots that marked the plague-stricken were called 'the Lord's tokens,' *Ant. & Cleo.*, 3.x; *death tokens*, like marks of the plague and so of death, *Troil. & Cres.*, 2.iii.
TONGUE, vote, *Cor.*, 2.iii; utter, *Cym.*, 5.iv.
TOP-GALLANT, the mast above topmast, so the utmost height, *Rom. & Jul.*, 2.iv.
TOPLESS, supreme, without superior, *Troil. & Cres.*, 1.iii. [*& Cres.*, 1.iii.
TORTIVE, twisted, contorted, *Troil.*
TOUCH, *the natural touch*, the instinct of a parent, *Mac.*, 4.ii; *one touch of nature*, *see* NATURE; *touch of hearts*, touchstone, *Timon*, 4.iii; *of noble touch*, proved by the touchstone of adversity, *Cor.*, 4.i; skill in playing a musical instrument, *Ham.*, 3.ii; in painting, a happy stroke, *Timon*, 1.i; feeling, *Cym.*, 1.i; occasion, incentive, *Ant. & Cleo.*, 1.ii; *verb*, test as with a touchstone, *Timon*, 3.iii; *Oth.*, 3.iii; *touch the estimate*, pay the price, *Timon*, 1.i; *thy thoughts touch their effects in this*, your fears are realized in this event, *Ant. & Cleo.*, 5.ii.
TOWARD, TOWARDS, in preparation, *Timon*, 3.vi; etc. [3.i.
TOWARDLY, accommodating, *Timon*,
TOWER, of a hawk, to mount above the quarry, *Mac.*, 2.iv.
TOY, *a toy in blood*, a passing fancy, *Ham.*, 1.iii; whim, *Rom. & Jul.*, 4.i; *Oth.*, 3.iv; a trifle, *Cym.*, 4.ii.
TRACE, *that trace him*, those who are his descendants, *Mac.*, 4.i.
TRACT, trace, trail, *Timon*, 1.i.
TRADED, experienced, *Troil. & Cres.*, 2.ii.
TRADUCEMENT, calumny, *Cor.*, 1.ix.
TRAIN, snare, plot, *Mac.*, 4.iii; *verb*, entice, lure, *Titus*, 5.i.

TRAITOR, *women's traitors*, deceivers of women, *Cym.*, 3.iv.

TRAMMEL, *trammel up*, to catch as in a trammel, a type of net, *Mac.*, 1.vii.

TRANC'D, in a swoon, *Lear*, 5.iii.

TRANSLATE, transform, *Timon*, 1.i; interpret, explain, *Troil. & Cres.*, 4.v.

TRASH, (1) poor specimen, with pun on (2), to weight a dog's collar to keep him from outrunning the pack, *Oth.*, 2.i. [*Oth.*, 1.iii.

TRAVERSE, military command: march!

TREACHER, traitor, *Lear*, 1.ii. [5.v.

TREATISE, tale, discourse, talk, *Mac.*,

TREATY, proposal for discussion, *Cor.*, 2.ii; *humble treaties*, proposals, *Ant. & Cleo.*, 3.xi.

TRENCH, wrinkle, *Titus*, 5.ii.

TRENCHER, wooden plate, *Ant. & Cleo.*, 3.xiii; *one which holds a trencher*, a servant, *Timon*, 1.i; *trencher-friend*, parasite, *Timon*, 3.vi. [against, *Ant. & Cleo.*, 2.i.

TRESPASS, *did trespasses to*, offended

TRIBUNAL PLEBS (for tribunis plebis), Tribune of the People, *Titus*, 4.iii.

TRICK, characteristic, type of temper, *Rom. & Jul.*, 1.v; jest, *Cor.*, 2.iii; a trifle, *Ham.*, 4.iv; natural or characteristic reaction, *Ham.*, 4.vii; *Ant. & Cleo.*, 5.ii; peculiarity, *Lear*, 4.vi; caprice, *Oth.*, 4.ii; *verb*, in heraldic illustration, to indicate colours by a conventional arrangement of lines and dots; Pyrrhus is variously marked with the one colour–blood, *Ham.*, 2.ii.

TRIFLE, to reduce by comparison to a trifle, *Mac.*, 2.iv.

TRIPLE, *the triple pillar*, one of three, *Ant. & Cleo.*, 1.i; *triple-turn'd*, thrice faithless, *Ant. & Cleo.*, 4.xii.

TRITON, Neptune's trumpeter, so spokesman, *Cor.*, 3.i.

TRIUMPH, procession of victorious general and his troops on return to Rome, *Jul. Caes.*, 5.i; *Ant. & Cleo.*, 5.ii; trump-card, *Ant. & Cleo.*, 4.xiv; *verb*, return with victory, *Cor.*, 2.i.

TRIUMPHANT, magnificent, *Rom. & Jul.*, 5.iii; splendid, *Ant. & Cleo.*, 2.ii.

TROPICALLY, figuratively, *Ham.*, 3.ii.

TROTH, truth, *Cor.*, 4.v; *Cym.*, 5.v; faith, *Cym.*, 1.i.

TROW, believe, *Lear*, 1.iv; *what is the matter, trow?* I wonder, *Cym.*, 1.vi.

TRUCKLE-BED, low bed on truckles (castors) for pushing under standing-bed, *Rom. & Jul.*, 2.i.

TRUE, well-proportioned, *Lear*, 1.ii; *true-bred*, courageous, *Titus*, 5.i; *truest manner'd*, honestly and kindly disposed, *Cym.*, 1.vi. [1.v.

TRUE-PENNY, honest fellow, *Ham.*,

TRUMPET, trumpeter, *Troil. & Cres.*, 4.v. [tail, *Lear*, 3.vi.

TRUNDLE-TAIL, dog with long curling

TRUST, trustworthiness, *Rom. & Jul.*, 3.ii; *men of trust*, seasoned reliable troops, *Cor.*, 1.vi; *verb*, *that trusted home*, the promise and all its implications accepted, *Mac.*, 1.iii.

TRUTH, loyalty, *Troil. & Cres.*, 3.ii; *Cym.*, 5.v.

TRY, test, *Timon*, 5.i; *verb*, *still been tried*, always been proved by his conduct however tested, *Rom. & Jul.*, 4.iii; *try the cause*, settle by combat, *Ham.*, 4.iv.

TUB, *tubs and baths*, for the sweating treatment for venereal disease, *Timon*, 4.iii; so *tub-fast*, restricted diet during the cure, *Timon*, 4.iii; *that tub both fill'd and running*, like the leaky jar the Danaides were condemned in Hades to fill, *Cym.*, 1.vi.

TULLY, *Tully's Orator*, Cicero's *De Oratore*, *Titus*, 4.i.

TURK, *turn Turk*, change completely, as if from Christian to infidel, *Ham.*, 3.ii; *the Turk*, the Sultan of Turkey, *Lear*, 3.iv.

TURLYGOD, apparently a name for a bedlam-beggar (*see* BEDLAM), *Lear*, 2.iii.

TURN, return, *Timon*, 2.i; be false to one's promise, turn to men, *Oth.*, 4.i. [3.ii.

TURTLE, turtle-dove, *Troil. & Cres.*,

TWAIN, *they two are twain*, not united by any feeling of love, *Troil. & Cres.*, 3.i; pair, *Ant. & Cleo.*, 1.i.

TWIGGEN, cased in wicker-work, *Oth.*, 2.iii.

TWIN, *twin in love*, close friends, *Cor.*, 4.iv; *twin with*, imitate perfectly, resemble completely, *Per.*, 5.*Prol.*; *twinn'd stones*, resembling each other, *Cym.*, 1.vi.

TYBALT, in *Reynard the Fox* the cat is called Tybalt, so *prince of cats*, *Rom. & Jul.*, 2.iv.

TYPHON, a giant that warred against the gods, *Titus*, 4.ii.

TYRANNOUS, cruel, *Ham.*, 2.ii.

TYRANT, usurper, *Mac.*, 3.vi.

UMBRAGE, shadow, *Ham.*, 5.ii.

UNACCOMMODATED, without the clothing, implements, etc., man has devised for his convenience, *Lear*, 3.iv. [*Rom. & Jul.*, 2.ii.

UNADVIS'D, without due reflection,

UNAGREEABLE, unsuitable, *Timon*, 2.ii.

UNANEL'D, without extreme unction, *Ham.*, 1.v.

UNBARB'D, unarmed; *unbarb'd sconce*, bare head, *Cor.*, 3.ii.

UNBATED, not blunted (the button being removed from the point), *Ham.*, 4.vii.

UNBENT, unprepared to strike the final blow (as if discharging an arrow), *Cym.*, 3.iv.

UNBITTED, unbridled, *Oth.*, 1.iii.

UNBLEST, wretched, *Oth.*, 5.i.

UNBODIED, *unbodied figure of the thought*, idea, *Troil. & Cres.*, 1.iii.

UNBOLT, reveal, *Timon*, 1.i.

UNBOLTED, unsifted, coarse, *Lear*, 2.ii.

UNBONNETED, without cover on his head, *Lear*, 3.i; *speak unbonneted*, speak without removing the cap, or showing any sign of inequality, *Oth.*, 1.ii.

UNBOOKISH, ignorant, *Oth.*, 4.i.

UNBORN, *all cause unborn*, without cause or reason, *Cor.*, 3.i.

UNBRAC'D, unlaced, *Ham.*, 2.i.

UNCHARGE, *uncharge the practice*, regard the deed as free from villainy, *Ham.*, 4.vii; *uncharged parts*, gates not yet attacked, *Timon*, 5.iv.

UNCLEW, unwind a ball (clew) of thread, so bankrupt, ruin, *Timon*, 1.i.

UNCOMPREHENSIVE, unsounded, *Troil. & Cres.*, 3.iii. [2.iii.

UNCOUTH, strange, disturbing, *Titus*,

UNCROSS'D, *his book uncross'd*, the account unpaid, not scored out as paid, *Cym.*, 3.iii.

UNCTION, ointment, so soothing notion, *Ham.*, 3.iv.

UNCTUOUS, oily, so gratifying to appetite, *Timon*, 4.iii. [*Mac.*, 5.vii.

UNDEEDED, having done nothing,

UNDER, *suffer'd under praise*, suffered in the sense that the praise given it puts it beyond the reach of a purchaser, *Timon*, 1.i; *this under globe*, the earth, *Lear*, 2.ii.

UNDERCREST, *to undercrest your good addition*, to show myself worthy of the distinction, *Cor.*, 1.ix.

UNDERGO, sustain, enjoy, *Ham.*, 1.iv; undertake, *Jul. Caes.*, 1.iii; take upon oneself, *Cym.*, 1.iv.

UNDERTAKE, answer for, stand as guarantor for, *Titus*, 1.i; *undertake every companion*, have to do with, answer the challenge of, *Cym.*, 2.i; enter, *Per.*, 2.v.

UNDERTAKER, *his undertaker*, see to him (by murdering him), *Oth.*, 4.i.

UNDERWRITE, submit to, *Troil. & Cres.*, 2.iii.

UNDO, solve a riddle, *Per.*, 1.i; prevent, be a bar to, *Per.*, 4.vi.

UNEQUAL, unjust, *Ant. & Cleo.*, 2.v.

UNFOLD, reveal, *Cym.*, 1.i; *Oth.*, 4.ii; *unfold yourself*, identify yourself, *Ham.*, 1.i; *unfolded*, exposed, *Ant. & Cleo.*, 5.ii; *unfolding*, proposal, *Oth.*, 1.iii.

UNFURNISH'D, deprived of, unattended by, *Titus*, 2.iii.

UNHANDSOME, unfair, failing to take the rough with the smooth in the soldier's life, *Oth.*, 3.iv.

UNHAPPILY, of a suspicious sort, *Ham.*, 4.v.

UNHAPPY, evil, fatal, *Rom. & Jul.*, 5.ii; of evil omen, *Cym.*, 5.v.

UNHEART, discourage, *Cor.*, 5.i.

UNHOUSED, free from domestic cares, *Oth.*, 1.ii.

UNHOUS'LED, without having received the sacrament, *Ham.*, 1.v.

UNIMPROVED, unused, not yet turned to account, *Ham.*, 1.i. [5.ii.

UNION, a large, splendid pearl, *Ham.*,

UNIVERSAL, *an universal wolf*, general greed; *an universal prey*, everything in the world its prey, *Troil. & Cres.*, 1.iii; *universal landlord*, of the whole earth, *Ant. & Cleo.*, 3.xiii.

UNJUST, false, *Troil. & Cres.*, 5.i.

UNKENNEL, reveal itself, *Ham.*, 3.ii.

UNKIND, unnatural, not humane, *Titus*, 1.i.

UNKNOWN, *the unknown Ajax*, his real qualities still underrated in public opinion, *Troil. & Cres.*, 3.iii.

UNLACE, *unlace your reputation*, divest yourself of your good name, *Oth.*, 2.iii.

UNLAID, *ghost unlaid*, active, not exorcised, *Cym.*, 4.ii; *unlaid ope*, concealed, *Per.*, 1.ii. [*Cleo.*, 3.vi.

UNLAWFUL, illegitimate, *Ant. &*

UNLEARN'D, ignorant, *Timon*, 4.iii.

UNLESS, except, *Titus*, 2.iii; *Oth.*, 1.i.

UNLIKE, *more unlike*, even more wonderful, *Cym.*, 5.v.

UNLIMITED, *poem unlimited*, a play that does not observe the unities of place and time, *Ham.*, 2.ii. [3.iii.

UNLUCKILY, boding evil, *Jul. Caes.*,

UNMANN'D, of falcon not yet trained by man, so of one not yet husbanded, *Rom. & Jul.*, 3.ii. [4.i.

UNMERITABLE, undeserving, *Jul. Caes.*,

UNNATURALNESS, lack of affection and its consequences, *Lear*, 1.ii. [3.v.

UNNOTED, undemonstrative, *Timon*,

UNNUMBER'D, innumerable, *Jul. Caes.*, 3.i; *Lear*, 4.vi.

UNPARAGON'D, matchless, *Cym.*, 1.iv.

UNPAVED, castrated, without stones, *Cym.*, 2.iii.

Unplausive, disapproving, *Troil. & Cres.*, 3.iii.

Unpolicied, devoid of sense for life, *Ant. & Cleo.*, 5.ii.

Unpossessing, without rights of inheritance, *Lear*, 2.i.

Unpregnant, *unpregnant of my cause*, barren, not quickened to action, *Ham.*, 2.ii.

Unprizable, beyond reckoning, *Cym.*, 1.iv.

Unpriz'd, *unpriz'd precious*, not valued by her family but precious to me, *Lear*, 1.i.

Unproper, not confined as they should be to their owner, *Oth.*, 4.i.

Unprovide, shake his resolution, disarm, *Oth.*, 4.i; *unprovided*, unarmed, *Lear*, 2.i.

Unqualified, deprived of resolution, sense of responsibility, *Ant. & Cleo.*, 3.xi.

Unread, *see* Artist.

Unreclaimed, untamed, *Ham.*, 2.i.

Unrecuring, incurable, *Titus*, 3.i.

Unrespective, *unrespective sieve*, a container which we might use indifferently for mere leavings, *Troil. & Cres.*, 2.ii.

Unrighteous, insincere, *Ham.*, 1.ii.

Unrough, smooth-faced, young, *Mac.*, 5.ii.

Unsanctified, wicked, *Lear*, 4.vi; accessible to the wicked, *Mac.*, 4.ii.

Unscann'd, *unscann'd swiftness*, thoughtless haste, *Cor.*, 3.i.

Unseam, rip open, *Mac.*, 1.ii.

Unseminar'd, castrated, *Ant. & Cleo.*, 1.v.

Unsifted, untried, *Ham.*, 1.iii.

Unsinew'd, weak, *Ham.*, 4.vii.

Unspeaking, wanting adequate powers of description, *Cym.*, 5.v.

Unsquar'd, not fitting, *Troil. & Cres.*, 1.iii.

Unstate, divest of rank and possessions, *Lear*, 1.ii; *unstate his happiness*, surrender the advantage of his fortune, *Ant. & Cleo.*, 3.xiii.

Untaught, rude, unmannerly one, *Rom. & Jul.*, 5.iii.

Untent, (1) issue from the tent, *Troil. & Cres.*, 2.iii; (2) *untented woundings*, wounds too deep to be cleansed by a tent (roll of lint), *Lear*, 1.iv.

Unthrift, prodigal, *Timon*, 4.iii; *unthrifty*, unlucky, *Rom. & Jul.*, 5.iii.

Untie, interpret, explain, *Cym.*, 5.iv; *untied my virgin knot*, in the classical sense of keeping the virgin zone untied, *Per.*, 4.ii.

Untraded, not in common use, *Troil. & Cres.*, 4.v.

Unvalu'd, of no social importance, *Ham.*, 1.iii.

Unwit, deprive of reason, *Oth.*, 2.iii.

Unyoke, *tell me that, and unyoke*, answer the problem and then you can relax (call it a day), *Ham.*, 5.i.

Up, in confinement, *Ant. & Cleo.*, 3.v.

Up-cast, a shot at bowls, *Cym.*, 2.i.

Uproar, throw into confusion, *Mac.*, 4.iii.

Up-spring, a kind of Teutonic dance, *Ham.*, 1.iv.

Upward, *extremest upward*, top, *Lear*, 5.iii.

Urchin, hedgehog, *Titus*, 2.iii.

Urge, *urge me in this act*, put forward my name as cover or excuse for the war, *Ant. & Cleo.*, 2.ii.

Urn, grave, *Cor.*, 5.vi.

Us, we, *Cym.*, 4.ii.

Use, *my uses*, my needs, *Timon*, 2.i; *all use of quittance*, what would be regarded as ample repayment, *Timon*, 1.i; *the use of nature*, the normal condition, *Mac.*, 1.iii; *the uses of this world*, the whole business of living, *Ham.*, 1.ii; habit, *Oth.*, 4.i; conduct, *Oth.*, 4.iii; *in use*, in trust, *Ant. & Cleo.*, 1.iii; *verb*, dispose of, *Titus*, 5.i; borrow from, *Timon*, 3.ii; make a habit of, adopt as a practice, *Lear*, 1.iv; *my so used a guest*, my habitual companion, *Per.*, 1.ii.

Usuring, profiteering, *Timon*, 3.v.

Usurp, encroach on, *Ham.*, 3.ii; *Per.*, 3.ii; *an usurp'd beard*, a beard you take upon yourself to wear, as if a soldier, *Oth.*, 1.iii.

Utter, sell, circulate, *Rom. & Jul.*, 5.i.

Utterance, *to th' utterance*, to the death of one of the combatants (*à l'outrance*), *Mac.*, 3.i; *keep at utterance*, keep even at the peril of death, *Cym.*, 3.i.

Uttermost, the latest hour, *Jul. Caes.*, 2.i.

Vacancy, the vacuum nature abhors, *Ant. & Cleo.*, 2.ii; leisure, *Ant. & Cleo.*, 1.iv.

Vail, perquisite, gratuity, *Per.*, 2.i; *the vail and dark'ning of the sun*, the going down of the sun, *Troil. & Cres.*, 5.viii; *verb*, bow in respect, *Per.*, 2.iii; do homage, *Per.*, 4.*Prol.*; *vailed*, downcast, *Ham.*, 1.ii; *vail your ignorance*, let your foolish minds bow down, *Cor.*, 3.i.

Valanc'd, bearded, *Ham.*, 2.ii.

Validity, strength, endurance, *Ham.*, 3.ii; dignity, worth, *Rom. & Jul.*, 3.iii; value, *Lear*, 1.i.

Valued, *the valued file*, a list indicating what gives each item its value, *Mac.*, 3.i.

Vanity, the illusion of earthly joys, *Rom. & Jul.*, 2.vi; *Vanity the puppet*, Lady Vanity was a character in morality plays, *Lear*, 2.ii.

VANTAGE, advantage, *Cor.*, 3.ii; *Cym.*, 5.v; opportunity, *Cor.*, 5.vi; *to the vantage*, in addition, *Oth.*, 4.iii; *with his next vantage*, at his earliest opportunity, *Cym.*, 1.iii; *coign of vantage*, corner that can be made use of, *Mac.*, 1.vi; *of vantage*, from a convenient place for listening, *Ham.*, 3.iii.

VANTBRACE, armour for the forearm, *Troil. & Cres.*, 1.iii.

VARIANCE, quarrel, *Ant. & Cleo.*, 2.vi.

VARLET, servant to a knight, *Troil. & Cres.*, 1.i; but frequently used to describe a knave or rascal; *varletry*, rabble, *Ant. & Cleo.*, 5.ii.

VARY, change of mood, *Lear*, 2.ii; *varying*, with the ebb and flow of fortune, *Ant. & Cleo.*, 4.xv.

VAUNT, beginning, *Troil. & Cres.*, 1.*Prol.*; *vaunt-courier*, forerunner, *Lear*, 3.ii.

VAWARD, vanguard, *Cor.*, 1.vi.

VEGETIVES, plants, *Per.*, 3.ii.

VEIN, *he rubs the vein of him*, encourages him in his vanity, *Troil. & Cres.*, 2.iii; *bloody veins*, the soldiers concealed within and intent on slaughter, *Per.*, 1.iv.

VENEREAL, amorous, *Titus*, 2.iii.

VENGEANCE, harm, injury, *Titus*, 2.iii; *adv.*, overwhelmingly, *Cor.*, 2.ii.

VENOM'D, *venom'd stuck*, thrust with poisoned rapier, *Ham.*, 4.vii.

VENOMOUS, harmful, *Cor.*, 4.i; *venomous wights*, those intent on evil, *Troil. & Cres.*, 4.ii.

VENT, opening, wound, *Troil. & Cres.*, 5.iii; *full of vent*, the eagerness of the hound that has picked up the scent, *Cor.*, 4.v; *vent of blood*, discharge of blood, *Ant. & Cleo.*, 5.ii.

VENTAGES, the holes or stops in the recorder, *Ham.*, 3.ii.

VENTURES, those whose trade exposes them to the risk of disease, *Cym.*, 1.vi.

VERBAL, *made she no verbal question?* did she not speak? *Lear*, 4.iii; *so verbal*, so insistent in your address, *Cym.*, 2.iii.

VERIFY, bear witness to, *Cor.*, 5.ii.

VERONESA, ship chartered from Verona, *Oth.*, 2.i.

VERSAL, universal, *Rom. & Jul.*, 2.iv.

VERY, complete, *Troil. & Cres.*, 1.ii; *Cym.*, 5.iv; beyond all doubt, *Cym.*, 4.ii; *a very pretence*, a deliberate intention, *Lear*, 1.iv; *very now*, at this instant, *Oth.*, 1.i.

VESSEL, *the weaker vessels*, women (*cf. I. Peter*, 3.7), *Rom. & Jul.*, 1.i; *Timon*, 2.ii; used, as in the Bible, of the human body, *Oth.*, 4.ii.

VESTAL, a priestess of Vesta, vowed to chastity, *Per.*, 4.v; *her vestal livery*, like that of the vestal virgins, *Rom. & Jul.*, 2.ii.

VESTURE, *the essential vesture of creation*, that is in form, moving, action, apprehension, *Oth.*, 2.i.

VEX, disturb in mind, *Jul. Caes.*, 1.ii; afflict, *Lear*, 3.iv; *the vex'd sea*, in commotion, *Lear*, 4.iv.

VICE, the Vice was a character in the morality plays, presented often as a buffoon, so in *Ham.*, 3.iv.

VICIOUS, mistaken, at fault, *Oth.*, 3.iii.

VIE, compete with, *Per.*, 4.*Prol.*; *nature wants stuff to vie strange forms with fancy*, nature cannot compete with fancy in the creation of strange forms, *Ant. & Cleo.*, 5.ii.

VIEW, *in his view*, in appearance, *Rom. & Jul.*, 1.i; gaze, *Troil. & Cres.*, 4.v; *to my sister's view*, to see my sister, *Ant. & Cleo.*, 2.ii.

VILLEIN, bondman, *Titus*, 4.iii.

VINDICATIVE, vindictive, *Troil. & Cres.*, 4.v.

VIOLENT, rage, *Troil. & Cres.*, 4.iv.

VIRGINAL, maidenly, *Cor.*, 5.ii.

VIRTUE, *an humble suitor to your virtues*, as we might say 'to your honours,' used of the senators, *Timon*, 3.v; authority, *Cor.*, 5.ii; *Oth.*, 1.iii; essential feature, *Timon*, 3.v; healing power, *Mac.*, 4.iii; *O infinite virtue*, bravest of the brave, *Ant. & Cleo.*, 4.viii; *thy single virtue*, your individual courage, *Lear*, 5.iii.

VIRTUOUS, *if his occasion were not virtuous*, the need of a man you have just described as virtuous, so an honourable necessity, *Timon*, 3.ii; *virtuously bound*, strongly (used hyperbolically), *Timon*, 1.ii; *by your virtuous means*, by your powerful help, *Oth.*, 3.iv.

VISITED, *strangely-visited*, mysteriously afflicted, *Mac.*, 4.iii.

VIZARDED, *degree being vizarded*, rank being masked, all ranks present the same uniform appearance, *Troil. & Cres.*, 1.iii.

VOICE, sound (of trumpet), *Troil. & Cres.*, 1.iii; *in second voice*, the voice of a deputy, *Troil. & Cres.*, 2.iii; *lose your voice*, speak in vain, unheeded, *Ham.*, 1.ii; report, *Jul. Caes.*, 2.i; *an imperial voice*, a judgement or opinion that is decisive, *Troil. & Cres.*, 1.iii; vote, *Cor.*, 2.ii; support, vote, *Cym.*, 3.v; authority, *Oth.*, 1.ii; *verb*, declare publicly a judgement on, *Timon*, 4.iii; nominate, *Cor.*, 2.iii.

VOID, *a place more void*, less crowded, *Jul. Caes.*, 2.iv; *verb*, emit, *Timon*, 1.ii.

'VOID, shun, avoid, *Cor.*, 4.v.

VOLLEY, bellow, *Ant. & Cleo.*, 2.vii.

VOLUME, *bear the knave by the volume*, suffer being called 'knave' so frequently that the repetitions would fill a volume, *Cor.*, 3.iii.

VOLUNTARY, willing, *Cym.*, 3.v; *a voluntary wound*, deliberately self-inflicted, *Jul. Caes.*, 2.i; *Ajax was here the voluntary*, the free agent, *Troil. & Cres.*, 2.i.

VOTARESS, woman vowed to the service of, *Per.*, 4.*Prol.*

VOTARIST, one vowed to chastity, *Oth.*, 4.ii; *no idle votarist*, not one who has taken a vow carelessly, *Timon*, 4.iii.

VOUCH, confirmation, *Cor.*, 2.iii; testimony, *Oth.*, 2.i.

VOUCHER, proof, *Cym.*, 2.ii; witness called to testify to a tenant's title, *Ham.*, 5.i; *double vouchers*, required the calling of two witnesses, *Ham.*, 5.i.

VOUCHSAFE, guarantee, *Jul. Caes.*, 3.i; *vouchsafe your rest here*, consent to stay here, *Ham.*, 2.ii; *vouchsafe my labour*, deign to accept my work, *Timon*, 1.i.

VULCAN, *Vulcan's badge*, Vulcan's wife Venus was unfaithful (with Mars), so the badge of the cuckold, *Titus*, 2.i.

VULGAR, plebeian, *Cor.*, 1.i; *a vulgar station*, a place among the crowd, *Cor.*, 2.i; common, *Ham.*, 1.iii; common knowledge, *Lear*, 4.vi; the common people, *Jul. Caes.*, 1.i.

WAFT, beckon, *Timon*, 1.i.

WAFTAGE, conveyance by water, *Troil. & Cres.*, 3.ii.

WAFTURE, wave, gesture, *Jul. Caes.*, 2.i.

WAG, move about, *Titus*, 5.ii; move, blink, *Ham.*, 5.i.

WAGE, stake, *Lear*, 1.i; take the risk of, *Oth.*, 1.iii; put to the test, try, *Ant. & Cleo.*, 3.vii; contend, *Lear*, 2.iv; *waged me with his countenance*, paid me with looks of favour or disfavour, *Cor.*, 5.vi; *the commodity wages not with the danger*, the profit does not equal the risk, *Per.*, 4.ii.

WAGGISH, sporting, frolicsome, *Cym.*, 3.iv.

WAGGON, chariot, *Titus*, 5.ii; *waggoner*, charioteer, *Rom. & Jul.*, 3.ii.

WAIT, be in attendance, *Rom. & Jul.*, 1.iv; attend, *Ant. & Cleo.*, 5.ii; *wait on fortune*, to await the outcome of the war, *Cor.*, 5.iii; *wait on*, accompany, *Mac.*, 3.iv.

WAITING-WOMEN (*Diana's*), the stars, *Troil. & Cres.*, 5.ii.

WAKE, festival on anniversary of a church dedication; such celebrations began the evening before, so all-night feast, *Lear*, 3.vi; *verb*, make a night of it, *Ham.*, 1.iv.

WALL-EY'D, glaring, *Titus*, 5.i.

WAN, grow pale, *Ham.*, 2.ii.

WANION, vengeance, *Per.*, 2.i.

WANTON, *towers whose wanton tops do buss the clouds*, frolicsome in that they kiss the clouds, unrestrained, *Troil. & Cres.*, 4.v; lascivious, *Troil. & Cres.*, 4.v; *noun*, a rabbit at the game, not a serious opponent, *Ham.*, 5.ii; sportive person, *Rom. & Jul.*, 1.v; *so citizen a wanton*, so pampered a person by my city life, *Cym.*, 4.ii; adulteress, *Oth.*, 4.i.

WANTONNESS, *pride fasting in his wantonness*, gorged with self-satisfaction, *Troil. & Cres.*, affectation, lasciviousness, *Ham.*, 3.i.

WARPEN'D, worn out, *Timon*, 4.iii.

WARD, to guard, *Troil. & Cres.*, 1.ii; *noun*, prison cell, *Ham.*, 2.ii; bolt for a door, lock, *Timon*, 3.iii.

WARRANT, *a fetch of warrant*, a device that is allowable, *Ham.*, 2.i; *hunt with modest warrant*, pursue the matter judiciously, *Cor.*, 3.i; *verb*, *our warranted quarrel*, our just war, *Mac.*, 4.iii; defend, maintain, *Troil. & Cres.*, 2.ii; assurance, *Oth.*, 3.iii; *the warrant of my note*, the assurance of your fidelity my knowledge of you gives me, *Lear*, 3.i; *out of warrant*, forbidden by law, *Oth.*, 1.ii.

WARRANTISE, authority, *Ham.*, 5.i.

WARRANTY, *with such general warranty*, in the way heaven permits all of us to love, *Oth.*, 5.ii.

WASTE, desert, blank hours, *Ham.*, 1.ii; the expenditure on so extravagant a scale, *Ant. & Cleo.*, 4.i; *verb*, wasted building, ruin, *Titus*, 5.i; *March is wasted fifteen days*, 15th March, *Jul. Caes.*, 2.i; destroy, *Cym.*, 5.v; annihilate, *Per.*, 4.iv; *till now some nine moons wasted*, till the last nine months, *Oth.*, 1.iii; expend, *Per.*, 1.*Prol.*

WATCH, sleeplessness, *Ham.*, 2.ii; *Cym.*, 3.iv; alertness, *Troil. & Cres.*, 1.ii; guard-duty, *Ham.*, 1.i; *whose howl's his watch*, the howl being the indication of the time to act, *Mac.*, 2.i; guard, group of soldiers on such duty, *Oth.*, 2.iii; *watch o' th' night*, period of time, generally associated with periods of duty, *Oth.*, 1.i; *verb*, keep awake, *Ham.*, 3.ii; *be watched*, kept awake, as hawks are tamed, *Troil. & Cres.*, 3.ii; so *watch him tame*, tame him, *Oth.*, 3.iii; *watch you for*, prevent you by my vigilance from, *Troil. & Cres.*, 1.ii.

WATER, *cast the water of my land*, diagnose its troubles, like the doctor diagnosing from his inspection of the patient's urine, *Mac.*, 5.iii; lustre of a diamond, *Timon*, 1.i; *Per.*, 3.ii; water-newt, *Lear*, 3.iv.

WATERFLY, showy, superficial being, *Ham.*, 5.ii.

WATER-RUG, rough-haired spaniel type of dog, *Mac.*, 3.i.

WAT'RY, *wat'ry palate*, sign of desire and expectation, *Troil. & Cres.*, 3.ii.

WAVE, waver, fluctuate, *Cor.*, 2.ii.

WAX, *a man of wax*, a model, *Rom. & Jul.*, 1.iii; *a form of wax*, lacking endurance in stress, *Rom. & Jul.*, 3.iii.

WAY, *give me way*, yield to my plan, humour, *Cor.*, 4.iv; *give him way*, yield to his fancy, *Per.*, 5.i.

WE, us, *Cor.*, 5.iii; *Cym.*, 5.iii.

WEAL, welfare, *Cor.*, 1.i; *purged the gentle weal*, made society civilized, *Mac.*, 3.iv; *a wholesome weal*, well-ordered commonwealth, *Lear*, 1.iv.

WEALSMAN, politician, *Cor.*, 2.i.

WEARY, *weary of all, shall want some*, shall want again what he has in his disgust discarded, *Lear*, 1.iv.

WEATHER, storm, *Cym.*, 3.iii; *mine honour keeps the weather of my fate*, the position to windward was the advantageous one in naval fighting; so his honour overcomes all risk or fear of death, *Troil. & Cres.*, 5.iii.

WEB, *the web and the pin*, the eye trouble now called cataract, *Lear*, 3.iv.

WEED, garment, *Cor.*, 2.iii.

WEET, know, *Ant. & Cleo.*, 1.i.

WEIGH, consider, allow for, *Jul. Caes.*, 2.i; *as they weigh*, according to their value, *Cor.*, 2.ii.

WEIGHT, *with weight*, in full measure, *Ham.*, 4.v.

WEIGHTY, *our weightier judgement*, our severer sentence, *Timon*, 3.v.

WEIRD SISTERS, goddesses of destiny, *Mac.*, 1.iii.

WELL, at rest (of the dead), *Rom. & Jul.*, 5.i; *Ant. & Cleo.*, 2.v; *well-advis'd*, sane, *Titus*, 4.ii; *well-a-near*, alas! *Per.*, 3.*Prol.*; *well-found*, achieved by skill or valour, *Cor.*, 2.ii.

WENCHLESS, without girls, *Per.*, 4.ii.

WENCH-LIKE, effeminate, *Cym.*, 4.ii.

WHARF, bank of a river, *Ham.*, 1.v; *Ant. & Cleo.*, 2.ii.

WHAT, why, *Titus*, 1.i; *Ant. & Cleo.*, 5.ii; how, *Rom. & Jul.*, 1.v; whatever, *Timon*, 4.ii; *Lear*, 3.vi; whoever, *Lear*, 5.iii.

WHATE'ER, whatever your name, *Troil. & Cres.*, 4.v.

WHEEL, *the spinning-wheel* as an accompaniment to the song, *Ham.*, 4.v; *go on wheels*, go smoothly, *Ant. & Cleo.*, 2.vii.

WHEELING, *wheeling stranger*, wandering, *Oth.*, 1.i.

WHELK'D, in ridges, as on the shell of the whelk, *Lear*, 4.vi.

WHERE, whereas, *Cor.*, 1.i.

WHEREABOUT, purpose, *Mac.*, 2.i.

WHEREAS, where, *Per.*, 1.iv.

WHEY-FACE, white with fear, *Mac.*, 5.iii.

WHILE, until, *Mac.*, 3.i.

WHINID'ST, most mouldy, *Troil. & Cres.*, 2.i.

WHIPSTER, whippersnapper, *Oth.*, 5.ii.

WHIPSTOCK, *practis'd the whipstock*, been a carter, *Per.*, 2.ii.

WHISTLE, with reference to the proverb, 'It is a poor dog that is not worth the whistling,' *Lear*, 4.ii; *whistle her off and let her down the wind*, like a falconer getting rid of an unsatisfactory hawk, *Oth.*, 3.iii.

WHITE, sign of cowardice, *Mac.*, 2.ii; *white herring*, fresh herring, *Lear*, 3.vi.

WHITE-LIN'D, whitewashed, *Titus*, 4.ii.

WHITTLE, clasp-knife, *Timon*, 5.i.

WHO, at times for 'whom.'

WHOLESOME, *wholesome days*, days of social soundness, *Mac.*, 4.iii; sane, reasonable, *Ham.*, 3.ii; well ordered, *Lear*, 1.iv; *in wholesome wisdom*, out of prudent considerations, *Oth.*, 3.i.

WHORESON, fellow, *Rom. & Jul.*, 4.iv; sometimes almost term of endearment, *Ham.*, 5.i; bastard, *Lear*, 1.i.

WIGHT, person, *Troil. & Cres.*, 4.ii; *Oth.*, 2.i.

WILD-GOOSE CHASE, form of cross-country horse-racing, *Rom. & Jul.*, 2.iv.

WILDNESS, madness, *Ham.*, 3.i; *Cym.*, 3.iv.

WILL, carnal desire, *Ham.*, 3.iv.

WILLOW, emblem of disappointed love, *Oth.*, 4.iii.

WIN, *win upon*, get the upper hand of, *Cor.*, 1.i; *win two days*, be ahead by two days, *Ant. & Cleo.*, 2.iv.

Winchester, the liberty of the Bankside, under the jurisdiction of the Bishop of Winchester, sheltered many brothels; so the disease and its victims were named Winchester goose and *goose of Winchester*, *Troil. & Cres.*, 5.x.

Wind, *recover the wind of me*, get to windward and frighten the game into the toil (windward was the commanding position in naval combat), *Ham.*, 3.ii; *have the wind of you*, retain liberty of action and so safety, *Titus*, 4.ii; *sits in the wind against me*, has the stronger position, *Ant. & Cleo.*, 3.x; sighs, *Troil. & Cres.*, 4.iv.

Windlass, roundabout approach, *Ham.*, 2.i.

Window, *eye's windows*, eyelids, *Rom. & Jul.*, 4.i; *Ant. & Cleo.*, 5.ii; *window-bars*, latticework either of dress or windows, *Timon*, 4.iii.

Window'd, looking from a window, *Ant. & Cleo.*, 4.xiv; *window'd raggedness*, full of holes, *Lear*, 3.iv.

Winking, a closing of the eyes, *Ham.*, 2.ii; with closed eyes, *Cym.*, 2.iii and 2.iv.

Winnowed, *winnowed opinions*, cultivated judgements, *Ham.*, 5.ii.

Winter-ground, protect from effects of winter, *Cym.*, 4.ii.

Wisdom, *the wisdom of nature*, science, *Lear*, 1.ii.

Wit, *five wits*, mental powers listed like the five senses, *Rom. & Jul.*, 1.i; *Lear*, 3.iv; *Dian's wit*, sentiment opposed to wedlock, *Rom. & Jul.*, 1.i; *brevity is the soul of wit*, wisdom, understanding, *Ham.*, 2.ii; judgement, *Rom. & Jul.*, 3.iii; cunning, *Lear*, 1.ii; *verb*, know, *Per.*, 4.iv.

Witch, sorcerer, male as well as female, *Ant. & Cleo.*, 1.ii; *a holy witch*, a man whose goodness enchants men's hearts, *Cym.*, 1.vi; *witching time*, suitable for unnatural happenings, *Ham.*, 3.ii.

With, by, *Jul. Caes.*, 3.ii; *Ant. & Cleo.*, 5.ii; on, *Mac.*, 4.ii; *not with himself*, beside himself, *Titus*, 1.i; *with you there*, quits, *Rom. & Jul.*, 2.iv; *are you there with me?* is that your meaning? *Lear*, 4.vi.

Within, *'tis better thee without than he within*, outside you than inside him, *Mac.*, 3.iv; *speak within door*, less loudly, vehemently, *Oth.*, 4.ii.

Witty, prudent, *Troil. & Cres.*, 3.ii; intelligent, cunning, *Titus*, 4.ii; clever, *Oth.*, 2.i.

Wolvish, *wolvish toge*, Coriolanus in the garment of a supplicant feels like the wolf in sheep's clothing, *Cor.*, 2.iii.

Wonder, admiration, *Mac.*, 1.iii; *wonder-wounded*, made motionless with astonishment, *Ham.*, 5.i.

Woodman, hunter, *Cym.*, 3.vi.

Woollen, plainly clad, *Cor.*, 3.ii.

Woo't, wilt thou, *Ham.*, 5.i; *Ant. & Cleo.*, 4.xv.

Word, *at a word*, indeed, in short, *Cor.*, 1.iii; motto, *Ham.*, 1.v; *Per.*, 2.ii; *the props of every word*, social intercourse, its laws, mutual obligations, etc., *Ham.*, 4.v; command, *Jul. Caes.*, 3.ii; *verb*, express, *Ant. & Cleo.*, 4.xiii; recite (instead of singing), *Cym.*, 4.ii; persuade, cajole, *Ant. & Cleo.*, 5.ii; *words him*, gives him a reputation, *Cym.*, 1.iv.

Work, *my brain was wrought with*, my mind was greatly disturbed by, *Mac.*, 1.iii; *what you would work me to*, what you would persuade me to do, *Jul. Caes.*, 1.ii; to bring it about that, *Rom. & Jul.*, 3.v; *let it work*, let the scheme continue, *Ham.*, 3.iv; *wrought upon*, bewitched, *Oth.*, 1.iii; become agitated, tempestuous, *Per.*, 3.i; *being wrought*, having his passions roused, *Oth.*, 5.ii.

Works, fortifications, *Oth.*, 3.ii.

World, *both the worlds*, this earthly life and the next, *Ham.*, 4.v; *a world elsewhere*, a place where one can live, *Cor.*, 3.iii; *this world*, this life, *Rom. & Jul.*, 3.i; *matter of the world*, any business or interest, *Troil. & Cres.*, 2.iii; *the world to come*, later generations of men, *Troil. & Cres.*, 3.ii; *how goes the world that*, how does it come about that, *Timon*, 2.ii; mankind, *Per.*, 3.ii; *his little world of man*, man regarded as the microcosm, a complete universe in miniature, *Lear*, 3.i.

Worldly, *worldly task*, your task in this life, *Cym.*, 4.ii; *an hour of love of worldly matter* (*of* meaning *from*), the private hour to be snatched from his duties as soldier, *Oth.*, 1.iii.

Worldly, mortal, *Titus*, 5.ii.

Worm, serpent, *Timon*, 4.iii; *Ant. & Cleo.*, 5.ii.

Worship, dignity, authority, *Ant. & Cleo.*, 4.xiv; *the worship of their name*, their honourable reputation, *Lear*, 1.iv; *this double worship*, this divided authority, *Cor.*, 3.i.

Worsted-stocking knave, contrasted with the better class wearing silk, *Lear*, 2.ii.

WORTH, riches, possessions, *Rom. & Jul.*, 2.vi; *his worth of contradiction*, get the best of the argument, *Cor.*, 3.iii; service of value, *Cym.*, 5.v; *adj.*, deserving (in bad sense), *Lear*, 1.i and 2.iv.

WORTHINESS, *the worthiness of praise*, well deserved praise, *Troil. & Cres.*, 1.iii.

WORTHLESS, *worthless praise*, being self-praise (*cf. Troil. & Cres.*, 1.iii), *Titus*, 5.iii; unworthy, *Jul. Caes.*, 5.i.

WORTHY, *no worthier than*, no more precious than, *Jul. Caes.*, 3.i; *worthy rage*, justifiable, *Cor.*, 3.i; *Oth.*, 3.iii; deserving of (in bad sense), *Cor.*, 3.i; honourable, *Jul. Caes.*, 5.v; *worthy to be a rebel*, fitted by his vices for the part, *Mac.*, 1.ii; *subdue my worthiest self*, since to live would be dishonourable, it is the honourable part that he will kill; honour calls for death, *Ant. & Cleo.*, 4.xii; *verb*, *that worthied him*, gained him credit, *Lear*, 2.ii.

WOT, know, *Cor.*, 4.i.

WOULD, *he would be crown'd*, Caesar's wish for the crown is indicated by *would;* it also, however, stresses the hypothetical nature of the argument, *Jul. Caes.*, 2.i.

WOUNDLESS, invulnerable, *Ham.*, 4.i.

WRANGLER, adversary, *Troil. & Cres.*, 2.ii.

WREAK, *a heart of wreak*, a spirit of revenge, *Cor.*, 4.v; *his wreaks*, vindictive actions, *Titus*, 4.iv; *verb*, avenge, *Rom. & Jul.*, 3.v.

WREAKFUL, vindictive, *Timon*, 4.iii.

WRENCH, a twist, in behaviour, *Timon*, 2.ii. [3.iii.

WREST, tuning-key, *Troil. & Cres.*,

WRETCH, often used affectionately, *Rom. & Jul.*, 1.iii; *Oth.*, 3.iii.

WRING, suffer in mind, *Cym.*, 3.vi.

WRINKLE, so to outmatch in comparison that the vanquished seems wrinkled and old, *Troil. & Cres.*, 2.ii.

WRIT, written document, *Ham.*, 5.ii; letter, *Titus*, 2.iii; *for the law of writ and the liberty*, plays according to strict classical rules and those that ignored the unities of time and place, *Ham.*, 2.ii; *holy writ*, the Scriptures, *Oth.*, 3.iii; *thinks all is writ he speken can*, all is as true as the 'gospel,' *Per.*, 2.*Prol.*; order, *Lear*, 5.iii; *verb*, *writ down in our duty*, prescribed by our duty, *Ham.*, 1.ii.

WRITE, *write happy*, count yourself fortunate, *Lear*, 5.iii; denounce, *Cym.*, 2.v.

WRONG, betray, *Ham.*, 5.ii; *wrong this presence*, offend by your behaviour this company, *Ant. & Cleo.*, 2.ii.

WRONGLY, *wouldst wrongly win*, win however unfairly, *Mac.*, 1.v.

WROUGHT, *see* WORK.

WRY, err, *Cym.*, 5.i.

YARD, *a clothier's yard*, the length of the arrow for the long-bow, *Lear*, 4.vi.

YARE, dexterous, quick, *Ant. & Cleo.*, 3.xiii; *yarely*, skilfully, *Ant. & Cleo.*, 2.ii. [*Ham.*, 5.ii.

YAW (of ship), to steer unsteadily,

YAWN, *yawning peal*, suggesting sleep, *Mac.*, 3.ii; to gape, *Cor.*, 3.ii; gape in wonder, *Ham.*, 4.v; as in an earthquake, open in terror, *Oth.*, 5.ii.

YEOMAN, freeholder, *Lear*, 3.v; *yeoman's service*, invaluable service (from the reputation the yeoman class had won in war), *Ham.*, 5.ii.

YERK, stab, *Oth.*, 1.ii.

YESTY, *yesty waves*, foaming seas, *Mac.*, 4.i; *yesty collection*, a frothy and superficial patchwork of items from their conversation with others, *Ham.*, 5.ii.

YIELD, assent to, *Cor.*, 2.ii; report of, *Ant. & Cleo.*, 2.v; *the gods yield you*, reward you, *Ant. & Cleo.*, 4.ii; *yielding of that body*, the assent of the state, *Ham.*, 1.iii.

YOKE-FELLOW, colleague, *Lear*, 3.vi.

YOND, yonder, there, *Troil. & Cres.*, 5.ii; yon, *Lear*, 4.vi.

YOUNG, *young in deed*, beginners in murder, *Mac.*, 3.iv.

YOUNGER, *two summers younger*, two summers ago, *Per.*, 1.iv.

YOUNGLING, a greenhorn, *Titus*, 4.ii.

YOUNGLY, early in life, *Cor.*, 2.iii.

YOUR, often used of what is known and common, without reference to person addressed.

YOUTHFUL, *youthful season*, spring (14th March), *Jul. Caes.*, 2.i.

Y-RAVISHED, delighted, *Per.*, 3.*Prol.*

YSLAKED, overcome, relaxed, *Per.*, 3.*Prol.*

ZED, described as unnecessary, since 's' often takes its place, *Lear*, 2.ii.

ZONE, *the burning zone*, the zodiac, *Ham.*, 5.i.

ZOUNDS, by God's wounds, *Titus*, 4.ii; *Oth.*, 1.i.